Handbook of Cultural Sociology

The *Handbook of Cultural Sociology* provides a comprehensive overview of contemporary scholarship in sociology and related disciplines focused on the complex relations of culture to social structures and everyday life. With 65 essays written by scholars from around the world, the book draws diverse approaches to cultural sociology into a dialogue that charts new pathways for research on culture in a global era.

Contributing scholars address vital concerns that relate to classic questions as well as emergent issues in the study of culture. Topics include cultural and social theory, politics and the state, social stratification, community, aesthetics, lifestyle, and identity. In addition, the authors explore developments central to the constitution and reproduction of culture, such as power, technology, and the organization of work.

This book is essential reading for undergraduate and postgraduate students interested in diverse subfields within Sociology, as well as Cultural Studies, Media and Communication, and Postcolonial Theory.

John R. Hall is Professor of Sociology at the University of California – Davis. His published works include *Apocalypse: From Antiquity to the Empire of Modernity* (Polity, 2009), *Visual Worlds* (Routledge, 2005, with co-editors), *Sociology on Culture* (Routledge, 2003, with co-authors), and *Cultures of Inquiry* (Cambridge University Press, 1999).

Laura Grindstaff is Associate Professor of Sociology at the University of California – Davis. She is the author of the award-winning *Money Shot: Trash, Class, and the Making of TV Talk Shows* (University of Chicago Press, 2002) and has published articles on various aspects of popular culture from reality programming to cheerleading.

Ming-Cheng Lo is Associate Professor of Sociology at the University of California – Davis. She is the author of *Doctors within Borders: Profession, Ethnicity and Modernity in Colonial Taiwan* (University of California Press, 2002). She has published various articles on the cultural processes of political and medical institutions.

Handbook of Cultural Sociology

Edited by
John R. Hall,
Laura Grindstaff,
and Ming-Cheng Lo

Routledge
Taylor & Francis Group

LONDON AND NEW YORK

First published 2010
Paperback edition first published 2012 by Routledge
2 Park Square, Milton Park, Abingdon, Oxon, OX14 4RN

Simultaneously published in the USA and Canada
by Routledge
711 Third Avenue, New York, NY 10017

Routledge is an imprint of the Taylor & Francis Group, an informa business

Typeset in Bembo by Taylor & Francis Books
Printed and bound in Great Britain by CPI Antony Rowe Ltd., Chippenham

British Library Cataloguing in Publication Data
A catalogue record for this book is available from the British Library

Library of Congress Cataloging in Publication Data
Handbook of cultural sociology / edited by John R. Hall,
Laura Grindstaff and Ming-Cheng Lo.
    p. cm
Includes bibliographical references.
1. Culture. I. Hall, John R. II. Grindstaff, Laura. III. Lo, Ming-Cheng.
HM621.H344 2010
306–dc22   2009049917

ISBN: 978-0-415-47445-0 (hbk)
ISBN: 978-0-415-54012-4 (pbk)
ISBN: 978-0-203-89137-7 (ebk)

Printed and bound in Great Britain by
CPI Antony Rowe, Chippenham, Wiltshire

Contents

Detailed contents

Acknowledgments

Contrary to popular stereotype, the process of producing a book is rarely a solitary one; it requires support and cooperation from others. That being said, some books are more collaborative in nature than others. This *Handbook* is a case in point. With 65 contributors and three editors, it bears the imprint of many hands, hearts, and minds. As editors, we are fortunate to have worked with so many good people, especially since the form of the *Handbook* – falling somewhere between an encyclopedia and conventional handbook – is somewhat unorthodox. For the engagement, patience, and good humor of our authors, we are grateful. Others we want to thank include graduate student researcher Geneviève Payne, who formatted the essays, Miranda Thirkettle, who coordinated the project at Routledge, and Lisa Williams, who copyedited the manuscript for Routledge. And a big "thank-you" to Gerhard Boomgaarden, Routledge's senior sociology commissioning editor, without whom the *Handbook* would not exist. Gerhard arranged for Routledge to provide the financial support to complete the project, and he respected our intellectual vision of what the *Handbook* should be. Finally, we editors acknowledge one another for the contributions each has made. None of us would have wanted to undertake this project alone, and we all feel that the *Handbook* is stronger for our collaboration. While John spearheaded the project and acted as the frontman with Routledge, all three of us participated equally in discussions that defined the project and carried it forward, we each worked as "lead" editor with approximately one-third of the contributors, and we shared in the editorial review of all the chapters. In short, editing the *Handbook* was very much a collective effort and we supported each other along the way. If we did not exactly achieve a state of "collective effervescence" during the course of our many meetings, we came pretty close.

Chapter 2 Tony Bennett's essay incorporates and elaborates upon text from "Making Culture, Changing Society", *Cultural Studies Vol. 21. Issue 4*, January 2007, reprinted with permission of the publisher, Taylor & Francis Group Ltd.

Chapter 15 Gene Ray's essay incorporates and substantially amplifies for the current volume parts of a text published as "History, sublime, terror: notes on the politics of fear" (Ray 2008). The author thanks John Hall for his skilful help with these alterations.

Chapter 45 Susan Silbey's essay incorporates and elaborates upon text from "After Legal Consciousness", *Annual Review of Law and Society Science*, 2005, with permission of The Annual Reviews, Palo Alto, California; and "Legal Culture and Consciousness", from the *International Encyclopedia of the Social and Behavioural Sciences*, 2001, with permission of Elsevier Science, Ltd.

Contributors

Jeffrey C. Alexander is the Lillian Chavenson Saden Professor of Sociology and a Director of the Center for Cultural Sociology at Yale. Among his recent publications are *The Civil Sphere* (2006), *Social Performances: Symbolic Action, Cultural Pragmatics, and Ritual* (with Giesen and Mast, 2006), *Interpreting the Holocaust: A Debate* (2009), and *The Performance of Politics: Obama's Victory and the Democratic Struggle for Power* (2010).

Victoria D. Alexander is Senior Lecturer in the Sociology Department at the University of Surrey. She has authored *Sociology of the Arts: Exploring Fine and Popular Forms* and *Museums and Money: The Impact of Funding on Exhibitions, Scholarship and Management*, and co-authored *Art and the State: The Visual Arts in Comparative Perspective* (with Marilyn Rueschemeyer). Her research interests include sociology of art and culture, organizational sociology, and mixed methods.

Sarah S. Amsler is Lecturer in Sociology at Aston University. She is author of *The Politics of Knowledge in Central Asia: Science between Marx and the Market* (Routledge, 2007) and various articles on cultural power, knowledge and social action, and education and everyday life. She is currently working on a project about the cultural politics of hope.

Divya Anand recently completed her Ph.D. in English and Sociology at La Trobe University, Melbourne, Australia. Her thesis was entitled "Re-imagining Nations and Rethinking Nature: Contemporary Eco-Political Controversies in India and Australia." She has completed her Masters of English Literature from the University of Kerala and Master of Philosophy from Jawaharlal Nehru University, New Delhi. She has also worked in the media and publishing fields in India and now resides in Chicago.

Marshall Battani is Associate Professor and Chair of Sociology at Grand Valley State University, Michigan. He teaches the sociology of art and has published articles on photography and cultural social theory. He is co-author of *Sociology on Culture* (2003).

Zygmunt Bauman is Emeritus Professor of Sociology, University of Leeds. His latest book publications are *Living on Borrowed Times* (2009) and *44 Letters from the Liquid Modern World* (2010).

Peter Beilharz is Professor of Sociology and Director of the *Thesis Eleven* Centre at La Trobe University, Australia. He is author or editor of twenty-three books, including books on Zygmunt Bauman and Bernard Smith, modernity and the postmodern, and, most recently, on socialism and modernity.

Tony Bennett is Research Professor in Social and Cultural Theory in the Centre for Cultural Research at the University of Western Sydney. He has published extensively in literary and aesthetic theory, cultural studies, museology, and cultural sociology. His most recent publications are *Critical Trajectories: Culture, Society, Intellectuals* (2007) and *Culture, Class, Distinction* (2009, with Mike Savage, Elizabeth Silva, Alan Warde, Modesto Gayo-Cal, and David Wright).

Denise D. Bielby is Professor of Sociology at the University of California, Santa Barbara, and holds affiliated appointments in the Department of Film and Media Studies and the Center for Film, Television and New Media. Her latest book is *Global TV: Exporting Television and Culture in the World Market* (NYU Press, 2008), with C. Lee Harrington.

Sam Binkley is Associate Professor of Sociology at Emerson College, Boston. He has published articles on the social production of subjectivity in varied contexts, from the lifestyle movements of the 1970s to contemporary anti-consumerist movements. His current work examines therapy and the happiness imperative through the lens of neoliberal governmentality. He is co-editor of *Foucault Studies*, and author of *Getting Loose: Lifestyle Consumption in the 1970s* (Duke University Press, 2007).

Nick Couldry is Professor of Media and Communications at Goldsmiths, University of London. He is the author or editor of nine books, including *Media Events in a Global Age* (2009, coedited with Andreas Hepp and Friedrich Krotz), *Media Consumption and Public Engagement* (2010, with Sonia Livingstone and Tim Markham), and *Why Voice Matters: Culture and Politics after Neoliberalism* (Sage, 2010).

Maxine Leeds Craig is Associate Professor of Women and Gender Studies at the University of California–Davis. Her latest research examines masculinities in the context of popular dance. She is the author of *Ain't I a Beauty Queen: Black Women, Beauty and the Politics of Race* (Oxford University Press, 2002).

Nina Eliasoph teaches in the Department of Sociology at the University of Southern California. She is the author of two books—*Avoiding Politics: How Americans Produce Apathy in Everyday Life* (Cambridge University Press, 1998), and *Empowerment Projects: How Good Ideas Turn Inside Out in Youth Volunteer Programs* (Princeton University Press, forthcoming 2010)—and numerous articles on political and civic participation.

Yen Le Espiritu is currently Professor and Chair of Ethnic Studies at the University of California, San Diego. Her latest book, *Home Bound: Filipino American Lives Across Cultures, Communities, and Countries* (University of California Press, 2003), received two national book awards. Her current research projects explore public and private "rememoration" of the Vietnam War and Vietnamese and Vietnamese American transnational lives.

Donald Fels is a visual artist and has been making art about trade since the 1980s. A Fulbright Fellow to Italy and a Fulbright Senior Research Scholar to India, Fels continues to theorize about and make visible the relationship between the exchange of goods, ideas, and culture around the world. He lectures at the University of Washington. Visit: www.artisthinker.com.

Gary Alan Fine is John Evans Professor of Sociology at Northwestern University. He has conducted a range of ethnographic research projects, including studies of Little League baseball, restaurant cooks, mushroom collectors, chess players, and professional meteorologists. He examines the development of small group cultures or "idiocultures" as they shape social interaction.

Carla Freeman is Winship Distinguished Research Professor of Anthropology and Women's Studies at Emory University. She is the author of *High Tech and High Heels in the Global Economy: Women, Work, and Pink Collar Identities in the Caribbean* (Duke University Press), a forthcoming book, *Neoliberal Respectability: Entrepreneurship and the Making of a New Caribbean Middle Class*, and numerous articles on the gender of globalization.

Joshua Gamson is Professor of Sociology at the University of San Francisco. He is the author of *Claims to Fame: Celebrity in Contemporary America, Freaks Talk Back: Tabloid Talk Shows and Sexual Nonconformity*, and *The Fabulous Sylvester*, winner of the Stonewall Book Award. He has received awards from the Speech Communication Association and the American Sociological Association. In 2009 he received a Guggenheim Fellowship.

David Gartman is Professor of Sociology at the University of South Alabama, where he teaches and researches in the areas of theory, culture, art, and architecture. He is the author of *Auto Opium: A Social History of American Automobile Design*, as well as, most recently, *From Autos to Architecture: Fordism and Architectural Aesthetics in the Twentieth Century*.

Jeffrey C. Goldfarb is the Michael E. Gellert Professor of Sociology at the New School for Social Research. He is the author of numerous books and articles, including *The Cynical Society: The Culture of Politics and the Politics of Culture in American Life*, *The Politics of Small Things: The Power of the Powerless in Dark Times*, and the forthcoming *Re-inventing Political Culture: The Culture of Power versus the Power of Culture*.

Mary-Jo DelVecchio Good is Professor of Social Medicine, Departments of Global Health and Social Medicine, Harvard Medical School and Sociology, Harvard University. She edited *Culture, Medicine, and Psychiatry*, with Byron Good, from 1986–2004. Her publications include *American Medicine, the Quest for Competence* (1995), "The Biotechnical Embrace" (2001), "The Culture of Medicine and Racial, Ethnic and Class Disparities in Healthcare" (2003), and *Postcolonial Disorders* (2008).

Philip Gorski is Professor of Sociology and Religious Studies at Yale University and Co-Director of the Center for Comparative Research and the MacMillan Initiative on Religion, Politics and Society. He is currently completing a book entitled *The Fall and Rise of American Civil Religion: From John Winthrop to Barack Obama*.

Kevin Fox Gotham is Professor of Sociology at Tulane University. His research focuses on the sociology of disasters, the political economy of tourism, and real estate and housing policy. He is author of *Authentic New Orleans: Race, Culture, and Tourism in the Big Easy* (New York University Press, 2007) and *Race, Real Estate, and Uneven Development* (SUNY, 2002).

David Grazian is Associate Professor of Sociology at the University of Pennsylvania. His work examines the public life of cities, with an emphasis on the production and consumption of urban entertainment and popular culture. He is the author of *Blue Chicago: The Search for Authenticity in Urban Blues Clubs* (2003), *On the Make: The Hustle of Urban Nightlife* (2008), and *Mix It Up: Popular Culture, Mass Media, and Society* (2010).

Liah Greenfeld is a University Professor, Professor of Sociology, Political Science, and Anthropology, and Director of the Institute for the Advancement of the Social Sciences at Boston University. She is the author of numerous publications on nationalism and on modern culture more generally, including the sequence *Nationalism: Five Roads to Modernity* (1992) and *The Spirit of Capitalism: Nationalism and Economic Growth* (2001).

Gary Gregg received a Ph.D. in personality psychology from the University of Michigan; he conducted five years' ethnographic fieldwork and a life-history study of identity in southern Morocco. Currently Professor of Psychology at Kalamazoo College, he is the author of *Self-Representation, The Middle East: A Cultural Psychology*, and *Culture and Identity in a Muslim Society*.

Laura Grindstaff is Associate Professor of Sociology and director of the Consortium for Women and Research at the University of California–Davis. She is the author of the award-winning *Money Shot: Trash, Class, and the Making of TV Talk Shows* (University of Chicago Press, 2002) and has published articles on various aspects of popular culture from reality programming to cheerleading.

Yifat Gutman is a Ph.D. Candidate in Sociology at the New School for Social Research. She is author of "Where Do We Go from Here: The Pasts, Presents and Futures of Ground Zero" (Memory Studies, 2009), and the forthcoming "Past before Future: Memory Activism in Israel" (working title). She is co-editor of *Memory and the Future: Transnational Politics, Ethics, and Society* (with Adam Brown and Amy Sodaro, forthcoming).

John R. Hall is Professor of Sociology at the University of California–Davis. His published works include *Apocalypse: From Antiquity to the Empire of Modernity* (Polity, 2009), *Visual Worlds* (Routledge, 2005, with co-editors), *Sociology on Culture* (Routledge, 2003, with co-authors), and *Cultures of Inquiry* (Cambridge University Press, 1999).

David Halle is Professor of Sociology at the University of California, Los Angeles. His books include *The Structure of Contemporary Art: A Global and Local Perspective via Chelsea, New York's Newest Dominant Gallery District* (University of Chicago Press, forthcoming), *New York & Los Angeles: Politics, Society and Culture* (Chicago, 2003), and *Inside Culture: Art and Class in the American Home* (Chicago, 1994).

Karen Bettez Halnon is Associate Professor of Sociology at Pennsylvania State University. She has researched heavy metal carnival culture, 420 marijuana smoker culture, stigma experiences, and is recently focused on the popular phenomenon known as "Poor Chic." In her work she explores multiple modalities of stratification, including segregation, gentrification, objectification, stigmatization, and carnivalization.

Gary G. Hamilton is a Professor of Sociology and of International Studies at the University of Washington. He specializes in historical/comparative sociology, economic and organizational sociology, and Asian societies. He is an author of numerous articles and books, including most recently *Commerce and Capitalism in Chinese Societies* (2006) and *The Market Makers: How Retailers Are Changing the Global Economy* (2010, co-edited with Misha Petrovic and Benjamin Senaur).

Martin Hand is an Assistant Professor in the Department of Sociology at Queen's University, Canada. He is the author of *Making Digital Cultures: Access, Interactivity and Authenticity* (Ashgate, 2008), co-author of *The Design of Everyday Life* (Berg, 2007), and is currently completing a book titled *Ubiquitous Photography*, to be published in 2011.

Seth Hannah is a Ph.D. candidate in the Department of Sociology at Harvard University. His awards include a NIMH Pre-doctoral Fellowship in the Department of Global Health and Social Medicine at Harvard Medical School and a Fellowship in the Multidisciplinary Program in Inequality and Social Policy at Harvard Kennedy School. Seth is completing a dissertation on culture in contemporary American psychiatry.

Nancy Weiss Hanrahan is an Associate Professor of Sociology at George Mason University, the author of *Difference in Time: A Critical Theory of Culture* (2000) and co-editor of *The Blackwell Companion to the Sociology of Culture* (2005). Her current research explores the consequences of the restructuring of the music industry and the new "media democracy" for jazz and popular music criticism.

Kirsten Henderson recently received her Ph.D. from La Trobe University, Australia. Her thesis is entitled "Rethinking the Politics of Water in Australia." She now works for the Australian Government Murray Darling Basin Authority developing a plan for the sustainable management of the Basin's water resources. Her research interests include social theory, and environmental, cultural, and rural sociology.

Ben Highmore is Reader in Media and Cultural Studies at the University of Sussex. He is the author of *Everyday Life and Cultural Theory, Cityscapes: Cultural Readings in the Material and Symbolic City, Michel de Certeau: Analysing Culture*, and *A Passion for Cultural Studies*. He also edited *The Everyday Life Reader* and *The Design Culture Reader*.

Trevor Hogan teaches in sociology at the School of Social Sciences, La Trobe University (Australia), where he is Director of the Philippines–Australia Studies Centre and Deputy Director of the *Thesis Eleven* Centre for Cultural Sociology. He is a co-ordinating editor of *Thesis Eleven: Critical Theory and Historical Sociology* (London, New Delhi, Thousand Oaks, CA: Sage). He writes on social theory, history of ideas, and cities.

Ronald N. Jacobs is Associate Professor of Sociology at the University at Albany, State University of New York. His research focuses on culture, media, and the public sphere. His current work is concentrated in two areas: (1) a study of media intellectuals and the social space of opinion; and (2) a study of entertainment media and the aesthetic public sphere.

Elihu Katz is Distinguished Trustee Professor of Communication at the Annenberg School of the University of Pennsylvania. He is Professor Emeritus of Sociology and Communication at the Hebrew University of Jerusalem, and former director of the Israel Institute of Applied Social Research. His most recent book is *The End of Television?* (edited with Paddy Scannell). He holds honorary degrees from six universities, and is winner of the McLuhan Prize of Canadian UNESCO, the Israel Prize, and the Ogburn Career Award of the American Sociological Association.

Rebecca Chiyoko King-O'Riain is Senior Lecturer in the Department of Sociology at the National University of Ireland, Maynooth. She has published in *Ethnicities*, *Sociology Compass*, *Journal of Asian American Studies*, and *Amerasia Journal*. Her most recent book is *Pure Beauty: Judging Race in Japanese-American Beauty Pageants* (2006).

Pei-Chia Lan is Associate Professor of Sociology at National Taiwan University. Her fields of specialty include gender, work, and migration. She is the author of *Global Cinderellas: Migrant Domestics and Newly Rich Employers in Taiwan*, which won the 2007 Distinguished Book Award from the Sex and Gender Section of the American Sociological Association.

Robin Leidner is Associate Professor of Sociology at the University of Pennsylvania and her scholarship focuses on the sociology of work and of gender. She is the author of *Fast Food, Fast Talk: Service Work and the Routinization of Everyday Life*. Her current research is on work and identity in theater.

Paul Lichterman is Professor of Sociology and Religion at the University of Southern California. A cultural sociologist and ethnographer, he has studied a variety of civic and political associations. Currently he is exploring how different styles of advocacy cultivate different definitions of housing and homelessness as social issues. Previously he was Associate Professor of Sociology at the University of Wisconsin-Madison.

Omar Lizardo is an Assistant Professor in the Department of Sociology at University of Notre Dame. His primary research interests are the sociology of culture and globalization, the sociology of knowledge, sociological theory, and organizational analysis.

Ming-Cheng Lo is Associate Professor of Sociology at the University of California–Davis. She is the author of *Doctors within Borders: Profession, Ethnicity and Modernity in Colonial Taiwan* (University of California Press, 2002). She has published articles on two broad topics: the cultural processes in non-Western civil societies, and medical encounters across cultural boundaries.

Kevin McElmurry is Assistant Professor in the Department of Sociology and Anthropology at Indiana University Northwest. He recently completed a Ph.D. dissertation entitled "Alone/Together: The Production of Religious Culture in a Church for the Unchurched." His areas of research include religion, gender, and media culture.

Scott McQuire is Associate Professor and Reader in the Media and Communication Program at the University of Melbourne. He has a strong interest in interdisciplinary research linking the fields of new media, urbanism, and social theory. His most recent book, *The Media City: Media, Architecture and Urban Space* (Sage/TCS, 2008) won the Urban Communication Foundation's 2009 Jane Jacobs Publication Award.

Eric Malczewski is on the teaching faculty in Social Studies and serves on the Committee on Degrees in Social Studies at Harvard University. He is also a member of the Institute for the Advancement of the Social Sciences at Boston University.

Joshua Meyrowitz is Professor of Communication at the University of New Hampshire, where he has won the Lindberg Award for Outstanding Scholar-Teacher in the College of Liberal Arts. He is the author of *No Sense of Place: The Impact of Electronic Media on Social Behavior* (Oxford University Press) and scores of journal articles and book chapters on media and society.

Murray Milner, Jr. is Senior Fellow, Institute for Advanced Studies in Culture, and Professor Emeritus of Sociology, University of Virginia. He is author of *The Illusion of Equality*, *Unequal Care*, *Status and Sacredness*, and *Freaks, Geeks, and Cool Kids*. His recent work focuses on the operation of status systems and he is currently completing a book on teenagers in India.

John W. Mohr is Professor of Sociology at the University of California, Santa Barbara. He is co-editor of *Matters of Culture* (2004, with Roger Friedland) and author of a number of articles concerned with the use of formal models in cultural analysis, the history of the welfare state, and the racial politics of affirmative action.

Vincent Mosco is Professor of Sociology and Canada Research Chair in Communication and Society, Queen's University, Canada. His most recent books include *The Political Economy of Communication*, second edition (2009), *The Laboring of Communication* (2008, with Catherine McKercher), and *Knowledge Workers in the Information Society* (2007, co-edited with Catherine McKercher).

Mary Jo Neitz is Professor of Women's and Gender Studies at the University of Missouri in Columbia, Missouri. She is the author of *Sociology on Culture*, with John R. Hall and Marshall Battani. Her main areas of research are religion, gender, and culture.

Jeffrey K. Olick is Professor of Sociology and History at the University of Virginia. His books include *The Politics of Regret: On Collective Memory and Historical Responsibility* (Routledge, 2007), and (with Andrew Perrin) a translation and critical edition of writings of Theodor W. Adorno, called *Guilt and Defense: On the Legacies of Fascism in Postwar Germany* (Harvard, 2010).

Jackie Orr is Associate Professor of Sociology at Syracuse University. She teaches and writes in the fields of cultural politics, contemporary theory, and critical studies of technoscience. She is the author of *Panic Diaries: A Genealogy of Panic Disorder* (Duke University Press, 2006), and practices "performance theory" as a way to re-invent sociology as a form of public culture.

Eileen M. Otis is Assistant Professor of Sociology at the University of Oregon. She has served as Assistant Professor at SUNY Stony Brook and postdoctoral fellow at Harvard University. Her research is published in the *American Sociological Review*, *Politics and Society*, and the *American Behavioral Scientist*. She is currently researching retail labor in two Walmart outlets in China.

Orlando Patterson, a historical and cultural sociologist, is John Cowles Professor of Sociology at Harvard University. His empirical works include the comparative study of ethno-racial inequality, slavery, and other forms of domination, as well as the culture and practice of freedom, democracy, and movements toward equality. He is the author of numerous papers and five books, including *Slavery and Social Death* (Harvard University Press, 1982), *Freedom in the Making of Western Culture* (Basic Books, 1991), *The Ordeal of Integration* (Civitas/Basic Books, 1998), and *Rituals of Blood: Consequences of Slavery in Two American Centuries* (Civitas/Basic Books, 1998).

Francesca Polletta is Professor of Sociology at University of California, Irvine. She studies social movements, storytelling, and experiments in radical democracy. She is the author of *It Was Like a Fever: Storytelling in Protest and Politics* (2006) and *Freedom is an Endless Meeting: Democracy in American Social Movements* (2002). She is also editor, with Jeff Goodwin and James Jasper, of *Passionate Politics: Emotions and Social Movements* (2001).

Mark Poster is a member of the Film and Media Studies Department and of the History Department at the University of California, Irvine, with a courtesy appointment in Comparative Literature. He is a member of the Critical Theory Institute, and his recent books include *Information Please: Culture and Politics in a Digital Age* (2006), *What's the Matter with the Internet? A Critical Theory of Cyberspace* (2001), and *The Information Subject in Critical Voices Series* (2001). He is Emeritus Professor as of 2009.

Alex Preda is Reader in Sociology at the University of Edinburgh. He is the author of, among other books, *Framing Finance: The Boundaries of Markets and Modern Capitalism* (University of Chicago Press, 2009) and *Information, Knowledge, and Economic Life: An Introduction to the Sociology of Markets* (Oxford University Press, 2009).

Nick Prior is Senior Lecturer in Sociology at the University of Edinburgh. His current research is on the impact of digital technologies on post-1980s popular music and on post-Bourdieuian conceptions of contemporary culture. He has published widely in the sociology of culture, including articles in the *British Journal of Sociology*, *Cultural Sociology, Space and Culture*, and *New Formations*.

Smitha Radhakrishnan is Assistant Professor of Sociology at Wellesley College. Her research interests lie at the intersection of gender, globalization, and nationalism. Radhakrishnan's most recent project examines the transnational class culture of Indian information technology (IT) professionals in India, the Silicon Valley, and South Africa.

Craig M. Rawlings is an Institute of Education Science (IES) postdoctoral fellow at Stanford University, where he is researching how faculty collaboration networks and organizational structures facilitate or inhibit academic knowledge innovation and diffusion processes. He received his Ph.D. in Sociology from the University of California, Santa Barbara in 2008.

Gene Ray is a critic and theorist living in Berlin. His published work targets the intersections of art and radical politics and has appeared in such journals as *Third Text*, *Left Curve*, and *Monthly Review*. He is the author of *Terror and the Sublime in Art and Critical Theory* (2005) and co-editor of *Art and Contemporary Critical Practice: Reinventing Institutional Critique* (2008).

Raka Ray is Sarah Kailath Chair of India Studies, Professor of Sociology and South and Southeast Asia Studies, and Chair of the Center for South Asia Studies at the University of California, Berkeley. Her areas of specialization are gender and feminist theory, domination and inequality, cultures of servitude, and social movements. Her publications include *Fields of Protest: Women's Movements in India* (1999), *Social Movements in India: Poverty, Power, and Politics* (2005, co-edited with Mary Katzenstein) and *Cultures of Servitude: Modernity, Domesticity and Class in India* (2009, with Seemin Qayum).

Kim Robinson is a doctoral candidate in sociology at the University of California, Los Angeles. She is currently writing her dissertation on globalization and community in emerging art worlds.

Hiro Saito is Assistant Professor in Sociology and a faculty member of the Center for Japanese Studies at the University of Hawaii, Manoa. His research examines cultural and political transformations of institutions of the nation-state, such as collective memory and education.

Barry Schwartz, Professor Emeritus of Sociology, University of Georgia, is author of several books and numerous articles. Since 1982, he has examined collective memory issues through his work on American presidents and in comparative studies of the United States, Germany, Japan, Korea, China, and ancient and modern Israel.

Susan S. Silbey is Leon and Anne Goldberg Professor of Sociology and Anthropology at MIT. Recent publications include *The Common Place of Law: Stories from Everyday Life* (1998, with P. Ewick), *In Litigation: Do the Haves Still Come out Ahead*

(2003, with H. Kritzer), *Law and Science* I, II (2008), and "Taming Prometheus: Talk about Safety and Culture" (2009).

Philip Smith is Associate Professor of Sociology at Yale University. For the past twenty years he has been an advocate of the Strong Program in Cultural Sociology. Recent books include *Why War?* (2005), *Punishment and Culture* (2008), and *Incivility: The Rude Stranger in Public* (2010, with T. Phillips and R. King).

Tammy Smith is Assistant Professor of Sociology at SUNY Stony Brook. Her research interests include the impact of war and displacement on social trust, historical narratives, gender inequalities, and the development of new formal institutions.

Ann Swidler is Professor of Sociology at the University of California, Berkeley. Her most recent book is *Talk of Love: How Culture Matters* (University of Chicago Press, 2001). Her current research explores how culture shapes institutions by analyzing global and local responses to the AIDS epidemic in sub-Saharan Africa.

Bryan S. Turner is concurrently the Alona Evans Distinguished Visiting Professor at Wellesley College (USA) and Professor of Social and Political Thought at the University of Western Sydney (Australia). He has edited the Routledge *International Handbook of Globalization Studies* (2009), the *New Blackwell Companion to Social Theory* (2009), and the *Cambridge Dictionary of Sociology* (2006). His current research is on globalization, religion, and youth cultures.

Robin Wagner-Pacifici is the Gil and Frank Mustin Professor of Sociology at Swarthmore College. She is the author of *The Art of Surrender: Decomposing Sovereignty at Conflict's End* and *Theorizing the Standoff: Contingency in Action*, winner of the 2001 American Sociological Association's Culture Section Best Book Award. Her work analyzes violent events and their mediations. An article on the "restlessness" of historical events is forthcoming (2010) in the *American Journal of Sociology*.

Suzanna Danuta Walters is Professor of Gender Studies at Indiana University and the author of numerous books and articles, including *All the Rage: The Story of Gay Visibility in America* (University of Chicago Press, 2001) and *Material Girls: Making Sense of Feminist Cultural Theory* (University of California Press, 1995).

Alan Warde is Professor of Sociology, University of Manchester, UK. His research interests include the sociology of consumption, particularly of food, and the sociology of culture. His publications include *Consumption, Food and Taste* (1997), *Eating Out* (2000, with Lydia Martens) and *Culture, Class, Distinction* (2009, with Tony Bennett *et al.*).

Daniel Winchester is a Ph.D. candidate in sociology at the University of Minnesota. His research agenda is broadly focused on better understanding the relations among human bodies, cultures, and forms of cognition and knowledge. His research on Muslim converts has appeared in the journal *Social Forces*.

David Wright works as an Assistant Professor in the Centre for Cultural Policy Studies at the University of Warwick, England. He has research interests in the sociology of taste, the cultural industries, and cultural policy. He is co-author of *Culture, Class, Distinction* (Routledge, 2009), a Bourdieu-inspired inquiry into the nature of cultural capital in contemporary Britain.

Xiaohong Xu is a Ph.D. candidate in sociology at Yale University. He is currently working on his dissertation, tentatively titled "Secularizing Revolutions? Remaking Moral Order in Revolutionary England and China," which compares moral reform movements in England and China.

Alford A. Young, Jr. is Arthur F. Thurnau Professor and Associate Professor of Sociology in the Center for Afro-American and African Studies at the University of Michigan. He has published *The Minds of Marginalized Black Men: Making Sense of Mobility, Opportunity, and Future Life Chances*, and co-authored *The Souls of W.E.B. Du Bois*.

Geneviève Zubrzycki is Associate Professor of Sociology at the University of Michigan. She's the author of *The Crosses of Auschwitz: Nationalism and Religion in Post-Communist Poland* (Chicago, 2006), which received three national book awards. Her research focuses on collective memory, commemoration, and the linkages between national identity and religion, as well as the role of symbols in national mythology. She is currently at work on a book on nationalism, religion, and secularism in Quebec.

Introduction

Culture, lifeworlds, and globalization

John R. Hall, Laura Grindstaff, and Ming-Cheng Lo

Let's start by considering some culture. In recent years, aided by the rise of the internet, the fascination with *animé* (animation) that started in Japanese *manga* (comics) has spread worldwide. Like many other forms of popular culture, *animé* generates interest ranging from casual engagement to organized fandom. But in Japan, a preoccupation with *animé* has intersected with another cultural reality—the difficulties that some adults have establishing friendships with people of the opposite sex. The convergence manifests in *moe*—intense imaginary relationships that some (typically male) Japanese establish with (typically female) *animé* characters. However, *moe* relationships are not always imaginary, private affairs. In one district of Tokyo, middle-aged men can be found carrying around body pillows with printed covers featuring full-size *animé* girls with their trademark doe eyes. One man, claiming to have been brought back from the brink of suicide by his 2-D relationships, touts the possibility of having more than one pillowcase and "dating around" (something he believes is discouraged in normal social life). Other men reportedly prefer 2-D over 3-D relationships because the former, unlike the latter, are "pure," unthreatening, and unconditional (Katayama 2009; http://www.anime-bliss.com/smf/index.php?action=printpage;topic=201.0).

In Japan and elsewhere, people will find elements both familiar and bizarre in *moe* culture; many will also no doubt be disturbed, just as people are variously disturbed by video games that supposedly blur fantasy and reality, by the popularity of staged "reality" television shows, or by the pursuit of status through lavish "lifestyle" purchases. Ultimately, what is considered normal, bizarre, fictive, or real is a cultural matter, and a socially constructed one—either on a broad public basis, in face-to-face social life, or both. As the anthropologist Clifford Geertz once wrote, people are animals "suspended in webs of significance" that they themselves spin (1973: 5).

Of course, how people spin "webs of significance" is culturally variable. Multiple social and cultural considerations shape the ethical, moral, and aesthetic sensibilities that yield perspectives on whether something appears strange, foreign, or bizarre. In particular, in a rapidly globalizing era, it is increasingly difficult to sustain the stereotypical assumption that such variations occur primarily along societal or national lines. Thus, the *moe* phenomenon may (for now) be localized among certain Japanese men, but we would be grossly mistaken to generalize it as characteristic of "Japanese society." By the opposite token, frustrations over love and romantic relationships are expressed in culturally diverse ways around the world. Although most of them do not involve dating one's pillowcase, we should not miss the widely shared social tension that underwrites alternative cultural expressions of frustration.

As the example of Japanese *moe* culture suggests, culture, social life, and social institutions are mutually implicated. Following any single strand of cultural analysis is likely to quickly open out into a broad set of considerations: of personal relationships, everyday life, economic institutions and their cultural bases, public etiquette, transnational differences, technology and culture, global diffusion, and more. The ways in which the social and cultural intersect and mutually constitute one another routinely connect lifeworlds and globalization. A specifically cultural sociology, as we editors envision it, takes up the challenge of understanding these analytic relationships. A cultural sociology, optimally, is sociology *tout court*.

A brief history of cultural sociology

Sociology is itself cultural, and triply so. First, the discipline has always involved cultural acts of social reflexivity, initially born of Enlightenment dreams confronting the possibilities and hard realities of the Industrial Revolution. Second, culture as an analytic issue can be found at the center of much classical and post-classical sociology—for example in Marx, Durkheim, Weber, Simmel, Veblen, Gramsci, Pareto, Mannheim, Horkheimer and Adorno, and Parsons. Third, although the nineteenth-century *Methodenstreit* (conflict over methods) in the social sciences will continue to be debated, there can no longer be any serious doubt concerning one contention in that debate: cultural meanings are fundamental to organization of the social and how it unfolds (Hall 1999: 10–11, 45–46).

Despite the importance of culture to the sociological enterprise, controversy about it has divided the discipline virtually from the beginning. Indeed, various sociological dismissals make the contemporary turn toward culture all the more striking. The antimonies evident during the high-modern epoch of sociology following World War II and the rapid eclipse of that epoch in the 1960s and 1970s are revealing. A wide variety of sociologists interested in social structure—including both positivists and marxists—when they discussed culture at all (typically by reference to ideas and values), dismissed it as ephemeral, lacking any robust role in social causation. Marxists were most emphatic, identifying an ideal "superstructure" as little more than a reflection of the material "base" of the society—constituted in the forces and relations that organize production. Differences between positivist and Marxist structuralist theories already suggest that the high moment of modernist sociology was not all of a piece. But there is more: even sociological approaches sympathetic to cultural analysis sometimes could have a dialectical tendency to undermine any project of cultural sociology. Thus, Durkheim's analysis of the transition from organic to mechanical solidarity might be read as a lament about the erosion of shared communitarian meanings binding people to the social order, and modern theorists of secularization made direct arguments about the declining importance of religion for public life, which left the status of the (e.g. Parsonian) idea of cultural values as an overarching societal subsystem in doubt.

Nor did the waning of the high modernist epoch of sociology eliminate antipathy to cultural analysis. Perhaps the most daring expression of a disinterested view was offered

2

by Theda Skocpol, who, in *States and Social Revolutions*, acknowledged that her hypotheses gave "short shrift" to any importance of revolutionary ideology in accounting for success of revolutions, because "Peasant goals in the French, Russian, and Chinese Revolutions were not intrinsically different from previous peasant aims in rebellions or riots" (1979: 114, original emphasis).

Yet those who would chart the emergence of cultural sociology could find stirrings long before Skocpol wrote her pithy dismissal. In the conventional division of academic labor before World War II, culture—whether understood as systems of ideas, meanings, and practices, or as material tools and products of human action—remained largely the purview of anthropologists. However, from World War II through 1970, as a perusal of Sociological Abstracts will show, things changed. Sociologists in Europe and North and South America were exploring the work of Thorstein Veblen, framing a sociology of comparative literature, studying issues of cultural relativity, and considering art, theater, radio, popular music, and the "jam session," as well as cultural aspects of individual consciousness, mass society, social and religious conflict, and even terror.

From the 1970s onward, to borrow Parsons's language, the differentiation of now conventional subfields—stratification, social movements, family, and so on—took place across the entire discipline of sociology. Following this pattern, the sociology of culture emerged as a distinct enterprise in the 1970s and 1980s, centered on questions about popular culture and high culture largely refracted in relation to conventional modern tropes of Culture (in a holistic sense), subcultures, and countercultures as relatively coherent packages; and increasingly focused on issues of the production of culture. But a puzzle remains. The big surprise was not that the sociology of culture, like other specialties, became a recognizable and increasingly coherent subfield, but that cultural issues began to permeate virtually all subfields of sociology, such that today people conventionally talk about a "cultural sociology"—that is, a general sociology that is cultural on every front, in every subdiscipline. How is it that cultural sociology has become so important so widely? There are both sociohistorical and intellectual shifts that help explain this development.

The sociohistorical shifts certainly include the broad transformation from a society organized along industrial lines to a society centrally ordered through a postindustrial logic. This shift created conditions in which leisure gained in importance relative to work, yielding an increased valuation to self-expression through cultural choices and practices, thus turbocharging sociological interest in the (often "popular") culture of everyday life.

Paralleling the socioeconomic shift, beginning in the late 1950s and more concertedly in the 1960s, eruptions of diverse, often broad-based, social and countercultural movements challenged the previously conventional assumption that culture could be viewed as a relatively coherent societal package. Both the anti-Vietnam War movement and civil-rights movements in the US and radical movements in Europe (France in 1968, for example) shifted away from strictly class-based issues. Moreover, emergent "new," non-classed-based social movements (e.g. concerned with gender, ethnicity, the environment) often focused not only on pursuit of political objectives but also on the construction of new cultural identities. The disruptions brought by such movements, including countermovements (for example of religious fundamentalism) unveiled the "arbitrary" and socially constructed character of previously conventional and taken-for-granted institutionalized cultural patterns. In short, under postindustrial conditions, cultural objects, practices, and processes arguably became more central to how the social works. Insofar as sociology is an empirical discipline, these shifts inspired new attention to culture as an object of sociological analysis.

As for intellectual developments, they subtend the essays in this handbook. In brief, a sociology that could be mapped fairly completely fifty years ago in relation to structural-functionalism, systems theory, quantitative empiricism, symbolic interactionism, and radical critique underwent an efflorescence that opened it up to wider intellectual currents. The consequences for cultural analysis in sociology became forged by appropriations of diverse approaches and thinkers—hermeneutics (e.g. Clifford Geertz, Paul Ricoeur), semiotics and symbolic structuralism (Ferdinand de Saussure, Claude Lévi-Strauss), phenomenology and social constructionism (Peter Berger and colleagues, and Dorothy Smith, all drawing on Alfred Schutz), poststructuralism (philosophically, Jacques Derrida; epistemologically and in a way that broke with all conventions while maintaining a program of substantive analysis, Michel Foucault), feminist theory and analysis (Judith Butler, Donna Haraway), and postcolonial theory (Franz Fanon, Edward Said, and, in a somewhat different vein, W.E.B. duBois).

These currents and their interminglings both threatened and at times enriched structural marxism and structuralist sociologies, but in the final analysis, historical events overwhelmed intellectual ones: the end of the Cold War spelled the end of any robust Marxist intellectual project. Arguably, this development sharpened the broad "cultural turn" that was by then already taking place. Because this turn occurred with near simultaneity across the human sciences, the importance of interdisciplinarity cannot be overstated: the cultural turn was both a cause and consequence of increasing dialogue across the social sciences and humanities. For cultural sociology and certain of its "sister fields" such as cultural history, cultural anthropology, and cultural studies, interdisciplinary dialogue was particularly fruitful.

Certain key developments carried inquiry along the cultural turn. One was what Lawrence Stone (1979) called a "revival of narrative." And with narrative came cultural history, itself something of a successor to the social history that in the 1950s and 1960s had begun to supplant grand metanarrative and political history. Amplifying this development, the cultural turn in the corridors of literary criticism and the humanities more generally encompassed a turn toward history, in the so-called "new historicism" championed by Stephen Greenblatt, and a turn toward social theory, in which Pierre Bourdieu gained a considerable following. The border crossings and poachings in all directions have proceeded apace ever since.

Given that the anthropological enterprise was fundamentally cultural from the beginning, the cultural turn there might seem a non-event. But just as empirical observation and structural analysis replaced armchair philosophizing during the early days of the discipline, feminist and postmodern critiques of objectivity challenged the modernist goal of theorizing case studies in relation to general social processes. Attention to the politics of meaning and representation, coupled with political critiques of asymmetrical power relations and exploitation of research subjects, has ushered in a more thoroughly "cultural" cultural anthropology, one increasingly concerned with the symbolic and ideological dimensions of both "objects" of inquiry and categories and modes of analysis. Similar concerns have informed the rise and development of cultural studies. From the emergence in the 1960s of the Birmingham School in Britain to current trends in post-colonial and queer scholarship both in the US and elsewhere, there has been an increasing recognition that social life is thoroughly constituted by language, subjectivity, and power.

This very brief account of the emergence of cultural sociology in relation to disciplines and interdisciplinarity can only serve as a placeholder marking complex developments detailed in the essays that follow. Nevertheless, the overall development is already clear: a fundamental shift has warranted the dramatic emergence of cultural sociology. "Culture," once theorized as a coherent system aligned (functionally or not) with a counterpart social system, no longer can be treated as a holistic "thing," but must instead be acknowledged to designate myriad socially produced, arranged, and employed symbolic and material aspects of the world that attain what coherence they might have in the invocations and practices of the social actors who develop or encounter them. The circumstance of intellectual ferment produced by this recognition warrants a cultural sociology that permeates every topic and issue of sociological analysis, and a cultural sociology elaborated in this way, by connecting culture directly and intimately to the social, has much to offer more widely.

The "Broad Program," the lifeworld, and globalization

Scholars routinely associate the turn from a "sociology of culture" to a "cultural sociology" with the "strong program" championed by Jeffrey Alexander and his colleagues. This account, however, takes too narrow a view of cultural sociology. We certainly would not gainsay the importance of the Strong Program: it is the subject of considerable discussion in the present volume. However, the many scholars who have embraced the turn toward a cultural sociology have sometimes formulated alternative analytic programs, and they have pursued diverse topics and questions subject to sociocultural analysis—in the study of work, emotions, the state, social movements, in short, in the widest range of social phenomena.

This handbook is thus based on a central thesis: the shift to cultural sociology encompasses more than any single program, and it is important precisely for its breadth. A "broad program" is necessary to constitute cultural sociology in a way that encourages controversy, debate, and research, and that speaks to scholars engaged in cultural analysis more widely. This Broad Program spans and connects two foci of analysis already before us in the example of *moe* culture discussed earlier—lifeworlds and globalization.

Most basically, a cultural sociology ought to be grounded in the analysis of everyday social life. As Georg Simmel recognized a century ago—and Charles Tilley (1984) reminded us more recently—"society" is not a thing. Instead, the social consists of networked relationships that develop through face-to-face and mediated interactions. All people live in the lifeworld—or, more accurately, in lifeworlds (plural)—where we enact our lives socially, episodically, in relation to other people. Taken seriously, this point has two implications. First, whatever the ways in which culture exists outside lifeworlds (an important topic in itself), culture that has any specifically sociological bearing would have to come into play within lifeworlds, that is, where "society" happens. Second, given the diversity of social phenomena that manifest in lifeworlds (work, leisure activities, bureaucracy, religion, markets, war, social movements, and so on), Simmel's (and our) concept of the social warrants the shift we have already described, to a cultural sociology concerned with all venues, processes, and meaningful activities of social life.

In itself, this broad tack does not settle the complex questions concerning (presumably myriad) relationships between cultural materials and lifeworldly manifestations. Nor does it presume either an essentialized lifeworld all of a piece or social lifeworlds that are

5

increasingly subordinated to "colonization" by a system (as Habermas 1987 argued). Rather, a cultural analysis suggests that lifeworlds, insofar as they are subject to systems of institutionalized practices, reflexively produce—through rules, laws, codes, and conventions of various sorts—whatever systematicity is to be found (Hall 2009: 127–28). In the Broad Program, and in the essays in this handbook, coming to understand the interdependent relationships between cultural practices, material culture, lifeworlds, and institutionalized systematicity is a central agenda.

Yet to fully consider how culture "happens" in lifeworlds, we must come to terms with the Eurocentric biases inherent in Western sociology. European economic, cultural, and political modernities developed in part through colonial expansions, yet sociology has largely failed to give adequate consideration to how colonial relationships have shaped its theorizations (Lo 2002; Steinmetz 2007). The early essentialized theorization of "the" lifeworld, for example, could have been produced only through sustained collective failure to account for difference in an intellectually honest way. Some early sociological writers unabashedly assumed the European self to be superior to the non-European others, describing the differences as based on the persistence of fading "tradition," thereby justifying their failure to take other viewpoints seriously. However, canonization as a process elided such racist overtones by largely disengaging scholarship from discussions about Europe's relationships with the colonies (Connell 1997). Western theorizations of the lifeworld in effect bracketed these difficult considerations (for an exception, see Berger *et al.* 1973). Similarly, the later Habermasian conceptualization of the public sphere—as desirable as it is in comparison to many alternative, explicitly oppressive theorizations—remains oblivious even to the existence of, to use the language of James Scott (1990), the "hidden transcripts" embedded in its conceptual framing.

Some four decades of feminist and postcolonial scholarship have pointed to the previously elided Western biases in sociological theory. Yet challenges remain, in relation to the lifeworld, the public sphere, and more generally. Chakrabarty poses the poignant question, "why can we [Third-World historians] not return the gaze?" (2000: 29). Why do non-Western scholars seem to have little option but to conceptualize their societies in theoretical terms generated by Europeans? To pursue the alternative—in Chakrabarty's vivid image, to "provincialize Europe"—does not involve celebrating cultural relativism. Rather, the task is to reveal the intricate connections, not only historically but also conceptually, between the multiple expressions of the "modern" and multiple expressions of the "traditional" (Eisenstadt 1999; Adams *et al.* 2005).

The West, however dominant it may be, does not define the only or even the dominant reference point in non-Western social lives. Recent scholarship offers a more nuanced picture of Western/non-Western interactions by attending on the one hand to global processes—sometimes of institutional isomorphism, sometimes not—and on the other, to local developments. Recent research on music ("world" music), visual culture (*animé*), the media (Bollywood), medical care (acupuncture), and many other topics explores the rise of non-Western centers of global cultural influence. This scholarship debunks the assumption that the West is the default center of forces of globalization.

Under multi-centric conditions, cultural sociologists need to ask new questions about cultural processes in relation to (increasingly globalized) lifeworlds. In a recent issue of the newsletter of the American Sociological Association Culture Section, Mark Jacobs put the issue concretely: "why is it so difficult for US and French sociologists to collaborate in studying 'culture'? Why do Brazilians read Gramsci differently than Europeans tend to? ... More generally, how do scholarly conceptions of culture differ, intersect, and

travel (or not) across national and regional borders?" (2009: 1) Underlying these important issues is the fundamental question that we must confront: is it possible for scholars to
conduct research without either using non-Western cases to service Western theories or
imposing Western conceptual categories—even revised and reflexive ones—on non-
Western cases? Taking this question seriously challenges us to move towards a dialogical
mode. In place of the Western hegemony over theories about the cultural and the social,
sociologists in the West need to engage with multiple non-Western gazes. In the present
handbook we have responded to these challenges by seeking participation by diverse
contributors, including especially those based outside the West, as well as Western
scholars whose works are in conversation with non-Western perspectives and cultural
phenomena. This endeavor is necessarily incomplete. To be published, an edited volume
reaches closure at some point prior to the total fulfillment of its goals. Yet the dialogue
will continue. We thus look forward to future conversations that we hope will further
encourage truly global approaches to cultural analysis.

Opening the handbook

If we have an overarching principle for the Routledge *Handbook of Cultural Sociology*, it is
the central importance of understanding lifeworlds in a global context. This emphasis
brings to the fore a variety of analytic issues about the relation of culture to diverse social
phenomena, ranging from the gendering of service work, through the ethics of consumption, to the politics of art and popular culture, and more. Rather than commission
fewer, longer essays on putatively central topics, we have chosen to inaugurate the Broad
Program by commissioning a larger number of somewhat shorter essays, thereby
increasing the range of participating authors. By bringing together established scholars
with emerging ones, by encouraging thematic connection and dialogue across essays, and
by acknowledging the importance of regional and international diversity to both cultural
practice and cultural analysis, we aim to widen the sociological conversation about
why and how culture matters in and around the world. We hope that the handbook
exemplifies the vitality and scope of discussion that we seek to encourage going forward.

Our effort to facilitate this discussion—revealed most obviously in our choice of topics
and authors but also in our organization of the sections and their relations to one
another—reflects many editorial discussions about how to structure and organize
the present volume. Because the essays discuss a wide array of overlapping phenomena,
there is no single "appropriate" ordering; indeed, the essays might have been displayed in
a hyperlinked sphere of network connections. But given that the essays exist in book
form, with its sequence of pages, we have chosen a single ordering, organizing the essays
in a series of ten thematic parts, and readers may fruitfully construct their own links
across topics. The first parts include essays that consider general programmatic, theoretical, and methodological topics, and then turn to issues of aesthetics, ethics, legitimacy,
and lifeworldy identities and performances. From these basic concerns, the section topics
shift to stratification and the production and consumption of culture. Subsequent parts
include essays concerning work and professions, political culture, and globalization *per se*.
The handbook concludes with a series of discussions of cultural processes and change.
In all cases, we asked authors to anchor their discussions in previous scholarship without
pursuing comprehensive reviews, and to take stock of emergent issues of importance.
We also encouraged them to engage with scholarship that either analyzes or has origins

outside the West, and, for all scholarship, to bring comparative cases and global processes into consideration where appropriate. The resulting handbook, with its diverse short essays, blurs genres: organized like a conventional handbook, it nevertheless covers topics in a way more encyclopedic.

We are indebted to various handbooks that precede and inform our approach. Lyn Spillman's (2002) *Cultural Sociology*, for example, is important not only for its representation of the field but also for its thoughtful discussions of how cultural sociology developed over time, and why the field differentiated as it did in response to various institutional pressures and disciplinary practices. Spillman employs the concept of meaning-making as her organizing principle, using it to connect cultural sociology's different analytic traditions—notably theoretical, institutional, and interactional/ethnographic—as well as contributors' different substantive foci. In a related vein, Jacobs and Hanrahan's (2005) *Blackwell Companion to the Sociology of Culture* employs aesthetics as a metaphor for understanding the operation of culture in society, and for holding in productive tension the various strands of cultural sociology as represented in their volume. For them, an aesthetic conception of culture highlights the ways in which culture mediates agency and structure, honoring difference while also facilitating social solidarity.

Both collections—and other scholarship as well—move sociological discussions beyond arguments about whether culture is derivative or autonomous—by insisting upon more complex, contradictory formulations in which culture is both the medium of everyday lived experience and the scaffolding on which institutions and systems emerge, cohere, and change. The authors contributing to the present handbook are in productive dialogue with this scholarship even as they expand the conversation. They address many different social manifestations with cultural aspects—discourses, identities, practices, material objects, systems, beliefs and values, and so on. Although this complexity makes the field of cultural sociology somewhat unwieldy, it also invites interdisciplinary cross-fertilization and disperses cultural authority. We do not presume to speak for our authors, but, for our part, we believe that this Broad Program of cultural sociology, connecting lifeworld and globality, is the basis on which both sociology and cultural analysis more generally can best proceed in the twenty-first century.

References

Adams, Julia, Clemens, Elisabeth, and Orloff, Ann. 2005. "Introduction: Social Theory, Modernity, and the Three Waves of Historical Sociology." Pp. 1–72 in Julia Adams, Elisabeth Clemens, and Ann Orloff, eds., *Remaking Modernity*. Durham, NC: Duke University Press.

Berger, Peter L., Berger, Brigitte, and Kellner, Hansfried. 1973. *The Homeless Mind: Modernization and Consciousness*. New York: Random House.

Chakrabarty, D. 2000. *Provincializing Europe: Postcolonial Thought and Historical Difference*. New Delhi: Oxford University Press.

Connell, R.W. 1997. "Why Is Classical Theory Classical?" *American Journal of Sociology* 102: 1511–57.

Eisenstadt, S.N. 1999. "Multiple Modernities in an Age of Globalization." *Canadian Journal of Sociology* 24: 283–95.

Geertz, Clifford. 1973. *The Interpretation of Cultures*. New York: Basic.

Habermas, Jürgen. 1987 (1981). *The Theory of Communicative Action*, Vol. 2: *Lifeworld and System*. Boston: Beacon Press.

Hall, John R. 1999. *Cultures of Inquiry From Epistemology to Discourse in Sociohistorical Research*. Cambridge: Cambridge University Press.

——. 2003. "Cultural History Is Dead (Long Live the Hydra)." Pp. 151–67 in Gerard Delanty and Engin Isin, eds., *Handbook for Historical Sociology*. Beverly Hills, CA: Sage.

——. 2009. *Apocalypse: From Antiquity to the Empire of Modernity*. Cambridge: Polity.

Jacobs, Mark. 2009. "Message from the Chair: Global Differences in Conceptualizing Culture." *Culture*, newsletter of the American Sociological Association Section on the Sociology of Culture 23(1): 1–3.

Jacobs, Mark D. and Hanrahan, Nancy Weiss. 2005. *The Blackwell Companion to the Sociology of Culture*. Malden, MA: Blackwell.

Katayama, Lisa. 2009. "Love in 2-D." *New York Times Magazine*. July 26: 19–21.

Lo, Ming-Cheng. 2002. *Doctors within Borders: Profession, Ethnicity, and Modernity in Colonial Taiwan*. Berkeley: University of California Press.

Scott, James. 1990. *Domination and the Arts of Resistance: Hidden Transcripts*. New Haven, CT: Yale University Press.

Skocpol, Theda. 1979. *States and Social Revolutions*. Cambridge: Cambridge University Press.

Spillman, Lyn. 2002. *Cultural Sociology*. Malden, MA: Blackwell.

Steinmetz, George. 2007. *The Devil's Handwriting: Precoloniality and the German Colonial State in Qingdao, Samoa, and Southwest Africa*. Chicago: University of Chicago Press.

Stone, Lawrence. 1979. "The Revival of Narrative: Reflections on a New Old History." *Past & Present* 85 (November): 3–24.

Tilly, Charles. 1984. *Big Structures, Large Processes, Huge Comparisons*. New York: Russell Sage Foundation.

Part I

Sociological programs of cultural analysis

The Strong Program

Origins, achievements, and prospects

Jeffrey C. Alexander and Philip Smith

The Strong Program is the most controversial advocate of the cultural turn in sociology. It is the least apologetic and ambiguous, the most transparent and ambitious. Yet, while proclaiming "without fear" that meaning really does count, the Strong Program is more than simply a powerful provocation. It is also a research program, along with a set of transposable modules—models, methods, and conceptual tools—that taken separately or together allow interpretation and explanation of the social world. With these it has relentlessly made the case for a switch from the "sociology of culture" towards a truly "cultural sociology."

The contours of this Strong Program were introduced some years ago in a polemic that underwent several iterations (Alexander 1996; Alexander and Smith 1998, 2001). Much water has passed under the bridge. The Strong Program has become the subject of special symposia, mini-conferences, journal articles, and textbook subheadings. We feel the time has now come for a more systematic accounting. Why was the emergence of the Strong Program regarded as significant? In what ways has it begun to deliver on its promises? What tasks remain?

Origins

As we see it the Strong Program is a major sociological carrier of the cultural turn, that sweeping arc of ideas that stretched over the latter part of the twentieth century. Wittgenstein's linguistic philosophy emerged in the 1940s and 1950s. The French structuralists and semioticians peaked in the 1950s and 1960s. The great cultural anthropologists Douglas, Turner, and Geertz wrote their most influential works from the mid-1960s to the early 1970s. These thinkers, assisted by selected texts from Durkheim and Weber, eventually provided the intellectual foundations for the Strong Program. None of this material was locked away in a vault marked "Top Secret." Why did it take twenty-five years for the implications of the cultural turn to be fully embraced in our discipline?

The answer lies in the peculiar intellectual history of the 1970s and 1980s. The revolt against Parsons in particular, and functionalism more widely, instigated a sharp turn away from culture as a valid mode of explanation. In the mid-1980s, things started to change, but the gesture towards culture in American sociology remained hesitant. Like a swimming lesson where the students stay in the shallow end, people wanted to talk about meaning but were unwilling to trust an elusive medium. They made certain their toes could still touch power, interests, and class, and all the other tiles at the bottom of the pool. Hence the growing influence during this period of the three big "weak programs" we identified in the initial Strong Program essay, those water wings and rubber rings that had been imported from Europe. Initially useful, such aids are eventually debilitating. Yet for all that, the writings of Bourdieu, Foucault, and the Birminghamers did serve the purpose of familiarizing a whole generation with new culturalist vocabularies. Challenging the tenor of mainstream American sociology, they also demonstrated the need for theoretically informed, non-empiricist explanations where concepts could play a stronger role than variables—a critique that was also anchored by the anti-cultural macro-historical sociologists like Mann and Tilly.

During this same period, there emerged from within American sociology influential middle-range nods to meaning that similarly revealed the uncertainties of this phase: John Meyer's neo-institutionalism, Ann Swidler's tool-kit theory, David Snow's "framing" concept, the work of Pete Peterson, Wendy Griswold, and others on the production of culture (for Strong Program critiques of such works, see Rambo and Chan 1990; Reed 2002; Eyerman and McCormick 2006). Even as these ambiguous programs emerged, however, there were important figures in American sociology who responded more deeply to the growing cultural fermentation outside it. We do not wish to make the Strong Program the only white knight in our tale. Viviana Zelizer's work, building on Durkheim and functionalism, looked to fundamentally challenge economic sociology's key assumptions by showing that pricing and exchange values are shaped by wider cultural codes. Robin Wagner-Pacifici began to engage in subtle reconstructions of political power and performance, using ideas from Victor Turner among others. Barry Schwartz probed issues of collective memory and national myth-making, stimulated by Halbwachs and Durkheim. Michele Lamont, inspired by Mary Douglas and Bourdieu, began a research program devoted to empirical studies of symbolic boundaries, an interest shared by Eviatar Zerubavel, who took off from cognitive psychology. We should also mention the "new cultural history," inside of which such figures as William Sewell Jr. and Lynn Hunt moved away from Tilly, walked over a bridge provided by Geertz, and in so doing enjoyed a major crossover influence in sociology. On the sociology side of the river, as early as 1987 John R. Hall's book on Jonestown was subtitled with the words "cultural history."

We must also acknowledge the longstanding and pervasive influence of ethnography and the Chicago School, as exemplified for example in the works of Howard Becker. For decades these approaches insisted that meaning is central to social life. To be sure, symbolic interactionism kept the torch burning during the darkest hours of abstract empiricism and quasi-materialist reductionism. We would suggest, however, that times have changed. By holding fast to the idea that concrete situations and interpersonal contacts are the building blocks of sociality, this tradition has never fully come to terms with the legacy of the more textual cultural turn—to understand that myth and meaning might structure and energize situations from above and without as well as from within and below (e.g. Fine *et al.* 2008).

As the 1990s unfolded, the pressure mounted. There began to be significant defections to cultural sociology from such theoretically minded Europeans as Ron Eyerman (2001) and Bernhard Giesen (2004), and such American mainstreamers as Roger Friedland (Friedland and Hecht 1996). To take one noted example, in the last years of his extra-ordinarily productive career Charles Tilly wrote books featuring words like "narrative" and "performance," describing these in Snow-like ways as powerful mobilizing devices. While such efforts seemed aimed more at co-opting rather cooperating with the cultural turn, they represented a tacit admission that the terms of debate had decisively changed.

Today the contemporary landscape looks very different from the one of the mid-1980s. This was when the first author of this essay and his then UCLA students first began Strong Program work. Twenty years ago, "cultural sociology" was regarded as an oxymoron, but now the term is a commonplace. This very ubiquity raises the question: How does the Strong Program distinguish itself from the work of its talented friends and fellow travelers, many of whom are, in fact, affiliated Faculty Fellows with the Yale Center for Cultural Sociology, the Strong Program's institutional base? What separates the Strong Program from that of Nina Eliasoph, Michele Lamont, Paul Lichterman, Margaret Somers, Lyn Spillman, Robin Wagner-Pacifici, Viviana Zelizer, George Steinmetz, Krishan Kumar, Mabel Berezin, Mustafa Emirbayer, John R. Hall, Richard Biernacki, Gary Alan Fine, and Julia Adams? All of these sociologists take meaning seriously too. Let us adumbrate some characteristics.

The Strong Program is a collective effort to put meaning center stage. By contrast with the model of the lone scholar working by candlelight, the Strong Program has the character of an intellectual social movement. Various scholars self-identify with the movement, and there is a sense of shared enterprise or common identity. It is, moreover, a movement with an increasingly global reach, e.g. with self-defined associates and/or partner centers in such places as Japan, Korea, Colombia, Hong Kong, Italy, Germany, Sweden, the Czech Republic, South Africa, and Australia. The creation of the Yale Center for Cultural Sociology in 2003 offered a symbolic home for this worldwide intellectual movement, with conferences and other gatherings. We see at least formal similarities here with other exercises in collective paradigm building, such as the Année Sociologique and the Vienna Circle. As Randall Collins has noted, such organized collective energy can often be effective in generating ideas and intellectual productivity.

The Strong Program is not field specific. Many contemporary cultural sociologists make contributions to a defined topic area. By contrast, the Strong Program orients itself towards sociology as a whole. Although individual studies are conducted in specific topic domains where the author has expertise, the major collective impetus is to change the sociological enterprise, to help create a new and different comprehension of social life. Such a radical ambition also marked the programs of Bourdieu, Foucault, and the Birmingham School, and it is also manifest by Randall Collins' interaction ritual theory today.

The Strong Program aims at explanation. Too much cultural work is theory of theory, history of theory, "compare and contrast" pseudo-theory, intervention, normative theory, or "readings" of meaning without long-term empirical investigation. By contrast, the Strong Program draws upon and reconstructs theory so as to engage in sociological explanation. The aim at the end of the day is to better understand the world, to know how society works and why certain outcomes eventuate.

Inside the Strong Program there is embedded a larger theory of modernity, a big picture behind all the individual studies. Inspired particularly by Durkheim's

15

religious sociology, but also by a cultural reading of Weber's political and institutional work, the Strong Program insists that social life is not fully or even mostly rational. It continues to be deeply meaningful, involves feelings about the sacred, good and evil, and has diffusely symbolic, theatrical, and often quasi-ritualistic qualities. For this reason, many Strong Program products set out to offer starkly alternative readings of presumed sites of instrumental rationality such as war, finance, punishment, or scientific information.

The Strong Program is omnivorous and promiscuous, looking far and wide for useful theories about culture, for concepts and exemplars. Others working in the field of culture (Wagner-Pacifici being a major exception) tend to pursue narrower agendas and drink mostly from one or two wells. Randall Collins, for example, uses Goffman to rework Durkheimian sociology, and Michele Lamont draws from Douglas and Bourdieu. The Strong Program incorporates the classical sociologies of Durkheim and Weber; the linguistic theories of Saussure and Jacobson; the literary theory of Northrop Frye, Peter Brooks, and Russian Formalism; the dramaturgic theory of Goffman and Schechner; the hermeneutics of Dilthey and Geertz; the anthropology of Turner and Douglas; the semiotics of Barthes and Lévi-Strauss; and more. Like recombinant DNA, these resources have generated continuous variations on the Strong Program's core mission, allowing evolutionary breakthroughs in models and research tools and allowing for generational or topic-specific adaptation.

The Strong Program has created new tools that allow generalization or create transposable theory: code, narrative, performance and so forth (we briefly describe these on pp. 16–19). While the ambition is not to construct a grand theory that explains everything from history to psychology, we confess a desire to move beyond intervention, relativism, and hyper-localism—hence an ambivalence about Geertz that might be surprising to some (Smith 2008b; Trondman 2008). In line with the Kuhnian model of the paradigm as an exemplar or concrete research strategy, the Strong Program has developed a series of middle-range theoretical concepts and models. These can be taken up and used by scholars in various local and topical settings. Modified and elaborated, new middle-range theorizing will be generated in turn.

Achievements

Doing cultural sociology is not as easy as it sometimes looks. Indeed, the late arrival of the cultural turn in sociology undoubtedly reflected the problem of translating resources from literary theory, philosophy, and anthropology into tractable idea-sets for explaining contemporary (and also historical) social life. This translation is necessary if we are to move beyond the impressionist hit-or-miss schools of esoteric, aesthetic, or impressionistic interpretation. We see the emergence and refinement of a range of middle-level resources over the past fifteen years as perhaps the single most important contribution to knowledge of the Strong Program. We set out below these research tools or paradigms.

Collective conscience, civil society and the mass media

Durkheim wrote many years ago about the collective conscience of a society. The idea is intuitively appealing, but also somewhat amorphous and plagued by metaphor.

Drawing from Habermas' ideas about the public sphere and rejecting his pessimistic conclusions, the Strong Program has argued since the late 1980s that we can see the collective conscience at work in a "civil sphere" (Alexander 2006). This is a place where the diffuse moral authority and pressure of public opinion are concretized and where the evaluation of actors and policies is made possible. With the civil sphere in mind, there can be a concerted effort to explore the public and observable speech acts through which claims are made, both in political and social movement arenas and in the mass media (Alexander and Jacobs 1998; Sherwood 1994).

Binary oppositions and the discourse of civil society

Binary opposition, of course, was a staple of the semiotic structuralism from Jacobson to Lévi-Strauss, Barthes, and Sahlins. A major step by the 1980s Strong Program pioneers was to understand public-sphere talk as shaped by strong binary logics. Emerging out of Alexander's Watergate research, we published studies about the "discourse of civil society" from the early 1990s. These offered a new way of reading politics (e.g. Alexander and Smith 1993; Smith 1991). Not only debate and public thinking but political action itself was shown to be organized around the codes through which sacred and profane motivations, relations, and institutions were defined and applied in a process of typification. President Nixon, for example, eventually came to be seen in terms of the negative side of the code (as secretive, emotive, non-rational, etc.) and was driven from office. While early critics suggested these civil codes were USA specific, Strong Program scholars have confirmed their distribution throughout liberal democracies (e.g. Smith 2005 for UK, Spain, and France) and in pro-democracy movements in less tolerant places (Baiocchi 2006 for Brazil, Ku 2001 for China). Further there have also been efforts to explore illiberal codes (fascism, authoritarianism, communism) and their relationship to this civil discourse (Baiocchi 2006; Edles 1998; Smith 1996b). Finally, the investigation of the binary opposition has by no means been restricted to political arenas. Strong Program members have identified them at work in more local institutional settings and lifeworld domains. The computer is coded by commentators as sacred or profane (Alexander 1992); concert performers are seen by their audiences as deeply musical or as robotic and shallow (McCormick 2009); in the men's movement any given masculinity can be read as regressive and hegemonic, or as sensitive and reformed (Magnuson 2008).

Narrative and genre

Binary oppositions are a critical intellectual tool but they do not exhaust the culture structures that form social life in a post-Geertzian world. To a certain extent they fail to capture fully the nuance and hermeneutic specificity of particular settings and struggles. Draft papers written by our members toward the end of the Cold War and during the build up to the Gulf War developed a model of narrative process in civil society (e.g. Sherwood 1994). The Strong Program argues that narratives, just like binary codes, circulate and are contested in the collective conscience/public sphere, and in this process can shape history. Watergate and Irangate, for example, are similar in that each involved an intensive deployment of the discourse of civil society, yet each also featured divergent efforts at storytelling. To understand the popular response to Watergate fully one needs to reconstruct the narrative that eventually became dominant: of the unshaven

Nixon and his "plumber" cronies engaging in secretive, un-American plotting in the White House. To account for the outcome of the Irangate scandal we would need to reconstruct the narrative of a patriotic Colonel Oliver North working with good intentions to help the "freedom fighters" in Central America.

Realizing that cognition is tied to storytelling, Strong Program members have developed two approaches to narrative. One is more inductive and historically embedded, even if it employs general theory of plot and character en passant. Thus Alexander (2002) demonstrates that the Holocaust was initially seen as a war crime and only later renarrated as universal evil. Eyerman (2001) traces continuous conflict between more optimistic and progressive narrations of slavery and more pessimistic and tragic ones in African-American history. The other approach is more ontological and Aristotelian, works more from the logic of culture structures, and has produced a more systematic model of narrative process. Jacobs (2000) and Smith (2005) employed Northrop Frye's theories of literary genre to show how powers of action, plot trajectories towards a happy society or its collapse, and other deep anxieties about future success vary systematically over a gamut of genre types (romance, tragedy, comedy, irony). These play out in predictable ways in struggles over legitimacy, authority, and reconciliation. Such models open the way towards a less idiographic mode of narrative inquiry, making a more systematic comparative cultural sociology possible. Tracking genres against outcomes, for example, Smith (2005) explains decisions in four nations as they encountered the same foreign policy crises, whereas Jacobs (2000) is able to predict the kinds of narrative that will accompany successful civic repair in a time of racial crisis.

Performance

A major problem of text-based approaches to culture is that agency tends to be squeezed out of the frame. Strong Program accounts of narrative and coding might leave us with a description of the distribution of signs and symbols relative to each other and to sponsors and constituencies, but not say enough about action patterns and projects. By developing a paradigm of social performance, the Strong Program has responded to this challenge by conceptualizing cultural pragmatics, thus building upon our more general understanding of political and social life as deeply dramatic. Ideas about performance were latent in our early studies that emphasized, as Wagner-Pacifici had already shown, liminal breaks in the political process, e.g. collective representations about "a new beginning" in the post-Franco era (Edles 1998). The work of Jacobs (2000) was still more explicit in the use of the "social drama" analogy for a city in crisis, as was Smith (1996a) in his account of the eighteenth-century public execution as a failed performance. Still, the main thrust of this early work was on the semiotics and narratology of the public sphere as reconstructed from texts, hence the subtitle of our original Strong Program essay— "Toward a Structural Hermeneutics." Today, there has been a change that, though at first glance slight, is rather significant, as this and the next two paradigms developed at Yale make clear.

Drawing on the philosophy of performativity, drama theory in the humanities, and the new discipline of performance studies, cultural pragmatics emerged in the early 2000s (Alexander *et al.* 2006) as a model that systematized formerly fleeting references. This new model provided a repertoire of transposable concepts—fusion/defusion/refusion, scripts and background representations, means of symbolic production, mise-en-scène, hermeneutical power—and showed how they could be employed in various settings to explain social dynamics. What separates the approach from the Goffmanian is not only its macro-orientation but its insistence that performances are oriented by and towards deep culture structures and myths, not only situational contingencies and interpersonal inter-action norms. This model has been especially effective in exploring political strategy and the ups and downs of political careers such as that of Bill Clinton (Mast 2006), various acts of political violence (Eyerman 2008), and the pivotal role of the Truth and Recon-ciliation Commission in South Africa (Goodman 2009), but it has also been turned back onto the arts themselves (Eyerman and McCormick 2006), even explaining how musi-cians communicate with audiences (McCormick 2009). Ideas about performativity also have enabled the return of a more Geertzian spirit of interpretation, allowing aesthetic play and historical locality (e.g. Reed 2007; Trondman 2008) to balance the structuralism that emanated from earlier, more text-based Strong Program writings.

Cultural trauma

The most problem-oriented paradigm of the Strong Program has focused on episodes of social trauma and their cultural reinterpretations (Alexander *et al.* 2004). The focus here is not on individual psychological process. Further, the approach takes aim at lay theories that view collective responses as rational or irrational adaptation. The spotlight, rather, is on meaning-work, how it orients painful experiences, constructs new collective iden-tities, defines moral responsibilities, and channels the course of future actions and events. Cultural trauma makes binaries about polluted others, even as it shapes narratives about past, present, and future confrontations between perpetrators and victims (Giesen 2004). These cultural processes are propelled by the ideal and material interests of carrier groups, powerfully mediated by the institutional field in which they unfold, and significantly affected by the existing distribution of vertical resources. So far, this trauma model has framed Strong Program investigations into war, genocide, mass murder, slavery, and political assassination.

Iconicity

A major challenge for cultural sociology lies in coming to terms with the non-discursive and non-verbal elements of social life. Evoking materiality, such aesthetic experience has primarily been approached by neo-Marxism. Materialist theories of commodification emphasize instrumental manipulation or posit that object meanings systemically reflect market processes and interests in oblique but generally shallow ways. Meanwhile "authentic" meanings from the lifeworld are taken to be a form of folk resistance to power. Introducing the idea of iconic consciousness (Alexander 2008), the Strong Pro-gram has most recently begun challenging the materialist vision, offering in its place a multidimensional vision of social materiality. We suggest how sensuous aesthetic surfaces remain powerful and how they are often experienced as seamlessly intertwined with the diverse social meanings or background scripts that establish an object's moral and intel-lectual depth. Often, we suggest, this process has very little to do with worldly power. Our ongoing work draws from less systematic earlier Strong Program surveys of the powerful meanings of visual culture (Emmison and Smith 2000), the iconic dimension of such punitive technologies as the guillotine and electric chair (Smith 2008a), and the sacral aura that inspires consumption and adheres to apparently mundane domestic objects (Alexander 1992; Woodward 2007).

19

Critiques and challenges

As the outspoken carrier of the cultural turn in sociology, the Strong Program has inevitably become subject to critique, increasingly so as its theorizing has so markedly extended into the middle range. One persistent charge has been idealism, an accusation that goes with the territory. This plaint turns out to have several dimensions: (1) we have an over-optimistic view of human nature; (2) we neglect strategic action by elites; (3) we fail to see that civil society is weak (Cutler 2006); (4) we ignore the situational interactions of concrete actors and groups in favor of a meta-discourse which goes about its business in a transcendental quasi-Hegelian way (Battani *et al.* 1997; Fine *et al.* 2008; Morris 2007); (5) we have little to say about the material bases of inequality or social life and should connect culture back to such foundations (Antonio 2007; Gartman 2007; McLennan 2004, 2005); and finally (6) we are anti-scientific, espousing a culturalist and anti-positivist relativism where interpretation replaces explanation (Boudon 2007; Steensland 2009), or more charitably we can't really explain why some meanings and performances stick and others don't (Emirbayer 2004; Kurasawa 2004).

Our critics have ignored our carefully worded caveats about power, interests, resources, and strategy, but they have pointed to real issues of balance, emphasis, and relative neglect. While there is not space to mount a protracted defense against these charges, we would maintain that Strong Program work has never departed from a multidimensional understanding of social life; that we do not assume real-world autonomy for culture structures just because we give them analytic autonomy (Kane 1992); that action can be fully strategic—but of course must still have due reference to meaning systems (Smith 2005); and that hermeneutical reconstruction need not abandon objectivity and efforts towards rational knowledge formation (Reed 2007). We add that pretty much every Strong Program exploration has been about struggles over meaning, not consensus. Indeed, power itself has become the object of intense examination, as something that energizes and directs, even as it is channeled by, cultural perceptions of geopolitical threat (Smith 2005); as something that attempts to deploy meaning as it goes about the task of controlling deviance (Smith 2008a); as something that is augmented and challenged by the deft performance of ideology and "character" (Mast 2006); and as the cultural outcome of ferociously aggressive political struggles (Jacobs 2000; Alexander 2009). Even the fighting effectiveness of troops in battle, the most raw of all forms of power, has been comprehensively explained using Strong Program resources (Smith 2008c). The trick as we see it is to understand the subtle distinction between an explanation that is "all about culture" and one that is "just about culture" (Smith 2005: 26), a semantic nuance that our critics are often unable to comprehend but towards which we are acutely sensitive.

Whilst most critics seem to wish the Strong Program to be something other than what it is, or to have not read our work carefully, we see two barbs against the Strong Program as potentially quite productive. The argument that we are Hegelians has alerted us to the problems of text-based research. While the early work of the program was more desk-driven and media focused and so vulnerable in this way, the younger generation has largely taken a different tack. It has generated more ethnographic and interview-based studies, tracing the interaction between symbolic structures and interaction at the local level. Magnuson (2008) looks at shifts in the cultural structuring of masculinity through the lens of a five-year study of micro-interactions inside a men's group. McCormick (2009) explores the meaning-making of classical music competitions through participant observation and interviews at multiple sites. Brad West (2008) employs ethnographic observation and interviews to explore the relationship of sacred collective memory narratives with the embodied activity of battlefield tourism. It is important to note that such work differs from that of more conventional ethnography or the Chicago School. Although attention is given to the local and situated meanings generated by participants in settings, the Strong Program ethnographers understand these as emerging dialogically with wider public culture structures of the kind captured by terms like myth, code, or narrative (Trondman forthcoming). So people bring prior ideas about masculinity, music, or national identity with them to the interpersonal encounter. Their ideas are modified in encounters, but we insist, contra Herbert Blumer, they do not emerge solely from the crucible of personal influence, group dynamics, or interaction ritual. The relationship is dialogical.

A second useful and somewhat fair critique has come from our fellow travelers who have conjured the specter of indeterminacy (Emirbayer 2004; Kurasawa 2004). This is a particularly sensitive issue for a cultural approach that aims to produce transposable and abstract models, that has ambitions to be a social science. Strong Program arguments typically explain outcomes by pointing to the rise and fall of cultural patterns. An apocalyptic narrative dogged Saddam Hussein in 1992; unable to shake this off, the "new Hitler" was driven out of Kuwait (Smith 2005). Mast (2006) tracks both the major failures of Clinton's Presidency to his "slick Willy" shadow. Likewise Edles (1998) links the successful post-Franco Spanish democracy to the emergence of three powerful sets of new representations, and Jacobs (2000) accounts for civil renewal in Los Angeles with reference to an ascendant Romantic genre. But just why does one cultural structure succeed and another fail? Traditional sociology would answer this question with reference to material resources, to information control, to networks, or to interests or manipulative elites—things or people that we can point to and measure because they seem somehow more "real" (Reed 2007; cf. Cutler 2006). These are the familiar default positions of mainstream sociology, an apparent bedrock of ontological faith where we can stop asking questions about origins. We could sleep easy if only we would admit that the narrative that won was propagated by a dense network, or the binary that stuck was promoted by an influential interest group.

The truth is that the Strong Program has chosen a bed of nails. We have avoided the easy choice of referring the triumph of one meaning system or another back to something that seems more concrete, insisting instead that there can be cultural factors behind cultural outcomes. So far as we are concerned there should be some equivalence of standards. If it is acceptable to the discipline to tether a cultural structure to a social structure as an explanatory move, it should also be acceptable to tether it to another cultural structure or to a performance or icon. So our explanations have continued to refer to the flexibility, plausibility, appeal, adaptability, attractiveness, fit, or instability of a discourse, trope, or performance as well as to the resources upon which the circulation of meaning depends. The challenge, as we have seen it, is to avoid two fates as we make this move. One is the destiny of framing theory in the social movement literature. While we certainly agree with its claim that a movement succeeded if a frame "resonated," failed if it did not, the concept of resonance looks a bit like a giant black box for post hoc explanation. The second fate is that of Geertz, who simply threw up his hands as he insisted that "it is turtles all the way down." We agree that everything is constructed and that meanings rest upon meanings, but we want an approach that is more systematic in explaining this piling up, and that also finds ways to incorporate those turtles into conflict, power, and institutional life. So we rejected what sometimes seems like Geertz's analytic fatalism, which has led many of his readers to conclude that a simple textual description of a meaning complex or setting is sufficient as an explanation.

Yet showing how meanings systematically build on meanings can easily result in a culturally mechanistic mode of explanation. If the Strong Program is to retain a belief in the relative autonomy of meaning, then of course there has always to be recognition of a moment of contingency that escapes crude explanatory ambitions. This is the act of interpretation through which people come to make sense of their world. We hope that the ethnographic and interactional studies by the next generation, and more historical methods as well, might be able to shed more light on such moments where persuasion and meaning-making take place, effectively linking large-scale cultural systems, such as those of civil discourse, to embedded situational contexts. That said, our belief is equally that our theoretical tools, by systematically mapping the structures of cultural life, will allow us to give more precise reasons for failure and success than the more inductive and somewhat descriptive "framing" theory was able to do. The performance paradigm provides a complex yet at the same time simplified model of the moving parts of cultural effect, of communicative intention and audience response, of background tradition and foreground script, of situation and mise-en-scène, of power in the productive, distributive, but also hermeneutical sense. Our structural models of code and narrative permit faulty discursive moves and absent component parts in wider myths to be identified and explained. Our theories of iconicity, trauma and civil discourse are also now developing to the point where there are core findings and patterns and where productive analytic comparisons can be made.

The Strong Program has been cumulative; it is a progressive research program in the Lakatosian sense. The conditions are more propitious than ever before for explaining outcomes with culture—if not exclusively with it, then never without reference to it. At the end of the day, this is what the Strong Program is all about.

References

Alexander, J. 1992. "The Promise of a Cultural Sociology." Pp. 293–323 in R. Munch and N. Smelser, eds., *Theory of Culture*. Berkeley: University of California Press.

——. 1996. "Cultural Sociology or Sociology of Culture?" *Culture* 10(3–4): 1–5.

——. 2002. "On the Social Construction of Moral Universals." *European Journal of Social Theory* 5(1): 5–86.

——. 2006. *The Civil Sphere*. Oxford: Oxford University Press.

——. 2008. "Iconic Experience in Art and Life." *Theory, Culture and Society* 25: 3.

——. 2009. "The Democratic Struggle for Power: The 2008 Presidential Election in the United States." *Journal of Power* 2: 65–88.

Alexander, Jeffrey C. and Jacobs, Ronald N. 1998. "Mass Communication, Ritual, and Civil Society." Pp. 23–41 in T. Liebes and J. Curran, eds., *Media, Ritual, and Identity*. London: Routledge.

Alexander, J. and Smith, P. 1993. "The Discourse of American Civil Society: A New Proposal for Cultural Studies." *Theory and Society* 22(2): 151–207.

——. 1998. "Sociologie culturelle ou sociologie de la culture? Un Programme fort pour donner à sociologie son second souffle." *Sociologie et sociétés* 30(1): 107–16.

——. 2001. "The Strong Program in Cultural Sociology: Elements of a Structural Hermeneutics." Pp. 135–50 in J. Turner, ed., *Handbook of Sociological Theory*. New York: Springer.

Alexander, J., Sherwood, S., and Smith, P. 1993. "Risking Enchantment: Theory and Method in Cultural Studies." *Culture* 4(4): 10–14.

Alexander, J., Eyerman, R., Giesen, B., Smelser, N., and Stzompka, P. 2004. *Cultural Trauma*. Berkeley: University of California Press.

Alexander, J., Giesen, B., and Mast, J., eds. 2006. *Social Performance: Symbolic Action, Cultural Pragmatics and Ritual*. Cambridge: Cambridge University Press.

Antonio, Robert J. 2007. "Locating 'The Civil Sphere'." *Sociological Quarterly* 48(4): 601–14.

Baiocchi, G. 2006. "The Civilizing Force of Social Movements." *Sociological Theory* 24(4): 285–311.

Battani, M., Hall, R., and Powers, D. 1997. "Culture's Structures: Meaning Making in the Public Sphere." *Theory and Society* 26: 781–812.

Boudon, R. 2007. "Nouveau Durkheim? Vrai Durkheim?" *Durkheimian Studies* 12(1): 137–48.

Cutler, J. 2006. "War Cultures and Culture Wars." *Contexts* 5(3): 52–54.

De La Fuente, E. 2008. "The Art of Social Forms and the Social Forms of Art." *Sociological Theory* 26(4): 344–62.

Edles, L. 1998. *Symbol and Ritual in the New Spain*. Cambridge: Cambridge University Press.

Emirbayer, M. 2004. "The Alexander School of Cultural Sociology." *Thesis Eleven* 79(1): 5–15.

Emmison, M. and Smith, P. 2000. *Researching the Visual*. London: Sage.

Eyerman, R. 2001. *Cultural Trauma: Slavery and the Formation of African-American Identity*. Cambridge: Cambridge University Press.

——. 2008. *The Assassination of Theo Van Gogh*. Durham, NC: Duke University Press.

Eyerman, R. and McCormick, L. 2006. *Myth, Meaning and Performance*. Boulder, CO: Paradigm Press.

Fine, G.A., Harrington, B., and Segre, S. 2008. "Tiny Publics and Group Practice." *Sociologica* 1: 1–6.

Friedland, R. and Hecht, R. 1996. *To Rule Jerusalem*. Cambridge: Cambridge University Press.

Gartman, D. 2007. "The Strength of Weak Programs." *Theory and Society* 36(5): 381–413.

Giesen, B. 2004. *Triumph and Trauma*. Boulder, CO: Paradigm Press.

Goodman, T. 2009. *Staging Solidarity: Truth and Reconciliation in the New South Africa*. Boulder, CO: Paradigm Press.

Hall, John R. 1987. *Gone from the Promised Land: Jonestown in American Cultural History*. New York: Transaction Publishers.

Jacobs, R. 2000. *Race, Media and the Crisis of Civil Society*. Cambridge: Cambridge University Press.

Kane, A. 1992. "Cultural Analysis in Historical Sociology: The Analytic and Concrete Forms of the Autonomy of Culture." *Sociological Theory* 9(1): 53–69.

Ku, Agnes. 2001. "The Public Up Against the State." *Theory, Culture and Society* 18(1): 121–44.

Kurasawa, F. 2004. "Alexander and the Cultural Refounding of American Sociology." *Thesis Eleven* 79 (1): 53–64.

McCormick, L. 2009. "Higher, Louder, Faster." *Cultural Sociology* 3(1): 5–30.

McLennan, G. 2004. "Rationalizing Musicality: A Critique of Alexander's Strong Program in Cultural Sociology." *Thesis Eleven* 79(1): 75–86.

——. 2005. "The New American Cultural Sociology: An Appraisal." *Theory, Culture and Society* 22(6): 1–18.

Magnuson, E. 2008. *Changing Men, Transforming Culture*. Boulder, CO: Paradigm Publishers.

Mast, J. 2006. "The Cultural Pragmatics of Event-ness: The Clinton/Lewinsky Affair." Pp. 115–45 in J. Alexander, B. Giesen, and J. Mast, eds., *Social Performance: Symbolic Action, Cultural Pragmatics and Ritual*. Cambridge: Cambridge University Press.

Morris, A. 2007. "Naked Power and 'The Civil Sphere'." *Sociological Quarterly* 48(4): 615–28.

Rambo, E. and Chan, E. 1990. "Text, Structure, and Action in Cultural Sociology: A Commentary on 'Positive Objectivity'." In Wuthnow and Archer, *Theory and Society* 19: 635–48.

Reed, I. 2002. "Review Essay on Ann Swidler, Talk of Love: How Culture Matters." *Theory and Society* 31(6): 785–94.

——. 2007. "Why Salem Made Sense." *Cultural Sociology* 1(2): 209–34.

Sherwood, S. 1994. "Narrating the Social." *Journal of Narrative and Life History* 4(1–2): 69–88.

Sherwood, S., Smith, P., and Alexander, J. 1993. "The British Are Coming. … Again! The Hidden Agenda of 'Cultural Studies'." *Contemporary Sociology* 22(2): 370–75.

Smith, P. 1991. "Codes and Conflict." *Theory and Society* 20(3): 101–38.

———. 1996a. "Executing Executions: Aesthetics, Identity and the Problematic Narratives of Capital Punishment Ritual." *Theory and Society* 25(2): 235–61.

———. 1996b. "Barbarism and Civility in the Discourses of Fascism, Communism and Democracy." Pp. 115–37 in Jeffrey Alexander, ed., *Real Civil Societies*. London: Sage.

———. 2005. *Why War: The Cultural Logic of Iraq, the Gulf War and Suez*. Chicago: University of Chicago Press.

———. 2008a. *Punishment and Culture*. Chicago: University of Chicago Press.

———. 2008b. "The Balinese Cockfight Decoded: Reflections on Geertz, the Strong Program and Structuralism." *Cultural Sociology* 2(2): 169–86.

———. 2008c. "Meaning and Military Power: Moving on from Foucault." *Journal of Power* 1: 275–93.

Steensland, Brian. 2009. "Restricted and Elaborated Modes in the Cultural Analysis of Politics." *Sociological Forum*. 24: 926–34.

Trondman, M. 2008. "To Locate in the Tenor of Their Setting the Sources of Their Spell: Clifford Geertz and the Strong Program in Cultural Sociology." *Cultural Sociology* 2(2): 201–21.

———. Forthcoming. "Burning Schools/Building Bridges: Ethnographical Touchdowns in the Civil Sphere." In J. Alexander, R. Jacobs, and P. Smith, eds., *Oxford Handbook of Cultural Sociology*. Oxford. Oxford University Press.

West, B. 2008. "Enchanting Pass." *Sociological Theory* 26(3): 258–70.

Woodward, I. 2007. *Understanding Material Culture*. London: Sage.

"Culture studies" and the culture complex

Tony Bennett

In *Reassembling the Social*, Bruno Latour argues that culture "does not act surreptitiously behind the actor's back" but rather is "manufactured at specific places and institutions, be it the messy offices of the top floor of Marshal Sahlins's house on the Chicago campus or the thick Area Files kept in the Pitt Rivers [*sic*] museum in Oxford" (Latour 2005: 175). He goes on to characterize this close attention to the sites where things are made as a distinguishing trait of work conducted in the tradition of science studies. In doing so, he counterposes these concerns to those of "sociologists of the social" who aim to bring to light hidden structures—of language or of ideologies, for example—in order to account for social actions in ways that social actors themselves are unaware of. This passes over the more mundane and material processes of making culture that Latour highlights. In what follows I explore the implications of Latour's approach for the analysis of the relations between culture and the social. I suggest that science studies and, more generally, actor–network theory (ANT) provide useful models for the development of forms of cultural analysis—which, analogically, I shall call "culture studies"—capable of illuminating how culture operates as a historically distinctive set of assemblages, the "culture complex" of my title, which act on the social in a variety of ways. I then relate these concerns to those of Foucauldian governmentality theory to suggest how the analysis of culture might best be approached when viewed as part of a field of government. Finally, I consider the implications of these approaches for the development of a properly historical approach to the tasks of cultural analysis. (In addressing these issues, I draw on, modify, and add to discussions in Bennett 2007a, 2007b.)

Culture studies

To look to Latour's work for guidance in analyzing the relations between culture and the social might seem quixotic given his opposition to the model of the two-house collective dividing the assembly of things (nature) from the assembly of humans (society) that he attributes to early modern science and political thought (Latour 1993). For the concern to distinguish culture from the social as a subdivision within the assembly of humans is a further aspect of the "modern settlement" that Latour has worked assiduously to unsettle. Latour makes this clear in *Politics of Nature*, where he suggests that we put aside the ideas of culture, nature, and society to focus instead on the processes through which humans and non-humans are assembled into collectives whose constitution is always simultaneously natural, social, cultural, and technical. Yet Latour also qualifies this position by arguing that although the division between nature and society as incommensurable realms has no valid epistemological foundations, it has real historical force if understood as referring not to "domains of reality" but to "a quite specific form of public organization" (Latour 2004a: 53).

Similarly, in *Reassembling the Social*, Latour is less iconoclastic in relation to the concept of the social than in many of his earlier formulations. The central difficulty, he argues, lies not in the concept of the social if this is thought of as a stabilized bundle of connections between human and non-human actants that might be mobilized to account for some other phenomenon—the connections between the middle classes, works of art, and the organization of class distinctions, for example (Latour 2005: 40). Rather, problems arise when the social is thought of as a specific kind of material—as if there were a distinctive kind of "social stuff"—that can be distinguished from other "non-social" phenomena and then be invoked, in the form of an encompassing social context or social structure, as an explanatory ground in relation to the latter (Latour 2005: 1–4). In place of this conception of the social, that informed the procedures of the sociology of science against which science studies pitted itself, Latour recommends that it be thought of as an assemblage of diverse components brought together via a work of connection on the part of a varied set of agents. John Law's formulations point in a similar direction, construing the social as the outcome of varied processes of translation through which different "bits and pieces" of the socio-material world are brought into association with one another in the context of relationally configured networks of people and things, a process that involves the deletion of other similarly constituted networks and their being held in place long enough to produce durable effects (Law 1994: 102–05).

Although it is not a move that either Latour or Law makes, the case for seeing culture not as made up of a distinctive kind of "cultural stuff," (representations, say) but as a provisional assembly of all kinds of "bits and pieces" that are fashioned into durable networks whose interactions produce culture as specific kinds of public organization of people and things, is readily perceptible. So, too, is the possibility of accounting for the historical emergence of culture as a result of the production of new assemblages of human and non-human actors through which its differentiation from the social and the economy was effected. Before pursuing this line of inquiry further, however, I want to consider some of the more general aspects of science studies and actor–network theory to identify the light they throw on the both the work that goes into the making of culture and the distinctive kind of work that it, in turn, performs. I shall focus on three issues here.

(1) The first concerns what Law characterizes as the "*semiotics of materiality*" of ANT, in which, given its focus on the "*relational materiality*" constituted by different assemblages of human and non-human actors, what matters is how the elements of such assemblages work together to order and perform the social (Law 1999: 4). Such practices of social ordering are, as Laws puts it elsewhere, "*materially heterogeneous*," made up of bits and pieces of talk, architecture, bodies, texts, machines, etc., all of which interact to construct

and perform the social. This relational materialism has much in common with the accounts of discursive or ideological articulation which have played such a significant role in cultural studies. In both cases, the identity and effectivity of elements derive not from their intrinsic properties but from the networks of relations in which they are installed. Yet, there is an important difference between these two positions, one of which, in my view, should be counted in ANT's favor. It concerns the expanded, and more convincingly materialist, field of analysis that results from ANT's incorporation of non-human actors into the networks that go to make up and perform the social. This has several advantages over the view associated with the "cultural turn"—that social relations are essentially cultural in form because they are informed by linguistic or meta-linguistic articulations of social meanings, positions, and identities. For it makes possible a non-tautological account of the constitution of culture, understood as a distinctive public organization of things and people, that is distinguished from the social rather than merged with it. When those whom Latour characterizes as "sociologists of the social" try to account for the durability of social ties, Latour argues, they typically appeal to the role of social norms and values, thus engaging in the "tautology of social ties made out of social ties" (Latour 2005: 70). A good deal of work in cultural studies proceeds similarly by defining culture's effects in terms of its properties: culture as a meaning-making system that makes meanings, for example. This is avoidable in an approach which focuses on culture as an assemblage of heterogeneous elements whose "culturalness" derives from, rather than precedes, their assembly.

(2) I take my second point from Andrew Pickering's characterization of the adjacent field of practice studies as amounting to a *"social theory of the visible"* (Pickering 2001: 164) that does not look for any deeper or hidden structures beneath the "the visible and specific intertwinings of the human and the nonhuman" (Pickering 2001: 167). This commitment to the analysis of natural/cultural/social/technical networks and assemblages as consisting only of visible surfaces, a single-planed set of wholly observable events, actions, and processes with no hidden, deep, or invisible structures or levels, stands in contradistinction to the dualistic ontologies of the social that still characterize those versions of the cultural turn that have most influenced the development of cultural sociology. Such ontologies provide the basis for ANT's opposition to the language of "cultural constructivism" since the very notion that culture constructs the social is at odds with ANT's focus on the complex entanglements of people and things in the intersecting networks through which the social is performed without any prior distinction between what might be allocated to culture and what to society. By locating intellectual work on a single-planed reality, this position also questions intellectual practices that aim to organize their own authority and distinctive forms of political intervention by claiming insight into another set of hidden or invisible processes and realities held to take place behind the backs of other actors. It construes intellectuals not as seers but as mobilizers and transformers, reshaping relations between things and people by the production of new entities and their mobilization in the context of the material-semiotic networks through which the social is made and performed.

(3) There is a strong focus in science and practice studies on the specific settings—most notably laboratories—in which scientific work is conducted, and on the transformations (purifications, reductions, translations, etc.) to which scientific practice subjects the materials it works with so as to produce new entities in the field of knowledge. This comprises an exemplary materialism in the attention it pays to the material settings and instruments through which such entities are made and mobilized. There is, as Law notes,

a good deal of common ground here between ANT and those readings of Foucault's concept of discourse which—somewhat against the authority of Foucault's own texts—stress its material and institutional properties (Sawyer 2002). But there is also a difference to the extent that ANT places a greater emphasis on analyzing the processes through which things are put together to comprise those ordering strategies that Foucauldian analysis calls discursive but whose formation—the processes of their making and remaking—it tends to occlude (Law 1994: 18–26). This opens up the space for a productive interchange between ANT and Foucauldian theory in its potential to add a denser materiality to Foucault's insistence on the need for an "ascending analysis of power" that would "begin with its infinitesimal mechanisms, which have their own history, their own trajectory, their own techniques and tactics, and then look at how these mechanisms of power, which have their solidity and, in a sense, their own technology, have been and are invested, colonized, used, infected, transformed, displaced, extended, and so on by increasingly general mechanisms and forms of overall domination" (Foucault 2003: 30). In a similar vein, Latour argues that "power, like society, is the final result of a process and not a reservoir, a stock or a capital that will automatically provide an explanation. Power and domination have to be made up, composed" (Latour 2005: 64). The task that this enjoins analytically is one of tracing the networks of associations through which particular forms of power are assembled, aiming for as dense a description as possible of the capacities that are folded into and accumulate within them.

The implication is that we should consider how distinctive kinds of cultural power are organized via the production of distinctive cultural assemblages—in museums, libraries, broadcasting, art galleries, heritage sites—which, as closely interacting components of the "culture complex," bring together persons, things, techniques, texts as parts of distinctive public organizations which, in turn, can be mobilized in distinctive ways to act on the social with a view to bringing about changes in conduct.

The culture complex and the analytics of government

I turn now to the implications of setting these concerns within the perspective of governmentality theory. Yet here, too, we need to probe whether there is any place in Foucault's account of governmentality for a set of concerns focused specifically on culture. The term is not one Foucault used except casually: it does not form a part of the system of concepts he used to lay out the field of governmental practices or of the techniques he proposed for their analysis. And a number of governmentality theorists have been wary of the concept. Nikolas Rose has expressed his doubts as to whether what he calls "the amorphous domain of culture" has any specific analytical purchase (Rose 1998: 24), while Mitchell Dean has also lodged his reservations concerning the thesis of "culture governance" associated with the role attributed to self-reflexive forms of individualization in relation to the agendas of neo-liberalism (Dean 2007). Both cautions are justified: Rose's because the logic of the cultural turn in construing culture, understood as meaning-making, as a component of all practices extends its reach at the price of depriving it of an analytical domain of its own; and Dean's because such accounts of individualization fail to identify the historically specific mechanisms through which its effects are produced.

Yet there is now a considerable body of work that explores the implications of the analytics of government for a wide range of cultural practices and institutions.

In referring to the "analytics of government" here, I draw on the terms proposed by Mitchell Dean in summarizing the perspective of governmentality:

> Government is any more or less calculated and rational activity, undertaken by a multiplicity of authorities and agencies, employing a variety of techniques and forms of knowledge, that seeks to shape conduct by working through our desires, aspirations, interests, and beliefs, for definite but shifting ends and with a diverse set of relatively unpredictable consequences, effects, and outcomes.
>
> (Dean 1999: 11)

Interpreted in this light, there is no shortage of studies examining how cultural practices and institutions are implicated in the processes through which this governmental concern with "the conduct of conduct" is organized. There is now a good deal of historical work focused on the roles played by the development of a new complex of cultural institutions—public libraries, exhibitions, museums, archives, art galleries, etc.—in the context of eighteenth- and nineteenth-century programs of liberal government (Bennett 1998, 2004; Joyce 2003). This, as Foucault elaborates it, refers to arts of governing which make the freedom and autonomy of individuals aspects of the very mechanisms of government—making them the means by and through which government works—by, for example, cultivating specific practices of the self through which they become responsible for managing their own conduct (Foucault 2007: 353). The relations between the development of literary education and popular schooling, and indeed the development of popular schooling more generally, have been examined from a similar perspective (Hunter 1988; Donald 1992). There is also a growing literature concerned with the role of broadcasting—and of its varied genres, from soap operas, through lifestyle programs, and reality TV—as a cultural technology of liberal government (Miller 1998; Ouellete and Hay 2008), with a number of collections addressing a range of popular media and cultural practices (Bratich *et al.* 2003; Dillon and Valentine 2002). And there is, finally, a considerable literature on the role of culture in colonial forms of governmentality (Mitchell 1989; Stoler 2002).[1]

What is less clear is how these different concerns might add up to a distinctive account of culture. I shall broach this question from two angles. The first derives from Foucault's account of governmental power as the result of a process which, in the West, "has led to the development of a series of specific governmental apparatuses (*appareils*) on the one hand, [and, on the other] to the development of a series of knowledges (*savoirs*)" (Foucault 2007: 108). I take two things from this definition. The first concerns the relations between culture and adjacent fields of government. If culture is to occupy a distinctive place within an analytics of government, it is necessary to identify it in terms of a distinctive set of knowledges connected to a set of governmental apparatuses, with these working together in ways that establish distinctive techniques of intervention into the conduct of conduct. The second is that these ensembles of knowledges and apparatuses should bring together persons, things, and techniques—ways of doing and making—that give rise to historically distinctive forms of power and modes of its exercise.

My contention, then, is that a distinctive field of cultural government has been shaped into being as an historically distinctive public ordering of things and people via the deployment of the modern cultural disciplines (literature, aesthetics, art history, folk studies, drama, heritage studies, cultural sociology, cultural and media studies) in the apparatuses of the culture complex (museums, libraries, cinema, broadcasting, universities, and schools, heritage sites, etc.) as distinctive technologies that connect particular ways of doing and making—particular regimes of cultural practice—to regularized ways of acting on the social to bring about calculated changes in conduct related to particular rationalities of government. This is not to suggest an absolute separation between cultural and other fields of government. We can, for example, see how the culture complex and the psy-complex overlap in the use of psychology alongside program-making expertise in the forms of cultural governance associated with reality TV (Ouellete and Hay 2008). Nor is it to suggest that the culture complex operates on one side of a historical dyke that separates it entirely from earlier forms of power. The scripts of many museums are clearly a mix of sovereign and governmental forms of power, while many contemporary cultural disciplines and apparatuses are still marked by their relations to earlier forms of pastoral power. However, these qualifications do not affect our capacity to distinguish the relations between the culture complex and the cultural disciplines as a distinctive ensemble of power relations and practices any more than the continuation of sovereign power alongside discipline and governmental power invalidates Foucault's identification of these as different modalities of power which, as he frequently emphasized, were often complexly mingled.

Analysis of the culture complex involves paying close attention to the assembly, to paraphrase Law, of those "*materially heterogeneous*" networks, made up of bits and pieces of talk, architecture, bodies, texts, machines, etc., which interact to construct and perform "culture" and to organize its relations to "the economy," "the social," and "the political." The issues at stake here can be illustrated by briefly reviewing the history of *Bildung*. Reinhart Koselleck has identified three main ways in which *Bildung*, as a practice of self formation, was connected to social and political programs through: first, its role in training the new corpus of experts, administrators, scientists, etc. who formed the nucleus of the bureaucratic state; second, its role in the internal forms of socialization through which the bourgeoisie—in marriage, in social life, in clubs, and at home—secured a specific identity for itself; and, third, its political mobilization in programs of public education (Koselleck 2002: 172–73). However, Koselleck offers little sense of what this work of connecting *Bildung* to public pedagogy amounted to or of the densely material processes that it involved. Yet it is clear that it entailed both the deletion of earlier networks and the organization of new ones, work in which new cultural knowledges (of art history and archaeology, for example) were centrally implicated (Marchand 1996). The articulation of *Bildung* as a program of public education thus involved a new ensemble of institutions (public libraries, concert halls, museums and art galleries, and exhibitions) that organized new networks of relations between human and non-human actors through the new publics they brought together with new assemblages of things, texts, and instruments in specially contrived architectural spaces. And, as Patrick Joyce (2003) shows, these spaces were themselves parts of new forms of socio-spatial ordering associated with the moral economy of the liberal city in which *Bildung* was hard-wired into the material environment. These new cultural assemblages were produced through the (partial) deletion of earlier networks in which particular configurations of the relations between people and things, between human and non-human actors, had organized differently structured networks. The material economy of the nineteenth-century city of culture thus depended not only on a new partitioning of urban space but on the severance of the nexus of the relations between people and things that had been inscribed in the quite different institutional nexus of the spa city and its practices (Borsay 1989).

This material economy of culture depended equally on the relocation of varied objects from their previous location in private settings (aristocratic and royal households) and, in thus being detached from earlier purely decorative functions or from their role in the spectacularization of power, on their acquisition of new properties that enabled them to be refunctioned for new purposes. The deployment of aesthetic discourses in art museums transformed works of art into resources for developing a new in-depth interiority on the part of the subject. This opened up an inner space within which a developmental relationship of the kind required by *Bildung* could be constructed (see, for example, Belting 2001; Bennett 2005). But, as Maiken Umbach (forthcoming) shows, the relationship between new forms of design and the restructuring of the bourgeois household also proved critical in reassembling the home as a space for the fashioning of new forms of interiority.

Historicizing culture

Here, then, are the rudiments of an account of the processes of assembling culture as a distinctive historical formation that is made up of specific networks of relations between human and non-human actors and which, through the distinctive assemblages that it effects, organizes and works on the social to bring about changes of conduct or new forms of social interaction. Its modes of engagement with the social, however, are not with a set of realities and processes that are somehow prior to those through which culture is assembled, or which in some way underlie these. They are rather forms of engagement with realities and processes of similar kinds, made up of similar kinds of stuff, whose differentiation from one another (the economy, the social, culture) is sectoral rather than substantive. For the materials from which they are assembled are all of a piece ontologically speaking: they are made up of the same kind of heterogeneous elements. Where they differ is in the form of the public organization into which they have been assembled, and it is this that "culture studies" should concern itself with.

There is no question in all of this of looking to develop an account of culture as an anthropological constant that operates in the same way in all kinds of societies. The remit of the program outlined above is limited to the forms of cultural assemblage that are associated with the development of secular forms of cultural knowledge, the institutions in which these are set to work, and the ways in which their operations—viewed in the light of the parallel development of the social and economic sciences—are related to the parallel emergence of the social and the economy as different public organizations of people and things. This is not to suggest a distinction of a fundamental kind between modern and pre-modern knowledge formations and the manner of their functioning. Similar principles of analysis can be used to study the makeup and operation of other knowledge systems and their implications for regulating social conduct. David Turnbull has thus interpreted medieval cathedrals as knowledge spaces which, like laboratories, brought together specific resources, skills, and labor in operating as "powerful loci of social transformation" (Turnbull 2000: 67), and he makes the same case for the knowledge assemblies of indigenous peoples. The distinctiveness of the ways of interrogating the relations between culture and the social that I am proposing thus consists in the focus on the operations of, and the interactions between, historically new forms of cultural and social knowledge in the context of the public differentiation of culture, the social, and the economy that is both their outcome and—so long as these differentiations remain durable—their condition.

31

Foucault comments usefully on these issues in his lecture series on *The Birth of Biopolitics*, a series which he begins with a methodological reflection on the status of so-called universals in the social and historical sciences. His method, he says, is not to start from the supposition that there are universals—the state, society, sovereign, subjects, and madness are the examples he gives—and to then put these "through the grinder of history" (Foucault 2008: 3) to examine the varied forms in which they are inflected. Rather, starting out from the opposite assumption that these universals do not exist, the task of historical analysis then becomes one of showing how, in the case of madness, for example, the conjunction of a set of practices and its coordination with a regime of truth could make something that did not exist before become something—a something that is made by the "set of practices, real practices, which established it and thus imperiously marks it out in reality" (Foucault 2008: 19).

And, in his earlier series of lectures on *Security, Territory, Population*, Foucault provides a clue regarding the implications of this move for a non-universalist approach to culture in his comments on the changing orientation to population associated with the historical transition from sovereignty to security. In the former, it is primarily the size of the population that matters, as a source and symbol of sovereign power, and of troops, and as a means of populating the towns and keeping their markets going. The primary aim of government in this context is to ensure that the population is obedient and animated by zeal in service of the sovereign. This requires an apparatus that will ensure that the population will work properly (labor laws), in the right place (immigration), and on the right objects. The transition to a regime based on the principle of security brings along a new conception of population according to which government is no longer primarily concerned with the formal or juridical adjudication of the rights and wills of subjects of the sovereign. Instead it is informed by the more general connect-ions between security and liberalism according to which government seeks to direct things by allowing them to go their own way. Population then appears in a new form, as something that is to be managed on the basis of its immanent properties. There are, Foucault argues, two different ways in which these immanent properties of population are constituted as new surfaces for the exercise of governmental power. The first, as a transformation connected to the development of the biological sciences, links the notion of population to that of species as something that is shaped by the conditions of life provided by a distinctive milieu. The second points toward the public: that is, "the population seen under the aspect of its opinions, ways of doing things, forms of behavior, customs, fears, prejudices, and requirements; it is what one gets a hold on through education, campaigns, and convictions." Putting these two together, Foucault continues:

> The population is therefore everything that extends from biological rootedness through the species up to the surface that gives one a hold provided by the public. From the species to the public; we have here a whole field of new realities in the sense that they are the pertinent elements for mechanisms of power, the pertinent space within which and regarding which one must act.
>
> (Foucault 2007: 75)

And it is in relation to this space that culture, understood as a set of new knowledges and technologies, is progressively assembled, producing its own new realities as a means of intervening in and acting on conduct.

Note

1 It is worth noting, in the light of the renewed interest in the work of Howard Becker occasioned by the republication of his *Art Worlds* (2008), the differences between Becker's concerns and those associated with this governmentality literature. Although Becker's approach shares with ANT a concern with the collective and institutional processes through which art works are produced, performed, and distributed as parts of specific art worlds, he does not offer an account of the ways in which such art worlds act on the social as itself a historically specific set of surfaces produced by, and for, governmental action of varied kinds.

References

Becker, Howard S. 2008. *Art Worlds*. Berkeley: University of California Press.

Belting, Hans. 2001. *The Invisible Masterpiece*. London: Reaktion Books.

Bennett, T. 1998. *Culture: A Reformer's Science*. Sydney: Allen and Unwin; London and New York: Sage.

——. 2004. *Pasts Beyond Memories: The Evolutionary Museum and Colonial Science*. London: Routledge.

——. 2005. "Civic Laboratories: Museums, Cultural Objecthood, and the Governance of the Social." *Cultural Studies* 19(5): 521–47.

——. 2007a. "Making Culture, Changing Society: The Perspective of Culture Studies." *Cultural Studies* 21(4–5): 610–29.

——. 2007b. "The Work of Culture." *Journal of Cultural Sociology* 1(1): 31–48.

Borsay, Peter. 1989. *The English Urban Renaissance: Culture and Society in the English Provincial Town, 1660–1770*. Oxford: Clarendon Press.

Bratich, Jack Z., Packer, Jeremy, and McCarthy, Cameron, eds. 2003. *Foucault, Cultural Studies and Governmentality*. New York: State University of New York Press.

Dean, Mitchell. 1999. *Governmentality: Power and Rule in Modern Society*. London: Sage.

——. 2007. *Governing Societies*. Maidenhead: Open University Press.

Dillon, Mick and Valentine, Jeremy, eds. 2002 "Culture and Governance," special issue of *Cultural Values: Journal for Cultural Research* 6(1–2).

Donald, James. 1992. *Sentimental Education: Schooling, Popular Culture and the Regulation of Liberty*. London: Verso.

Foucault, Michel. 2003. *Society Must Be Defended: Lectures at the Collège de France, 1975–76*. New York: Picador.

——. 2007. *Security, Territory, Population: Lectures at the Collège de France, 1977–1978* London: Palgrave Macmillan.

——. 2008. *The Birth of Biopolitics: Lectures at the Collège de France, 1978–9*. London: Palgrave Macmillan.

Hunter, Ian. 1988. *Culture and Government: The Emergence of Literary Education*. London: Macmillan.

Joyce, Patrick. 2003. *The Rule of Freedom: Liberalism and the Modern City*. London: Verso.

Koselleck, Reinhart. 2002. *The Practice of Conceptual History: Timing History, Spacing Concepts*. Stanford, CA: Stanford University Press.

Latour, B. 1993. *We Have Never Been Modern*. Cambridge, MA: Harvard University Press.

——. 2004a. *Politics of Nature: How to Bring the Sciences into Democracy*. Cambridge, MA: Harvard University Press.

——. 2005. *Reassembling the Social: An Introduction to Actor-Network-Theory*. Oxford: Oxford University Press.

Law, J. 1994. *Organising Modernity*. Oxford: Blackwell.

——. 1999. "After ANT: Complexity, Naming and Topology," in J. Law and J. Hassard, eds., *Actor Network Theory and After*. Oxford: Blackwell/The Sociological Review, 1–14.

Marchand, Suzanne L. 1996. *Down from Olympus: Archaeology and Philhellenism in Germany, 1759–1970*. Princeton, NJ: Princeton University Press.

Miller, Toby. 1998. *Technologies of Truth: Cultural Citizenship and the Popular Media*. Minneapolis: University of Minnesota Press.

Mitchell, Timothy. 1989. *Colonising Egypt*. Cambridge: Cambridge University Press.

Ouellete, Laurie and Hay, James. 2008. *Better Living through Reality TV*. Oxford: Blackwell.

Pickering, Andrew. 2001. "Practice and Posthumanism: Social Theory and a History of Agency," in Theodore R. Schatzki, Karin Knorr Cetina, and Eike von Savigny, eds., *The Practice Turn in Contemporary Theory*. London: Routledge.

Rose, Nikolas. 1998. *Inventing Our Selves: Psychology, Power and Personhood*. Cambridge: Cambridge University Press.

Sawyer, R. Keith. 2002. "A Discourse on Discourse: An Archaeological History of an Intellectual Concept." *Cultural Studies* 16(3): 433–56.

Stoler, Ann Laura. 2002. *Carnal Knowledge and Imperial Power: Race and the Intimate in Colonial Rule*. Berkeley: University of California Press.

Turnbull, David. 2000. *Masons, Tricksters and Cartographers: Comparative Studies in the Sociology of Scientific and Indigenous Knowledge*. Amsterdam: Harwood Academic Publishers.

Umbach, Maiken. Forthcoming. *German Cities and Bourgeois Modernism, 1890–1924*. Oxford: Oxford University Press.

3

The subaltern, the postcolonial, and cultural sociology

Raka Ray and Smitha Radhakrishnan

Theirs is no history of ideas, no calm Olympian narrative of events, no disengaged objective recital of facts. It is rather sharply contestary, an attempt to wrest control of the Indian past from its scribes and curators of the present, since, as we shall see, much of the past continues into the present. And if there can be no actual taking of power in the writing of history, there can at least be a demystifying exposure of what material interests are at stake, what ideology and method are employed, what parties advanced, which deferred, displaced, defeated.

(Said 1988: vii)

In the late 1970s, a group of Indian historians in England launched a movement that first came to public light in 1982 with the publication of a volume called *Subaltern Studies*, Volume 1. "The declared aim of *Subaltern Studies* was to produce historical analyses in which the subaltern groups were viewed as the subjects of history" (Chakrabarty 2000a: 15). Writing in the early 1980s against the backdrop of South Asian states' failure to live up to their promises thirty years after independence (and, indeed, the apparent failure of the postcolonial world)—"the historic failure of the nation to come into its own" (Guha 1982: 6)—subaltern historians sought explanations that lay outside of orthodox Marxist or developmentalist paradigms. They looked instead at the ways that postcolonial nations were imagined and understood, and at the failures of national elites to be genuinely inclusive of non-dominant groups that comprised most of their nations' populations. Their work was marked by simultaneous attention to questions of power, culture, and the politics of the dispossessed. Today, twelve volumes later, the project has spilled out of the bounds of South Asia and history, into other areas of the world and other disciplines, but it has stopped short of sociology. In this essay we make the case for how the *Subaltern Studies* approach to Indian history can enrich sociological understandings of culture, specifically with regard to thinking about nations, colonialism, and the production of knowledge.

Subaltern subjectivity

Central to the *Subaltern Studies* project was the Gramscian figure of the subaltern. As used by Gramsci, the term subaltern referred to those excluded from state power.

"The subaltern classes, by definition, are not unified and cannot unite until they are able to become a 'State'," Gramsci (1971: 52) wrote, but the term was commonly assumed to refer specifically to workers and peasants. Yet, in the essay in which he introduced subaltern studies to the world, Ranajit Guha defined the subaltern simply as those who were not among the elite, specifically, as the "demographic difference between the total Indian population" and the dominant indigenous and foreign elite (Guha 1982: 7). This capacious formulation opened up the possibility of bringing to the center those who had been excluded and marginalized—on the basis not just of class, but also of caste, gender, and indeed office. In widening the scope of subalternity, Guha facilitated the theorization of multiple forms of domination in ways that were not reducible either to pluralism or economistic Marxism (O'Hanlon 2000: 84).

In putting the subaltern at the center of their analysis, subaltern scholars intended to recuperate the subaltern as an agent. Indeed, in the early scholarly writings, subalterns seem to inhabit a separate sphere and capacity for self-determination—a characterization that has led to its share of criticisms, notably the charge of essentialism. Guha specifically argued that the politics of the people in the colonial period formed a culturally "autonomous" domain, parallel to the elite, but neither originating from it nor dependent upon it (1982: 3). In his formulation, peasants enjoyed the most powerful form of this autonomy. However, other scholars (Bhadra 1989; Amin 1984) represented the subaltern as possessing a more contradictory consciousness.

The loose definition of the subaltern permitted a reconceptualization of different modes of power, notably religious, colonial, caste-based, and the (otherwise invisible) power of marginal groups. Just as subaltern studies scholars documented multiple forms of domination, so too they documented multiple forms of resistance. In analyzing grain riots, small-scale peasant insurgencies, and the uprising of hill peoples (Sivaramakrishnan 2002: 217), studies—especially in the early volumes of *Subaltern Studies*—revealed the multiple workings of non-hegemonic cultural forms (e.g. magic, oral traditions, local religious customs, etc.) in shaping resistance. Simultaneously, this work reconceptualized resistant agency, holding that resistance was possible not only through violent conflict but also through cultural negation and inversion (see, for example, Sarkar 1989). The powerful but uneven structuring effect of colonialism, as well as the interactive effects of the precolonial and colonial on subaltern consciousness, were central ideas in the formulations of scholars engaged in *Subaltern Studies*.

The theoretical inspiration in the early years, certainly between Volumes I and IV, was the work of Antonio Gramsci. However, with Volume V, published in 1987, contributions came increasingly to draw on Foucault's conceptualization of knowledge and power, as well as Derridian deconstructionism—influences similar to those on British approaches to cultural studies. It was at this time both that Edward Said praised the project and that subaltern theorizing began to take on shades of postcolonial theory. In the words of Vinayak Chaturvedi, "what starts as a project trying to establish the autonomy of subaltern agency is now challenging the foundation of Enlightenment thought while attempting to hold on to a certain version of Marxism" (2000: xii–xiii). But the move from Gramsci to Foucault and postcolonial theory also pushed the work beyond the specificity of colonial India to the possibility of thinking about late twentieth-century imperialism (Chaturvedi 2000: xiii)—even as the core themes remained the exploration of agency, subject formation, and hegemony.

Whereas a Gramscian-inspired notion of subalternity highlighted the distinction between the dominant and the dominated, adapting a modified notion of hegemony, the turn to Foucault was accompanied by the increased use of discursive analysis and an understanding of power as diffuse and multilayered. These two strands of scholarship within the *Subaltern Studies* series did not go easily together, and each attracted its own share of critics. Historians of Latin America and Africa grappled with this tension as they engaged with the histories of colonialism and imperialism in their own areas (Cooper 1994; Mallon 1994). Scholars in literature departments, for whom subaltern studies was part of a larger turn towards study of the postcolonial, tended toward the more deconstructionist end of subaltern studies scholarship, while grappling with the work of subalternist writings published outside the series, most notably Gayatri Spivak's "Can the Subaltern Speak?" Indeed, the emergence of diverse interlocutors highlights what we would argue is a productive tension between Gramscian and poststructuralist conceptualizations of power.

This tension is most clearly illustrated in the divergent conceptions of the subaltern contained in Ranajit Guha's opening essay that introduced *Subaltern Studies* to the world, and Gayatri Spivak's "Deconstructing Historiography," initially published in Volume IV. Guha (1982) reworked Gramsci's notion of hegemony to conceptualize dominance that was possible without consent: in his formulation, neither those who mobilized against colonialism nor subalterns more generally consented to bourgeois rule. Even as Guha expanded and pushed the boundaries in his reworked notion of dominance by acknowledging diverse modes through which power is articulated, however, his conceptualization continued to distinguish clearly between the dominated and the dominating, and remained within a binary/dialectic framework. Spivak, in contrast, argued that subaltern studies as a project, while continuing to assert such binary dialectics in theory, was in practice and method deconstructionist, and had the potential to bring dominant historiography to the point of crisis precisely because it (implicitly) acknowledged that "subaltern consciousness is ... irreducibly discursive" (Spivak 1988: 11) Subaltern "voices," in this formulation, are inaccessible because they are already constituted through elite power.

How can these two approaches be reconciled with one another, if at all? On one hand, Guha's "autonomous sphere" of the subaltern is politically attractive because it asserts the existence of subaltern consciousness outside of colonial and nationalist power, and aims to articulate the specific actions, ideologies, and cultures of those outside the realm of elitist accounts of history. Spivak's approach, on the other hand, does not completely deny the existence of an autonomous sphere. Rather, she argues that such a proposition can never be verified, and that a truly radical historiography can only be deconstructionist—understanding the diffusiveness of power relations and the pervasiveness of elite power in constituting a subaltern consciousness that is perhaps *only* theoretically possible. Scholarship that continues the Guha line of argumentation can be found in the literature on resistance, while the Spivakian approach can be seen in postcolonial critiques of knowledge.

Among studies of consciousness, sociologists and anthropologists are most familiar with James Scott's (1985) analysis of resistance among Malay peasants, published almost simultaneously with *Subaltern Studies* in the mid-1980s. Scott sought to account for subaltern acts of resistance that did not result in peasant revolt, aiming to rethink notions of false consciousness and hegemony that dominated especially history and political science at the time. In many ways, notions of "subaltern agency" emerging from the writings of the Subaltern Studies collective resonated with Scott's core concepts and intent. However, although his account of resistance theorized an unconsenting peasant

37

subjectivity, Scott's idea of resistance included only intentional action aimed at under-mining superordinate classes (cited in Moore 1998). In contrast, subaltern studies questioned the ability to know and apprehend the intentionality of the subaltern. By questioning the relationship between the power of the subaltern and the knowledge we might come to acquire about her, subaltern studies provided a less positivist, more reflexive, and more multilayered account of agency, acknowledging not only the possi-bility of subaltern resistance, but also the extent to which the nature of that resistance may be hidden from view.

Historians of Latin America especially embraced the Subaltern Studies strategy of melding textual methods with a commitment to advancing the political aims of the poor (Mallon 1994; Rodríguez 2001). For those Latin American scholars who formed the Latin American Subaltern Studies collective, subaltern studies provided a rich set of "traveling theories," and thus offered an opportunity to borrow theory developed in the global South for advancing post-Marxist analysis of Latin American history, specifically to provide a set of tools for radical critique of dominant colonial cultures in Latin America. Most useful for sociology, perhaps, is the way the Latin American version of subaltern studies focused upon the history of societies' "Others" as a means of thinking through the limitations and incapacities of bourgeois knowledge production (Rodríguez 2001: 9). By de-centering the West and, in the same move, de-centering bourgeois ways of knowing and being, subaltern studies provided for Latin Americanists a critical episte-mology that bears important lessons for sociology as well. Overall, the Latin American project expanded upon the scope of the original collective to examine questions of citi-zenship and governance through the vehicle of radical critique, deconstructing cultures of dominance while retaining a political agenda meant to further counterhegemonic ideals.

Guha's founding claim of an "autonomous sphere" attracted as much criticism as admiration, and became a magnet for scholars in related fields to engage (Cooper 1994; Brass 1997). Related to the charge of essentialism is the charge that viewing subaltern politics as an autonomous sphere misleads by ignoring the dynamism and immediacy of subaltern subjectivity and struggle. Drawing from his own ethnographic work in rural parts of Eastern Zimbabwe, for example, anthropologist Donald Moore criticizes the idea of the autonomy of subaltern subjectivity and politics by arguing instead that "[s]ubalternity, understood as a relational process of identity formation and the crafting of agency within multiple matrixes of power, may shift" (1998: 370). Other critics of subaltern studies charge that the complexity of subaltern politics is not adequately theo-rized, although these same critics adapt the term "subaltern," choosing to interpret the term strictly in the context of Hall's notion of "articulation" (see, for example, Li 2001: 650–51; Escobar 2001). These interlocutors benefit from the revival that the term "subaltern" has enjoyed in the wake of subaltern studies, which becomes for them an important analytical concept.

The awareness of how elite power constitutes knowledge that is embedded within subaltern studies and the resulting critique of conventional historiography has led to a broader reflexivity about methods across disciplines. Anthropologists, for the most part, have welcomed the critique of ethnography and the position of the intellectual that subaltern studies demands, especially after Volume V, and have embraced new fields of inquiry under its influence (Pels 1997). Still, many have also found the apparent refusal of the ethnographic in favor of a discursive, deconstructionist approach to be politically troubling. In her critique of Spivak's reading of the debates surrounding satī, or widow-burning, in colonial India, for example, Sherry Ortner (1996) argues, "feminists who might want to investigate the ways in which *satī* was part of a larger configuration of male dominance in nineteenth century Indian society cannot do so without seeming to subscribe to the discourse of colonial administrators."

Sociology and subaltern studies

The most significant insight that subaltern studies and postcolonial theories bring to the sociology of culture is that analyses of the relations between the dominant and the dominated, including those between colonizer and colonized, must be made central to understandings of cultural forms of expression and knowledge. Here, we limit ourselves to three issues in which this insight manifests itself and in which sociology of culture and subaltern studies can have the most productive conversations—the relationship of culture to the nation, knowledge production, and marginalization and internal colonialism.

Culture and the nation

The cultural entity of the nation has been a point of critical focus for sociologists of culture. Subaltern scholarship provides tools with which to deepen this engagement while expanding our notion of the nation as a politicized cultural entity and, as such, a specific site of empirical study. Within cultural sociology, nationalism has been viewed most importantly as enacted through secular collective ritual, a display of Durkheimian solidarity. Lyn Spillman's work on centennial and bicentennial celebrations in the United States and Australia highlights this aspect of the nation, emphasizing that in "settler societies" like the United States and Australia a sense of collective solidarity had to be gradually built through specific kinds of rituals (Spillman 1997). Because such studies view rituals of the nation as being fundamentally similar to other types of collective rituals in "traditional" or "primordial" societies, understanding the nation as secular ritual problematizes the divide between "traditional" and "modern" societies in a way that resonates well with the political intent of subaltern studies (Hall *et al.* 2003). The work of subaltern scholars also feeds into and extends work on collective memory and nation as they show how the same events (such as within the anti-colonial struggle) may be memorialized differently in elite and subaltern cultural spheres, and yet how master narratives of these events may ultimately displace others to forge a powerful single narrative of the nation (Amin 1984; Pandey 1989).

Intersectional approaches within sociology are already engaged with questions of how race, class, and gender simultaneously figure into questions of personal identity. The work of subaltern studies scholars encourages us to add nationality as a vital axis of difference, as individuals are constituted through nationality or a sense of national belonging, even as they are simultaneously of a certain gender, class, and racial makeup. Subaltern and postcolonial studies posit the nation as more than ritual performance or even identity, treating the nation itself rather as an *embodied* practice that is lived out through gendered, classed, and raced bodies. In a well-known set of examples, the work of subaltern and postcolonial scholars signals the importance of women in the creation of postcolonial nations not just as actors but as *symbols* of the nation, historicizing this role in the context of particularly nationalist and colonial projects (Chatterjee 1990). This insight has yielded important synergies with a burgeoning literature on gender and the nation that acknowledges this gendered symbolic role as one of the central ways in which the nationalist project engages women (other ways include as biological producers and as overtly political actors) (Yuval-Davis and Anthias 1989; Enloe 1990; McClintock 1995; Walby 1996). Subaltern scholars have focused specifically on the ways in which women's bodies became icons for the nation in the South Asian context. For example, in the case of the debates surrounding *satī*, the immolation of widows, in colonial India, Lata Mani has famously shown how women were deployed in colonial and nationalist discourses *only* as symbols, never as subjects or potential citizens in their own right (1990). In this instance, the method of "reading against the grain" that is so embedded in subaltern studies yields a generalizable insight, which complements the broader theoretical and empirical work of the gender and nationalism literature by demonstrating how subaltern subjects figure into hegemonic discourses as objects even though they are apparently excluded as subjects. Such an insight opens up new areas of exploration for thinking through the embodied character not only of the nation, but also of "tradition" and "modernity," which are always constructed in relation to a sense of nation, and often configured through gender.

How might the bodies of women and men who are outside the realm of political discourse serve as symbols of national projects by virtue of their ostensible oppression or marginalization? Alternatively, how do gendered bodies become symbols in ways that support or undermine nation-building projects? To address this question, we can look, for example, to post-apartheid South Africa, where the public artistic, cultural, and political performances of South African Indian women may be a result of deeply felt individual choices, but they also take on much broader symbolic valences associated with the gendered and racial understandings of a "new" South Africa over which women themselves often have little control (Radhakrishnan 2005). By opening up these kinds of inquiries, subaltern studies extend the scope of our conceptualization of the nation, viewing it as a simultaneously symbolic and strategic site for the production and navigation of culture.

Knowledge production

Subaltern scholars' work on the politics of knowledge production speaks directly to the question of power by asking whose narratives contribute to a "universal" truth and whose authorial voices are given more credibility.

If sociology as a discipline came into existence at least in part to address the character of modernity, this dominant story has been told in a limited way from within the discipline. The analytic stories of the unfolding of modernity as narrated by Marx, Weber, Durkheim (whether the stories center on rationalization, increasing complexity of organization, or division of labor) assumed that a self-contained Europe formed the empirical crux; it was on the basis of this assumption that they generated their theories. Thus Raewynn Connell (1997) has recently argued that the engagements of nineteenth- and early twentieth-century sociologists with questions about the structure of world society emphasized differences between civilization (here) and primitiveness (there). Their methods—comparative and based on external examination—she suggests, reflected the viewpoint and methods of imperialism, a history that was erased with the self-conscious formation of the sociological "canon" in the 1920s. Although modern sociology, apart from World Systems Theory, continued to assume the same self-contained Europe, historians and postcolonial theorists have demonstrated that Europe was not self-contained, as previously imagined. Yet the story of modernity and capitalism as commonly narrated (except for the accounts by dependency theorists) ignored or glossed over the effect of Europe's relationship to its colonies in constituting both its capitalism and its modernity. In this vein, the sociological stories that we know, tell, and act upon, how we understand the constitutive parts of entire societies, or the roots of social problems, or even the consequences of social and political action—all these are at best incomplete and at worst inaccurate. Those of us in the West do not only misrecognize other parts of the world, but we misrecognize ourselves.

Subaltern historian Dipesh Chakrabarty (2000b) reminds us that Europe was a specific place with a specific history and that it has been costly for us to have universalized that story to create a single model of historical progress. If Western Europe developed certain forms of capitalist modernity, it did so because of its particular history, which makes its replication unlikely in other parts of the world. Thus, "provincializing Europe" would necessitate a shift away from belief in one model of the history of capitalism and of modernity, and toward an acceptance of multiple models. Much modern sociological theory took the opposition between tradition and modernity as given, such that it would only be necessary to understand the conditions under which tradition *per se* was transformed into modernity *per se*. Yet if we grant that there are multiple ways of being modern—in part due to the traditions that existed prior to colonialism and capitalism—then we can no longer treat the question of transition to modernity as linear or simply time-lagged from place to place.

The subaltern turn to Foucault refocused attention on the knowledge effects of colonial rule. One result of colonial rule was, in fact, the loss of earlier intellectual traditions in colonized countries: intellectual traditions in Sanskrit, Persian, and Arabic ceased to thrive, and whole categories of thought and analysis were relegated to history in a way in which, for example, Plato has not been (Chakrabarty 2000b: 5–6). Although European scholars generally have not engaged with these intellectual traditions' concepts of power, authority, and morality, they nevertheless live on and intersect with European traditions. For sociologists of culture, then, subaltern studies brings the challenge of understanding the coexistence of multiple traditions and the necessity of working with plural models of knowledge.

In *Provincializing Europe*, arguably the strongest statement about the subalternity of knowledge production, Dipesh Chakrabarty argues that given the asymmetries of power in global knowledge production and circulation, the very production of South Asian history occupies a subaltern position: "Third-world historians feel a need to refer to works in European history; historians of Europe do not feel any need to reciprocate. … The problem, I may add in parentheses, is not particular to historians" (2000b: 28). Thus, subaltern and postcolonial theorists challenge us to decolonize and democratize knowledge production.

Marginalization and internal colonialism

Sociologists of culture have been actively interested and engaged in the ways in which people construct "the Other." Subaltern studies offers opportunities to deepen that engagement in order to further nuance our understanding of the "Other" and its construction. Perhaps the greatest project of subaltern studies has been its multilayered effort to access, engage, and represent the voices of non-dominant groups. As we have shown

41

here, subaltern scholars highlight the ways in which regimes of power—whether colonial, nationalist, or bourgeois—structure and limit our ways of knowing about cultural "Others," whether external (as in the case of colonial productions of knowledge about India) or internal (as in the case of bourgeois Indian nationalists speaking on behalf of peasants). Borrowing these insights, as sociologists, we can extend our understanding of marginalization, which we tend to view in more or less dichotomous terms, towards a cultural theory of internal colonialism.

Although the expansive scholarship on cultures of globalization has focused extensively on the global South, little of it has examined how the dynamics of the global political economy have rendered marginalized communities in the United States and Europe invisible. Hurricane Katrina revealed to the world a subaltern sphere that appeared to be more of the "Third World" than of the "First World," and yet it is those who occupy that very sphere—low income, black, and lacking in political capital—whose worlds have been most affected by the deindustrialization of the US and the globalization of the economy. Subaltern scholars' emphasis on the structure of hegemony allows us to think about the United States as a political territory in which subaltern groups are ruled, but without consent or participation in the social and political mainstream.

"Othering" then becomes not just a question about the interactions between East and West, but also a question about layers of power and privilege within the West. We can then attempt to assess the effects of that power on how we come to know and characterize non-dominant groups. Linking this kind of marginalization to similar dynamics of colonialism and bourgeois nationalism can allow sociology to ask a new set of questions about subaltern groups around the world, while exploring the linkages between them. In using a set of sociological tools informed by subaltern studies to study, for example, marginalized communities in New Orleans's Ninth Ward, we could not only focus upon the relationships of power that constitute their everyday experiences, but also reflect upon *how* we come to know what we do about these communities. In so doing, we introduce (with full consciousness of the contradictions that such a conceptualization raises) explorations of the role of state power in the formation of subjects, and the possibility of political spheres existing "autonomously."

Such an exploration raises new kinds of questions, some of which could be transnational or multi-sited in scope. How, for example, does the Ninth Ward as an ethnographic field allow for some kinds of representation and not others? How might understanding the struggles of displaced subaltern groups in Mumbai or the Narmada Valley in India inform a global conversation on subaltern cultures and politics of displacement? By integrating an interest in the politics of representation with a broad conceptualization of political engagement, subaltern studies offer the field of sociology the tools with which to ask innovative questions that are relevant to our ethnographies of the contemporary world.

References

Amin, S. 1984. "Gandhi as Mahatma: Gorakhpur, Eastern Up, 1921–22." *Subaltern Studies* 3: 1–71.

Bhadra, G. 1989. "The Mentality of Subalternity: Kantanama or Rajdharma." Pp. 54–91 in R. Guha, ed., *Subaltern Studies*, Volume VI. Delhi: Oxford University Press.

Brass, T. 1997. "The Agrarian Myth, the 'New' Populism and the 'New' Right." *Journal of Peasant Studies* 24(4): 201–45.

Chakrabarty, D. 2000a. "Subaltern Studies and Postcolonial Historiography." *Nepantla: Views from South* 1(1): 9–32.

——. 2000b. *Provincializing Europe: Postcolonial Thought and Historical Difference*. New Delhi: Oxford University Press.

Chatterjee, P. 1990. "The Nationalist Resolution of the Women's Question." Pp. 233–53 in K. Sangari and S. Vaid, eds., *Recasting Women: Essays in Indian Colonial History*. New Brunswick: Rutgers University Press.

Chaturvedi, V. 2000. *Mapping Subaltern Studies and the Postcolonial*. London and New York: Verso.

Connell, R.W. 1997. "Why Is Classical Theory Classical?" *American Journal of Sociology* 102(6): 1511–57.

Cooper, F. 1994. "Conflict and Connection: Rethinking Colonial African History." *American Historical Review* 99: 1516–45.

Enloe, C.H. 1990. *Bananas, Beaches, and Bases: Making Feminist Sense of International Politics*. Berkeley: University of California Press.

Escobar, A. 2001. "Culture Sits in Places: Reflections on Globalism and Subaltern Strategies of Localization." *Political Geography* 20: 139–74.

Gramsci, A. 1971. *Selections from Prison Notebooks*, trans. and edited by Q. Hoare and G.N. Smith. New York: International Publishers.

Guha, Ranajit. 1982. "On Some Aspects of the Historiography of Colonial India." Pp. 1–9 in Guha, R., ed. *Subaltern Studies: Writings on South Asian History and Society*. Delhi; New York: Oxford University Press.

——. 1997. "Chandra's Death." Pp. 34–62 in R. Guha, ed., *Subaltern Studies Reader: 1986–1995*. Minneapolis: University of Minnesota Press.

Hall, J.R., Neitz, M.J., and Battani, M. 2003. *Sociology on Culture*. London and New York: Routledge.

Li, T.M. 2001. "Masyarakat Adat, Difference, and the Limits of Recognition in Indonesia's Forest Zone." *Modern Asian Studies* 35: 645–76.

McClintock, A. 1995. *Imperial Leather: Race, Gender, and Sexuality in the Colonial Contest*. New York: Routledge.

Mallon, F.E. 1994. "The Promise and Dilemma of Subaltern Studies: Perspectives from Latin American History." *American Historical Review* 99: 1491–515.

Mani, L. 1990. "Contentious Traditions: The Debate on Sati in Colonial India." Pp. 88–126 in K. Sangari and S. Vaid, eds., *Recasting Women: Essays in Indian Colonial History*. New Brunswick: Rutgers University Press.

Moore, D.S. 1998. "Subaltern Struggles and the Politics of Place: Remapping Resistance in Zimbabwe's Eastern Highlands." *Cultural Anthropology* 13(3) (August): 344–81.

O'Hanlon, R. 2000. "Recovering the Subject: Subaltern Studies and Histories of Resistance in Colonial South Asia." Pp. 72–115 in Vinayak Chaturvedi, ed., *Mapping Subaltern Studies and the Postcolonial*. London and New York: Verso.

Ortner, S. 1996. "Resistance and the Problem of Ethnographic Refusal." Pp. 281–304 in T.J. McDonald, ed., *The Historic Turn in the Human Sciences*. Ann Arbor: University of Michigan Press.

Pandey, G. 1989. "The Colonial Construction of Communalism: British Writings on Benaras in the Nineteenth Century." Pp. 132–69 in *Subaltern Studies*, Volume VI. Delhi: Oxford University Press.

Pels, P. 1997. "The Anthropology of Colonialism: Culture, History, and the Emergence of Western Governmentality." *Annual Review of Anthropology* 26: 163–83.

Radhakrishnan, S. 2005. "'Time to Show Our True Colors': the Gendered Politics of Indianness in Post-apartheid South Africa." *Gender and Society* 19: 262–81.

Rodríguez, I. 2001. *The Latin American Subaltern Studies Reader*. Durham, NC: Duke University Press.

Said, E. 1988. "Foreword." Pp. v–xii in R.Guha and G. Spivak, eds., *Selected Subaltern Studies*. Delhi: Oxford University Press.

Sarkar, S. 1989. "The Kalki-Avatar of Bikrampur: A Village Scandal in Early-Twentieth Century Bengal." Pp. 1–53 in R. Guha, ed., *Subaltern Studies*, Volume VI. Delhi: Oxford University Press.

Schwarz, H. and Ray, S. 2000. *A Companion to Postcolonial Studies*. Malden, MA: Blackwell Publishers.

Scott, J. 1985. *Weapons of the Weak: Everyday Forms of Peasant Resistance*. New Haven, CT: Yale University Press.

Sivaramakrishnan, K. 2002. "Situating the Subaltern: History and Anthropology in the Subaltern Studies Project." Pp. 212–55 in D. Ludden, ed., *Reading Subaltern Studies: Critical History, Contested Meaning, and the Globalization of South Asia*. London: Anthem.

Spillman, L. 1997. *Nation and Commemoration: Creating National Identities in the United States and Australia*. Cambridge and New York: Cambridge University Press.

Spivak, G. C. 1988. "Subaltern Studies: Deconstructing Historiography." Pp. 3–32 in R. Guha and G. Spivak, eds., *Selected Subaltern Studies*. Delhi: Oxford University Press.

Walby, S. 1996. "Woman and Nation." Pp. 235–54 in Gopal Balakrishnan, ed., *Mapping the Nation*. New York: Verso.

Yuval-Davis, N. and Anthias, F. 1989. "Introduction." Pp. 1–15 in F. Anthias and N. Yuval-Davis, eds., *Woman–Nation–State*. New York: St. Martin's Press.

4

The cultural turn

Language, globalization, and media

Mark Poster

In *The Cultural Contradictions of Capitalism*, Daniel Bell (1984), as early as 1976, discerned a new importance to culture as a social question, placing it high in the category of dangers, threats, and disruptive forces. Bell noticed recent changes in culture that implied a departure from the individualism of the rational self that had grounded the culture of modernity since the Enlightenment. Youth were moving away from the modern figure of the individual as autonomous and centered, toward avenues that Bell perceived only dimly but nonetheless did not like. Culture for him had become a general social problem. Others soon followed his lead in decrying the drift from rationality that was widespread and growing, notably Christopher Lasch in *The Culture of Narcissism* (Lasch 1979). The question of culture was thereby considerably raised in stature on the agenda of sociology, given the prominence of Bell as a leading social theorist. I believe Bell got it right in his perception of a deep change in culture but perhaps not for the reasons he gave, nor for the negative value he placed on the phenomenon. Surely the great theorists who founded sociology—Max Weber, Auguste Comte, Emile Durkheim—all considered culture as central to their domain of inquiry. Yet Bell was on to something new and distinct from the earlier theorists. I cannot trace in detail these changes in the discipline of sociology as they pertain to the question of culture, however important this project may be. Instead I will focus on three large trends that I believe have, in distinct but interrelated ways, altered at least for the time being, and probably well into the future, the way sociologists consider the question of culture. The three trends I shall discuss are the linguistic turn, globalization, and new media.

The first trend is theoretical and refers to what is often called "the linguistic turn" in philosophy. I argue this is best understood, from the standpoint of sociology, as a "cultural turn" since it conceives the individual as constituted by language, implying a new understanding of the cultural figure of the individual in society. (Fredric Jameson 1998 titles a collection of essays with this term but does not define it or discuss it.) The second trend is globalization. Here the persistent and massive crossing of cultures disrupts the sense of the local, the stability of any one culture. Finally, the rise and spread of new media, a third trend, transforms both the process of the cultural constitution of the self in language, as in the first trend, and the character and dynamics of globalization of the second trend. New media, I shall contend, position the individual in relation to information machines, altering the long-standing relation of humans to objects in the world.

In the social sciences, culture is often regarded as the body of meanings embraced by individuals in a given society. More broadly, the term is often distinguished from "nature" and understood as the sum of practices through which humans build their societies or worlds. The *Oxford English Dictionary*, for instance, gives this as one of its definitions of the noun "culture": "The distinctive ideas, customs, social behavior, products, or way of life of a particular society, people, or period." In a more restricted sense, culture often refers to refinement of taste or to the fine arts or to farming practices. In the discipline of sociology the term has been deployed in numerous ways and on countless objects of study, in far too many varieties for me to enumerate or analyze in this short paper. For my purposes I shall highlight one point: culture has become a chief problem for sociologists increasingly since the latter part of the twentieth century, continuing with ever more intensity in the current century. In the earlier period, say from the eighteenth to the mid-twentieth century, culture in Western societies was mainly naturalized under the sign of human rationality. The study of society did not focus sharply on culture because it was assumed to be a universal aspect of humanity, grounded in individual reason. After the discovery of reason as the essence of man by the *philosophes* in the eighteenth century, the question of culture was subordinated to more pressing issues. These were chiefly the formation of democratic nation-states and the development of industrial economies, two phenomena that preoccupied students of society until well into the twentieth century.

After World War II the assumed universality of culture came into question, especially in France, but more widely in the West, and finally in the rest of the world as well. Certainly the collapse of European empires contributed greatly to a new uncertainty about the naturalness of Western culture and its unquestioned supremacy, but the atrocities of the war—Nazi exterminations and the devastation of the American atom bombs dropped on Japan—also were part of the picture. If American science and the "rational" organization of German institutions were so deeply flawed, how could one argue for the universality of Western culture? Indeed, was not Western culture itself open for and in need of a thoroughgoing examination and critique?

Many intellectual currents contributed to this critique but the most comprehensive and convincing of them was no doubt the movement that came to be known, especially in the United States, as poststructuralism, and is sometimes called, especially in sociology, postmodernism (although I prefer the former term). Poststructuralism began in France and quickly spread to the United States and later more widely around the world. Its leading thinkers included Jacques Derrida, Michel Foucault, Jean-François Lyotard, Gilles Deleuze, Jacques Lacan, Louis Althusser, Pierre Bourdieu, Jean Baudrillard, and Michel de Certeau—a list that could be extended. These poststructuralists, whatever their sometimes considerable differences, developed an analysis of culture in which the rational, autonomous individual of the West was understood not as a value to be treasured, defended, and justified, but as a problem, a question to be pursued to define its limitations, restrictions, and confusions. In this way a path might be opened to construct a superior and less constraining vision of possible future cultural formations. Poststructuralists deepened and extended the insight of Ferdinand de Saussure (1959) that language is not simply a tool to be deployed by a fully conscious individual but that, on the contrary, to a considerable extent language constructs the individual. There was thus conceptualized a form of *unconsciousness* pervading the individual as he or she engaged in language practices.

For the discipline of sociology, poststructuralist arguments concerning the relation of language to the cultural construction of individuals opened a new project, a new manner of understanding and investigating cultural formations, and a new way of theorizing culture in relation to society. In Britain, this task was quickly taken up by Stuart Hall, a sociologist at the Birmingham School of Cultural Studies (Hall 1996); in France by Michel de Certeau and Pierre Bourdieu; in the United States by Larry Grossberg and many others. (See Jacobs and Hanrahan 2005 for a comprehensive interrogation of the question of culture for sociologists.)

The poststructuralist concept of the cultural construction of the individual enables sociologists to avoid imposing Western notions of individualism, assuming their universality, and projecting them throughout global cultures. For many groups are disadvantaged by Western precepts—women, ethnic minorities, working classes, children, and of course the non-Western world. Armed with a poststructuralist sense of the construction of individuals through languages and practices, sociologists study the historical formation of Western individuals as well as the formation of cultural groups outside the aegis of Western society. Although it is true that the pioneers of sociology such as Max Weber (1958) experimented with cultural analysis, they often fell into universalizing positions in part because of the absence of language theory in their work.

The second trend urging a repositioning of the problem of culture is globalization. Exchanges between cultures, even long-distance trade, characterize human society as far back as scholars have been able to determine. As transport and communications systems improved, such encounters only increased. In the wake of World War II, along with the ensuing overthrow of Western imperialist states, and finally with the emergence of neoliberal demands for unrestricted global trade in the 1980s, the process of globalization expanded exponentially. As late as the 1990s some economists cautiously pointed to the relative low percentages of global trade compared with intra-national movements of goods (Carnoy *et al.* 1993). But by the turn of the new century no one convincingly denied the prominence of an economically interconnected world. From the integration of major stock markets to the industrialization of Asian economies, from the instantaneous communication of news events by satellites circling the Earth to the startling unification of oil markets, globalization was recognized as a permanent and rapidly increasing feature of human society. At the economic level, globalization applied not only to commodity markets but to labor markets as well. Workers in one sector of national production now competed with others around the planet.

Economic globalization, whatever its benefits, also produced numerous discontents and resistances (Sassen 1998). Political responses to economic globalization have been and continue to be complex and in many ways unprecedented. From attacks on McDonald's outlets to the Seattle protests of 1999 against the meeting of the World Trade Organization, to the worldwide opposition movements against the Bush administration's war in Iraq in February 2003, globalization has not been greeted warmly by all groups. As a suggestion for further research, despite the often nationalist aspirations of some of these movements, one might find in the protests an emerging form of planetary political culture. Although it is tempting to understand contemporary globalization as yet another example of Western imperialism—and certainly George W. Bush's rhetoric about bringing democracy to Iraq lent itself to this interpretation—I find it too simple to reduce economic globalization to a new form of Western domination. If one limits oneself to that perspective, one would have to explain the eagerness of some nations, especially in Asia, to enter the global economy. Al Qaida and China arguably form two opposite poles on a continuum of responses to Western aspects of globalization. The former presents an absolute resistance (although, when it suits their purposes, al Qaida adopt Western originating technologies like the internet and the video camera); the latter constitutes a creative adaptation of Western economic practices, attuned to Chinese ways of doing things.

At the cultural level, globalization propelled images, sounds, and texts around the globe. Before the twentieth century, European colonialism as well as regional movements of groups established contacts and encounters between peoples of different cultures (Pratt 1992). In new spaces created in ports, border towns, and elsewhere, cultures confronted one another in face-to-face encounters, most often with unequal resources and disastrous results. Humans seemingly had great difficulty cognitively and emotionally when confronted by others, by those whose appearance, beliefs, languages, and practices were strange and incomprehensible. With more recent globalizing trends these mixings multiplied enormously, perhaps to the point that the coherence of individual cultures became no longer possible. In the late twentieth and early twenty-first centuries, trans-cultural encounters extended beyond face-to-face contacts to include flows of images, texts, and sounds in numerous media forms (Morely and Robins 1995; Castells 1996; Soares 1996). Sociologists would now have to account for culture not only at the level of individual societies but also at that of cultural contacts and exchanges, at the level of transnational national cultural phenomena, international cultural phenomena, and global cultural flows.

The third trend of a new sociology of culture—the globalization of media—follows perhaps from economic globalization. Texts, sounds, and images now flow across the globe with an unprecedented intensity and density. Trillions of bytes of information circulate continuously if unequally to every corner of the planet, with a full one-sixth of the human population using the internet, not to speak of television broadcasts and film audiences. Manuel Castells refers quite appropriately to this phenomenon as "the Internet Galaxy" (Castells 2001). It no longer comes as a surprise that instantaneous reception of news and other forms of information is an everyday occurrence. What may be less understood is that scientific knowledge, like the genome project, also is part of this global flow and indeed, as Eugene Thacker (2005) argues, this flow is essential to the success of genome research. The circulation of genome data, he argues, is an essential condition for their development and use. In his words, "the processes of globalization form a core component of biological knowledge and practice" (Thacker 2005: xvii). From financial markets to peer-to-peer file sharing, from scientific research to social networking, from online gaming to consumer buying, the global aspect of culture is now, and increasingly so, an integral part of human culture.

The chief challenge for the sociology of culture that takes the global flows of information into account is to theorize and analyze the specificity of different media forms in the process. At the same time, the relation of local cultures to the new media is also of critical importance. Compared with analogue broadcast media like print, television, radio, and film, the internet certainly provides an entirely different relation of the consumer/ user to the producer. The online receiver is also at once a sender, the consumer a producer, the audience is an author. What is more, the user/consumer is attached to an information machine in new ways. The human and the machine are integrated as an assemblage or ensemble so that the old Western individual no longer is configured as a "subject" over against a relatively inert "object." Further, the internet is the first medium of cultural exchange that consistently violates political borders. The posts that the nation-state established—paper mail, export control of book, magazines, film, and television—are bypassed to a great extent by the global network of computers.

Although new media introduce new cultural configurations, in good part as a consequence of their material structure, they also interact with social phenomena that are not *per se* new media. Two aspects of the relation of new media to culture that I discuss below, however briefly, are the nation-state and the corporation and adaptations of new media by non-Western cultures. First, the institutions that predate the internet, especially the nation-state and the industrial economy, appropriate the new media and attempt to shape it in their own image. China notoriously censors web sites, for example, attempting to retrofit the internet to state control of cultural dissemination. Corporations attempt to control the reproduction of cultural content, from software to music, film, and television. These actions form one end of a continuum of response by older institutions. A second level of adaptation of new media to older ways of doing things is cultural. Anthropologists have studied how some cultures extend existing practices and attitudes to the internet (Miller and Slater 2000). The innovative features of networked computing are in this case minimized. Older cultural patterns are simply brought to the internet, evaporating the opportunity for new patterns while reinforcing existing values.

Another and very distinct way that new media are adapted at the cultural level is one that makes fewer compromises with pre-digital worlds. Here the users throw themselves into the new domain, attempting to explore the differences it affords from analogue cultures. Massively, multiple online gaming, creating web sites, engaging in peer-to-peer exchanges of content, artist experiments with digital culture, and so forth are not simply substitutions for pre-existing behaviors (such as Skype for the telephone) but innovations in the basic conditions of culture. Of course these individuals and groups remain participants in their local cultures and are by no means born anew in their exploration of new media. Yet, especially the younger generation around the world is less socialized into analogue media forms than older generations and is perhaps more open to experimenting with new media.

These three large trends in the relation between global media and culture, as well as countless variations between them, open the salient political question of their resolution: which model will prevail? Will the internet become a mere extension of older social and cultural forms? Or will its innovative features emerge in relief, becoming the basis of new cultural configurations, in the context of wider aspects of globalization? Perhaps as a consequence in part of global media, "man," as Foucault says, will disappear. Or perhaps as Freud says at the conclusion of *Civilization and Its Discontents*, some new, unforeseen, and unforeseeable cultural form will arise in conjunction with global media, completely altering our sense of what is possible. The tasks are truly daunting for the sociology of culture in accounting for the impact of new media while at the same time giving due recognition of the multiple contexts of their dissemination.

One issue that, if pursued, might lead to some clarification of the question of a sociology of culture is that of media and self-constitution, and this is my main concern in this essay. Although the relations between the three trends affecting culture (the linguistic turn, globalization, and new media) might be studied in detail and are already being looked at, to be sure, my interest lies elsewhere. I mean the problematic developed with especial force by Michel Foucault throughout his works: the need to place the Western figure of the individual in question, in particular in historical question. Unless we understand how the self in the West is constituted by discourses and practices, we inevitably naturalize and universalize that self and consequently approach the context of globalization and multiple cultures with serious handicaps, blindness, and misrecognition of the others, of those with significantly different cultural figures. Of course this problem holds not only for the Western figure of the self but for all cultures. Yet the Western individual is the cultural form that accompanied the spread of Western power across the globe over the past half-millennium and is therefore especially implicated in the issue. If this problematic is accepted as pertinent, then one can focus on the role of media in the complex processes of self-constitution. One can move to this question without any sort of ontological privileging of media, any reliance on media determinism, but simply with the recognition that information machines have been and continue to be positioned in relation to human beings in such a manner that their imbrication is undeniable (McLuhan 1964). Man and machine are now, and surely will continue to be, joined at the hip, so to speak. Their relations are essential to a sociology of culture (Latour 1979).

The next step in the argument is to explore the question of media specificity: how are information machines implicated differently in the question of self-constitution? Do typewriters (Kittler 1986), print machinery (Johns 1998), telegraph (Carey 1989), telephone (Marvin 1988), film (Crary 1992), radio (Brecht 1979–80), television (Dienst 1994), and the internet (Poster 2006) create the same or different cultural forms, i.e. space/time configurations, imaginary registries, body/mind relations? How do these media interact with other everyday practices, with ethnicity, age, gender, and sexual preference? How do they interact in different national and regional cultures? How do they interact in different historic epochs? Without detailed analyses of these issues, the sociology of culture cannot contribute much to an understanding of our global, postmodern condition. Nor can it contribute much to a clarification of the important political matters that confront us. It is time, then, to take information machines—media—seriously into account in a developing and changing sociology of culture.

References

Bell, Daniel. 1984. *The Cultural Contradictions of Capitalism, and Beyond Mechanization: Work and Technology in a Postindustrial Age*. Cambridge, MA: MIT Press.

Brecht, Bertolt. 1979–80. "On Radio." *Screen* 20(3–4): 19.

Carey, James. 1989. *Communication as Culture: Essays on Media and Society*. New York: Routledge.

Carnoy, Martin and Castells, Manuel, Cohen, Stephen, and Cardoso, Fernando. 1993. *The New Global Economy in the Information Age*. University Park: Penn State University Press.

Castells, Manuel. 1996. *The Rise of the Network Society*. Cambridge, MA: Blackwell Publishers.

——. 2001. *The Internet Galaxy: Reflections on the Internet, Business, and Society*. New York: Oxford University Press.

Crary, Jonathan. 1992. *Techniques of the Observer: On Vision and Modernity in the Nineteenth Century*. Cambridge, MA: MIT Press.

Dienst, Richard. 1994. *Still Life in Real Time: Theory after Television*. Durham, NC: Duke University Press.

Hall, Stuart. 1996. "The Question of Cultural Identity." Pp. 595–634 in S. Hall, D. Held, D. Hubert and K. Thompson, eds. *Modernity: An Introduction to Modern Societies*. London: Blackwell.

Jacobs, Mark and Hanrahan, Nancy Weiss, eds., 2005. *The Blackwell Companion to the Sociology of Culture*. London: Blackwell.

Jameson, Fredric. 1998. *The Cultural Turn: Selected Writings on the Postmodern, 1983–1998*. New York: Verso.

Johns, Adrian. 1998. *The Nature of the Book: Print and Knowledge in the Making*. Chicago: University of Chicago Press.

Kittler, Friedrich A. 1986. *Grammophon, Film, Typewriter*. Berlin: Brinkmann & Bose.

Lasch, Christopher. 1979. *The Culture of Narcissism: American Life in an Age of Diminishing Expectations*. New York: Norton.

Latour, Bruno. 1979. *Laboratory Life: The Social Construction of Scientific Facts*. Beverly Hills, CA: Sage Publications.

McLuhan, Marshall. 1964. *Understanding Media: The Extensions of Man*. New York: McGraw-Hill.

Marvin, Carolyn. 1988. *When Old Technologies Were New: Thinking about Electric Communication in the Late Nineteenth Century*. New York: Oxford.

Miller, Daniel and Slater, Don. 2000. *The Internet: An Ethnographic Approach*. New York: Berg.

Morely, David and Robins, Kevin. 1995. *Spaces of Identity: Global Media, Electronic Landscapes and Cultural Boundaries*. New York: Routledge.

Poster, Mark. 2006. *Information Please: Culture and Politics in the Age of Digital Machines*. Durham, NC: Duke University Press.

Pratt, Mary Louise. 1992. *Imperial Eyes: Travel Writing and Transculturation*. New York: Routledge.

Sassen, Saskia. 1998. *Globalization and Its Discontents*. New York: The New Press.

Saussure, Ferdinand de. 1959. *Course in General Linguistics*. New York: Philosophical Library.

Soares, Luiz, ed. 1996. *Cultural Pluralism, Identity, and Globalization*. Rio de Janeiro: Conjunto Univerrsitário Candido Mendes.

Thacker, Eugene. 2005. *The Global Genome: Biotechnology, Politics, and Culture*. Cambridge, MA: MIT Press.

Weber, Max. 1958. *The Protestant Ethic and the Spirit of Capitalism*. New York: Macmillan.

5

Media evolution and cultural change

Joshua Meyrowitz

British colonial personnel first recorded the history of the state of Gonja in northern Ghana at the turn of the twentieth century. At that time, the Gonja explained the origin of the seven divisional chiefdoms of their territory by recounting how their founding father, Ndewura Jakpa, had traveled down from the Niger Bend in search of gold, becoming chief of the state after conquering its indigenous peoples, and placing his seven sons as rulers of seven territorial divisions. Yet, when the history of Gonja was recorded again sixty years later, following some territorial shifts, the story of origin had changed. Jakpa's family, as told at that time by the Gonja, had shrunk to only five sons, conveniently matching the then current five territorial divisions. As anthropologist Jack Goody and literary historian Ian Watt (1963) claim, such "automatic adjustments" of history to existing social relations were accomplished relatively easily by the Gonja because they functioned within an oral rather than a written tradition. Once the talk and memories of seven Jakpa sons faded, there were no written artifacts to contradict the new narrative of five sons. The spread of writing in a culture, argue Goody and Watt, has "consequences" that cannot be reduced to the content of what is written.

We human beings often distinguish ourselves from animals by pointing to the complex manner in which we communicate. Yet, most scholars have been hesitant to explore the intricate ways in which changes in the forms of communication—such as the addition of writing to oral societies, the addition of printing to scribal societies, the addition of radio to print cultures, and the subsequent wide use of television, the internet, and other electronic media—may encourage new forms of social organization and undermine old ones. Even in the field of media studies itself, the primary focus has been on the safer and simpler view of media as relatively passive conduits that deliver "messages." Most media research has focused on topics such as how audiences perceive and respond to media content or how political and economic forces shape dominant media messages. Content-focused research has led to many significant findings, but it has ignored larger questions about the ways in which changes in media, apart from messages, may alter the textures and forms of social life. At the same time, individual scholars from a variety of fields—including history, anthropology, literary studies, the classics, political economy, and legal studies—have tackled these larger questions. I have called their approach "medium theory" (Meyrowitz 1985: 16; 2009). I use the singular "medium" to highlight their focus on the distinct characteristics of each medium (or each type of media) and how those characteristics may encourage or constrain forms of interaction and social organization.

Medium theory can be divided into microlevel and macrolevel questions. Microlevel medium theory explores the consequences of the choice of one medium over another in a particular situation, such as initiating or ending a personal relationship, applying for a job, commanding troops, or interacting with one's children. Macrolevel medium theory explores larger questions about the ways in which changes in media have influenced modes of thinking, patterns of social organization, status differences, value systems, collective memory, and even the physical layout of the built environment. In this chapter, I provide a brief overview of the work of medium theorists. Then I outline four major communication/cultural phases as conceived of by macrolevel medium theory. And, finally, I describe a few key limits of the medium-theory perspective.

The medium theorists

The idea of studying media in themselves gained prominence in the 1960s with the publication of Marshall McLuhan's *The Gutenberg Galaxy* (1962) and *Understanding Media* (1994 [1964]). McLuhan's provocative puns and aphorisms helped to make him a media celebrity, with many passionate adherents and many savage critics. Most scholars fell into the latter camp. Indeed, the negative assessments of McLuhan's style of argument and bold claims have, unfortunately, tended to diminish, rather than increase, scholarly work in this area.

The history of medium theory, however, is much deeper and broader than McLuhan's work. Socrates (469–399 BC) was perhaps the earliest medium theorist. He argued that written communications were profoundly different from spoken ones. Writing, claimed Socrates, would alter humans' use of their memories, decrease interactive dialogue in favor of extended monologues, and lead to new forms of communication that were not tailored to specific local audiences. Socrates' negative assessment of these changes is mostly out of step with Western thought concerning the positive virtues of literacy. That evaluative disjuncture, combined with the irony that Socrates' critiques of writing survive only because his most famous student, Plato, wrote them down in the *Phaedrus*, has tended to mute appreciation for the basic accuracy of Socrates' descriptions of the differences between two forms of communication.

About nineteen hundred years after Socrates' death, the inventor of printing based on movable type, Johannes Gutenberg, expressed awareness of how different printing was from writing and how the religious information monopoly of the Catholic Church was being threatened as a result. The slow copying of texts by religious scribes was no match for the speed and accuracy of the printing press. In the closing inscription for a religious encyclopedia in 1460, Gutenberg boasted that it "has been printed and accomplished without the help of reed, stylus, or pen," that is, without the help of the Church's scribes. Gutenberg also hinted that his own invention was operating in the service of God, "who often reveals to the lowly what he hides from the wise" (quoted in Steinberg 1974: 19). Gutenberg's assessment of the potential impact of printing on the hierarchal control over religious information was made manifest by Martin Luther and his followers in the early sixteenth century. They employed the new communication technology to

53

circulate the Bible and religious commentaries and critiques in the "lowly" languages of the people, thereby orchestrating the first mass-media public-relations campaign and splitting the Church through the Protestant Reformation.

In the nineteenth century, an implicit medium-theory perspective underlay the birth of the field of sociology, whose founders understood that the influences of machines of mass production (the "media") could not be reduced to an inventory of the products (the "content") produced. Rather, they argued, the new means of production had to be measured in terms of new forms of social relations, such as urbanization and bureaucratization.

At the turn of the twentieth century, Scottish scientist and urban planner Patrick Geddes (1904) advanced the idea that interactions between social processes and the environment (both natural and constructed) brought about social change. Lewis Mumford (1934), a disciple of Geddes, explored the impact and mythology of "the machine," including the impact of the printing press. In the 1930s, gestalt theorist and film enthusiast Rudolf Arnheim (1957) articulated a medium-theory argument to defend the motion picture as an art form against critics who said that film was merely a mechanical reproduction of reality. In his *Materialtheorie*, Arnheim argued that "artistic and scientific descriptions of reality are cast in molds that derive not so much from the subject matter itself as from the properties of the medium—or *Material*—employed" (1957: 2).

In the 1930s, Canadian political economist Harold Adams Innis began to explore how his research on the fur trade and on the pathways and waterways that shaped the flow of staples could be extended into an exploration of the flow of information through different media. Innis' interest in economic monopolies led him to theorize that the characteristics of some media (such as very complex writing systems) supported hierarchal control over information, whereas other media forms encouraged more egalitarian communication systems. He also argued that different media were biased toward either lasting for a long time ("time-biased" media such as stone carvings) or traveling easily over great distances ("space-biased" media such as papyrus and paper), and he linked these contrasting biases to the differences between cultures that maintained stability over time in limited territory and empires that controlled large territories but were less stable and long-lasting. In two dense books written shortly before his death, *Empire and Communications* (1950) and *The Bias of Communication* (1951), Innis drew on these and similar insights to rewrite the history of civilization from the perspective of the impact of media on cultural forms.

Innis' theories of media were among the influences that led literary scholar and budding media theorist Marshall McLuhan to turn away from his analyses of advertising content (1951) to the study of media themselves. McLuhan played down Innis' concerns with political power and monopolies, however, emphasizing instead the ideas that different media altered the balance of the senses and changed patterns of perception and thought. Writing and printing, argued McLuhan, gave tribal peoples an "eye for an ear," in that writing emphasized the lineality of visual perspective over simultaneous, multi-sensory experience. Although McLuhan personally cherished literature, his dispassionate scholarly assessment was that electronic media were making print "obsolescent." He meant this not in the sense of ending book publishing or reading, but in the sense of electronic patterns undermining the "Gutenberg galaxy" of print-inspired forms, such as linear thinking, nationalism, standardization, fixed identity and narrowly defined "jobs," assembly-line mass-production and mass-education, cause-and-effect thinking, and fragmentation of knowledge into distinct disciplines. McLuhan tried to embody the changes he envisioned by using non-linear "probes" and trans-disciplinary arguments to investigate media and cultural change. Such approaches did not sit well with many of the guardians of literate modes of thinking and academic disciplinarity. With his often-misunderstood pun "the *medium* is the message," he chided media researchers for being too focused on media content and paying insufficient attention to the influences of each form of media, including the "change of scale or pace or pattern that it introduces into human affairs" (McLuhan 1994 [1964]: 8). In an electronic age, McLuhan argued, we often become "discarnate" beings whose communications are increasingly disembodied. McLuhan also claimed that electronic media were "retribalizing" the new generation and encouraging humans everywhere to become emotionally involved in affairs happening around the world in the electronically facilitated "global village."

Innis and McLuhan are unique in terms of their boldness of argument and the breadth of world history and human experience that they attempt to analyze. But many other scholars have offered more focused explorations of aspects of media evolution and cultural change. The shift from orality to literacy has been explored by J.C. Carothers (1959), Jack Goody and Ian Watt (1963), Eric Havelock (1963), and Walter Ong (1982). They suggest that literacy fostered new forms of social organization, modes of consciousness, conceptions of "knowledge," and individuality. Robert Logan (1986) argues that the phonetic alphabet, more than other writing systems (and particularly when amplified through printing), encouraged the development of abstract thinking that led to codified law, monotheism, formal, logic, and science—in short, the main hallmarks of Western civilization.

H.J. Chaytor (1945) and Elizabeth Eisenstein (1979) have explored the consequences of the shift from script literacy to print literacy. Chaytor argues that printing altered the psychological interaction of words and thought, created a new sense of "authorship" and intellectual property, reshaped literary style, and fostered the growth of nationalistic feelings. Eisenstein's massive study of printing supports Chaytor's claims and also presents detailed evidence and argument that the printing press revolutionized Western Europe by facilitating the Protestant Reformation and the growth of modern science.

The spread of electronic media has led to a surge of interest in medium theory. Building on his careful analyses of earlier communication shifts, Walter Ong (1967) argues that electronic media create a "secondary orality" that retrieves some aspects of the "primary orality" of preliterate societies, while also being distinct from all earlier forms of communication. Historian Daniel Boorstin (1973) compares and contrasts technological revolutions with political revolutions, and he describes how electronic media level time and space and reshape conceptions of history, nationality, and progress by "mass-producing the moment" and creating "repeatable" experiences. In my role-system version of medium theory (Meyrowitz 1985), I argue that electronic media tend to reshape everyday behaviors associated with group identity, socialization, and hierarchy by undermining print-era patterns of what different types of people know about, and relative to, each other. Electronic media, I claim, foster changes in roles by providing more shared access to information, breaking down the distinction between our public and private spheres, and weakening the age-old connection between physical location and social experience. Ethan Katsh (1989) details how electronic means of storing and processing information undermine print-era notions of legal precedent and monopoly over legal knowledge. Digital media, according to Manuel Castells (1996), facilitate the global dominance of "the network," an ancient form of connection that once could exist only on a small scale. In a medium-theory approach to changes in international relations,

Ronald Deibert (1997) reviews millennia of history to show how the "chance fitness" between the characteristics of a new medium and particular pre-existing social forces helped to bring those "media-favored" processes from the margin of society to the center. Deibert then demonstrates how the era of hypermediation is similarly facilitating major shifts in world order toward "de-territorialized communities, fragmented identities, transnational corporations, and cyberspatial flows of finance" (1997: ix). Mark Poster (2006) scrutinizes the cultural consequences of the unprecedented relations between humans and information machines. Among the many scholars studying the social ramifications of mobile media is Rich Ling (2008), who describes how mobile communications reshape the patterns of social cohesion and foster what he calls "bounded solidarity." In his *New New Media*, Paul Levinson (2009) details how blogging, Wikipedia, YouTube, FaceBook, and other media in which consumers are also producers are altering the texture of social and political life. This work extends Levinson's (1997) earlier analyses of the ways in which the development of new media throughout history has interacted with human decision-making and planning.

Although the above theorists would not necessarily consider themselves to be members of a common intellectual tradition, their work, when assembled into a single narrative, presents a surprisingly coherent and consistent view of the ways in which the use of various media of communication may contribute to large-scale cultural change. In the next section, I provide an outline of four communication/cultural phases as conceived of within medium theory. I have space here to present only broad sketches of each phase, stripped of nuance and qualification. Yet, the general exercise offers a preliminary sense of the promises and challenges of this perspective.

Cultural phases *à la* medium theory

Traditional oral cultures

In oral societies, sound and speech dominate as the forms of interaction. The culture's history, philosophy, and mores must be stored in memory and conveyed orally, supported by embodied action, song, dance, and ritual. This living storage system and biological delivery process tie members closely to each other. To facilitate memorization and transmission, cultural content is often put in the form of rhythmic poetry and mythic narratives that consist of familiar stories with formulaic actions and stock phrases. Because oral communication requires physical co-presence, oral cultures have few if any means of interacting with the experience or thinking of those who do not share the same time/ space arena. Such societies are "conservative" in the sense of working hard to conserve what they already know and are. People from other places are perceived as profoundly "strange." Moreover, the modern notion of the "individual" as the prime social unit has relatively little chance of developing. Members of the society tend to have very similar cultural experiences and knowledge. Novel ideas and complex original arguments can gain little traction because such concepts are difficult to remember (even by the people who develop them) and almost impossible to pass on to many others who have no means beyond memory through which to store them. Indeed, extreme individual creativity would be a potentially destructive force.

Because human beings naturally develop the abilities to utter and understand speech, oral societies have relatively few status distinctions, which would require different sets of social information and experience. Nomadic oral societies are particularly egalitarian, since they have limited opportunities to separate people of different ages, genders, and other categories into different information systems based on physical segregation. In oral agricultural societies, however, ties to locale make distinctions in status more feasible, since rudimentary separations of physical spheres allow for some segregation of male/female, child/adult, and leader/follower experiences and roles. Yet, even settled oral cultures find it difficult to isolate members into many different spheres. Children as a group can be partially separated from adults as a group, but year-by-year age distinctions are difficult to support.

In oral societies, words are not objects to be viewed or held, but time-bound *events*, much like thunder or a scream. It is difficult for a person to escape spoken words and other sounds in the way that one can look away from visual objects. (Humans have eyelids, but not earlids, and sounds come from all directions, not just from in front of us.) The shapes of the built environment in oral societies tend to mimic these circular contours of sound and hearing. In oral societies, both dwellings and villages are usually round. Oral peoples are always at the center of their communication world, with few opportunities or perceptual tools to stand back from it and analyze it.

The transitional scribal phase

The development of writing begins to change the structure of oral societies. Since writing is not a "natural" human ability, writing systems segregate those who can read and write from those who cannot. Different stages of mastery of writing and reading foster different levels of authority. Moreover, different types of writing systems have different influences. Writing systems that have many complex symbols support greater distinctions in status, whereas simpler writing systems encourage more egalitarian social roles. Additionally, pictographic writing systems (where each object or idea has its own "meaningful" symbol) sustain concrete thinking, whereas phonetic systems (where meaningless symbols represent each sound) tend to promote more abstract thinking.

At first, writing is used to record what was previously only spoken (poetry, dialogue, formulaic myths, etc.). In the long run, however, phonetic writing in particular tends to break down the tribal cohesion of oral societies because it offers a relatively simple way to preserve prose and construct extended strings of connected abstract thought that would be almost impossible for oral peoples to develop, memorize, or transmit to others.

Writing splinters and unites people in new ways. As writing spreads, people who live in the same places begin to know and experience different things, while those who read the same material begin to feel connected to each other regardless of their locations. Yet, the complexity of learning to read and write, combined with the initial scarcity of written materials, means that fledgling literate modes of social organization compete with powerful and enduring oral modes and have limited impact until the development of movable type and the printing press. Indeed, readers of early written texts have difficulty reading without speaking the words aloud.

Modern print culture

Although the Chinese developed the art of printing long before Gutenberg's fifteenth-century invention in Germany, the Chinese ideographic writing system, with thousands of different characters needed even for basic literacy, retards the impact of printing in that culture. In the phonetically alphabetized West, however, the growing availability of printed materials helps to reorganize social structures based on new patterns of shared and unshared communication. Conceptions of "them" versus "us" change. Literate readers and writers engage with ideas that their illiterate neighbors (and their own young children) cannot hear, speak, or remember, and different readers and writers develop different individual "perspectives." By allowing easy access to social information apart from face-to-face interaction, printing encourages retreat from the surrounding oral community and from extended kinship ties and greater isolation of the nuclear family. Yet, printing also bypasses the local community in the other direction with the development of larger intellectual, political, and religious units. The Protestant Reformation is facilitated by making the Bible and religious commentary and critique widely available in the vernacular, thereby bypassing the Catholic Church's monopoly over direct access to the word of God and to the paths to eternal salvation. The new patterns of sharing and not sharing religious texts foster new patterns of religious unity across vast distances and eras, along with growing disunity among those in the same places at the same time. "Strangers" are increasingly present in one's own midst.

Printing in the vernacular also permits readers to see on a printed page the larger "reality" of what were once only local voices, and this encourages the development of nationalism. Readers feel an abstract unity with all those who share the same language, wherever they may be, rather than feeling connections only to those who share the same concrete local space. Connections based on face-to-face loyalties—such as feudal ties based on oral oaths—yield over time to nation-states based on printed constitutions and other political, social, and legal documents that literally "constitute" the shared conceptions, customs, and laws of the nation.

Unlike the verbal events of oral societies, printed texts encourage the experience of words as objects, spatially fixed on a page. In oral interaction, even a delay of a few seconds in response can seem rude and inappropriate. With print, in contrast, a reader can stare at words, read them at his or her own pace, turn away from them, and re-read them. Most significantly, a reader is able to think about words before forming a reaction to them. And formal written responses can be revised and self-censored multiple times before being shown to other people. Utterances, in contrast, cannot be taken back or erased. These characteristics of reading and writing facilitate the growth of internal dialogue, introspection, and individualistic thinking. Moreover, literate persons' physical, social, and mental positions are no longer exclusively at the center of oral events; they can stand away from the communications of others and develop a more distant, refined, reflective, and individualized "point of view."

Print encourages modes of thinking and social organization that mimic its physical forms. "Rationality," highly valued in a print culture, is structured like the letters of type: step-by-step abstract reasoning along a continuous line of argument and analysis. In a print culture, the simultaneous, overlapping events and expressions of oral interaction must compete with a one-thing-at-a-time and one-thing-after-another world of linear thought. In place of "outmoded" views of human life as involving repeating cycles of nature, society comes to be seen as striving for constant linear development, improvement, and "progress." Visual and linear metaphors pervade modes of discourse: Do you see my point? I follow your line of thinking. "Circular reasoning" is dismissed as deficient.

As the quantity of information explodes in a print culture, features exclusive to print are used to manage the overload—page numbers, alphabetized indexes, cross-referenced category systems. Print's emphasis on sequence and on the segregation of one thing from another encourages the separation of topics and approaches into different disciplines, along with the ranking of material within each discipline in terms of degrees of mastery. Distinctions in "levels" of reading are seen as tied to natural differences in social identity and status. Modern conceptions of "childhood" and "adulthood" are invented in sixteenth-century Europe, and their spread follows the spread of literate schooling. Schools increasingly segregate children into year-by-year groupings based on different stages of reading skill and step-by-step access to adult information. Distinct literatures for each sex foster greater distinctions in gender roles. Leadership in print societies is based on distance and inaccessibility, delegated authority, and tight control over public image. Roles in businesses are structured via printed organizational charts with narrowly defined job descriptions in rectangular boxes connected by fixed "lines of authority."

New patterns of perception and thought are echoed in the built environment. Habitats evolve from round dwellings in round villages with winding paths to right-angle structures in linear rows on straight streets in grid-like cities. Outdoor marketplaces with non-linear arrangements evolve into stores with straight rows and labeled sections. Production of goods moves from holistic crafting to fragmented steps on assembly lines. Print-era classrooms are constructed with chairs bolted to the floors in rows that resemble the evenly spaced letters and words fixed on a printed page. Such arrangements of classrooms, offices, and other spaces generally discourage informal oral interactions, even among those in the same space.

Social passages—such as birth, aging, mental decline, and death—are increasingly denaturalized and removed from the center of community and family life and placed in isolated institutions. The physical and social membranes around such institutions thicken and harden as print culture matures. The school, hospital, prison, military barracks, and factory become highly distinct settings with restricted access and distinct rules and roles. The people within a single chamber of a single institution (fifth graders, assembly-line workers, bank tellers, etc.) are increasingly viewed as standardized interchangeable parts, while those in one institution (or in one subdivision of an institution) and those in another institution (or in another subdivision of the same institution) are increasingly seen as very different from each other. The world comes to be seen as naturally layered and segmented, with a distinct place for every thing and for every body, and with every thing and body in its designated place.

Postmodern global electronic culture

As with earlier communication shifts, the use of electronic media takes time to spread and saturate societies before having significant and visible influences on social forms. Indeed, the harbingers of a new media era, the telegraph and telephone, come into use as print culture is reaching its full power, with the push for universal literacy and the dominance of print-encouraged forms of thought and social organization.

In the long run, however, electronic media such as radio, television, the computer, the internet, and mobile devices undermine many features of print culture. They therefore have their most dramatic influences in the West, where the patterns of print culture became so pervasive. Electronic media retrieve some key aspects of oral societies, including the dominance of sensory experiences and the near-simultaneity of action, perception, and reaction. On radio and TV, the word returns as an event, rather than as an object. Unlike print media, which fostered new means of sharing knowledge,

59

electronic media tend to facilitate new forms of shared experience. Yet the secondary orality of the electronic era differs from pre-literate oral communication in multiple ways. Electronic interactions are not subject to the "natural" limits of time or space. Electronic communications can travel across great distances at the speed of light and they can be preserved beyond the lifetimes of the communicators. Electronic media also bypass the stages and filters of literacy. A child does not need to watch television shows or surf the internet in a particular order in the way that children typically need to read simple books before reading complex books. As a result, children are now routinely exposed to topics that adults spent several centuries trying to hide from children. Even those women who are isolated at home are able to observe closely the "male realms" of culture—business, war, sports, politics—that they have, until recently, been told are off-limits to them. Articulate, street-smart members of a studio audience (or radio listeners who call in) are often able to run circles around a talk-show guest with a Ph.D. or high political status. Electronic experiences thrust all of us among people with whom we have not shared the same literatures, territories, or even languages. As electronic patterns of interaction and experience diverge from the neat lines of print-supported sequences of ranks and hierarchies, there is a decline in the influence of political parties, unions, gender- and age-specific activities, organizational charts, and government and school bureaucracies. Digital media facilitate seemingly random patterns of collaborative and quickly shifting neo-feudal ties irrespective of territorial borders and traditional social groupings. "Wiki" formations, based on the power of open peer collaborations, change the notion of "authoritative" knowledge.

Unlike written and printed words, which emphasize ideas, many electronic media highlight feeling, appearance, and mood. Political and other figures in the public realm are increasingly judged by "dating criteria," in addition to "résumé criteria." That is, rather than primarily asking "What has he accomplished?" or "How well educated is she?" the public is also very concerned with the questions "What's he like?" and "Do I like her?" Even analyses of statements in televised political debates now tend to deemphasize print-era questions such as "Is it true or is it false?" with increasing attention to electronic-era questions such as "What impression does it make?" and "How does it feel?"

Along with the enhanced focus on feeling and emotion and other criteria of evaluation that require no special training, information implosion leads to the blurring of disciplinary boundaries, an appreciation for generalism, and the growing sense that everyone has the right to his or her opinion (whether "informed" or not!). The extended single "story line" yields to less linear forms in jokes, literature, and drama. And those who claim to be able to tap into the holistic thinking of the right side of their brains are now often praised as "advanced," rather than being dismissed as unsophisticated and primitive.

As with earlier changes in media, the shape of the built environment evolves to mimic the forms of electronic information flow. Classroom desks are unbolted and often set in circles and there is more mixing of the ages. Office walls are torn down and replaced with semi-open cubicles that let in sound from all directions. Management consultants suggest "quality circles" to improve productivity. Many once marginalized populations are "mainstreamed." The fanciest stores no longer have grid-like rows, but are arranged more like unpredictable pathways in oral villages. The membranes around institutions become more permeable. Birth and death are brought back into many homes at the same time as many birthing and hospice facilities welcome the whole family into spaces that are decorated to look like home bedrooms. Even those places that remain unchanged in appearance change in function. Sending a child to his or her room no longer serves as a punishment based on ex-communication from social interaction if the child's room is connected to others through radio, television, mobile phone, and computer. Similar changes in the relationship between physical place and social "place" occur for prisoners, minorities, the poor, and others in once informationally remote locations. There are more similarities between people in different locations and institutions, just as there is an acceptance of greater diversity and idiosyncrasy within the same places and institutions. Greater sharing of information and communication options increases demands for (and often tensions over) more equal roles and opportunities in the local, national, and global arenas.

Medium theory in perspective

The grand scope of macrolevel medium theory, as illustrated above, makes the theory difficult to test using typical "social-scientific" methods. This perspective is also susceptible to criticism for relative lack of attention to exceptions and variations within cultures, from culture to culture, and from one era to another. Or, put differently, a great deal more medium-theory work could certainly add needed detail and texture. Even in an electronic age, for example, some boundaries are blurred while others are reinforced; many institutions become more porous, yet others become more defended; and previously marginalized populations are mainstreamed unevenly and incompletely.

Such unevenness of change may be the result of many factors, including the coexistence of many different forms of communication within a culture, which obscures the differences among media. People in literate societies continue to speak, and those in electronic cultures still read, write, and use print. Technological convergence similarly complicates medium-theory work. Mobile phones, as one example, are now also type-writers, mail systems, news sources, voice and music recorders and players, alarm clocks, calendars, photo and video cameras and viewers, global positioning systems, and other devices.

Additionally, most medium theory has focused too narrowly on changes among the middle and upper classes in Western societies. Moreover, in trying to call attention to largely neglected dimensions of media experience, medium theory often commits complementary sins: it gives insufficient consideration to the influence of media content and media production variables and to the political, social, and economic forces that shape the development of new media and constrain the uses of media and the "stories" that are told through all of them (Meyrowitz 1998, 2006, 2008). In this chapter's opening illustration, for example, Goody and Watt (1963) are no doubt correct that the Gonja would have had a more difficult time "forgetting" about two of their founding father's sons had they relied on written rather than oral history. Yet even literate and post-literate cultures have manifested amazing feats of amnesia. Consider, as just one of many possible examples, how the stories in the corporate-owned American news media about the threats posed to the United States by the theocratic government of Iran rarely mention the CIA's role in overthrowing a democratic secular government in Iran in 1953, the US backing of the dictatorial Shah of Iran for twenty-six years, or the US's encouragement and military support for Saddam Hussein's bloody invasion of Iran after the popular Iranian revolt against the Shah in 1979. Similarly, many Americans' narrative of the origins of the American nation include only fuzzy and incomplete images of how much the country's Founding Fathers relied on African slave labor in support of their lifestyles and their revolution in the name of liberty.

Medium theorists wisely explore the under-studied role of media as distinct social environments and information systems. This perspective is essential to understanding one of the variables that influence the evolution of cultural forms. Yet medium theory is best used to supplement, rather than displace, other explorations of media, including analyses of the role of media as "disinformation systems" and as tools of both collective memory and collective amnesia.

Acknowledgments

The author thanks Peter Schmidt, Paul Heyer, Ruxandra Cristina Dumitriu, and the editors of this volume for their comments and suggestions. © 2009 Joshua Meyrowitz.

References

Arnheim, Rudolf. 1957. *Film as Art*. Berkeley: University of California Press.

Boorstin, Daniel J. 1973. *The Americans: The Democratic Experience*. New York: Random House.

Carothers, J.C. 1959. "Culture, Psychiatry, and the Written Word." *Psychiatry* 22: 307–20.

Castells, Manuel. 1996. *The Rise of the Network Society*. Oxford: Blackwell.

Chaytor, H.J. 1945. *From Script to Print: An Introduction to Medieval Vernacular Literature*. Cambridge: W. Heffer and Sons.

Deibert, Ronald J. 1997. *Parchment, Printing, and Hypermedia: Communication in World Order Transformation*. New York: Columbia University Press.

Eisenstein, Elizabeth. 1979. *The Printing Press as an Agent of Change: Communications and Cultural Transformations in Early-Modern Europe*, Vols. 1 and 2. Cambridge: Cambridge University Press.

Geddes, P. 1904. *City Development: A Study of Parks, Gardens, and Culture-Institutes*. Edinburgh, Scotland: Geddes and Colleagues.

Goody, Jack and Watt, Ian. 1963. "The Consequences of Literacy." *Comparative Studies in Society and History* 5: 304–45.

Havelock, Eric A. 1963. *Preface to Plato*. Cambridge, MA: Harvard University Press.

Innis, Harold Adams. 1950. *Empire and Communications*. London: Oxford University Press.

——. 1951. *The Bias of Communication*. Toronto: University of Toronto Press.

Katsh, M. Ethan. 1989. *The Electronic Media and the Transformation of Law*. New York: Oxford University Press.

Levinson, P. 1997. *The Soft Edge: A Natural History and Future of the Information Revolution*. London: Routledge.

——. 2009. *New New Media*. Boston: Penguin/Allyn & Bacon.

Ling, R. 2008. *New Tech, New Ties: How Mobile Communication Is Reshaping Social Cohesion*. Cambridge, MA: MIT Press.

Logan, R.K. 1986. *The Alphabet Effect*. New York: William Morrow.

McLuhan, Marshall. 1951. *The Mechanical Bride: Folklore of Industrial Man*. New York: Vanguard Press.

——. 1962. *The Gutenberg Galaxy*. Toronto: University of Toronto Press.

——. 1994 (1964). *Understanding Media: The Extensions of Man*. Cambridge, MA: MIT Press.

Meyrowitz, Joshua. 1985. *No Sense of Place: The Impact of Electronic Media on Social Behavior*. New York: Oxford University Press.

——. 1998. "Multiple Media Literacies." *Journal of Communication* 48(1): 96–108.

——. 2006. "American Homogenization and Fragmentation: The Influence of New Information Systems and Disinformation Systems." Pp. 153–86 in W. Uricchio and S. Kinnebrock, eds., *Media Cultures*. Heidelberg: Universitätsverlag.

——. 2008. "Power, Pleasure, Patterns: Intersecting Narratives of Media Influence." *Journal of Communication* 58: 641–63.

——. 2009. "Medium Theory: An Alternative to the Dominant Paradigm of Media Effects." Pp. 517–30 in Robin L. Nabi and Mary Beth Oliver, eds., *The Sage Handbook of Media Processes and Effects*. Thousand Oak, CA: Sage Publications.

Mumford, Lewis. 1934. *Technics and Civilization*. New York: Harcourt Brace.

Ong, W.J. 1967. *The Presence of the Word: Some Prolegomena for Cultural and Religious History*. New Haven, CT: Yale University Press.

——. 1982. *Orality and Literacy: The Technologizing of the Word*. London: Methuen.

Poster, M. 2006. *Information Please: Culture and Politics in the Age of Digital Machines*. Durham, NC: Duke University Press.

Steinberg, S.H. 1974. *Five Hundred Years of Printing*, 3rd edition. Harmondsworth, England: Penguin.

6

Re-imagining critique in cultural sociology

Nancy Weiss Hanrahan and Sarah S. Amsler

Orienting cultural sociology in a "post-critical" society

Critique and judgment were once regarded as the distinguishing features of an emancipatory social science, yet their role in the study of culture has become particularly contested in recent years. The growth of identity-based politics and the proliferation of new social movements in the 1970s and 1980s, and the accompanying cultural turn within social theory, highlighted the analytical and ethical limitations of the authoritative knowledge claims that are often associated with critique. Recognition of cultural difference, now widely regarded as crucial for advancing claims for social equality and analyzing many aspects of social life, challenged universal conceptions of human freedom, including those that had been the basis of an earlier generation of critical theory. The crisis and collapse of Soviet socialism during this period seemed only to mirror the exhaustion with Marxist conceptions of domination and liberation that had been central underpinnings of both normative social critique and struggles for social justice. Within cultural sociology, these developments opened up the field to a rich exploration of cultural practices across a wide range of social and cultural groups, many of which were not previously recognized as "legitimate" culture or legitimate subjects of cultural study. This "democratization" of both the culture concept and its analysis seemed to favor interpretive over critical methodologies. Indeed, by the end of the twentieth century, there was a strong "discourse of suspicion" in the field towards any normative claims that linked culture specifically to the expansion or denial of human freedom, beyond the basic theoretical observation that in practice it may do both (Reed 2007: 12).

However, although cultural sociologists may have become disenchanted with critical theory, culture itself is not yet "post-critical." During this same period, culture has become an "arena of intense political controversy" (Benhabib 2002: 1). From identity-focused struggles for political recognition and human rights to debates about localized cultural practices such as female genital cutting; from the symbolic mediation of terrorism to the political force of narratives about a geopolitical "clash of civilizations," both critiques of culture and cultures of critique proliferate in everyday social practice (Buck-Morss 2003; Calhoun *et al.* 2002; Eisenstein 2004; Fraser and Honneth 2003), and the future and possibility of critical judgment in global political life have become matters of theoretical concern (Couzens-Hoy 2004; Duncombe 2002; Pensky 2005). Within the global North, social critics have also expressed concern that the autonomy of culture is being increasingly weakened through the criminalization of political dissent, the closing down of democratic public spaces and activities, and the commercialization of artistic production in a "new cultural environment" shaped as much by the economic and political centralization of cultural production as by the postmodern disarticulation of social meaning (Bourdieu 2003; Kellner 2002; Wolf 2007).

The tension between a widespread disavowal of critique in cultural sociology and the persistence of critical judgment in cultural life raises several questions for sociologists. Can, and should, normative judgment be an integral part of a fully articulated approach to culture, one which values in equal measure the interpretation of meaning, its normative evaluation, and its relation to action in the social world? Does sociology best fulfill its "democratic imperative" (Reed 2007: 12) by renouncing critical theories of culture, or can the normative practices of critique and judgment be reconceptualized and renewed to pursue democratic goals of dialogue, interpretation, and an empathetic "ethic of engagement" with others (Kompridis 2005, 2006)? Cultural sociologists have answered these questions in part by highlighting the analytical and ethical dangers of deterministic approaches, which preclude dialogue and close down interpretive processes. However, they have also concluded that critical theories of culture inherently do the same things, thus leaving little scope for exploring how and why normative analysis is important for making sense of the complex relationship between culture and politics, on the one hand, and for orienting our action with others in the world, on the other.

Here, we offer an alternative perspective: that critical theory—including, and indeed particularly that within the Frankfurt School tradition—offers important insights for combining deep interpretations of meaning-making practices (which are essential for cultural understanding) with their normative evaluation, which is a necessary element of critical participation in political life. First, rather than essentializing critique as elitist and interpretation as democratic, critical theory demands that we continually problematize how particular forms of knowledge—including critique, judgment, and imagination— are legitimized or marginalized in practice. It therefore opens up new lines of reflective inquiry into the role of critique as a cultural practice. Second, although critical theorists regard autonomous culture as a potential space of freedom and possibility, they also argue that cultural autonomy must be understood as a political problematic rather than a social fact. In other words, while we may "uncoupl[e] culture from social structure" for analytical purposes and recognize its centrality in shaping actions and institutions (Alexander and Smith 2004: 13), we cannot overlook its relationship to the political and economic logics that have consequences for meaning-making and expressive action. Finally, in contrast with deterministic approaches to critique, critical theory challenges positivistic epistemologies in which knowledge is created in order to arrive at a single, absolute, empirical truth. It points to the limitations of claims to "total" knowledge, suggesting that it is difficult to develop rich understandings of cultural action without attention to other modes of understanding such as aesthetics, affect, and imagination.

Although these insights are developed in various ways throughout various feminist, postcolonial, and post-structuralist forms of critical theory, their clear articulation within the Frankfurt School tradition—some of which prefigures the later developments— makes this body of work an important point of reference for contemporary cultural sociologists. Before examining what critical theory has to offer, however, we want

65

to discuss its current status within cultural sociology, and to explain how critique has come to be interpreted as antithetical to culture, rather than as a cultural practice in its own right.

Situating the "cultural turn" in the sociology of culture

Jeffrey Alexander and Philip Smith (2004) recently argued that the study of culture has reached a new stage of professional maturity, overcoming the inadequacies of its critical predecessors. The emergence of the "Strong Program" in American cultural sociology and of post-critical theories appears to mark the beginning of a new intellectual era— one in which we can divest ourselves of the romanticism and reductionism of "weaker" traditions of cultural study and embrace the complexity, ambiguity, and autonomous power of culture itself.

Within this perspective, normative approaches to culture are often interpreted as both intellectually and politically regressive. Frankfurt School critical theory has also come to play a "traditional role in cultural studies … as a kind of negative or naive moment" which "has to be overcome for cultural studies to properly exist at all" (Nealon and Irr 2002: 3; see also Kellner 2002; Szeman 2002). However, the narrative of progress from reductionist approaches in the sociology of culture to the more intellectually and ethically advanced "structural hermeneutics" of cultural sociology is itself rooted in judgments about the nature of social scientific truth and the imagination of alternative possibilities: in other words, it is rooted in critical practices. The rhetorical devices deployed to structure this story, particularly the boundary drawn between normative judgments that impose objective meaning onto subjective experience, on the one hand, and descriptions of authentic cultural practice, on the other, indicate that critical judgment remains central to the analysis of culture itself.

Although the turn away from critical theory in the sociology of culture defies any simple explanation, it was rooted in a number of intersecting social and intellectual developments. By the 1970s, it became clear that neither critical theory nor the traditional sociology of culture, as they had been institutionalized, offered adequate conceptual tools for understanding how individuals experience, communicate, and negotiate the cultural resources that orient their being in the world. Although both critical theorists and cultural sociologists offered competent explanations of how culture is implicated in or used as an instrument of social domination, their work was rarely employed to develop analyses of culture as a separate space or practice of autonomy and possibility (Goldfarb 2005). Critical theorists were called upon by members of social movements to reflect on the viability of critique as a mode of action-oriented reflection and to develop theoretical approaches that could explain the emergence of new forms of cultural struggle. At the same time, sociologists of culture began to distance themselves from conceptions of culture grounded either in aesthetic discourse and hence considered abstract and elitist, or in theories of "the culture industry," which were deemed economically reductionist and deterministic.

Both projects in critical theory and the sociology of culture sought to clarify the possibility of autonomous cultural action and create alternative conceptions of culture that were sympathetic to subjective experience, contingent definitions of truth, and individual autonomy. However, neither seemed capable of reconciling the perceived antimony between subjective experience and objective truth without subordinating one to the other in epistemologically or even politically violent ways. Critique, which is always grounded in a normative claim to *some sort of* truth beyond individual self-understanding or culturally sanctioned knowledge, hence came to be regarded as inherently constraining, reifying, and anti-democratic. For in contexts where truth-claims are equated with determinate judgments or total representations of objective reality, both truth and judgment are "anti-critical" in the sense that they foreclose rather than open up possibilities for alternative thought and action.

Regarding criticality as a hopelessly flawed epistemological project, cultural sociologists therefore turned towards the "thick description" of ethnographic research and the descriptive reconstructions of social performance and meaning-making practices. But can critique justifiably be abandoned as a practice of dismissal and exclusion that is both intellectually and morally suspect? On the one hand, the critique of critique may be regarded as a positive shift, as authoritative claims to universal or hegemonic truth are antithetical to both critique and democratic deliberation. On the other hand, however, making judgments is vital not only for critical sociology, but also for cultural action and critical thought. The exercise of judgment, in which individuals participate in producing and deliberating claims to truth (or, as Horkheimer and Adorno once argued, "act as subjects in the truth") is a cultural practice—perhaps one of the very conditions of culture (1997: 244). It is practiced in various ways, from simple taste preferences to appeals to transcendent standards of ethics, justice, human rights, or aesthetics, to the systematic and rigorous analysis of social systems with respect to their potential for human freedom. Given the centrality of critique and judgment in everyday life, perhaps the question is not how they can be transcended or replaced but how they might be alternatively conceptualized and practiced in ways that advance cultural freedom.

The autonomy of culture as problematic

One way of answering this question is to examine how and why critique traditionally has been linked to concepts of freedom and cultural autonomy in critical theory. Given the importance of the autonomy of culture within cultural sociology, it is interesting that the Frankfurt School, for whose participants autonomy was a pressing social and epistemological problem, has been virtually written out of the "Strong Program's" history of the field (see, for example, Alexander 1990; Alexander and Smith 1993, 2004). References to the Frankfurt School's work tend to be oblique rather than specific, and lumped together with "Marxist" or "Leftist" analyses that reduce culture to its hidden material interests. Critical theory is presented as proceeding through "demystification" and "denunciation," through methods of ideology critique that are conducted from "on high" and deny the autonomy of culture (Eliasoph 2007; Lichterman 2005, 2007; Reed and Alexander 2007).

However, this characterization of critical theory is itself reductive, in that the Frankfurt School theorists wrote prolifically about the dangers of reductionism and absolutism in cultural critique. They also drew on other strands within Marxist theory, such as the conception of critique as a confrontation between norm and reality, as well as Kant's notion of critique as reasoned reflection on the conditions of rational knowledge, judgment, and action. Theodor Adorno specifically argued against the "barbarism" of reducing culture to its material interests, and for the need to proceed dialectically between transcendent and immanent positions when conducting cultural critique (1967: 32).

This position was asserted because autonomy, defined as human freedom, is not a given but rather enables "the single existential judgment" on which the whole project of critique depends (Horkheimer 1972: 227; see also Brunkhorst 1995: 82). The autonomy of culture is neither theoretically affirmed nor denied, but conceptualized as a possibility—one to be investigated, disclosed, or determined through critical analysis.

The links between the autonomy of culture and critique are visible throughout the diverse body of work in classical critical theory. Originally seeking to produce inter-disciplinary social research on the "great transformation" from liberal to monopoly capitalism, from democratic to authoritarian states, and from bourgeois to mass culture—in short, on the "transition to the world of the administered life," critical theorists aimed to analyze forms of social domination that threatened individual autonomy and reflective forms of thought (Horkheimer and Adorno 1997: ix). Culture entered these analyses both as an instrument of domination (through the distortion of language and cultural symbols as well as the manipulation of communication media that made mass mobiliza-tions of fascism possible), and as a relatively autonomous domain of thought and action. Art in particular held promise in that its specifically aesthetic forms and conventions embodied a non-instrumental form of rationality that could open space for reflection and allow both the articulation of utopian projects and the transcendent critique of social conditions.

The autonomy of culture in critical theory was therefore not a matter of disciplinary disposition that preceded analysis, but precisely a matter to be determined through the analysis of specific cultural configurations as against their historical possibilities and future potentials. Most importantly, because art and culture were implicated in both the reality of social domination and the possibility of eventual human freedom, distinguishing between these possibilities and making judgments about culture were crucial. For the Frankfurt School, judgment was therefore both a political imperative and a moment of autonomous culture itself. Yet what was clearly conceived as an act of subjective freedom, however contradictory and difficult to achieve, has come to be read as elitism or even domination.

Reflective, imaginative, and intimate critique

An alternative perspective can be obtained by problematizing critique as a complex and situated cultural practice. This approach enables us to raise more nuanced questions about how critique may be exercised to open or close down dialogue; why it may be inter-preted as "demystification" or "disclosure," evaluation or judgment, common sense or a specialized skill, and as oppressive or emancipatory; and under what conditions it engages or excludes and alienates others. To address these questions, we can explore how critical theorists have distinguished between critique and truth-claiming, determinate and reflective judgment, and the different ethics of engagement that these practices require. These issues are explicitly addressed in what has become the Frankfurt School's emble-matic and ironically most criticized text, *Dialectic of Enlightenment* ([1944] Horkheimer and Adorno 1997).

Much critical theory of culture has been criticized for taking a "god's-eye view" of culture and proceeding at an abstract "level of theorizing that does not address or attempt to document the *actual* mechanisms" of cultural mediation in social life (DeNora 2003: 40; 2005: 149). Interestingly, however, it is in *Dialectic of Enlightenment* that Horkheimer and Adorno inveigh most strongly against the very types of truth-claims and social scientific knowledge that they are accused of producing. Their analysis marks a turn away from authoritative social science and its positivistic methods of inquiry, which the authors believed had become implicated in the total administration of human beings. It is also a sustained reflection on the contradictions of Enlightenment thought itself: its potential for critical self-reflection remains a necessary condition for human freedom at the same time that its instrumentality undermines that very possibility.

As an alternative, in the opening essays of *Dialectic of Enlightenment*, the authors proceed mimetically, employing forms of presentation that challenge dominant expectations of scientific reason and mastery. Rather than undertaking a "positivistic search for information" about the nature of culture in their society, the authors use more hermeneutic and metaphorical methods to evoke, and persuade readers to consider, alternative representations of the social world (Horkheimer and Adorno 1997: x; Honneth 2007: 59). As Bernstein has argued, their aim was less to tell a truth than to raise questions about culture "from the perspective of its relation to the possibilities for social transformation" (1991: 2). In these terms, the question "remains open as to the kind of truth claims it can actually uphold" (Honneth 2007: 61). Far from being a factual description of social reality, therefore, the text may be interpreted as a "world-disclosing critique" of dominant interpretations of it (Honneth 2007).

This point is significant, for the argument within cultural sociology that critique is anti-democratic is based largely on the assumption that it stakes a claim, not only to *the* truth, but to a *superior* truth, and in particular one not recognized by, or accessible to, ordinary social actors. But this is not the assumption underlying the *Dialectic of Enlightenment*, which, while engaging in unmasking and demystification, does not simply presume that a final and absolute truth exists to be "uncovered." Indeed, the authors argued that "the proposition that truth is the whole turns out to be identical with its contrary, namely, that in each case it exists only as a part" (Horkheimer and Adorno 1997: 244). At a time when the authoritarian manipulation of "truth" was being used to justify highly "rationalized" forms of anti-Semitism, political conformity, and mass mobilization, critical theorists had purposes beyond unmasking the ideological underpinnings of fascist propaganda. They also aimed to open up spaces for autonomous, critical thought, and they did so by producing alternative interpretations of society that encouraged others to actively judge the merit and value of competing claims to truth (Horkheimer and Adorno 1997: 244). The philosophy of knowledge at work here is similar to that of Hannah Arendt (1954), who believed that establishing any claim to absolute truth is distinctly *un*-political because such finality is coercive and forecloses the very essence of politics—persuasion, performance, and the agonistics of speaking and acting in the presence of others.

Certainly there is a tension here between, on the one hand, opening space for autonomous thought and action by inviting others to participate in critical reflection about culture and, on the other, critical theory's self-understanding as a specialized practice able to produce unique insights and to reveal instances of domination otherwise obscured. Horkheimer and Adorno clearly struggled with this problem and the tension between the different strands of critique is not fully resolved in the text. Similarly, the precise relationship between critique and description is sometimes undeveloped, and in a later edition of the book the authors make explicit references to the "reality of the times" and social changes that require the reconsideration of their central arguments. Yet their intention as dialecticians was to reveal, however imperfectly, a world or possible

69

worlds that were not-yet-recognized in the facts—a world understood not through the observation of its particular temporal appearance, but through critical reflection on its actual and potential constellations of thought, emotion, relationships, imagination, values, and judgments.

Here, it is necessary to understand the influence of Kant's distinction between determinate and reflective judgment on the work of Adorno and Horkheimer. For Kant (2000), reflection was a form of reason positioned between the sensual and the cognitive. Frankfurt School theorists thus regarded it as an alternative to scientism, positivism, and instrumentality, on the one hand, and to raw sensation and impulse, on the other—both of which were implicated in the rise and consolidation of authoritarianism (Marcuse 1969). The reflective judgments that Kant associates with aesthetics differ from the determinate judgments of science because they can never be established as true or false in empirical or philosophical terms. Where the latter are coercive, reflective judgments are persuasive. Their validity can only be determined through a speaker's engagement with others, and through their agreement. Because reflective judgment is oriented toward this potential agreement, it is premised on an assumption that we judge *for* others, and on an expectation or even a hope that our own sense of beauty or right or good is shared by those from whom we seek agreement. Our judgment is therefore an appeal to universal norms, not in order to indict or oppress but to persuade.

Recently, new critical theorists have picked up this line of reasoning, re-conceptualizing critique as the reflective disclosure of social possibility, rather than the establishment of superior scientific truths. Nikolas Kompridis, for example, combines Kant's insights with a Heideggerian conception of "disclosure," arguing that empirical truth can never be the goal of any form of critique that is regarded as ongoing or unfinished, and oriented towards disclosing future possibilities. He also suggests that critique—when it is deliberately oriented towards learning with other people with whom we speak—may be practiced as an "intimate" form of engagement rather than an alienating one. The conception of critique as the reflective disclosure of possibility therefore operates on two levels—as the disclosure of possible solutions to social problems, and as the disclosure of possible selves. In an ideal relationship of intimate critique, Kompridis suggests, the aim "is not just the critical transformation of the object of critique, but also of the subjectivity of the critic" (2006: 175). In other words, rather than speaking authoritatively in ways that exclude others, "it is in the voice of the second person, not in the voice of the first, that critique must speak" (Kompridis 2005: 339). In order to disclose possibilities for the future, and to engage in cooperative problem solving, we have to listen, be receptive to others, and be willing to change our own self-understandings. For, as Kompridis argues,

> once we acknowledge that culture plays an irreducible and constitutive role in social and political life, once we acknowledge the irreducibility of reasonable disagreement, we may find that the critique of others with whom we must nonetheless find a way to live requires an intimate mode of criticism; a mode of criticism based on reciprocal recognition, on re-knowing one another in terms different from those on which we previously relied.
>
> (Kompridis 2006: 260)

It is of course tempting to suggest that critique is a practice of freedom when it is disclosing, intimate, reflective, and inclusive of others, and an exercise of domination when it is determinate and exclusionary toward others. Yet this view would be too simplistic. Indeed, although the theory of "intimate critique" is conceptually compelling, it reproduces some of the problems of Habermas's ideal speech situation: it is premised on face-to-face interactions in which imbalances of power must be bracketed, and it requires a degree of receptivity that may be difficult to achieve. Indeed, conceptualizations of intimate critique may be inappropriate in circumstances where relations of domination and subordination obtain, and it would be a mistake to discount other forms of critique that aim to speak truth to power as being inherently dominative. One form of critique cannot simply be substituted for another as being more "democratic" in principle, and there is no single model or criterion of "democratic" critique. Nevertheless, the reflective, inter-subjective, and indeterminate character of Kompridis's notion of intimate critique points to the alternative contributions that critical theory can make to a sociology which, in addition to understanding how cultural meaning is constituted in everyday practice, is also capable of explaining how it is implicated in the defense and expansion of human freedom. It also has particular importance for explaining how and why respect for cultural difference and the practice of normative understanding can, and perhaps should, be articulated together in new forms of critique. For whereas critique is often abandoned or rejected because it is thought impossible to carry out across cultural boundaries, Kompridis (2006: 145, 246) argues that disclosing critical practices in fact require radical differences that disrupt the horizons of our own taken-for-granted "cultural sensibilities" and that can, within facilitating conditions and in the spirit of learning, contribute to their transformation.

Conclusion

Throughout this chapter, we have argued that a normative interpretation of the "democratic imperative" is a valuable element of any democratically oriented and critical sociology of culture. Indeed, it is particularly important for any project that engages the complex cultural meanings, practices, and controversies that mark the current "global" era. The autonomy of culture was a central problematic for the Frankfurt School critical theorists, who believed that it was always possible and everywhere threatened. They developed their methods of critique as analytical strategies for assessing its possibility, and understood reflective judgment as one form of resistance to its closing down. Though the terms of their analysis were generated in response to particular social and historical conditions, the problem of cultural freedom remains urgent today. As long as it is possible for people to be arrested for posting dissenting material on a website, for public spaces to be closed or monitored in order to prevent peaceful political demonstrations, or for commercialization to infiltrate every aspect of artistic production—in other words, to the extent that the autonomy of culture remains a political problematic, critique must remain a central theoretical method for cultural sociology.

Hence, in political and intellectual contexts which are often "inhospitable to the practice of critique" (Kompridis 2005: 326), sociologists have a vital role to play in developing normative approaches to analysis that open up spaces for the reflective, intimate, and critical interpretation of culture. One of our main tasks is to work out how culture mediates judgment and how judgment mediates meaning; another is to critically evaluate our own practices of knowledge production in light of those more open, imaginative, and reflective possibilities. However, a critical theory of culture need not aim to *establish* the truth of such meanings and practices—not to understand them in an illusory "pure" form or to explain their causal roles as mechanisms for social change. Instead, as the *Dialectic of Enlightenment* so compellingly illustrates, and as new critical theorists such as Kompridis suggest, by disclosing how social life, and cultural sociology itself, could be otherwise, we might open up moments of autonomy in which the possibilities of culture can be critically evaluated and enlarged.

References

Adorno, T. 1967. "Cultural Criticism and Society." In *Prisms*. Cambridge, MA: MIT Press.

Alexander, J. 1990. "Analytic Debates." In J. Alexander and S. Seidman, eds., *Culture and Society: Contemporary Debates*. Cambridge and New York: Cambridge University Press.

Alexander, J. and Smith, P. 1993. "The Discourse of American Civil Society: A New Proposal for Cultural Studies." *Theory and Society* 22(2): 151–207.

———. 2004. "The Strong Program in Cultural Sociology." In J. Alexander, ed., *The Meanings of Social Life*. New York: Oxford University Press.

Arendt, H. 1954. "Truth and Politics." In *Between Past and Future*. New York: Penguin.

Benhabib, S. 2002. *The Claims of Culture: Equality and Diversity in the Global Era*. Princeton: Princeton University Press.

Bernstein, J.M. 1991. "Introduction." In *Theodor W. Adorno: The Culture Industry*. London and New York: Routledge.

Bourdieu, P. 2003. *Firing Back: Against the Tyranny of the Market 2*. New York and London: The New Press.

Brunkhorst, H. 1995. "Dialectical Positivism of Happiness: Horkheimer's Materialist Deconstruction of Philosophy." In S. Benhabib, ed., *On Max Horkheimer: New Perspectives*. Cambridge, MA: MIT Press.

Buck-Morss, S. 2003. *Thinking Past Terror: Islam and Critical Theory on the Left*. London: Verso.

Calhoun, C., Price, P., and Timmer, A., eds. 2002. *Understanding September 11*. New York: The New Press.

Couzens-Hoy, D. 2004. *Critical Resistance: From Post-Structuralism to Post-Critique*. Cambridge, MA: MIT Press.

DeNora, T. 2003. *After Adorno: Rethinking Music Sociology*. Cambridge: Cambridge University Press.

———. 2005. "Music and Social Experience." In M. Jacobs and N. Hanrahan, eds., *The Blackwell Companion to the Sociology of Culture*. Malden, MA and Oxford: Blackwell Publishers.

Duncombe, S. 2002. *The Cultural Resistance Reader*. London: Verso.

Eisenstein, Z. 2004. *Against Empire: Feminisms, Racism and the West*. London: Zed Books.

Eliasoph, N. 2007. "Beyond the Politics of Denunciation: Cultural Sociology as the 'Sociology for the Meantime.'" In I. Reed and J. Alexander, eds., *Culture, Society and Democracy*. Boulder, CO and London: Paradigm Publishers.

Fraser, N. and Honneth, A. 2003. *Redistribution or Recognition? A Political–Philosophical Exchange*. London: Verso.

Goldfarb, J. 2005. "Dialogue, Culture, Critique: The Sociology of Culture and the New Sociological Imagination." *International Journal of Politics, Culture, and Society* 18: 281–92.

Honneth, A. 2007. *Disrespect: The Normative Foundations of Critical Theory*. Cambridge: Polity Press.

Horkheimer, M. 1972 (1937). "Traditional and Critical Theory." In *Critical Theory: Selected Essays*. New York: Continuum.

Horkheimer, M. and Adorno, T.W. 1997 (1944). *Dialectic of Enlightenment*. New York: Continuum.

Kant, I. 2000 (1790). *Critique of the Power of Judgment*. Cambridge: Cambridge University Press.

Kellner, D. 2002. "The Frankfurt School and British Cultural Studies: The Missed Articulation." In J. Nealon and C. Irr, eds., *Rethinking the Frankfurt School: Alternative Legacies of Cultural Critique*. New York: SUNY Press.

Kompridis, N. 2005. "Disclosing Possibility: The Past and Future of Critical Theory." *International Journal of Philosophical Studies* 13(3): 325–51.

———. 2006. *Critique and Disclosure: Critical Theory between Past and Future.* Cambridge, MA: MIT Press.

Lichterman, P. 2005. "Civic Culture at the Grass Roots." In M. Jacobs and N. Hanrahan, eds., *The Blackwell Companion to the Sociology of Culture.* Malden MA and Oxford: Blackwell.

———. 2007. "Invitation to a Practical Cultural Sociology." In I. Reed and J. Alexander, eds., *Culture, Society and Democracy.* Boulder, CO and London: Paradigm Publishers.

Marcuse, H. 1969 (1934). "The Struggle Against Liberalism in the Totalitarian View of the State." In *Negations.* Boston: Beacon Press.

Nealon, J. and Irr, C., eds. 2002. *Rethinking the Frankfurt School: Alternative Legacies of Cultural Critique.* New York: SUNY Press.

Pensky, M., ed. 2005. *Globalizing Critical Theory.* New York: Rowman and Littlefield.

Reed, I. 2007. "Cultural Sociology and the Democratic Imperative." In I. Reed and J. Alexander, eds., *Culture, Society and Democracy.* Boulder, CO and London: Paradigm Publishers.

Reed, I. and Alexander, J., eds. 2007. *Culture, Society and Democracy.* Boulder, CO and London: Paradigm Publishers.

Seidman, S. and Alexander, J. 2001. "Introduction." In *The New Social Theory Reader.* London and New York: Routledge.

Szeman, I. 2002. "The Limits of Culture: The Frankfurt School and/for Cultural Studies." In J. Nealon and C. Irr, eds., *Rethinking the Frankfurt School Alternative Legacies of Cultural Critique.* New York: SUNY Press.

Wolf, N. 2007. *The End of America: A Letter of Warning to a Young Patriot.* Vermont: Chelsea Green Publishing.

Part II
Theories and methodologies in cultural analysis

7

Sociology and cultural studies

An interrupted dialogue

Nick Couldry

Nearly half a century ago, Raymond Williams (1961: 10) wrote that there was no academic subject that allowed him to ask the questions in which he was interested—questions of how culture and society, democracy, and the individual voice interrelate. The early tradition of cultural studies emerged into this gap, drawing in part on the resources of sociology. Looking back, the historical parallel between Williams and the critical sociology of C. Wright Mills was not accidental, since that too privileged the role of power in culture and cultural analysis (Mills 1959: 33, quoted in Hall *et al.* 2003: 2). From the beginning, then, the robustness of cultural studies' relationship with sociology was crucial to cultural studies' possibilities of success. This relationship has been interrupted, but can, I suggest, still be revived under today's very different circumstances.

What are the two poles of this interrupted dialogue? On the side of sociology, we must distinguish, first, between the field of sociology as a whole and domains of sociology more specifically interested in culture. Within the latter, I would distinguish between a formal sociology of culture (that places "culture" within a macro model of social organization) and a cultural sociology that takes a sociological approach to various aspects of cultural production and consumption. A dialogue between "sociology of culture" and cultural studies has never begun and perhaps was never feasible. In spite of some sympathetic calls for cultural studies to be "reintegrated" into sociology (Crane 1994; Long 1997), formal sociology of culture explicitly rejected a "power-based framework of analysis" (Smith 1998: 7), and so turned away from one of the key emphases common to all cultural studies. The position with cultural sociology is very different: the pluralism of cultural sociology as represented by the present volume derives from an attempt to mobilize the term "culture" across many domains of social analysis, foregrounding and certainly not suppressing issues of power. As a result, a dialogue between "cultural sociology" and cultural studies is without question feasible, even if for various reasons it has been interrupted.

What then do I mean by "cultural studies"? An important reference point remains the Birmingham school of cultural studies, with its origins in the earlier work of Raymond Williams, Richard Hoggart, and E.P. Thompson, even if it is important to emphasize that from the beginning this vision of cultural studies had international parallels (see Couldry 2000: 26–28 for discussion). But other important developments were under way also: from the 1980s onwards, aspects of the Birmingham school of cultural studies—particularly the strands of semiotics and Gramscian hegemony theory as taken up by Stuart Hall—were adopted in broader literature and the humanities in the US and elsewhere (Turner 1990); in the longer term, aspects of cultural studies became internationalized (Chen 1998). Given this huge expansion, you might ask: does "cultural studies" still stand for anything specific beyond a particular trajectory for introducing cultural analysis into academic work? If that were all the term stood for, then resuming at this late stage a dialogue between "cultural studies" and sociology would be of limited interest. So let me distinguish three ways, stemming from the early history of the Birmingham school of cultural studies, in which "cultural studies" might resume a productive dialogue with sociology, particularly cultural sociology.

The first substantive strand of cultural studies that we might identify for this purpose focused on giving serious attention to the forms and dynamics of contemporary popular culture. To be sure, there are sociological problems with isolating the "popular" as the focus of cultural studies in this way. For one thing, this excludes many important areas of taste and cultural consumption—the cultural experience of the old (Tulloch 1991; Riggs 1998), "middlebrow" culture (Frith 1986), the cultural experience of elites (Lamont 1992), and indeed any cultural experience that is not "spectacular" or "resistant" (for further discussion, see Couldry 2000: 58–62). Another point is that old debates about popular versus elite culture have failed to keep up with the de-differentiation of cultural taste, and the possibility, indeed importance, of cultural omnivorousness today (compare Strinati 1996 with Peterson and Kern 1996). Finally, an exclusive emphasis on "the popular" ignores the need to deconstruct the relation between what is designated "popular" and everyday "experience" (Hall 1981).

The second strand within early cultural studies that we might identify as a potential contact-point with sociology is the strand that prioritized ways of reading culture, especially those derived from semiotics and versions of post-structuralism. This is the strand most frequently emphasized in histories of cultural studies (Turner 1990; Barker 2003; Tudor 1999). But here too there are difficulties. On the one hand it becomes, in some versions, an attempt to read all culture as, indeed only as, text, an approach which is resolutely non-sociological and so inadequate to understand the multilayered but structured complexity of culture (Hannerz 1992). On the other hand, the use of semiotics and post-structuralist approaches to reading culture has largely been absorbed across all cultural sociology and humanities work (Hall *et al.* 2003), so it no longer comprises a distinct strand of cultural studies per se.

More promising for my purposes is a third strand within early cultural studies that focused cultural analysis on the particular question, and problem, of democratic culture. It is this strand—which develops furthest the concern for hidden power relations within culture, both inclusions and exclusions—that characterized cultural studies from the start. The early work of Raymond Williams identified a culturally embedded democratic deficit at the heart of societies such as late 1950s Britain (Williams 1958, 1961). Because of its concern with the broader conditions for sustaining something like a democratic culture, this strand had from the start a particular affinity with sociology; so it was that early cultural-studies work developed a cultural sociology within an intellectual legacy dominated by Marxism (Williams 1981). However, this strand of cultural studies has received less attention. The only recent scholarship engaging it (Hartley 2003) works exclusively through the analysis of texts, not employing a broader sociological approach to analyzing democratic culture.

Can this third stream of cultural studies provide the starting point from which we rebuild a dialogue between cultural studies and sociology? An affirmative answer will be my argument. In this chapter's second section (pp. 80–82), I explain how early cultural studies suffered from a "holism" that we must move beyond if a productive dialogue beyond cultural sociology and cultural studies is to be renewed. In the chapter's third section (pp. 82–84), I explore some recent developments that promise to reconnect cultural sociology and this third stream of cultural studies in ways that relate closely to today's challenges for a democratic culture. Those challenges can be summed up in three words: neoliberalism, mediation, and globalization. It is not difficult to see how concern with the conditions of democratic culture might have renewed relevance to a time of profound economic crisis. In addition, democratization is today inseparably linked with the emerging opportunities of digital media culture, such that no account of the conditions of contemporary democratic culture is adequate unless it thinks beyond the scale of the national and takes account of the multiple pressures of globalization (Beck 2001; Garcia Canclini 1995).

Before moving on, I should clarify one point. How is it that the potential dialogue between cultural sociology and cultural studies, particularly its third stream, has been so seriously interrupted? One reason is methodological choice. Some work within cultural studies that foregrounded democratic culture seemed uninterested in any specific dialogue with sociology because of its conscious refusal of disciplinarity. Indeed an overwhelming commitment to exposing the contradictions of the current "conjuncture" can sometimes seem to leave any questions of disciplinary method entirely to one side:

> Cultural studies always and only exists in contextually specific theoretical and institutional *formations* [which] are always a response to a particular political project based on the available theoretical and historical resources. In that sense, in every particular instance, cultural studies has to be made up as it goes along.
>
> (Grossberg 1997: 252, original emphasis)

My own work within cultural studies has questioned this suspicion towards disciplinarity (Couldry 2000, 2006); fortunately, Grossberg's recent work (2005) returns to terrain that is more plausibly sociological. Meanwhile other institutional factors have also worked to obscure possibilities for dialogue. Work from outside traditional disciplines— for example in queer theory and post-colonial studies—has revealed the silent exclusions within discourse that naturalize particular definitions of "normality," "home," "us," "the present," and so on (Berlant 1997; Warner 2002; Ganguly 2001; Gaonkar 2001). Such work has often identified with the broad label "cultural studies," and its insights into power and the complexities of democratic culture certainly align it with the third stream of cultural studies I identified earlier. But for reasons not yet fully disentangled, where such work has acknowledged links with the traditional disciplines, these have generally been anthropology, geography, or literary analysis, not sociology. So if it is a dialogue between cultural studies and sociology that we want to revive, we will need to look elsewhere.

The sociological limitations of subcultural theory

Raymond Williams's political and theoretical project was focused around one central insight, that "the making of a society is the finding of common meanings and directions" (1989: 4 [1958]); we should therefore see "the theory of culture as a theory of relations between elements *in a whole way of life*" (1958: 11–12, added emphasis). This approach inspired the attention in early British cultural studies to questions of cultural exclusion, particularly the studies of primarily male, working-class cultural life that inspired "subcultural" theory. (Cohen 1997 [1972]; Hall and Jefferson 1976; Hebdige 1979). Initially, this work focused on explaining subcultural style—mods, rockers, skinheads, and so on—as a resolution on the cultural level of conflicts experienced by British working-class youth at a material level. From the outset, this approach depended on seeing cultural experience and expression as systematic "unities." Phil Cohen's study of working-class culture in London's East End was typical, seeing "subcultures" as "attempt[ing] to work out through a system of transformations, the basic problematic or contradiction which is inserted in the subculture by the parent culture" (Cohen 1997: 100–101 [1972]). This approach reflected the legacy of Marxist functionalism. Dick Hebdige's analysis of popular style and music was more complex, emphasizing the role of ethnic relations to Britain's urban cultures and seeing the connection between popular culture and underlying social conflicts as mediated and to some extent arbitrary. Even so, Hebdige discussed subcultures such as British punk as systematic unities that "share[d] a common language" (1979: 122). Later critiques pointed to the highly gendered and "raced" nature (McRobbie 2000; Gilroy 1987) of the "unities" assumed by these early studies.

So far, the story is familiar. But early cultural-studies "holism"—its understanding of culture as a relationship between various unified systems—had other problematic consequences that we need to understand. Even at its most sophisticated, cultural studies' discussions of "the popular" formulated issues about culture exclusively at a structural level that ignored the complexity of individual cultural experience. The Australian cultural theorist Meaghan Morris formulated the difficulty well, arguing that the British cultural studies tradition failed to "leave much space for an unequivocally pained, unambivalently discontented, or momentarily aggressive subject" (1990: 25). In the mid-1980s, Richard Johnson—Stuart Hall's successor as head of the Birmingham Center for Contemporary Cultural Studies—criticized the structuralist approaches that then dominated cultural studies for being silent on "how ... social subjects ... produce accounts of who they are ... that is, constitute themselves politically" (Johnson 1996: 103 [1986–87]). Given this lacuna, it is hardly surprising that no links ever developed, for example, between cultural studies and the culturally sensitive work in France on the sociology of "actors" (Touraine 1981). Indeed for cultural studies, "identity," far from being a dimension of everyday life that we might investigate sociologically, became, under the weight of post-structuralism, the site of a theoretical problem of integrating psychoanalytic and sociological models that remains unresolved to this day (Hall 1996; Butler 1997).

There were exceptions. Carolyn Steedman's extraordinary double biography of her mother's life and her own childhood insisted on "a sense of people's complexity of relationship to the historical situations they inherit" (1986: 19). A crucial dimension of inequality, Steedman suggested, is precisely whether you are "outside" or "inside" the central narratives of your society and culture; to be of higher social status is, broadly, to be closer to those central narratives. So here was an account of inequality which identified the power relations at work in the distribution of symbolic resources that constitutes cultures and their boundaries. But by the mid-1990s the situation was clear: most cultural studies work that foregrounded power relations through cultural analysis was largely inadequate to analyze people's positions inside culture.

As "cultural studies" as an institutional site came under increasing, and often unfair, attack (Ferguson and Golding 1997), the momentum for enriching understandings of the interrelations of culture and power increasingly came from outside cultural studies. In terms of class, critical psychologist Valerie Walkerdine's work on young girls and popular culture argued against the assumption that working-class lives are "boring" unless inter-pretable as spectacular "resistance" to wider power structures (1997: 19); she insisted on the complex experience of "coping and surviving" with material and symbolic inequal-ities (1997: 21). For Walkerdine, the relations of individuals to popular culture are anything but "natural," shaped as they are by the lack of other means of legitimated self-expression. In terms of gender and class, sociologist Beverly Skeggs (1997) analyzed English working-class women's attempts to achieve social "respectability" via strategies of "passing" as middle class through various forms of performance. In this context, passing is not simply self-directed social advancement, but a consequence of something deeper— the fact that these women did not have available to them narratives through which they could speak positively about themselves as working-class women (Skeggs 1997: 95). Performing another class position represents not so much a desire to be middle class, as a desire not to be regarded as "merely" working class (Skeggs 1997: 87). Skeggs sees this as a complex "disidentification" (1997: 93) operating within a highly unequal class-based society, an insight that remains of great relevance given that class inequalities in Britain (as well as the USA) have increased in the era of neoliberal democracy. Yet such pro-cesses of disidentification could not in principle be grasped within the cultural "holism" of early cultural studies. In terms of ethnicity and "race," Pierre Bourdieu's important collection of interviews in *The Weight of the World* (1999) demonstrates that, without individual stories, our picture of the social terrain is inadequate. Meanwhile, sociologist Les Back's work on multiethnic London shows the value of listening closely to young people's reflections on cultural identity and the complexity of their identifications with "black" culture, music, and fashion (Back 1996). In relation to the apparently banal practice of media consumption, Ron Lembo, a US cultural sociologist, shows how the cheap, always available resource of television can provide a site of "disengaged sociality" for those whose tough work lives and lack of other resources give them few opportu-nities for engagement (Lembo 2000). Once again, this research greatly complicates our view of popular culture as something with which people simply "identify."

So in spite of its initial opening up of the implications of studying culture, cultural stu-dies' early promise to contribute to a broader sociological understanding of culture stalled because of an implicit early functionalism and a diversion from the mid-1980s into excessive theory. Innovative empirical research on individuals' complex place in wider cultural formations was largely conducted elsewhere. Let's now consider some more recent work, in cultural sociology and cultural studies, which develops these issues in

81

ways that connect back to the third strand of early cultural studies' concerns with the possibilities for democratic culture.

The promise of recent cultural sociology and cultural studies

The themes of mediation, globalization, and neoliberalism were already implicit in the work, for example, of Skeggs, Back, and Lembo just discussed, and they suggest the new dialogue between cultural sociology and cultural studies that is starting to emerge. The intensified mediation of everyday life—particularly through digitalization, which enables a vast intertext across multiple interfaces—promises to intensify the de-differentiation of cultural taste that has been progressing since the 1960s. At the very least, the increasing saturation of everyday life by media outputs requires us to find new ways of analyzing media cultures, and the ways in which such cultures acquire "depth." Sociologist Brian Longhurst's recent book *Cultural Change and Ordinary Life* helpfully clarifies the difficult issues here, attempting a wider reconciliation of sociology and media/cultural studies (2007: 4). As he puts it: "media and cultural studies ... are still not social enough ... by the same token, many aspects of sociological study have been insufficiently cultural" (Longhurst 2007: 121). Longhurst's approach, influenced by the sociology of taste (Peterson and Kern 1996) and by sociology and media studies' work on fandom (Harrington and Bielby 1995), identifies important areas where a cultural-studies attention to the experience of cultural consumption can be enriched by detailed sociological attention to everyday forms of performing/acting out audience engagement (compare Abercrombie and Longhurst 1998). It is also important to study the huge diversity of taste patterns across multiple media and the continued role of class in shaping taste and cultural capital (compare, for Australia, Bennett *et al.* 1999). Instead of limiting his analysis to the "popular," Longhurst insists that the object of cultural analysis must be the whole field of taste and the ways in which value is generated across social space.

Working at the boundary between cultural sociology and media/cultural studies, David Hesmondhalgh (2007), like Longhurst, looks to detailed fieldwork, in this case long reflective interviews with people about the trajectories of their musical tastes. Hesmondhalgh opens up an interesting new area for cultural sociology by exploring "what kinds of sentiments of social solidarity might lay within and beneath people's everyday discussions of what they value in music" (2007: 523). Hesmondhalgh wants to avoid the standard reduction of talk about aesthetics to the play of power or distinction; he argues this requires close attention to "the actuality of how people tend to talk about what they like and dislike" (2007: 524). Again, this research offers a plausible expansion of cultural sociology via detailed fieldwork that goes beyond some of cultural studies' previous narrow focus on celebrating "the popular."

Already from these two examples it is clear that mediated cultural consumption is sociologically very rich. However, much more remains to be done to understand its changing dynamics in a digital age. Meanwhile, the challenges posed by globalization go even deeper, affecting not only what we are doing with culture, but the boundaries of belonging and community on which previous territorial notions of "culture" implicitly relied. Particularly important here in opening up a common space of inquiry for cultural sociology and cultural studies in the face of globalization is Les Back's recent book *The Art of Listening* (2007). This book responds to the sociological challenges of the Bush administration's "global war on terror," intensified cross-border migration, and fear.

The study is striking also in its methodological sensitivity, drawing on both cultural studies' origins in a commentary on democracy (Back 2007: 167, discussing Raymond Williams) and recent calls by Michael Burawoy for a "public sociology" (Back 2007: 114, quoting Burawoy 2005). For Back, the methodological challenge for contemporary cultural analysis comes from the sheer difficulty of getting a perspective on the dense packing of stories and lives in multicultural cities such as London. Meeting the challenge requires "look[ing] for the outside story that is part of the inside story" (Back 2007: 9), cultivating a "global sociological imagination" (2007: 11) that is sensitive to underlying economic, political, and security pressures and the ordinariness of multicultural exchange. "There is a need," Back argues, "to find a language to speak of the unspectacular ways in which people live with and across the cultural complexities of sameness and difference" (2007: 148). Here, drawing on the resources of detailed fieldwork within the sociological and anthropological traditions, Back offers a way of reconnecting with Raymond Williams's vision of academic original work that addresses the promise of democracy.

At the same time, as cultural sociology revises its modes of analysis and styles of discourse, we must recognize certain forces—above all, neoliberalism's absolute prioritization of market values over all social or political values—as challenges to the projects of critical cultural analysis and democracy. Recent cultural studies that stay obsessed with the issue of the "popular" necessarily miss this wider development. However, there have been three recent contributions by writers within the original tradition of cultural studies that challenge neoliberalism directly. Larry Grossberg's book *Caught in the Crossfire* (2005) uses a variety of sources (sociology, documentary analysis, policy documents, and economic data) to clarify the history and provenance of neoliberal policies that in the US have discounted youth and education. Henry Giroux (2008), in his book *Against the Terror of Neoliberalism*, has identified the evacuation of politics and the devaluing of youth under neoliberalism as a key object of analysis for cultural studies. And Angela McRobbie (2009), in *The Aftermath of Feminism*, discusses contemporary women's and girls' media and argues that the suppression of feminism has produced a melancholia; the resulting loss of feminist voices reworks feminist freedoms into a consumerist rhetoric of sexualized performance.

In various ways, each of these writers is challenging the adequacy of today's democratic cultures through arguments that, even if they do not always draw on actual sociological fieldwork, imply the need for sociological inquiry into the workings of contemporary cultural experience on the ground. The potential dialogue between cultural sociology and cultural studies is already therefore being revived. Will it continue?

Conclusion

Clearly, as sketched here, much work within cultural sociology provides a basis for reviving the dialogue between cultural sociology and one strand within early cultural studies and, in doing so, reviving the momentum of cultural studies itself. For this potential dialogue to develop, perhaps an adjustment is needed on the side of cultural studies. Cultural studies needs to rediscover a focus that requires, once more, its distinctive attention to the power-laden complexity of culture. While certain observers claim that cultural studies is "dead," I have tried here to give a different sense of where those interested in reviving its fortunes should turn. The way forward lies in developing a renewed empirical understanding of how culture is lived that is adequate to the challenges of contemporary politics, of which one stands out: the threatened closure of democratic politics by neoliberal discourse that gives absolute priority to market values over social or political values. I have argued elsewhere that there is a crisis of voice under neoliberalism (Couldry 2008). Cultural studies may have a role in helping us to analyze and think beyond that crisis. If so, the third and largely neglected strand in cultural studies' origins—the analysis of the problems of democratic culture—would return to center stage.

Fortunately this moment of potential crisis for democratic culture (and cultural studies) is also a good time for cultural sociology to return to dialogue with cultural studies. Not only has there been, from many directions, revived interest over the past decade in analyzing the symbolic dimensions of politics (Melucci 1996) and their exclusions (Eliasoph 1998; Croteau 1995); rethinking the sites and purposes of democratic politics has itself become a topic of increasing urgency (Hardt and Negri 2004; Balibar 2004). Meanwhile, a new culturally oriented political sociology has emerged which problematizes the concept of "political culture" in ways that are quite compatible with the strand of cultural studies emphasized in this chapter (Somers 1993). Although some versions of this latest cultural turn may, once again, prove inhospitable to cultural studies' emphasis on power—for example Alexander's work (Alexander 2007; Alexander and Smith 1993: 196) that continues, even if in ever more complex ways, to see culture as "system"—others may prove more fruitful.

I have tried to see what signs of emerging dialogue can be discerned from the recent landscape of cultural research, but we must wait and see. Certainly this is no time to give up on the long-promised dialogue between sociology and cultural studies, however interrupted its trajectory. Indeed, its resumption may never have been more necessary.

References

Abercrombie, N. and Longhurst, B. 1998. *Audiences*. London: Sage.

Alexander, J. 2007. *The Civil Sphere*. New York: Oxford University Press.

Alexander, J. and Smith, P. 1993. "The Discourse of American Civil Society: A New Proposal for Cultural Studies." *Theory and Society* 22: 151–207.

Back, L. 1996. *New Ethnicities and Urban Culture*. London: UCL Press.

———. 2007. *The Art of Listening*. Oxford: Berg.

Bakardjeva, M. 2001. *The Internet and Everyday Life*. London: Sage.

Balibar, E. 2004. *We The People of Europe?* Princeton, NJ: Princeton University Press.

Barker, C. 2003. *Cultural Studies: Theory and Practice*. London: Sage.

Beck, U. 2001. *What Is Globalization?* Cambridge: Polity.

Bennett, T., Emmison, M., and Frow, J. 1999. *Accounting for Tastes: Australia Everyday Cultures*. Cambridge: Cambridge University Press.

Berlant, L. 1997. *The Queen of America Goes to Washington City*. Durham, NC: Duke University Press.

Bourdieu, P. 1999. *The Weight of the World*. Cambridge: Polity.

Burawoy, M. 2005. "For Public Sociology." *American Sociological Review* 70: 1–12.

Butler, J. 1997. *The Psychic Life of Power*. Stanford, CA: Stanford University Press.

Chen, K.-T., ed. 1998. *Trajectories: Inter-Asia Cultural Studies*. London: Routledge.

Cohen, Phil 1997 (1972). "Subcultural Conflict and Working-Class Community." In A. Gray and J. Mcguigan, eds., *Studying Culture*. London: Arnold.

Couldry, N. 2000. *Inside Culture*. London: Sage.

——. 2006. *Listening Beyond the Echoes: Media, Ethics and Agency in an Uncertain Age*. Boulder, CO: Paradigm Press.

——. 2008. "Media and the Problem of Voice." Pp. 15–26 in N. Carpentier and B. de Cleen, eds., *Participation and Media Production*. Cambridge: Scolars Press.

Crane, D., ed. 1994. *The Production of Culture: Media and the Urban Arts*. Newbury Park, CA: Sage.

Croteau, D. 1995. *Politics and the Class Divide*. Philadelphia, PA: Temple University Press.

du Gay, Paul. 1997. "Organizing Identity at Work." In P. du Gay, ed., *Production of Culture/Cultures of Production*. London: Sage.

Eliasoph, N. 1998. *Avoiding Politics*. Cambridge: Cambridge University Press.

Ferguson, Marjorie and Golding, Peter. 1997. "Cultural Studies and Changing Times: An Introduction." In M. Ferguson and P. Golding, eds., *Cultural Studies in Question*. London: Sage.

Frith, S. 1986. "Hearing Sweet Harmonies." In C. McCabe, ed. *High Theory/Low Culture*. Manchester: Manchester University Press.

Ganguly, K. 2001. *States of Exception: Everyday Life and Postcolonial Identity*. Minneapolis: University of Minnesota Press.

Gaonkar, D., ed. 2001. *Alternative Modernities*. Durham, NC: Duke University Press.

Garcia Canclini, Nestor. 1995. *Hybrid Cultures*. Minneapolis: University of Minnesota Press.

Gilroy, Paul. 1987. *There Ain't No Black in the Union Jack*. London: Routledge.

Giroux, H. 2008. *Against the Terror of Neoliberalism*. Boulder, CO: Paradigm.

Grossberg, L. 1997. "Cultural Studies: What's In a Name? (One More Time)." In L. Grossberg, ed., *Bringing It All Back Home*. Durham, NC and London: Duke University Press.

——. 2005. *Caught in the Crossfire*. Boulder, CO: Paradigm.

Hall, J., Neitz, M., and Battani, M. 2003. *Sociology on Culture*. London: Routledge.

Hall, S. 1981. "Notes on Deconstructing 'the Popular.'" In R. Samuel, ed., *People's History and Socialist Theory*. London: Routledge & Kegan Paul.

——. 1996. "Introduction: Who Needs Identity?" In S. Hall and P. du Gay, ed., *Questions of Identity*. London: Sage.

Hall, S. and Jefferson, T., eds. 1976. *Resistance through Rituals*. London: Hutchinson.

Hannerz, U. 1992. *Cultural Complexity*. New York: Columbia University Press.

Hardt, M. and Negri, T. 2004. *Multitude*. Cambridge, MA: Harvard University Press.

Harrington, L. and Bielby, D. 1995. *Soap Fans*. Philadelphia, PA: Temple University Press.

Hartley, J. 2003. *A Short History of Cultural Studies*. London: Sage.

Hebdige, Dick. 1979. *Subculture: The Meaning of Style*. London: Methuen.

Hesmondhalgh, D. 2007. "Audiences and Everyday Aesthetics." *European Journal of Cultural Studies* 10(4): 507–27.

Johnson, R. 1996 (1986–87). "What Is Cultural Studies Anyway?" In John Storey, ed., *What is Cultural Studies?* London: Arnold.

Lamont, M. 1992. *Money, Morals and Manners*. Chicago: Chicago University Press.

Lembo, R. 2000. *Thinking through Television*. Cambridge: Cambridge University Press.

Long, E., ed. 1997. *From Sociology to Cultural Studies*. Malden, MA: Blackwell.

Longhurst, B. 2007. *Cultural Change and Ordinary Life*. London: Sage.

McRobbie, A. 1998. *British Fashion Design*. London: Routledge.

——. 2000. *Feminism and Youth Culture*, 2nd edition. London: Routledge.

——. 2009. *The Aftermath of Feminism*. London: Sage.

Melucci, A. 1996. *Challenging Codes*. Cambridge: Cambridge University Press.

Mills, C. Wright. 1958. *The Sociological Imagination*. Harmondsworth: Penguin.

——. 1959. *The Sociological Imagination*. New York: Oxford University Press.

Morley, D. 1986. *Family Television*. London: Comedia.

Morris, M. 1990. "Banality in Cultural Studies." In P. Mellencamp, ed., *Logics of Television*. Minneapolis: University of Minnesota Press.

Negus, K. 1992. *Producing Pop*. London: Edward Arnold.

Peterson, R. and Kern, R. 1996. "Changing Highbrow Taste: From Snob to Omnivore." *American Sociological Review* 6: 900–07.

Riggs, K. 1998. *Mature Audiences*. New Brunswick, NJ: Rutgers University Press.

Silverstone, R. 1994. *Television and Everyday Life*. London: Routledge.

Skeggs, B. 1997. *Formations of Class and Gender*. London: Sage.

Smith, Philip. 1998. "Introduction." In *The New American Cultural Sociology*. Cambridge: Cambridge University Press.

Somers, M. 1993. "What's Political or Cultural about Political Culture and the Public Sphere?" *Sociological Theory* 13(2): 113–44.

Steedman, Carolyn. 1986. *Landscape for a Good Woman*. London: Virago.

Strinati, D. 1996. *An Introduction to Theories of Popular Culture*. London: Routledge.

Touraine, A. 1981. *The Return of the Actor*. Minneapolis: University of Minnesota Press.

Tudor, A. 1999. *Decoding Culture: Theory and Method in Cultural Studies*. London: Sage.

Tulloch, J. 1991. "Approaching the Audience: The Elderly." In E. Seiter, H. Borches, G. Kreutzer, and E.M. Warth, eds., *Remote Control*. London: Routledge.

Turner, G. 1990. *British Cultural Studies: An Introduction*. Boston, MA: Unwin Hyman.

Walkerdine, Valerie. 1997. *Daddy's Girl: Young Girls and Popular Culture*. London: Macmillan.

Warner, M. 2002. *Publics and Counter-Publics*. New York: Zone Books.

Williams, R. 1958. *Culture and Society*. Harmondsworth: Penguin.

——. 1961. *The Long Revolution*. Harmondsworth: Penguin.

——. 1981. *Culture*. London: Fontana.

——. 1989 (1958). "Culture Is Ordinary." In *Resources of Hope: Culture, Democracy, Socialism*. London: Verso.

8

Lost in translation

Feminist media studies in the new millennium

Suzanna Danuta Walters

Assessments—particularly of a work in progress—are always troublesome. To reflect on a field that is as amorphous as "feminist media studies" is akin to trying to pin down the truth in a Republican Party convention. Slippery business indeed. In addition, sometimes periods of enormous intellectual ferment are followed by periods of stasis or at least less explosive and reverberating innovations. For roughly twenty years—from the mid-1970s to the mid-1990s—the production of feminist media scholarship was both prodigious and pioneering. Many—myself included—have written about the (nonlinear, overlapping) heady shifts in this scholarship from a largely quantitative "images of women" approach through the many challenges and revisions wrought by psychoanalytic film theory, spectatorship studies, audience work, theories of the gaze, institutional and political economic framings, and beyond. Many of these histories frame the trajectory of the field through disciplinary logics, as humanities-based film studies debated/contested the more social-science oriented TV studies, or through logics produced through theoretical allegiances (psychoanalytic work vs. social structural) or, yet again, logics derived from the specificity of the medium itself (film, television, advertising). As helpful as these histories can be, they never quite resonated for me, largely because the more overarching frame of cultural studies (rather than, say, film theory or sociology of culture) was my entrée into the field, cutting across disciplinary logics, genres, and media. For many of us, this was indeed the main draw of Birmingham-style cultural studies—its deep and wide range, and its refusal to be cornered in by the demands of allegiances other than that of critical, political analysis. Formed in the post-1960s milieu of new social movements and institutional reevaluations, cultural studies couldn't afford the Marxist *longue durée* of avoidance; the barbarians were through the gate too quickly and the borders were too porous to begin with. Although in its early years cultural studies struggled mightily with the challenges posed by feminists and other others, I was surprised by how quickly the boys seemed to come around, or, at the very least, give ground so that cultural studies could begin to expand into something quite other than originally imagined (e.g. not just a working-class white boy's own story).

Cultural studies questions seemed tailor made for the new identity politics, focusing on the intricacies and variabilities of cultural resistance while continuing to reckon with the (older?) problems of commodification and cultural hegemony. Feminist cultural theorists seemed particularly astute. After moving quickly from the "images of women" approach that posited an "already there" meaning—filled with stereotype or rich with latent possibility—they produced some of the most challenging and explosive analyses to come out of the cultural studies tradition. From brazen inquiries into the pleasures of romance, to nuanced evidence of counter-reading in female fan culture, to sustained critiques of the persistence of masculinist ideologies in even the most avowedly progressive images, feminist media criticism ran wild and deep, taking male critics to task for their blithe refusal to reckon with sexual difference and offering up treatise after treatise that exposed the vexed intransigence of patriarchy while at the same time trumpeting the ever-present (or so we believed) possibilities of subversive readings and hidden feminist imagery.

Questions of visibility were at the heart of early feminist concerns, and not simply through the central concept of the gaze. For many a marginalized group, to simply be seen—to be part of the panorama of cultural vision—was at least part of the battle. But for all the complexities of cultural analysis, we often seemed to wind down to the conclusion "more and better." More people of color less confined to limited and narrow roles. More women, less stereotypically depicted. A reasonable goal perhaps, but one that ran up against both right-wing resistance and cultural studies innovations. More and better seemed so narrow a goal, so self-limiting, so crassly empiricist. And, of course, who is to say what better is? One person's feisty feminist warrior princess is another's sexualized bimbo. One person's subversive mainstreaming is another's shallow assimilation. Surely the decisive and transformative innovations of spectatorship theory problematized the "more and better" approach and made it increasingly difficult to make overly broad statements about the certain meaning of images or cultural moments.

Indeed, feminist cultural critics have always been wary of marking visibility as the easy sign of liberatory imaginings. The very theorizing of the male gaze—and attendant rejections of narrative logics and representation itself—explicitly argued that vision was not all it was cracked up to be and that, sometimes, being seen was itself the act of violation, the imprimatur of power. To be captured by the gaze was to be subject to it and to the power of imagining that the gaze implied. In later years, of course, the theory of the gaze came under increased scrutiny (for its assumption of only heterosexual desire, for its insistence that identification was at the heart of viewing pleasure, and for so much else!), and thus pushed even further against the futuristic promises of visibility politics. So feminists have maintained a healthy distance from that too-easy delight in being part of a scene/seen in which one has traditionally been absent or secondary. Even the most assiduous headcounters or devout Freudians seemed to realize that Woman's otherness could not be simply imaged away with a few healthy representations or revealed Oedipal moments.

For gay theorists and activists, visibility always seemed to hold out more promise. Perhaps we believed the illusion of visibility-as-transformation because our representational history has been so nasty, brutish, and short. Plagued by ugly stereotypes or crude indifference, we were the terrifying "others" of Hollywood's darkest fears—preying perverts, stealthy spies, simpering esthetes, ridiculous glam boys, sinister prison matrons, troubled youth. It was either some such portrayal or the despair of invisibility. If they could only see us, we seemed to believe, in all our normal glory, in all our proud sameness, society would slowly shift. If we could only just edge out from behind the thick curtain of invisibility, we would emerge into the bright sunshine of acceptance.

But, just like the singular (white, hetero) spectator was revealed as a fantasy, this too fell into disrepute as both queer theory and transnational feminism challenged the politics of visibility and recognition. Concerns with visibility have not wholly disappeared, but have surely receded or at the very least been reformatted to fit the new era of spectacularized identities.

New sites, old challenges

So if not visibility, if not more and better, if not accurate and true, then what is the (new) subject/object of feminist media criticism? In this brief essay, I want to try to sketch out what I see as some of the shifts or changes in feminist cultural studies. It is vital to note—as many have done—that the first great wave of feminist cultural studies emerged out of, and in dialogue with, the ferment of feminist activism, even when its relationship to that activism was tenuous at best. Not only was feminist cultural theory enmeshed with the vibrant women's movement but feminist media activism was itself central to the earliest definitions of the field, particularly in its more social-science orientations. So what happens to feminist media studies when feminism itself changes, morphing perhaps into a less singular and definable "movement" and becoming iterated differently across geographical borders? How to think feminist media studies when every instance of media activism seems so readily slurped up in the relentless commodification of dissent? It is true that alternative and subcultural forms still flourish and even find new homes in the world of internet bloggers and YouTube videographers. But mainstream media—and indeed even the alternative or at least more democratic forms mentioned above—remain resistant to challenges any deeper than postfeminism lite.

This is an historic moment, therefore, characterized by any number of political and intellectual shifts—including but not limited to the rise of a global media culture and the persistence of national forms; the increasing diversity of media forms and venues, including web and new media locations; the rise of new genres and the persistence of old ones; and the various posts (post-9/11 security states, putative postfeminism and its critics, postcolonialism). In an interesting essay that examines this much-debated phenomenon of postfeminism, Angela McRobbie situates the early 1990s as a crucial period in the academy for feminism and, specifically, for feminist cultural studies. Indeed, she articulates a kind of convergence where feminist self-criticism meets "popular feminism" via the work of postcolonial feminists, theorists such as Judith Butler, and the emergence of the body, subjectivity, and performance as key feminist tropes (McRobbie 2004: 256). Recent work has provocatively focused on how some attenuated, troubled, complicated versions of feminism come to circulate through popular culture, particularly in network television. Much remains to be done in this vein, however, as we need to pay more detailed attention to the mechanisms by which attenuated and desultory versions of feminism actually help demonize the more robust versions theorized and practiced around the world.

The biggest challenge, I think, has been to reckon with the ways in which new genres and new media forms—from "reality TV" to narrowcasting, the internet, and media interactivity—"speak" gender and gendered identities and politics in perhaps new and troublesome ways. These new genres and forms may not have produced new feminist methodologies but they have perhaps forged new emphases. For example, following wider recent trends in feminist theory, newer work often construes gender more broadly,

89

asking less how "women" are represented in any given film or TV show and more how a wide variety of gendered identities are invoked, produced, hailed, etc. Work on representations of trans-subjectivities has been particularly fruitful, in part because the questions raised (about the relationship between gender and sexuality, about authenticity and the body, about fluidity and constraint) more easily avoid the pitfalls of "positive/negative" media theories and narrowly textual and small-scale approaches. Indeed, one real appeal of transcultural scholarship—like diasporic scholarship—is, for me, methodological: the broadness of scope and vision is almost forced by the site of analysis.

Feminist scholars who work in television have been most challenged. While film as a medium has surely changed (e.g. with the rise of digital technology, the dominance of the blockbuster, the retreat of independent filmmaking and distribution, the increasing focus on international markets and nonpublic distribution sites, etc.), television has undergone dramatic revision in the years since feminists starting mining that particular vein. As Lynn Spigel writes:

> In one respect, television scholarship is changing because TV itself is so different from what it was in the past. The demise of the U.S. three-network system, the increasing commercialization of public-service/state-run systems, the rise of multi-channel cable and global satellite delivery, multinational conglomerates, Internet convergence, changes in regulatory policies and ownership rules, the advent of high-definition TV, technological changes in screen design, digital video recorders, and new forms of media competition—as well as new forms of programming (e.g., reality TV) and scheduling practices (e.g., year-long seasons or multi-plexing)—have all transformed the practice we call watching TV. This does not mean all of television is suddenly unrecognizable—indeed, familiarity and habit continue to be central to the TV experience—but it does mean that television's past is recognizably distinct from its present.
>
> (Spigel 2005: 83)

These changes—alongside other structural shifts, including the YouTube phenomenon and similar forms of DIY entertainment—have not only meant a necessary re-tooling of feminist scholarship but have provoked a more fundamental rethinking about the "site" of popular representations when the more public forms have receded or at least dispersed significantly. Indeed, if television has been so rigorously analyzed as a domestic, familial, and therefore (problematic) "feminine" medium, then it becomes necessary to rethink this chain of associations once narrowcasting, DIY TV, and other refigurings move TV away from the rigidly domestic realm in which feminist scholarship has staked such a major claim.

Reality TV—particularly the genres that emphasize the makeover—has proved to be a particularly fertile ground for these debates and feminist scholarship more generally. This should be no surprise, as these genres both target women as audiences and invoke them as subjects. The rise of reality TV may not have provoked substantially innovative theories or methodologies for feminist cultural studies, but it has forced a series of critical questions, including how to reckon with the increasingly direct address of consumerism and commodification in reality TV and how to signify bodily autonomy and ethics in an era of triumphant plasticity.

Another issue that remains current for feminist cultural theorists—indeed, one hopes it never disappears!—is that of pleasure. If critical cultural studies (and in particular post-Birmingham feminist work) reclaimed filmic and other pleasure from the dour Frankfurt School critics and orthodox feminists alike, then how has the renewed emphasis on the (hidden, dirty, bad) pleasures of popular culture altered the field? The pleasure question cuts through the new sites, and many critics "long to move outside the conceptual trap of 'guilty media pleasures' to develop a new third-wave feminist media theory that builds on the work of such innovative thinkers as bell hooks and Tania Modleski but works toward a less restrictive paradigm than the subversion/containment model that at times leads down a dead-end path" (Johnson 2007: 292).

Of course, we always want to be able to capture the complexity—the sometimes simultaneous expression of exhilarating liberation and teeth-gnashing containment—that characterizes high-end cultural artifacts of the early twenty-first century. We want to get past or get over or get beyond the either/or options of violation or liberation. Nonetheless, figuring out how to do this successfully is difficult at best. Too often, attempts to mediate between binaries results in a "little bit of victimization" and "little bit of empowerment" formulation, rendering the analysis very limp indeed, like Donny and Marie trying to merge country and rock aesthetics ("she's a little bit country, I'm a little bit rock 'n' roll") in their witless eponymous TV variety show of the late 1970s. Are there no more hegemonic forms in a culture of such dispersal? And has the emphasis on contestation and unevenness allowed us the illusion of a diversity that may exist only in our fantasies? What difference does difference make when it is attached at the hip to all the unhip machinery of neoliberal dominance?

Feminist cultural studies not only responds and shifts in relation to structural changes in media formations and innovations in media criticism, but—perhaps more importantly—also is deeply enmeshed in and responsive to larger shifts and currents in feminist theorizing writ large. Two of the most profound and thoroughgoing strands in feminist theorizing in recent years—transnational feminism and sexuality and queer studies—have enormously impacted both the objects of feminist cultural work and the analytic tropes used in the interpretation of those objects. Although it is an uneven and slow process, "scholars have begun paying attention to various media phenomena in order to examine the new gendered imaginations that are being articulated in the context of globalization and how they reproduce many of the earlier logics of colonialism and enact new ones. Indeed, a focus on how globalized media practices articulate gender enables scholars to produce more situated and empirically-driven research on globalization that can go beyond abstract and acontextual theorizations" (Shome 2006: 257). I would note that this seems a more accurate description of feminist film studies and, to a lesser extent, TV studies than the more tradition-bound (and US centric) field of "communications studies."

Importantly, the new transnational feminist cultural work is not narrowly anthropological in tenor. Rather, it addresses circulations of representation as they weave in and out of national locales, engaged by multiple constituencies in complicated ways. Thus, there has been an important shift not only in the presumptive "Westernness" of cultural forces but in the understanding of the uneven ways in which people experience popular culture—mediated by all the identities we already obsess about but also sometimes cutting across national/racial/sexual boundaries in ways that surprise and ignite. The most compelling renditions of this have come, I believe, from scholars working around questions of diaspora and borderlands, particularly when those questions are inflected with queer subjectivities. I think particularly here of work that examines how "feminine" identities slip precariously across borders in ways that show both their marked particularity and, simultaneously, their embeddedness in dominant ideological frames—for example in the scholarship of Gayatri Gopinath and Angharad Valdivia, who both engage with the movement of an eclectic and varied set of cultural texts, including Bollywood musicals and the complex icons of Latinidad.

Queer studies and its mellower twin, sexuality studies, has provided the second major challenge to feminist theorizing and, therefore, to feminist cultural/media studies as well. It would be a mistake, however, to characterize these challenges on a simple linear timeline; to do so perpetuates a tendency to set up a truncated (and simply inaccurate) history of feminist theorizing that starts out with the (dumpy) big, bad, white, middle-class, hetero essentialists and ends up in the funky garden of de-lite with the happy-go-lucky queer Asian/black/Latina sophisticates. Indeed, both transnational and queer cultural scholarship (and, by the way, US black feminism) came on the (feminist cultural) scene pretty early on. This is not to deny institutional resistances and continuous willful omissions, but rather to insist that we "break up" this romantic history, which always posits a transcendent true love that rescues the poorly matched lovers from years of desultory fumblings. Queer and diasporic emphases have been—for a quite a while—substantive if not equal players on the feminist cultural studies field.

So when gay, and later queer, theorists joined the cultural studies stew (or emerged as a distinct voice—we were, of course there from the outset), the project of cultural studies began to move even farther away from "representations of" and to hone in on a newly enhanced notion of the productiveness of popular images. Gayness, straightness, femininity, masculinity, ethnic, and racial categorizations became understood as essentially "fictive" categories that assumed a scary realness when produced in and through popular images and discourses. The vaunted authenticity of marginalized sexual identities necessarily gave way to analyses of fraught and deeply split subjectivities, at least in the world of cultural theory. Indeed, some of the most fruitful work in recent years has been located in the intersection of these interests, for example in analyses that examine the production of gendered and sexed subjectivities across and through national borders (see, for example, Maira 2002).

In many ways, feminist cultural studies found itself in the same boat as feminist theory more generally, called upon (and calling upon itself) to address the persistent assumptions of whiteness, Westernness, and heterosexuality in the figuration of representations of women and women audiences, spectators, and consumers. Just as feminist theory began to respond to the call with self-criticism and self-reflection, so too did the project of feminist cultural criticism begin to alter its object and subject—to attend to the global configurations of gendered representation, the intersecting lines of race and class across representational fields, and the complex interplay between shoring up a heterosexual imaginary and intimating at the sexually abject. In short, difference.

Maybe bigger is better?

So where is feminist cultural/media studies now? Has it simply matured, inevitably lost the luster of newness and rebellious nose-thumbing? Or is it lost in a wilderness of its own making, looking for love (in all the wrong institutional places) and unable to find its way back home? Maybe it never had a home and that's all to the good; maybe cultural studies is being simultaneously institutionalized and dispersed, continually and stoically refusing the canonization that would be its death knell? Or maybe we cultural critics are like Oz's bemused protagonists, vainly looking for someone, anyone, to hand us heart, brain, courage? Let me be clear: it is not that this period is without its wondrous works. And it just may be that we're good enough as it is, that new sites for analysis have emerged but that the old theories are more than adequate to address these new phenomena. Rather, the point I want to make here is that feminist media studies has yet to see the emergence of a fundamentally new theoretical or methodological framing even in the midst of quite substantive changes "on the ground."

If "more and better" are no longer legitimate political/cultural goals or supportable theoretical frameworks, then what is our project about? If the project of uncovering and revealing the workings of regressive and masculinist ideologies manifest in popular images seems redolent of a kind of hopeless, hypodermic determinism but the alternative of finding the subversive pleasure in every cultural haystack seems suspiciously naïve and glib, then what is an earnest (queer, feminist, whatever) cultural critic to do? Is Lynn Rakow right when she wonders if "feminist scholars [have] said all there is to say about the media? Is our work done? Do we now know enough about gender, representation, and technology to spend our time filling in details by looking at specific texts and specific audiences?" (Rakow 2001: 41). I wonder if we have returned (with new eyes perhaps) to some of the old questions that emerged from second-wave feminist work. I think here specifically of how the current focus on the body (the queer body, the mutilated body, the abject body, the diasporic body, the changeable body, etc.) has emerged as a key trope in recent feminist cultural criticism. Where once the body was seen as a simple template upon which patriarchy worked its objectifying magic, now the body becomes a site of complex negotiations and contestations. Particularly in queer, trans, and diasporic analyses, the body becomes not merely (only?) a location of enacted violence and control, but a more fluid space of potential and possibility. From musings on transnational makeover genres to discussions on the ("native") female body as signifier of a dangerous modernity, feminist cultural critics have reinvigorated discussions of the body in feminist theory. But I do wonder if we have gone a bit too far here, if in imagining the plasticity of body politics we have overlooked or avoided a continuing engagement with issues of commodification and objectification. For surely these are not transcended realities or simply the tired detritus of old (essentialist) theories of bodily wholeness and integrity. Women's bodies—transnationally—still serve far too often as the place to vent rage, to assert nationhood, to claim territory, to use with impunity. Just as cultural transgression and stolen pleasures may not imply transformation or challenge, neither does bodily plasticity and variability necessarily signal anything other than just that.

As Mary Ann Doane (2004: 1231) rightly notes, we abjure the large questions at our peril: "Current film feminisms often ally themselves with the logic of the local and its corresponding suspicion of abstraction. And this, to my mind, is a grave error. For there is at least one basic question that subtends the entire project of feminist film criticism and that has never been thoroughly addressed—the question of the relation between aesthetics and politics." I share her concerns that

> the current tendency to divide and subdivide subjectivities in an effort to avoid the overgeneralization or totalization of the concept of "woman" rests on the premise that this impact (of film on society or society on film) is potentially infinitely complex, but nevertheless there, as the substrate of the feminist endeavor. The logical outcome of such a process of division, which is ultimately based on the

premises of empiricism, is pure particularity, pure idiolect. This approach, which generates a great deal of discourse today, risks an aphasia of theory in which nothing can be said.

(Doane 2004: 1231)

This might be too strong a statement but divisions in the field are often less about the content of particular analyses than about territorial debates regarding the appropriate purview of feminist cultural work. The result is that, paradoxically, both too much and too little are claimed—too much, in the sense of making grand claims for small cultural moments, and too little, in the sense of refusing all generalities in the quest for local verifications. Like many critics who claim some origin story with British cultural studies, I still see enormous value in what may be called a synthetic approach (or, rather, a contextual and intertextual one). We may refer to it by any number of names (the one that seems most accurate, albeit awkward, is something like a "feminist social history of culture") but it has undoubtedly produced some very productive work in recent years, not only in reclaiming all the lost women filmmakers, videographers, spectators, etc. but in creatively integrating two of the central frames of early (Birmingham-style) cultural studies—the social and the historical—and infusing them with a deep sense of political immediacy.

Perhaps I am too pessimistic about the present, put off by narrowness as much as by misplaced hubris. Another way to understand this current moment is not as a lost girl in search of a paradigm but rather as the triumph of a sort of earnest eclecticism where traditional frameworks of cultural analysis have responded fruitfully and creatively to the challenges of postcolonial theory, critical race studies, queer studies, and other newer forms. True enough. But for all the talk of hybridity, contested readings, uneven patterns of cultural hegemony, revisioning, and other assorted tropes of the current moment, have we lost sight of large, impinging (and, yes, multifaceted) forms of masculinist domination? I like a resistant reading as much as the next girl and god knows I have my share of guilty pleasures, but so what? Wouldn't it be the case—truly—that the world would be quite different if all this supposed variability in media meaning were actually empowering, progressive, feminist? How do we account for the relationship between the truism that popular culture is a space of gender contestation and against-the-grain pleasures and the truism that dominative and damaging conceptions of (in this case) gender continue to rule the day, even as they morph and become, sometimes, more nuanced? Has the pluralization (femininities, masculinities) perhaps disenabled theorists to speak more broadly about dominant and hegemonic forms? For while it is true that pop culture provides a variety of gendered representations for us to consume/contest/engage, it is equally true that it does not provide an endless variety.

The question of how these pleasures, these resistances, these mis/readings translate seems to be have receded as cultural studies becomes at once more sophisticated and less sublime. Rest assured, I'm not invoking "translate" to imply a glib sense of political action (I see *Nip/Tuck* and I want to smash the corporate arm of plastic surgery!), but rather to provoke a sense of mattering, rendering, deciphering, decoding. In any good translation, there is a process of evaluation and adjudication: I choose this word over another possibility, this phrase expresses most pungently the passionate tone of the speaker, this intonation and not another. A compelling translation does not merely follow the intricacies of the language but locates that moment of utterance in larger contexts of culture, intention, identities of interlocutors, and history.

Although this synthetic approach certainly shouldn't and doesn't trump others, it has faded in prominence in recent years and does—particularly in these perilous times—need to find a way home again, if only because synthetic frameworks often ask questions that are left unaddressed in more modest work. Perhaps what I am bemoaning here is that true interdisciplinarity in feminist cultural studies still seems so elusive a goal. When you think of the pioneering work of a Mulvey or a Radway or a Brunsdon or a de Lauretis or any number of other scholars, you understand (and, yes, miss) their paradigm-shifting capacities. This reinvigoration of the synthetic can and should be just that: a reinvigoration. For if much of that earlier "grand theory" conveniently overlooked its own moorings, no such narrowness of vision need characterize a feminist "grand theory" for the twenty-first century.

Acknowledgments

Thanks particularly to Nick Clarkson for his able assistance in preparing this chapter.

References

Brundson, Charlotte and Spigel, Lynn. 2008. *Feminist Television Criticism: A Reader*, 2nd edition. Milton Keynes, England: Open University Press/McGraw-Hill Education.

Doane, Mary Ann. 2004. "Aesthetics and Politics." *Signs: Journal of Women in Culture and Society* 30(1): 1229–35.

Doyle, Jennifer and Jones, Amelia. 2006. "Introduction: New Feminist Theories of Visual Culture." *Signs: Journal of Women in Culture and Society* 31(3): 607–15.

Gallagher, Margaret. 2001. "The Push and Pull of Action and Research in Feminist Media Studies." *Feminist Media Studies* 1(1): 11–15.

Gopinath, Gayatri. 2005. "Bollywood Spectacles: Queer Diasporic Critique in the Aftermath of 9/11." *Social Text* 84–85, 23(3–4): 157–69.

Johnson, Merri Lisa. 2007. "Gangster Feminism: The Feminist Cultural Work of HBO's *The Sopranos*." *Feminist Studies* 33(2): 269–96.

Kaplan, E. Ann. 2004. "Global Feminisms and the State of Feminist Film Theory." *Signs: Journal of Women in Culture and Society* 30(1): 1236–48.

——. 2008. "A History of Gender Theory in Cinema Studies." In K. Gabbard and W. Luhr, eds., *Screening Genders*. New Brunswick, NJ: Rutgers University Press.

Kuhn, Annette. 2004. "The State of Film and Media Feminism." *Signs: Journal of Women in Culture and Society* 30(1): 1221–28.

Lee, Micky. 2006. "What's Missing in Feminist Research in New Information and Communication Technologies?" *Feminist Media Studies* 6(2): 191–210.

Lotz, Amanda D. and Ross, Sharon Marie. 2004. "Bridging Media-specific Approaches." *Feminist Media Studies* 4(2): 185–202.

McHugh, Kathleen and Sobchack, Vivian. 2004. "Introduction: Recent Approaches to Film Feminisms." *Signs: Journal of Women in Culture and Society* 30: 1205–07.

McRobbie, Angela. 2004. "Post-feminism and Popular Culture." *Feminist Media Studies* 4(3): 255–64.

Maira, Sunaina. 2002. *Desis in the House: Indian-American Youth Culture in New York City*. Philadelphia, PA: Temple University Press.

Rakow, Lynn. 2001. "Feminists, Media, Freed Speech." *Feminist Media Studies* 1(1): 41–44.

Shome, Rana. 2006. "Transnational Feminism and Communication Studies." *Communication Review* 255–67.

Spigel, Lynn. 2004. "Theorizing the Bachelorette: 'Waves' of Feminist Media Studies." *Signs: Journal of Women in Culture and Society* 30(1): 1209–21.

——. 2005. "TV's Next Season?" *Cinema Journal* 45(1): 83–90.

Walters, Suzanna Danuta. 1995. *Material Girls: Making Sense of Feminist Cultural Theory*. Berkeley: University of California Press.

——. 2001. *All the Rage: The Story of Gay Visibility in America*. Chicago: University of Chicago Press.

9

What is "the relative autonomy of culture"?

Jeffrey K. Olick

Among the myths one could tell about culture in recent American sociology is the following:

In the 1950s, the work of Talcott Parsons placed culture at the center of sociology. Culture, which Parsons discussed largely in terms of values, was for him the major integrative force of social life, the answer to sociology's foundational question—the Hobbesian problem of order. As critics in the 1960s and 1970s rejected Parsonsian theory, however, Parsons's version of culture often stood as a surrogate for culture analysis *per se*. In these years, cultural sociology thus went into a period of relative hibernation; although many continued to investigate culture sociologically in various circumscribed arenas (such as religion or the arts), culture was no longer easily accepted as an overarching or even significant force by the leading disciplinary figures of the time.

Beginning in the late 1970s and early 1980s, however, American sociology began returning to culture. In the early moments of this new cultural turn, the sociology of culture was largely a revival of the sociology of art, literature, popular culture, and knowledge. But since these early days, culture has recaptured center stage in the United States. In part, this was due to the exhaustion of the mono-causal or partial strategies (e.g. rational-choice theory and Marxist political economy, or phenomenology and interactionism) that many sociologists had pursued in reaction to, or merely instead of, Parsons's "grand" program. And in part it was due to the growing influence of European approaches—neo-Marxist, structuralist, and others—that had never faced the Parsonsian bugaboo. Moreover, the blurring of disciplinary boundaries in this period led to the importation of alternative culture concepts from fields like anthropology and literary theory, as well as from the linguistic turns in philosophy and historiography.

The current interest in culture—and its institutional expressions like the American Sociological Association's culture section, now the Association's second largest—thus began as a return of the sociology of culture, explaining cultural artifacts and ideologies in terms of their social backgrounds. But sociological interest in culture has in the meantime become something larger, a call for a *cultural* sociology, a sociology that sees anything and everything as including a cultural dimension, arguing that all social phenomena are structured by culture.

I call this a myth not because it is wrong, though it is certainly overly simplified, as well as told from a particular perspective: American sociology since the 1950s is not one coherent enterprise, nor have all its practitioners followed this trajectory. I call it a myth because it is a story with which many of us seek to understand and justify our contemporary efforts (Levine 1995).

Central to this supposedly new cultural sociology and its mythology has been the term "the relative autonomy of culture," which has become something of a shibboleth. With it, we seem to indicate at a minimum that we think that culture is an important, sometimes even the most important, topic for sociological analysis, and that we identify with others who share this view. The problem is that such use of "the relative autonomy of culture" often fails to specify anything beyond a general allegiance to "cultural" perspectives in sociology. The term itself and its casual uses do not specify what culture is supposedly autonomous from (the two major possibilities are structure and agency, though these clearly refer to distinct arguments in the philosophy of the social sciences) (Hays 1994). Moreover, "relative" is hardly a robust descriptor.

The term "relative autonomy," of course, has a long history in social thought. A wide variety of writers, including Durkheim, Lukacs, Sartre, and Elias, have employed it (Kilminster 1991: xxvii). Most famous is its use by Althusser and his followers, particularly Poulantzas, to reject economic reductionism in Marxist state theory. In cultural sociology, however, its most intentional and elaborated use was in a foundational essay by Jeffrey Alexander (1990) on culture and society. There and elsewhere in Alexander's so-called "strong program" for cultural sociology (Alexander and Smith 2003), "the relative autonomy of culture" has a more precise purpose than simply serving as an emblem for those who are interested in meaning and interpretation and who see themselves on the humanistic side of sociology. "The relative autonomy of culture," in Alexander's use, indicates a meta-theoretical argument about the role of culture in sociological analysis, namely one that insists on avoiding what Parsons, following Whitehead, called "the fallacy of misplaced concreteness." In this way, "the relative autonomy of culture" is an imprecise substitute for what is better described as an "*analytical* autonomy" argument, one that implies not only that meaning and interpretation are important, but that they are important in particular ways.

In this chapter, I outline this "autonomist" position, focusing on the arguments of Jeffrey Alexander (1990, 1995) and Margaret Archer (1988)—though to be sure there are differences between these authors and with others, like William Sewell (1992) or Nicos Mouzelis (1995), who also advance an autonomist position. Autonomists, I show, are concerned with avoiding not only the classical reduction of culture to other factors, but also the treatment of culture as a concrete force rather than as an analytical dimension. In fighting the enemy of misplaced concreteness (often referred to as the "concrete autonomy" argument), however, the autonomist position can lead to a misreading of yet another position, namely what I call "constitutive" theory, represented most prominently by Norbert Elias, Anthony Giddens, and Pierre Bourdieu, among others (e.g. Zygmunt Bauman). In contrast to the "autonomist" position, "constitutivists" reject the analytical distinction between culture and structure in favor of an approach that highlights mutual constitution over analytical autonomy. Because analytical autonomists are mainly concerned with distinguishing analytical autonomy from concrete autonomy, however, they mischaracterize constitutivists merely as failed autonomists and thus do not take on the constitutive argument in its own terms. But constitutivists are not bad analytical autonomists: for better or worse, they reject analytical autonomy intentionally in favor of a different set of meta-theoretical commitments.

The autonomist position

As with most issues in contemporary sociological theory, the question of cultural autonomy makes important reference to Max Weber. In contrast to reductionist arguments, particularly the Marxist claim that being determines consciousness, Weber argued in *The Protestant Ethic* that ideas can act as "switchmen," changing the course laid down by the dynamics of interest. This argument, however, is not quite the same as the one Weber made when he distinguished material and ideal interests. The former argument can be read as an example of what Anne Kane (1991), in a seminal article on the autonomy of culture, calls "concrete autonomy," ideas as determinative forces; the latter, in contrast, indicates a more profound epistemological dualism between material and ideal.

The contemporary "analytical autonomy" argument, however, owes its origins more directly to Parsons than to Weber, or at least to Parsons's interpellation of Weber's dichotomous approach in a less historical direction. As John Hall (1999: 108) puts it, "Parsons sought to displace (1) a broadly qualitative and historical-comparative case-oriented approach ... in favor of (2) a more abstract analytic approach focused on describing *variable elements* of action." How so? In the concluding chapter of his first major work, *The Structure of Social Action*, Parsons (1968) identified four basic epistemological stances, including: (1) *utilitarianism*, which reifies its analytical frame (rational self-interest) when it deduces reality from it; (2) *radical positivism*, which denies the existence of an analytical frame when it claims only to be generalizing on the basis of empirical induction; and (3) *idealism*, which allows for frames of reference, but does not accept that they are general and transcend a particular situation. A fourth frame Parsons associates with Weber, namely the belief that scientific concepts are merely "useful fictions"; "ideal types," for Parsons, are the prime example of Weber's advocacy for "useful fictions" as ways of organizing analysis.

Even though Parsons acknowledges "an element of truth" in this fourth, Weberian approach, he seeks to develop a fifth, distinct position, namely what he calls "analytical realism." Ideal types, he argued, must not be understood as merely useful fictions; they are as real as the empirical world they are used to describe. "Analytical realism" depends on Parsons's assertion—which as numerous commentators (e.g. Bershady 1973) note is close to that of Immanuel Kant—that we must distinguish between analytical and concrete aspects of reality. For Parsons (1968: 730), the concepts of science are analytical, and hence "correspond, not to concrete phenomena, but to elements in them which are analytically separable from other elements." For instance, we may be able to concretely dissect out the brain of an individual, but the distinction between mind and body is only an analytical one. Nevertheless, such analytical distinctions are essential to science, and are particularly appropriate to the social sciences, which must take into account the ideal element, lest they treat their objects as machines and hence cease to be social sciences at all.

Importantly, Parsons made clear that analytical categories are to be distinguished from "emergent properties." For Weber, normative patterns—e.g. the Protestant Ethic—must be understood to emerge from the accumulated actions of individuals; they are thus concrete emergences. For Parsons, in contrast, norms are an analytic element of action systems. When Parsons refers to "normative order" or to the "integrative powers of culture," norms or culture are thus not concrete elements but analytical dimensions. For Parsons, then, all explanations must be multi-dimensional, which is different from merely saying they must take into account emergence. To miss this is to succumb to the fallacy of misplaced concreteness.

Not every analytical autonomist has come to the position through a critical reading of Parsons. But that is certainly the case with Jeffrey Alexander, whose approach is quite explicitly neo- or post-Parsonsian. Nevertheless, Alexander points out the flaw in Parsons's conceptualization of culture: despite Parsons's emphasis on the analytical autonomy of culture and structure (conditions and norms, in his language), Parsons was in practice most interested in the concrete institutionalization of culture as values. In effect, in Alexander's view, Parsons's approach commits the sin of "internalized reduction," thus failing to fulfill the promise of his genuinely multi-dimensional theory. And indeed, multi-dimensionalism is the overriding principle of Alexander's analytical-autonomy position.

As Alexander's protégé Anne Kane (1991: 54) puts it, "analytical autonomy ... posits the complete and independent structure of culture; it is conceptualized through the theoretical, artificial separation of culture from other social structures, conditions, and action." The basic principle of the analytical-autonomy position is thus to overcome the elision of concrete and analytical autonomy: not only do ideas act as switchmen, ideal interests are always present, as part of an autonomous analytical dimension, even in the most material circumstances.

If "relative autonomy" thus refers to "analytical autonomy," it is a very poor choice of terms indeed, for the autonomy of culture is not meant in the sense that Althusser and his followers meant the autonomy of the state. The state is a concrete agency with buildings, resources, personnel, etc. The analytical autonomy of culture corresponds better to the distinction between, for instance, the political and economic aspects of a negotiation, which are not reducible to the presence of a politician and a banker. In Althusserian state theory, relative autonomy refers explicitly and clearly to concrete autonomy. Perhaps this is one reason why the overriding concern for the cultural analytical autonomists has been to distinguish their position from the fallacy of misplaced concreteness, which leads to the treatment of culture as emergent rather than as analytically autonomous. This urgency to reject concrete autonomy, however, leads analytical autonomists to misunderstand the argument of those who reject the durable status of such analytical distinctions, namely those I call "constitutivists."

Autonomy versus constitution

Bourdieu

The work of Pierre Bourdieu is perhaps the most prominent invocation of constitutivism in recent American theory discussions. Bourdieu constructs his positions as a response to what he sees as two failed sociological projects—structuralism (mainly Lévi-Straussian structural anthropology) and "subjectivism" (under which he includes phenomenology, existentialism, symbolic interactionism, and rational-choice theory). The problem with structuralism, according to Bourdieu, is that it reifies structure; structuralists claim to grasp structures as such clairvoyantly rather than through their appearance in human behavior. This position, Bourdieu argues, *a priori* creates a false dichotomy between structure and agency by positing an existence for structures that is completely external to individuals and that reduces agents to mere automatons.

In contrast, subjectivism ignores structuring processes, locating each interaction or decision in an immediate unstructured context. Subjectivists are thus unable to explain regularity and the reproduction over generations of the categories which agents draw on to "construct" social relations.

Bourdieu's response is that structures are not "real," but exist only in the regularities of human behavior. Similarly, agency is not the product of an unstructured subjectivity but of a structured set of dispositions, the "habitus." "Habitus," of course, is difficult to pin down because, consistent with his critique of idealism, Bourdieu is reluctant to specify concepts once and for all. Nevertheless, Bourdieu develops the notion of habitus as a method for grasping the inseparability of culture, structure, and agency. For Bourdieu, habitus gives expression to the dialectical relation between subjectivity and objectivity. The shared dispositions of the habitus generate certain groupings of attitudes and behavior: actors are "naturally"—by virtue of the habitus—oriented to what is conventionally called structure without consciously orienting themselves in this manner.

But it is not the habitus alone that ensures the reproduction of structuring processes. The concept of "field" designates a vast number of hierarchically structured arenas of social life. "A field," Bourdieu writes, "may be defined as a network, or a configuration, of objective relations between positions" (Bourdieu and Wacquant 1992: 97). Furthermore, "In a highly differentiated society, the social cosmos is made up of a number of such relatively autonomous social microcosms, i.e., spaces of objective relations that are the site of a logic and a necessity that are specific and irreducible to those that regulate other fields" (Bourdieu and Wacquant 1992: 97). Insofar as the field is a place of struggle, its very nature and its rules of operation are always either reproduced or changed, and thus cannot be taken for granted as fixed. Indeed, one major object and result of the struggle is not just the internal structure of the field, but the very boundaries of the field itself, its borders with and relations to other fields. Bourdieu's formulation thus suggests that institutions are themselves produced by the struggles that go on within them, and that the relations among fields also are always potentially fluid.

There are, however, two major points of criticism to be raised here, points that Alexander addresses powerfully. Despite the fluidity of Bourdieu's field concept, he seems to bring a hierarchical ordering in through the back door. Bourdieu "discovers" from his research that the most important condition for the development of the habitus is the distance from economic necessity. But then he seems to generalize this empirical "discovery" into an *a priori* condition: habitus, he writes, is "necessity internalized and converted into a disposition that generates meaningful practices and meaning-given perceptions" (Bourdieu 1984: 170). Furthermore, "Without ever being totally coordinated ... the dispositions and the situations which combine synchronically to constitute a determinate conjuncture are never wholly independent, since they are engendered by the objective structures, that is, in the last analysis, by the economic bases of the social formation" (Bourdieu 1977: 83). This assertion that economic structures are the main determinants of habitus, many critics have charged, compromises Bourdieu's claim that dimensions of the social world are mutually constitutive. If constitution is

101

mutual, then a single dimension (economic structure) must not be treated as primary and determining. This is Parsons's problem of internalized reduction redux.

Alexander's critique

Alexander's response to Bourdieu is thus shaped not by the claim that Bourdieu is insufficiently constitutive, but that he is too constitutive. Bourdieu's problem, according to Alexander (1995), is that he sees the habitus as the site of non-rational, practical consciousness: he wants to show that apparently non-economic realms of life are the objects of calculation. Bourdieu therefore needs to argue that the habitus is the location of strategic action. According to Alexander, this leads Bourdieu to conflate economy and culture. The habitus must not only structure action, it must explain why people tend to act in a way that, against their "interests," reproduces inequalities in various fields— "the regularities immanent in the objective condition of the production of their generative principle" (Bourdieu 1977: 78). In order to explain these regularities without falling back into a mechanistic model, Bourdieu insists that, instead of following rules, agents as knowing subjects are capable of deploying strategies. According to Alexander, Bourdieu's attempt to resolve his dilemma leads into a theoretical paradox. On the one hand, Bourdieu shows that structural analysis of cultural codes is inadequate to understanding action, since people possess varying degrees of mastery of these codes or ability to improvise within them. On the other hand, the habitus conceived as practical consciousness means repeated recourse to norms and habits, that is, to non-rational sources of motivation. According to Alexander, Bourdieu cannot have it both ways:

> Internalized, normative order and rational action are like oil and water; they can be placed beside one another but they cannot mix. If actors are simply calculating creatures, the objects of their calculation may certainly be norms; if so, then these same norms cannot form the character (habitus) of these calculating agents as well. Norms which are merely objects of calculation can only be the norms of others, not of the actor herself.
>
> (Alexander 1995: 155)

Thus, Alexander argues, Bourdieu has conflated dimensions of the social world. The cultural dimension of action, which allows people to exercise agency through interpretation, has been reduced to strategy, unconscious or not, which is at root an economic dimension.

Whereas Alexander sees this conflation as endemic to the constitutive project, however, it is also possible to see it as a particular problem of Bourdieu's that derives from his commitment to explaining reproduction rather than transformation of structures. Alexander's main concern is that distinctions between dimensions be preserved. However, it might also be possible to solve Bourdieu's conflationary problems by conceptually eliminating the problem of balance between structure and agency—in Bourdieu unbalanced in favor of structure—by eliminating the conceptual distinction between structure and agency. But before I explore such a possibility, it will be useful to examine Giddens's version of constitutive theory, which has the opposite weakness from Bourdieu's—over-balancing in favor of agency. By examining Margaret Archer's response to Giddens, we will gain an even clearer understanding of what the autonomist position entails.

Giddens

In the context of Anglo-American sociological theory, and independently of Bourdieu, Anthony Giddens has developed his own version of constitutive theory, which he refers to as structuration theory. Structuration theory, as Giddens conceives it, is an attempt to resolve the foundational Western sociological dualism between action and system. In contrast to Parsons's theory, which speaks of the internalization of norms, Giddens seeks to conceptualize the process whereby knowledgeable actors interact to produce and reproduce the systematicity of social relations. Into this "mutual constitution" of structure and agency, to avoid the interactionist pitfall of seeing all actors as equal in interaction, Giddens adds a broad concept of power.

Following Kilminster (1990), I offer the following two quotations as summarizing the core of structuration theory:

> All structural properties of social systems ... are the medium and outcome of the contingently accomplished activities of situated actors. The reflexive monitoring of action in situations of co-presence is the main anchoring feature of social integration, but both the conditions and the outcomes of situated interaction stretch far beyond those situations as such. The mechanisms of 'stretching' are variable but in modern societies tend to involve reflexive monitoring itself. That is to say, understanding the conditions of system reproduction becomes part of those conditions of system reproduction as such.
>
> (Giddens 1984: 195)

> Power is not, as such, an obstacle to freedom or emancipation but is their very medium ... The existence of power presumes structures of domination whereby power that 'flows smoothly' in processes of social reproduction (and is, as it were, 'unseen') operates. The development of force or its threat is thus not the type case of the use of power.
>
> (Giddens 1984: 257)

Giddens's point is to replace dualism with "duality," seeing neither structure (system) nor agency apart from the other. Structures, in this account, have only a "virtual existence." They are instantiated in action, and are perpetuated as "memory traces." This ontological observation is necessary, according to Giddens, to avoid reifying structures as entities when in fact they are only immanent orderings. Action instantiates and perpetuates structure.

Giddens's intention is to do away with what he sees as the ontological reifications inhering in dualistic theory. Dualism, for Giddens, is the assertion that agency and institutional structure are conceivable apart from one another. In contrast, he agrees that institutionalized practices and relations—more fluid and open categories—are where order is to be found. Sociology should study social practices and relations, not institutions and agents.

Archer's critique

"Institutions," in Giddens's account, as Margaret Archer (1995: 95) critiques it, "are never something concrete to which we can point but are essentially processual;

ever in a fluid process of becoming and never in a (temporarily or temporary) fixed state of being, because all structural properties and all actions are always potentially transformable." In her statement of an analytical-autonomy position, Archer (1988) characterizes structuration theory as a variety of what she calls "central conflationism," which can be read as a pejorative characterization of "constitutivism." The hallmark of central conflationism, she argues, is to insist on the mutual constitution of structure and agency, thus, according to Archer, precluding examination of their interplay. In contrast, Archer insists "that the two [structure and agency, individual and society] have to be related rather than conflated" (Archer 1995: 6). The crux of her argument is that central conflationism denies either structure and culture independent *causal* power:

> The endorsement of their mutual constitution precludes examination of their interplay, of the effects of one upon the other and of any statement about their relative contribution to stability and change at any given time. Conversely, social realism accentuates the importance of emergent properties at the levels of both agency and structure, but considers these as proper to the strata in question and therefore distinct from each other and irreducible to one another. Irreducibility means that the different strata are separable by definition precisely because of the properties and powers which only belong to each of them and whose emergence from one another justifies their differentiation as strata at all.
>
> (Archer 1995: 14)

One important reason for Archer's assertion of analytical autonomy is that it allows her to reintroduce separate temporal horizons for structure and agency—an independence denied by central conflation: "Properties and powers of some strata are anterior to those of others; they have relative autonomy; such autonomous properties exert independent causal influences in their own right and it is the identification of these causal powers at work which validates their existence, for they may indeed be non-observables" (Archer 1995: 14). Structuration, she argues, does not allow for this kind of analytical and temporal disentanglement.

The crux of Archer's critique is her assertion that "by enjoining the examination of a single process in the present tense, issues surrounding the relative independence, causal influence, and temporal precedence of the components have been eliminated at a stroke" (Archer 1995: 93). Two questions thus arise: What is left unexplainable by mutual constitution? And why should we believe that the components are indeed separate, analytically or otherwise? According to Archer, mutual constitution means that, despite an awareness of the unintended consequences of action, there are no emergent properties of the system that can vary independently of action. Moreover, "elisionists" "deliberately turn their backs upon any autonomous features which could pertain independently to either structure or agency. Otherwise such features could be investigated separately" (Archer 1995: 97). According to Giddens, structures have only a virtual existence, instantiated in action. For Archer, this means that structure exists only in people's heads; Giddens's account, therefore, cannot explain structures that exist clearly outside of people's heads. The example she gives is the knowledge contained in libraries.

A second unacceptable implication of mutual constitution for Archer is that seeing structure as having only virtual existence requires consigning its structuring influence to the moment of instantiation. This means, for Archer, that it is impossible to explain the persistence of structures that collectivities do not want. From the agency side, this approach is problematic as well: agents are denied autonomous properties and independent influences. In contrast, Archer asserts the value of emergent structural properties on the one hand and psychological and biological aspects of agency that are socially unmediated on the other. Duality of structure, according to Archer's critique, decenters the subject because it means that "human beings only become people, as opposed to organisms, through drawing upon structural properties to generate social practices" (Archer 1995: 101). Central conflationism, Archer argues, thus deprives both elements— structure and agency—of their "relative autonomy."

To defend the relative autonomy of the self from the social agent, Archer appeals first to Kant's "Transcendental Unity of Apperception," which she follows Kant in arguing stands as an *a priori* condition for the ordering of experience. This condition requires, she argues, the continuity of bodily experience through time for the identity of one continuous consciousness. Archer also asserts that the human body, which is essential to personhood, is pre-social: "the genetic characteristics of 'species being' are necessarily pre-social at any given point in time." She also argues that the things these pre-social selves sense are also not exclusively social: we can have non-social experience of non-social reality. The metaphysical nature of these musings, however, becomes most clear when Archer connects analytical autonomy and religious faith:

> whilst no spiritual experience (of itself) is auto-veridical, neither is it automatically a candidate for being explained away sociologically. After all, sociology can never be robust enough to substantiate and sustain the faith of the atheist. But what is at issue here is not verification or falsification ... but rather the possibility of authentic inner experience.
>
> (Archer 1995: 292–93)

My point in noting this connection in Archer's work is not to argue that all analytical autonomists are theists. It is to point out that, taken to its logical conclusions, analytical autonomy seems to imply some sort of metaphysics, more often a manifest belief not in God but in *a priori* concepts.

The view from the other side: Kilminster on Giddens

Before concluding, let us examine how the situation looks from the constitutivist side. Richard Kilminster (1990) provides a detailed critique of Giddens from a constitutivist perspective. In contrast to Archer, he argues that Giddens is insufficiently developmental and remains wedded to a solipsistic, aprioristic conception of agency. In other words, it is not that Giddens is too constitutive; he is not constitutive enough! According to Kilminster, Giddens's argumentative technique fails to appreciate the ways in which dualistic concepts have developed historically. Giddens's solution thus takes part in the same aprioristic logic that brought about the problem in the first place. In part, this is due to his discontinuist understanding of modernity as a world apart from other patterns of social organization, and of sociology as an enterprise distinctly formed to analyze that unique constellation. As a result, there is no historical, genetic device in Giddens's theory: "lacking a dynamic principle, he can only logically assess the cognitive value of the perspectives and schools [that comprise his theoretical synthesis], which he treats as comparable and equipollent" (Kilminster 1990: 108).

According to Kilminster's analysis, Giddens's ahistoricism leads him to preserve a solipsistic, aprioristic conception of agency: "despite his attempt to transcend the individual/society dichotomy by the duality of agency and structure, the ghost of the old dualism haunts the theory because his point of departure is action theory, which carries dualism at its core" (Kilminster 1990: 98). Giddens responds on the one hand to the functionalist conception of the actor as a "cultural dope" and on the other hand to the structuralist understanding of the actor as constructed by discourses. He is centrally concerned with articulating a concept of the actor as knowledgeable, possessing a capacity for discursive self-reflexivity as well as for practical consciousness. His actors are individuals acting knowledgeably and intentionally, bounded by both the unconscious and institutions. Giddens thus "ascribes vaunting power to human agency, including that of generating apparently social-structural properties, which are all said to be instantiated by action" (Kilminster 1990: 118). By theorizing structures as only virtual, and thus internal to the individual, Giddens makes it possible to analyze structures only through a process of methodological bracketing or an *Epoché* of agency. According to Kilminster (1990: 102), this "recommendation for methodological bracketing seems to embody a liberalistic timidity about the possibility of representing and theorizing social wholes, lest this procedure erases [*sic*] individuals."

According to Kilminster's analysis, "Structuration theory embodies a rationalistic image of people whose affective life is bracketed out by the methodological prescription that the reflexively monitoring actor is bounded by institutions on the one side and the unconscious on the other" (Kilminster 1990: 101). The image of the actor in structuration theory, according to Kilminster, thus "articulates, with an implicit normative stress, the dominant self-experience and public code of behavior of highly self-controlled individuals in advanced industrial societies" (Kilminster 1990: 101). Kilminster's alternative has two constituent elements: to show how this kind of individual came to develop in the first place, and to reconceptualize the understanding of relations among people.

In sum, then, Kilminster faults Giddens not for being conflationary, as Archer does, but for having an insufficient grasp on interdependence, one which brings a self-contained rationalistic agent in through the back door. Kilminster (1990: 98) agrees with Archer that Giddens is thus unable to grasp the properties of far-flung structures: "the interacting individuals in conditions of co-presence can only be visualized as connected to other individuals who are not present by using metaphors such as stretching of social practices (time–space distanciation) or by reference to their lateral properties or to the channeling of time–space paths of individuals in system integration." But unlike Archer, Kilminster does not pinpoint this shortcoming by claiming that Giddens insufficiently separates agent (and agency's constitutive elements) and structure, but by claiming that he separates them too much:

> despite the word relations, individuals are seen only in the first person, as positions. There is no conceptual grasp of the perspective from which they themselves are regarded by others in the total social web, nor of their combined relatedness. ... Giddens thus fails to grasp interdependence as a much more multileveled, complex, and relational structure. ... In analyzing such multidimensional functional nexuses,

one can show how the nature of bonds between individuals and groups changes over time as part of wider societal changes.

(Kilminster 1990: 121)

Kilminster's solution, inspired by theorists like Norbert Elias, is to see structural and agentic dimensions as historically, rather than philosophically, emergent. From the perspective of analytical autonomy, however, such a move appears to be a return to concrete autonomy, albeit one that emerges over a long course of history rather than within a situation.

Conclusions

I have argued that Alexander rightly critiques Bourdieu's constitutivism for tending, in the last analysis, to overemphasize an economistic determination. Alexander's response, however, is not to encourage a reconstruction of more faithful constitutive procedures but to use Bourdieu's errors as a basis on which to justify the analytical autonomist approach. In part, Alexander's approach can be appreciated if we remember the positions he is trying to avoid. In fact, Alexander is not arguing principally against constitutivism but against concrete autonomy (realism). In his much cited introductory essay on culture and society, for instance, Alexander (1990: 4) writes: "Parsons's insistence on the analytical autonomy of cultural, social, and psychological systems promises a way out of the mechanistic–subjectivistic dichotomy without giving up on either side. There is a place for culture, but it is only a relatively autonomous sphere." Alexander (1990: 5) warns: "The promise of this solution can be neutralized if the separation between these levels is taken in a concrete rather than an analytical way. By concretizing the social system as independent of culture, functionalism raises significant problems for an interpretive, culturally sensitive position." Elsewhere, Alexander refutes the concrete solution to the culture–agency problem as well, arguing that giving action pride of place may refute theories that give too much weight to the internal relations of symbolic elements, but that as a result "culture is reduced to a resource, a tool kit whose symbol supply is so elastic that the limits it imposes become largely irrelevant. The problem with such an approach is that it asks us to choose between cultural system and action. Such a choice can be avoided if an analytic rather than concrete approach to the action–environment relation is taken" (Alexander 1988: 329). In his critique of Bourdieu, Alexander seems to gloss over the elaborate relational and constitutive argument. He is not wrong about Bourdieu's faults, but his solution—which is to make an analytical distinction, surely the product of a long process of development and possible only at a particular point in history—is clearly Kantian, treating, that is, an historical development as an *a priori* distinction. Alexander thus does not seem to have engaged with the main point of Bourdieu's work, which is not accidentally constitutive, but intentionally anti-Kantian.

Archer is much clearer about her enemy. Nonetheless, she refutes Giddens's constitutivism not by engaging with it, but by using Giddens's inconsistent application of constitutivism to dismiss constitutivism in general. Where Alexander dismissed Bourdieu's constitutivism because Bourdieu overemphasized structure, Archer dismisses Giddens's constitutivism because Giddens overemphasized agency. By counterposing Kilminster's constitutivist critique of Giddens's residual solipsism, dualism, and apriorism, perhaps we finally can inaugurate a clear debate between a consistent autonomist and a consistent constitutivist position, a debate that is not well served by vague assertions about "the relative autonomy of culture."

Acknowledgments

The author is grateful to Matthew Morrison for comments on an earlier draft, and to Victoria Johnson for relevant discussions many years ago about the ideas expressed in this essay. This acknowledgment is not meant to imply that they agree with what I have written!

References

Alexander, Jeffrey C. 1988. *Action and Its Environments*. New York: Columbia University Press.
———. 1990. "Analytical Debates: Understanding the Relative Autonomy of Culture." In Jeffrey C. Alexander and Steven Seidman, eds., *Culture and Society: Contemporary Debates*. Cambridge: Cambridge University Press.
———. 1995. "The Reality of Reduction: The Failed Synthesis of Pierre Bourdieu." In *Fin de Siècle Social Theory*. London: Verso.
Alexander, Jeffrey C. and Smith, Philip. 2003. "The Strong Program in Cultural Sociology: Elements of a Structural Hermeneutics." In Jeffrey C. Alexander, ed., *The Meanings of Social Life: A Cultural Sociology*. Oxford: Oxford University Press.
Archer, Margaret S. 1988. *Culture and Agency: The Place of Culture in Social Theory*. Cambridge: Cambridge University Press.
———. 1995. *Realist Social Theory: The Morphogenetic Approach*. Cambridge: Cambridge University Press.
Bershady, Harold. 1973. *Ideology and Social Knowledge*. Oxford: Basil Blackwell.
Bourdieu, Pierre. 1977. *Outline of a Theory of Practice*, trans. Richard Nice. Cambridge: Cambridge University Press.
———. 1984. *Distinction: A Social Critique of the Judgment of Taste*, trans. Richard Nice. Cambridge, MA: Harvard University Press.
Bourdieu, Pierre and Wacquant, Loic J.D. 1992. *An Invitation to Reflexive Sociology*. Chicago: University of Chicago Press.
Giddens, Anthony. 1984. *The Constitution of Society: Outline of the Theory of Structuration*. Berkeley: University of California Press.
Hall, John. 1999. *Cultures of Inquiry: From Epistemology to Discourse in Sociohistorical Research*. Cambridge: Cambridge University Press.
Hays, Sharon. 1994. "Structure and Agency and the Sticky Problem of Culture." *Sociological Theory* 12(1): 57–92.
Kane, Anne. 1991. "Cultural Analysis in Historical Sociology: The Analytic and Concrete Forms of the Autonomy of Culture." *Sociological Theory* 9(1): 53–69.
Kilminster, Richard. 1990. "Structuration Theory as a World-View." In Christopher Bryant and David Jary, eds., *Giddens' Theory of Structuration: A Critical Appreciation*. London: Routledge.
———. 1991. "Editorial Introduction." In Norbert Elias, ed., *The Symbol Theory*. London: Sage.
Levine, Donald. 1995. *Visions of the Sociological Tradition*. Chicago: University of Chicago Press.
Mouzelis, Nicos. 1995. *Sociological Theory: What Went Wrong?* London: Routledge.
Parsons, Talcott. 1968 (1937). *The Structure of Social Action*. Glencoe, IL: The Free Press.
Sewell, William, Jr. 1992. "A Theory of Structure: Duality, Agency, and Transformation." *American Journal of Sociology* 98: 1–29.

10

The cultural sociological experience of cultural objects

Robin Wagner-Pacifici

How do cultural sociologists experience their objects of analysis? Does it even matter if they do come to know and experience them? Isn't it more the point that they understand how these objects operate in the social world, how they come to be produced, assessed, valued, and exchanged by individuals and organizations? Although the category of culture includes a vast array of objects, values, ideas, and relationships, I want to focus in this essay on aesthetic objects, objects like novels and paintings and photographs, in order to identify the types of cultural sociological knowledge of them available to analysts, as well as to consider the stakes in such knowing.

The essay makes a case for cultural sociologists knowing their objects from the inside out as well as from the outside in. Further, I will want to assert that it is only by gaining access to the operations and logics of the inner workings of cultural objects that any cultural sociology can begin to track the meanings and resonance of these objects in the social contexts in which they appear. And finally, I claim that such knowledge of aesthetic objects actually provides insight into the ways that these objects model social reality in their own turn. Human experience of art affects human experience of the world. This essay is thus written in much the same spirit as John Dewey when he wrote, in his book *Art as Experience*, "Aesthetic experience is always more than aesthetic. In it a body of matters and meanings, not in themselves aesthetic, become aesthetic as they enter into an ordered rhythmic movement towards consummation. The material itself is widely human" (1934: 248). Human materials require a human science.

Thus, adhering to the conception of such thinkers as Wilhelm Dilthey that sociology is a "human science" (2002: 92), with *interpretation* its signature modality, any analysis of the ways that cultural sociologists can know (or refrain from knowing) their objects of analysis must clarify what "knowing" means. When approaching a painting, for example, does the sociologist examine the painting's style, its participation in a particular school of rendering, its internal composition, its allegorical allusions? Or, alternatively, does the sociologist look around the painting—at its placement in a frame and a museum, as an object of exchange garnering a certain sum of money, as produced by way of patron's commissions, as extolled or decried as excellent or repugnant by critics and publics? If the interpretive role of the sociologist is highlighted, questions of style, composition, representational dynamics, and aesthetic genealogy will be paramount in the sociological analysis. Such emphasis does not mean that the social, economic, or political context in which the work appears is irrelevant. Rather, it means that such contextual concerns cannot substitute for an analysis of the object itself.

Diffidence toward an experiential approach to cultural objects, including, importantly, aesthetic objects, has diverse motives. On the one hand, the "production of culture" proponents are particularly interested in social uptake or rejection of cultural objects and thus "focus on how the symbolic elements of culture are shaped by the systems within which they are created, distributed, evaluated, taught, and preserved" (Peterson and Anand 2004: 1). Studies developed within this framework focus on the contexts of culture and on cultural change, especially rapid change: "Such rapid change exposes the constituent elements comprising a field of symbolic production composed of six facets. These include technology, law and regulation, industry structure, organization structure, occupational career, and market" (Peterson and Anand 2004: 1). It is certainly possible to track all of these facets without ever coming into direct contact with the produced objects themselves. And indeed, the production-of-culture proponents do not tend to engage with the produced objects in their analyses. Such avoidance points to yet another reason why some (critical) sociologists of culture eschew experience of the cultural objects at the heart of their studies. These scholars tend to reason that the objects are variable stand-ins for the ideologies (e.g. of class or gender) whose business they do. French sociologist Antoine Hennion takes aim at this critical sociological approach to cultural objects, an approach exemplified by Pierre Bourdieu. Hennion contends: "Direct contact with things, uncertainty of sensations, methods, and techniques used to become sensitive to, and to feel the feeling of, the object being sought—in the sociology of culture, these moments and gestures of taste are either neglected or are directly denounced as rituals whose principal function is less to make amateurs 'feel,' than to make them 'believe'" (2007: 98). For Hennion, by contrast, the pragmatic, sensual modalities by which amateurs *attach themselves* to the cultural objects of their worlds is of great and complex significance for understanding human relationships to that world and to each other.

On the other hand, many cultural sociologists, including Hennion, advocate a more intimate knowledge of the objects under investigation: some term this approach "endogenous explanation" (Kaufman 2004: 335). And the more Durkheimian of these approaches "ask not why a specific genre of art appears at a particular time and place but what the signs and symbols embedded in that genre say about that time and place" (Kaufman 2004: 337). Whether moving in the more phenomenological direction of Hennion or the more semiotic direction of the Durkheimian approaches, the direct experience of and with cultural objects is highlighted. This essay will push on such intimate knowledge to consider not only how aesthetic objects reflect or refract their times and places, but also to explore how they, themselves, act to temporalize and shape the very worlds in which they appear. The essay manages this task by way of a consideration of several (not mutually exclusive) choices confronting cultural sociologists—preoccupation with content or preoccupation with context; coming in close or keeping a distance from the objects of analysis; utilizing methods and theories developed primarily in the humanities or those developed primarily in the social and natural sciences. Resolutions of these choices can signal the diverse responses to appeals to either highlight or bracket the experience of the objects confronting cultural sociologists.

Arts and humanities as models

When cultural sociologists understand their discipline as fundamentally a "human science," they inevitably invoke the approaches to cultural objects forged by the arts and humanities. Such approaches assume the intrinsically hermeneutic dimension to all social research. Art historian Blake Stimson refers, for example, to the "affective grip given by the sensory experience of vision itself" (Hall *et al.* 2005: 2) lying at the junction of aesthetics and that cultural and historical sociology concerned with visuality. But the affective grip of an object or of the perception of the object must necessarily prompt the movement from inside to outside, one in which, I argue, the hermeneutic approach and the semiotic approach can actually join forces. How does this movement manifest itself?

Clearly, sociologists and humanists have divergent interests, questions, and methodologies (of course, there are divergences within sociology and within the humanities). And these divergences make explicit cross-overs or borrowings somewhat rare and epistemologically problematic. These rare, apparently hybrid forms of scholarship reconfigure aspects of our endeavor in significant ways. Do we even recognize them? Thinking about the ways that the social sciences and the humanities both coincide and diverge around apparently similar objects and topics involves thinking quite specifically about our choice of methods and objects. In the humanities, we find the methods of hermeneutics, semiotics, structuralism, deconstructionism, and the new historicism, and we find objects like paintings, sculptures, monuments, icons, novels, folk-tales, poems, and so forth. There are exceptions, of course. Some humanists use quantitative or network forms of analysis. Some humanists analyze medical or business texts rather than novels or poems (for example, see the work of Mary Poovey [1998, 2008] on double-entry book-keeping and on genres of the credit economy of nineteenth-century Britain). Sometimes, the methods and objects of social scientific and humanistic analysis appear to be identical. But a fundamental difference seems perduring—sociologists have different resting places, different states of satisfaction that their interests have been addressed, their questions answered. Sociological questions normally involve examining the relationships between what is going on in the work of art or cultural object and the world that generates and hosts (or resists) that work. Sometimes the differences between sociological questions and those in the arts and humanities are very subtle—they hinge on what is foregrounded, what is marginal, what is the main issue, and what is parenthetical. Given these differences within apparent similarity, what would it mean concretely to argue that sociologists need a *feeling for the text or the image* in the same ways that most literary theorists or art historians embrace?

Most cultural sociologists do not demonstrate a feeling for the text or image, regardless of what their actual experience of them may be. How and where do we find paintings, sculptures, or novels in sociology writing? This should be recognized as a fundamentally different question from that asking where we find the careers, networks, social milieux of painters, sculptors, writers in sociological studies—which we do in the work of Harrison and Cynthia White (1965), Natalie Heinich (1996), Howard Becker (1982), Pierre Bourdieu (1993), and Diana Crane (1987), among others. Some sociologists actually *feature* these cultural/artistic objects in their work (as opposed to featuring the worlds around the objects and their producers): Robert Witkin's (1997) article about Manet's painting "Olympia"; Emanuel Schegloff's (1998) article about body torque in which he features and briefly analyzes Titian's "Venus with the Organ Player"; Wendy Griswold's

(1987) cultural methodology article, in which she addresses the issue of genre via the Nigerian novel; Luc Boltanski's (1999) explorations of the sentimental novel and the writings of the Marquis de Sade; Chandra Mukerji's (1997) gorgeous intellectual foray into the gardens of Versailles; Andrew Abbott's (2007) appreciation of the lyric moment in sociological writing; Jeff Alexander's (2008) appreciation of Giacometti's sculptures in his analysis of icons; and my own coming to terms with the tensions in Diego Velazquez's painting "The Surrender of Breda" (Wagner-Pacifici 2005).

In spite of such examples, there is a paucity of direct contact scholarship among cultural sociologists. This paucity is noted by Robert Witkin (1997: 103) when he assesses a general desire to "distance sociological inquiry from direct contact with art objects themselves." Such practiced indifference to the objects of attention and consumption—objects powerful enough to move people to tears, awe, or anger—must be taken a little more seriously. Could there be some unconscious fear of contamination or enthrallment if the sociologist comes too close to the work's aura? The word "aura" evokes the name of Walter Benjamin, of course. And Benjamin seemed singularly able to walk this line, particularly in his evocative and moving analysis of Paul Klee's painting "The Angel of History" and his elegy for the disappearance of the storyteller (Benjamin 1969).

One current exception to this aesthetic diffidence is represented by Jeff Alexander's recent work on the iconicity of art objects. By addressing their iconic status and powers, Alexander is able to constitute a trading-zone between the domains and distinctions of the social sciences and those of the humanities. It is a zone where the analyst has a hybrid sensibility that matches the resonance of the objects: "Esoteric aesthetic objects become iconic by drawing us into the heart of the world … In the course of everyday life, we are drawn into the experience of meaning and emotionality by surface forms" (Alexander 2008: 6). Surface forms are thus anything but superficial in their resonance and consequentiality.

One useful way to get beyond disciplinarily conventional habits of thinking about this social science/humanities fault-line or mutual blind spots is by highlighting analyses that go against their given disciplinary grains. Two exemplars stand out here—one is that of Franco Moretti, a social-scientific oriented literary theorist, and the other is Andrew Abbott, who, in some recent work on what he calls lyrical sociology, demonstrates a humanistic orientation to sociology.

Among other sociologically inclined works, Moretti completed a study in which he claimed to reveal the deep structure of the social geographies of cities in nineteenth-century novels (statistically calculating where, for example, characters of particular social classes do and do not travel within these cities and where they do and do not encounter characters of other social classes) (Moretti 1987). To do this he needed to encompass literally hundreds of novels (and maps) in his study's methodology. The idea of iconic novels or a feeling for the text becomes irrelevant, and maybe a distraction in this framework. More recently, Moretti wrote three essays considering different abstract models for literary history—graphs, maps, and (genealogical) trees (Moretti 2005). In this most recent book of essays, the rural space and spatial patterns of villagers going out for walks in British and German "village novels" map the sociological transformations consequent upon nineteenth-century rural class struggles and industrialization "where a perceptual system centered in the isolated village is replaced by an abstract network of roads" (Moretti 2005: 84). Moretti asks: "What do literary maps do? … First, they are a good way to prepare a text for analysis. You choose a unit—walks, lawsuits, luxury goods, whatever—find its occurrences, place them in space ... or in other words: you reduce the text to a few elements, and abstract them, and construct a new, artificial object" (Moretti 2005: 84). This kind of analysis requires an abstracting and generalizing view from afar, one that seems to preclude a close, hermenueutic approach.

Moving in the opposite direction is Andrew Abbott's recent article, "Against Narrative: A Preface to Lyrical Sociology." Abbott appeals to the ability of certain works of sociological writing to recreate an "experience of social discovery," an experience that, unlike classical narrative forms of ethnography and other genres, "should not be the telling of a story but rather the use of a single image to communicate a mood, an emotional sense of social reality" (2007: 73). The key elements of a lyrical sociology are engagement, personal location (of the observer/analyst), and a moment of time (rather than a process that occurs over time and that has an outcome). While language is the medium for writing lyrical sociology, language seems to give way to images, or congeries of images. Causality and transformation over time give way to states of being. Among other examples, Abbott refers to Michael Mayerfield Bell's (1994) book, *Childerley*, in which the ringing of the church bells in the provincial village that Bell details in his book sociologically resonate in precisely the manner Abbott describes as "lyrical."

These two writers, Moretti and Abbott, are cognizant of the costs and benefits of coming in close or backing away when observing and analyzing cultural, aesthetic objects. A key issue here concerns the preoccupation with fundamental epistemological categories of time and place. Moretti assumes a readership of literary critics and scholars who begin with their experiences of (many) of the novels he analyzes—and he wants to pull them back in order to gaze about the social and political territories they map. Abbott assumes a readership of sociologists who begin with knowledge of social structures, institutions, and social movements—and he wants to pull them in close in order to catch moments of revelation or transformation that cultural objects identify and refract. Cultural sociologists may feel flummoxed in the face of such opposed vantage points and methodologies. How might they deal with the multiplicity of meanings of cultural objects? Ought they to be forced to choose? I would argue for alternations of approach that are contingent on the nature of the questions posed. Cultural sociologists can actually sustain *alternating* visions—those of revelation at the level of social structure and those of revelation at the level of being in time—as they work to transform discussions of revelation into analyses of social and political meaning, and, often, power. On this point, Blake Stimson refers to Walter Benjamin's claim that "the deep formation of 'political tendency' ... reveals itself only in the fissures of art history (and in works of art)" (Hall *et al.* 2005: 7). Thus it behooves us to head directly toward those fissures.

Art models reality—the case for images

The next step in cultivating an experiential cultural sociology involves assessing if, and how, art *models* social reality, rather then simply refracts it. Here, the claim is that one's perception of the world is changed by familiarity with stylized and aesthetic renderings of it. Visual art offers a particular cultural sociological opportunity. We perceive and shape the world through the images of it that we absorb. Art may be understood to offer itself as a tool for sociological analysis of social life, as sociological data, and as a cultural process that participates in the shaping of worldviews. How might this work?

In 1973, Paul Ricoeur published an article in the journal *New Literary History* that would serve as a touchstone for all hermeneutically inclined social scientists. It was titled: "The model of the text: meaningful action considered as a text." In it, Ricoeur raised the questions: "To what extent may we consider the notion of text as a good paradigm for the so-called object of the social sciences? And; 2) to what extent may we use the methodology of text-interpretation as a paradigm for interpretation in general in the field of the social sciences?" (Ricoeur 1973: 91). In this essay, the questions are similar, but the paradigmatic model is that of the artistic image, rather than the text. And rather than text-interpretation or hermeneutics, I want to raise the question of the use of a new iconology (sometimes termed "image science" or the "pictorial turn") as a model for cultural sociological investigation. What, then, might it mean to propose that the image is a good paradigm for the object of social sciences, to paraphrase Ricoeur? Surely images function and communicate differently than texts. They may thus provide us with a different purchase on social life, on power relations, on institutions than the purchase we attained via imagining social life as a text.

Images and texts are rather different creatures, with different carrying capacities. Texts are invested in the temporality of diachrony, and thus manage action and transformation. Images can present inaction, inasmuch as they capture a moment in time. In fact, social life itself is as replete with inaction, pauses, frozen moments, temporary congealings, as it is with action, progress, and change. While social scientists have been rightly preoccupied with getting an analytical handle on the dynamism of action and interaction, they have not been sufficiently concerned to understand the embodiments and informings of objects or revealed moments (or what I'm calling here inaction) that may have their own meanings and power, somewhat along the lines suggested by Abbott. We might even begin to ask what it would mean to see scenes of social life *as* works of art (in ways that neither trivialize nor reify them, but rather acknowledge their resonance). If we turn to art as a model for analysis in the sociology of culture, it is partly for its usefulness in getting at precisely those moments of inaction—moments that are critical and revelatory. But we cannot use images as models if we do not know how to read images.

There are several issues involved in developing this vantage point, and most of them have to do with finding the tools to discern the ways that art models life. Just as Ricoeur had to detail the hermeneutic strategies of textual analysis, we would have to detail the iconological strategies of pictorial analysis. But I want to make clear at the outset that such tools are not restricted to analysis of figurative art only—abstract art can also be approached as a model for cultural sociology. What tools have been developed to grasp these elements?

Semiotics, in the manner of Roland Barthes (1972) and others, can begin to illuminate the social and cultural meanings of images, by taking into account the structure of their internal relations—the figure and the background, the high and the low, the central and the peripheral, the dark and the light. But that is only the beginning. Scholars such as W.J.T. Mitchell (1994, 2005a, 2005b), Theo Van Leeuwen (Van Leeuwen and Jewitt 2001), and Hans Belting (2005) have pushed further, with iconologies that aim to grasp the social lives in and of images.

Some of the most pressing issues involve (1) the art-historical traditions brought to bear on singular creations, (2) the position, vision, and involvement of the spectator, and (3) the ability of the artistic object to both absorb aspects of the outer world and attach itself to (or, in a more aggressive idiom, impose itself on) that outer world. This involves, but is not restricted to, issues of the image-object's generalizability.

We have seen that pictures, unlike texts, present a scene "all at once." In theory, a spectator can take in an artistic image in a moment. In contrast to texts, which are fatally dependent on language's linearity (and thus a kind of implicit transformational syntax of cause and effect), images can appear outside of time, or capturing one moment of time. For example, history paintings anchor and orient their spectators with their vanishing points, their spatial simultaneity, and their frames. They also claim a particular trans-temporal purchase on a transformational historical moment. Alternatively, maps orient viewing subjects in terms of sovereign centers, routes of exchange, and boundaries. Specific pictorial genres are thus variably capable of representing and conjuring the world.

The spectator/witness/analyst is always an important figure in these new iconologies. Here, questions of proximity, involvement, and familiarity are key. In terms of the interactions among spectators and art objects, the worlds in the pictures and the world outside the frame, art historian Michael Fried (2007) has highlighted the critical moment of realist painting, what he calls the moment of the "magic of absorption" at the end of the sixteenth century (such painters as Caravaggio are key here), when painters represented figures literally absorbed in their own activities. Such paintings actually worked to deny the presence of any beholder outside the composed scene, including the spectator of the painting. They did so "in the first place by depicting personages [in the paintings] wholly absorbed in what they are doing, thinking, and feeling, and in multi-figure paintings, by binding those figures together in a single, unified composition—to establish the ontological fiction that the beholder does not exist. Only if this was accomplished could the actual beholder be stopped and held before the canvas" (Fried 2007: 500). Why does the spectator need to be ignored in order to be transfixed? Because only then do we know that the subjects in the painting (and by extension, in life itself) are not "acting" for the benefit of the spectator. Fried quotes Wittgenstein: "Nothing could be more remarkable than seeing someone who thinks himself unobserved engaged in some quite simple everyday activity. ... We should be seeing life itself" (Fried 2007: 517). Such a scene caught up in its own autonomy captivates and, paradoxically, frees the spectator while convincing him or her of its "reality" or "near-reality." Thus it functions as what Fried calls the "near-documentary mode," as true of contemporary photographs as it is of these realist paintings. Of course, the next, sociological, step might be to move from an apprehension of such nearly-real scenes in artistic renderings to an enhanced apprehension of the really-real scenes of everyday life—now re-familiarized by their resemblance to the nearly-real. If social scenes constitute our data—visible and tangible compositions and configurations of figures in space—our knowledge of artistic compositions and configurations is reflexively deployed to illuminate the stakes and the meanings of these scenes. But then, by analogy, do we sociologists need to be ignored in order to be able to see life itself? Issues of proximity and involvement remain key—how close up should we get to examine a scene, what distance brings most of a scene's elements and relationships to light? How singular is the scene: how generalizable? Are we as equipped to capture its stillness as we are to capture its dynamism (its origins, its exchanges, its trajectory)? Can we recognize the structure of relations that take shape? These are questions for sociology to take to heart as modes of inquiry incorporating images and scenes are brought forward by ethnographers and sociologists of culture, among others.

As points of reflexivity, artistic images certainly do act as models of and models for social relations. But, as I hope I am conveying, they do a lot more than that.

115

The relations presented within the artistic image may even absorb, contain, and displace the inchoate, sometimes violent, energy of actual social life. This may be particularly true for violent actions. Here, art can model relations of a more pacific nature, rendering hierarchy, charisma, and loyalty visible, among other things, appearing to put contentious matters to rest (but always temporarily). The in-action or stillness of images is potent here in that it provides a pause or break in action that needs such an outlet to desist. Of course, images can also carry forward the programs of violence. This is another reason it is so important to have the tools to interrogate them. Images are migratory. They inhabit one medium after another. Think of the pervasive, circulating, and disturbing images of Abu Ghraib. One of these images, in particular that of the "Hooded Man," made to stand balancing on a wooden box, "has become iconic for the American war on terror because it condenses … unspeakable scenarios [from the narrative of the life of Christ, to the Crusades] into an eloquent form whose simplicity and directness makes it ideal for duplication and repetition" (Mitchell 2005b: 305). Thus, part of thinking about art as a model for sociological analysis involves confronting the anxiety about images and their power, the alleged iconoclasm of a culture invested in discourse, suspicious of images. In the end, fear of or disdain for cultural texts or cultural images is simply not an option for cultural sociologists.

It behooves cultural sociologists to pause and consider the opportunities presented by prolonged direct contact with the objects they analyze. Theories and methods originating in the humanities and the early hermeneutically inclined social sciences provide several avenues of approach to objects that both live in the world and reshape that world in their own turn.

References

Abbott, Andrew. 2007. "Against Narrative: A Preface to Lyrical Sociology." *Sociological Theory* 25(1): 67–99.

Alexander, Jeffrey. 2008. "Iconic Experience in Art and Life: Beginning with Giacometti's 'Standing Woman.'" *Theory, Culture and Society* 25(5): 1–19.

Barthes, Roland. 1972. *Mythologies*, selected and translated from the French by Annette Lavers. New York: Hill and Wang.

Becker, Howard Saul. 1982. *Art Worlds*. Berkeley: University of California Press.

Bell, Michael Mayerfeld. 1994. *Childerley: Nature and Morality in a Country Village*, illustrated by Christian Potter Drury. Chicago: University of Chicago Press.

Belting, Hans. 2005. "Image, Medium, Body: A New Approach to Iconology." *Critical Inquiry* 31(2): 302–19.

Benjamin, Walter. 1969. *Illuminations*, edited and with an introduction by Hannah Arendt; trans. by Harry Zohn. New York: Schocken Books.

Boltanski, Luc. 1999. *Distant Suffering: Morality, Media, and Politics*, trans. by Graham Burchell. New York: Cambridge University Press.

Bourdieu, Pierre. 1993. *The Field of Cultural Production: Essays on Art and Literature*, edited and introduced by Randal Johnson. New York: Columbia University Press.

Crane, Diana. 1987. *The Transformation of the Avant-garde: The New York Art World, 1940–1985*. Chicago: University of Chicago Press.

Dewey, John. 1934. *Art as Experience*. New York: Minton, Balch & Company.

Dilthey, Wilhelm. 2002. *The Formation of the Historical World in the Human Sciences*, edited and with an introduction by Rudolf A. Makkreel and Frithjof Rodi. Princeton, NJ: Princeton University Press.

Fried, Michael. 2007. "Jeff Wall, Wittgenstein, and the Everyday." *Critical Inquiry* 33(3): 495–526.

Griswold, Wendy. 1987. "A Methodological Framework for the Sociology of Culture." *Sociological Methodology*, edited by Clifford Clogg, 17: 1–35.

Hall, John R., Stimson, Blake, and Becker, Lisa Tamaris, eds. 2005. *Visual Worlds* London and New York: Routledge.

Heinich, Natalie. 1996. *The Glory of Van Gogh: An Anthropology of Admiration*. Princeton, NJ: Princeton University Press.

Hennion, Antoine. 2007. "Those Things that Hold Us Together." *Cultural Sociology* 1(1): 97–114.

Kaufman, Jason. 2004. "Endogenous Explanation in the Sociology of Culture." *Annual Review of Sociology* 30: 335–57.

Mitchell, W.J. Thomas. 1994. *Picture Theory: Essays on Verbal and Visual Representation*. Chicago: University of Chicago Press.

——. 2005a. *What do Pictures Want? The Lives and Loves of Images*. Chicago: University of Chicago Press.

——. 2005b. "The Unspeakable and the Unimaginable: Word and Image in a Time of Terror." *English Literary History* 72(2): 291–308.

Moretti, Franco. 1987. *The Way of the World: The Bildungsroman in European Culture*. London: Verso.

——. 2005. *Graphs, Maps, Trees: Abstract Models for a Literary History*. London: Verso.

Mukerji, Chandra. 1997. *Territorial Ambitions and the Gardens of Versailles*. New York: Cambridge University Press.

Peterson, Richard and Anand, N. 2004. "The Production of Culture Perspective." *Annual Review of Sociology* 30: 311–34.

Poovey, Mary. 1998. *A History of the Modern Fact: Problems of Knowledge in the Sciences of Wealth and Society*. Chicago: University of Chicago Press.

——. 2008. *Genres of the Credit Economy: Mediating Value in Eighteenth- and Nineteenth-century Britain*. Chicago: University of Chicago Press.

Ricoeur, Paul. 1973. "The Model of the Text: Meaningful Action Considered as a Text." *New Literary History* 5(1): 91–117.

Schegloff, Emanuel. 1998. "Notes on Body Torque." *Social Research* 65(3): 535–96.

Van Leeuwen, Theo and Jewitt, Carey, eds. 2001. *Handbook of Visual Analysis*. London: Sage.

Wagner-Pacifici, Robin. 2005. *The Art of Surrender: Decomposing Sovereignty at Conflict's End*. Chicago: University of Chicago Press.

White, Harrison C. and White, Cynthia A. 1965. *Canvases and Careers: Institutional Change in the French Painting World*. New York: Wiley.

Witkin, Robert W. 1997. "Constructing a Sociology for an Icon of Aesthetic Modernity: Olympia Revisited." *Sociological Theory* 15(2): 101–25.

11

Formal models of culture

John W. Mohr and Craig M. Rawlings

By our accounting, a formal model of culture is, first of all, an output from a quantitative study of collected data that seeks to describe, explain, interpret, or otherwise represent some feature, aspect, or content of culture. As a model, the output has been transformed into a summary or a representation (in reduced form) of the data that purports to be analogous (in some fashion) to the phenomena under consideration. Thus, it is precisely the use of quantitative methods or the formal analysis of data that distinguishes work included in the present classification. In this essay, we trace some of the broad contours of change in the history of how culture has been modeled. We simplify this task in two ways. First, we focus on just one arena, American sociology in its first century or so of professional formation. Second, we highlight just one difference, distinguishing interpretative from non-interpretative intents. Thus, in the history presented here we look separately at models of culture that have explicitly hermeneutic goals in contrast to those that don't. Practitioners of the former sort want to use formal tools to make interpretations that they hope unlock useful readings of texts. Those of the latter persuasion usually seek robust measures of cultural forms that can be fitted onto other explanatory frames.

Our main goal is to describe important changes in how culture has been modeled by social scientists over the last century or so. We will also say something about the enduring frictions between qualitative and quantitative styles of social scientific research. In the final section of the essay (pp. 125–26) we take up the question of how these two different modalities of knowledge production have been linked in the history of American sociology, and we offer a preliminary interpretation of what this structure of articulation says about the recurrent "Methods Wars." We conclude with a few thoughts about the relevance of our analysis of culture modeling to other national intellectual milieux, and about the future prospects for the formal modeling of culture.

Two ways to know

The very possibility of using formal methodologies to study culture has long been the source of debate in the human sciences. There are those who hold to the centrality of interpretation, arguing that, more than anything else, it is the meaningfulness of human action that most essentially defines its character: social institutions are discursively structured in meaningful ways, and they must therefore be approached with a very specific and hermeneutically grounded method of interpretation. In contrast, formal modelers have long been convinced that there is much utility to measuring cultural phenomena, but they are divided as to whether the formal analysis of culture can (or should) be directed toward the problem of interpretation (Mohr and Rawlings forthcoming). Thus, there are (at least) three parties to the debate, qualitative scholars in pursuit of adequate interpretations of meaning, quantitative scholars who also seek interpretations of meaning (through other means), and quantitative scholars who want to measure culture without interpreting it. For a long while, this seemed to be a debate about the essential nature of the social world. If, for example, the discursive character of social institutions meant that they were historically contingent and thus variable, then it was argued that formalist procedures would bear no fruit because they were focused on finding "nomothetic" or law-like properties and these conditions did not apply in the world of culture. However, that specific debate is now moot. After the cultural turn, few if any sociologists still aspire to discover universal laws of the social. But this does not mean that the broader debate has subsided. On the contrary, if anything it has intensified and shifted to questions of method, and especially to the question of what is interpretation and how might we use the tools of formal analysis to advance a hermeneutic agenda.

A brief history of culture modeling in American sociology, 1900–2009

In American sociology, there have been significant changes in both the way that culture is understood and in the way that it is modeled. To simplify matters we divide the history of modern American sociology into six roughly equivalent time periods (see Table 11.1). For each period, we describe the ways that interpretative and explanatory models were used for analyzing culture.

Table 11.1 Types of formal models, relative strength of qualitative research community, and degree of methodologically based inter-group conflict across six historical periods of American sociology

Year	Period	Explanatory models of culture	Interpretive models of culture	Relative strength of qualitative research community	Degree of inter-group conflict by method
1900–1925	1. Pre-formal phase	—	—	+	L
1925–1940	2. Formalist turn	X	X	+	H
1940–1960	3. Institutionalization of formalist program	X	X	—	L
1960–1975	4. Fragmentation period	—	—	+	L
1975–1990	5. Cultural turn	X	—	+	M
1990–2010	6. Institutionalization of cultural turn	X	X	+	H
2010–?	?	?	?	?	?

Period 1: pre-formal phase

The first period runs from the origins of modern American sociology up to the mid-1920s. Quantitative methods were still quite primitive during this period. Two streams of formal modeling in which matters of culture figured are worthy of comment. First, social workers were in the early stages of professionalization and they were beginning to develop standardized procedures for gathering systematic data from clients on behaviors, cultural orientations, social situation, and the causes of economic failure. Mary Richmond (1917), director of the Charity Organization Department at the Russell Sage Foundation, contributed elaborate theories about how to assess and make inferences about the validity of information sources that social workers encountered. But Richmond sought to emulate the medical profession, and her systematizing efforts were devoted to abstract theorization of social pathologies and the diagnostic skills needed to identify them.

The second initiative of note was the Pittsburgh survey of 1907, which was followed by a flood of more than 2,500 similar endeavors over the next two decades. The Pittsburgh project followed in a line of work that extended back through W.E.B. DuBois's study of the Philadelphia black community and Jane Addams's studies of immigrant neighborhoods around Chicago's Hull House, to Charles Booth's studies of the London working class. With funding from the Russell Sage Foundation, the Pittsburgh initiative had seventy-four field staff compiling a mass of information about all manner of social and cultural processes. However, this was not a systematic door-to-door canvassing or questionnaire survey. "Rather it was an effort to provide an inventory and an overview of the state of the city, for which the investigators were omnivorous in their methods of data collection" (Converse 2009 [1987]: 24). Much of the data came in the form of the schedule, which "in the hands of the social surveyors was an instrument for making observations *or* for conducting interviews with respondents, or a mixture of both" (Converse 2009 [1987]: 34). But there was a seriousness to the survey task that reflected an appreciation for the relevance of qualitative distinctions. The checklist for clothing included check-off categories for "spotted ... dusty ... torn ... worn ... patched ... mussed ... wrinkled ... ". In one innovative development,

> John R. Commons (on the staff of the Pittsburgh survey and later a distinguished political economist) devised a Dwelling House Score Card, published in 1908, which featured a maximum of 100 possible points by the weighting of points added and subtracted for desirable and undesirable features. This method of quantifying qualitative observations, now so familiar in rating athletic and artistic competitions, was one that Commons borrowed from ratings used for stock animals, and it was apparently new to social science.
>
> (Converse 2009 [1987]: 34)

The researchers also borrowed from social work's methods by collecting "case-history interviews, which were gathered and then counted and compared among some dimensions, thus providing a 'casemounting' that represented a merger of the case study and statistical methods" (Converse 2009 [1987]: 34).

However, as Bulmer points out, "the Survey used quantitative data in more of an exploratory and descriptive than analytic way" (1996: 18). Here and elsewhere, "It was as if there was an intuitive sense of the value of collecting extensive data about individuals in the population being studied, without the necessary knowledge either about sampling or how to handle the data once collected other than to compute simple counts of characteristics and then treat respondents on a case-by-case basis" (Bulmer 1996: 26). Thus, with minor exceptions, culture was not subjected to systematic modeling during this period.

Period 2: the formalist turn

The second period marks a fundamentally important change in the field as—in what we call the formalist turn—sociology shifted toward a far more intense scientism (Ross 1991). A variety of factors contributed to this change, but a key influence was the emergence, spread, and professionalization of modern survey research technologies in the late 1920s and 1930s. Surveys offered sociologists for the first time a flexible, adaptable, convenient tool that could generate data to be used to create quantitative models of almost anything. Three developments were critical—statistical innovations in sampling theory, the rise of election and public opinion polling organizations, and the invention of attitude scaling. Sampling theory meant that it was possible (at relatively low cost) to ask a question to a reasonably sized group of respondents with some degree of confidence that extrapolating from those opinions would yield something valid to say about "the mood of the nation." Independent survey research broke the long-standing dependence of social scientists on the State as the provider of useful social statistical information.

The invention of attitude measurements provided the means to use surveys to measure cultural content systematically. W.I. Thomas is generally credited with having invented the modern notion of attitudes in his work with Znaniecki on *The Polish Peasant in Europe and America* (1918). Conceptualization of attitudes conveyed the sense of a deep structure of meanings and cultural orientations, which had direct consequences for action in the world. In 1925 both Floyd Allport and Emory Bogardus published independent approaches to developing formalized "attitude scaling." Later, Thurstone, Likert, and others produced rapid advances in the use of surveys for measuring subjective experience, including cultural orientation, values, systems of meanings and beliefs, and subjective understandings of social situations (Converse 2009 [1987]). In this period, both interpretative and explanatory models of culture were abundant and they were undergoing rapid innovation, development, and diffusion.

Period 3: institutionalization of the formalist program

The third period begins with the Second World War. Although the war was relatively short, its impact on developments in the social sciences was profound. Many sociologists were employed in support of the war effort and they were frequently mixed together with scientists from other disciplines—a situation that promoted interdisciplinary borrowing of methods and procedures. Large teams of coders went to work analyzing newspapers and other public communication systems to learn about enemy propaganda. Others used surveys to learn about both civilian and military populations. Stouffer surveyed over a half-million American soldiers during the war, asking a wide range of attitude questions about unit solidarity, the legitimacy of authority, social integration, and the like (Stouffer *et al.* 1949). Lazarsfeld later credited these developments as key catalysts for the institutionalization of formal methods in sociology. Stouffer's work in particular

121

represented a level of sophistication in survey methodology, which went far beyond previous efforts. As a consequence, "'survey analysis' now took on a broader connotation. It became the language of empirical social research, possessing its own rules for forming basic concepts and combining them into meaningful propositions" (Lazarsfeld 1968: vii).

In the postwar years, survey methodology underwent rapid growth in sophistication and legitimation. Lazarsfeld was the critical link. As Director of Columbia University's Bureau for Applied Social Research, he played a pivotal role in promoting and facilitating research projects, training and supporting quantitatively oriented sociologists, and developing the theoretical foundations for full-bodied quantitatively based formalist sociology.

Lazarsfeld's writings during this period constitute a systematic compendium of conceptual problems associated with the difficulty of grounding sociological inferences in a wholly quantitative system. He wrote relentlessly on how to conceptualize and operationalize variables, how to link indicators to concepts, how to use cross-tabulations to assess causality, how to measure latent structures, and the like. Most notably, for Lazarsfeld there was neither a hard and fast distinction between qualitative and quantitative methodologies nor a divergence in the phenomena to which they were to be directed. Rather, he envisioned a continuum from less to more formal modes of investigation and a theory of the social as a systemic totality that includes both social and cultural elements. He and those associated with him moved easily back and forth between efforts to model social organizational processes and research more directed toward the goal of understanding culture. Thus, American sociologists in this period aggressively drew on survey and content-analysis methodologies to pursue both interpretative and explanatory models of culture.

Period 4: fragmentation

The 1950s saw the ascendance and institutionalization of a formalist research project in the discipline, but it also witnessed the zenith of the theoretical hegemony achieved by Talcott Parsons and other "structural-functionalists." By the 1960s, the legitimacy of that theoretical framework was being subjected to significant challenges. In the wake of those challenges came stirrings of a fourth period of American sociology, one of "fragmentation." Robert Merton's notion of middle-range theorizing provided a kind of cover as the discipline turned its gaze downward, away from grand theory, towards a grounded focus and an emphasis on methods. This happened in both the qualitative and quantitative sides of the discipline. On the one hand, there were qualitative sociologists like Harold Garfinkel who became committed to an increasingly rigorous and phenomenologically anchored approach to interpretative sociology. On the other hand, there were formal modelers like Blau and Duncan (1967) who used multivariate analyses in new ways to demonstrate a foundational understanding about how social mobility and occupational-attainment processes are organized.

The fourth period was also something of a dead zone for formal models of culture. In part, this was because many semi-autonomous scholarly regions (or sub-professions) began to flourish, thus allowing qualitative and quantitative scholars to go their separate ways. Qualitative scholars increasingly embarked on sophisticated research programs that yielded ever more compelling findings, even as they developed more elaborate critiques of the methodological assumptions of quantitative sociologists. Meanwhile, formal modelers were turning away from culture. For one thing, the concept itself had fractured. Under structural functionalism, culture (operationalized as value and norm systems) was a system-level construct. With the demise of Parsonian system theory, culture had no natural home. In practice, a new appreciation for the interpretation of culture was being developed by emerging communities of qualitative sociologists, but that work was not getting picked up by quantitative scholars, who were focused on their own middle-range theoretical projects. Moreover, attitude measures (and other subjective constructs in formal models) were coming to be seen as less relevant in more and more fields. A fierce sort of objectivism had taken hold in many arenas of quantitative research. If you knew a man's father's occupation you could predict that man's own occupation, without knowing anything about what the man thought or how he was embedded in cultural systems of understanding. Organizational theory was focused on resource dependency relationships. Network analysts were content to emphasize the logic of material connectivity: real "empirical" relations were what mattered, not those conceptions of action generated after the fact as accounts that social agents offer to explain their behavior. And thus, in the fourth period of American sociology, qualitative and quantitative scholars went their separate ways, and culture (with a few notable exceptions such as political sociology, which was still focused on the role of opinions in generating outcomes) ceased to be an object for serious quantitative analysis.

Period 5: the cultural turn

The beginning of the fifth period marks off a second profound transformation in the field—a turn away from scientism, back towards culture. Interpretative scholars helped push the human sciences into a post-Wittgensteinian phase where it was presumed that the world is, in some utterly fundamental sense, grounded in a socially constructed reality. As the science wars of the 1990s clearly suggest, there was considerably less than full agreement about the scope conditions of this proposition. Rather, different subdisciplines came to operate within somewhat distinct intellectual frameworks for understanding the character of the social, and various discursive sub-communities engaged the cultural turn to move across that "*threshold of epistemologization*" in their own time, manner, and form (Agambin 2009: 15).

Formal models of culture staged a comeback during this period. Peterson and Berger (1975) initiated this development through their work on the popular song industry. Their goal was not hermeneutic: they were not concerned with interpreting the meanings of these cultural forms. Rather, they sought to find a solid and defensible metric for measuring variability in cultural forms, which could then be explained with respect to the conditions within a particular social domain, in this case in a sophisticated and elaborate theory of the social organization of the culture industry. The next step was taken by DiMaggio (1982), who expanded upon Peterson's detailed attention to the social structural terrain in which cultural forms are embedded. DiMaggio also developed a more sophisticated way to measure variations in the cultural forms themselves. In his work on cultural capital, for example, he used factor analysis to find patterns in the ways in which high school students are oriented with respect to their understanding of, appreciation of, and practical experience with elite cultural forms. Following Bourdieu, DiMaggio theorized that the ways students who have mastered the skills and knowledge associated with elite forms of culture deploy their cultural capital are causally linked to social structural outcomes: Specifically, the model could be used as an effective predictor of educational attainment.

123

DiMaggio's models are non-hermeneutic. Without relying on attitude measures or interpreting anyone's understanding of events or discursive meanings, he found a useful way of employing surveys to model important cultural processes. These measures were easy to sell to a skeptical quantitative community as objective, consequential, and having reasonable face validity. DiMaggio's models are, on the other hand, very much a reflection of a post-cultural turn sensibility in that they emphasized how culture is a force that shapes the social. The main innovation here was borrowed from Bourdieu—the idea of treating culture as something concrete, consequential as a status resource, and capable of producing useful models (measured by contributions to R-squared) in the same way that other status factors behave (within the Wisconsin tradition of social mobility research). Because DiMaggio's study featured cultural capital prominently as an independent variable, it became marked as one of the early successes of the new (American) cultural sociology project.

Perhaps not coincidentally, just as this new (non-interpretative) cultural modeling project was finding its footing, the old interpretative cultural modeling (using attitude measures from surveys) was entering a state of crisis. In 1977, a small group of survey research leaders met to discuss

> several events that caused some disquiet among people who collect and use survey data. One such event was the discovery of several instances in which seemingly equivalent survey measurements made at approximately the same time produced surprisingly different results. The discovery of these anomalies raised questions initially about the reliability, and ultimately about the meaningfulness, of commonly used survey data. The discovery of these anomalies coincided with a vigorous protest about the conduct of some particular surveys and with an apparent decline in public willingness to participate in surveys.
>
> (Turner and Martin 1984: xiii–xiv)

Thus, in the fifth period, culture was once again being modeled, but unlike in the previous periods the focus was almost exclusively on explanatory (rather than interpretative) models of culture.

Period 6: institutionalization of the cultural program

With the advent of a new generation of non-interpretative culture models, the use of quantitative tools for studying culture had, by the early 1990s, once again become a part of the normal practice of quantitative sociologists. To take one example, organizational sociologists of the new institutional school conceived of their project as a mapping of the effects of cultural processes in organizational fields. Their standard way to model organizational fields was to employ non-interpretative (explanatory) models of culture to illustrate, for example, the increasing homogenization of organizational forms within an organizational field (Powell and DiMaggio 1991). But as the implications of the cultural turn began to sink in, an increasing number of formal sociologists found themselves wanting to press beyond the use of explanatory models of culture in order to take on more fundamentally hermeneutic types of problems. Harrison White was probably the most conspicuous exemplar of this trend. A longtime leader in mathematical sociology and, especially, social network analysis, by the early 1990s White had come around to believe that an interpretative analysis of culture was a necessity for sociology because "in avoiding and sidestepping the interpretative—and thus any direct access to the con-struction of social reality—*mathematical models have come to an era of decreasing returns to effort. Another way to say the same thing is that interpretative approaches are central to achieving a next level of adequacy in social data*" (White 1997: 57–58).

Following White's lead, a number of social network scholars began to take up the interpretative study of culture as a focus for formal modeling. This group of "hermeneutic structuralists" has embraced two key principles. First, following in the path of semiotic theory, the new hermeneutic structuralists understand cultural meanings to consist of relational systems within which sign elements are linked together in networks of similarity and difference (Mohr 1998; Mohr and White 2008). So, for example, Gibson (2003) models conversations as social networks and Bearman and Stovel (2000) use network models to analyze the narrative structures buried in the life stories of Germans living inside Nazi Germany, while Smith (2007) develops similar procedures to compare and contrast models of the same historical narratives seen from two different perspectives—two ethnic communities living alongside the Yugoslovian/Italian border. Ruef (1999) employs text data to map the discursive logic of the health care industry, and Rawlings and Bourgeois (2004) do the same for higher education.

The second principle concerns how one domain is related to another, for example how systems of meanings are articulated with systems of practices. Here the focus is on the notion of a structurally ordered duality. According to this principle, two discrete institutional sub-domains have their own coherent (semi-autonomous) logics that are also mutually constitutive, so that the ordering of one substantively influences (indeed, constitutes) the ordering of the other (and vice versa). Thus, Mohr and Duquenne (1997) use Galois lattices to interpret the dual institutional logic of Progressive-Era poverty categories and their corresponding relief practices. Mische and Pattison (2000) use lattices to model the dualities that link political ideologies with the organizational histories of Brazilian youth activists. And Breiger (2000) generalizes these procedures into what he describes as a methodological toolkit for practice theory, which he then applies to an analysis of the dual logic of power and precedent within the US Supreme Court. Overall, Mohr and White theorize these relations as expressions of a general logic of institutional articulation that "links together different orders and realms of social life, notably the agentic with the structural, the symbolic with the material, and the micro with the meso and the macro structures of social organization" (2008: 485).

Thus, in this most recent historical period, formal modeling of culture has once again become an established practice among quantitative sociologists who are now actively pursuing both explanatory and interpretative models. However, in contrast to earlier periods, these recent efforts tend to highlight the power of culture as a force constitutive of the social, rather than (as traditionally was true) the other way around.

On the Methods Wars

We turn now to the question of why so much friction is generated between qualitative and quantitative scholars. Abbott's (1988) analysis of the roots of inter-professional conflict seems applicable. According to Abbott, professional communities come into conflict as a result of jurisdictional disputes—conflicts waged between two professional sub-communities that are vying for the authority to control the same region of institu-tional space. This suggests that variations in the intensity of methodological conflicts will reflect variations in the relative strengths of the two parties and the proportion of niche overlaps that are contested.

As a way to explore this idea we have gone back to Table 11.1 and coded each period in terms of the degree to which inter-group conflict around the qualitative/quantitative divide appears to be low, medium, or high. Thus, we have coded the first period—before quantitative sociology was firmly established—as having low levels of methods-based conflict, but period 2 as highly conflicted. Here, in part, we are drawing on the work of Platt, who used a close reading of textual materials to examine the methods debates in American sociology between 1920 and 1960 systematically. Platt notes: "The period up to the early 1940s shows a marked quantitative/qualitative, humanistic/ scientific controversy, with substantial technical work on both sides of the line. ... After the war, work on purely qualitative topics almost vanishes, though many issues relevant to qualitative work are still raised" (1996: 13). Accordingly, we have coded the level of conflict in period 3 as low, due largely to the diminished power of qualitative sociology during these years. Period 4, we coded as being relatively quiescent, at least with respect to debates over method. This is not to say that methods issues were not being debated, often heatedly, during these years, but it also seems as though the general mentality of middle-range theorizing served to mitigate the intensity of conflicts, at least those that pivoted on methodology. In contrast, period 5 was more clearly conflictual: we know that the literature of the time was filled with arguments about culture's proper role and, also, about the failures of naturalistic approaches to science. Still, we have rated this period as featuring only a medium level of conflict, if only because so much of the argumentation was one-sided, directed from cultural scholars towards quantitative practitioners who were themselves not necessarily engaged by the debate. In contrast, we have rated the most recent period as highly contentious, particularly around questions of interpretation and methodology. Again, one thinks of the science wars of the 1990s, or of the increasing prevalence of what might be called the "dirty methods" argument by some qualitative scholars who contend that, regardless of users' intentions, formal models are necessarily polluting and inherently incapable of being adapted to the kinds of intel-lectual (hermeneutic) tasks that are required for a proper social science.

Returning now to Table 11.1, our preliminary interpretation is that the shrillest conflicts over method occur during those historical periods when strong professional sub-communities are clashing over the same intellectual turf. The more actively quantitative models are being applied to the domain of culture, the more conflict will be generated over methodological issues. One qualification to this hypothesis is that conflict will subside during those periods in which weakness or disorganization permeates either the qualitative community (e.g. period 3) or the quantitative community (e.g. period 1). By contrast, whenever both quantitative and qualitative scholars are working in substantive ways on culture (e.g. periods 2, 5, and 6) we are likely to see more intense methodolo-gical conflicts. Moreover, if quantitative methodologies are aggressively applied to the analysis of cultural forms such that both interpretative and explanatory styles of modeling are in full swing (e.g. periods 2 and 6), that is when the Methods Wars really heat up.

Conclusion

In this essay, we have traced the lineage of formal models of culture, focusing in parti-cular on the history of American sociology. In the process, we highlighted one distinction in particular, differentiating between formal models that have interpretative or hermeneutic intentions from other types of formal models that are more explanatory in nature. As we have shown, the division between qualitative and quantitative methodologies has a dynamic character. For much of the history of sociology, formal modeling was directed at multiple goals (both explanatory and interpretative studies of culture). It was only during the period of theoretical fragmentation that quantitative methods came to be deemed unsuitable for cultural analysis by those who used such methods. Subsequently, the return to formal modeling of culture occurred in two stages, first, during the cultural turn period, with non-interpretative models of culture, and more recently with new types of interpretative models of culture coming on the scene. As more scholars, employing more kinds of methods, turn their attention to culture, the result is a kind of intellectual crowding, an intensification of jurisdictional conflicts that generate high levels of friction between sociologists from different methodological camps. This dynamic partially explains the waning and waxing of Methods Wars in the discipline.

Similar stories might be told about the history of formal models in other disciplines and other national milieux. In France, for example, Bourdieu aggressively pushed on developing interpretative models of culture (and he very much insisted on the duality of quantitative and qualitative approaches, applying correspondence analysis as the key method that allowed him to pursue his vision). There is also much sophisticated work in Germany and Italy that has highlighted the use of formal (lattice) models to analyze concept structures, and yet there appears to be little overlap between those projects and conventional sociological research in these same countries. Finally, a veritable explosion of formal modeling tools for analyzing systems of meanings has moved outward from the domain of computational linguistics into increasingly visible functions in our massively digitized world. In this context, it would seem deeply ironic not to pursue the formal modeling of culture at just this moment of history, when formalization and culture have merged in a very material and specific sense: our own computers are increasingly listening to us, interpreting us, trying to gauge what we mean in ever more sophisticated ways. In other words, just as our own experiences of culture, and indeed of the other and the self, have become increasingly mediated by the digitization of everyday life, when the very culture that we experience is increasingly itself a product of formal models of culture, this should be the moment to move forward—not to go back. For those who would want to smash the machines, we say to you, better to take them over, and to use them as best we are able to suit our own ends and needs. We believe a future sociology of culture would be well served by continuing to explore the ways in which formalism and hermeneutics can complement one another more fully than they do today.

References

Abbott, A. 1988. *The System of Professions: An Essay on the Division of Expert Labor.* Chicago: University of Chicago Press.

Agambin, G. 2009. *The Signature of All Things: On Method.* New York: Zone Books.

Bearman, P.S. and Stovel, K. 2000. "Becoming a Nazi: A Model for Narrative Networks." *Poetics,* 27: 69–90.

Blau, P. and Duncan, O.D. 1967. *The American Occupational Structure.* New York: Wiley.

Breiger, R.L. 2000. "A Tool Kit for Practice Theory." *Poetics* 27: 91–115.

Bulmer, M. 1996. "The Social Survey Movement and Early Twentieth Century Sociological Methodology." Pp. 15–34 in Maurine W. Greenwald and Margo Anderson, eds., *Pittsburgh Surveyed: Social Science and Social Reform in the Early Twentieth Century*. Pittsburgh: University of Pittsburgh Press.

Converse, J.M. 2009 (1987). *Survey Research in the United States: Roots and Emergence 1890–1960*. New Brunswick, NJ: Transaction Publishers.

DiMaggio, P.J. 1982. "Cultural Capital and School Success: The Impact of Status-culture Participation on the Grades of U.S. High School Students." *American Sociological Review* 47:189–201.

Gibson, D.R. 2003. "Participation Shifts: Order and Differentiation in Group Conversation." *Social Forces* 81: 1135–81.

Lazarsfeld, P.F. 1968. "Foreword." Pp. vii-x in Morris Rosenberg, *The Logic of Survey Analysis*. New York: Basic Books.

Mische, A. and Pattison, P. 2000. "Composing a Civic Arena: Publics, Projects, and Social Settings." *Poetics* 27: 163–94.

Mohr, J.W. 1998. "Measuring Meaning Structures." *Annual Review of Sociology* 24: 345–70.

Mohr, J.W. and Duquenne, V. 1997. "The Duality of Culture and Practice: Poverty Relief in New York City, 1888–1917." *Theory and Society* 26: 305–56.

Mohr, J.W. and Rawlings, C.M. Forthcoming. "The use of Formal Models in Cultural Sociology: Four ways to Measure Culture." In J.C. Alexander, R. Jacobs, and P. Smith, eds., *The Oxford Handbook of Cultural Sociology*, Oxford: Oxford University Press.

Mohr, J.W. and White, H.C. 2008. "How to Model an Institution." *Theory and Society* 37: 485–512.

Peterson, R.A. and Berger, D.G. 1975. "Cycles in Symbol Production: The Case of Popular Music." *American Sociological Review* 40: 158–73.

Platt, J. 1996. *A History of Sociological Research Methods in America: 1920–1960*. Cambridge: Cambridge University Press.

Powell, W.W. and DiMaggio, P.J. 1991. *The New Institutionalism in Organizational Analysis*. Chicago: University of Chicago Press.

Rawlings, C.M. and Bourgeois, M.D. 2004. "The Complexity of Institutional Niches: Credentials and Organizational Differentiation in a Field of U.S. Higher Education." *Poetics* 32: 411–37.

Richmond, M. 1917. *Social Diagnosis*. New York: Russell Sage Foundation.

Ross, D. 1991. *The Origins of American Social Science*. New York: Cambridge University Press.

Ruef, M. 1999. "Social Ontology and the Dynamics of Organizational Forms: Creating Market Actors in the Healthcare Field, 1966–94." *Social Forces* 77: 1403–32.

Smith, T. 2007. "Narrative Boundaries and the Dynamics of Ethnic Conflict and Conciliation." *Poetics* 35: 22–46.

Stouffer, S.A., Suchman, E.A., DeVinney, L.C., Star, S.A., and Williams, R.M. Jr. 1949. *Studies in Social Psychology in World War II: The American Soldier. Vol. 1, Adjustment During Army Life*. Princeton, NJ: Princeton University Press.

Thomas, W.I. with Znaniecki, F. 1918. *The Polish Peasant in Europe and America*. Chicago: University of Chicago Press.

Turner, C.F. and Martin, E. 1984. "Introduction." Pp. 3—21 in Charles F. Turner and Elizabeth Martin, eds., *Surveying Subjective Phenomena, Volume 1*. New York: Russell Sage Foundation.

White, H.C. 1997. "Can Mathematics Be Social? Flexible Representations for Interaction Process and Its Socio-cultural Constructions." *Sociological Forum* 12: 53–71.

12

Discourse and narrative

Tammy Smith

In an article in the *Annual Review of Sociology*, Roberto Franzosi (1998) asked why sociologists should be concerned with narrative. His answer stressed that social scientists regularly use some form of narrative as data and that narrators' stories possess rich accounts of action and social relations as embedded in linguistic practice. In contrast to variable-based approaches that impose researchers' pre-defined categories on subjects' responses and actions, analyses of narrative and other discursive forms provide clues to a more dynamic understanding of the mechanisms that transmit, maintain, and transform cultural frameworks through which actors derive meaning.

Both the general category of discourse and its more particular variant, narrative, denote a collection of communicative practices. Actors articulate their beliefs and thoughts, and conceive of appropriate actions to accompany those thoughts either through the deployment of speech acts and symbols in the back and forth of conversation or by the telling of a story with a beginning, middle, and end. Through these expressions, actors come to understand and construct their world, and their place within it.

Because of this connection with knowledge or truth, discourse and narrative both offer means to probe the micro-interactions of communicative processes between individuals, as well as broader macro- or institutional-level processes of meaning-making. Echoing C. Wright Mills's distinction between history and biography, an understanding of discourse and narrative in which actors emplot themselves and their experiences is crucial for observing the dynamics of historical change (Sewell 1992). Within research paradigms, however, examinations of discourse versus narrative typically yield different kinds of analyses. Whereas discourse may expose the interplay of power relations through conversation partners' utterances as they unfold, narrative reveals power through analysis of its structure and content: what gets mentioned and how it is mentioned are products of prefigured repertoires purposefully employed by narrators toward some communicative end that is known before a narrator begins his or her story. Though displaying these differences, both discourse and narrative analyses, with their attention to meaning through techniques that are semantic, pragmatic, or structural, have offered analysts a means of investigating social processes of mobilization, representations about the past, and especially identity formation, expression, and transmission.

Methodological innovations to the study of discourse and narrative such as content analysis and turn-taking analysis have been developed to add rigor to what is at heart an interpretive activity. Regardless of whether qualitative or quantitative methods are used, analyses of discourse and narrative have tended to focus exclusively on the said or marked. Comparatively less attention has been given to the unsaid, unmarked, or silenced. To the extent that social scientists are interested in comparing cultural frameworks or analyzing changes in these frameworks, however, what is forgotten or expunged from an account is as important as what is transmitted. By casting an analytic gaze upon only half of the data, discourse and narrative analyses remain necessarily incomplete. While arguing the strengths of discourse and narrative analysis, then, this chapter will make a case for the inclusion of both the remembered and the forgotten for a fuller understanding of how actors' discursive "tool kits" take shape and change over time.

What is discourse, what is narrative?

Discourse comprises the acts of language equal to or greater than the level of the sentence. These acts may include an argument, a speech, or a story, to name a few examples, which build progressively as actors string together concepts and events into chains of meaning in order to develop and/or communicate some understanding. A very basic level of interaction within discourse, then, is interaction between sentences in the production of meaning, which can take the form of emplotment, framing, or conversational turn-taking.

In examining how meaning builds from communicating partners, analysis of discourse sensitizes us to the frameworks with which actors enter into communication, and subsequently how these frameworks may be employed and altered within communication (Cicourel 1999). As Jaworski and Coupland (1999) suggest, the most basic sense of discourse analysis as "analysis of language in use" is inherently social, and is the way through which actors come to understand, classify, and build knowledge of the world around them. Discourse analysis is necessarily concerned with language, meaning, and context that is "relative to social, political, and cultural formations—it is language reflecting social order but also shaping social order, and shaping individuals' interaction with society" (Jaworski and Coupland 1999: 3). Language may be written, spoken, signed, or—as I argue below—discourse also may reveal significant aspects of social, political, and cultural formations through its notable absence.

Conceiving of discourse as encompassing both the means and products of interaction involves a notion that the social, political, and cultural formations with which we interact, though dynamic, nonetheless exist prior to interaction. The supra-personal character of these formations alerts us to the power of broader macro-level constructs in shaping our individual experiences and identities. Power, in this respect, as Lukes (2005 [1974]) conceptualizes it, can be considered as influence over others, the ability to control an agenda, and outright domination. Lukes's differentiation between the "power over" someone and the "power to" enact something—which includes the mere *potential* for action and the subtle exercise of domination from within—is especially helpful in moving between micro-encounters among individual actors and institutional environments in which action takes place. Observing the ways in which actors interact through the "talk and talk back" of social life (Steinberg 1999) offers analysts a means of exploring actors' identities and power, and the institutional settings and social groups or networks in which these are formed and practiced. In perhaps the strongest formulation, Foucault (2002 [1969]) observes that the power of such collectivities is not only in shaping what is known or true to actors, but in making that truth a reality for actors. Both truth and meaning, for Foucault, emerge through discourse. By indexing the meanings that emerge from sequences of sentences to institutional environments, discourse analysis, then, offers a powerful tool for examining how macro-structures of power and culture help orient actors' interactions by providing them with a framework for understanding their social worlds.

Exploring this continuity or change in both the form and the content of discourse is a means of revealing the complex link between individual actors and social structure. Grounded in Goffman's work on interaction, Harrison White's (1992) path-breaking *Identity and Control* opened a particularly important avenue for social-scientific discourse analysis through its examination of how power works through shifting relations that are encoded in stories. This approach blends the dynamic relationality of social network analysis with an awareness that identities and other cultural formations are articulated through stories that emerge, transform, and act back upon narrators to help shape their actions. White's work affords a view of actors as having complex sets of multiple and overlapping ties that are available as the basis for action and identity. The push–pull of narration is an effort at controlling the course of which ties are enacted, and which stories accompany those ties and signal which of the various available network domains are salient in the moment (White 1992: 68).

By investigating who controls a conversation or how conversation partners navigate their way through favorite retold tales or problematic events, discourse in social-science research has often been taken to signify a somewhat narrow notion of "talk in the moment." Such immediacy can create confusion or tension over meaning, since actors are engaged in interpretation on the fly. Discourse is malleable: meanings can be contested, ambiguous, or polysemic, stories frequently meander, and actors may attempt to steer conversations toward some topics and away from others. Therefore, talk in the moment often does not "hang together" (Freeman 2007: 232). An example from my own work, an interview with a man who was raised in Istria, a formerly contested border region in present-day Croatia, illustrates the contestation and fluidity found in discourse. In the following passage, the respondent is recounting his understanding of relations between ethnic Italians and Slavs in Istria just after the Second World War. Though I pointedly and repeatedly ask him to describe instances of Italian/Slavic violence, the respondent takes control of the conversation by actually changing my question and providing an account that stresses inter-ethnic cooperation.

SMITH: You keep mentioning Germans. Was there any fighting between Italians and the Slavic?

RESPONDENT: No, in Istria the war basically started after Italy got out of it. In fact my father and his generation of Istrian men were in the Italian army until Italy capitulated in September of 1943. And local Istrians just left, deserted. They joined the Yugoslavian fighters.

SMITH: Yes, I had heard about the cooperation between Yugoslav and Italian partisans, but then I've also read about a lot of the interethnic violence, particularly after the war.

RESPONDENT: There were Italian nationals from Istria who were part of the Yugoslav army. In fact, they were just part of Yugoslav units with all Italians in that

131

particular unit. Istrian Italians, they didn't like fascism, Mussolini, and they did revolt before … So there were—getting back to your question—there were Italian anti-fascists who were fighting either alongside and, in this case, they just fought under Tito's command within Yugoslavian units.

Despite the fact that my respondent had access to an enormous body of literature documenting rampant violence against ethnic Italians in the wake of Mussolini's defeat in 1943, I failed not once but twice to prompt him to mention any kind of inter-ethnic hostility. Instead, the respondent changed my question to redirect the conversation to cooperation in the fight against the Fascists, a story line that is consistent with the official Yugoslav version of events. This struggle over the direction of the story illustrates the effort at control described by White (1992) and demonstrates the indeterminate quality of discourse.

The process of unfolding meanings through the intersubjectivity of conversational give and take highlights one of the most salient differences between discourse analysis and studies of narrative: while discourse may be pregnant with meanings that are "in suspense" (Ricoeur 1984: 208) and co-constituted by conversation partners, narrative provides a framework where meanings have been worked out in advance by a narrator, who tells his account with beginnings, middles, and ends. Although narrative is sub-sumed under discourse as one of its four modes, the differences between the two in terms of structure and how they are produced yield unique opportunities and challenges for the social scientist.

A conventional understanding takes narrative to be structured by a sequence of non-random past events connected to each other through a plot in a way that schematizes the meaning for the listener or reader (Labov 1972; Ricoeur 1984; Toolan 1997). Narrative's structure—from the subject–verb–object relations of the sentence to the structured, sequential nature of the narrative as a whole—enables analysts to examine functions and patterns among constitutive units both within and across narratives (Franzosi 2004; Barthes 1975). To be considered a narrative, however, the story should provide a moral meaning that is gained through narrative closure (White 1987). This closure stands in contrast to the indeterminate quality of give-and-take discourse. Although the moralizing of narrative provides analysts with a window into narrators' interpretations and account-ing of action, such analysis is made possible by the structure of the narrative through its sequencing of events. An intelligible narrative does not include just any events in any order. Narrators grasp together selected events and order them within a certain tempor-ality through the overarching rubric of the plot. In this respect, meaning is derived as much from the content of the events that are noted as from the temporal order in which they appear. As Ricoeur (1984) notes, the narratives of our lives are structured through various kinds of temporality that interrelate with each other: human time is represented in the stories we tell about ourselves—what Ricoeur would later come to call narrative identity—which provides us with a framework for keying our inner time to the greater cosmic time of hours, days, and years. Through human time, people come to understand and transmit their individual experiences, the full measure of their joys and their suffering, by arranging or emplotting certain episodes within a sequence toward a specific end. Each episode, then, derives its meaning from its appearance at a certain moment of the story.

Precisely because of the temporal sequencing of events, narrative's form weighs in on notions of causality. Events do not merely follow each other, as in a chronicle, but flow from each other (Kvernbekk 2007). As events unfold within a narrative, their sequencing implies something about which events are necessary and contribute to a given outcome, while simultaneously lending meaning to each of the events (Ricoeur 1984). Scholars turn to narrative analysis in order to exploit this property of causality, though questions over whose perspective or vantage point for observing causality have produced two distinct veins of narrative analysis within the social sciences and humanities (Ewick and Silbey 1995). In the first approach, narratives are the product of the analyst's emplotment of events in order to understand historical processes. Here, the analyst mines the data—which may also take a narrative form—for information about events, which are then placed in some semblance of a "cosmic time" causal chain. This approach relates to questions seeking answers to historical causality, what Somers (1992) refers to as analytic narratives and metanarratives. Such an approach has been used for understanding social processes involved in lynching (Stovel 2001; Griffin 1993), and mobilization and counter-mobilization around workers' strikes (Franzosi 1997), to name just a few.

The other type, referred to by Somers as ontological and public, cultural, or institutional narratives, takes the temporality of the subject or informant's given narrative more forcefully—implicitly emphasizing that the way the narrator has emplotted events matters for the events' meanings. In this view, events may be creatively deployed by the narrator without regard to how they were sequentially experienced in lived time. Analysts here do not rearrange events to fit lived time for causal analysis, but interpret the meaning of the noted events by their placement in the sequence. Patterns in collected narratives, then, provide clues about the broader institutional environments in which such understandings were forged. Such approaches have yielded powerful insights into processes of identity (Lo 2002; Bearman and Stovel 2000), working-class formation (Somers 1992; Steinmetz 1992), and the construction of publics (Ikegami 2000; Eliasoph 1996), for example.

Through narratives, individuals select and order events in ways that help them give meaning to the otherwise idiosyncratic experiences in their lives (Riessman 2002). This process of emplotment is not only a matter of sense-making by an individual. It is the process by which historical events become defined and, in turn, provide individuals with broader classes of concepts through which to understand the meanings of their lives. For example, an individual driven out of his home initially may experience the act as a deeply individual violation, but later be able to place his experience within the broader framework of ethnic cleansing. This "narrativizing" of social life (Somers 1994) takes on particularly durable forms when embedded within the discourses of formal institutions such as educational systems, political organization and participation, science and medicine, and mass media (De Cilla *et al.* 1999; Anderson 1991). Such institutions have the potential to shape personal accounts, within a certain bounded space, by restructuring group narratives around new information and knowledge, and additional events, or by omitting previously told story elements (Smith 2007; Freeman 2002; Polletta 1998). Reconfigured narratives act back upon narrators and offer them opportunities to reshape their understandings of their social worlds (Ricoeur 1984). Examining the correspondence between individual and collective narratives provides a mechanism by which analysts can explore the dialogic relationship between individuals' narrations and the institutions that have shaped or transformed these accounts.

Although narratives may provide researchers with rich and creative descriptions of social events, Tilly (2002) cautions that narrators are woefully bad at identifying the structural forces that have helped shape their accounts. In other words, narrators are not necessarily good social scientists. Nonetheless, narrators' accounts as representations of culturally inscribed ideologies can be rich data. In particular, tracking and analyzing the ways in which the meanings of specific events have been transformed or omitted over time offers researchers clues into the effects of macro-structures over individuals' understandings, and how individual experiences or memories have been either expunged or drafted into the service of group accounts.

Though it may seem evident that the systematic omission of particular events from a group's account likely can be traced to processes of institutionalization—an American educational system that ignores the internment of Japanese-Americans while promoting a historical narrative of fighting for democracy and freedom during the Second World War, for example—social scientists by and large have focused on what is said rather than what is silenced. When they have turned attention to silences, scholars have tended to view silences as problematic missing pieces of information. As is clear from the internment example, however, what is remembered and what is forgotten work together to shape the meaning of people's collective representations, much like a painter's figurative subject and the negative spaces that help define it. The remainder of this chapter will argue for an integration of what is said and what is omitted within discourse and narrative analysis to gain a fuller sense of how actors' narratives expose the ways in which authoritative discourses have shaped personal accounts.

What is said and what is not said: toward a sociology of silence

To most social scientists, silence within a narrative is seen as problematic—as cover-up or refusal to admit an event (Zerubavel 2006; Beamish 2000; Minkley and Legassick 2000; Moore and Roberts 1990), as traumatic narrative ruptures (Pohlandt-McCormick 2000; Feitlowitz 1998), or as lack of coherence within a narrative (Steinmetz 1992). These responses are generated by our expectations that certain parts of a story be present in a narrative. When they are not, we determine that the narrative has been fractured and needs repair or that the narrator has been less than forthcoming. Returning again to the interview excerpt cited on pp. 131–32, however, demonstrates what is lost by this normative approach to narrative silence.

As noted, the excerpted interview demonstrates White's notion of control. I had approached this narrator because I wanted to know how people from Istria who came of age just after the Second World War interpreted post-war, inter-ethnic violence, and discrimination. My interview questions were directed toward that end. My respondent, on the other hand, had a very different story to tell, one that stressed cross-ethnic cooperation in the resistance against the Nazi–Fascist regime and included claims of victimization of ethnic Italians under Fascism. Our interview became a dance in which both partners struggled to lead. Because it was, in the end, his story to tell, my respondent won the battle for control. I recall leaving the two-hour interview feeling defeated in my attempt to learn about post-war violence, believing that I had recorded an interview that was useless for my research. Several weeks later, however, after a series of similar interviews with other Istrians, I came to see clear patterns in the way my respondents were avoiding discussion about certain events. Instead of recounting vignettes of inter-ethnic tension and discrimination, narrators populated their narratives with equally true and/or plausible events—such as joint participation of Italians and Yugoslavs in the wartime partisan brigades—that deflected attention away from episodes that contradicted their message of ethnic harmony.

The ways in which this set of narrators are silent about post-war violence illustrate that silence may be achieved through a variety of discursive strategies. Silence, for example, may not simply be the omission of certain events, or a tonally silent non-answer to a question, but the swamping of the story with other events. Recent work by linguists has begun to investigate the various practices and meanings of silence that can be traced, in part, to social organization and institutions. Some silences on concrete topics or events arise through implicit understanding or knowledge that the speaker presumes the listener possesses (Jalbert 1994; Sheriff 2000; Partee 1995). Alternatively, fear of capricious authority or outright hegemony can silence those being controlled, though an underlying current in this vein of research presupposes that actors maintain their ability to narrate their own lives despite the coercion or violence bearing down upon them (Cohen 2001; Green 1994; Scott 1990; Moore and Roberts 1990). In many cases, analysts point to the coercive state's obvious use of lies and propaganda, and citizens' ability to recognize these obfuscations as such, to demonstrate individuals' maintenance of a silenced but still present personal narrative (Jaworski 1993). Identity narratives of colonized subjects offer a variation on the coerced narratives of totalitarian regimes: as Ming-Cheng Lo (2002: 132) demonstrates in the case of Taiwanese doctors under Japanese colonialism, relatively privileged colonial subjects located in the liminal social space between colonizers and colonized may produce what she terms "fragmented consciousness." When states and institutions are more subtle in their exercise of power over public discourse, however, discerning silences becomes extremely difficult because of the seamlessness within the collective narrative, as anthropologist Andrea Smith (1994) has noted of Germans' "forgotten" history of past experience with foreign labor and present expressions of anti-foreigner sentiments (for other examples, see Norquay 1999 and Passerini 1980).

Linguist Thomas Huckin (2002) helpfully groups the range of silences noted above, what he calls "textual silence," into five categories:

- *speech act silences*, such as a pregnant pause or the "silent treatment";
- *presuppositional silences*, when narrators omit information they believe is known or understood;
- *discrete silences*, when narrators refrain from noting sensitive topics;
- *genre-based silences*, when the mention of certain types of stories preclude the telling of others; and
- *manipulative silences*, the intentional concealment of relevant information, i.e. secrets or lies.

This list indicates that silence may emerge in various ways within discourse, and that each of these ways will likely have different meanings and structures associated with it. By identifying both what is omitted and what is marked in narrators' accounts and mapping which other events these presences and absences are related to, one can begin to construct the structure of narrative silence. How silences are "articulated" and where they appear in an account, then, signal possible changes in narrative meaning that can be traced to group-level discursive processes. Analyzed in this way, silences are not necessarily problematic gaps that need to be filled in. Instead, silences motivate narrative change by reconfiguring the relations among the stories that are told. While some of these stories may be taboo elephants in the room, others certainly are relatively innocuous by-products of narrative processes over time. Their innocuousness, however, does not belie a lack of importance, as the roles of stories are pivotal in shaping the narratives around which communities mobilize to protest, fight, or contribute scarce resources to a common project. By examining what is said alongside what is silenced, then, analysts can begin to more fully explore the environments in which changes in discourse and narrative take place. And such change is necessarily about power, whether it is the crass power of authoritarian regimes that obviously muzzle certain accounts or the ways in which seemingly non-hierarchical systems contribute to more subtle forms of silencing.

Conclusion

As noted by Franzosi, much social-scientific data comes in some discursive form—from interviews, to legal transcripts, news accounts, and survey responses. Discourse and narrative analysis provide researchers with access to the macro-level processes of meaning-making in which actors are situated, and how their utterances in turn help shape group accounts.

Because of their different structures, narrative and discourse each have unique comparative strengths. Narrative, with its beginning, middle, and end of emplotted events, links an individual narrator's understanding of his/her position within a broader framework. Discourse, with its sequential talk in the moment, provides evidence for how actors engage and make sense as conversation unfolds by employing pre-existing cultural frameworks. So, while both the concepts of discourse and narrative enable us to acknowledge that actors are influenced by pre-existing cultural frameworks, discourse's meaning evolves through a process of give and take, while a narrative is presented as a worked-out whole. While an understanding of these two kinds of communicative strategies is necessarily about what is communicated, the relationship between what is told and what is not told is equally important, though very much understudied.

Considering what is omitted from accounts together with what is noted has the potential to open up new directions in studies of discursive practices. How stories are omitted, what, if anything, is mentioned in their place, and who drives the patterned omission of certain classes of stories all reveal acts of control. An actor's power to silence, by extension, links what is said or not said to the domains in which such power derives its authority.

References

Anderson, Benedict. 1991. *Imagined Communities*. London: Verso.

Barthes, Roland. 1975. "An Introduction to the Structural Analysis of Narrative." *New Literary History* 6: 237–72.

Beamish, Thomas. 2000. "Accumulating Trouble: Complex Organization, a Culture of Silence and a Secret Spill." *Social Problems* 47: 473–98.

Bearman, Peter and Stovel, Katherine. 2000. "Becoming a Nazi: A Model for Narrative Networks." *Poetics* 27: 69–90.

Cicourel, Aaron. 1999. "Interpretive Procedures." Pp. 89–97 in Adam Jaworski and Nikolas Coupland, eds., *The Discourse Reader*. London: Routledge.

Cohen, Stanley. 2001. *States of Denial: Knowing about Atrocities and Suffering.* Cambridge: Cambridge University Press.

De Cilla, R., Reisigl, M., and Wodak, R. 1999. "The Discursive Construction of National Identities." *Discourse & Society* 10: 149–73.

Eliasoph, Nina. 1996. "Making a Fragile Public: A Talk-Centered Study of Citizenship and Power." *Sociological Theory* 14: 262–89.

Ewick, Patricia and Silbey, Susan. 1995. "Subversive Stories and Hegemonic Tales: Toward a Sociology of Narrative." *Law & Society Review* 29: 197–226.

Feitlowitz, Marguerite. 1998. *A Lexicon of Terror: Argentina and the Legacies of Torture.* New York and Oxford: Oxford University Press.

Foucault, Michel. 2002 (1969). *The Archeology of Knowledge*, trans. A.M. Sheridan Smith. London: Routledge.

Franzosi, Roberto. 1997. "Mobilization and Counter-Mobilization Processes: From the 'Red Years' (1919–20) to the 'Black Years' (1921–22) in Italy: A New Methodological Approach to the Study of Narrative Data." *Theory and Society* 26: 275–304.

——. 1998. "Narrative Analysis—or Why (and How) Sociologists Should Be Interested in Narrative." *Annual Review of Sociology* 24: 517–54.

——. 2004. *From Words to Numbers: Words, Data, and the Social Sciences.* Cambridge: Cambridge University Press.

Freeman, Mark. 2002. "Charting the Narrative Unconscious: Cultural Memory and the Challenge of Autobiography." *Narrative Inquiry* 12: 193–211.

——. 2007. "Life and Literature: Continuities and Discontinuities." *Interchange* 38: 223–43.

Green, Linda. 1994. "Fear as a Way of Life." *Cultural Anthropology* 9: 227–56.

Griffin, Larry. 1993. "Narrative, Event-Structure Analysis, and Causal Interpretation in Historical Sociology." *American Journal of Sociology* 98: 1094–1133.

Huckin, Thomas. 2002. "Textual Silence and the Discourse of Homelessness." *Discourse and Society* 13: 347–72.

Ikegami, Eiko. 2000. "A Sociological Theory of Publics: Identity and Culture as Emergent Properties in Networks." *Social Research* 67: 989–1029.

Jalbert, Paul. 1994. "Structures of the 'Unsaid.'" *Theory, Culture and Society* 11: 127–60.

Jaworski, Adam. 1993. *The Power of Silence: Social and Pragmatic Perspectives.* Newbury Park, CA: Sage Publications.

Jaworski, Adam and Coupland, Nikolas. 1999. "Introduction: Perspectives on Discourse Analysis." Pp. 1–44 in Adam Jaworski and Nikolas Coupland, eds., *The Discourse Reader.* London: Routledge.

Kvernbekk, Tone. 2007. "Truth and Form." *Interchange* 38: 301–15.

Labov, William. 1972. *Language in the Inner City: Studies in the Black English Vernacular.* Philadelphia: University of Pennsylvania Press.

Lo, Ming-Cheng. 2002. *Doctors within Borders: Profession, Ethnicity, and Modernity in Colonial Taiwan.* Berkeley: University of California Press.

Lukes, Steven. 2005 (1974). *Power: A Radical View.* New York: Palgrave Macmillan.

Minkley, Gary and Legassick, Martin. 2000. "'Not Telling': Secrecy, Lies, and History." *History and Theory* 39: 1–10.

Moore, Donald and Roberts, Richard. 1990. "Listening for Silences." *History in Africa* 17: 319–25.

Norquay, Naomi. 1999. "Identity and Forgetting." *Oral History Review* 26: 1–21.

Partee, Barbara. 1995. "Allegation and Local Accommodation." Pp. 65–86 in Barbara Partee, ed., *Discourse and Meaning. Papers in Honor of Eva Hajicova.* Amsterdam: John Benjamins Publishing.

Passerini, Luisa. 1980. "Italian Working Class Culture between the Wars: Consensus to Fascism and Work Ideology." *International Journal of Oral History* 1: 4–27.

Pohlandt-McCormick, Helena. 2000. "'I Saw a Nightmare': Violence and the Construction of Memory (Soweto, Jun 16, 1976)." *History and Theory* 39: 23–44.

Polletta, Francesca. 1998. "'It Was Like a Fever … ' Narrative and Identity in Social Protest." *Social Problems* 45: 137–59.

137

Ricoeur, Paul. 1984. *Time and Narrative*, Vol. I. Chicago: University of Chicago Press.

Riessman, C. 2002. "Accidental Cases: Extending the Concept of Positioning in Narrative Studies." *Narrative Inquiry* 12: 37–42.

Scott, James. 1990. *Domination and the Arts of Resistance*. New Haven, CT: Yale University Press.

Sewell, William. 1992. "Introduction: Narratives and Social Identities." *Social Science History* 16: 479–88.

Sheriff, Robin. 2000. "Exposing Silence as Cultural Censorship: A Brazilian Case." *American Anthropologist* 102: 114–32.

Smith, Andrea. 1994. "Germany's Anti-foreigner Crisis: State Disunity and Collective 'Forgetting.'" *Journal of Historical Sociology* 7: 393–415.

Smith, Tammy. 2007. "Narrative Networks and the Dynamics of Ethnic Conflict and Conciliation." *Poetics* 35: 22–46.

Somers, Margaret. 1992. "Narrativity, Narrative Identity, and Social Action: Rethinking English Working-Class Formation." *Social Science History* 16: 591–630.

——. 1994. "The Narrative Constitution of Identity: A Relational and Network Approach." *Theory and Society* 23: 605–49.

Steinberg, Marc. 1999. "The Talk and Talk-back of Collective Action: A Dialogic Analysis of Repertoires of Discourse among Nineteenth-Century English Cotton Spinners." *American Journal of Sociology* 105: 736–80.

Steinmetz, George. 1992. "Reflections on the Role of Social Narratives in Working-Class Formation: Narrative Theory in the Social Sciences." *Social Science History* 16: 489–516.

Stovel, Katherine. 2001. "Local Sequential Patterns: The Structure of Lynching in the Deep South, 1882–1930." *Social Forces* 79: 843–80.

Swartz, David. 2007. "Recasting Power in Its Third Dimension." *Theory and Society* 36: 103–09.

Tilly, Charles. 2002. "The Trouble with Stories." Pp. 25–42 in *Stories, Identities, and Political Change*. Lanham, MD: Rowman and Littlefield Publishers.

Toolan, Michael. 1997. *Narrative: A Critical Linguistic Introduction*. London: Routledge.

White, Harrison. 1992. *Identity and Control: A Structural Theory of Social Action*. Princeton, NJ: Princeton University Press.

White, Hayden. 1987. *The Content of the Form: Narrative Discourse and Historical Representation*. Baltimore, MD: Johns Hopkins University Press.

Zerubavel, Eviatar. 2006. *The Elephant in the Room: Silence and Denial in Everyday Life*. Oxford: Oxford University Press.

138

13

The mechanisms of cultural reproduction

Explaining the puzzle of persistence

Orlando Patterson

One of the most challenging problems in the sociology of culture has been steadfastly neglected by the discipline—the puzzle of persistence. This may in part be explained by the discipline's preoccupation with change, its understandable disdain for cultural determinism, the well-based suspicion of essentialism, and the laudable need to acknowledge the role of meaning-making and agency in cultural analysis. These are all concerns that reflect the errors of an earlier generation of scholars, but they are erroneously associated with the question of cultural reproduction and persistence. Whatever the reasons, it is unfortunate that an understanding of the most fundamental feature of culture—that it is the prime source of the predictability and stability without which human society is impossible—is now largely left to other disciplines such as psychology (Nisbett and Cohen 1996), evolutionary studies (Boyd and Richerson 2005), cognitive anthropology (Cole 1996), and even economics (Barro and McCleary 2006)

It is not my objective to underplay the role of change in the understanding of culture. Indeed, my approach is processual and I see change as an inherent aspect of all cultural activity. The problem is to understand how persistence is possible in the face of such dynamism, and to account for the mechanisms that allow for this reconciliation.

A perdurantist view of cultural processes

Before examining how culture is persistently reproduced, one must first be clear about what it is. Culture is the production, reproduction, and transmission of relatively stable informational processes and their public representations, which are variously distributed in groups or social networks. The information is declarative and procedural, pertaining to ideas, beliefs, values, skills, and routinized practices as well as information about the transmission process. The transmission occurs both between and within generations; moreover, processes are shared unevenly, may be spread across non-localized groups, and may not be integrated.

Cultural processes allow for incremental changes that result from transmission errors and unwitting or deliberate alterations by learners. A perdurantist approach resolves the apparent paradox of how something can change incrementally—and over the long run quite substantially—yet maintain its identity. As philosopher Sally Haslanger (2003) explains, the persisting object does not undergo alteration by "gaining" or "losing" properties; instead, it changes like a lighted candle. That is, "contradiction is avoided by modifying the proper subject condition: the persisting thing (the composite) is not the proper subject of the properties 'gained' and 'lost' (the stages are), but the proper subjects of the properties are at least parts of the persisting thing" (Haslanger 2003: 318). Lévi-Strauss's (1963) treatment of a myth as the totality of all pre-existing and current versions is a classic example of this approach.

Culture is both internalized and externally represented in social relations, material structures, symbolic media, and other artifacts (Sperber 1996: 34). Although all structured behaviors and artifacts have a cultural dimension, many areas of culture—calculus, jazz, cricket, Hamlet—are delinked from their originating structures and can be limitlessly reproduced in varied contexts. A critical feature of all stable cultural processes is that their identities are collectively imputed, regardless of criterial properties—this being true of what W.V. Quine calls "time-extended objects."

There is a substantial literature on reproduction in sociology, but nearly all of it is devoted to the problem of structural and organizational stability rather than cultural reproduction (e.g. DiMaggio and Powell 1983). Social reproduction, which will not concern us here, refers to the means by which structural features of a society—class, gender, race, segregation, and other patterns of differentiation and organization—are maintained (see Hall *et al.* 2003: 1–15). When cultural reproduction is considered, most sociologists view it as social learning or socialization via family, schooling, and peers. Bourdieu, the most widely cited sociologist on the subject, is typical. His habitus concept does double duty, directly explaining cultural reproduction, which, in turn, explains "the reproduction of structures" (Bourdieu 1973: 71). Adopting a now dated view of social learning, circa 1950–75 (see Schonpflug 2009b: 11–14), Bourdieu goes no further in exploring the mechanisms of the reproductive process itself other than opaquely referring to an "internal law" by which external necessities are "constantly exerted" (1990: 278).

Drawing on the work of others, as well as my own, here I distinguish seven broad mechanisms of reproduction: enculturation, institutional, structural, frequency dependent, communication based, reinterpretive, and embedded.

The mechanisms of persistence

Enculturation or social learning

As indicated above, this is the most familiar mechanism of cultural reproduction. Often referred to as socialization, it is transmission through social learning and imitation both within and between generations. However, beyond stating the obvious—that people internalize culture through imitation and learning—we need to know why only some processes persist, while others change or disappear, and to identify what agents are more likely, and what less likely, to transfer different kinds of cultural processes.

In their seminal work, Cavalli-Sforza and his associates tackle the problem by modeling "who transmits what to whom, the number of transmitters per receiver, their ages and other relations between them" (Cavalli-Sforza *et al.* 1982: 19–20). Two distinctions undergird their model—the number of transmitters per recipient and the direction of transmission. Thus there can be many-to-one transmissions (for example a class or caste's influence on the naïve recipient), or one-to-many (such as a teacher's transmission to a class), and intermediate one-to-one or one-to-few transmissions (the last of which generate moderate rates of cultural change). The other distinction is that between vertical (parents and children), oblique (between non-parental adults and children), and horizontal (between peers). The authors argue that the rate of cultural reproduction (measured in terms of the rate of trait frequencies and variations over time), as well as the content of reproduction, will depend on the interaction of these two variables along with additional mediating factors such as age and transmitter–recipient gender differences. Among their more important findings is the fact that certain kinds of transmissions tend to be trait-specific; for example, among Americans, political and religious attitudes and sports preferences are strongly vertically transmitted, which largely explains their stability. Mothers and fathers account for the transmission of different cultural processes and, significantly, there is little interaction effect (Cavalli-Sforza *et al.* 1982: 218).

Researchers have theoretically developed and specified the precise psychological processes involved in the transmission process. Thus, in their review of psycho-logical studies of socialization, Putallaz *et al.* conclude that the "enabling materials of transmission" include primarily

> the proximity between caretaker and offspring, the quality of the emotional and interactional bond between them, the quality of the caretaker's life-long social relationship experiences, the translation of these experiences into schematized forms (such as memories), the presence of conflict among significant interaction partners in the family context, and the gender of both caretaker and child.
>
> (Putallaz *et al.* 1998)

Many studies have also documented the inter-generational transmission of parenting strategies (van Ijzendoorn 1992; Chen and Kaplan 2001). This research shows, unex-pectedly, that familial socio-economic status fails to predict the parenting strategies of adult children. It has also been shown that: intergenerational transmission is bi-directional, although the degree to which children influence parents varies with context (Kuczynski 2003); parent–offspring cultural similarity is strong only in some domains (Schonpflug and Bilz 2009: 212–39); and the degree of corroboration varies with class, region, immigrant status, the motivation of parents, and sibling position (Trommsdorff 2009).

Institutional reproduction: hegemonic and counter-hegemonic

Cultural institutions—ranging from simple salutations to complex formal rites—can be defined as routinized processes that have become normative. The main force of repro-duction and persistence is simply the fact that the process in question has become a part of the taken-for-granted, normative social world. They are part of the shared definition of a reality that is experienced as objectively and externally real. Hence "each actor fundamentally perceives and describes social reality by enacting it and, in this way, transmits it to other actors in the social system" (Zucker 1977: 728). A general principle is that the more institutionalized and complex a routine or belief, the less the reliance on childhood socialization or internalization, which, indeed, may not even be possible where the process is confined to adulthood and involves complex practices. Institutions are not strictly learned; they are enacted or performed. Their meanings may be accessible to only a few specialists. Thus, for over a thousand years, the single most important institutional rite in the Western world, the Catholic mass, was conducted in a language that the vast majority of participants did not understand.

How exactly do values and practices become institutionalized? "The key to institutionalizing a value," Stinchcombe (1968: 108–12) wrote in a seminal work, "is to concentrate power in the hands of those who believe in that value." Succeeding generations of power holders foster institutional self-reproduction "by selection, socialization, and controlling conditions of incumbency and hero worship." The powerful select those who share their values and other cultural preferences, and they control the processes of socialization. They also act as ego-ideals, as role models for ambitious younger persons, ensuring that the cultural processes they favor will be disproportionately imitated and re-enacted. And by arranging the institutional conditions under which later generations come to power, they ensure that there are independent forces that will keep potential deviants in line with their values. Power-backed beliefs and values also have a much greater chance of being popularly adopted, due to general admiration for the powerful and their proponents' greater access to communicative channels.

Stinchcombe's is really a well-argued theory of hegemony. However, it neglects the subaltern origins and replication of values (Spivak 1988). Though lacking legal, economic, and political power, some individuals are still able to exercise great influence and sometimes charismatic authority in the production and reproduction of subaltern cultures. African-American religious history provides a clear example of how a dominated group not only is able to resist cultural hegemony but can sometimes appropriate and transform the dominant creed to match their own likings and interests (Raboteau 1978; Genovese 1976). Levine (1970: part 6) documents the powerful role of charismatic counter-heroes—Stagalee, John Henry—in the rise of African-American folk and modern culture. In the extreme, the subaltern can turn the tables on elites and greatly influence the cultural beliefs and practices of dominant groups, as is best illustrated by the outsized influence of African-Americans on contemporary American popular culture. The same holds for Jamaica, where dancehall, Rastafarianism, Creole speech, and other areas of the previously denigrated Afro-Jamaican life-style now dominate popular culture (Thomas 2004).

Another powerful way that institutionalized processes are reproduced, especially over long periods, is through their mediation by deeply imbued culture-specific cognitive processes. Nisbett and his collaborators (2001) have found profound differences in tacit epistemologies and modes of thinking between Americans and Chinese, which the authors attribute to enduring institutional differences in the two societies. Social practices and cognitive ones, they argue, mutually maintain each other in very long-term equilibrium.

Structural reproduction

This mechanism refers to the process whereby a persisting structural condition continuously re-creates the cultural pattern in question even in the absence of cultural institutionalization. In America the intergenerational transmission of impoverished contexts, in which Blacks live in the same ghetto environment for generations, results not only in greatly reduced life chances (Sharkey 2008) but in persisting patterns of violence and victimization and impaired cognitive and educational functioning

(Sampson *et al.* 1997; Sampson 2008), as well as distinct speech communities (Labov and Harris 1986). In Jamaica, as elsewhere, chronic unemployment and extremely low wages often lead to a persistent pattern of seeming disdain for work, preference for hustling, and, especially in rural areas, a response to marginal increases in wages with less work (Patterson 1975). Many forms of property crime and prostitution may also be so reproduced. The non-institutionalized nature of many such cultural outcomes is evinced by their erosion in the face of changed structural environments. Thus Jamaicans recruited to work as farm laborers in America are noted for their work ethic. And the long tradition of prostitution in pre-revolutionary Havana disappeared for thirty years right after the revolution, then promptly returned after 1991 with the re-emergence of economic insecurity during the *periodo especial* following the collapse of Soviet aid (Clancy 2002).

The culture of honor in Mediterranean societies and the US South is perhaps the best-studied case of a long-term continuity of this kind. In the honorific cultural process, individuals (especially men) are extremely sensitive to real or perceived insults, and are inclined to react violently toward such perceptions. The culture is accompanied by a strong sense of shame, especially when people are unable to defend their honor. Scholars have found this cultural process primarily in herding or agri-pastoral societies, large-scale slave systems, conditions where centralized authority and law enforcement are weak, and especially where these conditions reinforce each other (Peristiany 1966; Wyatt-Brown 1982; Patterson 1982a: 77–101; Patterson 1984; Nisbett and Cohen 1996). The persistence of the process in modern Greece is one of the most durable cultural traditions on record, with scholars finding clear parallels between the tradition today and Homeric times twenty-seven centuries ago (Walcot 1996). In the deep South of the US, a durable honor culture accounts for, among other things, the region's much higher rate of violent crime (Nisbett and Cohen 1996).

An important aspect of the structural mechanism is that after a sustained period of reproduction, a given process may well become institutionalized and reproduced by both means in a pattern of mutual reinforcement, or independently of the structural context that originally generated it. Thus Sampson (2008) has found the persistence of neighborhood-induced reading impairment long after affected individuals have left the neighborhoods that generated it. And Nisbett has demonstrated in psychological experiments that students of Southern background living in the North are far more inclined to react honorifically to perceived threats to their manhood (Nisbett and Cohen 1996: 53). It is possible that a similar shift in the mechanism of reproduction from the structural to the institutional may have occurred in the honorific violence of inner-city African-American youth (Courtwright 1996: 225–46; Papachristos 2009) and in the familial patterns of poor Jamaicans (Patterson 1982b).

Frequency-dependent reproduction

Frequency-dependent reproduction occurs when individuals *disproportionately* select a variant of a cultural process either because it is the most or the least frequent. It is very important to distinguish this propensity from the more common situation where the most popular variant in a *population* is selected. Nature provides interesting examples of frequency-dependent choices. Predators, for example, prefer prey exhibiting the most common phenotypic trait, giving an advantage to conspecifics with a more rare phenotype, hence maintaining genetic polymorphism. Alternately, females in some polymorphic species disproportionately mate with males with more rare markings.

143

The models of Boyd and Richerson (1985: 227–40) indicate that, in spatially varying environments, conformist transmission provides individuals with a useful rule for acquiring the most locally adaptive behaviors. Applied to human populations, their line of analysis suggests one way of solving the puzzle of human cooperation. Thus, the sociologist Noah Mark (2002) argued that people disproportionately exposed to cooperative and exploitative behavior are more likely to replicate such behaviors, which in turn makes the cooperators more influential as role models (and those exposed to exploitation less influential), thereby creating an evolutionary cultural force toward cooperation (cf. Christakis and Fowler 2009: 217–23). Although the argument is suggestive, Mark's model is of limited generality and has been sharply criticized (Bienenstock and McBride 2004).

Frequency-dependent transmission has been more fruitfully, and empirically, applied to other areas of cultural reproduction. The most thorough analysis is Lieberson's (2003) study of naming practices among Americans and Europeans. Since the second half of the nineteenth century there have been two striking changes in Western naming practices—a growing turnover and diversity in names given children and a significant, though less pronounced, shift in the concentration of names. For centuries up to the early nineteenth century, half of all boys and girls were given one of the three most popular names, whereas today the most popular names are given to only a small minority of the population. This change cannot be explained by structural forces such as urbanization and growing ethnic diversity, nor by the rate of name turnover. Instead, Lieberson shows that the most likely explanation is what he calls "popularity as taste," in which there is a distribution of name choices made largely on the basis of their relative popularity, with some people choosing names mainly because they are popular, others because they are unpopular, and still others making choices in between. This results in a distinctive distribution in the reproduction of names that is consistent with the dynamics of frequency-dependent choices. Lieberson has suggested that this pattern characterizes the reproduction of other kinds of tastes such as music, the arts, and political ideas.

Path-dependent processes constitute yet another form of this mechanism. Sometimes, after originating in a specific period from a set of often quite adventitious initiating conditions, transmitted cultural practices become "locked in." The favorite, although disputed, example of this kind of persistence is the QWERTY keyboard layout. The process is maintained, once established, by mechanisms characterized by what economist Paul David (2005) calls "local positive feedback mechanisms," for example, factors such as sunk costs, the reluctance to learn new techniques, and coordination effects derived from aligning one's actions with others (Arthur 1994: 112–13). However, these factors are not peculiar to path-dependent processes, as critics of the whole idea of path dependence have insisted. Frequency-dependent selection would seem to be the critical factor (called bandwagon and reinforcing expectations in the path-dependent literature). It is when people begin to disproportionately choose a process based on its frequency (initially in conjunction with sunk- and learning-cost considerations) that it becomes locked in and, once locked in, frequency dependence alone explains its persistence, trumping other factors. In a compelling series of web-based experiments, Salganik and Watts (2009) have attempted to explain the winner-take-all puzzle of cultural markets, wherein books, songs, and movies that are only marginally different, and often judged to be inferior by experts, unpredictably outsell competing products by orders of magnitude. Hits emerge as the dynamic collective outcome of a path-dependent process driven by social influence and conformist individual behavior. After an initial chance lead, they get locked into a "cumulative advantage" in which success breeds success due to the "observation learning" of fans engaging in frequency-dependent decision-making. It is well known, too, that some consumers compulsively select cultural products because of their rarity and "cult" status.

Communication-based reproduction

We now come to a class of mechanisms that have in common the fact that the reproduction of culture is a direct result of the dynamics of communication itself and entails emergent population-level consequences of individual interactions.

The "common-ground" approach of Lyons and Kashima (2001: 374) explores how "information circulated through communication channels contributes to the information environment of individual members, influencing the availability of information to confirm or disconfirm cultural knowledge." They focus on the tendency of communicated knowledge to converge toward shared understanding. The basic idea is that when people communicate they are more interested in confirming their own established beliefs, values, and worldview than in accurately passing on what was communicated to them. Shared knowledge becomes "common ground," rather than a simple repository, which each person in the communicative chain believes others possess, and which they all use to make sense of new information. In this way, ambiguity and incoherence are minimized, creating an inherent tendency in information transmission toward weeding out messages that are inconsistent with established beliefs, and a force toward their propagation. Cultural stereotypes are typical of such common ground, and in an experiment simulating a serial communicative process Lyons and Kashima show how a story about an Australian football player converged toward the common-ground stereotype about footballers despite inconsistent versions transmitted in the early stages of the communicative chain.

The French anthropologist Dan Sperber (1996) draws analogously from virology to develop an epidemiology of representation. Durable cultural processes, he argues, are those that have become contagious. Populations are inhabited by vast numbers of mental representations, only some of which, under special circumstances, become public and enduring. This happens when a particular process becomes an "attractor" that provides the least costly way of achieving a given goal. Reproduction is not simple imitation, but rather one form of cultural production. Communication is a re-cognition of what one interprets the other person to mean, and in the process creates a person's own meaning in terms of what is most relevant to the person and the broader cultural context (Sperber 1996: 53). Micro variation achieves macro stability by movement toward attractors. "In the logical space of possible versions of a tale," Sperber writes of the reproduction of the Red Riding Hood folktale, "some versions have a better form: that is, a form seen as being without either missing or superfluous parts, easier to remember, and more attractive. The factors that make for a good form may be rooted in part in universal human psychology and in part in a local cultural context" (Sperber 1996: 106).

Sperber's attractor model is intuitively attractive but intellectually elusive. It owes more to Noam Chomsky than Charles Darwin. In the same way that a French child will converge toward standard French grammar no matter what French utterances she hears, Sperber argues, a child will be attracted to the "best" version of Little Red Riding Hood, no matter what incompetent versions she is exposed to. This clearly excludes my five-year-old, whose Disney version shuns the eating of all human beings! The question, then, is what constitutes the appropriate cultural context.

What is largely metaphor for Sperber becomes a literal social epidemiology in the empirically grounded network studies of Christakis and Fowler (2009). They have shown that behaviors and states such as smoking, over-eating, drinking, happiness, and voting are reproduced or spread through networks in remarkably patterned ways. By going far beyond the traditional emphasis on the structural component of networks (i.e. how people are connected) to large-scale empirical explorations of contagion (i.e. of what flows between the nodes), Christakis and Fowler have greatly extended our under-standing of cultural reproduction. What mainly flow through networks, their research suggests, are fundamentally cultural processes. Arguing that people shape and are shaped by their networks, that ideas, norms, behaviors, and even emotional states flow through chains of friends and acquaintances in hyperdyadic spreads of up to three degrees of influence (friends of friends of friends), and that these networks and contagions have emergent properties unknown to the individuals involved, they are explicit in the implications of such mechanisms for the nature and dynamics of culture (Christakis and Fowler 2009: 24–25, 31, 116–17). Not only have they powerfully demonstrated what the European sociologists Paul Willis (2004) and Dan Sperber (1996) could only surmise from their ethnographies—that the production and reproduction of cultural processes are intimately related—but they have given new life to the role of the superorganic in cultural systems, an idea that reaches all the way back to Emile Durkheim through Alfred Kroeber and Leslie White (see Chase 2006: 47–49). Thus, they write of the norm of quitting smoking: "What flows through the network is a norm about whether smoking is acceptable, which results in a coordinated belief and coordinated action by people who are not directly connected. This is an important way that individuals combine to form a superorganism" (Christakis and Fowler 2009: 117, also chapter 9).

Reinterpretation

Reinterpretation is the often-covert persistence or adoption of a cultural process through the representation of its meaning or practice in terms of another, established process. The mechanism was once widely recognized and studied by anthropologists after its identification and definitive analysis by Melville Herskovits (1937; 1950: 553–60), but was abandoned or viewed with hostility in the late twentieth century (Matory 2005: chapter 7). The classic case of reinterpretation is the identification of African deities with Catholic saints in the Creolization process underlying the formation of Black Atlantic religions such as Voudon, Santeria, and Condomble (Brandon 1997; Bastide 1978). However, the reinterpretive mechanism is found in all cultures, sometimes under other names, such as Brammen's (1992) description of the Japanese reinterpretation of Disneyland in Tokyo in terms of their own culture as "recontextualization." Native Americans, like West Africans and European pagans before them, used this mechanism as a way of retaining and camouflaging some of their traditions, and the Alaskan Tlingits did so as well when they secretly incorporated potlatch practices into Russian Orthodox and Protestant ceremonies (Nagel 1996: 201).

A good part of the fascination of reinterpretation is that it can operate as a mechanism of both change and persistence, accommodation and contestation, and domination and counter-domination, depending very much on the perspective of the agents involved, the context in which the interpretation takes place, and whether the issue is temporal connections in a single culture or lateral connections between different cultures. In the middle of the fourth century, Christian Church leaders reinterpreted the practices around the winter solstice as the birthday of the Christian son of God rather than the annual re-birth of the sun (Nissenbaum 1997). From the Christian perspective, this was a rather devious exercise in cultural reproduction; to the European pagans it was a hegemonic effort at changing their religious beliefs, which they strongly contested. In due course it became less and less clear which side had reinterpretively co-opted the other, so much so that eventually the American Puritans abolished Christmas as a heathen custom, admitting that the pagans had won!

Recently there has been a rediscovery of the reinterpretive mechanism. Hatch (2004: 199–201) has reprised Herskovits's concepts of focus and reinterpretation in her analysis of the dynamics of organizational culture. Anthropologist De Sardan (2005: chapter 9) sees development enterprise in Third-World countries as "an arena in which various logics and strategies come into confrontation," that of the development agent and that of the peasants. He calls this "innovation as reinterpretation," a cultural contest in which the new cultural package is "systematically disarticulated," selectively adopted, and often appropriated to ends that subvert the goals of the developer. Human-rights scholars and advocates who seek to improve the status of women in patriarchal societies have also rediscovered the value of "cultural reinterpretation" that "seeks to provide cultural 'ground' for the acceptance of women's rights by reinterpreting traditional gender ideologies that have been used to legitimate male domination and discrimination against women" (Bell et al. 2000: 180).

Sometimes what the mechanism of reinterpretation reproduces is a group's belief in its own identity and continuity, its sense of a living past that informs the present and leads into the future. In so doing a group may draw on a wide range of traditions from other groups, and even invent new processes. One of the most famous cases in point was the ghost-dance movement of Native Americans during the last decades of the nineteenth century, which reaffirmed a sense of continuity with Native Americans' past, however imagined. As Smoak (2008) shows, the movement was as much about persistence as innovation, a dynamic expression of an emerging pan-Indian identity that integrated reinterpreted aspects of Christianity and traditional beliefs in a fierce struggle against Euro-American cultural hegemony.

Embedded reproduction

We come, finally, to the most covert of all the means of cultural reproduction. Cultural embedding is the mechanism by which a process survives through its insertion into the core of a culture's dominant institution. Space constraints allow me to discuss only the most remarkable, though least apparent, form of this mechanism, what I call *embedded introjection*. This occurs when a cultural pattern persists by shifting from being an overt, secular belief to an inner, spiritual one, in which form it can remain, mainly dormant, for centuries. At any time, however, a reverse-introjection or projection may occur, in which the pattern is projected back into the secular, outer world. This, in brief, is the history of Western freedom from its introjection by Paul of Tarsus into the creedal core of the infant Christian religion during the first century of the modern era until its projective break-out during the sixteenth and seventeenth centuries.

I have shown elsewhere (Patterson 1991: 316–44; see also Martin 1990) that early Pauline Christianity took over the Roman secular notions of freedom (*libertas*) as liberation from slavery and as the exercise of absolute power, and made them the core doctrine of the religion. In his *Letter to the Galatians*, Paul reconceived sin as a kind of inner slavery and Christ's salvific crucifixion as the price paid to redeem mankind from spiritual thralldom (the Christian word *redemption* being derived from the Latin, *redemptio*, which literally means "to purchase someone out of slavery"). In the *Letter to the Romans*, the Augustan imperial notion of freedom as absolute power, into which secular worshipers could share by surrendering to the emperor's majesty, as freedmen did in the imperial cult, was reconceived by Paul as the spiritual freedom that came with surrender (Paul wrote "enslavement") to the absolute power and freedom of God.

From the beginning, Church leaders were fully aware of the explosive secular potential of Christianity's core doctrine and so worked hard to prevent its projection back into the secular world. When the doctrine became hegemonic following the conversion of Constantine in 312, the concealment took more elaborate form—in the tight and complex organizational structure of the Church, the careful screening and education of priests, and the use of an increasingly alien language, Latin, for the Mass. For the majority of European peasants, the introjection was only partly successful (Patterson 2007). Over the centuries there were radical expressions of freedom, in extreme cases expressed in servile revolts, the ideological bases for which were often secularized projections of the Christian doctrine of freedom revealed by renegade priests (Hilton 1973; Cohn 2006). In the late middle ages and early-modern Europe, we see the full projection back into the secular world of the Christian doctrine of freedom. As Ernst Kantorowicz (1957) has shown, nearly all political thought during the late middle ages and early-modern Europe were simply secularized Christology—a point that holds for the foundational text of liberalism, Locke's *Two Treatises*, the most authoritative recent reading of which sees it as essentially an exposition of Calvinist natural theology (Dunn 1983).

Conclusion

The mechanisms discussed above are not mutually exclusive. Indeed, we often find two or more interacting in the reproduction of cultural processes. Thus introjection involves reinterpretation, and in hegemonic persistence the powerful establish structures that reinforce the replication of favored values. We have also seen how cultural processes reproduced structurally can sometimes become institutionalized. Also, in the very long run, a similar tendency toward institutionalization characterizes many path-dependent reproductions.

It has not been my objective to underplay the role of socio-cultural change, which has garnered the overwhelming attention of social scientists. Rather, I have drawn attention to the neglect of the problem of cultural reproduction and persistence, which should be of equal importance for at least two reasons. First, social and cultural change on one level may be accompanied and powerfully influenced by deep underlying continuities, in much the same way that the Gulf Stream, one of the earth's most stable forces, has recently been shown to have profound effects on Northern Hemisphere weather patterns. Thus we have seen how quite radical changes in the turnover of American names have been accompanied by shifting but far more stable patterns of name concentration and even greater stability in the distribution of frequency-dependent preferences, and that volatility in criminal behavior and speech patterns are outward manifestations of deep-seated continuity in the pattern of racial segregation. Second, we need to study continuity, not only in its own right, but because a proper understanding of change itself is not possible without knowledge of the process of persistence against which it is measured and can only be properly understood.

References

Arthur, W.B. 1994. *Increasing Returns and Path Dependence in the Economy*. Ann Arbor: University of Michigan Press.

Barro, Robert, and McCleary, R.M. 2006. "Religion and Economy." *Journal of Economic Perspectives* 20: 49–72.

Bastide, Roger. 1978. *The African Religions of Brazil*. Baltimore, MD: Johns Hopkins University Press.

Bell, Lydia S., Nathan, Andrew, and Peleg, Ilan. 2000. *Negotiating Culture and Human Rights*. New York: Columbia University Press.

Bienenstock, Elisa J., and McBride, Michael. 2004. "Explication of the Cultural Transmission Model." *American Sociological Review* 69: 138–43.

Bourdieu, Pierre. 1973. "Cultural Reproduction and Social Reproduction." Pp. 71–112 in R. Brown, ed., *Knowledge, Education and Cultural Change*. London: Tavistock.

——. 1990. *The Logic of Practice*. Stanford, CA: Stanford University Press.

Boyd, Robert and Richerson, Peter J. 1985. *Culture and the Evolutionary Process*. Chicago: University of Chicago Press.

Boyd, Robert, and Richerson, Peter. 2005. *The Origins and Evolution of Cultures*. New York: Oxford University Press.

Brammen, M.Y. 1992. "Bwana Mickey: Constructing Cultural Consumption at Tokyo Disneyland." Pp. 216–64 in J.J. Tobin, ed., *Re-made in Japan*. New Haven, CT: Yale University Press.

Brandon, George. 1997. *Santeria from Africa to the New World*. Bloomington: Indiana University Press.

Cavalli-Sforza, L.L., Feldman, M.V., Chen, K.H., and Dornbusch, S.M. 1982. "Theory and Observation in Cultural Transmission." *Science* 218(1): 19–27.

Chase, Philip. 2006. *The Emergence of Culture*. New York: Springer.

Chen, Zeng-Yin and Kaplan, Howard. 2001. "Intergenerational Transmission of Constructive Parenting." *Journal of Marriage and Family* 63: 17–31.

Christakis, N. and Fowler, J. 2009. *Connected: The Surprising Power of Our Social Networks and How They Shape Our Lives*. New York: Little, Brown.

Clancy, Michael. 2002. "The Globalization of Sex Tourism and Cuba." *Studies in Comparative International Development* 36: 63–88.

Cohn, Samuel K., Jr. 2006. *Lust for Liberty: The Politics of Social Revolt in Medieval Europe, 1200–1425*. Cambridge, MA: Harvard University Press.

Cole, M. 1996. *Cross-Cultural Psychology*. Cambridge, MA: Harvard University Press.

Courtwright, David. T. 1996. *Violent Land: Single Men and Social Disorder from the Frontier to the Inner City*. Cambridge, MA: Harvard University Press.

David, Paul A. 2005. "Path Dependence, Its Critics, and the Quest for Historical Economics." Working Paper. Stanford, CA: Stanford University Department of Economics.

De Sardan, Jean-Pierre Olivier. 2005. *Anthropology and Development: Understanding Contemporary Social Change*. London: Zed Books.

DiMaggio, Paul and Powell, W. 1983. "The Iron Cage Revisited: Institutional Isomorphism and Collective Rationality in Organizational Fields." *American Sociological Review* 48: 147–60.

Dunn, John. 1983. *The Political Thought of John Locke*. Cambridge: Cambridge University Press.

Genovese, Eugene 1976. *Roll, Jordan, Roll*. New York: Vintage.

Hall, John R., Neitz, Mary Jo, and Battani, Marshall. 2003. *Sociology on Culture*. London: Routledge.

Haslanger, Sally. 2003. "Persistence through Time." Pp. 315–54 in M. Loux and D. Zimmerman, eds., *Oxford Handbook of Metaphysics*. Oxford: Oxford University Press.

149

Hatch, Mary Jo. 2004. "Dynamics of Organizational Culture." Pp. 190–211 in Marshall S. Poole and Andrew H. Van de Ven, eds., *Handbook of Organizational Change and Innovation*. Oxford: Oxford University Press.

Herskovits, M.J. 1937. "African Gods and Catholic Saints in New World Negro Belief." *American Anthropologist* 39: 635–43.

———. 1950. *Man and His Works*. New York: Knopf.

Hilton, Rodney. 1973. *Bond Men Made Free: Medieval Peasant Movements and the English Rising of 1381*. London: Routledge.

Kantorowicz, Ernst. 1957. *The King's Two Bodies: A Study in Medieval Political Theology*. Princeton, NJ: Princeton University Press.

Kuczynski, L. 2003. "Beyond Directionality: Bilateral Conceptual Frameworks for Understanding Dynamics in Parent–Child Relations." Pp. 1–24 in L. Kuczynski, ed., *Handbook of Dynamics in Parent–Child Relations*. Newbury Park, CA: Sage.

Labov, W. and Harris, W. 1986. "De Facto Segregation of Black and White Vernaculars." Pp. 1–24 in D. Sankoff, ed., *Diversity and Diachrony*. Philadelphia: John Benjamins.

Lévi-Strauss, Claude. 1963. "The Structural Study of Myth." In *Structural Anthropology*, trans. Claire Jacobson and Brooke Schoepf. Harmondsworth, England: Penguin.

Levine, Lawrence. 1970. *Black Culture and Black Consciousness: Afro-American Folk Thought from Slavery to Freedom*. Oxford: Oxford University Press.

Lieberson, Stanley. 2003. "Popularity as Taste: An Application to the Naming Process." *Onoma* 38: 235–76.

Lyons, Anthony, and Kashima, Yoshihisa. 2001. "The Reproduction of Culture: Communication Processes Tend to Maintain Cultural Stereotypes." *Social Cognition* 19: 372–94.

Mark, Noah P. 2002. "Cultural Transmission, Disproportionate Prior Exposure, and the Evolution of Cooperation." *American Sociological Review* 67: 323–44.

Martin, Dale B. 1990. *Slavery as Salvation: The Metaphor of Slavery in Pauline Christianity*. New Haven, CT: Yale University Press.

Matory, J. Leonard. 2005. *Black Atlantic Religion*. Princeton, NJ: Princeton University Press.

Nagel, Joane. 1996. *American Indian Ethnic Renewal: Red Power and the Resurgence of Identity and Culture*. Oxford: Oxford University Press.

Nisbett, Richard and Cohen, Dov. 1996. *Culture of Honor: The Psychology of Violence in the South*. Boulder, CO: Westview Press.

Nisbett, Richard, Peng, K.P., Choi, I., and Norenzayan, A. 2001. "Culture and Systems of Thought: Holistic vs. Analytic Cognition." *Psychological Review* 108: 291–310.

Nissenbaum, Stephen. 1997. *The Battle for Christmas*. New York: Vintage.

Papachristos, A. 2009. "Murder by Structure: Dominance Relations and the Social Structure of Gang Homicide." *American Journal of Sociology* 115: 74–128.

Patterson, Orlando. 1967. *The Sociology of Slavery: Jamaica 1655–1838*. London: Hutchinson.

———. 1975. *The Condition of the Low-Income Population in the Kingston Metropolitan Area*, Government Report. Kingston, Jamaica: Office of the Prime Minister, Jamaica.

———. 1982a. *Slavery and Social Death*. Cambridge, MA: Harvard University Press.

———. 1982b. "Persistence, Continuity, and Change in the Jamaican Working Class Family." *Journal of Family History* 7: 135–61.

———. 1984. "The Code of Honor in the Old South." *Reviews in American History* 12: 24–30.

———. 1991. *Freedom: Freedom in the Making of Western Culture*. New York: Basic.

———. 2007. "The Ancient and Medieval Origins of Modern Freedom." Pp. 31–66 in Steven Mintz and John Stauffer, eds., *The Problem of Evil*. Amherst: University of Massachusetts Press.

Peristiany, J.G. 1966. *Honor and Shame: The Values of Mediterranean Society*. Chicago: University of Chicago Press.

Putallaz, Martha, Costanzo, Philip, Grimes, C.L., and Sherman, D.M. 1998. "Intergenerational Continuities and their Influences on Children's Social Development." *Social Development* 7: 389–427.

Raboteau, Albert. 1978. *Slave Religion: The "Invisible Institution" in the Antebellum South*. Oxford: Oxford University Press.

Salganik, Matthew and Watts, Duncan. 2009. "Web-based Experiments for the Study of Collective Social Dynamics in Cultural Markets." *Topics in Cognitive Science* 1: 439–68.

Sampson, R. 2008. "Durable Effects of Concentrated Disadvantage on Verbal Ability among African-American Children." *Proceedings of the National Academy of Sciences* 105: 845–53.

Sampson, R., Raudenbush, S. and Earls, F. 1997. "Neighborhoods and Violent Crime." *Science* 227: 918–24.

Schonpflug, Ute, ed. 2009a. *Cultural Transmission*. Cambridge: Cambridge University Press.

——. 2009b. "Theory and Research in Cultural Transmission: A Short History." Pp. 9–30 in Ute Schonpflug, ed., *Cultural Transmission*. Cambridge: Cambridge University Press.

Schonpflug, U. and Bilz, L. 2009. "The Transmission Process: Mechanisms and Context." Pp. 212–39 in Ute Schonpflug, ed., *Cultural Transmission*. Cambridge: Cambridge University Press.

Sharkey, Patrick. 2008. "The Intergenerational Transmission of Context." *American Journal of Sociology* 113: 931–69.

Smoak, Gregory E. 2008. *Ghost Dances and Identity: Prophetic Religion and American Indian Ethnogenesis in the Nineteenth Century*. Berkeley: University of California Press.

Sperber, Dan. 1996. *Explaining Culture: A Naturalistic Approach*. Oxford: Blackwell.

Spivak, Gayatri. 1988. "Can the Subaltern Speak?" Pp. 271–313 in Cary Nelson and Lawrence Grossberg, eds., *Marxism and the Interpretation of Culture*. Urbana: University of Illinois Press.

Stinchcombe, Arthur. 1968. *Constructing Social Theories*. Chicago: University of Chicago Press.

Thomas, Deborah. 2004. *Modern Blackness*. Durham, NC: Duke University Press.

Trommsdorff, Gisela. 2009. "Intergenerational Relations and Cultural Transmission." Pp. 120–60 in Ute Schonpflug, ed., *Cultural Transmission*. Cambridge: Cambridge University Press.

van Ijzendoorn, M.H. 1992. "Intergenerational Transmission of Parenting: A Review of Studies in Non-clinical Populations." *Developmental Review* 12: 76–99.

Walcot, Peter. 1996. "Continuity and Tradition: The Persistence of Greek Values." *Greece and Rome* 43: 169–77.

Willis, Paul. 2004. "Cultural Production and Theories of Reproduction." Pp. 178–202 in Chris Jenks, ed., *Culture: Critical Concepts in Sociology*. London: Routledge.

Wyatt-Brown, Bertram. 1982. *Southern Honor: Ethics and Behavior in the Old South*. Oxford: Oxford University Press.

Zucker, Lynne. 1977. "The Role of Institutionalization in Cultural Persistence." *American Sociological Review* 42: 726–43.

Part III
Aesthetics, ethics, and cultural legitimacy

14

Social aesthetics

Ben Highmore

In his book *The Comfort of Things* the cultural anthropologist Daniel Miller presents thirty portraits of individuals and their relationship to things that they possess (and that, as he will suggest, possess them). He writes:

> There is an overall logic to the pattern of these relationships to both persons and things, for which I use the term "aesthetic." By choosing this term I don't mean anything technical or artistic, and certainly nothing pretentious. It simply helps convey something of the overall desire for harmony, order, and balance that may be discerned in certain cases—and also dissonance, contradiction, and irony in others.
>
> (Miller 2008: 5)

Miller uses the term "aesthetic" to describe his informants' intimate material worlds, but as soon as he does so, he energetically distances himself from the connotations of artiness and connoisseurship that often accompany the term "aesthetic." The story I tell about aesthetics does its share of distancing too, and although such pedantic positioning may seem overly fussy, it is, I will show, a necessary result of the history of aesthetics in intellectual thought.

But why does Miller want the term "aesthetic"? What is wrong with using a word like "style" or "lifestyle" to describe the pattern of our relations with the world of things? My guess is that, for Miller, "lifestyle" has become too easily associated with a one-dimensional critique of consumer capitalism, where material culture is merely a way of showcasing status and prestige. Aesthetics, on the other hand, suggests a world of sensual contact with things—a world of bodies perceiving themselves and other bodies, a world thick with emotion and sentiment. This gives the term "aesthetic" a lively visceral sense, in contrast to the seeming stifling snobbery of aesthetes. It is this sense of the term as corporeal—addressed to sensual perception and registering emotional intensities—that will make it useful to the sociologically informed study of culture. For social aesthetics, matter matters, and rationality and reason have to play second fiddle to the empirical world of sensation, affect, and perception. But before I offer examples of the productivity of social aesthetics, it is worth addressing the historical roots of the term "aesthetics" and the various paths this term has taken.

Historical roots and routes

From the mid-eighteenth century, the term "aesthetics" wavers between a limited sense as a reflection on beauty, taste, and art, and an extended sense more concerned with the everyday perception of the sensual, phenomenal world. If the former is driven by a desire to judge and appreciate, the latter is oriented to more general descriptive exploration. Writing in 1750, Alexander Baumgarten, who is usually acknowledged as coining the term "aesthetics," describes it as the "science of sensual cognition" (quoted in Hammermeister 2002: 7). From the start, aesthetics poses a problem: if we use the term "cognition" to primarily describe our dealings in the ideational world of thoughts and concepts, should we talk about "cognition" when we are dealing with the world of emotions and sensations? Baumgarten's insistence on the word "cognition" here is in keeping with his overall intention. For Baumgarten, our sensual "knowledge" of the world is neither to be trusted nor to be championed: "impressions received from the senses, fantasies, emotional disturbances, etc. are unworthy of philosophers and beneath the scope of their consideration" (Baumgarten 1998 [1750]: 490). In this, he sets the tone for numerous accounts of aesthetic knowledge: he recognizes that the world we live in is experienced sensually and passionately, but that this sensual engagement is often "base" and creaturely. The aesthetic task is not simply to explore the sensual realm but to transform it, to rescue it from its mere sensual form and to set it on a par with the higher purpose of reason. And it is here that poetry, theatre, novels, sculptures, or painting can work their magic—by transcending ordinary life and realizing the beauty of order and sensitive taste.

From the mid- to late eighteenth century onward, the sociological potential of aesthetics—its potential to attend to the full range of sensual experience—was effectively quashed by an overriding concern amongst philosophers and social commentators to concentrate on polite sensitivity and the categories of the beautiful and sublime. Other forms of sensual experience—for instance finding something unnerving, or being confused and anxious, or enjoying the comfort and familiarity of things, or finding something contemptible, and so on—simply got left out of the picture. Although the business of tasteful discrimination continued into the twentieth century, it was by then more obviously in conflict with a social paradox: philosophical attention to taste had sought to establish immutable laws for beauty, whereas the rising commercial culture and commodity exchange were also in the business of producing taste, yet for this production to provide endless cycles of new commodities beauty had to be profoundly mutable. As Jean Epstein wrote, "One talks of the eternal canons of beauty when two successive catalogs of the Bon Marché [a Parisian department store] confound this drivel" (quoted in Marcus 2007: 2).

The understandings of aesthetics as a form of art-theory or as a labyrinthine discussion of the beautiful and the sublime have been challenged by a much more generous understanding of what might count for aesthetic study. In his 1884 essay "What Is an Emotion?" the philosopher and psychologist William James described "the aesthetic sphere of the mind" as the mind's "longings, pleasures and pains, and its emotions" (James 1884: 188). Such a perspective connects to Baumgarten's original meaning for the term, but without the desire to rescue this sphere from our creaturely habits and desires. For James, the aesthetic sphere is the arena of our most visceral forms of life, our most insistently human domains: the task is not to transcend it but to explore it as our empirical reality. In this, James reconnects us to a moment, prior to Baumgarten's coinage, when philosophers talked about "the passions," and included the whole gamut of sense impressions and emotional reactions that would later be parceled out into discrete enclaves of aesthetics, psychology, ethics, and so on.

The first fully sociological use of the term aesthetics likely appears in the work of Georg Simmel. His 1896 essay "Soziologische Aesthetik" heralds an approach to the social that is attentive to the felt experience of social actors, attuned to the surface phenomena of culture (to be found in clothing and eating etiquette, as much as, if not more than, in elite culture), and expressly concerned with new forms of social life. Simmel's is an interest in the formal aspects of culture, in the ways that social life is patterned. Simmel doesn't ignore an interest in beauty; rather, our appreciation of certain formal shapes and arrangements is central to our ability to understand the world. Privileging symmetry and contrast, for instance, would determine (and be detrimental to) our understanding of the web-like complexity of modern life. Part of the task of sociology, in its social aesthetic role, is to appreciate new and more complex patterns: "the more we learn to appreciate composite forms, the more readily we will extend aesthetic categories to forms of society as a whole" (Simmel 1968 [1896]: 74).

In recent years the work of the French philosopher Jacques Rancière has prompted a new understanding of aesthetics that connects the sensual and affective orchestration of material life to the cultural forms we use to apprehend and manage material life. Rancière uses the phrase "the distribution of the sensible" ("*le partage du sensible*") to describe the orchestration of material and cultural life: the distribution of the sensible is "the system of a priori forms determining what presents itself to sense experience. It is a delimitation of spaces and times, of the visible and the invisible, of speech and noise, that simultaneously determines the place and stakes of politics as a form of experience" (Rancière 2004: 13). Here, Rancière's aesthetic thought is clearly political (what is and isn't perceivable matters socially), but it compellingly overcomes the distinction between an experience of sensorial life versus the cultural forms (novels, films, diaries, and so on) that are used to explain and describe such experience. The "distribution of the sensible" would include within its orbit the parceling out of the social world undertaken by, for instance, a realist novel, a school building, or a dietary practice. In this way, novels as much as herbs and spices "flavor" our world, and arrange it in sensorial ways.

The political and sociological orientation of Rancière's work points to a major accomplishment of social aesthetics: because it purposefully privileges practices, processes, and interconnections, it has the ability to overcome the separation of (human) subjects and (inhuman) objects. For Rancière, the social subject is constituted in a world patterned by arrangements of sensual and sensorial possibilities and impossibilities, and this arrangement is produced by human and non-human actions. Given that our societies, for all their differences, are structured unevenly (in terms of class, for instance, or gender), a radical social aesthetic perspective (Rancière's, for instance, but also Simmel's) would see this structuring as a product of aesthetic arrangements rather than seeing aesthetic arrangements as a product of a structuring that might be explained by, for instance, economics. Here, social aesthetics doesn't attempt to demote the importance of the distribution of wealth, but to insist that economic factors always take sensual, material forms and that these forms are aesthetic.

Such a short sketch of some of the roots and routes that the term "aesthetics" has taken cannot do justice to the many nuanced arguments that have been conducted in its name. One thing, though, seems obvious: social aesthetics simply can't afford to heed the limitations imposed on aesthetics by those whose main task is to protect the sanctity of the artwork. This is not to say that artworks aren't important for social aesthetics, far from it, but rather than aesthetics signaling the autonomous value of art, the flag of social aesthetics is raised in order to insist on the deeply embedded connections between art-works and creaturely, material life. Indeed, it could be argued that a social aesthetics places a higher value on the artwork than does an art aesthetics by seeing it as a gen-erative agent in the orchestration of the sensorial. Social aesthetics has a promiscuous interest in all sorts of manifestations—artworks, travel guides, furniture showrooms, plumbing, legal documents, and on and on and on. What keeps it focused is its over-riding interest in the "distribution of the sensible," the profoundly social and material work of patterning culture. But let me move away from these abstract discussions to offer some more concrete examples of the productivity, problems, and potential of social aesthetics.

Modern moods, modern modes

One way that social aesthetics has been enormously productive for cultural sociology has been in charting what might be called the moods and modes of modernity. Here, the work of German critics such as Walter Benjamin and Siegfried Kracauer during the 1920s and 1930s has been hugely influential in understanding the material transfor-mations of sensorial social life in the nineteenth and early twentieth centuries, as well as the cultural moods and modes that such transformations have generated. Both writers were profoundly indebted to the cultural sociology of Georg Simmel, and they followed his cue of finding deep structural changes within the surface phenomena of everyday culture. Both Kracauer and Benjamin paid attention to forms of popular entertainment (cinema, dance-troops, café-concerts, and so on), to the non-places of modern culture (hotel lobbies, moth-eaten shopping arcades, railway stations, etc.), and to the new technologies of communication and movement (trams and cars, cameras and telephones). Theirs was a diagnostic approach, scouring the surfaces of modern life for deep fissures that allowed them to glimpse both signs of sensual and perceptual change as well as the possibilities for new critical approaches to society that lay buried amongst commercial culture.

A central diagnostic argument put forward by both Benjamin and Kracauer was the claim that modern cultural forms solicited and encouraged new forms of attention. Thus in cinema (the new media of their day) they saw not only new cultural techniques but also new relationships between audiences and artwork. For Benjamin, if traditional art had been steeped in cult-value and aura, the art of cinema demanded a distracted spectator. Such new cultural forms reversed the relationship between the cultural object and the perceiving subject: instead of the viewer being absorbed by the artwork, the new cultural forms were absorbed into the viewers' orbits (their interests and concerns). This development heralds the birth of the modern mass audience. In cinema, audience members are less daunted by the auratic presence of the work and find themselves casually taking issue with the forms of representation that pass before them (the example of armchair sports critics springs readily to mind).

Both Benjamin and Kracauer were subtle, dialectical thinkers, and they would constantly reveal the simultaneous negative and positive possibilities within new cultural forms. So if the cinematic audience could potentially find a critical space in the new entertainment industries, it could also be lulled into a waking dream by the very same material. Distraction, then, has both negative and positive potential, suggesting a sense of overcoming cultural material (refusing its authority) while also being kept in a state of absent-mindedness (partly through the sheer abundance of cultural material). In this, cultural material (including road systems as much as cameras, office furniture as much as radio) is pedagogic—and this is its main aesthetic role. For Benjamin, cinema, funfairs, the click of the camera shutter, the crossing of the road, all serve as training manuals. Whether these phenomena train you for the factory floor or the role of social critic is uncertain; in Benjamin's understanding it was probably both. As a "training manual," aesthetic culture prepares the body, it readies our perceptional capacities, and it attempts to establish proclivities.

The focus on attention, on the perceptual capacities of the human subject in relation to changing social and material circumstances, has achieved renewed importance in recent decades. When looking at emerging patterns of feeling and perception, we tend to look backwards from the new to imagine a previous moment when things were different. Often, though, this looking back is itself a product of forces at work in the new. This is a crucial point: when looking at the emergence of modern moods like boredom or social anxieties like agoraphobia or nervous exhaustion, we need to keep in focus the forces at work in producing enthusiastic interest or urban dynamism or nervous stamina. For Jonathan Crary, distraction is a symptom of the attempt to produce concentration: "modern distraction was not a disruption of stable or 'natural' kinds of sustained, value-laden perception that had existed for centuries but was an effect, and in many cases a constituent element, of the many attempts to produce attentiveness in human subjects" (Crary 1999: 49). Although this adds a critical dimension to Benjamin and Kracauer's work, it does not contradict their positions. Rather it deepens the dialectic of absorptions and distraction that is also a mark of our present moment as we navigate working and domestic routines that demand sustained absorption in computer screens, gadgetry, and internet byways, while all around us leisure is offered to us in the shape of mobile sound technologies and computer graphics. The constant stream of journalism decrying the short attention span of today's youth (on what evidence?), or the over-prescribing of drugs like Ritalin, must be seen within a social demand for more and more fluid forms of concentration and promiscuous absorption.

Globalism in an aesthetic key

Although some social and cultural theorists might see globalization as a recent phenomenon, it is at least as old as Columbus's voyage across the Atlantic in 1492. Although there had been invasions and cultural appropriations prior to 1492, Columbus's voyage marked a new age of global power, a new age that has done much to constitute our contemporary world. We can get a quick sense of the extent of this longer history of globalization by looking at the spread of languages: The global languages (primarily English, Spanish, and French, but also to a lesser degree Portuguese and Dutch) are the languages of the colonizers. If language is sensual and sensorial consciousness, then the oral and aural texture of the modern world has been indelibly stamped with the aesthetics of colonialism to a very basic degree.

The sensual landscapes of global modernity have been marked by the comings and goings of people and things. In the United Kingdom, for instance, every town, every large village, and every city has a selection of Indian restaurants in its main street. The aesthetic registers of smell and taste within the UK have been shaped by Indian food, to the point where the unofficial English football anthem is named after the Goan dish vindaloo. To follow the sensual journey of this particularly spicy dish is to witness the aesthetic globalizing effects of colonialism and its neo-colonial persistence. Vindaloo is a dish that resulted from combining the Portuguese taste for pork (the Portuguese had colonized this part of India) with the spicing practices of local Goans. Yet what characterizes this dish, and many of the most globally well-known Indian dishes, is its use of chilies. And it was the Portuguese that introduced chilies into India when they transported them from South America (Collingham 2005). Yet, once designed, vindaloo doesn't remain unchanged as it moves around the globe, but takes on new textures and flavors as it textures and flavors in turn. This is not to privilege the agency of chilies over the practices of cooks or diners, but to claim that the experience of vindaloo eating in specific geographical and historical circumstances will always be a complex amalgam of sensual and symbolic social arrangements. Vindaloo eating cannot be adequately descri-bed or explained by recourse to socially symbolic values (for instance its association with male, white "lad" culture in Britain) without also recognizing its intense sensual effects and affects (see Highmore 2008).

If aesthetics is, following Baumgarten, sensual cognition, then the flavors, sounds, smells of everyday life should be social aesthetics' first port of call. Academic work on food culture usually only explicitly employs aesthetics when it wants to make claims for the culinary excellence of a certain cuisine, or, more often, of a highly select group of chefs. But social aesthetics should insist that elevating the ordinary to the level of art is a pointless game, and could instead respond by treating all sensual material as both worldly and singular. In this, social aesthetics is a form of close attention (to the specificity of things, to their phenomenal form) as well as a way of connecting specific things to lively worlds of other things and bodies. Elspeth Probyn's book *Carnal Appetites* (2000) is an exemplary instance of social aesthetics as it moves between localized bodies eating specific foods and patterns of economic and social power. Here, eating is never a solitary act: it materially connects to social and political realms. For social aesthetics, the "food chain" (in all its human, animal, industrial, chemical, and geographical complexity) is a materializing instance of what it means to be embodied. For Probyn, Pierre Bourdieu's analysis of social practices as unnervingly regular even when they seem to be most spontaneous and improvised is a compelling intellectual resource. But in her book the symbolic world of culture is made deeply physical and sensual through analytic descrip-tions that constantly move from actual bodies savoring flavors or turning up noses to the material actuality of larger patterns of food exchange and production (which also includes the production of ideas about food).

Philosophers and cultural critics, frustrated at the limitations of traditional aesthetics to consider sensual formations that don't correspond to the concentration on the beautiful and the sublime, have suggested that we focus on more "minor" aesthetic forms. Sianne Ngai, for instance, suggests that privileging emotions like irritation and envy (Ngai 2005a), and cultural forms like the cute and the zany, will provide a better understanding of our present times than maintaining a focus on strong feelings like anger and love and formal values like ugliness and beauty. In this, she follows philosophers like J.L. Austin (whom she acknowledges) who argue that ordinary life provides wonderful opportunities for studying language and that it might also provide a rich field for the study of aesthetics "if only we could forget for a while about the beautiful and get down instead to the dainty and the dumpy" (Austin, cited in Ngai 2005b: 811).

The dainty and the dumpy might need to take a back seat in any assessment of our contemporary world (like "frilly" they seem to have an early twentieth-century ring to them): more pertinent to today might be the shiny, the "buff," the fit, the cute, the connected, the fast, the mobile, and so on. Globalizing culture is constantly being refashioned and reshaped. In recent decades we have witnessed a globalizing trajectory manifesting from Japan. A key form has been characterized as "globalized cute." Cultural franchises like Pokémon, Hello Kitty, Digimon, Yu-Gi-Oh have spread across the globe by the billions—as trading cards, TV cartoons, computer games, brand identifiers, lunch boxes, stickers, toys, internet sites, clothing, bags, and so on. The round-eyed fairytale figures created by these franchises offer an image of smiling lovability and easygoing-ness in a world organized around complex and rigid rules. Their amazing success has created a transnational Japan that both maintains aspects of national cultural forms while also transforming them (there is a distinct lack of ethnic specificity in any of the brands). For social aesthetics, the emergence of "global cute" could be seen as both a softening of the phenomenal world and a hardening of its structuring abilities—for instance the ability to instill forms of compliance. But we would do well to remember Benjamin's insistence that we treat such materials dialectically, and refuse the easy option of treating them as having necessarily good or bad effects and affects.

Conclusion and future possibilities

In 1928, Mikhail Bakhtin and Pavel Medvedev declared, "it is necessary to overcome once and for all the naïve apprehension that the qualitative uniqueness of, say, art, could suddenly turn out to be something other than sociological" (1985 [1928]: 6). This suggests that socially oriented approaches to cultural objects like artworks need to be inoculated (from the start) against any transcendental understanding of aesthetics. This is the negative cargo of social aesthetics. While sociology has provided anti-transcendental accounts of the art world (for instance Becker 2008 [1982]), the less visible, positive challenge is for social aesthetics to apprehend the "qualitative uniqueness" of not just artworks but also cooking, gardening, media, furniture, business cultures, bureaucracies, and so on, sociologically. This means, I think, treating such cultural forms as agents of social life, rather than mediated reflections thereof; it means always asking how such forms distribute the sensible and what effects and affects such distribution has; it means looking at the feelings, moods, and modes that these forms generate. To give a concrete example, it means not simply recognizing that a plate of Bangladeshi food has a different meaning for a white racist than for a Bangladeshi cook, but acknowledging that the food will actually taste different: it will hit the taste buds differently, settle in the stomach in different ways, and so on. This is to recognize the sociality of our bodies and the way that our racial orientations are simultaneously ideas and bodily orientations. It is at the concrete level of experience that the real potential of social aesthetics lies, and its sociological power will not be guaranteed by treating food, for instance, as another marker of prestige or status, but by constructing sociological accounts of the qualitative

161

uniqueness of food as cultural phenomena that circulate in phenomenologically different ways than furniture or films. At present, much scholarship treats aspects of sensual and sensorial life sociologically (and at the cost of qualitative uniqueness), but few books treat the social distribution of sensual and sensorial culture aesthetically (examples like Probyn's work are a rarity).

The future of social aesthetics is not merely a matter of academic concern. Indeed, although social aesthetics is dedicated to forms of critical description, it also recognizes the way that aesthetic forms generate social experiences and social assimilation. In this regard, alongside providing analytic description, those practicing social aesthetics might consider their potential as cultural activists in producing new "distributions of the sensible." If aesthetics has always reflected on beauty, then the work of social aesthetics might require the active transformation of beauty. If beauty can be seen as the materialization of pleasure, then the displeasure invoked by the not-beautiful is of huge social and political significance. In an age when we are edging ever closer to environmental catastrophe, any aesthetic dispensation that automatically favors obsessive cleanliness and the brand-spanking-new over the worn, the crumpled, and the chipped will have serious long-term consequences. The social aesthetic challenges that climate change, for instance, brings us is to find new pleasures in the old, in refuse, and in the reused, and (perhaps more importantly) to find displeasure in the conspicuous waste generated by consumer culture. The trick here is for social aesthetics to sweep aside the language of moral duty to make way for the pleasurable reconfiguration of passionate aesthetic culture.

But this goal is meaningless if it merely reconnects aesthetics to the task of designating beauty (the central task of traditional aesthetics). One of the most compelling aspects of the social movements of the last fifty years is the liberation of certain social groups from mainstream (i.e. straight, white, male) standards of value, beauty, and worth. The ability to distribute new forms of cultural confidence among women, queer communities, and groups marginalized by race or class, is simultaneously political and aesthetic. Social aesthetics has political affectivity precisely because it has been socially aesthetic: this is a deep, grass-roots politics. And the work of social aesthetics is ongoing as long as the materialization of equality is still to be achieved.

References

Bakhtin, Mikhail and Medvedev, Pavel. 1985 (1928). *The Formal Method in Literary Scholarship: A Critical Introduction to Sociological Poetics*, trans. Albert J. Wehrle. Cambridge, MA and London: Harvard University Press.

Baumgarten, Alexander. 1998 (1750). "Prolegomena" [to Aesthetica]. Pp. 489–91 in Charles Harrison, Paul Wood, and Jason Gaiger, eds., *Art in Theory, 1648–1815: An Anthology of Changing Ideas*. Blackwell: Oxford.

Becker, Howard S. 2008 (1982). *Art Worlds*. Berkeley: University of California Press.

Benjamin, Walter. 2008 (1936). "The Work of Art in the Age of Its Technological Reproducibility." Pp. 19–56 in *The Work of Art in the Age of Its Technological Reproducibility and Other Writings on Media*. Cambridge, MA: Belknap Press, Harvard University Press.

Bourdieu, Pierre. 1990 (1972). *Outline of a Theory of Practice*, trans. Richard Nice. Cambridge: Cambridge University Press.

Collingham, Lizzie. 2005. *Curry: A Biography*. London: Chatto and Windus.

Crary, Jonathan. 1999. *Suspensions of Perception: Attention, Spectacle, and Modern Culture*. Cambridge, MA: MIT Press.

Dewey, John. 1980 (1934). *Art as Experience*. New York: Perigee.

Eagleton, Terry. 1990. *The Ideology of the Aesthetic*. Oxford: Blackwell.

Hammermeister, Kai. 2002. *The German Aesthetic Tradition*. Cambridge: Cambridge University Press.

Highmore, Ben. 2008. "Alimentary Agents: Food, Cultural Theory, and Multiculturalism." *Journal of Intercultural Studies* 29(4): 381–98.

Iwabuchi, Koichi. 2002. *Recentering Globalization: Popular Culture and Japanese Transnationalism*. Durham, NC: Duke University Press.

James, William. 1884. "What Is an Emotion?" *Mind* 9(34): 188–205.

Kracauer, Siegfried. 1995 (1930). *The Mass Ornament: Weimar Essays*, transl. Thomas Y. Levin. Cambridge, MA: Harvard University Press.

——. 1998. *The Salaried Masses: Duty and Distraction in Weimar Germany*, trans. Quintin Hoare. London: Verso.

McVeigh, Brian J. 2000. "How Hello Kitty Commodifies the Cute, Cool and Camp: 'Consumutopia' versus 'Control' in Japan." *Journal of Material Culture* 5(2): 225–45.

Marcus, Laura. 2007. *The Tenth Muse: Writing about Cinema in the Modernist Period*. Oxford: Oxford University Press.

Miller, Daniel. 2008. *The Comfort of Things*. Cambridge: Polity.

Ngai, Sianne. 2005a. *Ugly Feelings*. Cambridge, MA: Harvard University Press.

——. 2005b. "The Cuteness of the Avant-Garde." *Critical Inquiry* 31: 811–47.

Probyn, Elspeth. 2000. *Carnal Appetites: FoodSexIdentities*. London and New York: Routledge.

Rancière, Jacques. 2004. *The Politics of Aesthetics: The Distribution of the Sensible*, trans. Gabriel Rockhill. London and New York: Continuum.

Simmel, Georg. 1968 (1896). "Sociological Aesthetics." Pp. 68–85 in *The Conflict in Modern Culture and Other Essays*, trans. K. Peter Etzkorn. New York: Teachers College Press.

15

History, sublime, terror

Notes on culture's failure and the social catastrophe

Gene Ray

The problem of violence and its social origins is old and vexed. If it is not to be attributed to an imputed human nature already conceding inevitability, then violence must be grasped as the product of social forms and processes. However, the public debates following the attacks of September 11, 2001 and the subsequent invasion of Afghanistan and Iraq under the sign of a globalized "war on terror" have made clear that the long-standing disputes over the roots and springs of violence remain unresolved. Critical reflection on the social character of violence quickly touches the foundations and legitimacy of existing forms of society and their conflict-generating stratifications and concentrations of power.

In its traumatic character, violence has affinities with the traditional aesthetic category of the sublime, which names the mixed feelings of terror and pleasure triggered by encounters with excessive power or magnitude. That in the twentieth century, a period of unprecedented global violence, sublime strategies of "negative" or indirect representation reached new peaks of development in art should be no surprise. The Frankfurt critical theorist Theodor W. Adorno was among the first to explore this conjunction. His theory of modernism contains a coded rewriting of the sublime that positions it as the only adequate artistic response to historical catastrophe. However, as a cliché of contemporary cultural writing, the formula "after Auschwitz, no poetry" has been distorted and domesticated by its severance from Adorno's critique of enlightenment culture and capitalist modernity—a severance that allows it to be unjustly reduced to a moralizing judgment of taste. For Adorno the catastrophe is social, rather than some exceptional genocidal eruption within a continuing and reassuring historical progress.

The sublime: from first to second nature

In his 1757 book on aesthetics—published two years after the Lisbon earthquake—the young Edmund Burke proposed that anything connected to terror is potentially a source of the feeling of the sublime. Today, it seems timely to ask whether this category from eighteenth-century aesthetics still has anything relevant to say about the world.

The sublime names an aesthetic response to nature's capacity to strike us with fear, terror, awe, and astonishment. Terror is key. As Burke put it: "Terror is *in all cases whatsoever*, either more openly or latently *the ruling principle* of the sublime" (Burke 1990: 54, emphasis added). For Burke, there can be no sublime without terror, and wherever there is terror there is also, at least potentially, the feeling of the sublime. In Immanuel Kant's formulations, this moment of terror is specified as the power of raw nature to overwhelm and render helpless our faculty of imagination (Kant 1987: 106, 120–21). The exemplars of the sublime remained, at least through the nineteenth century, raging storms, earthquakes, erupting volcanoes, avalanches, and the like—what we now call natural disasters—or else the vast desolation of mountains, deserts or ice fields, the starry sky or the high seas.

A direct encounter with the violence or overwhelming immensity of nature could precipitate a plunge into pure, undiluted terror. But to contemplate such scenes from a position of relative safety renders the feeling of terror somehow delightful and fascinating. The sublime always has to do with terror, then, but not pure, immediate terror: It is rather terror mediated by a certain physical or temporal distance and compounded with enjoyment and fascination—a strange and singular mix of pleasure and pain.

In the twentieth century, however, the unprecedented scale and intensity of two world wars radically transforms the traditional category of the sublime. Over the course of this bloody century, eruptions of human violence come to displace nature as the exemplary object of the sublime. The catastrophic violence humans inflict on other humans becomes more terrible and terrifying than the power and size of nature. To inflect Georg Lukács's Marxist–Hegelian idiom, we could say that the sublime begins as an effect of *first nature*. But in the twentieth century these complex feelings become associated more with the self-made disasters of society, or *second nature*. This shift in the object of the sublime—from first to second nature—is a long time taking hold in critical discourses but is consolidated in the decades following 1945.

The trauma of the Second World War was decisive. By most estimates, this global bloodletting took between 50 and 60 million lives, although some recent accounts put the number as high as 70 million. Of the dead, something like two-thirds were civilians. I want to suggest that two events of violence in particular compelled the displacement of first nature within the category of the sublime. Auschwitz and Hiroshima both realize qualitative leaps in the human power and capacity for organized violence.

Very schematically: Auschwitz realizes the qualitatively new potential for systematic genocide inherent in the technics and logics of rationalized industrial commodity production, when these are put at the disposal of state administration and directed toward the aim of mass murder. Hiroshima realizes the qualitatively new potential for genocidal destruction inherent in the project of modernist science, when all the state-directed resources of research and development and rationalized production are mobilized for the war machine. The extermination camp or factory and the all-too-real doomsday weapon—the so-called weapon of mass destruction (WMD)—set the new standards for terror and sublimity. The shift, again, is from the power, violence, and size of first nature to the violent potentialities of second nature, or society itself. Viewed in this way, beyond all the obvious differences in their specific historical character and in the political forms and aims of the governments that realized them, Auschwitz and Hiroshima are shorthand for qualitatively new powers of violence gained by the nation-state. That these possibilities were historically realized is a new *social fact* (I follow Adorno [2000: 50]

165

here in his critical appropriation of Émile Durkheim's notion of "*fait social*") that quite properly should terrify us far more than the random natural disasters of old.

This shift is indeed a radical transformation of the sublime. In the traditional sublime—above all as formulated by Kant—the encounter with the power or size of first nature is ultimately the occasion for reaffirming human freedom and dignity. The helpless distress of the imagination before the power and violence of raw nature turns out merely to have been the trigger for a reassertion of the faculty of reason and for a reflection on man's supersensible dignity and destiny (Kant 1987: 106, 121). As the basis for moral freedom and human autonomy, reason is the capacity that ostensibly raises humanity above mere sensible nature and the blind play of forces, drives, and instincts. So humans need not be in terror of natural power, for they are reassured of their superiority over it. After 1945, however, this compensatory pleasure of self-admiration becomes highly improbable.

Poetry "after Auschwitz"

In light of the transformation of the sublime, we can read Adorno's argument concerning the predicament of culture "after Auschwitz" across the four passages in which it is advanced and revisited. The first occurs at the end of the programmatic essay "Cultural Critique and Society," written in 1949. In it, Adorno positions critical theory's dialectical approach to culture as a necessary corrective both to a "transcendental" ideology critique that rejects *Kultur* in toto and an "immanent" critique that restricts itself to the criteria that culture itself has generated. Cultural critics of this latter kind aim to reassert art's autonomy and deplore its corruption by commerce and other contemporary social forces. But because they never manage to attain a sufficiently critical position *vis-à-vis* culture as such, they ultimately contribute to its fetishization and reification as *Kultur*. "They help to weave the veil" (Adorno 1976: 9; 1992b: 20).

Critical theory shows the inadequacy of classic ideology critique, for contemporary culture tends to merge with society as a totality of processes—the untrue whole or *Ganzen*. The totality of life-processes tends to become *Kultur*. "Today ideology means society as appearance" (Adorno 1976: 25; 1992b: 31). Adorno and Horkheimer's term "*Kulturindustrie*," introduced in 1947 in *Dialectic of Enlightenment*, names this tightening nexus of relations and processes, which tends to eliminate artistic autonomy as it instrumentally valorizes, adapts, and absorbs culture (Horkheimer and Adorno 1969, 2002). With regard to the project of enlightened emancipation, these tendencies are disastrous, for they corrode and block the autonomous subjectivity that is the very condition of any critical enlightenment. It is this historical development that Adorno calls "integration society" (*Einheitsgesellschaft*) or, more provocatively, "absolute integration" (Adorno 1976: 30; 1992b: 34; 1966: 353; 1995: 362).

In this context, the place-name Auschwitz appears in the passage that ends the essay as a kind of eruption:

> The more total the society, so also the more reified the spirit [*Geist*] and more paradoxical its plan to wrest itself from reification on its own. Even the utmost consciousness of disaster threatens to degrade into chatter. Cultural critique finds itself facing the last stage of the dialectic of culture and barbarism: after Auschwitz, to write a poem [*ein Gedicht*] is barbaric, and this situation eats into even the

process of knowing and speaking about why it has become impossible to write poetry [*Gedichte*] today.

(Adorno 1976: 30–31; 1992b: 34, translation modified)

Auschwitz is not itself the disaster, but rather proof of the genocidal potential of the social tendencies toward absolute integration and the elimination of autonomous culture and its subjectivity. In social terms, the catastrophe has happened and is ongoing, and Auschwitz, as Adorno will put it in *Negative Dialectics*, is only its "first test-piece" or sample (Adorno 1966: 353; 1995: 362).

What is it about Auschwitz that thereafter makes writing poetry both barbaric and "impossible"? The claim entailed by the term "impossible" is obviously not empirical, for poems still are written. And there is more at stake than a simple judgment that writing poems would now be extremely distasteful. Adorno's reticence to say more makes the sentence rather cryptic. His later revisitations will clarify much. In the meantime, we are on notice: the social tendency to eliminate the autonomous subject is backed up by the capacity and willingness to murder categories of individuals industrially. Writing poems as if nothing has changed is so inadequate a response that it slips over into barbarism. Poetry seems to stand synecdochically for all of the inherited forms of art and culture. The passage implies a summary judgment—a social verdict against art.

Adorno's revisitations

Adorno reconsiders this verdict in the 1962 essay "Engagement." In a polemic against the committed writing of Jean-Paul Sartre and Bertolt Brecht, he writes:

> I am not inclined to relax the severity of the proposition, that to go on writing lyric poetry [*Lyrik*] after Auschwitz is barbaric; in it is expressed negatively the impulse animating committed literary work. The question of a character in [Sartre's] *Morts sans sepulture*, "Is there sense in living, when there are people who beat you until your bones break?," is also the question whether art should still exist at all; whether spiritual regression in the concept of committed literature is not urged on by the regression of society itself. But [Hans Magnus] Enzensberger's retort also remains true, that literature must withstand this very verdict, must be in such a way that it does not by its very existence after Auschwitz give itself up into the hands of cynicism. It is literature's own situation that is paradoxical, and not one's attitude toward it. The excess of real suffering tolerates no forgetting; Pascal's theological dictum "On ne doit plus dormir" is to be secularized. But this suffering, what Hegel called the consciousness of affliction, also demands the continuation of the very art it forbids; hardly anywhere else does suffering still find its own voice, the consolation that does not at once betray it.
>
> (Adorno 1981: 422–23; 1992a: 87–88, translation modified)

Whereas the first formulation only expresses the untruth of contemporary art, Adorno now begins to acknowledge the remnants of truth that may still belong to it. Art, he concedes, still gives suffering "its own voice." In *Negative Dialectics*, published four years later, he writes: "The need to let suffering be spoken is the condition of all truth" (Adorno 1966: 27; 1995: 17–18). Thus Adorno acknowledges that art must go on after

167

Auschwitz, even if it can only do so truthfully by finding a way to bear its failure without cynicism and to give suffering its own voice without immediately betraying it. Adorno begins, in the same essay, to unfold a case for a "negative" modernist art—exemplified by the unflinching but rigorously indirect work of Beckett—that would avow Auschwitz without ever speaking its name. This call for "negative presentation" of the social catastrophe is Adorno's rewriting of the sublime (Ray 2005: 19–32; 2009).

Philosophy too must find a way to bear culture's failure, in which it participates. Critical reflection on this predicament is the burden of *Negative Dialectics*. In "After Auschwitz," the first of the "Meditations on Metaphysics" that end this work, Adorno concedes the possibility that his first formulation may have been too one-sided:

> Perennial suffering has as much right to expression as the martyred one has to scream; thus it may have been wrong [to have proposed] that after Auschwitz not one more poem can be written.
>
> (Adorno 1966: 353; 1995: 362–63, translation modified)

The phrase "perennial suffering" here is remarkable. In Adorno, "perennial" points to the dynamic stasis of capitalist society, in which instrumental reason and universalized exchangeability drive the "ever new production of the always-the-same" (Adorno 1976: 13–14; 1992b: 23). Contrary to what a precipitous reading would expect, the suffering referred to here is not that of the victims of Auschwitz. Rather, it is the social misery generated continuously by "late capitalism"—by antagonistic society in the last stage of the dialectic of enlightenment.

In the second "Meditation," given the heading "Metaphysics and Culture," Adorno elaborates culture's aporia:

> Culture shudders at stench because it itself stinks; because its palace, as Brecht put it in a magnificent line, is built out of dog shit. Years after this line was written, Auschwitz demonstrated culture's failure irrefutably. That it could happen in the midst of all the traditions of philosophy, art, and the enlightening sciences says more than merely that these traditions—spirit—were unable to take hold of people and change them. In these branches themselves, in the emphatic claim of their autarky, untruth is squatting. After Auschwitz, all culture, including the urgent critique of culture itself, is garbage. In restoring itself after what took place without resistance in its own landscape, culture has become entirely the ideology it was potentially since the time when, opposing material existence, it presumed to inspire that existence with light—the same light refused it by the division of spiritual from manual labor. Those who plead for the preservation of this radically guilty and shabby culture make themselves its accomplices, while whoever spurns culture directly promotes the barbarism that culture revealed itself to be. Not even silence leads out of this circle; silence only rationalizes individual subjective incapacity with the status of objective truth, thereby once more degrading truth into lie.
>
> (Adorno 1966: 357–58; 1995: 367, translation modified)

Culture's failure, its complicity with untruth, has been exposed "irrefutably." To go on now, culture accommodates itself to a structural barbarism liable to genocidal explosions. But to give up and fall into silence cedes the field; to become hostile to culture gives barbarism a hand directly. Can't go on, go on. The echoes of Beckett are no accident. Adorno's negative modernism does not relieve art of its guilt or restore culture to its old glory. For him, it is the only reach for truth left for art after culture's exposure.

Adorno returns to his "after Auschwitz" verdict once more in 1967, in "Is Art Lighthearted?"

> Art, which if not reflective is no longer possible at all, must swear itself off of lightheartedness. Compelling it to do so above all is what happened in the recent past. The proposition that after Auschwitz not one more poem can be written does not hold utterly, but it is certain that after this event, because it was possible and remains possible into the unforeseeable future, lighthearted art is no longer tenable. Objectively, it degrades into cynicism, however much it would like to rely on the goodness of human understanding.
>
> (Adorno 1981: 603–04; 1992a: 251, translation modified)

Here, for Adorno, the provocation "after Auschwitz" is not an absolute prohibition, but it does mark the end of the old joy in artistic mimesis and representation. The element of semblance and free play is an inherent structural element of all art and cannot be revoked. But after Auschwitz it cannot be art's undiluted principle—at least not without collapsing into cynicism. Culture in class society has always been "subject to a historical dynamic" between the lightness of its impulse to autonomy and the seriousness that is not blind to social facts and so sees its own performative contradiction (Adorno 1976: 600–02; 1992a: 248–50). Art must now bear this tension consciously and seek forms that will be neither one nor the other alone.

State terror and capitalist modernity

The dialectic of culture and barbarism continues to unfold. Adorno would have been the last to exempt it from history. The task of a critical theory of culture is to track and analyze this unfolding in the ciphers of contemporary social facts and works of art. Adorno argued that Auschwitz was a kind of irreversible liquidation of metaphysical optimism. But for the reasons I have already indicated, we have to include Hiroshima to properly grasp what has changed. For these two events together accomplish a terrible and deep-reaching ruination that shakes—or should shake—human self-confidence and optimism to the core.

After 1945, we could say, a gap opens between, on the one hand, a fundamental uncertainty that surrounds our notions of humanity and the future, and, on the other hand, the officially proclaimed and manufactured optimism surrounding the over-production and consumption of commodities. Objectively, the meaning of what happened is that the myth of automatic progress is dead—the future will from now on be in doubt. But the postwar "economic miracles" of reconstruction and growth make it possible to repress the meaning of this history in everyday life: Despite what happened, I'm optimistic because I have a house full of things and next year I hope to buy a new car. For critical theory, in the wake of Auschwitz and Hiroshima, the Enlightenment notion of progress that informs Kant's sublime becomes naïve, when not obscene. For these staggering events establish that society, in its capacities for violence, has escaped rational, humane control and generated atrocities that cannot be folded back into any redemptive narrative of progress.

It is important to note that the new powers of violence out of the box after 1945 belong to the modern nation-state, with its monopoly on violence and its power to declare the *state of emergency* or *exception*—that is, as the rightwing legal theorist Carl Schmitt famously put it, the sovereign power to declare the existence of an absolute and intolerable *enemy* (Schmitt 1996: 27–45; 2006). The state, in declaring a state of emergency, invokes the rule of law *to exempt itself from the rule of law*: it gives itself permission to do whatever it deems necessary to crush the enemy, and the state alone will decide when it is safe to return to normality. It is the declared state of emergency that self-authorizes the state to take control of whole sectors of science and the economy and to mobilize all techno-instrumental capacities toward political ends, including the end of terror.

Whatever we are officially told today, terror remains above all the prerogative of the nation-state. Objectively, we have far more to fear from the state than from its challenging others, however brutal and excessive certain of those others—al-Qaeda and such—may be. The contemporary sublime is linked irreducibly to *state terror and violence*, and events since 2001 and the so-called "war on terror" do not change that at all. In the end, the terrible, sublime new powers that the state holds in reserve are products of *capitalist modernity* itself—that is, of techno-productive power and administrative reason developed within the frame of the modern nation-state and under the globally dominant logic of capitalist social relations. This is to say that *second nature is capitalist*: it is the society and world system that capitalist modernity produced. And so to speak of the sublime today is to speak of the terror of wars and genocidal eruptions, but also, necessarily, of the terror and violence of the nexus of social relations and processes as a global totality. It is no secret that the global logic of this totality is war—an unceasing and unforgiving war of all against all. When Thomas Hobbes penned this memorable phrase in the seventeenth century, he was describing a projected hell—the anarchic state of nature from which the modern state and the rule of law supposedly deliver us. But we will be excused, I trust, for having doubts about this kind of deliverance.

In the ideology of capital, competition is a social asset and spur to progress; war, in contrast, is a mistake, a slip into excess or miscalculation to be corrected by a return to the market. Unhappily, this distinction between competition and war is spurious. Under capitalism, competition is generalized and enforced. What I want to insist on is that the logic of competition is a *logic of war* that pushes against and takes aim at all values and logics that would constrain it—and for this reason it in fact leads to war, in the common sense of open armed conflict. This would be the structural barbarism that Adorno famously called "perennial catastrophe"—of which Auschwitz was only "the first test-piece" (Adorno 1976: 16; 1992b: 25; 1966: 353; 1995: 362).

One challenge for critical thought today is to grasp the current wars and occupations not merely as resource wars or imperialist adventures—they certainly are those—but more fundamentally as *wars of systemic enforcement*. In other words, we need to understand how violence is structurally generated by the very same social relations and logics that seemed to provide us with—or at least promise—material security and prosperity based on a superabundance of commodities. And more than that, we need to grasp how the brutal atrocities that strike us with fear today in fact function as means by which the global status quo maintains its power and hold over us—declaring and at the same time continuously generating the absolute enemy, from which, we are told, the state alone can protect us.

170

The "war on terror" is an efficient way of generating fear and maintaining the conditions of emergency—which perhaps have turned permanent war and crisis into a conscious *modus operandi* and new normality. After the atrocities of September 2001, Bush performed the speech acts of emergency, famously activating the friend–enemy distinction and invoking the reasons of state and language of exception—even as he enjoined Americans to go shopping. The laws granting expanded and exceptional powers quickly followed. The problem is that with such a schizophrenic normalization of emergency, it is difficult to see how the situation can end. According to the strategic calculation of the militarists of the "full spectrum dominance" school, the US has a better chance of maintaining its top position against rival nation-states and emerging blocs in a situation of generalized fear and terror and continuous emergency than in one characterized by a relative absence of war, in which democratic aspirations from below could hope and work for their global realization. It is the attempt to understand this new situation in terms of a logic of systemic enforcement that I admire about Retort's (2005) analysis, in *Afflicted Powers,* of what they call "military neo-liberalism" and the functions of failed states and weak citizenship.

Reinventing revolution

From these critical propositions I draw three conclusions:

First, unlike the sublime terror of first nature, that of second nature is *social in origin* and should in theory bear the openings for a *social solution*. However, since these capacities are the products of capitalist modernity and its relentless logics, if there is a way out for us, it can only be through a passage to a different social logic and order—a system of human relations not based on domination and exploitation. "Capitalism," Walter Benjamin warned us, "will not die a natural death"—though it may deliver us up to common ruin (Benjamin 1999: 667).

Second, the real terror is the threat that system change is no longer possible—the threat that there is no way out of this *capitalist thing*, this race to the bottom. This is the threatening claim of established power that history has ended, having realized itself in the current status quo. "There is no alternative," as Margaret Thatcher pompously put it. This is of course a claim, not a certain fact. The fact is we don't know—and can't know in advance—whether or not a system change to something better than capitalism is possible. But this absolute insistence that it isn't may be the most threatening terror of all, a paralyzing terror that would rob us at once of history and a future. This is indeed the terrifying, sublime, spectacular message continuously repeated by the voice of power today.

Third, as far as the power of art to respond to this predicament goes, we had better abandon all illusions before entering through the gallery gates. The promise of art to improve us and raise us out of barbarism was always overblown; Adorno in any case insisted that Auschwitz was the end of any claims for the power of culture; not even art's "right to exist" can be taken for granted today (Adorno 1997: 1).

I take as sound Adorno's dialectical verdict on culture and his formulation of its post-1945 predicament. His case for an astringent modernism of negative presentation is another matter. There are two compelling arguments for detaching the dialectical critique of culture from the modernist advocacy. In the first place, Adorno did not anticipate how much the forms of remembrance and representation would be instrumentalized and

171

sucked into the so-called culture wars over the course of the 1970s and 1980s. Here, the rise to dominance of Adorno's negative way within the administered art system becomes a sign of its neutralization. Even a sublime art of indirection loses its efficacy and power to avow truthfully when it becomes conventionalized and formulaic. The historical moment when a negative modernism could claim to be the most valid or even the only acceptable artistic response to the social catastrophe has passed (Ray 2005, 2009). It is an open question what can replace it.

Second, Adorno's rejection of committed artistic works is also subject to a historical dynamic. This aspect of Adorno's theory reflects the experiences of Stalinism and the Cold War; its assumptions must be revisited in light of the social struggles of 1968 and their subsequent defeat, the rise of globalizing neo-liberalism, and the collapse of Soviet-style bureaucratic regimes and social orders. Committed avant-garde cultural practices—above all those of the Situationist International (active from 1957 to 1972)— have demonstrated the blind-spots of Adorno's polemics against artistic engagement and shown the way beyond them (Ray 2007a, 2007b, 2007c).

Adorno circled the wagons around the remnant autonomy of the modernist artwork. This kind of retreat is an abandonment of the socially revolutionary impulses of the artistic avant-gardes. Even within the paradigm of the institutionalized and administered bourgeois artwork, Adorno's call for a sublime art of *negative presentation* on the model of Samuel Beckett's *Endgame* is a gambit whose time is past. Moreover, we have to acknowledge that the dialectic of public remembering and forgetting has to a very large extent been instrumentalized by power today. Practices of mourning adequate to this situation merge with the radical critique of existing society. This is so because violence is always traumatic; and everything that belongs to the critical processing of trauma is, in psychoanalytic terms, mourning. Mourning, however, cannot end so long as violence persists; and violence persists so long as it is installed in the dominant social logic.

At the level of representation, there certainly are counter-images to the images of state terror. As markers of a finally unrepresentable excess of trauma, such counter-images can be understood by means of a historicized notion of the sublime. The leaked images of Abu Ghraib are in this sense an answer to the officially disseminated images of the "shock and awe" night bombardment of Baghdad. This kind of image war is real enough: counter-images can produce real material effects and, as Retort (2006: 88) has suggested, can initiate at least momentary shifts in the balance of forces. And what Benjamin called "dialectical images" can generate energies for reigniting the social struggles we inherit as the unpaid debts of history (Benjamin 1999: 463–64; 2003: 390–91). But I doubt that art is any longer the privileged site for the production and circulation of such imagery. The internet would seem to be a far more important global medium for this today. And the fact is that art—even the most critical forms possible within institutions today— cannot in itself be the solution to our problem. What we need is to gain collective control over globalized social relations and processes, and this cannot be done within a differentiated sphere of relative autonomy that is only a subordinated part of a social totality. For this reason, the most effective forms of anti-capitalist art and culture will likely emerge not in the "art world," but in the openings created beyond the art institutions by social movements and struggles. These are in any case the very tough challenges that we—we latecomers, objects of capital, potential subjects of struggle, and a history beyond capitalism—inherit without wanting to. In the end, this is merely to say that terror will remain a central part of our reality unless and until we break its hold over us.

Acknowledgments

This essay incorporates and substantially amplifies for the current volume parts of a text published as "History, Sublime, Terror: Notes on the Politics of Fear" (Ray 2008). The author thanks John Hall for his skillful help with these alterations.

References

Adorno, T.W. 1966. *Negative Dialektik*. Frankfurt am Main: Suhrkamp.
——. 1976 (1955). *Prismen*. Frankfurt am Main: Suhrkamp.
——. 1981 (1958–65). *Noten zur Literatur*. Frankfurt am Main: Suhrkamp.
——. 1992a. *Notes to Literature*, Vol. 2, trans. S. Weber Nicholsen. New York: Columbia University Press.
——. 1992b. *Prisms*, trans. S. Weber and S. Weber. Cambridge, MA: MIT Press.
——. 1995. *Negative Dialectics*, trans. E.B. Ashton. New York: Continuum.
——. 1997. *Aesthetic Theory*, trans. R. Hullot-Kentor. Minneapolis: University of Minnesota Press.
——. 2000. *Introduction to Sociology*, trans. E. Jephcott. Stanford, CA: Stanford University Press.
Benjamin, W. 1999. *The Arcades Project*, ed. R.Tiedemann and trans. H. Eiland and K. McLaughlin. Cambridge, MA: Belknap/Harvard University Press.
——. 2003. "On the Concept of History." In H. Eiland and M. Jennings, eds., *Selected Writings, Volume 4 (1938–1940)*, trans. E. Jephcott *et al*. Cambridge, MA: Belknap/Harvard University Press.
Burke, E. 1990 (1757). *A Philosophical Enquiry into the Origin of our Ideas of the Sublime and Beautiful*. Oxford: Oxford University Press.
Horkheimer, M. and Adorno, T.W. 1969 (1947). *Dialektik der Aufklärung: Philosophische Fragmente*. Frankfurt am Main: Fischer.
——. 2002. *Dialectic of Enlightenment: Philosophical Fragments*, ed. G. Schmid Noerr, trans. E. Jephcott. Stanford, CA: Stanford University Press.
Kant, I. 1987 (1790/3). *Critique of Judgment*, trans. W. Pluhar. Indianapolis: Hackett.
Ray, G. 2005. *Terror and the Sublime in Art and Critical Theory*. New York: Palgrave Macmillan.
——. 2007a. "Avant-Gardes as Anti-capitalist Vector." *Third Text* 86: 241–55.
——. 2007b. "On the Conditions of Anti-capitalist Art: Radical Cultural Practices and the Capitalist Art System." Pp. 239–51 in A. Stopinska, A. Bartels, and R. Kollmorgen, eds., *Revolutions: Reframed, Revisited, Revised (Transpects: Transdisciplinary Perspectives of the Social Sciences and Humanities*, Vol. 5). Frankfurt am Main: Peter Lang.
——. 2007c. "Towards a Critical Art Theory." Pp. 85–97 in G. Raunig and G. Ray, eds., *Art and Contemporary Critical Practices: Reinventing Institutional Critique*. Essex and Vienna: Mayflybooks and European Institute for Progressive Cultural Policies.
——. 2008. "History, Sublime, Terror: Notes on the Politics of Fear." Pp. 23–35 in S. Kealy, ed., *Signals in the Dark: Art in the Shadow of War*. Toronto: Blackwood Gallery/University of Toronto. Revised for *Static* 07, Issue on Catastrophe. Available at http://static.londonconsortium.com/issue07 (accessed October 21, 2008).
——. 2009. "Hits: From Trauma and the Sublime to Radical Critique." *Third Text* 23(2): 135–49.
Retort. 2005. *Afflicted Powers: Capital and Spectacle in a New Age of War*, London: Verso.
——. 2006. "All Quiet on the Eastern Front." *New Left Review* 41: 88–91.
Schmitt, C. 1996 (1932). *The Concept of the Political*, trans. G. Schwab. Chicago: University of Chicago Press.
——. 2006 (1922). *Political Theology: Four Chapters on the Concept of Sovereignty*, trans. G. Schwab. Chicago: University of Chicago Press.

16

Modern and postmodern

Peter Beilharz

What is the modern, and the postmodern? And, why does this matter? What was the controversy about? For it was a controversy; and like others it may have generated more heat than enlightenment. Postmodern versus modern was the key debate in social theory from the 1980s on. In retrospect, it might be seen as a symptom of significant transformations within modernity itself. Likely it represented the anxiety of our age in that moment, and the need to name it. In an even larger proliferation of ways, we now mostly call this anxiety "globalization," though even the heat has gone out of that, too; what originally concerned us as globalization was loss, which now increasingly has been turned into the hope of "gain," that even the wretched of the earth will cheer up if they drink up. What was the fuss about?

There was a sense among intellectuals, anyway, that our world was changing; that there was a sea change, that the old modern ways would no longer do, that if we were still modern we should choose no longer to be. There was a sense of restlessness, of the need to begin anew.

The controversy over the idea of the postmodern was clearly one over naming, over naming our worlds, and ourselves, and of performing this act negatively, against the image of the postwar boom, Fordism, suburbia, the one-dimensional society of that abundance that grew into the 1960s and kept growing thereafter. Whether the postmodern itself is in any way responsible for this or not, the anxiety has in the meantime often turned into celebration, skepticism, into indifference as the progress-narrative of modernity is enthusiastically embraced throughout the world, not least in China and India. What this signals is that the idea of modernization still remains moot. The notion of progress through growth and development has somehow been revived unscathed even though the ecological scene has darkened considerably. Meantime, the semantics of modernity and modernism, kindred yet not identical, also still survive to extend the conceptual confusion.

Conventionally, modernity is understood as a philosophical or sociological term which refers to the idea that we moderns make ourselves, that societies self-constitute their forms, structures, institutions, and relationships. We make our worlds, large and small. And if we do not like the results, we believe we can remake them. Even if we fall easily back on reassurances about evil and human nature, we know that we can do better, that our social arrangements are at least in principle open. Anticipated by humanism, championed by the leading thinkers of the Enlightenment, modernity is viewed as coming historically closer to us with the Age of Revolutions—Industrial, French, American. Modernity comes to mean industrial, though modernization also means more than that, and modernization theory often presumes that industrialization brings all the other advantages of liberal–democratic development with it (not so).

Modernism, in contrast, is less often identified as the culture of modernity than as the aesthetic movement that becomes especially visible around the First World War and mainstreamed with more prominence into the 1960s. Associated in writing with Woolf and Joyce, in architecture with Corbusier, international style, and functionalism, in art with Picasso and Dada, modernism has a whole series of later correlates in industry, reflecting standardization and sleek design, from aerodynamic cars to flying refrigerators. Its high point can be best seen in an artist like Warhol, where avant-garde and mass consumption of repetitive icons merge. Coca-Cola rules (Gideon 1948; Conrad 1998; Gay 2008).

The postmodern is usually identified as a reaction against modernism, rather than modernity. In architecture, for example, functionalism is replaced by novelty, folly, dual-coding, ornament, pastiche; but these features might also be viewed as playfully (or earnestly) modernist. The postmodern involves an aspect of "up yours!" which results in the wider sense that "anything goes!" Semantically, the postmodern might then be identified as the critical rejection of tradition, rather than of modernity; but then there are also earlier traditions of the rejection of modernity, such as romanticism, which complicate all this reception and controversy.

The postmodern also coincides with a Western sense of "being after"; there are many posts, including postindustrialism, postcapitalism, postsocialism, postnationalism, post-structuralism, postcolonialism. The idea of the critique of progress might more precisely be called post-Enlightenment. But this then begs the question whether any of us can step out of modernity, especially in the West. To reject the modern may be impossible, not least because modernity is always anyway a mixed form, itself necessarily combining cultures of past, present, and future. And it is always changing. Modernity might be what Habermas called the unfulfilled project because it is unfulfillable; we are always carrying different traditions, some chosen, some inherited (Habermas 1989). Or as Bruno Latour put it, in a different register, we have simply never been thoroughly modern at all (Latour 1993). "Modernity" always necessarily includes the "premodern," and the postmodern cannot escape either of these.

Central to all of this, finally, is the idea of the decline or exhaustion of the West. If we do not progress, we decline, or else we are doomed to repetition. Each of the three scenarios is plausible. At best, we understand the world better, but no longer claim to know how to better it. Yet the new still continues; innovation and creation still persist. The postmodern is, or was, not only a refiguration of romanticism, reacting against its own image of modernity as hard-headed Enlightenment, but it was also that (Beilharz 1994; Murphy and Roberts 2004).

This much by way of introduction. In order better to map the controversy, we need to enter the labyrinth of some of its key arguments and sensibilities, here by visiting the views of some of its more eloquent and central interlocutors: Jean-François Lyotard, Ferenc Fehér and Agnes Heller, Zygmunt Bauman, Fredric Jameson, and David Harvey.

Where did it all begin, now that the postmodern is history? Is the postmodern indeed passé, history, or have we just grown weary of that particular debate or set of language games? Whatever the case, we need a text to start with. Lyotard's *Postmodern Condition: A Report on Knowledge* is as good a place to start as any. The original French edition, commissioned by the Canadian Conseils des Universitiés de Quebec, was published in 1979, and translated into English in 1984. With the passing of time, its purpose and substance have been forgotten, for it was a report on knowledge and society, explicitly on the knowledge society (Lyotard 1984). Its most famous claim was that the grand narrative of modernity was no longer viable. In this, Lyotard's was another installment in the long history of the critique of Enlightenment. The postmodern era, or attitude, signaled the contemporary incredulity towards metanarrative. Lyotard's target was the kind of project associated with Jürgen Habermas. In Lyotard's gaze, the defense of Enlightenment became the advocacy of Reason and Totalization. Habermas here was the Devil. The critique delivered here therefore echoed the broad sympathy of Foucault's critique of Enlightenment as totalitarian. What was overlooked, in its more generalized reception, was the substantive engagement of the book with the question of the status of knowledge in computerized societies. In retrospect, this particular work of Lyotard really extends McLuhan and anticipates the work of Manuel Castells more than that of Foucault. The distinction between modern and postmodern, here, was more like that between traditional and critical theory articulated in the 1940s by Horkheimer. The claim to truth led to totalitarianism; there would henceforth only be little or personal claims to truth. In a fragmented world, truth would also be fragmented.

Lyotard's missile at least implied a clear periodization: modern was, then, passé, postmodern now, even if the detail of his case occasionally indicated otherwise. Ferenc Fehér and Agnes Heller put a distinct interpretation upon this separation. As they wrote, in *The Postmodern Political Condition*—for Lyotard's title echoed—postmodernity is neither a historical period nor a cultural or political trend with well-delineated characteristics. Rather, postmodernity may be understood as the private-collective time and space, within the wider time and space of modernity, delineated by those who have problems with and queries addressed to modernity, who want to take it to task, and by those who make an inventory of modernity's achievements as well as its unresolved dilemmas. Those who have chosen to dwell in postmodernity nevertheless live among moderns as well as premoderns. For the very foundation of postmodernity consists of viewing the world as a plurality of heterogenous spaces and temporalities. Postmodernity can only define itself within this plurality, against these heterogeneous others (Fehér and Heller 1988: 1).

The issue opened up, or named, so to say, by Lyotard, had become a space or field; and the postmodern was now more fully to be contemplated as a way of thinking about the present. For postmoderns, anything goes. For Fehér and Heller, this told against Europe, and not only against modernity or tradition. Europe risked becoming a museum. The profound sense was one of "being after," being after history, after the modern, after Europe (Fehér and Heller 1988: 2–3). The postmodern in this optic was therefore profoundly aesthetic and cultural, but it had other coordinates as well. Politically it was often self-styled as the avant-garde, but that itself was a strong modernist resonance. As Fehér and Heller had argued earlier, modernity was characterized by three logics, often operating in tension: capitalism, industrialization, and democracy (Fehér and Heller 1983). Technology, science, and economy were also crucial (Heller 1999). The postmodern was not narrowly cultural, or to be read in culturalist terms alone, except in the broader sense that everything is culturally constituted. Postmodernity, in every regard, was parasitic on these dilemmas and achievements of modernity. Its culture fed back off high modern forms and then rebelled against some in particular, as, say, against uniform international style in architecture. But its politics could also look plainly romantic, Dada, in-your-face, the antimodern reacting against modernism within modernity itself.

For Fehér and Heller, then, the postmodern matters because of its impact on the lifeworld; it is a kind of counterculture in modernity. Zygmunt Bauman has also been given to the image of the counterculture, though historically he associates this with socialism as a current within modernity (Bauman 1976; Beilharz 2000, 2008). Bauman's most significant early intervention on the postmodern was *Legislators and Interpreters—On Modernity, Post-Modernity, and Intellectuals* (1987). It is the last term which is most telling here, for Bauman initially views the postmodern as an intellectual rather than popular ambit. The title also indicates the shift: the transition from legislators to interpreters as the dominant ideal type of intellectual coincides with the shift of intellectual focus from government to hermeneutics, from control to interpretation, from the avant-garde to the critic, or, as Bauman frames it, from gardeners back to gamekeepers. Bauman's book therefore includes the critique of modernity as a social engineering project, where the post-modern offers the implicit promise of something gentler. The modern intellectual desires to control cultural matters, taste, morality: These are the secular priests, *les philosophes*. The postmodern is the promise of what comes after this. Is this progress, for Bauman? The answer is both positive and yet somehow noncommittal, wait and see. Bauman already indicates his reservations regarding the seductive and regressive powers of postmodern culture, which after all is mediated by consumerism. He indicates his own deep ambivalence about the postmodern phenomenon by closing *Legislators and Interpreters* with two conclusions, one modern, one post-modern, one, so to say, with Habermas, one with Rorty, one with judgment, one with relativism.

Bauman's *Legislators and Interpreters* is also a shadow critique of communism, specifically of Bolshevism as Enlightenment (Beilharz 2000). For modernity and modernism are not only West European or American forms; every place will have its own modernity, from Melbourne to Montevideo, and Soviet-type societies also have a modern story to tell. Indeed, the Soviets and Nazis in some ways outperform all others at high modernity, where the state drives developmental patterns of destruction to the brink of extinction. Bauman's later writings open up onto the multiplicity of postmodern forms. In *Intimations of Postmodernity* the postmodern is viewed as the mixing of styles and genres, or as a state of mind. It is self-critical, or critical at least; but at the same time, "anything goes." Yet the postmodern also offers the possibility of reenchantment. The postmodern might also be global, or postnational; yet in this it nevertheless constitutes a development of modernity (Bauman 1992: 65, 187). As most critics in the field agree, the postmodern also corresponds with a series of other "afters," "ends," or posts— postindustrial, postcapitalist, later, posttraditional. Yet it remains, for Bauman, primarily an intellectual phenomenon—it throws light on intellectuals, and also on ethics. Thus, his subsequent works include *Postmodern Ethics* (1994) and *Postmodernity and Its Discontents* (1997), and across these the inflection shifts, as the emancipatory promise of the post-modern disappears into the shopping malls. The postmodern mind is tolerant, but then again, everything goes, including poverty and exploitation. Surplus tolerance leads to shared indifference.

For Bauman, as a sociologist, the postmodern is an inescapable phenomenon: whether it is superficial or deep, it is a presence, and therefore begs for interpretation. Nevertheless, Bauman makes his preference clear when he distinguishes between two different projects: a postmodern sociology and a sociology of postmodernity (Bauman 1989). Bauman is a life-long critic, not a celebrant. Yet we are all part of this phenomenon, at the same time. Something like a sense of postmodern fatigue perhaps eventually leads Bauman to coin a new term, "liquid modernity," this in contrast to the high, solid modernism of the postwar period. The analytical tension suggested by the postmodern nevertheless remains.

Two further approaches bring together culture and political economy, in exhaustive scope: these are the work of Fred Jameson and of David Harvey, both of whom reinstall Marx as a central figure for the postmodern, which just goes to show how modern we still are.

Jameson's central work here is *Postmodernism or, The Cultural Logic of Late Capitalism* (1991), built upon his pioneering *New Left Review* essay of 1984. The table of contents of the book indicates the ambition of the survey: it covers culture, ideology, video, architecture, sentences, space, theory, economy, and film. Jameson's broad sensibilities are in sympathy with others scanned here. It is safest to grasp the concept of the postmodern as an attempt to think the present historically in an age that has forgotten how to think historically (Jameson 1991: ix)—that is to say, a present of the present which has forgotten pasts and is blind to the possibility of other futures, or utopias. High commodification, here, is timeless: everything can be exchanged for everything else, as in Marx's critique, which means that at a certain level of abstraction everything becomes leveled, quality indistinguishable. Thus Jameson does seek to periodize the modern and postmodern, but only notionally, in terms of correspondences. He summons the idea of late capitalism, via the thinkers of the Frankfurt School and the Belgian Trotskyist Ernest Mandel, to argue this centrality of periodization. "Late," here, works with "post"; "post" is primarily aesthetic, but late capitalism involves the expansion of the aesthetic and visual. Van Gogh, Magritte, and Corbusier are central actors in this story, but especially Warhol, where standardization includes the aesthetic commodity-image and not only the old commodity-form. Postfunctional architecture, notoriously Portman's Westin Bonaventure Hotel in Los Angeles, offers fully playful and willful expressions of this wave. As Jameson puts it in conclusion, the postmodern is primarily based in visual culture, wired for sound (Jameson 1991: 299). Yet this cultural revolution is also homogenized and always "new." This is the acme of modernization's attack on nature (Jameson 1991: 310–11).

David Harvey works in a similar register to Jameson, even if the entry point is in political economy rather than culture. The title of Harvey's study, like that of Fehér and Heller, continues to echo back to Lyotard—Harvey's variation is *The Condition of Postmodernity* (1989). Harvey begins with the sense of sea-change in political economy from around 1972. The new capitalism brings with it postmodern culture and a further wave of the space–time compression that Marx uses to characterize capitalism's ongoing revolutions. The organizational focus in Harvey's work is the city—here, the postmodern city. Where Jameson tends to feature LA, Harvey's city at this point is Baltimore. His frame of reference is also Marxian, but it is less flavored by the Frankfurt School and more given to the frame provided by Marshall Berman in *All That Is Solid Melts into Air* (1984). From Baudelaire to Berman, this frame centers on aesthetics but also on the revolution in everyday life, on the experience of modernity and modernism on the street. Like Jameson, Harvey views the postmodern as the latest wave of the modernization process, which he connects to Schumpeter's idea of creative destruction, the emphasis here more heavily on noun than adjective (Harvey 1989: 106). The result is influenced by Berman, but is considerably less celebrative of the dizzying success of modernism or what follows. Rather than euphoria on the street, the core of modernism for Harvey is Fordism in factory and home (Harvey 1989: chapter 8). Fordism develops as a total way of life, based on mass production, mass consumption, and standardization. What follows is "flexible accumulation" and postmodern culture. Culture and economy, aesthetic and technological form here combine into one.

So what's new, in all this? Little, and yet so much. This is the world anticipated by Marx, Weber, and Simmel, where time accelerates and space contracts, the world ossifies, culture becomes hard as soon as it emerges, and yet it also seems that all that is solid melts into air. We no longer have a sense of foundations from which to work or to judge, and yet we go on, we rely on a daily sense that everyday life is a matter of business, or busyness as usual. Marx, Weber, and Simmel are all rediscovered or reinvented in the postmodern debate; this may be its most positive effect for the traditions of classical social theory. Durkheim, in turn, is called out again as we reconsider the extent to which (postmodern) cultures make or remake (modern) society or economy. More broadly, in terms of a sociology of everyday life or of cultural sociology in general, the great impact of the postmodern is to force the reconsideration of the root term and the broader horizons of modernity itself. Even if the idea of the postmodern now falls into disuse, its function as a thought-experiment has been to challenge moderns to reconsider the very idea of being modern at all. Even if the postmodern call to justify was often petulant, its results have been productive. To be postmodern, we need to embrace modernity in all its difference, diversity, and ambivalence. To be post, we first of all need to be modern.

References

Bauman, Z. 1976. *Socialism—The Active Utopia*. London: Allen and Unwin.

——. 1987. *Legislators and Interpreters—On Modernity, Post-Modernity and Intellectuals*. Oxford: Polity.

——. 1989. "Sociological Responses to Postmodernity." *Thesis Eleven* 23.

——. 1992. *Intimations of Postmodernity*. London: Routledge.

——. 1994. *Postmodern Ethics*. Oxford: Polity.

——. 1997. *Postmodernity and Its Discontents*. Oxford: Polity.

Beilharz, P. 1994. *Postmodern Socialism—Romanticism, City and State*. Melbourne: Melbourne University Press.

——. 2000. *Zygmunt Bauman—Dialectic of Modernity*. London: Sage.

——. 2005. "Postmodern Socialism Revisited." In P. Hayden and C. Ojeili, eds., *Confronting Globalization*. London: Palgrave.

——. 2008. *Socialism and Modernity*. Minnesota: University of Minnesota Press.

Berman, M. 1984. *All That Is Solid Melts into Air*. New York: Simon and Schuster.

Conrad, P. 1998. *Modern Times, Modern Places*. London: Thames & Hudson.

Fehér, F. and Heller, A. 1983. "Class, Democracy, Modernity." *Theory and Society* 12: 211–44.

——. 1988. *The Postmodern Political Condition*. Cambridge: Polity.

Gay, P. 2008. *Modernism: The Lure of Heresy from Baudelaire to Beckett and Beyond*. New York: Norton.

Gideon, S. 1948. *Mechanization Takes Command*. New York: Oxford University Press.

Habermas, J. 1989. *The Philosophical Discourse of Modernity*. Cambridge: Polity.

179

Harvey, D. 1989. *The Condition of Postmodernity*. Oxford: Blackwell.

Heller, A. 1999. *A Theory of Modernity*. Oxford: Blackwell.

Jameson, F. 1991. *Postmodernism or, The Cultural Logic of Late Capitalism*. London: Verso.

Jencks, C. 1996. *What Is Postmodernism?* London: Academy.

Latour, B. 1993. *We Have Never Been Modern*. Cambridge, MA: Harvard University Press.

Lyotard, J.-F. 1984. *The Postmodern Condition: A Report on Knowledge*. Minneapolis: University of Minnesota Press.

Murphy, P. and Roberts, D. 2004. *Dialectic of Romanticism*. New York: Continuum.

Smith, B. 1997. *Modernism's History*. New Haven, CT: Yale University Press.

——. 2007. *The Formalesque*. Melbourne: Macmillan.

17

New sociological narratives of morality under modernity

From subtraction to multiplicity

Mary Jo Neitz, Kevin McElmurry, and
Daniel Winchester

From its inception, sociology has been engaged with questions concerning the relationships between morality, religion, and the modern condition. Such questions are central to the sociologies of Durkheim and Weber as well as prominent contemporary scholars like Robert Bellah, Peter Berger, Zygmunt Bauman, and Robert Putnam. Despite the diversity of ideas within this long tradition of theorizing modern moral and religious life, both classical and contemporary accounts have largely been organized within a narrative of moral decline. It is a narrative of crisis and loss, a story with a rather tragic plotline. This story has been told, in various ways, by some of sociology's most eminent voices. It is a story that goes something like this:

> Once upon a time, in a social world far, far away, human beings lived under the yoke of moral orders. People lived short, hard lives working under the authority of various monarchs, feudal lords, and religious authorities. Literacy rates were low. Disease and morbidity rates were high. All social statuses were ascribed. Yet, despite all this, moral life flourished. People lived in close, integrated communities. They acted out of a sense of duty, obligation, and honor with regard to those around them. Steeped in a moral order based on rigid hierarchy and unwavering belief in a common religious culture, people knew where they stood in relation to what was good and valuable in life. There were no grand quests for meaning, no existential crises, no need for psychotherapists or guidance counselors. People lived their lives as characters in well-worn scripts. The good life was already spelled out; one only had to live out the script one's betters and one's gods had written.
>
> But then modernity brought profound changes unsettling everything people thought they knew about ethical and religious life. Capitalism replaced an agrarian economy with urban industry, alienating people from the land and the substantive value of their labor. Differentiation between church, state, home, and market stretched and strained the well-woven social fabric, leading to more individual freedom but also breeding feelings of anomie, narcissism, and distrust. Science and rationality disenchanted the world and reduced belief in the gods to superstition. As people turned away from their gods and toward their own powers

of reason, they gave up any sense of moral obligation beyond their own needs, wants, and desires.

Or so the story goes. Most readers will recognize the various threads of this narrative. This narrative of moral and religious decline amounts to what Charles Taylor (2007) calls a "subtraction story" of modernity: as societies become modern, "traditional" elements like faith, virtue, morality, and substantive ethics are inevitably subtracted from the mix of cultural life. It has certainly been a persuasive story, and while originally describing changes in Europe, it has influenced and directed sociological inquiry into ethical and religious life more generally for quite some time. But a good deal of contemporary thinking and research in cultural sociology and beyond has demonstrated that the subtraction narrative—for all its coherence and elegance—has failed to tell the whole story. In fact, research suggests that morality, ethics, and religiosity still matter a great deal in the late modern world, in the global North, and in the global South, but often in ways the subtraction narrative would not anticipate.

In this chapter, we bring together some of this research. We argue that research on contemporary moral and religious life is developing a new story, one not of subtraction but, rather, of multiplicity. This multiplicative story of modern moral life differs from the subtraction narrative in a number of important ways. First, as the numerical descriptor implies, a multiplicative narrative is a multivocal text; the story is not told from the position of a common moral culture (or lack thereof) but by a multiplicity of moral and religious voices coming together and moving apart in various degrees of harmony and conflict.

Second, a different theme characterizes a multiplicative story of modern moral and religious life. While the subtraction story is characterized by tragedy, the multiplicative narrative is best distinguished by suspense and sometimes mystery. In a multiplicative story, one does not always already know how the story will end. Indeed, the story could turn out to be tragic, but it could also be comedic, happy, violent, shocking, epic, mundane, etc. A multiplicative narrative is open-ended and unpredictable; one does not know how (or if) the story will take shape or end.

Third, being implicated in a multiplicative narrative of modern moral life places social actors (including sociologists) on a different normative terrain. In many ways, the subtraction story of moral life lets its characters off the proverbial hook. They may lament the condition of a fallen, disenchanted world; they may critique and rail against it in bellicose terms. But, ultimately, there is not much one can do about it. The story itself has already been written. Modernity will prevail, and morality, ethics, and the sacred will perish or be relegated to the periphery of life. A multiplicative story, however, demands that actors, situated as they are within the multiple moral and religious storylines that characterize contemporary life, make choices. Actors within a world characterized by moral multiplicity must exercise judgment, cultivate ethical sensibilities, confront, recognize, adopt, and disagree with different ways of being. Being a character in a multiplicative narrative means that one *can* act ethically in the modern world—even if doing so is complicated and even when a tragic outcome is always a distinct possibility.

Ultimately, we argue that telling a multiplicative story means moving away from grand narratives about a singular moral order and common religious culture (or lack thereof) and engaging in more grounded empirical work that examines how particular moral orders and identities are produced, negotiated, and put to use within and through specific sociocultural contexts. It also means attending to the ways that moral orders are produced outside the boundaries of institutional religion. It means, in short, telling a piece of the story, attending to a few of the many voices that make up contemporary moral and religious life with theoretical sophistication and empirical rigor. In what follows, we highlight research on moral orders that we believe represents this kind of work, research that opens up space for asking and addressing new questions about moral multiplicity and complexity. To illustrate these issues we highlight studies on (1) moral boundaries, (2) moral conflict, (3) hybridity, and (4) spirituality. Our examples point to general processes but show them at work among specific peoples and places, including evangelicals in the United States, Pentecostals in Nigeria, Hindi fundamentalists in India, and Thai immigrants in the United States.

Boundaries

Subtraction stories of moral decline might be understood from within their own contexts as reactions to a decline in the taken-for-granted universal authority of a moral ordering that developed in a particular time and place. In the United States that place was New England. As frontier settlements pushed further westward throughout the nineteenth century, the image of the New England town square anchored on one side by a substantial Protestant church became further removed from the daily experiences of citizens. This was especially true for immigrant populations caught between the cross-pressures of collective identity and assimilation. For regions of the United States settled apart from the eastern colonies, like the Northwest, the Protestant vision of moral order may not have held sway over popular imagination (Silk 2005). Regional comparisons highlight the particularity of a narrative genre that invokes themes of decline and loss. Comparisons such as these may afford scholars a more nuanced and critical view of religious hegemony (Long 2008).

Increasing urbanization in the east and (mid)west brought with it further growth within and contact among new populations, deepening the sense of loss of an over-arching moral order. However, this was a sense of loss rooted largely in the experiences of white, middle-class members of historically mainline Protestant communities. The work of moral ordering can be examined in the creation and maintenance of symbolic, social, and spatial boundaries like those that emerged historically in the US.

The study of boundary work, long part of the social science tradition, has blossomed in recent scholarship on collective identities, inequalities, social organization, and spatial borders (see Lamont and Molnar 2002 for a review). Lamont (1992, 2000) provides a framework for understanding how moral boundary work serves as an important component of racial and class divisions by examining the criteria people in France and the United States use to distinguish between others like and unlike themselves. She finds that the criteria used to distinguish "worthy persons" are rarely the same across social boundaries. For example, black and white working-class men evaluate their relationships to others like and not like themselves using largely incommensurable standards linked to social location (Lamont 2000). The scholarly focus on boundary-making activity emphasizes the negotiations that sustain multiple overlapping moral orders.

An assumption among observers of American culture has long been that religion is a constitutive carrier of moral order for society (Tocqueville 2000 [1835]). This is true even in a period of relative diversity and ecumenicist impulse in a nation where religion often takes multiple forms. Edgell, Hartmann, and Gerteis (2006) have observed that a scholarly meta-narrative of religious change in twentieth-century US is formed of three strands: (1) the positing of a foundational link between religious belonging and American-style democracy; (2) a focus on a Christian convergence around a common Judeo-Christian creed; and (3) a corresponding emphasis on pluralism. They suggest that this broadly construed formulation of "being religious" marks off wide spaces of inclusion while serving as a resource for personal and public identities. Edgell, Hartmann, and Gerteis focus on the rejection of atheists (religions' "Other") to provide content to cultural membership, highlighting unacknowledged assumptions linking religious identity, citizenship, and a moral worth in the US.

Contemporary trends among conservative US evangelicals provide an instructive example of boundary work in the production of exclusivist moral orders under conditions of increasing pluralism. As mainline Protestantism has ceased to be the taken-for-granted religious form and denominational affiliation has become less central to individual religious identification, large independent and non-denominational churches have grown in size and public stature. These conservative congregations often position themselves as a committed and contentious minority in a culture hostile to their vision of a good society. Even their location on the edge of many towns and cities suggests this outsider stance. But rather than adopt the high-boundary sectarian orientation of previous generations, many of these churches instead pursue their own "cultural Other," sometimes imagined, like the atheists described above, as an alienated non-believer seeking moral direction.

River Chapel (pseudonym) is one such conservative congregation, located in the midwest, with cultural and organizational roots in the Southern Baptist tradition (McElmurry forthcoming). Like many evangelical churches inspired by the success of the Chicago-area megachurch Willow Creek, River Chapel was imagined by its founders as a church where the morally unanchored "seeker" would feel welcome. Theologically, the founders are committed to an exclusivist vision of truth and moral order. Yet, in order to share their vision, they are equally committed to eliminating outward distinctions between themselves and those they perceive as others. Like missionaries to a foreign nation, the staff at River Chapel see themselves as engaging with an exotic and "Other" postmodern culture on its own terrain and in its own language. In their efforts to create an environment where people can experience a moral order that hinges on feeling a personal connection between themselves and god, they stage elaborate weekly productions emulating popular music concerts with a "culturally relevant" biblical message.

Pursuit of the seeker renegotiates boundaries between sacred and secular culture, believers and non-believers. Conservative churches like River Chapel have rejected much of the distinctiveness of earlier, more sectarian, fundamentalism in favor of relevance for and appeal to skeptical non-believers. Organizers imagine that intended audience members are intimidated by the language and symbols of a tradition with which they are not familiar and are more likely to participate if many of the outward symbolic boundaries marking the religious community are downplayed or eliminated. To this end, the seeker church eliminates much of the traditional language and symbols of the faith. In buildings that resemble light-manufacturing plants, crosses, stained glass, and pictures are replaced by state-of-the-art sound and video projection systems. Worship music is virtually indistinguishable from the adult oriented rock radio format, and moral principles are illustrated through excerpts from popular television programs like *Friends* or *ER*. In the seeker church the moral boundary is both widened (television programs and rock songs can symbolize god's love) and individualized (it is the profession of the faith that marks one as inside.) In this case, cultural content from outside is freely appropriated in the service of maintaining an exclusive identity (McElmurry forthcoming).

Conflict

In the evangelical US example, negotiating the boundaries between postmodern culture and moral conservatism results in embracing "outside" cultural forms while maintaining a distinctive identity, with little apparent conflict. However, our argument for a multiplicative story does not imply that all stories have equal weight or that the multiple stories always co-exist in an atmosphere of harmony and mutual respect. Multiple groups with diverse perspectives do not automatically constitute pluralism or imply some level of mutual acceptance (Wuthnow 2004). In history, it is easy to find examples of religious groups' intolerance and even violent persecution of members of other groups. In the current era, we also find traditionally based religious moral orders positioning themselves against each other and modernity itself. Yet those who rely on tradition and condemn modernity are often marked by the modern context in one way or another.

Thus, fundamentalism, as we understand it, is a reaction to modernity and the cultural pluralism that came with it. The word was first used to describe a dispute within US Protestantism at the beginning of the twentieth century between those who followed the new critical scholars who read the Bible as a historical text and those who opposed modernist thought. The latter published a series of pamphlets between 1910 and 1915 called "The Fundamentals," staking out their anti-modern position (Marsden 1980). This was a battle among seminary elites, and within the mainline denominations the modernist position by and large won out. After the Scopes trial in 1925, fundamentalists withdrew from public debates. By the 1970s, however, they reemerged with a strong institutional base from which to renew the fight against a society which violated their sense of moral order. In the United States, issues of sexuality, abortion, and gender roles were particularly salient, and in schools concerns about teaching evolution and prayer continued to be important. What is interesting is that the reemergence of a public battle between fundamentalists and secular humanism in the United States coincided with the emergence of fundamentalist movements in most of the world religions and in places as diverse as Israel, Iran, Egypt, India, and Indonesia. Although there is disagreement as to whether these diverse movements can all be captured under the generic frame of fundamentalism, nonetheless across the locales we see a defense of religion in response to secularism and modernity (Riesebrodt 2000).

We can only understand the moral programs of fundamentalism by locating particular expressions in relation to the modern secularizing movements and moral orders which they accompany (Emerson and Hartman 2006). For example, the recent conflict around the wearing of headscarves by female Muslim students is different in Turkey than in France, although it occurs in both places. Turkey and France have had their own particular battles between secularizing states and religious authorities; however, in France wearing the headscarf also constitutes an assertion of Muslim identity in families who have moved from countries in which to be Muslim was to be in the majority to a place where they are part of a cultural minority.

The drawing of boundaries by sectarian organizations can promote not only challenges, but violent conflicts. In India today competing movements combine ethnic, religious, and nationalist claims in their attempts to vie for cultural and political sovereignty. The largest Hindu nationalist movement, the *Rashtriya Svayamsevak Sanngh*, and its women's wing, the *Samiti*, believe that Hindu culture and religion should be the basis for citizenship; for them unassimilated Muslims constitute an unwelcome other. A study of Hindu nationalist paramilitary camps for women shows how middle-class women learn to think of themselves as potential victims of attack by Muslim males, reinscribing nationalist loyalties through intellectual, emotional, and embodied practices (Sehgal 2007). Physical training sessions occupy much of the time, with instruction in yoga, martial arts, fighting with wooden staves and daggers, marching, and games all included in the regimen. The camps propagate the three Samiti discourses—female empowerment, constructing Hindu women as active and powerful citizen agents and mothers to the nation, and an underlying nationalist discourse of duty and self-sacrifice for the nation. Sehgal argues that the physical training, however, brought to the surface women's generic fears of male violence, and portrayed that violence as occurring in public spaces and during riot-like circumstances: "Since these women had seldom directly encountered Muslim men in their daily lives, this depiction diverted their attention from harassment and violence in their homes and communities and focused it on a largely fictive threat" (2007: 177). The training taught routines that were more dancelike than defensive, and failed to teach maneuvers that would actually be of use to women in any confrontation. Yet through the use of political arguments, religious stories, and the embodied experience of imagining attackers, the women "internalized a bodily memory of a Muslim rapist against whom Hindu women needed to defend themselves" (Sehgal 2007: 180). While we characterize Samati as a right wing fundamentalist organization, even here a close look shows modern elements layered with the old in the production of the boundary that enforces the tradition of the moral Hindu woman.

Hybridity

In less antagonist circumstances, boundaries might be bridged rather than defended. In contrast with the above examples of cultural conflict, another response to cultural multiplicity is hybridity, a dynamic process of cultural change through incorporating elements of other cultures. One example is the diffusion of Pentecostalism in the non-Western world, especially South America and Africa. A religious movement originating in the United States at the beginning of the twentieth century among African-American and white practitioners of Holiness sects, the movement got off the ground with the Azusa Street meetings in Los Angeles. Speaking in tongues, prophesy, and faith healing are among the religious practices that mark Pentecostal services. It is arguably the fastest growing religious movement in the world. A globalization frame might emphasize Pentecostalism as one more cultural export from the United States, and assume that part of what is transmitted from the US institutional base is social and political conservatism. Yet the belief in following the "leadings of the spirit" that is central for Pentecostalism creates an opening for local responses. Across the global South, in addition to proliferating through worldwide denominations such as the Assemblies of God, Pentecostalism is growing through the emergence of local Pentecostal and charismatic churches. Although Christians in these places may take pains to distinguish their beliefs from indigenous ones, using a model of hybridity, we ask how Pentecostalism differs from the North American model in these locations. For example, how do Pentecostals incorporate indigenous religious practices such as prophecy, trance, and healing? We may also need to rethink the assumption that Pentecostals in the global South will be politically conservative (Miller 2007).

An example from a charismatic church in Nigeria shows the impact of charismatic evangelical movements on cultural models of women's sexuality (Pearce 2002). These charismatic groups tend to liberate women from limiting views prevailing in the previously established Christian evangelical churches and in the traditional culture. The charismatic groups encourage women to view sexuality as a sphere of pleasure and self-expression rather than merely a means of producing children. They encourage women to use contraception to limit and space their children as a means of increasing the health and welfare of mothers and children. The charismatic churches also offer an alternative cultural definition of women who do not have children. Instead of seeing these women as "barren" and unfulfilled, these churches offer a number of alternative interpretations and avoid the de-valuation of these women. In addition, the charismatic churches encourage women to consult physicians about issues of fertility, sexuality, and family planning. Finally, these churches support the strengthening of the nuclear family *vis-à-vis* the claims and demands of the extended family. Prophecy and other gifts of the spirit become tools in these Nigerian indigenous charismatic churches. Their complex message puts forth a new moral order that breaks the hold of the traditional society over the nuclear family and the sexuality of women, but at the same time offers clearly defined rules and practices that work for the women and men attracted to these churches.

As is evidenced in what we have said so far, moral orders under modernity are plural, existing in relation to one another and to modern secular culture. Even the most exclusive and fundamentalist sect is affected by the "Others" around it. While we lack the space to explore the question here, some researchers may ask why some groups consciously engage the Other, some hybridize, and others choose conflict. In our examples, we see that these categories are not exclusive and that the boundaries, even for the most sectarian, are continually negotiated in reference to the moral "Others."

Spirituality

Implicit in what we have presented so far is that we also see moral orders as constituted through embodied practices and feelings—the music at River Chapel or the physical training of young Hindu women—as much as through beliefs and values. Refocusing sociological thinking about moral orders on practices, and including what people are doing and feeling, becomes even more important when we begin to conceptualize moral orders outside of the boundaries of institutional religion. In this final section we consider the increasing numbers of people who do not identify with a denomination yet identify as "spiritual"—people who practice meditation, work in soup kitchens, and hear moral tales in contemporary film and television.

In their now classic study of moral community in America, Bellah *et al.* (1985) presented "Sheila Larson" and disparagingly quoted her description of her religion as "Sheilaism." Exemplifying a form of moral order that has become much more visible in recent years, Sheila, without affiliating with any congregation, denomination, or sect, had carefully constructed her own system of practices, beliefs, and values. Similar to others who do not identify with a denomination, Sheila affirmed the idea that "right living" means some kind of conscious attention to ethical life and, perhaps, engaging in some embodied activity.

The relationship between religious organizations and personal spiritual practices similarly demonstrates the multiplicative story. A comparison of two Theravada Buddhist temples, Wat Mongkoltempunee (Wat Phila) in the suburbs of Philadelphia and the Cambridge Insight Meditation Center (CIMC) in Cambridge, Massachusetts, shows that religious traditions do not alone determine what specific practitioners will do (Cadge 2005). The former temple was founded by first-generation Thai immigrants to the United States, while the latter was founded by "reverse messengers"—Americans who went to Asia, converted, and came back to the US to teach others to practice meditation. Different practices define doing Theravada Buddhism at the two centers. At Wat Phila, women give gifts to the monks to attain "merit." At CIMC the emphasis is on meditation. Community (Sangha), too, means different things in the two places. Thai immigrants go to Wat Phila to experience Thai ethnic traditions, while at the meditation center practitioners sit in silence. Both the Thais and the white converts have a hard time seeing what the other does as "practicing Buddhism," but both are concerned with making moral decisions. Whereas others have argued that religious groups thrive by creating tightly bounded subcultures within which individuals construct identities in tension with out groups, here we see groups thriving by crafting a weakly bounded subculture.

Recent explorations of lived religion give us insight into other ways that people co-construct moral orders: through seeking to understand their own embodied experiences, interactions with others, attending workshops, and reading on their own, many people, like Sheila Larson, have their own ways of exercising judgment and cultivating ethical sensibilities. When we try to understand how people become spiritual practitioners, it is clear that we need better tools for understanding religious experiences as sites for the religious imaginary as well as the connections between religious experience and theology (Bender 2007: 203–04).

Conclusion

Boundaries, conflicts, hybridity, diverse spiritual practices, and subjectivities—such are the phenomena constitutive of a multiplicative moral and religious landscape. This landscape is one in which a diverse array of social actors are situated, including, we think it important to note, social scientists. We too are part of the story, even as we attempt to analyze it, discern its numerous plotlines, and theorize its forms and contents.

Indeed, it has become increasingly apparent that a value-free social science is an impossible endeavor, that we cannot somehow extract ourselves from the moral orders that help constitute our social existence (see, for example, Haan et al. 1983; Harding 1986; Smith 2003). Social scientists, like all social actors, are implicated in moral orders and shaped by them, and they bring to their areas of inquiry moral values and sensibilities that cannot simply be left at the door. Given these circumstances, what is the ethical position of the sociologist of religious and moral life within a multiplicative narrative?

As religious historian Robert Orsi (2005) points out, the moral distinctions scholars have so often made between "good" and "bad" religion are not always the result of a sustained and reflective practice of understanding others' moral and religious worlds— and all the good and ugliness associated with those worlds in particular times and places.

Rather, they are often the products of long-held biases crafted within the Western academy and the wider society over the course of historical time. To engage in moral inquiry does not require that we redeem or denounce religious and moral others, even and perhaps especially those we initially find strange or even repugnant. To do so is also not to deny our politics and perspectives. Rather, it is to subject our moral positions to scrutiny, and to enter into moral conversation (which is not the same as conversion) with others, to allow them to subject our moral certainties to the same critical reflection as we often subject theirs. Moral inquiry means, in other words, adding our stories to the mix of moral life. "Understandings of morality represent an engagement in communication; we narrate what we know and we know what we narrate" (Orsi 2005: 204).

The study of moral and religious life, then, requires engaging in a project of understanding. Such a project is a "moral discipline in its commitment to examining the variety of human experience and to making contact across *boundaries*—cultural, psychological, spiritual existential" (Orsi 2005: 203, emphasis added). In a world characterized by moral multiplicity, by both conflict and cooperation, by both positive and tragic possibilities for human actors, this project of conversation and understanding is itself an ethical endeavor of the highest order.

References

Bellah, R., Madsen, R., Sullivan, W.S., Swidler, A., and Tipton, S. 1985. *Habits of the Heart*. Berkeley: University of California Press.

Bender, C. 2007. "Touching the Transcendent." Pp. 201–18 in N.T. Ammerman, ed., *Everyday Religion*. New York: Oxford University Press.

Cadge, W. 2005. *Heartwood*. Chicago: University of Chicago Press.

Edgell, P., Hartmann, D., and Gerteis, J. 2006. "Atheists as Cultural Other: Moral Boundaries and Cultural Membership in American Society." *American Sociological Review* 71: 211–34.

Emerson, M. and Hartman, D. 2006. "The Rise of Religious Fundamentalism." *Annual Review of Sociology* 32: 127–44.

Haan, N., Bellah, R., Rabinow, P., and Sullivan, W.S. 1983. *Social Science as Moral Inquiry*. New York: Columbia University Press.

Harding, S. 1986. *The Science Question in Feminism*. Ithaca, NY: Cornell University Press.

Lamont, M. 1992. *Money, Morals, and Manners: The Culture of the French and American Upper-Middle Class*. Chicago: University of Chicago Press.

——. 2000. *The Dignity of Working Men: Morality and the Boundaries of Race, Class, and Immigration*. Cambridge, MA: Harvard University Press.

Lamont, M. and Molnar, V. 2002. "The Study of Boundaries in the Social Sciences." *Annual Review of Sociology* 28: 167–96.

Long, C. 2008. "New Orleans as an American City: Origins, Exchanges, Materialities, and Religion." Pp. 203–22 in R.J. Callahan, Jr., ed., *New Territories, New Perspectives: The Religious Impact of the Louisiana Purchase*. Columbia, MO: University of Missouri Press.

McElmurry, Kevin. Forthcoming. *Feeling Jesus in the Backbeat: Music and Emotion in a Post-Modern Church*, Ph.D. Dissertation, University of Missouri: Columbia, Missouri.

Marsden, G. 1980. *Fundamentalism in American Culture*. New York. Oxford University Press.

Miller, D. 2007. "Progressive Pentecostals: The New Face of Christian Social Engagement." *Journal for the Scientific Study of Religion* 46: 435–45.

Orsi, R. 2005. *Between Heaven and Earth: The Religious Worlds People Make and the Scholars Who Study Them*. Princeton, NJ: Princeton University Press.

Pearce, T.O. 2002. "Cultural Production and Reproductive Issues: The Significance of the Charismatic Movement in Nigeria." Pp. 21–50 in S. Ellingson and M.C. Green, eds., *Religion and Sexuality in Cross-cultural Perspective*. New York: Routledge.

Riesebrodt, M. 2000. "Fundamentalism and the Resurgence of Religion." *Numen* 47: 266–87.

Sehgal, M. 2007. "Manufacturing a Feminized Siege Mentality: Hindu Nationalist Paramilitary Camps for Women in India." *Journal of Contemporary Ethnography* 36: 165–83.

Silk, M. 2005. "Religion and Region in American Public Life." *Journal for the Scientific Study of Religion* 44: 265–70.

Smith, C. 2003. *Moral Believing Animals: Human Personhood and Culture*. New York: Oxford University Press.

Taylor, C. 2007. *A Secular Age*. Cambridge, MA: Belknap Press.

Tocqueville, Alexis de. 2000 (1835). *Democracy in America*. Chicago: University of Chicago Press.

Wuthnow, R. 2004. "The Challenge of Diversity." *Journal for the Scientific Study of Religion* 43: 159–70.

18

Demystifying authenticity in the sociology of culture

David Grazian

The performance of authenticity pervades our popular culture and public arenas. In recent years "reality" television has proliferated not only because it is inexpensive to produce, but for its brazen attempts to capture "ordinary" people in unscripted moments of everyday life, warts and all (Grindstaff 2002). African American hip-hop music artists sell records on the basis of their ability to "keep it real" by remaining "true" to their neighborhood roots, even when they hail from middle-class suburbs (McLeod 1999). In American politics, highly stylized candidates perform authenticity to within an inch of their lives by emphasizing their working-class tastes, however manufactured. For example, during the early 1990s Tennessee Republican Fred Thompson's senatorial campaign reinvented the wealthy lobbyist "as a good old boy: it leased a used red pickup truck for him to drive, dressed up in jeans and a work shirt, with a can of Red Man chewing tobacco on the front seat" (Krugman 2007). Media elites act no differently, going so far as to downgrade their résumés for fear of seeming inauthentic and out of touch with "common" people. Conservative talk-show host Bill O'Reilly has asserted that "I understand working-class Americans. I'm as lower-middle-class as they come," even though he hails from the decidedly well-off neighborhood of Westbury, Long Island, and earned advanced degrees from Harvard and Boston University without financial aid (Murphy 2002).

Authenticity can refer to a variety of desirable traits: credibility, originality, sincerity, naturalness, genuineness, innateness, purity, or realness. Since the nineteenth century, the search for authenticity has been a bourgeois reaction to the ravages of industrial society and monopoly capitalism, whether expressed by Marx's critique of alienated labor, or Walt Whitman's and Henry David Thoreau's pastoral retreats. In our postindustrial age of high-tech frivolity—online shopping malls and Botox, email scams and edge cities, Hollywood artifice and boy-band pop, MySpace and virtual reality—citizen-consumers nostalgically seek out the authenticity suggested by symbols of agrarian simplicity (organic beets, folk music), or else the gritty charms of proletarian life (Pabst Blue Ribbon beer, trucker hats).

Like a badge of honor, authenticity connotes legitimacy and social value, but like honor itself, authenticity is also a social construct with moral overtones, rather than an objective and value-free appraisal. Given its socially constructed and thus elusive nature, authenticity itself can never be authentic, but must always be performed, staged, fabricated, crafted, or otherwise imagined (MacCannell 1976; Peterson 1997; Fine 2003; Grazian 2003). The performance of authenticity always requires a close conformity to the expectations set by the context in which it is situated. For instance, in American politics authenticity is marked by straight talk, plain speech, and working-class cultural sensibilities, whereas food writers measure the authenticity of ethnic cuisine by its closeness to national, local, or regional sources of tradition (Lu and Fine 1995; Johnston and Baumann 2007; Gaytan 2008). Audiences may employ a range of ambiguous criteria when evaluating the symbolic efficacy of such authenticity performances, which can lead to controversy. Examples include the ongoing debate among musicians and critics concerning the authenticity of jazz performed in Japan (Atkins 2000) and the contestation surrounding Columbian and Cuban salsa dance styles displayed in London nightclubs (Urquia 2004).

Given the constructed nature of authenticity, sociologists of culture are uniquely positioned to critically demystify its performance in popular culture and public life. The social construction and attribution of authenticity occur among culture-producing organizations, prestige-granting institutions, and other cultural authorities reliant on rhetorical and discursive strategies of classification, genre development, and reputation building (Bielby and Bielby 1994; Negus 1998; Fine 2003; Lena and Peterson 2008). Cultural producers from profit-seeking firms and entrepreneurs to artistic creators manufacture, stage, and promote authenticated artworks and entertainment within more extensive worlds of media and symbolic production (Hirsch 1972; Peterson 1997; Grazian 2003). Lastly, authenticity performances represent elaborate strategies of impression management, social interaction, and emotional control well suited for close dramaturgical analysis (Goffman 1959; Hochschild 1983).

In what follows I will take each of these strategies in turn—assigning authenticity through the production of discourse, staging authenticity as an integral part of the culture production process, and performing authenticity as an accomplishment of social interaction—in order to illustrate how the theoretical tools of cultural sociology can demystify the aura of authenticity surrounding the most hallowed of sacred cows and social myths. I conclude with a discussion of three emergent aesthetic practices—hybridity, irony, and transgression—that deconstruct or otherwise challenge the performance of authenticity as tradition-bound, pretentious, and essentialist.

Assigning authenticity

As a socially constructed myth, authenticity is produced through discourses that valorize certain qualities and assign or attribute them to cultural objects and symbols as a means of creating distinction, whether of status, prestige, or value; it is therefore ironic that authenticity is so often associated with hardship and disadvantage. Collectors assign legitimacy to the childlike artwork of uneducated, self-taught artists on the basis of its unmediated purity, its expression of the wild but innocent creativity of an unrefined mind (Becker 1982: 258–69; Fine 2003). Music fans and ethnomusicologists romanticize the Delta blues melodies of poor sharecroppers as rural expressions of African American primitivism, and Anglo-Saxon folk ballads for their association with country living and working-class populism (Roy 2002). For similar reasons, international tourists and consumers delight in their purchases of indigenous crafts handmade in developing countries such as Thailand and Costa Rica (Wherry 2008).

While these examples illustrate how the attribution of authenticity can serve as an exercise in snobbery or condescension, other cases reveal how authenticity claims can establish distinction through a more democratizing discourse. In gourmet food writing, culinary discourses validate ingredients, recipes, and dishes as authentic by associating them with a particular geographic region, whether Tuscan wild boar stew, Vietnamese beef wraps, Maryland crab cakes, or Nashville hot chicken. (The specificity of place serves as a marker of authenticity in discourses surrounding globally popular music as well, whether Punjabi bhangra or Jamaican reggae.) Other rhetorical strategies for legitimating foods as authentic include emphasizing the rustic quality of homegrown or organic produce—heirloom tomatoes, handpicked cilantro, shaved truffles—or else the modesty of handmade dishes such as black beans and rice, or mint cucumber salad (Johnston and Baumann 2007).

Whether generated out of self-interest or aesthetic convention, authenticity arguments are generally made by cultural authorities such as scholars, journalists, and critics, and commercial interests from local business entrepreneurs to city boosters. Given their invented quality, such claims must often be passionately defended, occasionally to ridiculous ends, if they are to masquerade as actual facts. Many locals insist that a truly authentic Philadelphia cheesesteak must be prepared with one of three kinds of cheese—American, provolone, or Cheez Whiz, even though the latter is perhaps the most artificial and synthetic of all foodstuffs, invented in a laboratory in 1952 (two decades after the introduction of the "original" Philly cheesesteak), and in Canada, no less. Food companies liberally draw on ideologies surrounding authenticity to euphemize the use of flavor additives and extracts as "natural flavors" (Schlosser 2002). Meanwhile, national supermarket chains such as Whole Foods market their processed meals, from frozen burritos and pizzas to TV dinners, as "organic," as if such dishes were grown on small family farms, rather than manufactured in industrial laboratories and packing plants (Pollan 2006).

Staging authenticity

Retail outlets and entertainment venues promote themselves on the basis of their staged authenticity and synthetic atmospherics. The Starbucks chain successfully transformed coffee into an upscale product by offering customers a thoroughly mediated experience steeped in the aesthetics of branded authenticity, as embodied in the wood-paneled décor of its stores, their soundtracks of folk, jazz, and indie rock, and a selection of coffees grown in exotic locales from Kenya to Indonesia. Their marketing materials promote their Burundi Kayanza coffee by emphasizing its authentic origins: "Juicy with herbal blackberry notes and tea-like flavors, this is a coffee unlike any African single-origin offering we've ever tasted. The microclimate of Burundi's rugged Kayanza Ridge is an ideal setting for farmers to grow this amazing coffee. Each farmer tends a small patch of just 50 to 250 coffee trees, making this a truly rare and special bean."

As Erving Goffman (1959) observes in *The Presentation of Self in Everyday Life*, although our social lives are most successfully performed on front stages deliberately designed for the purpose of impressing others, we prepare for those performances in more private backstage regions. Professors write up their classroom notes in their messy but draughty offices, and deliver their pearls of knowledge in stately looking university lecture halls; young romantic lovers prepare for dates in their clothes-strewn bedrooms, but encounter one another on the whirling dance floors provided by glamorous nightclubs and cocktail lounges. Of course, the privatized nature of backstage areas can make them seem particularly intimate and alluring as regions of authenticity lacking in pretense and superficiality. For this reason, restaurants sometimes offer customers the opportunity to observe their chefs and cooking staffs working in normally concealed backstage zones. Although diners inevitably enjoy the privileged views afforded by coveted seats alongside the counters of sushi bars, exhibition-style kitchens, and even at expensive tables placed inside the kitchen itself, such experiences mask how these "backstage" spaces represent little more than disguised front stages themselves, with all workers in performance mode, and potentially embarrassing eyesores such as flypaper and mousetraps hidden safely out of view (Grazian 2004).

The backstage areas of the city itself—its skid rows, segregated ghettos, corner taverns—offer similar thrills to the voyeuristically minded; this partially explains the fascination with local slaughterhouses, tobacco factories, morgues, and sewers shared among Parisian visitors and tour guides in 1900 (MacCannell 1976: 57–76). A century later, jazz and blues bars in Chicago attract curious tourists and other spectators in search of the authenticity marked both by their simulated ramshackle appearance and by bar menus offering Mississippi and Louisiana favorites like crawfish tails, fried okra, and slabs of pork ribs (Grazian 2003). Other urban entertainment venues are similarly staged, even when designed to appear abandoned and atrophied. Cloaked in the symbolic indicators of authenticity and subcultural credibility, rock clubs are commonly dilapidated affairs with beer-stained floors and graffiti-marred bathrooms in varying states of filth and disrepair, even as their box-office ticket sales bring in wildly enormous revenue sums. The dinginess of greasy-spoon eateries and dive bars located in affluent downtown neighborhoods can seem just as fabricated. According to a *New York Times* review of La Esquina, a latter-day speakeasy hidden behind an anonymous gray door in a down-town taco stand in Lower Manhattan:

> The décor, like the rabbit-hole descent, is so contrived as to feel uncontrived. …
> The rust on the wrought iron fence used decoratively throughout the restaurant
> was created by hydrochloric acid, not age. The brick walls were meticulously
> painted, scraped, and repainted to match the naturally decayed columns.
>
> (Lee 2005)

Along with urban entertainment, the staging of authenticity is particularly pronounced in US politics. National electoral campaigns stage local "town hall" meetings as excessively orchestrated affairs that attempt to recall an idyllic American past, while presidential visits to public schools, factories, poor neighborhoods, and flooded cities often serve as little more than opportunities to be photographed in working-class settings with ordinary citizens. Although a graduate of Phillips Academy, Yale, and Harvard, and a son of a former US president, George W. Bush pursued a political career that benefited from his handlers' ability to depict the scion as a rough-riding cowboy and all-around "regular guy." During President Bush's two terms in office, he customarily took his vacations at his ranch in Crawford, Texas—a more ruggedly populist setting than his family's oceanfront retreat in Kennebunkport, Maine:

President Bush has spent the last three Augusts at his ranch in the scorched flatlands of Crawford, Tex., where he has cleared brush, gone for runs in 105-degree heat, and summoned sweaty cabinet members to eat fried jalapeño peppers at the only restaurant in town. No one ever confused the place with that white-wine-swilling island in the Atlantic Ocean, to reprise the president's put-down of Martha's Vineyard, and so Mr. Bush has loved it all the more.

(Bumiller 2004: A12)

Similarly, after Alaska Governor Sarah Palin's selection as Arizona Senator John McCain's vice-presidential running mate in 2008, the campaign and media promoted the conservative Republican's credentials as an authentic frontierswoman—her small-town sensibilities, longstanding membership in the National Rifle Association, knack for aerial wolf hunting, and expert ability to properly field dress a moose. For a time McCain himself had been packaged as the candidate of authenticity—a self-proclaimed "maverick" who named his campaign bus the Straight Talk Express, and late in the campaign touted the support of a seemingly everyman figure named "Joe the Plumber" (a fellow who, as it turned out, was not actually a licensed plumber, nor named Joe).

Given that American consumers' valued authentic experiences are inevitably rooted in stereotypical images of reality rather than the messiness (and occasional unpleasantness) of everyday life as it is actually lived, the staging of authenticity can prove a risky balancing act. After all, few contemporary home buyers on the market for a "historically preserved" nineteenth-century Victorian carriage house are likely to desire one lacking indoor toilets. American diners at ethnic restaurants may crave exotic dishes from faraway lands, but not those foods so far removed from their customary palettes as to be deemed inedible—such as Swiss horsemeat, or Malaysian webbed duck feet, or bosintang, a Korean soup prepared with dog meat. In fact, the representation of cultural authenticity in dining and other entertainment settings almost always relies on a somewhat imaginary and aesthetically pleasing simulation of reality. In mainstream Chinese restaurants in the US, dishes like Mongolian Beef are prepared with lots of sugar to appeal to American tastes; soup is served as an appetizer course, rather than at the end of the meal (as it would be in China); and traditional Chinese dishes such as beef tripe, ox's tail, and pig's tongue are excluded from most menus (Lu and Fine 1995). Feigning authenticity, Mexican restaurants in the US serve tortilla chips before the meal, and burritos as a main course—not because traditional Mexican folkways demand it (they do not), but because Anglo customers do (Gaytan 2008: 325–26).

Within the culture industries, the production of popular music relies on similarly strategic methods of representation. In the early era of country–western music, record companies portrayed their actual artists as authentic old-timers, hillbillies, and cowboys (Peterson 1997). Contemporary labels rely on racially charged stock characters to market their rap and hip-hop acts as gang-bangers, street thugs, pimps, convicted felons, ex-cons, and drug users. Pop bands take their fashion cues from once-underground punk and skateboarding scenes in order to camouflage themselves in the symbolic authenticity of alienated youth and independent rock. Although blues club owners in Chicago occasionally employ musicians of varying racial and ethnic backgrounds, in response to audience demand for the authenticity represented by black culture, they almost exclusively hire African American bandleaders for profitable weekend gigs (Grazian 2003). According to one local guitarist:

It's because white audiences and owners are ignorant. The owners know that tourists will ask at the door, "Well, is the band playing tonight a black band, or is it a white band?" Because the tourists only want to hear black bands, because they want to see an authentic Chicago blues band, and they think a black band is more real, more authentic. When they come to Chicago, it's like they want to go to the "Disneyland of the Blues." You know, it's like this: people want German cars, French chefs, and well, they want their bluesmen black. It's a designer label.

(quoted in Grazian 2003: 36)

Performing authenticity

At an interactional level, authenticity performances require elaborate strategies of impression management and emotional control. During interpersonal encounters, we usually associate authenticity with sincerity and self-transparency. In other words, we assume that people are who they say they are, and that they actually believe what they claim to be true. Although Goffman observes that to a certain extent all social interactions are performed, he also distinguishes between cynical masquerades in which the actor intends to deceive his audience, and more genuine acts in which the performer "can be sincerely convinced that the impression of reality which he stages is the real reality" (1959: 17–18). Italian or Greek housewives who rely on traditional family recipes may sincerely believe in the authenticity of their cooking, just as folk and bluegrass songsters may genuinely embrace the authenticity attributed to Appalachian music. These examples illustrate how authenticity can be earnestly experienced as well as performed, even by the performers themselves. Indeed, comparative international research on prostitution in San Francisco, Stockholm, and Amsterdam reveals how sex workers sometimes perform "bounded authenticity" by providing genuine desire, affection, and erotic pleasure for their clients, at least within the temporal confines of a fleeting commercial sexual transaction (Bernstein 2007: 103).

On the other hand, workers in a range of occupations (including sex work) regularly engage in cynical authenticity performances that rely on tactics of misrepresentation and guile. Police detectives break down their suspects through a variety of deceptive strategies during interrogation proceedings (including performances of good/bad cop). Service workers from flight attendants to cocktail waitresses perform emotional labor by responding with feigned laughter and sympathetic smiles to their customers' often unsavory come-ons and rude requests (Hochschild 1983). In a turn toward what the public relations industry refers to as "reality marketing," paid female publicists pose as ordinary customers in urban bars and nightclubs for the purposes of engineering the fun and excitement that paying patrons cannot be relied on to generate for themselves (Grazian 2008: 86–90). More extreme examples of deceitful professionals include confidence artists, pool hustlers, double agents, fortune tellers, and used-car salesmen. Of course, as sociologist Ned Polsky reminds us, "Conning is only a matter of degree, in that all of us are concerned in many ways to manipulate others' impressions of us, and so one can, if one wishes, take the view that every man is at bottom a con man" (1967: 53).

While the feigning of sincerity represents one kind of authenticity performance, other contexts invite participants to play roles commensurate with dominant stereotypes of authenticity based on gritty images of the urban poor. Black middle-class youth pose as hoodlums on New York City subways as well as in rap music videos. Affluent white suburban teenagers cloak themselves in street fashion from baggy jeans to torn clothing, even going so far as to beg for change in wealthy neighborhoods of nearby cities. In February 2008, Riverhead Books published *Love and Consequences*, a memoir of a half-white, half-Native American girl from South-Central Los Angeles who grew up in a foster home and eventually sold illegal drugs for the Bloods gang. Later that year the book was revealed to be pure fiction, written by a white woman raised by her biological family in the upscale Sherman Oaks neighborhood in the San Fernando Valley.

These last examples emphasize the conscious elaboration of class, racial, or ethnic authenticity as an accomplishment of cultural performance and social interaction. Tabloid talk shows like Jerry Springer encourage working-class guests to overemphasize the performance of "trashy" stereotypes, and they oblige for the privilege of appearing on television (Grindstaff 2002), just as reality TV actors trade on clichéd stock characters (the effeminate gay man, the angry black woman, the sexy bimbo) for extra airtime. In Chicago blues clubs, African American musicians exaggerate the performance of blackness by appropriating racial caricatures reminiscent of antebellum black minstrelsy and more contemporary "blaxploitation" films—the country bumpkin, the cowboy, the sex machine, the dirty old-timer. In his club performances, one Mississippi blues singer "confesses" his passions for "blues, barbecue, watermelon, and pretty girls." Meanwhile, before his passing in 1998 James Ramsey, a popular Chicago blues figure dubbed the "Black Lone Ranger," strolled around local blues bars selling home-recorded tapes featuring his renditions of blues standards such as "I'm a Man," and invited customers to pay to have their Polaroid photograph taken with him in his minstrel regalia, replete with ten-gallon hat and black mask (Grazian 2003: 54).

The demystification of authenticity as cultural practice

Sociologists have the necessary theoretical and analytical tools to demystify the fabrication of authenticity in everyday life, whether through the examination of discourse and the social construction of knowledge, organizational analysis and case studies of cultural production, or dramaturgy and symbolic interaction. But in addition, as they become more common in popular culture and public life, authenticity performances are increasingly challenged by alternative aesthetic practices that devalue, deconstruct, or otherwise problematize such performances as tradition-bound, pretentious, and essentialist.

First, the social status of authenticity is challenged by the celebration of hybridity, represented by attempts to meld together otherwise disparate cultures in a self-conscious manner in order to generate new possibilities for creative expression. In many ways the history of popular music in the twentieth century is marked by attempts at synthesis and fusion. Blues and jazz developed as a mélange of African and European musical traditions; similarly, early rock 'n' roll pioneers developed the genre by blending together urban blues and country music. Such experiments in hybridity are also evident in: Bob Dylan's development of electric folk-rock (which signaled his supposed lack of authenticity among older folk music followers); Miles Davis's forays into free jazz, funk, and psychedelic rock on albums like *Bitches Brew* (1969) and *On the Corner* (1972); the appropriation of classical music techniques among 1970s and 1980s progressive rock and heavy metal artists like Rush, Deep Purple, Eddie Van Halen, Randy Rhoads, and Yngwie Malmsteen; and the emergence of rap rock, an amalgam of punk, hard rock,

197

and hip-hop music exemplified by 1990s acts such as Faith No More, the Beastie Boys, the Red Hot Chili Peppers, and Rage Against the Machine.

Like authenticity, adventures in cultural hybidity are popular among culinary artists, as evidenced by the pervasiveness of global fusion cooking in fine-dining establishments worldwide. In New York, San Francisco, Chicago, and even smaller cities such as Philadelphia, three- and four-star restaurants prepare fashionable exemplars of hybrid cuisine that combine French cooking with a mixture of ingredients from Japan, Italy, Mexico, and Morocco, among other regions. In local Philadelphia restaurants, fusion dishes include seared Kobe beef carpaccio, truffle-scented edamame ravioli, and spinach risotto with lemongrass sauce (Grazian 2003: 233; 2008: 12). By evading the traditions common to regional cuisines, chefs and diners alike reject the social construction of authenticity in favor of global hybridity and multiculturalism.

If the pursuit of hybridity represents a challenge to tradition, adventures in irony reject authenticity performances for their pretensions, as cultural creators and consumers play-fully mock what they regard as the self-importance of such displays. Since the early 1990s it has become fashionable for indie rock bands to rerecord pop hits as ironic jokes, as faithless covers that satirize rather than emulate the typically overwrought tone of their original versions. (Examples include Dinosaur Jr.'s 1990 cover of the Cure's "Just Like Heaven," Cake's 1996 rerecording of Gloria Gaynor's "I Will Survive," and Fountains of Wayne's 1999 remake of Britney Spears's " ... Baby One More Time.") Similarly, disc jockeys and recording renegades have built a cottage industry out of mash-ups, typically unauthorized remixes that combine the vocals from one recording with the instrumental track from another; the resultant cacophony serves a satirizing function by announcing itself as a kind of anti-authentic performance. (Examples include Destiny's Child singing "Bootylicious" over Nirvana's grunge-rock anthem "Smells Like Teen Spirit," and Christina Aguilera's "Genie in a Bottle" laid over the rock guitar tracks of the Strokes's "Hard to Explain.")

Similarly, the ironic embrace of kitsch in independent cinema (notably in John Waters's films, such as *Pink Flamingos* [1972]) and postmodern architecture (Venturi *et al.* 1972) suggests how camp can be employed as a repudiation of the performance of authenticity. Such moves can also be observed in the otherwise staid world of critical social theory, as illustrated by the strangely celebratory (or else severely sarcastic) writings of the French sociologist Jean Baudrillard, who proclaims in *America*:

> The US is utopia achieved. ... It is the world centre of the inauthentic ... it is Disneyland that is authentic here! The cinema and TV are America's reality! The freeways, the Safeways, the skylines, speed, and deserts—these are America, not the galleries, churches, and culture. ... Let us grant this country the admiration it deserves and open our eyes to the absurdity of some of our own customs. ... You have to have wondered, at least for a brief moment, "How can anyone be European?"
>
> (Baudrillard 1988: 77, 104–05)

Finally, through practices of transgression, participants baldly reject what they take to be the essentializing qualities of authenticity, fabrication, and performance. As a reaction to typecasting in theater and film and normative role assignment in everyday life, since 1993 the Los Angeles Women's Shakespeare Company has performed plays from *Hamlet* to *Romeo and Juliet* to *Richard III* with all-female casts. (Of course, Shakespeare's plays were originally staged with men performing all roles.) In recent years white actors have similarly been cast in traditionally black roles: Patrick Stewart played the title lead (without the offensive blackface makeup) in a 1997 staging of *Othello* by Washington, D.C.'s Shakespeare Theater. In *I'm Not There*, an experimental 2007 biopic of Bob Dylan and his multiple invented selves, the troubadour's many incarnations—each a riff off a different brand of authenticity and American myth—are performed by a cadre of actors varying in age, race, nationality, and gender, including Heath Ledger, Christian Bale, Marcus Carl Franklin, Richard Gere, and Cate Blanchett.

Conclusion

A central challenge among sociologists of culture remains the demystification of authenticity in entertainment, popular culture, politics, and public settings of everyday life. The construction of authenticity takes place in a context of collective involvement and social interaction, and requires the mobilization of a variety of interested actors, including: reputational authorities, prestige-granting organizations, and mass communications outlets; media-producing firms, art worlds, and cultural entrepreneurs; and public performers, creative personnel, and, naturally, their audiences. Along with the emergent aesthetic pursuits discussed above that deconstruct or otherwise challenge the performance of authenticity as tradition-bound, pretentious, and essentialist, the sociology of culture itself represents yet another critical practice designed to examine and debunk the dominant cultural myths of our time.

References

Atkins, E. Taylor. 2000. "Can Japanese Sing the Blues? 'Japanese Jazz' and the Problem of Authenticity." In Timothy J. Craig, ed., *Japan Pop! Inside the World of Japanese Popular Culture*. Armonk, NY: M.E. Sharpe.

Baudrillard, Jean. 1988. *America*, trans. Chris Turner. London: Verso.

Becker, Howard S. 1982. *Art Worlds*. Berkeley: University of California Press.

Bernstein, Elizabeth. 2007. *Temporarily Yours: Intimacy, Authenticity, and the Commerce of Sex*. Chicago: University of Chicago Press.

Bielby, William T. and Bielby, Denise D. 1994. "'All Hits are Flukes': Institutional Decision-Making and the Rhetoric of Network Prime-Time Program Development." *American Journal of Sociology* 99: 1287–1313.

Bumiller, Elisabeth. 2004. "White House Letter: When a Campaign Intrudes on Vacation." *New York Times*, 19 July.

Fine, Gary Alan. 2003. "Crafting Authenticity: The Validation of Identity in Self-Taught Art." *Theory and Society* 32: 153–80.

Gaytan, Marie Sarita. 2008. "From Sombreros to Sincronizadas: Authenticity, Ethnicity, and the Mexican Restaurant Industry." *Journal of Contemporary Sociology* 37: 314–41.

Goffman, Erving. 1959. *The Presentation of Self in Everyday Life*. New York: Anchor.

Grazian, David. 2003. *Blue Chicago: The Search for Authenticity in Urban Blues Clubs*. Chicago: University of Chicago Press.

——. 2004. "The Production of Popular Music as a Confidence Game: The Case of the Chicago Blues." *Qualitative Sociology* 27: 137–58.

——. 2008. *On the Make: The Hustle of Urban Nightlife*. Chicago: University of Chicago Press.

199

Grindstaff, Laura. 2002. *The Money Shot: Trash, Class, and the Making of TV Talk Shows*. Chicago: University of Chicago Press.

Hirsch, Paul M. 1972. "Processing Fads and Fashions: An Organization Set Analysis of Culture Industry Systems." *American Journal of Sociology* 77: 639–59.

Hochschild, Arlie Russell. 1983. *The Managed Heart: Commercialization of Human Feeling*. Berkeley: University of California Press.

Johnston, Josee and Baumann, Shyon. 2007. "Democracy versus Distinction: A Study of Omnivorousness in Gourmet Food Writing." *American Journal of Sociology* 113: 165–204.

Krugman, Paul. 2007. "Authentic? Never Mind." *New York Times*, 10 June.

Lee, Denny. 2005. "Remember, You Didn't Read About It Here." *New York Times*, 31 July.

Lena, Jennifer C. and Peterson, Richard A. 2008. "Classification and Culture: Types and Trajectories of Music Genres." *American Sociological Review* 73: 697–718.

Lu, Shun and Fine, Gary Alan. 1995. "The Presentation of Ethnic Authenticity: Chinese Food as a Social Accomplishment." *Sociological Quarterly* 36: 535–53.

MacCannell, Dean. 1976. *The Tourist: A New Theory of the Leisure Class*. New York: Schocken.

McLeod, Kembrew. 1999. "Authenticity within Hip-Hop and Other Cultures Threatened with Assimilation." *Journal of Communication* 49: 134–50.

Murphy, Cullen. 2002. "Lifosuction." *Atlantic Monthly* (February).

Negus, Keith. 1998. "Cultural Production and the Corporation: Musical Genres and the Strategic Management of Creativity in the U.S. Recording Industry." *Media, Culture and Society* 20: 359–79.

Peterson, Richard A. 1997. *Creating Country Music: Fabricating Authenticity*. Chicago: University of Chicago Press.

Pollan, Michael. 2006. *The Omnivore's Dilemma: A Natural History of Four Meals*. New York: Penguin.

Polsky, Ned. 1967. *Hustlers, Beats, and Others*. Garden City, NY: Anchor.

Roy, William G. 2002. "Aesthetic Identity, Race, and American Folk Music." *Qualitative Sociology* 25: 459–69.

Schlosser, Eric. 2002. *Fast Food Nation: The Dark Side of the All-American Meal*. New York: Perennial.

Urquia, Norman. 2004. "'Doin' It Right': Contested Authenticity in London's Salsa Scene." In Andy Bennett and Richard A. Peterson, eds., *Music Scenes: Local, Translocal, and Virtual*. Nashville, TN: Vanderbilt University Press.

Venturi, Robert, Brown, Denise Scott, and Izenour, Steven. 1972. *Learning from Las Vegas*. Cambridge, MA: MIT Press.

Wherry, Frederick F. 2008. *Global Markets and Local Crafts: Thailand and Costa Rica Compared*. Baltimore, MD: Johns Hopkins University Press.

19

Carnival culture

Karen Bettez Halnon

Long the territory of literary scholars, historians, and anthropologists, the study of "carnival" is gaining visibility in cultural sociology because of the analytic purchase it yields on questions of aesthetics, performance, and power. This essay begins by contextualizing carnival historically and describing carnival's two best-known manifestations, Brazilian *carnelevare* and North American Mardi Gras. I then elaborate on the concept of carnival culture by discussing its commodification and commercialization, from New Orleans's yearly festivities to shock music scenes. To plumb the conceptual depth of carnival, the body of the essay is divided into three parts, each of which integrates important recent scholarship on a distinct topic. The first (pp. 203–205) probes how carnival is traditionally understood as an instance of "liminality" that in these terms offers participants both a "second life" and a "second voice." The next part (pp. 205–207) elaborates on a debate that crosses nearly all carnival studies: whether carnival's "second life" fulfills positive or negative functions, and whether carnival reinforces or challenges oppressive features of the everyday status quo. The third part (pp. 207–208) delves into the more esoteric terrain where carnival and postmodernism meet and concludes with a discussion of how the supposed implosion of meaning—and therefore the absence of "safety valves"—in postmodern society gives way to a no-exit "Clockwork Orange" dispersion of carnival in haphazard and violent forms. The essay concludes by considering future directions for carnival culture studies.

Carnelevare (meaning literally "to lift up" or to say "farewell to the flesh") is a pre-Lenten meat-eating feast, dating back to about 965 CE (Kinser 1990). The years 1000 to 1300, the Christian middle ages, known as the "cradle of carnival," were followed between the 1300s and 1500s by carnival's fullest European development. There was subsequent diffusion through colonization. One of the world's most famous carnivals, *Carnevale*, originated in Brazil in 1641. It is held in late February or early March, four days before Ash Wednesday, in Rio de Janeiro and São Paulo, as well as other cities such as Salvador, Porto Seguro, and Recife. Highlights today include over 100 *blocos* (block parades) around Rio and the lavish, high-profile competition between "sambo schools" that lasts the entire four nights of the festivities at the *Sambodromo* open stage. Both McGowan and Pessanha (1998) and Peronne and Crook (1997) provide historically contextualized and vivid ethnographic vignettes describing people dancing and singing in the streets, in dance halls and clubs, and on beaches amidst an air of extroversion, sensuality, and frivolity (see also Peronne and Dunn 2002). These accounts convey carnival's roots in pre-Christian Greek and Roman celebrations and carnival's arrival in Brazil as a "chaotic Portuguese *entrudo*, in which celebrants would go to the streets and throw mud, dirt, water, flour balls, and suspect liquids at one another, often triggering violent riots" (McGowan and Pessanha 1998: 36).

The most widely known contemporary rendition of carnival in the United States is Mardi Gras, a yearly public festival held in New Orleans, Louisiana, and Mobile, Alabama, with tracings to Caribbean roots (not French roots, as commonly supposed). This pre-Lenten Gulf Coast celebration lasts from ten days to two weeks and is held before Ash Wednesday (the number of days depends on the date of Easter). Like *Carnevale*, Mardi Gras involves the grandeur of street masking, costuming, dancing, drinking, feasting, chanting, and cheering amid elaborate floats, bead tossing, and parade stripping. An air of sensuality and freedom from sexual repression takes hold, and it is common to see bodies barely covered with paint, stripes, glitter, or feathers. The festivities climax (no pun intended) on Fat Tuesday with two parades, one at midday featuring the pseudo-monarchs and one in the early evening showcasing the two oldest secret societies—Mobile's Order of the Mystics in Mobile and New Orleans's Krewe of Comus.

The commodification of carnival

Although Samuel Kinser's (1990) work stands as the authoritative text on Mardi Gras as American carnival, Kevin Fox Gotham's (2008) shorter and more recent chapter, "Contrast of carnival," complements and updates it with a substantively and theoretically rich account of the worldwide cultural dispersion of Mardi Gras. He argues that Mardi Gras "stands at the nexus of modernity and postmodernity." Put another way, Mardi Gras has been simultaneously transformed by forces of modernity—commodification and rationalization—and postmodernity—"the diversifying forces of difference and hybridity that constitute the postmodern condition" (Gotham 2008: 299). As a result of these complex forces, "local" features trace to global industries, as exemplified by one of the strongest icons of carnival, Mardi Gras beads, which are produced by a handful of factories in China and yield gross annual worldwide sales approaching $500 million (Gotham 2008: 306). Gotham also suggests that in reconstructing local culture "to appeal to and satisfy tourists' demands and interests," cities such as New Orleans and Mobile are transformed into "contrived tourist destinations." For Gotham, fantasy exceeds reality to such an extreme that the event becomes a hyper-real "model and ideal version of Mardi Gras," more real than the original (see Peronne and Dunn 2002 for a similar account of the globalization of Brazilian carnival).

Illustrating the applicability of carnival beyond the prototypes of *Carnevale* and Mardi Gras while furthering the commodification thesis, Brad Lucas's (1999) essay on the rock band the Grateful Dead—titled "Bakhtinian carnival, corporate capital, and the last decade of the Dead"—asserts that the 25-year history of the band exemplifies contemporary carnival. As evidence, Lucas points to album covers invoking circus high-wire acts, cover art depicting fire-eaters, circus animals, and trapeze-swinging skeletons, and lyrics connecting the band and its music with the natural world. He then focuses on the multiple factors—many having to do with commodification and commercialization—that led to the ultimate demise of the Grateful Dead's carnival culture. Ticketless fans were blocked from the concert vicinity, increasing concert violence; police presence was heightened; video screens were introduced during performances, effectively functioning as stage footlights; corporate vending replaced an open marketplace; the band incorporated and became Grateful Dead Productions; band merchandising became increasingly aggressive and expensive (e.g. $30 Bloomingdales neckties, $65 ladies scarves); ticket prices increased sharply in response to manufactured scarcity; and Grateful Dead revenue saw a staggering multi-million-dollar upsurge.

I, too, have studied the commercialization of carnival music cultures. Focusing on transgressive white artists and bands who gradually move into the mainstream, including Eminem, Marilyn Manson, Korn, Slipknot, and Kid Rock. In "Alienation Incorporated: 'F*** the Mainstream Music' in the Mainstream," I show how self-labeled "white trash," "rejects," "failures," and "freaks" delineate their experiences of alienation in lyrics and stage performances, and how anti-commercialistic youth consume alienation as authenticity in their quest for something "different" and "real" in a society of the spectacle (Halnon 2005). The ultimate critique posed by the concept of alienation incorporated—the commodification of alienated artists and their alienation experiences, along with the assimilation of potentially troublesome and estranged anti-commercialistic consumer youth—is that commodification not only transforms alienation (at both points of production and consumption) into a source of profit, it also forestalls more conscious, directed, and pragmatic avenues of rebellion.

As a counterpoint to research on commercialization, Garth Green, in his study of carnival in Trinidad and Tobago, criticizes what he calls "academic nostalgia," or "the propensity of academics ... to lament the supposed inauthenticity and commercialism that is said to accompany changes in Carnival" (2002: 283). He argues that this concern mirrors local critiques of carnival and is part of a larger recurring preoccupation in the twentieth century with the supposed negative effects of commercialization on cultural life.

"Second life" and "second voice" in Bakhtin's medieval carnival

Deriving from the Latin "*limins*," liminality means "a threshold passage betwixt and between two separate places," a "time filled with ambiguity" where there is "a confusion of all customary categories" (Carson 1997: 3–4). For anthropologist Victor Turner (1995), liminality—where the individual is positioned marginally and ambiguously, irreducible to one thing or another—is a middle place, marked in relation to two other locations in an overall passage: separation (where the individual is detached from a prior state) and incorporation (where the individual re-enters the community in an altered state). Birth, death, marriage, puberty, and circumcision rituals are typical anthropological examples of liminality.

As conventionally applied to carnival, the concept of liminality clarifies it as a ritually organized and socially licensed time outside time that suspends, releases, and potentially changes those who pass through it. For Bakhtin (1984 [1936]), the foremost authority on medieval carnival, the "carnival spirit" offers a "chance to have a new outlook on the world, to realize the relative nature of all that exists, and to enter a completely new order of things" (Bakhtin 1984: 89). An essential Bakhtinian understanding is that carnival is a festivity "giving birth to a reality of its own while being subject to its own utopian laws of freedom." For Bakhtin, "to degrade is to bury, to sow, and to kill simultaneously. Grotesque realism ... is the fruitful earth and the womb. It is always conceiving" (1984: 21). "Hence and to underline finally, through carnival's 'rebirth,' the 'world is destroyed so that it may be regenerated and renewed'" (1984: 48).

Bakhtin's studies, based on his reading of French author Rabelais, show that carnival peasant folk culture takes three distinct forms: (1) "ritual spectacles: carnival pageants, comic shows of the marketplace"; (2) "comic verbal compositions: parodies both oral and written"; and (3) "various genres of billingsgate: curses, oaths, popular blazons" (Bakhtin 1984: 5). Bakhtin emphasized that, whatever its form, carnival only exists so long as spectatorship does not. Insisting as emphatically on this point as he did on carnival being a form of rebirth, he wrote, "Carnival is not a spectacle seen by the people; they live in it, and everyone participates because its very idea embraces all the people" (Bakhtin 1984: 7). Hence, confusion and debate arise over whether certain writings, academic or mainstream, can be properly designated as "carnival." Although writing is performative (insofar as writers undertake the presentation of self for specific audiences) and participatory (at least insofar as there is engagement between authors and readers), it cannot be categorized as carnival unless it is performed publicly before an interactive crowd and located in a scene exhibiting carnival characteristics. Thus, in Bakhtin's conceptualization, contemporary comedic performances delivered via television, film, radio, or the internet—and specifically ones with carnival-grotesque dimensions that elicit laughter, shouting, revelry, and moral abandon—are better understood as carnivalesque than carnival per se.

In Bakhtin's description of public performances—notably, festive, pre-Lenten meat-eating feasts that bid "farewell to the flesh"—peasants let loose with dancing, parading, masking, drinking, hectoring, and sexual licentiousness. In such performances, the crowd becomes the "mass body." Rankings are obliterated, comically reversed, or inverted. Comic and grotesque "leaders" rule by consensus or by the immediate, fragile, and explicitly contingent will of the people. Barrier, boundary, and distance are replaced with absolute familiarity, with erotic and graphic exposure, with sensuous sweating, rubbing, and touching, and with equalizing farts and burps. Bakhtin's carnival rituals are centrally marked by the leveling, degrading, or "grotesque" exposure of what is otherwise hidden in or about the human body—genitals, breasts, orifices, fluids, and entrails. In Bakhtin's account of carnival's festive world of "grotesque realism," a fleeting and contained world with no other life outside it, there is "the lowering of all that is high, spiritual, ideal, abstract" (1984: 19–20). Baktinian carnival's symbol par excellence is the human body opened, exposed, and entirely unmitigated by repression or sublimation. The carnival body is distorted, deformed, degraded, decapitated, raped, sliced, mutilated, hacked, burned, desecrated, etc. etc.—all part and parcel of carnival's sundry and celebratory ludic violence. At the same time, however, the salivating, drooling, spitting, sneezing, defecating, urinating, bleeding, ejaculating, and violence that saturate Bakhtinian carnival are always consecrated with laughter.

Because carnival calls into question the sources and forces of repression and sublimation, it speaks as a "second voice," the voice of the people, articulating what is generally subverted, proscribed, or otherwise unstated about dominant cultural and social systems. In Bakhtin's medieval carnival, elites of Church and State are typically ridiculed and lampooned, moral boundaries from the political to the erotic are transgressed, and virtually all authority, morality, and rules are thrown to the wind. Thus, the "second life" of carnival suspends and releases, repudiates and rebels, and reverses and inverts through the degradation of all that is high, pure, civilized, and hidden. A central feature of the carnival grotesque is the death of seriousness, the emergence of unmitigated and fearless laughter, and the "comedic exaggeration of the improper." This characteristic is manifested in the clown's "laughing truth," the "election of the king of fools," the devil as "jovial fellow," and curses, abusive words, other billingsgate, travesties, parodies, and mock violence. As Bakhtin (1984: 91) affirms, the "awesome becomes the comic monster."

However, it is not enough in upending officialdom, Bakhtin says, to seek utopian freedom from the constraints of civility through festive rituals that trample temporarily over "official truth." Equally important is the suspension of conscience, judgment, superego, generalized other—what Bakhtin calls "the great interior censor." This latter process requires, for the entire duration of carnival, an exultant celebration of what in the first life of officialdom is typically repudiated as immoral, tasteless, deviant, or uncivilized. Carnival is thus a celebration of what Chris Rojek (2000) has termed "edgework," or what I refer to as "the reign of moral daredevils" (Halnon 2005, 2006). It is a celebration of everyday life beyond the pale.

The positive and negative functions of carnival

One of the basic tensions that cuts across studies of carnival cultures is the question of whether carnival's "second life" is conservative or transformative. Does it constitute a recuperative "safety valve" that releases pent-up steam only to ultimately preserve an oppressive status quo, or does it serve as a vehicle for challenging and potentially changing structural inequalities? Although Bakhtin regarded the opposition as a false one, subsequent scholars have nevertheless found it useful for analyzing contemporary instances of carnival culture.

The enduring applicability of Bakhtin's conceptualization of "second life" as "rebirth" is illustrated in my recent essay, "Heavy Metal Carnival and Disalienation: The Politics of Grotesque Realism" (2006), where I show how heavy-metal music and its carnival culture express a dis-alienating politics of resistance. Drawing on four years of fieldwork at concerts and extensive analysis of music media (focusing on "high underground" bands such as Cradle of Filth, GWAR, and Insane Clown Posse), I apply Bakhtin's multifaceted conceptualization of the carnival-grotesque to argue that heavy-metal music and heavy-metal performances constitute a proto-utopian liminal alternative to the impersonal, conformist, superficial, unequal, and numbing realities of a society driven by commercialism and spectacle. In heavy-metal carnival, the liminal second life is exemplified by grotesque bodies, inversion, experiences of collectivity and community, liberation from truth and order, liberation from interior censors, destructive humor, and rebirth. I argue, following Bakhtin, that liminal reality *is* reality—a creative medium for and by the people for imagining and living (at least for a few utopian hours) a radical difference from the everyday, oppressive status quo. The study concludes that the elaboration and celebration of this radical difference reflect a desire to reclaim and recreate local culture according to a new sensibility; participants experience the dark side of heavy metal as "pregnant death, a death that gives birth" (Halnon 2006: 46).

Chris Humphrey, in *The Politics of Carnival: Festive Misrule in Medieval England*, likewise makes the case that carnival is not simply "a controlled release of pent-up steam"

205

(2001: 6) in the service of perpetuating the status quo. However, rather than applying Bakhtinian concepts directly, Humphrey broadens the definition of carnival by replacing the term with "festive misrule" and defining it as any public and disruptive "custom" or "performance" that takes "place at a well-defined time of the year," and that turns "upside down" or breaks "some established rules or norms in some way" (2001: 40). He argues that instead of using Bakhtinian carnival concepts, scholars should apply a more general concept, "symbolic inversion" (or virtually any transgression of meaning). Using this broad framework, Humphrey pursues his interest in instances of "festive misrule" that produce specific political, economic, and/or social effects. For example, his archival case studies of Norwich and Coventry focus on mumming (festive cross-dressing), hocking (binding persons of opposite sexes with ropes and charging money for release), feast of the boy-bishop, feast of fools, May Day, summer games, and Gladman's riding. With these examples, Humphrey illustrates how symbolic inversion through festive misrule originated from a variety of sources and served a number of purposes, including complex and sometimes contradictory political and economic objectives.

A more critical position toward the putatively progressive potential of carnival is taken by Samuel Kinser (1990: 315), who argues that Mardi Gras rituals conserve black–white barriers and are marked by "unregenerate elitism." In his words, "the social peace which reigns in Carnival is puzzling. Sexual and racial loves and hates, taboo the rest of the year, are lavishly displayed. In fact, Carnival is peaceful because it is explosive" (Kinser 1990: 307). Phillip McGowan is similarly critical of carnival as egalitarian festive utopia. In "American Carnival: Seeing and Reading American Culture," McGowan suggests that carnivalesque forms may advance rather than eradicate inequality. Making comparisons between everyday conceptions of racialized "freaks" and their depiction in carnivalseque literary spaces, McGowan argues that such spaces operate as "sanctioned territories in which the (white) spectator or tourist can witness carnivalized representations of Otherness" (2001: xi). Departing from Bakhtin's temporal and spatial requisites for carnival, McGowan maintains that carnival is not limited in time and space. Rather, he sees it as a "symbiotic relationship of reinforcing belief systems … established between such overt locations as the side show, freak show, or World's Fair" and a "covert politics of seeing by which American society was categorized and interpreted" by a range of American literary figures, including Nathaniel Hawthorne, Stephen Crane, Saul Bellow, William Faulkner, Lindsay Gresham, Walt Whitman, Ernest Hemingway, and Paul Auster. In this conceptualization, carnivalesque forms (whether in literature or side shows) may be understood in fluid relation with the stratifying and objectifying mechanisms of everyday life. The particular point that McGowan stresses is that carnival's object is not an egalitarian eradication of inequality, but rather an inversion, reversal, or contestation of equalizing pressures. More specifically, his object is to show how equalities purported in "democracy's" "first life" are mitigated through the "second life" carnival form. This perspective resonates with that of Robert Bogdan, whose well-known *Freak Show* (1988) reveals in ethnographic detail the history of Barnum and Bailey, state fairs, and other traveling shows. Employing a symbolic interactionist lens, Bogdan shows how "sideshow freaks"—the tattooed man, fat woman, strong man, midget, sword swallower, and the giant—were constructed as spectacular human oddities for profit, and how carnival forms reconstruct and magnify the stigma associated with "deviance."

However, other scholars approach the question of oppression versus transgression by arguing that the carnivalesque is both simultaneously. Gamson, for example, in his research on tabloid talk shows, calls attention to the *"paradoxes of visibility* that talk shows dramatize with such fury: democratization through exploitation, truths wrapped in lies, normalization through freak show" (1998: 19, original emphasis). Gamson insists that there "is in fact no choice here between manipulative spectacle and democratic forum, only the puzzle of a situation in which one cannot exist without the other" (1998: 19).

Langman's (2008) study of body-adornment practices in "alternative" subcultures similarly calls attention to the double-edged nature of the carnivalesque. He argues that the "primitive" aesthetic exemplified by punk and heavy metal facilitates expressions of rage and protest, and that "porn chic" as a style implicitly critiques patriarchal codes of morality. At the same time, Langman (2008: 657) argues that such phenomena can serve as "repressive de-sublimations that shunt discontent from the political economy to the culture and incorporate potential dissidence." He reminds us that inequality for some (e.g. the asymmetric humiliation of women in pornography) can be a carnivalesque means of empowering others (e.g. relieving men of the everyday alienation they suffer under global capitalism). Langman's work foregrounds the thesis developed by Mike Presdee (2000) that postmodern carnivalesque forms tend to mask the pain of silenced or invisible subjects on whom the production of these forms depends.

Carnival and postmodernism

In "The Abnormal Forms of Leisure," sociologist Chris Rojek summarizes the "safety valve" thesis associated with carnival's "second life" in postmodern society.

> Traditional societies supported "antistructures" of time and space in which individuals could stand outside the axioms and conventions of the day. In these liminal zones, collective ritual and symbolic behavior enabled emotional discharge from the ordinary restraints of everyday life. The effect of liminal activity was not to transform society, but to reinforce it by providing a safety valve for the release of excess emotions and energies. The effect was cathartic inasmuch as excess energies were discharged and the readiness to capitulate to collective order was reaffirmed.
>
> (Rojek 2000: 161)

Rojek argues that in "highly specialized, secularized, and differentiated societies organized around performative, reservation cultures, liminal leisure ceases to be concentrated in time and space which has uniform, blinding power over individuals" (Rojek 2000: 161–62). He goes on to claim that even though "the spirit of the carnivalesque palpably remains in Western modern industrial society, the provision for a period of carnival in which the rules of everyday life are collectively overturned for an extended period of time is not common" (Rojek 2000: 162). Instead, liminal leisure is dispersed across a variety of diverse settings, and "edgework and the discharging of excess emotions and energy are chronically distributed" (Rojek 2000: 162).

Appearing in a plenitude of mundane settings, edgework takes forms such as speeding, charging through red lights, and imbibing excess alcohol. Rojek insists that these acts, which typically occur in banal settings, belong to the category of "liminal leisure." He conceptualizes what he calls a continuum of liminal "flow." This continuum includes "limit experiences," which (1) aim to achieve "moral transcendence from the collective restraints [chaining] behavior to standardized, routine practices"; (2) are characterized by various degrees of intensity; and (3) are typically fleeting and noncommittal, such that "most individuals drift in and out of edgework experience" (Rojek 2000: 161). According to Rojek, edgework is appealing because the dehumanizing conditions of everyday life in contemporary society invite escape. He also identifies three "abnormal" forms of leisure: "invasive," involving a lack of trust in or respect for one's own self (such as excessive drinking or taking LSD); "mephitic," involving a lack of trust in or respect for others (such as killing for recreation); and "wild," involving leisure practices that "push limit-experiences momentarily over the edge for the purposes of personal gratification and pleasure" (Rojek 2000: 186).

In *Cultural Criminology and the Carnival of Crime*, Mike Presdee (2000) elaborates on the conceptualization of wild zones as leisure. Like Rojek, he suggests that "without a partly licensed carnival forum to satisfy our second life, [the second-life impulse] emerges more haphazardly, unrehearsed, and often unannounced." Thus Presdee explores the "fragments and debris of carnival in our culture," where "the "second life" of the people is lived" (2000: 46). He seeks and finds evidence of second life in various forms of body modification, S&M, raving, recreational drug-taking, hotting and rodeo, gang rituals, online culture, festivals, and extreme sports. Presdee (2000: 3) emphasizes that "the context in which crime and violence are acted out is of paramount importance, and that an analytical 'cultural criminology' is necessary to achieve any in-depth understanding of crime, including violent and so-called 'senseless' acts."

Presdee maintains that in the present postmodern context "the carnival of crime" precludes any notion of festival closure; in other words, social reintegration, or a return to law and order, is no longer possible. For Presdee, we live in a world of endless consumption, including the consumption of violence for fun. The results are anarchy, disorder, and irrationality. Whereas carnival once had boundaries, the logic of postmodernism implodes boundaries. Carnival, consumption, and the postmodern have all become intertwined, making it impossible for carnivalesque forms to register dissent from dominant culture. Presdee's dismal diagnosis is that crime, violence, hatred, humiliation, and the various pleasures they yield are the products of a largely deadened, hyperrational, and shameless social life that produces an unquenchable passion for destruction. The carnival of crime is summarized as follows: "In its consumption, violence is simplified and reduces to a trivial act of instant enjoyment; it thereby becomes no different from, say, the eating of a chocolate biscuit or the drinking of a can of coke. There is no moral debate, no constraint, no remorse, no meaning." And since "social processes have contrived to suppress carnival in its 'authentic' sense," there is no safety valve, no substantial release of steam, no way out from the "Clockwork Orange" "iron cage" of postmodernity (Presdee 2000: 65).

Future directions for carnival culture studies

The study of carnival culture is a relatively new topic for sociologists and therefore fertile ground for future research. What will make sociology's mark on this topic especially distinctive is the prioritization of qualitative, ethnographic, and/or participatory approaches to research. Studying carnival at a distance seems to undermine the whole notion of carnival itself, as the philosophy of carnival emphasizes intimacy, dissolution of pretense, community, and commensality. Given that we live in a society where popular culture and consumer culture are intimately intertwined, it will be necessary for future carnival studies to stretch the traditional focus of ethnography and or ethnographic terrain into market relations while interrogating the slippery spaces of "utopia," "authenticity," and "dis-alienation."

Studies of specific carnival scenes may be guided by a number of fruitful topics of exploration and critique: the applicability and viability of traditional Bakhtinian carnival categories; the carnivalesque as a pervasive feature of popular consumer culture; the implications of understanding carnival as a temporary or seasonal "second life" beyond the cultural dictates of everyday life; carnivalesque consumption as an active response to alienation and/or dehumanization in a rationally organized and/or postmodern society; and the carnival production of "transgression" and "spectacle" as means of capitalizing on consumer desires for fun, escape, release, authenticity, difference, and enchantment (including the spiraling hegemonic effects of such production). Additional areas for exploration include the relationship between postmodernity, limit experiences, and the emotional consequences of rationally organized society; the various ways that commodified and commercialized renditions of the carnivalesque invert or reject efforts to achieve equalities of race, ethnicity, class, gender, sexuality, and religion (as well as the achievements resulting from such efforts); the dispersion of "Mardi Gras" and "Spring Break" festivities across numerous cities in the US and internationally; the meaning of carnival in specific traditions such as Halloween, the Dracula's Ball, and related festivities; and the carnivalization of social protest.

References

Bakhtin, Mikhail. 1984[1936]. *Rabelais and His World*, trans. Helene Iswolksy. Bloomington: Indiana University Press.

Bogdan, Robert. 1988. *Freak Show: Presenting Human Oddities for Amusement and Profit*. Chicago: University of Chicago Press.

Carson, Timothy L. 1997. *Liminal Reality and Transformational Power*. Lanham, MD: University Press of America.

Ehrenreich, Barbara. 2007. *Dancing in the Streets: A History of Collective Joy*. Metropolitan Book/Henry Holt & Company.

Gamson, Joshua. 1998. *Freaks Talk Back: Tabloid Shows and Sexual Nonconformity*. Chicago: University of Chicago Press.

Green, Garth L. 2002. "Marketing the Nation: Carnival and Tourism in Trinidad and Tobago." *Critique of Anthropology* 22(3): 283–304.

Gotham, Kevin Fox. 2002. "Marketing Mardi Gras: Commodification, Spectacle, and the Political Economy of Tourism in New Orleans." *Urban Studies* 39(10): 1735–56.

——. 2008. "Contrasts of Carnival: Mardi Gras between the Modern and Postmodern." Pp. 292–311 in Peter Kivisto, ed., *Illuminating Social Life: Classical and Contemporary Theory Revisited*, fourth edition. Thousand Oaks, CA: Pine Forge Press.

Halnon, Karen Bettez. 2005. "Alienation Incorporated: 'F*** the Mainstream Music' in the Mainstream." *Current Sociology* 53(4): 441–64.

——. 2006. "Heavy Metal Carnival and Disalienation: The Politics of Grotesque Realism." *Symbolic Interaction: Special Issue on Popular Music in Everyday Life* 29(1): 33–48.

Humphrey, Chris. 2001. *The Politics of Carnival: Festive Misrule in Medieval England*. Manchester and New York: Manchester University Press.

Kinser, Samuel. 1990. *Carnival American Style: Mardi Gras at New Orleans and Mobile*. Chicago: University of Chicago Press.

Langman, Lauren. 2008. "Punk, Porn, and Resistance: Carnivalization and the Body in Popular Culture." *Current Sociology* 56(4): 657–77.

Lucas, Brad E. 1999. "Bakhtinian Carnival, Corporate Capital, and the Last Decade of the Dead." Pp. 79–88 in Robert G. Weiner, ed., *Perspectives on the Grateful Dead: Critical Writings*. Westport, CT: Greenwood Press.

McGowan, Phillip. 2001. "American Carnival: Seeing and Reading American Culture." Westport, CT: Greenwood Press.

McGowan, C. and Pessanha, R. 1998. *The Brazilian Sound: Samba, Bossa Nova, and the Popular Music of Brazil*. Philadelphia: Temple University Press.

Peronne, Charles and Crook, Larry. 1997. *Folk and Popular Music of Brazil*. Albuquerque, NM: Latin American Institute, University of New Mexico.

Peronne, Charles and Dunn, Christopher, eds. 2002. *Brazilian Popular Music and Globalization*. London and New York: Routledge.

Presdee, Mike. 2000. *Cultural Criminology and the Carnival of Crime*. London and New York: Routledge.

Rojek, Chris. 2000. *Leisure and Culture*. New York: Palgrave.

Turner, Victor. 1995. *The Ritual Process: Structure and Anti-Structure*. New York, CT: Greenwood Press.

Twitchell, James B. 1992. *Carnival Culture: The Trashing of Taste in America*. New York: Columbia University Press.

Part IV

Individuals and groups, identities and performances

20

Group cultures and subcultures

Gary Alan Fine

Although it has once been conventional to treat culture as a "characteristic" or "feature" of societies, many cultural sociologists now emphasize the importance of examining grounded cultures. But this move has often lacked sufficient attention to what it entails. My intention here is to present the theoretical stakes of this shift to analyzing culture from a micro- or meso-level of analysis. Culture should be conceptualized as a set of actions, material objects, and forms of discourse held and used by groups of individuals. In this view culture is a tool that is situated in particular communities of action, shaping the contours of civic life (Fine and Harrington 2004). As a result, culture is tied to the existence of shared pasts and prospective futures.

Breaking from treating culture as belonging to large-scale social systems (macrocultures), an approach that emphasizes the "micro-" or "meso-"level of analysis needs to be specified. I examine how culture can be linked to interacting groups and to well-networked population segments, focusing on the development of idiocultures, subcultures, and countercultures. Such a perspective, grounded within social psychology, suggests that the locus of culture need not to be limited to society-based populations, but can be analyzed in light of social worlds and communication networks. I extend the idea of culture by emphasizing that it is a form of practice that is linked to local understandings and social relations. A microsociology of culture is a valuable addition to more structural, institutional, and societal views.

Sometimes social scientists, as well as the larger public, comfortably refer to the characteristics of American culture, French culture, or Brazilian culture. Such analyses have value in providing strategies to understand societies in the context of their exceptionalism, looking for means of differentiating a people or a nation from those who stand outside constructed boundaries. However, because of the cognitive, affective, and behavioral diversity within a geographically based population, any analysis that assumes a national culture is necessarily limited and imprecise. A national culture is in practice a many-splendored thing, splintered in various ways, while holding to an ideological claim of unity. In its totality a national culture is somewhat akin to a mist, everywhere and nowhere, sensed but invisible. Often culture is treated as something that people have—or are "given"—by virtue of their location within a spatial community, rather than something that they shape or construct.

Admittedly, nations and regions have elements of a "collective character" that reveal themselves in societal representations. However, the microsociological goal is to determine how these values and beliefs operate in group space and how multiple group cultures, similar to each other through a circulation of members, weak network ties, or common milieux, affect the belief in a national culture, given institutional support through media representations and collective commemoration. Locale matters through the interactions within groups, but also through the shared imagination of larger systems.

Ultimately cultural domains are transmitted and displayed through action, a recognition that privileges examining locales in which culture is performed. The study of culture properly belongs to the analysis of groups—from primary groups (including families) to interacting small groups (clubs, teams, cliques) to networked segments that are tied together through their ongoing interaction, communication, spatial co-presence, or consumption (populations based on age, race, gender, or region). I begin with the most molecular level of analysis—the domain of face-to-face groups and their linkage to group idiocultures—and then examine larger communities based upon socially differentiated networks that form subcultures and countercultures, the latter implying some level of resistance to hegemonic cultures.

Groups and their idiocultures

Every interaction scene, no matter how tiny, develops a set of common, meaningful referents. These bits of communal understanding—collective memories—are established from the opening moments of group life. This approach was presented in Fine's (1979) article on "Small Groups and Cultural Creation: The Idioculture of Little League Baseball" and subsequent studies that applied the "idioculture" model to other social domains, such as mental health organizations, congregations, workplaces, and social movements. The group-based analysis of culture reflects the human desire to create tight communities with shared pasts and prospective futures. Culture is to be found in all groups. Because these include policy makers (Janis 1982) and bureaucratic organizations (Herzfeld 1993), some group cultures have more external influence than others. Ethnographic accounts of "diggers" (who search for buried antiques) in Kaliningrad (Sezneva 2007), Israeli military units (Sion and Ben-Ari 2005), Argentinian opera lovers (Benzecry 2007), and Japanese motorcycle ("bosozuku") tribes (Sato 1991) all depict powerful local norms and shared images, demonstrating that group cultures are not limited to American culture, despite the preponderance of research done there. Wherever groups define themselves with common problems and the likelihood of continued interaction, group cultures are established. The microsociological approach, arguing for attention to the local conditions in which shared meaning is generated, suggests that the establishment of traditions, shared references, and customs is integral to identity and cohesion. Such creation depends upon ongoing performances that organize and routinize interaction, creating a group style (Eliasoph and Lichterman 2003). In turn, as Lawler *et al.* (2008) have argued, different group structures may produce distinctive "microsocial orders."

Any fully sociological understanding of the creation of group cultures must recognize the extensive institutional influences that impact the local scene, providing the conditions for shared action. The backgrounds (both demographic and habitus) of participants, coupled with the expectations that stem from group interaction, contribute to the expansion of a group's meaning system when a triggering event occurs—an event that sparks a recognition of collective experience. This process takes external cultural themes and incorporates them within group discourse and action. Once established, cultural elements provide a mechanism by which members recognize their group as salient and create cohesion with fellow participants. Every group has access to a combination of background culture (the known culture of the group), the moral standards of discourse (the usable culture), the instrumental goals that participants desire (the functional culture), and support for the status hierarchy (the appropriate culture). What eventually becomes recognized as characterizing group life is a result of immediate interactional demands (what becomes triggered).

Whether one accepts the processes that are claimed for this model of cultural development, which emphasize the functional needs of ongoing micro-communities, the focus of a group-based approach is to understand the creation of culture through processes of interaction, arguing for a *sociology of localism*. A sociology of localism emphasizes that the creation of group content depends upon the recognition of shared pasts and planned futures, and does not proceed by examining cultural products as divorced from social actors or by differentiating culture as a set of ideas that transcend time and space. Given that culture-creating processes are shaped by the knowledge, understandings, and goals of participants, they create not just random cultural elements, but an integrated and thematic content-based culture that stems from the past history, current desires, and imagined futures of members. The sociology of culture must analyze how traditions unite groups, providing a cultural grounding for trust, affiliation, and cohesion that then generates shared meaning and the creation of collective identity (Farrell 2001). Without this recognition, cultural content can become the basis on which groups divide or disintegrate. It is not only that tight-knit groups create culture, but that culture facilitates the establishment of tight-knit groups (and occasionally disrupts them). As Perrin (2005) argues, civic organizations depend on discussion based upon an understood political microculture that systematically varies among types of organizations as well as taking variant forms in particular spheres.

Idiocultures are evident in small groups in all institutional domains, including dyadic relations. The examination of families, gangs, sociometric cliques, workgroups, sports teams, cults, and fraternal organizations provides instances of how local cultures shape the content of social relations. The culture of the group provides a cognitive and emotional structure through which individuals recognize their collective pasts and plan for their shared futures (Katovich and Couch 1992). Put differently, microcultures—looking forward and backwards—have a temporal dimension. By recognizing their small group culture, participants understand that they share traditions. These traditions can be invoked with the expectation that they will be understood by other members. Thus, they can be used to address external challenges to the group.

This model of microcultures as structuring devices argues that social order is generated through the development of shared traditions and understandings. Following Collins (1981), collective attention constitutes a microfoundation for macrosociology. As I discuss later, groups build upon each other, creating expansive structures through their network linkages. Or as Collins (2004: xiii) remarked, "The aggregate of situations can be regarded as a market for interaction rituals." Collins's approach is consistent with the process that James Scott refers to as mētis, emphasizing the knowledge that derives from everyday, familiar experience. Scott writes, "Mētis resists simplification into deductive principles which can successfully be transmitted through book learning, because the environments in which it is exercised are so complex and nonrepeatable that formal procedures of rational decision making are impossible to apply" (1998: 316). This is what Scott refers to as "the art of the locality."

To borrow from Jeffrey Goldfarb's resonant image, this model of culture is linked to the sociology of small things, a perspective that captures the *place* of action. Goldfarb starts by theorizing the kitchen table—a microcultural space. His essential point is not simply that small, mundane cultures need to be theorized, but that the conditions of the environment under which they are produced provide for allegiance and shared perspectives. Through their tight-knit culture these domains motivate certain forms of action. The locale provides the basis for both social relations and the content of group life. In the words of Goldfarb, "When friends and relatives met in their kitchens, they presented themselves to each other in such a way that they defined the situation in terms of an independent frame rather than that of officialdom" (2006: 15). Flowing from the hearth, a framework of meaning is established that abounds with the agentic responsibility of the group. Communities can come to see their spaces, their microcultures, and their place in them in ways that have recursive effects. The hearth becomes a central symbol in the resistance against Eastern European authoritarianism, but kitchens and porches are found throughout the globe as meeting points in which primary relations are bolstered and discourse addresses modes of responding to local challenges. Hearths are widely duplicated, each with its own microculture that provides a remembered and referential past and encourages present talk. Similar discussions can be found in bookstores, salons, and clubs, and from there they can in time colonize public meetings and gatherings (Habermas 1991; Emirbayer and Sheller 1998: 732; Mische and White 1998: 706). In small places participants can assume that others share a history, emotional contours, and a sense of belonging. These are locales of likeness. Tiny publics (Fine and Harrington 2004), small cultures of shared interest, and experience provide the basis of a civil society and the creation of a shared and robust public culture.

An approach that focuses on local cultures addresses several critical theoretical problems in the sociology of culture. This strategy provides for understanding how innovation, socialization, affiliation, and change become manifested, revealed in action that, when successful, evokes an affiliative response. By understanding the dynamics of community and the creation of collective identities, an emphasis on local culture stands at the critical and often unexplored junction of the individual and the institutional, thus addressing forms of cohesion as well as disaffiliation. A sociology of the local emphasizes that routines that create community and identity are generated in place and time. If they are not explicitly part of a political project, they may respond to the political projects of others. The challenge for speakers within ongoing, unscripted interaction is to organize the unpredictable, interpreting it in light of beliefs in how society does and should operate. These shaping events that determine the culture of a group are not random. They are predictable in their broad contours, if not in their details. The challenge is that those events that shape collective life are readily understandable after the fact (reading backwards), but cannot be determined before they occur (looking forwards). Participants must shape their behavior, aligning ongoing interaction with established group standards. Even if we cannot predict the moments of everyday life—the jokes, insults, errors, or queries found in conversation—participants strive to make group interaction orderly and habitual. This commitment to the stability of interaction scenes—a commitment to a smooth flow of action—allows for members and analysts to feel comfortable in their expectations, even as new interpretations are generated.

Despite their fluidity and continual adjustment, conversations and collective action become routinized, grounded in shared practices, and embedded in group culture. Research within conversation analysis emphasizes this point, finding formal structures at the most granular level of talk (Schegloff 2007). Other scholars of conversation argue that practices of talk are responsive to external rules and pressures (Gibson 2008). Even when action sequences are altered in fact, we strive to persuade ourselves that they remain much the same, evolving incrementally. Given that action is unscripted, how readily coordinated lines of action can be established and maintained is both a startling and comforting achievement. Once a direction is established and understood, participants collaborate and collude in the hope that the outcome will satisfy all those with investments in it. Although conflict cannot always be avoided, under conditions of stability actors have considerable flexibility and leeway to shape performances. The desire to support the routines of an ongoing group and fellow members, keeping interaction flowing, means that negotiated agreements have weight, so much so that disruption often requires accounts from the perpetrator and produces avoidance from the audience.

Ephemeral micropublics ("Goffman publics") (Ikegami 2000: 997; White 1995) have a particular challenge in the creation of negotiated agreements to which participating social actors will adhere, but by means of establishing local cultures and practices self-referential groups can overcome the problem through shared expectations and a commitment to ritual. As a result, a local sociology is related to, but distinct from, the Goffmanian approach to the interaction order (Goffman 1983). Despite a shared concern with interaction ritual, *dramatism*, examining free-floating, untethered interaction, is contrasted to *localism*, the claim that action is shaped by and responsive to the salience of the group to participants. In contrast to a view that treats behavior as a response to the actions that have immediately proceeded it, seeing interaction as a form of continuous adjustment to an ever-changing and somewhat unpredictable stage, localism emphasizes the stability of group spaces with norms, standards, and expectations. The perspective of localism emphasizes the power and prominence of group rules. As a result, *practices*, actions understood by reference to local cultures, are central, in that such activity is linked to a bounded interactional domain, such as the kitchen table of Goldfarb's analysis. The response to situations as places in which social ties are displayed constitutes a grounded performance, shaped by the recognition of actors and audiences within a continuing and self-referential public that shares (albeit imperfectly) a recognition of norms, values, beliefs, and rituals. Treating groups as publics means that each ongoing group constitutes a local outpost of society. Even though actions extend beyond the interacting group, the boundary of the group—realized by the participants—establishes and perhaps consecrates the legitimacy of the actions within. The local scene represents a particular instance of the larger culture, with its style, rules, and beliefs defining how social relations should be transacted (Eliasoph and Lichterman 2003).

For a local sociology, culture operates as a form of group practice, linked to the meso-level of analysis—the space between individual action and the structural constraints of institutions. Interaction by itself lacks the specification of collective references through which action is transferred into routine. Local cultures organize action into a commitment to continuity, incorporating temporality and order into social life through the recognition of shared pasts and prospective futures (Katovich and Couch 1992). In other words, small group culture permits communities of actors to access tradition as part of their social field, displaying it in the forms of ritual and common references.

Networks and their subcultures

Although I have emphasized the linkage of culture to interacting groups, a social psychological approach to culture is not limited to intense, face-to-face microsocieties, but can be extended to larger social units by extending the small-group model. This involves treating cultures as being based upon a network of groups. Such an approach could theoretically be extended to the interpretation of national cultures because of the mass media and institutional support for widespread and mainstream cultural production and dissemination. However, the examination of subsidiary social domains that lack formal institutional support is likely to be particularly valuable because of the greater emphasis on creation of cultural forms within the context on ongoing interaction. Seeing subcultures manifest in group processes emphasizes that culture is not uniformly spread throughout a social system, but is embedded within tiny publics.

For the past half-century, social scientists have recognized that culture operates not only on the level of the nation, but within its subdivisions. These subdivisions can involve class, race, age, and gender—any domain that leads to a recognized common identity and a sense of "belonging" because of the placement of individuals within a demographic or cultural category. Such domains include the truffle trade in Provence (de la Pradelle 2006: 139–51), classical South Asian philosophy (Collins 1998: 177–271), and poetry in Tokugawa Japan (Ikegami 2005: 171–203). The underlying point for a microsociology of subcultural groups is not to emphasize the shared characteristics of the members in their biological or functional status, but to suggest how social characteristics shape the diffusion of cultural elements and the incorporation of those traditions within a set of social relations based on common affiliation.

The linkage of the process of diffusion with group identification is crucial. As a result, lines of communication are often linked to social categories. As Tamotsu Shibutani (1955: 566) remarked, "Culture areas are coterminous with communication channels." In this, Shibutani emphasized that subcultures do not depend only on physical co-presence, but rather on lines of communication, as a network perspective would suggest. These might consist of a set of gathering points (those "third places" that Ray Oldenburg (1989) describes) with continually changing attendees or open nodes of dissemination, such as internet websites or discussion boards. Such locations—physical or virtual—create spaces that draw certain types of individuals to them and, as a result, create knowledge boundaries in which some individuals are aware of cultural forms, while others are ignorant of them. Crucial are both the intersection of interacting groups that share cultural traditions with media transmissions and other communications networks that link these nodes. Weaker bridging ties connect knots of strong ties. The establishment of a common culture occurs through networks of small groups linked by media outlets that target population segments or through other forms of cross-group ties. We can conceptualize a process of differential association of social actors that links populations to cultural forms. As a result, where and whether cultural forms will be spread results from preferences and likelihoods of association within the segmental groups being considered.

Subcultural theory has traditionally focused on groups that were defined as standing outside "mainstream culture," often deviant groups, rejecting alignment with the established norms and values. While mainstream culture is itself internally differentiated, subcultural groups were seen as separate from what was defined as widely accepted by the society in which these groups were embedded. The concept of subculture was, in effect, a means of establishing a cultural boundary. As a consequence research has examined cultures of delinquency, cultures of poverty, or the Southern culture of violence. These analyses, popular in the middle decades of the twentieth century, were based upon the claim of an obdurate dialectic between categories of Us and Them. Subcultural theory has typically depended on recognizing an otherness that is coupled with a belief that those defined as Others conform to the norms, values, and rituals of their own social category. Even examinations of youth subculture have this focus in emphasizing the power of confrontational style (Hebdige 1981). Few if any scholars define their own cultures as subcultures. Not every social segment is said to have a sub-culture; the operating assumption is that some segmental groups are fully embedded in civil society, whereas others stand apart. Of course, mainstream culture (however that diverse domain is defined) does not reflect the only set of choices that is possible.

The interactionist perspective on subculture (Fine and Kleinman 1979) emphasizes the importance of webs of contact in the creation, activation, and perpetuation of cultural elements. This view suggests that cultural systems constitute social worlds, a concept that derives directly from the work of Anselm Strauss (1978). David Unruh (1980: 277) defines social worlds as "amorphous, diffuse constellations of actors, organizations, events, and practices which have coalesced into spheres of interest and involvement for partici-pants [and in which] it is likely that a powerful centralized authority structure does not exist." Without necessarily relying on demographic differences, the social-world approach emphasizes the importance of common interests and interpersonal contacts as the basis of community and the generation of culture. The existence of a subculture makes concrete the common concerns of the group in the absence of a clear authority structure, incorporating such elements as norms, values, beliefs, moral principles, and performances. This recognition of shared standards leads to embracing a collective identity.

This interactionist perspective locates culture within groups, but leaves open the challenge of explaining widespread understandings among population segments that are not in immediate contact. Although a small group can be studied as a closed system, group members do not interact exclusively with one another. We must theorize how groups intersect and how culture is diffused within population segments. Small groups are connected with numerous other groups through a system of *interlocks* or social connections. Such linkages take many forms, and can involve ties among individuals or small groups, but in each case the effect is to create a shared universe of discourse that can serve as the referent for each local establishment of culture. The contents of sub-cultures (what they are "about") are conceived of as emanating from group cultures and then subsequently shaping other group cultures through diffusion. Although interlocks can take many forms, I describe four: multiple-group membership, weak ties, structural roles, and specialized media diffusion.

Multiple group membership

Individuals rarely participate in a single group, but often are involved in several groups simultaneously. As a result, cultural elements that are accepted in one group can easily be introduced into others through overlapping memberships. Consider, for instance, the child who attends summer camp. Not only do camp cabins constitute groups with their own idiocultures, but each serves as an agora—a trading zone—in which local knowledges are transmitted. When campers return to a home community, these new cultures can potentially be shared and made traditional, expanding their range. The person who participates in two ongoing groups with only a few joint members serves as a crucial linkage for diffusion and cultural change. That many groups have these linkages permits ideas to transcend boundaries. The idea of the cultural "meme" emphasizes that certain elements will be seen as more transmittable (and more fit to survive) and will have a wider range (Dawkins 2006).

Weak ties

No matter how intense and densely connected their core social relations, most individuals maintain acquaintanceship relations outside of their stable and intense interacting groups. Networks based upon ongoing interacting groups are never fully bounded. Those external contacts or "weak ties" (Granovetter 1973; Collins 1998) are crucial for disseminating information widely and rapidly. Studies of rumor, of gossip, or of news in times of crisis demonstrate that information can spread quickly under favorable conditions—if the information is seen as significant and the relational structure is conducive to diffusion. Networks of weak ties have boundaries—racial, class, age, geography, or gender—limiting these pools of knowledge from being open to all. Further, different networks may transmit particular cultural genres, based on the assumed interest of the target (such as off-color humor, health information, or celebrity gossip).

Structural roles

Cultural information is also spread by those with particular structural positions in intergroup relations. Individuals who in their work or leisure roles intersect with multiple groups, organizations, or communities have the ability to spread information; these actors include motivational speakers, itinerant preachers, and standup comics. While their primary role obligation is not to diffusion culture from group to group, this constitutes an indirect result of their multi-group contact.

Media diffusion

The final interlocks that knit groups together are the specialized media. Media reach numerous groups simultaneously, providing the basis of shared knowledge. Media productions (opera, rock fests) are not accessed by random audiences. To the contrary, awareness results from prior interest, as interest shapes the boundary of exposure.

An important domain in the study of subcultures is that of countercultures, because, as noted, groups that are treated as subcultural are those that stand apart from the mainstream. However, in contrast to the traditional subculture, participants within countercultural groups typically share a consciousness that they are oppositional or counter-hegemonic (Yinger 1982). As typically defined, countercultures politicize or define their cultural themes as constituting a social critique. More explicitly than subcultural participation, embracing a counterculture suggests the explicit choice of an identity that differentiates a person from a dominant class. Fortunately for the stability of society, such groups are typically limited in participation. A countercultural perspective is inevitably historically and geographically situated, and, so, for example, countercultural movements were more prominent in the ferment of the late 1960s and early 1970s than currently, even though the distinctive styles of some youth groups (Goths, for instance) incorporate countercultural elements. In societies with strong youth movements, such as activist movements in Brazil (Mische 2007) or alienated youth in Japan (Sato 1991), these opposition networks can be quite robust.

Within the contemporary American context at least, the cultures of groups that oppose dominant systems are rarely fully oppositional; oppositional claims may constitute only a relatively small portion of a group's activity. Still, it is that rejection of dominant norms and values that both outsiders and insiders use to characterize the group. At issue is how a group's members come to treat their shared identity and activity: whether their identity is primarily internal to the group or whether—as in the case of countercultural groups— the subculture presents an active rejection of the mainstream culture.

Conclusion

Just as the culture concept in sociology can be linked to macro-sociological analysis, culture as a form of practice and as a negotiated order equally belongs to the micro- and meso-level. Culture ultimately comprised of actions that are performed and viewed or objects that are manufactured and consumed. This suggests that the locale and the timing of production are critical to its analysis. I began by describing culture as a behavioral domain that is constructed in and indigenous to small groups. Extending the analysis, I argued that society is comprised as a network of interlinked groups, which when it is segmented into networks of groups leads to the recognition of subcultures. Those sub-cultures that take an oppositional stance to the consensually recognized social order, and in which identities support this rejection, permit some cultures—as in the case of countercultures—to be sites of resistance, not only in their ideas and their collective action, but reflected in the selves of actors.

References

Benzecry, Claudio E. 2007. "Beauty at the Gallery: Sentimental Education and Operatic Community in Contemporary Buenos Aires." Pp. 171–92 in Craig Calhoun and Richard Sennett, eds., *Practicing Culture*. London: Routledge.

Collins, Randall. 1981. "On the Microfoundations of Macrosociology." *American Journal of Sociology* 86: 984–1014.

———. 1998. *The Sociology of Philosophies: A Global Theory of Intellectual Change*. Cambridge, MA: Harvard University Press.

———. 2004. *Interaction Ritual Chains*. Princeton, NJ: Princeton University Press.

Dawkins, Richard. 2006. *The Selfish Gene*, third edition. New York: Oxford University Press.

de la Pradelle, Michèle. 2006. *Market Day in Provence*. Chicago: University of Chicago Press.

Eliasoph, Nine and Lichterman, Paul. 2003. "Culture in Interaction." *American Journal of Sociology* 108: 735–94.

Emirbayer, Mustafa and Sheller, Mimi. 1998. "Publics in History." *Theory and Society* 27: 727–79.

Farrell, Michael. 2001. *Collaborative Circles: Friendship Dynamics and Creative Work*. Chicago: University of Chicago Press.

221

Fine, Gary Alan. 1979. "Small Groups and Culture Creation: The Idioculture of Little League Baseball Teams." *American Sociological Review* 44: 733–45.

Fine, Gary Alan and Harrington, Brooke. 2004. "Tiny Publics: Small Groups and Civil Society." *Sociological Theory* 22: 341–56.

Fine, Gary Alan and Kleinman, Sherryl. 1979. "Rethinking Subculture: An Interactionist Analysis." *American Journal of Sociology* 85: 1–20.

Gibson, David. 2008. "How the Outside Gets In: Modeling Conversation Permeation." *Annual Review of Sociology* 34: 359–84.

Goffman, Erving. 1983. "The Interaction Order." *American Sociological Review* 48: 1–17.

Goldfarb, Jeffrey. 2006. *The Politics of Small Things: The Power of the Powerless in Dark Times*. Chicago: University of Chicago Press.

Granovetter, Mark. 1973. "The Strength of Weak Ties." *American Journal of Sociology* 78: 1360–80.

Habermas, Jürgen. 1991. *The Structural Transformation of the Public Sphere*. Cambridge, MA: MIT Press.

Hebdige, Dick. 1981. *Subculture: The Meaning of Style*. London: Routledge.

Herzfeld, Michael. 1993. *The Social Production of Indifference*. Chicago: University of Chicago Press.

Ikegami, Eiko. 2000. "A Sociological Theory of Publics: Identity and Culture as Emergent Properties in Networks." *Social Research* 67: 989–1029.

——. 2005. *Bonds of Civility: Aesthetic Networks and the Political Origins of Japanese Culture*. New York: Cambridge University Press.

Janis, Irving. 1982. *Groupthink: Psychological Studies of Policy Decisions and Fiascos*. Boston: Houghton Mifflin.

Katovich, Michael and Couch, Carl. 1992. "The Nature of Social Pasts and Their Use as Foundations for Situated Action." *Symbolic Interaction* 15: 25–47.

Lawler, Edward, Thye, Shane, and Yoon, Jeongkoo. 2008. "Social Exchange and Micro Social Order." *American Sociological Review* 73: 519–42.

Mische, Ann. 2007. *Partisan Publics: Communication and Contention across Brazilian Youth Activist Networks*. Princeton, NJ: Princeton University Press.

Mische, Ann and White, Harrison. 1998. "Between Conversation and Situation: Public Switching Dynamics across Network Domains." *Social Research* 65: 695–724.

Oldenburg, Ray. 1989. *The Great Good Place: Cafes, Coffee Shops, Bookstores, Bars, Hair Salons, and Other Hangouts at the Heart of a Community*. New York: Paragon House.

Perrin, Andrew. 2005. "Political Microcultures: Linking Civic Life and Democratic Discourse." *Social Forces* 84: 1049–82.

Sato, Ikuya. 1991. *Kamikaze Biker: Parody and Anomy in Affluent Japan*. Chicago: University of Chicago Press.

Schegloff, Emanuel. 2007. *Sequence Organization in Interaction: A Primer in Conversation Analysis*. Cambridge: Cambridge University Press.

Scott, James C. 1998. *Seeing Like a State: How Certain Schemes to Improve the Human Condition Have Failed*. New Haven, CT: Yale University Press.

Sezneva, Olga. 2007. "'We Have Never Been German': The Economy of Digging in Russian Kaliningrad." Pp. 13–34 in Craig Calhoun and Richard Sennett, eds., *Practicing Culture*. London: Routledge.

Shibutani, Tamotsu. 1955. "Reference Groups as Perspectives." *American Journal of Sociology* 60: 562–69.

Sion, Liora and Ben-Ari, Eyal. 2005. "Hungry, Weary and Horny: Joking and Jesting among Israel's Combat Reserves." *Israel Affairs* 11: 656–72.

Strauss, Anselm. 1978. *Negotiations*. San Francisco: Jossey-Bass.

Unruh, David. 1980. "The Nature of Social Worlds." *Pacific Sociological Review* 23: 271–96.

White, Harrison. 1995. "Network Switchings and Bayesian Forks: Reconstructing the Social and Behavioral Sciences." *Social Research* 62: 1035–63.

Yinger, J. Milton. 1982. *Countercultures: The Promise and the Peril of a World Turned Upside Down*. New York: Free Press.

21

Culture and self

Gary Gregg

The sections on "culture and self" in the row of social and cultural psychology textbooks on my shelf all present the consensus that Westerners live in individualist cultures and develop "independent" or "egocentric" selves, whereas non-Westerners live in collectivist cultures and develop "interdependent" or "sociocentric selves" (see Cross and Gore 2003 for a review). This research was spurred by Hofstede's (1980) multi-national survey of IBM employees, by Shweder and Bourne's (1984) contrast of "sociocentric" Indian versus "egocentric" American selves, and by Geertz's discussion of the Moroccan "mosaic" self, in which he made the often-cited observation that "The Western conception of the person as a bounded, unique, more or less integrated motivational and cognitive universe ... [is] a rather peculiar idea within the context of the world's cultures" (1984: 126). Many of the textbooks illustrate the basic contrast with a diagram showing selves with "solid" versus "fluid" boundaries based on Markus and Kitayama's "Culture and the Self" (1991), and several illustrate it with photos contrasting idiosyncratically clothed American students in informal settings with Asian students at festivals in uniform. None, however, reports the well-established criticisms of the "we're egocentric/they're sociocentric" view, such as Spiro's (1993) observation that William James, G.H. Mead, and Erik Erikson all proposed sociocentric theories of the self, or the ample evidence that individualism (hereafter "I") and collectivism (hereafter "C") co-exist in most societies, as Triandis (1994) argued. In fact, Markus and Kitayama originally presented both a *boundary permeability* model (sociocentrics have less solidly bounded selves), and a *repertoire of schemata* model (people have both I and C self-schemas but sociocentrics more frequently activate C). The latter model points to the co-existence of I and C, but the textbooks continue to feature the boundary permeability view.

Takano and Osaka's (1999) literature review and Matsumoto's (1999) meta-analysis cast doubt on whether the I versus C contrast holds for Japan and America, and Oyser-man *et al.*'s (2002) meta-analysis found only limited support for I versus C as a core dimension of global cultural variation. A series of comments on this study called for abandoning or significantly modifying the I versus C construct. These developments bring cultural psychology—and especially the study of "culture and self"—to a point of crisis. The *repertoire of schemata* model may offer researchers a nuanced model for studying the "bicultural" or "hybrid" selves that often develop among ethnic minorities, immigrants, and others who live in multiple cultures. But the trouble with I versus C may run deeper, stemming from the project of identifying global dimensions of "self" on which cultures vary.

If I versus C does not provide a robust model of "culture and self," how should researchers proceed? One quandary that immediately arises concerns the many definitions of "self." As Spiro pointed out, researchers have used the term imprecisely to refer to (1) a culture's *explicit* "concept of personhood," (2) a culture's *implicit* "concept of personhood" as inferred from public rituals or etiquettes of daily interaction, (3) an individual's "persona" in key social roles, (4) an individual's "repertoire of self schemata," (5) an individual's fluid, constructed-by-discourse-in-the-moment "subject positions," (6) an individual's relatively stable "identity," or (7) the whole of an individual's personality. Other studies have described "self" as the ontological or existential core of subjective experience. Leary and Tangney (2003: 7) conclude that conflicting uses of "self" yield a "conceptual morass." A second quandary concerns the definition of "culture." Most researchers adopt the commonsense notion that culture consists of values and meanings that its members *share* (e.g. Lehman *et al.* 2004). In contrast, Wallace (1961) and Schwartz (1972) argue for a *distributed* notion of culture: that culture's elements are distributed unequally, with some individuals and groups internalizing features that others know only cursorily. Many "post-modern" ethnographers view culture as comprised of *intersecting discourses*, that some draw on Gramsci to describe as "hegemonic" and "counter-hegemonic," and others on Bakhtin to describe as a "polyphony" or "heteroglossia" of voices.

Back to the future: culture and personality?

How might cross-cultural researchers work through the quandaries? For all of its flaws, the much-maligned "configurationist" theory developed by Ruth Benedict, Margaret Mead, and Gregory Bateson offers a surprisingly sophisticated model of cultural influence on psychological development. Inspired by Boas's and Sapir's studies of the diffusion of linguistic and cultural "traits," this theory holds that the configuration of a culture develops when practices and beliefs are borrowed from neighboring cultures and revised to fit with a society's practical way of life and with the meanings conferred on it. As this borrowing and revision go on, a culture also consolidates around psychological traits from the "arc of human possibility" that affirm and accentuate some emotions and motives while suppressing others.

Several important implications follow. The configurationists' cultural relativism did *not* entail belief in the complete plasticity of the human psyche as an entity to be shaped by culture. Rather, the configurationists sought a model of psychological development in which temperament and culture interact. They believed that each cultural configuration favors those individuals born with temperaments well suited to it, but presents developmental obstacles for those born with less congruent temperaments. The model recognized that most individuals inevitably encounter developmental conflict with the adult selves that socialization to the culture encourages, and it provides a potentially powerful theory of deviance: Those with mismatched temperaments are most likely to become deviant. It thus differs from most contemporary models of culture-and-self that ignore developmental struggle and assume either that the twigs are bent gracefully by social learning processes or that the "pounding down" of potentially deviant nails (Markus and Kitayama 1991) creates no lasting structure of tension or conflict.

The "layered" genotype–phenotype theories of Lewin (1936) and LeVine (1973) seek to take account of these tensions. Both use "genotype" metaphorically, to capture the fact that important aspects of personality may not see public, "phenotypic" expression, and that "phenotypic" behaviors may be maintained by social roles or situational demands that do not express a person's core motives and emotions. Chodorow (1978), Herdt (1990), and Whiting (1994) adopt layered views when they theorize that some cultures create discontinuities in boys' development of masculinity, fostering an early "feminine/maternal" sense of self that boys must renounce and symbolically excise in order to become masculine men. They see misogynistic ideologies as strengthened insofar as they defend against the early "feminine/maternal" sense of self.

McAdams (1995) and Gregg (1991, 2005, 2007) have extended the genotype–phenotype models to propose three-level theories of psychological organization. McAdams's model derives from his synthesis of personality theories, and postulates Level I consisting of traits, Level II, of motives, and Level III, of identity as embedded in a life-narrative. Gregg's model derives from analyses of "study of lives" interviews with American and Moroccan young adults, and uses the term *core personality* to correspond roughly to LeVine's genotypic and McAdams's Level I, *social personality* to G.H. Mead's "social self" and McAdams's Level II, and *identity* to LeVine's phenotypic and McAdams's Level III. These layered models have much broader scope than "culture and self": they seek to describe the cultural shaping of psyches as a *developmental* process, one that creates culturally distinctive disjunctions, tensions, and conflicts between *levels* of psychological organization. They also suggest a resolution to the quandary of defining "self"—that "self" should not be used as a proxy for "personality," and that *self-concepts* should be distinguished from *identities*. That is, researchers may study the cultural shaping of *identity*, meaning the relatively permanent ideology/world-view that Erikson believed integrates personality by anchoring a life-project in a set of values and social relationships. Alternately, they may study the cultural shaping of *self-concepts*, that tend to be situation or role specific and relatively provisional (or, as discourse theorists describe, that shift as people take up varying "speaker positions" in social dialogues) (Wetherell and Edley 1999; Bamberg 2004). Bamberg (2006) captures this distinction by contrasting the representations constructed in the "little stories" of daily conversation with the "big stories" of life-histories. The "cultural construction of self" thus entails two quite different processes: the formation of role-, situation-, and discourse-specific *self-concepts*, and the development of relatively permanent and trans-situational *identities*. Certainly these are linked: identities are influenced by "small story" micro-social interaction, and daily self-presentations draw on "big story" identities. But it is crucial to recognize the differences between them.

As for the quandary of culture, ethnographies of even simple, pre-modern societies show the inadequacy of the "shared values and meanings" definition, and the need for *distributed* and *intersecting discourse* views. Here too, configurationist theory can help conceptualize how individuals fashion identities as "culture writ small": individuals selectively adopt elements from their distributed cultural heritage(s), and revise them in accordance with their social positions, their emotional styles, and the meanings they seek

225

to live by. Every "bit" of identity thus comes from culture, so that identity appears entirely "constructed" by appropriation of culture. But individuals have great latitude as to which elements of their culture to select and reject, and then to idiosyncratically re-fashion as they weave them into identities. Together, an intersecting discourse view of culture and a model of identity based on selection and adaptation of elements suggest that culture does not just stamp its imprint on its members' psyches. A great many life-histories show that even those who appear to most archetypically embody their culture's ideals often come to do so only after decades of struggle, and that it isn't so much cultural meanings that do the stamping but the harder realities of hunger, market forces, and authorities' fists.

Culture and self-conceptions

One direction beyond the I versus C approach comes from recent studies showing that members of ethnic minority groups and immigrants tend to form two "cultural frames" (Pouliasi and Verkuyten 2007) that entail self-concepts associated with majority and minority reference groups or with culture-of-origin and culture-of-residence. Psychological studies of "biculturalism" or "hybridity" generally endorse a "repertoire of self-schemata" view, according to which cultural priming—often by language (Schrauf and Rubin 2000) or cultural icons (Sui *et al.* 2007)—elicits self-schema and information processing congruent with the culture's regnant values. While these studies recognize the co-existence of I and C and the multiplicity of self-concepts, they rarely examine the specific cultural content of self-concepts.

Another direction beyond I versus C appears in ethnographic studies of what might be termed the micro-social construction of selves. There is a rich literature on this process in Japan that converges toward a consensus on basics. Nakane (1970), Lebra (2004), Doi (1973), and recently Bachnik (1994), Rosenberger (1989), and Quinn (1994) analyze situational constructions of "selves" in Japan in relation to an array of oppositions—*uchi* ("inside") versus *soto* ("outside"), *ura* ("in back") versus *omote* ("surface appearance"), *ninjoo* ("personal feelings") versus *giri* ("social obligation"), *honne* ("inner feeling") versus *tateme* ("surface obligations"), *kiryoku* ("disciplined ki energy") versus *kimochi* ("spontaneous ki energy")—that forge horizontal group bonds and vertical dyads through an emotional dialectic of *amae* (indulgence of dependence). There is a small but influential literature on this process in Arab-Muslim societies, mainly in Geertz's (1979), Rosen's (1984), and Eickelman's (1985) analyses of the micro-social construction of Moroccan self-conceptions. This work focuses on the building up of social structures from dyadic negotiations, constructing shifting "mosaic" selves in the process.

Many of the scholars conducting such research have, however, supported the I versus C hypothesis by claiming that the resulting "situated" and "relational" selves differ from Americans' independent selves (see, e.g., Geertz 1984; Lebra 2004). This claim seems unwarranted in light of symbolic interactionist and discourse-analysis studies showing how micro-social negotiations yield shifting, situated, and relational self-conceptions in the US and Britain (e.g. Bamberg 2004; Wetherell and Edley 1999), not to mention theories of Western women's relational selves (Chodorow 1978: Gilligan 1982). The evidence is strong that cultures differ in the "little stories" and meanings by which situated/relational self-conceptions are constructed, but *not* that Westerners do not construct situational and relational self-conceptions too.

Culture and identity

Most studies of Mediterranean and Arab-Muslim cultures have focused less on dyadic negotiation and more on the stratified and gender-based social structures that anchor cultural ideologies of honor and modesty, and on how these structures shape more permanent and less negotiable selves or *identities*. For men, honor-based values typically entail agonistic orientations to other men, intimidating-protective domination of women and junior men, and control of women's sexuality by surveillance and seclusion. Honorable manhood has been reported to be symbolized by the rhetoric of patriliny, "seed and soil" metaphors of reproduction, sacrilization of women as virgins and mothers, the architecture of dwellings, facial hair, clothing styles, rifles, raiding, and performances of dance and poetry (see Gregg 2005 for a summary). Herzfeld (1980, 1985) shows that Mediterranean communities differ in the traits seen to embody honor, but all entail projecting distinctly masculine performative styles. Women and junior men are excluded from many of the symbols and performances, but can accrue honor by displaying deference and self-restraint (Abu-Lughod 1986). El Messiri (1978) offers an analysis of the *ibn al-balad* ("son of the homeland") identity fashioned by residents of the "popular" quarters of Cairo that represents an elaboration of honor-based identities in a context of increasingly salient stratification. The son of the homeland embraces tough manliness and traditional clothing and speech styles in deliberate contrast both to the Westernized *ibn al-zawat* ("son of the upper class") style of the educated elite, and to the ignorant and crude style of the rural *fellahin* (peasants). As el Messiri glimpsed, a similar embracing of "authentic" tradition against both a "corrupt" Westernized elite and indigenous "backwards" groups has come to anchor many Islamist identities (Gregg 2005, 2007). In short, an individual's social "positioning" within a culture—especially based on age, gender, and class or caste—strongly influences both the set of identities he or she legitimately can adopt, and the constellation of rewards and punishments deployed to assure compliance (Holland and Leander 2004).

Similarly, Kondo's (1990) ethnography of workers in a Tokyo artisanal factory delineates the matrix of positions within which they "craft" selves (I suggest "identities"). She begins with the contrast between (1) the "downtown" traditionally Japanese Shitamachi district where the workers live and work long hours for low pay in small family firms, and (2) the "uptown" Westernized Yamanote area, home to professionals and "salarymen" who work in large corporations. Against the Yamanote stereotype of them as backward and vulgar (though also as "quaint anachronisms"), Shitamachi residents represent themselves as "more honest, more open, less pretentious," and closer to the true/traditional Japanese character (Kondo 1990: 73)—paralleling el Messiri's account of Cairo's "son of the homeland" identity. Kondo then describes the "disciplinary" combination of nurturance and coercion deployed to develop selves dedicated to duty. She focuses especially on (1) childrearing practices that foster a strong bond of protection and dependence, combined with deliberately induced fear of abandonment and with evocations of "indebtedness" to parents that is to be repaid by obedience and conformity; and (2) the reinforcement of this pattern at a week-long training the employees received at an "ethics school" that combines military discipline, physical hardship, group responsibility, meditation, and lectures on indebtedness to parents—all designed to foster a "sincere heart … a heart sensitive not to its own desires, but to the needs of others" (Kondo 1990: 105). She observes, however, that many workers ambivalently shift between embracing and rejecting the "sincere heart" self that these practices promote.

Kondo uses "selves" in many ways: as role- or situation-specific self-concepts, as concepts encompassing the whole of personality, and as cultural discourses that individuals draw upon to structure life-histories and define identities. But she also emphasizes the self's positioning *vis-à-vis* class, age, and gender, as well as its developmental history, showing that coercion is required to create and maintain the self, resulting in sometimes acute tension between the duty-to-others and company-as-family identities fostered by authorities, on the one hand, and the "selfish" subjects that sometimes resist, on the other. Shimizu similarly reports that many of the Japanese adolescents he interviewed either resist or cannot become the "sensitive to others," "sincere heart" selves that the culture prescribes; he argues that an "ontological self" "transcends culturally constructed selves" (2001: 225). In both Arab-Muslim and Japanese cultures, then, it appears that researchers can study either the micro-politics of dyadic negotiation of situated/relational *self-concepts* or the developmental history and macro-politics of more stable *identities*.

Culture and multiple identities

Katherine Ewing (1990) describes how her interviews with a Pakistani woman named Shamim show "rapidly shifting self-representations" between "two self-images based on inconsistent premises." She notes that when Shamim changes self-images she also changes her images of her parents and the personal memories that go with them, so that each of the two self-representations comprises a whole "frame of reference." Shamim generally remains unaware of her shifts, so each frame of reference creates a feeling that the self is whole, creating an "illusion of wholeness" that Ewing thinks may be universal:

> People construct a series of self-representations that are based on selected cultural concepts of person and selected "chains" of personal memories. Each self-concept is experienced as whole and continuous, with its own history and memories that emerge in a specific context, to be replaced by another self-representation when the context changes.
>
> (Ewing 1990: 253)

Like other Pakistanis whom Ewing (1991) interviewed, Shamim does not just shift among role- or situation-based *self-concepts*, but between two *identities* that correspond to the main culture war being waged in her society—one identity of an educated career woman with modern Westernist values and the other of a dutiful daughter loyal to her traditional Muslim family. The young Moroccans I interviewed often show a similar shifting of identities, between one that casts the narrator as fleeing the backward and constraining world of rural tradition for the cultured and Westernized world of urban modernity, and another rejecting the corrupt and insecure world of Westernized urban modernity for the authentic, simple, and secure rural world of family and religion (Gregg 2007). Like the Pakistani Shamim, some Moroccans did not recognize their shifts; a couple of them gracefully combined identities to express contrasting sides of their characters; several felt torn and paralyzed; one woman despaired that she had become a double personality, "a French Khadija and a Muslim Khadija." Similarly, Arab-Muslim novelists and scholars have described how the pervasive Westernist versus indigenist dualities create conflicting or even "schizophrenic" identities (Shayegan 1992; Barakat 1993; Ghareeb 1996).

Psychologists working in the "narrative study of lives" tradition have proposed three models of the multiplicity—and integration—of identities. McAdams (1988, 1995, 2001) draws on Erikson to view personality as differentiated into a small number of configurations—organized by imagoes and scripts—that achieve integration in an overall identity rooted in the plot structure of a life-narrative. Gregg (1991, 2007) draws on Lévi-Strauss to conceptualize personality as differentiated by a small number of contrasting identity discourses, each anchored in a set of often-reversible "Me" versus "not-Me" binary oppositions (i.e. "modern" = Me and "traditional" = not-Me that reverses to "traditional" = Me and "modern" = not-Me). These oppositions are integrated by structurally ambiguous "key" symbols (Ortner 1973) or metaphors (Turner 1967) that enable people to make figure/ground-like reversals in their meanings and thereby shift identity-defining discourses while preserving the illusion of wholeness. In an alternative approach, Hermans and Kempen (1991, 1998) draw on G.H. Mead and Bakhtin to view the self as a structure of dialogue among multiple subject-positions, with some voices typically displaying "dominance" over others. The three models—*plot structure*, *shifting discourses*, and *dialogue*—describe processes by which multiple identities can be differentiated and integrated, though it is not clear whether individuals tend to display all three forms or differ in which they mainly employ. All three treat identity as organizing personality, so that identity affirms and expresses some of a person's emotions, traits, and motives, and denies or "hypocognizes" (Levy 1973) others—which via projection then may appear as abject or villainous characters in one's life-story, as "not-Me" or "anti-self" figures in a discourse of identity, or as condemned or rejected voices in dialogue. These models thereby seek to account for (1) the inner tensions that an identity manages, (2) the representational centrality of "other" ethnicities, religions, genders, etc. to the definition of a person's identity, and (3) the organization of empathy or hostility directed at out-group ("not-Me") stereotypes. They suggest that a culture's predominant cleavages of status and power deeply shape identities, and that by linking the interpretation and management of affect with often-stereotypic representations of societal positions and groups, individual struggles for identity fuel culture wars.

Conclusion

In the wake of the meta-analyses and critiques of I versus C, it is important to emphasize that there are profound psychological differences between societies that, from birth, foster a life-long loyalty and subordination to parents, kin, and face-to-face groups, and those that raise children to leave home, become financially self-sufficient, and choose their own vocations, spouses, and life-styles. Many of these differences have been documented by researchers working within the I versus C framework (see Cross and Gore 2003). It may not, however, be appropriate to describe these as differences in *selves*. Even if cultures' predominant values and concepts of personhood can be arrayed on an I versus C continuum, there are good reasons to doubt that people's actual experiences, their repertoires of self-concepts, and their identities can correspondingly be scaled as independent versus interdependent or egocentric versus sociocentric. The early configurationists actually believed that the sort of cultural coherence typical of "collectivist" cultures better facilitates psychological individuation than do modern, fragmented cultures that celebrate individuality. A revised version of the "configura-tionist" view may in fact provide a sophisticated model for culture and self, as follows: (1) cultures—often subcultures in modern societies—select and combine elements from an "arc" of psychological characteristics, and seek to socialize individuals into con-formity with them; (2) individuals selectively adopt features from their *distributed* cultural heritage(s), and integrate them into life-styles and identities, often at odds with hegemonic cultural ideals; and (3) these processes frequently create developmental dis-continuities, resulting in lasting intra-psychic and interpersonal tensions that shifting identities seek to manage.

Beyond I versus C, then, ethnographic, discourse-analysis, and experimental studies of how *repertoires of self-concepts* organize behavioral flexibility will be even more important to understanding how these processes fashion the bi-culturalism and hybridity that globalization appears to be inducing. But these micro-social approaches will mislead if they do not recognize that people also form *identities* that are not organized only as repertoires of self-concepts, but as life-narratives, ideological discourses, and recurring dialogues. Identities may be developed in and deployed to negotiate dyadic interaction, but they are represented less in terms of micro-social roles and relationships than in terms of macro-social structure, specifically in representations of the moral, religious, and psychological characteristics stereotypically associated with macro-social positions: Shitamachi versus Yamanote; artisan versus "salaryman"; honorable man versus modest woman; *ibn al-balad* versus *ibn al-zawat*; French versus Moroccan-Muslim. The nature of the relationship between self-concepts negotiated in shifting dyads and "little stories," and identities anchored in "big stories" and political-religious ideologies lies open as a major frontier of research.

Finally, relatively few theories of "culture and self" give appropriate weight to the extent to which self-concepts and identities are formed in adaptation and resistance to the forces that "pound down" a society's young with powerful rewards and harsh coercion. Perhaps this issue was more salient for both Eastern and Western scholars in the post-World War II period. The first chapter of Minami's (1971 [1953]: 3) *Psychology of the Japanese People* is entitled "The Japanese Self," but it begins not with "social relati-vism" but with a section on "Be Submissive to Authority." Faced with despotic regimes and "neo-patriarchal" social relations, Arab-Muslim scholars have examined the role of intimidating authorities—from fathers to teachers to government officials to dictators—in shaping apparently sociocentric loyalty to family, kin, patrons, and rulers (Ammar 1964; Hijazi 1970; Sharabi 1988; Hammoudi 1997). They more often have used the term "personality" (*shakhsiyya*) than "self" (*dhat*), but most see identities ultimately built around defenses against vulnerability and fear that lead to identification with authorities. Kondo's analysis of the disciplinary techniques deployed to foster the crafting of dutiful "sincere hearts" appears unusual in recent research. Investigations of self-concepts and identities would do well to re-establish contact with studies of authority and obedience, on the one hand, and with prejudice and ethnocentrism, on the other. As Erikson has observed, the kind of ideological struggles that raged in Weimar Germany, in Taisho and Showa Japan, in post-1967 Arab societies, and in America in the 1990s serve to polarize identities, and recruit the passions of youths' identity-quests to both progressive and totalitarian movements. Political scientist John Sidel (2006: 13) argues that recent "riots, pogroms, and jihad" in Indonesia resulted from a confluence of group competition and struggles for identity in which the sensed deficits in one's self were attributed to "thefts" by ethnic/religious Others. The world of the 1920s and 1930s may not have been the laboratory of cultural variation in childrearing that Margaret Mead imagined, but the globalizing world of the new millennia may not be far from a laboratory of combustible identity politics.

References

Abu-Lughod, Lila. 1986. *Veiled Sentiments*. Berkeley: University of California Press.

Ammar, Hamid. 1964. *Fi bina' al-bashar (On Building Human Character)*. Cairo: Sirs Allayan.

Bachnik, Jane. 1994. "Self, Social Order and Language." Pp. 3–37 in Jane Bachnik and Charles Quinn, Jr., eds., *Situated Meaning*. Princeton, NJ: Princeton University Press.

Bamberg, Michael. 2004. "Form and Functions of 'Slut Bashing' in Male Identity Constructions in 15-Year-Olds." *Human Development* 47(6): 331–53.

——. 2006 "Stories: Big or Small." *Narrative Inquiry* 16(1): 139–47.

Barakat, Halim. 1993. *The Arab World*. Berkeley: University of California Press.

Chodorow, Nancy. 1978. *The Reproduction of Mothering*. Berkeley: University of California Press.

Cross, Susan and Gore, Jonathan. 2003. "Cultural Models of Self." Pp. 536–64 in M. Leary and J. Tangney, eds., *Handbook of Self and Identity*. New York: Guilford.

Doi, Takeo. 1973. *The Anatomy of Dependence*. New York: Harper & Row.

Eickelman, Dale. 1985. *Knowledge and Power in Morocco*. Princeton, NJ: Princeton University Press.

el Messiri, Sawsan. 1978. *Ibn al-Balad*. The Netherlands: E.J. Brill.

Ewing, Katherine. 1990. "The Illusion of Wholeness." *Ethos* 18(3): 251–78.

——. 1991. "The Dream of Spiritual Initiation and the Organization of Self Representation among Pakistani Sufis." *American Ethnologist* 17(1): 56–74.

Geertz, Clifford. 1979. "Suq: The Bazaar Economy in Sefrou." Pp. 123–244 in C. Geertz, H. Geertz, and L. Rosen, eds., *Meaning and Order in Moroccan Society*. New York: Cambridge University Press.

——. 1984. "From the Natives' Point of View." Pp. 123–36 in R. Shweder and R. LeVine, eds., *Culture Theory*. Cambridge, MA: Harvard University Press.

Ghareeb, Abdelkrim. 1996. *Ai namoudaj al-twafiq al-da al-shebab mathrebi? (What Model for Moroccan Youth?)* Pp. 117–34 in *A'lim al-nafs wa al-qadia al-mujtema' ma'ser (Psychology and Issues of Modern Society)*. Rabat: Mohammed V University.

Gilligan, Carol. 1982. *In a Different Voice*. Cambridge, MA: Harvard University Press.

Gregg, Gary. 1991. *Self-Representation*. New York: Greenwood Press.

——. 2005. *The Middle East: A Cultural Psychology*. New York: Oxford University Press.

——. 2007. *Culture and Identity in a Muslim Society*. New York: Oxford University Press.

Hammoudi, Abdullah. 1997. *Master and Disciple*. Chicago: University of Chicago Press.

Herdt, Gilbert. 1990. "Sambia Nosebleeding Rites and Male Proximity to Women." In J. Stigler, R. Shweder, and G. Herdt, eds., *Cultural Psychology*. Cambridge: Cambridge University Press.

Hermans, Hubert and Kempen, Harry. 1991. *The Dialogical Self*. San Diego, CA: Academic.

——. 1998. "Moving Cultures." *American Psychologist* 53(10): 1111–20.

Herzfeld, Michael. 1980. "Honour and Shame." *Man* 15: 339–51.

——. 1985. *The Poetics of Manhood*. Princeton, NJ: Princeton University Press.

Hijazi, Mustafa. 1970. *Al-takhaluf al-ijtima'i (Underdeveloped Society)*. Beirut: Ma'had al-inma' al-Arabi.

Hofstede, Geert. 1980. *Culture's Consequences*. Beverly Hills, CA: Sage.

Holland, Dorothy and Leander, Kevin. 2004. "Ethnographic Studies of Positioning and Subjectivity." *Ethos* 32(2): 127–39.

Kakar, Sudhir. 1981. *The Inner World*. Delhi: Oxford University Press.

Kondo, Dorinne. 1990. *Crafting Selves*. Chicago: University of Chicago Press.

Leary, M. and Tangney, J. 2003. "The Self as an Organizing Construct in the Behavioral and Social Sciences." Pp. 3–14 in M. Leary and J. Tangney, eds., *Handbook of Self and Identity*. New York: Guilford Press.

Lebra, Takie. 2004. *The Japanese Self in Cultural Logic*. Honolulu: University of Hawaii Press.

Lehman, Darrin, Chiu, Chi-yue, and Schaller, Mark. 2004. "Psychology and Culture." *Annual Review of Psychology* 55: 689–714.

LeVine, Robert. 1973. *Culture, Behavior, and Personality*. Chicago: Aldine.

Levy, Robert. 1973. *Tahitians*. Chicago: University of Chicago.

Lewin, Kurt. 1936. *Principles of Topological Psychology*. New York: McGraw-Hill.

McAdams, Dan. 1988. *Power, Intimacy, and the Life Story*. New York: Guilford.

——. 1995. "What Do We Know When We Know a Person?" *Journal of Personality and Social Psychology* 63(3): 365–96.

——. 2001. "The Psychology of Life Stories." *Review of General Psychology* 5(22): 100–22.

Markus, Hazel and Kitayama, Shinobu. 1991. "Culture and the Self." *Psychological Review* 98: 224–53.

Matsumoto, David. 1999. "Culture and Self." *Asian Journal of Social Psychology* 2: 289–310.

Minami, Hiroshi. 1971 (1953). *Psychology of the Japanese People*. Tokyo: University of Tokyo Press.

Nakane, Chie. 1970. *Japanese Society*. Berkeley: University of California Press.

Ortner, Sherry. 1973. "On Key Symbols." *American Anthropologist* 75: 1338–46.

Oyserman, D., Coon, H., and Kemmelmeier, M. 2002. "Rethinking Individualism and Collectivism." *Psychological Bulletin* 128(1): 3–72.

Pouliasi, Katerina and Verkuyten, Maykel. 2007. "Networks of Meaning and the Bicultural Mind." *Journal of Experimental Social Psychology* 43: 955–63.

Quinn, Charles. 1994. "Uchi/soto: Tip of a Semiotic Iceberg?" Pp. 247–94 in J. Bachnik and C. Quinn, eds., *Situated Meanings*. Princeton, NJ: Princeton University Press.

Roland, Alan. 1988. *In Search of Self in India and Japan*. Princeton, NJ: Princeton University Press.

Rosen, Lawrence. 1984. *Bargaining for Reality*. Chicago: University of Chicago Press.

Rosenberger, Nancy. 1989. "Dialectic Balance in the Polar Model of Self: The Japanese Case." *Ethos* 17(1): 88–113.

Schrauf, Robert and Rubin, David. 2000. "Internal Languages of Retrieval." *Memory and Cognition* 28(4): 616–23.

Schwartz, Theodore. 1972. "Distributive Models of Culture in Relation to Societal Scale." In *Scale and Social Organization*. Burg Warrenstein: Wenner-Gren Symposium No. 55.

Sharabi, Hisham. 1988. *Neopatriarchy*. New York: Oxford University Press.

Shayegan, Daryush. 1992. *Cultural Schizophrenia*. Syracuse, NY: Syracuse University Press.

Shimizu, Hidetada. 2001. "Beyond Individualism and Sociocentrism." Pp. 205–27 in H. Shimizu and R. LeVine, eds., *Japanese Frames of Mind*. Cambridge: Cambridge University Press.

Shweder, Richard and Bourne, E. 1984. "Does the Concept of the Person Vary Cross-culturally?" Pp. 158–99 in R. Shweder and R. LeVine, eds., *Culture Theory*. Cambridge, MA: Cambridge University Press.

Sidel, John. 2006. *Riots, Pogroms, Jihad*. Ithaca, NY: Cornell University Press.

Spiro, Melford. 1993. "Is the Western Conception of the Self 'Peculiar' within the Context of the World Cultures?" *Ethos* 21(2): 107–53.

Sui, J., Zhu, Y., and Chiu, C. 2007. "Bicultural Mind, Self-construal, and Self- and Mother-Reference Effects." *Journal of Experimental Social Psychology* 43: 818–24.

Takano, Yohtaro and Osaka, Eiko. 1999. "An Unsupported Common View: Comparing Japan and the U.S. on Individualism/Collectivism." *Asian Journal of Social Psychology* 2: 311–41.

Triandis, Harry. 1994. "Theoretical and Methodological Approaches to the Study of Collectivism and Individualism." Pp. 41–51 in U. Kim, H.C. Triandis, C., Kagitçibasi, S.-C. Choi, and G. Yoon, eds., *Individualism and Collectivism*. Thousand Oaks, CA: Sage Publications.

Turner, Victor. 1967. *The Forest of Symbols*. Ithaca, NY: Cornell University Press.

Wallace, Anthony. 1961. *Culture and Personality*. New York: Random House.

Wetherell, Margaret and Edley, Nigel. 1999. "Negotiating Hegemonic Masculinity." *Feminism and Psychology* 9(3): 335–56.

Whiting, John. 1994. *Culture and Human Development*, ed. E. Chasdi. Cambridge: Cambridge University Press.

22

From public multiculturalism to private multiculturality?

Rebecca Chiyoko King-O'Riain

Multiculturalism

Multiculturalism strives to celebrate and appreciate diverse cultures, races, and ethnicities. It is a social movement, an ideology, and a battleground for cultural ideas within legal, political, and national discourses. Multiculturalism in the United States is not an official government policy; it emerged from "below," out of the struggle for civil rights and on the back of the racial/ethnic "power" movements to gain equal representation and rights for people of color. For example, the 1964 Civil Rights Act was a result of this "bottom–up" process. Although multiculturalism is a relatively recent phenomenon, there have been heated debates about its efficacy as both an ideal and a policy in modern society. In the US, these debates—which address issues such as political correctness, reverse discrimination, colorblindness, etc.—are so heated because multiculturalism embodies a tension between the ideals of liberal equality, the autonomy of individuals/ groups, and notions of inclusion in the national whole. This essay briefly outlines the theories of multiculturalism in the US and applies them to international examples to see if multiculturalism plays out similarly in other parts of the world. I give examples of countries employing different models of multiculturalism—assimilationist (Japan), liberal (UK, Ireland), and cosmopolitan/social (France, Germany, and Sweden).

To build upon the concept of "multiculturality"—which has been defined as the lived experiences of cultural integration in various cultural contexts such as Hawaii (Finney 1963) and Germany (Zank 1998)—I then proceed to analyze an example of mixed–race people and the "problem" they pose to racial categorization in the US Census. Although multiculturalism signifies the coexistence of two or more preexisting cultures that are mutually exclusive, multiculturality implies a new cultural formation based on racial/ ethnic integration. Below, I draw on the concept to illustrate how mixed–race people are challenging state notions of "race" and "culture" in order to gain acknowledgment of multiplicity. I also seek to expand the concept of multiculturality in order to shift its application from personal cultural experience to cultural movements aimed at the state. Analysis along such lines shows how the agency of social actors transforms deeply embedded notions of culture (e.g. that racial identity is singular) in the state via the census. Through this example, we can see how cultural interaction redefines the idea of ethnic and racial communities, how specific processes shape both individual and interactional levels of identity, and how contact across groups (through multiracial people) can change the form and content of those groups.

Perspectives on multiculturalism

Hartmann and Gerteis (2005) have outlined three perspectives on multiculturalism—cosmopolitanism, fragmented pluralism, and interactive pluralism. They describe cosmopolitanism as an approach that "recogniz[es] the social value of diversity, but is skeptical about the obligations and constraints that group membership and societal cohesion can place on individuals." In cosmopolitan theories, the focus of multiculturalism is on the "lack of cultural specificity and resulting vagueness of its external boundary, and on tolerance and individual choice rather than mutual obligations. Group differences may well be important, but group identities are not to be totalizing or the source of public rights or obligations" (Hartmann and Gerteis 2005: 228). In turn, fragmented pluralism focuses on "the existence of a variety of distinctive and relatively self-contained mediating communities as a social reality, but also as a necessity and strength. Procedural norms rather than common moral bonds are important and a heavy emphasis is placed on the role of groups. This results in weaker macro-social boundaries but strong internal groups and boundaries" (Hartmann and Gerteis 2005: 229). In these theories, the role of the state is important for managing rights claims, but they assume the state is neutral. Finally, interactive pluralism "realizes the existence of distinct groups and cultures … it posits the need to cultivate common understanding across these differences through their mutual recognition and ongoing interaction" (Hartmann and Gerteis 2005: 231). The authors associate Hollinger (1995) with cosmopolitanism, Portes and Rumbaut (2001) with fragmented pluralism, and Taylor (1994) and Alexander (2001) with interactive pluralism. For Hartmann and Gerteis interactive pluralism is the most desirable option, but is interactive pluralism achievable? If so, how?

The above typology is helpful for organizing theories of multiculturalism, but the three theoretical approaches are based primarily on the US context and do not account for several "new trends" in multiculturalism around the world. Primarily, all the theories have difficulty accounting for the sense of connection and obligation that social actors may feel to more than one group or nation simultaneously (i.e. a sense of transnationality, multiraciality, hybridity, etc.). They assume homogeneity within groups/nations, when in fact such groups may have transnational connections and/or multiple racial backgrounds and may experience multiple allegiances to more than one group, national identity, and culture.

The approaches presented by Hartmann and Gerteis (2005) also falsely situate a strong internal group identity against a strong macro identity (in most cases, nationality). Again, this understanding of multiculturalism fails to account for individuals (and even whole cultural groups) who have both strong internal group identities and strong national identities prompted by dual allegiances, dual citizenship, and dual language identities. Some mixed-race people stand at exactly this intersection between multiple racial/ cultural groups, multiple nations, and multiple allegiances.

I will now consider how multiculturalism has played out abroad; after that, I focus on the case of multiracial people and racial/ethnic categorization in the US Census; this case shows that the project of multiculturalism has failed partly because it neglects the hybridity/transnationality of cultural identities and adopts a top–down approach to social diversity. I argue that—in order to influence state policy about rights and recognition—multiculturalism should be reframed as an issue of multiculturality from the bottom up, built upon the everyday lived practices of groups of people with multiple allegiances and backgrounds living together.

In the post-culture-war era, multiculturalism and its critics moved into Canada (see Kymlicka 2007), Australia (see Hage 2003), the United Kingdom, and to a lesser extent continental Europe and Asia. Examining these different national and cultural contexts allows us to see how different models of multiculturalism appear in different ways and how and when they can be linked to multicultural theories found in the approaches identified by Hartmann and Gerteis.

Cultural assimilation: Japan

Japan is an island nation believed to be historically, racially, and culturally "homogenous"—an example of cultural assimilation more than multiculturalism. Japan has a strong ideology of descent as linked to citizenship (e.g. one had to have a Japanese last or family name in order to register children for school or to become a citizen). Lie (2006) argues that Japan's changing economy draws immigrants and foreign laborers to the country, thus diversifying and making it a "multiethnic Japan." Burgess (2007) disagrees and finds that although Japan has more immigrants and guest workers than before, it is now only beginning to recognize "diversity." He argues that this recognition is often reluctant and driven by external pressure stemming from international relations rather than internal desires to appreciate cultural difference.

Siddle (2003: 1) finds that "the popular postwar notion of a 'unique' Japan with a mono-ethnic citizenry had served to marginalize and disempower the Ainu (a protected indigenous group)" and other minority groups in Japan such as Koreans, Chinese, and Japanese Brazilians. Keenly aware of the effects of ruling an island nation in a global economy, the Japanese state took measures to "recognize" Ainu in 1997 via the Ainu Cultural Promotion Act—but to protect only Ainu culture, not Ainu people as a distinct indigenous ethnic group. The Japanese state, even as its population reaches 10 percent non-Japanese, continues to deny citizenship to immigrants in Japan. Tarumoto (2003) argues that the Japanese government has made small changes to citizenship requirements but it has done so based not on an "internal multicultural logic" in response to increasing cultural diversity, but on an "external logic" stemming from international relations with other countries (mainly in the West). Changes in Japanese society are reluctant, and interactive pluralism is limited at best.

Liberal multiculturalism: the UK, Germany, and Ireland

In Europe the multicultural question is brought to the fore by the immigration of various groups, often postcolonial subjects from Africa and Asia. The question intensified in the post-9/11 era as Europe grew increasingly concerned with the presence of Muslims and the challenges they seemingly posed to "European culture." In the UK, Tariq Modood (2007) argues that the concern is misplaced: the rise of Islamic terrorism doesn't challenge

235

multiculturalism or lead to balkanization; rather, it shows that different groups need to be accommodated in diverse forms, not just by state actors but by other civil-society groups as well.

In the UK, immigrants come from former colonial outposts and citizenship is based on residency and knowledge of British culture, not bloodlines. Some argue that due to these historical factors and to current political attitudes towards multicultural-ism, immigrants and their descendants have "come to play a more important role in recent British history than their contemporaries in [countries such as] Germany, particu-larly if we examine their role in the political process and in popular culture" (Panayi 2004: 466).

In Ireland, there is no history of in-migration or of far-flung colonial subjects; discussions of multiculturalism and diversity are driven in large part by the "Celtic Tiger" economy, which brought rapid economic prosperity and significant and rapid increases in immigration. Today, many aspects of Irish society have been transformed by the presence of immigrants. The increasing cultural, linguistic, and religious diversity is happening largely without any formal policy regarding multiculturalism and with no formal approach to multicultural education. The rights of non-Irish workers and residents are protected under recent (1998) equality legislation and universal human-rights laws. However, for the most part, multicultural understandings emerge through everyday lived experience. Some argue that Ireland is more "open" to embracing cultural diversity because of its postcolonial past (Conway 2006). Yet although it is true that the country has no far right or white supremacist groups, certain constituencies (e.g. Immigration Control Platform) hold that immigration should be curtailed.

Boucher writes:

> It [the Irish government] simply assumes that these newer groups of EU [European Union] and non-EU immigrants will largely integrate into Irish society by themselves, through the neo-liberal modes of self-governance. … As such, the government does not need to abandon its present fragmented, cost-effective, de facto assimilationist, and laissez-faire integration policy.
>
> (Boucher 2008: 19)

There is no formal policy on the integration of immigrants into Ireland and Irish life, although services are offered in multiple languages (mainly Mandarin, Polish, and French) and since 2006 there have been attempts to enumerate the changing demographics of the country through a new racial/ethnic question on the census.

Cosmopolitanism or social multiculturalism? France and Sweden

Despite the presence of different ethnic groups in France, multiculturalism there is considered a "non-issue" as French citizens are integrated into "Frenchness" under the banner of "republican ideals"—through shared language and culture. But as the riots of the early 2000s made clear, not all French citizens are equal, nor are they the "same" type of French. Research by Pap Ndiaye (2009) clearly shows that skin tone and identification as a "visible minority" in France are highly correlated with socio-economic status, education, and occupation. In addition, the issue of wearing the hijab in public spaces (most controversially in schools) ignited a debate about the usefulness of maintaining the republican ideal that "we are all French, regardless of skin color or culture." Jennings writes:

> citizenship was grounded upon a set of democratic political institutions rather than upon recognition of cultural and/or ethnic diversity. Republicanism itself thus became a vehicle of both inclusion and exclusion. If, as can be argued, the existence of diverse cultural communities can be seen as a valuable element of a flourishing liberal society, republicanism needs to give a greater attention precisely to the claims of diversity, completing the move from recognition of the multi-ethnic nature of French society to the formulation of a multicultural conception of citizenship.
>
> (Jennings 2000: 597)

Sweden's history of progressive immigration policies has combined with a strong national identity to produce a highly developed rhetoric around multiculturalism and strong state support for "integrating" immigrants and culturally diverse groups into Swedish life (Pred 2000). However, there is a growing sense that "even in Sweden," racism is on the rise despite the country's low levels of immigration following the enlargement of the EU in 2001. Sweden, and countries like it, long considered socially progressive and tolerant of the multicultural agenda, are struggling with the "disjuncture between racist attitudes and behaviors and a widely held image of the self and the nation as altruistic and just" (Pred 2002: 1).

To deal with multiculturalism in Europe, Sweden and some other nations appear to be moving toward the concept of "diversity" and away from explicitly "multicultural" ideals *per se*. Titley and Lentin (2008) argue that the multicultural project, which is identified with the US and has been a basic failure in practice, is being transformed in Europe into a project of "diversity" which more easily accommodates different types of "differences" such as disability, gender, and age. "The drive towards diversity must therefore be seen as a way of overcoming the 'problem of difference': a solution to the perceived failure of multiculturalism" (Titley and Lentin 2008: 14).

Diversity, then, is one alternative to multiculturalism; it is also a more private social phenomenon, which holds open the promise of interactive pluralism because in its conceptualization of difference boundaries are more fluid and loyalties more complex.

Recognition and rights: instituionalizing diversity

If multiculturalism is on the wane, then why has the issue so sharply pierced the core of so many nations? One answer is that multiculturalism touches the very essence of what it means to be a nation in our post-national or post-ethnic (Hollinger 1995) world. Moreover, the fundamental questions that prompted the initial move toward multiculturalism remain: what or whose culture gets celebrated at a national level, and why? Can diversity as interactive pluralism be institutionalized?

To address these questions, I examine the case of racial/ethnic categorization in the US Census (including recent changes in the census) as an example of interactive plural-ism and as a way to understand the link between private identities and public institutions such as governments. Examining the census highlights ongoing identity politics because of the way that the "recognition" of cultural difference is embedded in the US state.

In 1977, in order to determine eligibility to participate in federal programs (not as scientific or anthropological data), Directive 15 of the US Census provided standard classifications for recordkeeping based on racial categorization. The push for "protected group" status under Directive 15 in the application of civil-rights legislation was the impetus for sorting who would qualify for federal programs and who would not. The result was the "racial pentagon"—American Indian/Alaskan Natives, Asian/Pacific Islanders, Blacks, Hispanics, and Whites—as the five categories of people recognized in the census. The directive encouraged a fusing of individual and collective identities around the construction of "race" as a precursor to gaining "rights." That is, a person needed to be identified as a member of a protected group in order to make claims for equal rights in housing, and employment, and against discrimination in voting. Because discrimination occurred along racial lines, it therefore was to be tracked along those same lines. Directive 15 then linked a certain understanding of "race" with "rights" (for more on the 2000 Census, see Williams 2008). Recognition and race were concomitant and the precursors to claims for "rights." Recognition and rights became attached to the same racialized identity—what we call today Asian Pacific American, African American, and the like. In other words, taking Asian Americans as an example, before Directive 15 there really was no term "Asian Pacific American." The state, in order to conduct civil rights compliance, and the Asian American community, via the Asian power movement of the 1970s, both pushed for "lumping" as a way to solve representational problems (King 2000). This practice inextricably linked individual identities along racial lines and simplified them so that the state (and some social movements) could utilize them.

In 2000, the census again changed the way it enumerated people based on race and ethnicity, allowing people to check multiple options. Interestingly, opposition to changing the racial/ethnic categorization in the 2000 Census came most strongly from groups of color (National Council de La Raza, National Association for the Advancement of Colored People, etc.), which held that they would lose numbers of Latinos and African Americans (both with large numbers of multiracial people in them)—and therefore resources—if the census allowed multiracial people to check more than one box. The move for "multiple checks" on the race question on the census therefore garnered support from conservatives, who saw it as a mechanism for reducing the salience of race, as well as some liberals, who saw it as a recognition of multiraciality. The racial/ethnic categories on the census were controversial not because of the categories or the people filling them out but because of the state resources linked to the categories, making some cultures recognized and valorized (worth) more than others. By offering a multiple-response option, the census was seen as "diluting" the salience of racial categories, thus making it harder for minority groups to retain distinctiveness, even as the census allowed for the recognition of multiraciality: in the end everyone could argue that in fact they were multiracial. Interestingly, less attention was focused on the fact that the racial/ethnic question on the census was self-determined and could prompt cases of "racial fraud" on the part of individuals hoping to gain access to resources.

The US Census is not unusual; an international study of 138 censuses from around the world found that 63 percent of them included some type of ethnicity question. About half of the censuses used the term "ethnicity" but others used terms such as "nationality" (in Eastern Europe) and "race" (most often in the Americas) (Morning 2008: 263). Most censuses that used the terms "ethnicity" and "race" did so in order to track, and in some cases to try to offer reparations for, inequality.

Multiculturality through multiraciality

State-sponsored multicultural policies and ideals that attempt to institutionalize diversity are rare. Wimmer reminds us that multicultural philosophy "does not distinguish between what political leaders say about the relevance and pervasiveness of ethnicity on the one hand, and the everyday lived experience of members of an ethnic category on the other hand" (2008: 257). Although we know that race is not genetically determined within racial/ethnic groups, it still has very real effects on people who live their lives classified as belonging to a minority racial group. Indeed, "first-wave" multiculturalists sought to bring this reality in to the public sphere (Takaki 2008). To work, a true model of interactive pluralism needs individuals and groups to interact on an everyday basis and these interactions, in turn, require informal spaces of association.

Traditional theories of multiculturalism have had trouble capturing the lived reality of mixed-race or multicultural people, who often have multiple allegiances that cross national boundaries and identities. Alternatively, multiculturality moves from the personal experience of mixed-race identities to the cultural experiences of multiraciality, and then to the racialization of political institutions (e.g. the racial/ethnic categorization on the census), thus encouraging the shifting of cultural and political as well as personal boundaries. Multiculturality also hybridizes—through groups' interactions, conceptions of cultural identity and the nation—a form of lived interactive pluralism.

Kimberly McClain DaCosta (2007) has studied the multiracial movement. She notes that it was successful in getting the 2000 Census changed largely due to its family and community base. A certain form of organic multiculturality sprang up out of the experiences of groups of multiracial people, and the existence of such people has long been used by advocates of multiculturalism—particularly in the media—as the "face of the future." But little scholarly attention has been given to how multiracial families negotiate and honor cultural differences both within their families and in their larger community affiliations.

Conclusion

The Japanese American community, which faces low immigration, high interracial marriage rates, and an aging population, opened up the definition of who is Japanese American and welcomed white parents and other non-Japanese Americans into the community. This example reveals the microfoundation of a different kind of multiculturalism—what I understand to be "multiculturality"—the everyday lived experiences of people in multicultural interaction. Here, there is recognition of both Japaneseness and whiteness, dual ethnic group membership, and porous boundaries of community seeking to encompass difference, not to exclude it. The implication is remarkably inclusive—that community membership is based on family, culture, and community, not just race. As a result, the criteria for community membership and collective self-identity shift, since the prior basis for collective identity rested on ethnicity and race. This does not mean that race ceases to matter. There is evidence that race continues to underlie ethnic concepts. But when race and ethnicity change, so too do the criteria for membership into the collectivity known as "the community" (King-O'Riain 2006).

By examining the boundaries of communities and the ways in which they are becoming more malleable, we can see that the multiracial lived experience is essentially about connection—the point at which one group ends and another begins. Mixed-race bodies stand at the intersection of two groups, forming the border in between. Mixed-race people, then, participate in collectivities where "us" and "them" meet, and in being both, participants create new definitions of community. It is at this touch-point that conflicts over the meaning of race, ethnicity, and culture in the US are thrown into clearest relief. The case of mixed-race people also exemplifies the frequent operation of more fluid multicultural relations at micro levels of social interaction.

What can we take from these examples of lived multiculturality by multiracial people and of changing state notions of race/ethnicity? First, that the redefinition of community membership and solidarity can happen through interactive pluralism; second, that such redefinitions operate at multiple levels of interactional and individual identities; and, third, that contacts between groups change the form and content of the groups themselves, which in turn can impact even such immovable practices such as the classification of race/ethnicity on the census.

In the future, the power of census numbers to constitute communities will weaken, because definitions of who is part of any given community—and of communities themselves—are changing. Officially defined racial and ethnic groups will remain, but these groups will be more porous than before and more open to claiming new members. What will this mean for society? It means that there will be uniquely defined groups, but they will be less rigidly defined than in the past. It also means that social groups will conflict, and the nature of their conflicts will change as membership in the groups overlaps in multiple ways.

This point leads us back to the concept of multiculturalism and the politics of recognition. Core to the politics of identity and recognition is the idea that everyone should be recognized for his or her unique identity, but in the past that "uniqueness" was predicated on exclusive group membership: people had to chose one "ethnic option" or race over another even if they were "mixed" (Waters 1990). The public recognition of the "differentness" of identities and groups is a difficult issue for mixed-race people because the basis of their identities is the borderland. They are not confidently "founded" in one group/ethnicity/race, but instead construct their identities primarily in relation to the spaces between groups. When they bring such private "borderlandness" to the collective public sphere and press its significance within monoracial or monoethnic communities, they force redefinition of all racial/ethnic groups.

The lived experiences of multiplicity (or hybridity) combined with strong group identification may emerge from spaces for multicultural interaction if multicultural interactive pluralism is a societal-level goal. Such spaces are crucial, and require structural support—policies to facilitate the racial integration of workplaces and schools, for example. Social actors have the agency to institute multiculturality, but multiculturality is slow to infiltrate state structures because opportunities for meaningful social interaction between racial groups are still relatively rare. For there to be lived multiculturality, it is necessary to eliminate structural segregation based on race, culture, and ethnicity. And even if this is done, political conflicts will threaten to destabilize any newfound multicultural understanding by demanding group loyalties whenever resources are at stake. Perhaps having a multiracial president of the US, who openly claims to be both black and white, and who managed to mobilize people across racial, ethnic, cultural, and class lines, is a first step towards a true multiculturality for all.

References

Alexander, Jeffrey C. 2001. "Theorizing the 'Modes of Incorporation': Assimilation, Hyphenation, and Multiculturalism as Varieties of Civil Participation." *Sociological Theory* 19(3): 237–49.

Boucher, Gerry. 2008. "Ireland's Lack of a Coherent Integration Policy." *Translocations: The Irish Migration, Race and Social Transformation Review* 3(1). Available at http://www.imrstr.dcu.ie/currentissue/Vol_3_Issue_1_Gerry_Boucher.htm.

Burgess, Chris. 2007. "The Discourse(s) of Migration: Changing Constructions of Other since 9/11." *Japan Focus* 22, posted March 24, 2007.

Conway, Brian. 2006. "Who Do We Think We Are? Immigration and the Discursive Construction of National Identity in an Irish Daily Mainstream Newspaper, 1996–2004." *Translocations: The Irish Migration, Race and Social Transformation Review* 1(1). Available at http://www.imrstr.dcu.ie/firstissue.

DaCosta, Kimberly McClain. 2007. *Making Multiracials: State, Family, and Market in the Redrawing of the Color Line.* Stanford, CA: Stanford University Press.

Finney, Joseph C. 1963. "Psychiatry and Multiculturality in Hawaii." *International Journal of Social Psychiatry* 9: 5–11.

Hage, Ghassan. 2003. *Against Paranoid Nationalism: Searching for Hope in a Shrinking Society.* London: Pluto Press.

Hartmann, Douglas and Gerteis, Joseph. 2005. "Dealing with Diversity: Mapping Multiculturalism in Sociological Terms." *Sociological Theory* 23(2): 218–40.

Hollinger, David. 1995. *Post Ethnic America: Beyond Multiculturalism.* New York: Basic Books.

Jennings, Jeremy. 2000. "Citizenship, Republicanism, and Multiculturalism in Contemporary France." *British Journal of Political Science* 30: 575–98.

King, Rebecca Chiyoko. 2000. "Racialization, Recognition, and Rights: Lumping and Splitting Multiracial Asian Americans and the 2000 Census." *Journal of Asian American Studies* 3(2): 191–217.

King-O'Riain, Rebecca Chiyoko. 2006. *Pure Beauty: Judging Race in Japanese American Beauty Pageants.* Minneapolis: University of Minnesota Press.

Kymlicka, Will. 2007. *Multicultural Odysseys: Navigating the New International Politics of Diversity.* Oxford: Oxford University Press.

Lentin, Alana. Forthcoming. "Europe and the Silence about Race." *European Journal of Social Theory.*

Lie, John. 2006. *Multiethnic Japan.* Cambridge, MA: Harvard University Press.

Modood, Tariq. 2007. *Multiculturalism.* London: Polity Press.

Morning, Ann. 2008. "Ethnic Classification in Global Perspective: A Cross National Survey of the 2000 Census Round." *Population Research and Policy Review* 27: 239–72.

Ndiaye, Pap. 2009. "Skin Tone Stratification and Its Social Consequences in France." Colloquia, "Beyond the Black/White Binary" African American Studies, Northwestern University, April 29, 2009.

Panayi, Panikos. 2004. "The Evolution of Multiculturalism in Britain and Germany: An Historical Survey." *Journal of Multilingual and Multicultural Development* 25(5–6): 466–80.

Portes, Alejandro and Rumbaut, Ruben. 2001. *Legacies: The Story of the Immigrant Second Generation.* Berkeley: University of California Press.

Pred, Alan. 2000. *Even in Sweden.* Berkeley: University of California Press.

——. 2002. "Somebody Else, Somewhere Else: Racisms, Racialized Spaces, and the Popular Geographical Imagination in Sweden." *Antipode* 29(4): 383–416.

Siddle, Richard. 2003. "The Limits of Citizenship in Japan: Multiculturalism, Indigenous Rights, and the Ainu." *Citizenship Studies* 7(4): 447–62.

Takaki, Ronald. 2008. *A Different Mirror: A History of Multicultural America.* New York: Back Bay Books.

Tarumoto, Hideki. 2003. "Multiculturalism in Japan: Citizenship Policy for Immigrants." *International Journal on Multicultural Societies* 5(1): 88–103.

Taylor, Charles. 1994. *Multiculturalism: Examining the Politics of Recognition.* Princeton, NJ: Princeton University Press.

Titley, Gavan and Lentin, Alana. 2008. "More Benetton than Barricades? The Politics of Diversity in Europe." In Gavan Titley and Alana Lentin, eds., *The Politics of Diversity in Europe*. Strasbourg: Council of Europe Publishing.

Waters, Mary C. 1990. *Ethnic Options*. Berkeley: University of California Press.

Williams, Kim M. 2008. *Mark One or More: Civil Rights in Multiracial America*. Ann Arbor: University of Michigan Press.

Wimmer, Andreas. 2008. "The Left-Herderian Ontology of Multiculturalism." *Ethnicities* 8(2): 254–60.

Zank, Wolfgang. 1998. *The German Melting Pot: Multiculturality in Historical Perspective*. New York: Palgrave Macmillan.

23

Bodies, beauty, and fashion

Maxine Leeds Craig

After years of relegating the study of bodies to other disciplines, sociologists have recognized the sociological relevance of the body as a site where status inequalities and boundaries are formed, suffered, upheld, and transgressed. During the past two decades, this work has taken institutional form as the sociology of the body. Scholarship on beauty and fashion should have a central place within the new sociology of the body. Scholars who write about beauty and fashion study the relationships between body ideals and structures of inequality; they also study the ways in which the body and fashion are used in identity work. Yet the large literature on beauty and fashion is marginal within the sociology of the body.

How can this marginalization be explained? Critical analyses of beauty ideals originated in feminist theory and regularly draw on theories of race and intersectionality. Analyses of fashion have a broader, longer history, but the recent scholarship of fashion routinely incorporates analyses of gender and race. A great deal of the work that is considered to focus on the sociology of the body acknowledges feminism, but does not seriously engage with the published work of feminist theorists and tends to ignore theories of race and intersectionality. Consequently, sociological scholarship on the body has developed in a way that leaves studies of race, along with those of beauty and fashion, at its periphery.

This chapter begins with a brief sketch of the theoretical foundations of the new sociology of the body and suggests that scholarship on beauty and fashion can provide a more inclusive way of thinking about those foundations. It then turns to the scholarship on beauty and fashion, considering, first, works about body ideals and structures of inequality and, second, research on fashion and identity.

Disregarded foundations

Although sociologists of the body often trace their genealogies to Norbert Elias, Marcel Mauss, Maurice Merleau-Ponty, Georg Simmel, Erving Goffman, and others, Pierre Bourdieu, Michel Foucault, Judith Butler, Bryan Turner, and Mike Featherstone are cited most often as the theoretical wellsprings of the new sociology of the body. Bourdieu directed attention to early learning and everyday repetition of postures, emotions, and movement as mechanisms of the social reproduction of inequality. Social origins become embodied through the inculcation of bodily dispositions. A disposition can be an orientation towards one's own body, such as, for example, the middle-class tendency to treat the body as an unfinished project. Bourdieu's theorization of embodiment has provided a starting point for studies of how class position is reproduced through the body.

Michel Foucault's writing is also a major touchstone for recent scholarship of the body. The body, in Foucault's work, is shaped and given meaning through disciplinary practices that arise from normalizing discourse. Although race and gender receive scant attention by Foucault, a few writers have used his work to understand embodied experiences of race, and more have drawn on it to explain the subjugation of women to normative bodily disciplines. Foucault's writing provides a point of departure for Judith Butler's theorization of the body as the product of discourse. Butler critiques Foucault's conception of the disciplined body and replaces it with a body that is the product of imitative performances for which there are no originals. Butler describes the performance of gendered subject positions as a series of endlessly repeated, imperfect citations. The process of imperfect citation generates play, resistance, and the possibility of transformation of gendered subject positions.

Inspired by both Foucault and Bourdieu, Featherstone and Turner have played a substantial role in establishing a place for the body within sociology. In the journal *Body & Society*, which they founded in 1995, and other publications, Featherstone and Turner frame personal body projects as labor extracted in a commodity culture. They trace their intellectual roots to Bourdieu and Foucault, as well as Nietzsche, Weber, Elias, and Goffman. Yet this theoretical foundation established a basis for analyses of the body in which attention to race or gender was optional.

The emergence of the new sociology of the body has given rise to numerous textbooks and literature reviews. In these overviews, feminist scholarship of beauty and fashion is usually overlooked, and specific theorization of race is absent. In a survey of the rapidly growing field, Anne Witz (2000: 2) noted that "sociological body building— the recuperation of the body in/for social theory—has been a predominantly male activity." We would have to add that it has also been predominantly white. Yet women, including numerous women of color, have put the body at the center of their work in studies of beauty ideals, the meanings attached to racialized bodies, beauty contests, beauty culture, and fashion. Thus, if the work of scholars who have theorized appearance is pulled into what we think of as the sociology of the body, the theoretical foundation of the sociology of the body must expand to include feminist and intersectional theorists of seeing, representation, and embodiment.

When in 1975 Laura Mulvey described women on screen as having the quality of "to-be-looked-at-ness," she provided a way for scholars of everyday women's experiences to explain the social compulsion women feel to meet beauty norms (1975: 11). Women saw themselves the way women were seen in films. In 1980 Iris Young went below the surface of appearance to the movement of the body when she explained the social constraints that produce physically timid girls who "throw like girls." Sandra Lee Bartky, working with but critiquing Foucault's gender-neutral conception of docile bodies, argued that women have been required to be more docile than men. She described three categories of disciplinary practices that govern and produce feminized bodies: "those that aim to produce a body of a certain size and general configuration; those that bring forth from this body a specific repertoire of gestures, postures, and movements; and those directed toward the display of this body as an ornamented surface" (Bartky 1990: 65).

The works of Mulvey, Young, and Bartky, and the scholarship initially inspired by them, theorized a general woman who was subjected to the power of a generalized male gaze. However, a woman's racial appearance filters how she will be seen and black men have been lynched for gazing. Patricia Hill Collins (1990: 67) brought race into the theorization of seeing and representation with the concept of "controlling images"—a way of describing the consequences of the meanings attached to black bodies. Similarly, Sander Gilman (1999: 220) theorized "systems of representation" that provide ideological support for gendered forms of racial domination. Thus, while Mulvey, Young, and Bartky described the power of a male gaze to shape the way women are seen and how they see themselves, Collins and Gilman describe the power of a racist gaze to differentiate, idealize, eroticize, and disparage bodies that are marked according to race as well as gender.

During the same period, Susan Bordo (1993) developed a Foucauldian analysis of women's dieting, eating disorders, and exercise that carefully attended to race and class, and to the complexities of contemporary standards of beauty. Her analysis of the shift in contemporary feminine body ideals toward limited muscularity opened the way to more nuanced research about women and weight. Raewyn Connell also built upon Foucault's theorization of the production of sexuality through knowledge regimes and joined it with Turner's theorization of the individual and social labor involved in producing bodies, to describe masculine bodies as the products of never-completed individual and collective projects (Connell 1995).

Studies of beauty and fashion, then, have never ignored the gender of bodies and increasingly recognize the consequences of race. Including these studies in the sociology of the body would require an expansion of its theoretical base to include the theorists who foreground gender and race. In other words, Mulvey, Young, Bartky, Collins, Gilman, Bordo, and Connell belong in the theoretical core of the sociology of the body.

Body ideals and structures of inequality

Critical analysts of beauty and fashion bring theorizations of gender and race to the study of bodies. Sociologists have often regarded the resulting scholarship as being primarily about gender or about race, while overlooking the contributions it makes to the sociology of the body. This section considers developments within the large and growing literature that analyzes beauty as a set of socially defined body ideals structured by, and contributing to, social inequality. It will show how the initial grounding of this scholarship in feminist theory and its later incorporation of analyses of racialized difference provide a model for a richer dialogue between theorists of the body, feminists, and scholars of race.

The scholarship on body ideals and inequality has extensively explored representations of women and girls in the media, the idealization of female thinness, the disparagement of the bodies of people of color, and the stigmatization of female aging. Historical research has been crucially important for the critical scholarship of beauty. Joan Jacobs Brumberg's (1997) research on the shift of girls' concerns from inner self-worth to outer

245

appearance in the early decades of the twentieth century demonstrates that there is nothing inevitable about the importance of appearance in young women's lives. Lois Banner's (1983) history of dominant beauty standards in the US and Kathy Peiss's (1998) history of the cosmetics industry show that beauty standards are culturally and historically specific.

Feminist critiques of beauty practices began with activists outside of academia who characterized women's beauty work as capitulation to male domination. In the 1990s a debate concerning beauty arose between scholars who characterized beauty ideals as components of women's oppression and those who saw beauty practices as vehicles for female pleasure and self-expression. The divide was often methodological. On one side were critical readings of women's beauty practices as oppressive and debilitating. On the other were researchers who used interviews, focus groups, and ethnographies to give voice to the pleasures women derived from dressing up, making themselves up, and transforming their bodies. The latter researchers, who complicated feminist critiques of beauty (Craig 2006), are referred to here as the "complicators." While noting the involvement of gender inequality in the production of women's anxieties regarding their bodies, the complicators refused to understand women's use of beauty culture solely in terms of gender oppression. The complicators listened to women who went to beauty parlors and plastic surgeons, and defended their actions as attempts to avoid stigma. Women who altered their appearance by various means sought to be normal, not beautiful. Some complicators described women as savvy consumers who demonstrated cultural expertise through their consumption of beauty products and shopped around for cosmetic surgeons who catered to their self-defined aesthetics.

Analyses of beauty ideals as forms of gender oppression have been further tested by the increased use of sexualized images of men in marketing and the entertainment media and the increased consumption of beauty products and appearance-altering drugs by men. Fashion historians have written of the late-eighteenth-century great renunciation (Kuchta 2002: 162–64), in which Western men gave up all that was irrational in fashion—color, lace, wigs, and powder—to put on the dignifying, rational, and empowering drab uniforms of masculine work. Is the great renunciation over? Did the characterization overstate male indifference to appearance? Recent studies of men in the US and Great Britain find that heterosexual men still tread cautiously into beauty work, careful to frame it as a business or health necessity. However, these studies describe and tend to generalize from the experiences of middle-class white men. More research is needed on how men of color are affected by appearance norms and bodily ideals, and the meaning of dress in their lives.

Debates about how to understand the pleasures that women derive from beauty, culture, and fashion—alongside their capacity to oppress—have continued. The divide between the beauty critics and the complicators is no longer a methodological one. Recent critical approaches to beauty and fashion as texts offer subversive readings that restore agency to women, while some empirical research has found that women do not resist beauty-culture ideology. The most useful recent work strives for a middle ground between false consciousness and autonomous, self-actualizing, individual shoppers. This scholarship takes seriously the possibilities for pleasure found in adornment, investigates beauty practices as identity work, and looks at beauty shops and beauty pageants as sites for the production of collective identities.

Banet-Weiser (1999), Craig (2002), and King-O'Riain (2006) have shown how beauty has been used to define group membership and to contest exclusion from national citizenship. Other scholars have examined the meaning of beauty beyond the US, and in the lives of US women of color, disabled women, and lesbians. Though any racial or ethnic group contains individuals with a wide range of physical features, racial and ethnic hatred is often expressed through disparagement of what are popularly taken to be typical racial or ethnic types. One of the manifestations of racism has been the depiction of racialized or ethnic minority women as ugly or exotic. Therefore, studies of racism have frequently been concerned with beauty ideals and with how race has shaped the meanings of beauty practices within minority communities. The collection of articles in Evelyn Nakano Glenn's 2009 *Shades of Difference* examines the favoring of light skin within non-white communities as a global phenomenon promoted through the marketing of skin-lightening products.

The reach of dominant norms, however, is rarely complete, and it is contested informally in everyday life and collectively through social movements. To the extent that dominant ideals are adopted, they are altered in local settings. Racial, sexual, and class communities can sustain alternative interpretations of popular representations. Research based on interviews, ethnography, and archival analysis can shed light on the meanings and significance of dominant representations in specific cultural and historical contexts. Thus, although an analysis of international beauty pageants as texts might indicate the dominance of a thin Western norm, Erynn Masi De Casanova (2004) interviewed young Ecuadorian women and found that they recognize the global beauty standards broadcast in foreign media without thinking that these standards are relevant to their own lives. Paula Black's (2004) ethnography of beauty salons in England shows how class shaped British women's judgments of the appropriateness of beauty practices. Craig (2002) shows how beauty ideals that circulate within US black communities are neither identical with, nor unaffected by dominant beauty ideals, and that social movements provide new ways of seeing beauty.

One of the reasons that the scholarship of beauty remains stalled in the oppression versus pleasure debate is that many of the complicators of feminist beauty critiques have worked with individualistic understandings of the meaning of beauty practices. Sociologists who locate their subjects socially, culturally, and historically avoid the pitfalls of viewing a practice as either wholly defined by a generalized male oppression or as individual, unassailable self-expression. If we understand that beauty ideals and the meanings of beauty practices are constituted within communities defined by race, class, and sexuality, we have a better chance of understanding the combination of suffering and pleasure that such ideals and practices can produce. Just as a sociology of the body that ignores gender is a partial and inadequate sociology, analyses of gendered bodies must account for race and class. In the next section I look at the everyday use of fashion as a vehicle for the expression of race, gender, and class identities.

Fashion and identity

Early studies of fashion suffered from the one-dimensionality that limited critiques of beauty culture. For instance, analyses that reduced fashion to an endless race for status or explained fashion in entirely sexual terms were criticized as reductive by Entwistle (2000) and Wilson (2003), who see fashion as simultaneously status-seeking and status-rejecting, sexual and asexual, pleasurable and oppressive, and much more. They argue that fashion is a decentralized medium through which all of us express the social contradictions of our

247

times, and call for research that looks at the ways ordinary people have worn clothing, moved in it, and felt about it. Calling fashion the "connective tissue of our cultural organism," Wilson (2003: 12) argues that fashion does the crucial work of saying who we are in an unstable social world.

Although Thorstein Veblen's characterization of fashion consumption as always and only a competition for status has been justifiably critiqued, one of fashion's uses is to achieve status distinction. Just as often, clothing has been an important signifier of identification with social movements, sexual cultures, and/or subcultures. A classic study of clothing's communicative power is Dick Hebdige's 1979 *Subculture: The Meaning of Style*. Hebdige argues that white working-class British youths used punk style to disrupt the normalization effected by dominant semiotic codes. When Hebdige studied punk culture, he drew on the methodological tools of semiotics to uncover the "hidden messages inscribed in code on the glossy surfaces of style" (Hebdige 1979: 18).

In a more recent ethnographic study of high-school girls in California's agricultural Central Valley, Julie Bettie (2003) explores the meanings of styles as markers of gendered race and class boundaries. Drawing on Bourdieu's work on the embodiment of class, Bettie argues that young Chicanas used beauty practices to distinguish themselves from their middle-class white classmates. Dark lipstick and revealing clothing, which teachers interpreted as expressions of sexuality, were worn by Chicana teenagers to mark their difference from the pale lipstick and boyish clothing worn by "preps." Dark lipstick was a way of rejecting a school system that gave higher value to white middle-class performances of femininity. This use of style may be interpreted as a form of resistance, yet the solidarity fostered through style had no power to weaken a racialized school-sanctioned status system or to garner resources. The girls' appearance was misread by teachers, who saw in it signs of sexual promiscuity and limited ambition, and who shunted them onto vocational tracks. In this research, dress and adornment are shown to provide an accessible means with which to assert collective identities, and non-dominant forms of dress may challenge dominant ways of seeing. However, the visibility of non-dominant dress and the likelihood that it will be misread by those in power frequently make communal forms of appearance the focus of social control. The moral and political panic regarding the use of head coverings by Islamic women in Europe provides a recent example. Head coverings, which may be worn to express religious faith or communal identity, have been banned by officials who read them as threats to the state (Duits and van Zoonen 2006).

Although difference-marking dress is often the focus of institutional forms of social control, it is just as often incorporated into fashion. The fashion industry, driven by the never-satisfied requirement to sell more clothing, feeds on difference. It depends upon and initiates change, and seeks new material everywhere. It finds innovation in the fabrics, styles, and practices of subordinated classes, minority cultures, and in those who have been excluded in various ways from positions of social acceptance. Thus the bindis and hennaed hands that in earlier periods had stigmatized South Asian women in England are now marketed to white women as decontextualized fashion (Puwar 2002). Fashion magazines use the bodies of non-white women as attention-getting devices. In July 2008 Italian *Vogue* released its "black issue," in which all of the featured models were black. The success of the issue—which received international press attention, sold out in the US and Great Britain, and had to be reprinted—arose from its novelty. White issues are published without notice.

Emerging issues

Two areas require additional study. Research on body ideals and structures of inequality, as well as work on fashion, bodily practices, and identity, have focused primarily on appearance at the surface. An underexplored area relating to beauty and fashion is the social origins of habits of movement. Movement has the capacity to beautify, stigmatize, and locate persons within grids of social inequality, and ways of dressing are inevitably connected with ways of moving. Glimpses of movement appear in studies of fashion and beauty but everyday forms of movement have not received sustained scholarly attention. Within the sociology of the body, attention to movement has been limited to studies of highly trained elites such as athletes and dancers. However, Young, Bartky, Bourdieu, and Connell have laid the theoretical groundwork for studies of everyday movement. Thus Helen Thomas (2003) calls for more dialogue between sociologists of the body and dance scholars. An example of how movement helps to embody racialized gender identities may be seen from the perspective of social and popular dance. At proms, at concerts and parties, and as they privately practice and experiment with movement styles at home, young men and women perform dances that are sexually, racially, and gender coded. When they learn to dance, dance publicly, and even when they avoid dance, youth take up particular forms of gender in their bodies. The meanings and practice of physical movement in everyday contexts are a vast area that has received little attention to date.

A second emerging area that warrants the attention of cultural sociologists is the increased acceptability of various forms of body modification. Susan Bordo (1993: 38) characterized contemporary conceptions of the body as "malleable plastic." Surgical, prosthetic, and pharmaceutical ways of altering the body have proliferated and have called into question the existence of a natural body. The use of braces to straighten teeth has become so normative that non-conforming teeth have become a stigmatizing marker of lower class position. The use of breast implants and Botox injections by women has gained a similar normative place within certain affluent communities. The boundaries between bodily beauty and fashion have diminished as body modifications such as tattooing and plastic surgery, which once were considered permanent, become routine, repeated, and temporarily worn. Sarah Banet-Weiser and Laura Portwood-Stacer (2006) suggest that beauty pageants have been replaced by reality shows, and in particular makeover shows, as sources of normalizing discourse. They argue that makeover shows rest on a post-feminist premise that offers women consumption as a path to female empowerment. By celebrating the surgical transformation of "average" women, the shows contribute to the normalization of plastic surgery and the stigmatization of women whose bodies deviate from youthful, white beauty ideals. In a study of plastic surgery in Australia, Meredith Jones (2008) describes a global makeover culture promoted through a new media narrative of the meaning of cosmetic surgery. In earlier years, cosmetic surgery was either a carefully hidden secret or a magical transformation documented in before/after pairs of photographs (Jones 2008: 16–18). Beauty derived from cosmetic surgery was widely regarded as disreputable and false. Makeover shows, which make a spectacle of the pain of cosmetic surgery and recovery, have replaced the false beauty narrative with a new narrative of surgically produced beauty as hard earned and well deserved.

Moreover, the medical modification of bodies is becoming a normal practice for the production of a middle-class body through techniques that minimize the appearance of ethnicity and age. Gilman has studied the pathologization of Jewish noses and their

249

"Americanization" by plastic surgeons; similarly, Kaw critiques the medical justification of surgery designed to make Asian women's eyelids appear more Western. The boundary between cosmetic surgery and surgery deemed medically "necessary" has thus become blurred in ways that pathologize racialized difference (Gilman 1999; Kaw 1993). Seeing connections between feminist and disability politics, Rosemarie Garland-Thomas wrote "The twin ideologies of normalcy and beauty posit female and disabled bodies particularly as not only spectacles to be looked at, but as pliable bodies to be shaped infinitely so as to conform to a set of standards called 'normal' and 'beautiful'" (2002: 11). As cultural sociologists attempt to understand the body in an era in which the natural body is no longer taken for granted, they can learn from disability theorists, who have taken the lead in critiquing processes of normalization and the medicalization of difference.

References

Banet-Weiser, Sarah. 1999. *The Most Beautiful Girl in the World: Beauty Pageants and National Identity.* Berkeley: University of California Press.

Banet-Weiser, Sarah and Portwood-Stacer, Laura. 2006. "'I Just Want to Be Me Again!' Beauty Pageants, Reality Television and Post-Feminism." *Feminist Theory* 7(2): 255–72.

Banner, Lois. 1983. *American Beauty.* New York: Knopf.

Bartky, Sandra Lee. 1990. *Femininity and Domination: Studies in the Phenomenology of Oppression.* New York: Routledge.

Bettie, Julie. 2003. *Women without Class: Girls, Race, and Identity.* Berkeley: University of California Press.

Black, Paula. 2004. *The Beauty Industry: Gender, Culture, Pleasure.* New York: Routledge.

Bordo, Susan. 1993. *Unbearable Weight: Feminism, Western Culture, and the Body.* Berkeley: University of California.

Brumberg, Joan Jacobs. 1997. *The Body Project: An Intimate History of American Girls.* New York: Random House.

Collins, Patricia Hill. 1990. *Black Feminist Thought: Knowledge, Consciousness, and the Politics of Empowerment.* Boston: Unwin Hyman.

Connell, R.W. 1995. *Masculinities.* Berkeley: University of California Press.

Craig, Maxine Leeds. 2002. *Ain't I a Beauty Queen: Black Women, Beauty and the Politics of Race.* New York: Oxford University Press.

——. 2006. "Race, Beauty, and the Tangled Knot of a Guilty Pleasure." *Feminist Theory* 7(2): 159–77.

De Casanova, Erynn Masi. 2004. "'No Ugly Women': Concepts of Race and Beauty among Adolescent Women in Ecuador." *Gender & Society* 18(3): 287–308.

Duits, Linda and van Zoonen, Liesbet. 2006. "Headscarves and Porno-chic: Disciplining Girls' Bodies in the European Multicultural Society." *European Journal of Women's Studies* 13(2): 103–17.

Entwistle, Joanne. 2000. *The Fashioned Body Fashion, Dress and Modern Social Theory.* Malden, MA: Blackwell.

Garland-Thomas, Rosemarie. 2002. "Integrating Disability, Transforming Feminist Theory." *NWSA Journal* 14(3): 1–32.

Gilman, Sander L. 1999. *Making the Body Beautiful: A Cultural History of Aesthetic Surgery.* Princeton, NJ: Princeton University Press.

Glenn, Evelyn Nakano, ed. 2009. *Shades of Difference: Why Skin Color Matters.* Stanford: Stanford University Press.

Hebdige, Dick. 1979. *Subculture: The Meaning of Style.* New York: Methuen.

Jones, Meredith. 2008. *Skintight: An Anatomy of Cosmetic Surgery.* New York: Berg.

Kaw, Eugenia. 1993. "Medicalization of Racial Features: Asian-American Women and Cosmetic Surgery." *Medical Anthropology Quarterly* 7(1): 74–89.

King-O'Riain, Rebecca Chiyoko. 2006. *Pure Beauty: Judging Race in Japanese American Beauty Pageants.* Minneapolis: University of Minnesota Press.

Kuchta, David. 2002. *The Three Piece Suit and Modern Masculinity: England, 1550—1850.* Berkeley: University of California Press.

Mulvey, Laura. 1975. "Visual Pleasure and Narrative Cinema." *Screen* 16(3): 6–18.

Peiss, Kathy. 1998. *Hope in a Jar: The Making of America's Beauty Culture.* New York. Metropolitan Books.

Puwar, Nirmal. 2002. "Multicultural Fashion ... Stirrings of Another Sense of Aesthetics and Memory." *Feminist Review* 71: 63–87.

Thomas, Helen. 2003. *The Body, Dance and Cultural Theory.* New York: Palgrave Macmillan.

Wilson, Elizabeth. 2003. *Adorned in Dreams: Fashion and Modernity,* revised edition. New York: I.B. Tauris.

Witz, Anne. 2000. "Whose Body Matters? Feminist Sociology and the Corporeal Turn in Sociology and Feminism." *Body & Society* 6(2): 1–24.

Young, Iris Marion. 1980. "Throwing Like a Girl: A Phenomenology of Feminine Body Comportment, Motility, and Spatiality." *Human Studies* 3: 137–56.

24

Gender performance

Cheerleaders, drag kings, and the rest of us

Joshua Gamson and Laura Grindstaff

Social theorists have long noted that people aren't simply male or female but rather they "do" gender. Thus, gender is neither a fixed nor an essential property of the self but an outcome of ongoing performances in various interactional and institutional contexts. Gender, along with other axes of social difference, helps constitute the culture of everyday life and is central to the implicit codes that guide "normative" identities and practices (Kessler and McKenna 1978; West and Zimmerman 1987; Butler 1990; West and Fenstermaker 1995). Sociologists have further noted that gender is a system, a social structure with concretized categories and hierarchies—most notably a patriarchal hierarchy in which men dominate and from which men benefit. Consequently, people don't import gendered selves into neutral institutions; rather, institutions themselves are gendered in their policies, practices, and ideologies (Connell 1987; Acker 1990; Martin 1990; Lorber 1994; Messner 2002). Martin (2003) has usefully distinguished between "practicing gender"—the micro level talk and action that signifies gender, but often fleetingly and/or unintentionally—and "gendering practices"—the institutionalized ideas, structures, and repertoires of conduct that help to organize gender in more or less systematic ways. The interplay between the doing of gender and the gendering of institutions is complex: each informs and shapes the other, the former reminding us of the possibilities of agency, creativity, and resistance, the latter reminding us of the macro structures that shape—and often constrain—individual conduct.

This essay works within and against these sociological traditions to explore the concept of "gender performance." On one level, the doing of gender is always performative, in a Goffmanesque sense: individuals repeatedly express and renew their taken-for-granted commitment to gendered scripts and ideologies as they go about their daily lives. Goffman's (1959) theatrical metaphor of social life—as a stage peopled by actors, in roles, enacting scripts, etc.—suggests that individuals manage their own conduct in light of normative expectations on the part of real or imagined audiences of what it means to be male or female. In this formulation, gender is always already a performance, and never entirely voluntary, even though it may feel "natural" and may be largely unconscious.

But what of those situations in which gender is not simply *accomplished* in everyday interaction but actively *displayed* before deliberately constructed audiences? What of those situations in which gender scripts are not implicit but explicit—in other words, when the theatrical metaphor is no longer metaphorical? With some exceptions (see Alexander 2004), sociologists have had less to say about this more literal version of gender performance, largely because of the need to establish the point that gender performances are not the occasional endeavor of particular actors but something we all do all the time.

In fact, it is useful to conceptualize two quite different, if overlapping, sorts of gender performance. On one end of the spectrum is *performing gender*, in which the doing of gender is an implicit dimension of everyday action oriented toward some other purpose (as when a woman smiles more often than her male counterparts in a business meeting); at the other end is *gender performance*, in which the main purpose of interaction is the explicit dramatization of gender (as in a strip show). In the latter scenario, although participants are also performing gender in the interactive sense, the expression of gender is heightened, exaggerated, codified, scripted, ritualized, and/or institutionalized in particular ways. Often there is a designated space for the performance, a collective organization of people to make it happen, a stage, costumes, props, and a clear distinction between performers and audience. These elements help construct a specific *culture* around and through which the gender performance works. Alexander's (2004) recent work on social action as performance is helpful here; while not focusing on gender *per se*, he posits a broad theory of social action that underscores both the wide-ranging and multi-dimensional nature of performance and the analytic force of privileging a theatrical frame.

In this essay we focus primarily on explicit gender performance, using the concept to highlight the ongoing negotiations, tensions, and conflicts involved in the doing of gender in the broader sense. Because gender performances are exaggerated and ritualized, they render the codes by which gendered norms and practices are constructed particularly visible, both to audiences and to participants themselves. Depending on the context, gender performances may either reinscribe traditional ways of doing gender or model new modes of gender enactment. Occasions for reflecting on—and critiquing—gender arise in either case, because exaggeration can foreground the power relations that tacit performances tend to obscure. Thus, far from merely calling attention to the gendered scripts at play in everyday life, gender performances do important cultural work of their own.

Of course, such gender performances do not all do the same kind of cultural work; the range of sites and practices that facilitate them is wide, and cultural work is more self-conscious in some gender performances than others. Certain cultural settings ritualize performance in ways that solidify the normal "rules" of gender, making these rules more apprehensible and encouraging their acceptance or embrace by both participants and audiences. We think of these as *inside-gender performances* because they tend to clarify rather than complicate traditional constructions of gender difference. In Alexander's (2004) terms, inside-gender performances appear more natural because they "fuse" their cultural scripts with the background assumptions of audiences. Consider beauty pageants, for example: typically, they embody normative ideologies about gender (in concert with race and nation) within carefully scripted institutional contexts. As Banet-Weiser (1999: 26) notes, the Miss America Pageant has for most of its history actively constructed a national feminine identity based upon notions of "respectable" femininity, "typical" (i.e. white, Western) beauty, and a neoliberal "tolerance" for diversity that accommodates rather than highlights cultural, ethnic, and racial difference. A similar woman-as-nation trope, in which an "idealized" femininity and an "idealized" national ethnic identity mutually constitute one another, is observable in pageants for women of specific ethnic subgroups within the US—including Chinese-Americans (Wu 1997), Japanese-Americans (King-O'Riain 2006), and African-Americans (Craig 2002)—as well as for pageants outside the West in countries such as Guatemala (McAllister 1996), Thailand (Van Esterik 1995), Tibet (McGranahan 1996), the British Virgin Islands (Cohen 1996), and Jamaica (Barnes 1994). Although definitions of womanhood and nationhood vary by time and place, beauty contests generally represent, in distilled form, what it means to perform gender "properly" on a given national or international stage. Other inside-gender sites such as proms (Best 2000), weddings (Nishimura 1996; Otnes and Pleck 2003; Ingraham 2008), bridal showers (Montemurro 2006), debutante balls (Lynch 1999), and the "institutional core" of men's professional sport (Messner 2002) likewise articulate traditional gender scripts.

By contrast, some gender performances aim solely or primarily to display, play with, challenge, critique, and/or expose the very construction of gender itself. Here, the social rules of gender are not necessarily fused with background expectations but are displayed to an audience for the purpose of subverting, transforming, or highlighting their constructed nature. We think of these as *outside-gender performances*. Drag shows are a prime example. As Taylor *et al.* (2004: 107) have noted, many drag shows are arranged precisely to "call attention to the role of cultural markers and practices such as dress, bodily style, gesture, and voice, in constructing gender and sexual difference," thus "destabilizing institutionalized gender and sexological classifications by making visible the social basis of gender and sexuality and by presenting hybrid and minority genders and sexualities" (see also Newton 1979; Schacht 2002). Similarly, various musical performance traditions—glam rock, for example (Auslander 2006), and some elements of "conscious rap" and "feminist hip-hop" (Collins 2006; Rose 2008), disco (Gamson 2005), and alternative rock (Schippers 2002)—intentionally undercut or critique gender assumptions.

It is worth noting that the same performance can simultaneously be "inside gender" in one sense and "outside gender" in another. For instance, Katherine Frank and others have pointed out that gender performances by sex-industry professionals—in strip shows, porn sets, and the like—often display gender in exaggerated ways that flatter a paying audience, thus reiterating and reinforcing gender norms and conventions, despite participants' conscious agnosticism about—or even resistance to—such norms and conventions (Frank 2002, 2007; Liepe-Levinson 2002). Similarly, one could argue that for all the ways beauty pageants normalize traditional gender difference, due to their public nature most of them also invite critique of that difference. Non-Western pageants in particular call attention to widely varying notions of "ideal" womanhood/nationhood (see Banet-Weiser 1999; Cohen *et al.* 1996). Moreover, in both the US and abroad, pageants undoubtedly have different meanings for different contestants, and still other meanings for audiences.

Indeed, it is likely typical for gender performances to be both "inside" and "outside" at once. The institutional context may generate an "inside" (i.e. gender-conformist) performance, while the performers' own conscious agency may add "outside" (i.e. gender-transgressive) elements; a performance intended as "outside" may be read by some audiences as "inside;" a performance may be "inside" in some of its ideological elements and "outside" in others. Understanding these inside–outside dynamics—the relative strengths of the traditional and transgressive aspects of the performance, and why the balance between them looks as it does—is our central analytic task. Through a detailed look at cheerleading (a predominantly inside-gender genre) and drag shows (a predominantly outside-gender genre), we hope to illustrate more fully the utility of analyzing gender performances as sites of tension between conformity and non-conformity—ultimately, sites of tension between accepting or challenging prevailing power arrangements.

Cheerleading: inside-gender performance

Cheerleading is ideally suited to analyzing the complexities of "inside-gender" performances both because it has changed significantly over time and because different constituencies of participants orient toward cheerleading in quite different ways. Of late-nineteenth-century, Ivy-League origins, cheerleading was once an all-male, exclusively white activity designed to foster and discipline spectator involvement in American collegiate football; it became gradually "feminized" and by the 1960s had come to symbolize feminine attractiveness and popularity (Hanson 1995). "Doing gender" in the context of cheerleading typically has meant enacting a feminine script that emphasizes supportiveness, enthusiasm, and sex appeal—what Connell (1987) has termed "emphasized femininity." By definition this script has also privileged middle-class whiteness in a cultural if not strictly demographic sense. For much of the twentieth century "the cheerleader" stood as an idealized symbol of "typical" American girlhood; becoming a cheerleader meant adopting an inside-gender performance.

However, conventional forms of cheerleading lost ground in the wake of second-wave feminism, when notions of "ideal" girlhood began changing to incorporate the "masculine" qualities of competitiveness and athleticism. Today cheerleading is more popular than ever precisely because it adapted to this new ideal. Although much school-based cheerleading still involves supporting sports teams from the sidelines, many school squads have embraced competitive cheerleading as well (executing routines before judges in competitions against other squads). Currently the fastest-growing segment of the cheer industry is "all-star" cheerleading, which occurs outside the school context altogether; participants join for-profit gyms for the sole purpose of competing with other all-star teams. Whether the venue is all-star or scholastic, the "skills" of cheerleading now include high-level tumbling, stunting, pyramid-building, and (often) dance. Once an auxiliary to sport, cheerleading has become more sport-like itself: Participants call themselves "cheer athletes," the term "team" is replacing the more traditional "squad," and some schools offer athletic scholarships to cheerleaders (Grindstaff and West 2006). Thus cheerleading remains an inside-gender performance, but only because social institutions—along with the wider culture—have accommodated historical changes in feminine ideals, such that assertiveness and physical toughness join the more traditional qualities of supportiveness and physical attractiveness. For female cheerleaders, the majority of whom are straight, white, and middle class, the "rules" of cheerleading and of normative femininity are therefore still more or less aligned. Performative script and cultural expectations remain fused.

Indeed, the cultural "work" of cheerleading may well be to continually reconcile old and new versions of emphasized femininity, to transform outside-gender scripts into inside-gender performances. As with women's figure skating (see Feder 1995), the athleticism required of women in contemporary competitive cheerleading tends to be gender-appropriate (emphasizing grace and flexibility as well as speed and strength, peppy enthusiasm as well as competitiveness) and packaged in gender-specific ways (short skirt, make-up, hair ribbons, etc.). Cheerleading allows young women to have their cake and eat it too, claiming the status of athlete but without anyone questioning their sexuality or their proper feminine credentials (Adams and Bettis 2004; Grindstaff and West 2006). It allows girls and young women to perform sexy girlishness and disciplined physicality at the same time; in fact, it now demands this combination, because without athleticism the sexy girl risks being labeled a slut, and without sex appeal the athlete risks being labeled a dyke.

Although cheerleading might be an inside-gender performance for young women overall, "insider-ness" is also a matter of gradation and degree. Working-class white women and women of color tend to have greater difficulty occupying the role of "authentic" cheerleader, in the eyes of others if not their own, because the codes of femininity underpinning it have historically been associated with middle-class whiteness (see Adams and Bettis 2003). Even for middle-class white women, the "fit" between performing gender in cheerleading and doing gender in everyday life is hardly seamless. Interviews with female cheerleaders, for example, reveal a more ambivalent relation to the activity than the uniformity of the outward performance might suggest, with some women inhabiting the requisite feminine script more or less effortlessly and others expressing a more instrumental stance in which the feminine appearance—and performance—demands are tolerated for the sake of getting around to the "real" business of winning competitions (Grindstaff and West 2006).

For male cheerleaders, the relations between "doing gender" and "gender performance," and between inside- and outside-gender performances, are more complex still. Since cheerleading is generally perceived to be feminine territory, the participation of men could be interpreted by audiences categorically as an outside-gender performance, in the sense that male involvement challenges what "real" men can or should do. At the same time, because Western gender regimes typically conflate gender and sexuality, it is widely believed that male cheerleaders are gay; that is, by virtue of their "wrong" sexuality, gay men gravitate "naturally" to "feminine" activities like cheerleading and dance (or, in the "real" world, nursing, beauty-care, or social work). Thus, to the degree that cheerleading is presumed gender-appropriate for gay men, male cheerleaders could be said to deliver an "inside-gender" performance.

A straight man might therefore seem to challenge the "typical" cheerleader image—to be performing gender outside of traditional masculine scripts. But this holds only if one privileges sexual orientation over the style of masculinity actually enacted. Whether a cheerleader gives an inside- or outside-gender performance is determined more than anything else by the cheerleading company with which his team affiliates. Cheerleading companies train coaches, run summer training camps, and host competitions, with different companies promoting different performative styles through their regulations and judging criteria. The largest and most profitable company, not surprisingly, is also the most gender-conservative, advocating a rigid division of labor between female and male cheerleaders and a highly "masculine" mode of performance for the latter (no dancing, no "flying," no specialized jumps, and minimal emotion work). Here, men deliver a traditionally masculine "inside-gender" performance despite the feminine valence of cheerleading overall. By contrast, other companies promote "outside-gender" performances to varying degrees by encouraging male cheerleaders—regardless of sexual orientation—to dance, execute jumps, and enact spirited enthusiasm; in these instances, despite their gender-specific attire, men deliver a type of gender performance traditionally aligned with women. They do so not necessarily because of personal disposition or identity but because masculinity has been institutionalized in different ways (see Anderson 2005; Grindstaff and West 2006).

Cheerleading also illustrates how inside-gender performances can provide tools and inspiration for outside-gender challenges. Precisely because its gender scripts are explicit and because, for women, cheerleading remains mostly an "inside-gender" activity, cheerleading has proved fertile ground for groups seeking to critique and challenge traditional gender norms and expectations. "Radical cheerleaders," for example, an international network of young third-wave feminists, use the concept and techniques of cheerleading in the context of political activism (marches, rallies, protests, and so forth). Instead of cheering for a sports team, they cheer about (or against) a range of gender-justice issues, from sexual violence and reproductive rights to global poverty and transnational unionization (Ferrar and Warner 2006; personal interviews). Radical cheerleaders sport "alternative" uniforms of combat boots, striped leggings, spiked hair, and multiple piercings; they sometimes use shredded garbage bags as pom–poms, and instead of precision and carefully cultivated enthusiasm, they prize loud, raucous, expletive-filled outbursts to generate crowd support for ideals of gender justice. As a predominantly outside-gender performance, radical cheerleading both exposes the politics at play in more traditional inside-gender performances and, not insignificantly, glosses over the nuances of these insider performances.

Drag shows: outside-gender performance

There is perhaps no gender performance more explicit. Drag—whether on the streets or on a stage—is intentionally a show about gender, in which participants treat gender as a costume and gender role as a theatrical character, and build their performances around gender scripts. Drag comes in many forms, of course, some that emphasize "passing" and others that reject that practice. The literature on drag queen performances, and a small but growing literature on drag king performances, reflects this diversity: as Shapiro summarizes it, some researchers conclude that "performances often draw on hegemonic gender norms and work to reinforce normative gender identities," while other researchers suggest that "drag queens pose a politicized challenge to beliefs about gender and sexuality in their performances" (Shapiro 2007: 251; see also Dolan 1985; Newton 1979; Rupp and Taylor 2003; Schacht 2002; Tewksbury 1993). And while there is overlap between the two cultures, drag queen shows do not necessarily do the same cultural work as drag king shows, which often eschew exaggeration for "the understatement of the male body" (Koenig 2002: 150) and build on the lesbian-specific history of butch–femme roles, which brings a unique set of tensions surrounding "authenticity, performance quality, and transgression" and a range of performances of female masculinity (Surkan 2002: 168; see also Halberstam 1998). These different forms of drag in themselves testify to the range of purposes to which gender performance can be put.

Historically, socially, and institutionally, however, drag shows are and have been primarily "outsider" performances, morphing from nineteenth-century female imperso-nation into central genres within marginalized sexual communities in the twentieth century, first at urban "balls" (Chauncey 1994) and later in gay male bar culture, only then becoming entertainment for straight audiences as well (Rupp and Taylor 2003). Drag kinging, with "female-bodied people performing masculinities," took hold in some

American lesbian communities in the 1990s (Shapiro 2007). Drag typically aims to disrupt the gender–sexuality order, to critique or at least call attention to the construction of gender. Indeed, even "impersonation" highlights the possibility that gender is an illusion. Drag performances have "a long history in same-sex communities as vehicles for the expression of gay identity and culture, the creation and maintenance of solidarity, and the staging of political resistance" (Taylor *et al.* 2004: 107); some in the US might even be considered a form of "counterpublic terrorism," calling attention to "the nation's internal terrors around race, gender, and sexuality" (Muñoz 1999: 100, 107).

The drag show is thus arguably the most outsider kind of gender performance, the mirror of cheerleading and beauty pageants. Indeed, Taylor *et al.* (2004: 113, 115–20) argue that the Key West drag shows they studied function as "protest episodes" and "oppositional performances" rather than "rituals of cultural affirmation." First, these performances *contest* the gender status quo, rejecting or mocking traditional gender and sexuality (as when one queen performs "The Wedding Bell Blues" in "a ripped-up wedding dress, coke-bottle glasses, and a mouthful of fake teeth"), and appropriating dominant gender and sexual codes but using them to "construct a hybrid and more fluid model of gender and sexuality" (as when a gay man in make-up and eyelashes lip-syncs "I Kissed a Girl" while skipping around the bar to kiss women). Second, the drag queens themselves *intend* to perform protest, consciously deploying sexuality to disturb gender and sexual categories, and making overt political points from the stage. Finally, the performances represent and enact collective identity for both the performers and the audiences, both by expressing gay solidarity and by challenging audiences to question, reach across, and expand gender and sexual-identity classifications. Bringing audience members with different gender and sexual identities up on stage to "do shots," for instance, the Key West drag queens arrange them in sexual poses that don't make conventional sense (e.g. a "lesbian" mounting a "gay man"). Audience members often described a utopian sense of unity across difference, a sense, as one man put it, of "the way it could be" (Taylor *et al.* 2004: 128). In such ways, drag shows like these serve as transformative outside-gender performances for performers and audiences alike.

Yet even within drag we can see the tension between conformity and transgression. While drag shows are recognizably outside-gender performances, they also clearly contain inside elements. The point is not simply that there is no "pure form," though that is certainly true; even the most radical drag performances do on occasion affirm conventional femininity and masculinity. More significant is that outside-gender performances always, unavoidably, also contain normative cultural assumptions about gender and sexuality—if sometimes only to counter them—and thus both articulate contradictory ideological components and leave room for a range of audience interpretations. For instance, drag performers "use the cultural equation of the penis with maleness to mix up gender categories" (Taylor *et al.* 2004: 118), juxtaposing the "male" body (revealed through nudity or facial hair) to women's costume and persona in order to generate gender confusion. Yet this equation of genitals and gender is precisely one of the bedrock assumptions of the gender order (Lorber 1994). Similarly, the project of creating and expressing gay solidarity and collective identity often requires a sort of gender essentialism, an assertion that, as one performer put it to the audience, "We may look like women, but we're all homosexual men" (Taylor *et al.* 2004: 125). For audience members, moreover, gender may not so much be radically destabilized or revealed to be a performance for all, but instead become integrated into a liberal message of unity and tolerance across stable gender and sexual categories.

258

In drag shows, we can again see how specific institutional locations impact gender performances and their reception. On the one hand, drag performances may take place within recognizably "gay spaces," where outside-gender consciousness is accepted and even encouraged. On the other hand, they may occur in more commercial venues profiting from a primarily "straight" clientele, where the location neither supports challenges to gender politics nor encourages audiences to see connections between their own everyday enactments of gender and that taking place onstage. Even here, however, political gender expression may enter under the cover of "just entertainment," as performers build their politics into their shows for audiences that might elsewhere be unreceptive (Taylor *et al.* 2004). Thus, particular venues structure gender performances in particular ways, reflecting differing degrees of fusion and de-fusion between scripts, performers, and audiences.

Shapiro (2007: 256–57) reaches a similar conclusion in her study of drag kinging within a feminist drag troupe, where the shows typically included both verbal and per-formed challenges to gender (cheerleading routines by "women" with facial hair, "men" in outfits revealing breasts, butch women, effeminate men, and so forth), and where members' gender identities were transformed because of their participation. It was not drag alone but drag in a particular organizational and ideological context that challenged the gender order; drag's "disruptive power" was harnessed mainly because the troupe had given organizational form to an oppositional, collective feminist identity. In a variety of significant ways, then, gender performances are structured—opportunities provided, limits set—by the synergy between performers' agency and the features of their institutional location.

Conclusion

We have argued here for the sociological relevance of explicit gender performances, in which an institutionalized performance culture codifies, scripts, and heightens gender expressions—along a range from "inside gender" to "outside gender" events. Explicit performances, through their exaggeration, can make visible the ongoing dynamics of "doing gender" in everyday life: they shine a spotlight on the gender scripts, codes, and norms to which we are routinely subject, and on the organizational and institutional mechanisms subtending these scripts. Along the way, they may model new, alternative ways of doing gender that lie outside taken-for-granted routines. Gender performances are not, therefore, merely exaggerated versions of everyday modes of gender enactment; in foregrounding the difference between doing and performing, they facilitate a distinctive type of cultural work. This work is centrally related to the question of power: whereas the everyday doing of gender typically renders power relations "natural" and therefore invisible, explicit gender performances can help reveal power—sometimes only to reaffirm it (as in certain forms of cheerleading) and sometimes to create new paths for change (as in certain forms of drag); significantly, they usually do both simultaneously to varying degrees. The cultural work a performance enables is shaped partly by the specific genres and institutional settings in which performances take place; as we have seen, generic conventions and institutional practices can encourage or discourage the affirma-tion or transgression of the gendered status quo. In this sense, the "gender code" and the "genre code" of a performance are related but not synonymous categories. While the former channels a certain set of ideas and practices related to the construction of gender scripts, the latter speaks to a specific framework and scaffolding within and upon which the construction takes place.

Gender performances also underscore the insight of queer theorist Judith Butler that gender is an iterative code predicated upon repetition and mimesis for its sense of solidity and consistency. To say, as she does, that gender is a copy with no original is not to deny its real presence and its real effects; rather, it is to insist that there is no fixed, objective ground from which to judge the relation between "normative" and "alternative" incarnations of gender. Masculinity presupposes, depends upon, and helps constitute femininity, and vice versa, just as heterosexuality presupposes, depends upon, and helps constitute homosexuality, and vice versa—regardless of whether or not these mutual interdependences are consciously acknowledged and understood. Gender repetition is necessary precisely because dependence on "the Other" puts "the Self" at perpetual risk of destabilization. And it is the possibility of destabilization—of recognizing that gender variance is always already there in "normative" and "alternative" gender scripts alike—that the concept of gender performance can, and often does, foreground.

References

Acker, Joan. 1990. "Hierarchies, Jobs, Bodies: A Theory of Gendered Organizations." *Gender & Society* 4: 139–58.

Adams, Natalie and Bettis, Pamela. 2003. "Commanding the Room in Short Skirts: Cheering as the Embodiment of Ideal Girlhood." *Gender & Society* 17: 73–91.

——. 2004. *Cheerleader!* New York: Macmillan.

Alexander, Jeffrey. 2004. "Cultural Pragmatics: Social Performance Between Ritual and Strategy." *Sociological Theory* 22(4): 527–73.

Anderson, Eric. 2005. "Orthodox and Inclusive Masculinity." *Sociological Perspectives* 48(3): 337–55.

Auslander, Philip. 2006. *Performing Glam Rock*. Ann Arbor: University of Michigan Press.

Banet-Weiser, Sarah. 1999. *The Most Beautiful Girl in the World: Beauty Pageants and National Identity*. Berkeley: University of California Press.

Barnes, Natasha. 1994. "Face of the Nation: Race, Nationalisms and Identities in Jamaican Beauty Pageants." *Massachusetts Review* 35(3/4): 471–92.

Best, Amy. 2000. *Prom Night*. New York: Routledge.

Butler, Judith. 1990. *Gender Trouble*. New York: Routledge.

Chauncey, George. 1994. *Gay New York*. New York: Basic Books.

Cohen, Colleen Ballerino. 1996. "Contestants in a Contested Domain: Staging Identities in the British Virgin Islands." Pp. 125–46 in Colleen Cohen, Richard Wilk, and Beverly Stoeltje, eds., *Beauty Queens on the Global Stage*. New York: Routledge.

Cohen, Colleen Ballerino, Wilk, Richard, and Stoeltje, Beverly, eds. 1996. *Beauty Queens on the Global Stage*. New York: Routledge.

Collins, Patricia Hill. 2006. *From Black Power to Hip Hop*. Philadelphia, PA: Temple University Press.

Connell, Robert W. 1987. *Gender and Power*. Stanford, CA: Stanford University Press.

Craig, Maxine. 2002. *Ain't I a Beauty Queen? Culture, Social Movements, and the Politics of Race*. Cambridge, MA: Oxford University Press.

Dolan, Jill. 1985. "Gender Impersonation Onstage." *Women & Performance* 2: 5–11.

Feder, Abigail. 1995. "A Radiant Smile from the Lovely Lady: Overdetermined Femininity in 'Ladies' Figure Skating." Pp. 22–46 in Cynthia Baughman, ed., *Women on Ice*. New York: Routledge.

Ferrar, Margaret and Warner, Jamie L. 2006. "Rah-Rah Radical: The Radical Cheerleaders' Challenge to the Public Sphere." *Politics & Gender* 2(3): 281–302.

Frank, Katherine. 2002. *G-Strings and Sympathy: Strip Club Regulars and Male Desire*. Durham, NC: Duke University Press.

——. 2007. "Thinking Critically about Strip Club Research." *Sexualities* 10(4): 501–17.

Gamson, Joshua. 2005. *The Fabulous Sylvester*. New York: Henry Holt.

Goffman, Erving. 1959. *The Presentation of Self in Everyday Life*. New York: Anchor Books.

Grindstaff, Laura and West, Emily. 2006. "Cheerleading and the Gendered Politics of Sport." *Social Problems* 53(4): 500–18.

Halberstam, Judith. 1998. *Female Masculinity*. Durham, NC: Duke University Press.

Hanson, Mary Ellen. 1995. Go, Fight, Win!: Cheerleading in American Culture. Bowling Green, OH: Bowling Green University Popular Press.

Ingraham, Chrys. 2008 (1999). *White Weddings*, second edition. New York: Routledge.

Kessler, Susanna J. and McKenna, Wendy. 1978. *Gender: An Ethnomethodological Approach*. New York: Wiley.

King-O'Riain, Rebecca. 2006. *Pure Beauty: Judging Race in Japanese American Beauty Pageants*. Minneapolis/London: University of Minnesota Press.

Koenig, Sharon. 2002. "Walk Like a Man: Enactments and Embodiments of Masculinity and the Potential for Multiple Genders." *Journal of Homosexuality* 43(3/4): 145–59.

Liepe-Levinson, Katherine. 2002. *Strip Show*. New York: Routledge.

Lorber, Judith. 1994. *Paradoxes of Gender*. New Haven, CT: Yale University Press.

Lynch, Annette. 1999. *Dress, Gender and Cultural Change: Asian American and African American Rites of Passage*. Oxford: Berg Publishers.

McAllister, Carolota. 1996. "Authenticity and Guatemala's Maya Queen." Pp. 105–24 in Colleen Cohen, Richard Wilk, and Beverly Stoeltje, eds., *Beauty Queens on the Global Stage*. New York: Routledge.

McGranahan, Carole. 1996. "Miss Tibet, or Tibet Misrepresented? The Trope of Woman-as-Nation in the Struggle for Tibet." Pp. 161–84 in Colleen Cohen, Richard Wilk, and Beverly Stoeltje, eds., *Beauty Queens on the Global Stage*. New York: Routledge.

Martin, Patricia Yancey. 1990. "Rethinking Feminist Organizations." *Gender & Society* 4(2): 182–206.

——. 2003. "'Said and Done' Versus 'Saying and Doing': Gendering Practices, Practicing Gender at Work." *Gender & Society* 17(3): 342–66.

Messner, Michael. 2002. *Taking the Field*. Minneapolis/London: University of Minnesota Press.

Montemurro, Beth. 2006. *Something Old, Something Bold: Bridal Showers and Bachelorette Parties*. New Brunswick: Rutgers University Press.

Muñoz, José Esteban. 1999. *Disidentifications*. Minneapolis: University of Minnesota Press.

Newton, Esther. 1979. *Mother Camp*. Chicago: University of Chicago Press.

Nishimura, Yuko. 1996. "South Indian Wedding Rituals." *Anthropos* 91: 411–23.

Otnes, Cele and Pleck, Elizabeth Hafkin. 2003. *Cinderella Dreams*. Berkeley: University of California Press.

Rose, Tricia. 2008. *The Hip-Hop Wars*. New York: Basic Civitas Books.

Rupp, Leila and Taylor, Verta. 2003. *Drag Queens at the 801 Cabaret*. Chicago: University of Chicago Press.

Schacht, Steven P. 2002. "Turnabout: Gay Drag Queens and the Masculine Embodiment of the Feminine." Pp. 155–70 in Nancy Tuana *et al.*, eds., *Revealing Male Bodies*. Bloomington: Indiana University Press.

Schippers, Mimi. 2002. *Rockin' Out of the Box*. New Brunswick: Rutgers University Press.

Shapiro, Eve. 2007. "Drag Kinging and the Transformation of Gender Identities." *Gender & Society* 21(2): 250–71.

Surkan, Kim. 2002. "Drag Kings in the New Wave." *Journal of Homosexuality* 43(3/4): 161–83.

Taylor, Verta, Rupp, Leila, and Gamson, Joshua. 2004. "Performing Protest: Drag Shows as Tactical Repertoire of the Gay and Lesbian Movement." *Research in Social Movements, Conflicts, and Change* 25: 105–38.

Tewksbury, Richard. 1993. "Men Performing as Women." *Sociological Spectrum* 13(4): 465–86.

Van Esterik, Penny. 1995. "The Politics of Beauty in Thailand." Pp. 203–16 in Colleen Cohen, Richard Wilk, and Beverly Stoeltje, eds., *Beauty Queens on the Global Stage*. New York: Routledge.

261

West, Candace and Fenstermaker, Sarah. 1995. "Doing Difference." *Gender & Society* 9(1): 8–37.

West, Candace and Zimmerman, Don. 1987. "Doing Gender." *Gender & Society* 1(2): 125–51.

Wu, Judy Tzu-Chun. 1997. "Loveliest Daughter of Our Ancient Cathay! Representations of Ethnic and Gender Identity in the Miss Chinatown USA Beauty Pageant." *Journal of Social History* 31(1): 5–31.

25

Rituals, repertoires, and performances in post-modernity

A cultural sociological account

Ronald N. Jacobs

In many respects, Cultural Sociology was established through the study of ritual. For Durkheim, ritual is the central social process that bonds the individual to society; at the same time, rituals serve to reinforce core social values, through the division or the world into the two basic categories of sacred and profane. As a particular mode of action, ritual serves to infuse culture with collective energy and affectivity, which increases its power and its ability to enact an identification of the individual with society.

In more recent times, however, scholars have criticized Durkheim's ritual theory for its functionalist assumptions; in the process, they have worked to rethink the connection between ritual and meaning in a way that is less mechanistic and more open to contingency, strategic action, and historical specificity. This essay provides a review of these attempts, through a critical examination of the work of Swidler, Bourdieu, Collins, and Alexander. Swidler and Bourdieu emphasize how ritual events facilitate strategic action as well as social integration. Collins and Alexander focus on the contingency of the ritual event, attempting to explain why some rituals are more successful than others. Throughout the essay, I illustrate the relative advantages that each approach offers, by focusing on a single empirical case, the Olympic Games.

Durkheim on ritual

For Durkheim, rituals serve to integrate individuals into society through the production of social solidarity. This social attachment occurs through two related social processes. First, ritual functions by marking off and separating the sacred from the profane. This is a spatial, temporal, and cognitive division. Rituals serve to identify sacred places, sacred times, sacred events, and sacred symbols. Profane things are kept at a distance from the realm of the sacred, through a series of prohibitions that Durkheim (1995: 303–20) called "negative rites." These prohibitions make it easier to separate sacred things from the mundane world, providing a heightened affective environment where the social group can more easily reaffirm itself (Durkheim 1995: 391). Ultimately—and this, for Durkheim, is the essential element of religion—the relationship between sacred things attains a systematic coherence, which is accepted and shared by all members of society. At this point, society becomes a collective reality acting upon individuals, stored as memories of the sacred within each individual.

In order for society to imprint itself through individual memories of the sacred, Durkheim insisted, these memories need to be re-established and energized by a continual cycle of ritual events. Rather than leaving the social bond as a purely cognitive entity, the cycle of rituals works to infuse social solidarity with emotion, affectivity, and collective effervescence. These events, which concentrate the public's attention on a common space, and which gather individuals into a shared communion of co-presence, are just as important for secular society as they were for earlier, more "religious" ones (Durkheim 1995: 429). Durkheim believed that it was possible to take the core integrative processes of religion and to transpose them onto the more secular society of the modern nation-state. This shift would require a new cycle of celebrations, in which citizens take time out from their daily lives in order to join in a common communion, a celebration of a common past and a common future, and an affirmation of a common system of sacred symbols and meanings. Increasingly, as Dayan and Katz (1992) have argued persuasively, these moments of communion would be coordinated in and through media.

Dayan and Katz point to the Olympic Games as an example of a media event that performs the kind of ritual functions that Durkheim identified. In the most recent Beijing Olympics, 4.7 billion viewers—roughly 70 percent of the world's population—tuned in to watch the Games. In China, more than 840 million people watched the opening ceremonies, and 94 percent of the country's population watched at least part of the Olympics. Similar concentrations of viewers could be found throughout Asia, and indeed in countries throughout the world.

There are a number of reasons why media events such as the Olympic Games are such powerful rituals, in a Durkheimian sense. First, they are announced through a marking off of sacred from mundane time, in this case through the interruption of normal broadcasting schedules. Furthermore, viewers tend to experience the Olympics as a form of communion, watching the events together with others in their society, in shared time as well as shared space. Indeed, one of the distinguishing features of media events, as compared to ordinary media consumption, is that audiences tend to gather in order to witness the event together, in the same social space, whether in a friend's family room, a hotel lounge, or a neighborhood bar. In the host city, in fact, it becomes common for viewers to gather by the thousands in designated parks and other common viewing areas, in order to share in the collective energy and the excitement of the ritual event. There is a fusion of society as people celebrate national triumphs, and reaffirm the core values that the Olympics symbolize—achievement, sacrifice, cooperation, national greatness, and a specific kind of competitive international solidarity.

Although Durkheim's ritual theory clearly has a lot of descriptive and explanatory power, it also displays a number of weaknesses. Lukes (1975) argued forcefully that the integrative effects of civic ritual tended to be assumed rather than demonstrated empirically. In fact, Lukes argued, many people in modern society are either apathetic to ritual events, or explicitly hostile to them. Lukes also argued, as did Tilly (1981), that Durkheim's ritual theory completely ignored power and conflict. For Lukes and Tilly, rituals are always organized by specific groups who have specific interests, and their meaning and authority is almost always challenged by competing groups. Indeed, this process was played out repeatedly throughout 2008 during the Olympic torch relay, as protesters used that ritual in order to challenge China on a variety of issues, most notably its humanitarian record and its treatment of Tibet. In other words, as these events demonstrated, ritual is a site of struggle, with no guarantee of success.

The contingent and strategic basis of ritual was emphasized in a different way by the work of Goffman, who focused on the work individuals need to do in order to manage their public image in interaction. Goffman's work (e.g. 1959, 1967) suggested a shift in orientation, away from the large public rituals that Durkheim emphasized and toward the small, everyday rituals in which individuals work to negotiate their own presentation of selves, as well as the small rituals of deference where they help others to create successful front-stage performances of self. Within this context, the shared meanings and the collective emotions of ritual are de-emphasized in favor of a focus on the strategic activities in which individuals use ritual events to their own personal advantage. This emphasis encouraged a conceptual shift: from ritual to repertoire, and from rule to strategy.

From ritual to repertoire: Swidler and the cultural toolkit

Swidler's main contribution to ritual theory lay in a conceptual shift, which focused on the way that culture provides a common repertoire of habits, skills, and styles from which people can develop their own specific "strategies of action." In other words, culture provides a pragmatic "toolkit," which "consists of symbols, stories, rituals, and worldviews, which people may use in varying configurations to solve different kinds of problems" (Swidler 1986: 273). Furthermore, according to Swidler, the model of a unified, systematic, and coherent cultural system was mistaken; in its place, she suggested (Swidler 1986: 277), there should be a theory that begins from the position that "real cultures" contain multiple and usually conflicting symbols and rituals, which actors draw upon in diverse ways in order to craft their own, context-specific guides to action.

The second component of Swidler's theory of culture and action is the distinction she made between "settled" and "unsettled" times. During settled times, there is a lower degree of commitment to the symbols and rituals that make up the common culture. This allows people to use the different elements of culture and ritual in more strategic ways, in a style that resembles the Goffmanian analyses of impression management. On the other hand, culture acquires an added significance and power during unsettled periods, when groups try to create new rituals that will reorganize the habits and modes of perception that individuals use to create their individual strategies of action. But these attempts are by no means guaranteed to succeed, because the fact that society is in flux also means that there will be competing groups deploying alternative rituals, designed to emphasize competing ideologies and cultural formations.

Returning to our case of the Olympic Games and its cultural impact, Swidler's distinction between settled and unsettled times can help to explain why different nation-states might have varying levels of effectiveness when they try to use the Games to reproduce a strong sense of national unity. In nations that are undergoing a period of stability, the commitment to the ritual should tend to be lower, as should the demand for cultural coherence. These conditions would create extra challenges for crafting a common cultural framework for a unified solidarity. The more likely scenario, in this situation, would be that individuals would deploy the Olympics in a variety of ways, in order to organize specific strategies of action. For example, many people watched streaming video of the Games while sitting at their desks—not as a ritual of solidarity, but rather as a way of avoiding work. Here, the Olympics provide them with a more legitimate justification for work avoidance than most other available justifications. At home, they avoid the communion aspect of the ritual, recording the broadcast so that they can watch it at their convenience, and so they can skip those parts of the broadcast they find boring. In this way, they rely on the same habits and strategies of action that regulate their everyday lives. There is no reinforcement of shared values, no collective effervescence, and no social solidarity.

This is not to say that ritualistic dimensions of the viewing experience are wholly absent in more "stable" societies. Many viewers do, in fact, experience a heightened emotional and cultural connection when watching the Games, just as a Durkheimian perspective would suggest. In other words, the putatively lower levels of cultural commitment that Swidler's theory suggests are not uniformly distributed across the population of a settled society. Nevertheless, the presence of these more deflated and strategic uses of the Games creates an additional integrative burden. Because viewers cannot be as sure in assuming that others share involvement in the ritual, they fear being ridiculed for their more pure and "naïve" experience of the events, and as a result they may limit their experience of the ritual to their own private spaces.

On the other hand, in countries that are experiencing more social change, the Olympics become a powerful and emotional battleground for competing ideologies. This was clearly the case in China, where debates raged about the meaning of the opening ceremonies of the Games. On one side was the official government position, which was that the opening ceremony was a display of government capability, the spirit of the Chinese people, and the distinctiveness of Chinese culture. On the other side was the competing position, circulated on blogs popular among Chinese intellectuals, that the mass display of thousands of drummers and soldiers represented an authoritarian aesthetic that was devoid of humanity. In this situation, the emotional involvement in the ritual was high, as was the degree of cultural coherence through which the ritual was interpreted. At issue was which cultural system of interpretation would prevail.

Although Swidler's distinction between settled and unsettled times can help to illuminate the general context in which strategies of action can be deployed through ritual, it has a more difficult time explaining how these different strategies of action are themselves structured. Instead, Swidler's work seems to adopt the perspective of pragmatism, in which action is guided by the immediate problem confronting the individual (see Swidler 2001). The difficulty is that this approach tends to overestimate agency, to underestimate structure, and to lead to the problem of the "randomness of ends" that Parsons (1967 [1937]) identified long ago as a risk for theoretical programs based on an instrumental action-orientation. Even from within an instrumentalist perspective, it is necessary to think about competing deployments of ritual as being themselves parts of other rituals.

From ritual to reproduction: Bourdieu and the strategic rituals of distinction

Although Bourdieu shares Swidler's concern for strategies and repertoires of action, his approach emphasizes a much more structural understanding of strategic action, and offers a stronger theory of ritual. For Bourdieu, strategic deployments of cultural repertoires are connected to the agonistic processes of social reproduction and social advantage, where the ritualistic deployment of these repertoires will be shaped by the actor's "feel for the game" (see Bourdieu 1990: 107–08).

For Bourdieu, the repertoires of action that an individual chooses are structured in significant ways by the *field* in which they are situated. Fields are "historically constituted areas of activity with their specific institutions and their own laws of functioning" (Bourdieu 1990: 87). Fields tend to produce these "laws of functioning" by providing dominant principles of distinction and division, organized around debates concerning what constitutes good art, who is a real intellectual, what makes up a great athletic performance, and so forth. The strategies of action that are available to an actor are shaped by that actor's position in the field, the distinctions she and her allies have deployed before, and the volumes of economic, social, and cultural capital she possesses.

There is also the possibility of employing socio-cultural distinctions that emerge from outside of the field itself: for example relying on market principles to define artistic success. Indeed, much of the conflict that animates the strategies of action within a given field is motivated by this distinction between autonomous and "pure" criteria of success, on the one hand, and heterodox criteria that emerge from other social sources, on the other. The development of this form of binary distinction is one of the most important characteristics of modernity: the aesthetic realm was successfully differentiated from the social realm, a new class of artists and critics emerged, and the pursuit of the pure aesthetic became a powerful new cultural repertoire that was increasingly available as a social resource for certain types of people. Indeed, conflict between aesthetic and heterodox principles of distinction gives most field-specific environments of action an "unsettled" character (to borrow Swidler's language), which increases the power of ritual as well as the force of cultural coherence.

In fact, the distinction between autonomous and heterodox principles helps to illuminate certain aspects of ritual that typically go unexamined—specifically, the choice between a social and an aesthetic mode of engagement with ritual. Thus, to continue with the example of the Olympic Games, social interpretations of the Games—emphasizing national unity, shared values, or even competing ideologies—are all examples of heterodox principles of cultural organization. To be sure, these are powerful modes of engaging with ritual, and they provide the most obvious ways in which ritual is linked to power. As Bourdieu (1996) argued, after all, heterodox principles of distinction typically emerge from the field of power.

On the other hand, rituals such as the Olympic Games can also be approached from an aesthetic mode of interpretation. Indeed, the professionals who are most involved with this sporting ritual—the athletes, the event organizers, and the broadcasters and journalists who cover the Games for the public—are much more likely to make aesthetic interpretations than social ones. For the Olympics, the aesthetic interpretations emphasize debates about what constitutes a great performance, as well as struggles to define the purity of sport itself. Furthermore, from the aesthetic mode of interpretation, the social interpretations—whether they are displays of political ideology or crass commercialism—are often seen as threats to the purity of the event and the success of the ritual.

In contemporary society, the aesthetic interpretation is always available as a cultural system for discussing the significance of a ritual. This is true even for more obviously political rituals, such as political inaugurations of new leaders, where the aesthetic features of the performance provide a constant source of discussion. Three groups are most likely to adopt the aesthetic mode of interpretation: (1) the professionals in charge of

267

organizing the ritual; (2) the cultural critics who provide the official aesthetic interpretation of public events; and (3) those who possess significant amounts of cultural capital, who adopt the aesthetic mode as a form of detached irony in order to distinguish themselves from their less sophisticated fellow citizens.

Through a consideration of the structures that organize strategies of action, a Bourdieuian perspective clearly extends the analysis of repertoires and ritual. But a purely strategic approach to ritual has important limitations. To begin with, the ability to see ritual as a source of social solidarity has disappeared altogether. Also obscured are the emotional and intimate aspects of ritual. For Durkheim, co-presence and collective effervescence are central to the ritual process, because they provide an immediacy that serves to block social distance and to replace it with a type of communion, which Victor Turner (1967) described as "communitas." But the calculating agents that Swidler and Bourdieu describe seem to lack any interest in this type of communion. Having no real commitment to the ritual's symbolic environment, and always scheming to figure out how they can turn the ritual to their own advantage, these actors define themselves only by distance and detachment.

Although the evaluation of a strategic model of ritual will in large part be based on the presuppositions that one adopts concerning the nature of social action and social order (see Alexander 1982), it nevertheless remains the case that the strategic model has certain empirical blind spots. Perhaps the most important among these is the difficulty in addressing the questions of why some rituals are more successful than others, or what constitutes a successful ritual performance. In their own ways, Randall Collins and Jeffrey Alexander have attempted to answer this important question in their recent works: Collins through his micro-theory of interaction ritual chains, and Alexander through his macro-theory of cultural performance.

Emotional energy and interaction ritual chains

In many respects, Collins's theory of interaction ritual chains returns to concerns that were central to Durkheim, but which were largely abandoned by later theories. Identifying important points of commonality between Durkheim and Goffman, Collins (2004: 7) defines a ritual as "a mechanism of mutually focused emotion and attention producing a momentary shared reality, which thereby generates solidarity and symbols of group membership." Central to this definition are the elements of *co-presence*, *mutuality* of focus, *emotion*, and *membership*. All of these elements vary in their intensity, resulting in a complex array of contingencies that, taken together, help to explain many of the varieties of social life (Collins 2004: 47). Included in these contingencies are diverse possibilities of failed rituals, which have their own distinctive social consequences.

Collins argues that a successful ritual is one where a high level of mutual focus and emotional entrainment develops among the participants in an interaction. When there is a low mutual focus and minimal emotional energy, the ritual is likely to fail. If an individual at an event only participates in "low intensity, perfunctory, or halting conversations," rather than being drawn into the mutual focus of the larger interaction ritual, she will not receive any emotional benefits from the interaction; in fact, if this style of interaction persists for too long, the individual is likely to find it tedious and emotionally draining (Collins 2004: 52). On the other hand, where there are high levels of focus and emotional entrainment, the result is a ritual that has powerful and durable cultural significance for the individual. Furthermore, because individuals tend to be drawn to those situations where they receive the most emotional energy, their identities and their associational life will be shaped in central ways by their ability to find situations where they can have regular access to successful rituals.

Collins's theory challenges the "strategies of action" approach in two important respects. First, it replaces Swidler's sweeping generalizations about "settled" and "unsettled" times with a focus on the contingencies and varying emotional intensities of specific situations. Collins suggests that low levels of symbolic commitment are less connected to macro-social dynamics than to the situation-specific failure of an interaction to produce a successful ritual. Second, and related to this, Collins shifts the focus away from the calculating individual, and places emphasis on the *situation*, "not as a cognitive construction but as a process by which shared emotions and intersubjective focus sweep individuals along by flooding their consciousness. It is not so much a matter of knowledgeable agents choosing from repertoires, as a situational propensity toward certain cultural symbols" (Collins 2004: 32). He goes on to argue that an examination of interaction ritual chains can help the analyst to predict when new cultural symbols will be created, when those new meanings will have a durable impact, and when their influence will be more fleeting.

Although Collins's work would seem to primarily provide a microsociology of rituals, it also makes some interesting macrosociological arguments about formal rituals and modernity. Of particular interest is his analysis of sporting ritual. Sporting events contain all the elements of a successful ritual. There is a large crowd gathered together, all focused on the same thing, with high levels of emotional involvement. The result is a strong feeling of social solidarity and the reinforcement of a strong group identity. This is why people prefer watching a sporting event in person, rather than on television. Even though the view on television is better, the mutuality of focus and the emotional entrainment tend to be weaker.

Collins's approach to the study of ritual is helpful in redirecting attention back toward emotion, mutuality of focus, and the contingency of particular situations. However, there remain important aspects in which it is less useful for cultural sociologists. First, and most problematic, is the way that the theory of interaction rituals represents a movement away from meaning. Although Collins is surely correct to argue that the ability of culture to have concrete causal force is connected to the emotional energy of interaction rituals, he does not have much to say about how these rituals are shaped or informed by culture. This critique is not only concerned with the need to consider the autonomy of culture. It also encompasses a historical argument about the way that cultural processes and formal rituals have come to be organized, since modernity, within a distinctively cultural realm that has taken over the creation, the production, and the official interpretation of most public culture. In other words, for many rituals today, a consideration of what makes them successful must include an examination of performers, critics, and audiences. This is the task that Alexander undertakes with his theory of cultural pragmatics.

The challenge of creating a successful ritual performance: Alexander and the theory of cultural pragmatics

With Alexander's (2004) theory of cultural pragmatics, the goal is to develop an understanding of culture and action that can incorporate the structural insights of ritual

269

theory as well as the arguments about repertoires and strategies of action that are emphasized more by contemporary practice theories. This theory involves a conceptual shift away from notions such as agency or practice and toward the concept of *performance*.

For Alexander, a ritual performance involves more than just the co-presence of individuals, or the simple enactment of a pre-existing cultural code. In fact, there are many "elements" of performance. One element consists of *systems of collective representation*, including background symbols and codes as well as the foregrounded "script." Another element comprises the *actors and performers*, who are involved in the enactment of the ritual performance. There is the *audience* to the performance, the *means of symbolic production*, and the *mise-en-scène*, or the general choreography of the performance. Finally, there is *social power*, which involves: (1) control over what kinds of texts are permitted, promoted, and encouraged; (2) what kinds of people are permitted to perform, and what kinds of people are permitted to attend, the performance; and (3) the extent to which the interpretation of the performance is controlled. The success of a ritual can be derailed by characteristics of any one of these elements of performance. Thus, the theory emphasizes the contingency of ritual, while also paying attention to the structural sources which inform that contingency.

Like most of the contemporary theorists discussed above, Alexander favors a historical theory of ritual. For Alexander, the key transformation of ritual that has taken place in modern times is the general movement from fusion to de-fusion, as the primary way that audiences initially engage with ritual performances. In earlier, less differentiated societies—the ones that make up most of the empirical referents in Durkheim's *Elementary Forms of the Religious Life*—rituals were characterized by fusion, in which there is no separation between actor and performance (Alexander 2004: 537). In contrast, modernity brings about an increasing social distance between the observers/audience and the other elements of performance, creating a situation of institutionalized "de-fusion." Indeed, many of the elements of performance have become institutionalized in particular ways by complex professional organizations, with the precise intention of creating this kind of distance. Professional writers have largely taken over the production of scripts. Professional actors have taken over many of the performance roles, and where they have not, the actors often receive professional coaching. Interpretations of ritual performances have become dominated by professional critics. Social power is centralized in an increasingly bureaucratic state, often with its own ministry of culture. The means of symbolic production are largely controlled by the state or by the cultural industries. In such a situation, performances can seem artificial, contrived, and unconvincing (Alexander 2004: 529).

Thus the challenge in modernity is the challenge of "re-fusion," of creating a successful ritual performance. This requires both an emotional and a cultural connection. "The aim," Alexander (2004: 547) argues, "is to create, via skillful and affecting performance, the emotional connection of audience with actor and text and thereby to create the conditions for projecting cultural meaning from performance to audience." Several challenging tasks must be successfully completed for this connection to occur, and for the audience members to feel that they are witnessing an authentic performance. For writers and other creative personnel, the challenge is to fuse the foregrounded script and the background representations (i.e. the underlying cultural codes and narratives). For performers, the challenge is to create a fusion between actor and role, whereas for choreographers or directors it is to enact a successful fusion between script, action, and performative space. Those who control the means of symbolic production must be willing to provide technological and distributional support, while those critics who control official interpretations must accept the legitimacy, power, and aesthetic quality of the performance. If all of this happens, then there is a much higher likelihood of a successful fusion of audience and text occurring, and of the ritual performance having a significant emotional and cultural impact.

Viewed from the perspective of Alexander's theory of cultural pragmatics, it becomes easy to see why the Olympic Games so frequently succeed as an authentic and meaningful ritual performance; at the same time, Alexander's theory points to specific ways that cultural fusion is likely to take place. One of the central features of the Olympics, as a contemporary ritual performance, is the fact that actor and role are already fused. Athletes spend their entire lives preparing for the Olympic competition. Their participation in the Games is the crowning achievement in their athletic lives, and the opportunity to represent their country is their greatest source of collective attachment and pride. As a consequence, there is no need to manufacture an emotional commitment to the role. There is also an easy fusion between script and background representation. In every competition, there are heroic moments of triumph and tragic moments of disappointment, and there are individuals who have had to overcome great obstacles in their Olympic quest. Finally, those who control the means of symbolic production are active and willing participants in the organization and broadcast of the myriad events that make up the Games. Even critics seem more willing than usual to emphasize the heroic and sacred character of the Games, whether that is the spectacle of the opening ceremonies or the superhuman feats of athletic performance.

As a consequence of these elements of cultural performance, most viewers of the Games are much more likely than usual to suspend their cynicism, to immerse themselves in the drama of the ritual, and to celebrate the scripts and the background representations that emerge. Importantly, the ritual performance of the Olympic Games provides two equally powerful and historically durable narratives for audience and script. On the one hand there are the narratives of national triumph and victory. When that more particularistic narrative is unconvincing, however, there is always a secondary set of more universalistic background representations, which are inscribed in the official Olympic Charter—"to place sport at the service of the harmonious development of man, with a view to promoting a peaceful society concerned with the preservation of human dignity" (see http://multimedia.olympic.org/pdf/en_report_122.pdf). Because performers, producers, official interpreters, audiences, the state, and the cultural industries are all working from this dual script, the likelihood of creating a successful ritual is increased immeasurably.

Conclusion

For a cultural sociology that is concerned to link meaning and action, the concept of ritual is one of the most useful conceptual resources. By providing a common horizon of meaning and attention, rituals bring actors together within a shared environment of action. This enables the production of social solidarity at the same time as it encourages a reproduction of common cultural codes and narratives.

However, most cultural sociologists are unwilling to accept the argument that rituals produce solidarity without conflict. They question how coordinated action can take place in the absence of strategic action. They pay much closer attention to the ways that rituals are connected to social power and to the reproduction of social advantage. These scholars reject the idea that all rituals are equally powerful, or even that rituals are destined to succeed. These challenges have produced a productive fragmentation in the cultural sociology of ritual, which has had the advantage of pointing to a number of important social processes and empirical questions. For those who are interested in the strategic elements of ritual processes, Swidler and Bourdieu provide useful resources. For those who are more interested in the contingent outcomes of ritual and the factors that explain the success of specific rituals, Alexander and Collins provide a provocative conceptual vocabulary.

What are still missing are empirical studies that allow us to make judgments and evaluations of these competing approaches. Indeed, many of the empirical claims about the Olympic Games that I have derived from these different approaches are in direct opposition to one another: for example Collins versus Swidler on the degree of emotional enchainment likely to be found at a sporting event in a "settled" society, or Alexander versus Bourdieu on the proportion of aesthetic interpretations that critics make of the Olympics. There is also the question of group boundaries. Most theories privilege the nation as the default boundary, but there may be instances when sub-national or transnational boundaries will be dominant. More studies are needed that can test these kinds of competing expectations.

References

Alexander, Jeffrey C. 1982. *Theoretical Logic in Sociology, volume 1: Positivism, Presuppositions, and Current Controversies*. Berkeley: University of California Press.
——. 2004. "Cultural Pragmatics: Social Performance Between Ritual and Strategy." *Sociological Theory* 22: 527–73.
Bourdieu, Pierre. 1990. *In Other Words: Essays Towards a Reflexive Sociology*. Stanford, CA: Stanford University Press.
——. 1996. *The Rules of Art: Genesis and Structure of the Literary Field*. Stanford, CA: Stanford University Press.
Collins, Randall. 2004. *Interaction Ritual Chains*. Princeton, NJ: Princeton University Press.
Dayan, Daniel and Katz, Elihu. 1992. *Media Events*. Cambridge, MA: Harvard University Press.
Durkheim, Emile. 1995 (1912). *The Elementary Forms of Religious Life*. New York: Free Press.
Goffman, Erving. 1959 (1956). *The Presentation of Self in Everyday Life*. New York: Doubleday.
——. 1967. *Interaction Ritual*. Chicago: Aldine.
Lukes, Steven. 1975. "Political Ritual and Social Integration." *Sociology* 9: 289–308.
Parsons, Talcott. 1967 (1937). *The Structure of Social Action*. New York: Free Press.
Swidler, Ann. 1986. "Culture in Action: Symbols and Strategies." *American Sociological Review* 51: 273–86.
——. 2001. *Talk of Love: How Culture Matters*. Chicago: University of Chicago Press.
Tilly, Charles. 1981. *As Sociology Meets History*. New York: Academic Press.
Turner, Victor. 1967. *The Ritual Process*. Chicago: Aldine.

Part V

Culture and stratification

26

Cultural capital and tastes

The persistence of *Distinction*

David Wright

Taste is variously invoked to describe a physical sensation, aesthetic sense, or moral sensibility, and it can be a characteristic of people or of things. It is a foundational concept in the sociology of culture, connecting accounts of the centrality of the choice and preference for goods in the struggle for status across the twentieth century with the various reflexive freedoms available for the construction of late-modern lifestyles. A pivotal reference in the development of this strand of study is *Distinction: A Social Critique of the Judgement of Taste* by the French sociologist Pierre Bourdieu, arguably the most influential and controversial piece of cultural sociology yet published. "Cultural capital" emerges from *Distinction* as the definitive Bourdieuian concept. This chapter will concentrate on the changing role of the concept in how processes of taste formation have been analyzed. I will argue for the continued centrality of Bourdieu's schema for the understanding of contemporary cultural production and consumption despite a range of transformations in the processes of taste formation themselves and in the ways in which these processes are researched and understood.

Although Bourdieu was not the first to reveal that an individual's taste is socially organized, the significant contribution of *Distinction* was to undermine the belief, stemming from Kant (1987 [1790]), that notions of cultural value are somehow ahistorical and reflective of a common sense of the beautiful. Bourdieu does more than merely reveal that tastes are socially constructed: he argues for a place for personal taste in struggles for social position—struggles ostensibly organized between class fractions. There are homologies for Bourdieu between hierarchies of "high" and "low" (or legitimate and popular) culture and the relative positions of people adhering to these forms in social and economic hierarchies. The appreciation of culture is constitutive of class relations. Taste, then, represents the lived experience of the power relations inherent in social structure— a manifestation, physically experienced or expressed, of an individual's stock of cultural capital, which can exist in three forms. First, cultural capital is institutionalized; that is, it emerges from forms of socially accredited institutions, nominally schools and universities, which bestow it in the form of qualifications but also denote it through the canonization of particular texts, pieces of music, or works of art as worthy of study. Second, it is objectified, and is accrued by the ownership or knowledge of specific works of art, books, and pieces of music. Finally, it is embodied and revealed by the correct comportment of the body in dress or styles of speech. Different forms of cultural capital can be traded or accumulated in different arenas, or fields, of social life, but within the structuring, overarching field of power, the possession of those forms of capital that have been legitimized or consecrated does most to determine one's social position.

Alongside his concern with the consumption of culture, Bourdieu makes a significant contribution to the understanding of the production of culture and, by extension, the production of tastes. In *Distinction*, this process is an interaction between (1) the consecration of legitimate culture by the educational system and reproduced in the family via the class system, and (2) the operation of taste-makers or cultural intermediaries. An emerging fraction of the middle class of 1960s France, cultural intermediaries are defined by Bourdieu (1984: 359) as, "all the occupations involving presentation and representation (sales, marketing, advertising, public relations, fashion, decoration, and so forth) and in all the institutions providing symbolic goods and services." If, as Bourdieu claims, this was a group with increasing importance in the understanding of cultural life in 1960s France, their significance has increased exponentially in contemporary Western societies, a point to which I will return in the final section of this chapter (pp. 297–82).

Elsewhere in his work, Bourdieu (1993, 1996) also placed cultural capital as central to the production of cultural goods. Fields of cultural production, he suggests, are variously organized according to the spread of cultural capital between two extremes or "poles." This spread maps onto the various commitments of producers and consumers as actors within fields to the concerns with art for art's sake on the one hand, the "autonomous pole," and the concern with art for the sake of economic profit on the other, "the heteronomous pole" (Bourdieu 1996: 124). The "game" of culture requires producers who are committed to the various positions in the field, with those richer in cultural capital tending towards the autonomous pole. It also requires consumers with similar commitments. Bourdieu describes the "universe of celebrants and believers" (Bourdieu 1996: 169) who are rich in cultural capital and ready to accept the ideas of "canon" or "classic" or avant-garde that emerge from producers. Boschetti (2006) suggests that it was Bourdieu's attempt to bring to light the role of the symbolic in the legitimation of the social order that accounts for the hostile reaction to his work in some circles. She explains:

> the cult of culture is such a deeply entrenched and shared belief that there was very little likelihood that a critical analysis would be well received or appreciated by either culture people, who profit by the prestige of culture, or those excluded, who in spite of the exclusion adhere to this cult.
>
> (Boschetti 2006: 139)

The charismatic belief in culture—the *illusio* that cultural taste is outside of social struggles that Bourdieu lays bare—has the persistent effect of preserving good taste as the property of those in the cultural know, thereby naturalizing relationships of class and power.

The model of cultural production that Bourdieu sketches, based upon the emergence of the literary market in the nineteenth century, clearly merits re-evaluation in the light of the contemporary cultural industries. Similarly the ways in which people consume, produce, and research culture have changed significantly since *Distinction*'s original insight. We might ask how an empirical study of the tastes of 1960s France can shed light on other times and places. Given new approaches to the complexity of popular culture, a model based upon apparently solid hierarchies of "high" and "low" culture appears outdated. Finally a model based upon the "rarity" and consecration of cultural activity and its policing by experts of various kinds fits uneasily into the contemporary experience of abundant culture, particularly activity wrought by the dispersion of the means of cultural production and consumption enabled by emerging technologies. Broadened access to the means of cultural production, rhetorically at least, allows the game of culture to be played out over a wider, more open field than Bourdieu anticipated. This chapter will argue that, despite these qualifications, the relationship Bourdieu establishes between taste and power retains considerable explanatory power.

Cultural capital and taste since *Distinction*

In the forty years since *Distinction* was written, and particularly in the thirty years since it was published in English, a number of researchers have engaged with Bourdieu's work, revealing important lacunae in the general relationships he uncovers. It is beyond the scope of this chapter to recount these debates, but their central thrust, nicely summarized and countered by Holt (1997), is that Bourdieu's schema is not generalizable across space and time. In particular, it is not applicable to the American context, where, so the story goes, a more egalitarian and mobile culture prevents the ossification of class and taste positions—although this culture does not, as Lamont (1992) notably reveals, prevent symbolic boundary-making of a different, moral, or racial kind. American sociology has generated its own "tradition" of research into the relations between culture and class and re-imagined the relationships that Bourdieu outlines.

What these developments and lacunae reveal is that any relationship between cultural capital and taste is a methodological and empirical as well as theoretical one. Holt tellingly implies that, in the context of answering a survey—the basis of *Distinction* and the dominant instrument in subsequent studies—informants' responses "are best understood as ideological accounts constructed for rhetorical purposes of the survey situation" (Holt 1997: 115). Similarly, Antoine Hennion, in a recent critical account of the dominant approaches to taste within cultural sociology, suggests that using judgments (whether positive or negative) as stand-ins for social characteristics is consistent with a kind of determinism. In the real world, Hennion argues, such a relationship between taste and social characteristics "is rarely observed," at least away from the survey setting (Hennion 2007: 101). Clearly, the items which are asked about in surveys of cultural activity as well as the ways in which researchers categorize class structure will affect the nature and shape of the relationships revealed. Such an emphasis on relationality is important for claims for the continued relevance of cultural capital. *Distinction* is an account of the process by which Bourdieu's respondents come to like things, based upon an assumption of their relative significance in relation to a vision of legitimate, consecrated, popular, or mass culture, organized into a hierarchy which is assumed, for good empirical reasons, to be somehow settled. Forty years later, evidence indicates that the hierarchy is fluid and changing.

The shape and direction of this change are partly addressed by the "omnivore" debate, sparked by Peterson and Kern (1996) and involving numerous researchers in the US, Europe, and beyond. This literature posits a very different relationship between class and cultural tastes. Researchers into "omnivorousness" have documented the selective incorporation of items of popular culture into the taste portfolios of the professional middle classes, thus challenging the homologous relationship between taste and social class suggested by Bourdieu and variously demonstrating a certain "openness" to the tastes of others amongst the professional classes of, mostly, Western societies. For Erickson (1996), the openness to a range of forms of culture exhibited by participants in her study of managers in the security industry reflects changes in the class structure evident in increasingly diverse workplaces and the more inclusive strategies used in managing them. Knowing about the arts and sport, for example, enables relationships between the boardroom and the shop floor, effectively unpicking the exclusivity that helped weave together cultural capital, class, and power. Erickson also points out that this new formation complicates the patterns linking culture and power. Although fifty years ago the rules of the game of culture were relatively transparent, "today, advantageous culture is no longer a short simple list of classy things. It is a complex combination: some high-status forms, some mid-level, some popular … Such subtle, variable cultural complexes are hard to identify and hard to learn" (Erickson 2008: 345). Recent contributions to this debate using British data (Bennett *et al.* 2009) suggest that, rather than being symptomatic of a fundamentally different relationship between class and taste, omnivorousness is instead one element of contemporary cultural capital at work in the taste profiles of the new middle classes.

Beverly Skeggs considers another aspect of new working arrangements. The knowledge and ability to range, selectively and critically, between legitimate and popular culture are one element of what Skeggs (2004) describes as the "entitled middle-class," a class that is mobile, free-floating, and cosmopolitan. A growing fraction of the class structure, this group is intimately concerned, via the exponential growth in the creative or symbolic economy within which it works, "to expand and legitimate its own particular dispositions and life-style" (Skeggs 2004: 141). An omnivorous taste profile can be contrasted with its discursive opposite, an immobile, less tolerant, less cosmopolitan working class, with less access to means of cultural production, as well as less certainty over the complex, shifting rules of cultural consumption. Working-class tastes might be selectively incorporated as "cool" or authentic but people rich in cultural capital still determine the strategies of legitimation. In the contemporary taste profile, knowing one ought to be eclectic and open replaces knowledge of the significance of the disinterested aesthetic gaze.

Changed class contexts, then, require qualification rather than dismissal of the relationships between taste and power that Bourdieu posits. Such qualification is also required in other areas, notably that of international comparability. In the light of processes of globalization, which often center on questions of cultural practice and the role of the cultural industries, an avowedly national study such as *Distinction* is bound to feel anachronistic. Few studies, though, have taken up the challenge of reflecting on the place of global flows of culture or people in shaping or re-working tastes. Danielle Kane (2003) attempts to address this gap by interrogating the coherence of Bourdieu's homology thesis through the analysis of international students newly arrived in the United States. Again, she finds that a taste for sport, rather than the arts, is a defining characteristic of legitimate culture amongst international elites, with emphasis on knowledge of and participation in sports that have global appeal (e.g. golf) providing the resources for symbolic boundary maintenance. In another attempt to complicate "the nation" as the site of cultural practice, Savage *et al.* (2005) recognize the increasing influence of global flows of culture across national boundaries and how these are incorporated into the taste profiles of the professional middle classes of the UK. This is a process also recognized by Bennett *et al.*'s (2009) study, where distinct relationships are mapped between different sections of the UK population and cultural items from around the world, with American television—once the epitome of "trashy" commercial culture in the British context—emerging as an important element of the taste portfolios of the younger British middle classes. These examples reveal that the ground upon which cultural hierarchies are built might be shifting as a result of processes of globalization, but they do little to dispel the idea that Bourdieuian hierarchies and homologies persist in Western societies. They do show, however, that the how and why of what "counts" as refined taste is perhaps less predictable than in Bourdieu's France of the 1960s. Gronow's (2003) study of the state-initiated re-casting of cultural hierarchy in Soviet Russia, whereby the mass availability of caviar and champagne was used as evidence that social distinctions had diminished in the post-revolutionary period, offers a tantalizing glimpse of an alternative basis for the social organization of taste. Beyond this we know relatively little of possible relations between cultural capital, taste, and power outside the Western context.

To complete this review of the necessary qualifications of the post-*Distinction* study of cultural taste, two further developments should be considered. First, the changed role, size, and scope of the media are significant. Although it only came to international prominence in the 1980s, the data collected in *Distinction* largely pre-dated, or at least failed to adequately anticipate, the forms of cultural participation enabled by the age of television, and although Bourdieu latterly attempted to engage with the media more directly (Bourdieu 1998), his effort possessed less empirical depth than his previous interventions. Television has a crucial role in providing access to a wide range of culture for a wide range of people, challenging the rarity of cultural items which might raise their cultural capital. Moreover TV has developed its own criteria of value and, increasingly, its own "canons" of good and bad, legitimate and popular, as well as its own arenas of academic consecration.

Second, but linked to this, is the development of a narrative from within the academy—initially generated by the British Cultural Studies tradition—about the relative merits of cultural items and the relative meanings of their use. This work reveals the ability of consumers or participants to bring unexpected meanings to their cultural lives in ways that challenge or resist their position in socio-economic, gender, or racial hierarchies on the basis of taste. Work inspired by de Certeau (1984), and latterly Fiske (1989), re-imagines popular, commercial culture not as the logical opposite of a disinterested avant-garde, as in Bourdieu's schema, but as complex in its own right. The ability of consumer-participants to have their own criteria of expertise and value (consider Thornton [1995] on dance-cultures) suggests that contemporary forms of cultural capital are organized around different norms, and that the ways of liking, crystallized in debates about active, passive, and creative users of popular culture, are important in appreciating the meanings attributed to these forms. In the following section, I will explore the particular impact of these changes in cultural production (and cultural research) to the production and understanding of cultural taste, and what they might mean for the continued relevance of cultural capital to understanding contemporary tastes.

New rules in the game of culture

One of the most robust criticisms of Bourdieu's work concerns the lack of an adequate vocabulary to deal with popular taste. The notion of "the culture of the necessary"—the idea that the tastes of those lacking in cultural capital are shaped by the drives (biological or financial) that emerge from their excluded position in the socio-economic hierarchy—implies that forms of popular cultural participation are reduced to the level of uncritical distraction. In light of innovations in the theoretical understanding of cultural consumption and transformations in the ways in which culture is circulated, this formulation denies the possibility of sophisticated critical engagement with forms of popular cultural production. Bourdieu's commitment to exposing the game of culture, by addressing the fields of both cultural production and consumption, however, continues to provide a robust framework with which to examine taste and the contexts of its formation, no matter how the rules of the game might change.

In the contemporary digital or information age, the ways in which we come to produce, know, like, or dislike cultural items are markedly different at the start of the twenty-first century than they were when Bourdieu was researching the processes of cultural consumption in the 1960s, or when he was theorizing the shape of the field of cultural production that emerged in France in the mid-nineteenth century. Even recent theoretical interventions into the contemporary media, though less directly concerned with questions of taste than with questions of power (Bourdieu 1998), appear somewhat dated in the emerging "media age 2.0," with all the characteristic quickening of information and value that accompanies it. Many received wisdoms in the social sciences, including those associated with the concept of cultural capital, are struggling to keep up with these changes.

Most fundamentally, the grip of legitimate culture as the means of shaping the tastes of the powerful has clearly weakened. In the recent past, the rarity of legitimate culture meant that arbiters of taste (such as artists, writers, academics, and critics of various kinds) could police access to it. In the contemporary context, such distinctions are less tenable: the accelerated circulation of culture—initiated by television but quickened again by digital technologies—generates a greater volume of culture than even the most dedicated celebrant can reasonably master. At the same time, technological innovations allow for the dispersal of the means of cultural production away from specialists based within the commercial cultural industries themselves and into the hands of enthusiastic amateurs able to produce and distribute music and film outside of the traditional circuits of cultural production and exchange. This shift might represent both increased access to cultural production and more intensive involvement on the part of privileged groups in society (notably well-educated young people), as technological expertise becomes a constituent element of contemporary cultural capital (Tepper 2008).

Moreover, the opposition between the avant-garde as the site of the exemplary "disinterested" aesthetic and commercial culture as site of the culture of the necessary is less coherent in societies characterized as "drenched" or saturated in culture. An excess of culture necessarily alters the position of the traditional high priests of taste and their ability to shape processes of taste formation. The cultural authority upon which pronouncements of taste rests does not disappear in this context; rather it is dispersed and fragmented between producers and consumers themselves, who range across digital and social networks in the pursuit of what is new, distinguishing, and "cool." Reflecting on the changing shape of cultural life in the information age, Jim Collins posits that "cultural value rests not on an imagined consensus of like-minded parties within the same 'taste culture' but on antagonistic relations between parties motivated by antithetical notions of cultural capital" (1995: 28). The conflict is especially significant in the case of popular culture, where numerous institutions with varying sources of cultural capital, including journalists, fans, and academics, all struggle to establish the relative merits of their particular claim to value.

In later work, Collins (2002) notes the transformation of items previously considered emblematic of high- or at least middle-brow culture into unapologetically popular entertainment, such as costume dramas, or blockbuster museum and art-gallery exhibitions. He suggests that the academy "has abandoned taste as an antiquated concept" (Collins 2002: 18), preferring to identify the ideological narratives that might underpin particular forms of cultural engagement rather than play a game of evaluation. This leaves the way clear for a new "evaluative dynamic" in which,

> a higher education is judged essential but incomplete, in need of the finishing that only high-end popular cultural authorities can now provide as they make taste into a process of converting one's stored cultural literacy into registers of personal preference articulated by the proper consumer choices.
>
> (Collins 2002: 18)

Here, the cultural intermediary, who in *Distinction* is a strategically important but marginal figure, gains significance as the technical skills of marketing, branding, and promotion become as important as the criteria of value that underpin academic critical judgment. Historically, symbolic and cultural capitals were allocated according to the criteria of academic experts, rhetorically disinterested but actually committed to the notion of *illusio*. In the game of culture in the contemporary context, taste-makers are more fundamentally embedded in the production of commercial culture, and, in whichever field of cultural production they operate, are more closely connected to the institutions of the media. Media attention becomes, as Couldry (2004) identifies, a form of "meta-capital," capable, through concerted attention on a particular field, of altering the criteria of value that shape claims to cultural capital within it.

The literary field, so central to Bourdieu's initial model of cultural production, is a particularly instructive site to examine the changing relationships between production and consumption that inform the changing dynamics of cultural capital and taste. First, the glacial core of "the canon" of good and bad literature has been fundamentally troubled by new literature studies aimed at revealing the gendered, ethnic, and class groupings excluded by traditional forms of canon-making. The revelations of this research have not flattened hierarchies completely, but have brought under the lens of academic inquiry material that would have been dismissed as commercial, trivial, frivolous, or middle-brow (consider Radway's [1984] work on romance novels or Gelder's [2004] study of popular fiction). Moreover the processes of the production and circulation of literary "stuff" have been transformed. The literary field itself upholds the narrative of excess and abundance characteristic of the contemporary cultural moment, with over a million titles published annually worldwide (according to UNESCO estimates). The management of this abundance through digital technologies (such as the catalogs of on-line book retailers and libraries) suggests that the role of the disinterested literary expert as an arbiter of taste is under threat. The threat comes not only from the alternative cultural capital of the journalist but also from the technical and marketing techniques that inform the advertising and branding campaigns central to the marketing of contemporary fiction (as well as the algorithmically generated recommendations of other readers exemplified by the "if you liked that, you'll love ... " formulation of Amazon.com). Even away from blockbusting authors such as J.K. Rowling or

John Grisham, the circuit of literary prizes reflects an increasing influence of the media field on what gets counted as good or bad in the literary field as it competes with other media fields for attention, significance, and money. Emblematic is the recent rise of television book clubs (Oprah in the US, Richard and Judy in the UK). Their success in transforming sales of established, canonical titles (in the case of Oprah) or adding to the marketing campaigns of new titles (in the case of Richard and Judy) reveals how, for producers and consumers, the distinctions between the autonomous and heteronomous poles of production are unclear and how, by extension, the sources of cultural authority and value in the formation of tastes are more fragmented than they were even two decades ago.

In the midst of transformations in production, though, there is an important continuity in patterns of literary consumption. Reading, particularly in the context of book cultures, is still almost exclusively the preserve of the educated middle classes. A review of recent research on reading in the US, Europe, and Australia by Griswold *et al.* (2005) suggests the presence of a numerically small but influential "reading class" characterized by the intensive activities of the highly educated. Tastes for reading, then, might well follow patterns similar to tastes for music or art in debates about omnivorousness. At the same time, the specific social location of participation in literary cultures implies a continued link between tastes and social position. The key point is that the relationship between cultural capital and tastes is no longer purely dependent upon a hierarchy of culture legitimated by disinterested writers or critics. Knowledge of the techniques of marketing and branding and the mastery of the technical means of circulating notions of cultural value become the elements of contemporary cultural capital, with the (mis)recognition of the importance of these processes in the formation of contemporary tastes for reading representing a new kind of *illusio*.

Conclusion

Despite the methodological and theoretical changes that have occurred in academic approaches to the study of culture since the publication of Bourdieu's influential work, cultural capital, as an explanatory tool, retains its purchase in examining processes of taste formation. Changes in the class dynamics of Western societies might alter the strategies of distinction, so researchers need to take a methodologically rounded approach in order to reflect both the active process of taste formation and the fluidity of cultural hierarchies. Inevitably, survey work alone can only "capture" these dynamics in an artificial way. More work is needed on the influence of global flows of both people and culture in altering the terrain upon which hierarchies of taste and class might be built in the West, and on how relations of taste, class, and power might operate in non-Western contexts.

The dispersal of cultural authority away from the high priests of legitimate culture—and the re-working of cultural hierarchies by the various institutions and technologies engaged in the circulation of cultural value—shift the foundations of cultural capital and power. The role of taste-makers (cultural intermediaries) as drivers of these changes and the abundance within the contemporary cultural realm are empirical realities that necessitate reconsideration of the narratives of scarcity and restriction underpinning *Distinction*. Researchers must account for these changed contexts in generalizing about social patterns of taste, nationally and globally. In the context of a quickened circulation of cultural value, the significance of the production of tastes, and the compunction to express them correctly as consumer choices still resonate with some groups more than others. Competing claims for cultural value are made and recognized in a more variegated and diffuse field of power, but it is still one in which processes of consecration and legitimation are ongoing. Although the terms of refined taste might have shifted from aesthetic disinterestedness towards eclectic omnivorousness and although the means of cultural production might be drifting from ennobled expert to enthusiastic amateur, there remains an implicit distance, marked by cultural capital, between those who get to play the game of culture and those who watch from the sidelines.

References

Bennett, T., Savage, M., Silva, E.B., Warde, A., Gayo-Cal, M., and Wright, D. 2009. *Culture, Class, Distinction*. London: Routledge.

Boschetti, A. 2006. "Bourdieu's Work on Literature: Contexts, Stakes and Perspectives." *Theory, Culture and Society* 23(6): 135–55.

Bourdieu, P. 1984. *Distinction: A Social Critique of the Judgement of Taste*. London: Routledge.

——. 1993. *The Field of Cultural Production*. Cambridge: Polity.

——. 1996. *The Rules of Art*. Cambridge: Polity.

——. 1998. *On Television and Journalism*. London: Pluto Press.

Collins, J. 1995. *Architectures of Excess: Cultural Life in the Information Age*. London and New York: Routledge.

——. 2002. "High-Pop: An Introduction." Pp. 1–31 in J. Collins, ed., *High-Pop: Making Culture into Popular Entertainment*. Malden and Oxford: Blackwell.

Couldry, N. 2004. "Media Meta-Capital: Extending the Range of Bourdieu's Field Theory." Pp. 165–89 in D.L. Swartz and V.L. Zolberg, eds., *After Bourdieu*. Dordrecht: Kluwer.

de Certeau, M. 1984. *The Practice of Everyday Life*. London: University of California Press.

Erickson, B.H. 1996. "Culture, Class, and Connections." *American Journal of Sociology* 102(1): 217–51.

——. 2008. "The Crisis in Culture and Inequality." Pp. 343–63 in S.J. Tepper and B. Ivey, eds., *Engaging Art: The Next Great Transformation of America's Cultural Life*. New York and London: Routledge.

Fiske, J. 1989. *Understanding Popular Culture*. Boston: Unwin Hyman.

Gelder, K. 2004. *Popular Fiction: The Logic and Practice of a Literary Field*. London: Routledge.

Griswold, W., McDonnel, T., and Wright, N. 2005. "Reading and the Reading Class in the Twenty-first Century." *Annual Review of Sociology* 31: 127–41.

Gronow, J. 2003. *Caviar with Champagne: Common Luxury and the Ideals of the Good Life in Stalin's Russia*. London: Berg.

Hennion, A. 2007. "Those Things that Hold Us Together: Taste and Sociology." *Cultural Sociology* 1(1): 97–114.

Holt, D.B. 1997. "Distinction in America? Recovering Bourdieu's Theory of Taste from its Critics." *Poetics* 25: 93–120.

Kane, D. 2003. "Distinction Worldwide? Bourdieu's Theory of Taste in International Context." *Poetics* 31: 403–21.

Kant, I. 1987 (1790). *Critique of Judgment*, trans. W.S. Pluhar. Indianapolis and Cambridge: Hackett Publishing Company.

Lamont, M. 1992. *Money, Morals, and Manners: The Culture of the French and American Upper-Middle Class*. Chicago: University of Chicago Press.

Peterson, R.A. and Kern, R.M. 1996. "Changing Highbrow Taste: From Snob to Omnivore." *American Sociological Review* 61: 900–09.

Radway, J. 1984. *Reading the Romance: Women, Patriarchy, and Popular Literature*. Chapel Hill: University of North Carolina Press.

Savage, M., Bagnall, G., and Longhurst, B. 2005. *Globalization and Belonging*. London: Sage.

Skeggs, B. 2004. *Class, Self, Culture*. London and New York: Routledge.

Tepper, S.J. 2008. "The Next Great Transformation: Leveraging Policy and Research to Advance Cultural Vitality." Pp. 367–85 in S.J. Tepper and B. Ivey, eds., *Engaging Art: The Next Great Transformation of America's Cultural Life*. New York and London: Routledge.

Thornton, S. 1995. *Club Cultures: Music, Media, and Sub-cultural Capital*. Cambridge: Polity Press.

27

Access to pleasure

Aesthetics, social inequality, and the structure of culture production

Ann Swidler

Pierre Bourdieu's (1984) preoccupation with cultural capital as a resource to be deployed in the competition for advantage or "exchanged" for other forms of capital has obscured the ways that aesthetic pleasure matters for its own sake. *Distinction* (1984) analyzes how the exercise of socially shaped cultural taste—the "distinctions" people make, which in turn "distinguish" them—advantages or disadvantages people in the competition for social advantage, especially in the educational system. Cultural knowledge and taste become a kind of "capital" that can be exchanged at specific "ratios" for capital in other realms. Even *The Rules of Art* (1992), which focuses on culture creators rather than cultural consumption, deploys vast erudition about Flaubert and his contemporaries to argue that culture creators are driven by concern about rivalries and sources of distinction in an existing artistic field, or by the aspiration to define a new artistic field in which they are supreme. Lost in Bourdieu's approach is the idea that a culture creator might be driven by the desire to create a certain aesthetic effect—to move, astound, delight, entertain, terrify, or simply *affect* an audience.

Here I explore a different, but no less significant form of cultural stratification: the differential availability of aesthetic pleasures to those with differing social resources. I focus on the production of cultural objects, performances, and meanings; on the ways audiences are brought into relationship with cultural creators; and on the organizations and practices that frame aesthetic experience.

I start from the premise that aesthetic pleasure is one of the great goods of life. The view that people participate in playful aesthetic experience only as a poor substitute for something else—politics, class struggle, the pursuit of power or status—is inadequate, both as an ideal of how people ought to live and as a description of how they do live (Stromberg 2009). I include under the broad category of "aesthetic pleasure" all forms of entertainment, from watching a wacky TV sit-com, to cruising YouTube for the latest political video, to the sometimes excruciating pleasures of serious drama, ballet, opera, or demanding music. Cultural expertise and the exercise of discriminating taste can serve to assert status, to intimidate others, and perhaps in some cases to gain access to material and other rewards. However, the Bourdieuian preoccupation with cultural distinction—both the amount of culture people "know" and the skills needed to decipher it—weakens cultural analysis by assuming that culture's major role is to reproduce inequality (by either mystifying class hierarchy, legitimating inequality, or serving as the opiate of the masses).

Taking the aesthetic function of culture seriously directs attention to the social-organizational factors that create differential access to aesthetic pleasure and to the social arrangements likely to produce such pleasure in greater or lesser measure. Social arrangements can stimulate or inhibit the creation of resonant cultural objects that appeal to particular sorts of audiences, and they can make the conditions for such enjoyment more and less available. Economic and educational inequalities matter partly because they deprive some groups of access to a full share of aesthetic pleasure—access to culture as a form of group expression and solidarity and access to intense, deep, rich, or thrilling cultural experience.

Meaning in social context

A sociologically useful approach to aesthetic pleasure focuses on "conventions"—the shared expectations that link culture creators and their audiences and allow them to communicate (Meyer 1956; Becker 1982; Griswold 1987; Olick 1999). As Becker argues, conventions help the producers of cultural works to coordinate their efforts, as when the conductor and members of an orchestra all know the conventions of musical notation or performance styles. But the deeper significance of conventions for aesthetic pleasure comes from what happens when conventions are broken—or rather when the aesthetic expectations that have emerged within a cultural genre allow creators and performers to create what Leonard Meyer called "emotion and meaning."

In *Emotion and Meaning in Music* (1956), Meyer argued that the arousal, violation, and resolution of expectations are fundamental to the creation of aesthetic "meaning." Conventions help to create expectations; slight violations of those expectations generate aesthetic tension—which, when resolved, produces aesthetic pleasure. When audiences and creators share conventions, creators have a set of expectations to work with to produce aesthetically powerful effects. Variations on a melodic theme, puzzlement about "whodunit" in a murder mystery, or suspense about the outcome in a well-matched sporting event (Geertz, 1973) produce just this sort of aesthetic tension and excitement for knowledgeable observers. Pleasurable anticipation, heightened attention, and absorbed involvement are the hallmarks of successful aesthetic engagement. For audiences who lack the relevant conventions, however, even a highly refined artistic product of an unfamiliar aesthetic tradition (Chinese opera for a Westerner unfamiliar with the genre, for example) may create no aesthetic pleasure.

The sociological question is: What allows some groups more than others (1) to develop a set of shared conventions and to refine or extend them so that variations on those conventions will be aesthetically meaningful, and (2) to support creators who will produce cultural objects or performances that respond to, develop, and continually renew those conventions? Since aesthetic pleasure depends both on shared expectations and on the creation of innovations that can surprise, unsettle, and delight, explaining differences in the availability and richness of aesthetic pleasure requires paying attention both to social forces that organize audiences and creators so that they share aesthetic conventions, and to social arrangements that stimulate extensions, refinements, and innovations that deepen or intensify cultural resonance.

If we examine class differences in aesthetic experience, we do not need to start from Bourdieu's (1984) essentializing claim that higher-class people, freed from material necessity, are inherently more likely to "aestheticize" experience (the fanciful "styling" of the dress of poor teenagers, or the stylized aesthetics that Tom Wolfe [1965] described in varied American subcultures easily demonstrates the fallacy of such an argument). Instead we can ask what resources different groups have to create and preserve cultural objects and practices that offer them depth, meaning, resonance, or excitement—objects and practices that can convey intense or gratifying aesthetic pleasure. Of course, such pleasure does not come from cultural objects alone, but from an interaction between an object and the educated skills, capacities, or interests of the appreciator (see Griswold 1986 on meaning as metaphor; Baxandall 1972 on the "period eye").

Revisiting the mass-culture debate

The debate over "mass culture," which roiled intellectuals in the 1950s and 1960s, has largely faded. In part this is the result of the important work of Paul DiMaggio (1982; see also Levine 1988), showing that the contemporary distinction between high and popular culture was socially constructed by particular groups, in a specific historical era. The history of how, in the mid-nineteenth century, popular performances might mix Shakespearean orations, popular song, ribald humor, and classical music, while by the end of the nineteenth century classical music and high art were carefully segregated in museums and symphony halls, seemed to show that the distinction between "high" and "popular" culture is a purely artificial one. By this logic, high culture is any culture created and monopolized by social elites who want to preserve their exclusivity and assert their superiority. Museums, orchestras, and ballet and opera companies then simply police the (arbitrary, artificial) boundary between a valued elite culture and a devalued popular culture.

A focus on cultural enjoyment, rather than cultural prestige, however, suggests the need to give attention to organizational and structural factors that shape opportunities for aesthetic pleasure. Groups differ in their access to satisfying cultural experiences due to systematic differences in the organization of cultural production and the structures that link potential audiences to culture creators.

Organizational bases for cultural pleasure

Two major, under-appreciated texts: Paul DiMaggio's (1987) "Classification in Art" and Robert Escarpit's (1971) classic, *The Sociology of Literature*, provide a starting point for analyzing social variations in access to aesthetic pleasure. DiMaggio argues that distinctive cultural genres emerge from groups' need to define or bound themselves. Cultural knowledge, including knowledge of specific cultural genres, he argues, operates not mainly to legitimate group claims to privilege, but to provide material for sociable interaction, for conversation, among those who want to enact or assert solidarity. This interpretation of cultural capital makes sense of the finding (one Bourdieu never explained satisfactorily) that social taste hierarchies are not exclusive. Higher status and more educated people have taste for and participate in all sorts of culture, including classically high culture, whereas the less educated participate in a narrower range of less high-culture activities (on the growing "omnivore" pattern in high-status groups see Peterson and Kern 1996; and for France, Coulangeon 2005). This makes sense if, as DiMaggio argues, higher-status people want to be able to form sociable bonds with people like themselves by signaling familiarity with high culture, but also to benefit from friendly relationships with people from all social strata (Erickson 1996, 2007). Of course, familiarity with a diverse array of cultural forms can itself be a status marker (Peterson and Rossman 2007; Sullivan and Katz-Gerro 2007), but the proliferation of artistic genres (Lena and Peterson 2008) and group and individual engagement with aesthetic experience suggest that much more is going on than the assertion of status distinctions. People seek aesthetic pleasure in entertainments that they share with others; and all sorts of groups have an interest in developing and promoting cultural genres that represent, express, and reproduce their collective life.

DiMaggio's perspective complements the valuable insights of Robert Escarpit in *The Sociology of Literature* (1971). Escarpit distinguishes not high and popular culture, but two ways of organizing communication between culture creators and their audiences—the "Cultured Circuit" and the "Popular Circuit." Although these two organizational forms may be associated with high versus popular culture, folk cultures grounded in a cohesive community may have the structural features of the cultured circuit, while certain elite cultural genres may lack them. The cultured circuit is characterized by extensive feedback from the consumers of cultural products to those who create them, usually via critics, who both shape audience taste and transmit critical understandings back to creators or producers. Escarpit notes that in the cultured circuit authors often receive active feedback on their work from likely audiences (these authors' friends tend to be the same sort of people as their readers) and from critics, who both respond to the work and organize and educate audiences. The popular circuit (mass-market paperbacks or network television, for example), in contrast, lacks feedback except through the market: culture producers for the popular circuit know what to create only by observing what has sold in the recent past (see Hirsch 1972). Culture produced for the popular circuit thus tends to imitate successful formulas, or, like the "recombinant" TV shows that Todd Gitlin (1985) describes, to combine currently popular themes in slightly new ways.

The distinction between popular and cultured circuits can be used to analyze groups' varying access to culture that reinforces group solidarities, responds to their tastes, and builds on shared tastes to innovate in ways that delight or entertain. And this organizational distinction may not always correspond to what we think of as high versus popular culture. Traditional high culture may stagnate—especially when those eager to maintain its boundaries rigidly patrol its content so that it does not evolve in response to the interests of its audiences. Some popular forms, such as jazz (especially in its formative period [Lopes 2002]), "indie" rock, or Hip-Hop dance parties, on the other hand, might bring culture creators face to face with knowledgeable, interested audiences who give direct feedback about what moves or excites them. Thus some popular genres are produced through structures resembling the cultured circuit, and some "high culture" genres may not have structures of production and distribution that generate vibrant cultural experience. In general, however, groups without wealth and leisure are also disadvantaged in their access to structures of cultural production that create the greatest possibilities of aesthetic pleasure.

What circumstances are likely to promote the discrete, bounded genres that DiMaggio (1987) analyzes or the responsive feedback circuits that Escarpit describes? DiMaggio points out that however much those who create a new genre would like to keep it exclusive (as the youth cultures that generate new musical styles try to do

[Hebdige 1979; Frith 1981]), commercial market interests seek to broaden audiences, thus diluting the symbolic exclusivity of a group's identification with a specific genre and weakening the link between culture producers and a specialized audience to whose sophisticated tastes they can respond. The commercial "massification" of any cultural genre is thus likely to make its cultural products more stereotyped, less innovative, and less exciting to the original fans, because now the genre also has to please less knowledgeable audiences, who are less experienced in the genre's particular conventions.

Diversity and innovation

Peterson and Berger's (1975) classic article "Cycles in Symbol Production" analyzed sources of innovation and diversity in culture production. They distinguished periods of market concentration (in which a small number of producers control production and distribution of cultural products and inhibit innovation) from periods in which many producers compete, creating more diverse and innovative cultural products. Building on Peterson and Berger, Lopes (1992) distinguishes not only between different degrees of concentration among producers, but between more segmented versus unified markets. In a segmented market, culture is distributed through specialized channels, reaching more homogeneous audiences. When, for example, radio diversified after television enticed away the mass audience, radio stations developed new formats geared toward small segments of the audience, creating specialized stations for jazz, soul, country, gospel, and rock (versus radio's pre-TV fare of variety shows, news, soap operas, dramas, and comedy). Diversified radio stations created specialized distribution channels for recorded music, which in turn led to a flowering of varied genres of music and to the creation of dynamic new genres. Market segmentation allows specialized producers to thrive and makes it more likely that cultural producers will be able to find those who share their tastes and appreciate their aesthetic conventions, encouraging the rapid development of cultural products that speak to those tastes.

Culture produced for a mass market is likely to satisfy average tastes reasonably well, since producers have an incentive to maximize their appeal to the broadest group of consumers. But such culture is not likely to develop a deepened aesthetic vocabulary, innovative variations on existing conventions, or enhanced power to move audiences (including the power to thrill, shock, or delight): creators cannot presume an audience whose aesthetic vocabulary they know and share, and the mass market does not have rich feedback mechanisms through which a knowledgeable audience can communicate its responses and thus stimulate cumulative development of intensified meanings. Jazz in its early development had all the structural advantages of a segmented audience and a "cultured" feedback circuit: it was played by musicians for musicians in after-hours venues, so audiences consisted largely of other musicians, who could respond immediately and knowledgeably to what they heard (Lopes 2002). "Massified" culture, in contrast, is not directed to a particular audience's taste; its aesthetic power is limited if there are few shared conventions that allow creators to pursue cumulative innovation by working new changes on "educated" tastes (by "educated" I mean, for example, the knowledgeable tastes of teenagers who have played many video games and are looking for the next heightened thrill, of movie-goers who have seen every horror film and are looking for a zombie-fest to top the last one, as well as of aesthetes who can appreciate the slightest variation in the movement of a ballerina's hand).

Structural sources of elite aesthetic advantage

If decidedly non-elite subcultures, like those of early punk rockers (Hebdige 1979) or Hip-Hop, can produce vibrant, aesthetically powerful culture, then why in general should those with greater wealth and privilege also have access to more aesthetic pleasure? The examples of punk music and Hip-Hop suggest one immediate reason: the subcultures that produce vibrant aesthetic experience have great difficulty maintaining control of that culture, which rapidly succumbs to commercial pressures that dilute the culture's meanings and separate culture creators from knowledgeable audiences.

Maintaining specialized relations between creators and audiences

The aesthetic advantages of elites go beyond simple freedom from pressures to "massify" their favored cultural products. Escarpit (1971) points to some obvious ways in which those with greater material resources secure for themselves the advantages of more deeply embedded cultural production. The wealthy are more likely to be able to pay for specialized cultural outlets (like bookstores, fashion houses, specialized magazines, or book review journals) that bring together audiences of those who share similar tastes. Second, they are more likely to be able to support specialists in feedback, like literary critics, who let producers know what audiences like, and who tell audiences what to watch out for. (Janice Radway [1984] described a bookstore owner who performed this function for women romance readers, but perhaps the fate of local bookstores makes the point about the disadvantages faced by non-elite culture consumers.)

DiMaggio (1982) describes how the nineteenth-century Boston upper class created an organizational infrastructure that set high culture apart. He also describes powerful aesthetic advantages that accompanied the new structure. Enormous organizational effort and considerable financial resources were required to create the organizational basis for a distinctive high culture—in the case of the Boston Symphony Orchestra, a canon purged of popular music, specialized musicians who performed only classical work, and special venues (a symphony hall) where audiences and performers or creators could reliably meet.

Aesthetic advantages of control over space and time

DiMaggio (1982) describes new norms that elites imposed in such venues as museums and symphony halls—sacralization, a hushed reverence (in contrast to the cacophony of a London theater, or the sometimes rowdy behavior of audiences in the vaudeville or popular performance circuit). Although the reverent decorum of high-culture venues is contested in some contemporary art, it is worth noticing what these audience norms permit aesthetically. Creators who know that audiences will spend time and effort trying to fathom their work can create subtle effects that those who have to grab their audiences' attention cannot afford. Both music and theater can use silences as expressive devices. Where audiences commit themselves to attentive engagement, a story can start slowly and build gradually. If audiences accept conventions of reverent waiting, art can create ambiguity, because audiences will tolerate it, waiting until the "meaning" seeps in. Of course these conventions can also lead to sterile, pretentious, or vacuous works, with audiences squirming miserably in their seats as they try to seem engaged by some piece of abstruse high culture. But the bounded spaces for cultural reception that elites can create—and the reverent attitude they inculcate—can give creators aesthetic resources with which to produce a range of effects, from the dramatic sound that shatters a silence, to the complexity of poetic language, to the exquisite variation in a soprano's aria that only an opera lover could appreciate.

Art "versus" market

It is part of the institutional delineation of "high" versus "popular" art forms—the "classification" and "framing" described by DiMaggio (1982)—that high culture is insulated from commercial pressures. From the poorest art-school student to the most eminent symphony conductor, the claim to be doing serious art has depended in part on (at least the pretense of) indifference to—or insulation from—market pressures. Indeed, the ideal of creators pursuing their autonomous aesthetic vision connotes indifference to or insulation from market forces. And the ideal of art as a purely aesthetic enterprise depends on the notion that someone somewhere—a wealthy patron, an endowed museum, an orchestra's wealthy board members—will protect the art from unmediated audience demands.

Why, however, should protection from market pressures be important for the creation of vibrant, aesthetically gratifying culture? After all, if people do not enjoy or appreciate a cultural form enough to pay for it, then it probably lacks the ability to move or excite them. For an answer to this question we have to return to DiMaggio's central point in "Classification in Art." The inability to buffer a genre against market pressures virtually guarantees that it will be diluted to satisfy a broader set of tastes than those of the group whose interests gave rise to it and brought initial success. It will then be less likely to have a rich set of shared conventions and to develop dynamic innovations and aesthetic intensification to delight a specialized group of skilled appreciators. At the same time, of course, culture that is so buffered from audience demands that it need move and excite no one at all—what is sometimes referred to as "academic" culture (Crane 1976)—can become sterile, providing very little aesthetic gratification. Nonetheless, the ability to buffer a genre against market pressures is not just a way of achieving the status of "art" (as Becker 1982 describes potters trying to do by slashing their ceramic bowls or making impossibly large or otherwise non-functional objects, to distinguish their "art" from "crafts"). Insulating one's genre against market pressures—as youth cultures from punks to "house" music aficionados try to do—is fundamental to being able to keep a genre dynamic and to preserving a direct relationship between culture creators and a specific audience that shares their conventions.

Collecting and preserving

The last critical element that has differentiated the high and popular arts is the ability to preserve and teach the history of the genre, adding what I would call cultural depth—a rich reservoir of potential associations—as an aesthetic resource that creators can draw upon. Artists who can visit museums—and who can take for granted that those who see their art have also visited museums and absorbed the history of the form—can make allusions, employ visual vocabularies, or challenge conventions that they know are shared.

291

Elites can afford to establish repositories for the history of their preferred genres, from the collections of antique batiks that wealthy Indonesian families preserve over centuries, to the collections of art museums, to the repertoires of theaters and orchestras. Elite institutions also maintain specialists who conserve and teach the inherited repertoire, analyzing it for new understandings and reproducing an educated audience of those who have studied "music appreciation" or "art history." Literature classes provide a background that those who write for educated readers can take for granted, even as universities and colleges revise and rearrange the canon that writers and educated readers share. Such "preservation" has typically been the way that new elites made claims for the value of "their" genre (as when new elites formed the Museum of Modern Art and, shortly after, the Whitney). It takes money to do this, and preservation—the attempt to raise the status of a genre by preserving its history and by having specialists catalog and analyze that history—is one of the fundamental acts that raises the stature, but also the shared aesthetic vocabulary, of a genre. The creation of the Academy of Motion Picture Arts and Sciences and the Academy of Television Arts and Sciences were attempts by cultural creators to raise the stature of their products. Film departments in universities create such a critical and canon-defining function for movies. The recognition of jazz as a serious art form (Lopes 2002) depended in part on the emergence of critics, collectors, and eventually academics, who preserve and interpret its history.

These elements of "art-ness"—special places and moods (which bring audiences and creators together as well), protection from commercial pressures, preservation of the history of the genre—all permit richer meaning making. And these are advantages that the privileged are more likely to be able to create and maintain for the genres that they favor.

Technological change and aesthetic pleasures (Yelp!)

If cultural vitality and aesthetic pleasure derive from the structural features of systems of cultural production and distribution, rather than from the supposed qualities of elite versus less-elite culture consumers, then technological changes can alter culture and the possibilities of aesthetic pleasure in fundamental ways. As the internet has made it possible for musicians to find and to produce music for tiny, geographically dispersed audiences—and as websites that critique and recommend music to those with shared musical tastes proliferate—there has been a revolution in the amount of musical creativity (and the consequent possibilities for powerful aesthetic experience for both creators and audiences) (see the examples in Tepper and Ivey 2007).

New technologies also make it possible for more genres to preserve their histories (movies and TV series on video) and thus for culture creators to presume a shared vocabulary of associations, references, and expectations. With the web's discovery of "customer reviews," many more subcultures can share tastes with bevies of like-minded others who revel in good local barbecue reviewed on Yelp!, or "swoon" (in Zagat's favorite terminology) at exquisitely subtle sushi. Almost any subculture can develop the shared conventions and the discriminating judgments that stimulate the creation of vibrant culture and intensified aesthetic pleasure. Such culture exercises pleasurable powers of discrimination, builds solidarities, and heightens appreciation. Such technologies widen the possibility of knowledgeable, cultivated taste, and its concomitant aesthetic delights.

To understand culture as a source of meaning and pleasure does not require that we ignore its important role in signaling group membership and enacting social hierarchy. But ignoring the social factors that shape possibilities for aesthetic enjoyment—and neglecting that enjoyment as one of the fundamental elements of a good life—also misses a major cost of social inequality.

References

Baxandall, Michael. 1972. *Painting and Experience in Fifteenth Century Italy*. Oxford: Oxford University Press.

Becker, Howard S. 1982. *Art Worlds*. Berkeley: University of California Press.

Bourdieu, Pierre. 1984. *Distinction: A Social Critique of the Judgement of Taste*. Cambridge, MA: Harvard University Press.

——. 1992. *The Rules of Art: Genesis and Structure of the Literary Field*. Stanford, CA: Stanford University Press.

Coulangeon, Philippe. 2005. "Social Stratification of Musical Tastes: Questioning the Cultural Legitimacy Model." *Revue française de sociologie* 46: 123–54.

Crane, Diana. 1976. "Reward Systems in Art, Science and Religion." *American Behavioral Scientist* 19: 719–34.

DiMaggio, Paul. 1982. "Cultural Entrepreneurship in Nineteenth-Century Boston, I: The Creation of an Organizational Base for High Culture in America" and "Cultural Entrepreneurship in Nineteenth-Century Boston, II: The Classification and Framing of American Art." *Media, Culture and Society* 4: 33–50 and 303–22.

——. 1987. "Classification in Art." *American Sociological Review* 52: 440–55.

Erickson, Bonnie H. 1996. "Culture, Class, and Connections." *American Journal of Sociology* 102(1): 217–25.

——. 2007. "The Crisis in Culture and Inequality." Pp. 343–62 in Steven J. Tepper and Bill Ivey, eds., *Engaging Art: The Next Great Transformation of America's Cultural Life*. New York: Routledge.

Escarpit, Robert. 1971. *The Sociology of Literature*, trans. Ernest Pick. London: Frank Cass.

Frith, Simon. 1981. *Sound Effects: Youth, Leisure, and the Politics of Rock 'n' Roll*. New York: Pantheon.

Geertz, Clifford. 1973. "Deep Play: Notes on the Balinese Cockfight." Pp. 412–53 in *The Interpretation of Cultures*. New York: Basic Books.

Gitlin, Todd. 1985. *Inside Prime Time*. New York: Pantheon Books.

Griswold, Wendy. 1986. *Renaissance Revivals: City Comedy and Revenge Tragedy in the London Theatre, 1576–1980*. Chicago: University of Chicago Press.

——. 1987. "A Methodological Framework for the Sociology of Culture." *Sociological Methodology* 17: 1–35.

Hebdige, Dick. 1979. *Subculture: The Meaning of Style*. London: Methuen.

Hirsch, Paul. 1972. "Processing Fads and Fashions: An Organization-Set Analysis of Cultural Industry Systems." *American Journal of Sociology* 77(4): 639–59.

Lena, Jennifer C. and Peterson, Richard A. 2008. "Classification as Culture: Types and Trajectories of Music Genres." *American Sociological Review* 73: 697–718.

Levine, Lawrence W. 1988. *Highbrow/Lowbrow: The Emergence of Cultural Hierarchy in America*. Cambridge, MA: Harvard University Press.

Lopes, Paul D. 1992. "Innovation and Diversity in the Popular Music Industry." *American Sociological Review* 57: 56–71.

——. 2002. *The Rise of a Jazz Art World*. Cambridge: Cambridge University Press.

Meyer, Leonard B. 1956. *Emotion and Meaning in Music*. Chicago: University of Chicago Press.

Olick, Jeffrey K. 1999. "Genre Memories and Memory Genres: A Dialogical Analysis of May 8th, 1945 Commemorations in the Federal Republic of Germany." *American Sociological Review* 64: 381–402.

Peterson, Richard A. and Berger, David G. 1975. "Cycles in Symbol Production: The Case of Popular Music." *American Sociological Review* 40: 158–73.

Peterson, Richard A. and Kern, Roger M. 1996. "Changing Highbrow Taste: From Snob to Omnivore." *American Sociological Review* 61: 900–07.

Peterson, Richard A. and Rossman, Gabriel. 2007. "Changing Arts Audiences: Capitalizing on Omnivorousness." Pp. 307–42 in Steven J. Tepper and Bill Ivey, eds., *Engaging Art: The Next Great Transformation of America's Cultural Life*. New York: Routledge.

Radway, Janice A. 1984. *Reading the Romance: Women, Patriarchy, and Popular Literature*. Chapel Hill: University of North Carolina Press.

Stromberg, Peter G. 2009. *Caught in Play: How Entertainment Works on You*. Stanford, CA: Stanford University Press.

Sullivan, Oriel and Katz-Gerro, Tally. 2007. "The Omnivore Thesis Revisited: Voracious Cultural Consumers." *European Sociological Review* 23(2): 123–37.

Tepper, Steven J. and Ivey, Bill, eds. 2007. *Engaging Art: The Next Great Transformation of America's Cultural Life*. New York: Routledge.

Wolfe, Tom. 1965. *The Kandy-Kolored Tangerine-Flake Streamline Baby*. New York: Farrar, Straus, and Giroux.

28

Status distinctions and boundaries

Murray Milner, Jr.

The thesis of this essay is that both general theories and attention to cultural variations are needed to understand patterns of social behavior. Such patterned behavior in turn reproduces and changes the form and content of the culture. I will illustrate this thesis by focusing on the operation of status systems. After defining a few key terms and outlining a general theory of status relationships, I show how the processes and tendencies identified by the theory are accentuated or retarded by the content of the particular culture in which they operate. Proposing a general theory does not imply that culture is simply derived from or a reflection of structural relations.

What is status?

Although status has several meanings in social science (see Milner 2006), as used here it refers to the distinctions of rank or stature attributed to a person, group, idea, or object. Such distinctions are rooted in the accumulated expressions of approval and disapproval of other actors in a social environment. For individuals, these are typically the expressions of approval and disapproval of one's friends, family, and co-workers. But a person's status can also be affected by more indirect expressions of approval and disapproval such as educational diplomas or criminal records. Organizations such as colleges, businesses, and voluntary associations can also have higher or lower levels of status. The same is true for cultural concepts and objects. Some are relatively abstract categories (e.g. occupation, ethnicity, gender) or principles (e.g. values, norms, or rules). Others are more concrete physical objects (e.g. automobiles, paintings, buildings, or cities). Status is a form of power and, like economic and political power, can become a generalized social resource, which can be thought of as a form of capital. (I do not attempt to deal with the notions of social and cultural capital since they are considered elsewhere in this handbook.)

Having economic power or wealth can give one status, but this is not necessarily the case. People may admire a successful entrepreneur, but they do not generally praise successful burglars and embezzlers. Tyrants and rich robber barons may receive deference, but they seldom have high approval ratings. The focus in this essay is on status that is relatively independent of economic and political power. This is a kind of power in its own right. The ability of the Pope, Martin Luther King, or John Dewey to influence people is not primarily because of their economic or political power. Hence, in addition to economic and political power, there is status power.

What are status systems?

Status is a relational concept: A person or thing has high or low status compared to someone or something else. Usually such relationships form a system, arena, or field. (Bourdieu's concept of "field" is widely used. It has, however, been subject to a number of critiques [e.g. Hall 1992] and is, in my opinion, unclear and problematic.) Each status system has its own specific status criteria. The attributes that give chess players high status are different from the ones that give a boxer high status; these are two different status systems, even though the same individual may be both a chess player and a boxer. Status systems vary in (1) how well defined their boundaries are, (2) how precisely they make status distinctions, and (3) how much these distinctions coincide with other forms of social inequality. For example, in most modern professional armies, the boundaries of the organization are quite clear, positions are unambiguously ranked, and these ranks are very highly correlated with how much people are paid and how much authority they have over others. In a baseball league, the win–loss rankings and boundaries of the league are clear. The ranking of a team may or may not be strongly correlated to the wealth of the team owner or the salaries of the players. For artists in a local community or for public intellectuals, the system boundaries, individual rankings, and correlation of ranking to income and authority are seldom unambiguous. Max Weber's notions of "status group" and "social class" both refer to status systems. The boundaries and rankings of the first are usually better defined than the second, while the second is more clearly linked to economic inequality.

How do status systems work?

The theory of status relationships is aimed at explaining the patterns of relationships that emerge when status is an important resource. The theory has two key assumptions. First, status is not simply reducible to economic or political power. Put concretely, the influence of Albert Schweitzer, Bach, Jesus, and Nelson Mandela is not primarily due to their economic or political power. Second, for someone or something to have a social status, it must have some level of social visibility. John Dewey has no social status in most Indian villages and the Hindu god Vishnu has no status in most American communities.

The theory has five elements. The first two elements focus on how status differs from other social resources.

Inalienability: Status is relatively inalienable. Although a person can give someone else their money, they cannot give away their status—nor can others simply appropriate it by force or purchase it with money. Hence, once a status is acquired—whether it be high or low—it tends to be relatively stable. This is why, in part, those who acquire new wealth or political power usually attempt to translate at least some of it into status, and why the status of those with "old money" may last longer than the actual money.

None of this is to suggest that status is absolutely stable. The approval ratings of politicians can change quickly; most movie idols and fashion models have relatively short careers; sports stars convicted of serious crimes are no longer seen as heroes. The stability of status is affected by other factors including the degrees of (1) institutionalization (i.e. being part of a long-organized, taken-for-granted pattern), and (2) insulation from economic or political rewards (e.g. politicians or preachers who become extravagantly rich lose their status and legitimacy). The key point is that holding other factors relatively constant, inalienability contributes to the stability of status. (For further clarification of the sources of status stability and the role of inalienability, see Milner 2004: 32, 206–07).

Inexpansibility: Status is relatively inexpansible compared to wealth or political power. If everyone is given a Nobel Prize or is made a member of the aristocracy, these are no longer bases of distinction. In contrast, the income of everyone can triple and their objective circumstances change significantly, even though their relative status remains unchanged. This relative inexpansibility of status has two important implications. First, if someone moves up in the status structure, someone else is likely to have to move down. Therefore, those with higher status tend to restrict and regulate upward mobility. If anyone could add their name to the Social Register or join the National Academies of Science, this would erode the status of all of their members. Second, one way of moving up is to put others down. This is the reason that teenage cliques, Indian upper castes, and country-club members often disparage those below them. It is also part of the reason that "critique," which, in part, is putdown by another name, is such an important element of intellectual life and high culture.

The next two elements of the theory focus on the sources of status.

Conformity: A key source of status is conforming to the norms of the group. As used here, this means not simply conforming to a set of rules, but also expressing the right values and beliefs, and using the proper symbols. Conformity to one set of norms may mean violating another set. The teenager who too enthusiastically follows official school norms violates the norms of his peers. That conformity to the group's norms is a source of status is obvious; it has a less obvious implication. Those who already have high status often complicate and elaborate the norms to make it difficult for others to conform. The elaborate manners and rituals of aristocracies are an obvious example. When it is relatively easy for those of lower status to copy the norms of higher status groups, those with higher status may change the norms frequently. This is why fashion is often important in status systems.

Association: Associating with higher-status individuals, groups, and objects raises one's status, whereas associating with people and things that are low reduces status. Especially important are intimate, expressive relationships as contrasted to instrumental relationships—particularly when the intimacy is officially recognized (e.g. a marriage versus an affair). Living in a Frank Lloyd Wright house gives more status than taking a tour of one. The status of one's parents has more impact than the status of one's third cousins. Sharing food and sex are near-universal symbols of intimacy. Hence, who you marry and who comes to your dinner parties has more effect on your status than which plumber you use. Nor is it accidental that teenagers are often preoccupied with who their peers are "going with" and who eats with whom in the lunchroom; they know these associations have much more impact on status than who sits next to you during class.

Pluralism: The theory also has implications for the sources of cultural pluralism. The larger the status system becomes, the greater are the pressures to develop subcultures or countercultures. In part this is because of the inexpansibility of status, but sheer numbers are also important. In a high school of two hundred, 10 percent, or twenty students, can constitute an elite "popular crowd." Virtually everyone in the school knows who they are. In order for other students to improve their own status, they often copy the behavior of the popular crowd and adopt their style and symbols. Moreover, a number of students have direct interpersonal associations with members of this elite: they were friends in elementary school or they attend the same church youth group. Such connections make the popular crowd seem less remote. These relatively intimate connections with a popular person can raise the other student's status. Some combination of such associations and careful copying of the elites' behaviors and symbols might lead to actual membership.

If, however, the school has two thousand students, the situation is quite different: 10 percent is two hundred individuals—far too many to be highly visible and known to everyone. Moreover, the odds of having any direct contact with members of the elite, much less being admitted to their group, are much lower. Consequently, excluded but talented individuals often attempt to create their own alternative crowds and cliques with different norms, values, beliefs, and symbols. This may involve reversals of previous values: white superiority is rejected and replaced by "black is beautiful." The restrained tailored elegance of the preps is countered by the "in your face" eclectic exhibitionism of punks or Goths.

The development of such alternative subcultures can lead to a near-complete rejection of the dominant subculture, and of the larger social entity. In the case of teenagers this can result in groups of resentful, alienated students or school drop-outs. Perhaps a parallel at the societal level is to be found in the 1960s protestors who became revolutionaries or emigrated to other countries. Such subcultures can obviously also lead to significant conflict between groups. Conflicts between ethnic, religious, and language groups are common within schools, prisons, and whole societies. The creation of such alternative cultures need not, however, result in total rejection and withdrawal. Rather, it can lead to a multicultural school or society in which individuals affirm being both Americans and African-Americans or both Frenchmen and strong supporters of the European Union. The key point: Expanding the size of status systems produces structural pressures toward cultural differentiation and pluralism. Globalism and the reactions to it are a contemporary example.

Finally, pluralism is one of the ways in which the inexpansibility of status is qualified, but not eliminated. Multiple status systems emerge: Being in the popular crowd is not the only way for teenagers to received respect and appreciation. Different individuals may receive respect in different status systems or the same individual may participate in several status systems. Nonetheless, the different systems themselves often develop a status; in the broader culture, it is more prestigious to be a grandmaster in chess than the domino champion.

Boundaries

The notion of boundary suggests an especially strong distinction that includes and excludes. A social boundary is a mechanism for reducing ambiguity. Intense conflict is one motivation for eliminating such ambiguity: "Are you with us or against us"? There are physical boundaries and symbolic boundaries. Sometimes these are strongly correlated (e.g. Jewish ghetto walls) and sometimes they are not (e.g. the state lines in many areas of the US, which do not demarcate social and cultural boundaries).

The boundaries of status systems vary greatly in their precision and rigidity. In most societies there would be little consensus about where to draw a clear line between smart and dumb, pretty and ugly, or moral and immoral. Of course people could be so categorized by some coercive authority, but such categories have little legitimacy. That is to say, the status of such status boundaries would be low.

As indicated above, intimate, expressive associations usually involve much stronger boundaries than instrumental ones. High-status executives may work closely with a wide array of relatively lower-status assistants—receptionists, computer support personnel, chauffeurs, etc. They may be on friendly terms with many of them. Rarely, however, are such subordinates invited home for dinner or to play golf. If they are invited to the superior's home, it is probably to assist with some urgent company project that requires working on the weekend. In racist societies, members of the dominant group may regularly interact with members of the subordinated group—but they do not intermarry. Stated another way, the manipulation of associations is a central mechanism of creating and maintaining social and cultural boundaries. As Michele Lamont (1992) has pointed out, the same culture may have different symbolic boundaries depending on whether the focus is on distinctions that are moral, socioeconomic, or cultural (in the sense of art, music, manners, etc.). The centrality and rigidity of status boundaries also vary with the cultural context, and we will consider such variations shortly.

So far, I have focused on processes that shape the structure and operation of status systems in most, if not all, cultural contexts. Now let us turn to how the content of cultures affects these processes.

What are the effects of culture?

Ideologies of equality and hierarchy

Perhaps the most obvious effect of a culture on status relations is whether its ideology emphasizes egalitarianism or hierarchy. Two polar examples are the US and traditional India. The American Declaration of Independence declares: "all men are created equal." Of course, it took from 1776 to 1964 before American ideology made explicit that this included women and Blacks; it still does not include homosexuals. Nonetheless, outside observers from Tocqueville on have noted that Americans are relatively egalitarian in their ideology and their interpersonal interactions compared to people in many other parts of the world. In contrast, throughout most of India's history, not only was a hierarchy of castes assumed, but a hierarchy of rulers existed, with the most powerful kings seen as an incarnation of the god Vishnu. In contemporary India, this is much less the case. Maharajas lost their political power in 1946 and their wealth, influence, and prestige have steadily eroded over time. Strongly egalitarian notions are incorporated in the Indian Constitution and regularly articulated by politicians. Most contemporary ideology in India is about the glory and solidarity of the nation and incorporates notions of equality of opportunity. Although conservative Hindu public figures often implicitly support traditional hierarchical assumptions about castes, in the public arena these ideas are articulated in relatively disguised form. Open expression of suspicion and hostility toward non-Hindu minorities is, however, not uncommon.

299

Similar contrasts have been noted between the US and Europe (Lipset 1996). Of course, there can be tremendous gaps between ideologies and actual social patterns, but there are limits to such contradictions. There is no question that the opportunities for upward mobility in the US have been much greater than in India—though this may be changing. The key point is that although the structural tendencies outlined in the theory of status relations are operative in most societies, their intensity is modified by the extent to which the culture legitimates equality or hierarchy.

The status of status and its correlation with economic and political power

Societies and other social units vary in the relative importance (i.e. the status) of political power, economic power, and status power. Political power was central in the Soviet Union; economic resources are the predominant form of power in most capitalist societies. Throughout much of the history of India and Tibet, religious and ritual status were central forms of power in their own right. The power of Brahmins and Tibetan monks was not reducible to whatever economic and political power they exercised.

Closely related but logically distinct from the relative importance of a form of power is its correlation with and convertibility to other forms of power. In traditional India, wealth could not easily overcome the stigma of being born into a low caste. Brahmins were ritually superior to others, but only in a few regions were they the richest or most powerful caste. That is, caste status was an important form of power, but it was loosely correlated with wealth or political power. In contrast, in a number of aristocratic societies, status and political power were highly correlated (Geertz 1980; Elias 1983). Similarly, in the Soviet Union political power was usually converted into status and economic privilege. Other forms of status, such as artistic accomplishment, might be converted into economic privilege, but were seldom the route to political power. In the US, new wealth can gain great respect relatively quickly, with Bill Gates, Warren Buffett, and George Soros being obvious examples.

To a very significant degree, these variations in the relative importance of forms of power, and their convertibility and correlation with other forms of power, seem to be rooted in historical cultural particularities. In India, caste status depended in large measure upon ritual purity and impurity (Dumont 1980; Milner 1994). In China, admission to the mandarin political bureaucracy was based on passing examinations on the Confucian classics. Differences in the levels of technology or wealth do not explain the centrality of caste in India or the centrality of the mandarin system in China. In each case, these key institutions were legitimized by particular ideological constructs, assumptions, and symbols that were both relatively unique and linchpins of their whole culture.

The content of culture

The different historical and cultural traditions of India and China meant that the content of their status systems was quite different: knowledge of Confucian classics was irrelevant in India and copying Brahmin purification rituals would do nothing to improve one's status in China. Less apparent is the way that relatively specific cultural notions can shape the details of social interaction and relationships and patterns of social change.

I will illustrate this with two examples. The first concerns the key symbols of intimacy, food, and sex.

Food, sex, and segregation

Racial segregation in the Old South of the US was frequently compared to the traditional Indian caste system (Cox 1948). In both cases there were rigid hierarchies that in principle allowed no mobility across race or caste lines. These lines were reinforced by notions of the purity of "superiors" and the impurity of "inferiors." In both situations, intermarriage and eating together were barred. In the Indian case, notions of social and physical purity were closely linked (Marriott 1976). Eating impure foods changed the nature of one's physical substances, which in turn decreased one's social standing. Consequently, who prepared the food was very important because the impurity of the cook was transferred to the food and in turn to those who ate the food. For the purity of a caste or an individual to be preserved, food must be prepared by someone of the same (or a higher) caste. At public events involving different castes, it was common for the cook to be a Brahmin, so that no one would be contaminated. Unsurprisingly, although such notions were common across most castes, they were emphasized much more by upper castes than lower castes. In Swidler's (1986) terminology, the idea that social and physical purity were inextricably linked—and even conflated—was part of the general cultural toolkit, but upper castes used this tool much more often and consistently than lower castes.

Now let us turn to America's Old South. Although restaurants, water fountains, and restrooms were segregated, a much clearer differentiation was made between social purity and physical purity—at least with respect to preparing and serving food. Who prepared the food was largely irrelevant and cooks were frequently black servants. Upper-class whites even competed to employ blacks who were noted for their culinary skills. With respect to sex and procreation, however, physical and social purity were less distinct. Although sex between white men and black women was common, whites had great concern about the status of the offspring of such liaisons. The result was the "one-drop" rule, which declared that anyone who had even "one drop of Negro blood" was considered black, and hence had low status. This rule was not restricted to conventions and prejudices, but was incorporated into many state laws. In contrast, in much of Latin America notions of pure and impure "blood lines" existed, but there was no "one-drop" rule: various mixtures of "racial" ancestry were recognized. These mixtures may have been ranked, but they did not result in the rigid racial boundary of the Old South. The point of these examples from traditional India, the Old South, and Latin America is that, although they all share the tendencies outlined in the theory of status relations, important differences in patterns of behavior are often shaped by seemingly esoteric variations in cultural concepts.

The market, individualism, and the therapeutic society

For the second example of how the content of culture affects patterns of behavior, I will focus on how psychotherapy moved from being a low-status marginal activity to a high-status central aspect of American culture. Not only does the status of individuals, groups, objects change over time, but worldviews (i.e. fundamental cultural assumptions) rise and fall in status. This section looks at such a change—specifically, a change concerning how one core cultural assumption is affected by the status and legitimacy of other core assumptions. My argument is that the early acceptance of psychotherapeutic perspectives in the US was due to the therapy's compatibility or elective affinity with the core economic and political assumptions of liberal capitalism.

Philip Rieff (1968) has noted and criticized what he calls "the triumph of the therapeutic"—the erosion of social and personal morality and an emphasis on individual choice and adjustment. Christopher Lasch (1978) shows that notions of therapeutic adjustment are not only applied to the mentally ill. Rather, they have become a widespread and even dominant cultural orientation that shapes the discourse in many realms of social life, including TV talk shows, self-help books, religious pastoral counseling, and interpersonal interactions. The result is a culture centered on personal fulfillment and thin notions of morality. Reiff and Lasch see this culture as having disturbing consequences—though others see the developments more positively (Marcuse 1974; Ziguras 2001). This is a well-known story that has been recounted more fully by others (see, e.g., Woolfolk 2003; Hall et al. 2003).

Here I do not want to debate the consequences or merits of these developments, but rather to highlight how they represent an enormous change in the status of alternative sets of core cultural norms and assumptions. This change was largely unopposed because the therapeutic perspective conformed to and was implicitly associated with the key assumptions of free-market capitalism, which had already become deeply institutionalized in the US. There have been moral ambiguities in every era, but certainly most Americans in the nineteenth century had a pretty sure sense that some things were "right" and some things were "wrong." Stated another way, it was relatively clear what would receive approval and disapproval—as were the moral boundaries that resulted. Arguably, the shift from Victorian morality to a therapeutic society is a more fundamental shift in the cultural ideas and norms than was the Protestant Reformation. Victorian cultural hallmarks such as Kipling's "You'll be a man, my son," Henley's "I am the captain of my soul," or Buchman's "moral rearmament" imply radically different moral stances than such late-twentieth-century maxims as "Go with the flow," "I'm okay, you're okay," "I am comfortable with that," or "Whatever." Second, compared to the resistance faced by other major cultural innovations (e.g. Darwinism or legalizing abortion), the shift to a therapeutic culture has been almost subliminal. Criticism and resistance were modest given the scope and implications of the cultural change. How do we explain why there was so little resistance?

Fundamental to Freudian theory is the idea that mental illnesses are caused by the repression of painful experiences. Individuals so traumatized cannot act rationally because they live in a world of distorted information and reality—in the form of neuroses, obsessions, and even psychoses. Psychoanalysis enables people to recover the past experiences that deformed them and face up to the present situation that actually confronts them. The choices they face may involve unavoidable tragedy (e.g. becoming alienated from a domineering parent or spouse), but the healed patient can now make such choices rationally. Other types of psychotherapy may attribute irrationality to other sources or propose other forms of therapy, but virtually all seek to help people overcome distorted and unrealistic ways of thinking by enabling them to have more and better information about themselves and their situation.

This is the same situation that the individual faces in the market: rational choices are dependent upon both opportunities to choose alternatives and receiving accurate information about the cost and consequences of the alternatives. These options may not be appealing—sell now at a loss or sell later at a bigger loss—but the better the information available, the more rational the decision. My argument is that both realms promote the ideal of the rational individual making choices that are undistorted by false information or irrational emotions.

In Weber's terms, there was an elective affinity between these two understandings of what constituted optimal circumstances. The resistance to the rise of therapeutic perspectives was so modest because "the Great Transformation" (Polanyi 1957) of earlier centuries had already overcome cultural resistance to the notion of individuals making free, rational choices in the economic and political realms. The "triumph of the therapeutic" simply extended this conventional wisdom to the emotional and moral realm. Stated in terms of the theory of status relations, the therapeutic perspective involved conformity to norms and values that already had enormous status in other realms of the culture. Similarly, "rationality," "freedom," and "choice" in the emotional and moral realm were given added legitimacy by their association with the same high-status notions in the economic and political realms.

The above argument suggests how existing cultural assumptions can shape the likelihood of new cultural innovations being accepted, that is, gaining a relatively high status. A more extensive test of the hypothesis would require not only much more detailed analysis of American society (e.g. Illouz 2007), but comparative analysis with other societies. There are existing studies of the reception of psychoanalysis and psychotherapies in India and Russia. Freud's ideas were enthusiastically accepted in the early years of the twentieth century in some intellectual circles in pre-Revolutionary Russia. Even after the Russian Revolution, Freudianism was initially respected, though eventually banned. The Indian Psychoanalytic Society was officially recognized by the International Psychoanalytic Congress in 1922—before there was a recognized branch in France. But in both cases, Freudian thought ran up against cultural assumptions that were antithetical to notions of the independent individual and the nuclear family, as well as other important cultural incompatibilities (Miller 1990; Hartnack 1990), and the overall impact of notions of psychotherapy was quite limited. This section, then, has had three key points. First, even extensive macro changes in cultural content can usefully be seen as cases of status transformation—a rise in the status of a set of core cultural assumptions. Second, such changes occur by various forms of conformity and association. Third, the likelihood of such a transformation is shaped by the content of cultural assumptions that already have high status and legitimacy.

Conclusion

- An adequate sociological analysis must conceptualize status as a distinct form of power, not reducible to economic or political power.
- It is useful to consider not only the status of and the relationships between individuals and groups, but also the status and relationships between cultural objects—from particular commodities to core cultural assumptions.
- Both general theories that focus on near-universal structural relationships and careful attention to the details of particular cultures, including the history of their development, are the best strategy for understanding the nature of status relations in concrete historical settings.

References

Cox, O. 1948. *Caste, Class, and Race: A Study in Social Dynamics.* New York: Doubleday.

Dumont, L. 1980. *Homo Hierarchicus: The Caste System and its Implications.* Chicago: University of Chicago Press.

Elias, N. 1983. *The Court Society.* New York: Pantheon Books.

Geertz, C. 1980. *Negara: The Theatre State in Nineteenth-Century Bali.* Princeton, NJ: Princeton University Press.

Hall, J.R. 1992. "The Capital(s) of Cultures: A Non-holistic Approach to Status Situations, Class, Gender, and Ethnicity." In M. Lamong and M. Fournier, eds., *Cultivating Differences: Symbolic Boundaries and the Making of Inequality.* Chicago: Chicago University Press.

Hall, J.R., Neitz, M.J., and Battani, M. 2003. *Sociology on Culture.* New York: Routledge.

Hartnack, Christiane. 2001. *Psychoanalysis in Colonial India.* New Delhi and New York: Oxford University Press.

Illouz, E. 2007. *Cold Intimacies: The Making of Emotional Capitalism.* Cambridge: Polity.

Lamont, M. 1992. *Money, Morals, and Manners: The Culture of the French and American Upper-middle Class.* Chicago: University of Chicago Press.

Lamont, M. and Fournier, M. 1992. *Cultivating Differences: Symbolic Boundaries and the Making of Inequality.* Chicago: University of Chicago Press.

Lasch, Christopher. 1978. *The Culture of Narcissism: American Life in an Age of Diminishing Expectations.* New York: Norton.

Lipset, S.M. 1996. *American Exceptionalism: A Double-edged Sword.* New York: Norton.

Marcuse, Herbert. 1974. *Eros and Civilization: A Philosophical Inquiry into Freud,* with a new preface by the author. Boston: Beacon.

Marriott, M. 1976. "Hindu Transactions." In Bruce Kapferer, ed., *Transaction and Meaning.* Philadelphia, PA: ISHI.

Miller, M.A. 1990. "The Reception of Psychoanalysis and the Problem of the Unconscious in Russia." *Social Research* 57(4): 875–88.

Milner, M., Jr. 1994. *Status and Sacredness: A General Theory of Status Relations and an Analysis of Indian Culture.* New York: Oxford University Press.

——. 2004. *Freaks, Geeks, and Cool Kids: American Teenagers, Schools, and the Culture of Consumption.* New York: Routledge.

——. 2006. "Status." In Austin Harrington, Barbara Marshall, and Hans-Peter Müller, eds., *Encyclopedia of Social Theory.* London: Routledge.

Polanyi, K. 1957. *The Great Transformation: The Political and Economic Origins of our Time.* Boston: Beacon Press.

Rieff, P. 1968. *The Triumph of the Therapeutic: The Uses of Faith after Freud.* New York: Harper & Row.

Swidler, A. 1986. "Culture in Action: Symbols and Strategies." *American Sociological Review* 51: 273–86.

Woolfolk, Alan. 2003. "The Therapeutic Ideology of Moral Freedom." *Journal of Classical Sociology* 3: 247–621.

Ziguras, Christopher. 2001. "Narcissism and Self-Care: Theorizing America's Obsession with Mundane Health Behavior." *Journal of Mundane Behavior* 2: 2.

29

Culture and stratification

Omar Lizardo

Canonical treatments of the link between culture and stratification in sociology typically focus on the role of culture as a resource for the formation and differentiation of status groups (Bourdieu 1984; Beisel 1997). The classical differentiation between status situation and class situation (Weber 1946: 300–01) provides the analytic foundation and the point of departure for current work on the subject. While often conflated, the terms class and status must remain analytically distinct in order for their empirical interrelationship to be meaningfully examined (Chan and Goldthorpe 2007). The class situation is best characterized by "opportunities to gain sustenance and income" (Weber 1946: 301). The status situation, on the other hand, entails "every typical component of the fate of ... individuals determined by means of a specific positive or negative social estimation" (Weber 1994: 113).

Status, in Weber's analysis, thus "expresses itself in the *specifically stylized way of life* to which all aspiring members [of the relevant group] are expected to adhere" (1994: 114, emphasis added). This way of conceptualizing the status situation implies that membership in status groups can only be sustained and temporally reproduced through the "monopolization of [access to] ideal and material goods" (Weber 1994: 117). Accordingly, whereas "classes stratify themselves according to their relation to the production and acquisition of goods," status groups do so according to "the principles of their consumption of goods" (Weber 1994: 119). It is therefore by molding the criteria of selection into status groups, as well as by providing the symbolic coordinates that differentiate lifestyles across the social landscape, that culture (and cultural goods) comes to be involved in the stratification process.

At the level of everyday experiential reality, status situations manifest mainly in individuals' differential ability to acquire informal entry into symbolically (and sometimes spatially) delimited arenas of association. The primary role of these circles of acquaintance is to provide a sense of membership and to serve as sites of "sociability" (Simmel 1949), that is—as Simmel defined it—sites of social intercourse explicitly dissociated from direct instrumental pursuits. This is a characteristic form of association "which does not have a strictly economic or business purpose" (Weber 1994: 114). In contemporary post-traditional, market-dominated societies with very little "formal" apparatus of social differentiation based on collectively defined "status orders" (Collins 1975), the primary way in which Weberian social honor is bestowed by members of one group to members of another is mainly through acceptance into informal networks of intimacy, friendship, and kinship (DiMaggio 1987).

After the analytical distinction between class and status has been made, the key question that emerges pertains to their relative causal priority. Most analysts agree with the general proposition that "[a] status situation can be the cause as well as the result of a class situation but it need be neither" (Weber 1946: 301). Accordingly, the relationship between class and status becomes a matter of empirical adjudication rather than a priori theoretical speculation. However, most American and European sociologists who theorize the culture–stratification link are not neutral on the question of whether status situations impact class situations. If some relation were not presumed to exist (especially going from status situation to class situation), it would diminish the warrant for being concerned with the culture–stratification link. The key question thus turns on specifying the concrete mechanisms through which status situations come to infiltrate or modify market-mediated systems for the determination of life-chances.

The emergence and reproduction of status cultures

Values, codes, and the emergence of status cultures

How do distinct class cultures emerge and reproduce themselves in post-traditional societies? Post-functionalist accounts of the culture–stratification link emphasize the crucial role of differences in socialization practices across status groups, which lead to the creation and intergenerational maintenance of distinct and sometimes antithetical values and conceptions of the world (Bourdieu 1984; Kohn 1989; Collins 1975; Lamont 1992). These "status cultures" function as the primary conduit through which partially self-reproducing lifestyle groupings obtain whatever coherence they have in post-traditional societies (Giddens 1991). "Social structure" in post-traditional societies is best conceived as a loose tapestry of status groups and income classes—each endowed with different cultural and material endowments—competing to exercise hegemony over the centers of cultural authority and prestige (Bourdieu 1984; Collins 1975; Ollivier 2000).

Contemporary theorists are almost unanimous in suggesting that distinct status cultures originate through cultural transmission processes set within the domestic sphere. Status-based socialization not only serves to demarcate group boundaries, but has functional implications for the generation of status-linked advantages outside of the household. This can happen in several (interrelated) ways.

First, there is the question of the origins and consequences of different approaches to childrearing by members of different status cultures. It is clear that differences may emerge because, depending on status-group membership, parents may be endowed with different "images" of the world that serve as cognitive templates in guiding their socialization practices (Kohn 1989). These divergent cognitive and moral orientations are reinforced by the pervasive experiences and opportunities for expression of those cultural patterns that people encounter during day-to-day activity at work (Kohn 1989; Collins 1975; Coser 1975).

These cognitive-evaluative orientations can be reinforced intragenerationally through the life-course as persons come to settle on one or another line of work. They are also reproduced intergenerationally through parental socialization practices, such that orientations play a key role in the status-reproduction process (Kohn 1989; Collins 1975; Goldthorpe 1996). For instance, members of culturally privileged status cultures come to place a heavy weight on the value of self-direction because it is reinforced in the white-collar workplace. In the very same way, members of routine white-collar and manual occupations come to weigh conformity positively because it is reinforced in the repetitive, low-autonomy work found in contemporary service establishments. This difference provides an explanation for the phenomenon of status-linked differences in work-values and career preferences (Kohn 1989).

Second, experience with a given status culture can come to define the way in which language is used inside and outside the home (Bernstein 1971, 1964). Differential acquisition of certain linguistic and cognitive skills in status-differentiated households links socialization practices set within the domestic arena with those competences that are rewarded in educational institutions. Children of middle-class parents are immersed in a distinct linguistic environment in the home, specifically in parents who belong to high-status occupations that presume difference and "spell everything out" directly, use a wider range of both syntactic and semantic resources (e.g. larger vocabulary, more complex syntax), and attempt to abstract out from both context and time.

Because school curricula are presented to students in a manner consistent with this status-differentiated style of linguistic encoding, pupils from middle-class backgrounds are able to more easily decode scholastic offerings as well as produce the specific styles of linguistic presentation favored by teachers, thus being more likely to be successful in academic environments, net of cognitive ability (Bernstein 1971). Members of high-status occupations are in this way more likely to provide their children with the linguistic and cognitive tools necessary to navigate social environments premised on encountering cultural diverse others (Bernstein 1964; Coser 1975).

Status and organizational skills

Status-linked parental socialization practices may serve to transmit cultural advantages not only directly (by rewarding those skills and value-orientations rewarded by educational institutions and high-status workplaces) but also indirectly, by providing children from privileged status backgrounds with a generalized competence for navigating complex bureaucratically organized institutions and effectively interacting with representatives of these organizations. It has been shown that the same formally organized environment (e.g. a school) can be used in a distinctive manner by parents and children of different class backgrounds, and that children of privileged status backgrounds are more likely to receive a "customized" experience (Lareau 2003).

Like other status-linked differences, inequalities in the ability to effectively navigate the institutions most likely to impact one's life-chances can be magnified when parents of high-status occupations adopt a distinct (ideal-typically characterized) orientation towards childrearing, which provides children from these status groups with a host of intended and unintended cultural advantages.

For instance, Lareau (2003) has found that in structuring their child-socialization activities, high-status parents tend to rely on a logic of "concerted cultivation," which involves the child's constant participation in structured extra-curricular activities outside the home. Through these forms of social and cultural participation, middle-class children come to be endowed with a set of habitual social skills—such as the ability to treat adults

307

in positions of authority as (relative) equals, and to demand customized treatment from representatives of bureaucratic institutions—that allow them to more deftly navigate those institutions most clearly linked to life-chances, such as schools. Parents from lower occupational status groups adopt a very different posture toward childrearing, what Lareau (2003) calls the logic of "natural growth." In this cultural script, the primary parental responsibility is to provide for the child's basic needs (e.g. food, shelter, safety). Because the natural-growth strategy sees children talents as inherent in their person and as following an "Aristotelian" logic of spontaneous maturation and expression (rather than a "Lockean" logic of cultivation and learning), there is less perceived need for constant, competitive cultivation of special skills.

This means that children from lower-status backgrounds tend to spend more of their time among familiar same-age kin in unstructured domestic activities; their parents are unable to provide their children with the same opportunities to develop the same set of social skills as their high-status counterparts. When it comes to interacting with adults and professionals in positions of power in established institutions, these children are thus at a distinct interactional disadvantage. They lack the ability to demand that institutional regulations be tailored to their particular needs. For both white and black children of less privileged status backgrounds, schools are perceived as impersonal and removed from everyday concerns; they are sites of constraint and not arenas designed for personal growth (Lareau 2003).

Class habitus

Parental socialization practices not only work at the level of value-orientations, the creation of future expectations, and "linguistic codes." Socialization into a status-linked environment affects persons in a deeper manner, at the level of unconscious dispositions, skills, and practices (Bourdieu 1984). The implicit immersion in status-linked home environments is driven both by the child's exposure to parental practices keyed to instruction and socialization, and by her active, bodily interaction with material objects and built environments, as well as her exposure to specific sensory experiences (Bourdieu 1990).

The acquisition of these tacit competences leads to the development of an unconscious, undirected (but ultimately systematically organized) set of expectations, styles of appreciation, schemes of perception, and systems of practical action in the world—what Bourdieu calls "habitus." Habitus can be thought of as an enduring (but dynamic) cognitive structure that produces thoughts, reactions (aesthetic, cognitive, and moral), and choices (e.g. what to buy, what to major in, whom to marry) that are in tune with and attempts (within constraints) to recreate the environment in which it developed (Bourdieu 1990). This explains why we can recurrently observe individuals socialized within distinct status environments "constructing ... positions for themselves ... without awareness that they ... [are] engaged in doing so" (Bettie 2003: 190).

Status cultures in post-traditional societies are thus recurrently generated and reproduced both within the household during the process of cultural socialization and outside the household in educational systems and the workplace. These status cultures fall into two general ideal-typical groups. The first is characterized by regularly occurring "interaction rituals" of high emotional intensity that are keyed to particularistic and concrete symbols of group membership (Collins 1975). The second is generated by way of membership in larger, loosely knit, more "cosmopolitan" networks with fuzzy boundaries which require more abstract and less context-specific forms of cultural currency capable of generating emotionally weaker but wider-spanning forms of membership across different social arenas (Coser 1975).

Cross-cutting institutional linkages

Institutions, capital, fields

In addition to exploring the nexus that connects status-linked socialization practices with success in key institutional sites outside the home, culture and stratification researchers have examined how implicit institutional linkages across seemingly disconnected societal domains contribute to the stratification process (Bourdieu 1984, 1996). This type of analysis combines the Weberian insight about the partial autonomy of status situations (and their ability to sometimes drive class situations), the Marxian emphasis on power and cultural hegemony, and Durkheim's concern with the social origins of shared systems of thought and classification. The key claim made by institutionally oriented theorists of the culture–stratification linkage is that status-based advantages (as produced within the family and in formal occupation-based class cultures) come to be inscribed in the very classificatory framework of the institutions in charge of sorting persons into positions that monopolize the extraction of Weberian class-based advantages and thus shape "life-chances."

All of the major institutions of post-traditional societies (e.g. education, science, art, the state) carry the "role imprint" (Bourdieu 1981; Burton and Beckman 2007) of the status-groups that were initially implicated in their emergence. It is therefore very difficult for social groups to achieve any type of "universal" (e.g. purely meritocratic) representation in, and access to, the institutions that determine life-chances that are not grounded in some delimited class culture. What can be shown is that different status groups compete for the claim to universal representation. This competition links to the process of status-group reproduction because, as we have seen, members of high-status occupational and professional fractions are able to impart those unofficial (and implicit) sets of habits, competences, mannerisms, and dispositions that provide their children with a probabilistic advantage of achieving success within dominant institutions. This circumstance partially guarantees some form of intergenerational transmission of the symbolic means of institutional authority and control, but also guarantees that this control will be subject to contestation (Bourdieu 1984).

This sensitizing framework carries with it major empirical implications. For instance, it should always be possible for the sociological analyst to empirically link even those fields of practice most apparently removed from status-group concerns (e.g. museums [Bourdieu and Darbel 1991]; research universities [Bourdieu 1996]) back to lifestyle-linked divisions in the wider social structure. This explains why we can observe robust cross-institutional linkages between fields that explicitly disavow being the instrument of status-group concerns (such as fields of cultural production and dissemination) and the audiences that incorporate the symbolic goods produced in those fields as a constitutive part of their lifestyle (Bourdieu 1984).

Cultural capital

The term cultural capital was first used in order to better understand patterns of inequality in educational outcomes in French schools—such as "educational inheritance" or the differential ability of the sons and daughters of educated parents to be judged as better students by their teachers (Bourdieu and Passeron 1977). The concept of cultural capital has nevertheless enjoyed much more flexibility in studies of the link between culture and stratification. In studies of the social bases of cultural taste, the notion of cultural capital has been generalized to explain differential rates of engagement in the arts (Bourdieu 1968, 1984; DiMaggio 1987). A key argument here is that the dispositions toward collectively validated symbolic goods function as cultural capital in post-traditional societies, because it is the most institutionally legitimated (e.g. through its reinforcement by educational institutions) form of appropriation of these goods (although it is not the only existing basis of reception).

More contemporary studies have challenged the notion that cultural capital is inherently linked to the arts or other forms of institutionalized "high culture." Instead, the empirical evidence shows that almost any set of status-based dispositions embodied by members of a privileged status group counts as "capital" when deployed to produce advantage in a concrete institutional setting. Thus, cultural aptitudes that facilitate the appropriation of locally valued cultural goods or the ability to master those forms of linguistic expression accorded the most value in the larger society—e.g. "idiomatic" English (Carter 2003)—can be thought of as dominant cultural or linguistic capital when they facilitate particular styles of self-presentation perceived (consciously or implicitly) by institutional gatekeepers to be markers of a superior student, endowed with sophistication and intelligence (Bourdieu 1996: 31).

In the Anglo-American literature, two primary conceptualizations of cultural capital inform contemporary theory and research on the culture–stratification linkage. One, partially based on Bourdieu's (1986) influential formulation, defines cultural capital as an aptitude or a generalized, transposable (across contexts) skill acquired in the combined realms of the upper-middle-class family and the school system (DiMaggio 1991: 134). The other major conceptualization of cultural capital perceives ambiguities in the Bourdieuian-inspired definition of cultural capital as "skill" or "proficiency." Instead, cultural capital is viewed from a "boundaries" perspective, and defined as "the institutionalized repertoire of high status signals" useful for purposes of marking and drawing symbolic boundaries in a given social context (Lamont and Lareau 1988: 164). This definition of cultural capital links to a Weberian theory of status-group closure; what counts as cultural capital is those symbolic resources that are actively mobilized by members of groups or class fractions to establish their difference from other groups and thus to devalue the cultural resources and symbolic practices of outsiders.

The context-specificity of cultural capital

Rather than being in competition or mutually exclusive, both definitions of cultural capital are empirically relevant and theoretically useful. This is because what "counts" as cultural capital in a given interaction setting is often determined by the local institutional context. For instance, minority youth from status-disadvantaged backgrounds can gain interactional advantages from command of both (1) dominant cultural patterns (institutionalized and associated with the "white middle class," e.g. the ability to speak in institutionally accepted ways)—cultural capital as competence—and (2) familiarity with minority cultural patterns ("black" slang; a taste for certain musical and sartorial styles associated with African-American oppositional youth cultures)—cultural capital as a boundary-marking resource (Carter 2003). The former allows minority youth to navigate their way through key institutions (schools, the workplace, the law), while the latter can be used to claim "authentic" membership in their ethnic subculture. Thus, cultural capital can be used not just as a boundary-drawing resource, but also as a way to claim ownership of desirable ethnic and racial identities. More importantly, precisely those youth who develop the ability to straddle the boundaries between dominant and non-dominant forms of cultural capital appear to reap the benefits of conventional success as well as acceptance by ethnic peers (Carter 2006).

Morals and manners

Contemporary research attempting to conceptualize the role of culture in marking divisions across status follows Weber and Bourdieu in keying in on the role of cultural aptitudes and lifestyle consumption patterns. However, this does not mean that taste and lifestyle are the only symbolic resources that serve to structure and mark the boundaries across status groups. As research demonstrates, certain moral ideologies may be as cogni-tively and affectively salient as tastes in serving as criteria for membership (and thus exclusion) from specific status-based collectivities (Lamont 1992, 2000; Sayer 2005).

For instance, boundaries based on moral qualities associated with socioeconomic pursuits tend to be more salient among culturally advantaged members of the American and French upper-middle class. Moral boundaries based on "honesty," however, are particularly salient in the US, whereas those associated with taste and broader cultural orientations are more salient in the French context. In addition, judgments of the worth of members of different status fractions (e.g. those who belong to occupa-tions closer to the market) made by members of culturally and economically distinct status fractions (culturally privileged but economically poor members of symbol-producing occupations) are structured by morally tinged conceptions of the propriety of profit-making versus dedication to more "transcendent," less materialistic pursuits (Lamont 1992).

In addition, nationally and ethnically specific "institutionalized cultural repertoires" (Lamont 2000: 243) regulate boundary-drawing strategies among members of less privileged status groups (Lamont 2000), such as when working-class white men draw boundaries between the "morally worthy" working-class and the morally unscrupulous upper-middle class, or when boundaries are drawn laterally in order to exclude the putatively undeserving members of racial and ethnic groups of comparable socio-economic status. It is impossible to understand these patterns of exclusion and inclusion and the role played by such key values as "hard work" or "honesty" in the discourse of the white working class (or the role of "caring" in the discourse of the black working class) without getting a handle of the distinct, context-specific cultural models deployed by different working-class fractions, both within a given national context (e.g. black versus white in the US) or across national societies (e.g. the relatively higher emphasis of the French working class on cross-racial solidarity based on trade unionism) (Lamont 2000).

Expanding the historical scope

The more institutionally oriented framework provided by cultural-capital theory has deeply affected Euro-American sociology (Savage *et al.* 2005). In particular, the concern with uncovering and delineating counterintuitive inter-institutional linkages connecting status-based pursuits with processes of economic advancement and class-reproduction remains a key theme. Some of the best work extends this line of research by looking at the role of both moral and cultural boundaries as they play out in the constitution of status-group cultures across different historical periods.

For instance, Beisel (1997) shows that attempts to impose specific forms of cultural hegemony on the part of competing fractions of the economic elite stand behind such seemingly disparate episodes as the panic over "obscene art" in late-nineteenth century America or the panic over the "corrupting influence" of literary curricula on (middle-class) children in schools. The historical evidence shows that in those cities in which elite groups perceived the most threat from mobile parvenus and newly arrived immigrants, projects of moral reform proved to have much more support than in those cities where the upper class was comparatively shielded from threats to its status position (Beisel 1997).

One of the primary ways in which status groups continue to reproduce themselves in post-traditional societies is by providing persons with (apparently status-neutral, but demonstrably status-linked) cultural templates that come to govern spousal choice. The evidence shows that spousal choice is robustly impacted by status-linked factors, including the education and occupational position of each spouse and their relative familiarity with institutionally legitimated culture (Kalmijn 1991, 1994; DiMaggio and Mohr 1985).

Sociological studies of the history of the notion and practice of romance show an even more complicated tapestry of inter-institutional linkages uniting informal behavior in the "dating market" with processes of class and status-group reproduction (Illouz 1997). Modern notions of romance have been historically constituted through multiple cross-linkages between various institutional actors (the market, fields of cultural production, mental health). In this way, different conceptions of the "romantic" as forms of status culture become even more salient in determining status-based reproduction precisely at the point at which people experience themselves to be making the most autonomous of "choices"—whom to fall in love with. Preferences for a "soul-mate" are inseparable from other systems of preferences acquired and transmitted in the same sites dedicated to status-group reproduction, such as schools and the home (Bourdieu 1984). In this respect, homogamy based on status continues to be produced within a system dedicated to the discourse of love as an overwhelming (non-rational) emotional force or as an idiosyncratic (status-neutral) individual experience (Illouz 1997).

Problems and prospects in culture and stratification research

Contemporary analysts of the culture–stratification link have continued to develop the classical legacy by producing innovative lines of research. They have attempted to explore new dimensions of the culture and stratification links in two ways: "extensively," in terms of historical nuance and scope, complexity, and the number of institutional linkages through which class cultures come to acquire hegemony over a given set of authoritative discourses; and "intensively," in terms of uncovering process-based mechanisms through which status-based advantage is intergenerationally transmitted or produced and reproduced in concrete contexts.

A lot of this work, even that which takes a more comparative approach (e.g. Lamont 1992, 2000), is centered on the Euro-American West, and is thus not as fully geographically and cross-culturally representative as it could be (Kane 2003). Recent moves toward a more comparative approach to the study of "repertoires of evaluation" are a commendable way to radicalize the extensive strategy (Lamont and Thévenot 2000). Nevertheless, we still have very limited knowledge of how the relationship between status and class situations is manifested outside of the Euro-American context. Exceptions to this general claim include scholarship that explores the relationship between arts consumption and social stratification, a field of study that has experienced a very healthy expansion of late (Peterson 2005). This work has extended the "cultural-capital" framework for the study of lifestyle consumption patterns to Latin America and the transition economies of Russia and the former Soviet block (e.g. Zavisca 2005; Torche 2007).

We know even less about how cultural repertoires deployed for the demarcation of symbolic boundaries operate in non-Western developing countries. Outside of sociology, there is a vibrant and exponentially growing literature on cultural consumption and global media in anthropology and communications. In it, researchers make use of fundamental sociological insights on the relationship between status-based stratification and lifestyle. Some of this research indicates that the cultural-capital framework can certainly be used to understand the relative appeal of global versus local cultural products (Straubhaar 2007). For instance, in the case of Brazil, evidence shows that membership in distinct status fractions shapes media and other culture-consumption choices: members of culturally advantaged status groups gravitate towards "global" (English-language) culture and those endowed with less cultural capital prefer regional and local ("cultural proximate") materials rendered in the national language. This work represents a good first step toward greater dialogue between scholars of globalization and scholars of culture and stratification.

It is clear that progress in the field requires both a continuation and a radicalization of extensive and intensive strategies. For the extensive strategy, it is important to examine the ever-changing and increasingly complex inter-institutional linkages through which status systems connect to class systems of rank both in contemporary "network" societies and during the transition to neoliberalism throughout the globe. Furthermore, it is important to begin to theorize the interstitial sites in which status-based cultural practices are beginning to become objectified and institutionalized (see, for instance, Illouz 2007 on "emotional capital") so that we may continue to illuminate the sometimes surreptitious ways in which institutional logics based on delimited class cultures come to acquire society-wide cultural authority across and within contemporary contexts.

In terms of the intensive strategy, we need research designs that highlight the fine-grained processual mechanisms and processes responsible for the transmission of cultural resources within generations and across institutional sites (e.g. Carter 2003; Lareau 2003; Bettie 2003). We still know woefully little about the concrete realization and operation of the cultural and interactional mechanisms that generate status-based privilege and are therefore responsible for intergenerational transmission of cultural advantage. The intensive strategy may be harder to pursue than the extensive one but is equally essential. For only by having a clear handle on the micro-mechanisms and processes of status-based reproduction can we understand the origins of the apparently "natural gifts" that allow members of privileged status groups to more effectively navigate key institutional settings—settings that certify some cultural competencies as more legitimate than others and that therefore shape life-chances in post-traditional societies.

References

Beisel, Nicola Kay. 1997. *Imperiled Innocents: Anthony Comstock and Family Reproduction in Victorian America*. Princeton, NJ: Princeton University Press.
Bernstein, Basil. 1964. "Elaborated and Restricted Codes: Their Social Origins and Some Consequences." *American Anthropologist* 66: 55–69.
——. 1971. *Class, Codes, and Control: Theoretical Studies Towards a Sociology of Language*. London: Routledge and Kegan Paul.
Bettie, J. 2003. *Women without Class: Girls, Race, and Identity*. Berkeley: University of California Press.
Bourdieu, Pierre. 1968. "Outline of a Theory of Art Perception." *International Social Science Journal* 20: 589–612.
——. 1981. "Men and Machines." Pp. 304–17 in Aaron V. Ciccourel and K.D. Knorr-Cetina, eds., *Advances in Social Theory and Methodology*. Boston: Routledge and Kegan Paul.
——. 1984. *Distinction: A Social Critique of the Judgement of Taste*. Cambridge, MA: Harvard University Press.
——. 1986. "The Forms of Capital." Pp. 241–58 in John Richardson, ed., *Handbook of Theory and Research for the Sociology of Education*. New York: Greenwood Press.
——. 1990. *The Logic of Practice*. Cambridge: Polity Press.
——. 1996. *The State Nobility: Elite Schools in the Field of Power*. Cambridge: Polity Press.
Bourdieu, Pierre and Darbel, Alain. 1991. *The Love of Art*. Cambridge: Polity Press.
Bourdieu, Pierre and Passeron, Jean-Claude. 1977. *Reproduction in Education, Society, and Culture*. Beverly Hills, CA: Sage.
Burton, M.D. and Beckman, C.M. 2007. "Leaving a Legacy: Position Imprints and Successor Turnover in Young Firms." *American Sociological Review* 72(2): 239.
Carter, Prudence L. 2003. "'Black' Cultural Capital, Status Positioning, and Schooling Conflicts for Low-Income African American Youth." *Social Problems* 50(1): 136–55.
——. 2006. "Straddling Boundaries: Identity, Culture, and School." *Sociology of Education* 4: 304–28.
Chan, T.W. and Goldthorpe, J.H. 2007. "Class and Status: The Conceptual Distinction and Its Empirical Relevance." *American Sociological Review* 72(4): 512.
Collins, Randall. 1975. *Conflict Sociology*. New York: Academic Press.
Coser, Ruth Laub. 1975. "The Complexity of Roles as a Seedbed of Individual Autonomy." Pp. 237–63 in Lewis A. Coser, ed., *The Idea of Social Structure*. New York: Harcourt.
DiMaggio, Paul. 1987. "Classification in Art." *American Sociological Review* 52: 440–55.
——. 1991. "Social Structure Institutions and Cultural Goods: The Case of the United States." Pp. 133–55 in Pierre Bourdieu and James Coleman, eds., *Social Theory for a Changing Society*. Boulder, CO: Westview Press.
DiMaggio, P. and Mohr, J. 1985. "Cultural Capital, Educational Attainment, and Marital Selection." *American Journal of Sociology* 90: 1231–61.
Giddens, Anthony. 1991. *Modernity and Self-identity: Self and Society in the Late Modern Age*. Stanford, CA: Stanford University Press.
Goldthorpe, J.H. 1996. "Class Analysis and the Reorientation of Class Theory: The Case of Persisting Differentials in Educational Attainment." *British Journal of Sociology* 47: 481–505.
Illouz, Eva. 1997. *Consuming the Romantic Utopia: Love and the Cultural Contradictions of Capitalism*. Berkeley: University of California Press.
——. 2007. *Cold Intimacies: The Making of Emotional Capitalism*. London: Polity.
Kalmijn, M. 1991. "Status Homogamy in the United States." *American Journal of Sociology* 97: 496–523.
——. 1994. "Assortative Mating by Cultural and Economic Occupational Status." *American Journal of Sociology* 100: 422–52.
Kane, Danielle. 2003. "Distinction Worldwide? Bourdieu's Theory of Taste in International Context." *Poetics* 31(5–6): 403–21.
Kohn, Melvin L. 1989. *Class and Conformity: A Study in Values*. Chicago: University of Chicago Press.

Lamont, Michèle. 1992. *Money, Morals, and Manners: The Culture of the French and American Upper-Middle Class*. Chicago: University of Chicago Press.

——. 2000. *The Dignity of Working Men*. New York: Russell Sage Foundation.

Lamont, Michèle and Lareau, Annette. 1988. "Cultural Capital: Allusions, Gaps and Glissandos in Recent Theoretical Developments." *Sociological Theory* 6: 153–68.

Lamont, Michèle and Thévenot, L. 2000. *Rethinking Comparative Cultural Sociology*. Cambridge: Cambridge University Press.

Lareau, Annette. 2003. *Unequal Childhoods: Race, Class, and Family Life*. Berkeley: University of California Press.

Ollivier, Michèle. 2000. "Too Much Money off Other People's Backs: Status in Late Modern Societies." *Canadian Journal of Sociology* 25: 441–70.

Peterson, Richard A. 2005. "Problems in Comparative Research: The Example of Omnivorousness." *Poetics* 33: 257–82.

Savage, M., Warde, A., and Devine, F. 2005. "Capitals, Assets, and Resources: Some Critical Issues." *British Journal of Sociology* 56(1): 31–47.

Sayer, R.A. 2005. *The Moral Significance of Class*. Cambridge: Cambridge University Press.

Simmel, Georg. 1949. "The Sociology of Sociability." *American Journal of Sociology* 55: 254–61.

Straubhaar, Joseph D. 2007. *World Television: From Global to Local*. Newbury Park, CA: Sage.

Torche, Florencia. 2007. "Social Status and Cultural Consumption: The Case of Reading in Chile." *Poetics* 35: 70–92.

Weber, Max. 1946. "The Social Psychology of the World Religions." Pp. 267–301 in H.H. Gerth and C. Wright Mills, eds., *From Max Weber: Essays in Sociology*. New York: Oxford University Press.

——. 1994. *Sociological Writings*. New York: Continuum.

Zavisca, Jane. 2005. "The Status of Cultural Omnivorism: A Case Study of Reading in Russia." *Social Forces* 84: 1233–55.

30

The conundrum of race in sociological analyses of culture

Alford A. Young, Jr.

In what may very well be the most recognized statement in the history of social scientific inquiry on race, W.E.B. Du Bois (1903) wrote in his classic book *The Souls of Black Folk* that the problem of the twentieth century is the problem of the color line. In making this claim, Du Bois forecast what ultimately became a major social preoccupation. Throughout the twentieth century and beyond, race became a central factor in social conflicts that emanated around the globe, and in the formation and (in some cases) re-formation of various nation-states—many of those on the continent of Africa (McKee 1993; Rex 1986; Winant 2001).

A great deal of sociological investigation of race throughout the twentieth century was rooted in a vision of race as a formidable structural force that divided social groups into hierarchies and afforded them differential access to societal resources and rewards. An effect of such dividing and positioning was the production of cultural traits and properties (e.g. attitudes, worldviews, and practices) that were presumed to be directly linked to the social categories (or structural positions) that people occupied. In the latter decades of the twentieth century, however, cultural sociologists and other scholars of race began exploring how race operated as a dynamic cultural artifact as much as (if not more than) an element of the structural arrangements of society. Scholars began seriously examining the centrality of race in various patterns of action, meaning-making, and representation at both individual and collective levels and exploring how these patterns ultimately reshaped as well as reinforced the structural dimensions of society.

Cultural approaches to race attempted to explain how people consciously or inadvertently construct new meanings or interpretations about racial categories, how perceptions of self and of others as racial beings come to surface, how people perform and represent themselves as racial beings, and how people employ discursive and inter-actional strategies to downplay or diminish the significance of race in their under-standings and interpretations of social reality. These research initiatives reveal the ways in which race shapes what people think and do in ways that sometimes challenge and sometimes affirm the structural positions they occupy (whether by choice, imposition, or some combination of the two). It also reveals the extent to which racial categories remain fluid despite the durability of race itself as a social construct. The panoply of concerns and issues suggests that there is an expansive terrain for cultural analyses of race in contemporary sociology.

In documenting cultural analyses of race in modern sociology, this essay first will explore sociology's late-twentieth-century break from early understandings of race as a static dimension of social life and the move toward a logic based upon fluidity and dynamism. I will then consider how cultural analyses have addressed the transformation in racial categories and the meanings attached to them, and how cultural inquiry into racial identity, subjectivity, and representation has reshaped our understanding of everyday lived experience.

Diversifying and loosening of racial categories at the end of the twentieth century

Since its origins and during the first half of the twentieth century, sociologists committed to the study of race and race relations consistently employed classifications such as white, black, Asian, Hispanic, and Native American in ways that promoted the idea that such categories reflected natural and durable distinctions among people (Winant 2000, 2001). As racial categories were strongly associated with geographic regions (white with Europe and subsequently the Western Hemisphere, black with Africa, and Asian with Asia), they maintained fairly durable and consistent meanings because individuals were linked by their racial lineage to one of these regions. As sociology matured from a speculative and reflective field of inquiry into a more structured discipline with formalized research methods and analytical schemes, it was often taken for granted that peoples' identification or association with a geographic arena was central to the formation of their racial identity (Alba 1990; Glazer and Moynihan 1975; Jenkins 1997). Hence, much attention was given to analyzing how the degree of intensity of individuals' racial identification might be associated with social outcomes such as their desire for group boundary maintenance or their commitment to certain notions of collective socio-political outlook or ideology.

Ultimately, the strong turn taken toward cultural analysis in sociology over the past two decades has created opportunities to more fully inject, assess, and problematize the voices of those being studied. As a consequence, sociologists learned that people of color often maintained vastly different orientations and outlooks about social reality compared to white majorities (i.e. those classified as white in the United States and Europe) or compared to Whites with political power irrespective of numerical status (i.e. those classified as white in South Africa, and Latin and Central America). Furthermore, cultural inquiry has demonstrated the wide-ranging differences in how social reality in general, and identity in particular, is defined, interpreted, and made meaningful by people who share a racial classification—differences previously too often masked by research efforts that either falsely or minimally depicted the true diversity of lived experience (see Calhoun 1994; Lemert 2004, 2005).

Both racial boundaries and racial categories are increasingly understood as porous and flexible. Accordingly, critical sociological research increasingly explores how people locate and make sense of themselves rather than simply defining them according to accepted categories. It also highlights the tremendous within-category racial diversity that exists in many communities.

For instance, research has documented that many individuals throughout the world who have been classified as black and who regard such classification as central to their

317

self- and social consciousness may come to quite different understandings of what it means to be black (Frederickson 1995; Gilroy 2000; Winant 2001). Thus, while race may play a salient and pervasive role in the social consciousness of the sub-category of black people labeled African Americans, it takes a wholly different form for many Blacks in Africa, especially as they have not lived as racial minorities in their respective nation-states.

In his analysis of the genocidal actions that took place in 1994 in Rwanda, Mahmood Mamdani (2001) argues that any notion of a collective racial consciousness was irrelevant in assessing why members of a black ethnic group, the Hutu, committed to killing so many members of another black ethnic group, the Tutsi. In effect, colonization by the Belgians created a logic of difference that overrode any capacity for collective racial cohesiveness in twentieth-century Rwanda. This logic of difference was rooted in references to body types, facial features, and other demarcations between the two groups even though there never were any biological grounds for making such distinctions. The maintenance of this logic provided Belgian colonizers with a means of maintaining social control without having to maintain an explicit presence in the region. In essence, those classified as Tutsi were put in a trustee-status so that the social, political, and economic affairs of Rwanda would continue to benefit the colonizers. As Mamdani reported, animosity between the two groups was so intense that, following the massacre in Rwanda, appeals by South African President Nelson Mandela for racial unity struck Rwandans of both ethnic groups as incomprehensible.

In his book *In My Father's House*, Anthony Appiah (1992) also challenges the notion that collective racial consciousness is a predominant feature of social life in Africa. Appiah criticizes what he calls the "Western fiction" of depicting Africans as uniform and homogenous regarding manners of cultural expression and socio-political perspective. This same one-dimensional vision of Africans is also explored in Mamdani's (1996) discussion of race-making in Africa.

Recent sociological attention to other regions largely populated by Blacks underscores the complexity of racial meaning-making in modern life. Consider South Africa, where extreme social differences among black South Africans, often reflecting the numerous ethnic divisions within that racial group, drive patterns of social consciousness in which race plays a secondary or minimal role in how black South Africans think about social identity and cultural commonalities (Frederickson 1995). Brazil represents another nation-centered model of racial complexity, where a much larger scaffolding than the now common black–white–bi-racial troika (still to some measure alive and well in the United States) exists for documenting the variant forms of racial consciousness and identity in that country (Winant 2001).

Analyses of racial meaning-making outside the United States have driven the notion that blackness, as a racial category, not only comes to have different meanings for people situated in vastly different places in the world and in different positions in social hierarchies, but also holds different degrees of relevance for forming interpretations of social reality. It is an insight that applies equally well to the US context. Research on Afro-Caribbeans, for example, shows that many in this ethnic grouping do not read racial conflict or understand race relations in the ways that many African Americans do (Kasinitz *et al.* 2004; Waters 1999). This is because Afro-Caribbeans, like black Africans, lack extensive social experience living as racial minorities, and thus come to possess different kinds of subjective orientations about race in comparison to African Americans. As sociologist Mary Waters (1999) argues, Afro-Caribbeans experience relations with a white world through a lens viewed from their own history of colonization, which is based upon a much more socially distant relationship with Whites given the independence that many Afro-Caribbean nations achieved in the early to mid-twentieth century.

Clearly, cultural analyses that rethink the extent to which cohesion and consistency apply to the meanings attributed to racial categories have not been restricted to the study of blackness. They extend across the other formal racial categories mentioned earlier. For instance, much of the early research in what has become known as "whiteness studies" suggests that a defining feature of whiteness is an engagement with racism and/or racial privilege (Mcintosh 1989). This research tradition thus explores the extent to which people classified as white embrace, reject, or work to transform themselves given the salience of their racial identity (Hartigan 1999; Lewis 2003; Mcintosh 1989). More recently, scholars studying whiteness have focused more directly on the explication of social power. They explore the complex variability of whiteness depending on its inter-section with socioeconomic status and its degree of access to social power and societal resources (see Hartigan 1999). For example, by demonstrating how certain privileged white Americans deem certain lower-income Whites to be "white trash," and, therefore, not legitimately white, Matt Wray (2006) analyzes the ways in which class difference functions simultaneously to diversify white racial identity while reaffirming white racial superiority. Breadth and complexity also characterize comparative research on Whites who do, on the one hand, and who do not, on the other, maintain a highly conscious sense of themselves as white (Perry 2002).

In similar fashion, emerging cultural and culturally informed analyses of people labeled Asian and Asian American have broadened the template within which race is investigated and examined in cultural sociology. Kim (2008) and Prashad (2000, 2001) both highlight (and critique) the extent to which earlier scholarship placed Asians and Asian Americans at the mid-point of the black–white racial classification continuum. They provide a new perspective for exploring Asian and Asian American racialization that attends to historical and cultural specificity: racial identities are forged through varying degrees of attachment to particular ancestral homelands and by the different socio-political climates of the various geographic regions through which people move; moreover, the construction of "Asian-ness" may not correspond in obvious ways to the construction of blackness, and this lack of correspondence challenges the often-implicit assumption that racial subordination in the US be read in relation to the African American experience (African Americans representing the paramount subordinate group).

Indeed, perhaps the most robust challenge to the notion of rigid racial categories has been provided by scholars studying the experiences of bi-racial and multi-racial people. Such research has shifted from efforts to determine how such people locate themselves along a linear continuum ranging from white to black identity (DaCosta 2007; Daniel 2002; Rockquemore and Brunsma 2008) toward a recognition of the continuum's irrelevance to many (and perhaps most) bi- and multi-racial people. Some sociologists have explored the extent to which the very meanings attached to race by multi-racial individuals may shift radically throughout a given day (Harris and Sim 2002). The case of the Colored in South Africa, who are bi-racial in the genealogical sense, further demonstrates the diversity of racial meaning-making. As a result of apartheid, the Colored have cultivated a distinct ethnic and cultural sensibility that does not reflect the kind of contingencies to black or white racial categories that bi-racial citizens

319

in the United States have often had to contemplate, reconcile, or explicitly reject (Frederickson 1995).

De-emphasizing race and racial categories at the end of the twentieth century

Cultural studies of the transformation of meanings attached to racial categories have largely been centered on numerical minorities in various nations or black people in Africa and the Afro-Caribbean region (spaces marked as highly racialized). However, a growing body of work is now focusing on the discursive practices employed to de-emphasize race as a significant feature of social reality. More specifically, some scholars are considering how whites in Europe and the US increasingly avoid talking about race altogether in public debates on socio-political issues—debates in which the very criteria for what constitutes a just or moral society (and how best to achieve it) reflect the interests of dominant racial groups.

Paul Gilroy (1987) early on pursued an analysis of this sort, arguing that the cultural politics of late-twentieth-century Britain increasingly denied black Britains a voice in articulating a sense of nation, national identity, and national destiny. This conservative political project, best exemplified by the leadership of Margaret Thatcher in the 1980s, was characterized by a lack of explicitly racial language in civic discourse about what properly constitutes an English person, yet the end-result was the exclusion of people of color, especially Blacks, from that constitution. The work of Paul Gilroy (1987, 1993a, 1993b, 2000), Stuart Hall (1988, 1997; Hall and du Gay 1996), and others involved with the Birmingham School of Cultural Studies played a crucial role in developing analyses of race as a dynamic, fluid, and ever-changing construct; they also paved the way for making sense of how racial inequality can be sustained in social life precisely through its omission in civic and public discourses concerning mobility, opportunity, and national identity.

Today, sociologists continue to investigate these practices, especially in the United States, where the cultural politics of race took a dramatic turn after the Civil Rights Movement. That turn left many black Americans and other people of color strongly cognizant of the social power and significance of race not only as a tool of oppression, but as a means of galvanizing social change (Carmichael and Hamilton 1967; Collins 1990; Cruse 1967, 1987; Dawson 1994, 2001), even while some white Americans became concerned, if not threatened, by the heightened emphasis on race promoted by people of color (Weisbrot 1990; Blauner 1989; Carson 1981; Hodgson 1976; Sitkoff 1981). Consequently, sociologists such as Michael Omi and Howard Winant (1994) argue that public discussion of race has been transformed since the 1960s, making it harder for formal organizations and groups to use race-specific arguments to encourage government intervention or redress for race-based inequalities. This argument has been more fully elucidated by Stephen Steinberg (1995), who suggests that a defining feature of contemporary socio-political thought concerning race is the absence of substantive public discussion on the matter.

A leading concept used to define the contemporary discourse in which race-based privileges are maintained—while race itself is rarely invoked—is color-blind racism. Although there are seemingly as many definitions of color-blind racism as there are scholars who have explored the phenomenon, the language of Eduardo Bonilla-Silva (2003) captures it well. According to Bonilla-Silva, color-blind racism is constituted by four central frames: abstract liberalism (e.g. blanket claims that all people are equal, and thus preferential treatments of any sort are inherently racist); naturalization (e.g. explaining social segregation as the result of individuals' "natural" preference for homophily); cultural racism (e.g. privileging certain groups not on assumptions of inherent superiority but on assumptions of their more appropriate social functioning or adaptation); and the minimization of racism (e.g. claiming that acts of discrimination or prejudice are actually based upon some other factor or condition).

According to a masterful summary of relevant scholarship by Amanda Lewis (2003), color-blind ideology presumes as well as asserts racial neutrality when such neutrality does not necessarily exist. Moreover, it often stigmatizes attempts to seek redress for racial inequality: those who raise objections are accused of "playing the race card" or of being committed to an outdated and disdained identity politics. All of this unfolds in the course of a robust denial of the salience of race in social interaction and other forms of social experience. So although racism is alive and well, it is not much talked about by those who benefit most from its persistence. Of course, for many African Americans and other people of color, race continues to be extraordinarily well embedded in public discourse about equality and opportunity (Dawson 2001; Hochschild 1995; May 2001).

New considerations of racial performance and representation in the modern world

The consideration thus far has been restricted to how racial categories have been expanded, revised, or challenged by cultural sociologists, and how race has been deployed in public discourses in modern social life. Another body of work examines how race is performed and represented in everyday life.

Carter (2003, 2005), for example, has studied the behavior of adolescents in school and indicated the wide-ranging ways in which blackness is read by Whites as a problematic, if not dangerous, construct that threatens the effective functioning of the institution. Similarly, Bettie's (2003) ethnographic analysis of young Latinas in high school documents the extent to which race-based styles of dress and behavior solidify for the girls an oppositional, class-conscious identity even while ensuring their continued exclusion from the avenues of social mobility afforded by schooling. This work complicates and extends the cultural-structural analysis of Paul Willis in his classic study *Learning to Labor* (1977), about the agentic capacities of low-income British youth in cementing their troubled outcomes in regard to schooling.

Perry (2002) has explored how whiteness is performed differently by adolescents depending on the degree to which their educational context is racially and ethnically diverse: Caucasian students enrolled in racially diverse institutions are able to reflect on how they are "acting like white people," whereas Caucasian students in predominantly white schools remain unaware of how their racial identity might be guiding their actions and choice-making. Other recent work examines how upwardly mobile and professional-class African Americans understand, identify with, and "perform" blackness in different organizational settings such as higher educational institutions (Willie 2003) and in neighborhood contexts characterized by high degrees of racial diversity and intra-racial class difference (Lacy 2007).

321

Yet another important intervention in addressing the cultural politics of representation addresses how people in specific racial categories understand morality, in both personal and collective terms (see Lamont 2000; Young 2004). This body of work demonstrates that cultural inquiry into race need not be restricted to studies of whether and how people think about race, but may focus instead on how people's racial classification informs their thinking about concepts such as dignity, respectability, and selfhood in a more general sense.

Making meaning of race in the future: a cautionary word

Through studies of the flexibility, fluidity, and dynamism of racial categories, of the changing public and civic discourses pertaining to race, and of ways of thinking about, and enacting, racial difference, cultural sociology has significantly advanced our understanding of the social significance of race. The subfield has produced an impressive body of work that recognizes and explores the complexity and diversity of racial-formation processes among people who share the same racial classification and who, in the recent past, might have been thought to share a common identity and politics. The mandate for continuing cultural inquiry into race is supported by social developments that underscore the importance of thinking anew about race. One obvious development is the presidency of Barack Obama. As a black/white bi-racial man whose black ancestry is one generation removed from Kenya, who has a half-sibling of Asian ancestry, and who did not explicitly articulate a racialized political agenda or ideology when he campaigned for the office that he now holds, President Obama is certainly representative of a new, complex understanding of race and racialization in the modern world. He is a prominent public figure whose life story and present situation challenge, if not rupture, the ways by which early generations of sociologists understood race to operate. Although it is unwise to attempt to forecast the future, it appears evident that race will continue to play a significant and prominent role in social processes of meaning-making, identity-formation, and collective consciousness. It may also take unforeseen directions, which may require new nomenclatures for labeling racial categories or new ways of interpreting how race relates to individual and collective thought and action.

References and further reading

Agger, Ben. 2002. *Postponing the Postmodern: Sociological Practices, Selves, and Theories*. Lanham, MD: Rowman and Littlefield.

Alba, Richard D. 1990. *Ethnic Identity: The Transformation of White America*. New Haven, CT: Yale University Press.

Appiah, Kwame Anthony. 1992. *In My Father's House: Africa in the Philosophy of Culture*. New York: Oxford University Press.

Best, Steven and Kellner, Douglas. 1997. *The Postmodern Turn*. New York: Guilford Press.

Bettie, Julie. 2003. *Women without Class: Girls, Race, and Identity*. Berkeley: University of California Press.

Blauner, Robert. 1989. *Black Lives, White Lives: Three Decades of Race Relations in America*. Berkeley: University of California Press.

Bobo, Lawrence, Kluegal, James R., and Smith, Ryan A. 1997. "Laissez Faire Racism: The Crystallization of a 'Kinder, Gentler' Anti-Black Ideology." Pp. 15–42 in Steven A. Tuch and Jack K. Martin, eds., *Racial Attitudes in the 1990s: Continuity and Change*. Westport, CT: Praeger.

Bonilla-Silva, Eduardo. 2003. "New Racism, Color-Blind Racism, and the Future of Whiteness in America." Pp. 271–84 in Ashley Doane and Eduardo Bonilla-Silva, eds., *White Out: The Continued Significance of Racism*. New York: Routledge.

Calhoun, Craig J. 1994. *Social Theory and the Politics of Identity*. Cambridge, MA: Blackwell.

Carmichael, Stokely and Hamilton, Charles V. 1967. *Black Power: The Politics of Liberation in America*. New York: Random House.

Carson, Clayborne. 1981. *In Struggle: SNCC and the Black Awakening of the 1960s*. Cambridge, MA: Harvard University Press.

Carter, Prudence L. 2003. "Black Cultural Capital, Status Positioning, and Schooling Conflicts for Low-Income African American Youth." *Social Problems* 50(1): 136–55.

——. 2005. *Keepin' It Real: School Success beyond Black and White*. Oxford: Oxford University Press.

Collins, Patricia Hill. 1990. *Black Feminist Thought: Knowledge, Consciousness, and the Politics of Empowerment*. Boston: Unwin Hyman.

Cruse, Harold. 1967. *Crisis of the Negro Intellectual*. New York: William Morrow.

——. 1987. *Plural but Equal: A Critical Study of Blacks and Minorities and America's Plural Society*. New York: William Morrow.

DaCosta, Kimberly McClain. 2007. *Making Multiracials: State, Family, and Market in the Redrawing of the Color Line*. Stanford, CA: Stanford University Press.

Daniel, G. Reginald. 2002. *More than Black: Multiracial Identity and the New Racial Order*. Philadelphia, PA: Temple University Press.

Dawson, Michael. 1994. *Behind the Mule: Race and Class in African American Politics*. Princeton, NJ: Princeton University Press.

——. 2001. *Black Visions: The Roots of Contemporary African American Political Ideologies*. Chicago: University of Chicago Press.

Du Bois, W.E.B. 1969 (1903). *The Souls of Black Folk*. New York: The New American Library, Inc.

Farley, Reynolds. 1984. *Blacks and Whites: Narrowing the Gap?* Cambridge, MA: Harvard University Press.

Farley, Reynolds and Allen, Walter R. 1989. *The Color Line and the Quality of Life in America*. New York: Oxford University Press.

Frederickson, George. 1995. *Black Liberation: A Comparative History of Black Ideologies in the United States and South Africa*. Oxford: Oxford University Press.

Gans, Herbert. 1995. *The War against the Poor: The Underclass and Antipoverty Policy*. New York: Basic Books.

Gilroy, Paul. 1987. *Ain't No Black in the Union Jack: The Cultural Politics of Race and Nation*. Chicago: University of Chicago Press.

——. 1993a. *The Black Atlantic: Modernity and Double Consciousness*. Cambridge, MA: Harvard University Press.

——. 1993b. *Small Acts: Thought on the Politics of Black Culture*. New York: Serpent's Tail.

——. 2000. *Against Race: Imagining Political Culture Beyond the Color Line*. Cambridge, MA: The Belknap Press of Harvard University Press.

Glazer, Nathan and Moynihan, Daniel P., eds. 1975. *Ethnicity: Theory and Experience*. Cambridge, MA: Harvard University Press.

Hall, Stuart. 1988. *The Hard Road to Renewal: Thatcherism and the Crisis of the Left*. London: Verso.

—, ed. 1997. *Representation: Cultural Representations and Signifying Practices*. London: Sage Publications.

Hall, Stuart and du Gay, Paul, eds. 1996. *Questions of Cultural Identity*. London: Sage Publications.

Harris, David R. and Sim, Jeremiah Joseph. 2002. "Who Is Multiracial? Assessing the Complexity of Lived Race." *American Sociological Review* 67(4): 614–27.

Hartigan, John, Jr. 1999. *Racial Situations: Class Predicaments of Whiteness in Detroit*. Princeton, NJ: Princeton University Press.

Hochschild, Jennifer. 1995. *Facing Up to the American Dream: Race, Class, and the Soul of the Nation*. Princeton, NJ: Princeton University Press.

Hodgson, Godfrey. 1976. *America in Our Time*. Garden City, NJ: Doubleday.

323

——. 2004. *More Equal Than Others: America from Nixon to the New Century*. Princeton, NJ: Princeton University Press.

Jenkins, Richard. 1997. *Rethinking Ethnicity: Arguments and Explorations*. London: Sage Publications.

Kasinitz, Phillip, Mollenkopf, John, and Waters, Mary C., eds. 2004. *Becoming New Yorkers: Ethnographies of the 'New' Second Generation*. New York: Russell Sage Foundation.

Kim, Nadia. 2008. *Imperial Citizens: Koreans and Race from Seoul to LA*. Palo Alto, CA: Stanford University Press.

Lacy, Karyn. 2007. *Blue Chip Black: Race, Class, and Status in the New Black Middle Class*. Berkeley: University of California Press.

Lamont, Michèle. 2000. *The Dignity of Working Men: Morality and the Boundaries of Race, Class, and Immigration*. New York and Cambridge: Russell Sage Foundation Press.

Lemert, Charles C., ed. 2004. *Social Theory: the Multicultural and Classic Readings*. Oxford: Westview Press.

——. 2005. *Postmodernism Is Not What You Think: Why Globalization Threatens Modernity*. Boulder, CO: Paradigm Publishers.

Lewis, Amanda E. 2003. *Race in the Schoolyard: Negotiating the Color Line in Classrooms and Communities*. New Brunswick, NJ: Rutgers University Press.

Mcintosh, Peggy. 1989. "White Privilege: Unpacking the Invisible Knapsack." *Peace and Freedom* (July/August): 10–12.

McKee, James B. 1993. *Sociology and the Race Problem: The Failure of a Perspective*. Urbana: University of Illinois Press.

Mamdani, Mahmood. 1996. *Citizen and Subject: Contemporary Africa and the Legacy of Late Colonialism*. Princeton, NJ: Princeton University Press.

——. 2001. *When Victims Become Killers: Colonialism, Nativism, and Genocide in Rwanda*. Princeton, NJ: Princeton University Press.

Massey, Douglas and Denton, Nancy. 1993. *American Apartheid: Segregation and the Making of the Underclass*. Cambridge, MA: Harvard University Press.

May, Reuben. 2001. *Talking at Trena's: Everyday Conversations at an African American Tavern*. New York: New York University Press.

Morley, David and Chen, Kuan-Hsing, eds. 1996. *Stuart Hall: Critical Dialogues in Cultural Studies*. New York: Routledge.

Omi, Michael and Winant, Howard. 1994. *Racial Formation in the United States: From the 1960 to the 1990s*, second edition. New York: Routledge.

Perry, Pamela. 2002. *Shades of White: White Kids and Racial Identities in High School*. Durham, NC: Duke University Press.

Prashad, Vijay. 2000. *Karma of Brown Folk*. Minneapolis: University of Minnesota Press.

——. 2001. *Everybody Was Kung Fu Fighting: Afro-Asian Connections and the Myth of Cultural Purity*. Boston: Beacon Press.

Rex, John. 1986. *Race and Ethnicity*. Philadelphia, PA: Open University Press.

Rockquemore, Kerry Ann and Brunsma, David. 2008. *Beyond Black: Biracial Identity in America*. Lanham, MD: Rowman and Littlefield.

Sitkoff, Harvard. 1981. *The Struggle for Black Equality*. New York: Hill and Wang.

Steinberg, Stephen. 1995. *Turning Back: The Retreat from Racial Justice in American Thought and Policy*. Boston: Beacon Press.

Waters, Mary C. 1999. *Black Identities: West Indian Immigrant Dreams and American Realities*. New York: Russell Sage Foundation; Cambridge, MA: Harvard University Press.

Weisbrot, Robert. 1990. *Freedom Bound: A History of America's Civil Rights Movement*. New York: Norton.

Willie, Sarah Susannah. 2003. *Acting Black: College, Identity, and the Performance of Race*. London: Routledge.

Willis, Paul. 1977. *Learning to Labor: How Working Class Kids Get Working Class Jobs*. New York: Columbia University Press.

Winant, Howard. 2000. "Race and Race Theory." *Annual Review of Sociology* 26: 169–85.

———. 2001. *The World is a Ghetto: Race and Democracy since World War II*. New York: Basic Books.

Wray, Matt. 2006. *Not Quite White: White Trash and the Boundaries of Whiteness*. Durham, NC: Duke University Press.

Young, Alford A. Jr. 2004. *The Minds of Marginalized Black Men: Making Sense of Mobility, Opportunity, and Future Life Chances*. Princeton, NJ: Princeton University Press.

31

Culture

Liquid-modern adventures of an idea

Zygmunt Bauman

In (the utterly unlikely) case his name does not ring an enormous bell, here is a handful of hints about his current (AD 2008) cultural standing in London, its surroundings, and its extensions: Stephen Fry, a hugely popular actor, wit, and raconteur, is a most coveted guest to any London party with an ambition of the "talk of the town" rank, and a most coveted address in the directory of any "network" with a reasonable pretense to prestige and significance. Trying to explain the phenomenal success of the Facebook website (attracting 55 million users and the price evaluation of $15bn), the top British Sunday paper noted that "the crowd" of its users, uncharacteristically for "social networking" sites, "included lots of famous types," and suggested that this happened since "how else could you ask Stephen Fry to be your friend?"[1]

Stephen Fry, a personality looked up to by anybody who wishes to be somebody in the world of connoisseurs of the latest cultural fashions, felt it necessary to explain and justify to *Guardian* readers[2] why it is all right for a person like him, acclaimed as a paragon of most refined and sublime culture credentials, to slip once a week into "dork" garb and dedicate his column to the latest electronic gadgets: contraptions deemed to belong to the "popular" (in the past, in times blissfully unaware of "political correctness," known as the "mass"), rather than to the high or high-brow culture (denominations no longer used in the present "politically correct" vernacular, except as a snub—in derision and inverted comas). Fry begins his plea with a confession: he owns a quality which, as he suspects, may be held against him by at least some slow-to-move-on-with-the-times *Guardian* readers: "Digital devices rock my world. This might be looked on by some as a tragic admission. Not ballet, opera, the natural world, Stephen? Not literature, theatre or global politics?" And he hurries to pre-empt the potential charges:

> Well, people can be dippy about all things digital and still read books, they can go to the opera and watch a cricket match and apply for Led Zeppelin tickets without splitting themselves asunder. ... You like Thai food? But what is wrong with Italian? Woah, there... calm down. I like both. Yes. It can be done. I can like rugby football and the musicals of Stephen Sondheim. High Victorian Gothic and the installations of Damien Hirst. Herb Alpert's Tijuana Brass and the piano works

of Hindemith. English hymns and Richard Dawkins. First editions of Norman Douglas and iPods. Snooker, darts, and ballet. ... [A] love of gismos doesn't make me averse to paper, leather, and wood, old-fashioned Christmases, Preston Sturges films, and country walks. Nor does it automatically mean that I read Terry Pratchett, breathe only through my mouth, and bring my head slightly too close to the bowl when I eat soup.

Some limits are still respected and their trespassing is ill advised: Pratchett is left beyond the pale (because of being the second most widely read author in Britain, and therefore too common? As common as some table manners, like bowing head over a soup bowl, instead of lifting hand?). *In toto*, however, this public confession and plea beg to be read as a point-blank challenge to Pierre Bourdieu's idea of "distinction" that ruled and streamlined our thinking of "culture" for the last three decades.

Stephen Fry is known to be a trend-setter, but he is also a most reliable spokesman for (and walking embodiment of) the trends set; he may be trusted to speak not just in his own name, but in the name of hundreds of thousands of card-carrying and millions of aspiring members of the "cultural elite"—people who know the difference between *comme il faut* and *comme il ne faut pas*, and are first to note the moment when that difference becomes different from what it used a moment earlier to be. He did nor err this time either. According to the report written by Andy McSmith and published in the online edition of the *Independent*,[3] authoritative academics gathered in the most authoritative university—Oxford—have proclaimed that a "cultural elite does not exist."

Here, however, McSmith, searching for an adequately hard-biting and stirring title, got it wrong: what John Goldthorpe, the most reputable Oxford social-science researcher, and his team of thirteen have concluded from the data collected from the UK, Chile, Hungary, Israel, Netherlands, and the US, is that what can be found no longer are top people distinguishing themselves from their inferiors by going to the opera and admiring whatever currently has been branded "high arts," while turning up their noses at "anything as vulgar as a pop song or mainstream television." The leopard of the cultural elite is very much alive and biting—it has only changed its spots. Its new spots can be called, since Richard A. Peterson of Vanderbilt University coined the word (Peterson and Simkus 1992), "omnivorousness"—opera *and* pop songs, "high arts" *and* mainstream television; a bit from here, a morsel from there; now this, now that. As Peterson recently put it, "we see a shift in elite status group politics from those high-brows who snobbishly disdain all base, vulgar, or mass popular culture ... to those highbrows who omnivorously consume a wide range of popular as well as highbrow art forms."[4] In other words: *Nihil* "cultural" *a me alienum puto*, though there is nothing "cultural" with which I'd identify unswervingly and uncompromisingly—to the exclusion of other enjoyments. I am everywhere at home, though (or because) that somewhere I'd call my home is nowhere. It is no longer one (refined) taste against another (vulgar). It is omnivorousness against univorousness, the readiness to consume-it-all against a selective disgust. Elite is alive and well, livelier and busier than ever before, too engrossed in all things cultural to have time to proselytize and convert. Apart from "stop fussing, be less selective" and "consume more," it has no message to convey to the crowds of the univores down the cultural hierarchy.

Artistic offers, Bourdieu memorably insisted just a few decades ago, are all class-addressed and class-selected; the triple effect of the separation of classes, of class-assignment, and signification of class membership is their main *raison d'être*, the most seminal of social functions and even perhaps their latent, even if not the manifest, purpose.

In Bourdieu's view, *objets d'art* meant for aesthetic consumption indexed, signaled, and protected class divisions, legibly marking and fortifying the borders that kept classes apart. To sign the borders unambiguously and to guard them effectively, all or most *objets d'art* had to be assigned to mutually exclusive sets—sets that couldn't be mixed, nor should be appreciated and/or possessed conjointly. What counted was not so much their substance and intrinsic virtues or their absence, as their mutual intolerance and the prohibition to mix them—misrepresented as their inherent resistance to gel. There was a high-brow, middle-brow, and low-brow artistic taste—and they could be jumbled together no more than could fire and water. From Bourdieu's *Distinction*, culture emerged chiefly as a contraption used, and possibly also meant, to signify the differences between classes and to keep them different: as a technology deployed in building and protecting class difference, separation, and *hierarchy*. It emerged in much the same condition in which it was situated almost a century earlier by Oscar Wilde: "Those who find beautiful meanings in beautiful things are the cultivated. ... They are the elect to whom beautiful things mean only Beauty."[5] The *elect*. People who set the tune, and set it in a way certain to bring them victory in the song contest. They would surely *find* beautiful meanings, since it was up to them to *decide* what things are beautiful. Before it came to finding those meanings, who if not the elect must have decided where the beautiful meanings were to be sought?

To put it in a nutshell, culture (the set of culturally prompted and "culturally relevant" choices) was a *socially conservative* force. And to acquit itself properly of that function, it needed to apply with equal zeal each of the two apparently opposite expedients: it needed to be similarly, if not yet more resolutely, strict and uncompromising about *exclusion* as it was about *inclusion*. Alongside the signifiers that marked its "inside," culture needed other signifiers that branded/stigmatized the "outside"—markers with the warning label *hic sunt leones* attached. Just like that shipwrecked man from the ostensibly ironic yet morally edifying English story, who when marooned on an uninhabited island needed to build three huts to re-establish and retain his full identity: the first to live in, the second to be used as a club that needs to be attended on evenings, and the third as the club whose threshold should not, and would not, ever be crossed.

When it was published almost forty years ago, Bourdieu's *Distinction* turned upside down the original, Enlightenment-born, and bequeathed idea of "culture." The cultural practice that Bourdieu discovered, revealed, and put on record was a far cry from the inherited model of "culture" construed at the time when the concept was coined and ushered into public vocabulary in the third quarter of the eighteenth century, almost simultaneously with the English concept of "refinement" and the German of "*Bildung*."

At its birth, the idea of "culture" was intended to stand for an instrument of the (power-assisted) progress towards a universal human condition. "Culture" denoted then a *proselytizing* mission, intended to be undertaken and adumbrated in the form of a resolute and sustained effort of *universal* cultivation and enlightenment, of social amelioration, and spiritual uplifting, and the promotion of the "lowly" to the level of those "on top." Or, in Matthew Arnold's inspired and widely echoed phrase from the book under a telling-it-all title, "Culture and Anarchy" (1920 [1869]: 31), as a labor that "seeks *to do away with classes*; to make the best that has been thought and known in the world current everywhere; to make all men live in an atmosphere of sweetness and light"—unpacked in the preface of "Literature and Dogma" (1873) as the job awaiting the seekers: "Culture is the passion for sweetness and light, and (what is more) the passion of *making* them prevail" (emphases added).

"Culture" entered the modern vocabulary as a declaration of *intent*—as a name of an intended *mission* yet-to-be-undertaken. Similarly to the idea from which the intended action drew its metaphorical name—that of *agri*-culture, which juxtaposed the farmers and the field-full of plants they farmed—it served a writ on prospective missionaries, designating in one go the relatively few called to cultivate and those many who waited to be the objects of cultivation: wardens and their wards, teachers and the taught, producers and their products.

"Culture" stood for the planned and hoped-for compact between those in the know (and above all confident to be in the know) and the ignorant (or defined as ignorant by those confident to be knowledgeable); a compact signed unilaterally and put into operation by the emergent "knowledge-class" seeking its setting-the-tune role to be duly respected in the emergent new order about to be built on the ruins of the *ancien régime*. The declared intent was to educate, enlighten, improve, and ennoble *le peuple* freshly re-cast as *les citoyens* of the newly established *état-nation*: the marriage of the emergent nation self-elevating into a sovereign state with the emergent state claiming the role of the nation's guardian. "The project of Enlightenment" allocated to culture (understood as the *labor of cultivation*) the status of a principal tool of nation, state, and nation-state *building*; simultaneously, it appointed the knowledge-class as that tool's principal operator. In its travels from political ambition to philosophical ruminations and back, the two-pronged objective of the enlightenment venture (whether explicitly proclaimed or tacitly presumed) had promptly crystallized as the discipline of *state-subjects* and the solidarity of *nationals*.

The emergent nation-state felt emboldened by the fast-swelling numbers of "the people," since the rising number of potential worker-soldiers was believed to raise its power differential. As the nation-building efforts, conjointly with economic progress, sedimented growing numbers of "redundant" individuals (indeed, entire categories of population that urgently needed to be disposed of, lest the sought-after order fail to come up, or its growth be severely disturbed; see Bauman 2005), the newly established nation-state was also soon pressed to start looking for spaces outside its borders fit to accommodate the excess of products and people it could not absorb itself. The resulting empire-building and colonizing efforts gave a powerful boost to the Enlightenment-born idea of "culture"—and an altogether new dimension to the proselytizing mission which that idea implied. In the likeness of the "enlightening the people" vision, the concept of the "white man's burden" and "lifting the savages out of their savagery" was shaped. It was soon to be given a theoretical gloss in the form of "cultural evolution theory," which assigned to the "developed" part of the globe the role of the "most advanced" pattern, to which the rest of the planet was destined sooner or later to rise (or be risen) and which they ought to be actively helped (or coerced) to follow; the theory of "cultural evolution" cast the "developed societies" as the planetary center with a missionary role toward the rest of humanity. The future role of that center was conceived after the pattern of the function claimed by and/or assigned to the knowledge elite in its relation with "the people" inside the colonial metropoly.

Bourdieu designed his study, collected his data, and interpreted his findings at a time when the above job by and large had been completed—at least inside the "center" in which the maps of the world and its anticipated/postulated futures were drawn (though not in its imperial extensions, from which the expeditionary forces of the "center" were ever more spectacularly forced into retreat well before bringing the realities up to its standards). Inside the center, the two-centuries-old declaration of intention had spawned a wide-ranging and comprehensive network of mostly state-conceived and state-run institutions, strong enough to rely for their continuous operation on their own momentum, entrenched routine, and bureaucratic inertia. The intended product ("the people" reincarnated as "citizens") was in place, and the position of knowledge-classes in the new order was, or at least was believed to be, secure. Rather than as a bold, iconoclastic adventure, a crusade, and a mission, culture looked (and could be credibly talked about) as a homeostatic contraption, a sort of gyroscope rendering the established nation-state resistant to cross-winds and keeping it on a steady course (or, in the influential Talcott Parsons's phrase, making the "system" "self-equilibrating").

In a nutshell: from a weapon of modern revolution, "culture" turned into a preservative/stabilizer, a homeostat or a gyroscope, of the modern status quo. In this moment precisely (a brief and transient moment, as it was soon to become clear) it had been caught—immobilized and frozen snapshot-style, explored, and recorded—in Bourdieu's *Distinction*. Bourdieu's report belonged to the Owl of Minerva's type of wisdom: it scanned the landscape bathing in the light of the setting Sun, thrown on the contours already starting to dissolve in the darkness of night. It caught the status-servicing, homeostatic, society-reproducing, and system-equilibrating culture on its way to the imminent and already fast-approaching redundancy.

That redundancy was the outcome of several processes contributing to the passage from the "solid" to the "liquid" form of modernity (the term "liquid modernity" denotes the presently prevailing state of the modern condition, also called by other authors by the names of "postmodernity," "late modernity," "second modernity," or "hypermodernity"). What makes modernity "liquid" is the compulsive and obsessive, unstoppably accelerating "modernization," through which—just like liquids—no forms of social life are able to retain their shapes for long. "Melting of solids," an endemic/defining feature of *all* modern forms of life, continues—but melted solids are no longer intended, as before, to be replaced by "new and improved," "more solid" solids, hoped to be immune to all further melting.

The realities about to be "dissolved in the darkness" at the time Bourdieu's study was published were those viewed and described through the prism of the "self-equilibrating system"—the ideal model which the nation-states of the "solid" phase of the modern era repeatedly declared it to be their intention to attain, and a condition which they time and again, with keen help from their learned panegyrists, pretended to have reached. Since properly functioning homeostatic appliances (that is, such as effectively fight back, or better yet pre-empt, all and any deviation from the chosen systemic model— and promptly restore the temporarily lost balance) are crucial to the survival of self-equilibrating systems, the impulse to define/evaluate all and any part or aspect of social totality in terms of their homeostatic capacity and effect was a natural tendency of societies that believed themselves to be, or intended to become, such a system. It was also natural for them to view all deviations from the chosen model with suspicion—as factors adding avoidable stress to the labors of systemic self-equilibration, and potentially throwing the totality out of balance. As long as nation-states entertained their initial ambitions, that tendency seemed well founded; taking the stabilizing effects for the criterion of "functionality" seemed therefore self-evident and immune to questioning. Since the nation-states have been forced/encouraged/determined to abandon those ambitions, however, foundations no longer look unshakable; measuring "functionality" of institutions by the strength of their system-stabilizing effects has stopped therefore seeming like the obvious way to proceed.

As long (but only as long) as the ambitions to construe a self-equilibrating system stayed alive, the homeostatic vision of culture did not need to fear serious contestation. But the ambitions started to fade and eventually had to be, reluctantly at first but later willingly, abandoned under the pressure of globalization. Dissipation of ambitions gradually exposed the vulnerable and increasingly fictional nature of system boundaries and in the end called the bluff of territorial sovereignty—and so also of the self-sustained and self-equilibrating systems confined to the nation-state territory.

Most seminal impacts of globalization (above all, the divorce of power from politics, and in its consequence the progressive surrender of its traditional functions by weakening states and their ensuing exemption from political control) have been by now thoroughly investigated and described in great detail. I will confine myself therefore to one aspect of the globalization process—too seldom considered in connection with the paradigmatic change in the study and theory of culture—namely, the changing patterns of global migration.

There were three different phases in the history of modern-era migration. The first wave of migration followed the logic of the tri-partite syndrome: territoriality of sovereignty, "rooted" identity, gardening posture (subsequently referred to as TRG). That was the emigration from the "modernized" center (read: the home of order-building and of economic-progress—the two main industries turning out and off the growing numbers of "wasted humans"), ca. 60 million people altogether, to "empty lands" (read: lands whose native population could be struck off from most calculations and accounts; be literally "uncounted" and "unaccounted for," presumed either non-existent or irrelevant), founding there new and hopefully perfected replicas of England, Scotland, or Wales, and London, Berlin, Amsterdam, or Warsaw. Whatever had remained of the indigenous population after a spate of wholesale murders and similarly massive epidemics has been cast as another edition of "the people" awaiting "acculturation"—and dealt with as suggested by the "white man's mission."

The second wave of migration can be best modeled as an "Empire emigrates back" case. With the dismantling of colonial empires, a number of indigenous "people" in various stages of their enlightenment and "cultural advancement" followed their colonial superiors to the metropolis. Upon arrival, they were cast in the only worldview-strategic mold available: one construed earlier in the nation-building era to deal with the categories earmarked for "assimilation," that is, a process aimed at annihilation of cultural difference and casting the "minorities" at the receiving end of crusades, *Kulturkämpfe*, and proselytizing missions (currently renamed, following the rules of political correctness, as "citizenship education" aimed at "integration"). This story is not yet finished: time and again, its echoes reverberate in the declarations of intent of the politicians following the habits of Minerva's Owl, known to spread its wings at dusk: just as in the first phase of migration, efforts to squeeze the drama of the "empire migrating back" into the frame of the now outdated TRG syndrome are in vain.

The third wave of modern migration, now in full force and still gathering momentum, leads into the age of *diasporas*—a world-wide archipelago of ethnic/religious/linguistic settlements oblivious to the trails blazed and paved by the imperialist-colonial episode and following instead the globalization-induced logic of the planetary redistribution of life resources. Diasporas are scattered and diffused, they extend over many nominally sovereign territories, ignore territorial claims to supremacy (and preferably exclusivity)

331

of the local demands and obligation, and are locked in the double bind of "dual (or multiple) nationality" and dual (or multiple) loyalty. Present-day migration differs from the two previous phases by moving both ways (virtually no countries are nowadays exclusively "immigrant" or "emigrant"), and privileging no routes (routes are no longer determined by the imperial/colonial links of the past). It differs also in exploding the old TRG syndrome and replacing it with a EAH one (extraterritoriality, "*a*nchors" displacing the "roots" as primary tools of identification, *h*unting strategy).

The new migration casts a question mark upon the bond between identity and citizenship, individual and place, and neighborhood and belonging. Jonathan Rutherford (2007: 59–60), acute and insightful observer of the fast-changing frames of human togetherness, notes that the residents of the London street on which he lives form a neighborhood of different communities, some with networks extending only to the next street, others which stretch across the world. It is a neighborhood of porous boundaries in which it is difficult to identify who belongs and who is an outsider. What is it we belong to in this locality? What is it that each of us calls home and, when we think back and remember how we arrived here, what stories do we share?

Living like the rest of us (or most of that rest) in a diaspora (how far stretching, and in what direction(s)?) among diasporas (how far stretching and in what direction(s)?) has for the first time forced onto the agenda the issue of "art of living with *a* difference"—which may appear on the agenda only once the difference is no longer seen as merely temporary, and so now, unlike in the past, urgently requiring arts, skills, teaching, and learning. The idea of "human rights," promoted in the EAH setting to replace/complement the TRG institution of territorially determined citizenship, translates today as *the right to remain different*. By fits and starts, that new rendition of the human–rights idea sediments, at best, *tolerance*; it has as yet to start in earnest to sediment *solidarity*. And a moot question remains as to whether it is fit to conceive group solidarity in any other form than that of the fickle and fray, predominantly virtual "networks," galvanized, and continually re-modeled by the interplay of individual connecting and disconnecting, calling and messaging initiatives, and their termination.

The new rendition of the human–rights idea also disassembles hierarchies and tears apart the imagery of upward ("progressive") evolution. Forms of life float, meet, clash, crash, catch hold of each other, merge, and hive off with (to paraphrase Simmel) equal specific gravity. Steady and stolid hierarchies and evolutionary lines are replaced with interminable and endemically inconclusive battles of recognition; at the utmost, with eminently renegotiable pecking orders. Imitating Archimedes, reputed to insist (probably with a kind of desperation which only the utter nebulousness of a project might cause) that he would turn the world upside down if only given a fulcrum, we may say that we would tell who is to assimilate to whom, whose dissimilarity/idiosyncrasy is destined for the chop and whose is to emerge on top, were we only given a hierarchy of cultures. Well, we are not given it, and unlikely to be so anytime soon.

Indeed, in the part of the world where pleas on behalf of culture, including Fry's, are composed and voiced, avidly read and hotly debated, the arts have lost (or at any rate are fast losing) their function of the handmaiden of social hierarchy struggling to reproduce—just as some time earlier culture as a whole lost its original function of the handmaiden of emergent nations, states, and class hierarchies. One by one, all such tasks have either lost their application and topicality, or come to be performed by other means and using different instruments. Emancipated from the obligations imposed on the culture-creators and culture-operators from a missionary at first, and later the homeostatic functions of their labors, the arts (in the expanded meaning that in the era of intense individualization and widening sphere of "life politics" came to include the art of life) are free to serve the individual concerns with self-identification and self-assertion, that shift the issue of "belonging" from the "before" to the "after" of individually made choices. We may say that culture (and most conspicuously, though not at all uniquely, its artistic branch) is in its liquid-modern phase made to the measure of (willingly pursued, or endured as obligatory) *individual* freedom of choice. And that it is *meant* to service such freedom. And that it is meant to insure that the choice remains *unavoidable*: a life necessity, and a duty. And that responsibility, the inalienable companion of free choice, stays where the liquid-modern condition forced it—on the shoulders of the *individual*, now appointed the sole manager of "life politics."

This is not a mere paradigm *shift*, one might say; we could and should speak instead of a "paradigm *earthquake*." One might say that, were it not a fact that having moved to the liquid-modern setting together with the realities to which it referred in the solid-modern past, the term "paradigm" has joined the fast-growing family of the (as Ulrich Beck would say) "zombie concepts" or (as Jacques Derrida would prefer) concepts which need to be used *sous rature*—or better yet not used at all. Liquid modernity is a permanent war of attrition waged against any and all paradigms—and indeed any other homeostatic, conformity-and-routine-promoting contraptions, meant to sustain monotony and repetitiveness of events. That concerns the paradigmatic (bequeathed by solid modernity) *concept* of culture as much as it does the *culture* itself (the sum total of human-made, intentional artifices), which that concept intended to grasp and render intelligible.

Today culture consists of *offers*, not *norms*. As already noted by Bourdieu, culture lives by seduction, not normative regulation; PR, not policing; creating new needs/desires/wants, not coercion. This society of ours is a society of consumers, and just as the rest of the world as-seen-and-lived by consumers, culture turns into a warehouse of meant-for-consumption products—each vying for the shifting/drifting attention of prospective consumers in the hope of attracting it and holding it for a bit longer than a fleeting moment. Abandoning stiff standards, indulging indiscrimination, serving all tastes while privileging none, encouraging fitfulness and "flexibility" (the politically correct name of spinelessness), and romanticizing unsteadiness and inconsistency is therefore the proper (the only reasonable?) strategy to follow; fastidiousness, raising brows, stiffening upper lips is not recommended. The TV reviewer/critic of the same pattern-and-style-setting organ in which Fry's apology was published praised the New Year's Eve 2007/08 broadcast for promising "to provide an array of musical entertainment guaranteed to sate everyone's appetite." "The good thing" about it, he explained, "is that its universal appeal means you can dip in and out of the show depending on your preferences."[6] A commendable and indeed a seemly quality in a society in which networks replace structures, where the attachment/detachment game and an unending procession of connections and disconnections replace "determining" and "fixing."

The current phase of the graduated transformation of the idea of "culture" from its original Enlightenment-inspired form to its liquid-modern reincarnation is prompted and operated by the same forces that promote emancipation of the markets from any remaining constraints of a non-economic nature—social, political, and ethical constraints among them. In pursuing its own emancipation, liquid-modern consumer-focused economy relies on the excess of offers, their accelerated aging, and quick dissipation of their seductive power—which, by the way, makes it an economy of profligacy and waste. Since there is no knowing in advance which of the offers may prove tempting

333

enough to stimulate consuming desire, the only way to find out leads through trials and costly errors. A continuous supply of new offers and a constantly growing volume of goods on offer are also necessary to keep circulation of goods rapid and the desire to replace them with "new and improved" goods constantly refreshed—as well as to prevent the consumer dissatisfaction with individual products from condensing into the general disaffection with the consumerist mode of life as such.

Culture is turning now into one of the departments in the "all you need and dream of" department store into which the world inhabited by consumers has turned. As in other departments of that store, the shelves are tightly packed with daily restocked commodities, while the counters are adorned with the commercials of latest offers, destined to disappear soon together with the attractions they advertise. Commodities and commercials alike are calculated to arouse desires and trigger wishes (as George Steiner famously put it, for "maximum impact and instant obsolescence"). Their merchants and copywriters count on the wedding of the offers' seductive power with the ingrained "one-upmanship" and "getting an edge" urges of the prospective customers.

Liquid-modern culture has no "people" to "cultivate." It has instead the clients to seduce. And unlike its "solid modern" predecessor, it no longer wishes to work itself, eventually but the sooner the better, out of job. Its job is now to render its own survival permanent—through temporalizing all aspects of life of its former wards, now reborn as clients.

Notes

1 See Ian Tucker, "Facebook Makes a Lot of New Friends," *Observer Magazine*, December 23, 2007: 35.
2 See "Welcome to Dork Talk," *Guardian Weekend*, October 27, 2007.
3 http://news.independent.co.uk.this_britain/article3266586.ece.
4 See his summary of, and illuminating reflection on, two decades of his own and related studies in "Changing Arts Audiences: Capitalizing on Omnivorousness." Presented at a workshop on October 14, 2005 (culturalpolicy.uchicago.edu).
5 See Oscar Wilde, *The Picture of Dorian Gray*, Wordsworth Editions, 1992: 3.
6 See Philip French, "A Hootenanny New Year to All," *Observer Television*, December 30, 2007–January 5, 2008: 6.

References

Arnold, Matthew. 1920 (1869). *Culture and Anarchy*, first edition text. New York: Macmillan.
——. 1873. *Literature and Dogma*. London: Smith, Elder.
Bauman, Zygmunt. 2005. *Wasted Lives*. Cambridge: Polity Press.
Peterson, Richard A. and Simkus, Albert. 1992. "How Musical Tastes Mark Occupational Status Groups." Pp. 152–86 in Michele Lamont and Marcel Fournier, eds., *Cultivating Differences: Symbolic Boundaries and the Making of Inequality*. Chicago: University of Chicago Press.
Rutherford, Jonathan. 2007. *After Identity*. London: Laurence & Wishart.

Part VI
Making/using culture

32

Environment and culture

Trevor Hogan, Divya Anand, and
Kirsten Henderson

The nature–culture dialectic

Nature is fate, culture is destiny. Nature is the condition of our material existence, culture is our only means of encountering and re-forming nature. At the outset of a new millennium, we are beginning to understand that the collective fate of humankind is in our own hands but if we continue to ignore our natural limits we shall experience the consequences in ways beyond existing cultural capacities.

Once upon a time, plastic trees were planted along a freeway in LA then uprooted by protesting citizens. But it might be asked: "What's wrong with plastic trees?" (Krieger 1973). We live after the "end of nature" (McKibben 1989). It is we moderns who first learned to privilege artifice over nature and now imagine post-nature. No part of the planet remains untouched by humans. All landscapes are enculturated, which is to say we see, reflect, inscribe, and act upon the natural worlds that surround us (which we call environment or that which environs us) (Hogan 2003; Seddon 1997). We experience nature but our senses are mediated by our own languages, social imaginaries, and technologies. For humans, nature is cultural and not only in ways of our choosing. It can be said that it is in our human nature to be cultural. We have the material resources to mass produce the simulacra of natural things. In mimicking the ways and forms of nature we also change our meanings and values of nature, and of our own appropriations, significations, imaginaries, and interventions.

We not only mimic nature, we consume it (Flannery 1995). Yet, we are still embodied, material beings that depend upon, and use, our "environment" for survival. Being near the top of the food chain we are beginning to face the consequences of centuries of *homo sapiens*' domination of other species, a domination that has led to the extinction of many other species of flora and fauna. Some of the animals under threat of extinction compete with human populations for resources. Not only do we have these problems with untamed animals, we have also made a massive imprint on the earth's surface with domestication programs—of livestock through to pets. Animals used for food production have radically reshaped nature, turning parts of all continents from wilderness areas into landscapes. But the process of enculturation is never one way; human societies that work with animals are shaped by this close alliance that is at once cooperative and exploitative (with the power heavily weighted in favor of the *homo sapiens* masters). Pastoralist, agri-cultural, and industrial-urban societies alike have for many centuries worked with animals in taming nature for productive purposes. These relationships in turn have reshaped collective social imaginaries, institutions, and cultures—to name but three examples, the Olympic Games, circuses, and horse-racing industries. In each of these areas of human endeavor and play, *homo sapiens* is deploying animals that reflect our collective identities as *homo faber* even as we exhibit our own capacities and characters as *homo ludens*. So too our everyday conversation and jokes remind us of our codependencies and taboos (e.g. sheep jokes in pastoralist societies).

If thinking human culture *vis-à-vis* our environment were not complex enough in relation to animals, our domination of nature in food production extends the challenge to vegetarians, omnivores, and carnivores alike. This is especially the case since the industrialization of the countryside from at least the eighteenth century in England, exported to the world by the beginning of the twentieth century, not least in the mass production of food. It is another sign of our times: once mighty rivers dammed and reduced to streams and mass storage lakes to irrigate thousands of hectares of mono-cultures for mass consumption elsewhere, e.g. the tomato, the potato (for chips), maize (for corn syrup) are but three famous examples in the US. These foods are genetically modified, processed, and then distributed and consumed in contexts and settings very different from their original points of production. But the story of our use and depen-dency on nature is not only about production. Even the most humble of foodstuffs, such as cereals and "root" vegetables, are highly enculturated objects that go to the very center of human significatory practices and social imaginaries (see Gallagher and Greenblatt 2000). A plethora of recipe books, celebrity chefs, global food histories, and genealogies of particular food types (the curry leaf, the tomato, the potato, and the coffee bean) in recent decades underscores this critical insight.

In this essay, we address this dialectic of nature and culture by first defining the key terms "nature" and "environment." Because the elemental forces of nature are the absolute conditions of our material being, becoming, and dying (individually and col-lectively), it is a common-sense view to presuppose that nature is underlying and impervious to human being and action upon it. "Nature is natural: it just is!" Over the past century, social theory and the social sciences more generally have gone a long way to shifting this common sense to a critical sense of nature: these days it is relatively uncontroversial to assert the enculturation of nature. We affirm this achievement but add the rider that we are in danger of creating a new common sense that loses purchase on the radical otherness of nature that both forms and informs our very existence and destiny. The nature–culture dialectic demands that we read our own culture in and through nature, and that we understand nature as that which is not ultimately subordinate to human action. Having first restored our critical appreciation of nature/environment, we then seek to rethink "culture" in the active present tense of human being and becoming.

Our essay then shifts register to put our discussions of key concepts to work on two regional case studies involving a key element—water—in order to display the differing and changing meanings, stories, institutions, and actions that shape human engagement with ecological settings. We hope that these examples not only illustrate the value of what Jeffrey Alexander and Philip Smith (2001) have called "a strong program of cultural sociology," but promote a cultural sociology that places the nature–culture dialectic at the forefront of a rethinking of culture as performative, autonomous, creative, and in continuous movement.

Defining "nature" and "environment"

We use the terms "nature" and "environment" interchangeably, with the former the generic term, and the latter as its sub-set—a specific example or expression of nature as a whole. In doing so, we are reflecting the bias of the greater part of Western literature and specifically of the English language. "Environs" is a Middle English word that depicts that which surrounds us. Thomas Carlyle, a renowned coiner of many new words and trafficker of exotic terms into common English-language parlance, is said to have been the first—in the 1820s—to turn "environment" from a verb to a noun: his specific innovation was to give the term a sociological application from its original natural life-sciences context (*Oxford English Dictionary on Historical Principles* 1993).

But it is "nature" rather than "environment" that has dominated debates about modernity, and for the very good reason that nature points us back to the material terms of being and becoming and dying—something that is tangibly beyond human mastery, an objective and critical horizon above and beyond our own interests and concerns. To put the matter in common-sense terms, "human nature" is only a bit part of "nature" writ large. The term "environment," on the other hand, too readily keeps an uncritical (i.e. unthinking, unselfconscious) focus on ourselves. We humans have been too readily given to speaking of "our" environment as if it is simply a background context that we own and which we deploy for our own interests, uses, and pleasures alone.

One of the most familiar—and enduring—understandings of nature in culture is that of nature as an infinite storehouse of wealth upon which industrial capitalism and the consequent flourishing of human culture are built. The famous exponent of this idea is Karl Marx. Far from viewing the progressive technological exploitation of nature for societal reproduction and change as a problem, Marx shares with the political economists from Adam Smith onwards an enthusiasm for the liberation of humanity from dependence on nature—as a liberation from "nature idolatry" and "rural idiocy." For Marx, the capitalist mode of production uses nature as object, subordinate to human interest and mastery. The potential that these new material conditions of plenty offer for *homo faber* to obtain the just conditions of good work and freedom from exploitation, alienation, and immiseration was the hope of the young Marx. Capitalism's technological revolutionary potential for freeing humans from work itself is the hope of the late Marx (Rabinbach 1998). As for Marx, so too the dreams of "progress" and "development" in the twentieth century.

By the time the Frankfurt School theorists, Horkheimer and Adorno, came to write *Dialectic of Enlightenment* in 1944, however, they had witnessed two world wars, a great depression, and the rise of Bolshevism and Fascism. Consequently, they were less sanguine about human prospects. The paradox of human domination of nature in modernity is for Horkheimer and Adorno the tragedy of development first grasped by Goethe's *Faust*. Far from liberating human beings from the vagaries of superstition, scarcity and want, the development of instrumental reason and the systematic separation of human culture from its natural basis had produced a fundamental contradiction. Horkheimer and Adorno recognized that human mastery via instrumental reason not only led to alienation from nature but to the domination of one human group over another (i.e. of masters over slaves, from, between, and across classes, races,

339

and genders). The rule of reason was founded on a myth of reason that was ultimately tyrannical.

As Murphy and Roberts (2004) highlight, however, modernity is characterized by a dialectic not just of enlightenment but also of romanticism. There is more than one way to be modern: nature is not only subjected to an instrumental rationality of domination, exploitation, and alienation, but is also a complex semiotic well-spring for a radical alteration in human self-understanding and engagement with the non-human world, embracing the sciences, religions, aesthetics, and new versions of subjectivity and reflexivity. This dialectic of romanticism *vis-à-vis* the non-human worlds involves various contradictory constructions of its otherness—as the sublime (wilderness) and as the projection of human affectivities and individuated self-formation. The significance of romanticism in all its various instituted cultural formations as a quintessentially modern phenomenon is underscored by the rise of various social movements of reform, from preservation and conservation to anti-urbanism and urban reform, along with their associated new institutions, professions, and bureaucracies of management.

It is in this context (mainly "First World" trans-Atlantic), that "environment" as a popular term of discourse has emerged since the mid-twentieth century. The rise of environmentalism manifested in social movements and ecological politics has brought the term "environment" into popular consciousness and everyday use. As demonstrated in the work of the Australian eco-political theorist and activist Robyn Eckersley (1992), these movements and ideas have deep roots in the emergence of romanticism in the late eighteenth and early nineteenth centuries. Eckersley develops a typology of contemporary environmental movements and ideas that connects the historic emancipatory promise of the dialectic of enlightenment and the deep ecological values of the dialectic of romanticism as revealed in contemporary left socialist, anarchist, feminist, and ecological movements. She grades them according to their normative orientations—from anthropocentricity to eco-centricity, and from mono-dimensional to comprehensive eco-political policies and programs. This exercise is helpful insofar as it highlights the intrinsic importance of ontological, epistemological, and aesthetic dimensions of cultures and repositions the ideological and material interests of political movements *vis-à-vis* the question of culture itself.

Defining "culture"

"Culture" is the abiding preoccupation of sociology. The contrast with "environment" is substantial. Environment is at best outside the house of society. It has been an "external environment," as it were, to a century of conceptual and methodological struggles concerning social structure and agency. Compared to the somewhat tortuous journey of the concept "culture," "environment" has not been a conceptual problem for sociology. Rather it has been treated as an external variable. The rise of a sub-discipline called "environmental sociology" represents a reflexive anxiety and ethical response by sociologists rather than a critical re-conceptualization of sociology's own terms of discourse. Even where a leading English environmental sociologist, Steven Yearley (2005), looked at the *Cultures of Environmentalism*, he undercut his own cultural turn by expressing a suspicion of theory and rhetorically resorting to concept-free empiricism. We are left with an undialectical appreciation of both "nature" and "culture" alike, let alone a dialectic of the nature–culture relation. Even sociologists' attempts to conceptualize the environment—most famously, Ulrich Beck's risk theory—whilst empirically rich in application persist in viewing collective social action and decision-making as matters of calculative reason, and as power struggles between contesting stakeholders and vested interests (Lash *et al.* 1996).

So, how best can we think about culture so that environmental concerns and the question of the nature–culture dialectic can be brought into the house of sociological theory? At the risk of simplification and in potted form, we nominate four ways to think about culture:

1   *Culture is performed.* This is the ordinary anthropological sense of culture as something held and practiced in common—a whole way of life. Culture is something humans do. Therefore, we need to keep the critical focus on our doing and our thinking of our doing. This means paying more attention to narrative, to place and time, and finding ways of talking about the practice of culture and less on identifying factors, variables, and abstract ratios of power.

2   *Culture is autonomous.* Culture is viewed here as signs, customs, symbols, codes, and texts of meaning. It thus is not reducible to power structures or social construction itself (Alexander and Smith 2001). Sociology, as the in-house professional discipline of trans-Atlantic modernity, has too readily held culture hostage to power—modernization, social action, and systems theories. We think that in the twentieth century sociological theorists became so obsessed with structures and the science of power that they lost purchase on understanding culture as creation, reflexivity, and expressivity.

3   *Culture is creative.* Human cultures are expressive, reflexive, and creative. Collective creativity in turn needs to be explained as socio-historical yet unfounded by any external agency and not reducible to logics of material or social power (Castoriadis 1997). Hence the notion of the "social imaginary" is intrinsic to any self-respecting cultural sociology.

4. *Culture travels.* And in its movement it is transformed. So culture is not only hybrid (Bhabha 1994; Canclini 1995), it is embedded in a series of relationships and exchanges across time and place that are asymmetrical but reflexive and transformative (Beilharz 1997; Smith 1960). The classic text here is William McNeill's *The Rise of the West* (1963), which in turn is a reply to Oswald Spengler's theory of self-enclosed civilizations in *The Decline of the West* (1922–23 [1980]). McNeill treats Eurasia as a single civilization defined by cultural exchange. Moreover, the more hybrid and impure the culture, the further it travels (Sassoon 2006).

Towards a strong program of environmental cultural sociology: two case studies

Let us see if we can seek some potential ways of developing a strong program of cultural sociology—that is, one that views culture as performative, autonomous, creative, and in continuous movement—by putting the program to work on the nature–culture dialectic. To do so, we look at a natural resource essential to human survival and security, namely "water." Water is one of the most powerfully symbolic elements across all human cultures. It is used in "baptisms, libations, holy ablutions, fertility rites, for blessings and protection, and mortuary rituals" (Strang 2004: 85). When it is flowing, it is characterized as the "river of life," as a metaphor for the passing of time. In many locations such as

341

Lourdes, Bath, and the Ganges, it is believed to have healing properties. By considering a ubiquitous and quintessential natural element that is absolutely and universally essential to human survival and flourishing, we can tease out and highlight how human beings enculturate water in our naming, imagining, institutions, and uses of it. Moreover, recovering the centrality of nature to our survival and the meanings we give to nature in our social stories and traditions is, we believe, central to the task of interpreting contemporary environmental political struggles within and across nations and regions. We examine just two examples in the Asia–Pacific region—the Sundarbans in the Bay of Bengal (an eco-region that crosses a nation-state border), and the Australian island-continent (a set of social imaginaries, cultural practices, and policy regimes within a federated polity). Important to our argument, these two examples incorporate and cut across the standard sociological structuralisms of class, ethnicity, and gender that inform most environmental political and sociological analyses. They demonstrate a more general point—that any regional analysis today involves respect for civilizations, empire-colonies, nation-states, local governments, and global, national, and regional markets. In sum, they point to the need for a cultural sociology of environmental struggles even if we have not yet provided the means to its achievement.

Case study I: the Sundarbans, Bay of Bengal—a mangrove forest delta swamped by human problems

The Sundarbans is the world's largest mangrove forest area. In it, continent meets ocean in a maze of rivers spawning thousands of islands. Water is the primary element of the ecology, sustaining varied ecosystems where islands change shape with every turn of the tide. In turn, water shapes the ecological and political history of the region. Our case study reveals how creativity functions along multiple paths in the construction of social imaginaries in a unique water ecology. To tell this story we must unravel the issues of human migration, political geography, and economic development before we can understand the nature of the water issue that saturates the environment and human imaginations alike.

In this complex and dynamic water ecology can be found the largest contiguous population of tigers in the world (their man-eating trait is attributed to the physical properties of the water), living in uneasy alliance with a human population of seven million. The divisions are not merely between humans, animals, and flora, but are political also. The Partition of India and Pakistan in 1947 meant that 60 percent of the Sundarbans was apportioned to East Pakistan (Bangladesh after 1971), triggering an exodus of refugees into India. The majority of early refugees were the upper-caste, educated elite (*bhadralok*), who with their social mobility easily integrated with mainstream Calcutta society. Unlike the *bhadralok*, the lower-class, lower-caste refugees (*nimnobarno*) were met with grossly inadequate rehabilitation practices and forcible relocation. In a specific instance, refugees seeking a familiar water ecology occupied the island of Morichjhapi. The island was part of the tiger-reserve buffer zone, and to "protect" the tiger the government forcibly evicted the refugees, leaving several thousand dead (Biswas 1982: 19). The Morichjhapi episode of 1979 found its way into local narratives reconciling the violence perpetrated on the islanders by the state and the man-eating tigers. The people believe that the idyllic relationship between humans and tigers was broken after the Morichjhapi incident, when—following the lead of the *bhadralok* mistreatment of the *nimnobarno* and the government protecting the tiger at the cost of human lives—the tigers began eyeing the poor as "tiger-food" (Jalais 2005: 1758). The cultural interpretation of the tiger–human conflict tied up with the class/caste struggle points to the dynamism with which the physical environment continuously refashions cultural narratives. The villagers rationalize and adapt to their social past and to the changes in their immediate physical environment by a creative reinvention of traditional beliefs. Culture and environment emerge as interlinked parts of a system of relationships that embraces the transformation of both the natural and cultural environment.

In 2002, the state government entered into a joint venture with a private corporation to set up an ecotourism project in the Sundarbans, with tiger tours having pride of place. Despite the inclusion of local people in the venture, almost every ecotourism claim made was contested, and the project was abandoned in 2005. One of the strongest voices that protested against the project was that of Amitav Ghosh. The publication of his novel *The Hungry Tide* in 2004, with its seamless narratives of the many histories of the Sundarbans, put the controversy into perspective for a global audience, especially with the poignant fictionalization of the Morichjhapi incident. *The Hungry Tide* was successful in highlighting the diversity and uniqueness of the Sundarbans, interweaving its social and ecological histories as against the homogenized vision of the ecotourism project. The novel was political as a cultural product that stood for an environmental ethos and a vehicle of social change that refashioned a particular "environmental" outlook. Above all, the title of the book—*The Hungry Tide*—pointed back to the central challenge facing the region: water is both the source of life but, with rising sea levels, also a threat to the survival of its inhabitants. The Sundarbans faces an immediate threat from climate change, with studies predicting that more than 15 percent of the existing islands will be submerged by 2020, leaving 70,000 people homeless.

Rising sea levels are a global problem, and governments and societies are fretting about the need to increase the heights of their dykes (Netherlands) or to build them (Thailand). Venice and Bangkok were already sinking cities, but now they face more permanent flooding. Island states in the Indian and Pacific Oceans are now assessing their options. The Maldives government recently announced an interest in buying land in India or Australia to house its population. The irony is that the Maldives is flush with cash from the ecotourism of the world's rich, who have come there in droves to admire the atolls of coral. Whole nation-states in the Pacific archipelagos are also facing this threat. The twenty-first century looks to be one characterized by ecological refugee movements that will add to the waves of forced migrations of the past century for economic and political reasons. The increasing threat of islands permanently disappearing further exacerbates the impasse of limited spaces and rising populations, decreasing standards of living, and depleting resources.

Case study II: Australia—not enough water?

In contrast to the water civilizations of its neighboring archipelagos of the Indian and Pacific Oceans (Jumsai 1988), Australia is a continent characterized by extensive arid zones, unpredictable rainfall patterns, and large underground aquifers. It has much in common with the arid regions of the Middle East and Northern Africa and now, increasingly, Southern Europe. In all other respects, however, Australia is more readily compared to the other New World settler-societies that emanated from the British empire, namely North America, New Zealand, and South Africa. It has been "made" by a number of influences that relate to the circumstances of its settlement, its historical path through modernity, and the relationship between itself, Britain, and the rest of the world.

Water in Australia, despite being intimately associated with the cultural activities of food production, reproduction, and religion, was always regarded by European settlers as an "external variable" with no bearing on (settler) culture. Water is "irrigation," an "environmental flow" or an "entitlement." In other words, water is an abstract entity, as something without a history or a culture. Yet, water is neither ahistorical nor acultural: it has human meaning attached to it. It evokes peace and serenity, or terror and violence. Especially in Australia, its absence—as drought—can elicit powerful cultural responses (West and Smith 1996, 1997).

These tensions have played out in the history of water management in Australia. After the settlers came to terms with a hydrological environment that differed substantially from European conditions and expectations, the initial haphazard and uncoordinated delivery of water for mainly individual benefit was subjected to explicit state control of the resource, and managed for the collective good of all citizens.

Engineers had a unique position within this national water/irrigation culture. They held and controlled the knowledge about water flow, volumes, pressures, and evaporation rates, and they combined this knowledge with bureaucratic skills. They played an integral role in realizing water benefits through the actions of the state. Centralized, state-run enterprises carried out a range of activities well outside their main jurisdiction of water supply—including settlement of families on irrigation blocks, financial assistance, housing, education, marketing advice, and even moral guardianship. Water engineers were the embodiment of the notion that the principles of engineering could be applied to social issues. But they did not act in isolation. There was widespread societal consensus that the technological transformation of rivers and use of water for population settlement and economic growth was a worthwhile exercise. What emerged from all this was a complex mix of nation-building ideals, attempts to reconcile diverging foundational myths and material interests, and responses to the imperatives of statecraft. In essence, what was built (over and above dams, locks, and weirs) was a stable conglomeration of ideas and institutions—not exactly the state, the nation, or communities, but organizations and conventions that invented, re-invented, and responded to all three.

Today, the certainties of the "national Australian waterscape" are rapidly being "washed away." Changing social priorities, political philosophies that favor the market over the state, and the challenge of climate change have ushered in a new management regime. Water is now understood as an entity with a use-value in its own right, as a commodity to be bought and sold in the marketplace. The potential exists here for water to be used solely for wealth creation detached from production *and* detached from any concept of it as a public good. As the price of water rises rapidly, however, the general population of suburbanites and country folk alike are devising both private and public solutions to perceived threats to water infrastructure, systems, and flows.

The challenge and the promise of a cultural sociology of nature

This essay has argued several things. First, nature is a better concept than environment to think with about the question of ecology, sustainable development, and human flourishing. Second, sociology has always had a realist appreciation of the materiality of

344

culture and this has informed its critical understanding of the nature–society dialectic. Nevertheless this emphasis has been at the cost of an appreciation of the autonomous power and creative value of culture that is performed as it moves. Third, culture is our only means of expressing ourselves in our material worlds. So, although nature is beyond human control, and therefore is a critical horizon of our own material being, it can only be grasped in and through our human imaginings and actions. Demonstrating this was our purpose in examining the two regional case studies by considering their cultures and engagements with their ecologies *vis-à-vis* water. We think our two case studies point towards the promise of a strong program of cultural sociology for understanding more about struggles in the cultural politics of the environment, but our analysis is leavened with a salty recognition that human ordering and society are but a part of larger ecology that we call nature and that is neither ably described as "our environment" nor reducible to our needs, fantasies, and uses.

At the outset of the twenty-first century, we know what the main ecological challenges are: climate change, species diversity, non-renewable resource depletion, entropy, population control, sustainable development, waste management, and livability. Most of these issues are no longer even controversial in scientific circles, or now even amongst the world leadership elites. Moreover, we have many tools at hand to solve and apply the solutions to these challenges. Turning these knowledges and scientific innovations and technologies to systemic, institutional, and economic ends is the central conundrum of human collective life. There are no simple techniques of market or states that can easily solve the challenges or apply the solutions. There are no structures, systems, or hidden hands of nature to fix things. The politics of environment cannot short-circuit the radical diversity of contexts and instituted forms of cultures across the globe. The cultural politics of environment is intrinsic to the definition and practice of the cultural transformations of world environment.

Paradoxically, conceptualization of culture has proven harder work than understanding the environment—at least for sociologists. Yet all forms of representation of nature—mythic, aesthetic, moral, and scientific—are but the work of culture itself: as socio-historical imagination and creation, instituted culture, and autonomous modes of meaning, symbolism, and interpretation. Innovative technologies, new cultural adaptations, and ultimately new stories and new systems are being developed. That at least is the challenge and the promise. Whether or not our collective cultural reflexivity is fast enough in adapting to the demands of our natural environments is the central question of our times, and one faced by all humankind—at once and as one—for the first time in world history.

References

Alexander, J. and Smith, P. 2001. "The Strong Program in Cultural Sociology." In J. Turner, ed., *The Handbook of Sociological Theory*. New York: Kluwer.

Beilharz, P. 1997. *Imagining the Antipodes*. Melbourne: Cambridge University Press.

Bhabha, Homi. 1994. *The Location of Culture*. London: Routledge.

Biswas, A. 1982. "Why Dandakaranya a Failure, Why Mass Exodus, Where Solution?" *The Oppressed Indian* 4(4): 18–20.

Canclini, N.G. 1995. *Hybrid Cultures: Strategies for Entering and Leaving Modernity*. Minneapolis: University of Minnesota Press.

Castoriadis, C. 1997. "The Imaginary: Creation in the Social-Historical Domain." In David Ames Curtis, ed., *World in Fragments. Writings on Politics, Society, Psychoanalysis, and the Imagination.* Stanford, CA: Stanford University Press.

Eckersley, R. 1992. *Environmentalism and Political Theory: Toward an Ecocentric Approach.* New York: SUNY/UCL Press.

Flannery, T. 1995. *The Future Eaters.* Melbourne: Cambridge University Press.

Gallagher, C. and Greenblatt, S. 2000. *Practicing the New Historicism.* Chicago: University of Chicago Press.

Hannigan, J. 1995. *Environmental Sociology.* New York: Routledge.

Hogan, T. 2003. "'Nature Strip': Australian Suburbia and the Enculturation of Nature." *Thesis Eleven* 74: 54–75.

Horkheimer, M. and Adorno, T. 1973. *Dialectic of Enlightenment.* London: Allen and Unwin.

Jalais, A. 2005. "Dwelling on Morichjhanpi: When Tigers Became 'Citizens,' Refugees 'Tiger Food.'" *Economic and Political Weekly*, 1757–62.

Jumsai, Sumet. 1988. *Naga: Cultural Origins in Siam and West Pacific.* Singapore: Oxford University Press.

Krieger, M. 1973. "What's Wrong with Plastic Trees?" *Science* 179: 446–55.

Lash, S., Szerszynski, B., and Wynne, B., eds. 1996. *Risk, Environment, and Modernity: Towards a New Ecology.* London: Sage.

McKibben, B. 1989. *The End of Nature.* New York: Random House.

McNeill, W. 1963. *The Rise of the West: A History of the Human Community.* Chicago: University of Chicago Press.

Murphy, P. and Roberts, D. 2004. *Dialectic of Romanticism: A Critique of Modernism.* New York: Continuum.

Oxford English Dictionary on Historical Principles. 1993. Revised edition. Oxford: Oxford University Press.

Rabinbach, A. 1998. "The End of the Utopias of Labor: Metaphors of the Machine in the Post-Fordist Era." *Thesis Eleven* 53: 29–44.

Sassoon, D. 2006. *The Culture of the Europeans.* London: HarperCollins.

Seddon, G. 1997. *Landprints: Reflections on Place and Landscape.* Melbourne: Cambridge University Press.

Smith, B. 1960. *European Vision and the South Pacific 1768–1850: A Study in the History of Art and Ideas.* London: Oxford University Press.

Spengler, O. 1980. *The Decline of the West.* New York: Alfred A. Knopf (English translation).

Strang, V. 2004. *The Meaning of Water.* Oxford: Berg.

West, B. and Smith, P. 1996. "Drought, Discourse, and Durkheim: A Research Note." *Australian and New Zealand Journal of Sociology* 32(1): 93–102.

——. 1997. "Natural Disasters and National Identity: Time, Space, and Mythology." *Australian and New Zealand Journal of Sociology* 33(2): 205–15.

Yearley, S. 2005. *Cultures of Environmentalism: Empirical Studies in Environmental Sociology.* New York: Palgrave Macmillan.

33

Culture and the built environment

Between meaning and money

David Gartman

The environment that humans construct for habitation has always been more than mere utility. From the beginning, groups have invested their domiciles and cities with meanings, making their built structures symbolic of their beliefs and values. And although the built environment may express a shared worldview, just as often it inscribes into space the divisions and inequalities of the social structure. For example, Pierre Bourdieu (1990: 271–83) argues that the spatial structure of the Kabylian house unconsciously embodies the gendered division of labor of the Berber community, thus facilitating an early apprenticeship in and acceptance of the unequal roles of men and women. And Chandra Mukerji (1997) convincingly asserts that the famous gardens of Versailles symbolically displayed the ability of the emerging absolutist state in France to impose its power on the landscape and create a sovereign territory of order and control.

It is only with the rise of modern capitalist societies, however, that the artifacts of the built environment take on another status beyond either utility or symbol—that of the commodity. The usefulness of buildings and infrastructure in meeting material needs makes them an important part of the economy of every society. But only with the advent of capitalism is this economic utility confounded with and eventually dominated by the built environment as a commodity—a product to be sold on the market for profit. In capitalist societies, then, the built environment has a hybrid character, shaped by both money-making and meaning-making. The design of buildings and cities has for centuries been considered an art—architecture—with aesthetic rules autonomous from considerations of economic utility or profit. Yet in capitalist economies the construction industry also participates in the real estate market, in which developers and investors are driven by economic profits. To be built, a building must be not only aesthetically pleasing and meaningful in the culture but also profitable enough to attract capital.

These imperatives of meaning-making and money-making may sometimes conflict, as is illustrated by the controversies over rebuilding the World Trade Center site in the aftermath of 9/11. Most New Yorkers and other Americans wanted the Ground Zero site to contain a memorial, the most meaning-laden type of structure. But the Port Authority of New York and New Jersey, which owned the land, and the leaseholder of the destroyed World Trade Center, Larry Silverman, also insisted on building as much rent-producing space as was destroyed. Bowing to the public's symbolic need for remembrance, the Port Authority sponsored an architectural competition for the design of Ground Zero that mandated a memorial. The competition was won by Daniel Libeskind, whose design memorialized victims with a void at the center of the site. Silverman, however, hired his own architect to produce a design that maximized rent, not remembrance. A protracted battle over the final design ensued between the two parties, representing the conflicting demands of money and meaning on the built environment (Goldberger 2004).

Once having recognized these two distinct and potentially contradictory social forces shaping the built environment in most modern societies, sociologists—especially cultural sociologists—must specify their interaction. Is one more powerful than the other? If so, under what conditions? Are their effects on the environment independent or interactive? And at what level are these effects generated and experienced—at the macro level of national economics and politics, the meso level of institutions and organizations, or the micro level of individuals and small groups? Current scholarship on the built environment answers these questions in different ways, some of which are more informative than others.

Built environment as capitalist commodity

Some sociologists emphasize the overwhelming importance of the built environment as a commodity shaped by the market imperative for profit. The most powerful argument for this position is John Logan and Harvey Molotch's *Urban Fortunes: The Political Economy of Place* (1987). The authors argue that real estate in market societies simultaneously has exchange value, generating rent for owners, and use value, providing accommodations for residents, and that these two functions conflict. Those interested in land as commodity unite into a "growth machine," a group of interlocking pro-growth associations and agencies that seek to increase the exchange value of real estate through growth. Those interested in land as use value often organize to fight growth, which drives up rents and displaces residents. But even though houses and neighborhoods provide to residents not merely utilities like physical shelter but also cultural meanings like "home" and "security," Logan and Molotch's economic model provides no place for the influence of cultural factors on the built environment.

The work of Marxist geographer David Harvey (1985a, 1985b) also offers a conception of the built environment as commodity, but one that pays more attention to the cultural dimension. Like Logan and Molotch, he sees the landscape in capitalist societies as a social product molded by the contradiction between space as a means of exchange and space as a place of human community and consumption. The two capitalist imperatives—to move commodities rapidly over the landscape for exchange and to make land itself a commodity of exchange—both tend to level and homogenize space, destroying its differentiated qualities valued by human occupants. Thus, capitalism generates struggles not merely in the workplace but also in the landscape, as people resist homogenization of the built environment and seek to build distinctive communities. Unlike Logan and Molotch, however, Harvey mentions cultural needs beyond mere shelter that shape consumers' demands on the built environment. He argues (Harvey 1985a: 53–55) that consumers want homes and communities that, through images of an unspoiled, pastoral nature, provide an escape and respite from the alienation of the factory. Capitalists are driven to meet these cultural needs in the built environment, not just to sell real estate but also to make workers happy and docile for their production work. So the landscape is shaped by both economic and ideological needs. And the fulfillment of both needs requires responding, as least superficially, to the cultural demands of consumers.

Despite these insights on culture, however, Harvey's conception of the built environment is, like Logan and Molotch's, driven mainly by an overwhelming macroeconomic logic in which capitalists manipulate the built environment for their economic interests. So, for example, he suggests that the American state's massive subsidy for suburban housing after World War II was undertaken as a Keynesian solution to the under-consumption problem of an economy of Fordist mass production (Harvey 1985b: 203–11). The importance of the culture in stimulating consumer demand for suburban housing goes largely unexplored. But not all Marxists have been blind to the independent role of culture in the built environment, as demonstrated by the critical discourse around the topic of postmodernism.

Cultural Marxism and the space of postmodernism

The tradition of cultural Marxism, pioneered by Georg Lukács and the Frankfurt School, transcends the deterministic base-superstructure model offered by Harvey and others, and thereby assigns culture a more autonomous role in society. Thinkers in this tradition hold that the main influence of the economy on culture is found in its unconscious rather than conscious forms. So they examine a culture not for overt legitimations of the economy and its dominant class, but for its forms of expression, which they see as unconsciously reflecting the contradictions of economy and class. Thus Fredric Jameson (1971, 1981), an important contemporary exponent of cultural Marxism, argues that every mode of production generates social contradictions that shape human experience. Cultural producers grapple with these contradictions, seeking to resolve them in artistic forms. Artists unconsciously legitimate class hierarchy because their work is shaped by their own class interests. So for cultural Marxists, the meanings of the built environment are not directly dictated by the economic interests of bourgeois producers. They are unconsciously molded by the attempts of bourgeois artists, especially architects, to symbolically solve the social contradictions of the day, especially the contradictory experiences of space and time in a class society.

Perhaps the most influential application of cultural Marxism to the built environment is Jameson's analysis of postmodern architecture as a symbolic response to the contradictions of late capitalism (Jameson 1991, 1994). The postmodern aesthetic, he argues, is an attempt to aesthetically resolve the problems created by the new post-Fordist capitalism that emerged in the mid-1970s to replace the Fordist economy of mass production and mass consumption. Fordism had produced a modernist built environment that addressed the contradictions of its day. The rapid introduction of new technologies like the assembly line and the automobile undermined any sense of permanence by accelerating and objectifying time and generating the "shock of the new." However, the constant improvement of mass-produced goods created within these rapid changes a unifying sense of technological progress. Modern architects reflected this ideology of progress in a functionalist, rectilinear aesthetic that promised to increase both the efficiency and order of the built environment. Fordist innovation also compressed and

349

objectified space, turning once separated, heterogeneous places into simultaneous, homogeneous units of real estate. But rural and peripheral landscapes of difference still existed to relieve leveling, and architects accentuated these spatial differences with an organic aesthetic in order to compensate for the machine aesthetic of urban areas. By formally addressing the temporal and spatial contradictions of their times, modern architects unconsciously produced a landscape that culturally furthered bourgeois interests.

Jameson argues, however, that the aesthetic resolutions of the modernist built environment were unraveled by the rise of post-Fordist capitalism, characterized by the disintegration of mass markets and the rise of global systems of flexible production. This new economy produced new experiences of time and space that demanded new aesthetic resolutions. On the dimension of time, changes in diversified goods became so rapid and arbitrary that any sense of unified technological progress was lost. On the dimension of space, the spread of the homogenizing market into rural areas and under-developed countries caused the landscape to lose its differentiated use value. Postmodern architecture arose to resolve these problems. When people could no longer believe in progress, they turned to the past for meaning, so architects created an eclectic mix of historical styles to give them a reassuring place in time. And to compensate for a world losing its spatial differences to globalization, postmodern architects superficially differentiated spaces for diverse cultures and markets, often drawing on popular culture.

Jameson's analysis is nonreductionist in its treatment of the form of the built environment as an unconscious cultural response to the experiential contradictions created by the economy. But he only vaguely ties these responses to concrete classes and their interests. Although he states that the postmodern built environment ideologically corresponds to the new professional-managerial class (Jameson 1991: 407), he does not detail what its interests are. And Jameson remains exceedingly vague about how economic forces are translated into cultural changes in the built environment. He implies that economic shifts change individual artists' psychological experiences of time and space, which motivates them to create new aesthetic solutions. But this short-circuited link between macro-economics and micropsychology leaves out important mediating relations at the meso or institutional level. As sociologists have shown, artists are not isolated individuals responding separately to macro forces but social actors in a profession whose structure mediates their responses to the larger society. Both the extent of competition in a field of art and its autonomy from outside social forces affect how and whether they respond to macro changes. And these responses are not uniform but vary by artists' positions in the profession, which are often related to the class divisions of the larger society. Only by examining the professional structure of the art form most important to the built environment, architecture, can we give a full accounting of its changing aesthetics.

Institutional analysis of the built environment

Several sociologists focus on the architectural profession to specify more concretely how economic and political macro trends impact the aesthetics of the built environment. Their general argument is that architecture is a partially autonomous profession that affects aesthetics through its internal structure and struggles. But the larger society affects this structure by determining both the supply of qualified practitioners and the demand for architectural services. For example, Mauro Guillén (2006) argues that even though some sponsors in industry or the state were required, modern architecture's aesthetic of technological efficiency and rationality was not merely a reflection of the industrialization of the larger economy. Modernism was strong only where engineers and their scientific management movement substantially influenced the profession of architecture. The modernist aesthetic thus emerged in countries where architects were trained in engineering schools, not art schools, and based their claims of professional expertise on technological knowledge, not aesthetics. So even though the United States and Britain were far more advanced economically than Germany, only the latter was an important breeding ground for modernism because of the influence of engineering and scientific management on architecture.

David Brain's (1989) institutional analysis helps to explain why engineering was not influential on architecture in the US. He argues that by the mid-1800s American architects were losing control over aesthetics to clients from the emerging commercial and financial elite, whose demand for ornamental excess to display their wealth resulted in stylistic chaos. In 1857 architects seized control back from clients and achieved autonomy by establishing the American Institute of Architects, which institutionalized the Beaux-Arts aesthetic. Thus, architecture and its claims to expertise were already professionalized around a particular aesthetic by the time, later in the century, that engineers and scientific management rose to prominence.

In treating aesthetics as a tool in struggles for professional control, however, Guillén and Brain largely ignore the demand for architecture in the larger society, on which cultural Marxists focus. This problem is addressed by Magali Sarfatti Larson (1993) in her institutional analysis of the rise of postmodern architecture in the American built environment. Although she has a similar focus on the internal dynamics of the architectural profession, she recognizes that the external demand of a changing economy also shapes internal aesthetic struggles. Larson argues that an opportunity to challenge the dominance of modern architects, who had risen to power in the postwar profession, was created by post-Fordist capitalism, which economically devastated many urban areas through deindustrialization. Many cities responded by seeking to attract middle-class consumers back downtown with new consumption venues such as convention centers, shopping malls, and upscale housing in historic neighborhoods. But the competition between cities for consumer dollars forced each to differentiate its "urban product" from those of others. This demand in turn pressured architects to produce eye-catching buildings while simultaneously holding down costs, thus favoring an aesthetic of superficial, often historical, ornamentation that became known as postmodernism.

Postmodern architecture was produced, Larson argues, by the confluence of this external demand with the internal dynamics of the profession. In the late 1960s and early 1970s, young architects inspired by the broader youth movement began to challenge the complicity of the modernist establishment in creating a divided and unequal built environment. Their challenge was strengthened by a mismatch in the profession between supply and demand. In the 1970s a flood of young architects trained in an expanded system of higher education poured into a profession suffering from declining demand due to recession. To compete in this crowded field required heightened aesthetic innovation, which was steered by market demand into superficial decoration (Larson 1993: 243–50).

Larson's model, however, seems to suffer from unexplained contingency. Although she incorporates the preferences or needs of both producers and consumers of architecture, Larson does not explain whose interests matter more, and under what circumstances.

She seems to subscribe to the general rule of the production-of-culture perspective (DiMaggio 1977) that the more competition there is between cultural producers, the more important consumer demand is in shaping products. Yet, neither she nor the other institutionalists really address what producers or consumers desire aesthetically, or where these desires come from. Just about any exclusive body of technical or aesthetic knowledge, whether modernist, Beaux-Arts, or postmodern, would suffice for the purpose of monopolizing professional expertise. What factors select one over the others? Competition encourages innovation, but where do new aesthetics come from? Do larger class interests play a role, as cultural Marxists postulate? If so, how do these interests interact with producers' professional interests? These questions can only be answered by a perspective which simultaneously takes into account the cultural demands of both producers and consumers, how these demands are affected by the larger economic organization of society, and how all of the above factors are filtered through the institutional structure of professions. To my knowledge, the only theory of culture that does all this is Pierre Bourdieu's.

A Bourdieu model for the built environment

Pierre Bourdieu (1984) offers a powerful theory that helps to explain the effects of both money-making and meaning-making on the built environment. First, he gives an explanation of cultural preferences that is grounded in the economy and its class structure. Individuals growing up in different classes are exposed to different material conditions that ingrain different sets of unconscious preferences, within what Bourdieu calls habitus. The abundant resources of those in the upper class condition them to be unconcerned with the material necessities of life, and thus to privilege form or aesthetics over material function. In the built environment, such a habitus determines a taste for accommodations formally designed in classical styles that are sedately indulgent. The meager resources of those in the working class condition them to be constantly concerned with material necessities, and thus to privilege function over form. Such a habitus manifests itself in the built environment as a taste for accommodations that are comfortable and convenient, but also incorporate a kitschy prettiness. Because society as a whole validates the superiority of the tastes of the dominant class, the cultural consumption of this class makes its members seem personally superior, thus justifying their superior resources.

Thus, class habitus shapes consumer demand in the built environment, which in turn helps determine what producers like architects and developers build. But do producers simply give the largest group of consumers what they demand in order to maximize profits? Or do their own cultural preferences, which might differ from those of consumers, also mold their productions? For Bourdieu (1993, 1996), the answer depends on where the producers are located in the cultural field. He argues that the cultural field is divided into two subfields that are distinguished by the degree of producer autonomy from the economic market. In the subfield of large-scale or mass production, producers possess more economic capital (money) than cultural capital (education and knowledge), and thus seek to maximize economic profits by catering to the cultural preferences of consumers in the market. Markets within this subfield are usually stratified, with some producers filling the demand of high-class consumers, and others producing for petty-bourgeois or working-class tastes.

The subfield of small-scale or restricted production is composed of the high arts, and is autonomous from the market. Having more cultural capital than economic capital, producers here seek not to make money but to make works that receive recognition from other cultural producers on the basis of internal aesthetic standards. They thus cater to what Bourdieu calls the dominated fraction of the dominant class or the intellectual bourgeoisie, whose members have a taste for "aristocratic asceticism," that is, goods that deny indulgence in the name of cerebral appropriation. There are two factors, Bourdieu states, that determine the cerebral standards on which these autonomous producers base their productions—the habitus of producers and the dynamics of the field. Producers often originate from different class backgrounds, which give them different habitus that determine preferences for different styles of art (Bourdieu 1996). These habitus initially distribute producers between the competing stylistic positions in a field. But competitive dynamics also influence aesthetic standards. When competition is high, often as a result of new entrants, producers are more likely to pioneer new styles of art, creating niches that distinguish them from competitors and that bring recognition or symbolic profits. Ultimately, however, the new styles must also find consumers among other cultural producers whose habitus are predisposed to them.

Bourdieu's model clearly recognizes that the economic and cultural dimensions of the built environment interact at the macro, meso, and micro levels. The macro-economic structure not only produces specific cultural tastes in individual consumers and producers, but also determines the relative impact of these tastes on culture by affecting the autonomy of professional fields.

Applying Bourdieu's model to modern architecture

I will demonstrate the power of Bourdieu's model by applying it to the differential development of modern architecture in the United States and Europe. As we saw above, Mauro Guillén (2006) seeks to explain the differential development of modernism in the built environment with an institutional model that focuses on the influence of engineering and scientific management on the professionalization of architects. But his model cannot account for the fact that although American engineers pioneered and applied scientific management in industry, they were not influential within architecture. In Europe, by contrast, engineers and scientific management were largely uninfluential in industry, but did influence architecture toward modernism. This disjuncture between economic and cultural influence can be explained, however, if we examine important variables in Bourdieu's model, namely, the autonomy of the profession from the market and the cultural preferences of consumers themselves.

I argue that the modern movement in architecture reflected the culture of not merely engineers but the larger professional-managerial class, whose positions depended more on cultural capital than economic capital (Gartman 2000, 2009). The stark, recti-linear, unadorned aesthetic of modernism was a form of "aristocratic asceticism," which Bourdieu argues is characteristic of this intellectual bourgeoisie. Modern architecture arose mainly in Europe, not the US, because the position of this class was different there. Around the turn of the twentieth century, the professional-managerial class in both regions gave rise to a technocratic movement glorifying knowledge over wealth, of which modern architecture was a part. In the US, two architects attached to this move-ment, Frank Lloyd Wright and Louis Sullivan, pioneered the style of the Chicago School, a protomodern architecture characterized by relatively functional and unadorned forms. Both architects had habitus and tastes conditioned by middle-class intellectual backgrounds and technical training, which distinguished them from the upper-class backgrounds and Beaux-Arts training of the architects dominating the American profession. The habitus of Wright, Sullivan, and other American protomodernists placed them at the periphery of the architectural field, where they struggled to displace the established Beaux-Arts elite. The latter architects were motivated by money-making to supply members of the industrial and commercial bourgeoisie of the day with sedate but decorative historical forms that revealed their wealth but hid that wealth's industrial origins. Wright and Sullivan, by contrast, often found clients among the emerging professional-managerial class, whose members sought to assert through functional forms the preeminence of their efficiency and rationality over the money of industrialists.

In America, however, the technocratic movement of the new professional-managerial class was cut short, depriving the Chicago School of supporting clients. Early in the century, modernizing capitalists integrated these knowledge professionals, including designers and architects, into mass-production corporations in order to increase profits and contain conflict. Once integrated into these economic organizations, professionals lost autonomy, moving from the cultural subfield of restricted production into the subfield of large-scale production. There, their creations were subjected to the market demand of the working masses, who rejected ascetic functionalism in favor of the kitschy decoration that is characteristic of this class. This demand affected urban architecture because most workers lived in cities and visually consumed the aesthetics of buildings like movie theaters, department stores, and corporate headquarters. To cater to this mass market, American architects created an expressive, decorative aesthetic known as Art Deco, which replaced the protomodernism of the Chicago School.

In interwar Europe, however, the technocratic movement of the professional-managerial class was stronger. This class's incorporation into industry was blocked by a capitalist class reluctant to modernize due to its alliance with the Old Regime. So educated professionals mounted an autonomous technocratic movement to rationalize industry, and modern architecture was an important part of it. The pioneers of modernism argued that architects and designers should cooperate with industrial engineers to design housing and other products that were compatible with mass production. These products, they argued, would help placate restless workers and forestall revolution. Finding no support for their program among industrialists, the intellectual bourgeoisie turned to social-democratic governments, which launched programs to encourage industrial rationalization. One such state program funded the building of mass-produced public housing designed by modern architects such as Ernst May and Bruno Taut. This state support meant that architecture remained in the subfield of restricted production, subject to the tastes not of the mass market but of architects and others in the intellectual bourgeoisie. Unlike in the US, where the built environment was shaped by the market and subject to mass demand, in Europe workers were forced to accept the modern aesthetic favored by the habitus of the educated elite.

Conclusion

Bourdieu's model holds out the possibility of incorporating both cultural and economic determinants into explanations of the built environment. Unlike those who see the landscape merely as an economic commodity, he reveals that commodities too have cultural meanings, which are conditioned by the economic positions of both their producers and consumers. And unlike the cultural Marxists, who postulate short-circuited connections between economic interest and cultural meaning, Bourdieu shows these connections to be mediated by the meso structure of potentially autonomous fields that organize the work of cultural producers like architects. But the model has its limitations, as critics have suggested. I have argued that Bourdieu's theory of culture as class distinction is valid mainly in more unequal societies, while in more equal ones distinctive class cultures become leveled and hybridized (Gartman 2002). For example, the more equitable distribution of both economic and cultural capital in post-World War II Western societies seems to have undermined elite modernism and given rise to a postmodern architecture that combines elite and popular culture. Keynesian economic programs not only gave the lower classes more money to buy cultural goods but also more education to appreciate high culture. Upwardly mobile individuals have developed a hybrid habitus that combines a childhood taste for mass culture with an acquired knowledge of high arts. Such a habitus inclined both architectural producers and consumers toward the combination of high and low symbols that became known as postmodernism.

The applicability of Bourdieu's model may also be limited to Western societies, but it is difficult to know due to the paucity of research on the built environment in non-Western societies. The little research that exists is distorted by the battles of the Western architecture field. For example, from their research on Lagos, Nigeria, and China's Pearl River Delta, Rem Koolhaas and his students in the Harvard Design School Project on the City (2000) have concluded that a new urbanism of contingency and difference is emerging in the developing world that cannot be understood by Western models. But the unqualified praise they sing to real estate speculation in China and proliferating squatter villages in Lagos implies that Western architects view the "undeveloped" world through the struggles of the architectural field of the "developed" one. Koolhaas became an architectural star in the 1980s by denouncing modernism's rational planning in favor of postmodernism's difference and contingency. By viewing the built environment of the developing world through this polemical position within Western architecture, he mistakes the poverty and overcrowding of Lagos for vitality and diversity. We can determine the applicability of Bourdieu's model to the non-Western world only by viewing it through its own social structures and institutions, not through the struggles of Western ones.

References

Bourdieu, P. 1984. *Distinction: A Critique of the Social Judgement of Taste.* Cambridge, MA: Harvard University Press.

———. 1990. *The Logic of Practice.* Stanford, CA: Stanford University Press.

———. 1993. *The Field of Cultural Production.* New York: Columbia University Press.

———. 1996. *The Rules of Art.* Stanford, CA: Stanford University Press.

Brain, D. 1989. "Discipline and Style: The Ecole des Beaux-Arts and the Social Production of an American Architecture." *Theory and Society* 18: 807–68.

DiMaggio, P. 1977. "Market Structure, the Creative Process, and Popular Culture: Toward an Organizational Reinterpretation of Mass-Culture Theory." *Journal of Popular Culture* 11: 436–52.

Gartman, D. 2000. "Why Modern Architecture Emerged in Europe, not America: The New Class and the Aesthetics of Technocracy." *Theory, Culture and Society* 17(5): 75–96.

——. 2002. "Bourdieu's Theory of Cultural Change: Explication, Application, Critique." *Sociological Theory* 20: 255–77.

——. 2009. *From Autos to Architecture: Fordism and Architectural Aesthetics in the Twentieth Century*. New York: Princeton Architectural Press.

Goldberger, P. 2004. *Up From Zero: Politics, Architecture and the Rebuilding of New York*. New York: Random House.

Guillén, M. 2006. *The Taylorized Beauty of the Mechanical: Scientific Management and the Rise of Modernist Architecture*. Princeton, NJ: Princeton University Press.

Harvey, D. 1985a. *Consciousness and the Urban Experience: Studies in the History and Theory of Capitalist Urbanization*. Baltimore, MD: Johns Hopkins University Press.

——. 1985b. *The Urbanization of Capital*. Oxford: Basil Blackwell.

Jameson, F. 1971. *Marxism and Form*. Princeton, NJ: Princeton University Press.

——. 1981. *The Political Unconscious*. Ithaca, NY: Cornell University Press.

——. 1991. *Postmodernism, or, the Cultural Logic of Late Capitalism*. London: Verso.

——. 1994. *The Seeds of Time*. New York: Columbia University Press.

Koolhaas, R. *et al.* 2000. *Mutations*. Barcelona: Actar.

Larson, M.S. 1993. *Behind the Postmodern Façade*. Berkeley: University of California Press.

Logan, J. and Molotch, H. 1987. *Urban Fortunes: The Political Economy of Place*. Berkeley: University of California Press.

Mukerji, C. 1997. *Territorial Ambitions and the Gardens of Versailles*. Cambridge: Cambridge University Press.

34

The rise and fall of cyberspace, or, how cyberspace turned inside out

Martin Hand

As the Internet becomes more pervasive—as it moves off desktops and screen and becomes embedded in things, spaces, and minds—cyberspace will disappear.
Alex Soojung-Kim Pang (http://www.endofcyberspace.com/, accessed 15 July 2009)

The term *cyberspace* has been a key metaphor in both academic analyses of cultural change and wider popular discourse for around two decades. The coupling of Norbert Weiner's cybernetics with a notion of space has provided the most pervasive representation of "where" electronic data is and what our relations with it are. Its etymology of "steering" or "navigating," translated into "surfing" and "mapping," has shaped research agendas and precipitated new ways of thinking about what "culture" is. At this key site for theorizing cultural change in recent years, debates about what is happening and what is at stake have often cleaved into utopian and dystopian narrative clusters (Hand and Sandywell 2002). In this essay I want to trace the fate of cyberspace as a metaphor for conceptualizing the relations between electronic media technologies and culture in its broadest sense. Rather than debating the various merits and pitfalls of internet-related research, I will point to how the term cyberspace itself has morphed and what the implications are for theorizing the relations that constitute the internet and associated technologies. There are substantial changes in the nature of electronic and digital media alongside epistemological and methodological problems of cyber-research. It would be a Herculean and somewhat unwieldy task to review the entire spectrum of cyberspace research here. I have condensed much of this material into what I see as three largely heuristic variants, each of which has been periodically dominant: cyberspace as an immaterial cultural autonomy, as a central myth of Western culture, and as turned inside out, becoming the "materiality of cultural practice."

Cyberspactial autonomies

During the late 1980s and early 1990s the metaphor of cyberspace most commonly referred to an autonomous cultural environment. This autonomy, for some, was and

357

perhaps still is intensely theological. In an explicit form, cyberspace *transcends* the materialities and spatiotemporal constraints of bounded cultures: "The Web ... has no need for the presence of a real world beyond, because it replaces it with its own world beyond, that is, with its own virtual world" (Apolito 2005: 16). In discourses of transcendence, the "space" element of cyberspace is conceptualized as a non-physical environment (Bolter and Grusin 1999: 181). The ability to evade the markers of physical embodiment suggests transcendence of "the bloody mess of organic matter" (Wertheim 2000: 19) and the limitations implied by containment within the "meat" of human flesh (Flichy 2007: 130). The important implication was that the ethnic, gendered, embodied nature of sociocultural life might therefore be transcended and deconstructed. Popular-science magazines such as *Wired* and some cyberpunk fiction similarly articulated cyberspace through a specific rejection of embodiment (Flichy 2007).

More sociologically, those who debated the kinds of interaction or "life" emerging within cyberspace as environment looked toward concepts of "community" and "identity" in trying to situate novel forms of interaction and representation. Many of the interventions were interested accounts of cultural autonomy, not simply descriptions of on-line activity or of technical capacity. They were efforts by enthusiastic participants to discursively establish open democratic cultural practices outside of state, corporate, or what might be taken to be "closed regimes" of one kind or another.

Virtual community and identity

The text-based bulletin board systems of the 1980s were imagined as communities. According to this view, communities are not simply temporally reproducible expressions of mutual reliance and shared cultural values, but can emerge in a strong form through fleeting "moments" when "enough people carry on those public discussions long enough, with sufficient human feeling, to form webs of personal relationships in cyberspace" (Rheingold 1993: 5). In the context of late modern "disembedded" community, it is not a matter of "where" individuals might be physically, but whether the interactions between them are sufficient to form "webs of personal relationships." Although mostly about discussion forums on the Net, this idea also characterized "virtual reality" environments, role-playing games such as the "virtual worlds" of MMORPGs and MUDs (Multi-User Dungeons), all of which involve participants who never meet outside of the screen and are, in this view, unrelated to place. Ironically, such a conception of autonomous virtual culture was reproduced through its initial critique. Jones (1997) and Sardar (1996) argued that community is not simply a matter of communication; the fact that connections are formed through bonds of transient mutual interest rather than mutual obligation or proximity makes them *simulations of community*.

If community was disembedded, then identity was disembodied. It has been argued that "self-identity" has become a dominant "reflexive project" in late modern culture (Giddens 1991). Self-identity is an *endeavor* that is continuously worked at and reflexively reconstructed, particularly as it is increasingly tied to patterns of consumption (Featherstone 2007). As performed in cyberspace, virtual identity allows for an anonymous identity choice to be made and it positions users as "authors"; in other words, they do not simply *enact* their given identities but *re-write* them in a "post-social" world (Hayles 1999). To take one example, Turkle argued that MUDs offered the opportunity for players not only to create the text (or graphics) of the game but also to construct "new selves though social interaction" (1997:12), giving themselves alternative or non-human characteristics in on-line texts or "avatars." Our interactions with networked machines encourage performances of multiple selves, and are further enhanced when we recognize the possibility of non-linear identities and a "distributed presence" (Turkle 1997: 12–13).

Indeterminacy and virtuality

the Internet is more like a social space than a thing, so that its effects are more like those of Germany than those of hammers … the problem is that modern perspectives tend to reduce the Internet to a hammer.

(Poster 2001: 176–77)

Commentators drawing explicitly upon poststructuralist theory and/or analyses of postmodernity have conceptualized the technologies of cyberspace as decidedly indeterminate (Lash 2002; Manovich 2001; Poster 2006). Mark Poster argues that we simply misunderstand the internet unless we appreciate its non-representational character, where the "flow of signifiers" disrupts the fixed categories associated with earlier oral and written cultures. The mistake of modern theorizing is to think exclusively in terms of either the emancipatory effects of digitization upon pre-existent identities, or the irrevocable "loss" of the human subject to all-encompassing convergent media/technology (Taylor and Harris 2005). The sheer contingency of cyberspatial interaction inaugurates a democratization of communication where "The magic of the Internet is that it is a technology which puts cultural acts, symbolizations in all forms, in the hands of its participants" (Poster 2001: 184).

In a broad sense "culture" is thus simultaneously received, mediated, and manipulated. The flows of information are always open to reconfiguration, because they are never concretized in specific time–spaces (unlike, say, print objects). Web pages are always in process, always deferred, as new links are created and followed, old links disappear, and endless ways of navigating through appear possible. In cyberspace, there is no central authority that can fix symbolic forms in material time and space, and therefore actualize them. Moreover, where the subject is constituted and reconstituted within electronic databases, it is both disembodied and disembedded from the traditional anchorage of social and cultural institutions and territories. Exploration of the resulting possibilities of "e-topia" has not been limited to cultural theory of this kind but has been embraced by Western governments, transnational agencies, non-governmental organizations (NGOs), and so forth, as a sphere within which political arrangements could be redrawn and a "citizen-based" democratization of communication might be fostered. But the significance of theorizing cyberspace as a zone of cultural autonomy has been its impact upon how we think about digital technology and culture as "less material" or even immaterial.

Mythologies of cyberspace

Indeed, we are in the midst of a worldwide effort, organized by many different companies and governments in many different ways, to make computer communication a transcendent spectacle.

(Mosco 2004: 41)

359

Theorizing cyberspace can be considered in dialectical terms where the promise of transcendence is met with the threat of colonization. The imagined outcomes of postmodern information machines appear a little celebratory and the possibilities of subjectivity have been limited to individual, disembodied self-transformation. Where initial critiques of virtual community and identity as the "darker side of the West" left the ideology of cultural autonomy largely untouched, a series of interventions that became dominant from the mid- to late 1990s—including the political economy of communication, ethnographic explorations of the internet, and the integration of the Web in social network analyses—all had the effect of *disaggregating* cyberspace as a distinctive cultural formation.

Production of cyberspace

Post-Marxist analyses of "cyberculture" have been concerned with the digital divides laundered by the more celebratory accounts of community and identity formation, but they have also operated as a means of critiquing postmodern and poststructuralist conceptions of culture in light of web commercialization. If cyberspatial autonomy privileges cultural discontinuity, from this perspective it is clear that "Continuity is painfully apparent in everything" (Robins and Webster 1999: 234). The "culture industry" is now extended through cyberspace. The penetration of advertising, marketing, and e-commercial applications has rendered any sense of cultural autonomy moot. The sheer *production* of cyberspace as proliferating new markets—and the accompanying efforts to regulate and monitor internet traffic, and to enforce laws of private property—represents a perfected alignment between technology, capital, and culture (Taylor and Harris 2005). The central concern of productionist analyses was thus to reintroduce modern conceptions of capitalist power to the study of cyberspace. Notions of disembodiment and virtuality represented the worst excesses of immaterial models of power relations; in them, the modern state and corporation seemed to have little impact upon the playful realm of cyberculture, at least for intellectuals. Research in the productionist vein has directed our critical attention to the longer military and commercial history of information processing and the rhetorics of novelty at work in cyberspatial narratives, especially as wielded by government departments, corporate bodies, and the computing industries. As Mosco (2004) observes above, it is in the interests of very material organizations to construct cyberspace as immaterial and transcendent.

From this perspective, cyberspace as cultural autonomy is spectacle and commodity. The questions now turn to how such a spectacle has been generated, whose interests it serves, and what kind of cultural significance these developments have. The apparent immaterialism of cyberspace and the related assumption of a kind of cultural separatism are revealed as necessary mythologies of informational capitalism. For Sassen: "much of what happens in electronic space is deeply inflected by the cultures, the material practices, and the imaginaries that take place outside electronic space" (2006: 344).

Integrative practices

The political economy of electronic communication dismantled the speculative assumptions about cybercultures at the level of state and corporation. A second trajectory of analysis has dismantled cyberspace from the ground up. The idea that cyberspatial practices are divorced from the dynamics of everyday life came under sustained critique from anthropological perspectives. In the most prominent example, concepts of "cyberspace" or "virtuality" are bracketed in favor of exploring how the practices of everyday life incorporate and integrate (or not) elements of internet technology into the rhythms of everyday practice (Miller and Slater 2000). The internet was dissolved into its multifarious components, which may or may not be assembled into "cyberspace" by individuals in daily life. A significant element to Miller and Slater's ethnographic work was its location in Trinidad, which exposed the ways in which Euro-American assumptions about individualized computer use, alienation, and postmodern identity politics had structured previous polarized models of cyberspace. Instead of conceptualizing the internet or cyberspace as a vehicle for identity performance or of disembedded and dematerialized community building, research convincingly showed, people incorporate elements of media into existing material-symbolic arrangements and, in this case, counter-intuitively use the internet to "make concrete" rather than virtualize *national* identities.

The attempts to "contextualize cyberspace" through detailed ethnographic exploration have been a complex arena for debate (Hine 2000) because of the shifting ground of where access to cyberspace takes place (home, library, cybercafé, cell phones) and the proliferating range of possible uses related to ever-evolving technologies and techniques (chat, games, education, shopping). Moreover, efforts to understand the "contexts" of cyberspatial activity reveal their inseparable interrelation with cyberspace and the ongoing reconfiguration of both (see Green *et al.* 2005).

The aforementioned debates about cyberspace and community revolved around utopian transcendence *or* dystopian simulation, both of which maintained the autonomy of cyberspace as a cultural space in its own right. In contrast, like those doing ethnography, those concerned with social network analysis have argued that such a distinction is deeply problematic, as in reality the so-called "on-line world" is an extension and often an enhancement of pre-existing social relations, which themselves have become increasingly orientated through "networks" rather than spaces or places (Wellman and Haythornthwaite 2002). The metaphor of autonomous "space" was thus challenged by a model where internet activity was enveloped in wider practices of network formation and maintenance. This theorization also entailed the recasting of "community" itself as a network formation, resting upon a conception of "networked individualism" where people find themselves spatially dislocated and seek to maintain social ties with dislocated others (Barney 2004). In accounting for the material bases of power, the texture of everyday life, and the integration of networked communication practices, all these rather different approaches questioned the conception of "cyberspace" as a useful, accurate, or generative way of researching cultural forms and practices.

The fall of cyberspace and the rise of everyware

The polarized dialogue about cyberspace has been transcended by theoretical and technical developments. For some time, analysts have recognized that the distinction between "on-line" and "off-line" cultures is highly problematic on conceptual and methodological grounds, reifying technology or culture and making little sense experientially or phenomenologically (Hine 2000; Miller and Slater 2000). In what follows,

361

I highlight three emergent challenges to dominant conceptions of cyberspace that extend and problematize the critiques discussed so far.

The materials turn

The idea of "cyberspace" (on-line) on the one hand and "users" ("off-line") on the other has been subject to serious critique. But further to that, the work of Latour (2005) and others in the "sociology of associations" has shifted the agenda in cultural sociology by asking us to rethink our relations with things *per se*. Latour wants to extend the capacities and dynamism of things themselves in a relational materialism so that "things might authorize, allow, afford, encourage, permit, suggest, influence, block, render possible, forbid, and so on" (2005: 72). For Latour, technologies do not so much "reflect" or even "represent" the intentions of designers, manufacturers, the interests of capitalist organizations, or the claims of social actors. He argues that "Their action is no doubt much more varied, their influence more ubiquitous, their effect much more ambiguous … even as textual entities objects overflow their makers, intermediaries become mediators" (Latour 2005: 85). The issue here is one of recognizing that the social is technical, that "action" is the outcome of sociotechnical associations, and that we should take a route beyond the semiotics of technologies and their content as being simply "reflective" of cultural meanings or "projectors" of hegemonic interests. The significance, then, is more than "cultural appropriation" versus "ideological domination" and concerns the dynamics of mutual interdependence—the consideration given to *how* technical objects actively "define a framework of action together with the actors and the space in which they are supposed to act (Akrich 1992: 222)."

There are three dimensions of relevance here. First, technologies co-evolve with the dynamics of systems of which they are part. The characteristics and agency of specific technologies, such as laptops, HTML text, and databases, shift and change alongside changes in the computer industry, the socioeconomic and financial ebbs and flows of the capitalist marketplace, the patterns of demand in a given market, and so on. Second, technical characteristics can be said to evolve in tandem with shifting conventions and practices of use (Oudshoorn and Pinch 2002). Third, we should consider how whole "suites of technology" operate (Shove *et al.* 2007). The latter point has real significance in the present because increasing numbers of technologies are designed to be compatible with others, thereby creating systems or networks of interdependence (for example between computers, printers, software, and digital cameras). The dynamics of *uses* will have different kinds of impacts upon trajectories of both production and consumption. Moreover, digital cultural objects as mediators are more or less designed to facilitate multiple interpretations and uses (Lash and Lury 2007). In other words, digital technologies are "inscribed" with open-ended ambivalence in symbolic, practical, and material ways. Current digital information technologies are mobile, additive, and adaptable, *designed to be active*. This is "material vitalism" (Kuchler 2008).

Knowing materials

The rethinking of what "things" are and how they are relationally defined is augmented by the new technicality of material-informational things. Indeed, one of the most striking aspects of contemporary culture is the sheer number of electronic and digital devices through which information is said to flow. From personal computers and laptops, to cell phones and iPhones, image capture machines, MP3 players, BlackBerries, "smart" fabrics, and the like, a proliferating materialization *and* informationalization of culture emerges via the mobility of bodies. Recent accounts of an "internet of things" and of the "automatic production of space" (Thrift 2005) suggest that these devices are also increasingly interactive and constitutive of everyday life in the form of interoperable mobile environments. Citizen-consumers are now *expected* to interact with them and "produce cultural objects" (Hand 2008). The significance here, as Thrift (2005) has argued, is that the technical is becoming the surface and the exterior. In other words, what was once cyberspace—a cultural space to be accessed and entered through the PC—is now, in Thrift's terms, a material "screenness" that is portable and independent of any particular container. It is everyware. What was once a theoretical proposition about technological agency has become *explicit*.

This development raises important issues. First, the range of technological devices is radically different, enabling different cultural practices to emerge. Where the desktop PC was once the primary interface, there are now entire interconnected suites of technologies designed to engender continual movements of information. The shift is perhaps most clear when we consider how the global circulation of digital images is enabled through cameraphones, laptops, social networking sites, and so on, which position users as "interfacing" rather than "using" or "entering." The emerging practices of continual archiving *and* constant transmission that these technical devices make possible— and are themselves enfolded within—are quite different from the kinds of "virtual life" or "networked individualism" discussed earlier.

Second, the characteristics of Web 2.0 applications are, to some extent, novel (O'Reilly 2005). Mash-ups, social networking sites, wikis, and the like enable vast amounts of user-generated content to be uploaded, often in the form of private information (thought, personal information, images, tastes) placed in the public domain, encouraging a reversal of the relation between "public" and "private" life that characterized the modern archive (Gane and Beer 2008). Bauman (2007) sees this reversal as conjoining consumption and confession—and it is, at the least, resolutely non-anonymous. Others speak of how the Web 2.0 technologies seem to necessitate the ever more detailed codification of habitus (Burrows and Gane 2006). The graphics, moving images, sounds, shapes, spaces, and texts incorporated in mash-ups and re-formed through metadata "tagging" in Facebook and Flickr have "become computable; that is, they comprise simply another set of computer data" (Manovich 2001: 20). The resulting new cultural objects are liquid in form. In contrast to the objects of Benjamin's mechanical reproduction, they can produce infinite *variations* not copies. This development might appear to result in a radical democratization of cultural production. However, some of the choices are delegated in advance to software, and performed by them in ways that mute democratic possibilities.

Third, it is not that "we" access cyberspace, but that software has come to intervene and mediate nearly all aspects of everyday life, whether we know it or not (Thrift 2008). Instead of searching for our preferences in virtual community, we are presented with our preferences as the result of algorithmic assessment of previous interests or purchases. We now live in an "age of the portal" where "the data find you" (Lash 2006: 580). The materials of cyberspace are now infrastructural and anticipatory, "knowing" where to find us (Thrift 2005). For example, in marketing, "deep packet inspection" software, running through ISP servers, "tunnels in" to individual hard drives and "looks at" packets in order to generate the finest-grained knowledge of user activity. Software intercepts packets leaving the user's computer (this requires software installed by, for example, *Phorm*, and running on the ISP's server system) and redirects them in transit to its own servers where the page request (sender's data) is tagged with a unique ID. This ID catalogues multiple/all/any subsequent page visits and then redirects the information to companies who want to serve targeted ads back at the user in "real time." This software development allows companies to customize preferences to an extraordinary degree in a post-privacy world, but for our purposes it represents a radical reversal of the previously dominant conception of who is accessing what and vice versa.

Territories and zones

If the computer screen through which one "entered" cyberspace is now a distributed mobile "webtop" where the data find you, then what happened to the territorial notions of space and network? It is the increasingly sophisticated software of geodemographics that provides some sort of answer. Instead of existing as an externality (cyberspace) or set of extensions (networks), information now re-structures actual geographic territories (city, neighborhood) through automated classification systems such as neighborhood profiling, Google Maps, GPS systems, loyalty cards, public wi-fi, and so on (Burrows and Gane 2006). The flows of information produced through ordinary practice (made visible as "consumption patterns") are classified by software. As individuals, we are increasing "socially sorted" (Lyon 2003) *and* encouraged to "sort ourselves out." The notion of cyberspace as cultural autonomy conceptualized physical spaces as irrelevant or unimportant. What we see here are invisible processes of structuring and re-structuring due to the proliferation of software—as it becomes materialized in more devices—and, given that the data produced do not "represent" but perform *judgment* in Latour's sense, the increasing significance of classification. One of the key criticisms of cyber-theory in its most technophilic variant centered on the hidden, rather stark stratification of access through inequality—locally, regionally, nationally, and globally. This inequality remains a significant issue, but, as I have shown by example above, such a "digital divide" has been overlain with many other divides. The general concern about enabling equitable access to, and use of, software machines now has to incorporate a third layer of divisions performed by the software that determines who can access local "premium networked spaces" linked with other global premium networked spaces.

If the space of cyberspace was once thought a "place" to enter, live, and construct democratized culture, or simply the latest spectacle produced by informational capitalism, it has now become the hidden technical apparatus of Euro-American societies, producing an "automated spatiality" (Thrift 2005). Software increasingly organizes the flows of people *and* things; it produces new forms of control and domination but also innovation, experimentation, and play. It is becoming the very materiality of contemporary cultural practices.

Conclusions

I have not provided an exhaustive review of cyberspace scholarship, far from it. Rather, the modest task here has been to document some dominant conceptions of cyberspace over the last twenty years and comment on changes in the character and theorization of "technological culture" more generally. It is certainly not the case that conceptions of cyberspace as a specific cultural realm have disappeared (think here of Second Life, the "3D virtual world imagined and created by its users"). Neither is the political economy of information technology (the re-shaping of the cultural economy by Google, Microsoft, Apple, Nintendo, and so on) no longer relevant for cultural sociology. I think each of these phenomena has become even more pervasive and exaggerated precisely because what was previously visible as the hardware of technoculture and information culture is now increasingly invisible as the *infrastructure* of contemporary culture. *Culture*, in terms of shared symbolic and material resources and relations, increasingly circulates *as* information, where, for example, the "new volunteerism" associated with YouTube, Facebook, Wikipedia, and such like appears to usher in a flattened form of cultural production, or at the very least a blurring of the differences between cultural production and consumption (Beer and Burrows 2007). But such information or data is no longer confined to the realm of cyberspace. It does not have external spatial qualities *in that sense*. The consequences of information-driven reflexivity are that "culture" is no longer "out there" as ideological, symbolic or representational, but rather:

> [Culture] is so ubiquitous that it, as it were, seeps out of the superstructure and comes to infiltrate, and then take over, the infrastructure itself. It comes to dominate both the economy and experience in everyday life.
>
> (Lash and Lury 2007: 4)

Most analyses of cyberspace are consistently skewed toward Euro-American cultures in this way. There have historically been good reasons for this; most obviously, the sites of technological development have been primarily located in the global North, as have the dominant users of such technologies. This state of affairs may now be subject to considerable shifts in interesting and important ways. First, although I have argued that the global North has undergone the fall of cyberspace and the rise of everyware, this is not necessarily the case elsewhere. Although advanced market economies across Asia see similar increases in the mobility of internet use (Minges 2005), notions of linear development in relation to internet infrastructure and the cultural embeddedness of uses are highly problematic. This is most clear in relation to the largely market-driven governmental idea of Africa "leapfrogging into Modernity" via cyberspace—an idea which simultaneously resurrects cyberspace as virtuality, ignores material-structural inequities between North and South (Alden 2003), and pays little attention to the dynamics of consumption and production. In other words, transition in the global North is historically, technologically, and culturally specific.

Second, it is arguably the case that much of the invisibility occurring when cyberspace becomes infrastructural is related to some elements of the material production and laboring of that infrastructure shifting to the global South. For example, much of the material work (manufacturing, service industries, data collection) enabling ubiquitous computing and mobile communication to occur in the North is conducted in the new information processing centers in India and Latin America. In other words, the experience of seamless digitization and convergence in the North often rests upon the specific concentration of its materiality in other centers (Sassen 2006). Third, the automatic production of cultural-spatial classifications discussed above has serious implications for how people in non-Western regions are categorized by the software machines of the global North, and what the implications are for the movement of peoples, allocation of capital, the dynamics of globalization, and the circulation of culture.

Finally, the understandings of cyberspace here, and all that is suggested by them, are "in play" in contemporary cultures. It is the relations between them that raise so many more important issues. Indeed, one of the most pressing issues of our time will be how the application of specific material law now predicated on the notion of territorial "cyberspace" comes to terms with the cultural dynamics of ubiquity, flow, and invisibility inaugurated by the softwaring of culture. Moreover, the shifting relations between materiality and immateriality discussed above raise important research questions around the significance of past and present cyberspatial activity as it will be understood in the future. Where the internet as cyberspace was positioned as autonomous, anonymous, and "immaterial," it was thought that digital texts, objects, and images leave no memory traces. The turn to informational materiality, both in theory and in practice, is producing some rather different trajectories. For example, it is becoming clear that the materiality of networked digital traces is partly one of an *impossibility* of erasure (think of Abu Ghraib) and the increasing possibility of resurrection because everything has been *routinely* archived. In terms of what and how societies remember, as increasing domains of cultural life are enacted through digital information machines, individuals and cultural institutions are presented with dilemmas of how to store, manage, and preserve the vastness of "cyberspatial" activity (van Dijck 2008). In contrast to the dialectic of liberation and domination implied in earlier accounts, if cyberspace is becoming the infrastructure of ordinary cultural practice, then it is also becoming the archive of everyday life.

References

Akrich, M. 1992. "The De-Scription of Technical Objects." Pp. 205–24 in W. Bijker and J. Law, eds., *Shaping Technology/Building Society: Studies in Sociotechnical Change*. Cambridge, MA: MIT Press.

Alden, C. 2003. "Let Them Eat Cyberspace: Africa, the G8 and the Digital Divide." *Millennium—Journal of International Studies* 32(3): 457–76.

Apolito, P. 2005. *The Internet and the Madonna: Religious Visionary Experience on the Web*. Chicago: University of Chicago Press.

Barney, D. 2004. *The Network Society*. Cambridge: Polity.

Bauman, Z. 2007. *Consuming Life*. Cambridge: Polity.

Beer, D. and Burrows, R. 2007. "Sociology and, of and in Web 2.0: Some Initial Considerations." *Sociological Research Online* 12(5). Available at http://www.socresonline.org.uk/12/5/17.html.

Bolter, J.D. and Grusin, R. 1999. *Remediation: Understanding New Media*. Cambridge, MA: MIT Press.

Burrows, R. and Gane, N. 2006. "Geodemographics, Software and Class." *Sociology* 40(5): 793–812.

Featherstone, M. 2007. *Consumer Culture and Postmodernism*. London: Sage.

Flichy, P. 2007. *The Internet Imaginaire*. Cambridge, MA: MIT.

Gane, N. 2006. "Speed-up or Slow Down? Social Theory in the Information Age." *Information, Communication and Society* 9(1): 20–38.

Gane, N. and Beer, D. 2008. *New Media: The Key Concepts*. Oxford: Berg.

Giddens, A. 1991. *Modernity and Self-Identity*. Cambridge: Polity.

Green, S., Harvey, P., and Knox, H. 2005. "Scales of Place and Networks." *Current Anthropology* 46(5): 805–18.

Hand, M. 2008. *Making Digital Cultures: Access, Interactivity, and Authenticity*. Aldershot: Ashgate.

Hand, M. and Sandywell, B. 2002. "E-Topia as Cosmopolis or Citadel." *Theory, Culture & Society* 19 (1–2): 197–225.

Hayles, N.K. 1999. *How We Became Posthuman*. Chicago: Chicago University Press.

Hine, C. 2000. *Virtual Ethnography*. London: Sage.

Jones, S., ed. 1997. *Virtual Culture*. London: Sage

Kuchler, S. 2008. "Technological Materiality: Beyond the Dualist Paradigm." *Theory, Culture & Society* 25(1): 101–20.

Lash, S. 2002. *Critique of Information*. London: Sage.

———. 2006. "Dialectic of Information? A Response to Taylor." *Information, Communication & Society* 9(5): 572–81.

Lash, S. and Lury, C. 2007. *Global Culture Industry: The Mediation of Things*. Cambridge: Polity.

Latour, B. 2005. *Reassembling the Social: An Introduction to Actor-Network Theory*. Oxford: Oxford University Press.

Lyon, D. 2003. *Surveillance as Social Sorting*. London: Routledge.

Manovich, L. 2001. *The Language of New Media*. Cambridge, MA: MIT Press.

Miller, D. and Slater, D. 2000. *The Internet: An Ethnographic Approach*. Oxford: Berg.

Minges, M. 2005. "Is the Internet Mobile? Measurements from the Asia-Pacific Region." *Telecommunications Policy* 29(2–3): 113–25.

Mosco, V. 2004. *The Digital Sublime: Myth, Power, and Cyberspace*. Cambridge, MA: MIT Press.

Mosco, V. and McKercher, C. 2008. *The Laboring of Communication: Will Knowledge Workers of the World Unite?* Lexington, MA: Lexington Books.

O'Reilly, T. 2005. "What Is Web 2.0: Design Patterns and Business Models for the Next Generation of Software." *O'Reilly*. Available at http://oreillynet.com/1pt/a/6228 (accessed December 7, 2006).

Oudshoorn, N. and Pinch, T., eds. 2002. *How Users Matter*. Cambridge, MA: MIT Press.

Poster, M. 2001. *What's the Matter with the Internet?* Minneapolis: University of Minnesota Press.

———. 2006. *Information Please: Culture and Politics in the Age of Digital Machines*. Durham, NC: Duke University Press.

Rheingold, H. 1993. *The Virtual Community*. Cambridge, MA: Addison-Wesley.

Robins, K. and Webster, F. 1999. *Times of the Technoculture*. London: Routledge.

Sardar, Z. 1996. "Cyberspace as the Darker Side of the West." In Z. Sardar and J. Ravetz, eds., *Cyberfutures*. London: Pluto Press.

Sassen, S. 2006. *Territory, Authority, Rights*. Princeton, NJ: Princeton University Press.

Shove, E., Watson, M., Hand, M., and Ingram, J. 2007. *The Design of Everyday Life*. Oxford: Berg.

Taylor, P. and Harris, J. 2005. *Digital Matters: The Theory and Culture of the Matrix*. London: Routledge.

Thrift, N. 2005. *Knowing Capitalism*. London: Sage.

———. 2008. *Non-Representational Theory*. London: Routledge.

Turkle, S. 1997. *Life on the Screen: Identity in the Age of the Internet*. New York: Simon and Schuster.

Urry, J. 2000. *Sociology Beyond Societies*. London: Routledge.

van Dijck, J. 2008. *Mediated Memories in the Digital Age*. Stanford, CA: Stanford University Press.

Wellman, B. and Haythornthwaite, C., eds. 2002. *The Internet in Everyday Life*. Oxford: Blackwell.

Wertheim, M. 2000. *The Pearly Gates of Cyberspace*. New York: W.W. Norton.

35

Public institutions of "high" culture

Victoria D. Alexander

This chapter focuses on institutions that distribute "high" culture via public, or quasi-public, mechanisms. High culture includes the fine arts, such as classical and contemporary visual arts, opera, classical music, and theatre. I discuss art museums, symphony orchestras, and opera, drama, and dance companies. These organizations comprise the "supported arts sector" as they are reliant, to some degree, on public (governmental) funding for their continued operations.

After noting the difficulties inherent in the concept of high culture, I discuss the organizational forms used to distribute high culture, which include nonprofit and non-governmental organizations, and government agencies. I then look at the public funding of fine-arts institutions and consider several issues facing these organizations. These include the conflict among (internal) missions and the effects of various external pressures. The chapter concludes with a discussion of topics which may be fruitful in the continuing study of public institutions of high culture.

"High culture" as a problematic term

"High" culture tends to refer to those art forms traditionally associated with the upper social classes. High culture stands in contrast to "low" or "mass" culture, which includes the popular arts produced by cultural industries and distributed to large audiences, and the folk arts, produced and consumed by people in local settings. Scare quotes often accompany the term to highlight the problematic, and usually elitist, nature of its definition.

The creation of institutions of "high culture" took active work on the part of social elites, and required that certain forms of art be seen as better (higher) than others (DiMaggio 1992, 1991, 1982a, 1982b). Levine (1988) discusses this "sacralization" of the arts, which occurred in the United States toward the end of the nineteenth century. And, of course, in Europe, the history of museums is connected to treasures amassed by royalty, and aristocratic traditions played a role in the institutionalization of other forms of high culture. A common thread running through these examples is prestige.

"High culture" is socially situated. It is always defined (favorably) against other types of culture (cast as inferior), and it allows patrons to claim status honor, or "distinction" (Bourdieu 1984).

Interestingly, while the concept of high culture became strongly institutionalized at the end of the nineteenth and the beginning of the twentieth centuries, at the end of the twentieth century and into the twenty-first, distinctions between high and low arts have weakened. High culture, therefore, is a concept situated in a particular historical period. It is, moreover, a Western concept. Consequently, the term may have little meaning in many regions of the world. (From a first-world perspective, terms commonly used about non-Western culture include "folk art" or "indigenous culture," but these draw on Western concepts and carry distortions when they are applied elsewhere.) There is no good formal definition of high culture, as any definition must be made relative to specific times, places, and art forms.

Crane (1992) argues that the concepts of high culture and popular culture are "outmoded," and suggests replacing them with a more useful division of the arts by production context: the national-level commercial arts (which encompass popular culture) and the "urban arts" (where fine arts—but also various local and folk arts—are produced for local audiences). Although this is a useful suggestion which deserves serious attention, hierarchies of cultural forms persist (even though they may be weakened) and so the term "high culture" remains a useful short-hand.

The "high culture model"

In the United States, most institutions of high culture are nonprofit organizations. They are legally incorporated as 501(c)(3) organizations, which means that they are exempt from some kinds of taxes and can receive charitable contributions that attract tax relief for the donor. DiMaggio (1992) describes the nonprofit organizational form as the "high culture model" of producing or distributing the arts. (The nonprofit corporation, of course, has other functions in other sectors.) DiMaggio (1982a, 1982b) shows how elites in Boston established the Museum of Fine Arts and the Boston Symphony Orchestra, in 1870 and 1881 respectively, as a way of claiming cultural capital and status for themselves. Prior to this time, the demarcation between the fine and popular arts, or, more accurately in this case, between the high and low arts, had not been clearly drawn. The Boston Brahmins, by establishing charitable institutions to house and showcase only the fine arts, and to "educate" the populace in the superiority of these forms, were "cultural entrepreneurs" who worked to draw symbolic boundaries between cultural forms of different social classes.

Museums and symphony orchestras were established as nonprofit enterprises through-out the United States in the late nineteenth and early twentieth century (DiMaggio 1992). Nonprofit theatres, dance companies, and opera houses were founded subse-quently, in the early half of the twentieth century, following the model of the museum and symphony, as charitable (not profit-seeking) organizations that showcased high culture (DiMaggio 1992). During the founding process, champions of each art form needed to create a boundary between the high-status version of the art form and its more popular and commercial relatives, and they needed a way to protect high-status art from the pressures of the marketplace. The marketplace works against distinctions in culture, as it "drives entrepreneurs to elide aesthetic distinctions in order to create larger audiences

369

and discourages canon formation by providing incentives for presenters to differentiate their products" (DiMaggio 1992: 43–44). DiMaggio's work highlights the importance of social action in the creation of boundaries between high culture and other, "lower" forms:

> The stories of the progress of opera, theater, and dance to 'high cultural' status remind us that, even though systems of cultural classification present themselves as based on natural and enduring judgments of value, they are products of human action, continually subject to accretion and erosion, selection and change.
>
> (DiMaggio 1992: 43)

Nonprofit organizations are technically private forms, but their nonprofit charters require that they operate in the public interest: I therefore include them in this consideration of public institutions of high culture. The "high culture model" (the nonprofit organizational form coupled with boundary work to establish certain types of cultural expression as superior) is culturally located in the American context, though other countries may also rely on voluntary organizations in the distribution of the fine arts.

In other nations, public institutions of high culture may be governmental organizations, or they may be quasi-non-government organizations (QUANGOs). In the United Kingdom, for instance, museums and galleries are non-governmental organizations, governed by boards of trustees. As charitable organizations, they can receive covenanted gifts that are tax sheltered (Alexander and Rueschemeyer 2005). In contrast, most French institutions of high culture are government owned, although since the 1980s the management of many of these institutions has been delegated to private, nonprofit groups. Many French institutions, including the major museums and the state theatre sector, continue to be both owned and run by central or local government (Toepler and Zimmer 2002).

Public funding of fine arts institutions

A key element in the public nature of fine-arts institutions is the fact that these institutions receive, in one form or another, government support. Public funding of arts institutions in the United Kingdom is channeled through "arms-length" organizations such as the Arts Councils and through the Department for Culture, Media, and Sport (DCMS). Government provides funding for the DCMS, which in turn provides grants-in-aid to the National Museums and to the Arts Council of England. (The Arts Councils of Scotland and Wales are funded through the Scottish and Welsh governments.) The DCMS has a say in who is appointed to the boards of museums. Government grants-in-aid do not cover all of the costs associated with running museums and galleries, however, so these organizations are required to fundraise from other sources. In the United Kingdom, the Arts Councils (in England, Scotland, Wales, and Northern Ireland) provide funding for performing-arts organizations, and for literature and visual arts. The Arts Councils evolved from the Arts Council of Great Britain, which was established in 1946. (On British cultural policy, see Alexander 2007, 2008; Gray 2000.)

In the United States, the federal government supports the Smithsonian Institution museums and also funds the National Endowment for the Arts (NEA). The NEA was established in 1965. It provides grants directly to artists and arts organizations, and to the fifty state arts councils. The NEA follows the British model of the Arts Council, as a body that makes funding decisions independently of Congress and party-political influence. After the "culture wars" of the 1990s, however, Congress constrained the remit of the NEA and cut its funding (Alexander and Rueschemeyer 2005; Dubin 1992). Private initiative plays an important role, even in NEA funding, as grants must always be matched by funding from other sources. The most notable feature of American public funding of the arts, however, is that a large portion of it is indirect, through tax relief (Schuster 1985, 1986). The United States government spends a relatively paltry sum on direct financing of the arts and culture, compared to other developed nations. But the American tax system, along with a strong philanthropic tradition, encourages individual and corporate patronage of the arts. Americans receive tax deductions on charitable giving, including gifts to cultural organizations. Because the government forgoes taxes on these donations, it is said that government is indirectly funding the recipients in the amount of the forgone tax.

Toepler and Zimmer (2002) contrast this "Anglo-Saxon" model of public funding with the "Continental European" model and the "Nordic" model. The Continental model, as typified by France, is a centralized, top-down, bureaucratic system in which the state plays a central role in the provision of culture, especially high culture. Relatively high levels of public funds are committed to culture, which is seen as an important element of national identity. Private funding of culture "remains undeveloped" due to "the traditional antimarket and antibusiness attitudes of policy makers" (Toepler and Zimmer 2002: 36). The Nordic model, as typified by Sweden, is a decentralized, corporatist approach in which national government takes responsibility for financing the arts and culture, but devolves decision-making to regional and local institutions. Like France, Sweden does not rely on private funding of the arts; in contrast to France, Swedish funding includes a broad array of "popular and grass-roots cultural activities," as well as high culture (Toepler and Zimmer 2002: 39).

Issues in public institutions of high culture

A crucial issue in public institutions of high culture involves what Zolberg (1986) calls "tensions of missions." Zolberg describes the conflict within art museums between, on the one hand, elitist and curatorial goals and, on the other hand, populist and educational goals. This conflict has been inherent in art museums since their inception: they were founded to conserve and display works of art, and they have been run by curators with scholarly goals. At the same time, they were also founded as educational institutions that were supposed to benefit the public. DiMaggio (1991) discusses the increasing ascendancy of curatorial goals at the expense of educational goals in American museums of the 1920s. In the United Kingdom, the Arts Council of Great Britain was established (in 1946) with similar tensions, summed up by the phrase "raise or spread" (Minihan 1977). The debate was whether public taste should be raised to the highest standards, with only excellent art supported, or whether art should be made available to a wide audience across the geographic spread of the nation.

Such tensions continue to exist for most institutions of high culture, although in recent years the emphasis has been to move the balance more toward the popular, inclusive role of arts institutions, and away from the seemingly elitist, curatorial, and esoteric visions of goals of arts organizations. Ballé (2002), for instance, discusses the contemporary

371

"democratization" of French art museums. She traces the roots of this process back to the French Revolution, which "codified the democratic concept of the museum as a public institution, encompassing the state's responsibility for its heritage and the museum's obligation toward the citizens" (Ballé 2002: 134). While the pressure for democratization has deep roots, more recent, and complex, events (since the 1980s in Europe, earlier in the United States) have pressed cultural institutions towards more inclusive policies.

In addition to the problem of balancing excellence and access, art museums and other public institutions of culture have been increasingly subject to other pressures, most notably a new emphasis on managerialism (Alexander 1996; Hewison 1987, 1995). Glynn (2000), for instance, describes symphony orchestras as "dual identity" organizations in which the business side of the organization stands in contrast to the musical/artistic side, and often conflicts with it. Increasing, managerialism has many roots, including the introduction of new types of personnel in the organization, pressures for accountability from funders (both governmental and corporate), and general societal trends and neo-conservative political tastes favoring the use in all charitable, nonprofit, and governmental organizations of particular managerial styles drawn from the business world. Many arts organizations face chronic budget shortages, and managerial approaches are seen as a solution.

Artists and curators often decry managerialism as it puts emphasis on earned income, fundraising, commercial projects, and "value for money" in ways that seem to pull against artistic interests and press toward popularism over excellence. Performing-arts organizations experience this tension when balancing the need to produce the most popular and familiar works from the traditional repertoire (Bach, Beethoven, and Brahms; Shakespeare comedies; the Nutcracker Ballet) to attract audiences—often described as "warhorse programming"—with the need to present other works (new and old), both for the sake of innovation *per se* and to ensure that musicians, actors, or dancers can be challenged or, at least, not get bored (McCarthy *et al.* 2001).

McCarthy *et al.* (2001) argue that these and other pressures will lead to the demise of medium-sized cultural institutions. They suggest that, in the future, cultural organizations will be divided into two groups: a small number of large, nonprofit organizations in major cities and a much larger number of small, nonprofit organizations aimed toward local, specialized markets. Small organizations will be able to survive because their costs are relatively low. The large organizations, particularly, will adopt business strategies from the profit-seeking sector:

> Like their large commercial-sector counterparts (and for many of the same reasons), these organizations too will seek to maximize their earned revenues from ticket sales and related business income. They will rely on advertising and marketing campaigns promoting celebrity performers and traditional materials designed to attract the broadest share of what appears to be a relatively stable market— those individuals who can pay premium prices to attend the highest-quality live performances.
>
> (McCarthy *et al.* 2001: 108)

A crucial issue for cultural institutions relates to difficult funding climates. In 1966, Baumol and Bowen identified the problem of "cost disease" in performing-arts organizations. They argued that these organizations run into trouble because their chief costs are for personnel. This distinguishes them from those sectors which are able to gain efficiencies in production over time. The costs of producing, say, a computer can be brought down over time, allowing prices to drop or profits to increase. But the performing arts are not able to realize such productivity gains. A Shakespeare play has exactly the number of characters specified by the script today as in the past. A symphony orchestra needs roughly 100 musicians to play the classical repertoire, and a quartet is always four. These facts mean that there will always be intrinsic cost pressures in performing-arts organizations, because their personnel costs rise along with increases in other sectors, but are not accompanied by productivity gains. Baumol and Bowen's discussion underpins a "market-failure" argument for public support of performing-arts organizations (i.e. the market will produce a financial shortfall over time, so the state should step in).

In addition to implicit financial pressures, arts institutions may face financial problems due to policy shifts. In the 1990s, the US Congress slashed funding for the arts during the "culture wars," in which visual and performance arts were particularly implicated. This meant that private sources, or earned income, had to fill the gap. The economic crisis that began in 2008 will make both fundraising and earning income even more challenging.

Public institutions of high culture also face political pressures that can accompany public funding. The financial cuts in the NEA were a direct result of political intervention in the cultural arena. In the UK, Margaret Thatcher dramatically reduced funding for the arts in the 1980s with the express purpose of encouraging cultural organizations to find alternative funding. Tony Blair's government encouraged such organizations to increase social inclusion, a political aim that does not necessarily relate to their main aims (Alexander 2008). Britain's current Prime Minister, Gordon Brown, believes that funding for the arts is important to the extent the arts contribute to the growth of the "creative economy."

Relatedly, cultural organizations that rely on funding from non-governmental sources find they have to accede to funders' desires in order to win grants. Wu (2002) is particularly concerned about the influence of corporate sponsors on the arts. And it is clear, in the museum field, that while funders do not actually request changes to individual exhibitions, their interests increase the number and proportion of more popular and "blockbuster" shows such as international, traveling exhibitions (Alexander 1996).

The American "system," in which government funds are supplemented by private grants and earned income, is now viewed by many European governments as the correct direction in which to take cultural funding. For instance, so-called "plural funding" or "mixed economy" support for high culture institutions is increasingly prevalent in the United Kingdom. "Privatization" has become a keyword for fine-arts institutions across Europe. Regardless of the previous level of state support for the fine arts, most European governments have cut back public funds, requiring arts institutions to seek more earned income and private sponsorship. Many have instituted other reforms to reduce the influence of the state, such as transferring management functions from the state to nonprofit entities (Boorsma et al. 1998).

Future directions

There are many questions remaining about public institutions of high culture. Here, I suggest four areas where future study may be most promising.

First, what happens to institutions of "high" culture as boundaries between different genres of art become blurred, both in wider society and within fine-arts institutions themselves? Many institutions of high art have become more populist. Some reasons for this include the marketization of arts institutions and increasing commercial pressures—both of which may lead to weakened boundaries between high and popular art forms and encourage performances or exhibitions that have the potential to attract larger audiences (DiMaggio 1987). Government policies and funding patterns, along with particular pressures from commercial funders, as we have seen, may push arts institutions towards more populist goals. It may also be that contemporary audience members have broadened their cultural repertoires, as is argued in theories about high-status "cultural omnivores" who have eclectic tastes (Peterson and Kern 1996).

Second, to what extent are these institutions affected by where the money comes from? This question relates to state sponsorship and private philanthropy, both individual and corporate, as well as to the extent that public institutions of high culture are subject to the marketplace. How do arts organizations respond as governments attempt to shape their artistic policies (e.g. by requiring institutions to foster social inclusiveness) or management structures (e.g. by requiring institutions to prepare strategic plans, by appointing directors or boards, or by shifting governance structures from public to private entities)? What influence do business corporations have on cultural institutions in countries where corporate philanthropy is common? How do the different strategies of privatization affect cultural institutions? The effect of most of these policies is to increase the degree to which these institutions are subject to the marketplace. In this regard, the second area for future research relates to the first, because market-based systems appear to erode symbolic boundaries among cultural forms. In addition, some theorists suggest that large organizations may be best positioned to present high culture in marketized systems, as they can capture income and audiences that are not available to smaller organizations (Hewison 1987; McCarthy et al. 2001). Since 2006, for example, the Metropolitan Opera has simulcast high-definition transmissions of live performances to hundreds of cinemas in many countries. This affords the Met a revenue stream not readily available to smaller, less prestigious companies.

Third, what happens to artistic production, especially in terms of innovation and artistic autonomy, as governments provide less insulation from the marketplace and public institutions of high culture become embedded in more market-based systems? Large, "heritage" arts organizations may be best positioned to attract audiences and sufficient funding for high-quality programs. However, these programs will of necessity either lean toward the popular, or favor well-established, traditional repertoires and unproblematic canonical work in order to retain audience numbers. We may hypothesize that offering innovative or controversial work will be left to smaller organizations, but these organizations will find access to funding challenging. Related to this are changes in the governance of public institutions of high culture, as senior personnel are increasingly drawn from the business rather than the art world. Nation-states have pushed in this direction, too. In November 2008, for instance, the Italian government appointed as Director General of Museums and Archeological Sites a man whose most recent position had been McDonald's head of operations for Italy. The appointment of a fast-food expert to Italy's highest post for museums has, of course, been controversial, and it remains to be seen what policies will be implemented during his three-year term.

Fourth, how do the concepts of high culture and institutions dedicated to high culture translate or travel from the West to other regions of the world? Many Western art forms (e.g. classical music) have become firmly rooted in non-Western nations, and so have some institutions for the display of cultural artifacts (e.g. the museum). In the past, colonial officials exported cultural ideas. And Tomooka *et al.* (2002) show that, in the late nineteenth century after the Meiji Restoration of 1868, Japan looked to the West as a "reference point" for its own culture. Japan imported such concepts as culture, visual arts, and fine arts, and reconceptualized some of its own cultural forms in these terms, specifically to increase the prestige of Japan abroad. (Of course, although contemporary Japanese high culture may have been influenced by Western ideas during the Meiji period, it is not a Western product, and is deeply embedded in Japanese history; see Ikegami 2005.) In today's post-colonial world, what other factors play into the creation of high-arts institutions in non-Western societies? For instance, in December 2007, China opened its National Center for the Performing Arts in Beijing. The building, colloquially called "the Egg," includes three venues, each with a large seating capacity to display both Western and Chinese performing arts. In November 2008, Qatar opened its Museum of Islamic Art in a building designed by I.M. Pei. These prestige venues, with impressive and distinctive architecture (created by so-called "starchitects"), are clearly designed to generate esteem for the increasingly successful nation-states they represent. They also draw on ideas, institutionalized in Western settings, about how to display culture, and on Western notions of high culture as prestigious and worthy of distinction. But why have non-Western nations adopted these institutions, and do the institutions function differently depending on national context? As the world system changes, these differences may become more relevant.

Let me close with one final example which draws together several themes. Abu Dhabi is currently building a cultural district on Saadiyat Island. In addition to a concert hall and a performing-arts centre, the island will feature a Guggenheim Museum (to be designed by Frank Gehry) and a Louvre Museum. The Guggenheim has built several "branch" museums since the 1990s. The new Guggenheim strategy has not been particularly controversial, but this is not the case with the so-called "desert Louvre." The French Government has licensed the Louvre "brand"—which includes twenty-year use of the Louvre name, curatorial expertise, and a selection of its art treasures—for an undisclosed sum rumored to be in the vicinity of $1 billion. Critics believe that the French government has sold the soul of the Louvre through this agreement to rent out works of art rather than loaning them. Traditionally, France has protected its culture from commercial pressures, but the government's agreement with the United Arab Emirates seems, to critics, to have done away with France's crucial anti-market stance. If France accedes, in the cultural sphere, to the commercial logic of global capitalism, what hope is there for public institutions of high culture in other nations?

Conclusion

Public institutions of high culture take different organizational forms in different countries. Government policies also vary by nation. Nevertheless, these institutions share a broad definition, formulated in the West (and relatively recently), of what "high culture" is (status-enhancing fine arts) and how it should be displayed (in museums or performing-arts venues where audiences consume culture "seriously"). Moreover, in recent years, public institutions of high culture in many nations face similar situations—decreased government funding and increased pressure to attract audiences through more popular fare. They find themselves operating with more managerial and business-world strategies in increasingly marketized and commercialized settings. And although the concepts of high culture were institutionalized in the West, non-Western nations play an increasing role in the production and display of high culture in our globalized world.

References

Alexander, Victoria D. 1996. *Museums and Money: The Impact of Funding on Exhibitions, Scholarship, and Management*. Bloomington: Indiana University Press.
——. 2007. "State Support of Artists: The Case of the UK in a New Labour Environment and Beyond." *Journal of Arts Management, Law and Society* 37(3): 185–200.
——. 2008. "Cultural Organizations and the State: Art and State Support in Contemporary Britain." *Sociology Compass* 2(5): 1416–30. Available online at: http://www3.interscience.wiley.com/journal/118902502/home.
Alexander, Victoria D. and Rueschemeyer, Marilyn. 2005. *Art and the State: The Visual Arts in Comparative Perspective*, St Antony's Series. London: Palgrave Macmillan.
Ballé, Catherine. 2002. "Democratization and Institutional Change: A Challenge for Modern Museums." Pp. 132–45 in Diana Crane, Nobuko Kawashima, and Kenichi Kawasaki, eds., *Global Culture: Media, Arts, Policy, and Globalization*. London: Routledge.
Baumol, William J. and Bowen, William G. 1966. *Performing Arts: The Economic Dilemma*. New York: Twentieth Century Fund.
Boorsma, Peter B., van Hemel, Annemoon, and van der Wielen, Niki, eds. 1998. *Privatization and Culture: Experiences in the Arts, Heritage and Cultural Industries in Europe*. London: Kluwer.
Bourdieu, Pierre. 1984. *Distinction: A Social Critique of the Judgement of Taste*. Cambridge, MA: Harvard University Press.
Crane, Diana. 1992. *The Production of Culture: Media and the Urban Arts*. London: Sage.
DiMaggio, Paul. 1982a. "Cultural Entrepreneurship in Nineteenth-Century Boston: The Creation of an Organizational Base for High Culture in America." *Media, Culture and Society* 4: 33–50.
——. 1982b. "Cultural Entrepreneurship in Nineteenth-Century Boston, Part II: The Classification and Framing of American Art." *Media, Culture and Society* 4: 303–22.
——. 1987. "Classification in Art." *American Sociological Review* 52: 440–55.
——. 1991. "Constructing an Organizational Field as a Professional Project: U.S. Art Museums, 1920–40." Pp. 267–92 in Walter W. Powell and Paul J. DiMaggio, eds., *The New Institutionalism in Organizational Analysis*. Chicago: University of Chicago Press.
——. 1992. "Cultural Boundaries and Structural Change: The Extension of the High Culture Model to Theater, Opera and the Dance, 1900–940." Pp. 21–57 in Michèle Lamont and Marcel Fournier, eds., *Cultivating Differences: Symbolic Boundaries and the Making of Inequality*. Chicago: University of Chicago Press.
Dubin, Steven C. 1992. *Arresting Images: Impolitic Art and Uncivil Actions*. New York: Routledge.
Glynn, Mary Ann. 2000. "When Cymbals Become Symbols: Conflict over Organizational Identity within a Symphony Orchestra." *Organization Science* 11(3): 285–98.
Gray, Clive. 2000. *The Politics of the Arts in Britain*. London: Macmillan.
Hewison, Robert. 1987. *The Heritage Industry: Britain in a Climate of Decline*. London: Methuen.
——. 1995. *Culture and Consensus: England, Art and Politics Since 1940*. London: Methuen.
Ikegami, Eiko. 2005. *Bonds of Civility: Aesthetic Networks and the Political Origins of Japanese Culture*. New York: Cambridge University Press.
Levine, Lawrence W. 1988. *Highbrow, Lowbrow: The Emergence of a Cultural Hierarchy in America*. Cambridge, MA: Harvard University Press.
McCarthy, Kevin F., Brooks, Arthur, Lowell, Julia, and Zakaras, Laura. 2001. *The Performing Arts in a New Era*. Arlington, VA: Rand.

Minihan, Janet. 1977. *The Nationalization of Culture: The Development of State Subsidies to the Arts in Great Britain*. New York: New York University Press.

Peterson, Richard A. and Kern, Roger M. 1996. "Changing Highbrow Taste: From Snob to Omnivore." *American Sociological Review* 61: 900–07.

Schuster, J. Mark Davidson. 1985. *Supporting the Arts: An International Comparative Study*. Unpublished Report, funded by the Policy and Planning Division, National Endowment for the Arts.

——. 1986. "Tax Incentives as Arts Policy in Western Europe." Pp. 320–60 in Paul DiMaggio, ed., *Nonprofit Enterprise in the Arts: Studies in Mission and Constraint*. New York: Oxford University Press.

Toepler, Stefan and Zimmer, Annette. 2002. "Subsidizing the Arts: Government and the Arts in Western Europe and the United States." Pp. 29–48 in Diana Crane, Nobuko Kawashima, and Kenichi Kawasaki, eds., *Global Culture: Media, Arts, Policy, and Globalization*. London: Routledge.

Tomooka, Kuniyuki, Kanno, Sachiko, and Kobayashi, Mari. 2002. "Building National Prestige: Japanese Cultural Policy and the Influence of Western Institutions." Pp. 49–62 in Diana Crane, Nobuko Kawashima, and Kenichi Kawasaki, eds., *Global Culture: Media, Arts, Policy, and Globalization*. London: Routledge.

Wu, Chin-tao. 2002. *Privatising Culture: Corporate Art Intervention since the 1980s*. London: Verso.

Zolberg, Vera L. 1986. "Tensions of Mission in American Art Museums." Pp. 184–98 in Paul DiMaggio, ed., *Nonprofit Enterprise in the Arts: Studies in Mission and Constraint*. New York: Oxford University Press.

36

Contemporary art and cultural complexity

The case of Chelsea

David Halle and Kim Robinson

Much social-scientific writing on specific cultural phenomena has tended to foreground one or two analytic frames of reference from the variety of those that have been developed in the field. Here we draw on findings from a case study of a local art scene in a global context—Chelsea, Manhattan, the most important contemporary art-gallery district in the world. We argue that our empirical material concerns a highly complex situation for which one or two analytic frames cannot alone do justice. We further suggest that this may be true now of many other central cultural phenomena, partly because of the increasingly "global" context in which they exist. As complex phenomena (like art worlds) change over time, the analytic approaches that work best also change, with new ones coming to the fore and older ones needing modification in key ways.

We pursue these points via a discussion of four main analytic frameworks—globalization, market theory, analysis of the meaning of the cultural works for those who view them, and class and status theory, especially the debate between the "class homology" and the "omnivore" hypotheses. Overall, our approach is consistent with that of other cultural analysts (e.g. Griswold 2004; Battani and Hall 2000; Mann 2007) who have likewise stressed the need for theoretical complexity and eclecticism to do justice to a complex and changing empirical situation.

Chelsea in global context

Chelsea, on Manhattan's Far West Side, became the most important contemporary art-gallery district in the world with startling speed. Between 1996 and the summer of 2008, the number of commercial galleries in Chelsea grew from 12 to at least 270, dwarfing other art districts in the United States and elsewhere and supplanting SoHo, once the most dynamic gallery neighborhood in New York City (of course, the number of galleries in Chelsea began to decline in the fall of 2008 as a result of the economic crisis, dropping by 10 percent by February 2009). One indicator of Chelsea's predominance in the contemporary art world is the number of Chelsea galleries exhibiting at Art Basel, the world's leading annual fair for contemporary art, which operates a ferociously competitive admissions process for galleries that wish to exhibit there. At Art Basel 2007, the 31 galleries from Chelsea comprised by far the largest contingent selected, with the next largest contingent, from Berlin, way behind with 22 galleries, followed by London with 18. Marveling at the Chelsea phenomenon, the *New York Times* art critic Roberta Smith (2004) wrote that "a contemporary art scene on this scale has never happened before, and it's hard to imagine it ever happening again."

This mega-gathering of publicly accessible Chelsea galleries offers a magnificent opportunity for systematic research on contemporary art—on the art works, their audiences, the galleries, and the artists. At the same time, in today's world, a local case, however important, obviously cannot be properly understood outside a "global" context, which, in the world of contemporary art, certainly includes the internet, international art fairs, and international auction houses.

In this account, therefore, we first view Chelsea in the context of the international contemporary art market, looking in particular at art fairs, auctions, and the internet. We then discuss detailed material from Chelsea. We integrate into this account a discussion of the four main analytic frames mentioned above, and show how we need their various perspectives, and more, to understand what is going on.

Clarifying "globalization"

It is hard these days to analyze cultural phenomena of major importance without drawing on the concept of "globalization." Yet it is important at the outset to clarify the concept of "global." It is not, for example, fruitful to classify everything with an international dimension as "global." Discussing this issue, Michael Mann (2007) has usefully distinguished six geographical/spatial interaction networks, five of which are less than "global." These include local (any sub-national network of interaction), national (networks bounded by states, though not necessarily organized by states), international (between national units), macro-regional (transnational but regionally bounded), transnational (transcending the boundaries of the national and potentially global), and global (the extension and intensification of social relations over the globe). In what follows, we argue that many relevant phenomena that are often referred to as "global," such as international art fairs, are more accurately classified as "macro-regional." On the other hand, in our discussion of efforts to sell art on the internet, we will suggest that the term "global" in its strict sense is probably appropriate.

International art fairs

The growth of annual international art fairs is one key development underlying the perception that the art world is becoming increasingly international and "global." These fairs, with displays primarily by commercial art galleries, in principle allow galleries from any country to sell their art abroad during the few days the fair lasts, thereby promoting a gallery's stable of artists in a market/country outside its home base(s). Art fairs, therefore, constitute one suitable terrain for examining "globalization" in the contemporary art market.

Art Basel (in Switzerland) bills itself as "the world's premier modern and contemporary art fair," and few in the art world would disagree. Competition among galleries for selection (by an admissions committee) at Art Basel is ferocious. Analysis of the geographic origins—by nation, city, and neighborhood—of the galleries selected for Art Basel in June 2007 is illuminating. Considering first national origins, there is a clear concentration of galleries from a handful of countries located in two regions— the United States and Western Europe—which together account for 90 percent of the 242 galleries selected. Although Art Basel's claim to showcase galleries from all five continents is formally correct, representation is tiny from Africa (one gallery from South Africa), small from Latin America (just two galleries from Mexico and three from Brazil), and modest from Asia, despite the burgeoning economies of China and India (four galleries from Japan, two from South Korea, one from China, and none from India). Analysis of galleries at the Armory Show (New York) or Frieze (London) confirms this.

Turning from national to city data, New York City clearly tops the hierarchy. It accounted for 21 percent of all the galleries accepted at Art Basel 2007, over twice as many as Berlin, the second largest city represented, with 9 percent of all the galleries, followed by London (7 percent), Zurich (6 percent), and Paris (5 percent). Finally, analysis within New York City shows Chelsea's dominance over other gallery districts there. Galleries located in Chelsea account for 63 percent of all New York City galleries selected for Art Basel.

These findings demonstrate that the world of art fairs basically involves circulation around a select group of fairs by a select number of art galleries, mostly from a few key cities in Western Europe and North America, with New York's Chelsea gallery neighborhood at the apex. In Mann's spatial typology, these relationships are "macro-regional," not strictly "global." In a superb discussion based on empirical research, Quemin (2006) has generalized this point beyond art fairs and commercial art galleries. As he puts it, despite enormously increased international mobility,

> the world of contemporary art thus clearly has a center, because it functions very much as a duopoly formed by, on the one hand, the US and, on the other … a few countries in Western Europe … In contrast to this emphatically Western center, there is an 'artistic periphery' that … includes all those countries that do not appear in the preceding list, and in particular the countries of the Third World, but not only them, as can be seen from the cases of Japan, Canada, and Spain.
>
> (Quemin 2006: 542–43)

Selling art on the internet

At the same time, some of the main attempts to sell contemporary art via the internet do seem truly global in Mann's sense as "the extension and intensification of social relations over the globe." For example, Charles Saatchi, whose 2008 Museum of Contemporary Art in London is one of the largest physical spaces in the world for displaying contemporary art, is now at the forefront of the movement to sell art on the internet. Starting in May 2006, his website, Saatchi online, allowed artists, free of charge, to create tailored home pages on the site featuring their art work. A central aim was to help little-known, typically young, artists to display their works. The site currently displays the work of 65,000 artists. The artists can field email inquiries from any potential buyers visiting their pages, negotiate directly and without any further Saatchi Gallery involvement, and keep all proceeds from any art sales. Purchasers around the globe with an internet connection can contact artists anywhere, on a 24/7 time-line. It is not clear how far this process will undercut the traditional role of commercial galleries as mediators between artists and purchasers (collectors), but the potential for significant inroads is clearly there.

This site, with its low—in many cases, almost zero—transaction costs for artists wishing to use it to sell their art, seems to fit the designation "transnational" (transcending the boundaries of the national and potentially global) and probably "global" (the extension and intensification of social relations over the globe). Our data thus suggest that the concept of globalization needs to be used carefully and with an eye to making distinctions between the "strictly global" and various situations that are somewhat less so.

The local market and organizational analysis

We now set the previous analysis alongside the detailed Chelsea material. In this discussion, first we stress the analytic perspectives of market and organization theory. Later we discuss the content and meaning of the works for those who view them. And finally, we introduce class and status theory. Our basic argument, we repeat, is that we need these multiple perspectives in order to grasp a complex and changing situation.

The multiplication and persistence of small galleries

Despite the presence of a sizeable contingent of elite, global galleries, Chelsea would not be the dense art-gallery neighborhood that it is without the plethora of small, boutique-size galleries (owned by individuals not corporations) that make up the majority of the galleries. This co-existence of elite and small operations in the same environment has some parallels to dominant centers in other creative industries, for example Silicon Valley. Thomas Crow (1996: 34) too has commented on the fact that so much of the gallery system exists at the "artisanal level." Our interviews in Chelsea found that gallery owners, often motivated by "art for art's sake," may be willing to settle for less profit than "humdrum entrepreneurs," which also helps explain why there are so many small galleries. As the economist Richard Caves commented about art galleries generally, "The motivation of business owners makes a difference. Many art gallery dealers appear to share art for art's sake preferences and hence are willing to settle for less profit than humdrum entrepreneurs. That factor probably makes for a denser population of galleries than if they were run by profit-seekers" (2000: 44).

The best free show in town

Unlike the established art museums in New York City, which charge admissions (entry to the recently re-opened MoMA is $20), Chelsea galleries impose no entry charge, do not pressure onlookers to buy, and provide an open and welcoming ambience. Of course, most retail organizations such as galleries do not charge admission, but the Chelsea galleries have moved considerably in the direction of free museums in their modes of display. Data from our interviews with samples of the audience show that the vast majority (over 95 percent) come just to look, with absolutely no intention of purchasing art. The major purchasers (serious collectors) typically attend private showings arranged specially for them and even buy works based on photos via the internet. The overwhelming majority of the audience is therefore comprised of viewers but arguably not "consumers," if that term refers to people whose role is to purchase goods

381

in the market. Free admission runs counter to the strong tendency in the modern world toward the "commercialization of leisure life," whereby a growing proportion of leisure time is devoted to events for which admission is paid. A large commercial locus such as Chelsea offers, ironically, a substantial, no-charge benefit for the public.

Further, in other cultural spheres when the "show" is free, audiences typically pay another price—for example waiting in long lines for admission or enduring second-rate performers. What is interesting, and perhaps even unique, about Chelsea is that the elite galleries are the ones that display the very best of contemporary art in the most easily accessible form. Audiences simply step right off the street into these galleries, whereas most (non-elite) galleries usually display their art on upper floors. This feature appears to distinguish Chelsea from other key "cultural enterprises" such as Hollywood and Silicon Valley. Whether Chelsea's free-show approach is "rational" for the galleries or something that just emerged is not yet clear. "Buzz" theory suggests that it is rational. Several studies have confirmed the importance of "buzz" (defined as a critical mass of favorable, or at least involved, discussion) in the sale of creative goods generally. A favorable "buzz" is likely to reach many potential buyers and also influence critics (Caves 2000: 81; DiMaggio 1987; Collins 1979; Frith 1998: 4–5).

Commercial galleries as opportunities for artists

Although nearly every Chelsea gallery is commercial, almost all the artists, whether successful or struggling, say that the Chelsea galleries generally offer them far more freedom and opportunity than do nonprofit museums and other institutions, in New York or elsewhere. Artists mostly consider museum directors and curators to be more conservative—focused on established art and less open to new art and artists—than the typical gallery owner/director. Above all, the artists that we interviewed do not, on the whole, see the gallery system as a structure of dominance or oppression.

An occupational community of "gallerists"

Chelsea is not a residential community of artists. From the time it started as a gallery district in the mid-1990s, few artists could afford to live there, and they certainly cannot now. (SoHo was, by contrast, an occupational and residential community of artists who produced art from their lofts/homes.) Yet Chelsea has developed into an occupational community of people who work in/run/own galleries, and a special term, "gallerists," has emerged to characterize this phenomenon. Chelsea's gallerists are not well described as an impersonal set of atomistic units locked in ferocious competition, to employ one stereotype of market relations. Rather, they arguably have many of the positive aspects associated with the idea of "community."

The local commercial real estate market: will Chelsea go the way of SoHo?

Above all, every Chelsea gallery must deal with Manhattan's ferocious real estate market. Indeed, Chelsea's very rise was real estate-driven. Rents soared in SoHo from 1995–99, fueled by an influx of clothing boutiques, forcing a mass exodus to Chelsea of galleries that could not afford the new rents.

Not surprisingly, a much debated topic among Chelsea gallery owners and other observers is whether real estate developments will eventually cause a similar, SoHo-style debacle. Learning from SoHo, most of those galleries that came to Chelsea with sufficient capital bought their spaces so as to insulate themselves from the commercial rental market. The other galleries, the vast majority, signed leases and are at the mercy of the commercial real estate market, which, in Manhattan, has no controls. At the end of a typical five-year lease, plus a five-year option to extend, landlords can charge whatever they can get. Here, the huge influence of the real estate market in determining Chelsea's future as a gallery district is apparent.

Emerging gallery–auction house conflict

Chelsea, too, is a site where it is possible to study an emerging challenge by auction houses to the long prevailing division of labor in the art market between art galleries and auction houses. Recently, auction houses have begun to move into the galleries' lucrative market for primary works. The brashest—and most successful—such challenger is located in Chelsea. Phillips de Pury, an auction house founded in London in 1796, in 2003 moved its headquarters to a spectacular space in Chelsea just north of the Meatpacking district on 15th Street. In 2006, Phillips began what it called "Selling Exhibitions," where it displayed and sold brand new works that had never been on the market before. To emphasize its new, dual role as both gallery and auction house, Phillips repackaged itself as an "art company that does auctions" (of contemporary art, photography, design, and jewelry), not just an auction company.

The intrusion into the gallery world by Phillips de Pury was followed by Christie's 2007 purchase of Haunch of Venison, a contemporary art gallery in London and Zürich, with plans announced to open a gallery in New York later that same year, in Rockefeller Center. This move was less drastic than Phillips's, since Christie's was not (yet) itself selling new works, and auction houses have owned galleries in the past, though never successful ones. Still, given Christie's size, the move garnered enormous attention (and anxiety) in the gallery world.

The shift in the function of auction houses merits close study. For example, will the auction houses drive the gallery world towards the kind of oligopolistically structured industry long present in other creative industries such as publishing and movie production and of which the auction world, long dominated by the Sotheby's/Christie's duopoly, is an extreme form?

In summary, from the analytic perspective of market and organization theory, the overall picture is complex. There is an enormous literature discussing market and related organizational perspectives; our argument is that, to properly understand the gallery scene in Chelsea, we need to draw on much of this literature and use it in subtle and nuanced ways. Some important studies, in addition to those already cited, are Getty Research Institute (2004), Moulin (1967), Velthius (2005), New Museum of Contemporary Art (2007), and Miller (1987).

The art works and their meaning for those who view them

To understand the meaning of art works for those who view them—a crucial but exceedingly complex topic—yet a different perspective is needed. Here we challenge

383

much popular discussion which collapses the issue of meaning into the topic of markets and money, implying that art basically appeals as a lucrative investment—an argument that might seem to find some support in Chelsea's growth as an art-gallery district in the context of what was probably the most effervescent art market ever.

Content analysis of the art displayed in Chelsea galleries, combined with interviews of audience members about what the art means to them, suggests that people are drawn to art that speaks to ongoing issues in their lives. (Fiske [1989] presents a similar perspective in relation to cultural consumption more generally. He argues that cultural texts/objects of all kinds typically need to resonate with people's everyday experiences in order to be popular.) In brief, five categories dominate the content of the art displayed in Chelsea. Each of these categories represents at least 13 percent of all the works in the sample.

The first category—depictions of landscapes/nature—constitutes 25 per cent of all the works sampled and it divides into three main types. There is the classic "good stretch of countryside/water/sky" type (15 percent of all works), which has been featured prominently in Western landscape art over the last 200 years and remains immensely popular.

The second type within the overall category of landscapes, constituting 5 percent of all works, we label "radical environmental." These landscapes foreground concern, and often alarm, about the deterioration of the natural environment. This type is in many ways new since the 1960s and clearly reflects a widespread alarm, even social panic, at the environmental damage caused by humans. The third type of landscape is conceptual. It implies a narrative scene, and also constitutes 5 percent of all works sampled.

The second most common category (accounting for 23 percent of all works) is the decorative/mostly pure design. Grouped under the umbrella of "abstract" art, this category was considered by the "modernist avant-garde" in the twentieth century to be the apogee of art, superior in almost every way to all forms of representative or figurative art. Such claims are now widely seen as exaggerated (e.g. Kleiner and Mamiya 2005). In the Chelsea art scene, the abstract/decorative category has assumed a more modest, though still important, position as (just) one among five categories.

A third category is the nuclear family, typically depicted with a critical or satirical edge as a troubled institution (13 percent of all works). Serenely confident families and individual family members of the kind depicted by Norman Rockwell are so rare as to be almost taboo. This category—the problematic family—is a new genre in art history. Although troubled families have obviously existed in actuality throughout history, artists or patrons did not depict them in a sufficiently systematic way so as to make them a recognizable genre.

Sex is the fourth most popular category of contemporary art, constituting 8 percent of all those displayed. About half of these images depict sexual activity—most often intercourse between men and women. The other half of the images classified as "sex" here just depict people naked or semi-naked, usually women—akin to the classic nude of art history. Like "radical environmental art," sexual intercourse is unusual in Western art, at least for the last two millennia. Although naked or semi-naked men and women pervade the history of Western art, they have rarely been depicted as engaged in sexual activity (exceptions include Indian art, for example, which has a well-known tradition of eroticism, as did classical Greek pottery). The remaining category includes the miscellaneous topics of politics, raw/basic materials, the poor and disadvantaged, religion, and mass/commodity production.

The general picture suggested by considering the five major categories does not fit the view that the art is primarily about trading and making money in a global market.

On the contrary, the categories are mostly rooted in modern life and in the varied ways that people (artists and audience) experience today's world. For example, environmental landscapes seem rooted in post-1960s alarm about the deteriorating natural environment. The troubled nuclear family mimics today's high divorce rate and reflects a variety of adaptational challenges, such as the growing prominence of single-headed households, blended families, and same-sex relations. Sexual intercourse seems to mimic current interest in pornography, especially promoted by the web.

Interviews with audience members attending particular art shows likewise suggest that these themes flourish because they resonate with everyday life in an ongoing, creative, and interactive way. For example, audience interviews at shows where the works are abstract/decorative suggest that the main attraction of these works is their ability to brighten up people's lives.

It is true that the small minority of audience members who intend to purchase art—namely the "collectors"—may do so as a financial investment. But even here, a conflation of the market-oriented analysis with an analysis of art's meaning short-circuits the question of how certain works and artists come to be sufficiently attractive in the first place to constitute a promising investment. The central answer suggested here is that the works resonate with the lives of audiences.

We now discuss a fourth set of approaches: "class homology" and "omnivore" arguments.

"Class homology," "omnivorism," and their limits

Considerable cultural theory and debate have revolved around the "class homology" theory and its major rival, the "omnivore" hypothesis. We argue that both approaches are helpful, but that the data suggest a more complex situation than either perspective usually allows.

The homology argument basically claims that social stratification and cultural stratification map closely onto each other. Individuals in higher social strata prefer and predominantly consume "high" or "elite" culture, and individuals in lower social strata prefer and predominantly consume "popular" or "mass" culture—with, usually, various intermediate situations also being recognized. For a restatement of the argument, see Gans (1999). However, more elaborate versions of the homology argument exist, notably that developed by Bourdieu (1984).

There is certainly some support in the Chelsea data for "class homology." For example, the audience and collectors for contemporary art are typically economic and cultural elites, comprising primarily managers, professionals, entrepreneurs, and the independently wealthy, as well as individuals working in the cultural field (art students, art administrators, and artists). Strikingly absent are blue-collar workers and lower-white-collar employees. In this sense, the taste for contemporary art is class specific.

Yet the data are also consistent with the omnivore approach. The broad hypothesis is that, in modern societies, the homology argument is outmoded, not because cultural consumption has lost all grounding in social stratification but because a new relationship is emerging. Rather than cultural stratification mapping straightforwardly onto social stratification, the cultural consumption of individuals in higher social strata differs from that of individuals in lower strata chiefly in being much wider in its range—comprising not only more "high-brow" culture but more "middle-brow" and more "low-brow" culture as well. Thus, the crucial contrast is not that of "snob versus slob" but that of cultural omnivore versus cultural univore (Chan and Goldthorpe 2005, 2007a, 2007b, 2007c). Further, the strong implication of omnivore theory is that omnivores pursue a broad range of cultural interests above all because doing so enables them to advance in a wide variety of contexts.

This argument is both supported by our data and incapable of really dealing with all the important complexities. On the one hand, those who engage with contemporary art could plausibly be classified as "omnivores" since they engage with this art and, probably, a broad range of other art too. Yet on the complexity side, it is increasingly difficult to distinguish "high" from "popular" art, and thus to differentiate the apparent omnivore from the apparent univore. In other cultural spheres, we can still probably construct high–popular differences (e.g. classical music versus the many varieties of popular music), but in the art world it is less clear what is "low brow" or "popular" these days. Also, it is unclear that people who engage with contemporary art are doing so primarily for reasons of status and/or class advantage, as the "omnivore" hypothesis strongly implies. On the contrary, many of those who engage with contemporary art just seem to like it, plausibly enough because much of it, as we have argued, resonates with aspects of their lives. Further, if high-status people—those who may be most likely to travel and interact with a variety of transnational individuals—consume a greater variety of cultural genres and forms than low-status individuals, this may reflect the variety of culture they encounter rather than a concerted effort to differentiate themselves from others, as older versions of status theory would have predicted.

Conclusions

A case study of Chelsea, Manhattan, the most important contemporary art-gallery district in the world, set in a "global" context, suggests a complex and changing situation to which one or two analytic frameworks cannot alone do justice and which demands new combinations of theoretical perspectives. "Globalization" theory, organization and market theory, the analysis of the meaning of art works as considered from the audience's point of view, and "class homology" and "omnivore" theory can all illuminate some aspects of our data, but only when presented in a cautious form with many caveats and qualifications. Overall, we emphasize the need for theoretical complexity, flexibility, and eclecticism in order to do justice to a complex empirical situation. Although our topic has been the contemporary art scene in Chelsea as set in a global context, we suspect that a similarly eclectic and multi-dimensional perspective is needed for many other major cultural phenomena in the contemporary world.

References

Art 38 Basel. 2007. www.artbasel.com/ca/bt/kh/.

Battani, M. and Hall, J. 2000. "Richard Peterson and Cultural Theory: From Genetic, to Integrated, to Synthetic Approaches." *Poetics* 28(2–3): 137–56.

Bourdieu, Pierre. 1984. *Distinction: A Social Critique of the Judgement of Taste*, trans. Richard Nice. Cambridge, MA: Harvard University Press.

Caves, Richard. 2000. *Creative Industries*. Cambridge, MA: Harvard University Press.

Chan, T.W. and Goldthorpe, J.H. 2005. "The Social Stratification of Theatre, Dance, and Cinema Attendance." *Cultural Trends* 14(3): 193–212.

——. 2007a. "Social Status and Newspaper Readership." *American Journal of Sociology* 112(4): 1095–1134.

——. 2007b. "Social Stratification and Cultural Consumption: Music in England." *European Sociological Review* 23(1): 1–19.

——. 2007c. "Social Stratification and Cultural Consumption: The Visual Arts in England." *Poetics* 35(2–3): 168–90.

Collins, Randall. 1979. *The Credential Society: An Historical Sociology of Education and Stratification.* New York: Academic Press

Crow, Thomas. 1996. *Modern Art in the Common Culture.* New Haven, CT and London: Yale University Press.

DiMaggio, Paul. 1987. "Classification in Art." *American Sociological Review* 52: 440–55.

Fiske, John. 1989. *Reading the Popular.* New York: Routledge.

Frith, Simon. 1998. *Performing Rites: On the Value of Popular Music.* Cambridge, MA: Harvard University Press.

Gans, Herbert. 1999. *Popular Culture and High Culture: An Analysis and Evaluation of Taste*, revised and updated editioin. New York: Basic Books.

Getty Research Institute. 2004. *The Business of Art: Evidence from the Art Market.* Los Angeles: Getty Research Institute.

Griswold, Wendy. 2004. *Cultures and Societies in a Changing World*, second edition. Thousand Oaks, CA: Pine Forge Press.

Kleiner, Fred and Mamiya, Christin. 2005. *Gardner's Art through the Ages.* Boston: Thomson-Wadsworth.

Mann, Michael. 2007. "Globalizations: An Introduction to the Spatial and Structural Networks of Globality." Unpublished paper.

Miller, Daniel. 1987. *Material Culture and Mass Consumption.* Oxford: Basil Blackwell.

Moulin, Raymond. 1967. *The French Art Market: A Sociological View.* New Brunswick, NJ: Rutgers University Press.

New Museum of Contemporary Art. 2007. *Unmonumental: The Object in the Twenty-first Century.* New York: Phaidon.

Quemin, Alain. 2006. "Globalization and Mixing in the Visual Arts: An Empirical Survey of 'High Culture' and Globalization." *International Sociology* (July) 21(4): 522–50.

Saatchi Online. 2008. http://www.saatchi-gallery.co.uk/yourgallery/register/.

Smith, Roberta. 2004. "Chelsea Enters Its High Baroque Period." *New York Times*, November 28.

Velthius, Olav. 2005. *Talking Prices: Symbolic Meaning of Prices on the Market for Contemporary Art.* Princeton, NJ: Princeton University Press.

37

Pop culture institutions

From production to aesthetics

Marshall Battani

The study of popular culture institutions developed into a legitimate sociological specialty as sociologists of culture harnessed conceptual toolkits already developed for the study of organizations and occupations to focus on the systemic institutionalized nature of the creation, distribution, and valuation of popular culture. The production of culture perspective (Peterson 1976) is emblematic of this orientation. Other approaches informed by ambitious classical studies of culture, and by critiques of cultural hegemony, persist as well, and have influenced sociologists taking up the study of audience "reception" and uses of popular culture (Press 1994). This chapter outlines the field of production, reception, and critical studies, and more recent moves to incorporate aesthetic argument into sociological studies of pop culture institutions. Reviewing the field this way illustrates the development of increasingly complex views of culture in social life and suggests that the incorporation of aesthetic argument provides an important next step in that development.

The production of culture

The production perspective is typically unconcerned with distinctions between popular culture and high culture, and the quintessential production study is, without doubt, Howard Becker's *Art Worlds* (1984), in which he applies the sociology of occupations to the artistic case. In this perspective, production tends to explain culture as a direct outcome of the structures within which it is created. Studies of news production, for example, illustrate how the organization of news-gathering into "beats," in combination with the conventions of a given news medium (column inches, server space, live-feeds, deadlines, news cycles, etc.), creates a "news-net" (Tuchman 1978) that will capture only a very particular and narrow vision of the world. News-making studies of this sort have been one of the most active areas of inquiry in popular culture institutions (see Altheide 1976; Tuchman 1978; Gitlin 1980; Fishman 1980; Hallin 1986; Kannis 1997; Hoynes 1997; Clayman and Reisner 1998; Schudson 2001, 2003; Miladi 2003).

Much like news content, the narrow range of content in prime-time television programming can be explained by focusing one's attention on the constraints imposed on production by the everyday and routine organization of work (Gitlin 1983; Bielby and Bielby 1994; Scott 2004). Workplace interactions become normalized, institutionalized, and routinized over time, and, as a result, particular conventions of style and meaning emerge, predominate, and become institutionalized. The production perspective has been employed to explain the style and content of Hollywood movies (Kerr 1990; Baker and Faulkner 1991; Bauman 2001), Bollywood movies (Desai 2003; Dudrah 2006), the economic viability and cultural relevance of French cinema (Scott 2000), the organization of radio broadcasting (Leblebici 1995), the work of book reviewers (Janssen 1997), the form and content of magazines (Haveman 2004), photographic meanings in the US (Rosenblum 1978; Battani 1999; Aspers 2006) and Japan (Edwards and Hart 2004), as well as music production in Korea (Shin and Oh 2002), India (Manuel 1993), Israel (Perelson 1998), Britain (Frith 2000; Brownrigg and Meech 2002), Zimbabwe (Scannell 2001), France (Tinker 2002) and the US (Peterson and Berger 1971; Peterson 1978, 1997; Kealy 1979).

The production perspective emerged from a perceived impasse as grand functionalist and Marxist theorists had failed to recognize their potential shared interest in empirical studies of culture (Battani and Hall 2000). The grand and critical work of the classics like Tocqueville's (2004) take on "middling" values, Weber's (1998) famous protestant ethic thesis, Simmel's (1950) objective and subjective spirit, David Riesman's (1950) "other-directed" personality types and Bellah *et al.*'s (1985) summation of American middle-class culture are anathema to the production perspective and to prevailing norms in much contemporary sociological practice which tend to dictate sharp empirical focus and modest generalizable findings (Alexander 2003). Still, ambition persists in critical work today. For example, there is McVeigh's (2000) "How Hello Kitty Commodifies the Cute, Cool, and Camp," Anne Allison's "Cuteness as Japan's Millennial Product" (2004), and Larissa Hjorth's (2003) "Cute@Keitai.com." Ritzer's McDonaldization thesis (2008), like the classics, makes a grand and sweeping gesture as it reinvigorates Weber's theories of bureaucracy by identifying and critiquing processes of "McDonaldization" and "Starbuckization" to better understand how rationalization, as a cultural imperative, permeates social life.

Hegemonic and affirmative culture

Sociological analysis of pop culture at its most critical (and least subtle) generally investigates the substance of popular culture (the content of news, advertising, and television, for example) to reveal the powers working to perpetuate the appearance of social solidarity that is, in reality, an ideologically and materially self-interested effort to maintain the status quo. Drawing on Frankfurt School concepts of affirmative culture (often implicitly) this work tends to focus on the political economy of mass media and their biases (Bagdikian 1983; Herman and Chomsky 2002), on advertising and public relations, (Ewen 1976, 1988, 1996; Nelson 1989; Leiss *et al.* 1997), and on corporate control of public culture (Schiller 1989, 1996). The critical theoretical distinction between authentic culture (emergent, fulfilling, open to human agency) and popular culture (rigidly structured, empty, reifies structures) informs work ranging from the analyses of the commodification of rock and roll (Seiler 2000), to the intimate connections between bookstores, shopping malls, amusement parks, and cities (Miller 1981; Fjellman 1992; Hannigan 1998; Gottdiener *et al.* 2000; Miller 2006).

A significant body of critical work draws its inspiration from the Birmingham School of cultural studies to examine hegemonic power and the potential for ideological resistance. The classic examples are Hall and Jefferson (1976) and Hebdige (1979). Current studies in this tradition often delineate the creation and management of ambivalent identities within particular institutional settings. Laura Grindstaff (2002) and Joshua Gamson (1998) have studied television talk shows and illustrate how practices in the institutional field of TV talk intersect and overlap with US traditions of the public sphere. The resulting interactions in the production and airing of TV talk shows give voice to stigmatized members of society while at the same time recreating and reinforcing status structures of sexuality, class, and ethnicity. Amy Best's ethnographic studies of US teenagers' emergent identities in relation to high school prom traditions (Best 2000) and car subcultures (Best 2006) illustrate this ambivalence as well. In her studies one sees teens constructing identities for themselves that embrace and resist social structures of gender, class, and ethnicity at play in the popular institutions central to their lives.

The skateboarder and documentary filmmaker Stacy Peralta takes a similar approach in *Dog Town and Z-Boys* (2002) as he chronicles the transformation of skateboarding from a Southern California fad into a subculture, which, in turn, became institutionalized as a multi-billion-dollar global industry in the late 1970s via the marketing of the identities of a small group of skaters from Santa Monica, California. Along the way the skaters are transformed as well, some leaving behind their working-class lives to become celebrities, others embracing their working-class identity in a fatalistic rebellion much like the English school boys described by Paul Willis in his study of institutionalized class reproduction in British schools (Willis 1977). The conclusions of such studies often depict a mutually reinforcing relationship between emerging and established cultural institutions and social structures. In another case, for example, Battani (1999) shows how the emerging institutional field of popular photographic practices and industry in the nineteenth-century US was constructed around newly powerful notions of middle-class respectability and how photographic products, practices, and aesthetic assessments gave consequential institutional form and meaning to status distinctions.

Active audiences and the complexities of meaning

The tendency to explain culture as an outgrowth of social structure or as a "negotiation" engaged in by social actors in relation to social structures has come under criticism for being "weak" in relation to a "strong" program of cultural sociology (Alexander 2003). Although presented as a corrective to the sociology of culture generally, the strong program critique is better thought of as a commentary on only the most simplified production studies or clumsy applications of critical theory. Even so, and despite a healthy debate over its merits (Emirbayer 2004; Kurasawa 2004; McLennan 2004, 2005; Joas 2005), the strong program is an important directive to treat the complexities of culture with due respect. The strong program critique points out two potential weaknesses with which sociologists of culture have grappled, and continue to grapple. The first is a failure to give culture the analytic autonomy and causal force that it deserves, and the second is an insufficiently thick description and thus lack of hermeneutic complexity. Just how the strong program will inform the study of pop culture institutions is not yet clear.

Strong program proponents advocate replacing current approaches, including production traditions, with a "structural hermeneutics" capable of accomplishing the ambitious theoretical goal of explaining culture as a product of cultural rather than social structures. So far, strong program culture studies tend to be less focused on particular pop culture institutions and more concerned with theories of culture (Alexander and Smith 1993; Alexander 1996; Smith 1998a, 1998b) and the foundational meanings of civil society (Alexander 1993, 2003; Smith 1996, 1998c). As pop culture scholars continue to expand the scope of their analyses and embed their institutional studies within the larger webs of cultural structures of meaning they would do well to keep in mind the strong program's admonition to focus on what is specifically cultural about our pop culture institutions.

Even before Alexander's critique, sociologically informed analyses of audiences taught pop culture investigators to look carefully and critically at how people collectively make aesthetic judgments and create meaning (Radway 1984; Jenkins 1992; Press 1994). The women in Janice Radway's (1984) study of romance novel readers, for example, construct empowering gendered meanings and edifying reading practices in everyday life that run counter to what literary elites read as patriarchy-reinforcing content in popular romance novels. Elites and book club participants employ very different aesthetic standards and it is a mistake to presuppose the predominance of one over another. Audiences, it would seem, don't always interpret things in ways wholly predicted by social structures. Consider JoEllen Shively's (1992) study of the Hollywood Western genre, in which Native American audience members identified more closely with cowboy characters than did Anglos. Similarly, studies of audience reception demonstrate that the notion of "cultural imperialism" is more complex than the term implies, because local audiences actively interpret global media and do not simply absorb their meanings and assimilate to them. See, for example, Liebes and Katz (1990) and Ang (1991) on the world-wide popularity of the US soap opera *Dallas*, Sakr (2001) and Hafez and Paletz (2001) on mass media, globalization, and patterns of political and social change in the Middle East, and Denise Bielby and C. Lee Harrington's (2004) explanation of how the concept of genre facilitates cross-cultural interpretations of television shows on the global market.

Sociological studies of culture continue to be inspired by the production perspective's sharp focus on the collective work of symbol production but take an increasingly complex view of the social and cultural contexts that facilitate and are affected by such production. Crane's (2001) study of fashion addresses the United States, the United Kingdom, and France in both the nineteenth and twentieth centuries as she examines fashion as an industry and as a meaningful territory of contested identities. In her institutional analysis of an industry (defined as including consumers), she is able to delineate major cultural shifts from modernism to postmodernism—from clothing as social control to clothing in the service of identity-formation. Not unlike Crane, Zukin (2004) proposes that we study consumption as an institutional field by essentially transposing the analytical tools developed for institutional analysis onto a practice, or set of practices, of social actors who are more typically studied as if they lie outside the boundaries of productive organizations and institutions. There are good reasons for doing this, and she compellingly demonstrates the expertise of shoppers and their varied understandings of their practices that include both the human-scale interactions of local farmer's markets and the totalizing (if not total) institutions of K-Mart and Wal-Mart. Wendy Griswold (1986) similarly bridges the divide between production and reception/consumption. Her analysis of English drama examines four centuries of revival theater to show the intimate connections between a society and its cultural products, as evolving conceptions of justice and order find expressive form in the revivals of the City Comedy and Revenge Tragedy genres. Turning to the study of Nigerian readers and writers, Griswold (2000) explains the operations of a macro-level modernist literary system—what she calls the "Nigerian fiction complex"—as part of a social setting that is both pre- and postmodern. In doing so she paints an intimate picture of the everyday struggles with social structures and cultural practices actualized in the production and reception of the novel.

Aesthetics

Most audience studies attribute meaning to the discursive resources that audience members bring to their encounters with popular culture. Discursive resources, in turn, are attributed to the stocks of knowledge engendered by a person's social location (ethnicity, class, gender, age, sexual orientation, etc.). Such an approach risks reproducing the "weakness" of the production perspective by reducing cultural meanings to outcomes of social structure. However, in "Audience Aesthetics and Popular Culture," Bielby and Bielby (2004) move beyond a social structural explanation of meaning and argue for treating the emergent collective understanding among audiences as an aesthetic phenomenon. They insist that the appreciation of popular culture be treated by the researcher as an expressive and emotional experience and the Bielbys have created a large body of collaborative work devoted to engaging production principles and meaningful interpretation of pop cultural institutions simultaneously (Bielby and Bielby 2002, 2003a; Bielby et al. 2005; Harrington and Bielby 2005). The most sophisticated of these studies examine a nexus of production processes, audience reception, and aesthetics at play in a given institution or institutional field.

Acknowledging the importance of aesthetic experience to analyses of popular culture, as the Bielbys have done, does not automatically signal a critical approach. It is still quite possible to undertake a sociology of aesthetics as opposed to engaging with an aesthetic argument. Sociologists of culture typically accept the aesthetic concepts and judgments of their research subjects at face value (Crane 1987, 2001). Mark Gottdiener's (2001) analysis of the built environment points in an alternative, aesthetic, direction by asserting a critical concept of its own. In McDonald's restaurants and sites such as Planet Hollywood and Hard Rock Café restaurants, shopping malls, theme parks, and Las Vegas, Gottdiener identifies what he calls "theming"—a practice whereby people make their culture concrete as they infuse their built environment with dreams, values, ideas, and cosmologies. As ancient Athens revolved around its gods, contemporary pop culture institutions circulate mediated fantasies. Today's Disneyland or Las Vegas functions in much the same way as did a cathedral positioned at the center of a medieval city. Because the "theme" is a meaningful concept that identifies and critiques a cultural practice cutting across history and societies, it creates an opportunity to engage with critical aesthetic discourses in architecture and urban design.

Important cases of sociological informed cultural and aesthetic critique lie outside the traditional boundaries of the sociological discipline as well. Lutz and Collins's (1993) critique of *National Geographic*, Maren Stange's (1989) critique of late nineteenth- and early twentieth-century social documentary photography, and Richard Steven Street's (2008) visual history of California farm workers are all excellent examples. They come from outside sociology's disciplinary boundaries but nevertheless employ a production approach to delineate the complex structural constraints on photographic production and reception while simultaneously engaging critical aesthetic discourse. For instance, Street (2008) offers up, in great historical detail, the social, cultural, and institutional contexts from which our images of California farm workers emerge. In the process he offers a critical and cultural perspective on politics, ideology, and economics, while making an aesthetic argument extolling the humanitarian values of photographic styles that took shape in the 1930s.

Conclusions

The production perspective has dominated the study of institutionalized popular culture and yet its tendency to explain culture in social terms (political, ideological, economic, etc.) has opened it to criticism and calls for a more fully cultural approach. Critical traditions informing production and reception studies open up complementary approaches that engage in critical argument coupled with aesthetic judgment. Moving in this direction might reinvigorate an already present impulse stemming from a sense that cultural practice and critique are, in many ways, synonymous (Adorno 2000). Arguments over the place of cultural critique in sociology are complex and beyond the scope of this chapter, but if our studies of pop culture audiences tell us anything they tell us that to engage in cultural practice is to interpret, to argue, to be critical, and to make judgments. It seems logical, then, that the practice of cultural sociology would require the same.

References

Adorno, Theodor. 2000. "Cultural Criticism and Society." Pp. 195–210 in Brian O'Connor, ed., *The Adorno Reader*. Oxford: Blackwell.

Alexander, Jeffrey, C. 1993. "Citizen and Enemy as Symbolic Classification: On the Polarizing Discourse of Civil Society." Pp. 289–308 in Marcel Fournier and Michèle Lamont, eds., *Where Culture Talks: Exclusion and the Making of Society*. Chicago: University of Chicago Press.

—, ed. 1996. *Durkheimian Sociology: Cultural Studies*. Cambridge: Cambridge University Press.

——. 2003. *The Meanings of Social Life: A Cultural Sociology*. Oxford: Oxford University Press.

Alexander, Jeffrey C. and Smith, Philip. 1993. "The Discourse of American Civil Society: A New Proposal for Cultural Studies." *Theory and Society* 22(2): 151–207.

Allison, Anne. 2004. "Cuteness as Japan's Millennial Product." Pp. 34–49 in Joseph Tobin, ed., *Picachu's Global Adventure: The Rise and Fall of Pokémon*. Durham, NC: Duke University Press.

Altheide, David L. 1976. *Creating Reality: How TV News Distorts Events*. Beverley Hills, CA: Sage.

Ang, Ien. 1991. *Desperately Seeking the Audience*. London: Routledge.

Aspers, Patrick. 2006. *Markets in Fashion: A Phenomenological Approach*. London: Routledge.

Bagdikian, Ben. 1974. *The Effete Conspiracy and Other Crimes by the Press*. New York: Harper.

——. 1983. *The Media Monopoly*. Boston: Beacon.

Baker, Wayne E. and Faulkner, Robert R. 1991. "Role as Resource in the Hollywood Film Industry." *American Journal of Sociology* 97: 279–309.

Battani, Marshall. 1999. "Organizational Fields, Cultural Fields, and Art Worlds: The Early Effort to Make Photographs and to Make Photographers in the 19th-Century United States." *Media, Culture, and Society* 21: 601–26.

Battani, Marshall and Hall, John R. 2000. "Richard Peterson and Cultural Theory: From Genetic, to Synthetic, and Integrated Approaches." *Poetics* 28(2): 137–58.

Bauman, Shyon. 2001. "Intellectualization and Art World Development: Film in the United States." *American Sociological Review* 66: 404–26.

Becker, Howard. 1984. *Art Worlds*. Chicago: University of Chicago Press.

Bellah, Robert, Madsen, Richard, Sullivan, William M., Swidler, Ann, and Tipton, Steven M. 1985. *Habits of the Heart: Individualism and Commitment in American Life*. New York: Harper and Row.

Best, Amy. 2000. *Prom Night: Youth, Schools, and Popular Culture*. London: Routledge.

———. 2006. *Fast Cars, Cool Rides: The Accelerating World of Youth and Their Cars*. New York: New York University Press.

Bielby, Denise D. and Bielby, William T. 1994. "All Hits Are Flukes: Institutionalized Decision-Making and the Rhetoric of Network Prime Time Television." *American Journal of Sociology* 99: 1287–1313.

———. 2002. "Hollywood Dreams, Harsh Realities: Writing for Film and Television." *Contexts* 1(4): 21–27.

———. 2003a. "Beyond Contexts: Taking Cultural Objects Seriously in Media, Popular Culture, and the Arts." *Sociological Perspectives* 46(4): 429–33.

———. 2004. "Audience Aesthetics and Popular Culture." Pp. 295–317 in Roger Friedland and John Mohr, eds., *Matters of Culture: Cultural Sociology in Practice*. Cambridge: University of Cambridge Press.

Bielby, Denise D. and Harrington, C. Lee. 2004. "Managing Culture Matters: Genre, Aesthetic Elements, and the International Market for Exported Television." *Poetics: Journal of Empirical Research on Literature, the Media and the Arts* 32(1): 73–98.

Bielby, Denise D. and Moloney, Molly. 2008. "Considering Global Media: Sociological Contributions." Pp. 269–300 in Ron Rice, ed., *Media Ownership: Research and Regulation*. Cresskill, NJ: Hampton Press.

Bielby, Denise D., Moloney, Molly, and Ngo, Bob. 2005. "Aesthetics of Television Criticism: Mapping Critics' Reviews in an Era of Industry Transformation." Pp. 1–43 in Candace Jones and Patricia Thornton, eds., *Research in the Sociology of Organizations: Transformations in Cultural Industries*, Volume 23. London: JAI Press.

Bielby, W.T. and Bielby, D.D. 2003b. "Controlling Primetime: Organizational Concentration and Network Television Primetime Programming Strategies." *Journal of Broadcasting & Electronic Media* 47(4): 573–97.

Brownrigg, Mark and Meech, Peter. 2002. "From Fanfare to Funfair: The Changing Sound World of UK Television Idents." *Popular Music* 21(3): 345–55.

Clayman, Steven E. and Reisner, Ann. 1998. "Gatekeeping in Action: Editorial Conferences and Assessments of Newsworthiness." *American Sociological Review* 63(2): 178–99.

Crane, Diana. 1987. *The Transformation of the Avant-Garde: The New York Art World, 1940–85*. Chicago: University of Chicago Press.

———. 2001. *Fashion and Its Social Agendas: Class, Gender, and Identity in Clothing*. Chicago: University of Chicago Press.

Desai, Jigna. 2003. *Beyond Bollywood: The Cultural Politics of South Asian Diasporic*. London: Routledge.

Dudrah, Rajinder Kumar. 2006. *Bollywood: Sociology Goes to the Movies*. Thousand Oaks, CA: Sage.

Edwards, Elizabeth and Hart, Janice. 2004. *Photographs Objects Histories: On the Materiality of Images*. London: Routledge.

Emirbayer, Mustafa. 2004. "The Alexander School of Cultural Sociology." *Thesis Eleven* 79(1): 5–15.

Ewen, Stuart. 1976. *Captains of Consciousness: Advertising and the Social Roots of the Consumer Culture*. New York: McGraw-Hill.

———. 1988. *All Consuming Images: The Politics of Style in Contemporary Culture*. New York: Basic Books.

———. 1996. *PR!: A Social History of Spin*. New York: Basic Books.

Fishman, Mark. 1980. *Manufacturing the News*. Austin: University of Texas Press.

Fjellman, Stephen M. 1992. *Vinyl Leaves: Walt Disney World and America*. Boulder, CO: Westview.

Frith, Simon. 2000. "Music Industry Research: Where Now? Where Next? Notes from Popular Music." *Popular Music* 19(3): 387–93

Gamson, Joshua. 1998. *Freaks Talk Back: Tabloid Talk Shows and Sexual Nonconformity*. Chicago: University of Chicago Press.

Gitlin, Todd. 1980. *The Whole World is Watching: Mass Media in the Making and Unmaking of the New Left*. Berkeley: University of California Press.

——. 1983. *Inside Prime Time*. New York: Pantheon.

Gottdiener, Mark. 2001. *The Theming of America: American Dreams, Media Fantasies, and Themed Environments*. Boulder, CO: Westview Press.

Gottdiener, Mark, Collins, Claudia, and Dickens, David R. 2000. *Las Vegas: The Social Production of an All American City*. Oxford: Blackwell.

Grindstaff, Laura. 2002. *The Money Shot: Trash, Class and the Making of TV Talk Shows*. Chicago: University of Chicago Press.

Griswold, Wendy. 1986. *Renaissance Revivals: City Comedy and Revenge Tragedy in the London Theater, 1576–1980*. Chicago: University of Chicago Press.

——. 2000. *Bearing Witness*. Princeton, NJ: Princeton University Press.

Hafez, Kai and Paletz, David L., eds. 2001. *Mass Media, Politics, and Society in the Middle East*. Cresskill, NJ: Hampton Press.

Hall, Stuart and Jefferson, Tony, eds. 1976. *Resistance through Rituals: Youth Subcultures in Post War Britain*. London: Hutchinson.

Hallin, Daniel C. 1986. *The Uncensored War: The Media and Vietnam*. Berkeley: University of California Press.

Hannigan, John. 1998. *The Fantasy City: Pleasure and Profit in the Postmodern Metropolis*. London: Routledge.

Harrington, C. Lee and Bielby, Denise D. 2005. "Global Television Distribution: Implications of TV 'Traveling' for Viewers, Fans, and Texts." *American Behavioral Scientist* 48(7): 902–20.

Haveman, Heather A. 2004. "Antebellum Literary Culture and the Evolution of American Magazines." *Poetics* 32: 5–28.

Hebdige, Dick. 1979. *Subculture: The Meaning of Style*. London: Routledge.

Herman, Edward S. and Chomsky, Noam. 2002. *Manufacturing Consent: The Political Economy of the Mass Media*. New York: Pantheon.

Hjorth, Larissa. 2003. "Cute@Keitai.com." Pp. 50–59 in Mark McLelland and Nanette Gottlieb, eds., *Japanese Cybercultures*. London: Routledge.

Hoynes, William. 1997. "Journalism as a Balancing Act: Direct and Indirect Pressures on the News." *Sociological Imagination* 34(2–3): 72–87.

Janssen, Susanne. 1997. "Reviewing as Social Practice: Institutional Constraints on Critics' Attention for Contemporary Fiction." *Poetics* 24: 275–97.

Jenkins, Henry. 1992. *Textual Poachers: Television Fans and Participatory Culture*. London: Routledge.

Joas, Hans. 2005. "Cultural Trauma? On the Most Recent Turn in Jeffrey Alexander's Cultural Sociology." *European Journal of Social Theory* 8(3): 365–74.

Kannis, Phyllis. 1997. *Making Local News*. Chicago: University of Chicago Press.

Kealy, Edward R. 1979. "From Craft to Art: The Case of Sound Mixers and Popular Music." *Management and Organization Studies* 6(1): 3–29.

Kerr, Catherine E. 1990. "Incorporating the Star: The Intersection of Business and Aesthetic Strategies in Early American Film." *Business History Review* 64: 383–410.

Kurasawa, Fuyuki. 2004. "Alexander and the Cultural Refounding of American Sociology." *Thesis Eleven* 79(1): 53–64.

Leblebici, Huseyin. 1995. "Radio Broadcasters." Pp. 308–31 in Glenn R. Carroll and Michael T. Hannan, eds., *Organizations in Industry: Strategy, Structure, and Selection*. New York: Oxford University Press.

Leiss, William, Kline, Stephen, and Jhally, Sut. 1997. *Social Communication in Advertising: Persons, Products, and Images of Well-Being* 2nd ed. London: Routledge.

Liebes, Tamar and Katz, Elihu. 1990. *The Export of Meaning: Cross-Cultural Readings of "Dallas."* Oxford: Oxford University Press.

395

Lutz, Catherine A. and Collins, Jane L. 1993. *Reading National Geographic*. Chicago: University of Chicago Press.

McLennan, Gregor. 2004. "Rationalizing Musicality: A Critique of Alexander's 'Strong Program' in Cultural Sociology." *Thesis Eleven* 79(1): 75–86.

——. 2005. "The 'New American Cultural Sociology:' An Appraisal." *Theory Culture & Society* 22(6): 1–18.

McVeigh, Brian. 2000. "How Hello Kitty Commodifies the Cute, Cool, and Camp: 'Consummutopia' versus 'Control' in Japan." *Journal of Material Culture* 5: 225–45.

Manuel, Peter. 1993. *Cassette Culture: Popular Music and Technology in North India*. Chicago: University of Chicago Press.

Miladi, Noureddine. 2003. "Mapping the Al-Jazeera Phenomenon." Pp. 149–60 in Daya Thussu and Des Freeman, eds., *War and Media—Reporting Conflict 24/7*. London: Sage.

Miller, Laura J. 2006. *Reluctant Capitalists: Bookselling and the Culture of Consumption*. Chicago: University of Chicago Press.

Miller, Michael B. 1981. *The Bon Marché: Bourgeois Culture and the Department Store*. Princeton, NJ: Princeton University Press.

Nelson, Joyce. 1989. *Sultans of Sleaze: Public Relations and the Media*. Toronto: Between the Lines Press.

Peralta, Stacy, director. 2002. *Dogtown and Z-Boys: The Birth of Extreme* (motion picture). Sony Pictures Classics.

Perelson, Inbal. 1998. "Power Relations in the Israeli Popular Music System." *Popular Music* 17(1): 113–28.

Peterson, Richard A. 1976. "The Production of Culture: A Prolegomenon." Pp. 7–22 in Richard Peterson, ed., *The Production of Culture*. Beverley Hills, CA: Sage.

——. 1978. "The Production of Cultural Change: The Case of Contemporary Country Music." *Social Research* 45: 292–314.

——. 1994. "Culture Studies through the Production Perspective: Progress and Prospects." Pp. 163–90 in Diana Crane, ed., *The Sociology of Culture*. Cambridge, MA: Blackwell.

——. 1997. *Creating Country Music: Fabricating Authenticity*. Chicago: University of Chicago Press.

Peterson, Richard A. and Berger, David G. 1971. "Entrepreneurship in Organizations: Evidence from the Popular Music Industry." *Administrative Science Quarterly* 16: 97–107.

Press, Andrea. 1994. "The Sociology of Cultural Reception: Note Toward an Emerging Paradigm." Pp. 221–45 in Diana Crane, ed., *The Sociology of Culture*. Cambridge, MA: Blackwell.

Radway, Janice. 1984. *Reading the Romance: Women, Patriarchy, and Popular Literature*. Chapel Hill: University of North Carolina Press.

Riesman, David. 1950. *The Lonely Crowd*. New Haven, CT: Yale University Press.

Ritzer, George. 2008. *The McDonaldization of Society 5*. Thousand Oaks, CA: Pine Forge Press.

Rosenblum, Barbara. 1978. *Photographers at Work: A Sociology of Photographic Styles*. New York: Holmes and Meier.

Sakr, Naomi. 2001. *Satellite Realms: Transnational Television, Globalization, and the Middle East*. London: I.B. Tauris.

Scannell, Paddy. 2001. "Music, Radio and the Record Business in Zimbabwe Today." *Popular Music* 20(1): 13–27.

Schiller, Herbert I. 1989. *Culture Inc.: The Corporate Takeover of Public Expression*. Oxford: Oxford University Press.

——. 1996. *Information Inequality: The Deepening Social Crisis in America*. London: Routledge.

Schudson, Michael. 2001. "The Emergence of the Objectivity Norm in American Journalism." Pp. 165–85 in Michael Hechter and Karl-Dieter Opp, eds., *Social Norms*. New York: Russell Sage Foundation.

——. 2003. *The Sociology of News*. New York: W.W. Norton.

Scott, Allen J. 2000. "French Cinema: Economy, Policy, and Place in the Making of a Culture-Products Industry." *Theory, Culture & Society* 17: 1–38.

———. 2004. "The Other Hollywood: The Organizational and Geographic Bases of Television-Program Production." *Media, Culture & Society* 26: 183–205.

Seiler, Cotten. 2000. "The Commodification of Rebellion: Rock Culture and Consumer Capitalism." Pp. 203–76 in Mark Gottdiener, ed., *New Forms of Consumption*. New York: Rowan and Littlefield.

Shin, Eui Hang and Oh, Joong-Hwan. 2002. "Changing Patterns of Social Network Structure in Composer–Singer Relationships: A Case Study of the Korean Popular Music Industry." *East Asia: An International Quarterly* 20: 24–53.

Shively, JoEllen. 1992. "Cowboys and Indians: Perceptions of Western Films among American Indians and Anglos." *American Sociological Review* 57: 725–34.

Simmel, George. 1950. "The Metropolis and Mental Life." Pp. 409–24 in Kurt H. Wolff, ed., *The Sociology of George Simmel*. New York: Free Press.

Smith, Philip. 1996. "Executing Executions: Aesthetics, Identity and the Problematic Narratives of Capital Punishment Ritual." *Theory and Society* 25(2): 235–61.

———. 1998a. "The New American Cultural Sociology." Pp. 1–14 in P. Smith, ed., *The New American Cultural Sociology*. Cambridge: Cambridge University Press.

—, ed. 1998b. *The New American Cultural Sociology*. Cambridge: Cambridge University Press.

———. 1998c. "Barbarism and Civility in the Discourses of Fascism, Communism and Democracy." Pp. 115–37 in J. Alexander, ed., *Real Civil Societies*. London: Sage.

Smith, Philip and Alexander, Jeffrey C. 1996. "Durkheim's Religious Revival." *American Journal of Sociology* 102(2): 585–92.

Stange, Maren. 1989. *Symbols of Ideal Life: Social Documentary Photography in America 1890–1950*. Cambridge: Cambridge University Press.

Street, Richard Steven. 2008. *Everyone Had Cameras: Photography and Farmworkers in California 1850–2000*. Minneapolis: University of Minnesota Press.

Thussu, Daya and Freeman, Des, eds. 2003. *War and Media—Reporting Conflict 24/7*. London: Sage.

Tinker, Chris. 2002. "A Singer-Songwriter's View of the French Record Industry: The Case of Léo Ferré." *Popular Music* 21(2): 147–57.

Tocqueville, Alexis. 2004. *Democracy in America*. New York: Library of America.

Tuchman, Gaye. 1978. *Making News: A Study in the Construction of Reality*. New York: Free Press.

Warren, Stacy. 1994. "Disneyfication of the Metropolis." *Journal of Urban Affairs* 16: 89–107.

Weber, Max. 1998. *The Protestant Ethic and the Spirit of Capitalism*. Los Angeles: Rothbury.

Willis, Paul. 1977. *Learning to Labor: How Working Class Kids Get Working Class Jobs*. New York: Columbia University Press.

Zukin, Sharon. 2004. *Point of Purchase: How Shopping Changed American Culture*. New York: Routledge.

Zukin, Sharon and Maguire, Jennifer Smith. 2004 "Consumers and Consumption." *Annual Review of Sociology* 30:173–97.

38

The rise of the new amateurs

Popular music, digital technology, and the fate of cultural production

Nick Prior

A studio reverie

I recently spent some time in a popular-music recording studio. Not quite Abbey Road but a professional recording studio nevertheless. At its center, like an altarpiece, lay the mixing desk, its aura reinforced by a ring of synthesizers the likes of which I'd only read about in music magazines—a Roland TB-303, an old Mellotron, a Juno 106, a Yamaha DX7, a Moog. Next to the mixing desk sat a computer screen, with blocks of colorful data hinting at a mixing and mastering session that was to be more about software than hardware. For all their kudos as hardware classics, the synthesizers and outboard gear had been replaced by simulated versions in the form of "soft synths," all-in-one studios, and software programs like "Band in a Box," which allows users to generate music by inputting chord names, genres, styles, and rhythms. It was the sound engineer's job to negotiate, via a series of menus and mouse clicks, a virtual desktop replication of the very equipment that surrounded him.

And here, propelled by my professional myopia, I encountered a group of sociologists of culture. Howard Becker (1982) explained to me that the studio setting and its personnel satisfied a conception of art as collective activity. Even the student who made the coffee, he said, was a key link in an elaborate chain of cooperation that made the music world possible. In broad agreement, Paul Hirsch (1972) and John Ryan and Richard A. Peterson (1982) elaborated. The studio, they suggested, is part of a complex organizational system of popular music characterized by market structures, reward systems, and decision chains that work to reduce demand uncertainty. It's likely, they explained, that the cultural work put into the demo CD would make the songs sound more polished and professional, but it was gatekeepers further down the production chain who would really determine whether they would get airplay.

With varying degrees of detail, a group of sociologists of music refined my knowledge of the process, their responses displaying great diversity. Some, of a more Marxist persuasion, pointed to the interpenetrations of genre formation and niche marketing in a music industry that was increasingly part of a globalized market of taste, talent, and rights (Frith 1978); others dismissed the studio outright as a cultural factory peddling repetitive dross to a manipulated mass of consumers. Others still identified a trend towards the fragmentation of music networks and a patchwork of micro-industries, from small record labels and unlicensed nightclubs to urban music scenes and amateur radio broadcasts. These less visible networks, they said, blurred boundaries between producers and consumers, professionals and amateurs, in ways that suggested historical fluidity in the organization of cultural work (Kealy 1979).

Finally, there was a group of scholars who wanted to talk specifically about the studio technologies—the microphones, the cables, the acoustic insulation, even the door closers (Kealy 1979; Latour 1988). Some took a shine to particular synthesizers in the studio, such as the Moog, whose history as a technological artifact was shown to be bound up with the practices, discourses, and biographies of designers and engineers (Pinch and Trocco 2002). A few gravitated towards the computer and waxed passionately about the potential for new digital technologies of cultural production such as software studios and samplers to promote vernacular creativity amongst an untrained mass of new producers (Chadabe 1997). Others pointed to the rise of virtual studios and virtual music scenes made possible by globalized networks of communication, mobile digital devices, and the internet (Bennett and Peterson 2004). In years to come, they explained, the locality of this recording studio, its connections to place, will be softened, perhaps even threatened, by its insertion into a global space of flows (Théberge 2004). Sure enough, around the time the music-based social networking site MySpace took off, the studio was forced to close down due to lack of demand. Still, at least it played host to all these cultural sociologists whose own work had enriched my experience of being there.

Digital transformations of popular music

The studio is not the only place where digital transformations are afoot in popular music, of course. The digital lies at the center of claims regarding root-and-branch changes in the way culture is produced, disseminated, and consumed. Sometimes lauded as a revolutionary new set of creative practices, sometimes denigrated as a technological beast responsible for destroying music, the digital has become a technocultural *leitmotif* for the twenty-first century. Most spectacularly, the globalized circulation of music in ones and zeros has been implicated in a radical overhaul of the music industry. The practice of digital downloading via peer-to-peer networks and file-sharing programs, it is claimed, is dissolving the hegemony of major entertainment conglomerates, replacing product-based economies of scale and control with gift-like networks of de-materialized exchange (Leyshon 2003). Mainstream channels of distribution have been joined by user-organized networks of creation and distribution that potentially undermine chains of production based upon rights and ownership.

Meeting these undercurrents of "disintermediation" are the first signs that mainstream musicians are taking their cue from bottom-up developments in digital consumption. Recently, high-profile acts like Prince, Nine Inch Nails, and Jay-Z have distributed content direct to consumers via the internet, through newspapers or in constituent digital parts to allow fans to re-version tracks. The release of Radiohead's album *In Rainbows* was (initially at least) not only an all-digital affair, but fans were permitted to download the album at whatever price they thought fair, including for free. Meanwhile, consumers are increasingly invested in loops of feedback, commentary, and customization in the digital spaces of new music media, from music blogs to cell phone clips. They are

399

making use of digital infrastructures to pool knowledge with other music fans—annotating, filtering, and linking content and creating their own dissemination channels.

The implication is clear: If the classic model of the 1950s and 1960s saw a few firms and various independent labels involved in controlling the flow of production to sale, the contemporary model is much more diffuse and multiplicitous. The power that once resided in record companies to control the infrastructure and techniques needed to produce, promote, and disseminate commercial products is certainly less universal and, for many of them, has hemorrhaged (Ryan and Hughes 2006). In its wake has emerged a decentralized system of post-industrial cells—individually insignificant, but collectively powerful in providing alternatives to the mainstream commercial industry. In short, of all the identifiable trends that might be significant harbingers of systematic change in music over the last thirty years, from the rise of hip-hop and sampling to portable tape machines and CDs, the most vivid and far-reaching can be subsumed under umbrella processes and practices associated with digitalization—the turning of continuous information (sound) into discretely scanned symbols (binary data).

This chapter pursues the shifting terrains of popular music as they are nudged and shaken by the movements, constructions, and uses of digital technologies. Specifically, it will suggest that our understanding of the structure and culture of popular music needs to change if we are to analyze post-1980s developments in fast-paced, highly technologized societies with precision. Diagnosing change always has its perils, of course, and this is particularly apparent with new technologies, where the idea of transformation (*viz.* digital "revolution") is often overplayed, as if digitalization is a new "year zero" in popular music's history. Clearly, older industry structures of rights, contracts, and high-value capital remain largely intact, if only in adaptive or "residual" form, to use Raymond Williams' (1977) term. Moreover, an infrastructure of bedrooms, clubs, gigs, studios, festivals, rehearsal rooms, and record companies continues to be significant in the cultural life of any music scene, virtual or not. To assume nothing has changed, however, is exactly the mistake made by centralized firms in the music industry, shocked and overtaken by less than superficial changes in consumer practices. Although not just in consumer practices.

The rise of the new amateurs

For all the attention heaped upon Napster and music piracy, there is a less obvious, but by no means unimportant shift in the way music is created and circulated—a quieter, more subtle evolutionary process at work, threaded through these developments. It is a shift that brings into question the very separation between production and consumption as well as traditional boundaries around cultural expertise. If the "direct access relationship" between musicians and fans is fulfilling an ideal of unmediated contact between the two constituencies, another ideal is being serviced by digital technologies, that of the self-sufficient "amateur" producer. Digital technologies and corresponding practices have twisted, stretched, and radicalized older tendencies in modern culture, for sure, but they have also extended the very notion of production into realms previously estranged from academic and cultural analysis.

When *Time* Magazine made "you" the person of the year in 2006, it bucked the popular trend of identifying "great men" as sole influential agents of history, placing ordinary people, instead, at the center of an upsurge of productivity and innovation.

"You" were the passionate producers of a range of cultural forms and media, from home videos to personal blogs, bedroom songs to podcasts. Harbingers of a "digital democracy," ordinary people are making culture with an energy and in quantities never seen before, *Time* suggested. They are forming collaborative communities, customizing their own content, and shifting the principles upon which creativity rests.

The dizzying proliferation of digital folk culture is nowhere more apparent than on the new digital repositories of demotic creativity such as YouTube (for videos), MySpace (for social networking and music), and Flickr (for photos). This is content dominated by non-specialists at a range of levels and in a range of forms, circulated through rapidly expanding global networks of communication. Beyond the hype of "web 2.0" and the fact that leisure time, technical capital, and access to a computer are still fundamental passports to this form of creativity, the underlying point is incontrovertible. Huge swathes of the population are making, filtering, editing, and distributing digital culture, creating micro-organizational worlds with systematic, macrological effects.

It is a point that should not be lost on cultural sociologists, not least because it has implications for how we see production, expertise, and modes of creativity. If those previously considered non-specialists are actively producing websites, on-line photography galleries, radio broadcasts, and the like, not only are they failing to fit models of passive consumers suggested by the Frankfurt School and "hypodermic syringe" models of consumption (media and technology studies scholars have known about this poor fit for a long time), but they are threatening the very boundaries around professional and amateur, expert and non-expert, so central to modern social configurations. The welling up of small-scale, specialized, and participatory projects is, in other words, meeting top-heavy delivery of content head on, potentially chipping at the surety bestowed upon modern credentialism and the status of the modern professional.

In historical terms, this valorization is actually a return. Just over a century ago, the amateur was lauded as the epitome of virtue, respectability, and grace. In eighteenth- and nineteenth-century Britain, the evaluative standards of the aristocratic amateur were central to the development of "polite culture." By dint of their supposed disinterestedness and adherence to neo-platonic truths—both of them, ideological products of a privileged structural location—amateurs were, it was believed, exclusively qualified to act as arbiters of taste, shaping the contours of public virtue, and the ideals of civic heroism. Processes of modern professionalization and commercialization inverted this status hierarchy, however, consigning the amateur to the status of dabbler whose expertise was weakened both by lack of time dedicated to their pursuit and by institutional affiliation, training, and credentials. Indeed, for most of the twentieth century, the amateur was a fringe figure, propping up hierarchies of quality in a normative system dominated by professional groups.

In the last two decades or so, the status and position of the amateur have been redeemed and a new, less aristocratic, breed of amateur has emerged. These are technologically literate, seriously engaged, and committed practitioners working to professional standards but often without the infrastructural support or conventional credentials of the professional. Disproportionately, though not exclusively, drawn from the educated middle classes, they deploy their cultural capital in projects and self-organized cultural milieux (Bourdieu 1990; Leadbeater and Miller 2004; Battani 1999). They are unlikely to earn much of their total income from their activities, but their sense of identity is firmly attached to the pursuit of "serious leisure" (Stebbins 2007).

If the twentieth-century professional was defined partly by a monopoly over a specialized field of knowledge, objects, and esoteric skills, such monopolies are mutable and under erosion. This has partly to do with material and technological processes: the objects and tools that once separated amateur and professional now travel between them more readily. The complex machines and spaces that once imposed financial barriers to production are no longer the necessary prerequisites for quality. And boundaries around technical expertise are more permeable with the rise of mass higher education and dispersed digital technologies of communication. It is nowadays a fairly straightforward exercise to find out how to make your own movie, add expressive filters to your photos, or publish your own newsletter. If only a decade ago we saw computers as esoteric business machines and word-processors, we now think of them as cultural devices for generating images, editing movies, and mixing tracks.

Convergence and the fate of "DIY" music production

In the domain of music, the idea of the "amateur" has been given especially short shrift. Indeed, with the exception of Ruth Finnegan's (1989) now classic ethnography of music-making in a small English town, very few studies have tackled the amateur in any detail. Finnegan herself notes how musicological analysis has gravitated to the "best" or "highest" forms of music-making. In popular music studies this has meant skewed attention to the highly commodified and spectacular domains of the large-scale sub-field (Bourdieu 1993). A careful stock-take of music-related activity, however, reveals a diverse set of amateur networks, practices, and creative forms outside the commercial domain, from choirs and brass bands to family gatherings and karaoke. In the UK, arts surveys suggest that around 9 percent of the population play musical instruments, 2 percent play to audiences, and 5 percent sing to audiences at least once a year (Leadbeater and Miller 2004). Indeed, many of the musical organizations noted in Finnegan's study still exist, including formal music-making communities and local groups.

Electronic and digital technologies have expanded these networks, not just by bringing like-minded musicians together, but by establishing alternative modes of creativity through non-institutional means. In an initial phase of distribution in the 1980s and 1990s, the development of affordable technology for music production significantly lowered thresholds for making professional-sounding music. As the prices of four-track recording devices, drum machines, effects boxes, and synthesizers dropped, so they migrated from high-end studios to the bedrooms of non-professional producers. Associated techniques like multi-tracking, once the preserve of experimental producers and super-studios like Abbey Road, became relatively normalized practices outside the studio.

In a subsequent phase, an expanding global market for domestic personal computers and music-authoring software (in some cases, as with Apple's *GarageBand*, shipped free with the computer) has transferred a colossal bulk of recording equipment onto the desktops and laptops of ordinary musicians. All-in-one software studios like *Cubase*, *Logic*, *Acid*, *Ableton Live*, and *Reason* combine the functions of a range of hardware separates such as mixers, compressors, sequencers, and samplers into a single virtual unit. Whole orchestras—indeed music's whole sonic palette—can be conjured up in these digital spaces, giving rise to new stylistic combinations and borrowings not just in hip-hop, but in pop and rock generally. What a multi–million-dollar recording studio once contained as its top-end equipment is now actively appropriated in simulated form by non-professionals, many of whom have never set foot in a "real" studio—or, indeed, had a music lesson.

The new amateurs are taking advantage of music promotion and dissemination sites like MySpace to reach audiences directly, bypassing the mediating chains populated by gatekeepers, marketers, A&R men, and label bosses. In effect, the internet has become the stage for a continuous performance and audition, a space for hopeful musicians to arrange gigs or try out songs. But it is only one of the stages. As well as live performances, musicians are taking advantage of CD-burning capabilities to create their own demo CDs for distribution amongst local communities, friends, and fans, potentially turning their homes into processing plants. This was unthinkable little more than a decade ago, when the music business had a monopoly over factory production, the pressing of vinyl, and CDs.

Such developments are convergent in nature. What is, after all, distinctive about the computer is that it is a meta-device—the first device in the history of popular music to converge production, distribution, and reception. Operations and techniques that were once separate have been unified in the digital spaces of sequencing software and Digital Audio Workstations, making it possible (and in some respects expected) for musicians to write, record, mix, master, upload, distribute, promote, download, and listen to music using a single unit. Convergence is also, by implication, an occupational folding. Tasks that were discretely allocated in modes of production have collapsed, giving new amateurs the opportunity to become specialists in a range of professional occupations.

Kealy (1979) provides a benchmark for comparison. He sketches the occupational transformation of the sound mixer from craftsman to artist in the United Stated during the 1950s and 1960s as this group became professionalized and unionized. This shift was dependent upon protectionist strategies and boundary work designed to stave off the encroachments of other emerging audio professions. Nowadays, however, sound mixing is just one of a range of practices undertaken by self-producers whose amateur CVs are boasting expertise in all phases of production—from composition and sound engineering to promotion and distribution. They are learning their multiple trades in formal educational establishments, as well as through informal networks of friends, on-line databases, consumer magazines, and discussion forums.

All this makes for a denser cultural life, where pluralized expressions of creativity are bubbling up amongst a diversifying body of creators. With cultural gatekeepers relatively displaced, musicians are getting closer to fulfilling the "do-it-yourself" ideologies of punk and hip-hop, reinstating practices of homemade art that existed long before the rise of transnational media conglomerates and mass distribution. And they are making a difference, not just in the dark corners of the internet but throughout the cultural system. For, although non-professionals and independent producers have always been active producers of music, they rarely matched the success of those sponsored by the established culture industries. Today, they still suffer structural disadvantages, not least in advertising, promotion, and marketing. But they are making up some ground.

Band in a boxroom

Here's a case in point. In the summer of 2008, I interviewed a British Asian musician called Jyoti Mishra, otherwise known as the band White Town. For a short moment in the late 1990s, Mishra was the poster boy of musical geeks and bedroom musicians everywhere. In 1997, whilst studying for a film and sociology degree at the University of Derby, UK, Mishra produced a song, "Your Woman," in a nine-foot-square spare bedroom, using an eight-track recorder, a £35 microphone, and some free computer software. The song, a 1980s-inspired chunk of electro-pop, was arranged around a catchy 1930s trumpet sample from a song by Lew Stone and the Monseigneur Band called "My Woman."

In October 1996, Mishra sent a demo of this song to BBC Radio1 DJ Mark Radcliffe, who liked it so much he made it his "record of the week." This meant it was played every day that week on Radcliffe's evening show. A series of institutional contingencies followed. Radcliffe went on holiday, but his replacement continued to play the track. Chris Evans, a prime-time breakfast DJ, became ill and had to be replaced. Radcliffe replaced him, but kept plugging the song. Music journalists jumped on the homespun origins of the track and consumers became captivated by the catchy sample hook. Record companies queued up to sign White Town and in just a few short weeks, in January 1997, the record reached number one in the UK charts, eventually selling around 400,000 copies. It went gold in Canada, sold 250,000 copies in the United States, and proceeded to reach number one in eight different countries. "Bedroom to Big Time," *Wired* magazine put it (Pemberton 1997). Mishra signed to EMI/Chrysalis, went on to record an album, promptly fell out with the record company, but had made enough money on the basis of "Your Woman" to give up his studies and continue his life as an independent musician, self-producing, marketing, and distributing his own material.

This is a satisfying narrative, an antidote to the top-heavy, stitched-up ruthlessness popularly attributed to the record industry. If one can avoid the "never give up on your dreams" sentimentalism that Mishra's label promoted at the time, then it is still remark-able that an unknown Asian man in his thirties could single-handedly write and produce a hit song without huge commercial backing or support. It shows how cheap, modern musical technologies can be used to make professional-sounding tracks, and it demon-strates the viability of a grassroots mode of production. Musicians have always sought ways to "make do" in the sense implied by de Certeau (1984). In many respects, they are the consummate "creative consumers," improvising resourcefully with whatever materi-als and channels are available to them. In the past, this has meant sourcing equipment from unusual places, financing the recording, designing the sleeve, pressing and distributing the record, or even setting up a micro label. In other words, this DIY system has always been a viable option.

The difference today is one of global reach, speed, ease of use, and absolute scale. One might even suggest that the DIY ethic so cherished by punk rockers is no longer an activist ideology, but a systematic, structural condition of the production of music itself. And not just in the developed West either. For whilst the digital divide between rich and poor countries undoubtedly exists in a climate where "ethnic sounds" are sampled and fetishized by the likes of Missy Elliot and Madonna for their "exotic" quality, impover-ished musicians in places like the Dominican Republic are managing to find access to digital recording facilities in order to record and press CDs on very tight budgets (Hernandez 2004). Meanwhile, digitalization has undoubtedly accompanied a creative cross-pollination of styles from around the world in a context of intensified migration, displacement, and mobility. Contemporary Bhangra, for instance, remixes Punjabi folk dance with Western popular music—rock, hip-hop, rap, and house music, in particular—in an articulation of the hybrid identities of Asian migrants and their descendants in English and North American cities (Maira 2002). Here, the evolving complexity of diasporic identities is a product not only of urban or national settings but also of global soundscapes embedded within increasingly tangled webs of mass-mediated, transnational communication systems, including the internet (Connell and Gibson 2003).

Add to this the material affordances of wireless laptop computers and these global hybridities and DIY processes are infinitely flexible and geographically mobile. Musicians are making music on the move with others, in the spatial and temporal interstices of life, on a little-and-often basis. They are untethering cultural production from fixed locations and sending music into a fluid network of exchanges (Prior 2008). As broadband communication infrastructures become more widespread, they are collaborating remotely with other musicians (via email, virtual worlds, teleconferencing, or streaming audio technologies), displacing the need to be physically co-present with collaborators. Finally, they are finding new spaces in which to play and consume music, in the domains of interactive media forms such as video games, where mainstream music-making overlaps with music simulations, virtual gigs, and rhythm-action games like *Guitar Hero*. Production has truly evolved into "prosumption" (a combination of the words "production" and "consumption").

Conclusion: why 1983?

Stock histories of popular music often gravitate to a "golden age" of rock, usually located in the late 1950s or early 1960s—a period of rapid socio-economic change that begat a pantheon of rockers, from Elvis Presley to the Beatles. In an article titled "Why 1955? Explaining the Advent of Rock Music" (1990), Richard A. Peterson points to that as the year consolidating legal, technological, and organizational developments conducive to the birth of rock music in the United States. These included the development of a "dual structure" industry of small firms and oligopolies, the spread of network radio programming, and the development of 45 rpm vinyl records (Peterson 1990). Even if there is a whiff of nostalgia about this analysis, the point is sound: a unique confluence of occupational, technological, and cultural elements in the mid-1950s comprised a system of production geared to the total transformation of the music industry.

What, then, of the last twenty-five years? If popular music is a moving object, how much has it moved during this time, how significant has this era been in transforming the auspices of pop, and what role have digital technologies played in catalyzing these developments? It is clearly perilous to assume that free-floating technologies in themselves have revolutionized music. New technologies do not create music worlds from scratch. But they have facilitated or afforded new possibilities.

The period 1982–83 was a particularly propitious one for pop. First, two of the most influential musical works of recent times were produced and disseminated around this time. One, Michael Jackson's album *Thriller*, remains the biggest selling album in history and turned Jackson into a global superstar. The other, New Order's *Blue Monday*, is widely perceived to be the biggest selling UK 12-inch record of all time and presaged a shift to dance-based pop of the 1980s. Second, in production terms, 1983 saw the invention of several influential musical devices and processes—their presence emblematic of a fundamental shift in the global structure of the electronics industry towards East and Southeast Asia (Gregory 1985). Such devices included the first commercially successful

405

digital synthesizer—the Yamaha DX7—affordable drum machines, commercial audio software packages, and the first desktop computers with monitors and graphic user interfaces. The year 1983 also witnessed the invention of MIDI, or "Musical Instrument Digital Interface," an industry-standard protocol set up by Japanese electronics corporations to enable different instruments to communicate streams of algorithmic data with one another (Kakehashi 2002). Like the spread of any universal language or technical standard, MIDI unified what could have potentially become a fragmented landscape of musical instruments, "locking in" subsequent technological developments around a new paradigmatic frame of recording and performing. Third, CDs and CD players were introduced to the mass market in late 1982—another step in a long line of format shifts in the history of music that changed how we listened to music, one that cemented the idea of the audio file as a unitary piece of digital information capable of being stored, catalogued, manipulated, and endlessly reproduced in chunks of binary data. Finally, 1983 was the year that ARPANET and its associated protocols (the first manifestation of internet technologies) were switched over to the TCP/IP protocol, establishing networking capabilities across different and hitherto incompatible computers. Today, the world wide web is largely based upon TCP/IP software that connects different networks of computers.

None of these four developments was independently responsible for creating the momentum necessary for wholesale changes in popular music. In many respects, they replicated and attended to an already emergent series of global processes that ushered in advanced, high-tech, networked societies favoring a re-ordering of modes of cultural production. In other words, they articulated with contemporary social, economic, and political practices to emplace key struts of a reconfigured system of cultural production and consumption—one that has blurred this very separation. The digital is many things: a rhetoric, a claim, a set of technologies. But it is also a shorthand, a formation, a condition—one that opens up creative agency, unhooks it from place, and sends it into flows of global information. What we hear, where we hear it, how we listen to new music, who produces it: these have all traveled. Musical styles have diversified and novel ways of making music have emerged. But in many ways, these are no more than the latest twists in popular music's history in the *longue durée*, a cat-and-mouse story of conservation, innovation, and subversion, a reconfiguration rather than a revolution. There is no last word to be had on these changes, not just because disagreements abound over their character and extent, but also because the pace of change leaves the analyst invariably trailing behind. What is for sure is that the struggle between technology, use, and control over protean networks and colonizing organizations will continue. As will the music.

References

Battani, Marshall. 1999. "Organisational Fields, Cultural Fields, and Art Worlds." *Media, Culture and Society* 21(5): 601–26.
Becker, Howard S. 1982. *Art Worlds*. Berkeley and Los Angeles: University of California Press.
Bennett, Andy and Peterson, Richard A. 2004. *Music Scenes: Local, Translocal, and Virtual*. Nashville, TN: Vanderbilt University Press.
Bourdieu, Pierre. 1990. *Photography: A Middle-brow Art*. Stanford, CA: Stanford University Press.
——. 1993. *The Field of Cultural Production*. Cambridge: Polity.
Burgess, Jean E. 2007. "Vernacular Creativity and New Media." Unpublished Ph.D. thesis, Queensland University of Technology.

Chadabe, Joel. 1997. *Electric Sound: The Past and Promise of Electronic Music*. Englewood Cliffs, NJ: Prentice-Hall.

Connell, John and Gibson, Chris. 2003. *Sound Tracks: Popular Music, Identity and Place*. London: Routledge.

De Certeau, Michel. 1984. *The Practice of Everyday Life*. Berkeley: University of California Press.

Finnegan, Ruth. 1989. *The Hidden Musicians: Music-Making in an English Town*. Middletown, CT: Wesleyan University Press.

Frith, Simon. 1978. *The Sociology of Rock*. London: Constable.

Gregory, Gene. 1985. *Japanese Electronics Technology: Enterprise and Innovation*. New York: John Wiley and Sons.

Hernandez, Deborah Pacini. 2004. "Building Bridges across the Digital Divide: An Interview with Giovanni Savino." *Journal of Popular Music* 16(1): 99–108.

Hirsch, Paul. 1972. "Processing Fads and Fashions: An Organisation-Set Analysis of Cultural Industry Systems." In S. Frith and A. Goodwin, eds., *On Record: Rock, Pop and the Written Word*. London: Routledge.

Kakehashi, Ikutaro. 2002. *I Believe in Music: Life Experiences and Thoughts on the Future of Electronic Music by the Founder of the Roland Corporation*. Milwaukee: Hal Leonard.

Kealy, Edward R. 1979. "From Craft to Art: The Case of Sound Mixers and Popular Music." *Sociology of Work and Occupations* 6(1): 3–29.

Latour, Bruno. 1988. "Mixing Human and Nonhumans Together: The Sociology of a Door-Closer." *Social Problems* 35(3): 298–310.

Leadbeater, Charles and Miller, Paul. 2004. *The Pro-Am Revolution: How Enthusiasts Are Changing Our Economy and Society*. Demos report.

Leyshon, Andrew. 2003. "Scary Monsters? Software Formats, Peer-to-Peer Networks, and the Spectre of the Gift." *Environment and Planning D: Society and Space* 21: 533–58.

Maira, Sunaina Marr. 2002. *Desis in the House: Indian American Youth Culture in New York City*. Philadelphia: Temple University Press.

Pemberton, Daniel. 1997. "Bedroom to Big Time." *Wired* 5.06 (June).

Peterson, Richard A. 1990. "Why 1955? Explaining the Advent of Rock Music." *Popular Music* 9(1): 97–116.

Pinch, Trevor and Trocco, Frank. 2002. *Analog Days: The Invention and Impact of the Moog Synthesizer*. Cambridge, MA: Harvard University Press.

Prior, Nick. 2008. "OK Computer: Mobility, Software and the Laptop Musician." *Information, Communication and Society* 11(7): 912–32.

Russell, Dave. 1995. "Amateur Musicians and Their Repertoires." In Stephen Banfield, ed., *Music in Britain: The Twentieth Century*. Oxford: Blackwell.

Ryan, John and Hughes, Michael. 2006. "Breaking the Decision Chain: The Fate of Creativity in the Age of Self-Production." In Michael D. Ayers, ed., *Cybersounds: Essays on Virtual Music Culture*. New York: Peter Lang.

Ryan, John and Peterson, Richard A. 1982. "The Product Image: The Fate of Creativity in Country Music." Pp. 11–32 in J.S. Ettema and C.D. Whitney, eds., *Individuals in Mass Media Organizations: Creativity and Constraint*, vol. 10, *Sage Annual Reviews of Communication Research*. Beverly Hills, CA: Sage.

Stebbins, Robert. 2007. *Serious Leisure: A Perspective for Our Time*. Edison, NJ: Transaction Publishers.

Théberge, Paul. 2004. "The Network Studio: Historical and Technological Paths to a New Ideal in Music Making." *Social Studies of Science* 34(5): 759–81.

Williams, Raymond. 1977. *Marxism and Literature*. Oxford: Oxford University Press.

39

Consumption and critique

Alan Warde

Only recently have sociologists used the concept of consumption extensively. It remains primarily a topic of interdisciplinary attention, with the related concept "consumer" more widely deployed, especially in economics, psychology, and marketing. That said, terms like consumer culture and consumer society have come to play an important role in some sociological characterizations of contemporary social arrangements. Many accounts suggest that central features of industrial capitalism—where disciplined labor in manufacturing goods was the key axis of social order in the face of material scarcity—are receding, replaced for most people in affluent societies by the appeal of consumption in a context where leisure, shopping, and the home become the focal points of everyday life. In this chapter I describe some features of the emergence of a specialized sociological sub-discipline, paying particular attention to oscillations between the normative and the empirical analysis of this crucial component of social life.

Consumption is something of a chaotic concept and few sociologists have been prepared to define it. Campbell (1995: 102) proposed a working definition of consumption "as involving the selection, purchase, use, maintenance, repair, and disposal of any product or service." Compared to its use in economics, where consumption typically indicates the act of purchase in market exchange, it has much wider application, for instance raising issues of how people use and dispose of items. Campbell noted difficulties in this broader definition gaining acceptance because it has been pre-empted in everyday language by the economists' notion. However, a broad definition serves to recognize the two separate historical roots of the concept, both of which continue to resonate for sociological purposes. The first, emerging from Latin into early English, had a negative connotation—to destroy, to waste, to use up. Only later, with the emergence of political economy in the eighteenth century, did a neutral sense develop in description of market relationships, in which consumer is distinguished from producer and, analogously, consumption from production. This second meaning focused more on the changing value of items being exchanged rather than the purposes to which goods and services might be put. These two meanings have existed in tension ever since.

For most of the twentieth century, sociological analysis of consumption was driven largely by normative and quasi-political considerations about the threats it posed to pursuit of "the good life." Puritan and Protestant cultures in particular have displayed negative and hostile attitudes towards consumption because of their suspicion toward luxury and waste. Conspicuous consumption, a term coined by Veblen (1925 [1899]), describes the competitive pursuit of social status through display of possessions by a section of the American middle class. Other scholars studied processes involving invidious comparisons between groups, employing such concepts as imitation, emulation, and the trickle-down effect. Attitudes towards mass consumption also tended to be critical, the Frankfurt School among others declaiming its uniformity, mediocrity, and tendency to induce passivity. Often such critique was associated with a more general and abstract critique of Western capitalist modernity, focusing especially on the fundamental process of commodification. According to Schudson's (1993) summary, during the twentieth century consumption was condemned not only for encouraging cultural mediocrity and pandering to status concerns but also for promoting hedonistic materialism, creating excessive waste, causing privatization, and obscuring the relationship between producers and consumers to the detriment of working conditions.

Such normative diagnoses of the nature and consequences of modern consumption were rarely supported by evidence from systematic empirical study of consumer behavior. The one notable exception to this generalization, although usually conceptualized in other terms, was research on "under-consumption" driven by a concern that many people consumed too little to achieve socially acceptable standards of physical reproduction and cultural participation. Studies of poverty and inequality, in a long empirical tradition stretching back to the mid-nineteenth century, are precisely concerned with consumption in its wider remit. Studies of the circumstances of private households were complemented in the 1970s by analyses of collective consumption, involving examination of the role of the state in delivering to citizens' income, goods, and public services. Supplementing or supplanting provision through the market, which implies de-commodification, was a *raison d'être* of the modern welfare state. However, the policies of the New Right from the 1980s gradually re-commodified (privatized), or subjected to quasi-market mechanisms (marketized), such provision. Sociologists have intensively monitored the resulting tendency to increase inequality and fragment social relations.

Consumption and the "cultural turn"

The sociology of consumption developed in part from reservations about the perceived priority accorded to production, sociology having presumed in the 1960s and 1970s that economic forces had a powerful determining effect on how societies operated. The critique of "economism" became widely accepted in Europe in the 1980s—witness, for example, the demise of neo-Marxism—and attention focused on cultural forms and practices instead. Goods and services delivered in abundance through commercial channels came to be analyzed less in terms of their role in the accumulation of profit, and more in terms of their symbolic meanings. Commodification and its consequences remained very important, but the presumption that production determines consumption, or that producers are overwhelmingly powerful and influential, receded.

As part of the "cultural turn" in the 1970s and 1980s, attention increasingly shifted from the instrumental aspects of consumption, from use-values, to the symbolic dimension of the process, to sign-values. Baudrillard's (1998 [1970]) critique of Marx for concentrating too much on the use of goods at the expense of their capacity to convey social meaning was particularly influential. The intellectual presence of cultural studies, whose roots lay in literary studies and European neo-Marxism, was a major stimulus to the evolution of a sociology of consumption in Europe. It was responsible for contesting the earlier moral condemnation of consumer behavior. (By contrast, in the US there had been, from the late nineteenth century but particularly from the 1930s, a much more optimistic understanding of consumption. The idea that growth in production increased consumption, which improved standards of living and created further demand, was widely welcomed.) The view of the consumer as a passive victim of processes associated with mass production, of which advertising was the epitome, was countered by demonstrations of how people actively and creatively engaged with items, appropriating them for their own purposes. Not only did mass-produced goods and services provide comfort and entertainment, they also expanded cultural experience for many people, supplied materials to be used in personal self-development and self-expression, and, as with the example of gifts, established and consolidated social relationships (Warde 2002).

Increasingly, consumption came to be seen as a means by which individuals and groups expressed their identities. When combined with diagnoses of postmodern culture stressing the fluidity and malleability of identity, consumption was pronounced a key element in a process of continually renewed self-constitution or self-assembly. Zygmunt Bauman (1988) was not atypical in pronouncing consumption to be an arena of unprecedented individual freedom for affluent majorities in Western societies. The slogan that now "there is no choice but to choose," which has frequently been applied to consumer behavior, captures the sense in which individuals are attributed with an autonomy previously denied them by both lack of resources and the weight of group or community conventions. This view was adapted and modified by Beck (1992) and Giddens (1991), helping to entrench within Europe a highly influential individualization thesis that described dominant forms of action consistent with the construction of the sovereign consumer.

The individual agent exercising supreme self-control over personal destiny, a key figure in the discourse of late modernity, offers a seductive model. People like to think about themselves in this way, or at least privileged and successful people do. Such a view is constantly on the brink of reverting to a paradigm for understanding consumption that presumes the sovereignty of consumer choice and reduces explanation to the reasons why individuals make particular choices. Yet how people think about themselves, although one precondition of their behavior, is not sufficient to explain what they do. It is therefore necessary to note some alternative perspectives on consumption. Although sociology has often been complicit in the promotion of versions of rational-action theory, it now possesses an extensive and increasingly multifaceted, but still minority, critique of the idea of individual choice.

An empirical sociology of consumption

Despite the social scientific significance of, and widespread public concern about, the impact on economic, social, and cultural activities of substantial increases in consumer spending in affluent societies, the sociology of consumption has been slow to emerge as a sub-discipline with targeted research programs or an empirical corpus of findings.

Developed most purposefully in northern Europe, it initially had little impact in the US, where the prior establishment of a vigorous research tradition focused on consumer behavior apparently resisted sociological encroachment. In Europe, however, textbooks and general reviews of the field were published in the 1990s (e.g. Lury 1996; Slater 1997), journals like *Journal of Consumer Culture* and *Journal of Material Culture* were launched, and professional bodies like the European Sociological Association sponsored research groups on consumption. Among their key features was the rejection of explanations based on consumer sovereignty and on the premise of free individual choice.

Leading the challenge to the individualization thesis were studies proclaiming the continuing influence of socio-demographic characteristics, particularly social class, on cultural knowledge and practice. Bourdieu's classic study *Distinction* (1984 [1979]) demonstrated a strong association between class position and cultural taste in France; specifically, he explored differences in taste between the commercial and professional bourgeoisie, the intellectual fraction of the middle classes, and the working classes. These groups differed in what they ate, drank, and wore, and in their preferences in interior decoration, music, and the arts. Such class differences were widely presumed to characterize other industrialized societies. However, many scholars subsequently argued that taste is less socially determined and lifestyle less strongly associated with class than Bourdieu argued; moreover, there is no longer a marked hierarchical ordering of cultural activities, as implied in his contrasts between high-brow and low-brow, or elite and mass, cultures. Testing the wider applicability of Bourdieu's analysis has generated considerable empirical research (Bennett *et al.* 1999; Holt 1997; Halle 1993; Lahire 2004; Prieur *et al.* 2008; Bennett *et al.* 2009), which has revealed considerable national variation in cultural consumption, including variation in how cultural consumption confers prestige or distinction (Lamont 1992; Peterson and Kern 1996; Warde and Martens 2000). Although the impact of class remains contested, it is now established that other, previously underestimated, socio-demographic characteristics (e.g. gender, generation, and ethnicity) are also significant influences on cultural consumption (Bennett *et al.* 2009).

Re-examination of Bourdieu's arguments has also served to emphasize the extent to which societal cultures matter. Reflecting on the topic of distinction from a comparative perspective, Daloz (2007) showed that the ways in which elites consume, and the social meanings associated with their consumption, differ in different contexts. What in one society is a source of symbolic superiority is, in another, a sign of vulgarity. Thus, for example, rich Norwegians conceal their wealth, "conspicuous modesty" being a collective ethical imperative; Americans are much more likely to make material display of their personal opulence, while the ostentation of the "Big Men" of Nigeria serves to express the collective standing of their clients. Here is a reminder of the diversity of cultural expression, and a diversity not solely apparent in the postmodern West. There are many ways to exhibit distinction depending on the societal setting.

Symbolically significant topics attracting the attention of sociologists of consumption include possessions, cultural participation, and aesthetic preferences. In the absence of comprehensive plausible sociological theories of consumption, many of the most informative studies are framed in terms of particular processes or practices like fashion, cultural classification, enthusiasms, body maintenance, television viewing, and collecting.

The burgeoning studies of material culture have focused on specific objects. Most examine the meanings attached to symbolically charged items like cars and scooters, houses and gardens, pictures, and clothes, but others emphasize the functional role of technological devices in daily life (Miller 1998). In addition, mundane and unspectacular

411

items like water and electricity attract increasing attention, signifying a shift to concerns with inconspicuous or ordinary consumption and the normalization of standards of comfort (see Gronow and Warde 2001; Shove 2003). Items of this kind have come to the fore partly for theoretical reasons, because of prior generalizations about consumption seemingly focused on a narrow range of products, and partly for political-economic reasons, because of new normative concerns about the environmental impact of current levels of consumption.

Fifteen years of empirical research that explicitly addresses processes of consumption have made a significant difference. Sociology now has a more balanced critique of markets than in the 1980s, when they were seen as a fatal threat to public welfare provision. The condescension once expressed towards popular culture has been more or less eliminated. We also have detailed knowledge of everyday practices which entail multiple forms of consumption. The social and practical dimension of consumption, and its role in maintaining social relationships, has been re-emphasized, reversing a tendency to see it primarily as a form of symbolic communication. In addition, as the following sections suggest, consumption has developed a role in contemporary political mobilization.

Consumer politics

Associations and movements for the protection and promotion of the interests of consumers have grown. As these movements flourished, governments began speaking and acting on behalf of "consumers"—rather than of, say, classes, citizens, or the nation—so that political discussion increasingly refers to consumer sovereignty, consumer choice, and consumer rights. In other words, political discourse increasingly echoes the understandings of neo-classical economics. This was not always the case. Recently, historians have made a major contribution to the understanding of the construction of "the consumer" (Trentmann 2006). They show that alternative ways of understanding the roles of consumers in the past have been forgotten and that this collective amnesia has facilitated a particular form of contemporary consumer politics in the present. Cohen (2000) makes a rather ungainly distinction, but an effective one, between the citizen-consumer and the customer-consumer. The former are "consumers who take on the political responsibility we usually associate with citizens to consider the general good of the nation through their consumption, and the latter [are] consumers who seek primarily to maximize their personal economic interests in the market place" (Cohen 2000: 204). She shows how that distinction has played out in US development, with the former orientations being fairly prominent in the first half of the twentieth century but largely disappearing thereafter. A labor and consumer alliance, which emerged as part of the New Deal, with its Keynesian considerations about maintaining demand and dealing with poverty during the Depression, and which had its apotheosis in collective restraint during World War II, was replaced by a quite different politics in the subsequent period of abundance. This changed discourse, agenda, and policies. The move (during the mid-1980s) to viewing the consumer in the context of public service delivery is the last, or latest, stage in the shift from consumption as a citizenship issue to one of consumer choice. The power relations underlying these shifts are highlighted by Jacobs (2000) and Cross (2000), who document the ways in which conservative republican business interests cemented in law their prejudice in favor of free markets.

412

The shifting balance of opinion in favor of the framing of consumption as a private matter most satisfactorily accomplished in market exchange has affected most Western countries to some degree, although the US probably most of all. The relationship between state and market provision is constituted and understood differently in societies with stronger welfare traditions, as in the Nordic countries. The relationship between consumption, saving, and debt is much different in East Asia: the Japanese, the South Koreans, and other populations in the Far East saved for genuinely patriotic reasons after the World War II, a fortiori in Singapore where saving was compulsory for thirty years (Garon and Maclachlan 2006: 177). Nevertheless, even within those Western societies most committed to the paradigm of the autonomous sovereign consumer, there is considerable evidence of continued resistance to commodification. Sassatelli (2006) describes the emergence and spread of "critical consumerism," which looks beyond the instrumental issues of market regulation typically pursued by established consumer associations in seeking to "reform" consumption. The Fair Trade movement, the organization of a "No shopping day," and voluntary simplicity, each an expression of the current attention devoted to ethical consumerism, indicate a continued awareness of the moral deficiencies of the market economy. These are practical critiques of consumption. They reflect ambivalence about the experience of commodification which, if surfacing only intermittently, suffuses most people's everyday lives and political discourse. People are not seduced all the time by the promise of the market and value highly gifts, self-provisioning, and collective entitlements. In scholarly discussion too, the concept of "moral economy" is invoked ever more often.

Sustainable consumption

Another area of considerable political disquiet is marked by the escalating reference to "sustainable consumption." The goal of making consumption "sustainable" arrived on the political agenda about ten years ago, to heavy contestation (Cohen 2001). The potential exhaustion of finite natural resources and the challenge of climate change drew attention to the practical and ethical feasibility of the continued increases in standards of material living that have accompanied consumer culture. The ramifications of a (perceived) need to retard, halt, or even reverse trends in consumption are enormous in social terms, potentially highly conflictual, and disruptive, not least because of the legitimate future expectations of countries like China, India, and Brazil. As Cohen (2001) points out, rich countries tried for a couple of decades to attribute global environmental problems to population growth in developing countries. However, since the 1990s, policy analysts have increasingly acknowledged that it is the West, and particularly the US, which emits most greenhouse gases and thus puts most stress on the planet's eco-systems—as a consequence of lifestyles built upon heavy use of domestic energy, dependence on a global agro-industrial food industry and supply chain, suburban patterns of residence requiring private automobiles, and increasing air travel.

Individuals, social movements, economic organizations, and states apparently, if ambivalently, hope for change. Mainstream political parties have proved unprepared to canvas electorates on policy platforms that include halting economic growth or reducing material standards of living. Proposed solutions seem largely inadequate to the scale of the implied task, relying primarily on optimistic expectations about either technological solutions—making more efficient use of resources by means of less damaging

413

technologies—or giving citizens more information and encouragement so that they might voluntarily curtail their more damaging habits or practices. These can be construed as increasingly unsuccessful attempts to deflect responsibility from governments and corporations. Calls for "sustainable production and consumption" are meanwhile climbing up the political agenda in Europe.

Much intellectual and political energy is currently devoted to devising means to moderate consumption. Although there is no consensus about the most desirable direction of change, one challenge for social science is to clarify how, even if goals were shared, change might be effected. Political strategies that are currently advocated focus heavily on altering individual behavior, but they have proved relatively ineffective: giving people information does not often result in changed behavior; changing their values so that they wish to act more considerately proves extremely difficult; and people tend to resist state regulation and to protest against any taxation that would reform their consumption patterns. Mostly the aim is to get people to buy different commodities, a framing of the problem that relies predominantly on market exchange. Perhaps, however, the object of policy is misconstrued. Perhaps what matters first and foremost is not what people buy, but what they do, and how they use things. As the economist Alfred Marshall observed, the expansion of demand is a process whereby activities generate wants, rather than vice versa. The purchase of goods and acts of final consumption are often not the best points upon which to focus because they are mere props to other more meaningful and purposeful social engagement. Anthropologists especially have insisted that consumption involves a process of appropriation that is achieved not in the moment of exchange, but in the singularization of products as part of their adoption and use (Kopytoff 1986; Appadurai 1986). De Certeau (1984) famously applied this insight to understanding the tactics of resistance in daily life. Viewing consumption as tactical use offers a different perspective on the problem.

In this regard, the recent renewal of interest in theories of practice (e.g. Schatzki *et al.* 2001) suggests alternatives to analyses based on consumer choice. As individuals we often have limited control over what things we use and how we use them. Convention, infrastructure, and shared goals constrain everyone. Types and levels of consumption tend to be determined socially and collectively. A practice-theoretical approach acknowledges these factors, proposing that consumption is less a matter of individual personal display or an expression of self-identity, and more a corollary of the conventions of the specific, socially organized practices deemed necessary to live a good life (Warde 2005). For much of the time, participation in a practice means nothing more than the requisitioning of familiar items and their routine application to well-understood activities. Performances recognized as competent—for example in the fields of dress, interior design, motoring, or listening to music—are orientated by and toward collectively accredited and locally situated conventions associated with such practices. Hence, efforts to change behavior targeted at the individual point of purchase are unlikely to be sufficient. New ways of intervening are needed, with less emphasis on personal education or ethical conversion and more on reviewing the social organization and infrastructure of particular practices.

References

Appadurai, A. 1986. *The Social Life of Things: Commodities in Cultural Perspective*. Cambridge: Cambridge University Press.

Baudrillard, J. 1998 (1970). *The Consumer Society: Myths and Structures*. London: Sage.

Bauman, Z. 1988. *Freedom*. Milton Keynes: Open University Press.

Beck, U. 1992. *Risk Society: Towards a New Modernity*. London: Sage.

Bennett, T., Emmison, M., and Frow, J. 1999. *Accounting for Tastes: Australian Everyday Cultures*. Cambridge: Cambridge University Press.

Bennett, T., Savage, M., Silva, E., Warde, A., Gayo-Cal, M., and Wright, D. 2009. *Culture, Class, Distinction*. London: Routledge.

Bourdieu, P. 1984 (1979). *Distinction: A Social Critique of the Judgement of Taste*. London: Routledge and Kegan Paul.

Campbell, C. 1995. "The Sociology of Consumption." Pp. 96–126 in D. Miller, ed., *Acknowledging Consumption: A Review of New Studies*. London: Routledge.

Cohen, L. 2000. "Citizens and Consumers in the United States in the Century of Mass Consumption." Pp. 203–22 in M. Daunton and M. Hilton, eds., *The Politics of Consumption: Material Culture and Citizenship in Europe and America*. Oxford: Berg.

Cohen, M. 2001. "The Emergent Environmental Policy Discourse on Sustainable Consumption." Pp. 21–38 in M. Cohen and J. Murphy, eds., *Exploring Sustainable Consumption: Environmental Policy and the Social Sciences*. Oxford: Pergamon.

Cross, G. 2000. "Corraling Consumer Culture: Shifting Rationales for American State Intervention in Free Markets." Pp. 283–300 in M. Daunton and M. Hilton, eds., *The Politics of Consumption: Material Culture and Citizenship in Europe and America*. Oxford: Berg.

Daloz, J.-P. 2007. "Elite Distinction: Grand Theory and Comparative Perspectives." *Comparative Sociology* 6(1–2): 27–74.

de Certeau, M. 1984. *The Practice of Everyday Life*. Berkeley: University of California Press.

Gabriel, Y. and Lang, T. 1995. *The Unmanageable Consumer: Contemporary Consumption and Its Fragmentation*. London: Sage.

Garon, S. and Maclachlan, P., eds. 2006. *The Ambivalent Consumer: Questioning Consumption in East Asia and the West*. Ithaca, NY: Cornell University Press.

Giddens, A. 1991. *Modernity and Self-Identity*. Cambridge: Polity.

Goodwin, N., Ackerman, F., and Kiron, D., eds. 1997. *The Consumer Society*. Washington, DC: Island Press.

Gronow, J. and Warde, A. eds. 2001. *Ordinary Consumption*. London: Routledge.

Halle, D. 1993. *Inside Culture: Art and Class in the American Home*. Chicago: Chicago University Press.

Holt, D. 1997. "Distinction in America? Recovering Bourdieu's Theory of Tastes from Its Critics." *Poetics* 25: 93–120.

Jacobs, M. 2000. "The Politics of Plenty: Consumerism in the 20th Century United States." Pp. 223–40 in M. Daunton and M. Hilton, eds., *The Politics of Consumption: Material Culture and Citizenship in Europe and America*. Oxford: Berg.

Kopytoff, I. 1986. "The Cultural Biography of Things: Commoditization as Process." Pp. 64–94 in A. Appadurai, ed., *The Social Life of Things: Commodities in Cultural Perspective*. Cambridge: Cambridge University Press.

Lahire, B. 2004. *La Culture des individus: Dissonances culturelles et distinctions de soi*. Paris: Editions la Découverte.

Lamont, C. 1992. *Money, Morals, and Manners—American and French Middle-Classes*. Chicago: University of Chicago Press.

Lane, R.E. 1991. *The Market Experience*. Cambridge: Cambridge University Press.

Lury, C. 1996. *Consumer Culture*. Cambridge: Polity.

Miller, D., ed. 1998. *Material Cultures: Why Some Things Matter*. London: UCL Press.

Peterson, R. and Kern, R. 1996. "Changing Highbrow Taste: From Snob to Omnivore." *American Sociological Review* 61: 900–07.

Prieur, A., Rosenlund, L., and Skjott-Larsen, J. 2008. "Cultural Capital Today: A Case Study from Denmark", *Poetics* 36(1): 45–71.

Sassatelli, R. 2006. "Virtue, Responsibility, and Consumer Choice: Framing Critical Consumerism." Pp. 219–50 in J. Brewer and F. Trentmann, eds., *Consuming Cultures, Global Perspectives: Historical Trajectories and Multicultural Conflicts*. Oxford: Berg.

Schatzki, T., Knorr-Cetina, K., and von Savigny, E., eds. 2001. *The Practice Turn in Contemporary Theory*. London: Routledge.

Schor, J. 1992. *The Overworked American: The Unexpected Decline of Leisure*. New York: Basic Books.

Schudson, M. 1993 (1984). *Advertising, the Uneasy Persuasion: Its Dubious Impact on American Society*. London: Routledge.

Shove, E. 2003. *Comfort, Cleanliness and Convenience: The Social Organization of Normality*. Oxford: Berg.

Slater, D. 1997. *Consumer Culture and Modernity*. Cambridge: Polity.

Trentmann, F. 2006. "The Modern Genealogy of the Consumer: Meanings, Identities, Political Synapses." Pp. 19–70 in J. Brewer and F. Trentmann, eds., *Consuming Cultures, Global Perspectives: Historical Trajectories and Multicultural Conflicts*. Oxford: Berg.

Veblen, T. 1925 (1899). *The Theory of the Leisure Class: An Economic Study of Institutions*. London: George Allen and Unwin.

Warde, A. 2002. "Changing Conceptions of Consumption." Pp. 10–24 in A. Anderson, K. Meethan, and S. Miles, eds., *The Changing Consumer*. London: Routledge.

——. 2005. "Consumption and the Theory of Practice." *Journal of Consumer Culture* 5(2): 131–54.

Warde, A. and Martens, L. 2000. *Eating Out: Differentiation, Consumption, and Pleasure*. Cambridge: Cambridge University Press.

Part VII

Cultures of work and professions

40

Work cultures

Robin Leidner

Frameworks of meaning shape work experiences as surely as do organizational structures, technology, and patterns of ownership. Motivation, effort, discipline, group identifications and boundaries, and self-understanding all depend on work cultures. These factors are molded in obvious ways by structural and material factors both within and beyond the workplace, yet work cultures do more than express and embody differences in power, authority, interests, and advantage. They have their own effects on how work is done, how organizations operate, how people understand themselves, to whom they feel loyal. While drawing on elements of the broader culture that order solidarities and identities, whether based on nation, gender, or other social distinctions, cultures of work can also affect surrounding cultural milieux.

Work cultures, broadly defined, are sets of values, beliefs, norms, and sentiments about work and the symbols and rituals that express them. Sociological and historical work demonstrates the significance of work cultures that operate at a variety of levels, from specific workplaces and occupations to organizations to nations and supranational systems. These cultures are neither static nor uncontested. They can provide the impetus and resources for struggles over control of work, inclusion and exclusion, goals, and rewards.

This essay emphasizes the continual interplay between culture and economic conditions, structures, and practices. It first argues that cultural frameworks always guide economic activity, even as changes in the structures and practices of work shape consciousness, identities, and ideologies. The discussion then moves from large-scale cultural shifts to the operation of culture within more sharply delineated structures of work, noting change over time in the significance of occupational cultures, workplace cultures, and organizational cultures. At all of these levels, workers aim to maintain control over their tasks and their environment, sometimes offering resistance to efforts by others, especially bosses, to interfere with the norms of their work culture. Yet solidarity among those who share an occupation or a workplace may be weakened by cultural distinctions imported from beyond the workplace. The chapter concludes with a discussion of how changing conditions of work—currently driven by globalization—transform elements of culture at all levels, providing ongoing challenges to sociologists seeking to understand the complex interplay of economic structures, everyday work experiences, and surrounding cultures.

Culture and economics

Weber called attention to the ways that preexisting cultures shape orientations to new kinds of work, noting, for example, that efforts to motivate peasants to work longer hours at harvest time by increasing wage rates had the opposite effect because they did not see material gain as a route to a better life. *The Protestant Ethic and the Spirit of Capitalism* (Weber 1958 [1904–05]) points to the rise of a novel cultural framework—a system of religious beliefs—as a necessary part of the causal chain leading to the development of capitalism. Weber's approach complicates the Marxist view of culture as part of the superstructure that derives from the material, economic base.

The nature of the relation between cultural frameworks and economic developments remains open to debate, but historical and sociological research, especially cross-cultural studies, demonstrates that these realms cannot be separated. Social structures stimulate and limit aspirations and ideas about how to fulfill them, but the mixture of motivation and compulsion employers use to control their workers depends in part on the workers' cultural frameworks. In addition, cultural settings shape workplace practices; economic relations help determine individual and group identities; and structures of work affect the surrounding cultures.

Economists and organizational theorists often treat individualistic rationality and efficiency as primary and unproblematic principles of action. The aggressive spread of bureaucracies around the world may seem to be the result of inherent efficiencies, but rationality and efficiency take form only within particular ideological traditions and social contexts. Neither timeless values nor constants of human behavior can explain the variable workings of the economy in general or of particular organizations. In reality, cultural frameworks with their own histories always guide economic activity. Neo-institutional theorists explain the nearly ubiquitous reach of bureaucracies as the result of a kind of cultural imperialism—the creation of a world culture dominated by Western ideas (Meyer *et al.* 1997, cited in Morrill 2008: 26) consonant with the bureaucratic organization of work.

Still, even in the same bureaucratized industry, work cultures may vary across nations. In his detailed historical account, Biernacki (1995) demonstrates that disparate understandings of labor as a commodity developed in Germany and Britain in the nineteenth-century textile industry, apparently as the result of differential timing in the emergence of wage labor. He argues that culture is an autonomous force, but that in each country cultural assumptions came to be embedded in work practices which in turn conveyed and reproduced the logic upon which they are based. These nationally distinctive principles, he writes, produced distinctive patterns of industrial relations.

Once such cultural assumptions are built into social structures and practices—the length of the working day, how pay is calculated—they are reproduced by the practices of everyday life, shaping the consciousness, the taken-for-granted, the common sense of all involved. Whenever and wherever the labor market moves people into the unfamiliar world of industrial or bureaucratic work and they prove recalcitrant to its demands, owners and managers try to reform them and generally succeed. Populations of newly industrializing countries, immigrant workers, rural people drawn into industrial work, former welfare recipients, people from neighborhoods lacking models of steady employment, and former housewives all must give up familiar notions about who is entitled to organize their time, determine their effort, and decide the best ways to do things. Showing up for work every day, on time, dressed appropriately, with a proper willingness to accommodate oneself to workplace regulations and norms does not come naturally to people who previously regarded work as properly regulated by tradition, family members, the dictates of the weather and hours of daylight, their own needs and standards, or community scrutiny.

Methods of acculturating workers have become more sophisticated with time but the essential program has not changed. When the International Harvester Corporation hired immigrant Polish laborers in the United States a century ago, it set about teaching them how to live by the demands of the industrial order. Lesson One included a text that provided guidance for the workday: "The whistle blows at five minutes of starting time. I get ready to go to work. I work until the whistle blows to quit" (Gutman 1975: 6). Ultimately, these Poles learned to abandon their old ways and conformed to the new order of highly rationalized work. Contemporary firms making use of new pools of labor now do the same kind of things in a great variety of cultural settings all around the planet.

Occupational and workplace cultures

Historically, *occupational* groups have elaborated work cultures for many workers. Occupations, including professions, typically develop specific sets of norms that are passed on to novices both during training and on the job. Some have extensive periods of training and socialization during which initiates' sense of themselves and their status relative to others is remade. They learn and internalize not only knowledge and skills, but also the occupation's ideology, ethos, traditions, and norms, including criteria for judgment, craft pride, and rules for interacting among themselves and with various others. Strong occupational cultures delineate social boundaries, affect patterns of inter-action, and generally intensify struggles over status and autonomy *vis-à-vis* coworkers, workplace superiors, customers and clients, occupational groups that have related mandates, and the general public (Hughes 1984a [1959]).

Much of what Hughes called "the social drama of work" (Hughes 1984b [1951] derives from efforts by the members of an occupation to act on their values in order to maintain their prerogatives and their dignity rather than comply with others' standards. Jazz musicians who resent attempts of "squares" to influence the performance (Becker 1951), male firefighters who refuse to abandon sexist practices to make women feel welcome (Chetkovich 1997), and professionals who consider some kinds of work beneath them are all defending occupational self-determination.

However, those who share an occupation do not necessarily share a culture. *Workplaces* often have their own distinctive cultures—what industrial sociologists once called shop-floor cultures—which can alter occupational values or override occupational barriers. Moreover, within and across occupational boundaries, differences based on race and ethnicity, gender, language, nationality, and citizenship status may be imported into the workplace or developed there—their significance magnified or downplayed in part by how they map onto job placement, organizational hierarchy, and seniority. Such features of everyday work life as dress, patterns of interaction, and topics of conversation depend

421

on workers' cultural background and their incorporation into workplace groups. For example, the radically different workplace cultures of elementary-school teachers and coal miners can be explained in large part by the distinct demands of the work, but the gender order beyond the workplace has a significant impact as well.

Both occupational and workplace cultures often reproduce patterns of exclusion, although some people are relatively accepting of cultural differences sexism, racism, and, ethnocentrism flourish in many occupations and at many work sites. Barriers to entry into an occupation have often had disparate effects, intentionally or not. Within the workplace, traditional forms of cultural expression can be used to carry out disputes between competing groups. A dispute may be limited to a struggle for control over expression, as when Latino athletes want to hear salsa music in the locker room and African-Americans want to hear rap, but a dispute may also carry forward battles about material interests. Hostile joking, obscenity, religious rituals or proselytization, and political symbols and slogans all can be used by one group to make the workplace uncomfortable for potential newcomers, thus to preserve control over jobs.

As in many other circumstances, the degree of solidarity among members of an occupation or among co-workers at a particular workplace is influenced by the salience of boundaries between in-group and out-group members and of struggles over access to resources. When outsiders, be they customers, bosses, members of other departments, or those in allied jobs, act in ways that threaten workers' autonomy, convenience, or self-regard, we can expect to see relative solidarity among those who are similarly situated. Divisions among co-workers and members of occupations are most likely to surface when access to jobs, promotions, and preferred tasks is threatened from within or when newcomers challenge existing elements of workplace culture.

Organizational culture

Traditionally, decisions about how to carry out daily tasks came from occupational groups, but organizational forms such as guilds and craft unions that formerly upheld occupational cultures have disappeared or lost their relevance. Professional associations still flourish, but professionals are far less likely to set up practices for themselves than they once were and are therefore less autonomous. Most work now takes place in organizations, which have sharply undercut the strength of occupational cultures by taking over control of work and distributing it with scant regard for traditional divisions of labor, and also by trying to impose *organizational* cultures that reorder solidarities and values.

Some aspects of *occupational* cultures, including hostile attitudes between different kinds of workers, can be useful to management insofar as they undermine worker solidarity. In general, however, when organizations bring together workers with a strong occupational ethos, owners and managers seek to override group norms so that they can exercise control over the distribution of tasks, workers' level of effort, work standards, pace, and technique. Braverman (1974) argued that the indispensability of workers' knowledge, experience, and skill was dramatically diminished by managements' successful imposition of work systems that deskilled the work. Reallocation of the right and ability to control work processes undercuts not only workers' power and wages but also their occupational identities and cultures. But managerial control measures do not typically eliminate struggle over the conduct and rewards of work. Rather, the weakening of occupational bonds can strengthen class solidarity within and across organizations, such that the work site remains contested terrain (Edwards 1979).

Occupational subcultures do often survive within organizations as sources of norms and values which contrast with those of management (Trice 1993). They can serve as bases of struggle over status and workplace control and provide communities of resistance to managerial dictates. Although professionals increasingly work in bureaucracies, they do not altogether abandon their formally prescribed ethics and standards or their carefully cultivated worldviews when subjected to organizational discipline. Similarly, distinctive elements of gender or ethnic cultures can uphold priorities and solidarities that challenge management's cultural impositions.

Morrill (2008) describes how managerial attention to culture as a means of improving production and winning workers' commitment surged and ebbed throughout the twentieth century, intermittently countering or complicating more straightforward emphasis on hierarchy and bureaucratic efficiency. Some firms took a paternalistic stance toward employees, aiming to foster identification with the organization by promoting a familistic culture and providing programs and facilities that strengthened workers' commitment to and dependence on the company. The Hawthorne experiments of the 1920s and early 1930s demonstrated that simply paying attention to a specific work group could increase its productivity, forming the basis of the human-relations approach to management that emphasized consideration of workers' emotional well-being as part of the organization's strategy for building loyalty and increasing output. Edwards (1979) argues that elaborate bureaucratic systems of job ladders fostered not only identification with the company but also an individualistic culture in which workers focused on their own mobility opportunities. All of these approaches were intended to lead workers to identify with the organization as a whole rather than form class-based or occupation-based identifications.

In the last decades of the twentieth century, several significant trends made culture an even more central managerial concern in the US. Foremost among them was competition from abroad, in particular from Japan, where corporate cultures and production processes differed markedly from those in the United States in emphasizing employee participation and responsibility, teamwork across barriers of rank, and activities aimed at building solidarity. Many US corporations experimented with similar practices, while among management consultants, "corporate culture" became a buzzword. Acknowledging that companies varied greatly in ethos, the consultants urged corporate executives to make culture an explicit focus of leadership. Top–down cultural strategies might center on customer satisfaction, on continual innovation, or on a given company's tradition of quality, but the shared goal was creating a positive, unifying ethos that motivated workers and contributed to corporate success.

The expansion of high-tech and service industries also prompted renewed attention to business culture. High-tech companies dependent on the creative work of young technical workers developed famously informal yet intense work cultures that promoted long hours of self-driven labor. Companies whose success requires attracting and pleasing customers strove to create cultures of service that called on workers to reshape their orientations and self-presentations. As Hochschild (1983) argues, service workers are frequently required to perform "emotional labor" in order to produce a desired feeling state in those on the receiving end of services. Such labor is shaped in large part by norms of gender and class. Since customers are necessarily involved in this sort of work, often as participants as well as evaluators, the practices of service businesses both draw on and exert influence over the surrounding culture.

Organizational efforts to manage work cultures do not go unchallenged. Workers often consider such efforts manipulative and see them as potentially lessening their dignity, their independence, and their class or other loyalties. Class-based resentment and a pervasive suspicion of managerial intentions can generate resistance to such attempts, and resistance also can arise in defense of informal workplace practices. Oppositional stances do not necessarily undermine managerial aims, however, as has been demonstrated in a range of workplaces from manufacturing to engineering. Cultures of resistance may take forms that subtly elicit acquiescence to exploitation (Burawoy 1979) or that support ironic distancing rather than creative engagement (Kunda 1992). Women's work cultures and their associated rituals may uphold alternative values and justify a degree of autonomy, but employers can also draw on codes of femininity to manipulate workers (Salzinger 2003).

Managerial emphasis on controlling organizational culture varies by setting and fluctuates over time for a variety of reasons. The costs of creating and imposing a culture, the relative effectiveness of other kinds of controls, including material incentives, the difficulty of attracting and keeping desirable employees, and management fads are all significant factors. Recent structural changes in the corporate economy have, on the whole, made organizational cultures a less important managerial strategy. In general, under pressure of international competition, rapid technological change, and market uncertainty, companies increasingly limit their commitment to employees. When companies lay off large numbers of employees, outsource work, hire workers on short-term contracts, or otherwise match skill and labor precisely to demand at a given moment, the resulting instability of careers within particular organizations means that management is less apt to rely on a unified culture to spur motivation and to create long-term loyalties. Corporate mergers, increasingly frequent late in the twentieth century, have also had an effect because of the difficulties of meshing contrasting cultures. Besides, mergers almost always entail uncertainty and layoffs, which produce a workplace culture marked by cynicism and disaffection. Dubious that workers' loyalty to the company yields significant benefits, some managers have taken to cultivating an employee ethos of competitive individualism, readiness to redefine oneself, and personal entrepreneurship (van Maanen and Kunda 1989).

Thus, changing contexts of work have eroded some of the conditions that support organizational cultures, as well as occupational and workplace ones—conditions that previously could be taken for granted. The physical isolation of telecommuting workers, the brief communities created by short-term contracts, the individualism promoted by the replacement of fixed employment with independent contracting, as well as the movement of work across national borders—these all undercut the kinds of face-to-face interaction and the awareness of a community of fate that promote workplace and occupational cultures and that can attach workers to the organizational culture.

Yet surprisingly powerful work cultures can be maintained under unlikely circumstances. Actors and other theater personnel form tight communities for strictly limited time periods and preserve professional traditions regardless of employment; direct selling organizations create intense cultures that bind together independent contractors (Biggart 1989); even temporary production workers can identify strongly with an organizational culture (Smith 2001). In none of these cases, however, is the occupational culture a significant source of resistance to managerial power. Moreover, the growth of service work, which often incorporates non-employees into the labor process, encourages employers to take control of workers' attitudes and presentation of self in dramatically more thoroughgoing ways (Leidner 1993).

Work cultures in an era of globalization

In the contemporary world, the increasingly swift movement of capital, organizational processes, technology, and cultural products has wrought many changes in cultures of work and in the relevant elements of surrounding cultures. The power of the globalizing economy to effect great changes in work cultures is notable throughout the world, even where there has been highly organized resistance to market economics. In the formerly socialist nations and in China, globalization, which has exposed workers to market forces once unimaginable, has provided vivid evidence of how rapidly work cultures shift when state regimes change. Lee's collection of ethnographies of work in contemporary China (Lee 2007) documents how employment insecurity and new demands for attracting and keeping customers undermine familiar cultural suppositions, disorienting workers who must play by new rules. The lack of preparation of those who emigrate from rural areas in search of work replicates the disorienting experiences of agricultural and small-town people in other parts of the world in the earlier stages of industrialization and capitalist development.

Globalization and advanced rationalization are modifying and perhaps transforming not only work cultures but local and national cultures as well. The consequences are quite variable and difficult to predict. Two examples illustrate this indeterminacy: the effects of globalization on women's identities and the cultural consequences of service corporations' worldwide expansion. Sociological research on the ways that women workers employed by transnational corporations express their gender identities amply demonstrates the variability of globalization's cultural effects. Even as companies are pursuing their own ends, women employed by foreign-owned firms reshape their identities as women while participating actively in creating work cultures that draw on the surrounding culture, affect their home culture, and make use of the norms and resources of their employers. Radhakrishnam (2007), for example, describes women employed in information technology in India who understood themselves to be participating in a global business culture yet took pride in asserting their "Indianness" in ways that shook expectations about what traditional Indian women were like. Salzinger (2003) shows that transnational manufacturing firms moved factories to Mexico to make use of the "productive femininity" of the subservient women assembly workers they believed would be found there. Yet her fieldwork reveals that, rather than drawing on preexisting character types, each of four assembly plants produced a distinctive "gendered subject," ranging from docile to combative. Freeman (2000) finds that data-entry workers employed by foreign companies in Barbados collectively generated a new style of femininity that asserted a status superior to other workers and that flaunted their womanliness and creativity. The complex and elusive cultural effects of outsourcing and similar transfers of jobs out of highly industrialized nations form an especially promising subject for further research.

The cultural effects of service companies such as McDonald's that have spread around the world are also more complicated than might be assumed. They export not only products but also physical settings and styles of interaction that have numerous cultural effects. They do not simply superimpose the organizational culture onto the receiving culture, however. Cultural imperialism is too gross a concept to capture the interplay of

425

myriad influences on either the culture of the workplace or the surrounding culture. Watson's edited volume on McDonald's outlets in East Asian countries (Watson 1997) shows that customers in various countries make use of the facilities in ways that fit their own cultural patterns, sometimes forcing the owners to adapt to their preferences. Similarly, although the business model of McDonald's and other fast-food companies grew out of a legal environment that provides workers with virtually no voice and few rights, their efforts to impose their workplace cultures in countries in which workers have more power often run into both legal and informal resistance (Royle and Towers 2002).

Conclusion

The uncertainty about the interplay of nearly incessant economic change and culture presents sociologists with a challenging and perhaps daunting research agenda. The task facing sociologists of work and culture is to understand that interplay in a global economy with massive and sometimes apparently overpowering international transfers of capital, technology, personnel, and organizational and occupational cultures. The research agenda includes specifying the effects when societies experience the arrival of large numbers of workers from unfamiliar cultures, when significant sectors of the economy come under the control of foreign corporations, or when new technologies disrupt occupational traditions.

Outcomes are likely to be quite variable, with national differences in responses to economic restructuring providing evidence of the enabling and constraining powers of longstanding cultural and structural patterns. But in all societies, the changing character of work raises many questions about culture. On the one hand, existing cultures variably shape people's capacity to cope with the fluidity of work arrangements. On the other, changes in the structures of work and career can give rise to cultural innovation. They also may lead to changes in beliefs about what workers are owed, about who is to blame for individual occupational failure, and about who should bear the costs of change.

Cultural resources undoubtedly shape individuals' capacity to cope with fluidity in work arrangements. In turn, changes in the structures of work and career can be expected to give rise to cultural innovation. If, for large numbers of workers, work no longer takes place in relatively stable groups and large numbers of people switch occupations during the course of their working lives, work and occupational cultures may well decline in importance as significant bases of personal identity. What will replace them? Societal notions of the place of work in individual lives, the proper orientation toward work, and the kinds of qualities assumed to be required for success at work will still be important, but their content may shift markedly, as is happening in China.

The study of work cultures draws together sociological studies of work and economic life and studies of culture. Understanding the reciprocal impact of structural economic change, everyday experiences of work, and the surrounding culture is the major task facing students of work culture.

References

Becker, Howard S. 1951. "The Professional Dance Musician and His Audience." *American Journal of Sociology* 57: 136–44.

Biernacki, Richard. 1995. *The Fabrication of Labor: Germany and Britain, 1640–1914.* Berkeley: University of California Press.

Biggart, Nicole W. 1989. *Charismatic Capitalism: Direct Selling Organizations in America.* Chicago: University of Chicago Press.

Braverman, Harry. 1974. *Labor and Monopoly Capital: The Degradation of Work in the Twentieth Century.* New York: Monthly Review Press.

Burawoy, Michael. 1979. *Manufacturing Consent: Changes in the Labor Market under Monopoly Capitalism.* Chicago: University of Chicago Press.

Chetkovich, Carol A. 1997. *Real Heat: Gender and Race in the Urban Fire Service.* New Brunswick, NJ: Rutgers University Press.

Edwards, Richard. 1979. *Contested Terrain: The Transformation of the Workplace in the Twentieth Century.* New York: Basic Books.

Freeman, Caroline. 2000. *High Tech and High Heels in the Global Economy: Women, Work, and Pink-Collar Identities in the Caribbean.* Durham, NC and London: Duke University Press.

Gutman, Herbert G. 1975. *Work, Culture, and Society in Industrializing America: Essays in American Working-Class and Social History.* New York: Vintage Books.

Hochschild, Arlie. 1983. *The Managed Heart: Commercialization of Human Feeling.* Berkeley: University of California Press.

Hughes, Everett C. 1984a (1959). "The Study of Occupations." Pp. 283–97 in *The Sociological Eye; Selected Papers.* New Brunswick, NJ and London: Transaction Books.

——. 1984b (1951). "Work and Self." Pp. 338–74 in *The Sociological Eye: Selected Papers.* New Brunswick, NJ and London: Transaction Books.

Kunda, Gideon. 1992. *Engineering Culture: Control and Commitment in a High-Tech Corporation.* Philadelphia, PA: Temple University Press.

Lee, Ching Kwan, ed. 2007. *Working in China: Ethnographies of Labor and Workplace Transformation.* New York: Routledge.

Leidner, Robin. 1993. *Fast Food, Fast Talk: Service Work and the Routinization of Everyday Life.* Berkeley: University of California Press.

Meyer, John W., Boli, John, Thomas, George M., and Ramirez, Francisco. 1997. "World Society and the Nation-state." *American Journal of Sociology* 103: 144–81.

Morrill, Calvin. 2008. "Culture and Organization Theory." *Annals, AAPSS* 619: 15–40.

Radhakrishnam, Smitha. 2007. "On the Cusp of the National and Global: Gender and the Making of a New India." Paper presented at the annual meetings of the American Sociological Association, New York.

Royle, Tony and Towers, Brian, eds. 2002. *Labour Relations in the Global Fast-Food Industry.* London: Routledge.

Salzinger, Leslie. 2003. *Genders in Production: Making Workers in Mexico's Global Factories.* Berkeley: University of California Press.

Smith, Vicki. 2001. *Crossing the Great Divide: Worker Risk and Opportunity in the New Economy.* Ithaca, NY: ILR Press.

Trice, Harrison M. 1993. *Occupational Subcultures in the Workplace.* Ithaca, NY: ILR Press.

van Maanen, John and Kunda, Gideon. 1989. "'Real Feelings': Emotional Expression and Organizational Culture." Pp. 43–103 in L.L. Cummings and B.M. Staw, eds., *Research in Organizational Behavior.* Greenwich, CT: JAI Press.

Watson, James L., ed. 1997. *Golden Arches East: McDonald's in East Asia.* Stanford, CA: Stanford University Press.

Weber, Max. 1958 (1904–05). *The Protestant Ethic and the Spirit of Capitalism.* New York: Charles Scribner's Sons.

41

Cultures of service

Eileen M. Otis

In 2007 the service sector became the largest employer worldwide (International Labour Organization 2007). Services are now an employment mainstay not only in advanced economies but also in many developing countries around the globe. Despite the regional and international proliferation of services, cultural diversity has thus far largely been neglected in the analysis of interactive service labor. The expansion of services across regions and cultural domains, as well as the export of services from Western nations, reveals a seemingly obvious yet frequently overlooked fact: service labor requires workers to be culturally competent. A central component of most service labor is inter-action between a worker and a client or customer. This interaction requires that workers recognize and manipulate culturally dominant forms of civility and etiquette. In common parlance, we often restrict our use of "culture workers" to the cultural elite—artists, musicians, actors, and writers. Yet service workers are also culture workers.

The inattention to cultural processes in service has led to a blind spot in scholarship, which overlooks culturally variegated norms of interaction and expectations for social exchange that are the basic substance of service interactions. By assuming these norms to be universal, scholarship not only misses variation in the substance of service interactions but also inadequately grasps processes of cultural diffusion. For example, scant attention is paid to ways in which Western transnational service retailers serve as conduits of cultural globalization by introducing new standards of interaction based upon culturally specific norms of civility to new domains. And as locally operated services proliferate, employers adopt repertoires from international firms because they are proxies for reliability, credibility, and trust. These repertoires necessarily become absorbed into existing orga-nizational and interactive practices. Such cultural transactions are rarely addressed in the service work literature. In this essay I explain why culture is left out of studies of service and why culture matters for service labor. I show how we can bring culture into our understanding of service work without abandoning the search for patterns and explanations, even as a cultural analysis unveils a bewildering array of practices, norms, and beliefs.

The essay proceeds as follows. I first assess the utility and limits of existing frameworks for the study of interactive service work across diverse cultural settings, reviewing central concepts in the study of interactive service. These concepts tend to illuminate generic organizational dynamics without regard to cultural variation across space and time. In particular, I explore three bedrock assumptions in the sociology of service that present limitations to extending our analytic reach to new domains of culture. The notions of separate spheres, method acting, and metaphors of performance that inform prevailing theories of service work limit the applicability of these concepts across cultural arenas. Finally, I address the problem of cultural diversity. Once we open the Pandora's box of culture and find endless cultural variety, are we left to merely inventory the myriad cultural practices observed in service labor? How are we to appreciate patterns and explain differences in service labor practices? I suggest two heuristic concepts that can help make comparative sense of cultural heterogeneity within interactive service labor— embeddedness and consumer markets. These concepts promise to bring order to an otherwise bewildering array of cultural norms practices, meanings, and beliefs that unfold in the service labor. Data on service work in China illustrates these ideas.

The emergence of labor studies of service work

In the 1970s, the service sector in the US began outstripping manufacturing as a source of revenue and employment (Block 1990). Other advanced economies were also fast becoming "service societies," as they moved their manufacturing to export-production platforms in newly developing countries. The service sector was employing more Americans than ever, often in low-wage, insecure work. And US firms were exporting services abroad, with the global development of hotels, fast-food chains, and retail stores. The tectonic shifts occurring in the employment landscape begged for new theories and new concepts. With these shifts sociologists gradually began to examine service-sector labor processes.

But unpacking the basic competencies of interactive service labor proved a daunting task because the product is intangible and ephemeral. As a category of economic activity, service is defined by what it is not. Unlike its cousin sectors, manufacturing and agriculture that produce items of physical substance, the service sector produces products that are not tangibly material. Moreover, service "products" cannot be separated from the people who produce them; services involve direct interaction between the producer and the consumer. Especially in lower-wage consumer-service occupations, the primary content of labor is interaction with customers.

Service labor unfolds in the fugacious realm of human sentiment, sensibility, and culture. The product is not material; it is not a bolt, a handbag, a car, or a kitchen appliance. Rather, the product item is an affective response created in a consumer (Hochschild 1983). Service workers are paid to produce a range of affect for customer consumption: a sense of security, happiness, calm, delight, excitement, or even titillation. Although the product contains value to be exchanged on a market, it is quite literally immaterial. Therefore the conditions, the production, and the outcome of interactive service labor easily elude empirical analysis.

For this reason, ethnography is often the method of choice for examining service work (although an important exception is Wharton 1993). As an "embodied" methodology that engages the researcher's multiple senses, ethnography requires immersion in the work setting. The ethnographer ventures close to experiencing firsthand how workers "do interaction" and navigate social relationships with customers and managers. In-depth

429

interviewing allows ethnographers to explore how workers themselves understand the process of producing a range of affect in their work. Using ethnography, sociologists began to make legible types of work that had been taken for granted, naturalized, often feminized, sexualized, and assumed to be low skilled. With their studies, scholars have developed a variegated repertory of concepts for analyzing the labor dynamics of the service sector.

In particular, Arlie Hochschild's book *The Managed Heart* (1983) dramatically altered labor scholars' perception of service work. She cast light on the mental-emotional proficiency required of service workers who interact with customers. She termed the emotional adjustments that service workers perform on their own moods "emotion work." The concept illuminated a set of competencies that had previously been invisible. Service laborers do not assemble parts, or build bridges, or solder or weld, she explained. They labor on the self, exercising a profound degree of control over their emotional states with the objective of producing affective responses in customers. Hochschild compared the flight attendants she studied to method actors who do intense emotional labor to actually self-induce the sentiments that they seek to portray in their characters. Through similar methods of emotional labor, workers replace their own learned emotional responses with the affective imperatives of the firm. Hochschild argued that such deep work on the self, enacted in the interest of profit, threatens the authentic selfhood of workers.

Multiple adjustments, specifications, elaborations, and applications of Hochschild's work followed. Scholars investigated the labor of security guards, secretaries, paralegals, waitresses, fast-food workers, hotel workers, beauticians, and retail sales people. One major adjustment in Hochschild's original framework stemmed from a study of fast-food workers at McDonald's. In this research, Leidner (1993) argues that the routinized interactive scripts employees are required to follow are not so much a compromise to a deeply felt sense of authenticity, as Hochschild's work suggests. Instead workers use scripts as a shield to protect their private senses of self. Scripts provide interactive armor against the endless streams of customers with whom workers contend, by allowing employees to control and process service interactions.

In another critical contribution, Lan (2001) shows that retail service workers not only perform emotion work, but also do "physical" labor that requires using the body as a vector of symbols and codes to promote products to customers. Service workers' bodies are highly controlled: they become objects of display for commodities—like cosmetics— so that customers can inspect the use of products directly. Furthermore, the workers' body is a vehicle for messages about status and sexuality that become associated with the service product and the firm (see also Kang 2003).

In research on nursing-home attendants, Lopez (2006) revisits the issue of authenticity, showing that instead of depriving workers of an authentic sense of self, some employers actually create an employment environment that incubates, encourages, and rewards authenticity. In contrast to Hochschild's contention that service firms eliminate the possibility for workers to enact authentic selfhoods (sets of emotions that express their own underlying dispositions and interests) as they interact with customers, Lopez finds that some nursing homes do in fact strive to create social and material conditions that enable workers to enact authentic selfhoods, that allow them to draw upon their own empathy and compassion as they care for the elderly.

Not only have labor studies of service investigated the reshaping of selfhoods in pursuit of labor control, they have also complicated dualistic worker–manager models of the labor process that derived from industrial labor. They do so by recognizing the central role of the customer in the disciplinary dynamics of labor. These analyses reveal the triangles of potential conflict and cooperation between consumers, managers, and workers, as actors forge situationally strategic two-way alliances to gain an advantage over the third party. To optimize control over this three-way labor interaction, management attempts to recruit customers into the labor process as both objects and agents of discipline (Fuller and Smith 1991). Employers coordinate control of employees and customers by enlisting customers for surveillance (Fuller and Smith 1991), using tipping systems (Sallaz 2002), routinizing interactions (Leidner 1993), and transforming the identities and bodies of workers to influence customer behavior (Leidner 1993; Macdonald and Sirianni 1996).

Sociologists' analyses of service-sector labor processes tend to capture generic organizational dynamics of service, but overlook the rich variation in cultural norms of service across communities of interaction. The neglect is in part a byproduct of disciplinary practice: sociology's predominant geographical focus is the US, and practitioners often generalize (often implicitly) about multiple settings based on observations derived solely from the US. Moving studies of service beyond the US, including following US service firms across national boundaries, can address these shortcomings.

Bringing culture in

Since few sociological analyses of service work venture beyond US borders or explore the cultural presuppositions of service interactions, they tend to take for granted regionally and historically specific norms of civility and etiquette (exceptions include Gottfried 2003; Hanser 2006; Poster 2007). Given its affective nature, interactive service work is particularly subject to longstanding cultural practice, including rules of etiquette, norms regarding how and when to express feelings, and guidelines for maintaining appropriate social boundaries. To enact service labor successfully, the worker must have expertise in shared understandings of what, for example, is considered pleasant, appropriate, and respectful behavior. In the arena of service labor, where work tasks require interaction and, more specifically, induce an emotional effect in a customer, cultural ideals informing appropriate, satisfying, and aesthetically desirable interaction are particularly central to producing emotionally resonant service interactions with customers.

One limitation in transposing Hochschild's innovative analysis to other settings stems from its roots in Western institutional and normative traditions. She bases her central critique of emotion work on a notion of separate spheres—a non-commercial, domestic, private sphere, and a commercial, public sphere. She argues that service work enters and defiles a sanctum of human authenticity otherwise protected in the private sphere, which is presumed to be non-commercial. Yet the domestic sphere is a preeminent site of the consumption of commercial products and a place where money entwines with and enables intimate relations (Zelizer 2007). But the extent to which a private/public divide (a byproduct of Western industrialization) is maintained or how the lines between spheres are drawn in other social settings remain open questions.

Another impediment to applying Hochschild's analysis across cultural settings is a definitional reliance of the core concept of emotion work on Stanislovskian performance theory, popularly known as method acting. Emotion work is defined as the labor of displaying an emotion so as to elicit an intended feeling in a customer. Hochschild draws

431

an analogy between method acting and emotion work to illuminate the latter's basic psychological mechanics. Simply put, the method involves conjuring a memory with emotional resonance to prompt the expression of a desired emotion, which in turn allows the actor to create a highly naturalistic display of feeling. Actors can induce the most natural display of emotions, it is assumed, by drawing upon deeply affective memories.

The theory reflects a strongly individualist disposition in that it focuses solely on the personal interior as the wellspring of emotions and affective displays. Other schools of acting, such as the Brechtian method and traditional Chinese performance theory, are less individualistic approaches to performance. For example, the Chinese performance tradition, which extends from the fourth century BCE to Mao's twentieth-century socialist realism, focused less on the actor than on the relationship between the actor and audience, which was understood as a pedagogical relationship. Actors focused more intently on the reception of the performance by the audience, and their own relationship to the audience, than on the degree of authenticity or naturalism displayed. As Schechner observes:

> From an early day, theater was seen as a way of reaching ordinary people who could not read. And at various times, theater served Confucian or Taoist thought, disseminated imperial edicts regarding proper behavior, helped people understand their place in the social hierarchy, or sowed revolutionary ideas.
>
> (Schechner 1999: x)

Service workers whom I interviewed in China echoed the pedagogical orientation. Thus, as one waitress at a luxury hotel in Beijing described her interactions with customers, "I teach them through my smile, so they can improve their breeding" (Otis 2008: 28). If interactive service performance in the US is measured by a standard of naturalism and authenticity, in China service interaction tends to be viewed as a conduit for displaying appropriate social norms and values. The alternative Chinese school of performance theory also diverges from method acting in its focus on the social context rather than emotional memory as a source of feeling. Rather than manufacture an emotion by enlisting individual memories that are resonantly affective, a Chinese approach (and a Brechtian one as well) places the actor in a social environment, or some semblance thereof, which allows the desired character to emerge.

There are also limits to the analogy of drama and interactive service labor. We can gain leverage on understanding the labor politics of service work by recognizing the differences as well as the similarities between acting (for an audience) and interacting (with a paying customer). Unlike service workers, actors do not anticipate or respond to the needs of paying patrons. Actors are not required to do the bidding of customers. On the contrary, actors are more likely to exercise control and influence over the audience through their arts. Actors create a world apart for their audience, a world that the audience enters. Indeed, actors have been deemed "elite emotion managers" (Orzechowicz 2008). Workers, on the other hand, are more likely to enter into and navigate the class and cultural worlds created to appeal to their customers. These service environments are more likely to reflect the tastes and aesthetics of the customers than the employees. Although the theater analogy has been useful for highlighting certain elements of interactive service work, it presents limits for the study of service by diverting attention away from the specific emotional and interactive content of service interactions as well as the power hierarchies formed in particular service contexts.

Although the dictionary of concepts developed by labor scholars of interactive service reveals some of the key organizational dynamics of this type of work, it is time we trained our analytic lens on the cultural content rather than the more formal organizational properties of service labor. If interactive labor is defined by emotion work, then *which* emotions are produced and under what conditions? If it is routinized and scripted, what exactly are the interactive forms that are subject to standardization? If interactive labor is "authentic," what is the behavior that is considered to reveal authenticity? Furthermore, exactly how valued a cultural norm is authenticity across cultural spheres? By focusing on how and why specific emotions, gestures, and actions are produced in particular service contexts, researchers can more clearly perceive the micropolitics of service labor processes, as workers negotiate new contexts of interaction. But this promise of "bringing culture in" comes with the peril of facing a perplexing assortment of norms, meanings, beliefs, and understandings in the study of service "culture work."

Analyzing and comparing routine culture work: consumer markets and embeddedness

How can we make sense of the potentially wide-ranging cultural practices that services in diverse settings encompass? How can we adapt existing concepts to better understand cultural variation and interaction, as firms develop within—and move between—diverse cultural settings? To address these issues, I suggest two heuristic concepts. The first is a notion of institutional embeddedness that points to articulations between the relatively formalized organizational dimensions of service work and those attributes of labor that are particular to time and place. The second is a working definition of consumer markets, which configure service-labor regimes.

I propose applying the concept of embeddedness to understand and compare the cultural substance of service labor. Embeddedness is used by economic sociologists to reveal the non-economic substrate of economic organization and exchange (Block 1990; Polanyi 1957). The concept helps to show the mutual constitution of formal market processes and cultural institutions, at the same time countering the belief (widely held by neoclassical economists) that modern economies are highly rationalized organizational forms that transcend "non-rational" modes of human activity like religious, ritual, and informal cultural practices.

Service firms codify, systematize, choreograph, and even routinize forms of interaction between customers and workers. To do so they draw on widely accepted social understandings of interaction that are considered pleasant, appropriate, and civil. Hence firms tap into, or embed within, culturally resonant symbols, meanings, gestures, and language in order to elicit a given desired response in customers. As hotels, fast-food chains, and other international service firms export operations to new regional settings, they introduce novel organizational models, forms of civility, and norms of interaction that are part of the interactive service product. But to implement these novel protocols service firms inevitably adapt to localized markets, institutional legacies, and the local cultural schema of employees.

Service work is particularly prone to embeddedness because it is not as peripatetic as industrial labor (Otis 2008). Service is an industry that directly follows and serves its consumer markets; therefore it must be spatially proximate to those markets. In other words, consumer service workers "produce" in the same place and at the same time that consumption occurs. The spatial proximity contrasts sharply with manufacturing, where the customer's purchase and consumption of items takes place far from the point of production. This means that, unlike manufacturers who nimbly dart about the globe in search of low-cost labor, service firms cannot readily relocate (Silver 2003).

In short, manufacturers follow labor markets, whereas service firms follow consumer markets. Because service firms operate in the midst of their consumer markets, it is nearly impossible for these firms to threaten to relocate if workers and managers do not accede to firm demands. The locational commitment, along with the fact that service workers deliver the product directly to consumers, means that service firms experience much greater pressure than manufacturing firms to adapt to pre-existing employment practices and the cultural schema that local employees bring into the workplace.

Service firms' decisions about location are shaped by their strategies for appeal to the status aspirations (or distinction struggles) of particular sets of customers—in other words, consumer markets. Economists use the term "consumer market" to refer to the purchasing preferences of individuals. They conceive of consumer preferences as highly individualistic, driven by rational self-interest, and cemented long before individuals are exposed to advertising and marketing. On the other hand, social scientists tend to view consumer markets as driven by marketing; consumers' choices are deeply influenced by the elaborate marketing and promotion activities of corporations (Marcuse 1964). A way of recognizing both the "agency" of the consumer and the "structure" of marketing is to employ Bourdieu's (1984) concept of distinction struggles. For Bourdieu (1984) class struggles for distinction occur in the realm of consumption. Accordingly, the way that consumers exhibit taste through consumption preferences is a preeminent means that groups draw on to position themselves within a class hierarchy and to naturalize and legitimate class inequalities. This positioning involves perpetual struggle, as Bourdieu writes:

> Because the distinctive power of cultural possessions or practices ... tends to decline with the growth in the absolute number of people able to appropriate them, the profits of distinction would wither away if the field of production of cultural goods ... did not endlessly supply new goods or new ways of using the same goods.
>
> (Bourdieu 1984: 230)

In other words, struggles for distinction pivot around exclusive consumption of goods and services. Firms enter into these distinction struggles by promoting goods and services as status-enabling—and often exclusive—in an effort to generate revenue. Drawing on these ideas I define consumer markets as the institutionalization of struggles for distinction between social groups by firms. As firms adapt services to distinction rivalries, they organize labor accordingly—to provide experiences that resonate with the culturally based distinction strategies of different classes, genders, and nationalities of consumers.

Although technically we can say that labor practices are embedded in local consumer markets, it is useful to distinguish between the strategic, profit-driven activity involved in designing labor practices to appeal to a consumer market, and the embedding of these practices within pre-existing, local cultural and institutional conditions. In other words, the design of labor practices may originate in firms' appeals to distinction struggles among status groups that in effect constitute consumer markets. But they are then adapted to, or embedded within, local institutional legacies as well as cultural expectations and practices of employees (schema).

Hence the actual implementation of labor practices is organized in relationship to pre-existing institutional legacies, that is, longstanding practices that shape relationships between employers and workers. I observed these processes at an international, luxury hotel in China, the Beijing Transluxury (a pseudonym). The hotel was connected to a US-based hotel conglomerate that imported Western executive managers to operate the hotel. During my ethnographic research I found that managers organized workers to provide individually customized services to their wealthy, high-profile clientele of Western businessmen, diplomats, and professionals (Otis 2008). Female interactive workers (waitresses, hostesses, butlers, and room attendants) were taught to adopt US middle-class, feminine dispositions: smiling, making eye contact, and walking "like ladies." They were required to adopt new bodily treatments, including makeup, daily showers, and use of deodorant. Yet a set of collectivist work legacies from the earlier Mao era affected the implementation of these new work practices: workers received generous monetary benefits, including healthcare, housing subsidies, and regular distribution of in-kind welfare, like large bottles of cooking oil as well as twice-daily meals in the staff canteen. Managers coordinated regular events for workers like collective weddings, singles parties, holiday soirees, and outings to plays. The Chinese Communist Party recruited members from among staff and held regular meetings at the hotel. These practices fostered a collegial environment that allowed middle managers to comment on the intimate details of worker appearance with the objective of standardizing service delivery. Managers carefully informed workers that they should wear deodorant to suppress body odor, brush their teeth to eliminate garlic breath, learn new ways of walking to act like ladies, and take birth control to adhere to the one child per family policy and avoid out-of-wedlock childbirth. In the end, managers successfully transformed young women workers by embedding new body and interactive processes in more familiar Mao-era relationships and language. But the transformation was not total; these workers filtered new service protocols through their own particular cultural dispositions.

Because interaction with customers is a form of production that draws from workers' own personality and emotions, the labor necessarily engages (or embeds within) workers' own pre-existing cultural dispositions—their perceptions, values, expectations, and physical demeanors. Despite the firms' highly choreographed designs for interaction with customers, workers continued to tailor interactive practices to suit their own needs for respect on the service floor. In other words, workers filtered new interactive protocols through their own norms of civility and etiquette. In so doing, they adapted, tempered, and reworked interactive routines introduced by management to pursue their own culturally defined standards of dignity and respect. It is these locally defined frames of meaning and practice that root service work in employees' everyday cultural worlds.

To return to the example of the Beijing Transluxury Hotel, female staff members frequently viewed it as their job to teach customers how to act appropriately, by being paragons of proper behavior themselves. In other words, they held a view of their work as pedagogical. They also combined the imported, US middle-class femininity learned at the hands of managers with local cultural schema of "face." "Giving face" refers to a conferral of status and honor involving semi-ritualized, culturally encoded enactments of deference. It is a hierarchical model of interaction (Yang 2002). Repeatedly, Transluxury workers told me that it was their job to "give face," that is, to confer status upon the customer. They did not view their work as making customers feel comfortable or happy or satisfied but, rather, as giving face. As a form of emotion work (Hochschild 1983) "giving face" is not conditioned by an expectation of individual authenticity; workers at the Beijing Transluxury tended not to view giving face as offering care or nurture. Since these workers were not striving for authenticity in interactions, they achieved greater scope to interact strategically, potentially to exploit their own construction of customer status, and to acknowledge the centrality of their status-giving to revenue. Giving face reflects a hierarchical, and ritual, mode of interaction that departs dramatically from US service-work models that are more democratic and reciprocal (Sherman 2007). Labor may be designed with consumer struggles for distinction in mind, but service workers absorb new interactive protocols into their own cultural understandings and expectations. And they do so within organizational contexts affected by historical legacies of employment. The concepts of consumer markets and embeddedness facilitate comparison of the cultural adaptations of service across time and space.

Looking ahead

Some sociologists are using case studies from cultural contexts outside the US to understand contemporary shifts in service work as well as the specific cultural underpinnings of service in diverse contexts. Of particular note is Winifred Poster's (2007) work on call centers in India, where managers subject workers to immersion in American cultural practices, which she terms "national identity management." Hanser (2006) examines the impact of socialist organization on a department store in China. Gottfried (2003) uses the term "aesthetic labor" to grasp service labor in Japan, a term that leaves capaciously open the possibility of inquiring about the cultural and historic specificity of the aesthetic of service labor. Collectively, these are promising points of departure, first, for reaching beyond US boundaries and addressing some of the culturally bound assumptions that have been part of US-focused labor studies of service work, and, second, for specifying how and under what conditions the more generic properties of the labor process occur, as well as how they combine with local forms of organization. The task remains, though, to build these studies into comparative frameworks that can explain how cultural practices are reshaped by and reshape service labor in diverse time and places.

An embeddedness framework can help us develop systematic cross-cultural analyses of these and future case studies, which in turn promises to enrich our capacity for developing theories of labor that respond to the particularities of service work, which has fast become the most common type of labor on the planet. The concepts of embeddedness and consumer markets allow researchers to compare and discover order in the otherwise bewildering and variegated proliferation of practices, norms, and beliefs introduced by bringing culture into the service-work equation. Use of the meso-level heuristic concepts can allow researchers to recognize cultural diversity without abandoning systematic analysis and search for patterns in the face of a panoply of cultural forms. It can help us fully appreciate the myriad ways in which service workers are, in fact, culture workers.

References

Block, Fred. 1990. *Postindustrial Possibilities: A Critique of Economic Discourse*. Berkeley: University of California Press.

Bourdieu, Pierre. 1984. *Distinction: A Social Critique of the Judgement of Taste*. London: Routledge & Kegan Paul.

Fuller, Linda and Smith, Vicki. 1991. "Consumers' reports—Management by Customers in a Changing Economy." *Work Employment and Society* 5(1): 1–16.

Gottfried, Heidi. 2003. "Temp(t)ing Bodies: Shaping Gender at Work in Japan." *Sociology: Journal of the British Sociological Association* 37: 257–76.

Hanser, Amy. 2006. "A Tale of Two Sales Floors: Changing Service-Work Regimes in China." Pp. 77–98 in Ching Kwan Lee, ed., *Working in China: Ethnographies of Labor and Workplace Transformation*. London: Routledge.

Hochschild, Arlie Russell. 1983. *The Managed Heart: Commercialization of Human Feeling*. Berkeley: University of California Press.

International Labour Organization. 2007. *Key Indicators of the Labour Market*. Geneva: International Labour Organization.

Kang, Miliann. 2003. "The Managed Hand: The Commercialization of Bodies and Emotions in Korean Immigrant-Owned Nail Salons." *Gender and Society* 17: 820–39.

Lan, Pei-Chia. 2001. "The Body as a Contested Terrain for Labor Control: Cosmetics Retailers in Department Stores and Direct Selling." Pp. 83–105 in Rick Baldoz, Charles Koeber, and Philip Kraft, eds., *The Critical Study of Work: Labor, Technology, and Global Production*. Philadelphia: Temple University Press.

Leidner, Robin. 1993. *Fast Food, Fast Talk*. Berkeley: University of California Press.

Lopez, Steven H. 2006. "Emotional Labor and Organized Emotional Care: Conceptualizing Nursing Home Care Work." *Work and Occupations* 2: 133–60.

Macdonald, Cameron Lynne and Sirianni, Carmen. 1996. "The Service Society and the Changing Experience of Work." Pp. 1–26 in Cameron Lynne Macdonald and Carmen Sirianni, eds., *Working in the Service Society*, Philadelphia: Temple University Press.

Marcuse, Herbert. 1964. *One Dimensional Man*. London: Abacus.

Orzechowicz, David. 2008. "Privileged Emotion Managers: The Case of Actors." *Social Psychology Quarterly* 71: 143–56.

Otis, Eileen. 2008. "Beyond the Industrial Paradigm: Market-Embedded Labor and the Gender Organization of Global Service Work in China." *American Sociological Review* 73: 15–36.

Polanyi, Karl. 1957. *The Great Transformation*. Boston: Beacon Press.

Poster, Winifred. 2007. "Who's on the Line: Indian Call Center Agents Pose as Americans for U.S.-Outsourced Firms." *Industrial Relations* 46: 271–304.

Sallaz, J.J. 2002. "The House Rules: Autonomy and Interests among Service Workers in the Contemporary Casino Industry." *Work & Occupations* 29: 394–427.

Schechner, Richard. 1999. "Forward." In *Chinese Theories of Theater and Performance: From Confucius to the Present*. Ann Arbor: University of Michigan Press.

Sherman, Rachel. 2007. *Class Acts: Service and Inequality in Luxury Hotels*. Berkeley: University of California Press.

Silver, Beverly. 2003. *Forces of Labor: Workers' Movements and Globalization since 1870*. Cambridge: Cambridge University Press.

Wharton, Amy. 1993. "The Affective Consequences of Emotion Work." *Work and Occupations* 20: 205–32.

Yang, Mayfair. 2002. "The Resilience of *Guanxi* and Its New Deployments." *China Quarterly* 170: 459–76.

Zelizer, Viviana. 2007. *The Purchase of Intimacy*. Princeton: Princeton University Press.

42

Cultures of carework, carework across cultures

Pei-Chia Lan

Carework refers to the work of caring for others, including unpaid care for family members and friends, as well as paid care for wards and clients. As a form of reproductive labor, carework is necessary to the maintenance of individuals, families, and communities. It includes emotional and nursing care for children, elders, the sick, and the disabled, as well as domestic work such as cooking and cleaning (Misra 2007). By deploying the term "carework," scholars and advocates emphasize that care is hard work—physically and emotionally—whose value is nevertheless overrated and underpaid. Viewed in this way, care is no longer an expression of women's natural feelings or endowments, but concrete labor performed in society.

This chapter discusses how culture constitutes the ways we understand and conduct carework. "Culture" designates two meanings here. First, the cultures of carework refer to the ideologies, values, norms, customs, and common senses about how care should be organized and done. They provide a "tool kit" of cultural resources (Swidler 1986) from which individuals and families develop strategies of actions. Second, the scripts and practices of carework vary and travel across socio-cultural contexts. Here culture designates worldviews and lifestyles shared by particular ethnic groups, religious communities, or nation-states.

Previous scholars have widely discussed the privatization of care as a dominant cultural framework, but they have used the term "private" with a variety of significations. I will identify and distinguish its various connotations, including domesticity, emotionality, feminization, and marketization. I argue that we need to reject binary thinking about the public and private, love and money, and paid and unpaid. To avoid ethnocentric assumptions about familial intimacy and private domesticity, we need to look into how carework is embedded in particular institutional regimes and cultural contexts. And we should analyze carework as a terrain of power struggles that shape the stratified division of labor and as a contextualized practice of constructing the family with intertwined meanings across the realms of market and intimacy.

Privatization of care as a cultural framework

Privatization is a cultural framework that characterizes people's thinking about and orientation toward care in many parts of the world. However, the loaded term "private," along with its opposite pair "public," connotes multiple meanings in association with different theoretical presuppositions across various historical and social contexts (Weintraub 1997). When describing care as "private," people refer to the public/private distinction in four different ways, which are analytically distinct and yet intertwined in reality.

First, the privatization of care describes the view that care is a family responsibility and is, preferably, conducted in private homes. Here the "private" refers to the domestic realm as opposed to the space outside it. The doctrine of "separate spheres," which became influential in nineteenth-century Europe and America under the impact of industrial capitalism, placed a moral value on the private household in contrast to the commercial world. In addition, the public domain outside the family also comprises law and state administration. To what extent and on what circumstances can the government intervene family life, including care for vulnerable family members like abused wives and neglected children, is a moral and policy debate in negotiating the boundary between the public and private.

Despite the various ways of restructuring the public and private, what is consistent across forms is that reproductive labor is constructed as "female" (Nakano 1992). This reveals the second meaning of private care: caregiving is viewed as women's natural endowment and social calling, either at home or in the labor market. Here the "private" refers to the feminine as opposed to the masculine as the "public." Some people even use the public/private categories as synonyms for men and women (Hansen 1987). The gendered division of carework is historically linked to the feminization of domesticity and emotions. The "cult of domesticity" as a Victorian cultural heritage made woman's household occupation her vocation and associated carework with maternal love and feminine virtues (Cott 1977). Although, increasingly, men, straight and queer, are getting involved in parenthood and paid carework, women are still burdened with the major share of carework.

Third, the privatization of care designates the emotionalization of care, a construct in parallel to the cult of female domesticity. Carework is considered a "labor of love," which is distinct from regular forms of waged labor. Here the public/private binary distinguishes intimacy from economic rationality and market transactions. Neoliberal economists, along with lay observers, assume that care workers, whether paid or unpaid, have altruistic motivations and receive moral rewards from their caregiving; this "prisoners of love" argument explains the low wage and devaluation of carework (England 2005).

Finally, the privatization of care also refers to the marketization or commodification of care. This line of thinking views the public/private distinction in terms of the divide between state administration and market economy. Marketization of care describes the processes that replace public services and welfare provisions with care services bought and sold in the market. This trend is particularly salient in Europe now. The market principle is introduced as a neoliberal solution to the restructuring of welfare states in facing the critique that public services are too costly and lead to care dependence (Knijin 2000).

The cultural framework of privatizing care orients people's preference about the arrangements of care and shapes their capacities for actions—habits, emotions, and sensibilities—while caring for others and being cared for. It also offers discursive frames and a moral ethos in policy debates about how to properly distribute resources among the state, market, family, and voluntary sector. Moreover, its multifaceted connotations demonstrate that the cultures and arrangements of carework are—as outcomes of conflicts between social groups with competing interests—subject to negotiation and transformation (Laslett and Brenner 1989).

Next, I will explain how the cultural framework of privatizing care leads to the paradox that the moralization of unpaid care stands hand in hand with the devaluation of paid carework, and how women reconcile this paradox by engaging in a stratified division of care labor between themselves and their market surrogates. In the following two sections, I will look into the macro/institutional contexts and the micro/interpersonal dynamics that complicate the public–private, paid–unpaid, and love–money dichotomies. Finally, the care of elderly immigrants is used as an example to demonstrate how the cultures, meanings, and practices of carework are constantly transformed by human agency and institutional circumstances.

Stratified divisions of carework

An increasing number of upper-middle- and middle-class households, in both the global North and global South, are hiring maids and nannies at home, who are largely women of ethnic minorities or immigrant status. Meanwhile, the ideological importance of motherhood and care has become more intensive than ever in these societies. Sharon Hays (1996) coins the term "intensive mothering" to observe that childrearing is viewed as child centered, expert guided, emotionally absorbing, and financially expensive. The enhanced moral values of unpaid care greatly contrast with the monetary and symbolic devaluation of paid carework. As Hochschild (2003: 2) put it, "Ideologically, 'care' went to heaven. Practically, it's gone to hell." How do we explain such a paradox? How do people reconcile the intensified moral elevation of care with the reality of marketization and racialization of carework?

The expanding recruitment of migrant domestic workers is a result of the privatization of care. Care is still considered a family duty and women's responsibility in many societies, wherein facilities of social care remain in shortage and husbands' share of labor is limited. Women seek market surrogates to be their "shadow laborers" (Macdonald 1998); they rely on the invisible labor of other women to achieve their duties as wives, mothers, and daughters-in-law. Besides, women prefer hiring live-in helpers because they consider in-home care a better arrangement that approximates the ideal of care provided by stay-at-home mothers and family members. The arrangement of market outsourcing, nevertheless, stirs a sense of guilt, jealousy, or deprivation (Lan 2006). These anxious women turn to the strategies of redefining the meanings of carework and micromanaging the division of labor.

Carework is composed of a series of practices. Tronto (1993) distinguishes four components: caring about (recognizing the necessity of care), taking care of (assuming some responsibility for the identified need and determining how to respond to it), care-giving (directly meeting needs for care), and care-receiving (the object of care responding to the care she receives). The market transfer of care has divided the labor while maintaining the hierarchical order between different agents along the divides of gender, class, race/ethnicity, and citizenship: "Caring about, and taking care of, are the duties of the powerful. Care-giving and care-receiving are left to the less powerful" (Tronto 1993: 114).

Scholars have documented how mothers who hire caregivers for the purpose of childcare maintain a hierarchical division of labor by distinguishing the "menial" and "spiritual" aspects of carework. This split enables middle-class women to magnify the significance of mothers at home and to minimize the presence of nannies (Macdonald 1998); as mothers they can transfer part of carework to colored or working-class women without disturbing the norm of female domesticity or the moral meaning of home (Roberts 1997).

The privatized notion of carework—as domestic, feminized work—greatly impacts the labor conditions of hired care workers (underpaid, deskilled, low status, and highly feminized) and their emotional and cognitive experiences (diverted motherhood, fictive kin). When a society continues to define caring labor as women's duties in the family, a female employer tends to treat the worker as "an extension of the more menial part of herself rather than an autonomous employee" (Rollins 1985: 183). She transfers to the surrogate not only the work but also the social expectations placed upon women associated with unpaid carework. As it is, she often makes requests that are unreasonable by the standards stipulated in employment contracts, and she ignores that the worker's labor performance is not bound by moral norms tied to emotional commitment or family responsibility.

Policy parameters and care regimes

Sociological studies of carework, especially those produced in North America, have paid great attention to the micropolitics of employment relations. The discussion has centered on the dyad relationship between maid and madam, mother and nanny, plus personal links with other women involved in global care chains, including local maids of migrant domestics and other female kin (Parrenas 2001). The roles of husband and children have been overlooked. And the macro context—the institutional embeddedness of carework—has somehow faded into the background.

By contrast, social policy studies, especially those produced in the United Kingdom and Scandinavia, have focused on the policy parameters of care. To compare institutional differentiation across countries, scholars in this field have established various typologies of *care regimes*. A "regime" embodies values, norms, and rules that provide a regulatory framework to shape behaviors and policies (Sainsbury 1999: 77). These studies illustrate the cultures of carework in two ways: first, they shed light on how carework is embedded in particular institutional regimes which organize the public and private in distinct patterns; second, they offer comparative perspectives about the variations of care regimes across cultural and policy contexts.

The discussion of care regimes extends and modifies the influential work of Gosta Esping-Anderson (1990), who uses three dimensions to characterize welfare regimes— the relationship between state and market in providing welfare, the effects of welfare state on stratification, and the character of social rights (decommodification). Feminist scholars have criticized the gender blindness of his theory, especially the concept of decommodification, which is based on formal, waged labor, excluding unpaid carework in the family. Scholars have reconstructed this framework by incorporating the family and the voluntary sector into the state–market nexus, examining the stratification effects on gender relations, and considering care as an essential social right (Daly and Lewis 2000; Orloff 1993).

Different care regimes can be distinguished by their specific policy logics associated with particular cultural scripts about gender and family. Jane Lewis (1992) differentiates care regimes based on their commitment to the male breadwinner model (men as workers and women as wives and mothers); she contrasts Germany, Ireland, and the UK as strong breadwinner regimes, with France in the middle and with Sweden and Denmark at the opposite end, where the dual-breadwinner family is the norm. Diane Sainsbury (1999) identifies three different kinds of care regimes: male-breadwinner regime (carework is privatized, unpaid), separate-gender-roles regime (women receive state benefits for caring responsibilities in the family), and individual-earner-carer regime (care in and outside of the family is subsidized by the state).

Notably, the social rights of immigrants had been a neglected topic in comparative research on welfare states until very recently. To complicate the analytic framework for the institutional embeddedness of carework, Helma Lutz (2008) adds in the concept of *migration regime*, which concerns a multitude of state regulations that promote or discourage the entry and employment of migrants. The various ways of interweaving care regime and migration regime result in distinct policy patterns. To help female nationals reconcile work and family, some European states have released quotas for the recruitment of migrant care workers (Spain, Italy, Greece) or have opened their borders to them (Britain and Ireland). Others, such as Germany, the Netherlands, and the Nordic states, have hardly acknowledged the need for such labor migration. This, however, does not mean that migrant care workers are absent in these countries; they only live and work in illegal circumstances (Lutz 2008).

Without exception, the studies cited above have focused on Western industrialized states. There are few comparative studies about care regimes in non-Western regions or across regions. The familialistic model of care has existed widely in East Asia, where states have provided limited public care. However, East Asian state policies regarding the recruitment of migrant care workers differ. Hong Kong and Singapore share a similar model of migration regime: both states opened immigration gates for foreign domestic workers in order to push local women into the labor force. By contrast, South Korea and Japan have not encouraged the employment of local housewives, and they did not welcome the recruitment of migrant workers (with the exception of overseas Koreans and Japanese) until recently (Oishi 2005).

It is important to note that the policy parameters of a care regime are prone to transition and change. In Japan, according to Ito Peng (2002), the welfare state expanded in the 1970s but underwent restructuring in the 1980s that reemphasized the family's care responsibilities. The crisis of declining fertility since the 1990s—which can be seen as a silent protest of younger cohorts of women—has pushed the government to adopt policy reform toward the socialization of care. The care regime has shifted from a needs-based care provision model to a rights-based universal social insurance scheme. However, the expansion of social care has gone hand in hand with the marketization of service, including the plans of recruiting care workers from Indonesia and the Philippines.

In addition, because the unit of analysis in care-regime research is the nation-state, the formulation of domestic regimes is prone to the pitfall of methodological nationalism. Nicola Yeates (2005) has raised the concept "global care regime" to encompass transnational processes of care transfer and the influence of supranational organizations. As important as the global political economy of care is the everyday practice of transnational caregiving, such as long-distance motherhood and elder care. In a later section (pp. 445–46), I will use the care for immigrant elders as an example to reveal the articulation between the cultural scripts of care and the institutional allocation of care in a transnational context that links the macro level of policy regimes and the micro level of family relations.

Intertwined meanings and contexualized practices

Paying for care often raises concerns about possible corruption and disruption of informal relations, leading to the harmful consequence of commercialization of intimacy or commodification of care. Viviana Zelizer (2005) calls this line of thinking "separate spheres" or "hostile worlds." In it, economic activities and intimate relations are viewed as distinct arenas, such that their mixing will result in inevitable disorder. On the one hand, market compensation would contaminate and undermine moral obligation. On the other hand, emotional ties may complicate and even undermine business-like service relations.

Zelizer rejects the assumption that only profit and self-interest rule in the market; instead, she calls for an alternative approach of "connected lives," in which moral obligations can be confirmed and assured by market compensation. For instance, spending money to purchase intensive and quality care provided by trustworthy non-family caregivers is perceived as an act of care and an expression of love. Paula England (2005: 394) also contests the dichotomy between love and money. She suggests that we need empirical research to identify "which particular structural or cultural features of behavior in market, families, or states have which consequences, rather than assuming that solving these problems is impossible as long as care is done as waged work in private-sector firms."

I agree with these opinions and would like to further argue that the dichotomous thinking about market and intimacy, or love and money, is rooted in Western cultural scripts of familial intimacy. Existing carework studies, as criticized by Tsai Yen-Ling (2008), posit a particular *a priori* notion of domestic intimacy based on the ideal of the European bourgeois family. In line with the cannon of separate spheres, the home was defined, first, as a haven from the uncertainties and calculation of commercial life and, second, as "the locus of social and personal morality" (Laslett and Brenner 1989: 387). Besides, the studies unwittingly presume the nuclear family—composed by the conjugal union between husband and wife as well as their offspring—as the fundamental form of domestic organization. The normalization of the nuclear family contradicts the reality that the nuclear household is actually a recent form of social organization most highly concentrated in white, Protestant, north-west Europe and the United States (Dalley 1988: 30–31).

Gillian Dalley (1988) argues that the ideals of the bourgeois family encapsulate the principle of "possessive individualism," which privileges self-determination, personal autonomy, privacy, and freedom from intrusion. This notion of private domesticity is not only Western and modern but also classed and gendered (Armstrong and Armstrong 2005). Conjugal-family intimacy is preferred as a middle-class ideal over both "the 'vain' ... sociability of the rich and the promiscuous sociability of the poor" (Cott 1977: 92). The proverb "An English man's home is his castle" perfectly illustrates how the aspiration for familial intimacy is centered on the autonomy of the family head (husband/father) from the subordinated family members, including women and children.

The combination of individualism and familist ideology, along with the gendered construct of separation of spheres, normalizes the model of the nuclear family and the feminization of carework.

Dalley (1988) then proposes the model of "collectivist care" as an alternative, in which *the community* as the collectivity takes on responsibility for all its members, especially dependent members. The community may be formed by primordial bonds, including kin-based extended family or traditional villages; or there are communities consciously formed on religious or politico-economic grounds, including welfare regimes practicing the ideal of social care.

The ideas and practices of familism and collectivism differ in some other parts of the world, where intergenerational cohabitation is still common. The familist ideology in these countries is not linked to the principle of individualism but to that of *collectivism*. The family takes on the responsibility to care for dependent members with the values of sharing, commitment, and cooperation. However, the collectivity is not immune to power inequalities, especially along the lines of gender, age, and generation. The ideologies and operation of carework could also be grounded on domination, subordination, and power struggles *within* the family.

I have coined the term "subcontracting filial piety" to describe how Taiwanese adult children transfer the filial duty of caring for their aging parents to non-family employees (Lan 2006). By incorporating the care workers to be their filial agents and fictive kin, adult children may maintain the traditional family form of three-generation cohabitation as well as the cultural ideal of filial piety. Meanwhile, kinship analogies enable adult children to place on care workers kin expectations beyond the assigned duties in a contractual relationship.

Paying for carework can also become a means for the nuclear family to achieve the ideal of private domesticity. Many Taiwanese daughters-in-law maneuver the employment of nannies or caretakers to avoid cohabitation with mothers-in-law. Traditionally, a Taiwanese grandmother plays a crucial role in the care of her son's children; it remains a common practice for a mother-in-law to take care of her grandchildren if her daughter-in-law is working outside the home. This arrangement, however, may cause tension across generations regarding different childcare styles and encroach upon the parental autonomy of young mothers.

In Han Chinese societies, *taking care of* aging parents is traditionally considered the duty of sons, although the actual work of caregiving is mostly shouldered by the sons' wives. The traditional idea of caregiving is associated with the hierarchical concept of "serving" rather than the more egalitarian notion of "caring" (Liu 1998). Hiring a migrant caregiver becomes a strategy of "patriarchal bargaining" that Taiwanese daughters-in-law can use to avert subordination to the patrilineal family authority. In other words, there is a "transfer chain of filial care" consisting of two linkages—first, *gender transfer* of the filial duty from the son to the daughter-in-law, and, second, *market transfer* of carework from the daughter-in-law to non-family employees, who are still predominantly women.

Paying for carework thus becomes a practice for Taiwanese middle-class families to maintain what they perceive as the ideal arrangements of domestic intimacy. By incorporating a live-in caregiver into the family, the conjugal couple can maintain the filial ideal of three-generation cohabitation without doing the actual work of caregiving. Or, by outsourcing childcare to a waged worker rather than the grandmother, the conjugal couple can avoid cohabitation with or intervention from the older generation; in this way they achieve their ideal of private intimacy based on the model of nuclear family as a cultural transfer of Western modernity.

Carework in immigration contexts

Carework in the context of immigration offers a critical case to explore how the discursive frames and institutional arrangements of carework vary across cultural and social contexts, and how the cultures of care are transplanted or transformed after traveling across borders. The analysis in this section is based on my study of elder care among Taiwanese immigrants in North California (Lan 2002).

Scholars analyzing the US census data found that immigrants from Asia and Latin America, compared with US-born Americans, display stronger patterns of co-residence between elder parents and adult children (Kritz et al. 2000). This difference is largely explained by the collectivist and familial norms of the sending countries from which immigrants arrive. Yet, the ethnic practices of elder care also show a tendency to wane with acculturation across time and generations (Pyke 2004).

Immigrant seniors, like other elderly people, need care not only for their physical frailty and emotional loneliness, but also to achieve independence and autonomy. The latter goals may become more difficult for them to achieve because of the increase of linguistic and cultural barriers and the decline of parental authority in a foreign country. Their dependence on their grown children may foster their submissiveness and deference to their children (Treas and Mazumdar 2002).

Taiwanese immigrants in my study often refer to the individualistic norms in the US to justify their residential separation from their elderly parents. Kevin Li (pseudonym) says: "You know American laws are like this: children grow up and leave their parents, so they are not obligated to take care of their parents. But our civil law is different. In Taiwan, if you don't support your parents, you are guilty of abandoning them. This is a crime."

Taiwan's family law stipulates that children should respect and support parents filially. Attached to the criminal charge of abandonment, family law honors and enforces the moral contract of patrilineal familism. Childrearing is viewed as a social investment with an expectation of delayed repayment. Sons, in particular, are obligated to return the debts through caring for their aging parents. Delegating carework to the domestic sphere, Taiwan's government did not introduce any social security or welfare programs for senior citizens until the mid-1990s.

Relocated to a new land and a new care regime, Taiwanese elderly immigrants found themselves an "American filial son"—a term they applied to the California state government—who sends them monthly allowances without delay or complaint. Since most of them own few assets and earn no income in the US, they are eligible for low-income elderly benefits. Many prefer living in senior apartments under public subsidy to living with their adult children in a suburb, because the former provides them with convenient access to public transportation and peer social circles. These public care programs provide new institutional resources that help some immigrant elders to empower themselves on foreign soil.

The state of California also provides the elderly with in-home care services through the program of In-Home Supportive Services (IHSS). Notably, IHSS not only subsidizes care services provided by non-family workers, but also compensates previously unpaid caring labor offered by family members, mostly women. Adult children who accommodate their low-income parents can also apply for food and housing subsidies. These programs contrast with the familial model of care in the Chinese cultural context, and for this reason some of my informants criticized the programs as "ridiculous" or "not right." Their perspective adheres to the cultural scheme of privatized care—as familial and emotional work—and thus resists the intervention of the state and market.

Cash subvention from welfare states to family caregivers helps achieve the progressive ideal of social care and the autonomy of female kin from care responsibilities in the family. Yet, it can also stir controversy about the consequence of marketization of care. Such concerns, as mentioned earlier, are rooted in a dichotomous thinking about love and money, market, and intimacy.

We cannot take the marketization of intergenerational relationships at face value. For instance, some Taiwanese immigrant adult children charge rent to parents who stay in their houses. In addition to facilitating a rental subsidy from the government, paying rent becomes a means for the elderly to transfer income to their children so the parents can still maintain their eligibility for low-income benefits. The trading of economic resources among kin would be impossible without strong family bonds.

On the surface, the conditions for receiving public care indicate a lack of familial care according to Chinese filial norms; yet, under the table, immigrant families circulate financial resources among kin to make their parents eligible for low-income benefits. They are engaged in a family conspiracy to extract welfare provisions in the new care regime, whose policy logic is based on an individualistic assumption that parents and adult children are financially independent. As a result, the marketization of care does not weaken family bonds but actually reinforces kin connections as economic ties.

Conclusion

The cultures of carework are part of a tool kit from which social agents construct the everyday practice of interpersonal relations as well as the policy logic of welfare regimes. The privatization of care as a dominant cultural framework connotes complex and sometimes contradictory meanings. The cultures and arrangements of carework are subject to transformation as the outcome of power struggles, but ideological consistency and historical continuity are found across various modes of labor division. Feminization and racialization characterize the hierarchical divisions of carework between men and women, madams and maids, and rich nationals and poor migrants.

The scripts and practices of carework vary and travel across cultural and social contexts. The example of care for immigrant elders shows that culture is not a static heritage but is constantly transformed by human agency and institutional regimes. The changes in care arrangements after crossing borders demonstrate how immigrant families negotiate cultural norms and kin relations in response to different care regimes, which distribute care responsibilities between state, family, market, and community in various ways. Paying for carework, or receiving payment for carework, does not necessarily interrupt domestic intimacy or the quality of care, but it can become a means for the family to negotiate the meanings of care by articulating love and money, the private and the public.

It is crucial to situate the micro dynamics of maid–madam interactions and love–money negotiations in the macro processes of care regimes. Only by doing so can we examine how the multifaceted organization of the public and private is mediated by specific cultural contexts and policy parameters, and contextualize people's strategies of actions in particular structural circumstances that offer cultural and social resources to enable or constrain their choices. We need more research that combines micro and macro inquiries. In particular, cross-national comparison and transnational cases are fruitful research designs for exploring the formation and transformation of carework across cultures.

References

Armstrong, P. and Armstrong, H. 2005. "Public and Private: Implications for Care Work." *The Sociological Review* 53(2): 167–87.

Cott, N.F. 1977. *The Bonds of Womanhood: "Woman's Sphere" in New England*. New Haven, CT: Yale University Press.

Dalley, G. 1988. *Ideologies of Caring: Rethinking Community and Collectivism*. Basingstoke, UK: Macmillan Education.

Daly, M. and Lewis, J. 2000. "The Concept of Social Care and the Analysis of Contemporary Welfare States." *British Journal of Sociology* 51: 281–98.

England, P. 2005. "Emerging Theories of Care Work." *Annual Review of Sociology* 31: 381–99.

Esping-Anderson, G. 1990. *The Three Worlds of Welfare Capitalism*. Princeton, NJ: Princeton University Press.

Glazer, N. 1993. *Women's Paid and Unpaid Labor: The Work Transfer in Health Care and Retailing*. Philadelphia, PA: Temple University Press.

Hansen, K.V. 1987. "Feminist Conceptions of the Public and Private: A Critical Analysis." *Berkeley Journal of Sociology* 32: 105–28.

Hays, S. 1996. *The Cultural Contradictions of Motherhood*. New Haven, CT: Yale University Press.

Hochschild, A.R. 2003. *The Commercialization of Intimate Life: Notes from Home and Work*. Berkeley: University of California Press.

Knijin, T. 2000. "Marketization and the Struggling Logics of (Home) Care in the Netherlands." Pp. 232–48 in M.H. Meyer, ed., *Care Work: Gender, Class, and the Welfare State*. New York: Routledge.

Kritz, M., Gurak, D.T., and Chen, L. 2000. "Elderly Immigrants: Their Composition and Living Arrangements." *Journal of Sociology and Social Welfare* 27: 84–114.

Lan, P.-C. 2002. "Subcontracting Filial Piety: Elder Care in Ethnic Chinese Immigrant Households in California." *Journal of Family Issues* 23: 812–35.

——. 2006. *Global Cinderellas: Migrant Domestics and Newly Rich Employers in Taiwan*. Durham, NC: Duke University Press.

Laslett, B. and Brenner, J. 1989. "Gender and Social Reproduction: Historical Perspectives." *Annual Review of Sociology* 15: 381–404.

Lewis, J. 1992. "Gender and the Development of Welfare Regimes." *Journal of European Social Policy* 3: 159–73.

Liu, Z.-D. 1998. *Women's Medical Sociology* (in Chinese). Taipei: Feminist Bookstore.

Lutz, H. 2008. "Introduction: Migrant Domestic Worker in Europe." Pp. 1–10 in H. Lutz, ed., *Migration and Domestic Work: A European Perspective on a Global Theme*. Burlington, VT: Ashgate.

Macdonald, C. 1998. "Manufacturing Motherhood: The Shadow Work of Nannies and Au Pair." *Qualitative Sociology* 21: 25–53.

Misra, J. 2007. "Carework." In G. Ritzer, ed., *Blackwell Encyclopedia of Sociology*. Malden, MA: Blackwell.

Nakano, Glenn E. 1992. "From Servitude to Service Work: Historical Continuities in the Racial Division of Paid Reproductive Labor." *Signs: Journal of Women in Culture and Society* 18(1): 27–69.

Oishi, N. 2005. *Women on the Move: Globalization, State Policies and Labor Migration in Asia*. Stanford, CA: Stanford University Press.

Orloff, A.S. 1993. "Gender and the Social Rights of Citizenship: The Comparative Analysis of Gender Relations and Welfare States." *American Sociological Review* 58: 303–28.

Parrenas, R.S. 2001. *Servants of Globalization: Women, Migration and Domestic Work*. Stanford, CA: Stanford University Press.

Peng, I. 2002. "Social Care in Crisis: Gender, Democracy, and Welfare Restructuring in Japan." *Social Politics* 9(3): 411–43.

Pyke, K. 2004. "Immigrant Families in the US." Pp. 253–69 in J. Scott, J. Treas, and M. Richards, eds., *The Blackwell Companion to the Sociology of Families*. Malden, MA: Blackwell.

Roberts, D. 1997. "Spiritual and Menial Housework." *Yale Journal of Law and Feminism* 9: 49–80.

Rollins, J. 1985. *Between Women: Domestics and Their Employers*. Philadelphia, PA: Temple University Press.

Sainsbury, D. 1999. "Gender and Social-Democratic Welfare States." In D. Sainsbury, ed., *Gender and Welfare State Regimes*. New York: Oxford University Press.

Swidler, A. 1986. "Culture in Action: Symbols and Strategies." *American Sociological Review* 51(2): 273–86.

Treas, J. and Mazumdar, S. 2002. "Older People in America's Immigrant Families: Dilemmas of Dependence, Integration, and Isolation." *Journal of Aging Studies* 16: 243–58.

Tronto, J.C. 1993. *Moral Boundaries: A Political Argument for an Ethic of Care*. New York and London: Routledge.

Tsai, Y.-L. 2008. "Strangers Who Are Not Foreign: Intimate Exclusion and Racialized Boundaries in Urban Indonesia." Ph.D., diss., Department of Anthropology, University of California, Santa Cruz.

Weintraub, J. 1997. "The Theory and Politics of the Public/Private Distinction." Pp. 1–42 in J. Weintraub and K. Kumar, eds., *Public and Private in Thought and Practice: Perspectives on a Grand Dichotomy*. Chicago: University of Chicago Press.

Yeates, N. 2005. "A Global Political Economy of Care." *Social Policy and Society* 4: 227–34.

Zelizer, V.A. 2005. *The Purchase of Intimacy*. Princeton, NJ: Princeton University Press.

43

Science cultures

Alex Preda

Any sociologist writing on the topic of science cultures is almost immediately confronted with an apparent paradox: while the study of culture(s) has become increasingly popular among sociologists (for instance, the American Sociological Association's sociology of culture section is one of the largest), culture has apparently been increasingly marginalized in sociological inquiries of science. To give but one example, the third edition of the *Handbook of Science and Technology Studies* (Hackett *et al.* 2007), a work of over one thousand pages giving a state of the art overview of the field, mentions culture only in a few places, mostly in describing the relationship between the usage of technologies and law or health movements. The lack of attention to culture is even more intriguing if we take into account that the new sociology of science emerging in the late 1970s has substantially contributed to investigating the role of culture in the production and adoption of forms of scientific knowledge, as well as in the dynamics of scientific disciplines.

How can we explain this conspicuous absence of culture? Has it become irrelevant in relationship to science? The answer is straightforward—not at all. Culture is perhaps more relevant than ever in the study of scientific knowledge. What has happened, though, is that a series of conceptual and methodological shifts, triggered by the very preoccupation with scientific cultures, has led to significant terminological changes which, in their turn, are consequential for the study of other domains. Let's examine them one by one.

The debates about the cultural significance of science were triggered in the German-speaking world after World War I, in relationship to the perceived capacity of science to provide a progressive conception of the world, as an alternative to retrograde ones (Turner 2007: 40). Among the better known elements of these debates are Max Weber's interventions: in two lectures, Weber (1970 [1919]) contrasted science and politics as characterized by specific sets of behavioral norms and ethical values. His position significantly influenced Robert King Merton's (1973 [1942]) argument that science is characterized by the norms of communalism (initially called communism), universalism, disinterestedness, and organized skepticism.

In this view, science was seen as a particular culture (different from political or economic ones), having at its core a restricted set of specific norms and values.

In a structural-functionalist account, then, culture consists of norms characteristic of a domain of social activity, norms that determine behavioral patterns. Thomas Kuhn's *The Structure of Scientific Revolutions* (1962) challenged the claim of universalistic norms of science, as well as the progressivist view according to which better scientific theories always replace lesser ones. Kuhn argued instead that scientific disciplines are organized around paradigms—that is, specific views, definitions, and explanatory frames supported by social relationships within concrete scientific communities. These views and frames resist falsification attempts and cannot be dismantled other than on the basis of changes within (and across) the scientific communities in question. The latter communities would then compete for a central position within their domain, ensuring that the explanatory paradigm they embrace is dominant. In this perspective, the approach to culture shifted from concern with ethical norms to broader explanatory, empirically resistant frames. Kuhn's arguments played a seminal role in the emergence of a whole research program that broke away from Merton's view on culture, while seeking to specify, both empirically and theoretically, the character of scientific paradigms (Zammito 2004: 128–31).

The notion of scientific culture was re-formulated in works published in the late 1970s and early 1980s, among which probably the most prominent are Bruno Latour and Steve Woolgar's *Laboratory Life* (1979), Karin Knorr-Cetina's *The Manufacture of Knowledge* (1981), and Michael Lynch's *Art and Artifact in Laboratory Science* (1985). These empirical studies of scientific laboratories in disciplines such as molecular biology and astrophysics departed from the understanding of the scientific paradigm as a (mental) framework shared by scientists, and focused instead on the practical actions through which new knowledge is produced in a specific setting (the lab), characterized by material configurations (such as instruments and devices), and by the interactions of scientists. These, as well as subsequent studies, also departed from any ethnic or national undertones that might be associated with the notion of culture: the culture of scientific laboratories (and more generally, of science) is characterized precisely by the irrelevance of any national or ethnic distinctions with respect to the practical actions through which knowledge is produced. Studies of large-scale collaborations involving hundreds of scientists from different countries (e.g. Knorr-Cetina 1999; Collins 2004) have highlighted that ethnic and national distinctions do not impact the interactions and science-specific social structures within which knowledge is generated. Karin Knorr-Cetina highlights the ways in which multi-ethnic scientific communities are built and maintained around a specific project (such as the Large Hadron Collider). Harry Collins (2004), who has studied the Laser Interferometer Gravitational Wave Observatory, analyzes how competitions among groups of scientists are shaped by alternative research programs rather than nationality: groups of scientists from different countries compete against other multi-national groups by developing alternative research paths for conducting research on one and the same issue.

This is not to say that the interests of particular groups are insignificant in the choice of their respective research programs, or that there is no competition among groups of scientists working on the same topic. Quite the contrary: as the above-mentioned ethnographic studies have shown, competition and group interests play a significant role here, yet both interests and competition are shaped by the logic of scientific knowledge production, and not by ethnic or national factors.

These arguments run counter to the Mertonian view of science as determined by a restricted set of ethical norms: in scientific groups and communities, prestige, reputation within specific research communities, as well as adherence to and identification with a specific research program, and the capacity to mobilize funding resources are much more relevant factors.

Competition for prestige and high ranking within scientific communities can also lead in specific circumstances to the emergence of anomic forms of behavior, as manifested, for instance, in claims of scientific discoveries based on forged laboratory protocols. Such cases, indeed, have repeatedly come to attention since the late 1980s; a recent example is that of South Korean molecular biologists falsely claiming in 2005 to have produced the first human embryonic stem cells from cloned embryos. In many instances, scientific frauds have been exposed only after an initial period of public enchantment with the fraudulent claims (see also Gieryn 1999). These instances run counter to the Mertonian view that scientific cultures are characterized by disinterestedness. They show that pres-tige-seeking competitions (in many cases associated with national pride as well), together with the financial incentives provided by the potential commercialization of applied research, can create an environment conducive to deviant behavior.

We should expect therefore to find particular science cultures centered on specific research programs within different scientific disciplines. These science cultures are then anchored not only in particular material arrangements (provided by the technologies of scientific experiments, for instance) but also in the skills and abilities required by manipulating such arrangements, and in the communication processes and interactions related to manipulations. Science cultures are dynamic: whereas the notion of paradigm has been very often interpreted as emphasizing stability and lack of or slow change, in the above understanding scientific cultures are in flux, simply because the material arrangements in which they are anchored represent not only resources, but also constraints with respect to human action. The actions of scientists have to overcome these constraints by constantly adjusting and rearranging experimental technologies, for instance. Agency (including the making of new scientific discoveries) arises out of reciprocal adaptations of human actions and technological arrangements (Pickering 1995: 204). Culture, then, designates the "specific ensemble of conditions that allow the generation of unprecedented events" (Rheinberger 1997: 140), that is, scientific discoveries. Within a scientific discipline, groups may have similar technological sets (used, for instance, in replicating experiments), similar skills, and shared commitment to a research program. Or, they may compete with each other—on the basis of technologies, skills, and concepts.

Consequently, the micro-dynamics of knowledge production will translate into the meso- and macro-dynamics of scientific groups and institutions. Factors such as influence, interests, and prestige intervene in groups coalescing and competing against each other but, ultimately, the underlying dynamics will be those of knowledge production. For instance, Karin Knorr-Cetina (1999: 238–39) emphasizes that disciplines such as molecular biology and high-energy physics have different structures of competition versus collaboration, due mainly to the specific constraints of production discussed above. In high-energy physics, the very expensive and complex character of technology (an experimental machine can cover thousands of acres) requires collaboration concentrated in a few centers. In molecular biology, scientific projects are seen as individual—not collective—undertakings: they involve minute, individualized work, which can be coordinated across a team, but which nevertheless can be broken down into distinct, quasi-independent projects. Project-specific individualization would be much more difficult to achieve in the case of high-energy physics. Hence the culture of collaboration in physics contrasts with that of competition in molecular biology.

If the natural sciences have different cultures structured not only along disciplines, but mainly along different modes of knowledge production (determined by material arrangements, interactions, and communication), do we then encounter different cultures within the social sciences as well and, more importantly, within the same discipline—say, within sociology or within economics? For instance, is there a particular scientific culture centered upon modeling in economics, different from one centered upon economic experiments? Although the general feeling is that the social sciences are characterized by different cultures too, there is surprisingly little research in this area. Recent ethnographic investigations (Yonay and Breslau 2006) suggest that economic models are interpreted in specific ways by their academic audiences, the aim being not so much to represent reality as to represent entities and processes as plausible economic forces. Taking into account the recent rise of, for instance, experimental economics, a task for future research will be to compare experimental cultures in the natural sciences and in economics, in economics and in other social sciences such as psychology, as well as to investigate experimental and theoretical cultures in economics. All in all, we still know very little about scientific cultures in the social sciences as compared with the natural sciences.

The more general picture is one where culture means "the aggregate patterns and dynamics that are on display in expert practice and that vary in different settings of expertise" (Knorr-Cetina 1999: 8). Scientific discoveries are cultural in the sense that they are "extracted" from socio-technical interactions within specific settings (Lynch 1992: 249). "Culture" becomes dependent on the (inter)actions through which knowledge is produced within expert settings. Since the word "expert" plays here a central role, the question arises how to distinguish scientific cultures from non-scientific ones. The issue becomes then the cultural boundaries among different forms of expertise, as well as between scientific expertise, on the one hand, and other forms of knowledge, on the other hand. If we take into account the relentless proliferation of experts and expertise in contemporary societies, the question of cultural boundaries acquires a larger relevance.

We can distinguish here at least the following kinds of boundaries, with direct relevance for scientific cultures. First, there are the boundaries defining the realm investigated by science; for instance, what are the boundaries of natural phenomena, as investigated by physics or by biology? Second, there are the boundaries between science and other forms of knowledge production. What are the characteristic features of scientific facts? How can we distinguish between scientific expertise and other forms of expertise? What is more, to what extent is scientific knowledge informed by non-scientific elements? These questions have profound implications for a whole series of ethical and political issues. To give but a couple of examples, they have profound implications for science education, as witnessed in the recent controversies about teaching "intelligent design" alongside evolution theory, or for environmental policies, as seen in the debates about how to counteract global warming. Third, there are the boundaries of science within society. To what extent, for instance, should (political) decisions be informed by science and expertise? To what extent should ethical considerations be taken into account? The debates about cloning or about stem cell research are cases in point here.

Due to its particular relevance, the notion of cultural boundaries requires more extensive unpacking here. Although this notion oftentimes has been taken to mean a distinction or divide, boundaries should not be seen as given, absolute, or based on a lack of communication. Any set of distinctions between science and non-science, for instance, would be the product of specific communicational processes, involving definitional procedures (e.g. what constitutes scientific evidence?), narratives, evaluations, and judgments, among others. Communicational processes include formal events (e.g. conferences, symposia) and informal occasions (e.g. conversations in the lab); they can entail a variety of actors (scientists and non-scientists alike) and audiences (e.g. lay, economic, or political publics). Communication-generated distinctions include debates, conflicts, or negotiation; they can involve the mobilization of what Bruno Latour (2004: 73–75) calls networks of human and non-human actors—that is, of various social resources (for instance the mobilization of networks of influence, but also of material evidence). Boundary issues can arise not only in the communication between scientific and non-scientific groups, but also within scientific communities. For instance, scientific debates and controversies often imply defining specific evidence (lab data, or measurements) as unreliable, or as tainted—in other words, as not up to scientific standards. Establishing such boundaries through communication implies persuasive interventions in debates—interventions in which resources (rhetorical or otherwise) are mobilized, and alliances of scientists/non-scientists are formed. The processes through which such science-relevant boundaries are established and accepted in society involve "strategic practical action" (Gieryn 1999: 23). They are essential with respect to how scientific groups establish their authority and legitimacy within society.

Let us first examine the boundaries between the natural and the social world, boundaries that are so relevant with respect to the disciplinary and methodological makeup of the modern sciences. Although these boundaries would seem self-evident, the sociology of science has long pointed out that they are the result of complex social processes, involving scientists as well as political and economic groups. Several studies undertaken since the 1980s by the French anthropologist Bruno Latour have highlighted how the distinction between natural and social facts is constituted in the practice of scientific research, and how this distinction becomes consequential for our ways of understanding social order. Latour (2004: 234) argues that if we take the distinction between society and nature for granted, we automatically ascribe natural facts to the domain of science, and interests to the domain of politics. This differentiation, however, tends to ignore the fact that the production of scientific knowledge is an inherently cultural enterprise, one that cannot be separated from politics. Instead of trying to insulate science from political interventions (be they initiated by social movements or political groups), Latour proposes to bring the sciences in conversation with various social groups and thus allow a multi-voiced "political ecology" (2004: 235). This approach, which turns Weber's distinction between science and politics upside down, is not without its own pitfalls. The plea for multiple voices of authority (instead of a single, scientific voice) could be interpreted as relativizing scientific authority. Such authority, however, is anchored in the generation of discoveries and therefore cannot be replaced with something else (this something would not be science). In the end, the notion of a public dialogue of interests and positions vis-à-vis scientific knowledge must acknowledge the unique character of the latter. Nor can we imagine the authority of scientific knowledge being replaced, in such a dialogue, by, say, political or religious authority. Especially in light of the recent debates about science teaching, or about global warming, a public, multi-voiced dialogue can take place only with science as a *sui generis*, non-substitutable voice.

What we take as "nature" is the result of complex material and communicational distinctions, inextricably linked with modern state formations *and* with modern science. Thus, Patrick Carroll (2006: 6–7) argues that modern science and modern state formations are cultural co-products of the same process through which the distinctions between nature and society are inscribed in scientific-political programs, correlated with transformations of the material environment, and supported both by groups of scientists and by political elites.

This recognition raises at least two questions, relevant to modernization processes as well to processes of scientific knowledge production. If modern states and modern science are inextricably linked, how can scientific cultures contribute to socio-political modernization processes in developing countries? All too often, modernization has been understood as economic development; investigations such as Carroll's, however, show that development is conditioned by the successful constitution of a "science–state plexus" (Carroll 2006: 4), with cultural components at its core, provided by a culture of inquiry and a discourse of ingenuity, together with associated practices. Development and modernization efforts should take these factors into account, encouraging and supporting local scientific projects and groups. We still know very little about scientific cultures in developing countries. The issue's relevance with respect to how development works (or does not) calls for intensifying research on this topic.

The second question concerns how extraneous factors intervene in the establishment of scientific research programs and the making of scientific facts. Although the sociology of science has traditionally given considerable attention to these factors, the catalyst leading to their more systematic investigation was the AIDS crisis of the 1980s and early 1990s. The medical controversies and debates about AIDS, as well as its mediatization, have included, among others, various conflicting theories about the causation mechanisms, arguments about the role of cultural and geographical factors in these mechanisms, heated debates about the most appropriate preventive measures, and controversies about whether cultural factors influence the character of the infectious agent. Activist groups began appropriating medical knowledge and using it in debates (and sometimes conflicts) with policy makers and with scientists alike. These controversies have demonstrated that the production of scientific expertise is, in the words of Steven Epstein (1996), an "impure" process, involving the participation of heterogeneous groups and movements, from scientific as well as from political domains. Such groups appropriate and interpret aspects and applications of scientific knowledge in ways which cannot be centrally controlled. They use this knowledge in policy debates and develop their own authority in scientific matters. Epstein (1996: 350) argues that the science-based expertise of social groups and movements contributes to the democratization of policy making. This does not mean a wholesale challenging of scientific authority, but rather implies appropriations and modifications of specific aspects, often in the context of scientific controversies. These examples show that the cultural boundaries of science are not given, but the result of communication processes involving heterogeneous groups. Such processes take place in the public sphere, where media representations of debates and controversies can be mobilized as resources by the very parties involved in them.

If the cultural boundaries of science are not exclusively constituted in the laboratory or the conference room, but in the public sphere as well, where they involve heterogeneous groups and media interventions, then a question arises about the relationship among various forms of expertise, as well as between scientific authority, on the one hand, and other forms of authority (e.g. political or religious), on the other hand. Forms of expertise have proliferated in modern societies. Not all of them are associated with applied science, and not all of them are in harmony with established scientific positions. Examples are not difficult to find. Think of homeopathy as a form of medical expertise often at odds with academic medical knowledge, or of chartism as a form of financial expertise at odds with financial economics. What is the boundary between science and these forms of expertise, and how do such alternative cultures, or countercultures, of expertise position themselves in the public sphere, in relationship to science?

Harry Collins and Robert Evans (2002: 252), following Stephen Turner, distinguish among five kinds of expertise situated along a continuum. First, there is the expertise of established scientific disciplines, such as physics, the authority of which is universally acknowledged. A second type of expertise is that which is legitimated with respect to a particular following (theology would be a case in point here). The third type of expertise creates its own following (think chiropractics, for instance). Types four and five have their followers created by third parties (such as governmental agencies). Decisive is whether types II–V can enter a dialogue with type I; this dialogue can be contributory or interpretive (Collins and Evans 2002: 254). For instance, contributory expertise in molecular biology or aircraft engineering would mean that somebody from outside the field would have acquired so much knowledge (as an autodidact, for instance) as to be able to make a material contribution within that field of research. By contrast, interpretive expertise means that a person or a group has acquired enough experience within a domain (or about an issue) as to be able to interact with scientists investigating that domain. Patients taking an experimental drug have acquired experience about the effects of the drug and about the ways in which it affects everyday life; they thus are able to interact with pharmacologists researching the said drug in a way that is meaningful for the issue at stake—in that it can lead to informed decisions. A concrete example is that of participants in HIV patient groups investigated by Steve Epstein (1996: 216–19), who, without having formally studied medicine, had acquired enough medical knowledge and accumulated experience about the effects of antiviral drugs as to enter into meaningful dialogue (not necessarily devoid of tensions) with researchers, and thus influence clinical trials and drug administration policies.

Types of expertise need not be at odds with each other, and they need not contest each other's authority. In order to achieve alignment, however, types II–V of experts need to acquire interaction expertise—that is, experience and/or knowledge relevant to the issue at stake so as to be able to sustain a substantive dialogue with type I experts (i.e. scientists). The issue of boundaries then becomes one of communication: different types of expertise need not be in conflict, but do not align automatically either. Alignment will rather be seen in those cases where interaction expertise is accumulated, a process that must involve type I experts as well. In other words, scientists too need to learn about the experiences, viewpoints, and knowledge of groups affected by the issues they engage.

The implication is that democratic participation in decision-making regarding scientific matters cannot be separated from informed communication across heterogeneous groups. For instance, in September 2008, when physicists at the European Organization for Nuclear Research in Geneva, Switzerland, were about to start the Large Hadron Collider (LHC—the largest particle accelerator in the world), the media perpetrated fears that the LHC would create black holes and that these would destroy the planet. Calls were made to stop the experiments. Did such calls constitute legitimate democratic participation in decisions about scientific research? The answer is no: the callers did not have any interaction expertise related to field experience (after all, high-energy physics has been around for a while) on the basis of which to initiate substantive communication with groups of physicists. Another illustrative case is that of calls for teaching creationism alongside evolution theory in schools, on the grounds that they have a similar status. Most proponents of teaching creationism, however, cannot claim interaction expertise in the field of evolutionary biology, an expertise that should form the basis of opening a dialogue and participating in decision-making about science teaching. Intelligent design and evolution theory cannot therefore be seen as meaningful alternatives to each other, as competing theories, or as an extension of expertise (from type I to type II). In this case, the two forms of expertise (and the associated forms of authority) appear as rather incommensurable.

The use of expertise in public debates raises the issue of science education, especially in terms of the ways in which it can contribute to increasing public awareness and knowledge of scientific issues. This crucial issue is still awaiting a more thorough investigation: we know relatively little about how science education influences public engagement with scientific problems. Nevertheless, the issue of democratic decision-making involving scientific issues remains an important one, even more so if we think of the potential of scientific research to improve human life, but also of the pitfalls and unintended consequences that can be associated with some areas of scientific research. Among the more recent prominent issues are those involving stem cell research, cloning, and genetically modified crops. But it should also be noted here that ethical issues related to scientific research have been around for a while, and that scientific institutions, as well as policy makers, have set in place mechanisms for dealing with them (for instance ethical boards which must approve research grant applications). It is rather the potential commercial applications of research results that raise additional ethical questions here. This concern leads us to examine the boundaries between science and the economy, which have been blurred in recent years through the increased integration of applied research and commercialization. Aspects of these boundaries need closer public scrutiny, including attention to the ethical issues raised by the commercialization of applied research (e.g. cloning) and the maintenance and expansion of basic, "non-profitable" research. It is often around boundary issues that debates take place. But such debate depends upon informed democratic participation, which in turn requires increased scientific education. The same kind of dynamic can be found in social-science research as well: the growing volume of science studies based on field research has provided many social scientists with the kind of understanding (i.e. interaction expertise) that allows meaningful interventions in public debates. Overall, then, the cultural boundaries of science can be seen as akin to tectonic plates: they overlap with economic and political domains and shift due to internal dynamics (scientific discoveries), or when encountering other tectonic plates (e.g. economic or religious groups and their interests).

Going back to the initial question: Do science cultures matter? Yes, and more than ever. The conceptual shift from norms and values to the practical actions that support knowledge production, as well as investigations concerning the boundaries between science and other knowledge forms, has uncovered the cultural dynamics that make science a motor of social and political change in modern societies.

References

Carroll, Patrick. 2006. *Science, Culture, and Modern State Formation*. Berkeley: University of California Press.

Collins, Harry. 2004. *Gravity's Shadow: The Search for Gravitational Waves*. Chicago: University of Chicago Press.

Collins, Harry and Evans, Robert. 2002. "The Third Wave of Science Studies: Studies of Expertise and Experience." *Social Studies of Science* 32(2): 235–96.

Epstein, Steven. 1996. *Impure Science: AIDS, Activism, and the Politics of Knowledge*. Berkeley: University of California Press.

Gieryn, Thomas. 1999. *Cultural Boundaries of Science: Credibility on the Line*. Chicago: University of Chicago Press.

Hackett, Edward J., Amsterdamska, Olga, Lynch, Michael, and Wajcman, Judy, eds. 2007. *The Handbook of Science and Technology Studies*, third edition. Cambridge, MA: The MIT Press.

Knorr-Cetina, Karin. 1981. *The Manufacture of Knowledge: An Essay on the Constructivist and Contextual Nature of Science*. Oxford: Pergamon.

——. 1999. *Epistemic Cultures: How the Sciences Make Knowledge*. Cambridge, MA: Harvard University Press.

Kuhn, Thomas. 1962. *The Structure of Scientific Revolutions*. Chicago: University of Chicago Press.

Latour, Bruno. 2004. *Politics of Nature: How to Bring the Sciences into Democracy*. Cambridge, MA: Harvard University Press.

Latour, Bruno and Woolgar, Steve. 1979. *Laboratory Life: The Social Construction of Scientific Facts*. Beverly Hills, CA: Sage.

Lynch, Michael. 1985. *Art and Artifact in Laboratory Science: A Study of Shop Work and Shop Talk in a Research Laboratory*. London: Routledge & Kegan Paul.

——. 1992. "Extending Wittgenstein. The Pivotal Move from Epistemology to the Sociology of Science." Pp. 215–65 in Andrew Pickering, ed., *Science as Practice and Culture*. Chicago: University of Chicago Press.

Merton, Robert King. 1973 (1942). "The Normative Structure of Science." Pp. 267–78 in Norman W. Storer, ed., *The Sociology of Science: Theoretical and Empirical Investigations*. Chicago: University of Chicago Press.

Pickering, Andrew. 1995. *The Mangle of Practice: Time, Agency & Science*. Chicago: University of Chicago Press.

Rheinberger, Hans-Jörg. 1997. *Toward a History of Epistemic Things: Synthesizing Proteins in the Test Tube*. Stanford, CA: Stanford University Press.

Turner, Stephen. 2007. "The Social Study of Science before Kuhn." Pp. 33–62 in Ed Hackett, Olga Amsterdamska, Michael Lynch, and Judy Wajcman, eds., *Handbook of Science and Technology Studies*, third edition. Cambridge, MA: The MIT Press.

Weber, Max 1970 (1919). *From Max Weber: Essays in Sociology*, ed. and trans. H.H. Gerth and C. Wright Mills. London: Routledge & Kegan Paul.

Yonay, Yuval and Breslau, Daniel. 2006. "Marketing Models. The Culture of Mathematical Economics." *Sociological Forum* 21(3): 345–86.

Zammito, John. 2004. *A Nice Derangement of Epistemes: Postpositivism in the Study of Science from Quine to Latour*. Chicago: University of Chicago Press.

44

Medical cultures

Mary-Jo DelVecchio Good and Seth Hannah

Social and cultural studies of contemporary biomedicine have flourished over recent decades, enriching our understanding as well as generating new questions about the vast domain of contemporary medicine. The social sciences have long and robust traditions analyzing the myriad ways that medical knowledge, training, and care are deeply embedded in social relations as well as imbued with profound and often soteriological cultural meanings (Good 1994). Our essay addresses culture and biomedicine, distinguishing between studies of "the culture *of* medicine" and studies of "culture *in* medicine."

Medical cultures are socially constructed worlds of illness and healing that vary across local and national contexts. They stem from the dynamic relationship between the local and global worlds of knowledge production, technologies, markets, and clinical standards. Modern biomedicine, often popularly conceptualized as "Western medicine," is frequently regarded as a universalized domain of science and technology largely devoid of cultural variations at its bioscience core. Contemporary biomedicine or "cosmopolitan medicine," to follow terminology popularized in medical anthropology by Charles Leslie (1976) and Fred Dunn (1976), has become an integral part of scientific as well as popular cultures worldwide. And although biomedicine is fostered through an international political economy of biotechnology and by the investment in medical knowledge by an international community of medical educators, academic physicians, clinical investigators, and bioscientists, medicine is taught, practiced, organized, and consumed in local contexts (Good *et al.* 1999).

Cultural approaches to the study of contemporary biomedicine are rooted in the work of mid-twentieth-century anthropologists and sociologists who began to examine the social construction of health and illness and the institutional and cultural foundations of healing systems around the world. In the 1960s, involvement in public health projects led anthropologists to investigate how biomedical knowledge is received and understood. They argued that individuals are not "empty vessels" waiting to be filled and that medical "habits and beliefs" constitute elements in elaborate "cultural systems" (Paul 1955). In the 1970s, social scientists engaged Leslie's (1976) comparative agenda, studying medical systems across a variety of cultural settings from small pre-literate villages to the great traditions of practice in Ayurvedic/Indian and Chinese classical and folk medicine (see also Kleinman *et al.* 1976). The comparative agenda challenged assumptions that medical cultures are closed systems that develop autonomously; rather, it was shown that diverse medical traditions were pluralistic, evolving from dynamic, transnational flows of knowledge and practices integrated into local cultures, and that "cosmopolitan medicine" was a parallel system to the classical traditions.

Cultures in and of medicine

Drawing from Geertz (1973), social scientists popularized culture as an analytic lens to understand the diverse and complex worlds of biomedicine, often in comparison with other contemporary medical systems. Sociologists enthusiastically built upon the work of Talcott Parsons (1951) and Renee Fox (1988 [1979]): leading scholars engaged in studies of medical work, biomedical research and clinical practice, patient experience, and the culture of contemporary medicine (Bosk 2005 [1979]; Conrad 1992; Glaser and Strauss 1968). In anthropology, cultural studies of biomedicine flourished, as did new journals, including *Culture, Medicine, and Psychiatry: A Journal of Cross-cultural and Comparative Research* (Good and Good 1980; Good 1994; Good 1995a, 1995b, 2001, 2007; Hahn and Gaines 1985; Kleinman 1980).

Social scientists writing on the culture of medicine also influenced how the concept of culture is used in and for medicine to enhance relations between the worlds of medicine and the lifeworlds of patients, to promote health policies and define the modernist projects of biomedicine in contemporary societies (Mechanic 1978; Mishler 1984). A key development was the move to understand patients' "explanatory models" (Kleinman *et al.* 1978) and to explore how clinicians could better incorporate these models into treatment regimens. Currently, we are witnessing a robust effort by medical institutions to shape the meaning of culture *in* medicine for political and marketing purposes and to respond to the needs of increasingly diverse patient populations. This effort is taking multiple forms: (1) defining new "cultural" diagnoses, particularly in mental health; (2) setting standards for "cultural competence" in response to civil rights and identity politics agendas; and (3) developing politically generated health policy agendas, including the Surgeon General's Report *Mental Health: Culture, Race and Ethnicity* (2001), which emphasized "culture counts," and the Institute of Medicine's *Unequal Treatment*, on racial and ethnic disparities in healthcare (Lewis-Fernandez and Diaz 2004; Lo and Stacey 2008; Chang 2003; Smedley *et al.* 2002–03; Good *et al.* 2002–03). Cultural experts advocate for changes in clinical medicine to increase access to care at national, state, and local levels (Betancourt *et al.* 2003). Olafsdottir and Pescosolido (2009) identify a new turn toward culture in medical sociology due to the growing influence of cultural sociology; yet, they too recognize a long tradition of scholarship on the "culture" of medicine and the "culture" of patients in medicine and psychiatry.

The culture of medicine

Classics in mid-twentieth-century medical sociology include Fox and Merton's work in *The Student Physician* (Merton *et al.* 1957), Becker *et al.*'s *Boys in White* (1961), Hafferty's *Into the Valley: Death and the Socialization of Medical Students* (1991), and Bosk's *Forgive and Remember* (2005 [1979]). These works explore the process of acculturation in medical education and training whereby medical students are transformed into doctors and residents become surgeons. Building upon this work, our cultural analyses of late-twentieth-century medical education document historical depth and continuity in the culture of medicine. Students come to embody a medical gaze and persona during their initial training. Developing a professional way of seeing and speaking is essential to entering the clinical world. We explored "how medicine constructs the 'objects' to which clinicians attend" and how it formulates "the human body and disease in a culturally distinctive fashion." Students learn visually "biology's natural hierarchical order" via "modern imaging techniques [that] give a powerful sense of the authority of biological reality" (Good 1994: 65–75). In clinical training, speaking and writing practices through case presentations and medical records teach students how to "construct" the patient through medically relevant narratives. Such practices authorize students' clinical interactions with patients, even as they legitimize an "editing out" of medically irrelevant data. Through experiences such as these, many of them recognized by physicians trained around the globe, students are socialized into contemporary clinical biomedicine. The cultural core of medical education persists despite a sea change in the gender, race, and ethnicity of medical students, the extraordinary transitions in disease burdens, morbidity, and mortality rates, the revolutionary innovations in biotechnologies, and the major reorganization and financing of healthcare.

Variations in "transnational" cultures of medicine arise through distinctive local practices, such as understandings about responsibility and obligation within professional hierarchies between attending physicians and residents, residents and medical students, and nurses and physicians. Notable crises in coverage, teaching, and oversight have occurred, for example in Kenya's national teaching hospitals and to a lesser extent in Indonesia's leading medical schools. These crises highlight different cultures of obligation and expectations about attending availability and responsibility that are common or idealized in most American academic medical settings. Variations in standards of clinical practice and obligations to patients, along with errors in practice and compromises in quality of clinical care, are common difficulties which also vary by locality within societies as well as among societies. Moral and ethical dilemmas in medicine range from the mundane to the spectacular and include problems ranging from the dilemma of disclosing AIDS diagnoses to spouses to the challenge of halting the commoditization of body parts for the international organ trade (Sanal 2004; Cohen 1999).

Policy contests over use of financial resources, organizational cultures of healthcare systems, and programs to promote equitable healthcare coverage are ideologically driven and related to the degree to which societies tolerate inequalities. Even among specialty practices following national practice guidelines, significant differences occur in rates of various procedures. Breast-conserving surgery and radiation, for example, are conducted more frequently than mastectomies in the northeastern states than the western states of the US (Good 1995b). Invasive and expensive medical tests are performed much more often in one Texas town than in surrounding towns (Gawande 2009). Such stories are legion, and they remind us of the salience of local medical cultures in determining how treatment is delivered.

Local and cosmopolitan worlds of biomedicine

When we write about contemporary biomedicine, cosmopolitan medicine, or Western medicine, the realities of local contexts compel us to ask what is culturally, politically, and economically specific as well as what is truly cosmopolitan. Indeed, the brute facts of local practice oftentimes overwhelm even the best that biomedicine can offer—for example when professional prestige among American academic physicians is measured by the skillful use of experimental high technology therapeutics, and at times "salvage therapies"; when a British trained Kenyan oncologist knows how to cure most children on his pediatric oncology ward, such as those with Burkitts, but does not have the wherewithal to access to the necessary chemotherapies; or when East African doctors face wards so full of patients suffering HIV and multiple-drug-resistant tuberculosis (MDR-TB) that they become "overwhelmed by disease entity" even when they have some access to the latest antiretrovirals. In such cases, the brute facts of local practice and political economies defy any reified analysis of a singular category "biomedicine" (Good 1995a).

In *Cultural Studies of Biomedicine*, Mary-Jo Good proposed an agenda to focus on (1) "the dynamics, tensions, and exchanges between local and global worlds of knowledge, technology, and practice," (2) "the integration of interpretive and cultural analyses with investigations of the political economies of biotechnology and the biosciences," and (3) "how local and international political economies of medical research and biotechnologies shape clinical medicine's cultural, moral, and ethical worlds" (1995b: 461). Since then, a massive sea change—a true biotechnical revolution—has occurred in AIDS research, leading to the development of effective HIV antiretroviral therapies and a concomitant burgeoning of multi-donor global health projects infused with social justice ideologies devoted to treating people afflicted with HIV, MDR-TB, and malaria (Farmer 2003; Kim and Farmer 2006).

A complementary revolution in treatment delivery has evolved through what Biehl (2008) terms the "pharmaceuticalization" of public health. For example, in the Brazilian response to the HIV epidemic, social activists and a liberal central government developed programs aiming to treat all HIV patients with antiretroviral therapies. In post-genocide Rwanda, governmental partnerships with non-governmental organizations (NGOs) such as Partners-In-Health and the Clinton Foundation have encouraged a modest improvement in the delivery of primary healthcare services necessary to support HIV treatment programs. In comparatively wealthy South Africa, after nearly a decade of efforts to demonize antiretrovirals and AZT, the central government recently agreed to support pharmaceutical treatments for some of the approximately 5.7 million people infected with HIV (18 percent of South Africa's 18–49 age group are infected with HIV [Fassin *et al.* 2007]).

The antiretroviral (ART) stories underscore how local cultures of medical practice are influenced by biotechnological innovation as well as by transnational systems of patents, World Trade Organization policies, laws governing the production of generics, and the policies of the World Health Organization (WHO). The "3 × 5" agenda designed by anthropologist/physician Jim Yong Kim for WHO urged governments to work toward enrolling three million HIV patients in ART by 2005 (Kim and Farmer 2006). This agenda had a profound influence on the global cultures of medical care as treatments became increasingly deliverable and effective even in societies with limited existing healthcare systems. Antiretroviral therapies and other "technically sweet" innovations from the biosciences have recast local medical cultures even as they have introduced new moral and ethical dilemmas, challenging ultimate questions of who "should" receive medications and care. How will treatments be financially supported and care efficiently organized? At this writing, the global community is suffering a severe recession, which poses the question: Will the public and private global funds which poured into HIV treatment over the past decade encouraging the "pharmaceuticalization of public health" be reduced? Some in the AIDS research community are working to develop vaccines and efficient technologies of delivery such as nano-techniques for longer-acting and more compact medication doses; however, many goals are as yet unrealized (Walker 2009). Local meanings are overlaid by global standards and technologies in nearly all aspects of biomedicine, as in the HIV examples. We see this local–global connectedness throughout cultural studies of biomedicine.

Theoretical approaches to this connectedness resonate with Marcus (1995: 3) and Fischer's (1991) notions of "multiple regimes of truth," in which they urge multi-sited ethnographies. Their approach is evident in much empirical research examining the transnational political economy of biomedicine and the cultural traffic of the biosciences across national boundaries. Works in this vein include Marcus's edited collection *Technoscientific Imaginaries* (1995), Rabinow's (1996) ethnography of a biotechnology firm and the "making of PCR," Dumit's (2004) analysis of PET and how new medical imaging technologies relate to wider cultural imaginaries, and a vast body of research on organ donation. Many studies document locally specific medical practices that disregard the legal and ethical stances of American and European organ transplantation standards, which conceive of organs as gifts from "donors" rather than as commodities procured from prisoners or the poor (Fox and Swazey 1992; Cohen 1999; Sanal 2004). In the arena of genetics, Heath and Rabinow (1993) were among those who first turned anthropological attention to the culture of the human genome project and related genetic technologies. An astonishing twenty-first-century global revolution in techno-logical capacities has made possible rapid and relatively inexpensive mapping of indivi-dual genomes, thereby profoundly influencing genetic/medical research (Church 2009).

Comparative perspectives and interpretive concepts

Our research on oncology and high technology medicine has been enriched by colla-borations and conversations with academic medicine colleagues from Europe, the Middle East, Africa, and Southeast Asia—particularly Indonesia. A comparative perspective encourages several questions: How do local and international political economies of medical research and biotechnology shape medicine's scientific imaginary, its cultural, moral, and ethical worlds, and the distribution of medicine's material and cultural products? How do local and international ideologies about population health and indi-viduals' rights to healthcare influence professional and institutional responses to specific needs of particular societies—from the HIV epidemic to post-conflict trauma to extreme scarcity of resources? What form does "the political economy of hope" take in contexts of great wealth as well as in contexts of extreme poverty? Questions such as these led to four interrelated interpretive concepts to guide explorations of how the culture of medicine "lives" in respective societies. These are the medical imaginary, the political economy of hope, the biotechnical embrace, and the clinical narrative (Good *et al.* 1990; Good 1995a, 2001, 2007).

Ethnographic studies of high technology medicine suggest ways that the affective and imaginative dimensions of biotechnology envelop physicians, patients, and the public in a "biotechnical embrace." The medical imaginary—that which energizes medicine and makes it a fun and intriguing enterprise—circulates through professional and popular culture, creating the potential to "embrace" and to "be embraced by" medicine. Clinicians and their patients are subject to "constantly emerging regimes of truth" in medical science, and those who suffer serious illness become particularly susceptible to the hope generated by the medical imaginary. The connection between bioscience and patient populations can be measured in part by the degree of support for disease-specific philanthropies (Farber 2009), the power of political health action groups (for AIDS, breast cancer), and taxpayer support for government financing of the National Institutes of Health ($27.9 billion in 2004, $40.4 billion in 2009–10). Americans clearly invest in the medical imaginary—the "many possibilities" enterprise—culturally, emotionally, as well as financially. Enthusiasm for medicine's possibilities arises not only from products of therapeutic efficacy but also through the production of ideas about potential but as-of-yet unrealized therapeutic usefulness (such as an HIV vaccine, designer anti-cancer therapies, or stem-cell-generated treatments for debilitating diseases). As an officer in one of the most successful biotechnology firms in America told us, biotechnology firms are in the business of producing ideas about potential therapeutics.

At more mundane levels, Americans live in a media world in which the medical imaginary has star billing. *ER* has been among the most popular television shows not only in the US but also in Indonesia and China and other parts of the world. The circulation of knowledge and products of the medical imaginary is uneven, and the robustness of local scientific and medical communities influences how people use globalized medical knowledge. Videos of Tanzanian teenagers acting in popular community theatrical performances designed to teach about the biology of the HIV virus and how antiretroviral therapies combat the virus illustrate the global appeal of the twenty-first century's medical imaginary (Earls and Carlson 2009). Recent studies on HIV in Brazil (Biehl 2008), on French cutting-edge science (Rabinow 1999), and on the elevation of community-health workers into twenty-first century deliverers of high technology therapeutics (Kim and Farmer 2006) attest to the cultural power of medicine. Medical errors, fraud, and failures are also a part of the medical imaginary, yet these negative components are often hidden by the larger narrative of hope that energizes modern medicine.

The "biotechnical embrace" brings into relief the subjective experiences of clinicians and their patients, and it pays particular attention to the affective dimension of clinical relationships. "Embracing" and "being embraced by" science and medicine fundamentally link high technology bioscience to the wider society, and clinicians to patients in their care. Whether new reproductive technologies, therapies for infectious disease, innovative organ transplantation procedures, progress in gene manipulation, or breakthroughs in cancer and heart disease research, the medical imagination drives the political economy of hope as well as society's investment in medical adventures and, occasionally, misadventures.

Clinical narratives capture the dynamics of clinical interactions between physicians and their patients. Narrative analysis and related literary concepts—plot, emplotment, and narrative time—introduce new ways of making sense of everyday clinical life and the plotting of a therapeutic intervention and course. Narrative analysis also illuminates how affect and desire play out in clinical narratives through which evidence-based medicine is incorporated into clinical culture, seducing patients and clinicians and enveloping both in a world of the medical imagination and therapeutic action. Although physicians drive the clinical story for patients and utilize a variety of narrative strategies to convey meaning and hope, patients also shape the clinical narratives, as they read their own bodies and disease processes in light of narratives of treatment. Narrative analysis also highlights specialty power by incorporating findings from the latest research and clinical trials to justify choices among treatment options. In radiation and medical oncology in particular, the aesthetics of statistics—how clinicians convey odds and chances of treatment actions—are central in clinical narratives, addressing the immediacy of therapeutic activities, even as ultimate questions of death are avoided. In the American culture of oncology, patients expect their physicians to invite them to enter the world of experimental therapeutics when cancer is resistant to standard therapies. Through these invitations to salvage therapies, such as autologous stem-cell treatments, clinical narratives wed the experimental to the therapeutic, directing the meaning of technological interventions and inscribing treatment experiences on patients' psyche and soma (Good 1995a; 2007; see also Mattingly and Garro 2000).

Culture in medicine: addressing healthcare disparities

In 2001, the Institute of Medicine requested a background paper for *Unequal Treatment* on the culture of medicine and how it might produce disparities in medical care (Good *et al.* 2002–03). We argued that the culture of medicine taught physicians to embody the "medical gaze" and to focus on medically relevant data. Patients whom physicians consider social "trainwrecks," who might "derail the smooth workings of the medical machine," threaten time and efficiency, which is highly prized; thus illness narratives are minimized. Physicians interviewed hypothesized that patients who resist being patients or are distrustful of clinicians and institutions of care may indeed receive less than equal treatment. When asked who these patients might be, "no shows" and "drug users and abusers" were most often mentioned rather than any particular cultural group or social identity. What *was* evident in these discussions was that "culture" was a salient category for many physicians and for the institutions where they work. Culturally tailored services and language translation were policy mechanisms designed to attract potential patient populations in the clinics' catchment areas. Our current study—*Shattering Culture: American Medicine's Responses to Hyperdiversity* (funded by the Russell Sage Foundation)—investigates ways that "culture" is used by medicine in response to increasingly diverse patient populations.

Cultural responses as correctives to disparities in care

The US Surgeon General's *Mental Health: Culture, Race, and Ethnicity* (2001), followed by the Institute of Medicine's *Unequal Treatment* (Smedley *et al.* 2002–03), built political cases to redress disparities in mental health services and quality medical care for ethnic minorities. "Culture" became equated with social identities, most often race and ethnicity. Institutions of medical care and training were mandated by local and national governments to address disparities and to respond to increased diversity of patient populations. These recent political mandates reenergized attention to patients' culture, which had long been a mainstay of cultural psychiatry. Cultural differences between patients and providers have been debated as one source of possible disparities and inequalities in care, with language differences identified as the ultimate barrier to a therapeutic alliance (Lopez 2003; Willen *et al.* 2010). Burdens of difference have been attributed to "ethnic" cultural beliefs, behaviors, and fears of stigma (Guarnaccia and Rodriguez 1996; Santiago-Irizarry 2001; Lewis-Fernandez and Diaz 2004).

Attending to ethnicity and culture has a long tradition in American medicine, exemplified by the ethnic community health clinics established in the 1960s. In the past decade, aggressive marketing and packaging of "culture" have led to "cultural competence" and "diversity" training for hospital staff. The recent politicization of "culture"—for example in "Culture Counts" in mental health care and "race and ethnicity count" in *Unequal Treatment*'s documentation of disparities in healthcare—has led to a reexamination of standards of practice and clinical norms. Newly revised culturally based educational programs and culturally specific services have been introduced by physician leaders in medicine's efforts to shape the meaning and appropriate uses of "culture" (Betancourt *et al.* 2003; Sue 1998; Lo and Stacey 2008; Hinton and Good 2009). Hospitals routinely track the racial and ethnic composition of their patient populations, and during the past decade many adopted the goal of providing high quality and equitable care for all racial, ethnic, and cultural groups (Kagawa-Singer and Kassim-Lakha 2003).

These efforts by medical institutions rely on the existence of group-bounded cultural characteristics in order to offer culturally tailored services (Kirmayer and Sartorius 2007; Hunt 2005). However, it is unclear to what extent cohesive group identities are among the most salient social categories in today's US, and to what extent such social categories are clinically relevant (Appiah and Gutman 1996; Idler 2007; Sundstrom 2002; Root 2000; Zack 2002).

Our recent research explores the cultures of medicine in highly diverse settings where the cultural identities of patient populations are often fluid and ambiguous (Hannah 2009). We hypothesize that cultures of clinical practice would vary depending on the diversity of patient populations and cultures and the salience of identified inequalities or disparities in care. We found that some clinics provided rich layers of cultural and linguistic services as essential to the core mission of the practice. Others attended minimally to cultural matters, yet cared for highly diverse patient populations and staff. Clinicians and support staff at both types of clinics were often culturally attuned to racial and ethnic groups, cultural traditions, and languages. In these complex social environments, broad identity categories such as African American, Hispanic, West Indian, Russian-Jewish, or Asian failed to capture the most salient cultural characteristics of individual patients. Often there were greater cultural differences among individuals within ethnic or racial groups than between them.

We developed a theoretical concept to illustrate these findings, referring to the treatment settings above as "cultural environments of hyperdiversity" (Hannah 2009). Five scenarios illustrated how the use of culture to address disparities in care was challenged by the complex interaction of culture and identity: (1) *multiplicity*, where the sheer number of different racial-ethnic groups makes organizing services based on identity impractical; (2) *ambiguity*, where racial-ethnic group membership is not easily labeled or understood; (3) *simultaneity*, where labeling is difficult because individuals occupy multiple racial/ethnic categories at once; (4) *misidentification*, where a patient is mistakenly labeled a member of a particular racial/ethnic group; and (5) *misapplication*, where an individual's racial-ethnic group membership is correctly identified, but the individual does not share significant cultural characteristics with others from that group.

These scenarios suggest that culturally specific services based on census racial or ethnic categories were difficult to design due to ever shrinking degrees of cultural similarity and increasingly blurred boundaries. In the cultural environments of hyperdiversity that we observed, clinicians and staff often eschewed the use of racial/ethnic categories as proxies for cultural characteristics in the treatment of immigrant and minority patients. Instead, they were more likely to regard language, need, disadvantaged class status, nativity, illness, or individual behaviors such as drug use of greater relevance to their clinical tasks than race or ethnicity.

Conclusion

We close by reflecting on the tension between universalism and particularism inherent in the culture *of* medicine and how culture is used *in* medicine. A psychiatrist colleague devised ways to bring "culture" into the diagnostic process in psychiatry through his commitment to revising the cultural components of the Diagnostic and Statistical Manual (DSM 5.0). For him, "culture" has become a political trope, a way to argue for public support for adequate and culturally sensitive mental care for Hispanic populations in need. At a professional meeting, he discussed the tension in much of contemporary medicine and psychiatry between universalism and cultural specificity. Arguing for greater clinical attention to the uniqueness of *ataques de nervios* the psychiatrist resolved, "I am not anti-universalism in psychiatry, but for a *more informed universalism*" (Lewis-Fernandez, personal conversation, 2009). It is this tension we observe in the way "culture" is used in medicine today.

From the perspective of clinicians, universalism is the heart of the culture of medicine. Yet we see from cross-national variation the influence that particular cultural traditions have in shaping local practices of medicine. It is these local practices that reshape the universal culture of medicine itself—creating an evolving, more informed cosmopolitan standard.

References

Appiah, K.A. and Gutman, A. 1996. *Color Conscious*. Princeton, NJ: Princeton University Press.

Becker, H., Geern, B., Hughes, E.C., and Strauss, A. 1961. *Boys in White: Student Culture in Medical School*. Chicago: University of Chicago Press.

Betancourt, J.A., Green, J.E., and Ananeh-Firempong, O. 2003. "Defining Cultural Competence." *Public Health Reports* 118(4): 293–302.

Biehl, J. 2008. *Will to Live: AIDS Therapies and the Politics of Survival*. Princeton, NJ: Princeton University Press.

Bosk, Charles. 2005 (1979). *Forgive and Remember*. Chicago: University of Chicago Press.

Chang, D.F. 2003. "An Introduction to the Politics of Science: Culture, Race, Ethnicity and the Supplement to the Surgeon General's Report on Mental Health." *Culture, Medicine and Psychiatry* 27: 373–83.

Church, G. 2009. "Sequencing Whole Genomes: How and Why." Lecture presented to HST 934: Introduction to Global Medicine, Harvard Medical School.

Cohen, L. 1999. "Where It Hurts: Indian Material for an Ethics of Organ Transplantation." *Daedalus* 128(4): 135–65.

Conrad, P. 1992. *Deviance and Medicalization: From Badness to Sickness*. Philadelphia, PA: Temple University Press.

Dumit, J. 2004. *Picturing Personhood Brain Scans and Biomedical Identity*. Princeton, NJ: Princeton University Press.

Dunn, F. 1976. "Traditional Asian Medicine and Cosmopolitan Medicine as Adaptive Systems." In C. Leslie, ed., *Asian Medical Systems*. Berkeley: University of California Press.

Earls, F. and Carlson, M. 2009. "Working with Children Affected by HIV/AIDS in Tanzania." Lecture presented to HST 934: Introduction to Global Medicine, Harvard Medical School.

Farber, A. 2009. LAM Treatment Alliance website: http://lamtreatmentalliance.org.

Farmer, P. 2003. *Pathologies of Power*. Berkeley: University of California Press.

Fassin, D., Jacobs, A., and Varro, G. 2007. *When Bodies Remember: Experiences and Politics of AIDS in South Africa*. Berkeley: University of California Press.

Fischer, M.J. 1991. "Anthropology as Cultural Critique." *Cultural Anthropology* 6: 525–37.

Fox, R. 1988 (1979). *Essays in Medical Sociology: Journeys into the Field*. New York: John Wiley and Sons.

Fox, R. and Swazey, J. 1992. *Spare Parts: Organ Replacement in American Society*. New York: Oxford University Press.

Gawande, A. 2009. "The Cost Conundrum: What a Texas Town Can Teach Us about Health Care." *New Yorker* (June).

Geertz, C. 1973. *The Interpretation of Cultures*. New York: Basic Books.

Glaser, B. and Strauss, A. 1968. *A Time for Dying*. Chicago: Aldine Publishing.

Good, B.J. 1994. *Medicine, Rationality, and Experience: An Anthropological Perspective*. Cambridge: Cambridge University Press.

Good, B.J. and Good, M.D. 1980. "The Meanings of Symptoms: A Cultural Hermeneutic Model for Clinical Practice." In *The Relevance of Social Science for Medicine*. Dordrecht: Reidel.

Good, M.D. 1995a. *American Medicine: The Quest for Competence*. Berkeley: University of California Press.

——. 1995b. "Cultural Studies of Biomedicine: An Agenda for Research." *Social Science & Medicine* 41(4): 461–73.

——. 2001. "The Biotechnical Embrace." *Culture, Medicine and Psychiatry* 25: 395–410.

——. 2007. "The Medical Imaginary and the Biotechnical Embrace." In J. Biehl, Byron Good, and Arthur Kleinman, eds., *Subjectivity*. Berkeley: University of California Press.

Good, M.D., Good, B.J., Schaffer, C., and Lind, S.E. 1990. "American Oncology and the Discourse on Hope." *Culture, Medicine and Psychiatry* 14: 59–79.

Good, M.D., Mwaikambo, E., Amayo, E., and Machoki, J.M. 1999. "Clinical Realities and Moral Dilemmas: Contrasting Perspectives from Academic Medicine in Kenya, Tanzania, and America." *Daedalus* (Fall): 167–96.

Good, M.D., James, C., Good, B.J., and Becker, A.E. 2002–03. "The Culture of Medicine and Racial, Ethnic, and Class Disparities in Healthcare." In B.D. Smedley, A.Y. Stith, and A.R. Nelson, eds., *Unequal Treatment: Confronting Racial and Ethnic Disparities in Health Care*. Washington, DC: National Academy Press.

Good, M.D., Gadmer, N.M., Ruopp, P., and Lakoma, M. 2004. "Narrative Nuances on Good and Bad Deaths: Internists' Tales from High-technology Work Places." *Social Science & Medicine* 58: 939–53.

Guarnaccia, P. and Rodriguez, O. 1996. "Concepts of Culture and Their Role in the Development of Culturally-Competent Mental Health Services." *Hispanic Journal of Behavioral Sciences* 18: 419–43.

Hafferty, F. 1991. *Into the Valley: Death and the Socialization of Medical Students*. New Haven, CT: Yale University Press.

Hahn, R. and Gaines, A. 1985. *Physicians of Western Medicine*. Dordrecht: Reidel.

Hannah, S. 2009. "Clinical Care in Environments of Hyper-diversity: Race, Culture, and Ethnicity in the Post-Pentad World." *Manuscript Under Review*.

Heath, D. and Rabinow, P., eds. 1993. "Bio-Politics: The Anthropology of the New Genetics and Immunology." *Culture, Medicine and Psychiatry* 17(1) Special Issue.

Hinton, D. and Good, B., eds. 2009. *Culture and Panic Disorder*. Palo Alto, CA: Stanford University Press.

Hunt, L. 2005. "Health Research: What's Culture Got to Do With It?" *Lancet* 366: 617–18.

Idler, J.E. 2007. *Officially Hispanic*. Lanham, MD: Lexington Books.

Kagawa–Singer, M. and Kassim-Lakha, S. 2003. "A Strategy to Reduce Cross-Cultural Miscommunication and Increase the Likelihood of Improving Health Outcomes." *Academic Medicine* 78(6): 577–87.

Kim, J.Y. and Farmer, P. 2006. "AIDS in 2006—Moving Toward One World, One Hope?" *New England Journal of Medicine* 355(7): 645–47.

Kirmayer, L. and Sartorius, N. 2007. "Cultural Models and Somatic Syndromes." *Psychosomatic Medicine* 69: 832–40.

Kleinman, A. 1980. *Patients and Healers in the Context of Culture.* Berkeley: University of California Press.

Kleinman, A., Kuntadter, P., Alexander, E., and Gale, J., eds. 1976. *Medicine in Chinese Cultures: Comparative Studies of Health Care in Chinese and Other Societies.* Washington, DC: US Government Printing Office for Fogerty International Center, NIH.

Kleinman, A., Eisenberg, L., and Good, B.J. 1978. "Culture, Illness, and Care: Clinical lessons From Anthropologic and Cross-Cultural Research." *Annals of Internal Medicine* 88: 251–58.

Leslie, C., ed. 1976. *Asian Medical Systems: A Comparative Study.* Berkeley: University of California Press.

Lewis-Fernandez, R. and Diaz, N. 2004. "The Cultural Formulation: A Method for Assessing Cultural Factors Affecting the Clinical Encounter." *Psychiatric Services* 73(4): 271–95.

Lo, M.M. and Stacey, C.L. 2008. "Beyond Cultural Competency: Bourdieu, Patients and Clinical Encounters." *Sociology of Health & Illness* 30(5): 741–55.

Lopez, S. 2003. "Reflections on the Surgeon General's Report on Mental Health, Culture, Race, and Ethnicity." *Culture, Medicine and Psychiatry* 27(4): 419–34.

Marcus, G. 1995. *Technoscientific Imaginaries: Conversations, Profiles and Memoirs.* Chicago: University of Chicago Press.

Mattingly, C. and Garro, L. 2000. *Narrative and the Cultural Construction of Illness and Healing.* Berkeley: University of California Press.

Mechanic, D. 1978. *Medical Sociology.* New York: Free Press.

Merton, R.K., Reader, G.G., and Kendall, P.L. 1957. *The Student Physician; Introductory Studies in the Sociology of Medical Education.* Cambridge, MA: Harvard University Press.

Mishler, E. 1984. *The Discourse of Medicine: Dialectics of Medical Interviews.* Norwood: Ablex.

Olafsdottir, S. and Pescosolido, B. 2009. "Drawing the Line: The Cultural Cartography of Utilization Recommendations for Mental Health." *Journal of Health and Social Behavior* 50(2): 228–44.

Parsons, T. 1951. *The Social System.* Glencoe, IL: The Free Press.

Paul, B. 1955. *Health, Culture, and Community: Case Studies of Public Reactions to Health Programs.* New York: Russell Sage Foundation.

Rabinow, P. 1980. "The Meanings of Symptoms: A Cultural Hermeneutic Model for Clinical Practice." In *The Relevance of Social Science for Medicine.* Dordrecht: Reidel.

——. 1996. *Making PCR: A Story of Biotechnology.* Chicago: University of Chicago Press.

——. 1999. *French DNA.* Chicago: University of Chicago Press.

Root, M. 2000. "How We Divide the World." *Philosophy and Science* 67: S28–S639.

Sanal, A. 2004. "'Robin Hood' of Techno-Turkey or Organ Trafficking in the State of Ethical Beings." *Culture, Medicine and Psychiatry* 28: 281–309.

Santiago-Irizarry, V. 2001. *Medicalizing Ethnicity: The Construction of Latino Identity in a Psychiatric Setting.* New York: Cornell University Press.

Smedley, B.D., Stith, A.Y., and Nelson, A.R., eds. 2002–03. *Unequal Treatment: Confronting Racial and Ethnic Disparities in Health Care.* Washington, DC: National Academy Press.

Sue, S. 1998. "In Search of Cultural Competence in Psychotherapy and Counseling." *American Psychologist* 53(4): 440–48.

Sundstrom, R. 2002. "Racial Nominalism." *Journal of Social Philosophy* 33(2): 193–10.

Surgeon General. 2001. *Mental Health: Culture, Race, and Ethnicity. A Supplement to Mental Health: A Report of the Surgeon General.* Washington, DC: United States Department of Health and Human Services.

Walker, B. 2009. "Setting up Science Labs in Resource Poor Places." Lecture presented to HST 934: Introduction to Global Medicine, Harvard Medical School.

Willen, Sarah, Bullon, Antonio, and DelVecchio Good, Mary-Jo. 2010. "'Opening up a Huge Can of Worms': Reflections on a 'Cultural Sensitivity' Course for Psychiatric Residents." *Harvard Review of Psychiatry* (November/December).

Zack, N. 2002. *Philosophy of Race and Science*. New York: Routledge.

45

Legal culture and cultures of legality

Susan S. Silbey

Culture is a hotly debated and contested construct, evidenced by the existence and content of this handbook. The importation of this term into legal scholarship is fraught with unfortunate confusion. The meaning of the word "culture" alone is unstable, theoretically and empirically; adding "legal" to "culture" only exacerbates the conceptual tumult. Some confusion derives from intermingling two meanings of culture. One meaning names a particular world of beliefs and practices associated with a specific group. The second meaning is analytic rather than empirical, referring to the outcome of social analysis—an abstracted *system* of symbols and meanings, both the product and context of social action. In the former use, referring to the distinctive customs, opinions, and practices of a particular group or society, the term is often used in the plural, as in the legal cultures of Japan and China, or in reference to African or Latin cultures. In the latter analytic sense, the word is used in the singular, as in legal culture, or the culture of academia.

Since the cultural turn of the 1980s, use of the word culture has proliferated so much that the historic confusion has infested scholarship in almost every field of inquiry where it is invoked. In addition to the thousands of journal articles, one can find hundreds of books with "law" and "culture" or "legal culture" in the title. Some of these call for cultural study of law as if it had not been going on for decades; others entitle collections of diverse essays under a general rubric of law and culture; yet others do treat culture as a serious theoretical concept (e.g. Benton 2002; Bracey 2006; Rosen 2006). The unprecedented and rapidly proliferating use of the concept has unfortunately exacerbated the traditionally unruly discourse. In this essay, I hope to offer helpful clarification, distinguish alternative uses, and provide a short lexicon to some of the concepts of legal culture's progeny in legal scholarship—legal ideology, legal consciousness, legality, and cultures of legality.

A concise conceptualization

Contemporary cultural analyses have moved beyond conceptions of culture as either everything humanly produced or as only what calls itself culture (e.g. arts, music, theater, fashion, literature, religion, media, and education) to conceive of culture as a system of symbols and meanings and their associated social practices. In its most effective and theoretically plausible uses, the concept of culture is invoked (1) to recognize signs and performances, meanings, and actions as inseparable; yet (2) *"to disentangle, for the purpose of analysis* [only], the semiotic influences on action from the other sorts of influences— demographic, geographical, biological, technological, economic, and so on—that they are necessarily mixed with in any concrete sequence of behavior" (Sewell 2005: 160, emphasis added). (3) Although formal organizational attributes and human interactions share symbolic and cognitive resources, many cultural resources are discrete, local, and intended for specific purposes. Nonetheless, (4) it is possible to observe general patterns so that we are able to speak of a culture, or cultural system, at specified scales and levels of social organization. "System and practice are complementary concepts: each presupposes the other" (Sewell 2005: 164), although the constituent practices are neither uniform, logical, static, nor autonomous. (5) As a collection of semiotic resources deployed in interactions (Swidler 1986), "culture is not a power, something to which social events, behaviors, institutions, or processes can be causally attributed; it is a context, something within which [events, behaviors, institutions, and processes] can be intelligibly—that is, thickly—described" (Geertz 1973: 14). (6) Variation and conflict concerning the meaning and use of these symbols and resources are likely and expected because at its core culture "is an intricate system of claims about how to understand the world and act on it" (Perin 2005: xii; cf. Silbey 2009).

Genesis of the term legal culture

Despite often abstruse debate, many scholars find the concept of culture particularly useful when they want to focus on aspects of legal action that are not confined to official legal texts, roles, performances, or offices. Lawrence Friedman (1975) is credited with introducing the concept as a means of emphasizing the fact that law was best understood and described as a system, a product of social forces, and itself a conduit of those same forces. Friedman was a founding father of American (socio-legal) law and society scholarship and as such was intent on making explicit the unofficial, and what otherwise would have been thought of as non-legal, behaviors as nonetheless important for shaping what is more conventionally understood as legal. Although law can be defined as "a set of rules or norms, written or unwritten, about right and wrong behavior, duties, and rights" (Friedman 1975: 2), according to Friedman this conventional notion attributed too much independence and efficacy to the law on the books and acknowledged too little the power and predictability of what is often called the law in action. To advance a social scientific study of law in action, Friedman adopted the model of a system—a set of structures that processes inputs (demands and resources) from an environment to which it sends its outputs (functions) in an ongoing recursive feedback loop. He identified three central components of the legal system: (1) the social and legal forces that, in some way, press in and make "the law," the inputs; (2) the law itself—structures and rules that process inputs; and (3) the impact of law on behavior in the outside world, the outputs or functions of the system. "Where the law comes from and what it accomplishes—the first and third terms—are essentially the *social* study of law" (Friedman 1975: 3, emphasis added).

Friedman chose the phrase legal culture to name the subject of this social study of law, the "social forces ... constantly at work on the law," "those parts of general culture—customs, opinions, ways of doing and thinking—that bend social forces toward or away from the law" (1975: 15). As an analytic term, legal culture emphasized the role of taken-for-granted and tacit actions that operated on and within the interactions of the legal system and its environment. As a descriptive term, it identified a number of related phenomena—public knowledge of and attitudes toward the legal system as well as patterns of citizen behavior with respect to the legal system. These included judgments about the law's fairness, legitimacy, and utility. To the extent that patterns of attitudes and behaviors are discernible within a population and vary from one group or state to another, it was possible, Friedman said, to speak of the legal culture(s) of groups, organizations, or states (1975: 194). As an example of variations within legal cultures, Friedman distinguished the internal legal culture of professionals working in the system from the external legal culture of citizens interacting with the system. As the "ideas, values, expectations, and attitudes toward law and legal institutions, which some public or some part of the public holds," legal culture was meant to name a range of phenomena that would be, in principle, measurable (Friedman 1997: 34). Although Friedman never elaborately theorized the concept of legal culture even as he reformulated it several times in different texts, he remained convinced that the concept was useful as a way of "lining up a range of phenomena into one very general category" (1997: 33).

Confusions and debates

Following the concept's introduction, researchers began using it in a range of empirical projects, including studies of children's knowledge of and attitudes to law (Tapp and Kohlberg 1971; Tapp and Levine 1974), rights consciousness among Americans (Scheingold 1974), the practices of criminal courts (Nardulli et al. 1988; Kritzer and Zemans 1993), comparative analysis of different groups and nation-states (Kidder and Hostetler 1990; Tanase 1990; Hamilton and Sanders 1992; Bierbrauer 1994; Barzilai 1997; Gibson and Gouws 1997; Gibson and Caldeira 1997; French 1998; Chanock 2001). For those who attempt to measure variations in legal cultures, the indicators include such diverse phenomena as litigation rates and institutional infrastructures (Blankenburg 1994, 1997) or crime rates (Kawashima 1963).

Predictably, given the historic confusion surrounding the term, debates have arisen among researchers who have attempted to use the concept in empirical projects (Nelken 1997a, 1997b). The most persistent divide and heated dispute seem to align with the distinction named earlier, between those who use culture as an analytic concept within a more developed theory of social relations and those who view legal culture as concrete, measurable phenomena. Those who attempted to use the concept as a focus for comparative research moved quickly toward measurement and a more limited concept. For some of these researchers, when the concept of legal culture is used with insufficient specificity the distinction between all of culture and legal culture is unclear, and what constitutes the legal seems unspecified (Blankenburg 1994, 1997). Some researchers insist that legal culture is that which is produced and studied most effectively among professional legal actors, while others insist that such a narrow definition belies the theoretical utility of the concept of legal culture as a way of mapping the connections between law and everyday life—exactly the analytically conceived feedback loop that Friedman posited in his notion of a legal system.

Cotterrell has produced one of the most sustained critiques of the concept (1997, 2006). He insists that "everything about law's institutions and conceptual character needs to be understood in relation to the social conditions which have given rise to it. In this sense law is indeed an expression of culture" (Cotterrell 1992 [1984]: 26). Nonetheless, Cotterrell is unwilling to accept a concept of legal culture if it is indistinguishable from other forms of social control or normative ordering. Somewhere between a "thoroughgoing legal pluralism" (Cotterrell 1992 [1984]: 42) in which "law can be distinguished from other social norms only in vague terms" and a too narrow, too simple conception of state law, Cotterrell seeks a middle ground that recognizes the cultural influences on and from law but yet retains a recognition of the distinctiveness of legal forms and doctrines.

To some extent, these socio-legal debates reproduce controversies plaguing the concept of culture generally. The most important issues are less empirical than theoretical. The measurement problems decried by those studying national legal cultures derive from the theoretical questions. How is legal culture evident and measurable and yet diffuse and abstract? What is the relative importance of causal explanation as against description and interpretive understanding? How central is formal legal doctrine in understanding participation in, support for, and consequences of law?

Constitutive theories of legal culture

The cultural turn that swept across the humanities and social sciences in the 1980s brought some clarification to the analytic concept, if not entirely for those seeking precise quantifiable measurement. In the interdisciplinary community of law and society scholars, psychologists, anthropologists, sociologists, historians, geographers, and law professors spoke across traditional divides, even if they often spoke from and retreated back to their disciplines. They worked in the crosshairs of different disciplinary lenses, tacking back and forth, and producing—I think much before it happened in most of the disciplines—a new set of theories and methods, exemplifying some of the most important insights that would eventually emerge in most social science fields. What was that insight? That the "site" of social action matters to the meaning and organization of that action, whether that site was legal, scientific, or organizational. There was a turn away from large-scale theory development and abstract modeling to more situated, contextualized analyses of sites of social action. Researchers were finding ways to bridge the epistemological and theoretical paradigms that had both fueled their knowledge production and simultaneously created deep chasms between and within disciplines. The emergence of cultural analysis signaled an effort to synthesize behavioral and structural as well as micro and macro perspectives.

In socio-legal scholarship the cultural turn had three components. First, it abandoned a "law-first" paradigm of research (Sarat and Kearns 1993). Rather than beginning with legal rules and materials to trace how policies or purposes are achieved or not, scholars turned to ordinary daily life to find, if they were there, the traces of law within. They were as interested in the absences and silences where law could have been and was not as they were interested in the explicit signs of positive law. Law and society had already moved beyond what Friedman (1985: 29) had identified as lawyer's law ("of interest to legal practitioners and theorists") to legal acts ("the processes of administrative governance, police behavior") and legal behavior (the unofficial work of legal professionals).

Cultural analysis added a new focus on the unofficial, non-professional actors—citizens, legal laymen—as they take account of, anticipate, imagine, or fail to imagine legal acts and ideas. It shifted empirical focus from a preoccupation with legal actors and legal materials to the everyday life-world of ordinary people.

Second, the cultural turn abandoned the predominant focus on measurable behavior that preoccupied those who wanted to compare national legal cultures and reinvigorated the Weberian conception of social action by including analyses of the meanings and interpretive communication of social transactions. From this perspective, law is not merely an instrument or tool working on social relations, but also a set of conceptual categories and schema that help construct, compose, and interpret social relations. The focus on actors' meanings brought into the mainstream of law and society scholarship a stronger commitment to a wider array of research methods, drawing particularly from anthropology and qualitative sociology that had long been studying actors' meaning-making in other than legal domains.

Third, and perhaps most fundamentally, the turn to everyday life and the cultural meanings of social action demanded a willingness to shift from the native categories of actors as the object of study, e.g. the rules of the state, the formal institutions of law, the attitudes and opinions of actors, to *an analytically conceptualized unit of analysis, the researcher's definition of the subject: legal culture.* We had been studying law with insufficiently theorized concepts. We were using our subject's language as the tools for our analysis and in the course finding ourselves unable to answer the questions our research generated, fueling that conceptual muddle that has characterized deployment of the word culture. New theoretical materials and research methods were necessary (cf. Gordon 1984; Munger and Seron 1984). These involved more intensive study of local cultures, native texts, and interpretive hermeneutical techniques for inhabiting and representing the quotidian world to construct better accounts of how law works, or, to put it another way, how legality is an ongoing structure of social action (Ewick and Silbey 1998: 33–56). The new research efforts also involved attention to and appropriation of the venerable traditions of European social theory that had been addressing questions of consciousness, ideology, and hegemony in an effort to understand how systems of domination are not only tolerated but embraced by subordinate populations.

What became known as the constitutive perspective, or cultural turn, recaptured some of the critical tradition of law and society research that had been waning after decades of path-breaking scholarship. Focused on the everyday life of citizens, scholars also began to interrogate the ideals and principles that legal institutions announce. Even if they fail to consistently implement them, might these policy efforts and abstract principles nonetheless play important roles in everyday life and be a part of how legal institutions create their power and authority? The ideals of law, such as open and accessible processes, rule-governed decision-making, or similar cases being decided similarly—despite being incomplete as descriptions of how law works—might be part of the popularly shared understandings of what law is. They might serve as aspirations that help shape and mobilize support for legal institutions. They might also be part of what allowed the system to appear to be what Hannah Arendt (1972: 178) labeled a headless tyrant. In this approach, researchers reconceived the relations between legal texts and actions and the commonplace events and interpretations through which, they theorized, legality circulates.

From the mid-1980s to the present, a steady stream of empirical literature described the mediating processes through which local practices are aggregated and condensed into systematic institutionalized power (cf. Silbey 1992, 1998, 2005a, 2005b, 2009). Unfortunately, multiple uses of similar terms recreated the conceptual confusion that had achieved, for a while, quiescence through constitutive/cultural theories. Within the more general discourse on legal culture, however, one can find four strong threads:

1 *Legal ideology*: Without necessarily using the term legal culture, research on legal ideology explores "the power at work in and through law. Studies of law and ideology also suggest that the power associated with signs and symbols is being exercised unjustly." Thus, in studies of legal culture, "adopting and deploying the term ideology is a form of social criticism" (Silbey 1998; cf. Ewick 2006).

2 *Legal consciousness*: One can also find studies of legal consciousness, defined as participation in the construction of legality, where legality refers to the meanings, sources of authority, and cultural practices that are commonly recognized as legal, regardless of who employs them or for what ends (Ewick and Silbey 1998: 22). As with legal culture, however, we can also find many and confusing uses of the term legality, which is an English language term, meaning "that which is within the specifications and boundaries of formal law." Many law review articles use the term this way, specifically distinguishing culture and legality as two independent social phenomena, exactly what constitutive theories of legal culture are meant to overcome. Constitutive socio-legal theories treat legal culture and/or legality as a set of schema or narratives circulating in popular discourse, sustaining legal hegemony and creating, or failing to create, opportunities for resistance. Such research is not limited to the US (see Cowan 2004; Cooper 1995; Hertogh 2004; Pelisse 2004; cf. Silbey 2005a), although work focused on the discourses of law and legality in colonial and post-colonial "theatres" more often refers to the "cultures of legality ... constitutive of colonial society" (Comaroff 2001; Maurer 2004).

3 *Legalities, cultures of legality, and counter-law*: Very recent work invokes the phrase cultures of legality to identify and highlight the fetishization of popular constructions—such as legality or rule of law—that are actively and broadly mobilized for diverse political (national and international) projects. In discussions of corporate capitalism, financial transparency, globalization, state-building, as well as analyses of resistance movements, law is invoked for legitimation not simply of itself but for the specific interests or institutions being promoted. Comaroff and Comaroff (2004, 2006) ask why the discourse of law and disorder are so often conjoined, especially marking analyses of post-colonial situations. Why is law posed as the alternative of disorder? Do legal procedures and discourses offer mechanisms of commensuration (Espeland and Stevens 1998), real or otherwise, to manage what seems disordered among globally diverse norms, structures, and processes? Does legality suggest the universal availability of historically successful, although limited, transactional channels and mechanisms—so much so that legality's myriad forms and cultural instantiations can be both buried and fetishized under the universal rubric of the rule of law? Some authors, also writing from a critical position, talk about the cultures of legality through the term counter-law, emphasizing the illiberal use of law (Ericson 2007; Levi 2008). By using the phrase cultures of legality, authors call attention to the excess meanings that are being deployed for purposes and interests not limited to law or legality.

475

The unruly slippage in the language may derive as much from authors' normative commitments (wanting to both valorize different cultures yet identify common ground, to both relativize and normatively support) as well as from professional interests in carving distinct communities through terminological variation. Some of the linguistic variation may also indicate an attempt to differentiate studies of legal culture from research on legal attitudes and opinions that fail to theorize or attend to the aggregation or cultural system in which persons are participating (see Silbey 2005a).

4 *The structure of legality*: Finally, Ewick and Silbey (1998) describe a general pattern in legality, which they refer to as the structure of legality; they also suggest that the narrative and normative plurality characteristic of legality is apparent in other institutions and social structures (Ewick and Silbey 2002). Legal culture, or the schematic structure of legality, is a dialectic composed of general normative aspirations and particular grounded understandings of social relations. A general, ahistorical, truth (the objective rational organization of legal thought, disinterested decision-making) is constructed alongside, but as essentially incomparable to, particular and local practices (unequal quality of legal representation, the inaccessibility of bureaucratic agents, the violence of the police). The apparent incomparability of the general and the particular conceals the social organization linking the ideals of due process to diverse, uneven material practices, including unequal access and the mediating role of lawyers. Thus, legality becomes a place where processes are fair, decisions are reasoned, and the rules are known beforehand, at the same time as it is a place where justice is only partially achieved, if at all—where public defenders don't show up, sick old women cannot get disability benefits, judges act irrationally and with prejudice, and the haves come out ahead (Ewick and Silbey 1999).

Any singular account of legality, or the rule of law and the global spread of its rationality, for example, conceals the social organization of law by effacing the connections between the concrete particular and the transcendent general. Because legality has this complexity—among and within its several schema—legality can be a hegemonic structure of society, embracing the range of conventional experiences of law. Any particular experience or account can fit within the diversity of the whole. Rather than simply an idealized set of ambitions and hopes, in the face of human variation, agency, and interest, observation suggests, legality operates as both an ideal as well as a space of practical action. As a consequence, power and privilege can be preserved through what appears to be the irreconcilability of the particular and the general. Thus, this analysis of legal culture argues that instead of resting with one account, legality or legal culture should be understood in its plaited heterogeneity.

Further study of legal culture

Although one of the themes of this essay has been the unfortunate conceptual confusion that has accompanied the widespread use of the concept of legal culture, the research has been unusually generative. Promising avenues for further study have been suggested. First, a well-designed project might help to resolve continuing debates about the theoretical definition and modes of analysis of legal culture. An ambitious project of common data collection using a standard protocol developed for cultural analysis across national sites might help to systematically map cultures of legality, resolve inconsistencies in the current literature, and advance theory on the spread, support, or resistance to the rule of law. In other words, by adopting some of the sampling strategies of large comparative projects but deploying the close observation, in-depth interviewing, and discursive analysis of cultural studies, a comparative project might produce important theoretical as well as empirical advance.

Second, Maurer (2004) suggests that some of the confusion and theoretical exhaustion apparent in studies of legal culture might be addressed by adopting a conceptual innovation from social studies of science. Through close empirical inquiry, socio-legal scholars had discovered law everywhere, not only in courtrooms, prisons, and law offices, but in hospitals, bedrooms, schoolrooms, shops, and certainly in theaters, films, novels, as well as outer space (Silbey 1997). They also noted the places where law ought to be but is not. Similarly, "in *socializing* the natural facts with which scientific inquiry contends," Maurer (2004) worries that social studies of science may have come up against the same theoretical exhaustion, discovering more and more sociality in science just as law and society scholars discovered that "the law is all over" (Sarat 1990). However, science studies have a unique insight, which legal scholars are now only beginning to pick up (Valverde 2008). Social studies of science push against theoretical exhaustion and anthropocentric accounts of scientific culture by providing analyses of the "network of human and nonhuman agents that, together, push back against" the orthodoxy of social construction, and "in the process make their own moral—as well as material—claims known" (Maurer 2004: 848). Studies of legal culture need to do the same (Latour 2004).

Third and finally, Ewick and Silbey (2002) suggest that cultural analyses might provide avenues for studying long-term institutional and social change—a central question in sociology. If we observe cultural heterogeneity and contradiction in a variety of social institutions, is it possible that competing and contradictory accounts sustain those institutions as structures of social action? Is it possible that the alternative narratives not only create a protective covering that inures institutions against more systemic challenge, but that structures actually rely upon the articulation and polyvocality of each distinct narrative in order to exist? As a corollary, might the absence of that polyvocality, or what we might call significant imbalances in the narrative constitution of social structures, create vulnerability and increase the likelihood of structural transformation? If cultural analyses show that social structures rely on the contradictory rendering of experience for both legitimation and durability over time, it should be possible to trace the cultural ascendance of institutions and social structures such as law to the degree of contradiction they encompass. By taking a broad historical view, we should be able to trace the rise and fall of institutions to the sorts of stories people tell, or are enabled to tell by the availability of diverse, and sometimes contradictory, discursive referents or schemas.

References

Arendt, H. 1972. *Crisis of the Republic*. New York: Harcourt Brace Janovich.

Barzilai, G. 1997. "Between the Rule of Law and the Laws of the Ruler: The Supreme Court in Israeli Legal Culture." *International Social Science Journal* 49, 2(152): 143–50.

Benton, L. 2002. *Law and Colonial Cultures*. Cambridge: Cambridge University Press.

Bierbrauer, G. 1994. "Toward an Understanding of Legal Culture: Variations in Individualism and Collectivism between Kurds, Lebanese, and Germans." *Law and Society Review* 28(2): 243–64.

Blankenburg, E. 1994. "The Infrastructure of Legal Culture in Holland and West Germany." *Law and Society Review* 28(4): 789–809.

——. 1997. "Civil Litigation Rates as Indicators for Legal Cultures." Pp. 41–68 in D. Nelken ed., *Comparing Legal Cultures*. Brookfield, VT: Dartmouth Publishing Company.

Bracey, J.H. 2006. *Exploring Law and Culture*. Long Grove, IL: Waveland Press.

Chanock, M. 2001. *The Making of South African Legal Culture 1902–1936: Fear, Favour and Prejudice*. Cambridge: Cambridge University Press.

Comaroff, J. 2001. "Colonialism, Culture, and the Law: A Foreword." *Law and Social Inquiry* 25: 305–14.

Comaroff, J. and Comaroff, J. 2004. "Policing Culture, Cultural Policing: Law and Social Order in Postcolonial South Africa." *Law and Social Inquiry* 29: 513–45.

—, eds. 2006. *Law and Disorder in the Postcolony*. Chicago: University of Chicago Press.

Cooper, D. 1995. "Local Government Legal Consciousness in the Shadow of Juridification." *Journal of Law and Society* 22(4): 506–26.

Cotterrell, R. 1992 (1984). *The Sociology of Law: An Introduction*, second edition. London: Butterworth.

——. 1997. "The Concept of Legal Culture." Pp. 13–32 in D. Nelken ed., *Comparing Legal Cultures*. Brookfield, VT: Dartmouth Publishing Company.

——. 2006. *Law, Culture and Society*. Aldershot, UK: Ashgate Publishers.

Cowan, D. 2004. "Legal Consciousness: Some Observations." *Modern Law Review* 67(6): 928–58.

Eisenstein, J., Flemming, R.B., and Nardulli, P.F. 1988. *The Contours of Justice: Communities and Their Courts*. Boston: Little, Brown.

Ericson, R. 2007. *Crime in an Insecure World*. Cambridge: Polity.

Espeland, W. and Stevens, M. 1998. "Commensuration as a Social Process." *Annual Review of Sociology* 24: 313–43.

Ewick, P. 2006. *Consciousness and Ideology*. Aldershot, UK: Ashgate Publishers.

Ewick, P. and Silbey, S. 1998. *The Common Place of Law: Stories from Everyday Life*. Chicago: University of Chicago Press.

——. 1999. "Common Knowledge and Ideological Critique: The Importance of Knowing Why the 'Haves' Come Out Ahead." *Law & Society Review* 33(4): 1025–42.

——. 2002. "The Structure of Legality: The Cultural Contradictions of Social Institutions." Pp. 149–65 in Robert A. Kagan, Martin Krygier, and Kenneth Winston, eds., *Legality and Community: On the Intellectual Legacy of Philip Selznick*. Berkeley: University of California Press.

French, J.D. 1998. "Drowning in Laws but Starving (for Justice?): Brazilian Labor Law and the Workers' Quest to Realize the Imaginary." *Political Power and Social Theory* 12: 181–218.

Friedman, L.M. 1975. *The Legal System: A Social Science Perspective*. New York: Russell Sage Foundation.

——. 1985. *Total Justice*. Boston: Beacon Press.

——. 1997. "The Concept of Legal Culture: A Reply." Pp. 33–40 in D. Nelken ed., *Comparing Legal Cultures*. Brookfield, VT: Dartmouth Publishing Company.

Geertz, C. 1973. *The Interpretation of Cultures*. New York: Basic.

Gibson, J.L. and Caldeira, G.A. 1997. "The Legal Cultures of Europe." *Law and Society Review* 30(1): 55–85.

Gibson, J.L. and Gouws, A. 1997. "Support for the Rule of Law in the Emerging South African Democracy." *International Social Science Journal* 49, 2(152): 173–91.

Gordon, R.W. 1984. "Critical Legal Histories." *Stanford Law Review* 35: 57.

Hamilton, V.L. and Sanders, J. 1992. *Everyday Justice: Responsibility and the Individual in Japan and the United States*. London and New Haven, CT: Yale University Press.

Hertogh, M. 2004. "A 'European' Conception of Legal Consciousness: Rediscovering Eugen Ehrlich." *Journal of Law and Society* 31(4): 455–81.

Kawashima, T. 1963. "Dispute Resolution in Contemporary Japan." Pp. 41–72 in A. von Mehren ed., *Law in Japan*. Cambridge, MA: Harvard University Press.

Kidder, R.L. and Hostetler, J.A. 1990. "Managing Ideologies: Harmony as Ideology in Amish and Japanese Societies." *Law and Society Review* 24: 895–922.

Kritzer, H.M. and Zemans, F.K. 1993. "Local Legal Culture and the Control of Litigation." *Law and Society Review* 27(3): 535–57.

Latour, B. 2004. *La Fabrique du droit: Une Ethnographie du conseil d'état.* Paris: Editions Decouverte.

Levi, R. 2008. "Making Counter-Law: On Having No Apparent Purpose in Chicago." *British Journal of Criminology* 49: 131–49.

Maurer, B. 2004. "The Cultural Power of Law? Conjunctive Readings." *Law & Society Review* 38: 843–49.

Munger, F. and Seron, C. 1984. "Critical Legal Theory versus Critical Legal Method: A Comment on Method." *Law and Policy* 6: 257–99.

Nardulli, P.F., Eisenstein, J., and Flemming, R.B. 1988. *The Tenor of Justice: Criminal Courts and the Guilty Plea Process.* Urbana: University of Illinois Press.

Nelken, D. 1997a. "Puzzling Out Legal Culture: A Comment on Blankenburg." Pp. 69–92 in D. Nelken ed., *Comparing Legal Cultures.* Brookfield, VT: Dartmouth Publishing Company.

——. 1997b. *Comparing Legal Cultures.* Brookfield, VT: Dartmouth Publishing Company.

Pelisse, J. 2004. "From Negotiation to Implementation: A Study of the Reduction of Working Time in France (1998–2000)." *Time & Society* 13(2/3): 221–44.

Perin, C. 2005. *Shouldering Risks: The Culture of Control in the Nuclear Power Industry.* Princeton, NJ: Princeton University Press.

Rosen, L. 2006. *Law as Culture.* Princeton, NJ: Princeton University Press.

Sanders, J. and Hamilton, V.L. 1992. "Legal Cultures and Punishment Repertories in Japan, Russia, and the United States." *Law and Society Review* 26(1): 117–38.

Sarat, A. 1990. "' ... The Law Is All Over': Power, Resistance, and the Legal Consciousness of the Welfare Poor." *Yale Journal of Law and Humanities* 2(2): 343–79.

Sarat, A. and Kearns, T. 1993. "Beyond the Great Divide." Pp. 21–61 in A. Sarat and T. Kearns, eds., *Law in Everyday Life.* Ann Arbor: University of Michigan Press.

Scheingold, S.A. 1974. *The Politics of Rights: Lawyers, Public Policy, and Political Change.* New Haven, CT: Yale University Press.

Schutz, A. and Luchman, T. 1989 (1973). *The Structures of the Life-World.* Evanston, IL: Northwestern University Press.

Sewell, W.H. 2005. *Logics of History.* Chicago: University of Chicago Press.

Silbey, S.S. 1992. "Making a Place for Cultural Analyses of Law." *Law and Social Inquiry* 17(1): 39–48.

——. 1997. "Let Them Eat Cake: Globalization, Postmodern Colonialism, and the Possibilities of Justice." *Law & Society Review* 31(2): 207–35.

——. 1998. "Ideology, Justice, and Power." Pp. 272–308 in Bryant Garth and Austin Sarat, eds., *Justice and Power in Law and Society Research.* Evanston, IL: Northwestern University Press.

——. 2005a. "After Legal Consciousness." *Annual Review of Law and Social Science* 1: 323–68.

——. 2005b. "Everyday Life and the Constitution of Legality." In Marc Jacobs and Nancy Hanrahan, eds., *The Blackwell Companion to the Sociology of Culture.* Oxford: Blackwell Publishing.

——. 2009. "Taming Prometheus: Talk of Safety and Culture." *Annual Review of Sociology* 35: 341–69.

Swidler. 1986. "Culture and Action: Symbols and Strategies." *American Sociological Review* 51: 273–86.

Tanase, T. 1990. "The Management of Disputes: Automobile Accident Compensation in Japan." *Law and Society Review* 24: 651–91.

Tapp, J.L. and Kohlberg, L. 1971. "Developing Senses of Law and Legal Justice." *Journal of Social Issues* 27(2): 65–91.

Tapp, J.L. and Levine, F.L. 1974. "Legal Socialization: Strategies for an Ethical Legality." *Stanford Law Review* 27: 1–72.

Valverde, M. 2008. "The Ethic of Diversity: Local Law and the Negotiation of Urban Norms." *Law & Social Inquiry* 33(4): 895–923.

Part VIII

Political cultures

46

Making things political

Nina Eliasoph and Paul Lichterman

In this short essay we focus on the everyday situations in which people politicize or depoliticize issues. By "politicizing" we mean action, collective or individual, that makes issues or identities into topics of public deliberation or contestation. Depoliticizing means making once-salient issues or identities inaccessible to deliberation or contestation.

Until recently, political scientists and sociologists examining political culture have focused either on society-wide traditions or on consciousness. Research on society-wide traditions has emphasized the role of shared values or widespread discourses of the good citizen or good society (Almond and Verba 1963; Bellah *et al.* 1985). Studies of consciousness have emphasized propaganda, agenda-setting, or subtle media effects (Lukes 1974; Gaventa 1980; Hall 1977; see Gramsci 1971). Both approaches, at bottom, have assumed the conventional definition of power as A's ability to make B do something against B's will, or to prevent B from even thinking of alternatives.

Our definition of political culture, in contrast, is a communication-centered and setting-sensitive definition. Rather than conjure up a society's culture in general, we focus on situated communication. Rather than make individual or collective actors the subjects of politics, we focus on relationships and speech genres in settings that actors usually can recognize and "typify" already (Cicourel 1981), using their own understandings. While we could not possibly deny the horrific power of the media to convince people of half-truths, neither do we reduce political culture to ideological domination. Our research shows that people can express and think thoughts in one situation that they cannot easily express or even think in another. Similarly, we do not deny that a relatively few political and moral discourses may circulate widely in a society, but people in complex, diverse societies use them in too many different ways, in different settings, for the notion of shared traditions to be very useful for research purposes. The differences between two societies may very well be in how they distribute situations, how people learn what it is possible to say and do in a union versus a political party versus a charity group, or even in different kinds of political parties (Faucher-King 2005). Focusing on how people in various societies learn the proper etiquette for a political party versus a religious charity is different from asking how different societies create a certain kind of taken-for-granted consciousness in people. On this point our view differs also from some uses of Foucault's work which equate power with the creation of subjectivities, without talking about how the creation, maintenance, and transformation of identities vary from one situation to another.

Rather than assuming that some issues or groups are inherently more political than others, we call for examining how and where, if at all, people acting in concert make things political. We argue that before asking, "Who is wielding power over whom," researchers have to take a prior step, to ask how people, groups, or institutions politicize and depoliticize issues or people. Rather than reading off amounts of power from people's race, class, gender, or other social positions in the same way wherever the people go, and rather than assuming that these categories mean the same thing and weigh the same everywhere, we investigate how and where, if at all, inequalities are not just reproduced and transformed, but also formed in everyday interaction. We investigate how inequalities *materialize* differently in different everyday situations. That is why our approach to cultures of politics focuses on interaction in everyday situations, whether in institutions, formal organizations, or informal settings.

With our focus on interaction, we say that cultures of politics are shared methods of politicizing or depoliticizing. Like other cultural sociologists, we maintain a "strong" sense of culture as a relatively autonomous force in social life—symbolic patterns that cannot be explained away by relations of domination and subordination. We agree with cultural sociologists who say that symbols exert their own enabling and constraining influence on action. We depart from some cultural sociologists, however, when we follow culture's effects all the way down to the level of everyday interaction.

Shared methods of politicizing: elements of a cultural analysis

First, following Durkheim (Alexander 1988; Durkheim 1995 [1915]), we start by focusing on a society's "collective representations," though we do not suppose all members of a society share or affirm collective representations uniformly. By collective representations we mean conventional vocabularies or moral narratives that put people's motives into words and stories that others easily can apprehend. In interviews, in pamphlets and position statements, at pitched moments of conflict in groups, Americans tell each other that it is good to be active in community life because "I am doing God's work," or "We are giving back to the community," or "It feels good to help other people," or because "The people united will never be defeated." These are structured vocabularies of motive, moral languages we use to make our acts meaningful and compelling to others, as sociologists such as Robert Wuthnow (1992) would point out. To understand collective representations such as these, we look to Geertz (1973), Ricoeur (1991), Burke (1945), or Frye (1957) for models of culture's durability, its patterned qualities. As cultural sociologists, we start with these symbols. However, we do not end with them because the symbols sometimes absorb radically different meanings from the contexts in which people invoke them. The same words mean different things depending on who is saying them, to whom, in what situation. The differences are not simply random.

Discourses or representations become meaningful in specific settings, in relation to the organizational style of action that people share in the setting. An *organizational style* is members' routine ways of coordinating action and defining the meaning of membership in some collectivity, as the group is acting (Eliasoph and Lichterman 2003).

Organizational styles are enduring, often structure-like, cultural forms, not momentary improvisations. To find organizational style, a researcher can notice several broad areas of action and meaning-making. First, organizations draw *boundaries* around themselves on a wider social map; those boundaries bring "the organization" itself into being, defining what is "inside" or "outside" it. Second, organizations sustain *bonds* that define a set of good members' obligations to each other that may vary according to the category of person—a man's obligations versus a woman's, for example, or a volunteer's versus a paid staff member's. Third, organizations observe speech norms that define the meaning of speaking differently in different face-to-face situations within the overall organization— in the coffee room versus in the boardroom, for instance. The fact of organizational style implies that organizations cannot be reduced to an unpredictable flow of emergent definitions of the situation, as some symbolic interactionists (e.g. Blumer 1969) might argue. Rather, people quickly have to recognize what kind of meaning-making situation they have entered, or else everyone would be constantly learning from scratch how to act differently at school versus in a courtroom versus in a volunteer group. And finally, words, gestures, or images are not the only bearers of meaning. Important symbols solidify into material conditions, or what we call "equipment" (Thévenot 2006; Glaeser 2000)—architectural spaces, bureaucratic forms, furniture, zoning patterns, highways, for example, that are products of previous meaning-making, but are hard to ignore once they are built, even if they no longer bear the meanings that the original creators intended. Equipment helps materialize style in interaction.

In this short essay we will focus much more on organizational style than collective representations since style inflects representations in everyday interaction, and our concept of style makes our approach quite different from other approaches to political culture. The equipment is part of an organizational style, but we focus on the other aspects of the concept to highlight how our approach to meaning differs from others'. Readers interested in fuller treatments of our approach can consult other works (Eliasoph and Lichterman 2003; Lichterman 2005; Eliasoph 2010). Here we use ethnographic illustrations from our studies of church-based community service groups (Lichterman 2005) and youth civic engagement projects (Eliasoph 2010)—both in a mid-sized, Midwestern US urban area.

Politicizing is more than "sounding political"

Many studies have used the concept of "framing" to investigate political culture in social movements, civic organizations, and legislative assemblies (Snow *et al.* 1986). Originally used by Erving Goffman to denote the implicit assumptions about speech that operate in a particular setting, the concept often refers to the ideological theme or worldview said to motivate some instance of communication. This renovated frame concept is one popular means of studying collective representations. Organizational style helps us explain the successes or frustrations of politicizing, whereas the currently widespread notion of framing would not. The concept of organizational style also keeps us from assuming that "political"-sounding language must be a sign that only politicization and not also depoliticization is happening.

One example is the case of the Justice Task Force, a local group of liberal church representatives in a Midwestern US city who wanted to publicize the dangers of welfare policy reform in the 1990s. Members of the task force shared a vocabulary of social criticism familiar to many US grassroots progressives; they criticized corporate capitalism. Yet the way they communicated about corporate interests often scared away people who did not share their style, *even people who likely agreed with their viewpoints*. The Justice Task Force's communication style encouraged members to talk angrily whenever possible (speech norms), reject people who did not have the same intense commitment to left ideology (group bonds), and think of the group as lonely prophets poised against corporate power, complacent state officials, and false images circulated by the mass media (group boundaries).

The Justice Task Force put together educational workshops intended to teach churchgoers that welfare reform benefited the rich and the corporations at the expense of the poor. At one meeting, twelve members listened as one member delivered an hour-long, ideologically sophisticated critique of corporate neoliberalism. The host of a radical radio talk show came to the meeting, sat silently for a long time, and finally he told us in a rising voice that he represented "a race [African American] that doesn't live as long. ... There are lots of Blacks who don't care a lot about ideology." He thought the group should be able to "act on our faith underpinnings." And at last he blurted out, "We know who the number-one activist is, the one who risked everything—Jesus!" There was an awkward silence. No one else spoke up for Jesus. The radio announcer did not come back to another meeting. The Justice Task Force thought any association that was serious about welfare policy should be bound together by leftist solidarity, not faith in Jesus. They did not consider whether or not some African Americans would be more accustomed to and comfortable with a different *style* of group, with more religious bonds, in order to voice the same criticisms of welfare policy, and their response to the radio announcer in effect depoliticized racial identity. Customary ideas about what makes a good group kept the Justice Task Force small, marginal, and socially homogenous, unable to talk even with people who would agree with much of its collective representations of welfare reform "on paper." Their method of politicizing disempowered the message.

Another example, from the youth civic engagement projects in the same city, shows that how people do or do not politicize their actions can diverge remarkably from the image one would get if one only analyzed the representations or frames in their public statements. Part of the agenda for these projects was, at least in some organizers' minds, to make a connection between volunteering and political activism. Organizers spoke about not just feeding the hungry, for example, but of encouraging young people to ask, "Why is there hunger in such a wealthy country?" From the organizations' written statements, and from organizers' discussions, it would look like these projects were "politicizing" young people by framing issues in terms that would link social change with individual caring. Moral vocabularies of compassion and social justice lived together on paper and in organizers' discussions.

Yet, youth participants never actually did talk about why there was hunger in the US. One of the extremely rare moments of political controversy arose when a girl tried to flirt with a boy but got the organizational style wrong and also failed at flirting: her gambit was to get his attention by vehemently telling him that she was anti-abortion and pro-capital punishment. Acting as a typical member of the organization, the boy politely tried to avoid saying that he disagreed with her positions. Talking politics had to be out of place in these organizations if they were to be welcoming to all. Controversy would divide people, not bring them together. Although nearly all the organizers were vaguely liberal, they did not consider it fair to impose their ideas on young people, because they did not want to exclude any participants, even the anti-abortion, pro-capital punishment girl. The organizational style called for smoothing out differences—including political disagreements—in the name of inclusive group bonds, extremely permeable boundaries, and polite, upbeat speech.

Organizers encouraged their program members to attend County Board hearings, to testify that their programs deserved money. This may look like an unequivocal example of "politicizing," because youth participants were putting pressure on the state. But from our perspective, what is most interesting is the how—how this activity, which looks, from the outside, to be direct political activism, came to appear to youth as uncontroversial and apolitical. Every year of the study a new group of youth filled the programs, and each year's members thought that if they won they would get money instead of other county programs, such as those for old people or disabled babies. Every year, youth wondered if there would be a way for everyone to get what they needed, and every year adult organizers neglected to address this question. Every year the question quickly died, and a potentially political set of hearings became depoliticized when controversy was removed from the conversational docket.

Depoliticizing is more than social-structural domination

The adult organizers and funders of the Regional Youth Empowerment Project (YEP) hoped that volunteer work would bring diverse youth together, make them better citizens, and make them feel more like equals who could even help usher in a more egalitarian society. Even though participants were not equals in the rest of their lives, organizers hoped they could leave their unequal pasts behind when they joined hands together as volunteers. Organizers spoke in the language of can-do volunteering, another widespread civic vocabulary in American life (Eliasoph 1998; Lichterman 2006), and linked it to social critique. They often said that getting one's hands dirty, doing the work, walking the walk, would set participants on an equal footing in a volunteer group. So, talking about members' inequality was certainly taboo in the Regional YEP's monthly meetings and in the service projects that members planned and attended.

The inequality was unavoidably noticeable even to the casual observer. Most of the poor and minority youth who participated in the meetings of the civic engagement projects, which were in the evening, came to them from their afternoon, after-school "prevention programs." The non-poor, middle-class or affluent volunteers were almost all white, with only a very small handful of Latinos and Asians, and no Blacks, thus reflecting the overlap of racial and class inequality in the region at the time. Rather than coming as members of prevention programs, these volunteers came partly for the purpose of plumping up their CVs for college admission.

Creating this haven from inequality meant learning how to ignore the differences. Members could not talk about how they got there or why they perceived the same activities differently. Yet, organizers had to talk about youth participants as members of categories when communicating with important outsiders—the government agencies and big nonprofit organizations that funded them. Hybrid organizations (Hall 1992) like YEP are supposed to serve the needy, not just the privileged. Diversity helped justify the volunteer projects' existence, and, indeed, they were much more diverse than typically homogenous voluntary associations (Verba et al. 1995; Popielarz and McPherson 1995).

487

Typical voluntary associations create, in other words, one kind of social inequality; these "hybrid" (Hall 1992) projects created their own.

A purely social-structural analysis might ask if YEP projects "reproduced" inequality or cultivated "resistance" to oppression, to echo Michael Burawoy's (Burawoy *et al.* 1991) or Paul Willis's (1981) dichotomy. However, the sum of all these differences was not a simple reproduction of pre-existing inequality. YEP projects *created a specific kind* of inequality in everyday interaction, one that materializes in organizations when they bid participants speak as if they are equals when they know they are not. Minority youth participants knew where they stood partly because they had heard statistics about people like them—from organizers themselves who had to chase funding by publicizing how effective their programs would be in lowering the high drop-out rate for black teens. Organizers had to document that their programs helped minority youth defy the odds, statistically speaking, for crime, teen pregnancy, and drug abuse, for example. Organizers had to make sure that members' inequality was visible, literally, so it was always important in public events to put visibly non-white youth on the podium, while poor, rural white youths' presence was not as urgent. Youth participants inevitably overheard all this, yet most organizers considered it a mistake when a black thirteen-year-old who was asked to speak from personal experience recited statistics about the drop-out rates for black males in town, and described how it felt to be treated like someone who would fulfill that prediction. He breached the organizational style that encourages people to act as if they are socially equal and proscribes talk that puts people in (unequal) social categories.

Statistics can politicize or not, depending on who is using them, and for what ends—to denounce, as other black speakers did, or to document for fundraising purposes, as organizers did, or to describe the feeling of being treated as a failure waiting to happen, as the black boy did, for example. Whites and non-whites talked about statistics for different purposes, for different audiences, with different meanings, and different political implications. White organizers most often mustered statistics in grant applications to convince funders to fund the after-school and summer programs—a political, social project for the organizers, who wanted to improve the life chances of the low-income, minority youth in their programs. In contrast, non-white, especially African-American speakers, mustered statistics in emotionally powerful public speeches, for the purpose of raising consciousness among an audience of potential activists—a different kind of politicization.

The over-arching point here is that in organizations like these inequality feels different and has different effects than it has in an organization in which inequality happens in other ways—through separation of participants, rejection of participants, or outright stigmatizing of participants, for instance. Each of these different ways of creating inequality in organizations can lead people to different political ends, with potentially different political effects. Certainly class and racial inequality mattered in YEP projects and structured the experiences of participants. At the same time, organizational styles politicized and depoliticized inequality in patterned ways that we could not simply read off from the class and race positions of YEP organizers and volunteers.

Even if class and race inequalities by themselves do not offer a complete guide to power relations, can't we assume that differences between ordinary citizens and state agencies translate reliably into a story of power and domination? What can a focus on "cultures of politics" teach us regarding this kind of structural inequality? It shows that elements of organizational style—in this case group boundary-drawing—can have unintended depoliticizing consequences even apart from what external, state entities force groups to do or avoid doing.

Two other congregation-based community service alliances will illustrate our point. In the first case, members of the Humane Response Alliance (HRA) *assumed* from the beginning that their association was an adjunct to the state and would work inside the categories of state policy. As one of HRA's leaders said, the group needed to find a role within policies "set by the local government." No one pressed the issue further.

Of course churchgoers could not simply offer their own social services and usurp government authority without consequences. Yet they did not need to define themselves so strongly in terms of the state's own categories, especially in the US context, in which people assume that citizens are free to organize civic efforts apart from state mandates. They did not have to propose doing the state welfare service's job in order to come up with some other role beyond that "set by the local government," and one state employee came up with just such a role. He suggested that the HRA organize forums that would enable people newly cut off from financial assistance to speak directly to state agents and describe their troubles. In our terms, the state employee was suggesting that HRA help people *politicize* welfare reform in new ways, while HRA leaders already had *depoliticized* welfare reform—removing it as a potential object of deliberation or contention. To find power working inside the HRA's own style, its own definition of its boundaries and relationships, is a more nuanced, useful story of power relations than to say, as some critical observers might (McKnight 1995; Habermas 1975), that "the state colonized the HRA."

In the other example—an evangelical-sponsored support program for former welfare-receiving families—many volunteers considered the program nonpolitical, even though the program director conceived the program as a church-based complement to welfare reform. It would be easy for a researcher to assume the volunteers enlisted in this "Adopt-a-Family" program because they were ideologically or politically invested in welfare reform. Some researchers would assume, on the contrary, that our job would be to show how ideologically manipulated these volunteers were.

Both approaches would impute silent motives to people by fiat, and neither attends to the volunteers' own ways of distinguishing "political" from "not political," so neither can offer much help in understanding how ordinary citizens make sense of policy agendas. Many of these volunteers were strikingly indifferent to the various political ideologies surrounding welfare policy. They sounded neither supportive nor critical of welfare reform; it was not very salient to them one way or the other. They articulated their motives much more in terms of an evangelical Protestant-inflected version of compassion. They said that volunteering for this program was a way to perform "Christ-like care." They enacted Christ-like care in a very particular style; they imagined themselves and their adopted families acting in a pure world of caring and gratitude beyond the realm of politics altogether. They saw Adopt-a-Family as one service opportunity among others their pastor told them about, and not an opportunity to step into history and take a stance on the enormous change in the social contract, as many social scientists might view the program. Attributing ideological or political motives to these volunteers would have produced a very distorted picture of their participation. The volunteers' own ways of politicizing or depoliticizing welfare reform became clear only from following their own communication and their own relationship-building in the program.

Cultures of politics in global perspective

Given our attention to how people draw lines between political and nonpolitical, our approach is especially useful for understanding "politics" in places where an already sedimented political culture does not define some relationships and forms of speech as "politics" *a priori*. In Albania, for example (Sampson 1996), or Uzbekistan (Makarova 1998), figuring out what to count as "politics" is not easy for the analyst, much less the actors. Would an Islamic gathering place in Uzbekistan—a *mahalla*—that plans funerals, doles out something that looks to a Westerner like social welfare, and builds schools be a "political" entity, making political decisions? Asserting that it is or is not "political" is not as interesting as saying *how* it becomes political, how issues or identities become topics of public deliberation or silencing, and how the process of politicizing creates and recreates the typical *mahalla* in Uzbekistan. When squatters in India siphon water from the city's water mains without paying, is it more "political" if they do it visibly to make a public statement, or if they make under-the-table deals with local politicians, or if they simply take what they consider to be rightfully theirs (Chatterjee 2004)? Along with many scholars in the "post-colonial studies" tradition, we argue that they might all be "political" in different ways that highlight different aspects of the issue, shape different arguments and, eventually, different outcomes.

In Brazil, on the other hand, we find the opposite situation: a crammed-full public sphere, with profuse and big distinctions between positions. Members of youth activist organizations in Brazil carry different, practical definitions of a good member and a good group (Mische 2008). Depending on the organization, good members are ones who plot and argue, or value harmonious, consensus-building members, or prize rational deliberation. Argument, feelings, and rational discourse characterize all of these organizations to some extent, but groups vary widely in whether they put these different kinds of communication front-stage or back-stage. As Mische argues, newcomers can recognize one of these group styles by observing how members push some feelings, ideas, and relationships off the horizon here, but spotlight them there. Once again, politicization is more than sounding political. The variety of styles cannot be placed on a single spectrum of more or less politicization by group; rather, they represent different definitions-in-practice of "politics."

Conclusion: qualities of political engagement in everyday interaction

Our interaction-centered approach to cultures of politics differs from prominent alternatives of the past twenty-five years. Older approaches have ignored differences in setting and reduced political culture to dominant ideology that social elites use consciously to manipulate subordinates completely (Ewen 1976; Lasch 1979). A more nuanced version of this argument holds that people carry dominant ideologies ambivalently, and sometimes contest domination. In Stuart Hall's example, a working-class person who is watching the national news on TV hears "the national interest" and decodes that message as "the interest of the ruling elite," but may identify partially with the ruling elite's interest too because it seems so commonsensical. In contrast, a member of the ruling elite assumes what the newscaster assumed when writing the piece, which is that the national interest is the same as his or her own interest. Hall's Gramscian approach improves greatly on the "dominant ideology" approach, but still ignores settings and assumes that the listener's social background is all we really need to know. Political culture is, for these analysts, a process of either accepting or resisting dominant ideology, albeit ambivalently, a lot of the time.

Pierre Bourdieu's sociology of political culture (Bourdieu 1984) advances a step by not reducing political culture to class. In his framework, different groups—which themselves result from struggles to define collective identities—compete to politicize or depoliticize issues. For him, different political languages are more or less prestigious and convincing depending on the prestige and skills of the group that uses them. In Bourdieu's approach, then, interaction serves largely to reproduce inequalities in power between actors competing in grossly slanted fields. "Field" is a concept that seems, at first glance, to resemble our notion of setting. Bourdieu says that he treats fields as games, within which different moves have different meanings: what is deemed worthy for fine, museum art, for example, is not considered worthy for cool graffiti-inspired art. But in most of his work, hierarchical power struggles appear in the end to be the only really important game; after his earlier ethnographic studies (Bourdieu 1977) he rarely got close enough to the ground to see how people create fields and make moves in them, in everyday interaction. Settings and styles reduce to hierarchical positions.

Our examples show, in contrast to these two approaches, that it is difficult to describe actual instances of politicizing and depoliticizing completely in terms of domination, resistance, or relative group position. Methods of politicizing and depoliticizing are more situation-specific, more a product of organizational style, than these other approaches presume. We do not argue that people all have the same chances to politicize issues. Rather, our focus on cultures of politics helps us ask how and when people decide they are doing something "political," instead of defining individuals, organizations, or issues as political, powerful, or not powerful by scholarly fiat. Instead of being absolutely certain about which inequalities matter where, or which side should win, a focus on cultures of politics asks how people learn to create situations that politicize or depoliticize issues. Of course, sometimes it seems obvious to any fair or good-willed person which side should win, but how they play the game also matters.

References

Alexander, Jeffrey. 1988. *Durkheimian Sociology: Cultural Studies*. Berkeley: University of California Press.

Almond, G.A. and Verba, S. 1963. *The Civic Culture: Political Attitudes and Democracy in Five Nations*. Princeton, NJ: Princeton University Press.

Bellah, R.N., Madsen, Richard, Sullivan, William, Swidler, Ann, and Tipton, Steven. 1985. *Habits of the Heart: Individualism and Commitment in American Life*. Berkeley: University of California Press.

Blumer, Herbert. 1969. *Symbolic Interactionism: Perspective and Method*. Englewood Cliffs, NJ: Prentice-Hall.

Bonilla-Silva, Eduardo. 2002. "The Linguistics of Color-Blind Racism: How to Talk Nasty about Blacks Without Sounding 'Racist.'" *Critical Sociology* 28(1–2): 1–24.

Bonilla-Silva, Eduardo and Forman, Tyrone. 2000. "'I'm Not a Racist, but … Mapping White College Students' Racial Ideology in the USA." *Discourse and Society* 11(1): 50–85.

Bourdieu, Pierre. 1977. *Outline of a Theory of Practice*, trans. R. Nice. Cambridge: Cambridge University Press.

——. 1984. *Distinction: A Social Critique of the Judgment of Taste*, trans. R. Nice. Cambridge, MA: Harvard University Press.

Burawoy, Michael, *et al.* 1991. *Ethnography Unbound: Power and Resistance in the Modern Metropolis.* Berkeley: University of California Press.

Burke, Kenneth. 1945. *A Grammar of Motives.* New York: Prentice Hall.

Chatterjee, Partha. 2004. *The Politics of the Governed: Reflections on Popular Politics in Most of the World.* New York: Columbia University Press.

Cicourel, A.V. 1981. "Notes on the Integration of Micro- and Macro-Levels of Analysis." Pp. 51–80 in Karin Knorr-Cetina and Aaron Cicourel, eds., *Advances in Social Theory and Methodology.* London: Routledge and Kegan Paul.

Durkheim, Emile. 1995 (1915). *The Elementary Forms of Religious Life*, trans. K.E. Fields. New York: Free Press.

Eliasoph, N. 1998. *Avoiding Politics: How Americans Produce Apathy in Everyday Life.* Cambridge: Cambridge University Press.

——. 2010. *Making Volunteers: How Nonprofits are Transforming Intimacy and Civic Life after Welfare's End.* Princeton, NJ: Princeton University Press.

Eliasoph, N. and Lichterman, P. 2003. "Culture in Interaction." *American Journal of Sociology* 108(4): 735–94.

Ewen, Stuart. 1976. *Captain of Consciousness: Advertising and the Social Roots of the Consumer Culture.* New York: McGraw-Hill.

Faucher-King, Florence. 2005. *Changing Parties: An Anthropology of British Political Party Conferences.* New York: Palgrave Macmillan.

Frye, Northrop. 1957. *Anatomy of Criticism: Four Essays.* Princeton, NJ: Princeton University Press.

Gaventa, John. 1980. *Power and Powerlessness: Quiescence and Rebellion in an Appalachian Valley.* Chicago: University of Chicago Press.

Geertz, Clifford. 1973. *The Interpretation of Cultures: Selected Essays.* New York: Basic Books.

Glaeser, Andreas. 2000. *Divided in Unity: Identity, Germany and the Berlin Police.* Chicago: University of Chicago Press.

Gramsci, Antonio. 1971. *Selections from the Prison Notebooks*, trans. Q. Hoare and G. Smith. New York: International Publishers.

Habermas, Jürgen. 1975. *Legitimation Crisis.* Boston: Beacon Press.

Hall, Peter. 1992. *Inventing the Nonprofit Sector and Other Essays on Philanthropy, Voluntarism, and Nonprofit Organizations.* Baltimore, MD: Johns Hopkins University Press.

Hall, Stuart. 1977. "Culture, the Media and the Ideological Effect." In J. Curran, M. Gurevitch and J. Woollacott, eds., *Mass Communication and Society.* London: Edward Arnold.

Lasch, Christopher. 1979. *Culture of Narcissism.* New York: Warner Books.

Lichterman, Paul. 2005. *Elusive Togetherness: Church Groups Trying to Bridge America's Divisions.* Princeton, NJ: Princeton University Press.

——. 2006. "Social Capital or Group Style? Rescuing Tocqueville's Insights on Civic Engagement." *Theory and Society* 35(5/6): 529–63.

Lukes, Steven. 1974. *Power: A Radical View.* London and New York: Macmillan.

Makarova, Ekatarina. 1998. "The Mahalla, Civil Society, and the Domestication of the State in Uzbekistan." Paper presented at the annual conference of the Association for the Study of Nationalities, New York, April.

McKnight, John. 1995. *Careless Society: Community and Its Counterfeits.* New York: Basic Books.

Mische, Ann. 2008. *Partisan Publics.* Princeton, NJ: Princeton University Press.

Popielarz, P.A. and McPherson, J.M. 1995. "On the Edge or in Between: Niche Position, Niche Overlap, and the Duration of Voluntary Association Memberships." *American Journal of Sociology* 101(3): 698–720.

Ricoeur, Paul. 1991. "Life: A Story in Search of a Narrator." In Mario J. Valdés, ed., *Reflection and Imagination: A Paul Ricœur Reader.* Toronto: University of Toronto Press.

Sampson, Steven. 1996. "The Social Life of Projects: Importing Civil Society to Albania. Pp. 127–42 in Chris Hann and Elizabeth Dunn, eds., *Civil Society: Challenging Western Models.* New York and London: Routledge.

Snow, D.A., Rocheford, E. Burke, Worden, Steven K., and Benford, Robert D.. 1986. "Frame Alignment Processes, Micromobilization, and Movement Participation." *American Sociological Review* 51(4): 464–81.

Thévenot, Laurent. 2006. *L'Action au pluriel: sociologie des régimes d'engagement*. Paris: La Découverte.

Verba, Sidney, Schlozmann, Kay, and Brady, Henry. 1995. *Voice and Equality: Civic Voluntarism in American Politics*. Cambridge, MA: Harvard University Press.

Willis, Paul. 1981. *Learning to Labor: How Working Class Kids Get Working Class Jobs*. New York: Columbia University Press.

Wuthnow, Robert, ed. 1992. *Vocabularies of Public Life: Empirical Essays in Symbolic Structure*. New York: Routledge.

47

The cultural constitution of publics

Yifat Gutman and Jeffrey C. Goldfarb

The public sphere, or, as we prefer, the sphere of publics (Calhoun 1997: 100), appears as a structure of a particular place and time. As a fundamental support in the making of democracy, both historically and in contemporary polities, it has spread and developed, and has become multiple and global. To understand these propositions, we must remember that publics appear metaphorically as structures. They are given their structural appearance through regularized patterns of social interaction. They are culturally constituted in human interaction. Publics form as people meet as equals in their differences, and develop together a capacity to act among themselves and with other publics. Democracy is created in the interactive life of publics.

To substantiate this position, we will review the changing history of publics and the different theoretical approaches to the subject. We will analyze the cultural constitution of publics. *We will move from the analysis of the structural transformation of the public sphere toward the analysis of the making of publics and spheres of publics.* We will also move from a consideration of the public as a specific site for rational deliberation toward the analysis of other key cultural forms of public action: appearance, display, embodiment, contestation, competition, and other forms of political participation. As we proceed, the normative dimension of publics and their study will be addressed.

Habermas's public sphere

One of the starting points in contemporary discussions of publics is Jürgen Habermas's *The Structural Transformation of the Public Sphere* (1989). Habermas identified a distinctively modern development, the emergence of the autonomous public sphere in discursive gatherings and communication via the print media of bourgeois men in late-seventeenth- and eighteenth-century Europe. He saw that this sphere was one of the central structures of the modern order, along with the modern economy (capitalism) and the modern state. The participants in this sphere, according to Habermas, read, wrote, and discussed matters of state and economy in coffee shops and salons, at a distance from the public institutions of the state (1989: 23, 25, 27, 106). Engaged in rational communicative action, suspending their individual interests, these men were able to reach a consensual understanding about the common good (Habermas 1984: 328–30). Their free (from the state as well as self-interest) rational debate led them to knowledge that balanced and limited state power (Habermas 1989: 54–56).

Habermas's approach to this public sphere contains a radical change from the classical Greek notion of the public sphere. In the Greek polis, freedom was public—the realm of autonomous citizens which is free from the necessity that characterizes the private household. By contrast, in the public sphere, Habermas observes, individuals become capable of public action in their homes, and freedom is found in the private realm, or at least the unofficial space, separated from the state and protected from its authority (Calhoun 1993: 6–7; Habermas 1989: 50–52). Habermas's public sphere "appropriates" the classical concept of participation in the polis and applies it to complex modern societies with differentiated spheres of the economy, law, family, culture, and politics. Seyla Benhabib, developing the implications of Habermas's approach, has mapped out the substantial consequences, not fully specified by Habermas. In modern societies, participation is widened to other spheres of life, and is made possible by the formation of a discursive will (Benhabib 1993: 86). According to this conceptualization, residents' initiatives to create a more sustainable urban environment are considered political participation, and so are families' protests against the plans to rebuild Ground Zero (Gutman 2009). According to Benhabib, participation, for Habermas, emphasizes the practical debate among those who are affected by general norms and decisions. Emphasizing practical debate allows or even assumes various publics and debates, even as many publics as there are debates (Benhabib 1993: 86–87). Considering multiple publics, then, grows out of Habermas's approach.

Arendt's public domain

Hannah Arendt—most extensively in her *The Human Condition* (1998 [1958])—presents a different, but related, way of considering the problem of the public domain in modern societies in light of ancient Greek experience. Her position, although not as directly recognizing the special modern circumstance and structure of modern public life, explicitly opens up the analysis to publics (in the plural) and to cultural activities beyond rational discourse. Using the Athenian polis as the definitive public space, she describes the public as the space of appearances. In the public domain, people meet as equals, according to Arendt, in their differences. In public, they see, hear, and talk to others and in the process initiate action, bringing something new into the world. In this way, they form their individual identities and realize the power of the public—the power of people acting in concert—political power, as the opposite of coercion (Arendt 1998: 57).

Arendt's approach opens the analysis of public life to a broad array of cultural actions and representations. How we appear, how arguments are embodied, visual grace and power, and much more are all part of public life and are central to the primary political ideal of freedom. Unlike Habermas, Arendt insists upon the Greek connection between freedom and the public sphere, asserting that individuals interacting in public are free from the necessity of the private home, which includes the social and economic. They reach informed opinion, not truth, by viewing a matter from the many different perspectives of individuals in different social positions (Arendt 1998: 57). Such communicative and discursive acts in public are for Arendt synonymous with the political—the ongoing activity of citizens coming together so as to exercise their capacity for action and to conduct their lives together by means of free speech (broadly understood, beyond rational discourse), appearance, and persuasion (Arendt 1998: 26, 179; Benhabib 1993: 78). Publics are the very center of politics and its primary ideal. Arendt's distinctive political theory suggests a complementary normative approach to that of Habermas, something which he recognized (Habermas 1977). Social theorists and historians have been exploring such complementarity in their critiques of Habermas's seminal approach.

The bourgeois public sphere: theoretical and historical revisions

While Habermas has pushed his argument for the rational-critical nature of the discursive interaction in the public sphere in his later work on communicative action and the "ideal speech situation" (Habermas 1990), he has received critical responses from scholars who searched for a broader notion of public debate. While he has worked for a more philosophically sound basis for public life as rational discourse, many critics suggest moving in a different direction, pointing toward a new and more culturally inflected approach to the study of publics that meets with Arendt's position.

They start from the position that rational judgment as the single model for discursive interaction in the public sphere is problematic. Centrally, it underplays the importance of other forms of communicative action such as rhetoric and play, and by so doing limits public participation and debate. By emphasizing and prioritizing rational-critical debate, Habermas problematically theorizes a binary opposition between information/informed publics and entertainment/uninformed publics that excludes many people from participation. Put bluntly, it conceptualizes participation in the public sphere as limited to those with advanced graduate degrees, whereas realistically a democratic public life includes a broad array of persuasion.

Moreover, Habermas's conception of the public sphere does not do justice to what is most interesting and significant about publics—social movements operating in ways that challenge the codes of social orders. They publicly and culturally enact alternative commitments through their very appearance on the public stage (as Arendt would emphasize) and in their performances, once they appear (see Touraine 1981; Melluci 1989). This is true especially for movements that reveal the normative hierarchies hidden behind the "rational." For these groups, which are often discriminated against by the "neutral" and commonsensical, by what appears to be the rational, the over-rationalized public sphere is a principal example of the problematic social relations that they fight to change and disrupt (Warner 2005: 54).

The consensual mutual understanding that is the goal of Habermas's critical-rational public debate is confronted by the notion of counterpublics—publics that are defined by conflict and tension with the larger or dominant public (Warner 2005: 56). It is also confronted by competing public spheres, such as the routes constructed by North American women in the nineteenth century, as contemporaries of the bourgeois public sphere (Ryan 1993: 272–73; see also Eley 1993: 330–31).

Ironically, the very universal rationality that is supposed to keep the public sphere accessible to all humans, suspending hierarchies of status, class, and gender, has been deployed as a strategy of exclusion (Fraser 1993: 115). According to revisionist historiographers, from its very beginning this rationality was part of an ethos and practice that marked the distinction of the bourgeois class from other, competing classes and publics (Eley 1993: 297–306; Ryan 1993: 272–73; Landes 1998: 89; Fraser 1993: 114). This observation suggests the existence, from the start, of a sphere of competing publics, sometimes in conflict, with different degrees of power. The very idea of a single public sphere has been criticized for conceptually excluding, or at least limiting, the participation of marginal groups, and thus opposing the ideal of full participatory equality. According to Fraser, the problem of the public sphere conceptualized as a singularity stems, first, from the impossibility of isolating the public sphere from its social context of inequalities, and, second, from the tendency of the deliberative process to benefit dominant groups, whose cultural expression of ethos and rhetoric lenses are central to it even in the absence of formal exclusions (Fraser 1993: 122–28).

How should we revisit the bourgeois public sphere today in light of these critiques? The bourgeois public sphere can be viewed as a moment in an extended "chain" of partial or "damaged" but real discursive public spheres (Warner 2005: 50–51). Another moment with even greater potential is the current one of modern social movements. These movements can be seen as operating in the same "public sphere environment" that Habermas drew or even emerging from that context, while they make right the faults of the bourgeois public sphere (Warner 2005: 50–51, 56; Lee 1993: 407).

Furthermore, the existence of multiple publics and counterpublics demonstrates that the sphere of publics is not just a stage for representation and discussion of the interests of the group, but also an important space for the formation, shaping, and reinforcement of identities, which can reopen Habermas's division between public and private, undo the hierarchical dichotomy between the problems of equality (private) and freedom (public), and enable connections between the two (Warner 2005: 57; Calhoun 1997: 82, 86; Benhabib 1993: 89–90).

Social interaction and the formation of publics

Habermas's critics help establish publics as plural and culturally constituted, yet attention should also be paid to publics in their formation and actions. To investigate them requires the sort of philosophical and macro sociological approaches reviewed above (pp. 494–97), but it also requires that we look more closely at the details of social interaction and its cultural fabric.

Erving Goffman has studied this dimension of publics and their constitution systematically. Appearance, meeting and speaking to each other, significant gestures, and the like are common concerns of Arendt and Goffman, though they address these concerns from radically different intellectual traditions. Goffman's sociology is focused phenomenologically on the life of the public as Arendt understands it. Goffman sociologically analyzes the social texture of what people do when they meet and act in each others' presence. People perform and constitute their selves and their situations. They communicate with one another not only through speech acts but through gestures, and they engage in interaction rituals (Goffman 1971: x; 1967: 77). These activities enact the social order, but also can yield an alternative order of social institutions, the under-life of the social order, since even large institutions are made of interacting individuals. Usually individuals conform to social rules and norms, but not always. In studies of prisons and asylums, where patients and prisoners are locked in, Goffman illuminates acts of resisting and breaking the rules (1967: 48–49). From our point of view, this analysis points in the direction of the creation of alternative public spaces, not only in distinct and independent frameworks of regularized interaction, i.e. alternative institutions and movements, but also beyond the reach of command in formal institutions of many different sorts (this point is discussed systematically in Goldfarb 2006a, which develops a theory of "the politics of small things," built upon a synthesis of Goffman and Arendt's theories of public life).

The attention of Habermas and Arendt was focused on official public space, but in fact social movements and the under-life of social institutions are no less important for ongoing publics. This becomes apparent in an interactionist perspective.

Goffman researched public life in the most peculiar of circumstances, total institutions. But its very peculiarity, an extreme space where free interaction is the most constrained, stands as compelling evidence that public life is a general aspect of organizational life. In Goffman's analysis of total institutions, he recognizes the complexity of the politics of public interaction in a way that is implicit in much of his work but never really fully developed. He in this way presents central insights into the cultural constitution of publics.

Total institutions are places that radically disrupt a definitive characteristic of modern societies—social differentiation. In the modern order, people in different social positions do different things, at different times, with different people. How we present ourselves to others changes when we are at home, at work, at a place of worship, in a political institution, and so forth. We interactively give definition to each of these situations as we present and define ourselves in them, and we tend to keep these social definitions of self and situation separate. Total institutions—from asylums to boarding schools, to military organizations to prisons—break the separation. They process unified definitions of self that break down modern complexities. But in the conclusion of his study of the under-life of total institutions, Goffman highlights interesting limits to this process, and comes to a telling observation, illuminating what we might call the sociological setting of public-making capacity:

> Without something to belong to, we have no stable self, and yet total commitment and attachment to any social unit implies a kind of selflessness. Our sense of being a person can come from being drawn into a wider social unit; our sense of selfhood can arise through the little ways in which we resist the pull. Our status is backed by the solid buildings of the world, while our sense of personal identity often resides in the cracks.
>
> (Goffman 1961: 320)

With the solid buildings at our backs, we have the support to present ourselves in everyday life and create our persona for ourselves and for others. In the cracks, we constitute our distinctive identities. In these cracks, publics are born. Alternative presentations and definitions of self and situation are developed.

Public interaction of the sort that Arendt had in mind is built into the modern institutional structure. This has been especially true in the formation of publics associated with modern social movements. Social movements are directed against some aspect of the institutional order. They often emerge from cracks in the order, but they create places where people meet and discuss, appear, and reveal who they are and how they can act together. This is characteristic of new social movements generally, e.g. the feminist movement, the civil rights movement, the green movement, the antiwar movement, and much more. Each is about specific ends, but, just as important, each is about exploring in the emerging publics who the participants are as individuals and as groups—as a woman and with other women, as an African American with other African Americans (Melluci 1989). There are patterns of deference and demeanor that define what it means to be a woman (Goffman 1956), but emerging from those patterns women define themselves not only within institutionalized patterns but also against them. As women do so together, an alternative public is formed, supporting alternative politics, emerging in everyday interaction, developing in social movements (see Duplessis and Snitow 1998). And as the publics form, as the movements' members speak and act in each others' presence, committed to their freedom, their autonomous action (Arendt's definition of public freedom), they develop a capacity to act in concert (Arendt's definition of political power). They then address not only each other, but also those outside their immediate circle, i.e. other publics and a more general sphere of publics. In this way, interacting individuals develop publics and political power, as John Dewey outlined in his opening pages of *The Public and Its Problems* (Dewey 1954).

Media and the cultural constitution of publics and the sphere of publics

No approach to the question of publics, particularly one that is centered on social interaction and cultural constitution, can avoid the analysis of media. Indeed it is notable that casual and unreflective analysis of media leads to major mistakes in the evaluation of publics and their problems. This is most evident in Habermas's seminal study *The Structural Transformation of the Public Sphere* (1989). The development of media forms— from public life centered on the spoken word to one that is centered on the interaction between the spoken and the written—is a key part of his analysis. But when it comes to listening and watching through the electronic media, Habermas abandons objective analysis, and sees a determined decline. Rationality is not possible. Commodity exchange prevails over intellectual exchange. Years later, he revised this determinist position, but that he made it is indicative of not systematically considering the relationship between media and publics (Habermas 1982).

In the place of face-to-face interaction, electronic media usually facilitate virtual or no interaction, and instead offer visibility (Dayan 2005). If print media operate along a linear timeline—writing, reading, and talking are lined up in time—electronic media operate in space, as all the information is displayed immediately and simultaneously, often visually. These inverted features influence the capacities of media to facilitate publics and public debate. Electronic media bring people together for discussion, as print media have done in the past, but they also offer types of interaction and appearance that were not available before. These developments have a significant effect on the constitution of new publics.

Two views prevail. There is the view that Habermas assumed in his masterwork and revised later on: the electronic media give an illusion of democracy but in fact legitimate the reproduction of a social system of inequalities (the state, the capitalist market). TV "amuses us to death" (Postman 1986), "manufacturing consent" (Chomsky 1989), and creating a society of spectacles and simulations (Debord 1994; Baudrillard 1988). These critiques highlight how the present media regime substitutes entertainment for enlightenment, or at least confuses the two, owned as it is by the corporate elite, serving its interests, distancing people from their immediate circumstances, making illusions seem more real, or at least as real, as perceptions and human experiences. On the other hand, electronic media continue to make publics and to constitute alternative ones, e.g. the aforementioned social movements—the women's and civil rights movements—and their publics. Most spectacularly recently, there are the movement and publics created by the Obama political campaign (Goldfarb 2009). The media have facilitated all of these developments, even more than they have undermined them.

Walter Benjamin (1998 [1936]) and Marshall McLuhan (1964) are classical thinkers who revealed this media potential. They understood the shift of media forms as opening new possibilities for democratic debates within and among publics, as well as between different media forms. Electronic media have not replaced print media, but enjoined them. In McLuhan's seminal work "The Medium Is the Message" (McLuhan 1964), media are viewed first and foremost as transformative forces that not only extend our senses and knowledge, but also introduce new scales and paces that bring new patterns of social relations. Walter Benjamin revealed the political potential that underlies the new visual media in "The Work of Art in the Age of Mechanical Reproduction" (Benjamin 1998 [1936]). He described new media technologies as enabling people to gain a more realistic understanding of their social life and to introduce a new scope of collective action (Benjamin 1998: 237–38). This was an expansion of the political potential found in appearance as Arendt studied the matter.

While spectacle and the eclipse of the public are certainly one side of the electronic media coin, the other side is new forms of participation. John Dewey highlighted the critical point: "Vision is a spectator. Hearing is a participator." He insisted that even if the press (and radio, film, and television, we should add) provides partial information, this is not the basis of democracy. The conversation of local publics and communities is what gives public opinion reality (Dewey 1954: 219). The message of the media is defined by the interactive communities that live with them. Daniel Dayan and Elihu Katz beautifully develop this point in *Media Events* (1992), showing how the centered publics of nation-states engage in rituals of public confirmation through a certain type of media presentation. Breaking the rhythms of television presentation and flow, the same sorts of rituals associated with transfers of power, celebration of collective values, and political authority that existed before television now are enacted through television. It is done differently and involves conflicts and competition over visibility in addition to unity and public deliberation (think of presidential campaigns and inaugurations), but it is not fundamentally different. This is the case not only in the central publics associated with national television, but also in the formation and development of multiple publics and counterpublics—strikingly, through the internet.

The internet enables publics to communicate without face-to-face interaction. The locality of publics and communities transcends countries and continents. This is a new form of interaction that accommodates kinds of debates and of publics that were not available or possible before. The antiwar movement and the Dean Campaign formed alternative publics capable of action that seriously challenged the previously existing consensus in favor of the Bush administration's policies concerning the war in Iraq and the global war against terrorism. Their discussions and mobilizations online formed an alternative public sphere and the grounds for critical action that turned the position of the Democratic Party and eventually the larger American public (Goldfarb 2006a, 2006b). Although John Kerry lost the election of 2004, the alternative publics that developed during his campaign were a significant result of the campaign. Text messaging also has become a popular means of public formation and political mobilization: most famously, it helped to bond citizens in the Orange Revolution in the Ukraine in 2004 and to gather hundreds of students in downtown Seoul in 2005. Even publics that conduct their activities in local spaces to promote a public issue—such as in the case of non-profit associations in Israel today—use the internet not just to arrange their gatherings but to interact among themselves and with other publics, in the nation-state and abroad (Gutman forthcoming).

Conclusion

The political potential of visual and electronic media to facilitate public debates and mediate publics brings us back to the central argument of this essay. Arendt's political realm of appearance extends and complements Habermas's notion of the deliberative public sphere. In the midst of the electronically mediated new sphere of publics are performance, visibility, and interaction. These practices of publics maintain the ideal of a deliberative public sphere, as Habermas first described it, in an age of new media and global circulation of powers, people, and ideas. The deliberative ideal is grounded in empirical reality and new media forms.

There is also and crucially a normative side. Publics have a normative edge and the investigations of publics have practical political consequences. If you believe that the norms of public life are the ones that Habermas identifies, your politics will be of one sort. Believe that they are more like the norms identified by his critics and you will engage in politics in a different, though related, way. Believe that Arendt has it right and your political judgment and action will be of yet another related but different variety. The place of expert knowledge, rationality, images, identity politics, the mass media, and the like will be differently evaluated and acted upon following the different conceptualizations.

Therefore, publics are culturally constituted as social phenomena, not simply structures or discursive orders. Publics are formed through human interactions in everyday life and in formal occasions, in more and less official public spaces, in social movements, and in the under-life of total institutions and regimes. In the context of modern power relations and social control, these interactions have two aspects: *empirically*, people are unequal and they appear in their differences in public, express their different views in each other's presence; *normatively*, they develop a capacity to act as equals. Not all publics are equal, but they form and operate against one another within a sphere of publics that they cannot transcend. This makes media doubly important, as they not only facilitate the formation and interaction of publics, but may amplify or diminish their cultural capacities.

In this view, those who see decline in the sphere of publics could be said to have a narrow view of culture. On the other hand, from our point of view, in the distance from the Habermasian ideal there is not distortion or a loss, but the gain of the cultural complexity of public life today. We believe we have not only demonstrated empirical qualities of modern publics, but also staked out a normative position that opens public life to new kinds of participation, of different publics and counterpublics.

Conflict and competition, play and display, embodiment and appearance, aesthetics and belief are all parts of the life of publics, as these publics look inward at themselves and outward at other publics through a variety of different media and cultural forms. Our sociological lens to publics, different from philosophical or political theories that make a claim to universality, studies publics as a social problem. The problem of constituting a sphere of publics is, in fact, one of the fundamental social problems of modernity. The process began in a specific place and time and spread all over the world, carrying with it not just new empirical realities, but also a range of normative positions, with practical political consequences regarding the modern democratic project. From Arendt to Goffman to Benjamin, we have traced a cultural richness that has developed together with new media forms and has opened up new democratic possibilities that are not available through a strictly rational, exclusive, and universal debate on public life.

References

Alexander, Jeffrey C. 2006. *The Civil Sphere*. New York: Oxford University Press.

Arendt, Hannah. 1966 (1958). *The Origins of Totalitarianism*, second edition. New York: Harcourt, Brace & World.

——. 1982 (1963). *On Revolution*. Westport, CT: Greenwood Press.

——. 1998 (1958). *The Human Condition*. Chicago: University of Chicago Press.

Baudrillard, Jean. 1988. *Selected Writings*, ed. Mark Poster. Stanford, CA: Stanford University Press.

Benhabib, Seyla. 1993. "Models of Public Space: Hannah Arendt, the Liberal Tradition, and Jurgen Habermas." Pp. 73–98 in Craig Calhoun, ed., *Habermas and the Public Sphere*. Cambridge, MA: MIT Press.

Benjamin, Walter. 1998 (1936). *Illuminations*. New York: Schocken Books.

Calhoun, Craig. 1993. "Introduction." Pp. 6–8 in Craig Calhoun, ed., *Habermas and the Public Sphere*. Cambridge, MA: MIT Press.

——. 1997. "Nationalism and the Public Sphere." Pp. 75–102 in Jeff Weintraub and Krishan Kumar, eds., *Public and Private in Thought and Practice: Perspectives on a Grand Dichotomy*. Chicago: University of Chicago Press.

Chomsky, Noam. 1989. *Necessary Illusions: Thought Control in Democratic Societies*. Boston, MA: South End Press.

Dayan, Daniel. 2005. "On Mothers, Midwives and Abortionists: The Genealogy and Obstetrics of Audiences and Publics." In S. Livingstone, ed., *Audiences and Publics*. San Francisco: Intellect Press.

Dayan, Daniel and Katz, Elihu. 1992. *Media Events: The Live Broadcasting of History*. Cambridge, MA and London: Harvard University Press.

Debord, Guy. 1994. *The Society of the Spectacle*. New York: Zone Books.

Dewey, John. 1954. *The Public and Its Problems*. Chicago: Swallow Press.

Duplessis, Rachel Blau and Snitow, Ann. 1998. *The Feminist Memoir Project: Voices from Women's Liberation*. New York: Three Rivers Press.

Eley, Geoff. 1993. "Nations, Publics, and Political Cultures: Placing Habermas in the Nineteenth Century." Pp. 289–339 in Craig Calhoun, ed., *Habermas and the Public Sphere*. Cambridge, MA: MIT Press.

Fraser, Nancy. 1993. "Rethinking the Public Sphere: A Contribution to the Critique of Actually Existing Democracy." Pp. 109–42 in Craig Calhoun, ed., *Habermas and the Public Sphere*. Cambridge, MA: MIT Press.

Goffman, Erving. 1956. "The Nature of Deference and Demeanor." *American Anthropologist* 58(3): 131–63.

——. 1961. *Asylums*. New York: Knopf.

——. 1967. *Interaction Rituals*. Garden City, NY: Anchor Books.

——. 1971. *Relations in Public: Microstudies of the Public Order*. New York: Basic Books.

Goldfarb, Jeffrey C. 1978. "The Social Bases of Independent Public Expression in Communist Societies." *American Journal of Sociology* 83(4): 920–39.

——. 1980. The Persistence of Freedom: *The Sociological Implications of Polish Student Theater*. Boulder, CO: Westview Press.

——. 1982. *On Cultural Freedom: An Exploration of Public Life in Poland and America*. Chicago: Chicago University Press.

——. 2006a. *The Politics of Small Things: The Power of the Powerless in Dark Times*. Chicago: University of Chicago Press.

——. 2006b. "The Politics of Small Things: The Left Finds Its Voice, the Right Responds, Democratic Prospects." *Contexts* (May): 26, 28.

——. 2009. "On Barack Obama." *Constellations* 16(2) (June).

Gutman, Yifat. 2009. "Where Do We Go from Here: The Pasts, Presents and Futures of Ground Zero." *Memory Studies* 2(1): 55–70.

——. Forthcoming. "Past before Future: Enacting Contested Memories as a vehicle for Conflict Resolution in Israel and Palestine." Ph.D. diss. New School for Social Research.

Habermas, Jürgen. 1977. "Hannah Arendt's Communications Concept of Power." *Social Research* (Spring): 5–24.

——. 1982. "A Reply to My Critics." Pp. 219–317 in John B. Thompson and David Held, eds., *Habermas: Critical Debate*. London: Macmillan.

——. 1984. *The Theory of Communicative Action*, Volumes 1 and 2. Boston: Beacon Press.

——. 1989. *The Structural Transformation of the Public Sphere*, trans. Thomas Burger. Cambridge, MA: MIT Press.

——. 1990. *Moral Consciousness and Communicative Action*. Cambridge, MA: MIT Press.

Horkheimer, Max and Adorno, Theodor W. 1972. "The Culture Industry: Enlightenment as Mass Deception." Pp. 121, 136, 158 in *Dialectic of Enlightenment*. New York: Herder and Herder.

Landes, Joan. 1998. *Women and the Public Sphere in the Age of the French Revolution*. Ithaca, NY: Cornell University Press

Lee, Benjamin. 1993. "Textuality, Mediation, and Public Discourse." Pp. 402–20 in Craig Calhoun, ed., *Habermas and the Public Sphere*. Cambridge, MA: MIT Press.

McLuhan, Marshall. 1964. *Understanding Media: The Extensions of Man*. New York: McGraw-Hill.

Melluci, Alberto. 1989. *Nomads of the Present: Social Movements and Individual Needs in Contemporary Society*. Philadelphia: Temple University Press

Postman, Neil. 1986. *Amusing Ourselves to Death: Public Discourse in the Age of Show Business*. New York: Penguin Books.

Ryan, Mary P. 1993. "Gender and Public Access: Women's Politics in 19th Century America." Pp. 259–88 in Craig Calhoun, ed., *Habermas and the Public Sphere*. Cambridge, MA: MIT Press.

Touraine, Alain. 1981. *The Voice and the Eye: An Analysis of Social Movements*. New York: Cambridge University Press.

——. 1983. *Solidarity: The Analysis of a Social Movement: Poland, 1980–1981*. New York: Cambridge University Press.

Warner, Michael. 1993. "The Mass Public and Mass Subject." Pp. 377–401 in Craig Calhoun, ed., *Habermas and the Public Sphere*. Cambridge, MA: MIT Press.

——. 2005. *Publics and Counterpublics*. New York: Zone Books.

48

Cultures of democracy

A civil-society approach

Ming-Cheng Lo

As a political system, democracy generally derives its legitimacy through the claim of broad popular participation. Although many social scientists have examined how socio-economic factors facilitate or erode the institutional basis for public involvement in democratic politics, recent discussions of the cultural dimension of democratic engagement raise questions that need to be addressed. One dominant conceptualization, often employed in large-scale surveys, views culture in terms of subjective, individual-level orientations toward political values or social trust. But such approaches cannot easily come to terms with the puzzle of how discriminatory, racist, and expansionist collective narratives—even to the point of ethnic cleansing—could develop and become dominant in societies where most members share some commitment to democratic values (see, e.g., Mann 2005). In contrast, those who consider political cultures as fundamentally hegemonic and therefore exclusionary tend to focus on tracing the macro processes that shape dominant discursive constellations. But here, too, an important question arises: How is democratic consolidation to develop if hegemonic struggles are inevitable? What, in general, are the cultural conditions or mechanisms that would facilitate democratic consolidation in the face of ongoing social domination or counter-hegemonic struggles?

The question about democratic consolidation amidst serious social divisions appears particularly pressing in many young, fragile democracies in post-colonial Asia and Africa. Few of these countries have achieved the desired outcome of stable, multicultural civil society; many have experienced either outbreaks of civil war, tribalism, or regression into authoritarian rule (Moore 2001; Magnusson and Clark 2005). Faced with the challenge of building a coherent society after decades of colonialism, dictatorship, and anti-colonial struggles, most post-colonial democracies are stretched between addressing legacies of profound anger and inequality and envisioning a civil community capable of communication and cooperation across deep racial and political divides (Monga 1995). Overall, these diverse societies have followed, sometimes in combination, three paths: "to separate along the lines of their differences, to repress their differences, or to constitute their unity through discourse across the lines of their differences" (Calhoun 1995: 268–69). While the "third option" is no doubt the most desirable, its realization is also the most difficult. "One of the crucial questions of the modern era," then, is precisely "how often and under what circumstances the third option—meaningful, politically efficacious public discourse without fragmentation or repression—can be achieved" (Calhoun 1995: 269).

With the possibility of civil solidarity as one of its central theoretical and empirical puzzles, scholarship on civil society often is focused on advancing discussions about "the third option," or the possibility of democratic consolidation amidst hegemonic struggles. On a general conceptual map, civil society can be broadly described as (1) located in a social sphere of associations or informal networks that is autonomous from the state and the family, and (2) sharing a ubiquitous culture of civility that informs individuals' participation in this social sphere (Hall 1995; Bryant 1995; see Alexander 2006 for a detailed discussion of the concept). Although most contemporary students of civil society trace the origin of the concept to the Scottish Enlightenment thinkers, scholars differ over how to properly conceptualize civil society, e.g. whether the idea of an autonomous sphere of association should encompass or exclude the economy and religion, whether legacies of rational individualism are essential to the definition of the culture of civility or merely one of its numerous possible empirical manifestations, or how well the concept of civil society can travel outside of its Western birthplace. Books devoted to discussions of these issues fill shelves at libraries, extending far beyond the scope of this essay. Nevertheless, the diverse approaches generally agree on the importance of civil solidarity, or a sense of "we-ness" that sustains a healthy tension between differences and social integration, either as a defining cultural feature or a desired goal of civil society.

Towards the possibility of civil solidarity

Largely inspired by Habermas's influential *The Structural Transformation of the Public Sphere* (1989 [1962]), much discussion of civil solidarity challenges any assumption of "the public" or "the people" as a natural category waiting to be released in political expression. Instead, the debate establishes the premise that a public has to constitute its own identity as both the subject and the object of democratic representation. In other words, members of "the public" have to negotiate and debate over exactly who is or isn't part of this public (e.g. "Should illegal immigrants be considered part of the public?"), as well as deliberate what the public thinks (e.g. "Should we provide health-care for illegal immigrants and why?"). The articulation of civic identities entails the process of delineating a symbolic, collective community, a sense of "we-ness" as Alexander (1992) describes it. At the same time, in a democratic community, this sense of we-ness must also acknowledge its internal divisions. Cultural practices of civil society must sustain a sense of integration as well as a meaningful engagement with internal differences.

This tension between integration and differences has challenged Habermas's formulation of a unitary public sphere and, subsequently, stimulated competing approaches. Habermas's own notion of the ideal speech community is itself a conscious attempt to address this tension. In his view, all people, across cultural, racial, and gender lines, hold the capacity for rational-critical thinking. As long as democratic rules and procedures protect every citizen's right to speak up and make her case, participants in the public sphere have the capacity to rationally evaluate any argument in terms of its merits rather than by reference to the status of the speaker. Habermas argues that the foundations of this public sphere remain universal because they are communicative. As Rabinovitch observes, "Any individuals or groups may argue for continued incorporation into the decision-making process simply by demonstrating their ability to reason and to express their point of view" (2001: 347). Habermas describes the potential for inclusiveness as the self-transforming quality of the bourgeois public sphere. For him, only communicative action can achieve the social integration necessary for a democratic public sphere without suppressing social and cultural differences.

Subsequent scholars engaging with Habermas's thesis have questioned his faith in communicative action. Historical studies show that some social groups appear to be more likely to form separate publics than to join a dominant public (Eley 1992; Ryan 1992); as a result, actual rational-critical discourses become embedded in unequal and relatively separate symbolic systems. Thus, even when a civil society is formally open and inclusive to all, its dominant cultural vocabulary often becomes an informal mechanism of exclusion, as it is composed of styles of speech and discursive codes that have been shaped by legacies of power inequality. Fraser argues that recognizing the cultural hegemony of public discourses is part of how "true" (or, in her words, "radical") democracy works. Fraser proposes the concept of "subaltern counter-publics" as a way to signal that there are parallel discursive arenas where members of subordinated social groups invent and circulate counter-discourses to "formulate oppositional interpretations of their identities, interests, and needs" (Fraser 1992: 123). The relationships between subaltern counter-publics and hegemonic publics are posited to be hierarchical and conflictual; their cultural difference remains largely irreconcilable through communicative action (Young 1990).

Alexander, Rabinovitch observes, takes up the challenge of explaining "exactly that which both Habermas and Fraser omitted: how it is that people successfully argue that they are in fact members of the symbolic community of 'common humanity' without losing sight of their distinct cultural identities" (2001: 351). To conceptualize this possibility, Alexander shifts the basis of integration from Habermas's universal rationality to a notion of fundamental discursive binaries. Reminiscent of Durkheim's argument about the elementary forms of religion, Alexander argues that the binary normative code of sacred and profane provides the fundamental cultural language for discourses on democratic ideals. The public resorts to characteristics associated with the sacred/civil and the profane/uncivil in their shared cultural repertoire to make sense of social events and construct narratives about them. Rather than seeing marginal groups as enjoying a fair hearing in universal, critical-rational discourses or operating with completely different cultural systems of their own, Alexander (2006) contends that they are often unfairly coded with stigmatized/uncivil categories within a shared system of meaning, or what he calls the codes of liberty. In a multicultural civil society, marginal groups can potentially succeed in their struggle to gain the freedom and resources to argue in front of the general public that their stigmatized qualities are in fact a different and valued manifestation of characteristics of the sacred/civil. This mode of counter-hegemonic struggle amounts to a process of multicultural incorporation rather than separatism, because the opposing groups are theorized to operate with shared binary systems. Empirically, at least in the case of the United States, such struggle is often undertaken through social movements—a form of "civic repair" in Alexander's terms. If such struggle is successful, women, racial minorities, or other previously marginalized groups eventually become recognized as possessing specific cultural qualities that manifest broad democratic ideals, e.g. rationality, justice, altruism, etc. Through such ongoing processes that "particularize the universal," cultures of civil society become broader and richer, and core civic values are reinforced across social groups. But even in this process, social groups continue to operate with a binary semiotic structure, defining the civil self in opposition to some anti-civil other. The construction and reconstruction of civil society, in this perspective, is a never-ending process.

All civic ties are not equal

Even in societies with relatively strong legacies of liberty codes, broad civil ideals alone do not dictate *how* cultures of civil society will develop. Although cultural codes provide the underlying "grammar" of civil society discourses, it is when social groups employ these codes to structure their narratives and arguments that concrete patterns of democratic cultural practices take shape. Group-level ties, styles, and narratives must be recognized as crucial cultural mechanisms for the formation and transformation of civil-society cultures.

As much as individual autonomy is valued by academic as well as non-academic advocates for democracy, an atomized society threatens to weaken the very social fabric of democracy. As Putnam (2000) and other neo-Tocquevillian scholars have warned, cynicism, apathy, or other forms of political disengagement of citizens signal a decline in civility and foretell a story of collective democratic non-participation. This insight has inspired much recent research on American and other civil societies focused on measuring the density of group ties in the associational sphere. Although critics complain that this approach tends to quantify civic ties at the expense of their content and meanings, the emphasis on civic ties is useful in establishing the premise that practices of group-level association and interaction nurture a sense of social connectedness, which in turn is foundational to political engagement. More broadly, horizontal group ties can become social mechanisms against state monopoly of power in non-democratic settings (Ryan 2001). For example, Ikegami (2005) argues that the Japanese "aesthetic publics," or loose cultural circles devoted to tea ceremonies, poetry, music, and other arts that developed during the Tokugawa period, constituted realms of sociability that brought together strangers from drastically different social backgrounds. These horizontal networks not only eroded the Tokugawa hierarchical social order but nurtured social capital that was later mobilized in democratization movements after the collapse of the Tokugawa Shogunate.

Not all associational ties are equal, however. *How* people associate with each other matters as much as *how often* they do so. Although a corrupt or authoritarian state provides a common target that can temporarily unify forces of resistance from various social strata and political corners, eventually civic groups will face tests of their capacity for mutual engagement of differences without dissolving into shouting matches. So, are certain group ties more conducive to nurturing reflexive consideration of differences than others? In a series of studies based on ethnographic work on everyday talk and interaction in civic groups, Lichterman takes up this important question. He argues that "group customs"—informal, group-specific styles of interaction that shape how members carry out conversations and handle differences and criticisms—are crucial in nurturing or limiting a group's capacity for social reflexivity. The capacity for social reflexivity, in turn, mediates how a civic group "maps" its own position in relation to others, negotiates bridging ties with them in the civil sphere, or reconsiders and redefines its social role or collective identity (Lichterman 2008, 2005). Thus, group customs that enable rich social reflexivity—not the act of associating, interacting, or deliberating alone—facilitate tolerance and mutual understanding in a multicultural civil society. Along similar lines, Mische (2008) develops a typology of four modes of communication (Habermasian, Gramscian, Deweyian, and Machiavellian), arguing that it is important to analyze social actors' skills for flexible "discursive switching" across institutional settings rather than to regard one mode of communicative action as inherently more virtuous than another.

Group cultures and styles of associating can also be important expressions of agency and creativity by members of civil society. As a corrective measure for the exaggerated public/private and rational/expressive distinctions found in the work of some Habermasian scholars, we should understand civil society not only as an arena for expressing fairly established identities but also as the realm of sociability where identities develop, change, and articulate creatively with the social world (see, e.g., Calhoun 1992). In processes of sociability, social groups produce songs, symbols, narratives, and so forth as the means both to think through and to express their identities. For example, "submerged networks" (Melucci 1989) or "free spaces" (Evans and Boyte 1986) in social movements can be considered as cultural laboratories where social groups experiment with new expressions. Sometimes, in these spaces, participants struggle to make sense of the tensions and contradictions in the multiple social positions that they simultaneously occupy, e.g. as both African Americans *and* women (Robnett 1997) or as both colonial subjects *and* high-status professionals (Lo 2002), producing narratives and ideas not reducible to social structures but rather registering their creative responses to what I have elsewhere called the "messiness of modernity" (Lo 2005).

Thus far I have discussed how specific cultural mechanisms or expressions are important resources for individual civic groups to negotiate the dual tasks of self-reflexivity and self-empowerment. In turn, it is useful to consider how the cultural narratives that these groups produce contribute to the larger social narratives beyond their own group boundaries, e.g. in shaping the commonly shared narratives of national trauma, honor, or tragedy. To be sure, such collective narratives are never singular or static; they may be repeatedly subjected to some form of hegemonic contestation. But even when a consolidated position is more or less settled about certain issues in a society (e.g. slavery is inhuman; apartheid is uncivil; Hiroshima is a reminder of the cruelty and absurdity of war), diverse group narratives may continue to encourage and enrich reflexive understandings of national events. When various groups and multiple publics experience or reflect upon shared histories, they do so within the matrix of social relationships where they are situated, thereby developing explanatory stories that connect, highlight, suppress, and rearrange chronological events in different ways (Somers and Gibson 1994). For example, mainstream media and black newspapers in Los Angeles reported the 1992 Rodney King controversy in drastically different ways. Although both sides shared a critical stand against police brutality and a commitment to racial equality, they described two very different stories of who the heroes and villains were and what the romance/tragedy of civic repair was about (Jacobs 1996). Similarly, the recent attempts to archive black women's pictorial and written testimony in a "Memory Cloths" program in South Africa were crucial steps in fleshing out the marginalized aspects in the collective memory of apartheid. These representations of the past by black women are not only important—and overdue—for black women themselves, but also for the unrealized potential embodied within collective narratives about past wrongs (McEwan 2003). In both examples, the multiple and diverse accounts of "storied life" add nuanced layers of meaning to the larger social narratives about shared histories and consolidated political positions. For a democratic polity, it is desirable that big national narratives be multi-stranded and multi-layered, as their discursive richness renders them more inclusive and flexible, better able to accommodate future reinterpretations and revisions without an immediate threat of cultural fragmentation.

Beyond the codes of liberty

As I have argued thus far, the codes of liberty provide the broad cultural vocabulary for civil-society discourses, and group ties, styles, and narrations constitute the meso-level mechanisms of mediation therein. If these arguments hold, must the same cultural properties be reproduced in non-Western societies that aspire for democratic consolidation? Historically, many societies have been forced into confrontation with Western imperialist powers, eventually acquiring "a skeleton of institutions similar to those ... [in] the West." However, the West's culture of rational individualism "has not become the dream of these societies" (Mardin 1995: 295). Therein lies the question, both academic and political, of whether and how such societies might develop their own cultures of civility or alternative cultural vocabularies for civil solidarity. Many civil-society scholars are skeptical, not so much because they are convinced of Western cultural superiority, but because they tend to see civility as intrinsically tied to rational individualism. Alexander describes the binary codes of liberty most clearly, grounding his theory in empirical analyses of the United States. Gellner (1994) argues a strong functionalist position, asserting that a prevalent notion of "modular individuals" provides the essential cultural foundation for non-authoritarian communal bonds. But can there exist a culture of civility that differs in origin and content from rational individualism, yet is functionally similar and thus recognizable as one of its variants?

To recall Alexander's conceptualization, the capacity of a cultural system to treat differences as legitimate by constructing them as variations on the theme of common humanity is only possible if "the particular is viewed ... as a concrete manifestation of the universal" (Alexander 2006: 259). Gellner does not see other cultural systems—which he famously describes as "cousin-ridden" on one occasion—as possessing this crucial capacity. Similarly, Alexander ponders, if an alternative ethics such as caring "bases itself on such ties as love ... , then there is no theoretical room for compelling commitment to abstract social rules. ... Such an ethic is well and good for the intimate sphere, but can it actually be extended to the civil one?" (Alexander 2006: 261). But going beyond Gellner and Alexander, I have argued elsewhere (Lo and Fan forthcoming) that *relationality* can and does exist as an abstract principle that is detached from concrete *relational ties*, informing abstract, universalistic civil society ethics. This relationality is made possible when cultural systems undergo the historical process of what Gellner terms "modularization."

In Gellner's insightful but Western-centered observation, modularization describes a process of the ascendance and subsequent collapse of a strong cultural center. Historically, the cultural system we know as rational individualism is a product of the fragmentation of the cultural center of the Roman Catholic Church. The collapse of the center liberated individuals from institutionalized ideological control, while the remnants of this shared cultural legacy provided them with a flexible cultural motif. In other words, strangers find it easy to form associational ties because they more or less share the same abstract cultural values and rules, but they are able to enter relationships or exit from

509

them voluntarily, free from the supervision of specific ideological or political centers. What's important for the discussion at hand is that parallel examples have been documented in the absence of the Church or the legacies of rational individualism. As a corrective to Gellner's ethnocentrism, we find that the family-state in pre-war Japan also represented a political and cultural center that subsequently underwent a similar process of fragmentation. A familial culture became a shared legacy that was detached from a totalizing center, and was afforded voluntary and flexible application in the formulation of social relationships in post-war Japan (Lo and Bettinger 2001). Having become modularized, familial-civility developed into a culturally specific ethics of relationality, which requires *not* that individuals pledge loyalty to the familial-state or remain attached to specific particularistic relationships, but that they honor the obligations, cultures, and well-being of the groups in which they have voluntarily chosen to participate in the civil sphere. Familialism may or may not continue to regulate relationships in the private sphere, but what needs to be recognized is that another form of familialism, a "generalized particularism," now operates generally and broadly in post-war Japan as a civil ethics, beyond the confines of primordial relationships. Just as rationality is not inherently public even if it was historically regarded as the cultural logic of the public sphere, relationality is by no means an inherently private culture despite past histories or cultural biases. Certainly, not all cultures of relationality become modularized and develop explicitly *civil* ethics. But while civil solidarity refers to *civic*, rather than *particularistic* bonds, we must also recognize that there can be cultural variations in how such civic relationships are defined (e.g. a civic community of rational, independent social actors, or a civic community of caring, compassionate individuals).

The Japanese example documents cultural modularization in a non-Western context through which a civil ethics *not* grounded in rational individualism has emerged. But instead of assuming diverse civil ethics to always develop in isolation from one another, it is more fruitful intellectually to consider when and how different cultures of civil society may interact across porous, fluid national boundaries. For example, in their pursuits of democratization, social groups in emergent civil societies often import and appropriate the code of liberty for their own use. Sometimes, we witness competition or mutual displacement between democratic and authoritarian codes, raising challenges as to whether and how a civil ethics will indeed take root (Ku 2001). In other cases, social groups hybridize between different systems of culture that have become available to them. We have yet to engage in systematic studies of empirical cases in order to develop a good understanding of the patterns and conditions of hybridized civil ethics. But a few compelling cases suggest that sometimes, e.g. in the face of severe social polarization or unspeakable past wrongs, social actors find it challenging to sustain the inclusive potential of civil-society discourses solely with the code of liberty. When the appropriate application of the principles of justice and rationality would lead to daunting consequences, sometimes these consequences are eclipsed by alternative visions of social groups' making, e.g. forgiveness, reconciliation, caring, or a shared future. For example, in the two small and fragile "off-shore democracies" in the greater China region, it has been shown, social groups in Taiwan and Hong Kong both structure political debates and other civil-society discourses by employing imported codes of liberty. Yet as challenges in democratic transition brew deep political polarization or profound cynicism, democratic ideals are invoked almost entirely to figure out who is uncivil and deserves exclusion from society. To remedy this lopsided discourse of democracy, some social groups have turned to the ethics of caring and relationality as they contemplate how political opponents may still recognize their common humanity (Lo and Fan forthcoming). In the case of post-apartheid South Africa, the exclusion of all past per-petrators would be tantamount to enforcing a mass exodus from the nation; instead, the civic repair processes have proceeded with the vision of a deep moral transformation (as in the example of the Truth and Reconciliation Commission). The hybridization of the liberal ethics of justice and truth and the religious virtues of reconciliation and grace makes it possible to talk about a coherent vision of nation-rebuilding. But the delicate tension between responsibility and vilification, reconciliation and denial, also remains a difficult challenge and unsettling force in the South African culture of democracy as well as in the lives of many individuals (Nagy 2004).

Conclusion

With its focus on the tension between difference and integration, the civil-society approach offers a useful conceptual tool for analyzing the cultural processes of democratic consolidation. Alexander's civil-society discourse approach theorizes how the ethics of civil solidarity, concretely manifested in the American case as a code of liberty, offers a universalistic cultural vocabulary through which hegemonic struggles can be carried out without leading to social fragmentation. Although most theoretical work on the topic to date has come from a Western context, this possibility of democratic con-solidation is especially crucial in various fragile young democracies. In turn, the works of Putnam, Lichterman, and other scholars specify meso-level cultural mechanisms that shape how the general code of liberty might be invoked concretely. While the act of associating provides a foundation for political engagement and social movement net-works facilitate resistance, self-empowerment, and creative cultural expressions, group customs and styles shape the group's capacities (or lack thereof) for social reflexivity and self-restraint. At an inter-group level, these discourses of resistance and reflexivity can potentially contribute to larger, commonly shared social narratives about national pride or trauma. Recently, studies of non-Western cases further suggest that codes of liberty are not the only bases of civil ethics. Cultural vocabularies that share similar functions but differ in content have developed elsewhere historically, through the process of mod-ularization. This insight opens up questions about code competition and hybridization. Of particular interest are questions about how hybridized cultural discourses may facil-itate, limit, or otherwise shape processes of democratic consolidation in fledgling civil societies.

Looking forward, research can benefit from a more systematic comparison between different cases. We need more empirical work comparing civil-society discourses inspired by liberty codes and alternative civil ethics in order to better understand their varying potential and limitations. As paradoxical as it might seem, such empirical studies will illustrate concretely the historical construction of universalistic ideals. Furthermore, research on how meso-level cultural mechanisms work in non-Western contexts to balance between empowerment and reflexivity, or resistance and cooperation, has been relatively under-developed, perhaps because striking such balances—the desired but difficult "third option," to recall Calhoun's phrasing—is particularly challenging in young democracies. But precisely because of this, it is particularly important for us to study such mechanisms. Finally, with the insights learned from Asian and African cases, we are encouraged to ask if civil-society participants in the United States or other Western contexts resort to non–liberty ethics in their civil-society discourses as well. If so, under what conditions, and with what consequences? Issues of code hybridization—e.g. between religious values and democratic ones; between the ethics of caring and that of liberty—may inspire new research questions about cultural practices in established democracies. The cross-fertilization of insights from Western and non-Western contexts, one hopes, will effectively move us beyond the West/non-West divide, towards broader and more rigorous theoretical understandings about cultures of civil society.

References

Alexander, Jeffrey C. 1992. "Citizen and Enemy as Symbolic Classification: On the Polarizing Discourse of Civil Society." Pp. 289–308 in Marcel Fournier and Michèle Lamont, eds., *Where Culture Talks: Exclusion and the Making of Society*. Chicago: University of Chicago Press.

——. 2006. *The Civil Sphere*. New York: Oxford University Press.

Bryant, Christopher G.A. 1995. "Civic Nation, Civil Society, Civil Religion." Pp. 136–58 in John A. Hall, ed., *Civil Society: Theory, History, Comparison*. Cambridge: Polity Press.

Calhoun, Craig. 1992. "Introduction: Habermas and the Public Sphere." Pp. 1–48 in Craig Calhoun, ed., *Habermas and the Public Sphere*. Cambridge, MA: The MIT Press.

——. 1995. "Nationalism and Difference: The Politics of Identity Writ Large." Pp. 231–82 in Craig Calhoun ed., *Critical Social Theory*. Cambridge, MA: Blackwell.

Eley, Goeff. 1992. "Nations, Publics, and Political Cultures: Placing Habermas in the Nineteenth Century." Pp. 289–339 in C. Calhoun, ed., *Habermas and the Public Sphere*. Cambridge, MA: MIT Press.

Evans, Sara M. and Boyte, Harry C. 1986. *Free Spaces: The Sources of Democratic Change in America*. New York: Harper & Row.

Fraser, Nancy. 1992. "Rethinking the Public Sphere: A Contribution to the Critique of Actually Existing Democracy." Pp. 109–42 in C. Calhoun, ed., *Habermas and the Public Sphere*. Cambridge, MA: MIT Press.

Gellner, Ernest. 1994. *Conditions of Liberty: Civil Society and Its Rivals*. London: Hamish Hamilton.

Habermas, Jürgen. 1989 (1962). *The Structural Transformation of the Public Sphere*, trans. Thomas Burger with the assistance of Frederick Lawrence. Cambridge, MA: MIT Press.

Hall, John A. 1995. "In Search of Civil Society." Pp. 1–31 in John A. Hall, ed., *Civil Society: Theory, History, Comparison*. Cambridge: Polity Press.

Ikegami, Eiko. 2005. *Bonds of Civility: Aesthetic Networks and the Political Origins of Japanese Culture*. New York: Cambridge University Press.

Jacobs, Ronald N. 1996. "Civil Society and Crisis: Culture, Discourse, and the Rodney King Beating." *American Journal of Sociology* 101(5): 1238–72.

Ku, Agnes S. 2001. "The 'Public' Up Against the State—Credibility Crisis and Narrative Cracks in Post-Colonial Hong Kong." *Theory, Culture and Society* 18(1): 121–44.

Lichterman, Paul. 2005. *Elusive Togetherness: Church Groups Trying to Bridge America's Divisions*. Princeton, NJ: Princeton University Press.

——. 2008. "Religion and the Construction of Civic Identity." *American Sociological Review* 73(1): 83–104.

Lo, Ming-Cheng M. 2002. *Doctors within Borders: Profession, Ethnicity, and Modernity in Colonial Taiwan*. Berkeley: University of California Press.

——. 2005. "Professions: Prodigal Daughter of Modernity." Pp. 381–406 in Julia Adams, Elisabeth S. Clemens and Ann Shola Orloff, eds., *Remaking Modernity: Politics, Processes and History in Sociology*. Durham, NC: Duke University Press.

Lo, Ming-Cheng M. and Bettinger, Christopher P. 2001. "The Historical Emergence of a 'Familial Society' in Japan." *Theory and Society* 30: 237–79.

Lo, Ming-Cheng M. and Fan, Yun. Forthcoming. "Hybrid Cultural Codes in Non-Western Civil Society: Images of Women in Taiwan and Hong Kong." *Sociological Theory*.

McEwan, Cheryl. 2003. "Building a Postcolonial Archive? Gender, Collective Memory and Citizenship in Post-Apartheid South Africa." *Journal of Southern African Studies* 29(3): 739–57.

Magnusson, Bruce A. and Clark, John F. 2005. "Understanding Democratic Survival and Democratic Failure in Africa: Insights from Divergent Democratic Experiments in Benin and Congo (Brazzaville)." *Comparative Studies in Society and History* 47: 552–82.

Mann, Michael. 2005. *The Dark Side of Democracy: Explaining Ethnic Cleansing*. Cambridge: Cambridge University Press.

Mardin, Şerif. 1995. "Civil Society and Islam." In John A. Hall, ed., *Civil Society: Theory, History, Comparison*. Cambridge: Polity Press.

Melucci, Alberto. 1989. *Nomads of the Present*. London: Hutchinson Radius.

Mische, Ann. 2008. *Partisan Politics: Communication and Contention across Brazilian Youth Activist Networks*. Princeton: Princeton University Press.

Monga, Celestin. 1995. "Civil Society and Democratisation in Francophone Africa." *Journal of Modern African Studies* 33(3): 359–79.

Moore, David. 2001. "Neoliberal Globalisation and the Triple Crisis of 'Modernisation' in Africa: Zimbabwe, the Democratic Republic of the Congo and South Africa." *Third World Quarterly* 22: 909–29.

Nagy, Rosemary. 2004. "The Ambiguities of Reconciliation and Responsibility in South Africa." *Politic Studies* 52(4): 709–27.

Putnam, Robert D. 2000. *Bowling Alone: The Collapse and Revival of American Community*. New York: Simon & Schuster.

Rabinovitch, Eyal. 2001. "Gender and the Public Sphere: Alternative Forms of Integration in Nineteenth-Century America." *Sociological Theory* 19: 344–70.

Robnett, Belinda. 1997. *How Long? How Long? African-American Women in the Struggle for Civil Rights*. New York: Oxford University Press.

Ryan, Mary. 1992. "Gender and Public Access: Women's Politics in Nineteenth-Century America." Pp. 259–88 in C. Calhoun, ed., *Habermas and the Public Sphere*. Cambridge, MA: MIT Press.

——. 2001. "Civil Society as Democratic Practice: North American Cities During the Nineteenth Century." In Robert Rotberg, ed., *Patterns of Social Capital: Stability and Change in Historical Perspective*. New York: Cambridge University Press.

Somers, Margaret R. and Gibson, Gloria D. 1994. "Reclaiming the Epistemological 'Other': Narrative and the Social Constitution of Identity." Pp. 37–99 in Craig Calhoun, ed., *Social Theory and the Politics of Identity*. Cambridge, MA: Blackwell.

Young, Iris M. 1990. *Justice and the Politics of Difference*. Princeton, NJ: Princeton University Press.

49

National culture, national identity, and the culture(s) of the nation

Geneviève Zubrzycki

Until relatively recently, scholars of nationalism primarily used *culture* to stand for language, ethnicity, and broadly defined traditions. Culture was that stuff out of which nations were built and which nationalists sought to protect and perfect under the aegis of the modern nation-state. Alternatively, culture was regarded as a "thing" requiring invention in order for people to care about and fight for the establishment of nation-states. By embracing the so-called cultural turn, a new generation of scholars changed both the lens and the focus of the field: the object of study shifted from an emphasis on nationalism to one on national identity. From this new vantage point, the nation is not a reified object but a symbol competed over by social actors, nationalism is a field of debates about the symbol of the nation, and national identity is a relational process enacted in social dramas and "events" as well as in everyday practices.

This essay analyzes the various ways in which culture has been conceptualized in the literature on nations and nationalism. It then discusses the import of the "cultural turn" on the field, with a specific focus on recent contributions and new directions. Visualizing that turn, however, presupposes some knowledge of the road and the maps by which we navigated before. To that end, I begin with a brief consideration of the pre-history of "national culture."

Archaeology of the field: esprit, character, civilization

Long before the advent of nationalism—and even longer before it became a topic of scholarly interest—philosophers reflected on what differentiated one people from another. That "nations" had distinctive "spirits," "souls," "genius," or "characters" was widely taken for granted; what remained to be explained was what was at their source. For Hobbes (1588–1679), Kant (1724–1804), Herder (1744–1803), Montesquieu (1689–1755), and Rousseau (1712–78), to name only the most prominent thinkers on the issue, it was the idiosyncratic configuration of a variety of factors that produced moral traits specific to a people, the unique *Geist* of a given nation. Those factors ranged from the physical characteristics of the inhabitants, the geophysical properties of the soil, the landscape, and the climate; to the language, folk traditions, and art of the population; to the form of political institutions and laws; to religious beliefs, mores, and rituals. Montesquieu, for instance, saw climate as especially significant in shaping a nation's *esprit*. As he argued in *The Spirit of the Laws*, it influenced personality, social dynamics, and political systems, so that people in very warm regions tended to be "hot-tempered" and politically unstable, whereas those living in northern parts of the world were overly stiff and passive. France's temperate climate similarly explained the unusual qualities of the French people.

If some thinkers were concerned about the origins of specific national cultures, others considered their impact on political life and international relations. Rousseau, for example, argued that a well-defined, coherent "national character" was a necessary condition for national self-awareness and patriotism, and in turn a key step toward political sovereignty. Since national character played such a crucial role in the establishment of sovereignty and free government, he insisted, it would have to be created in places where it did not already exist—presciently anticipating the arduous work of cultural imagination and institutional invention that nation-builders all over the world applied throughout the nineteenth and the early part of the twentieth centuries.

Whereas Rousseau understood national character as the result of a dynamic interplay between culture and politics and in terms of the role it played in fostering national consciousness and the general will, the notion of national character later evolved into a static and often stereotypically descriptive and normative category. The reified fusion of individual moral traits and national culture was then used as an alleged predictor of political behavior. For example, influenced by Freudian theory, the "culture and personality school" in the 1930s to 1950s United States took as its point of departure the view that, through their culturally determined child-rearing practices, different societies tend to foster specific personality types. National character studies, primarily associated with the work of Ruth Benedict and Margaret Mead, took this argument even further. They claimed that these personality types, taken as an aggregate, constituted distinct national characters that would shape political organizations and influence, for example, military versus more pacific propensities.

The psycho-cultural approach has since been discredited for its impressionistic tone, selective use of evidence, and looseness in empirical demonstration. Still, some scholars have tried to salvage the idea that different nations have specific attitudes and values that constitute distinct "national characters." This agenda has been carried forward most prominently by political scientist Alex Inkeles, who sought to demonstrate the empirical existence of national characters through innovative survey instruments and sophisticated quantitative analysis. Although the 1997 publication of a book of essays on the subject largely fell on deaf ears, one could argue that the notion persists, albeit in new form, in its incarnation as the thesis of the "clash of civilizations." That controversial theory of global conflict rests on the idea that culture—and more specifically religion—drives how people see themselves and understand their place in the world. "Civilizational" fault lines, according to Huntington (1996), draw the battle lines of the future.

This reification of culture and the division of the world into different and conflicting civilizations are reminiscent of the distinction made in the aftermath of World War II by the early theorist of nationalism, Hans Kohn (1946), who distinguished between what he termed "Western" and "Eastern" types of nationalism. For Kohn, nationalism in the West was the product of the Age of Reason and its ideas of liberty, equality, and fraternity, and was closely related to individualism, liberalism, constitutionalism, and

515

democracy more generally. As nationalism spread eastward and developed in closed, authoritarian societies, however, it morphed into a collectivist ideology that rejected the ideas of the Enlightenment and embraced xenophobia instead. Whereas in the West, for Kohn, nationalism was a force promoting liberal ideals through political institutions, in the East it found expression in the concept of the *Volk* and its "authentic" culture.

In this lineage, national culture is seen as an enduring, relatively impermeable *substance* defining the nation and its identity; a substance predating political projects and therefore a valued resource for building and legitimizing them. This "substance" idea of national culture is what nationalists later on sought to define, protect, and to elevate under the aegis of national states. In the contemporary literature on nations and nationalism, this last argument has been made most forcefully and often over the last three decades by Anthony D. Smith, who locates the origins of modern nations in pre-modern cultures (what he calls *ethnies*). Ethnies constitute the basis for, and provide the original cells from which, the modern nation and its defining ally, the nation-state, were allegedly hatched.

The recent "turn" in the study of national culture began as an angling off from the lineage described above. But what direction did scholars turn *to*? They turned toward the idea that national cultures, far from being ancient and coherent wholes that shaped national identity and built nation-states, had to be somehow created in the first place.

Culture as construction tool: inventing national culture and promoting a culture of the national

Ernest Gellner's theory of nationalism, initially articulated in a chapter of *Thought and Change* in 1964, rigorously questioned the putative causal power of a pre-existing culture in the formation of nations and nationalism. In what is now a famous reversal of commonsensical understandings of the relationship between culture and nationalism, he insisted that it is not "the nation"—a bounded national culture—that creates nationalism, but the other way around. Nationalism, he argued, was the process *through which* homogeneous high cultures were created in modernity. In fact, Gellner explained, nationalism came into being in the modern era in order to fulfill that specific function. With industrialization and the erosion of traditional social structures, a common "high culture"—defined as a unified language and literacy—became increasingly important to facilitate communications and economic exchanges, as well as to shape social relationships. To achieve these goals, a standardized education system was needed. Such a system, Gellner argued, could only be created and sustained in a modern nation-state; a political unit larger than local-regional political organizations, but smaller than imperial structures. Nationalism, then, was the pragmatic push toward such political entities, and toward their ideological justification in the claim that the political and cultural units should be congruent.

Although Gellner's theory of nationalism was wedded to modernization theory and suffered from many problems commonly attributed to functionalism, it nevertheless offered a novel way to think about the relationship between culture and nationalism. Instead of taking national culture for granted, as a "pre-existing condition" reified as something that elites manipulated in the service of nationalism, or as something that they evoked to mobilize support for nationalism because it needed to be saved, protected, or promoted, Gellner showed that nationalism actually came into being for national culture's very creation.

Eric J. Hobsbawm took up the issue of national culture's creation in his canonical *The Invention of Tradition* (1983), where he carefully documented that process and explained the various motivations behind it. He convincingly showed that most of what people consider part of their national culture was invented in a specific historic period (1870–1914) by self-interested actors. Government agencies applied themselves to create traditions, myths, and symbols that would foster affective horizontal bonds at a moment of social and political unrest, and vertical allegiance to newly created nation-states and their political elites. The establishment of public collective celebrations such as national holidays and memorial days honoring those who died for the nation, the creation of public spaces and construction of monuments, as well as the designing of national symbols such as flags and national anthems were all are part of that broader project.

The intensity with which a national culture had to be forged depended, according to Hobsbawm, on the strength of the initial national project. In the case of France, the "Revolution had established the fact, nature and the boundaries of the French nation and its patriotism" (Hobsbawm and Ranger 1983: 278). Therefore the need for extensive symbols and traditions was relatively small. In the German case, however, the national definition was still vague, the unity shaky, and the identification with the Second Empire less precise, and as a result there was a greater need to establish the "national fact" (Hobsbawm and Ranger 1983: 278). To achieve unity, Germany had to rely on the intensive production of traditions. John R. Gillis corroborated this insight, finding that the fragility of new nations intensifies their commemorative efforts (1994: 9). Similarly, Karen Cerulo (1995), who studied the syntactic structure of national symbols, found that "younger," or less established nations often show an expansiveness in the content of their national symbology, and that the more intense the cognitive focus of the target (as in post-1789 France), the less elaborate the accompanying symbolic structure. The key point shared by all of these scholars is that national identity needs to be created, supported, intensified, and periodically reasserted. The role of national culture in that process cannot be overemphasized: it simultaneously creates and encapsulates national identity, builds affective bonds, motivates patriotic action, honors the efforts of citizens, legitimates authority, and, under certain conditions, becomes a tool for popular political protest (Cerulo 1995: 13).

If all these are "constructive" byproducts of national culture's creation in the nineteenth and early twentieth centuries, one must not forget the darker side of that process. Indeed, the creation of national identity through the production of a homogeneous national culture and a master narrative of the nation necessarily implied the repression of alternative memories, discourses, identities, and loyalties (local or religious, for example). As the historian of China Prasenjit Duara rightly pointed out, "the attention devoted to the process whereby national identities are formed has neglected to see that it is the same process whereby other identifications and nation-views are repressed and obscured" (1995: 164). This hegemonization of national culture through its homogenization, however, is not merely discursive in a textual sense, but "pictorial" as well. In *Siam Mapped*, Thongchai Winichakul (1994) showed that Western, modern conceptions of space, geography, and territoriality led to "national" map-making, and that the creation of such "geo-bodies," represented on paper and thereby reified, *de facto* created nations where they previously did not exist.

It is therefore vital to recognize the dual constructive and destructive processes involved in the creation of national culture. If mandatory primary education, commemorations, public monuments, museums, and maps were critical in forging a uniform national culture and creating a unified national identity, they also participated in the annihilation of other (local) cultures, memories, traditions, geographies, and identities. Eugen Weber (1976), to take one prominent example, showed how public primary schools simultaneously imposed a particular version of the French language and (often violently) repressed *patois*, local dialects. Museums collect certain objects deemed valuable, while ignoring or discarding others as merely so much flotsam and jetsam. The investigation of forgotten, silenced, or repressed stories is crucial not only to restore the voices that allow a fuller understanding of local histories, but also because these investigations expose an ineluctable aspect of nation formation, namely its annihilative power.

National culture as discourse and structure of meaning

Whereas the works of Gellner, Hobsbawm, and Benedict Anderson were all determinative in establishing social constructivist approaches to the study of nations and nationalism as the new orthodoxies in the field, Anderson's *Imagined Communities* must be flagged as especially significant with regard to the role of culture. Here is where the most dramatic turn was made. *Imagined Communities* moved the center of the discussion on nationalism from Europe to the so-called "periphery," and it more strongly centered the field on cultural analysis. The advent of nations and nationalism in modernity, Anderson argued, had been possible because of epochal cultural transformations, on the one hand, and because of daily practices, on the other. This intervention stimulated a new generation of researchers and theorists, and generated fruitful approaches to the study of the national question, approaches which remained sociologically grounded, but which henceforth paid attention to the *discursive* formation of the nation and the production of meaning.

Rogers Brubaker, in his classic *Nationhood and Citizenship in France and Germany* (1992), directed attention to "idioms of nationhood"—ways of thinking and talking about one's nation that shape the institutional realities of statehood, inform immigration policies, and affect integration practices. These cultural idioms, he insisted, are not merely speech acts; they originate in cultural and political geography, and are reinforced and activated in specific historical and institutional settings. Once established, however—and this is key—cultural idioms not only acquire causal force, they also are sedimented to become thoroughly resilient. Brubaker's comparative analysis of French and German national cultures was also important in that it highlighted varied ways of thinking about "culture." It examined, for example, the historical constitution (and the cultivation) of a "culture of the national," as well as the meaningful discursive practices that shape how people understand their nation.

Just as the paradigm shift from primordialism to social constructivism in the 1980s had entailed a shift from the study of nationalist movements and conflicts to that of the nation and its making, the discursive turn inaugurated by Anderson initiated the redefinition of the very object of study, from the nation to national *identity*. In the wake of *Imagined Communities*, the field moved even further away from "objectivist" stances and toward "subjectivist" ones. Duara, for example, sees national identity as a "subject position produced by representations in relation to other representations," the national self being constituted "within a network of changing and often conflicting representations" (1995: 7). In that context, nationalism is neither a unified ideology nor movement, but is rather a discursive field where different views of the nation compete and negotiate with each other. The ultimate outcome of these discursive struggles—which are embedded in social and political structures and backed by institutional power—is the creation of the nation as a compelling symbolic configuration. Though it may therefore be regarded as a "productive" process, one should not overlook the fact that the process also necessarily entails the use of power, including the discrediting, dislocation, repression, and even destruction of alternative visions and the marginalization of social actors representing them. Understanding the nation as a symbol competed over by different groups maneuvering to monopolize its definition and enjoy its legitimating effects, scholars of nationalism must identify the global, societal, and institutional contexts in which different groups fight for the exclusive control to define the nation, and to what ends (Verdery 1993: 39; cf. Bourdieu 1991). The focus on the conflict *within* the nation over the nation's meaning and identity, its project, and destiny is where some of the most interesting discussions may now be found.

In my own work on post-communist Poland (Zubrzycki 2006), I show that national identity is constituted through specific social dramas and events in which the meaning of the nation is contested and potentially transformed. Events like the war of the crosses at Auschwitz—when ultranationalist Poles erected hundreds of crosses just outside the former death camp to mark the site as one of *Polish* martyrdom (as opposed to one of the Jewish Shoah) and to stridently affirm Poles' *Catholic* identity—are meaningful and consequential in that they sporadically create, re-create, define, and refine national identity through social contestation. But such events are embedded within and caused by *longue durée* social, political, and cultural environments. Although the immediate context of the war of the crosses was post-communism, I argue that the period itself could not be understood without considering how Poles interpret and narrate the historic transformations taking place in the 1990s. It is by first historicizing the fall of communism, that is, by placing it within the context of Polish history and of Poles' *interpretations* of that history, that the meaning of the transition emerges. Indeed, Poles inject communism into a long series of narratives of conquest, occupation, and oppression by powerful neighbors, and of their own historical struggle for independence. The long decade between the fall of communism in 1989 and Poland's accession to the EU in 2004 was thus emplotted as merely the latest chapter in the epic of Poland's fight for independence. The year 1989 was—and is—commonly evoked as the "recovery of national independence," and historical linkages are constantly forged between the interwar period, when Poland reappeared on the European map, and the re-mapping of post-Soviet Europe.

The post-communist transition was therefore first and foremost understood by Poles as a *national* one; it was a period characterized not merely by democratization and marketization, but primarily by the construction of a national state, a state *of* and *for* Poles, to borrow Rogers Brubaker's apt formulation (1996). Given this project, the issue of what exactly constitutes "Polishness" is a recurring theme in public discourse; in the debates, Polish national identity's "traditional" association with Catholicism has been seriously questioned. It is in this broader context that the planting of crosses at Auschwitz takes on a fuller meaning, and that the analysis of such an event can shed light on the relationship between national identity and religion. One point here is that without considering the *meaning* of the post-communist transition, much of the public debates that have punctuated the decade, as well as the *type* and *pace* of institutional reforms that took place then, remains incomprehensible. But the point is also that meaning

519

is constituted through perduring narratives of the nation that have been sedimented into a national culture—canonized in history books and maps, inscribed onto the landscape, allegorized in poetry, folktales, popular sayings, and music, visualized in paintings, monuments, and popular art, materialized in vestments, jewelry, and other embodied practices, and memorialized in family photographs and memoirs. These multiple sites and forms not only establish a canonical national culture in the traditional sense of the term, but also constitute a specific culture of the nation, a prism through which national subjects see institutions, understand political transformations, and *feel* themselves to be related to historical events.

In the end, I show that nationalism is the result of perceptions of history and their aesthetic representation in material symbols and performance in rituals that succeed in taking hold as a "thinly coherent" national culture, to borrow William H. Sewell Jr.'s (1999) apposite phrase. Paying attention to this process is important because it is through symbols and the narratives they carry that people become emotionally invested in the nation and, potentially, mobilized or recruited into nationalist action. As a coveted symbol constructed out of sub-symbols, events, and narratives—that is, a thinly coherent national culture—the nation is constituted through the intersection of diverse discourses and practices, with political and cultural actors struggling to determine the direction of advance. Instead of the nation as a "thing" or as a historical and sociological fact, we have the nation as a constant work in progress constituted through debates about what constitutes "its" culture, its key symbolic representations.

As mentioned earlier, the continual process of nation-making is far from harmonious. It is instead characterized by conflictual debates as to what defines the national "self," as well as by "othering" practices. If the exclusion of "others" can be expressed through institutional-legal channels and even sometimes through violent means, it can also be enacted through more "subtle" discursive practices and symbolic violence (Bourdieu 1991). In Poland, for example, Catholicism is used by certain groups to define the symbolic boundaries of the "Polish nation": one is said to "truly" belong depending on one's commitment to the religion and to a very specific—and narrow—vision of Polishness that is symbiotically fused with Catholicism. Jewishness, in that discourse, is configured as the polar opposite of "true Polishness" through its association with secularism and civic nationalism. Through a complex chain of associations and double entendres, then, a "Jew" is anyone who does not adhere to a strictly exclusive ethno-Catholic vision of Poland. From this perspective, Poland is believed to be ruled by "Jews"; by *symbolic* Jews. Hence, we witness the strange phenomenon of anti-Semitism in a country virtually without Jews, but also its mirror-image, *philo*-Semitism. Indeed, the recent emergence and increasing popularity of Jewish festivals, the opening of Jewish restaurants, and the popularization of klezmer music in Poland index not merely the folklorization of Jews and things Jewish in that country but also the attempt to reclaim a past that was eradicated with the Holocaust and that had been ideologically erased and suppressed by the socialist state. Although tourism and other economic considerations certainly play an important role in that recent development turned "cultural phenomenon," I argue that a key objective of the cultural entrepreneurs engaged in these festivals is actually to create a *plural* Polish national culture. For, if "Jews," for the ethno-religious Right, symbolize a pernicious civic vision of the nation that destroys national culture, for the secular Left "Jews" serve as the symbol of an *emancipating* civic vision, defined by "post-national" national culture (Zubrzycki 2010).

520

New lines of research: everyday practices, material culture, and the senses

Hobsbawm rightfully insisted that nations and their associated phenomena, although "constructed essentially from above, ... cannot be understood unless also analyzed from below, that is in terms of the assumptions, hopes, needs, longings, and interests of ordinary people" (1990: 10). This is, of course, easier said than done.

The daunting empirical challenge of analyzing "everyday nationalism" has been taken up recently by Rogers Brubaker and his colleagues, who investigated the daily, routine construction of national identity and the nation by "ordinary" people in the Transylvanian town of Cluj, Romania (Brubaker *et al.* 2006). Cluj is an interesting place to study how subjects are "nationalized" in political discourses and by institutions, on the one hand, and through everyday practices, on the other, as the city is populated by a majority of Romanian-speakers and a significant Hungarian minority. The city in fact is the symbolic kernel of Transylvania, a borderland region between (and competed over by) Hungary and Romania; a city at the heart of Hungarian and Romanian national imaginations, and thus the object of passionate nationalist claims on both "sides." In a liminal geographic space construed as the respective cultural "core" of neighboring nations, *whose* national culture is to be dominant in the public sphere in bi-national Cluj, and how each group's national culture is maintained, disseminated, and reproduced become key social and political issues. The questions Brubaker and his colleagues pose, however, are whether, when, and how (ethno)national culture and (ethno)national identifications matter for "ordinary people." They therefore analyze the processes through which ethno-nationality becomes a significant modality of experience for individuals, situating "nation-ness" in the broader social worlds that its subjects inhabit—from the schools they go to, the churches they attend, the newspapers they read, and the stores they patronize to the partners they marry and the languages they speak at home, at work, and in the street. The researchers' observations also encompass subjects' everyday lives—from common preoccupations such as "getting by" in a rapidly transforming economy to workplace habits, from patterns of sociability to the uses of symbolically charged public spaces.

The study is part of a broader theoretical agenda proposed by Brubaker in influential essays published throughout the last decade—to develop a constructivist and "non-groupist" framework that views ethnicity and nationhood as relational, processional, and dynamic categories instead of as bounded entities comprising "collective individuals" and self-conscious actors. This agenda has impelled Brubaker to shift his empirical focus away from large-scale historical comparisons, in which national culture was constituted by, and shaped through, discursive idioms of nationhood, to the micro-analysis of everyday life, where national culture plays out in myriad small acts through which webs of belonging are spun. By showing in great detail how and when ethnicity matters for ordinary people in a "mixed" setting, the authors offer an incisive and novel way to think about national culture and provide a methodological guide to research other cases.

Another area where the challenge of studying "everyday" constructions of the national self is being taken up is in relation to material and visual culture, aesthetics, and consumption. If the discursive turn pressed scholars to consider national identities as partially shared ways of speaking and reading, the recent profusion of works on material culture invites reflection on the ways national cultures are made and maintained through a broader sensory range of images, sounds, textures, smells, and even tastes.

Visual culture, to take only one example, provides an interesting point of entry into national identity and its transformation because images have a special ability to mediate imaginary, linguistic, intellectual, and material domains (Morgan 1998: 8). By grabbing our attention and acting as concrete substitutes for abstract discourse (Agulhon 1981), images become agents of socialization. Because of their immense rhetorical power, they can also influence thought and behavior, which is why images play such an important role in marketing and propaganda (Bonnell 1997). Deciphering the various components of what French historian Maurice Agulhon (1981) has called "pictorial discourses" set forth by institutions and social actors is therefore another way to learn how subjects are nationalized and how they become emotionally invested in the abstract idea of "the nation." It is also a useful way to track conflicts about, and changes in, national visions. Another reason why visual culture is important for scholars of nationalism to study is that it binds individuals into a community, and it *bounds* that community. Visual culture indeed delineates the borders of imagined communities— whether religious, national, or other—by providing a shared repertoire of images and objects that shape memory and identity (Morgan 1998: 8). Because images are employed as "vehicles for shaping a collective sense of social belonging" (Stimson 2006: 8), they often become the object of struggles between groups promoting different ideologies or identities—a process referred to as iconomachy—which sometimes leads to iconoclasm, the discrediting and displacing of rivals through the destruction of their symbols (Morgan 2005). This process was indeed key, as I show in my latest work, in reshaping national identity and its relationship to Catholicism in 1960s Quebec (Zubrzycki in progress).

The question of producing and reproducing the senses of national identities has been pushed forward in part by the issue of spatial dislocation. Whether under the rubric of diaspora, the transnational, or any of many other terms, the question of how non-territorial national affiliations are maintained and transformed over time is, while not new as such, a proliferous area of contemporary research (Johnson 2007). Satellite television allows viewers to, in a sense, consume national identity via subscription, paying a monthly fee to have programming from a given region broadcast to their new home from thousands of miles away. Music is similarly mobile. However, other material features of national culture—say, agricultural techniques or the choreography of large-scale ritual events—are less transmissible. This means that long-distance or diasporic national cultures may take on quite different material forms and performative qualities from territorially based national cultures. As multiple versions of "the same" national culture emerge, they present new lines of fracture and change, and call for close attention.

Consider, for example, the Black Caribs of the Caribbean, also known as the Garifuna. The group is descended from both Africans and Amerindians, speaks an indigenous tongue, and has members residing in at least four different states—Honduras, Belize, Guatemala, Nicaragua, and the United States. Thus the Garifuna possess multiple plausible national affiliations and multiple historical horizons available for activation. As Paul Christopher Johnson's (2007) work has shown, as one-third of the group (an estimated 100,000) migrated from the Caribbean basin to US urban centers in the last half-century—especially to New York City—many adopted a heretofore mostly unknown "African diasporic" identity. In part this occurred because they came to be read as simply "black" within strictures of American racial codes, and in part due to their adoption of a diasporic self-understanding as a form of cultural resistance to that racial reduction.

Much of the shift occurred through religious practice, as the Garifuna in the Bronx and Brooklyn began to frequent rituals of Afro-Cubans, Haitians, Dominicans, and Jamaicans, gradually constructing a meta-national African diasporic self-understanding. In the process, they began to rethink the parameters of their own historic "Black Carib" identity, restructuring those parameters in relation to their African roots and privileging them over their Amerindian heritage. Yet, Johnson shows, when these Garifuna "cosmopolites" return to their homeland villages, they often find that their novel identity holds little resonance for those they left behind, and that in fact this identity is often actively resisted, since it confounds indigenous meanings and histories of Garifuna-ness. Through the spatial relocation of a significant portion of the population, then, two versions of the "national culture" emerge, one claiming a cosmopolitan authority of newly acquired multicultural awareness and skills, the other relying on the indigenous authority of superior "traditional" knowledge and direct contact with the central American "homeland."

This case shows, for our purposes, the malleability of what constitutes national culture but also the limits of that malleability, for although selectively remembering the past and the "homeland" (Central America or Africa?) can create new opportunities for social and political alliances of those who emigrated, these new identifications and affiliations fashioned "in diaspora" may become sources of social conflict when they are remitted to countries of origin and juxtaposed with local practices, resulting in distinct "indigenous" versus "cosmopolitan" forms of even an allegedly single nation.

Conclusion

Research on nationalism and national identity since the 1980s has left behind the old notions of culture as a static "thing." Instead, national culture is now approached as a set of meaningful discursive and ritual practices that are shared by individuals, but only shared sufficiently to allow for contest and debate. National cultures, moreover, do not exist outside of history, but rather "are" only as a series of interventions and enactments— in social dramas and "events," as well as everyday practices. National cultures are therefore neither reified "things" nor rarified abstractions. Rather, they are created and are instantiated in material objects and symbols, located in everyday practices, and rendered meaningful in specific social worlds. The space where the ideal/discursive and the material/practical meet is where, I believe, our continued efforts to understand national identity and its relationship to national culture should focus. Important works discussed in this essay have already laid the flagstones of that path.

References

Agulhon, Maurice. 1981. *Marianne into Battle: Republican Imagery and Symbolism in France, 1789–1880*. Cambridge: Cambridge University Press.

Anderson, Benedict. 1991. *Imagined Communities: Reflections on the Origins and Spread of Nationalism*. London and New York: Verso.

Billig, Michael. 1995. *Banal Nationalism*. London: Sage.

Bonnell, Victoria. 1997. *Iconography of Power: Soviet Political Posters under Lenin and Stalin*. Berkeley: University of California Press.

Bourdieu, Pierre. 1991. *Language and Symbolic Power*. Cambridge, MA: Harvard University Press.

Brubaker, Rogers. 1992. *Nationhood and Citizenship in France and Germany*. Cambridge, MA: Harvard University Press.

———. 1996. *Reframing Nationalism: Nationhood and the National Question in the New Europe*. Cambridge: Cambridge University Press.

Brubaker, Rogers, Feischmidt, Margit, Fox, Jon, and Grancea, Liana. 2006. *Nationalist Politics and Everyday Ethnicity in a Transylvanian Town*. Princeton, NJ: Princeton University Press.

Cerulo, Karen A. 1995. *Identity Designs: The Sights and Sounds of a Nation*. New Brunswick, NJ: Rutgers University Press.

Duara, Prasenjit. 1995. *Rescuing History from the Nation: Questioning Narratives of Modern China*. Chicago: University of Chicago Press.

Fox, Jon E. and Miller-Idriss, Cynthia. 2008. "Everyday Nationhood." *Ethnicities* 8(4): 536–76.

Gellner, Ernest. 1964. "Nationalism." Pp. 147–78 in *Thought and Change*. Chicago: University of Chicago Press.

Gillis, John R. 1994. "Memory and Identity: The History of a Relationship." Pp. 3–24 in J.R. Gillis, ed., *Commemorations: The Politics of National Identity*. Princeton, NJ: Princeton University Press.

Hall, John R., Stimson, Blake, and Becker, Lisa Tamiris, eds. 2006. *Visual Worlds*. New York: Routledge.

Handler, Richard. 1988. *Nationalism and the Politics of Culture in Quebec*. Madison: University of Wisconsin Press.

Hobsbawm, E. 1990. *Nations and Nationalism since 1780: Programme, Myth, Reality*. Cambridge: Cambridge University Press.

Hobsbawm, Eric J. and Ranger, Terrence, eds. 1983. *The Invention of Tradition*. London: Verso.

Huntington, Samuel P. 1996. *The Clash of Civilizations and the Remaking of World Order*. New York: Touchstone.

Inkeles, Alex. 1997. *National Character: A Psycho-Social Perspective*. New York: Transaction Publications.

Johnson, Paul Christopher. 2007. *Diasporic Conversions: Black Carib Religion and the Recovery of Africa*. Berkeley: University of California Press.

Kohn, Hans. 1946. *The Idea of Nationalism: A Study in Its Origins and Background*. New York: Macmillan Company.

Morgan, David. 1998. *Visual Piety: A History and Theory of Popular Religious Images*. Berkeley: University of California Press.

———. 2005. *The Sacred Gaze: Religious Visual Culture in Theory and Practice*. Berkeley: University of California Press.

Sells, Michael A. 1996. *The Bridge Betrayed: Religion and Genocide in Bosnia*. Berkeley and Los Angeles: University of California Press.

Sewell, William H. Jr. 1999. "The Concept(s) of Culture." Pp. 35–61 in V.E. Bonnell and L. Hunt, eds., *Beyond the Cultural Turn*. Berkeley: University of California Press.

Smith, Anthony D. 1986. *The Ethnic Origins of Nations*. New York: Blackwell.

Stimson, Blake. 2006. "Introduction: Visual Cultures and Visual Worlds." Pp. 1–10 in John R. Hall, Blake Stimson, and Lisa Tamiris Becker, eds., *Visual Worlds*. New York: Routledge.

Verdery, Katherine. 1993. "Whither 'Nation' and 'Nationalism'?" *Daedalus* 122(3): 37–46.

Weber, Eugen. 1976. *Peasants into Frenchmen: The Modernization of Rural France, 1870–1914*. Stanford, CA: Stanford University Press.

Winichakul, Thongchai. 1994. *Siam Mapped: A History of the Geo-Body of a Nation*. Honolulu: University of Hawai'i Press.

Zubrzycki, Geneviève. 2006. *The Crosses of Auschwitz: Nationalism and Religion in Post-Communist Poland*. Chicago: University of Chicago Press.

——. 2010. "What Is Pluralism in a 'Monocultural' Society? Considerations from Post-Communist Poland." In Courtney Bender and Pamela Klassen, eds., *After Pluralism: Re-imagining Models of Interreligious Engagement.* New York: Columbia University Press.

——. In progess. "'A People Learns Through Its Eyes': Visual Symbols and the Remaking of National Identity in Quebec."

50

Nationalism as the cultural foundation of modern experience

Liah Greenfeld and Eric Malczewski

For several years, the authors of this essay have begun their classes on nationalism by asking students to draw a pictogram of their "world"—the reality that they experience as significant. These pictograms usually consist of some indication of our globe, often with national flags on it, houses representing homes or schools, and figures of generic humans, often drawn in one or another way that stresses their basic interchangeability. The striking feature of these telegraphic representations has been their uncompromising secularism: they are focused on this mundane experiential world; transcendental forces appear nowhere on these drawings. God, clearly, is absent from these students' thoughts, even though many of these students would define themselves as religious. Their image of significant reality differs dramatically from the image we find represented in Western art even as late as El Greco, the canvases being filled with the depiction of God and his saints, canvases in which all of the action—everything of significance, that is to say, everything to which the artist strives to attract attention—takes place above the heads of diminutive mortals crowded into the lower quarter (or less) of the painting. The second salient characteristic of the students' images is the stressed equality of the humans, again contrasting with the representations of humanity in the art of the thirteenth to sixteenth centuries, in which the size of the figure quite often serves as the indication of the person's social status.

Our students' pictograms invariably reflect the *modern* form of consciousness—the secular and egalitarian image of reality that was brought into being by *nationalism* (Greenfeld 2006: 64–92). Nationalism is the constitutive element of modernity, and it provides the foundational form of consciousness in all societies defined as nations (Greenfeld 1992: 3–26). The perspective of nationalism is the cultural (i.e. symbolic) foundation of modern reality and the foundation on which our students build their identities (Greenfeld 1992; Greenfeld and Eastwood 2007). Our students live in the world created by nationalism.

In a short essay such as the present one, the best way to define culture is by analogy to DNA (for a detailed discussion of culture and the nature of social science, see Greenfeld and Malczewski 2009; Greenfeld 2006: 115–34, 203–23; Greenfeld 2005: 101–16). In human society, culture is the functional equivalent of the genetic code in animal species: whereas animal social orders are replicated genetically, the bases of our social orders are transmitted symbolically, or culturally. This means that the information contained in a particular form of culture is represented in various social, political, economic, and other arrangements in human society, just as the information contained in a particular genetic code is represented in the patterned behaviors of animals in various situations. Understanding the form of culture that serves this function in a particular society is, therefore, the central task in understanding that society, just as understanding the genotype of a species is the central basis for understanding that species (Durkheim 1995; Greenfeld and Malczewski 2009; Greenfeld 2007: 132–36). An accurate understanding of nationalism brings us much closer to the accurate understanding of the culture of modern society—its politics, economy, and all other aspects of modernity—than any other approach we can take.

Nationalism: the context of its birth

The form of consciousness known as nationalism emerged in sixteenth-century England in the aftermath of the War of the Roses (Greenfeld 1992: 3–87). As a result of the war, the feudal aristocracy was decimated, thereby creating a vacuum at the top of the social hierarchy. The new, Tudor, dynasty, however, needed an aristocracy, and so a new aristocracy was created out of especially talented and educated individuals coming from the lower social strata. In the form of consciousness characteristic of the medieval society of orders, such social mobility was impossible; social reality was envisioned as a hierarchical arrangement in which the three fundamental orders of men—the military nobility, the clergy, and the toilers—were as closed to interpenetration as the different species of life are to interbreeding (Greenfeld 2001b: 886). The experience of the new English aristocracy contradicted this image of reality, and its members sought to rationalize this experience—i.e. explain it and render it legitimate—in some other terms.

Needing a new form of consciousness to explain their experiences, these Englishmen appropriated the term "nation"—a term which in the context of the medieval church councils referred to a "political and cultural elite." The word "nation," used in this very dignified sense, became the synonym of "people" (which designated the general population of commoners, but specifically had the connotation of "rabble," or the least respected classes), and this equation had the effect of elevating the populace—all of the "people"—to the status of an elite. The implication of this conceptual innovation was that all Englishmen were thereafter imagined as being, and thus seen as, equal. In addition, since the term "nation" in particular meant "political elite" (which is to say the bearer of sovereign authority) the people thus saw themselves as, and so became, sovereign, too. The concept of sovereignty, however, only permitted one supreme authority; sovereignty could not be shared, and so the people replaced God as the bearer of sovereignty. Nationalism—at its root being the definition of the people as a nation—thus offered a fundamentally secular and egalitarian view of the world based on the principle of popular sovereignty. This new form of consciousness provided an acceptable, positive interpretation of the new aristocrats' experience. Thus emerged a new cultural framework through which experience was imagined and shaped.

Nationalism became the characteristic form of consciousness in England by 1600, then spreading first to the English colonies in America, then to France and Russia in the eighteenth century, and extending throughout Europe in the nineteenth century and around the world by the end of the twentieth century (Greenfeld 1992: 397, 89, 189, 275; Greenfeld 2001b: 897; Eastwood 2006). As the cultural foundation of modernity, nationalism provides the essential meaningful orientation to reality (a symbolic map, if you will) and a blueprint of the social order in all modern societies (those societies defined as nations). For this reason, all the institutional structures of these societies are shaped by it.

Implications of nationalism

To reiterate, there are three qualities that constitute nationalism's form of consciousness: (1) the picture of reality that it offers is essentially secular; (2) it is fundamentally egalitarian in its view of members of the nation; and (3) it assumes popular sovereignty. Each one of these features has important implications. We shall list some of them briefly.

To begin with, because nationalism is essentially secular, the value of the experience of this world is heightened and so is the value of an individual's life. Gone are the times of impatient waiting for communion with the eternal and an eternal existence that follows death—a characteristic feature of the experience of the religious society that modern society replaced. Life on this earth is all there is, and suffering and discontentment in this reality are thus intolerable. Modern individuals must take control of their fates, change arrangements that they find unacceptable, pursue happiness here, and mitigate suffering that is no longer seen as a part of a divine plan. Concerns about this world and this life interest all members of the nation (all of whom are interchangeable in their generalized capacity to occupy the available social positions), and their interest and subsequent activism are viewed as legitimate. Nationalism's principles of egalitarianism and popular sovereignty reinforce the effects of secularism.

Given the secular quality of national communities, we understand such terms as "Jewish nation" and "Islamic nation" designating groups that are understood to be fundamentally oriented to a transcendental reality to be very different; typically, such terms are indicative of forms of religious nationalism, with religion itself existing on nationalism's sufferance (Greenfeld 2006: 93–114, 135–44). Unlike forms of consciousness that limit activism or political participation to members of select social strata, nationalism legitimates and fosters universal participation.

Nationalism's most important political implication is *the state* (Greenfeld 2006: 77). This characteristically modern form of government is impersonal and necessarily bureaucratic: its legitimacy is not tethered to the individuals who staff it. Individuals are socially mobile within nationalist society and in its central institutions, and nationalism's egalitarian principle legitimizes staffing the various positions in the state with anyone qualified for the job. The state stands in stark contrast to personal government (such as kingship). The state both demands a flexible system of stratification and strengthens such a system. What is more, with the principle of popular sovereignty placing the source of authority in the national community, the government is necessarily representative. The officers who occupy positions in the state do so on behalf of the people, who maintain the right of recall of their public servants. Even in exceptional cases in which the state is seen to be personalized (Hitler and Stalin are two striking examples), the apparent autocrat is merely a remarkably powerful bureaucrat representing the authority of the people. Processes of democratization are manifest in nationalist societies to a degree not seen in other forms of society; the fundamentally egalitarian society based on the principle of popular sovereignty by definition and in practice yields democracy, which, of course, may take different forms. Liberal or individualistic democracies (such as those found in the US or Britain) differ from social or popular democracies (as in the USSR or Nazi Germany); popular dictatorships are a type of democracy, differing from liberal democracy in the form of the implementation of the same fundamental principles (Greenfeld 1993: 327).

Modern economy (i.e. the economy oriented toward growth, or capitalism) is also a product of nationalism (Greenfeld 2001a, 2006: 176). Despite common belief to the contrary, it can develop in the most liberal of democracies (e.g. Britain and the United States) as well as in dictatorships and authoritarian regimes (e.g. 1930s Germany, Chile under Pinochet, and, today, China); the historical record (indeed, a mere survey of the daily papers) demonstrates, emphatically, that it is so. The competition for economic growth is one of the forms of competition for prestige manifest in nationalist culture. Membership in a nation endows the individual with a sense of dignity and pride that is shared with the perceived dignity of the nation itself, thereby fueling the inter-national competition for prestige. Prestige is, however, a relative value, which makes such competition endless; in nations competing for prestige in the economic sphere, the result is the striving for ever-increasing wealth. Not all nations choose the economy as the sphere of international competition; some, such as Russia, may value military power, or something else—the choice depends on which sphere the nation in question feels most comfortable in at the outset. The open social structure implied in nationalism (so important for staffing the state bureaucracy) provides ideal conditions under which mobile labor can develop; therefore, it favors economic competition.

Another product of nationalism is science (Greenfeld 2006: 43–63, 145–61). Indeed, as a social institution, science emerged as a direct result of burgeoning national consciousness in seventeenth-century England. Science was advocated as the proof of English *genius*, serving to increase the nation's glory. As it did not exist at the time anywhere else, science provided a field on which the English could compete successfully for prestige. (It is interesting as well as important to note that in the seventeenth century England was the only nation on Earth, the only society with a national consciousness; this did not stop English contemporaries, however, from assuming that the rest of the world had national consciousnesses, too.) Additionally, of course, the secular focus of nationalism invested empirical reality with deep meaning, and what intellectual endeavor was better qualified to decipher this meaning than science—oriented to the understanding of empirical reality, which, to boot, rejected the intellectual authority of privileged estates and declared every man to be capable of this understanding? Today, the international competition for scientific advancement is as robust as ever, and many of the answers to questions concerning the nature of reality come from this institution.

Nationalism, however, made society exceedingly confusing: all nationalist societies are *anomic*. The concept of *anomie*, one of Emile Durkheim's best known contributions to our understanding of culture, refers to a state of cultural insufficiency, a systemic problem in the process of culture reflecting inconsistency between or the lack of coordination among various institutional structures or concretized culture, which results in the sending of contradictory messages to individuals: in a state of anomie, one is left devoid of a model for behavior (Durkheim 1951; Greenfeld 2006: 211–13). Given that culture shapes the ends to be desired by humans and provides the means for their attainment, the failure of culture to perform its function leaves individuals groping for solutions. Anomie is thus rightly understood as a culture-generative force, being the spur to symbolic imagination and, thereby, the premier cause of cultural change. Although nationalism, providing the foundation of modern social structure, proved to be an effective form of consciousness for those who adopted it, it also left them with the responsibility to fill in the details that their nationalist culture did not provide, such as finding one's place in this new reality. The noble doctrine that all men (and later women, too) were created equal was not very helpful: When everybody was defined as being as good as anyone else, every relationship of authority and every reward for individual achievement became problematic. Above all, a guide to this egalitarian, anomic world needed to include instructions for modern people charged with shaping their own individual identities and, trying, with varying success (and often without success at all), to figure out how to live in it—that is to say, to figure out what behavior is expected and appropriate.

It was literature, specifically the genre known as the *modern novel*, which for a long time provided such a guide. The premise of the modern novel is that to live in modern society is not simple. The modern novel depicts the social labyrinth negotiated by everyone from harlots, scullery maids, and orphans, to squires, men of the world, and fashionable young ladies—and the often terrible personal cost of such negotiation. The novel developed in early eighteenth-century England (although elements important to its genesis, such as casuistical literature, autobiography, travel literature, and romance, were known before), at a time when English society, including the full complement of its institutions and patterns of behavior, was being reshaped from the perspective of nationalism. The tremendous social mobility that was clearly extant in the time of Shakespeare was building to its acme in the late seventeenth century and early eighteenth century. This development placed a burden on those mobile social actors who struggled to learn how to behave in their new social positions, those actors seeking to negotiate the split in terrain created by the radical shift in the social order and the absence of clearly established hierarchies. The novel provided English readers with models for behavior, providing illustrations of contemporary life and the unfolding and resolution of various problems characteristic of it. The attention paid by authors such as Daniel Defoe and Samuel Richardson to the depiction of true-to-life experience was typical of the preoccupation with understanding the new social order; what was equally typical was the degree to which the English public devoured novels. The advent of the French novel followed identical lines: the novel flourishes after the advent of nationalism in France, with interpreters of social experience such as Honoré de Balzac and Gustave Flaubert penning what are nothing less than guides to life in modern society (whatever the artistic merits of their work might be). Today, our students typically look to popular music, television, and film for models of behavior and for interpretations of their experience and a language for describing it; until about World War II, literature was the chief, if not the only, source of such knowledge.

Much of the modern novel is devoted to the subject of love—another, perhaps most surprising, product of nationalism, which also emerged in sixteenth-century England (Greenfeld forthcoming). The story of Abelard and Eloise is well known, of course, proving that the capacity for "love" existed; however, any mental experience characteristic of a particular culture—be it reading, writing, enjoying the taste of a particular delicacy, or falling in love—can be experienced only on the condition that the capacity for such experience exists within human nature itself. The existence of a capacity, nevertheless, while it may explain certain cases of deviance (such as was the unique and, therefore, tragic story of Abelard and Eloise), cannot account for the virtual universalization in a particular period and society of what was earlier a deviant experience. Yet, this is what happened with love in sixteenth-century England. "Love" was an old word which was commonly used before the sixteenth century with a meaning similar to that of the original concept of *eros* in Hesiod—an ecstatic, self-transcendent, desire. It is because of this general meaning that "love" could be used to express both the lofty sentiment of Christian love and even the divine love of God itself (*agape, caritas, eros* as used in Christian theology) and the base (because carnal, essentially sinful) sexual lust. The sixteenth-century English concept of love—which is our concept—was dramatically different. While it implied the very opposite attitude to sex from the one that characterized Christian thinking, it retained clear sexual connotations. Thus the connection of love to lust seems obvious, but the other older usages were completely eclipsed, becoming foreign to us.

The new, as it came to be known later, "romantic" love was defined as a central expression of the sovereignty of the self, the supreme movement of the sovereign human spirit. Social arrangements that contradicted it became, by definition, inauthentic—false, wrong, morally abhorrent. Love made it possible for free and therefore rootless modern individuals, defined only as equal to all other individuals, to find their proper place and to define themselves. It was, therefore, an identity-forming device; this feature, above all else, explains the tremendous importance of the emotional complex of love in our lives. Love requires no effort whatsoever; as Shakespeare's Juliet says: "God join'd my heart to Romeo's." Love happens to one, one falls into it, thus leading to the discovery of one's true identity directly, filling life with meaning and at once reconciling one to it, even to the inevitability of death. What makes love an expression of the self nevertheless is the immediate recognition of the true love's object, the One, that particular her or him who is one's destiny and yet, paradoxically, is most freely chosen. One's identity, one's true self, is found in that other person and in what he or she sees in one. The unrivalled importance of love in the modern life cannot be explained by the fact that it delivered sex in a new package (adding to its legitimacy when sanctioned by marriage as well as the legitimacy by association with the ultimate expression of the authentic self). No, it is the invaluable aid that love provides to us in defining who we are that is responsible for such centrality.

For four centuries since Shakespeare we have been taught the lesson of *Così fan tutte*—that true love is a chimera, that we are fools to pine for it, that we should reconcile ourselves to this fact and be satisfied with what there is, some sexual infatuation growing into habitual attachment under the protection of social norms. But, despite all the lessons, people continue to believe that—to quote the Beatles' very famous distillation of Shakespeare's message put to music—"All you need is love/All you need is love/All you need is love, love/Love is all you need" (Lennon and McCartney 1967).

The modern family is a result of the advent of marriage for love and the egalitarian conception of society implied in nationalism. A society in which the bond of love between two individuals is seen as the only legitimating force behind marriage is dramatically different from a society in which marriage is seen as fulfilling the needs of a familial collectivity or some larger social obligation. What is more, nationalism has shaped the roles within marriage such that the duties and responsibilities of the husband and wife are matters of personal choice: fathers may be primarily responsible for childcare and wives may be the breadwinners; that is to say, the ancient institution of the family falls under the influence of egalitarianism and the increased value of the individual. Marriage is sanctioned by an impersonal entity (the state) that derives its force from the nation itself, religion playing a secondary role as a legitimating institution. And, as we know so well from the current debates over the question of gay marriage in the US and the steadily growing support for it in the general public, the influence of nationalism continues to grow.

Alternative perspectives

Studies of the nature of modern society have not always born fruit that has sated appetites for understanding the social systems under question. The classical dichotomies such as Feudalism/Capitalism, *Gemeinschaft/Gesellschaft*, and Organic versus Mechanical solidarity that have been bequeathed to us by our disciplinary forebears fail to grasp the constitutive element of modern society and, therefore, do little to describe accurately, much less to explain, the nature of the world we live in (Greenfeld 2006: 64–92; Marx 1978; Toennies 1963; Durkheim 1964). Additionally, theories of society and, therefore, theories of modernity that are based on some form of historical materialism—such theories being widespread in the social sciences (seen now and seen frequently in the variants of economic determinism, for example the modernization theory of the 1950s and 1960s) that were developed upon a particular view of history, a view in which history was understood to progress teleologically, advancing through a series of stages culminating in modernity (a point at which all societies would eventually converge)—are theoretically unjustified, given the problems of logic inherent in the perspective, the failure to explain how transitions between stages occur, and, most importantly, the universe of empirical evidence that contradicts the specific arguments being advanced. The theory of nationalism advocated in this essay, with the explanatory power it provides, differs markedly from other theories that have recently met with interest, such as those offered by Ernest Gellner and Benedict Anderson. The theory advanced here is logically sound and falsifiable, is based on empirical study of the societies in question, therein accounts for the phenomena being investigated, and is not based on that remnant of speculative philosophy—the deterministic, teleological view of humanity, and, therefore, of culture. The latter has provided no explanatory power to date, has no proof advocating for it (indeed, *quod erat demonstrandum* remains a begged question), and, thus, has no justifiable place in any science whatsoever.

As argued elsewhere in greater detail, grave problems are manifest in certain of the dominant interpretations of nationalism (Greenfeld 2005, 2006: 64–92). (For a detailed discussion of the state of the art, see Eastwood 2006: 1–22.) The main trouble with Ernest Gellner's argument in *Nations and Nationalism*, an argument which continues to be popular in the social sciences, is that it omits the one element central to the empirical sciences: empirical evidence itself (and Gellner's imaginary Ruritarians, Megalomanians, and blue people mirror known human societies very poorly, being, therefore, less-than-ideal ideal types, however understood). Gellner's underlying argument that nationalism is a systemic requirement of the capitalist (or industrial) economy is forcefully contradicted by the empirical evidence—England, France, Germany, Japan, and America, to name a few not unimportant cases, were nationalist societies *before* a capitalist economy arose in those societies. In addition to the evidence calling the authority of Gellner's work into question, other problems include the tautological nature of Gellner's definitions, which, obviously, presents logical problems, and his teleological conception of human development, which remains patently unjustified (Greenfeld 2005: 101–03; Greenfeld and Eastwood 2005: 247–50).

Anderson's argument in *Imagined Communities*, another work on nationalism that remains in vogue, does not differ much from Gellner's in substance insofar as nationalism is seen as systemic and determined: It is a retelling of history from the standpoint of classical historical materialism. In it, nationalism is, expectedly, taken as being epiphenomenal. Contrary to what the title might suggest, *Imagined Communities* does not emphasize the role of imagination (arguably the central ingredient in culture and the primary means by which members of national communities experience their nationality); instead, it focuses on the advent of print capitalism, seen as an economic development that gave birth to new political structures as it facilitated the imagining of linguistic universes as nations. The historical process said to be captured—and, therefore, the body of empirical evidence purported to be explained—by this logic is left unaccounted for in Anderson's work, and the logic itself is riddled with gaps (e.g. by regarding the process as fundamental, for example, the process could then be left unexplained—and it was). Anderson's work suffers from other problems with evidence—for example, Anderson's location of Latin America as nationalism's birth site is not sustained in his book, but the evidence against this claim is overwhelming (Bell 1995; Colley 1992; Eastwood 2006; Greenfeld 1992)—and fails to account for why the groups that came to be known as nations imagined themselves as such and not in some other way (such as churches or classes, for instance). In his later work, *The Spectre of Comparisons: Nationalism, Southeast Asia and the World* (1998), Anderson leaves no doubt of the role that imagination plays in his conception of the world: it follows "objective" social forces—in the case of national communities the social force is "capitalism" (Anderson 1998: 62). The evidence suggests otherwise (Greenfeld 2001a).

Conclusion

Nationalism is and has been the most important social, political, and economic force in the last five hundred years: it is such a force because it is the order-defining culture of our time. The equation of "people" and "nation" half a millennium ago effected a revolution in consciousness, compared to which all great modern revolutions, whether political or economic, pale in significance. All modern history, from the sixteenth century until today, is the history of the gradual institutionalization of the cultural precepts of nationalism, i.e. of the implementation of this form of culture in social, economic, political, and other arrangements, and its expression in the intellectual traditions characteristic of modern society. Such representation of the cultural blueprints of nationalism proceeds in different nations at different paces, but the direction of institutional change remains the same—towards greater consistency with secularism, egalitarianism, and popular sovereignty. Nationalism is the cultural foundation of modernity: it is the framework which gives meaning to our ideals and aspirations, and, insofar as modern humanity is concerned, it is our equivalent of DNA. We are defined, constructed, and made by nationalism—it is high time we start understanding it even better.

References

Anderson, Benedict. 1983. *Imagined Communities: Reflections on the Origin and Spread of Nationalism*. London: Verso.

——. 1998. *The Spectre of Comparisons: Nationalism, Southeast Asia and the World*. London: Verso.

Bell, David. 1995. "Lingua Populi, Lingua Dei: Language, Religion, and the Origins of French Revolutionary Nationalism." *American Historical Review* 100(5): 1403–37.

Colley, Linda. 1992. *Britons: Forging the Nation 1707–1837*. New Haven, CT: Yale University Press.

Durkheim, Emile. 1964. *The Division of Labor in Society*, trans. George Simpson. Glencoe, IL: The Free Press.

——. 1951. *Suicide*, ed. George Simpson, trans. John A. Spaulding and George Simpson. New York: The Free Press.

——. 1995. *The Elementary Forms of Religious Life*, trans. Karen E. Fields. New York: The Free Press.

Eastwood, Jonathan. 2006. *The Rise of Nationalism in Venezuela*. Gainesville: University Press of Florida.

Gellner, Ernest. 1983. *Nations and Nationalism*. Ithaca, NY: Cornell University Press.

——. 1997. *Nationalism*. New York: New York University Press.

Greenfeld, Liah. 1992. *Nationalism: Five Roads to Modernity*. Cambridge, MA: Harvard University Press.

——. 1993. "Nationalism and Democracy: The Nature of the Relationship and the Cases of England, France, and Russia." In *Research on Democracy and Society*, Vol. 1. Stamford, CA: JAI Press Inc.

——. 2001a. *The Spirit of Capitalism: Nationalism and Economic Growth*. Cambridge, MA: Harvard University Press.

——. 2001b. "Western Europe." In *Encyclopedia of Nationalism*, Vol. 1. San Diego and London: Academic Press.

——. 2005. "The Trouble with Social Science." *Critical Review* 17(1–2): 101–16.

——. 2006. "Nationalism and the Mind." *Nationalism and the Mind: Essays on Modern Culture*. Oxford: Oneworld Publications.

——. 2007. "*Main Currents* and Sociological Thought." Pp. 125–42 in Brian-Paul Frost and Daniel J. Mahoney, eds., *Political Reason in the Age of Ideology: Essays in Honor of Raymond Aron*. New Brunswick, NJ: Transaction Publishers.

——. Forthcoming. "The Cradle." Work in progress; an unfinished manuscript on modern culture and mental disease.

Greenfeld, Liah and Eastwood, Jonathan. 2005. "Nationalism in Comparative Perspective." Pp. 247–65 in Thomas Janoski, ed., *The Handbook of Political Sociology: States, Civil Societies, and Globalization*. Cambridge: Cambridge University Press.

——. 2007. "National Identity." Pp. 256–73 in Carles Boix and Susan Stokes, eds., *The Oxford Handbook of Comparative Politics*. Oxford: Oxford University Press.

Greenfeld, Liah and Malczewski, Eric. 2009. "Politics as a Cultural Phenomenon." In Craig Jenkins and Kevin Leicht, eds., *The Handbook of Politics*. New York: Springer.

Lennon, John and McCartney, Paul. 1967. "All You Need Is Love." From *Magical Mystery Tour*, Capitol Records.

Marx, Karl. 1978. "Manifesto of the Communist Party." Pp. 469–500. And "Preface to A Contribution to the Critique of Political Economy." Pp. 3–6 in Robert C. Tucker, ed., *The Marx–Engels Reader*. New York: W.W. Norton.

Toennies, Ferdinand. 1963. *Community and Society*, trans. Charles Loomis. New York: Harper & Row.

51

The cultural of the political

Towards a cultural sociology of state formation

Xiaohong Xu and Philip Gorski

In the human sciences, the study of culture and the study of the state are usually separate enterprises. In the disciplinary division of labor, the state is assigned to political science and (diplomatic) history, while culture is placed in the care of anthropology and (cultural) sociology. This division of labor has been underwritten and legitimated by aligning the state/culture opposition with various other binaries—state and nation, self-interest and solidarity, institutions and culture, power and language, and so on. These oppositions are quite old and stable.

This division of labor has come under challenge during the last two decades. The challenge arose from multiple conjunctures and can be observed across multiple fronts. The historical turn within anthropology (Comaroff and Comaroff 1997 [1991]) and the cultural turn within sociology both generated a number of "culturalist" studies of the state (Geertz 1980; Corrigan and Sayer 1985; Steinmetz 1999). The Foucauldian impact within the humanities led some literary scholars to roam far afield. Among early modern historians, the "confessionalization paradigm" generated much research interest in state-building. Even within political science, there is some evidence of a similar erosion of binary divides (e.g. Laitin 1986).

Certainly, there are plenty of counter-trends. These days, the buzz in history is about "political economy" and empire. In political science, formal models, quantitative methods, and experiments are the order of the day. In sociology, meanwhile, the once busy intersection of cultural and historical work is less traversed. Research informed by cultural and historical perspectives certainly generated impressive works of individual scholarship but—thus far—not a coherent research program. In retrospect, it looks more like a patchwork than a wave. As for cultural sociology, it has always been somewhat presentist and Americanist in orientation.

Is state formation just a bridge too far for cultural sociology? Not in principle. Many of the aforementioned binaries can be, and have been, challenged. Culturalist approaches have yielded considerable insight on other, seemingly unpromising topics, such as money and scientific institutions (e.g. Zelizer 1994; Vaughan 1996). Moreover, as state-building enters into discussion of foreign policy (e.g. Fukuyama 2004; Chandler 2005), it is important that historical and cultural sociologists counter naïve forms of neo-conservatism, which imagine that liberal democracies simply sprout up out of the scorched earth left behind by the slash-and-burn politics of regime change.

In this chapter, we will first review the theoretical threads in sociological lineages that can inspire cultural approaches to state formation; second, examine the state of affairs and the problematics in current literature on state and culture; and, lastly, tease out four subject areas in which a cultural sociology of state formation may bear fruit.

Cultural approaches to the state in sociological lineages

Karl Marx

Although most cultural Marxists have been more interested in "hegemony" and "ideology" (e.g. Gramsci 1971; Althusser 1971), Philip Corrigan and Derek Sayer's by-now classic work *The Great Arch* (1985) shows what a Marxist cultural sociology of state formation might look like. By linking English state formation back into the process of the "long making of bourgeois civilization" and the embourgeoisement of English society, they have paid much attention to the changes in social relations and human subjectivity that shaped the English state. Into this line of inquiries of culture, class formation, and state formation also falls Jürgen Habermas's early work *The Structural Transformation of the Public Sphere* (1989 [1965]), which tracked the emergence—and decline—of a "bourgeois public sphere" in early capitalist societies.

Max Weber

Strangely enough, the best starting point for a Weberian theory of culture and the state is not his political sociology, but his sociology of religion. Consider two of his most famous metaphors: the "switchman" and "elective affinity." The "switchman" metaphor arises out of Weber's attempt to grasp the long-term impacts that subtle differences in religious doctrine have on economic conduct, but a similar mode of analysis can be, and has been, employed in thinking about the impact of culture and/or religion on *political* conduct, the *locus classicus* being Michael Walzer's (1965) analysis of Puritanism, selfhood, and revolution in seventeenth-century England. There, Walzer argues that the Puritan movement forged a disciplined self capable of extraordinary feats of world-transformation.

Weber's second metaphor, "elective affinity," is an attempt to grapple with the same problem. In this case, however, the relationship is not between a realm of abstract ideas on the one hand and the sphere of individual interests on the other, but between two cultural constructs or "historical individuals"—the "spirit of capitalism" and the "Protestant ethic." This mode of analysis can also be applied to the relationship between culture and the state, if we focus on potential affinities between religio-cultural and political ethics or spirits. For example, Gorski (2003) has argued that Calvinism and bureaucracy have such an affinity, and Van Kley (1996) has made a similar argument for Calvinism and French republicanism.

Weber's sociology of religion contains two other concepts that are potentially useful for a cultural theory of the state—value spheres and carrier groups. In his version of differentiation theory, Weber makes "ultimate values" the gravitational force around which the various spheres take shape. These ultimate values are transmitted and elaborated by "carrier groups" that have strong interests, material and ideal, in the preservation and influence of these values. The value spheres concept is useful insofar as it allows us to pose questions about cultural boundaries—between the political and the religious, say, or the political and the aesthetic. In addition, it instructs us to conceive of such boundaries as the result of ongoing struggles between carrier groups that are seeking to expand the reaches of their cultural authority. This line of analysis is further elaborated in Bourdieu's theory of "fields" and "classification struggles."

We conclude with Weber's well-known definition of the state as an organization that claims a "monopoly of legitimate violence" within a particular territory or community. Although this definition appears non-culturalist at first glance, Norbert Elias (1994) has spelled out its underlying cultural significance, in that the historical process of monopolization of legitimate use of physical violence involved a radical cultural change in terms of both the disposition of the governed and the relationship between the state and the individual life. Moreover, as Ikegami (1995) has shown, the civilizing process is not a purely Western phenomenon.

Emile Durkheim

Although Durkheim is often charged with ignoring power and politics, Durkheimian political sociology is not an oxymoron. For example, Durkheim's theory of ritual (1995) can help to solve the "collective action problems" that arise within rationalist accounts, which transform obedience into the "principal–agent problem," cooperation into the "collective action problem," and institutional reproduction into an "equilibrium problem." A Durkheimian approach suggests that these "problems" are more easily solved if we attend to collective rituals, collective emotions, and collective identity. The fruitfulness of this neo-Durkheimian political sociology is evident in works on court ritual, political festivals (Ozouf 1988), "political religion" (Gentile 1996; Falasca-Zamponi 1997), and "civil religion" (Bellah 1975).

The second possible starting point for this research program is the analysis of law in Durkheim's *The Division of Labor in Society* (1984), particularly the discussion of criminal punishment as a mechanism for articulating and reproducing the social norms that make up the "collective conscience." Historical criminologists of a neo-Durkheimian bent— and that includes Foucault—have effectively shown how changing practices of punishment can be used to track changes in the character and efficacy of state power (Smith 2003; Garland 2006; Spierenburg 1984; Foucault 1995).

A third possible starting point for a neo-Durkheimian political sociology is a pair of lesser known works: *Moral Education* (1961) and *Professional Ethics and Civic Morals* (1958). Little read and often out of print, these writings anticipate themes that are now drawing increasing attention. One is the relationship between state formation and subjectivity. Whereas the standard trope suggests that the growth of state power is associated with a devaluation of the individual, Durkheim strongly rejects this view. Insofar as the growth of the state goes together with an increasing "division of labor," it is in fact accompanied by a higher degree of individuation as well as by a greater respect for "the abstract individual," that is, with respect for, and protection of, human rights. If Durkheim is right, a cultural sociological analysis of state formation will not be complete without serious inquiry into the ideologicization of the individual (Koselleck 1988), as the formulation of autonomous political judgments

537

has become both an important right and duty of the modern, democratic citizen (Schneewind 1998).

Michel Foucault

Few contemporary social theorists have had a greater impact on state theory than Michel Foucault. Contrary to the commonplace understanding of state power as top-down, centralized, coercive, legal, and ideological, Foucault asserts that power is diffuse and productive. Real state power, he argues, operates at the micro-level (as capillary power). It works on the body, not the mind, and it does so through the organization of space rather than the promulgation of laws (disciplinary power). It is more concerned with bringing the lost sheep back into the fold (pastoral power) than with building fences. Given the secularist impulse that underlies Foucault's work, unsurprisingly he refuses connection between ideas (beliefs, ideologies, etc.) and practices, and altogether ignores the history of Christendom, focusing instead on pre-Christian antiquity and the post-Reformation. Still, as Gorski (2003) has shown, Foucault's theories of "disciplinary power" and "governmentality" can be adapted and applied to religious movements and to the pre-Enlightenment era. Timothy Mitchell's (1999) well-known work on "the state effect" suggests another possible direction for Foucauldian analysis. He maintains that it is precisely through its self-conscious separation and disentanglement from the "society" by its management of space, uniforms, routines, and specialized organization that the state manages to (mis)represent itself as a unifying structure and achieve the "state effect."

Pierre Bourdieu

Insofar as Bourdieu's work represents a synthesis of the classical traditions, it is a fitting way to conclude such a survey. Like Weber, Bourdieu is preoccupied with the relationship of the ideal and the material or, as he usually frames it, the "subjective" and the "objective," and his programmatic aim is to do justice to both. This is particularly evident in his approach to class. Like Marx, he formulates a political sociology that highlights class conflict and capital accumulation. Like Durkheim (and Mauss), however, he gives considerable attention to systems of classification as well. The result is his theory of "classification struggles," in which the stakes are not simply power relations between already existing classes, but the very reality of competing bases of group formation, what Bourdieu (2000) calls "principles of vision and di-vision." The outcome of such struggles, he argues, is determined not solely by material conditions, but also by symbolic struggles. If this outcome influences the state, the reverse is also true. In one famous formulation, Bourdieu refers to the state as the "central bank of symbolic credit" (Bourdieu 1996: 376). What does he mean by this somewhat cryptic phase? Simply put, the state is often the final arbiter of classificatory systems, through its authority over language and the law. Like Weber, Bourdieu traces the emergence of the state field mainly to intra-elite conflicts, first within royal households, and then between religious and secular intellectuals and administrators. He also links the formation of the state to the differentiation of various species of capital (Bourdieu 2004). The separation of the political rule, first from economic production, and then from ideological production (i.e. religion), is accompanied by the primitive accumulation of three species of capital— symbolic, economic, and cultural (Loveman, 2005).

Research agendas

As should be clear from the foregoing discussion, a "cultural sociology of state formation" could be many different things. Just what it is depends on just how one defines "culture" and "the state," as well as on the direction of the causal arrow between them. In this context, we can only outline a few of the main questions and approaches. The first question concerns the ontology of culture—what culture *is*. Here, we can distinguish three basic approaches. The first conceives of culture as a kind of grammar, as the "code" that underlies and structures language and ritual. In this conception, the key task of the cultural sociologist is to discover the rules and crack the codes that structure cultural expression. The second approach conceives of culture as "values." From this perspective, the main task of the cultural sociologist is to identify the central values of a culture and specify their relationship to world-pictures. There is also an intermediate view, which understands culture as a "map" or a "script," which people use to orient themselves. Here, the key task of the cultural sociologist is to identify the various types of cultural performances.

The second major question concerns the relationship between culture and action. In the first tradition, the relationship between culture and action is analogous to the relationship between grammar and speech. Action simply manifests and reproduces culture. Culture is *en*acted. In the second tradition, the relationship between culture and action is one of ends to means. Culture provides one set of ends, material interests another, and action arises out of the clash between them. Culture exerts a force *on* action. In the third tradition, the relationship between culture and action is one of means to ends. Culture provides scripts for performing a role or maps for traveling to a destination.

A third and final area of difference concerns the relationship between culture and social structure. On one view, broadly Durkheimian, the relationship is homologous and unitary. Social boundaries are cultural boundaries. On a second view, broadly Marxist, the relationship is homologous but stratified. Class boundaries are also cultural boundaries, but the dominant class dominates the culture. On a third view, more Weberian in inspiration, the relationship is fractured and stratified. Societies are divided into autonomous and antagonistic value spheres, and the value spheres are dominated by a class of "virtuosos."

We can distinguish three broad categories in theories of the state as well: neo-Marxian, neo-Weberian, and neo-Smithian. For the most part, neo-Marxian approaches conceptualize the state as an instrument of class domination, putting the focus on state–society relations and state policies. There is little attention to institutional structures or inter-state relations. These are precisely the principal concerns of many neo-Weberians, for whom state formation is synonymous with state organization and geo-political conflict the key catalyst. Finally, in the neo-Smithian approach, the state is conceptualized as a hierarchy of self-interested principals (i.e. rulers) and agents (officials) engaged in various forms of predation and deception. Not much culture here. The dominant approach to the state within contemporary sociology is undoubtedly the neo-Weberian one. Insofar as culture figures at all in comparative-historical work on the state, it is mainly as a "dependent variable." Thus states build nations, construct ethnicities, legitimate professions, etc.

What would be the most promising and fruitful direction for a new cultural sociology of the state? Some of the possible paths between cultural theory and state theory are already well trodden. Surveying the terrain, we see two paths that are both passable and under-traversed. The first leads from Weber's theory of value spheres to the study of "the state effect" and "the political" more generally, and involves looking at how conflict within carrier groups and between ultimate values affects state/society boundaries (one could also map this path in Bourdieuian terms by focusing on the state's role in constituting and regulating an encompassing "field of power"). The second leads from Durkheim's sociology of religion to the study of political rituals and classifications. Each path can also be trodden in reverse as well. This yields the following four subject areas: (1) state ideas, (2) state boundaries, (3) state rituals, and (4) state classifications.

State ideas

The concept of the impersonal state as the object of universal service and respect, from both rulers and ruled, is a modern invention (Shennan 1974). The historical formation of this concept and the drawing and redrawing of boundaries between the state and other spheres—many of which are also modern constructions—were not epiphemonenal to the formation of the "class state" or "fiscal-military state." Instead, these processes independently took part in shaping the symbolic power and organizational de-limitation of the emerging state. A cultural sociology of state formation thus needs to address the cultural constructions of the state idea and its relationship with other spheres.

For cultural sociologists, the formation of state ideas itself must be part and parcel of "real" state formation. Here, a fruitful starting point may be found in Bourdieu's analysis of the *noblesse de robe* and their republican inheritors, who have their private interests in public interest, and who have played a role in constructing the centrality of the state idea in France's political life. A similar analysis might be made of, say, the revival of Roman law from the late medieval period to the Renaissance (Anderson 1974: 26–29; Berman 1983) and the emergence of "reason of state" around the same period (Shennan 1974; Viroli 1992; Skinner 1989; Oestreich 1982). Both developments helped augment the symbolic power of the central authority and transform the "king's house" into an impersonal state. Meanwhile, the symbolic power of the state also encountered its organizational de-limitation with the emergence and autonomization of other spheres, helping to forge the functionally differentiated world we know today.

State boundaries

There are two dimensions of boundary-makings in this process—external and internal. Both are involved in long-term processes of state-making. Territorial states must bind themselves off both from sub-state social formations such as kinship networks, as well as from larger-scale social formations such as religious networks. The idea of "sovereignty" was integral to this process, and jurists played a particularly important part in its articulation (Spruyt 1994). With the "rise of the West," the territorial nation-state became *the* legitimate model of political organization (Meyer 1999). The state–empire relation should not be conceived in stadial terms, however: The consolidation of Western nation-states was succeeded by a long period of empire-building, too. The same might be said of the relationship between state-building and nation-building. The old adage that the one follows the other—"We have made Italy, now we must make Italians"—is only one of the forms it can take. Nationalism can also be a tool for empire-building—or empire-smashing. Once a territorial state has been consolidated, a new problem of internal boundary formation emerges—the boundary between state and society. The problem was first posed by Cassirer (1946) and posed anew in recent years by Philip Abrams (1988) and Timothy Mitchell (1999). But it has not received sustained and systematic attention from them or anyone else.

A culturalist account may need to first ask if it even makes sense to speak of "state–society relations" in historical contexts where these are not operative political categories. In early modern Europe, such relationships were above all marked by the emergence of the pre- or non-political public space that early Enlightenment thinkers understood as "civil society" or simply "society" (Koselleck 1988) and that today's scholars refer to as "civil society" or the "public sphere" (Habermas 1989 [1965]). This "society" was characteristic of the equality between contracting agents or conversational partners and its rejection of the logic of hierarchy that was usual in families, corporations, political patronage, or any other social relations. Its emergence made a huge impact on the dynamics of politics and the form of state power that could be legitimately exerted (Knights 2005; Ikegami 2005).

The boundary between state and economy has been quite contested and variable as well. As Foucault (1991) reminds us, "economy" was originally private or household economy and only gradually came to be redefined in impersonal terms that legitimated state involvement ("governmentality"). However, we should not imagine that the boundaries of state power are always expanding. The upshot of the eighteenth-century debate between mercantilist and *laissez-faire* theories of political economy was to contract the boundaries of the state and free the economy from political control.

Similarly, the boundaries between state and religion can also be problematized in cultural sociological terms. How shall we explain the historical relationship between the emergence of the modern state and the separation of church and state in the context of confessional strife in early modern Europe? Which kinds of cultural refashioning in political theories as well as in political theologies had made possible the autonomization of these two fields from each other? To what extent can we compare the Western experience with those of other parts of the world? These are questions that have received too little attention from sociologists. The church/state relationship has also not been as simple as modernist narratives would lead us to believe. True, the dominant trend in most Western countries has been towards the transfer of various "social functions" from the church to the state ("secularization"). But there have been local counter-trends as well—the expansion of religious schools and colleges, for example, or the growth of "faith-based initiatives"—which have shifted boundaries in the other direction.

State rituals

In comparison to the study of state boundaries, this is a relatively developed field of inquiry. One seminal work is Ernst Kantorowicz's study (1957) of the funereal rituals designed to contain the contradiction between the immortality of kingship and the mortality of kings with the (to us) peculiar doctrine of "the king's two bodies." Others include Mona Ozouf's monograph on "French Revolutionary Festivals" (1988), which staged the revolutionary break and connected the new regime to transcendent purposes by means of elaboration processions and deistic liturgies; Emilio Gentile's (1996)

541

fine-grained analyses of Mussolini's use of ritual to legitimate his new regime, and Falasca-Zamponi's (1997) and Berezin's (1997) re-theorizations of it; and finally Robert Bellah's (1975) analyses of "American civil religion." Nor are these the only studies that might be mentioned (e.g. Hobsbawm and Ranger 1992; Geertz 1980; Shils and Young 1953). One limitation of this work, however, has been its focus on social stability and reproduction. That ritual analysis can also be used to understand processes of historical rupture and transformation has recently been shown by William Sewell, Jr.'s study (1996) of the cultural improvisation and invention that occurred during the storming of the Bastille and the subsequent influence of these events and their construction on the French Revolution as a whole.

Contemporary cultural sociology has offered two major strains of thought, both deriving from the Durkheimian heritage, which may bear fruit in studying state rituals. Jeffrey Alexander's social performance theory (2004) can be employed to analyze how state actors (symbolic persons such as figureheads, diplomats, etc.) succeed or fail in "re-fusing" the elements of successful social performance in front of their audiences. Even in stable democracies, the maintenance of state power cannot dispense with the façade of these "stately" performances. Randall Collins's interaction ritual theory (2004) focuses on collective, rather than individual, performances, and could be fruitfully applied to political life. Although Alexander and Collins both emphasize the "higher rituals" of the state, its "lower rituals" (e.g. bureaucratic rituals) can also be studied in light of Goffman's work.

State classifications

In the seminal work of Durkheim and Mauss, the theory of ritual was closely associated with a theory of classification. Strangely, the latter subject has received relatively little attention. One important exception to this rule is Chandra Mukerji's study of *Territorial Ambitions and the Garden of Versailles* (1997). In seventeenth-century France and other early modern states, she shows, the building of states went hand in hand with a reshaping—or rather, a reconstitution—of the "natural" environment. Whereas conventional, realist accounts might be more apt to portray the Garden of Versailles as a symbol of fiscal irresponsibility. Mukerji suggests that such projects were symbols of something else—the centralization and territorialization of political power. Nor were such projects "merely" symbolic: for instance, there was considerable synergy between gardens and garrisons. If Durkheim and Mauss argued that group boundaries underwrote and naturalized epistemological categories, Murkerji shows that groups' boundaries were themselves "planted" in the material environment. The "construction" of the French state and the French nation was not just linguistic, then, but aesthetic as well.

The limits of such construction projects are ably demonstrated in another work, James Scott's *Seeing Like a State* (1998). By the nineteenth century, for economic and fiscal reasons, rulers were looking to reshape landscapes and cityscapes so as to increase their efficiency and output. To that end, state managers and planners sought to rationalize the natural and built environments. State-owned forests were reconfigured to maximize timber harvests. State-managed housing developments were constructed to maximize labor productivity. As Scott reminds us, however, such schemes rarely worked for long. The reason, he argues, is that the hyper-rationalist models of "high modernist" aesthetics failed to capture many aspects of natural and social ecologies—aspects that turned out to be crucial to their long-term vitality. That such utopian schemes were ever implemented had to do with their "elective affinity" with the ethos and interests of managerial elites, on the one hand, and the weakness of civil society, on the other.

Of course, one of the most important forms of state classifications is individual identification and the issuance of corresponding documents. John Torpey (2000) uses the history of the passport to track the state's gradual monopolization of control over movement across borders and its use of civil registration as a means of public mobilization (e.g. in mass conscription). This project is also subject to failure, as shown by Mara Loveman's study (2007) of popular opposition to civil registration in Brazil's "war of the wasps." The "primitive accumulation of symbolic power," she argues, is in a sense prior to, and constitutive of, other forms of state power and requires a certain degree of cooperation and collusion on the part of local elites, which it did not receive in the Brazilian case, partly because state managers refused to ally themselves with the traditional holders of classificatory authority in Brazil—the Catholic clergy. And with far-reaching consequences: Absent such basic information, the Brazilian state was unable to establish a "modern" army and forced to rely on semi-feudal systems of military recruitment. Here again, symbolic power proved all too "real."

Conclusion

The "third wave" of comparative-historical sociology arose out of a powerful confluence of trans-disciplinary currents during the late 1980s, when the "second wave" of neo-Marxian and left-Weberian work intersected with cultural sociology, cultural history, Geertzian anthropology, and historicist forms of literary scholarship. The result was a dramatic upsurge in culturally inflected historical analysis. But many of these currents have now weakened or receded. This is not to say that the sands have not shifted in their wake. Historians now routinely do comparative work. Comparative methods are *de rigueur* in such diverse areas as urban ethnography and international relations. Historical anthropology is a stable sub-field. Still, the center did not hold. It never does.

A new wave of cultural work on state formation, and cultural analysis of politics more generally, would probably have to draw its energy from other sources. Which ones? Surveying the horizon, we see three possibilities. One, of course, is cultural sociology itself, a field which has been remarkably Americo-centric and presentist in its orientations, but where trans-national scholarly networks have become denser and cross-national comparison is becoming somewhat more common (Lamont and Thévenot 2000). Another is political theory, where old-school exegesis of classical texts has been increasingly supplanted by empirically informed (if methodologically unsystematic) philosophical reflection on citizenship, cosmopolitanism, toleration, minority rights, public and private, and other subjects closely related to the research program sketched above (Benhabib 2002; Walzer 1997; Kymlicka and Norman 2000). The last is historical work by literary scholars, which increasingly engages topics such as publicity, secularism, civil religion, state subjectivity, and so on (Warner 2002; Visconsi 2008).

In a sense, promoting a cultural sociology of state formation means not only reclaiming the analytical territories that sociologists have surrendered to other disciplines by engaging substantive questions about the state and its historical formation, but also reinventing sociology itself in this process.

References

Abrams, Philip. 1988. "Notes on the Difficulty of Studying the State." *Journal of Historical Sociology* 1: 58–89.

Alexander, Jeffrey C. 2004. "Cultural Pragmatics: Social Performance between Ritual and Strategy." *Sociological Theory* 22(4): 527–73.

Althusser, Louis. 1971. "Ideology and Ideological State Apparatuses." Pp. 127–86 in *Lenin and Philosophy and Other Essays*, trans. Ben Brewster. New York and London: Monthly Review Press.

Anderson, Perry. 1974. *Lineages of the Absolutist State*. London: NLB.

Bellah, Robert N. 1975. *The Broken Covenant: American Civil Religion in Time of Trial*. New York: Seabury Press.

Benhabib, Seyla. 2002. *The Claims of Culture: Equality and Diversity in the Global Era*. Princeton, NJ: Princeton University Press.

Berezin, Mabel. 1997. *Making the Fascist Self: The Political Culture of Interwar Italy*. Ithaca, NY: London: Cornell University Press.

Berman, Harold J. 1983. *Law and Revolution: The Formation of the Western Legal Tradition*. Cambridge, MA: Harvard University Press.

Bourdieu, Pierre. 1994. "Rethinking the State: Genesis and Structure of the Bureaucratic Field," trans. Loic J.D. Wacquant and Samar Farage. *Sociological Theory* 12(1): 1–18.

——. 1996. *The State Nobility: Elite Schools in the Field of Power*, trans. Lauretta C. Clough. Oxford: Polity Press.

——. 2000. *Pascalian Meditations*, trans. Richard Nice. Cambridge: Polity.

——. 2004. "From the King's House to the Reason of State: A Model of the Genesis of the Bureaucratic Field." *Constellations* 11(1): 16–36.

Cassirer, Ernest. 1946. *The Myth of the State*. New Haven, CT: Yale University Press.

Chandler, David. 2005. "How 'State-Building' Weakens States." Available at http://www.spiked-online.com/Articles/0000000CADDB.htm (last accessed June 25, 2008).

Collins, Randall. 2004. *Interaction Ritual Chains*. Princeton, NJ and Oxford: Princeton University Press.

Comaroff, Jean and Comaroff, John L. 1997 (1991). *Of Revelation and Revolution*. Chicago: University of Chicago Press.

Corrigan, Philip and Sayer, Derek. 1985. *The Great Arch: English State Formation as Cultural Revolution*. Oxford and New York: Blackwell.

Durkheim, Emile. 1958. *Professional Ethics and Civic Morals*, trans. Cornelia Brookfield. Glencoe, IL: The Free Press.

——. 1961. *Moral Education: A Study in the Theory and Application of the Sociology of Education*, trans. and ed. Everett K. Wilson and Herman Schnurer. New York: Free Press.

——. 1984. *The Division of Labor in Society*, with an introduction by Lewis Coser, trans. W.D. Halls. New York: The Free Press.

——. 1995. *The Elementary Forms of Religious Life*, trans. Karen E. Fields. New York: The Free Press.

Elias, Norbert. 1994. *The Civilizing Process: Sociogenetic and Psychogenetic Investigations*, trans. Edmund Jephcott. Oxford and Malden, MA: Blackwell Publishers.

Falasca-Zamponi, Simonetta. 1997. *Fascist Spectacle: The Aesthetics of Power in Mussolini's Italy*. Berkeley: University of California Press.

Foucault, Michel. 1988. "Politics and Reason." Pp. 57–85 in *Politics, Philosophy, Culture: Interviews and Other Writings, 1977–1984*, trans. Alan Sheridan and others. New York: Routledge.

——. 1991. "Governmentality," trans. Rosi Braidotti and revised by Colin Gordon. Pp. 87–104 in Graham Burchell, Colin Gordon, and Peter Miller, eds., *The Foucault Effect: Studies in Governmentality*. London: Harvester Wheatsheaf.

——. 1995. *Discipline and Punish: The Birth of the Prison*, trans. Alan Sheridan. New York: Vintage Books.

Fukuyama, Francis. 2004. *State-Building: Governance and World Order in the 21st Century*. Ithaca, NY: Cornell University Press.

Garland, David. 2006. "Concepts of Culture in the Sociology of Punishment." *Theoretical Criminology* 10(4): 419–47.

Geertz, Clifford. 1980. *Negara: The Theater State in Nineteenth Century Bali*. Princeton, NJ: Princeton University Press.

Gentile, Emilio. 1996. *The Sacralization of Politics in Fascist Italy*, trans. Keith Botsford. Cambridge, MA: Harvard University Press.

Gorski, Philip. 2003. *Disciplinary Revolution: Calvinism and the Rise of the State in Early Modern Europe*. Chicago and London: University of Chicago Press.

Gramsci, Antonio. 1971. *Selections from the Prison Notebooks of Antonio Gramsci*, ed. and trans. Quintin Hoare and Geoffrey Nowell Smith. New York: International Publishers.

Habermas, Jurgen. 1989 (1965). *The Structural Transformation of the Public Sphere: An Inquiry into a Category of Bourgeois Society*, trans. Thomas Burger and Frederick Lawrence. Cambridge, MA: MIT Press.

Hobsbawm, Eric and Ranger, Terence, eds. 1992. *The Invention of Tradition*. Cambridge and New York: Cambridge University Press.

Ikegami, Eiko. 1995. *The Taming of the Samurai: Honorific Individualism and the Making of Modern Japan*. Cambridge, MA: Harvard University Press.

——. 2005. *Bonds of Civility: Aesthetic Networks and the Political Origins of Japanese Culture*. Cambridge and New York: Cambridge University Press.

Kantorowicz, Ernst H. 1957. *The King's Two Bodies: A Study in Mediaeval Political Theology*. Princeton, NJ: Princeton University Press.

Knights, Mark. 2005. *Representation and Misrepresentation in Later Stuart Britain: Partisanship and Political Language*. Oxford: Oxford University Press.

Koselleck, Reinhart. 1988. *Critique and Crisis: Enlightenment and the Pathogenesis of Modern Society*. Cambridge, MA: The MIT Press.

Kymlicka, Will and Norman, Wayne, eds. 2000. *Citizenship in Diverse Societies*. Oxford and New York: Oxford University Press.

Laitin, David. 1986. *Hegemony and Culture: Politics and Religious Change among the Yoruba*. Chicago: University of Chicago Press.

Lamont, Michèle and Thèvenot, Laurent, eds. 2000. *Rethinking Comparative Cultural Sociology: Repertoires of Evaluation in France and the United States*. Cambridge and New York: Cambridge University Press.

Loveman, Mara. 2005. "The Modern State and the Primitive Accumulation of Symbolic Power." *American Journal of Sociology* 110(6): 1651–83.

——. 2007. "Blinded Like a State: The Revolt against Civil Registration in Nineteenth-Century Brazil." *Comparative Studies in Society and History* 49(1): 5–39.

Meyer, John W. 1999. "The Changing Cultural Content of the Nation-State: A World Society Perspective." Pp. 123–43 in George Steinmetz, ed., *State/Culture: State Formation after the Cultural Turn*. Ithaca, NY and London: Cornell University Press.

Mitchell, Timothy. 1999. "Society, Economy, and the State Effect." Pp. 76–97 in George Steinmetz, ed., *State/Culture: State Formation after the Cultural Turn*. Ithaca, NY and London: Cornell University Press.

Mukerji, Chandra. 1997. *Territorial Ambitions and the Gardens of Versailles*. Cambridge and New York: Cambridge University Press.

Oestreich, Gerhard. 1982. *Neostoicism and the Early Modern State*, ed. Brigitta Oestreich and H.G. Koenigsberger, trans. David McLintock. Cambridge and New York: Cambridge University Press.

Ozouf, Mona. 1988. *Festivals and the French Revolution*, trans. Alan Sheridan. Cambridge, MA: Harvard University Press.

Schneewind, Jerome. 1998. *The Invention of Autonomy: A History of Modern Moral Philosophy*. Cambridge: Cambridge University Press.

Scott, James C. 1998. *Seeing Like a State: How Certain Schemes to Improve the Human Condition Have Failed*. New Haven, CT and London: Yale University Press.

Sewell, William Jr. 1996. "Political Events as Structural Transformations: Inventing the Revolution at the Bastille." *Theory and Society* 25: 841–81.

Shennan, J.H. 1974. *The Origins of the Modern European State, 1450–1725.* London: Hutchinson.

Shils, Edward and Young, Michael. 1953. "The Meaning of Coronation." *Sociological Review* 1: 63–81.

Skinner, Quentin. 1989. "The State." Pp. 90–131 in Terence Ball, James Farr, and Russell L. Hanson, eds., *Political Innovation and Conceptual Change.* Cambridge: Cambridge University Press.

Smith, Philip. 2003. "Narrating the Guillotine: Punishment Technology as Myth and Symbol." *Theory, Culture and Society* 20(5): 27–51.

Spierenburg, Pieter. 1984. *The Spectacle of Suffering: Executions and the Evolution of Repression: From a Preindustrial Metropolis to the European Experience.* Cambridge and New York: Cambridge University Press.

Spruyt, Hendrik. 1994. *The Sovereign State and Its Competitors.* Princeton, NJ: Princeton University Press.

Steinmetz, George, ed. 1999. *State/Culture: State Formation after the Cultural Turn.* Ithaca, NY and London: Cornell University Press.

Torpey, John. 2000. *The Invention of the Passport: Surveillance, Citizenship, and the State.* Cambridge and New York: Cambridge University Press.

Van Kley, Dale. 1996. *The Religious Origins of the French Revolution: From Calvin to the Civil Constitution, 1560–1791.* New Haven, CT: Yale University Press.

Vaughan, Diane. 1996. *The Challenger Launch Decision: Risky Technology, Culture, and Deviance at NASA.* Chicago: University of Chicago Press.

Viroli, Maurizio. 1992. *From Politics to Reason of State: The Acquisition and Transformation of the Language of Politics, 1250–1600.* Cambridge and New York: Cambridge University Press.

Walzer, Michael. 1965. *The Revolution of the Saints: A Study in the Origins of Radical Politics.* Cambridge, MA: Harvard University Press.

——. 1997. *On Toleration.* New Haven, CT: Yale University Press.

Warner, Michael. 2002. *Publics and Counterpublics.* New York: Zone Books.

Visconsi, Elliott. 2008. *Lines of Equity: Literature and the Origins of Law in Later Stuart England.* Ithaca, NY: Cornell University Press.

Zelizer, Viviana. 1994. *The Social Meaning of Money.* New York: Basic Books.

52

The "soul of the citizen," the invention of the social

Governing mentalities

Jackie Orr

Michel Foucault's notion of governmentality has a significance for us today because it suggests alternative ways of thinking the activity of politics. The forces of power that subject us, the systems of rule that administer us, the types of authority that master us—do not find their principle of coherence in a State nor do they answer to a logic of oppression or domination.

(Rose 1993: 286)

My last point will be this: The emergence of social science cannot ... be isolated from the rise of this new political rationality and from this new political technology.

(Foucault 1988b: 162)

Governmentality, writes Michel Foucault, is an "ugly word" (2007: 115) for articulating the political rationality, or the practices and reason of rule, which constitute the field of operations for political power today. Sifting the archives from early modern Europe through twentieth-century post-war economic thought, Foucault identifies the "birth of a new art" (2000a: 217) for exercising power in the name—and in the vital interests—of "society," bringing the heterogeneous life of populations and an ever widening range of individual behaviors into the realm of explicit political calculation (Foucault 2000a, 2007, 2008). An historical hypothesis, an "experiment of method" (Foucault 2007: 358), a challenge to Left political cultures, a genealogy of contemporary power—"governmentality" marks out a remarkably generative conceptual space launched by Foucault in 1978 in his annual series of public lectures at the Collège de France. In the face of the "failure of the major political theories nowadays," Foucault pursues a turn "not to a nonpolitical way of thinking but rather to an investigation of what has been our political way of thinking during this century" (1988b: 161). Governmentality, then, like so much of Foucault's intellectual project, offers a history of the present, an "ontology of ourselves" (1988a: 95) aimed at countering a form of power that "not only rules but produces us" (Brown 2001: 109):

My project is ... to bring it about, together with many others, that certain phrases can no longer be spoken so lightly, certain acts no longer ... so unhesitatingly, performed; to contribute to changing certain things in people's ways of perceiving and doing things. ... I hardly feel capable of attempting much more than that.

(Foucault 1991: 83)

Belying such modesty, Foucault will also announce: "Liberation can only come from attacking ... political rationality's very roots" (Foucault 1988c: 85). As a political ration-ality animating contemporary architectures of power and of experience, governmentality must be historically grappled with on the way to imagining radically other forms of experience, and practices of freedom.

My task here is to trace this enormously influential notion of "governmentality" as it is theorized first by Foucault in the late 1970s, and then elaborated by an early group of scholars interested, in part, in how neoliberal governmentality is reconfiguring political, social, and market relations today. Next, I turn to two specifically cultural sites where the problematic of governmental reason creates new and potentially important visibilities: the "therapeutic cultures" of well-being broadly disseminated within post-World War II liberal (and neoliberal) Euro-North American societies, and recent "cultures of resistance"—feminist and disability activism in particular. Then, taking up the limits of Foucault's original conception, I look at notions of "colonial" and "transnational" governmentality that critically reorient the concept to address histories of colonial power, and current practices of governance complexly networked across state and national boundaries. Throughout, I foreground the implications of governmentality for the poli-tics of knowledge-production itself, and I end with some questions we might want to ask ourselves, as cultural sociologists, in the face of the historical and analytic implications of Foucault's work.

Power's double itinerary: "policing" and pastoral care

At the heart of Foucault's analysis of the emergence of a "new governmental reason" is an image of the social as a new surface, a previously unintelligible and not-yet-politicized space of relationships, across which techniques of governance can extend their reach and geography of effects. If governmentality is clearly entangled with the constitution of the early modern state, as a general technology of power "at once internal and external to the state" (Foucault 2000a: 221), then (less clearly perhaps) the constitution of "society" becomes a "necessary correlate" to the governmentalizing state (Foucault 2007: 350). The state, itself "an episode in governmentality," works to reveal "a new reality with its own rationality"—civil society, a "reality" materializing for the first time as "a possible domain of analysis, knowledge, and intervention" for which the state has responsibility (Foucault 2007: 348–50). Here, after the defamiliarizing gesture that a history of the present performs, "it is the social that suddenly looms as a strange abstraction ... [so that] perhaps the most surprising thing is the status that 'the social' has thus won in our heads as something we take for granted. A strange aquarium that has become ... the reality principle of our societies" (Donzelet 1979: xxvi).

Tracking the reality principle of the social back to its historic invention, Foucault identifies the seventeenth- and eighteenth-century "science of police" as an experimental site for producing a newly governable real (Foucault 2007: 311–54). "Policing" (predecessor not only to today's police but to "policy" and public administration as well) attempts to deploy a vast, detailed regulatory apparatus across proliferating domains of social activity: the circulation of people, goods, wealth; the surveillance of the birth, death, value, health, and productivity of individual citizens and aggregate populations; the administration of the security, competitiveness, and expansion of state and non-state institutions. Dismantled and redistributed over the next century into the discrete governing practices embedded in population management, in political economy and market analyses, in law and the regulation of "freedom," and in a police apparatus as we know it today (Foucault 2007: 354), "policing" establishes for the first time "population" as the target and the rationale of governmental reason (see Foucault 1988b; Pasquino 1991b). Population as the scene of a newly "real" social body in its calculable, its statistically communicable, its policy-oriented and evermore policed form.

Even as eighteenth-century liberal thought secures the well-being of the "social"—measured via the happiness and prosperity of the population—as the central problematic of modern governmentality (Foucault 1997a), Foucault continues to trace the double itinerary of a power that moves between managing social relations and governing individual conduct. As a strategy of state and social regulation and a "political technology of individuals," governmentality is historically entwined not only with the science of the police, but with that "strangest form of power, the form of power that is most typical of the West"—Christian pastoral power (Foucault 2007: 130). An "individualizing" power at its core, pastoral power demands a knowledge of the "truth" of one's self in exchange for the spiritual guidance and protection of a pastoral figure. The role of pastoral power, buried deep in the logic of today's political rationality, is "to constantly ensure, sustain, and improve the lives of each and every one" (Foucault 1988c: 67).

Here, at the intersection of a science of administering society in its totality, and the pastoral task of perpetual care for the flock through an individualizing knowledge of each member, the paradoxical power of governmental technologies operating "in whole, and in detail" takes shape (Foucault 1988c: 62). The simultaneously totalizing and individualizing effects of governmental power are, for Foucault, precisely the source of its peculiar efficacy and its particular violence: at the same time that the Christian West has produced "the most creative, the most conquering, the most arrogant, and doubtless the most bloody" of societies, the individual has also "learned to see himself as a sheep in a flock" (Foucault 2007: 130). How to address the "political 'double bind'" of this "individualization and totalization of modern power structures" (Foucault 2000b: 336)—and the consequent "coexistence in political structures of large destructive mechanisms and institutions oriented toward the care of individual life" (Foucault 1988b: 147)—becomes a profoundly troubled question for contemporary social struggles, as well as for those individualized, historically situated effects of governmental agencies: our selves.

A neoliberal turn

The multiple provocations of "governmentality" became evident more than a decade before its conceptual and archival elaboration in Foucault's 1977–79 lectures started to circulate in English translation. In 1991, *The Foucault Effect: Studies in Governmentality*, edited by Graham Burchell, Colin Gordon, and Peter Miller, assembles a collection of essays announcing the early, influential preoccupations of "governmentality studies": the social management and rationalization of everyday life via insurance practices and new "technologies of risk" (Defert 1991; Ewald 1991); the governmentalizing aims and effects of expert knowledges such as criminology (Pasquino 1991a), social economy

549

(Procacci 1991), and statistics (Hacking 1991); and the constitution of new forms of political and social identity as the target and the medium of liberal governance (Burchell 1991).

Threaded through several of these essays—most of them written in the late 1970s—is a critical concern with "neoliberalism" as an emergent mutation in governmental rationality, introducing potentially radical changes to the terrain of contemporary politics and the contours of an effective counter-politics. Foucault (2008) devoted the bulk of his public lectures in 1979 to an analysis of post-World War II neoliberal thought in Germany and the United States, and the notion of "neoliberal governmentality," amplified by *The Foucault Effect*, has had a prolific trajectory into the present moment (see Gordon 1991: 41–46; Brown 2003; Raffnsøe *et al.* 2009). Through a relentless extension of market values and logics into non-economic realms, neoliberalism practices a kind of "economic administration of the social" (Donzelet 1991: 278) in which governance and entrepreneurial models of cultural and political activity become inextricably linked. With neoliberal reason, the "promotion of an 'enterprise culture' as a new model for social and economic citizenship" paves the way for a social reality in which "individual citizens should be the entrepreneurs of themselves and their lives" (Gordon 1987: 315). Governed by our freedom to choose, regulated by the responsibility to optimize our own value as "human capital," neoliberal subject-citizens live at the crossroads of an expansive demand for self-development and the stark attempt to implement immigration policies, global economic policies, penal policies, fiscal policies, military/diplomatic policies, education policies, and health care policies that privatize social inequalities while corporatizing the public "commons" as a for-profit venture.

Therapeutic cultures and the governance of happiness

This neoliberal blend of entrepreneurial pastoralism with macropolicies of market expansion and selective state withdrawal from liberal or welfare-based governing mentalities produces a cultural politics that is as entangled as ever with technologies of care and the targeting of psychic/affective/physical well-being as key strategies of governance. "[The] happiness of individuals," Foucault writes, "is a requirement for the survival and development of the state. ... It is an instrument" (1988b: 414). Therapeutic cultures organized around the health, happiness, and fulfillment of individualized body-minds constitute today, as throughout much of the twentieth century, a significant and seemingly "de-politicized" site of governmentality's political reach. Historically, such cultures emerged out of liberal technologies of governance exercised through the "'psycho' knowledges" (Rose 1992) or "psy world" (Castel *et al.* 1982) of post-World War II forms of therapeutic expertise that tried to calibrate the exercise of power with the "subjective commitments, values, and motivations of those over whom authority is to be exercised" (Rose 1992: 360). Today, therapeutic cultures popularize an aggressive "will to health" amplified by consumer advertising and marketing practices, where the maximization of well-being (mental, emotional, physical, sexual, economic) becomes the responsibility of individual customer-patients (Rose 2001: 17–18). In these therapeutic scenarios of neoliberal governance, technologies of care coordinate individual well-being not only through population-level measures of aggregate risk for depression, diabetes, anxiety disorders, breast cancer, and so on (coupled with disease prevention campaigns targeted at risk-stratified populations and individual behaviors), but also

550

through techniques of self-governance increasingly coordinated at the "pre-individual" or "molecular" level of genetic function and affective matter (Deleuze 1991; Rose 2001; Clough 2007).

With self-esteem legislated as a political obligation (Cruikshank 1993), and self-empowerment circulating as an antidote to individualized unhappiness, the "subject" and (governmentalizing) "power" are choreographed together in ways that blur the boundaries between consent and coercion, desire and control, through a political subjection that may be "all the more profound because it appears to emanate from our autonomous quest for ourselves, it appears as a matter of our freedom" (Rose 1989: 256). If a therapeutic culture of the "desiring, relating, actualizing self" is, as Nikolas Rose (1989: xii) suggests, an invention of the latter half of the twentieth century, then what to make of the early twenty-first-century appearance of a kind of "therapeutic patriotism" in the wake of September 11, 2001, when US citizens were encouraged to experience the attacks as a psychological "trauma" for individuals and the entire nation (see Orr 2004: 476–79)? Therapeutic behaviors such as strenuous exercise, listening to calming music, and expressing grief were advised by political authorities, educators, psychological experts, and the mass media as soothing balm for traumatized selves. As the historical and political relay of catastrophic violence intensified with the US attacks on Afghanistan and Iraq, the simultaneous deployment of governmental technologies of individualized care and of systematic slaughter—that puzzling "antinomy of our political rationality" that first leads Foucault to theorize governmentality and its "death and life game" (1988b: 147–48)—is in full evidence. "What are we today?" Foucault asks in 1982, and the question lingers (1988b: 145). How to name—or address—the cultural politics of a governmental reason that produces individualizing forms of therapeutic experience and empowering agency in tandem with a neoliberal triage of social securities against a backdrop of increasingly militarized political formations and popular cultures? What counter-therapeutics might heal the wounds of a body politic that turns to yoga practice in astounding numbers as the state produces and discounts hundreds of thousands of Iraqi dead? "What are we today?" after having read Foucault, who once wrote: "it would probably not be worth the trouble of making books if ... they did not lead to unforeseen places, and if they did not disperse one toward a strange and new relation with himself" (1997b: 205). To what unforeseen places have Foucault's writings led us? What new relation with our selves becomes possible today, perhaps strangely necessary, in pursuing a collective counter-therapeutics of what, indeed, "we" have become?

Rethinking cultures of resistance

The problem and challenge of creating effective cultures of resistance to the current reach of governmental rationality directly follows the insight that governance works intimately in the spaces where particular subjects "cultivate 'their own' selves and identities" (Inda 2005: 10). Collective political identities and forms of agency, too, are "cultivated" via governmental practices; a cultural politics of resistance doesn't necessarily escape "complex 'machines' for government" that assemble together diverse strategies of power across explicitly "political" and, seemingly, "non"-political spaces (Rose 1993: 286–87). If politics, as Foucault offers, is "no more or less than that which is born with resistance to governmentality, the first uprising, the first confrontation" (2007: 390), then identifying a new configuration of governance demands attention to the "modalities of resistance it outmodes" (Brown 2003). Recent scholarship questions whether and how the rights-based identity movements of the last several decades have become incorporated into neoliberal, market-oriented governing mentalities that offer forms of social inclusion and cultural citizenship as a way to manage, not contest, power-charged histories of exclusion and disenfranchisement. Inderpal Grewal cites the "marketization" of new social movements—feminist, multicultural, ethnic—whereby "lifestyles of empowerment" are made available through consumer market segmentation, with consumer "choice" operating as a strategy for individual and collective identity-making (2005: 16). Here, contemporary feminist cultures become visible as technologies of government that produce specific forms of subjectivity and self-regulation: "Empowerment, self-esteem, and self-help through spiritual and new age movements, exercise and health club attendance, and talk shows and books on the topic ... become key to dominant feminist practices in the United States" (Grewal 2005: 27, 16). At the level of transnational politics, feminist activisms today can demonstrate a disturbing interdependence between "rationalities of governance and forms of contestation" (Grewal 2005: 125) as struggles to establish "women's rights as human rights" lean—unevenly, and with consequential exceptions—on the accelerating professionalization and rationalization of non-governmental organizations (NGOs), and their role in extending transnational governmentalities to new populations (Grewal 2005: 138–45).

In the still vitalized and shifting field of contemporary disability politics, Shelley Tremain (2005) argues that current understandings of what is necessary for the liberation of people with disabilities are deeply unsettled by Foucault's analysis of governmentality. Foregrounding Foucault's claim that power governs human actors by "guiding, influencing, and limiting their conduct in ways that accord with the exercise of their freedom," Tremain re-examines the grounds of entitlement (to civil rights, access, and inclusion) and the goals of liberation (from discrimination and social death) animating the politics of disability (2005: 10–12). Rather than liberating people with disabilities from the cultural and political constraints of discrimination, the terms of struggle in disability activism may actually promote a set of "choices" that extend governmental rationalities and legitimate the very social arrangements activists want to contest; the social gains associated with access and inclusion may be cut through with governmentalizing forces that regulate and rationalize conduct in ways that accord with the exercise of freedom. In particular, in the context of a neoliberal governmentality reshaping US education policy, the institutional and cultural politics of "inclusion" becomes "a permanent target of government," and inclusion may now consist of "the opportunity for one to obtain those skills of participation and communication that are required in order to operate in the community of entrepreneurs ... to choose or construct an identity, to invest in oneself and others" (Simons and Masschelein 2005: 217). Here, students with disabilities can find themselves "included" in a governmentalization of education driven by a neoliberal dream of individualization "act[ing] upon a totality of individuals who all exercise freedom in the same way" (Simons and Masschelein 2005: 221).

Colonial governmentality

While "governmentality" has been put to work critically questioning historically specific forms of subjectivity and experience, as well as recent formations of political and cultural resistance, governmentality itself has of course been an object of criticism, perhaps most usefully from those most committed to Foucault's project of a history of the present that might intervene in possible futures. Noting Foucault's conspicuous silence regarding modes of governmentality operating outside the geographies of Europe, scholars from a range of inter/disciplinary sites—including anthropology, history, cultural studies, and postcolonial studies—have challenged the historical and conceptual limitations of his thought (Stoler 1995, 2002; Scott 1999; Venn 2000; Ferguson and Gupta 2005; Inda 2005). At the same time, these scholars elaborate ethnographically and theoretically rich notions of "colonial," or "imperial," or "transnational" governmentality that deploy elements of Foucault's analytics to understand the complexities of colonial rule and a volatile, heterogeneous postcolonial present.

Starting from the assumption that the expansion by European nation-states into colonial territories necessarily shadows and reshapes Foucault's history of governmentalities from the late sixteenth into the twentieth century, "colonial governmentality" gives name to those processes of political rule that—beside and beyond the brutal logics of military conquest or the political economies of enslaved or indentured labor—were exercised "in relation to new targets, new forms of knowledge, and new technologies, and ... [the] production of new effects of order and subjectivity" (Scott 1999: 51). What practices of affective investment, of cultural regulation and the creation of intimate desires characterized colonial inventions of the "social" as a strategic space for enacting effective forms of collective and individual "subjection"? While Foucault's turn to "governmentality" in 1978 marks a "clean erasure of the question of racism from his project" (as he turns away from a focus on the biopolitics of state racisms), how to frame ongoing research on colonial governance in relation to nuanced and dramatically stratified constructions of racialized sexualities, racialized genders, and race-specific formations of family and childhood (Stoler 1995: 25)? Refusing Foucault's presumption of the state as a discrete analytic space, how to rethink "transnational governmentality," and its recombinant technologies of state and non-state practices, in relation to the spatial reordering of geographies of authority and power (Ferguson and Gupta 2005)? What sense to make of the simultaneity of local, national, and global institutions operating across multiple scales to produce "the rapid, deterritorialized point-to-point forms of connection (and disconnection) that are central to both the new communications technologies and the new, neoliberal practices of government" (Ferguson and Gupta 2005: 120)? How to use Foucault, without reproducing his selective "forgettings," to theorize a specifically modern "imperial" governmentality that machines together forms of governance described by Foucault along with governing forces that he largely ignores, including "the visible deployment of military force and ... indigenous structures of power founded on different, traditional mechanisms of legitimation" (Venn 2000: 55)? How, in short, to make Foucault's "governmentality" speak in the language of colonial studies, postcolonial politics, and "transnational connectivities" (Grewal 2005: 23–24)—a language for which it was not originally trained but with which so much of use and necessity might be said.

(In)conclusions: the cultural politics of cultural sociology?

The measure of genealogy's success is its disruption of conventional accounts of ourselves—our sentiments, bodies, origins, futures. It tells a story that disturbs our habits of self-recognition, posing an "us" that is foreign.

(Brown 2001: 106)

Like much of his work which consistently turns and re-turns to the "political entailments of knowledge production" (Stoler 2002: 141), Foucault's genealogy of governmentality carries with it a demand to (dis)locate our selves—not only as potentially governmentalized subjects, but as sociologists whose disciplining is deeply implicated in a political rationality that depends, from its eighteenth-century emergence, on practices of knowledge that come to be called the "social sciences" (Foucault 1988b: 162). As governmentality invents the social "as a new field for producing effects of power" (Scott 1999: 38), it also promotes and provokes a field of new knowledges—statistics, political economy, demography, sociology, criminology, psychiatry—for policing the new "real" which governmental reason both manages and produces.

Genealogy becomes a "vertiginous knowledge when developed and practiced within the culture it aims to unravel" (Brown 2001: 98). What forms of vertigo are most productive for a contemporary cultural sociology engaged with governmentality's present history? Certainly, Foucault's genealogy makes the disturbing suggestion that the first strategic practitioner of a cultural politics may have been, strangely enough, the governmentalizing state, as political rationalities of rule began to reach into every domain of cultural practice and individual conduct. Clearly, "governmentality" as an analytic contributes, along with several decades of cultural studies scholarship, to undoing the foundational dualisms that structure several critical grammars of cultural theory: economy/culture, coercion/consent, private/public, domination/freedom, society/market, etc. Without a doubt, Foucault's work challenges those of us engaged in contemporary cultural struggles and critique to consider seriously their potential complicity with governmentalizing forces, while calling us out to imagine different, more politically promising forms of social and self-governance.

But none of this captures the dizzying sense of uncertainty, the disorienting genealogical descent, that it is possible to feel while reading Foucault. "[A] ground has crumbled away beneath our feet," writes Pasquale Pasquino in a 1978 essay published in *The Foucault Effect*, "the ground upon which there emerged ... [the] practice of what for a century at least has been known in Europe, and for us, as the 'left'. ... On what ground are we standing now? I do not think any of us really knows" (1991b: 117). That was over thirty years ago. On what grounds do "we" stand today, as cultural workers and researchers of culture, as the possibilities for collective transformation remain radically uncertain and "our" ways of producing knowledge—about culture, about power, about our own relations to both—remain resolutely individualized and increasingly driven by the professionalized, entrepreneurial demands of a neoliberalizing university? How might a history of governing mentalities, bound to a story of power's relentless search for new methods of extension and intensification, offer to "us" (an "us" now made somewhat foreign to our selves?) other sensations of what's possible, other signposts toward different methods for making up and remaking again what's real?

References

Brown, W. 2001. *Politics Out of History*. Princeton, NJ: Princeton University Press.
——. 2003. "Neo-Liberalism and the End of Liberal Democracy." *Theory and Event* 7(1).
Burchell, G. 1991. "Peculiar Interests: Civil Society and Governing the System of Natural Liberty."
    Pp. 119–50 in G. Burchell, C. Gordon, and P. Miller, eds., *The Foucault Effect: Studies in Governmentality*. Chicago: University of Chicago Press.

Burchell, G., Gordon, C., and Miller, P. 1991. *The Foucault Effect: Studies in Governmentality*. Chicago: University of Chicago Press.

Castel, R., Castel, F. and Lovell, A. 1982. *The Psychiatric Society*. New York: Columbia University Press.

Clough, P. 2007. "Introduction." Pp. 1–33 in P. Clough, ed., *The Affective Turn: Theorizing the Social*. Durham, NC: Duke University Press.

Cruikshank, B. 1993. "Revolutions Within: Self-government and Self-esteem." *Economy and Society* 22(3): 327–44.

Dean, M. 1999. *Governmentality: Power and Rule in Modern Society*. London: Sage Publications.

Defert, D. 1991. "'Popular Life' and Insurance Technology." Pp. 211–33 in G. Burchell, C. Gordon, and P. Miller, eds., *The Foucault Effect: Studies in Governmentality*. Chicago: University of Chicago Press.

Deleuze, G. 1991. "Postscript on the Societies of Control." *October* 59: 3–7.

Donzelet, J. 1979 (1977). *The Policing of Families*, trans. R. Hurley. New York: Pantheon Books.

——. 1991. "Pleasure in Work." Pp. 251–80 in G. Burchell, C. Gordon, and P. Miller, eds., *The Foucault Effect: Studies in Governmentality*. Chicago: University of Chicago Press.

Ewald, F. 1991. "Insurance and Risk." Pp. 197–210 in G. Burchell, C. Gordon, and P. Miller, eds., *The Foucault Effect: Studies in Governmentality*. Chicago: University of Chicago Press.

Ferguson, J. and Gupta, A. 2005. "Spatializing States: Toward an Ethnography of Neoliberal Governmentality." Pp. 105–31 in J.X. Inda, ed., *Anthropologies of Modernity: Foucault, Governmentality, and Life Politics*. Malden, MA: Blackwell.

Foucault, M. 1988a. "The Art of Telling the Truth." Pp. 86–95 in L.D. Kritzman, ed., *Michel Foucault: Politics, Philosophy, Culture*, trans. Alan Sheridan and others. New York: Routledge.

——. 1988b. "The Political Technology of Individuals." Pp. 145–62 in L. Martin, H. Gutman, and P. H. Hutton, eds., *Technologies of the Self: A Seminar with Michel Foucault*. Amherst, MA: University of Amherst Press.

——. 1988c. "Politics and Reason." Pp. 57–85 in L.D. Kritzman, ed., *Michel Foucault: Politics, Philosophy, Culture*, trans. Alan Sheridan and others. New York: Routledge.

——. 1991. "Questions of Method." Pp. 73–86 in G. Burchell, C. Gordon, and P. Miller, eds., *The Foucault Effect: Studies in Governmentality*. Chicago: University of Chicago Press.

——. 1997a. "The Birth of Biopolitics." Pp. 73–79 in P. Rabinow, ed., *Michel Foucault: Ethics*, Vol. 1, trans. R. Hurley and others. New York: The New Press.

——. 1997b. "Preface to The History of Sexuality, Vol. 2." Pp. 199–205 in P. Rabinow, ed., *Michel Foucault: Ethics*, Vol. 1, trans. R. Hurley and others. New York: The New Press.

——. 2000a. "Governmentality." Pp. 201–22 in J.D. Faubion, ed., *Michel Foucault: Power*, Vol. 3. New York: The New Press.

——. 2000b. "The Subject and Power." Pp. 326–48 in J.D. Faubion, ed., *Michel Foucault: Power*, Vol. 3. New York: The New Press.

——. 2007 (2004). *Security, Territory, Population: Lectures at the Collège de France, 1977–78*, trans. G. Burchell. New York: Palgrave Macmillan.

——. 2008 (2004). *The Birth of Biopolitics: Lectures at the Collège de France, 1978–79*, trans. G. Burchell. New York: Palgrave Macmillan.

Gordon, C. 1987. "The Soul of the Citizen: Max Weber and Michel Foucault on Rationality and Government." Pp. 293–316 in S. Lash and S. Whimster, eds., *Max Weber, Rationality and Modernity*. London: Allen and Unwin.

——. 1991. "Governmental Rationality: An Introduction." Pp. 1–51 in G. Burchell, C. Gordon, and P. Miller, eds., *The Foucault Effect: Studies in Governmentality*. Chicago: University of Chicago Press.

Grewal, I. 2005. *Transnational America: Feminisms, Diasporas, Neoliberalisms*. Durham, NC: Duke University Press.

Hacking, I. 1991. "How Should We Do the History of Statistics?" Pp. 181–95 in G. Burchell, C. Gordon, and P. Miller, eds., *The Foucault Effect: Studies in Governmentality*. Chicago: University of Chicago Press.

Inda, J.X. 2005. "Analytics of the Modern: An Introduction." Pp. 1–20 in J.X. Inda, ed., *Anthropologies of Modernity: Foucault, Governmentality, and Life Politics*. Malden, MA: Blackwell.

Orr, J. 2004. "The Militarization of Inner Space." *Critical Sociology* 30(2): 451–82.

Pasquino, P. 1991a. "Criminology: The Birth of a Special Knowledge." Pp. 235–50 in G. Burchell, C. Gordon, and P. Miller, eds., *The Foucault Effect: Studies in Governmentality*. Chicago: University of Chicago Press.

——. 1991b. "Theatrum Politicum: The Genealogy of Capital—Police and the State of Prosperity." Pp. 105–18 in G. Burchell, C. Gordon, and P. Miller, eds., *The Foucault Effect: Studies in Governmentality*. Chicago: University of Chicago Press.

Procacci, G. 1991. "Social Economy and the Government of Poverty." Pp. 151–68 in G. Burchell, C. Gordon, and P. Miller, eds., *The Foucault Effect: Studies in Governmentality*. Chicago: University of Chicago Press.

Raffnsøe, S., Rosenberg, A., Beaulieu, A., Binkely, S. Kristensen, J. E., Opitz, S. 2009. "Neoliberal Governmentality." Special issue of *Foucault Studies* 6: 1–4.

Rose, N. 1989. *Governing the Soul: The Shaping of the Private Self*. London: Routledge.

——. 1992. "Engineering the Human Soul: Analyzing Psychological Expertise." *Science in Context* 5(2): 351–69.

——. 1993. "Government, Authority, and Expertise in Advanced Liberalism." *Economy and Society* 22(3): 285–99.

——. 2001. "The Politics of Life Itself." *Theory, Culture & Society* 18(6): 1–30.

Rose, N. and Miller, P. 1992. "Political Power Beyond the State: Problematics of Government." *British Journal of Sociology* 43(2): 171–205.

Scott, D. 1999. "Colonial Governmentality." Pp. 23–52 in *Refashioning Futures: Criticism after Postcoloniality*. Princeton, NJ: Princeton University Press.

Simons, M. and Masschelein, J. 2005. "Inclusive Education for Exclusive Pupils: A Critical Analysis of the Government of the Exceptional." Pp. 208–28 in S. Tremain, ed., *Foucault and the Government of Disability*. Ann Arbor: University of Michigan Press.

Stoler, A. 1995. *Race and the Education of Desire: Foucault's History of Sexuality and the Colonial Order of Things*. Durham, NC: Duke University Press.

——. 2002. *Carnal Knowledge and Imperial Power: Race and the Intimate in Colonial Rule*. Berkeley: University of California Press.

Tremain, S. 2005. "Foucault, Governmentality, and Critical Disability Theory." Pp. 1–24 in S. Tremain, ed., *Foucault and the Government of Disability*. Ann Arbor: University of Michigan Press.

Venn, C. 2000. *Occidentalism: Modernity and Subjectivity*. London: Sage Publications.

Part IX
Global cultures, global processes

53

Consumerism and self-representation in an era of global capitalism

Gary G. Hamilton and Donald Fels

"What a difference a century makes," observed the distinguished anthropologist G. William Skinner (1999: 56). A century ago cities in China looked Chinese. Buildings had a distinctively Chinese architecture. The cities were laid out with a distinctively Chinese sense of space and propriety. The shops lining the streets sold distinctively Chinese products that were to be consumed in distinctively Chinese ways. And the people walking up and down the street looked distinctively Chinese, dressed in characteristic clothes and shoes, and talked in an array of local dialects. A century later, the outer appearance of things is no longer uniquely Chinese.

Today, in Chinese cities, high-rise buildings, urban space, and public propriety seem completely at home with culture found in newly constructed cities throughout the world. The ubiquitous shopping malls are filled with products that could be bought most anywhere; the people in the stores and on the street wear the same clothes and shoes that are worn by stylish and not-so-stylish people throughout the world; and although people still speak Chinese, they most likely use Mandarin in their daily life, which has become the standardized form of communication throughout the Chinese-speaking world today. Skinner's point is well taken: in the past century, China has been transformed.

The same set of observations could be made for most countries. A century ago, the way of life in cities everywhere resonated with local culture. A century later, there is considerable uniformity in the look and feel of most major cities around the world. Today, urbanites dress and act in similar ways—shopping in malls and supermarkets, buying more or less the same standardized products that are worn or otherwise consumed in similar ways. The use of local dialects is declining everywhere in favor of official languages, and English is rapidly becoming the standardized form of communication on the internet, in meetings, and at international conferences.

The easy conclusion to these observations is that we are witnessing a global cultural convergence. Indeed, in many spheres of their lives, people around the world have embraced a common vision of what it means to be modern and they have adopted an increasingly similar range of ideal and material goods to signify that modernity. And this modernity is fundamentally, if not exclusively, Western—based overwhelmingly on patterns of American consumerism, or, as George Ritzer (2008 [1993]) would say,

"McDonaldization," resulting in the "globalization of nothing." This conclusion is indeed easy, but in fact it is incorrect.

Theories of cultural convergence are deceptive, as we suggest in this chapter. Still, the observations on which such theories are based certainly beg for our attention: the last half of the twentieth century was a period of profound and ongoing global transformations in the culture of everyday life. It may be easy to dismiss these transformations as merely a convergence towards the emptiness of Western consumerism. Yet if we examine the actual changes wherever they occur, then we should feel a lot less confident that a global convergence is underway. Instead, it is more accurate to view these global transformations as laying a foundation for a new global diversification of world cultures. Although we subscribe neither to Samuel Huntington's "clash of civilizations" thesis (1996) nor to the subaltern theories of the postcolonial theorists (Said 1978; Spivak 1987), we do see, in progress, a reconfiguration of world cultures, centering on similar cultural spheres, but leading to an increasingly sophisticated articulation of social and cultural differences.

The theories of cultural convergence

Although the various theories of cultural convergence are quite different from one another, they all make the same basic assumption: the forces of globalization are so powerful and pervasive that local cultures necessarily have to bend, if not to break, to accommodate Western patterns of consumption. Theorists are often so confident in making this assumption that they confine their analyses to the irresistible forces causing the change and largely ignore the consequences of those same forces not only in non-Western societies, but in Western societies as well.

One of the best known theories of global convergence is George Ritzer's thesis on "the McDonaldization of society." In a series of books and articles dating from the 1980s, Ritzer (1983, 2008 [1993], 2007 [2004]) argues that modern societies are becoming increasingly rationalized, a process that he identifies as being similar to that used by McDonald's, the fast-food chain. Citing Weber's theory of rationalization as the source of his inspiration, Ritzer (2008 [1993]) submits that McDonaldization is a process in which efficiency, calculability, predictability, and centralized control pervade the organization of all kinds of activity, ranging from the production of food to the delivery of health care, education, and family life.

Ritzer's concept plays on a clever analogy. McDonald's is a worldwide success, and the McDonald's model of fast-food delivery has been widely imitated. At the core of this model, however, is the logic of scientific management, the same logic that Fredrick Taylor (1911) put a name to and that factory owners have widely applied to the production of whatever they make. This logic of using a division of labor to achieve an efficient system of mass production was first outlined in Adam Smith's example (1976: chap. 1) of organized production in a pin factory. McDonald's merely, but very successfully, applied this logic to an area in which it had not previously been employed, to the efficient production and delivery of hamburgers. To apply this logic (think of it as "factorization"), McDonald's created upstream supply lines to obtain the necessary components (beef, potatoes, and the other accoutrements) to make the products that they sell in their small, widely dispersed, but highly efficient factories. What Ritzer brings to this discussion is a certain shock value that comes in using McDonaldization as the analogy for global convergence.

Ritzer's use of this analogy is similar to Karl Marx's attempt to argue that factory production is inherently better—that is, more efficient and profitable, and therefore more likely to survive—than any previous system of production. Marx's concept, which he called "capitalism," included a factory system of production very much like the one Smith described, but, unlike Smith, Marx believed that this system of factory production depended on the exploitation of labor. Still, like Smith, Marx also believed that capitalist factories produced products that were obviously superior and cheaper than handicrafts made by artisans. However, neither Marx nor Ritzer attempts to understand "factorization" from the viewpoint of those buying the products. Instead Marx and Ritzer simply assume the factory system to be a force producing irresistibly priced goods. As Marx (1959: 11) put it, "Cheap commodity prices are the heavy artillery with which (the bourgeoisie) batters down all Chinese walls and forces the barbarians' obstinate hatred of foreigners to capitulate. ... It compels them to introduce what it calls civilization in their midst, i.e., to become bourgeoisie themselves." To paraphrase Marx, Ritzer is arguing that McDonaldization produces goods for the Chinese that introduce Western civilization in their midst, i.e. so that they become Western consumers themselves.

A more subtle account of globalization is found in the theories of global institutional convergence developed by John Meyer and his colleagues (Meyer and Hannan 1979; Drori *et al.* 2006). According to these theories, countries around the world are converging on certain institutional ideals emanating from the West. The range of institutionalized organizational spheres, such as the nation-state or the US system of higher education, creates normative ideals that other countries are drawn into emulating. They emulate these ideals because of coercive pressures from international agencies (i.e. the United Nations) or because, in conditions of uncertainty, they want to imitate the best practices of leading nations and leading universities. This process of isomorphism (think of it as global "normalization") generates an irreversible global, cultural, and institutional convergence leading to the most profound type of Westernization—a transformation in the meaning of modernity.

Like McDonaldization, however, this concept maps global "normalization" as a one-way street, where all forces of globalization come from one direction on their way to all other locations, with uniform and irresistible consequences. Normalization, then, is the prescriptive process of conforming to organizational forms and organizational ideas upon which those forms are based. In terms of globalization, these forms and ideas happen to come from the West and particularly from the United States. And they are "consumed" by people who find them irresistible because they symbolize and therefore represent the very essence of modernity. Western organizational forms are the heavy artillery that batters down all non-Western walls and that force the non-Western Others to introduce civilization in their midst, i.e. to become Westerners themselves.

The obvious problem with both of these and other similar theories of global convergence is that they do not take into account the perspectives of those who buy or who otherwise take hold of these ideal and material goods that are introduced from the outside. In economic terms, these are supply-side interpretations of globalization with no corresponding theories of demand. These theories do not take consumers into account; they merely assume uniformity in consumption without conceptualizing consumers as agents in their own right.

It is certainly true that McDonald's and other fast-food franchises are diffusing throughout the world. It is equally clear that officials in many societies have decided to adopt the American model of higher education because, for whatever reason, they

561

believe there are advantages in doing so. Theorists need to deal with these and a wide range of similar facts, because they are aspects of a global diffusion of ideal and material goods. But, rather than creating theories about the objects being diffused, a better way to examine this diffusion is to analyze the process of diffusion itself, and to recognize that buyers, in one form or another, are increasingly essential agents in this process, a process we can label "consumerization."

The retail chain: the link between suppliers and buyers

To conceptualize the process of consumerization, we will examine one of its most important organizational components—the rise of global retailing and brand name merchandising (Hamilton 2006: chap. 6; Feenstra and Hamilton 2006). Relying on point-of-sales data, global retailing is increasingly organized "backwards" from the consumer to the manufacturer. Retailers are the intermediaries and the most important players in this process. On one side of their business, they create, maintain, and attempt to stabilize *consumer markets* for their products. They locate their stores so that consumers will find them easily; they select, display, and price their goods so that consumers will find it easy to buy what they offer. The sellers seek out and tantalize consumers through advertising, and reassure them by offering money-back guarantees and warranties on the goods they sell. Consumers are the target. On the other side, sellers create *supplier markets* in order to acquire the goods they sell. They need to find purchasing agents and manufacturing firms that can supply them with the products that they wish to sell. They are the "big buyers" (Gereffi 1994) who negotiate with manufacturers or their agents a price and level of quality that allows them to earn a profit at the point of sales. They need to find shippers, truckers, and other logistic suppliers to deliver these goods efficiently to the stores. With point-of-sales information, they can instantly track which goods are selling and which are not, adjusting their orders and their supply chains accordingly.

Retail stores were not always able to operate in this fashion. Before the 1960s, retailers were, by today's standards, small, locally or regionally based, and privately owned stores. With a few exceptions, such as Sears, Roebuck and J.C. Penney's, these retail stores were unable to greatly influence either consumer or supplier markets. In the last half-century, however, a "retail revolution" has occurred, a revolution that has changed the global economy, as well as retailing. The retail revolution has been described elsewhere at some length (Feenstra and Hamilton 2006), but the main elements can be easily outlined. Starting in the 1960s, retailers began substantially to reorganize the way they did business. This process of reorganization began first with retailers in the US, but soon retailers in Europe and Japan followed suit.

At the core of this phenomenon in the US was a rapid commercial building boom, especially in less expensive outlying areas, fed by supportive tax reform. In a relatively short time, the number of shopping malls in the US jumped from about 500 small malls in 1954 to 7,600 in 1964, of which nearly 400 were very large regional shopping malls, accounting for about 30 percent of all retail sales in the US. At the same time that this building boom occurred, the interstate highway system was constructed and widespread suburbanization began. Less than forty years later, in 2002, there were over 50,000 shopping malls in the US alone. In the same interval, tens of thousands more shopping malls were built around the world, some as large as or even larger than the largest malls in the US.

562

A main component of these shopping centers is the chain store. The same stores began to pop up in malls all across the US and now are seen all across the world. Downtown department stores such as Macy's, J.C. Penney's, and Sears were common retail chains before malls became widespread. They were among the first stores to anchor the large new shopping centers, but they were soon joined by several new types of stores. First came the general discount stores. Wal-Mart, Kmart, Kohl's, and Target all started discount retailing in the same year, 1962. Then came the specialty retailers, chain stores like The Limited (founded in 1963), The Gap (1969), TJX (1977), and Best Buy (1983). In the twenty-year span between 1975 and 1995, every major retail segment consolidated into large chains—hardware by Home Depot (1978), drugs by CVS (1963), Rite Aid (1968), and Walgreen's, consumer electronics by Circuit City (1968) and Best Buy (1983), toys by Toys 'R' Us (1978), books by Barnes and Noble and Borders (1971), office supplies by Staples (1986) and Office Depot (1986), and warehouse stores by Costco (1983). In the US, the two or three chains in each segment, together with the general discounters (e.g. Wal-Mart) that sell across all segments, account for nearly 90 percent of all sales in these retail segments.

In the 1970s, when chains began to expand rapidly, they needed to locate or otherwise establish large and reliable suppliers to stock their shelves. Many retail chains were eager to stock their shelves with brand-name products, which they could sell at a discount. This eagerness promoted the creation and rapid growth of brand-name merchandisers without factories, such as Ralph Lauren (1967), Anne Klein (1968), and Nike (1972), as well as the rapid growth of existing brands, some of whom were initially manufacturers in their own right, such as Levi's, Schwinn, Eddie Bauer, Sony, and Panasonic. Other retail chains, such as The Limited, The Gap, and even Macy's and J.C. Penney's, needed suppliers for in-house or private-label brands. General discounters, such as Wal-Mart, and specialty retailers, such as Home Depot, needed huge quantities of a considerable range of branded and non-branded goods. To obtain these goods, all of these brand-name merchandisers and retailers became what Gereffi (1994) calls "big buyers."

Starting in the late 1960s and rapidly increasing in the 1970s, big buyers began to source both brand-name and private-label goods from factories in Asia (Gereffi and Pan 1994; Feenstra and Hamilton 2006). Most of these buyers established offices in Asia that specialized in locating and, at times, creating suppliers. They worked closely with Asian manufacturers, transferring technology, lending them capital, and giving them large orders. In the 1970s and 1980s, most of the goods produced under these arrangements came from factories located in Taiwan, South Korea, Hong Kong, and Japan. Economies in these countries became *demand responsive*; that is, a great portion of the entire economy was organized around export production based on big buyers' orders for goods (Feenstra and Hamilton 2006; Hamilton and Gereffi 2009). In the 1980s, these core countries began to move portions of their production to other Asian countries. In the 1990s, Southeast Asia and especially China began to grow very rapidly in response to the intra-Asian movement of capital, expertise, and big-buyer orders.

One of the key factors in the 1990s restructuring of Asian economies was the spread of lean retailing (Abernathy *et al.* 1999). In the 1970s, Uniform Product Codes (UPC) were established, bar codes and scanners invented, and computerization began in earnest. By the 1980s, most chains had established computerized inventory systems and transfer stations instead of large warehouses. These changes allowed reorganization to make them more responsive to point-of-sales information. These changes were made possible by the simultaneous creation of a global logistics system, which included widespread containerization, container terminals, and trucking companies—all of which facilitated the integration of Asian factories into the big buyers' organizations for selling products (Bonacich and Wilson 2008). With all the pieces in place, supply chains, instead of distribution channels, became the standard methodology of organizing the global economy. And at the core of this methodology is the retail chain—the feedback loop between retailers and customers—in which the consumer serves both as the final purchaser of goods and also as the initiator of the next round of decisions about what to sell in the future.

The expansion of global retailing

For the global economy, the 1990s was when the tail began to wag the dog. In the early days of capitalism, when consumers could buy any color of car as long as it was black, there was a very large gap between manufacturers' production and consumers' demand. Factory owners always had to guess what final demand for any product would be, and consumers had limited if any influence over what goods were available for them to buy. When producers overshot the mark, they had fire sales, and when they undershot they lost business. It was usually one or the other. Lean retailing has closed that gap considerably, but in so doing it has shifted the balance of power between manufacturers and retailers decisively towards retailers. With that shift, the consumer plays a larger and larger role in determining which products are actually offered for sale.

In 1990, having built large, reliable, and flexible supply chains, retailers consolidated consumer markets in their home territories and expanded their consumer markets internationally. With modest-sized home markets, European retailers were the first movers. The largest retailers in France (Carrefour), England (Tesco), and Germany (Metro, Aldi) all expanded beyond the home country and beyond Europe to found international operations. Wal-Mart soon followed suit, first in Mexico, and then around the world, as did other US retailers such as Costco and Home Depot.

The main driver of this global expansion was food retailing. Before 1990, people in most countries around the world, especially outside of the US, Europe, and Japan, bought food products from local markets and small sundry stores. Starting in the 1990s, however, supermarket chains began to penetrate and then to dominate food retailing in most countries around the world (Reardon *et al.* 2007). Starting in the early 1990s, the first waves occurred in much of Northern and Central Europe, South America, and East Asia outside of China and Japan. In these countries about 60 percent of all food products are purchased in supermarket chains. The second wave began in the mid-1990s in Mexico and Central America, Southeast Asia, and Southern Europe, with supermarkets now accounting for about 50 percent of the food purchases in these countries. The third wave, in the late 1990s and early 2000s, extended supermarkets to China, India, Russia, and parts of Africa. In these countries, supermarkets now make up about 20 percent of total food purchases. Reardon and his colleagues (2007) show that the diffusion of supermarkets is completely revamping the organization of suppliers of food products, creating rationalized supply chains and larger and more reliable suppliers, with small farmers losing and large agro-businesses winning a place in the chain. Many of these supermarkets also sell a range of other goods beside food, moving them towards becoming more like general discounters than simply grocery stores.

At first glance, it seems that the world's largest retailers, stores like Wal-Mart and Carrefour, would grow at the expense of other retailers. Although these firms have expanded exponentially in recent years, they are also creating new markets for goods that other retailers are now providing. The large firms create a new consumer market by presenting a model and building the infrastructure that other, smaller firms then use to good advantage. McDonald's may have been among the first fast-food firms to establish themselves globally, but now it has many, many competitors everywhere. The same is true for Wal-Mart and Carrefour. Even the threat of Wal-Mart's entry into a new location has spurred mergers between, and a comprehensive reorganization of, local firms to use lean retailing techniques to create and to respond to local demand.

Stratification, lifestyles, and the art of self-representation

The rapid growth and global presence of all types of retailers, both large and small, ranging from supermarkets to fast-food franchises, have increasingly created new types of consumers as well as new types of retailers that cater to these consumers. Retailers have been able to create new consumer markets throughout the world not simply because they offer cheaper prices, for that is usually not the case, but rather because they promise a new way of life for people, who come to see themselves in a new light.

Social scientists have known for a long time that people consume what they do as a means of conveying to others a sense of who they are as individuals. Thorstein Veblen, in *The Theory of the Leisure Class* (1953), was the first social scientist to develop a demand-driven theory of the economy. He showed that the logic of consumption was to convey a sense of self-worth to others by means of making invidious distinctions. People who regard themselves as privileged in one way or another will use status-marking objects and actions as a way of establishing their distinctiveness. For Veblen (1953), writing in the Gilded Age, this distinctiveness was based on a class identity: to establish oneself in the upper class was to create an image of non–utilitarian consumption of goods and time, which is what Veblen called "conspicuous consumption" and "conspicuous leisure."

A long line of sociologists have substantiated Veblen's insights: consumption and stratification go hand in hand. But more recent researchers have also qualified these insights by showing that class stratification is not what it used to be. When asked, almost everyone in the US with any means whatsoever puts him- or herself into the middle class. Although the actual items of consumption vary greatly from person to person, the invidiousness attached to objects and actions cannot be comfortably ranked by class position. Instead of class, objects and actions increasingly attach themselves to lifestyles, which are only indirectly associated with class and income. Today, not class, but rather lifestyles are the vehicles of self-representation and of stratification, too (Holt 1997).

The key to understanding this phenomenon is to see that retailers today, in whatever business, have entered into a virtual, and sometimes an actual, conversation with their customers. Customers discover who they are by exploring what is being offered to them, and once those identities form and once those identities signify a lifestyle filled with ideal and material goods, retailers strive to supply those goods, and in so doing expand the lifestyle. Demand-driven retailing responds to buying. What is bought gets made, and more and more of it, establishing the feedback loop.

What only the very rich could afford to do in Veblen's time has now become available to people of a wide range of income categories. Instead of being synonymous with class, lifestyles themselves become stratified according to levels of income. Eating foie gras in France and bird's nest soup in Hong Kong, playing golf at Pebble Beach and doing yoga at Borobudur, climbing the Matterhorn, and snorkeling off the Great Barrier Reef—all these are conspicuous activities that people can do today, even with modest incomes. And the very rich may not even have the most fun anymore. Only the very poor and dispossessed get left out, and the knowledge of their exclusion makes their plight all the more unbearable. For everyone else, an array of lifestyles is there for choosing. Select the lifestyle that suits you, refine that lifestyle in terms of reachable goals, Google those goals on the web, and, presto, there they are: travel agents to help you arrange your trip, retailers to give you a price and a delivery date for the objects you want to buy, clubs to join to help you become sophisticated consumers of a given activity, even friends and potential friends with whom to enjoy your way of life.

This is not Veblen's world: it is the world we live in today, a variegated and expanding world of diverse lifestyles and identities that go with them. However anachronistic, these lifestyles and identities are necessarily contemporary ones. They are up to date precisely because retailers and other purveyors provide the necessary accoutrements to establish a contemporary way of life. Without these retailers, a particular lifestyle might be difficult if not impossible to establish—difficult to find the right stuff, difficult to find others to associate with, difficult even to know about. Demand-driven retailing helps define and fill out lifestyles that would hardly exist otherwise.

It is also clear that, outside of Europe and the United States, the feedback loop between retailers and the new consumers has helped to create new identities out of the apparent convergence that so many people have observed. Music, movies, the internet, technology hardware and software, vacations and tourism, strategic English, standardized national languages, houses that call for interior decoration, cuisines that require specialized kitchenware, occupations that require a standardized education—the list of convergences goes on. But what this listing obscures is the fact that these are the very media of differentiation.

Demand-driven retailing allows consumers to create distinct worlds out of standardized points of entry. The youth of each country use cell phones to text to their friends and create their own rap songs; in turn, both media relay to the audience what it means to be young and in a particular place. Bollywood helps Indians to understand who they are or might be, a fact that can be shared with movie-goers around the world, who in turn can understand who they are not. Google and other internet search engines are strictly speaking demand driven; they rely on information fed by its users. They adapt to each locale, and they help to differentiate among locales.

The standardization of entry points encourages cultural differentiation, and encourages the formation of new worlds filled with new identities to explore. Mathews and Lui (2001) show in their fine collection on consumerism in Hong Kong that shopping there has become a way of life, not a Western way of life, but an new Hong Konger way of life. Chua, in *Life Is Not Complete without Shopping* (2003), makes the same argument for Singapore. In both locations, a unique consumer culture has emerged, including styles of clothing, home décor, movies, and food. Mona Abaza (2001) lets us see that shopping malls in Cairo offer a new space for Egyptians, not as Westerners, but as Egyptians forging new identities to fit the times, for women who are finding a space away from Islamic restrictions, for couples who can look into each other's eyes longingly and without shame. In *Golden Arches East: McDonald's in East Asia*, James Watson and colleagues (2006) look at variations in how customers in different Asian societies respond to McDonald's, and make it clear that there is nothing uniform in the diffusion of McDonald's in Asia. Like everything else, McDonaldization is a source of differentiation, the globalization of differentiation.

When one examines only the objects of diffusion, it is easy to jump to the conclusion that a global convergence is underway, for indeed carriers of identity are becoming standardized around the world. Ready-made apparel, accessories and shoes, cuisines, cultural media (television, movies, DVDs, and the internet), communication systems (cell phones and the internet), and even languages—all become vehicles that people use to identify with and at the same time to distinguish themselves from others. These standardized vehicles are the very media that greatly expand the range of choices individuals are able to make about how to represent themselves in relation to others, both the real ones close by and the imagined ones further away. The range of accessible choices encourages people everywhere to develop an awareness of who they are—of a personal identity rooted in a locale or perhaps even of what Kuah-Pearce (2006) calls a "transnational self." Whatever the choices people make, the awareness of making choices about their lives also encourages them to develop some "artfulness" to their self-representation, some distinctive touch that distinguishes one individual from another, one group from another.

The awareness of the necessity to make choices about one's life and the lives of others nearby is producing something equivalent to an existential crisis in many societies around the world today. Rather than simply living a traditional life because no other options are known or are available, now people, offered an array of choices, have to opt in if they are to embrace traditionalist and fundamentalist ways of living. The necessity of choosing one's way of life transforms such taken-for-granted routines into lifestyle choices, which niche retailers can in turn target with specialized products, with everything from videos, music, and books having religious themes to armaments to fortify and defend a way of life.

The art of representation is essential and integral to the feedback loop that modern retailing establishes. By listening closely to customers, global retailers turn customers into consumers, people who use ideal and material goods to establish who they are in a modern world. This is a world of both convergence and differentiation, and both processes are intimately connected with each other.

References

Abaza, Mona. 2001. "Shopping Malls, Consumer Culture and the Reshaping of Public Space in Egypt." *Theory, Culture, and Society* 18(5): 97–122.

Abernathy, Frederick H., Dunlop, John T., Hammond, Janice H., and Weil, David. 1999. *A Stitch in Time: Lean Retailing and the Transformation of Manufacturing—Lessons from the Apparel and Textile Industries.* New York: Oxford University Press.

Bonacich, Edna and Wilson, Jake B. 2008. *Getting the Goods: Ports, Labor, and the Logistics Revolution.* Ithaca, NY: Cornell University Press.

Chua, Beng Huat. 2003. *Life Is Not Complete without Shopping: Consumption Culture in Singapore.* Singapore: Singapore University Press.

Drori, Gili S., Meyer, John W., and Hwang, Hokyu, eds. 2006. *Globalization and Organization: World Society and Organizational Change.* New York: Oxford University Press.

Feenstra, Robert. C. and Hamilton, Gary G. 2006. *Emergent Economies, Divergent Paths: Economic Organization and International Trade in South Korea and Taiwan*. Cambridge: Cambridge University Press.

Gereffi, Gary. 1994. "The Organization of Buyer-Driven Global Commodity Chains: How U.S. Retail Networks Shape Overseas Production Networks." Pp. 95–122 in G. Gereffi and M. Korzeniewicz, eds., *Commodity Chains and Global Capitalism*. Westport, CT: Greenwood Press.

Gereffi, Gary and Pan, Mei-Lin. 1994. "The Globalization of Taiwan's Garment Industry." Pp. 126–46 in E. Bonacich, L. Cheng, N. Chinchilla, N. Hamilton, and P. Ong, eds., *Global Production: The Apparel Industry in the Pacific Rim*. Philadelphia: Temple University Press.

Hamilton, Gary G. 2006. *Commerce and Capitalism in Chinese Societies*. London: Routledge.

Hamilton, Gary G. and Gereffi, Gary. 2009. "Global Commodity Chains, Market Makers, and the Rise of Demand-Responsive Economics." Pp. 136–62 in Jennifer Bair, ed., *Frontiers of Commodity Chain Research*. Stanford, CA: Stanford University Press.

Holt, Douglas B. 1997. "Poststructuralist Lifestyle Analysis: Conceptualizing the Social Patterning of Consumption in Postmodernity." *Journal of Consumer Research* 23(4): 326–50.

Huntington, Samuel P. 1996. *The Clash of Civilizations and the Remaking of World Order*. New York: Simon and Schuster.

Kuah-Pearce, Khun Eng. 2006. "Transnational Self in Chinese Diaspora: A Conceptual Framework." *Asian Studies Review* 30(3): 223–40.

Marx, Karl. 1959. *Basic Writings on Politics and Philosophy*. New York: Anchor Books.

Mathews, Gordon and Lui, Tai-lok. 2001. *Consuming Hong Kong*. Hong Kong: Hong Kong University Press.

Meyer, John W. and Hannan, Michael T. 1979. *National Development and the World System: Educational, Economic, and Political Change 1950–1970*. Chicago: Chicago University Press.

Reardon, Thomas, Henson, Spencer, and Berdegue, Julio. 2007. "'Proactive Fast-Tracking' Diffusion of Supermarkets in Developing Countries: Implications for Market Institutions and Trade." *Journal of Economic Geography* 7: 399–431.

Ritzer, George. 1983. "The McDonaldization of Society." *Journal of American Culture* 6(1): 100–07.

——. 2008 (1993). *The McDonaldization of Society*, eighth edition. Thousand Oaks, CA: Pine Forge Press.

——. 2007 (2004). *The Globalization of Nothing*, second edition. Thousand Oaks, CA: Sage.

Said, Edward. 1978. *Orientalism*. New York: Pantheon.

Skinner, G. William. 1999. "Chinese Cities: The Difference a Century Makes." In Gary G. Hamilton, ed., *Cosmopolitan Capitalists: Hong Kong and the Chinese Diaspora at the End of the Twentieth Century*. Seattle: University of Washington Press.

Smith, Adam. 1976. *An Inquiry into the Nature and Causes of the Wealth of Nations*. Oxford: Clarendon Press.

Spivak, Gayatri Chakravorty. 1987. *In Other Worlds: Essays in Cultural Politics*. New York: Methuen.

Taylor, Frederick. 1911. *The Principles of Scientific Management*. New York: Harper and Brothers.

Veblen, Thorstein. 1953. *The Theory of the Leisure Class*. New York: Mentor Books.

Watson, James, ed. 2006. *Golden Arches East: McDonald's in East Asia*. Stanford, CA: Stanford University Press.

54

The political economy of cultural production

Vincent Mosco

Political economy examines the social relations, especially the power relations, that mutually constitute the production, distribution, and exchange of resources. This essay focuses on the cultural resources that are turned into commodities for sale in the converging broadcasting, telecommunications, and new media industries. By definition, political economy distinguishes itself by examining the use of power in society. In particular, it takes up how power is used in three social processes—commodification, spatialization, and structuration.

Commodification examines the transformation of goods valued for their use into commodities valued for what they can bring in exchange. A story that a parent tells a child contains use value. When that story is dramatized on a commercial television program, it carries exchange value, which can be measured by how much a television station or distributor will pay for it in the marketplace. The process of commodification extends beyond cultural content to include audiences, whose attention is marketed to advertisers, and media workers, whose labor is sold for a wage.

The process of spatialization encompasses the transformation of space with time. In the political economy of communication, studying this process entails identifying the ways cultural products and information technologies define spaces. For example, television overcomes distance by bringing images of world events to every part of the globe, and companies increasingly use computer communication to organize business on a worldwide basis, thereby allowing them greater access to markets and the flexibility to move rapidly when conditions make it less favorable for them to stay in one place. Communication is central to spatialization because media and information technologies are processes that promote flexibility and control throughout industry, but particularly within the media, communication, and information sectors. Spatialization encompasses the process of globalization, including the worldwide restructuring of industries, companies, and other institutions. Restructuring at the industry level is exemplified by the development of integrated markets based on digital technologies and at the firm level by the growth of the flexible or networked company, which makes use of communication and information systems to continuously change structure, product line, marketing, and relationships to other companies, suppliers, its own workforce, and customers.

Finally, structuration describes a process by which structures are constituted out of human agency, even as they provide the very "medium" for that constitution. It is the process of creating social relations, mainly those organized around social class, gender, race, and social movements. For example, with respect to social class, political economy describes how access to the mass media and new communication technologies is influenced by inequalities in income and wealth, with some able to afford these technologies and others not (Mosco 2009).

Traditionally, the political economy of communication has focused on the power of large media companies to control the process of cultural production. Specifically, this included firms that operate internationally across most of the major media platforms—including print, broadcasting, film, telecommunications, and the internet. Time-Warner, Disney, Viacom, General Electric, News Corp., Sony, Bertelsmann, and now perhaps Google, Microsoft, Apple, and AT&T would inevitably find their way onto such a list. These are companies that take advantage of converging technologies making use of a common digital language to build their profit and their share of the market, and to shape decisions about what cultural products are produced and how they are distributed. This influence often extends into wider economic and political domains. Such a line of analysis succeeded in explaining a great deal about how power works in global cultural production (McChesney 2007). However, it is increasingly recognized that a focus on media concentration, while still important, was more applicable to a Fordist economic model and provides only a partial picture in the emerging post-Fordist global economy.

Fordism refers to an economic system based on mass production for mass consumption (Harvey 1989). It evolved out of the New Deal in the United States and from social democracy in Europe to comprise what some would describe as an informal social contract between capital, labor, and the state. Large, near monopoly enterprises win control over major economic decisions in return for providing a living wage and secure employment to workers, an arrangement that is overseen and regulated by a supportive government. In cultural production in the US, this was the era of three dominant American broadcasting networks and one giant telephone monopoly, most of whose workers were organized in large national unions, and all of which were overseen by the Federal Communications Commission and other regulatory bodies. In essence, political economy traditionally emphasized the concentration of media power in a handful of corporate conglomerates made up of functionally interdependent divisions. These companies were vertically integrated in the sense that they contained the entire process of production and distribution in-house. NBC studios produced for the NBC television network, which distributed programs to its owned and operated stations and to its many affiliates, which had little choice but to accept what the network provided.

But Fordism depended on clear US global hegemony, which began to erode when foreign competition across the global political economy, especially from Asia and the Middle East, began to undermine the social contract in the 1970s. Out of the global economic turmoil of the 1980s and 1990s emerged what some call a post-Fordist economic model. Giant corporations remain but their success depends less on cozy arrangements with national governments and labor unions than on their ability to respond quickly to changing markets and technologies. As a result, large companies are in an almost constant process of restructuring internally and are constantly establishing new relationships with companies in and around their lines of business. For example, in 2000 the merger of Time-Warner and AOL was widely considered "the deal of the century" because it would bring together a leading global cultural producer with what was then considered the dominant internet company (Rushe 2008). It did not take long for the arrangement to sour because the pieces did not fit very well and because Google overtook most of the competition for control of the internet. In 2008, with technology permitting massively decentralized distribution, legally and illegally, Time-Warner declared that content production was becoming central to its mission as it looked to focus on television, film, and online content and to downgrade, if not sell off entirely, its cable distribution and AOL holdings (Arango 2008). Post-Fordism means that success derives from customized production for customized markets. The hierarchical firm drawing support from monopoly control over a national market gives way to the global networked corporation making use of advanced technologies to adjust production and distribution to rapidly shifting and increasingly differentiated tastes and audiences (McKern 2003; Sirkin *et al.* 2008).

Today the pressures of flexible accumulation and the risks of global instability are leading to a new set of structural patterns. These include the loosely integrated multi-divisional form, the networked corporation, and networks of distinct corporations that come together in strategic alliances and other teaming arrangements for specific projects. Moreover, in spite of their differences, these forms share important characteristics. They are primarily concerned with maximizing commercial gain through flexible accumulation, and they draw from an increasingly precarious workforce of immaterial labor (Mosco and McKercher 2008). The challenge for the political economy of cultural production is how to understand and assess the significance of the shift from Fordism to post-Fordism. The remainder of this chapter takes up the range of forms that make a difference for cultural production today and the differences they make for the political economist.

Post-Fordism presents fundamental challenges for the businesses involved in cultural production. Companies have greater opportunities to profit from global markets and technologies that expand the options for commodification, but these also present major risks that have to be faced without many of the regulatory supports that once ensured control over markets. When they try to retain the Fordist characteristics of one large enterprise with functionally interdependent parts, firms risk failure because they are unable to respond to changing global conditions and changing technologies. For example, Microsoft remains powerful, but its tightly centralized structure based on control over computer operating systems and business software has made it difficult for the firm to anticipate markets that Google captured. One response is modest but organizationally important: develop a strong market within a large corporation and operate each unit as a quasi-independent profit centre. This multi-divisional form provides the overall financial authority to central management but with opportunities for cross-pollination among divisions which operate as separate units expected to meet specific profit goals (Riahi-Belkaoui 1995). Time-Warner is a single entity but it operates separate divisions for its print, broadcasting, film, cable, internet, and other holdings. But, as the company's recent decision to cut some of its distribution divisions attests, the multi-divisional format is often insufficient to maintain market share, let alone market dominance, in a post-Fordist economy. Additional steps involve moving out of the corporation itself to build new relationships with units loosely tied to, or entirely outside, the parent firm.

One way to "externalize" the corporation is to move production outside the company by establishing or building ties to independent cultural producers. Sometimes that means retaining an ownership share, as have Fox and Disney with their in-house independent production companies. Sometimes that means arranging short-term, project-specific deals with fully independent companies or the subsidiaries of other large firms. Whatever the specific arrangement, the purpose is to externalize some of the risk brought about by a turbulent global environment (Scott 2004).

Until recently, one of the dominant forms of post-Fordist cultural production was founded in the formal coproduction that brought together private capital, global networks of film and video producers, along with government representatives who, meeting at the many international festivals and trade shows, produce new cultural products. In the course of this activity, they have formed a new power bloc that promotes strong intellectual property laws and other cultural policies that protect the wider interests of private capital. Some of these coproductions are decidedly formal, the result of treaty arrangements among national governments. Others are less formal, often one-off deals negotiated at the constant flow of meetings that bring together this diverse group of participants. The challenge for such work is to produce local cultural specificity while drawing support from global sources (Baltruschat 2008). For example, the film *In Bruges*, a UK–Belgium coproduction, brought together an international cast in a hybrid buddy–crime narrative that featured a picturesque medieval city.

Coproductions are still important in the global political economy of cultural production but are declining in significance because their success in pooling risk is offset for the largest players by challenging longstanding power hierarchies in the industry. How, these companies wondered, can they retain power, externalize risk, and benefit from the spread of global cultural production? One of the most important answers is to be found in the growing practice of global format licensing, whereby a major cultural producer develops a video format which, if successful, is marketed as a format throughout the world. In essence, a format refers to a program or to program dimensions that can be licensed for export. It might refer to an entire program such as *American Idol*, *Who Wants to be a Millionaire?*, or *The Weakest Link*, or it can address specific elements of these programs such as the ideas behind them, their characters, designs, or music. What makes format licensing possible is strong, globally enforceable copyright laws that protect the right to own not just a program but the idea for a program and many of its component parts. Through organizations like the Format Recognition and Protection Association (FRAPA), which represents the interests of major format creators and license holders, popular brands are protected and violators punished. The leaders of this association develop formats, sell them abroad (as when *American Idol* becomes *Canadian Idol*), and make certain that all of the key content, character, music, and design characteristics are emulated even as the licensee sees to it that the program is adapted to local conditions (Baltruschat 2008).

The practice of dealing in formats is not particularly new. I grew up with television programs like *Beat the Clock* that originated as radio shows but were subsequently licensed to television producers for what was then a new medium. In fact, the popular program *Wheel of Fortune*, a major beneficiary of format licensing, developed as a radio broadcast in the 1950s. Moreover, there is nothing new about exporting cultural products for the global market. Much of the early research in political economy addressed the extent to which film and television exports sent from the United States to developing nations constituted cultural imperialism. What makes today's global format licensing significant is that a global system of cultural production is now led by the world's major media firms, which market ideas and help to shape their application to local conditions. In essence, a large company can now market a program concept or the pieces of a concept, thereby expanding the potential for commodification. Moreover, it can spatialize the product by controlling the interplay of its global pattern and local application. Finally, in a primary example of structuration, format licensing maintains a hierarchy within the global system of production that clearly defines who has power (those who own and copyright the format) and who is so dependent that they must give up all control over the concept in order to share its local profits.

These new developments in the political economy of cultural production comprise important changes to traditional practice. But all of them focus on content production. There are also important developments in the social and power relations of audiences for cultural products and of cultural labor. One of the central challenges faced under the Fordist model was the potential for new technologies to help empower audiences by providing them with the tools to control the flow of programming and, more importantly, the flow of commercials. Companies continue to grope for solutions but have made significant progress in recent years by creating formats, programs, and ancillary products that give them more control over their audiences. One of the most important innovations is the growth of cultural products that directly involve the audience. The fundamental premise of *American Idol* is that the audience is the star. Yes, celebrities make up the famous or infamous judges, but the show is based on the view that an ordinary person can become a celebrity. Those lacking this aspiration can participate in the voting, which, in an interesting wrinkle on spatialization, connects celebrity with community by pitting cities and towns in a competition for which of them will have bragging rights to the next Idol. When a finalist for *Canadian Idol* from my town of Kingston, Ontario competed, all of our local media and many of our community organizations mobilized support. Indeed, "reality" programming in general aims to make the daily lives of the audience a central premise of television content. So, for example, in *Wife Swap*, one of the major successes in global format licensing, mothers trade families and cameras chart the consequences.

As anyone who recalls such outrageous programs of the 1950s as *Queen for a Day*, in which audiences voted to reward the woman with the saddest life story, there is nothing entirely new about audience participation. Furthermore, a program created in 1948, which was eventually made into the popular television show *Candid Camera*, is credited with originating the reality format. However, today's programs occupy more video time and make extensive use of new media and information technology to generate support and participation of all sorts. For example, fandom has found a home on the web, from sponsored web pages to audience-generated social networking sites, which build program communities that extend well beyond the actual television show. These sites join other media to build networks of merchandising ties that market products connected to celebrities and to celebrity culture. Just at a time when audiences gained the tools to win some control over programming, determined companies advanced a post-Fordist solution. Instead of generating revenue by delivering a mass audience to a national advertiser—a mainstay of the Fordist era—firms build programs that create customized audiences and use those audiences to reduce programming costs by replacing paid (and often unionized labor) with audience performers. The result is a series of program communities commodified in real and virtual space (Gray *et al.* 2007; Jenkins 2006).

Intimately connected to these new developments in the political economy of the audience are new approaches to cultural labor. No longer as protected by government policy, technological limitations, or low levels of economic development, production companies now compete in a global market for product, for audiences, and for labor. They are responding by transforming their relationships to their workforce. Faced with a more highly skilled national workforce positioned to demand high wages and creative control, companies respond by shifting production abroad and by increasing the technology content of programming (special effects, animation). The two are often combined as new technologies enable producers to reshape foreign locations to simulate the required venue. For example, it is no longer necessary for a cost-conscious producer to physically "dirty up" the streets of Toronto to turn it into New York. Furthermore, nations, cities, and even small communities eagerly reach out to cultural producers and provide all sorts of incentives, including low-cost labor, to attract productions which provide both immediate revenue and branding opportunities for the location. Large cities have built substantial departments whose sole task is to attract cultural producers. Taking a lead among small towns, Marfa, Texas, dubbed the "desolation capitol of the United States," has provided the location for two Oscar nominated films, *There Will Be Blood*, and the best-picture winner *No Country for Old Men*. Moreover, when big companies produce in a high-wage nation, they typically produce programs such as audience participation shows that employ few skilled workers or programs such as reality television shows that employ non-union labor (Wasko and Erickson 2008).

The similarity between controlling audiences and controlling workers goes just so far because the latter have a long tradition of unionization. On the one hand, cultural producers face audiences that begin as isolated individuals and generally come together for collective action against a company only over a very specific issue like the cancellation of a favorite program or the treatment of a popular star. On the other hand, from the start, many of the workers that cultural producers face are organized into unions that negotiate contracts. These include both technical workers who operate cameras, build sets, and manage electronics, as well as writers, performers, and directors.

Political economists have paid closer attention to labor relations in the cultural industries because the shift to post-Fordism has created enormous tensions and because of new developments in labor's response. New media has not only created production opportunities in low-wage and non-union locations, it has also muddied the waters for unionized cultural workers. There have always been struggles over how to compensate workers for additional use of their work, as when a television program goes into syndication or when a film moves to television. However, new technology expands the potential for ancillary revenue enormously, especially when high speed connections make downloading cultural material relatively easy and certainly very lucrative. The insistence among major producers that they retain most of the revenues from programs viewed on the internet led to a long strike by members of the Writers' Guild of America and threatened strikes by the Directors' Guild, the Screen Actors' Guild, and the American Federation of Television and Radio Artists (AFTRA). Some of the unions have also taken action to stop moving cultural work abroad (what they call "runaway production"), and to curtail the expansion of revenue streams, such as product placements, that they believe violates their professionalism (Mosco and McKercher 2008).

On the other hand, the changing cultural production industry has also exacerbated rivalries and tensions among cultural workers. Should they emulate the Writers' Guild by taking a strike action? Should they demand that government penalize producers engaged in "runaway production"? How much should they demand in revenues from reuse of their work on the internet? These and other issues have created conflicts among unions that make it much more difficult for them to pressure cultural producers to meet their demands. One obvious solution is to follow the lead of management and merge these and other separate unions into large unions, perhaps even one big union representing the cultural industry workforce. This is not as farfetched as it may appear, despite the long-term decline in union representation (in the United States trade union density is down to about 12 percent overall and less than 9 percent in the private sector).

The most important new development is the formation of large unions that bring together previously separate organizations across the communication, knowledge, and service industries. In the United States the model is the Communication Workers of America (CWA), with 600,000 members. The CWA began as a telephone-workers' union but over the years has expanded to include newspaper, broadcasting, and telecommunications workers as well as some high-tech and service workers. It has crossed the US border to organize print and broadcast workers in Canada, using its resources and influence to win in a 2005 labor action that pitted workers at Canada's national broadcaster against a management team that wanted to downsize and contract out labor. Canada has its own version of the CWA in the Communication Energy and Paperworkers' Union, which ranges even more widely to include forest workers who cut down trees for newsprint, as well as journalists, broadcast workers, and much of the telecommunications industry workforce. The major holdouts in all of these efforts to build a united front in cultural labor are the unions that represent Hollywood workers and their counterparts abroad. Whether these workers unite will go a long way to answering the question of whether cultural workers can get a better working relationship with cultural producers. But even if somehow the Screen Actors' Guild and AFTRA can bury the hatchet and merge unions that have come within a few votes of achieving this in the past, the question will remain as to whether some version of international trade union convergence can be achieved in the culture industries. With cultural production moving to Asia (Reuters has moved over a thousand wire-service jobs to India) and Eastern Europe, no measure of national trade union harmony will stop the flow of workers abroad. Nor, some argue, should it, since no one nation is entitled to monopolize work in the industry. Opponents argue, however, that when jobs move abroad they are also degraded and deskilled, lowering the quality of work and its rewards for all workers.

There are signs that worker organizations are following their corporate counterparts in expanding internationally. In the field of cultural production, the most important development is the formation of the Union Network International (UNI), a global labor federation that specializes in media and information-technology workers and operates throughout the world. UNI has been particularly active in trying to bridge the chasm separating workers in rich nations from those in nations that are the providers of most outsourced labor. It has also established Global Framework Agreements with transnational corporations that commit the firms to guaranteeing basic standards of pay and work quality. These are important developments, but even the federation admits that such actions represent just the beginning of an effort to bring communication and cultural workers together (Mosco and McKercher 2008).

Political economists from different perspectives now focus on the significance of these changes in the social relations of cultural labor. Some see the expansion of precarious labor insofar as benefits in wages and working conditions won in the Fordist era degrade with the inevitable expansion of global capitalist production. Others see the potential for resistance as more workers are united in their experience of immaterial labor or work based on the production and distribution of communication, culture, and informational products.

References

Arango, T. 2008. "Holy Cow Batman! Content Is back." *New York Times*, August 9. Available at http://www.nytimes.com/2008/08/10/business/media/10warner.html?scp=14&sq=time%20warner%20aol& st = cse (accessed August 31, 2008).

Baltruschat, D. 2008. "Film and Television Formats: The Cross-border Adaptation of Interactive Media Productions." Pp. 299–332 in J. Wasko and M. Erickson, eds., *Cross-border Cultural Production.* Amherst, NY: Cambria Press.

Gray, J., Sandvoss, C., and Harrington, C.L., eds. 2007. *Fandom: Identities and Communities in a Mediated World.* New York: NYU Press.

Harvey, D. 1989. *The Condition of Postmodernity.* Oxford: Blackwell.

Jenkins, H. 2006. *Fans, Bloggers, and Gamers.* New York: NYU Press.

McChesney, R.W. 2007. *Communication Revolution.* New York: The Free Press.

McKern, B., ed. 2003. *Managing the Global Network Corporation.* London: Routledge.

Mosco, V. 2009. *The Political Economy of Communication*, second edition. London: Sage.

Mosco, V. and McKercher, C. 2008. *The Laboring of Communication.* Lanham, MD: Lexington Books.

Riahi-Belkaoui, A. 1995. *The Nature and Consequences of the Multidivisional Structure.* New York: Quorum Books.

Rushe, D. 2008. "AOL and Time-Warner Split after 'Deal of the Century' Goes Bad." *Sunday Times*, February 10. Available at http://business.timesonline.co.uk/tol/business/industry_sectors/media/article3340944.ece (accessed August 31, 2008).

Scott, A.J. 2004. *Hollywood: The Place, the Industry.* Princeton, NJ: Princeton University Press.

Sirkin, H.L., Hemerling, J.W., and Bhattacharya, A.K. 2008. *Globality.* New York: Business Plus.

Wasko, J. and Erickson, M., eds. 2008. *Cross-border Cultural Production.* Amherst, NY: Cambria Press.

55

Analyzing culture through globalization

Carla Freeman

The need of a constantly expanding market for its products chases the bourgeoisie over the whole surface of the globe. It must nestle everywhere, settle everywhere, establish connections everywhere. *The bourgeoisie has through its exploitation of the world market given a cosmopolitan character to production and consumption in every country … In place of the old wants, satisfied by the productions of the country, we find new wants … the products of distant lands and climes.* In place of the old local and national seclusion and self-sufficiency, we have intercourse in every direction, universal interdependence of nations.

(Karl Marx in Marx and Engels 1979 [1848]: 476–77, italics added)

Globalization is arguably today's favorite buzz-word, and as with all buzz-words, there is both substance and vacuity in the degree to which it signals everything from the purported homogenization of life-ways and "world culture" to the primacy of world markets and the transnational flow of finance capital, and the supposed decline of the nation-state. The vastness of globalization as both a concept and a set of contemporary processes makes it difficult to grasp in all of its complexity and its apparent embrace of virtually all domains of life and corners of the world. Indeed, globalization and neo-liberalism, in many ways its economic synecdoche, have become, to use Henrietta Moore's term, "concept-metaphors that float between and across popular and academic domains … as theoretical concepts and as descriptive referents to a seemingly endless range of contemporary processes and experiences" (2005: 25).

Ironically, although because of its scope, globalization would seem to demand analytical holism, in fact it has often been tackled from the primary perspectives of *either* economy *or* culture, and contained within debates about homogenization or hybridity (Hannerz 1991; Yudice 2003; etc.). To boot, academic discourse has largely accepted a division of labor between economic and cultural perspectives such that macro processes are explored in political-economic terms, while attention to culture more often appears in micro or "local" case studies. Economic systems of globalization are portrayed as causing a range of effects that take shape both economically and culturally on "local" or national ground. Concomitantly, it has been the realm of *production* that has constituted an early and dominant site of globalization analysis, while efforts to examine

577

the *cultural* dimensions of globalization have inclined toward the growing circulation and *consumption* of new media, commodities, and technologies, and the culture industries of film, television, and internet communications, etc. (Pieterse 2004; Featherstone 1990; Friedman 1994). The tendency to polarize macro, masculinized forces of the global capitalist economy against micro, feminized spheres of local culture has also subtly but powerfully privileged the former, macro scaled, analysis as bearing the weight of globalization *theory*, while treatments of the latter, local, and particular domains are generally ascribed the status of illustrative ethnographic case studies (see, for examples, the theoretical and historical works of Jameson 1991; Harvey 1989; Robertson 1992; and recent ethnographic works of Liechty 2003; Lan 2006; Pun 2005, to mention but a few).

Efforts to examine the convergences, clashes, and knotty articulations of the scale, dimensions, and expressions of globalization have been suggested in such various concepts as "glocalization" (Robertson 1992), "frictions" (Tsing 2005), and "global assemblages" (Ong and Collier 2004). However, retaining both dialectical complexity and a nuanced reading of the particulars of globalization—the gendered and racialized permutations of economy/culture, production/consumption amid what Harvey (1989) evocatively called the "time–space compression" of postmodernity—remains a challenge in the enterprise of globalization theory (Comaroff and Comaroff 2000: 305). Where Jameson (1991) and Harvey have arguably contributed the most weighty and enduring treatises on late capitalism as a distinctive phase of capitalist accumulation and commodification, it is not only in the provocative spheres of high art, literature, architecture, and "mass" or commercial culture that these complex processes are to be seen. Whereas for Jameson and Harvey the cultural logic of postmodernity is inextricable from its economic fragmentation and form, the questions of *where* culture is located and *how* it gets articulated and contested in people's lived experience are harder, and yet essential, to address. Globalization is enacted in the particulars of social, cultural, and economic life, in the "otherness" or "difference" that Harvey himself concedes has been under-recognized. It is precisely to understanding such realms of particularity that much of the recent ethnography contributes, and in so doing, I would suggest, it contributes indispensably to our very capacity to theorize globalization.

This essay promises neither definition nor conclusion as to globalization's limits, threats, or promises. Instead, my discussion takes as its focus the relationship between culture and "the global"—what is "cultural" about globalization and how does "the global" work in and through the stickiness and particularities of culture? What I propose at the outset is simply that we question the pervasively generic pretense of globalization. Globalization is always both imagined and manifested in and through cultural and historical particulars. My premise is not that globalization threatens and refashions culture, but that globalization itself is imbricated within various cultural forms and meanings that come into increasing and intensified contact with one another. This argument can be broken down into two very simple but critical parts. The first is a refusal to read globalization as a singular and monolithic force that operates outside the fabric of culture, in the US, India, China, or anywhere else in the world. The second is a purposeful engagement with culture/economy not as dual spheres—as they are often portrayed—but rather as mutually constitutive forces, and domains of practice and meaning. Economic relations themselves are understood as embedded in specific cultural understandings and constructs (e.g. what kinds of people do what kinds of work and why, how these people are situated within class and other hierarchies, and how they can move within and outside these groupings). Cultural forms and meanings involve both structural economic, affective dimensions, and meanings. I highlight in this essay the dialectics of culture/economy across the domains of production/consumption in order not only to examine the political economy of global labor and commodification, but to provide a window into the changing contours of "selfhood" the project of identity-making. Exploring how globalization works in and through culture to foster new concepts of the self—and, specifically, how the notion that under neoliberal capitalism the person becomes an "entrepreneur" of the self—offers a particularly powerful lens on the simultaneity of cultural/economic forces and meanings.

Toward a dialectic of globalization

As prescient as Marx was in the quotation on p. 577, to anticipate the global expansion of wants and goods in the capitalist system, his and Engels's understanding of labor and capital lay largely outside the specificities of culture, arguably limiting their imagination as to the manifestations and meanings this globalization would entail. Indeed, what many of the case studies of global production suggest is that although multinational capitalists have criss-crossed the globe with assembly lines whose goods bear no marks of their makers, production is not generic in the organization of labor, the recruitment and discipline of laborers, or the meanings and identities attached to these complex processes. However much multinational corporations have attempted to minimize the interfering "noise" of culture as they set up assembly plants across the world, culture and historical legacies resurface at every juncture, whether as challenges to the mandate that "global" workers be uniformly young, single, and childless women (Freeman 2000), in the form of spontaneous production stoppages due to outbreaks of spirit possession and calls for local religious mediation (Ong 1987), or in numerous other ways. Indeed, dominant discourses of globalization have often portrayed the weighty and powerful engines of a masculinized global capitalism as tapping into local and feminized labor and incorporating it into a highly disciplined and standardized orbit of production. However, ethnographic accounts reveal that such imagined "docile" and "available" labor pools are often already, or soon become, agents of globalization capable of reshaping not only production processes, but also their ideological foundations and future possibilities. That cultural forms and expressions—whether religious rituals, structures of kinship, styles of music and art, ideologies, or ethics of labor—are increasingly entangled within a global consumer marketplace prompts a broader interpretation of how "the global" is articulated in people's lived experience. This interpretation entails not only discussion of the ways in which people come to understand and experience their own identities through specific cultural idioms and relations of production, but at the same time, increasingly, how consumption represents a potent medium through which dimensions of self are enacted and experienced.

The yearning for new goods, media, and styles as a medium for modern self-expression—especially among the youth and aspiring middle classes of the world—offers a window into some of the most fascinating and daunting aspects of globalization. Not only is global consumption in the popular domain full of arresting expressions of juxtaposition—the Maasi warrior sporting Ray-Ban glasses, burka-clad women enjoying a refreshing Coca-Cola, the outpacing of salsa over ketchup in the American diet—but it also represents an especially fertile ground in which to analyze the tensions and inversions inherent in the familiar binaries of global/local, homogeneity/hybridity, modernity/ tradition, macro/micro.

According to some observers, new modes of consumption offer liberating pleasures and creative identity-making projects for a growing number of social actors. Others see a never-ending swirl of desire, trapping youth in a ceaseless hunger to adorn themselves with the signs of modernity, offering little to address the chasm between rich and poor, and proving ephemeral in their satisfactions at best. Some have argued that in the de-industrialized West, consumption has trumped production as the basis for class consciousness and identity and therefore "class" as we knew it is dead (Pakulski and Waters 1996). I suggest that precisely the ambiguities—anxieties, desires, and dreams— introduced by new modes of consumption beg for deeper analysis. And the increasingly complex interconnections between consumption and production as sources of self-identification and social/economic practice offer a critical opportunity to re-examine how such meanings and boundary projects are reframed under globalization.

Clearly influenced by Marx, one model that first drew attention to the critical juncture of production and consumption under globalization was proposed by Maria Mies (1986). Path-breaking at the time, her study not only characterized the active dialectic of dom-ination/dependency entailed in the First/Third World dyad of industrialization and development, but located the gendered deployment of women as a key nexus of this exploitative relationship. She proposed that the emerging global system was predicated upon the simultaneous *proletarianization* of Third-World women and what she called the "*housewifization*" of First-World women. In short, Mies argued that what was then referred to as the "new international division of labor" rests simultaneously upon the creation of cheap feminine labor forces in developing countries and the creation of an active pool of eagerly consuming "middle-class housewives" in the West. However, what Mies could not have anticipated was the rapid rate at which mass consumption, mass media, and information would circulate multidirectionally. The neat boundaries of Mies's model—in which the "Third" World represented a repository of poor women workers and the "First" World represented the site of middle-class (feminine) consump-tion and domesticity—failed to imagine both the internal complexities of labor and consumption within "First" and "Third" Worlds, and the ways in which these articula-tions would become increasingly dynamic.

Indeed, both global assembly lines and global commodity markets have become increasingly diversified and complex. In an expanding array, labor-intensive industries in search of cheaper labor are migrating to developing countries. The movement of jobs from "global north" to "global south" has extended from agricultural extraction and low-level manufacturing to include "white collar" services like graphic design, accounting, and even medicine. At the same time, other global circuits have stimulated a flow in the opposite direction, from "developing" to "post-industrial" nations, of jobs in seasonal agricultural labor, temporary domestic work, to highly trained IT and other professional arenas. Within these movements, the powerful reach of global consumption has expanded to include all corners of the world—from those people in flux to those who stay put, those whose labor is directly tapped by global industries and those aspiring to new middle-class status, to those who remain in the hungry shadows either un- or under-employed. We now see in abundant ways that what appeared to be unidirectional circuits of production and consumption are increasingly multidirectional and in constant flux.

Pei-Chia Lan (2006) illustrates, for example, the critical importance and contradictory meanings of cell phones for Indonesian and Filipino domestic workers in Taiwan.

On the one hand, they serve as highly valued status markers and key communicative devices to maintain contact with children and kin networks oversees and to foster social ties with new friends. On the other hand, the cell phone becomes a monitoring device used by employers intent to keep tabs on their employees—both while minding their children and on their ostensible "free" time. Thus, cell phones are both highly desired signs of modernity and mechanisms of surveillance and control. For Ngai Pun (2005), young Chinese factory workers urgently embrace new modes of consumption (fashion, makeup, accessories) as much desired elements of leisure in order to ease the exhaustion and alienation of production and to disguise their rural migrant marginality in the modern city. Many find, however, that rather than achieving their consumerist dream of transformation, such consumption instead reinforces the very gendered and localized peasant identities they seek to overcome.

If, as Marx argued, production is an alienating process in which workers lose control of themselves by losing control over their labor, Pun suggests that it is in the realm of consumption that producers attempt to rectify their alienation, and that therein is to be found the dialectic of production/consumption (Pun 2005: 163).

Like Lan and Pun, I want to draw attention not only to the ways in which globalizing modes of consumption are inextricable from global production but how together these forces come to bear upon new dialectical articulations of gender, class, race, culture, and location. To do so, I turn to the Caribbean island of Barbados, long understood to be not simply steeped in a history of globalization but created by its very forces.

Producing/consuming culture and globalization in a Caribbean context

Shaped by British conquest and colonial settlement in the name of colossal export production (sugar), peopled entirely by migrants—enslaved, indentured, and free—Barbados offers a vivid example of the central dialectics of globalization. In this region long spurned by social scientists for its apparent lack of "pure" cultures, the now popular concepts of "creole" and "hybridity" find evocative renderings, and local–cultural paradigms offer powerful clues for interpreting contemporary globalization and locality. To illustrate a rich and complex conjuncture between Caribbean cultural history and the contemporary forces of globalization, I introduce a group of social actors I have studied over the past decade who represent an emergent fraction of the Barbadian middle class, as well as, in essence, a new direction in the national development strategy for a small island economy in the changing tides of global capitalism. Their lives and dreams give expression to many of the global dialectics mentioned above, and illustrate the cultural complexities and particularities of globalization itself.

This group of new middle-class entrepreneurs is made up of a wide variety of women and men who have departed from a longstanding Barbadian tradition in which upward mobility and middle-class status have been associated with the pursuit of education, stable long-term employment, and a heavily bureaucratized public sector. By eschewing higher education, or leaving secure jobs in established public-sector or private-company domains, and entering into entrepreneurial endeavors that often depend upon global imports, exports, and styles of management, these individuals mark both a new social landscape of the middle-class in the Caribbean, and also a new and growing subject of globalization—the "global" middle classes. Indeed the new entrepreneurs challenge boundaries and understandings of social class in ways that hinge upon changing relationships between production/consumption and illustrate not only structural economic transformations but transformations in people's intimate and emotional lives and self-images. Intricate convergences between their productive labor and a growing sphere and intensity of consumption actively reconfigure the forms and meanings of work and self amid neoliberal globalization. The manifestations of this convergence are wide-ranging. They include new modes of travel, new styles of dress and comportment, changing religious and spiritual practices, new therapeutic interventions, and new forms and expectations of intimacy, marriage, and parenthood. And they provide evocative renderings of the ways in which contemporary globalization is articulated in and through local cultural practice.

In order to unpack these convergences and challenges, and their particular significance for women forging new entrepreneurial livelihoods and identities, I make use of one of Caribbean region's most powerful and controversial gate-keeping concepts—that of "reputation–respectability," first proposed in the 1960s by anthropologist Peter Wilson (1973: 9). I want to suggest that this regional cultural paradigm provides an indispensable tool for challenging the notion of globalization as a singular or homogenizing force of contemporary social change comprehensible through a singular epistemological frame. Wilson argued that the Anglophone Caribbean region can be broadly understood as steeped within the structures and ideologies of two competing but dialectically related value systems or cultural models: respectability—the inescapable legacy of colonial dependence through which patterns of social hierarchy are upheld and reproduced; and reputation—a set of responses to colonial domination and the elusiveness of respectability through which people enact creative individualism and at the same time achieve a social leveling, or "communitas." Although this formulation has been critiqued by scholars of the region as too rigidly binary, it has also retained enduring analytical valence as a heuristic for the contemporary context.

Respectability, for Wilson, encodes a set of colonially defined values and mores endorsed and practiced largely by the middle class (women, in particular, and old or married men as well). Ideals of social order, propriety, monogamy, and domesticity are enacted through the institutions of formal marriage, schools, and the Anglican Church. Respectability sanctions the nuclear patriarchal family over the more fluid "visiting union" and casual sexual relations, and enshrines the white Christian church over other nascent syncretic denominations. The essence of *reputation*, by contrast, is a kind of improvisational adaptability or flexibility associated primarily with a lower-class and masculine public sphere of performance and sociality, encompassing such venues as street corners, the political platform, the rum shop, the market, and the musical stage—all associated with such attributes as sexual prowess, verbal wit, musical flair, and economic guile. Whereas the path of respectability in Barbados historically has been marked by formal education leading to a place in the secure hierarchy of the civil service or the crowning professional achievement of a career in law or medicine, the qualities that Wilson describes as central to reputation can be thought of as the embodiment of an entrepreneurial esprit—always adaptive, self-defined, and in opposition to bureaucratic hierarchy. How this Caribbean model brings into relief the dialectics of culture/economy integral to contemporary globalization is evocatively demonstrated by considering emerging entrepreneurs who seek to navigate new paths of economic mobility and personhood.

Neoliberal entrepreneurship of the self

No figure better embodies the demands and qualities of neoliberalism than the entrepreneur—whose flexible capacity for self mastery, responsiveness to market changes, and willingness to retrain and retool make the entrepreneur a widely celebrated hero of global capitalism and the epitome of modern individualism (Beck 1992; Bourdieu 1998). De Toqueville and Schumpeter, among others, equated economic adventurism and entrepreneurship with the essence of American Protestant culture from its inception. However, in the Barbadian cultural and historical context, the entrepreneur has had a different resonance. Here, this figure has signified a more marginal identity—of economic survival and a path of last resort more than one of leadership and status. Because of the recent decline of the island's sugar industry—its economic backbone for some three hundred years—and a precarious position in the global marketplace of tourism and off-shore services, entrepreneurship has been identified by the state as the new-found key to economic growth, and has become not just a new profile of economic possibility, but a new framework for Barbadian selfhood.

The growth of entrepreneurship today is encouraged zealously by the Barbados government, NGOs, and the local private sector, which have all introduced a wide range of initiatives, from youth training programs to small-credit schemes, to spur new entrepreneurial endeavors. Simultaneously, government efforts to restructure and whittle down the social-welfare system and the public sector (the single largest employer) mirror such steps elsewhere in the developing world, compelling people to look for new economic directions. Indeed, a government sector that once demonized the informal economy as an unauthorized (untaxed) drain on the formal economic structure now eagerly promotes self-employment and independent business not just for "micro-entrepreneurs" but for members of the middle class—black as well as white. This local promotion of entrepreneurship closely resembles the global capitalist agenda of neoliberalism at large—market-driven competition spurring individuals toward self-propelled economic enterprise that is flexible and responsive to changing conditions and demand, and industriously operates outside the support and unwieldy bureaucratic intrusion of the state.

However, for Barbadian women and men, entrepreneurship represents a dramatic departure from traditionally idealized paths of upward mobility and respectable middle-class status. Where former generations emphasized education, a university degree, a secure and long-term job in government or a large private company, today young people increasingly set their sights on business and resist the rigidity of large institutional hierarchies. The Oxbridge tradition of the region's early prime ministers—including Eric Williams, Norman Manley, and Grantley Adams—once set the standard for achievement to which children even of the island's poorest families might aspire. But now, in a radical turn, the aspirational goals have shifted toward American icons of self-invention like Oprah Winfrey, Tiger Woods, and Bill Gates. Titans of American entrepreneurship who have made their own way in the world without the imprimatur of prestigious credentials now capture the imagination and dreams of Barbadian youth and parents alike. The shift constitutes a decisive break with the past for this post-colonial nation known both proudly and mockingly as "Little England" for its Anglophilic culture of bureaucratic order, conservatism, and respectability. As the government sector and corporate arena are shrinking and unstable, individuals are forging new paths of economic enterprise, embracing the discourse of neoliberal self-sufficiency, industry, and flexibility—all key aspects of the local cultural tradition of "reputation." In so doing, they are actively both redrawing the local profile of the middle class and giving new shape to the Barbadian landscape of respectability, middle-class lifestyles, and culture (Freeman 2007).

The "global" frames these transformations in unmistakable ways. New business owners quote familiar US business gurus like the late Peter Drucker and the Microsoft giant Bill Gates; they make contact with US firms to source materials and supplies, and they view US business culture as a goal to be achieved while fashioning regional and even global circuits of distribution. Nevertheless, they simultaneously employ social networks and cultural resources that can only be understood within national and regional frames. Entrepreneurship, for them, represents a new promise of upward mobility and social esteem once perceived to be the preserve of other, more "respectable" occupations. Entrepreneurial pursuits are motivated frequently by the goal of creativity and self-regulation, dispensing with hierarchy, bosses, and the "establishment" in ways that are reminiscent of reputation's longstanding anti-colonial, anti-capitalist, and oppositional qualities. Entrepreneurship also allows for middle-class women to enter fields (manufacturing, transportation, etc.) that would otherwise be viewed as unsuitable for "respectable" Barbadian ladies. For these entrepreneurs, increasingly, flexibility is being decoupled from its lower-class associations with reputation, and is being harnessed to the goals of class mobility, economic security, and middle-class self-invention in the context of the contemporary global economy. Flexibility thus embodies simultaneously the marks of neoliberal capitalism and the local cultural value of reputation.

Yet, if entrepreneurship is strongly associated with the values of "reputation" in the constant demand for adaptability, travel, and the capacity to navigate various public domains and a wide range of social groups, "respectability" continues to be sought and romanticized in the realms of marriage and church. In a country known for its kinship tradition of "matrifocality," I discovered a striking reversal of this national profile at work. For, whereas according to the latest census, only about 25 percent of the adult population are reported to be married and nearly half of all households in the country are headed by women, an inverse of this picture emerged from my research: roughly 60 percent of the entrepreneurs I studied (n = 85) were married and only 15 percent were female heads of households. In the realm of religion, too, intriguing transformations speak to the reaches of globalization. Most entrepreneurs I interviewed eschew the Anglican Church of their childhood in favor of a range of new individualized spiritual activities as well as Pentecostal and "new-age" churches. We see in these patterns that some longstanding codes of respectability associated with middle-class life in Barbados are being upheld not only as ideals but in practice, albeit in new guises. Entrepreneurial women are strongly invested in the institutions of marriage and the church. Notably, however, the forms of marriage and expressions of religious practice that they are keen to enact—and the close relationship of these new practices to a general spirit of entrepreneurialism—have imbued these revered institutions of respectability with signature elements of reputation.

Women and men entrepreneurs use the language of "partnership" to describe their marriages and enact relationships in new ways that prioritize the couple over traditional single-sex social groups of friends and "crews" and in a new range of associated activities meant to enhance romantic and emotional compatibility, all of which they describe as new, "modern," and less typical among their parents' generation. Based on active rejection of the traditional patriarchal household, these new partnerships are forged around the ideal of sharing responsibilities, economic support, decision-making, household expenses, and leisure time. At least as important is an emphasis on sharing feelings, values, intimacy, and the stresses and pleasures of life. Like entrepreneurship and the consumption of new goods and media, companionate marriage and ideals of romance are rich domains of global cultural practice, unmistakably familiar but situated in the particular complexities of each cultural context (Hirsch and Wardlow 2006).

The emphasis on romance, intimacy, and emotional needs, as expressed especially powerfully by entrepreneurial women, is also reflected in the kinds of new business they themselves initiate and frequent—from cafes and romantic wine bars to catering services and prepared foods for dual-career couples who wish to entertain but have little time, and to small specialty boutiques and art/craft galleries; from day spas and beauty services to personal (and personality) trainers, therapeutic massage, health and nutrition consultation, therapists specializing in holistic healing, iridology, and religiously inspired psychology, marriage counseling and yoga studios, organized transportation services, and team building exercises for high-end tourists and for the children of busy working parents—all newly expanding niches of this middle-class marketplace geared toward soothing/nourishing/adorning new middle-class subjects and fostering new middle-class selves. Not only are new businesses reflecting a new cultural economy of globalization in which increasing domains of life are becoming embedded in market relations, but personhood itself is increasingly understood as a project forever under construction.

Such reconfigurations of marriage and transformations of religious practice and spirituality signal a subtle but powerful re-crafting of respectability. The new entrepreneurs are, in growing numbers, attending US-style charismatic churches whose "prosperity gospel" preaches economic flourishing and individualism to middle-class congregations and whose interactive style departs from the "stiffness" and "formality" of traditional, mainline churches. Others favor a range of individualized forms of spirituality—from yoga and meditative practices melding elements of Eastern religions to rigorous daily exercise infused with Christian belief and biblical reading. Meanwhile, patriarchal marriage ideals (though certainly not all patriarchal practices) are giving way to a vision of intimate partnership and the extended family veers toward nuclearization and the primary "investment" in and cultivation of children, while the bureaucratic order and hierarchy of the Anglican Church and government sectors are ceding to Pentecostalism, living-room churches, and both economic and personal entrepreneurialism.

The pressure to become not only an economically self-sufficient entrepreneur but an "entrepreneur of the self" by retooling one's intimate relationships, spirituality, parenting style, and manner of marking social class challenges some of the nation's longstanding bureaucratic conventions, models of matrifocal kinship, patriarchal marriage, and hierarchical Anglican traditions. These dialectical convergences of economic, cultural, social, individual, and emotional spheres in which such self-making unfolds call for new tools of analysis that transcend a rigidly binary treatment of production/consumption, economy/ culture, and global/local. It might be tempting to read the transformations I have described as illustrations of the homogenizing force of globalization; however, by applying the local cultural matrix of reputation/respectability, we see that such a reading is both partial and inadequate.

Conclusions

One might easily feel a "déja-vu" sensation as one glimpses seemingly ubiquitous signs of neoliberal globalization that have recently emerged in Barbados as a post-colonial nation.

Others described similar transformations in the globalizing logics of production and consumption recasting selfhood through the particular prisms of history and culture (Liechty 2003; Pun 2005; Fernandes 2006; Walkerdine 2003). In Pun's (2005) account, we see that self-invention is central to Chinese women's passionate desires when they migrate to urban factory centers. The wide range of evening classes, self-help books, romantic possibilities, and religious offerings are both familiar signs of globalization, and framed within particular Chinese characteristics. In Lan's (2006) study, state-sponsored circuits of migration cast domestic workers as dutiful long-distance mothers and "ambassadors" whose remittances are integral to both their family's livelihood and their homeland's national economy; at the same time these women are actively engaged in fashioning themselves as savvy, independent, and feminine subjects in both their privatized workplaces and the global marketplace.

However, it is precisely the ways in which apparent similarities are framed within the particular contours of culture—in the case of Barbados, the rubrics of a dynamic cultural logic of Barbadian reputation/respectability—that reveal the most complex and in some ways most important cultural meanings of globalization. Globalization is driven by economic forces, and is increasingly expressed and mediated through new technologies, it is true. But many facets of the global are enacted through the textured fabric of culture by people who in effect create new social relations and new selves embedded in the particulars of place, culture, and time. The creation of new subjectivities cannot be accomplished *ex nihil* but instead is achieved by people who mobilize existing fragments of cultural practice and invest them with new meanings in new configurations and contexts.

As prophetic as Marx and Engels were in foreseeing the tremendous reach that global capitalism would attain, even they might have been surprised by the intricate ways in which production and consumption would become inextricable economic and cultural forces. The implications of these dialectics for redefining personhood and for redrawing the contours and class, gender, and race as lived, felt, and imagined through the particulars of culture remain some of the most potent questions of this "global" age.

Acknowledgements

I thank the editors Ming-Cheng Lo, John Hall, and Laura Grindstaff for their patient and generous engagement and conversation surrounding the broad themes of globalization and culture in the various stages of my article's emergence. Thank you to Robert Goddard, Cory Kratz, Viranjini Munasinghe, and David Nugent for their close reading of and helpful suggestions with several longer versions of this paper, and to Gul Ozyegin, my ever generous interlocutor, who has sharpened my prose and collaborated in the development of my thinking on these matters of particularity and globalization. The Barbados fieldwork presented in this paper has been generously funded by the National Science Foundation, the Institute for Comparative and International Research at Emory University, and the Alfred P. Sloan Foundation's MARIAL (Myth and Ritual in American Life) Center. I am grateful to them all for supporting this research, and to the brave and generous entrepreneurs who shared their time and experiences.

References

Beck, U. 1992. *Risk Society: Toward a New Modernity*. London: Sage.

Bourdieu, P. 1998. "The Essence of Neoliberalism." *Le Monde Diplomatique*, December 8. Available at http://mondediplo.com/1998/12/08bourdieu.

Comaroff, J. and Comaroff, J.L. 2000. "Millenial Capitalism: First Thoughts on a Second Coming." *Public Culture* 12: 291–343.

Featherstone, M., ed. 1990. *Global Culture: Nationalism, Globalization, and Modernity*. London: Sage.

Fernandes, L. 2006. *India's New Middle Class: Democratic Politics in an Era of New Economic Reform*. Minneapolis: University of Minnesota Press.

Freeman, C. 2000. *High Tech and High Heels in the Global Economy: Women, Work, and Pink Collar Identities in the Caribbean*. Durham, NC: Duke University Press.

Freeman, C. 2007. "The 'Reputation' of Neoliberalism." *American Ethnologist* 34: 252–67.

Friedman, J. 1994. *Consumption and Identity*. New York: Harewood.

Hannerz, U. 1991. "Scenarios for Peripheral Cultures." In A.D. King, ed., *Culture, Globalization, and the World-System: Contemporary Conditions for the Representation of Identity*. Binghamton, NY: Department of Art and Art History, State University of New York at Binghamton.

Harvey, D. 1989. *The Condition of Postmodernity*. London: Blackwell.

Hirsch, J. and Wardlow, H., eds. 2006. *Modern Loves: The Anthropology of Romantic Courtship and Companionate Marriage*. Ann Arbor: University of Michigan Press.

Jameson, F. 1991. *Postmodernism or the Cultural Logic of Late Capitalism*. Durham, NC: Duke University Press.

Lan, P.C. 2006. *Global Cinderellas: Migrant Domestics and Newly Rich Employers in Taiwan*. Durham, NC: Duke University Press.

Leichty, M. 2003. *Suitably Modern: Making Middle-Class Culture in a New Consumer Society*. Princeton, NJ: Princeton University Press.

Marx, K. and Engels, F. 1979 (1848). "Manifesto of the Communist Party." In R.C. Tucker, ed., *The Marx Engels Reader*, second edition. New York: W.W. Norton and Company.

Mies, M. 1986. *Patriarchy and Accumulation on a World Scale: Women in the International Division of Labor*. London: Zed Books.

Moore, H.L. 2005. "The Future of Gender or the End of a Brilliant Career?" In P.L. Geller and M.K. Stockett, eds., *Feminist Anthropology: Past, Present, and Future*. Philadelphia: University of Pennsylvania Press.

Ong, Aihwa. 1987. *The Spirits of Resistance and Capitalist Discipline: Factory Women in Malaysia*. Albany, NY: State University Press.

Ong, A. and Collier, S.J., eds. 2004. *Global Assemblages: Technology, Politics and Ethics as Anthropological Problems*. London: Blackwell.

Pakulski, J. and Waters, M. 1996. *The Death of Class*. London: Sage.

Pieterse, J.N. 2004. *Globalization and Culture: Global Melange*. Lanham, MD: Rowman and Littlefield Publishers.

Pun, Ngai. 2005. *Made in China: Women Factory Workers in a Global Workplace*. Durham, NC: Duke University Press.

Robertson, R. 1992. *Globalization: Social Theory and Global Culture*. London: Sage.

Tsing, A. 2005. *Friction: An Ethnography of Global Connection*. Princeton, NJ: Princeton University Press.

Walkerdine, V. 2003. "Reclassifying Upward Mobility: Femininity and the Neo-liberal Subject." *Gender and Education* 15: 237–48.

Wilson, P. 1973. *Crab Antics: The Social Anthropology of English-Speaking Negro Societies of the Caribbean*. New Haven, CT: Yale University Press.

Yudice, George. 2003. *The Expediency of Culture: Uses of Culture in the Global Era*. Durham, NC: Duke University Press.

56

Globalization and cultural production

Denise D. Bielby

Among the many transformations in the world economy during the last quarter-century is the expanded trans-nationalization of cultural production. The industry trade publication *The Hollywood Reporter* (Turner 2008) reported that in 2007 the major US studios alone generated an estimated $6 billion in international program sales, and as a singular measure this figure is but one small indicator of how the robust production and distribution of cultural products that include film, radio, television, books, music, and new media now constitute an overwhelmingly vibrant global economic sector. Although world markets are not new, what has changed is the rapid acceleration of the globalizing world economy, and, in particular, the organizational arrangements that underlie it. As organizations have become increasingly transnational in scope, industrial arrangements of production and distribution have become more complex. Social theorists (Weber 1978 [1921]) recognized that globalization of industrial forms would be the end-point of modernity, itself the outgrowth of scientific technology and industrial production that has yielded a world of economic markets, legal settings, and political organizations in which social institutions operate under rational organizational principles. In the study of these arrangements, however, organization scholars found that when firms expand into less familiar cultural locales, they are often confronted with ambiguous marketplaces and no clear route to success, and it is within those contexts that firms collectively develop conceptualizations of how their market is structured along lines of, for example, competitive strategies (Fligstein 1996), labor relations (Dobbin *et al.* 1993), and organization boundaries (Davis *et al.* 1994) to augment familiar institutional strategies for action. Strategic corporate leaders play a pivotal role in this process (Fligstein 2001).

According to neo-institutionalists (Scott and Meyer 1994), the global spread of organizational forms leads to growing interdependencies among countries, with social institutions eventually resembling one another through worldwide adoption of shared cultural understandings of economic and legal systems. These claims pertain to some extent to the production of cultural products in a global context, but their applicability is less straightforward. As global theorists have observed, incorporating the concept of culture, "the signifying system through which necessarily (among other means) a social order is communicated, reproduced, experienced, and explored" (Williams 1981: 13),

into understanding societal, national, or organizational levels of development is complicated by the many ways in which culture itself is understood as a focus of study (Pieterse
2006). Concepts such as national identity and national culture, for example, are no
longer regarded as unitary, and likely never could be (van Elteren 1996). Although discussions among globalization theorists themselves about the theoretical adequacy or utility of their own conceptualizations of culture (see Connell 2007, for example) are
beyond the scope of this chapter, such discussions do affect how we understand the significance of an increasingly globalizing industrial system of cultural production because,
while cultural products are circulated by powerful corporations, the symbolic creativity
they organize, produce, and distribute is not immune from the inequalities of class,
gender, and ethnicity present in the industries of contemporary capitalist societies; in
addition, cultural products are increasingly significant as sources of wealth and employment in many economies (Hesmondhalgh 2007).

Because cultural production as an industrial system encompasses "outputs [that]
are marked by high levels of aesthetic and semiotic content in relation to their purely
practical uses" (Scott 2000: 2), and symbolic content plays an increasingly important
role in how countries, nations, regions, and cultures interconnect on organizational
levels, this chapter addresses what sociologists understand about globalization and cultural production, that is, the trans-national institutional arrangements that are associated
with the creation or execution, reproduction, circulation, and exhibition of cultural
products.

Studying globalization and cultural production

The political economic perspective is perhaps the best known scholarly approach to
understanding how global cultural production is embedded in economic systems that are
interrelated with political, social, and cultural life. Insights by scholars who assume an
overtly critical stance about the consequences of these interconnections have tended to
dominate this approach to the field, especially in the study of media (e.g. Miller *et al.*
2005; McChesney 2004): they have deeply influenced broader interpretations of the
interplay between cultural production and global markets, nations, and development.
A perhaps unintended consequence of an overtly critical perspective is that it can
encumber empirical approaches to the study of cultural production at the global level
(Scott 2005: chap. 6), although that is less the case in scholarship on national industries,
especially of those in the US, Europe, and Australia. That research, which focuses on
local contexts of cultural production, offers keen insights from the study of cultural
industries, organizations, and markets, and about the social organization of the creative
labor of art worlds that contributes to cultural production at the global level (e.g.
Cunningham and Jacka 1996). Yet even as the research has much to say, others have
observed how the characteristically democratizing thrust of US scholarship, in particular,
in its aim to contextualize the contribution of creative workers adequately, has muted
understanding of the ways in which the work of cultural industries intersects with issues
of power and structure (Hesmondhalgh 2007). Taking these considerations into account,
at this juncture, I characterize the field of globalization and cultural production as a
composite of scholarship that on the one hand consists of grounded empirical work,
usually at the national level, whose implications for understanding the political economic
contexts of globalization and cultural production are under-theorized, and on the other

hand relies upon top-heavy conceptual perspectives that over-theorize the hegemony of cultural industries in a world economy (see also Guillen 2001).

Increasingly, however, scholars in the US, Australia, and Europe, especially those who study the television, film, and music industries, have begun to call for middle-range theoretical approaches that bridge this divide by targeting meso-level conceptualization, evidence, and analysis (Bielby and Moloney 2008). This intermediate approach emphasizes the importance of grounded analysis of institutional logics—the cultural determinants of organizational decisions (Douglas 1986), alongside production logics—the social contexts and historical contingencies that shape markets and mediate the effect of concentration and competition on product homogeneity (Dowd and Blyler 2002). Analysis of institutional logics focuses on, for example, which organizational issues and problems stakeholders attend to in order to survive, or what answers and solutions are available or deemed appropriate (Thornton 2004), while examination of production logics considers, for example, how new technologies transform markets and how successful strategies toward technology (rather than the technologies themselves) are what prompt market changes (Dowd 2002).

Although studying institutional and production logics of markets as such is very important to better understand the mechanisms by which they operate, it is also increasingly necessary to bring evidence of organizational, institutional, or economic issues into cultural explanations. Scholars seeking a middle ground, where matters such as technological development or institutional transformation are placed alongside aspects of the political economy rather than subordinated to it, have also been increasingly turning to an explicitly cultural emphasis in traditional organizational and institutional analysis (Friedland and Mohr 2004). Granovetter's (1985) seminal insight, that market action is influenced by its embeddedness in a web of networked social roles and relations, was important to launching this line of thinking. More recently, economic sociologists Biggart and Beamish (2003) have extended Granovetter's insights, arguing that it is also necessary for the study of market arrangements to focus on how institutional and organizational structures, practices, customs, and modes of operation in market contexts are themselves socially and culturally constructed—an approach that redirects attention to the agency of institutional actors in marketplaces and the factors that account for their actions. In sum, a shift to a middle-range theoretical approach to global cultural production would invite a different set of questions, ones that would advance an empirically grounded understanding of the mechanisms and dynamics as well as the structures that constitute the vibrant economic sector of global cultural production.

Culture industries

Nearly four decades ago, organizational sociologist Paul Hirsch (1991 [1972]) identified the distinctive characteristics of the organizations that make up cultural-products industries. Today, understanding the social organization and dynamics of the creative worlds in which cultural production takes place is crucial to achieving a more nuanced and empirically informed approach to the study of global cultural production. Cultural products are shared significance embodied in form (Griswold 2000), meaning that they are expressive in nature and may be transcendent in effect. Hirsch himself described them as embodying live, one-of-a-kind performances and/or containing a unique set of ideas (Hirsch 1991 [1972]). Such products originate from art worlds (Becker 1982), which are themselves organized around shared understandings among artists and their associates about materials, performance, expertise, criteria for evaluation, quality of production, and so forth. Thus, the properties of cultural products, unlike strictly utilitarian ones, encompass aesthetic or expressive functions that differentiate them from other manufactured ones. Because of this character, products flow in and out of fashion due to the changing tastes, preferences, and patronage of consumers, creating unpredictable cycles of demand and tremendous business uncertainty as a result. Although Hirsch's particular focus at the time was national-level industries, his insights are just as relevant to those at the level of global cultural production.

As symbolic forms that connote, suggest, or imply expressive elements that may be appropriated for creation of social meanings, cultural products not only face demand uncertainty, their innovation can be uncertain as well. This added dynamic has implications for understanding cultural production at the level of the organization, whether it occurs at the global or the local level: the oversight of artistic origination, creation, and production is difficult to regulate bureaucratically because it relies upon intangible expertise—a situation akin to craft administration (Stinchcombe 1959), where the quality of the work cannot be unambiguously evaluated based on technical and measurable features of the finished product. Instead, the quality of the work and the competence of its creator are evaluated *post hoc* based on the acceptance and success of the work within the marketplace—an arrangement that significantly complicates the implementation of the rational bureaucratic organizational form and its control over the creative labor of employees.

The production–of–culture perspective, which is the prevailing conceptual approach to studying contexts of production (Peterson and Anand 2004), points to the importance of the effect of market structure (Dowd 2004a), embeddedness of organizations (Dowd 2004b), industry transformation (Jones and Thornton 2005), and classification of cultural industries (Janssen *et al.* 2008) as central determinants of product range and diversity. Although this perspective has been widely utilized for the study of national industries and contexts, it has yet to be extensively applied to analyses of cultural production at the global level. In particular, there is a need to study the cultural spaces of creative labor, especially how access to collaborative arrangements is formulated and interacts with the conduct of day-to-day work practices (McRobbie 2004).

In describing just how uncertain the demand for cultural products is, Hirsch (1991 [1972]) highlights the complexity of organizational control over the process of distribution. Manufacturers overproduce and from that abundance selectively sponsor large-scale promotion of new items in order to surmount the uncertainty of the market, an aspect of culture industry systems that necessitates specialized, labor intensive approaches to product dissemination. Other scholars expand on this insight in specifically cultural ways. Because cultural products are symbolic and expressive, and their complex aesthetic properties resonate differently in different contexts, their marketing is based upon establishing meaningful social relationships that utilize personalized or charismatic strategies (Biggart 1989), which are more effective at revealing the potential personal utility (i.e. the pleasure, transcendence, or resonance) of such products (Hirschman 1983). However, as particularistic transactions, they introduce vast interorganizational complexities into the mix. These go beyond mere interconnections and interdependencies among firms and individuals comprising culture-industry systems and extend to the contribution of individuals in key roles and the actions they take at the "input" and "output" boundaries of organizations (Hirsch 2000).

Observing such interorganizational dependencies associated with distribution of cultural products, especially at the global level, can be a challenge because they may include activity that is not readily visible to outside observers. This might encompass, for example, intra-organizational product modification following manufacturing—which can fundamentally transform a product from its original form to another for use in other locales (Bielby and Harrington 2008)—or complicated co-production agreements between firms from different countries. Such arrangements are intended to reduce uncertainty by anticipating the tastes of consumers in different nations, but they still can fail miserably (see Hubka 2002). Conglomerates may modify product repertoires for different locales (Negus 1999), but ever shifting tastes may overtake the market, circumventing well-developed corporate strategies altogether. In short, although enterprising producers and distributors of cultural products can come to dominate a nation, global region, or even the global market itself, cultural production and dissemination do not occur in an unfettered way. Although these complexities in cultural production were not directly anticipated in Hirsch's seminal contribution, his work continues to make possible keen insights about the organization of cultural industries.

Consideration of further constraints to cultural production adds yet another layer to the conceptual and empirical complexities that a middle-range theoretical approach can bring to the field. Peterson (1982) pointed out that cultural production at the national level is constrained by at least five factors—law, technology, market, organizational structure, and occupational careers. By identifying these hurdles, Peterson explicitly intended to problematize the production-of-culture perspective, organizational analysis, and institutional or economic perspectives, which do not always recognize such limits or constraints as central to the analysis of production in cultural industries. Important work by others adds factors to Peterson's list, a pivotal one being cultural policy *per se* (Crane 2002). As the location where social power writ large is brought into the mix of global cultural production (Pieterse 2006), cultural policy is the site where national interests are developed and enacted as formal instruments to facilitate cultural standing and to protect cultural authority within and across national borders or regions. In arguing for its inclusion when studying globalization and cultural production, Crane (2002) identifies three observable strategies or lines of action available to national governments, urban governments, and cultural organizations for preserving, protecting, and enhancing their cultural resources on the international level—protecting the country's culture, creating and maintaining images, and developing and protecting international markets and venues.

Crane's suggestions are important when considering the study of globalization and cultural production because nations vary in the degree to which they subscribe to a cultural policy—if one even exists. The US, for example, offers minimal oversight of forms of high culture, whereas other nations such as France are vigorous in protecting encroachment upon their national cultural identity. As of 2006, there were several dominant international policy agencies, each with its own membership and agenda: the European Union (EU), North American Free Trade Association (NAFTA), Mercado Commun del Sur (MERCOSUR), Association of Southeast Asian Nations (ASEAN), General Agreement on Tariffs and Trade (GATT), World Trade Organization (WTO), and General Agreement on Trade in Services (GATS) (Hesmondhalgh 2007). All were created to encourage free (or freer) trade between member countries but also in some instances to set quotas on the export of content to forestall overwhelming one nation or a set of nations. How such associations foster trade that creates advantages for wealthier nation-members is an empirical question. These organizations notwithstanding, there are other less formal but equally concerted strategies within nations that are intended to manage cultural products at the local level. These, according to Crane (2002), include the process of culturally "reframing" aspects of specific national urban and historical sites so that they are more (or less) accessible to non-locals. Such strategies can blunt national efforts to maintain a balance between local and global exposure (Tinic 2006).

Commodity chains and regionalism

Work by cultural geographers holds promise for advancing middle-range sociological approaches to globalization and cultural production. To some geographers, global production occurs through seemingly straightforward ties between manufacture and distribution—so-called commodity chains, which are the networks of labor, production, trade, and service activities that yield commodities (Hopkins and Wallerstein 1986: 159). Transnational chains array components of the production process across the world economy by relying upon key nodes of operation in different locations in the production process (Gereffi 1992: 94). Within the chain structure, business transactions and intra-firm transfers contribute or "add" the value that moves production along to conclusion (Appelbaum and Gereffi 1994).

While the imagery of a chain structure is a very useful mechanism for organizing understanding of how elements of cultural production flow across borders, for some who study cultural industries it is just a starting point because of the vastly more complicated nature of cultural products with complex aesthetic properties. To some geographers, especially those whose focus is the industries of television and film, basic concepts such as commodity chains are supplanted by the importance of geographic regions to sustaining synergies among workers with the creative skills necessary for the creation, production, and distribution activities that make up cultural industries. As sites of economic activity, geographic regions shape how development (the process of building and rearranging economic resources in the interests of enhanced productivity) and growth (the expression of that enhancement in terms of increments to gross product) actually occur (see Scott 2002). Because of the interconnections among creative workers in art worlds, regional economies exhibit "efficiency promoting properties" among transactions at the local level, and particularly successful regions can effectively "push" national development and growth because of their strong network structure of production, technology systems, local labor markets, and regional business cultures (Storper 1997). Hollywood is a particularly successful example of regional agglomeration, as is France's film industry, Latin America's telenovela production, and India's Bollywood. The concept of agglomeration—the concentration of capital and labor comprising modern production systems—is crucial here. According to Scott, the synergy of agglomeration—coupled with strong industry marketing and distribution capabilities sustained by the influx of capital and labor to magnet-like metropolises such as Milan, Vancouver, Paris, Miami, or Hong Kong—is what accounts for a region's unshakable competitive advantage despite an increasingly dispersed, polycentric global media commodity chain and strong national and regional industries elsewhere around the globe (Scott 2004). In short, the concept of regional agglomerations of cultural production offers considerable explanatory power for understanding globalization and cultural production in the absence of a culture industry's ability to bureaucratically manage creative labor or control the conventions that organize and sustain art worlds where creative production takes place.

Although some would agree with these arguments, others would question the strength of their claims by pointing to evidence of the counterbalancing effect of cultural and political policies upon local, regional, and national economies. Scott acknowledges these factors as relevant but secondary to his emphasis on the concept of agglomeration as a fundamental explanation for the strength of regional production centers. An analysis relevant to this unresolved matter is found in Curtain's (2005) study of how the institutional logics of politics, market, and cultural production and distribution in China thwarted Rupert Murdoch's attempt to completely penetrate that country with his STAR satellite system of television distribution. In spite of neighboring Hong Kong's unquestionable influence as a regional center of cultural production—a robustness that is due to its unique position at the periphery of China and its strong links to the West, primarily Europe—China's openness to Hong Kong's influence did not extend to an acceptance of STAR's organizational mechanisms (its business strategy for growth, expansion, and development), which were fundamentally disrupted by China's culturally distinct expectation that the market be subordinate to political institutions and ideologies. In this instance, Western conventions about the interconnections between the market and corporate growth were not shared because the cultural assumptions underlying transnational co-orientation were absent, miscommunicated, out of reach, unknown, or unattainable. In short, the business plan could not proceed as Murdoch intended because it ran counter to China's practice of subordinating the business of its economy to government interests. Further work that counterposes these important lines of research is clearly necessary.

Conclusion

The study of globalization and cultural production is ready for a focused theoretical integration. Such a project will necessarily bring evidence of organizational, institutional, or economic issues into cultural explanations, consistent with the "cultural turn" in sociology. Studies of organizations and institutions ably document the forms and structure of conglomerates and consolidation, but it is those who study the structure of markets and the cultural specificities that affect them who often come closest to conceptually engaging what is most relevant to theoretical integration—particularly when they go beyond strictly national-level interests. Such efforts frequently entail reading across disciplinary boundaries. Although media scholars may be more inclined to consider topics of particular relevance to globalization and cultural production, such as industry concentration, they can just as easily overlook the relevance of market context and institutional forms for understanding the phenomenon under consideration.

Empirical study of the impact of cultural policy on globalization and cultural production is crucial to advancing theoretical integration, but it remains to be seen how useful the valorization of the local–global dichotomy and attention to top–down effects of media institutions can be in moving the field forward. Moreover, in order to more effectively address the connections between globalization, cultural production, and political economy, scholars will need to reconsider Western assumptions that saturate thinking about modern organizational forms in light of challenges by religious nationalisms, differences in business relationships (such as Asian expectations that they be based on personal networks and relations of mutual obligation—*guanxi*), and political cultures that foreground policy over institutional mandates (Gessner *et al.* 2001).

With a revised agenda in mind, Hesmondhalgh (2007: 51–79) offers several useful questions to guide our thinking as the field of globalization and cultural production develops. To what extent, he asks, have the cultural industries become increasingly important in national economies and local business? What are the implications of the further commodification of culture? To what extent have changes in conglomeration and integration led to recognizably new and distinct forms of ownership and structure? What are the effects of the growth in size and power of cultural industry corporations on cultural production and wider society? To what extent have international cultural flows changed sufficiently for us to speak of a new era in cultural production and circulation? To what extent does the increasing global reach of the largest firms mean an exclusion of voices from cultural markets? Finally, given the emergence of new media, are we in a new era of cultural production?

References

Appelbaum, Richard and Gereffi, Gary. 1994. "Power and Profits in the Apparel Commodity Chain." In Edna Bonacich, Lucy Cheng, Norma Chinchilla, Nora Hamilton, and Paul Ong, eds., *Global Production: The Apparel Industry in the Pacific Rim*. Philadelphia: Temple University Press.

Becker, Howard. 1982. *Art Worlds*. Berkeley: University of California Press.

Bielby, Denise and Harrington, C. Lee. 2008. *Global TV: Exporting Television and Culture in the World Market*. New York: NYU Press.

Bielby, Denise D. and Moloney, Molly. 2008. "Considering Global Media: Sociological Contributions." Pp. 269–300 in Ron Rice, ed., *Media Ownership: Research and Regulation*. Cresskill, NJ: Hampton Press.

Biggart, Nicole. 1989. *Charismatic Capitalism: Direct Selling Organizations in America*. Chicago: University of Chicago Press.

Biggart, Nicole and Beamish, Thomas. 2003. "The Economic Sociology of Conventions: Habit, Custom, Practice, and Routine." *Annual Review of Sociology* 29: 443–64.

Connell, Raewyn. 2007. "The Northern Theory of Globalization." *Sociological Theory* 25(4): 368–85.

Crane, Diana. 2002. "Culture and Globalization: Theoretical Models and Emerging Trends." Pp. 1–25 in Diana Crane, Nobuko Kawashima, Kenichi Kawasaki, eds., *Global Culture: Media Arts, Policy, and Globalization*. New York: Routledge.

Cunningham, Stuart and Jacka, Elizabeth. 1996. *Australian Television and International Mediascapes*. Cambridge: Cambridge University Press.

Curtain, Michael. 2005. "Murdoch's Dilemma, or 'What's the Price of TV in China?'" *Media, Culture, and Society* 27(2): 155–75.

Davis, G.F., Diekmann, K.A., and Tinsley, C.H. 1994. "The Decline and Fall of the Conglomerate Firm in the 1980s." *American Sociological Review* 59: 547–70.

Dobbin, Frank, Sutton, John, Meyer, John, and Scott, Richard. 1993. "Equal Opportunity Law and the Construction of Internal Labor Markets." *American Journal of Sociology* 99: 396–427.

Douglas, Mary. 1986. *How Institutions Think*. Syracuse, NY: Syracuse University Press.

Dowd, Timothy. 2002. "Culture and Commodification: Technology and Structural Power in the Early U.S. Recording Industry." *International Journal of Sociology and Social Policy* 22(1/2/3): 106–40.

——. 2004a. "Concentration and Diversity Revisited: Production Logics and the U.S. Mainstream Recording Industry, 1940–90." *Social Forces* 82(4): 1411–55.

——. 2004b. "Introduction: The Embeddedness of Cultural Industries." *Poetics* 32(1): 1–3.

Dowd, Timothy and Blyler, Maureen. 2002. "Charting Race: The Success of Black Performers in the Mainstream Recording Market, 1940 to 1990." *Poetics* 30(1–2): 87–110.

Fligstein, Neil. 1996. "Markets as Politics: A Political-Cultural Approach to Market Institutions." *American Sociological Review* 61: 656–73.

——. 2001. "Social Skill and the Theory of Fields." *Sociological Theory* 19(2): 105–25.

Friedland, Roger and Mohr, John. 2004. "The Cultural Turn in American Sociology." Pp. 1–68 in Roger Friedland and John Mohr, eds., *Matters of Culture: Cultural Sociology in Practice*. Cambridge: Cambridge University Press.

Gereffi, Gary. 1992. "New Realities of Industrial Development in East Asia and Latin America: Global, Regional, and National Trends." Pp. 85–112 in Richard Appelbaum and Jeffrey Henderson, eds., *States and Development in the Asian Pacific Rim*. Newbury Park, CA: Sage.

Gessner, Volkmar, Appelbaum, Richard, and Felstiner, William. 2001. "Introduction: The Legal Culture of Global Business Transactions." Pp. 1–36 in Richard Appelbaum, William Felstiner, and Volkmar Gessner, eds., *Rules and Networks: The Legal Culture of Global Business Transactions*. Oxford: Hart Publishing.

Granovetter, Mark. 1985. "Economic Action and Social Structure." *American Journal of Sociology* 91(X): 481–510.

Griswold, Wendy. 2000. *Cultures and Societies in a Changing World*. Thousand Oaks, CA: Pine Forge Press.

Guillen, Mauro F. 2001. "Is Globalization Civilizing, Destructive, or Feeble? A Critique of Five Key Debates in the Social Science Literature." *Annual Review of Sociology* 27: 235–305.

Hesmondhalgh, David. 2007. *The Cultural Industries*, second edition. London: Sage Publications.

Hirsch, Paul M. 1991 (1972). "Processing Fads and Fashions: An Organization-Set Analysis of Cultural Industry Systems." Pp. 313–34 in Chandra Mukerji and Michael Schudson, eds., *Rethinking Popular Culture*. Berkeley: University of California Press.

——. 2000. "Cultural Industries Revisited." *Organization Science* 11: 356–61.

Hirschman, Elizabeth C. 1983. "Aesthetics, Ideologies and the Limits of the Marketing Concept." *Journal of Marketing* 47: 45–55.

Hopkins, Terence K. and Wallerstein, Immanuel. 1986. "Commodity Chains in the World-Economy Prior to 1800." *Review* X(1): 157–70.

Hubka, David. 2002. "Globalization and Cultural Production." Pp. 233–55 in Diana Crane, Nobuko Kawashima, and Kenichi Kawasaki, eds., *Global Cultures: Media, Arts, Policy and Globalization*. New York: Routledge.

Janssen, Susanne, Kuipers, Gislelinde, and Verboord, Marc. 2008. "Cultural Globalization and Arts Journalism: The International Orientation of Arts and Cultural Coverage in Dutch, French, German, and U.S. Newspapers, 1955 to 2005." *American Sociological Review* 73(5): 719–40.

Jones, Candace and Thornton, Patricia. 2005. "Transformation in Cultural Industries: Introduction." In Candace Jones and Patricia Thornton, eds., *Research in the Sociology of Organizations: Transformations in Cultural Industries*. Greenwich, CT and London: JAI Press.

McChesney, Robert W. 2004. *The Problem of the Media: U.S. Communication Politics in the Twenty-First Century*. New York: Monthly Review Press.

McRobbie, Angela. 2004. "Making a Living in London's Small-Scale Creative Sector." Pp. 130–43 in Dominic Power and Allen J. Scott, eds., *Cultural Industries and the Production of Culture*. New York: Routledge.

Miller, Toby, Govil, Nitin, McMurria, John, Maxwsell, Richard, and Wang, Ting. 2005. *Global Hollywood 2*. London: British Film Institute.

Negus, Keith. 1999. *Music Genres and Corporate Cultures*. New York: Routledge.

Peterson, Richard A. 1982. "Five Constraints on the Production of Culture: Law, Technology, Market, Organizational Structure and Occupational Careers." *Journal of Popular Culture* 16: 143–53.

Peterson, Richard A. and Anand, N. 2004. "The Production of Culture Perspective." *Annual Review of Sociology* 30: 311–34.

Pieterse, Jan Nederveen. 2006. *Development Theory: Deconstructions/Reconstructions*. London: Sage.

Scott, Allen J. 2000. "French Cinema: Economy, Policy and Place in the Making of a Cultural-Products Industry." *Theory, Culture & Society* 17(1): 1–38.

——. 2002. "A New Map of Hollywood: The Production and Distribution of American Motion Pictures." *Regional Studies* 36(9): 957–75.

——. 2004. "The Other Hollywood: The Organizational and Geographic Bases of Television-Program Production." *Media, Culture, and Society* 26(2): 183–205.

——. 2005. *On Hollywood*. Princeton, NJ: Princeton University Press.

Scott, W. Richard and Meyer, John. 1994. *Institutional Environments and Organizations: Structural Complexity and Individuality*. Newbury Park, CA: Sage.

Stinchcombe, Arthur. 1959. "Bureaucratic and Craft Administration of Production." *Administrative Science Quarterly* 4: 168–87.

Storper, Michael. 1997. *The Regional World: Territorial Development in a Global Economy*. New York: Guildford Press.

Thornton, Patricia H. 2004. *Markets from Culture: Institutional Logics and Organizational Decisions in Higher Education Publishing*. Stanford, CA: Stanford University Press.

Tinic, Serra. 2006. "Global Vistas and Local Reflections: Negotiating Place and Identity in Vancouver Television." *Television & New Media* 7(2): 154–83.

Turner, Mimi. 2008. "Broad Casting: U.S. Studios Looking Overseas for Growth." *The Hollywood Reporter*, March 14–16: 1, 14–15.

van Elteren, Mel. 1996. "Conceptualizing the Impact of US Popular Culture Globally." *Journal of Popular Culture* 30(1): 47–89.

Weber, Max. 1978 (1921). *Economy and Society: An Outline of Interpretative Sociology*. Berkeley: University of California Press.

Williams, Raymond. 1981. *Culture*. London: Fontana.

——. 1992 (1974). *Television: Technology and Cultural Form*. Hanover, NH: Wesleyan University Press.

57

Media technologies, cultural mobility, and the nation-state

Scott McQuire

It's August 2008 and I'm in Melbourne watching a live telecast of sprinter Usain Bolt winning the 100 meters gold medal at the Beijing Olympics. I'm not at home, or even in front of a television set, but peering at the screen on a friend's mobile phone as we walk down the street. Suddenly a message arrives from friends in London with the first photos of their newly born baby. We look at them, and then ring a colleague to discover that the place we're heading for is actually just around the corner. I text my partner to let her know where I am, and then glance at the first news coverage of Bolt's record-breaking run.

Although the details of the above account are imagined, exchanges along these lines are increasingly commonplace, albeit more common in some places than others. The point of my story is to highlight the way in which routine social interactions now often involve complex technological mediations operating across a number of levels. At one level, global events are screened on a variety of media platforms, including television, internet, and mobile phones. These events garner massive audiences across the world: the Beijing Olympic opening ceremony claimed the largest ever "live" screen audience— around two billion. In addition, the process of responding to and interpreting events has accelerated; instead of news cycles defined by the arrival of the morning paper or the broadcast of the evening news, we now have journalism metered by the speed of pervasive "real time" media. The blurring of the lines between event, live presentation, and interpretation gives rise to the rolling twenty-four-hour news coverage that characterized the attacks of September 11, 2001 and the invasion of Iraq in 2003.

At a second level, private communication now routinely occurs across great geographic expanses, enabling widely dispersed communities to maintain forms of "distant intimacy" stitched together by the frequent exchange of small messages. If the content of such messages often seems mundane to outsiders (and even to participants), the significance of the process of exchange should not be underestimated. Media have become integral to the enactment of social ties via social networks distributed over vast territories. As Scott Lash (2002: 15) puts it, "because my forms of social life are so normally and chronically at-a-distance, I cannot navigate these distances, I cannot achieve sociality apart from my machine interface." Moreover, routine communication not only bridges vast distances but reconfigures local practices, such as visiting friends. The fact that these different scales and trajectories are now dependent on the same complex technological systems shifts our understanding of the coordinates of "public" and "private" and alters the space–time texture of our everyday lives.

Finally, we might note that media not only enable new forms of mobility through their capacity to bridge time and space, but they are increasingly becoming mobile themselves. This shift from fixed and discrete points of production and consumption— centered around key sites such as studio, home, and office—to pervasive networks that can be accessed on the run is reconfiguring the characteristic spatial experiences and rhythms of social life. Foundational presumptions of sociology, such as the emphasis on structure and "solids," are being challenged. Indeed, the social is reconceptualized as "liquid" (Bauman 2000), "mobile" (Urry 2007), and composed of "flows" (Castells 1989).

In this chapter, I will analyze some of the ways in which media technologies have contributed to the transformation of social relations of space and time. To conceptualize space and time as social relations is, first of all, to insist that they are neither "natural" nor "objective" systems. Rather, understandings and valuations of space and time emerge from complex interactions involving technologies, institutions, material infrastructures, forms of knowledge and imagination, embodied experience, and social practices.

My analysis here will trace the historical role played by different media technologies in helping to constitute the nation-state as a dominant frame for modern culture and social life. After identifying some of the tensions in this project, I will conclude by arguing that contemporary developments, such as the emergence of global digital networks, have accentuated gaps in the alignment of territory, culture, and sovereignty that once defined the ideal nation-state, incubating new patterns of cultural affiliation and belonging not yet solidified into formal institutions.

Clearly, media comprise only one force at work in contemporary debates over globalization, and they need to be assessed in the context of other dynamics, including new processes of economic exchange affecting trade, investment, and production; new patterns of migration affecting the movement of people; and new "global risks" such as climate change that increasingly drive demands for "post-national" forms of governance. Nevertheless, focusing on media offers strategic insights into emergent relations between national and global formations at a number of levels. Media not only form a primary source of information and images about both "home" and "foreign" territories—helping to orchestrate complex processes of identification and belonging—but media flows offer visible demonstrations of the impact of global processes on national sovereignty. National regulatory regimes are more difficult to maintain in the face of satellites and the internet, as China found during the Beijing Olympic Games, while national regulation of intellectual property is increasingly challenged by digital "piracy," on the one hand, and standards established by powerful content producers such as the United States, on the other. These examples serve to remind us that media, in the broad sense, underpin globalizing processes in most other sectors, enabling the rapid, ubiquitous, and distributed forms of communication that are becoming the taken-for-granted backdrop to social life in the twenty-first century.

Space, time, and modernity

The period of "modernity" is often characterized by distinctive shifts in the social relations of time and space. The most influential political economist of the nineteenth century,

Karl Marx, identified territorial expansion of markets and the acceleration of capital circulation as central to the dynamic of industrial capitalism. For Marx (1973: 539), "the more developed the capital, therefore, the more extensive the market over which it circulates, which forms the spatial orbit of its circulation, the more does it strive simultaneously for an even greater extension of the market and for greater annihilation of space with time." New transport technologies such as railways and steamships played key roles in beginning to link the world as a global entity. Increased mobility powered the extension of industrial capitalism and altered the patterns of human habitation. At a national level, migration from country to city became the dominant demographic trend, providing the conditions for the urbanization of social life. At a transnational level, new forms of technological mobility underpinned the colonization of much of the globe by the West, and ushered in the "age of migration" characterized by the flow of Europeans to "settler societies" such as the US, Canada, and Australia. Both trajectories produced significant collisions in space–time patterns, as the slower, cyclical rhythms of rural existence and the supposedly "backward" condition of indigenous populations increasingly became measured against the emerging norms of uniform linear time and urban speed (McQuire 1998).

Similar disjunctions in space–time experience have been observed in recent years. Sociologist David Harvey (1990) has theorized the experience of "space–time compression" to be at the heart of contemporary life. Harvey argues that the new capacity to bridge distance at high speed "so revolutionize[s] the objective qualities of space and time that we are forced to alter, sometimes in quite radical ways, how we represent the world to ourselves" (1990: 240). Similarly, Anthony Giddens describes contemporary global society "as expressing fundamental aspects of time–space distanciation"; he goes on, "globalization concerns the intersection of presence and absence, the interlacing of social events and social relations 'at distance' with local contextualities" (1991: 21). For Giddens, space–time distanciation is not simply about the heightened capacity for distant events to intrude into everyday consciousness via avenues such as news media; it also concerns the ways that intimate exchanges with family and friends are now routinely mediated across vast distances.

Media technologies such as telephone, television, and the internet cannot be regarded simply as the "cause" of contemporary "space–time compression" or "time–space distanciation." As I have indicated above, other factors must be considered—the impact of technologies such as new transport systems, and logics such as the emergence of abstract forms of knowledge, bureaucratic systems of organization, urbanization, patterns of migration, and the systemic expansion of industrial capitalism into a global market. Nevertheless, media technologies play a significant role in conditioning the current global order, by coordinating dispersed sites of production and consumption essential to expanded markets, by underpinning the rapid data-processing and exchange essential to the global financial system, and by promoting the rapid circulation of cultural and symbolic forms across transnational circuits.

Print media and the formation of the nation-state

Towards the end of his career, Canadian economic historian Harold Innis examined how different modes of human communication exerted a wider impact on social existence, including forms of economic life, politics, religion, education, and culture. Innis (1951) proposed that different media were "biased" according to whether they favored distribution in space or time, and he argued that changes in dominant media platforms were a significant factor in explaining major shifts in social organization. At one extreme, media such as stone and clay tablets are time biased—durable, but heavy, bulky, and hard to transport. At the other end of the spectrum, paper is space biased—light and easily transportable, but also fragile and susceptible to the depredations of time. Innis (1951: 116) argued that whereas time-biased media such as clay "helped sustain centralized religious forms of tradition, transportable media favored the growth of administrative relations across space, thereby facilitating the decentralized growth of secular and political authority." In his account, the invention of paper, and its spread from China to the Middle East and then to the West, was a central factor in the decline of traditional oral culture, and the subsequent emergence of spatially extensive forms of political authority such as the Roman Empire.

Innis's work proved influential on another Canadian scholar, literary professor Marshall McLuhan, who shot to fame in the 1960s on the back of his provocative argument concerning the transformative effects of television. McLuhan has often been criticized, notably by Raymond Williams (1990), for espousing a form of technological determinism that treats technology as an autonomous cause of social change. Williams insisted that new technologies and their patterns of use were not simply "invented," but depended upon the interplay of a range of specific conditions—such as corporate power to determine patterns of investment or the settings of government policy—in conjunction with more general conditions relating to the enhanced importance of mobility in an expanding capitalist system.

Although it is true that McLuhan pays scant attention to questions of power, he nevertheless offers important insights into the impact of modern media. Prior to McLuhan, the dominant paradigm of communication studies tended to treat the medium as "neutral" and to limit debate largely to questions of "content." In contrast, McLuhan (1974: 27) insisted, "the effects of technology do not occur at the level of opinions or concepts, but alter sense ratios or patterns of perception." He followed Innis in extolling the importance of print media—the so-called "Gutenberg Galaxy"—and in particular the newspaper, which he dubbed the "architect of nationalism." McLuhan (1974: 158) also recognized the rise of print culture as one of the conditions for the growth of modern rationality and individualism. But spatial extension came at a cost. Although print functioned to fragment and compartmentalize the individual human mind, in organizational terms it promoted a centralized, "top–down" culture governed by bureaucratic forms with rigid hierarchies.

A similar thesis concerning the integral relation between the newspaper and the nation-state was advanced in far more historical detail by critical theorist Jürgen Habermas (1989) and sociologist Benedict Anderson (1983). For Anderson, the rise of print culture was the structural condition that enabled "vernacular languages" to undermine the dominance of Latin and the central authority of the church. By creating unified zones of communication and exchange, print became the joint vehicle of both the emerging national economy and novel forms of national consciousness, resulting in the spread of what Anderson dubs "print capitalism." In Anderson's account, the expanded circulation of printed information is fundamental to the construction of the "imagined community" that characterizes the modern nation-state. The modern community is "imagined" because it comprises a mass of citizens who will never all meet "face to face," but who nevertheless develop forms of affective attachment and political solidarity mediated by media such as the newspaper and the book.

Jürgen Habermas (1989) also stresses the relation between expansion of markets for goods and for news, which have jointly functioned to "nationalize" the town-based economy and thereby constitute the nation-state. In his influential account of the formation of the "public sphere," Habermas locates its emergence in the transition from feudal to proto-democratic systems of political authority. The public sphere names the arena in which the ascendant bourgeoisie were able to find a political voice, as the legitimacy of noble "birthright" waned in favor of new modes of authority based on the will of "the people." "Public opinion"—a term that first entered the Oxford Dictionary in 1781—and the press as the "fourth estate" played key roles in the emergent democratic system. For Habermas, the press became the key instrument through which private citizens engage in rational public discourse to comment on "society" as a public affair. However, this ideal scenario has only rarely existed in reality. The increasing commercialization of the press, which helped to secure its independence from state control, also created the conditions for what Habermas terms a "re-feudalization" of the public sphere. Instead of articulating a broader public interest, public opinion comes to be dominated by coalitions of private interest.

Although the debates generated by Habermas's work are important, the key issue here is the role of media in establishing the nation-state as the primary frame for modern culture and social life. Spatially extended and temporally compressed communication circuits such as those established by mass daily newspapers help to create the conditions in which locally based forms of identity cede ground to widespread identification of citizens as national subjects. In Giddens's terms, the modern nation-state involved the "disembedding" of traditional, locally based social systems and a "stretching" of social relations, so that local markers of time and space such as places and seasons give way to more abstracted forms of knowledge such as news cycles and railway timetables. Like McLuhan and Anderson, Giddens (1991: 25–26) recognizes the mosaic form of the newspaper page as an index of the way that modernity produces both fragmentation and continuity. Disparate events are juxtaposed on the same page, unified only by the time of their occurrence (the present) and by the authority of the medium—an authority that is itself partly based on the novel speed and reach of the newspaper as a communication form.

Electronic media and national space

McLuhan's astounding popularity and influence in the 1960s was predicated on his spectacular extension of Innis's thesis concerning the spatial and temporal "bias" of electronic media. The "big flip" initiated by the spread of electronic media such as television involved displacement of the private detachment fostered by print by an imploding "global village" in which everyone is profoundly "involved" with everyone else. McLuhan's analysis remains contentious in terms of its sweeping claims about the effects of specific media, but it does serve to highlight the profound ambiguity of electronic media in relation to the space of the nation-state. As Thomson (1995) points out, while the late nineteenth-century newspaper gained mass distribution and was able to draw on dispersed sources of information via the telegraph, the logistics of physical distribution meant its primary audience was restricted to a single city or region. Electronic broadcasting is bound by no such limits. The capacity of radio waves to cross national borders was a key reason for the urgency with which different national governments moved to assert control over radio spectrums in the early twentieth century, often subordinating civilian to military use. Terrestrial television signals were initially more circumscribed. However, following the launch of geostationary satellites in 1962, television could not only relay "live" events from locations across the world, but also develop networks that bore no necessary relationship to the physical bounds of the nation-state.

Despite their technical capacity to travel across borders with relative impunity, radio and television remained primarily national industries and institutions into the 1980s. Individual nation-states sought to assert control over radio and television within their territories through a combination of licensing and regulation, and (with the notable exception of the United States) the provision of funding for public service broadcasters. This system, in which the media space of most nation-states was dominated by one or, at most, a handful of television broadcasters, proved remarkably stable across the major geo-political divides of the period. In fact, unified national programming arguably became a key means by which the "imagined community" was enacted in the second half of the twentieth century. As Colin McCabe (1986: 8) argues, "Just as national literature in the vernacular tongue was an essential component in the constitution of the ruling classes of post-Renaissance Europe, so a national broadcasting system is a crucial element in the current political settlement of the capitalist West."

This political function of broadcasting situates the major debates that emerged in the 1960s and 1970s concerning "media imperialism" and the need for a "new world information and communication order" (NWICO) as a response to the domination of media content by the West in general and the United States in particular. The character of these debates, which began from concern over the physical importation of program-ming as well as the dominance over communication infrastructure, began to change in the 1980s as new technologies opened gaps in the established fit between national terri-tory and media regulation. Fiber optics allowed cables to carry many more channels, while satellite distribution enabled cable operators to cover much larger territories. The launch of HBO as a national cable network in the US in 1975 was followed by the establishment of the first "global" channels, such as CNN (1980) and MTV (1981), which signalled the beginning of the shift away from nationally based television services. In Europe, the expansion of the number of channels coincided with growing privatization of television services and the formation of new policy settings, such as the "Television without Frontiers" Directive (1989) advocating greater cross-border media circulation within the European Union. By the close of the 1980s, direct satellite broadcasting began to provide growing competition to cable. Rupert Murdoch's News Corporation relaunched Sky Television (later BSkyB) in the UK in 1989, as the first node in his ambitious attempt to cover the globe with satellite television services. However, this ambition was itself outflanked by the rapid expansion of the internet, particularly the explosion of the "world wide web" (which married hypertext to the internet, enabling easy access to linked "pages" via web browsers) from around 1994.

Digital networks, global media, and post-national space

By the late 1980s the increasing influence of the internet led scholars such as urban sociologist Manuel Castells (1989: 6) to posit "the emergence of a space of flows which dominates the historically constructed space of places." Similarly, in his influential essay

"The Overexposed City," French social theorist Paul Virilio (1991: 13) argued that pervasive electronic media fundamentally dissolved traditional spatial dimensions in favor of instantaneous interactions: "From here on, people can't be separated by physical obstacles or by temporal distances. With the interfacing of computer terminals and video monitors, distinctions of here and there no longer mean anything." As the dot-com boom gained momentum in the late 1990s, economists such as Frances Cairncross (1997) announced the "death of distance," while the "Magna Carta for the Knowledge Age," written by Dyson et al. (1994: 26), proclaimed: "the central event of the twentieth century is the overthrow of matter." Borders, distance, and solid structures seemed not only less constraining, but virtually irrelevant, and the alignment of culture and national territory seemed poised to be entirely overtaken by global processes.

However, in contrast to widespread assertions that "cyberspace" necessarily involved the "annihilation" of distance and space, others insisted on the need to recognize the material embeddedness of digital networks. In her pioneering work on the global city, sociologist Saskia Sassen (1991) argues that "global cities," which form the command-and-control centers of contemporary global capitalism, have a critical dependence on digital infrastructure. If the global city is partly defined by its ability to attract skilled workers in sectors such as finance, management, and legal services, it also demands high-speed communication networks to control globally dispersed corporate systems. Instead of the wholesale disappearance of physical space that Virilio, Cairncross, and others prophesied, digital networks have a distinct geography. It is no accident that the "fattest pipes" (enabling the fastest data exchange) are those linking New York and London. Sassen contends that the spatial impact of digital networks involves simultaneous processes of concentration and dispersion. In this context, Sassen (2006) contends there is a partial disaggregation of national space in favor of the emergence of new sub-national (global city) and supra-national (global market) configurations. This does not entail the wholesale dismantling of the nation-state, but does challenge the logic of the national as the primary container for economic, cultural, social, legal, and even political processes at a number of strategic points.

Sassen's analysis is useful for conceptualizing the new patterns and trajectories that characterize contemporary media flows. On the one hand, we can point to the formation of supra-national broadcasting networks based on a combination of cable and satellite. Although some of these networks, such as News Corporation's Star Television, which covers fifty-three countries in Asia, testify to the persistence of older patterns of media dominance, others, such as the formation of al Jazeera in 1996, suggest their complication and potential transformation. At another level, we can point to the heightened frequency and visibility of transnational exchanges, ranging from the highly integrated international banking system—which now enables a single swipe card to access ATMs around the world using (relatively) secure private networks—to the sort of rolling global protests coordinated via the public internet that marked the onset of the Iraq war in 2003. The proliferation of media platforms, combined with new patterns of user-generated production and dissemination of content, means that the "public sphere" of most nation-states is increasingly defined by multiple channels and sources at a national level, but also by increased frequency of cross-border flows. This development has led to new hopes for a regeneration of the public sphere—because entry barriers to media access have been substantially lowered—but also to new concerns about the fragmentation and splintering of public discourse, insofar as customized media enable users to filter out information that might challenge their own world view. Is the public sphere expanding to include previously marginalized voices, and thus moving closer to its claim to universality, or is it being reduced to what Todd Gitlin (1998) calls "public sphericules"—atomized bubbles of opinion which lack the transversal connections which might animate sectional discussions into an active discourse about the public good? How might a transnational or global public sphere be established? These key questions now demand serious consideration.

The new global information order is by no means egalitarian, and the "digital divide" at both national and international levels remains a major issue. Nevertheless, media and cultural flows in the twenty-first century have assumed a growing level of complexity. The partial and uneven shift away from Western, and especially US, dominance of communications infrastructure—such as the use of satellites and the electromagnetic spectrum, micro-electronics, remote-sensing capabilities, and direct satellite broadcasting—is also increasingly evident in relation to the internet. Fifteen years ago there was substantial concern that the hardware, software, and content of the internet were following established patterns of global information flows. In 1993, nearly 94 percent of internet data flowed through just four countries: the US, Canada, the UK, and Australia. India accounted for 0.01 percent, China for so little it didn't register. However, recent years have seen substantial growth of the non-English-language internet, so that predictions of English as the universal "operating system" of global communication no longer seem so well founded. By 2008 English language content on the internet had dropped well below 30 percent. Internet theorist Geert Lovink (2008: xi) notes: "the majority of internet traffic these days is in Spanish, Mandarin, and Japanese, but little of this seems to flow into the dominant Anglo-Western understanding of Internet culture." Equally important, the internet is becoming much less dependent on US telecommunications infrastructure, with the amount of traffic routed through the US dropping from 70 percent to around 25 percent over the last decade. If this development was partly spurred by the draconian security provisions of the 2001 US Patriot Act, it is also an effect of increased investment in internet backbone by countries such as India and China.

The cultural implications of these new patterns are significant. Diasporic communities, as well as many other dispersed "communities of interest," which previously fell below the threshold of a national broadcast system with few outlets, have been able to shift media communication from the physical exchange of tapes, CDs, and DVDs to the establishment of specialist cable and satellite channels. Such communities are also able to use the internet to access national media, and to support new modes of private and semi-private communication across national borders using email, skype, blogs, and social networking websites. The increased availability of such circuits facilitates new modes of cultural belonging and cultural exchange, in which place of residence is no longer the threshold condition for awareness of, or participation in, one's "home" culture.

Homi Bhabha (1994) pointed out long ago that the legacy of colonialism and a century of mass migration, whether intended or not, was that the space of the national homeland became increasingly fractured from within. Now, new, more turbulent patterns of migration and "people movement" (Papastergiadis 2000) and the rise of what Ong (1999) calls "flexible citizenship" demand that we consider the increased significance of transnational exchanges. Kleinschmidt (2006) argues that, in order to map new regional patterns of cultural exchange, we need to move away from the paradigm of what he terms "residentialism" as the default setting for understanding mobility. Because residentialism treats mobility principally in terms of the threat it creates to national borders and state sovereignty, it tends to obscure the productive agency of migrants as the

605

creators of transnational social spaces of varying scales, durations, and structures. Contemporary media technologies exercise a similar migratory effect, accentuating the sense in which "home" is no longer bound to a particular place, synonymous with a single language, homogeneous people, or unified culture. Such mediatization of social life is a significant part of the condition which leads Urry (2007) to call for sociology to shift its focus and its concepts to address new forms of mobilities, many of which are not constrained by national boundaries.

In the present context, in which neither the internal nor the external borders of the nation as "home" remain secure, new possibilities for breaking away from fixed and exclusionary stereotypes are emerging. Instead of identity being circumscribed by a subjectivity dictated by place of origin, identity might be redefined to include the over-lapping, interpenetrating spaces and contradictory affiliations we inhabit in the present. The consequences of refusing to rethink the relations between identity and alterity, home and exile, familiar and foreign, and self and other have been all too evident in recent decades. Aggressive definition of a national culture based on primordial associa-tions between blood and land often leads to discrimination, segregation, and apartheid, and to the horror of ethnic cleansing operations in Bosnia, the walling off of the West Bank, and the fencing of the Mexico–US border. On the other hand, as power leaches away from the state to other entities such as transnational corporations, the nation can become a strategic point of resistance. In his meditation on "Europe," Derrida (1992: 37) pointed out that current ruptures mean that no radical politics can afford to define itself simply in opposition to the nation-state: "in certain cases the old state structures help us to fight against private and transnational empires."

In a world facing problems such as climate change that can only be resolved through concerted global action, a transnational public sphere is not a luxury but a necessity. However, a genuinely transnational public sphere can no longer afford the pretense of a universalism that masks the imperialism of powerful nations. It requires instead the development of lateral, horizontal exchanges that emphasize both cultural locatedness and cultural exchange as dynamic processes. This is the promise and challenge of how networked digital media might contribute to what Manray Hsu (2005) aptly terms "networked cosmopolitanism."

References

Anderson, B. 1983. *Imagined Communities: Reflections on the Origin and Spread of Nationalism*. London: Verso.

Bauman, Z. 2000. *Liquid Modernity*. Cambridge: Polity Press.

Bhabha, H. 1994. *The Location of Culture*. London and New York: Routledge.

Cairncross, F. 1997. *The Death of Distance: How the Communications Revolution Will Change Our Lives*. Boston, MA: Harvard Business School Press.

Castells, M. 1989. *The Informational City: Information Technology, Economic Restructuring, and the Urban–Regional Process*. Oxford and Cambridge, MA: Blackwell.

Derrida, J. 1992. *The Other Heading: Reflections on Today's Europe*, trans. M.B. Naas and P.A. Brault. Bloomington: Indiana University Press.

Dyson, E., Gilder, G., Keyworth, G., and Toffler, A. 1994. "A Magna Carta for the Knowledge Age." *New Perspectives Quarterly* 11: 26–37.

Giddens, A. 1991. *Modernity and Self-Identity: Self and Society in the Late Modern Age*. Stanford, CA: Stanford University Press.

Gitlin, T. 1998. "Public Sphere or Public Sphericules?" In T. Liebes and J. Curran, eds., *Media Ritual and Identity*. London: Routledge.

Habermas, J. 1989. *Structural Transformation of the Public Sphere: An Inquiry into a Category of Bourgeois Society*, trans. T. Burger. Cambridge, MA: MIT Press.

Harvey, D. 1990. *Condition of Postmodernity: An Enquiry into the Origins of Cultural Change*. Oxford and Cambridge, M.A.: Blackwell.

Hsu, M. 2005. "Networked Cosmopolitanism—On Cultural Exchange and the International Exhibition." In N. Tsoutas, ed., *Knowledge + Dialogue + Exchange*. Sydney: Artspace.

Innis, H. 1951. *The Bias of Communication*. Toronto: University of Toronto Press.

Kleinschmidt, H. 2006. "Migration and the Making of Transnational Social Spaces." Paper presented at the "Mobility, Culture, and Communication," symposium, University of Melbourne, 11 June. Available online at www.spatialaesthetics.unimelb.edu.au/pdfs/Symposium/Migration%20and%20Transn.pdf.

Lash, S. 2002. *Critique of Information*. London: Sage.

Lovink, G. 2008. *Zero Comments: Blogging and Critical Internet Culture*. London and New York: Routledge.

McCabe C, ed. 1986. *High Theory/Low Culture*. Manchester: Manchester University Press.

McLuhan, M. 1974 (1964). *Understanding Media: The Extensions of Man*. London: Abacus.

McQuire, S. 1998. *Visions of Modernity: Representation, Memory, Time, and Space in the Age of the Camera*. London: Sage.

Marx, K. 1973. *Grundrisse: Foundations of the Critique of Political Economy*, trans. M. Nicolaus. London: Allen Lane/NLR.

Ong, A. 1999. *Flexible Citizenship: The Cultural Logics of Transnationality*. Durham, NC: Duke University Press.

Papastergiadis, N. 2000. *The Turbulence of Migration: Globalization, Deterritorialization, and Hybridity*. Malden, MA: Polity Press.

Sassen, S. 1991. *The Global City: New York, London, Tokyo*. Princeton, NJ: Princeton University Press.

———. 2006. *Territory, Authority, Rights: From Medieval to Global Assemblages*. Princeton, NJ: Princeton University Press.

Thomson, J. 1995. *The Media and Modernity: A Social Theory of the Media*. Cambridge: Polity Press.

Urry, J. 2007. *Mobilities*. Cambridge and Malden, MA: Polity.

Virilio P. 1991. *The Lost Dimension*, trans. D. Moshenberg. New York: Semiotext(e).

Williams, R. 1990. *Television, Technology, and Cultural Form*, second edition. London: Routledge.

58

Tourism and culture

Kevin Fox Gotham

Over the decades, scholars have sought to understand and explain the changing institutional, political, and socio-economic linkages between culture and tourism. Researchers have long theorized some of the central features of tourism and tourist experiences, and examined the impact of tourism development on local culture. Much scholarship has also investigated the ways in which local cultural practices and identities shape the production and organization of tourism at a grassroots level. In conventional accounts, tourism is a set of discrete economic activities, a mode of consumption, or a spatially bounded locality or "destination" that is subject to external forces. In contrast, recent research conceptualizes tourism as a highly complex set of institutions and social relations that involve capitalist markets, state policy, and flows of commodities, technology, cultural forms, and people. In this conception, tourism is embedded within broader patterns of societal transformation as well as local networks and cultural practices.

My scholarship examines the ways in which tourism affects culture (both positively and negatively), how culture structures the development of tourism in a particular locale, and how tourism and culture transform each other as different actors and organized interests compete for access to and control over political and economic resources. Both tourism and culture are multidimensional, heterogeneous, and fluid categories that attain their significance in relationship with each other. Moreover, the boundaries between tourism and culture are porous and ever changing, in part because these categories become both sites and objects of political struggle among different groups.

In what follows, I have developed and applied the concept of "touristic culture" as a heuristic device to illustrate the ways in which culture and tourism share similar themes, symbols, discourses, and interpretive systems. Whereas a "culture of tourism" showcases local culture to attract tourists, a "touristic culture" blurs boundaries between tourism and other major institutions and cultural practices. Specifically, touristic culture is a process by which tourist modes of staging, visualization, and experience increasingly frame meanings and assertions of local culture, identity, authenticity, and collective memory. Exploring the concept of touristic culture can provide novel insights into several areas of scholarship, including: (1) the relationship between tourism and culture, ethnicity and race; (2) processes of cultural erosion and invention; and (3) tourism as a catalyst and expression of socio-cultural transformation.

Conceptualizations of the tourism–culture nexus

Scholars have developed typologies of tourism and theories of tourist experience, and investigated the impact of tourism on local economies and modes of cultural creation, among other concerns. Tourism has been conceptualized as a search for authenticity (MacCannell 1976), an expression of leisure and performative identity for the post-modern consumer (Urry 1995), a malevolent form of colonialism, conquest, and imperialism (Krippendorf 1984; Crick 1989), an opportunity for sexual exchange, sexual trafficking, and/or sexual exploitation (Cabezas 2004; Desmond 1999; Ryan and Hall 2001), a form of pilgrimage to culturally significant places (Gladstone 2005), a type of ethnic relation (van den Berghe 1980), a force for historical and cultural commodifica-tion (Watson and Kopachevsky 1994; Britton 1991; Kirschenblatt-Gimblett 1998), and a process of mobility and demographic migration (Cohen 1972). In John Urry's (1990) famous concept of the "tourist gaze," tourists view or gaze upon particular sites and sights because "there is an anticipation, especially through day-dreaming and fantasy, of intense pleasures, either on a different scale or involving different sense from those customarily encountered" (Urry 1990: 132). Influenced by Michel Foucault, Urry argues that a variety of non-tourist sites, such as film, newspapers, TV, magazines, records, and videos, construct tourist experiences and circulate the signs and symbols by which consumers are coached to view tourist attractions and understand their experiences as tourists.

In *Tourism Mobilities: Places to Play, Places in Play*, Mimi Sheller and John Urry (2006) show how places to play are also places in play—made and remade by the mobilities and performances of tourists and workers, images and heritage, the latest fashions, and the newest diseases. For Sheller and Urry, culture is not just anchored in a particular place but constituted by various mobilities and performances. Places and cultures "move" as they are put into play in relation to other places. In addition, tourism itself is in motion, becoming less predictable as changing processes of leisure and entertainment reshape global mobilities. From a mobilities perspective, tourism is about the mobilization of collective memories, performances, and identities. In leaving a place, residents carry its culture, including local beliefs, values, and sentiments that they use in new places to create new cultural forms. According to Sheller and Urry, cultures and places are not static and fixed in place but are embedded within complex networks by which hosts, guests, and cultural objects are continually interacting to produce new perfor-mances, ideologies, identities, and solidarities in different places and different times. In this sense, a mobilities perspective complicates binary distinctions between "residents" and "tourists" and blurs distinctions between demographic and migration processes and tourism development.

Several scholars have noted that cities are important sites for examining the theoretical and empirical connections and manifestations of the tourism–culture interplay. In the past few decades or so, city leaders and economic elites around the world have worked tirelessly to create new networks and promotional strategies to encourage the growth of tourism in their communities (Rath 2007; Hoffman *et al.* 2003). Indeed, in many cities and rural areas tourism has become the main strategy of urban revitalization: local governments and the tourism industry forge close institutional and financial ties to "sell" the city to potential "consumers" and invest in costly infrastructure to support tourism (Eisinger 2000). Whether the focus is celebrations like Mardi Gras, music festivals, or casino gaming, tourism-oriented urban regeneration and festival production remain a source of much debate and controversy around the world. On the one hand, proponents claim that tourism improves urban aesthetics, enhances leisure facilities for residents, enlivens and valorizes local culture, and democratizes travel. For Picard and Robinson (2006), tourism-oriented festivals and celebrations are markers of cultural and social life, akin to a series of rituals that local people perform to affirm their community identity. However, others maintain that tourism promotes the growth of low-wage jobs with few benefits, diverts public monies from addressing crucial local problems, and produces a form of mass seduction that alienates and disempowers consumers (for overviews, see Alsayyad 2001; Fainstein and Judd 1999; Kearns and Philo 1993). Whether they celebrate or condemn, the burgeoning discussions of urban tourism point to a broader concern with the changing nature of consumption and media, the repackaging of cities as sites of tourist consumption, and the ways in which local festivals become key motivators for tourism investment in cities.

Tourism, ethnicity, and race

The concept of touristic culture draws attention to the role that tourism discourses and practices play in constructing and reproducing ethnic identities and ethnic relations, a concern shared by other scholars. For Dean MacCannell (1973; 1992: 168), tourism systematically purveys a "reconstructed" ethnicity, meaning a rhetorical and symbolic expression of cultural difference that is packaged and sold to tourists. Robert E. Wood's (1998) analysis of ethnic groups in Asia and the Pacific Rim, Jane Desmond's (1999) examination of tourism in Hawaii, and Diane Barthel-Bouchier's (2001) study of the Amana Colonies in southeastern Iowa suggest that ethnicity can be constructed and strategically deployed by different groups for instrumental purposes, including confronting the values, categories, and practices of the dominant culture, challenging the dominant culture's depiction of a minority group, and contesting public policy within the political arena. A major component of sex tourism, for example, involves men of various racial and ethnic backgrounds interacting with poor women of color. As scholars have pointed out, in sex tourism issues of race and ethnicity interlock with conceptions of gender and sexuality to influence how tourism is conceptualized, organized, and experienced (Cabezas 2004; Desmond 1999; Sheller 2003). Today, ethnic group interaction with tourism is an integral part of the construction and reproduction of ethnic identity. Local meanings of ethnicity shape and are shaped by tourism advertising and promotional strategies. In these processes, the tourism creates new bases of struggle and conflict over meanings of ethnicity (Picard 1996; Picard and Wood 1997).

Today, ethnicity is taking on an expanded role in urban economies and is increasingly becoming a fundamental theme of tourist destinations and entertainment-enhanced developments. My work on New Orleans suggests that assertions and constructions of ethnicity reflect a dual process of globalization and localization. That is, tourism is a force for globalizing ethnicity—delocalizing and disembedding ethnicity from place—and a force for localizing ethnicity—producing and reinforcing ethnic distinctiveness in place through indigenous networks and place-bound social bonds. These points support the findings of Ulf Hannerz (1996; 1992), Zygmunt Bauman (1998), and Arjun Appadurai (1996), who maintain that the emergence of diasporic communities and hybrid cultures resulting from global migration intimates that tourism is one of the key factors shaping modern ethnic identities. For Appadurai (1996), tourist sites around the world are the archetype of translocalities, where a variety of circulating populations create new types of communities and contribute to the development of diasporic ethnic neighborhoods. In other words, the notion of touristic culture suggests that tourism is a major structuring element of ethnic culture and identity and not something that is external, *a priori*, or outside of these social categories (see also Crang 2004; Hannam 2006; for a programmatic statement, see Franklin and Crang 2001).

In addition, tourism boosters and promoters use sophisticated niche-marketing techniques to define local ethnic cultures and attract diverse kinds of ethnic tourists (Gotham 2007c). Niche marketing refers to the development of new forms of cultural fragmentation, differentiation, and specialization that split consumers and markets into ever smaller segments or niches, resulting in heterogeneity rather than homogeneity. Niche marketing is simultaneously about diversity and homogeneity, or "homogenized diversity." Place marketers and tourism officials seek to create and exploit niche markets by erasing the diversity of social groups and defining and thus homogenizing families, baby boomers, senior citizens, African and Hispanic Americans, and gays and lesbians as consumers. Here terms such as "diversity," "culture," and "ethnicity" have a great deal of symbolic value and utility for cities. Their use does not rule out any particular group, and they can be used to refer to almost any artistic or entertaining activity associated with tourism. More important, the terms "culture" and "ethnicity" are not actively resisted by consumers and tourists because they do not carry the negative connotation that the term "race" often does. For tourism boosters and promoters, "race" signifies inequality, oppression, domination, and subordination. To neutralize the negative image of race and racial inequality, place marketers deploy the terms "diversity," "ethnicity," and "culture" to create the impression that cities are both non-hierarchical and egalitarian. What the local tourism industry seeks to promote is a simulated or ersatz culture and ethnicity of no offense. Tourism discourses highlight ethnic differences and diversity while ignoring social divisions, conflicts, and struggles. Thus, whether ethnic and cultural differences are real or false is irrelevant, for tourism marketing seeks to efface social categories and identities of all meaning except the signification of pleasure (see Gotham 2007c).

Cultural erosion and invention: authenticity in tourism

Two prominent arguments in the study of tourism and culture focus on the quest for authenticity in the tourist experience and the construction of authenticity to attract tourists to cities. First, according to the cultural-invention model of tourism, tourism provides a set of symbols, imagery, and discourses that local people can (re)interpret and integrate into their tactics of invention to produce new expressions of local culture. In this conception, tourism can accentuate local particularity by making possible unique appropriations of culture and heritage, thus encouraging the proliferation of difference and diversity. As a positive force for communities, tourism can help build and sustain important cultural linkages, institutional connections, and global–local networks that bring a wealth of new products, ideas, and economic opportunities to local people and visitors.

611

Second, and in contrast, according to the cultural-erosion model of tourism, tourism is a global process of commodification and rationalization promoting the serial reproduction of corporate tourist spaces that undermine local culture and erode place distinctiveness. Commodification is the conversion of local products, cultures, and social relations and identities into products that can be profitably sold by businesses. Rationalization implies a process whereby social actions and interactions become based on considerations of efficiency and calculation rather than on motivations derived from custom, tradition, or emotion. In the cultural-erosion model of tourism, commodification implies the rationalization of urban space to enhance tourist consumption and the prepackaging of tourist experiences for economic gain. According to this view, entertainment corporations and tourism organizations hollow out the rich texture, spontaneity, and uniqueness of local culture and thereby corrupt authentic cultural spaces. As a result, local culture and heritage become abstract, manufactured, and simulated social forms estranged from communal life. The image is that of a hostile and combative relationship in which tourism contaminates, spoils, or "bastardizes" a "pure" and "authentic" culture and place—an image popularized by Daniel Boorstin (1964), who lamented the spread of so-called "pseudo-events" in the United States, and Guy Debord (1994), who derided the rise of the "society of the spectacle."

Closely related to the cultural-erosion model of tourism is the view that tourism is a global process of simulation that reflects and reinforces people's alienation from society and social relations. Early on, Dean MacCannell (1973) developed the concept of "staged authenticity" to refer to the manufacturing of local culture to create an impression of authenticity for a tourist audience. MacCannell conceived of culture as primordial and viewed tourists as alienated consumers who strive to experience "authentic" encounters with "authentic" sites, objects, or events. In contrast, Ritzer and Liska (1997) maintain that rather than seeking authenticity, as MacCannell suggests, people prefer inauthentic and simulated tourist attractions and experiences because they are highly predictable and efficient vehicles for delivering fun and entertainment. Thus, for Ritzer (2006: 6), tourism is about the global production of "nothing," by which he means a social form "centrally conceived, controlled, and comparatively devoid of distinctive content." Other scholars have used the concept of Disneyification to examine the spread of Disney theme-park characteristics to cities and urban culture. This city-as-theme-park explanation suggests that urban cultural spaces are being refashioned to attract visitors and enhance entertainment experiences through the production of fake histories and phony cultures that masquerade as "authentic" (Sorkin 1992; Eeckhout 2001; Bryman 1999; Reichl 1999).

The cultural erosion model is not without critics, who see it as theoretically misleading and factually incorrect. Terms like "staged," "fabricated," or "simulated" authenticity assume that commodification and rationalization processes are imposed from the top down onto passively accepting people who are swindled into accepting the dominant ideology. Susan Fainstein and David Gladstone (1999: 29–30) contend that although the analysis of commodification is important for understanding tourism, it is "incomplete, since it does not explicitly examine the assumptions governing the production of culture and its connection to social relations in space." Simon Coleman and Mike Crang's (2003) discussion of tourism as "between place and performance" positions tourism as a set of localized practices that frame meanings of local culture and help constitute place identities and authenticity. Erik Cohen's (1988) notion of "emergent authenticity" suggests that authenticity is a mutable and negotiated category whose meaning varies by time and context. Going further, Cohen argues that local people may initially view certain tourism products and images as contrived and artificial but over time redefine them as authentic representations of local culture and heritage. Scholars holding this view imply that not all tourism involves the staging of authenticity, nor does the staging of local culture amount to a massive deception that dupes local people or visitors (Shepherd 2002).

Elsewhere, I have elaborated on the touristic-culture concept to examine the actions of local elites in using tourism practices, images, symbols, and other representations to build a New Orleans community identity during the first half of the twentieth century (Gotham 2007c). It is important to note that the terms "culture," "authenticity," "community," and "identity" are not created by abstract collectives but are fashioned in the struggles of factions and groups to create and control material resources and collective representations. The social construction of culture, community, authenticity, and related urban representations is always a contested process. Powerful groups and organized interests often deploy symbols and imagery in attempts to unite local citizens and build supportive constituencies for tourism development. Used in a political strategy, the symbol of "community" contains a multiplicity of meanings that provide social actors with a strategic vocabulary, but one that leaves specific content deliberately ambiguous. In this sense, we can view terms like "authenticity," "community," and "identity" as resources of cultural capital that elite groups wield more or less self-consciously in their social and political struggles to influence local meanings of authenticity and shape urban culture.

Overall, I suggest that tourism practices can support and invigorate existing modes of authenticity, help reconstruct old forms of authenticity, and promote the creation of new meanings of authenticity and local culture. Rather than viewing authenticity as immutable and primordial, I examine the process of authentication, focusing on how and under what conditions people make claims for authenticity and the interests that such claims serve. This conception is at odds with Peterson's (1997) argument in his study of the historical development of country music that authenticity is an inherently "renewable resource." Such a conception has trouble explaining the ways in which power relations, structures, and inequalities demarcate the content, form, and trajectory of the processes by which authenticity is constructed. In my analysis, pre-existing social structures—including values, norms, beliefs, interpretive systems, and formal and informal organizations—can shape and constrain the availability of symbols and themes that people use to construct meanings and definitions of authenticity. Such a conception resonates with the work of David Grazian (2003), who suggests that authenticity construction is akin to a collective performance, a presentation of "community self." For Grazian, Chicago's claim as the home of blues music is embedded within the active production of blues culture as a major pillar of the tourist economy. In short, social structural forces shape and frame assertions of authenticity in the production of culture and tourism. An adaptable and hybrid phenomenon, authenticity is continually recreated, ironically because social movements, cultural authorities, and other groups struggle to legitimate selective and idealized perceptions of local culture as fixed and immutable. The implication is that tourism discourses, practices, and framings can mobilize people to create new authenticities, reinvent culture, and foster new conceptions of place identity.

Tourism as a metaphor of cultural transformation

The linkages between tourism and culture are complex and ever-changing. Global transformations and local actions produce tourism development and encourage the proliferation of new modes of consuming local culture via tourism. Diverse scholars—including John Hannigan (1998), Paul Chatterton and Robert Hollands (2003), Chris Rojek and John Urry (1997), Mark Gottdiener, Claudia Collins, and David Dickens (1999), Sharon Zukin (1996), Richard Lloyd (2005), and Terry Nichols Clark (2003)—all foreground the centrality of cultural concerns in the rise of urban entertainment and tourism over the past several decades (for an overview, see Lloyd and Clark 2001). As I pointed out earlier in this essay, the concept "touristic culture" suggests that because tourist modes of visualization, staging, and discourse are now central to understanding cities, they cannot be marked off as discrete activities (Gotham 2007a, 2007b).

On the one hand, touristic culture involves enhanced spatial flows of people, commodities, capital, and cultures. On the other hand, touristic culture is a set of codes or repertoires that structure people's ability to think of places as objects of tourism, and to see themselves as reflective and active agents who use tourist practices to affirm identities and construct culture. In the case of New Orleans, tourism is an amalgam of global/local processes that can disempower some people, empower others, transform meanings of local authenticity, and create new pressures for local autonomy. Yet present constructions of local cultures are not simply historical residuals, sets of meanings and traditions inherited from the past. Nor are meanings and assertions of authenticity arbitrarily fabricated and deployed at will. Rather, people construct culture by appropriating some images and symbols from the past, discarding others, and adding new ones to fit the opportunities and constraints of the present. In contrast to prevailing conceptions that treat authenticity as either stable and durable or malleable and fabricated, the relationship between tourism and authenticity is contingent, contested, and conflictual.

Overall, the dramatic expansion of tourism and the intensification of government and corporate efforts to commodify place and culture in cities around the world have triggered an explosion of authenticities over the last several decades. Assertions of place identity, cultural distinctiveness, community solidarity, and neighborhood uniqueness proliferate in cities, reflecting people's engagement with tourism discourses, imagery, and representations. These authenticities are embedded within discourses about racial and ethnic identities, culture and heritage, and struggles over access to and control over political and economic resources. On the one hand, the rise and expansion of tourism over the last century or so are a product of global transformations, including widespread demographic movement, new modes of travel, corporate restructuring, and the re-fashioning of cities as places of entertainment and leisure. On the other hand, doing tourism involves an array of culturally specific practices, including the production of nostalgia, the mobilization of collective memories and heroic imagery, the estheticization and theming of space, and the circulation of people to particular places to consume culture, history, nature, and otherness. Today, tourism, culture, and authenticity share similar vocabularies, symbols, imagery, and interpretive systems.

References

Alsayyad, Nezar, ed. 2001. *Consuming Tradition, Manufacturing Heritage: Global Norms and Urban Forms in the Age of Tourism.* London: Routledge.

Appadurai, Arjun. 1996. *Modernity At Large: Cultural Dimensions of Globalization.* Minneapolis, MN: University of Minnesota Press.

Barthel-Bouchier, Diane. 2001. "Authenticity and Identity: Theme-Parking the Amanas." *International Sociology* 16(2): 221–39.

Bauman, Zygmunt. 1998. *Globalization: The Human Consequences.* New York: Columbia University Press.

Boorstin, Daniel. 1964. *The Image: A Guide to Pseudo-Events in America.* New York: Harper-Row.

Britton, S. 1991. "Tourism, Capital, and Place: Towards a Critical Geography of Tourism." *Environment and Planning D: Society and Space* 9: 451–78.

Bryman, Alan. 1999. "Disneyization of Society." *Sociological Review* 47: 25–47.

Cabezas, Amalia. 2004. "Between Love and Money: Sex, Tourism, and Citizenship in Cuba and the Dominican Republic." *Signs: Journal of Women in Culture and Society* 29(4): 987–1015.

Chatterton, Paul and Hollands, Robert. 2003. *Urban Nightscapes: Youth Cultures, Pleasure Spaces, and Corporate Power.* London and New York: Routledge.

Clark, Terry Nichols, ed. 2003. *The City as an Entertainment Machine.* New York: Elsevier Press.

Cohen, Erik. 1972. "Towards a Sociology of International Tourism." *Social Research* 39: 164–82.

——. 1988. "Authenticity and Commodification in Tourism." *Annals of Tourism Research* 15: 371–86.

Coleman, Simon and Crang, Mike, eds. 2003. *Tourism: Between Place and Performance.* London: Berghahn Books.

Crang, Michael. 2004. "Cultural Geographies of Tourism." Pp. 74–84 in Alan Lew, Michael C. Hall, and Allan Williams, eds., *A Companion to Tourism.* Malden, MA: Blackwell.

Crick, Malcolm. 1989. "Representations of International Tourism in the Social Sciences: Sun, Sex, Sights, and Savings, and Servility." *Annual Review of Anthropology* 18: 307–44.

Debord, Guy. 1994. *The Society of the Spectacle,* trans. Donald Nicholson-Smith. New York: Zone Books.

Desmond, Jane C. 1999. *Staging Tourism: Bodies on Display from Waikiki to Sea World.* Chicago: University of Chicago Press.

Eeckhout, Bart. 2001. "The 'Disneyification' of Times Square: Back to the Future?" In Kevin Fox Gotham, ed., *Critical Perspectives on Urban Redevelopment.* New York: Elsevier Press.

Eisinger, Peter. 2000. "The Politics of Bread and Circuses: Building the City for the Visitor Class." *Urban Affairs Review* 35(3): 316–33.

Fainstein, Susan S. and Gladstone, David. 1999. "Evaluating Urban Tourism." In Dennis R. Judd and Susan S. Fainstein, eds., *The Tourist City.* New Haven, CT: Yale University Press.

Fainstein, Susan S. and Judd, Dennis R. 1999. "Global Forces, Local Strategies, and Urban Tourism." Pp. 1–20 In Dennis R. Judd and Susan S. Fainstein, eds., *The Tourist City.* New Haven, CT: Yale University Press.

Franklin, Adrian and Crang, Michael. 2001. "The Trouble with Tourism and Travel Theory." *Tourist Studies* 1: 5–22.

Gladstone, David. 2005. *From Pilgrimage to Package Tour: Travel and Tourism in the Third World.* London: Routlege.

Gotham, Kevin Fox. 2007a. *Authentic New Orleans: Race, Culture, and Tourism in the Big Easy.* New York: New York University Press.

——. 2007b. "Ethnic Heritage Tourism and Global–Local Connections in New Orleans." In Jan Rath, ed., *Tourism, Ethnic Diversity and the City.* London: Routledge.

——. 2007c. "Selling New Orleans to New Orleans: Tourism Authenticity and the Construction of Community Identity." *Tourist Studies* 7(3): 317–39.

Gottdiener, Mark, Collins, Claudia C., and Dickens, David R. 1999. *Las Vegas: The Social Production of an All-American City.* Malden, MA: Blackwell.

Grazian, David. 2003. *Blue Chicago: The Search for Authenticity in Urban Blues Clubs.* Chicago: University of Chicago Press.

Hannam, Kevin. 2006. "Tourism and Development III: Performances, Performativities, and Mobilities." *Progress in Development Studies* 6(3): 243–49.

Hannerz, Ulf. 1992. *Cultural Complexity.* New York: Columbia University Press.

——. 1996. *Transnational Connections.* London: Routledge.

Hannigan, John. 1998. *Fantasy City: Pleasure and Profit in the Postmodern Metropolis.* New York: Routledge.

615

Hoffman, Lily K., Fainstein., Susan S., and Judd, Dennis R., eds. 2003. *Cities and Visitors: Regulating People, Markets, and City Space.* New York: Blackwell Publishing.

Kearns, Gerry and Philo, Chris, eds. 1993. *Selling Places: The City as Cultural Capital, Past and Present.* Oxford: Pergamon Press.

Kirschenblatt-Gimblett, Barbara. 1998. *Destination Culture: Tourism, Museums, and Heritage.* Berkeley: University of California Press.

Krippendorf, Jost. 1984. *The Holiday Markers: Understanding the Impact of Leisure and Travel.* Oxford: Butterworth/Heineman.

Lloyd, Richard. 2005. *Neo-Bohemia: Art and Commerce in the Postindustrial City.* London: Routlege.

Lloyd, Richard and Clark, Terry Nichols. 2001. "The City as an Entertainment Machine." In Kevin Fox Gotham, ed., *Critical Perspectives on Urban Redevelopment.* New York: Elsevier Press.

MacCannell, Dean. 1973. "Staged Authenticity: Arrangements of Social Space in Tourist Settings." *American Journal of Sociology* 79(3): 589–603.

——. 1976. *The Tourist: A New Theory of the Leisure Class.* New York: Schocken Books.

——. 1992. *Empty Meeting Grounds: The Tourist Papers.* New York: Routledge.

Peterson, Richard. 1997. *Creating Country Music, Fabricating Authenticity.* Chicago: University of Chicago Press.

Picard, David and Robinson, Mike, eds. 2006. *Festivals, Tourism, and Social Change: Remaking Worlds.* Buffalo and Toronto: Channel View Publications.

Picard, Michel. 1996. *Bali: Cultural Tourism and Touristic Culture.* Singapore: Archipelago Press.

Picard, Michel and Wood, Robert E., eds. 1997. *Tourism, Ethnicity, and the State in Asian and Pacific Society.* Honolulu: University of Hawaii Press.

Rath, Jan, ed. 2007. *Tourism, Ethnic Diversity, and the City.* London: Routledge.

Reichl, Alexander J. 1999. *Reconstructing Times Square: Politics and Culture in Urban Development.* Lawrence: University Press of Kansas.

Ritzer, George. 2006. *The Globalization of Nothing*, second edition. Thousand Oaks, CA: Pine Forge Press.

Ritzer, George and Liska, Allan. 1997. "'McDisneyization' and 'Post-Tourism': Contemporary Perspectives on Contemporary Tourism." In *Touring Cultures: Transformations in Travel and Leisure.* London: Routledge.

Rojek, Chris and Urry, John, eds. 1997. *Touring Cultures: Transformations of Travel and Theory.* London and New York: Routledge.

Ryan, Chris and Hall, C. Michael, eds. 2001. *Sex Tourism: Marginal Peoples and Liminality.* London and New York: Routledge.

Sheller, Mimi. 2003. *Consuming the Caribbean: From Arawaks to Zombies.* London and New York: Routledge.

Sheller, Mimi and Urry, John. 2006. *Tourism Mobilities: Places to Play, Places in Play.* London: Routledge.

Shepherd, Robert. 2002. "Commodification, Culture, and Tourism." *Tourist Studies* 2(2): 183–201.

Sorkin, Michael, ed. 1992. *Variations on a Theme Park: The New American City and the End of Public Space.* New York: Hill and Wang.

Urry, John. 1990. *The Tourist Gaze.* Thousand Oaks, CA: Sage.

——. 1995. *Consuming Places.* London and New York: Routledge.

van den Berghe, Pierre. 1980. "Tourism as Ethnic Relations: A Case Study of Cuzco, Peru." *Ethnic and Racial Studies* 3: 375–92.

Watson, G. Llewellyn and Kopachevsky, Joseph P. 1994. "Interpretations of Tourism as Commodity." *Annals of Tourism Research* 21(3): 643–60.

Wood, Robert E. 1998. "Touristic Ethnicity: A Brief Itinerary." *Ethnic and Racial Studies* 21(2): 218–41.

Zukin, Sharon. 1996. *The Culture of Cities.* London: Blackwell.

Part X
Cultural processes and change

59

Culture and collective memory

Comparative perspectives

Barry Schwartz

Shame is sometimes difficult to fathom. When South Korean university students were recently asked to name the three events that "arouse in you as a citizen (rather than a private individual) a sense of dishonor, disgrace, shame, and/or remorse," they listed, in order of frequency, Japanese colonial rule, the International Monetary Fund loan, the Korean War, wrongdoings of former presidents, and the collapse of the Sung Soo Bridge and Sam Poong Department Store. One of the investigators, an American, found the Korean response bizarre. Why should occupation by an overwhelmingly powerful neighbor and acceptance of a loan to support a troubled economy be deemed sources of shame rather than anger or distress? Why should an approximately equal proportion of respondents consider the crimes of individual politicians, the Korean War—which preserved the existence of their country, and the collapse of a bridge and department store, as instances of national disgrace?

Ghanaians, like Koreans, find in economic dependency a source of disgrace; success in international sports, a basis of national pride. But Ghanaians rarely mention colonial exploitation, and they take the enslavement of their ancestors more lightly than do Westerners.

That the field of collective memory contains too few surprises like these is a sign of its provincialism. In the Western stockpile of collective-memory concepts, nothing makes these findings comprehensible, let alone generalizable. For the past quarter-century, it is true, many scholars around the world have labored over the sources and consequences of national memory, but efforts to build a collective-memory discipline have been confined to the West. The present essay addresses this imbalance by using non-Western memories as tools for widening existing concepts, and, in so doing, moving collective memory scholarship intellectually—not just topically—into a global field.

History, commemoration, and memory

The distinction between history and memory is now part of our common vocabulary, although the distinction itself remains vague. That *history* tells about the reality of the past while *memory* misrepresents the past is, in certain respects, plausible. But that statement needs clarification and expansion—clarification because it makes memory synonymous with lies and misperception; expansion because collective memory scholarship, vibrant and creative for so many years, is approaching a plateau, contenting itself with empirical enrichments and theoretical variations on precisely the themes that have concealed some of memory's important functions. Exploring memory across cultures clarifies these functions by transcending theories based solely on Western experience.

Culture is conceived here as "an *historically* transmitted pattern of meanings embodied in symbols, a system of *inherited* conceptions expressed in symbolic forms by means of which men communicate, perpetuate, and develop their knowledge about and attitudes toward life" (Geertz 1973: 89, emphasis added). Collective memory, then, as a means for the preservation of cultural forms as well as information, enables us to engage the past in at least two ways. First, collective memory is a model *of* society—a reflection of its present problems and mentalities. Second, collective memory is a model *for* society—a program that determines the content of its values and defines the meaning of its experience.

However, the adjective "collective" does not mean that a "group memory" exists independently of its constituents. Nor does it mean that everyone perceives the past in the same way. Collective remembering refers to variant individual expressions of culturally induced beliefs, feelings, and moral judgments about the past.

In modern societies, oral traditions persist, but history and commemoration are collective memory's main repositories (Assman 1992). Historical accounts include research and analytic monographs, textbooks, and encyclopedia entries. Commemorative symbolism includes eulogy and ritual oratory, monuments, shrines, relics, statues, paintings, and ritual observances. Clearly, history and commemoration perform different functions. History enlightens by revealing the causes and consequences of events. Commemoration designates the significance of events by lifting from the historical record those which embody a community's distinctive values. History and commemoration, however, cannot be empirically separated: just as history dramatizes the values that commemoration sustains, commemoration is rooted in historical knowledge.

Two perspectives

In the early decades of the twentieth-century, many scholars explored the social contexts of history, commemoration, and belief, but Maurice Halbwachs's work was the most profound. His influence, on the other hand, has been sporadic. Between 1945—the year of his execution by the SS—and the early 1980s, American sociologists ignored him. After 1980, Halbwachs was cited time and again, even though his two major books, *The Social Frames of Memory* and *The Legendary Topography of the Gospels in the Holy Land*, had not been translated into English. (Lewis Coser's selection and translation of Halbwachs's collected works did not appear until 1991.) Halbwachs was therefore dragged into a wave of research that arose independently of him.

Two perspectives on collective memory, the *presentist* and *traditionalist*, organize this late twentieth-century groundswell. These perspectives are neither verifiable nor falsifiable; they are analytic fictions in terms of which observations of experience and memory can be compared. In the presentist perspective, inferred from constructionist, political, and postmodern models of memory, different elements of the past become more or less relevant as circumstances change. The most inclusive term, "presentist," emphasizes what the specific models have in common, namely a focus on concrete situations as the basis for the past's perception and representation. In this perspective, memory is always in transition, always precarious. Memory is a dependent variable insofar as each social unit forges a past compatible with its own needs and problems (See, for example, Bodnar 1992).

The second, traditionalist, perspective refers to realist models depicting the past as a standard and frame for the present. Assuming the historical record to be reasonably authentic, such models construe collective memory as a source of energy and moral direction—in short, an independent variable. The effect of independent variables is, of course, irregular: in one time and place their influence is strong; in other times and other places, weak. At all times and places their influence is real. Because traditionalism places so much weight on the reality of the past, collective memory appears, in its light, to be inherited rather than self-created. History and tradition constantly revise themselves, but they are modifying the essence of existing ideas rather than creating new ones (Schudson 1989, 1992).

The carriers of the traditionalist perspective—from Edmund Burke to Edward Shils (1981)—are sensitive to differences *within* cultures but find the most significance in differences *between* cultures. The latter difference—and there is no way to overemphasize the point—consists of central tendencies governed by an "axial principle": cultures of self-denial thus distinguish themselves from cultures of self-fulfillment; Apollonian cultures from Dionysian; inner- from tradition-directed; communitarian from individualist. The traditionalist perspective asserts a discontinuity in kind among cultures, distinguishing itself from theories that derive macro-content from such micro-processes as metaphor narrative structures, texts, classifications, and boundary-making (Alexander 2003; Wertsch 2002; Zerubavel 2003).

Is memory really a *construction*

Presentism shaped early collective memory scholarship, including Maurice Halbwachs's, and dominates the field today. It arose in the West as an effort to systemize post-World War I disillusionment and doubt. Almost twenty years after that war ended, Louis Wirth observed:

> At a time in human history like our own, when all over the world people are not only merely ill at ease, but are questioning the bases of social existence, the validity of their truths, and the tenability of their norms, it should become clear that there is no value apart from interest and no objectivity to hold tenaciously to what one believes to be the truth.
>
> (Wirth 1936: xxv)

For the first time, ordinary people, as well as intellectuals, began to believe there were no longer absolutes of time and space, of good and evil, or even of knowledge.

"Demystifying" knowledge was central to social science in the 1920s and 1930s, and its implications were broad. The "unmasking turn of mind," which refutes ideas by revealing their functions, inevitably challenges the authority of the past, for once one sees the interests concealed by an idea, it loses its efficacy (Mannheim 1952 [1928]: 140).

The cynical science of memory construction, with its emphasis on a past that is unreal or, at best, disputable, transparent, and temporary, prospers in a world of reciprocal distrust.

By the late 1960s, the past became more meaningless to more people than ever. The young not only thought about it differently; they thought about it less often, remembered less, and felt less strongly about what they remembered. The past's reality and relevance diminished together as identification with tradition weakened (Nora 1996). Underlying this erosion was the discrediting of grand narratives—the legends and myths that once inspired and consoled nations (Lyotard 1984 [1979]). What distinguishes the West, then, is not new or revised historical narratives but an unprecedented sense that all such narratives are irrelevant.

Innovations

By the 1980s and 1990s, a great wave of research had linked collective memory to power relations, relativism, and the "production" of culture. Conceiving the past as a mask for the interests and hegemony of the privileged led to great excesses. Memory became something "manufactured," "invented," "fabricated," "created," and "remade." Its favorite topics included victims, unpopular wars, and other reprehensible events. Holocaust and slavery topics abounded. This pattern accompanied the late-twentieth-century rise of multiculturalism, recognition of minorities' entitlements, diversity, and erosion of beliefs that once legitimated separation of racial, religious, and ethnic groups.

Three recent developments, however, limit presentist bias. First, there has been a reaffirmation of the obduracy of history, convincingly demonstrated rather than asserted. Michael Schudson's (1992) analysis of the "resistance of the past" and Gary Fine's (2001) treatment of "cautious naturalism" and of historical events as "action templates" react against models that reduce collective memory to unbridled fabrication. What is known about the past limits what can be done with it interpretively.

Second, collective memory scholarship need no longer infer individual beliefs from historical and commemorative contents. Many scholars, most prominently Howard Schuman, move forward with new lines of inquiry—including national surveys—that explore what individuals believe and feel about the past and how they judge it morally.

Application of the dialogical perspective, which defines collective memory in terms of both cause and consequence, is the third new development. Individuals holding beliefs about the past are not passive end-links on some chain of social causation; they reinforce and modify the oral messages, texts, and symbols they consume. If "culture creation" and "culture reception" are inseparable, then collective memory, an aspect of culture, must be a context for and against which historians and commemorative agents react (Schwartz and Schuman 2005). In this sense, memory is path-dependent: earlier representations of the past affect the availability and resources required for present representations. Collective memory can be seen as an ongoing process of meaning-making (Olick 1999).

The influence of these developments has been limited, but in different research settings they can redirect theoretical trends. As we move from Western to Eastern cultures, we see collective memory and its problems under new lights. In Asia (including China, Japan, and Korea), there exists a surfeit rather than a deficit of meaningful remembrance, and this condition fixates nations, preventing them from coming to terms fully with the dilemmas of the day.

Memory and culture

"Western" and "Asian" are shorthand for two clusters of nations, each having a definite core but indefinite boundaries. Western nations are exemplified by Central and Western Europe, Great Britain, and its three major settler societies—the United States, Canada, and Australia. Northeast Asia is exemplified by three core nations—China, Japan, and Korea. No homogeneity is claimed for these nations, but the differences *among* them—in religion, philosophy, literature, the visual arts, architecture, music, moral values, and worldviews—are small compared to differences *between* them and the nations of the West. This "East–West" divide is not to be dismissed as a product of Eurocentric history and interests; it is palpable and consequential. The cultural contrast between Asia and the West is evident in the constituent beliefs of their histories and memories. (For convenience, the term *Asia* will henceforth abbreviate *Northeast Asia*.)

In recent years, Asian memory has been studied within a presentist framework (Fujitani *et al.* 2001; Jager and Mitter 2007) applied directly or indirectly to World War II. But to say that World War II memories are constructed, then manipulated to strengthen the state and flatter the public, ignores important questions: Why do elites choose a 75-year-old war as their hegemonic tool? Are any parts of this war remembered but not used for the purpose of manipulation? Which parts of the war justify indignation; which require expressions of regret? In this connection, the "politics of regret," a sub-field of collective memory, now grows rapidly in the West (Olick 2007), but our understanding of regret itself assumes a conception of guilt only partially felt by most Asians.

That memory runs deeply and vitally through Asia is evident in the concept of "the history problem." Ordinary citizens recognize and feel this problem in their own lives. Nowhere is the tone and texture of the history problem more evident than in Asia's "textbook incidents." When, in 1982, the Japanese Ministry of Education demanded that an author revise his textbook to show that Japan "advanced" into rather than "invaded" Chinese cities, the Chinese and Korean governments reacted explosively: they withdrew ambassadors, condemned the Ministry's action, and declared that bilateral relations would never be the same. In the streets, angry Chinese and Korean students demonstrated their indignation. Japan's Chief Cabinet Secretary issued a statement assuring that the error would be corrected. Later, in November, 1982, the Ministry adopted a "Neighboring Country Clause" to make history textbooks consistent with international harmony. Because this clause was only a symptom of the history problem, future textbook crises were inevitable. Such crises continue to inhibit transformative politics, slow the pace of national and regional growth, and obscure the importance of relations with the widening world community.

No comparable "history problem" exists in the West. True, Westerners remember their own nations' difficult pasts, but in every sphere of international relations— technology, popular culture, politics, trade—the past is a second thought, not the first. Because America's relations with former enemies are free of recrimination, for example, international business proceeds without reference to the sins of earlier generations.

The Asian history problem is both a historiographical and commemorative matter; it concerns the way Asians invoke the past, play the history card in their relations with one another, how they conceive and symbolize the historical dimensions of events. National surveys commissioned by two Japanese newspapers (*Asahi Shimbun* and *Yomiuri Shimbun*) asked, "Do you think the history issues are important for Japan's relations with China and South Korea?" If a question about "history issues" were asked in the United States

623

about America's relations with its neighbors, no one would understand it. Japanese respondents, no less than Chinese and Korean, were familiar with the issue: 67 and 75 percent replied "important" in 2001 and 2005, respectively. In 2005 a comparable sample was asked, "What should Japan do to better relations with China?" In their replies 66.3 percent mentioned "respect Chinese culture and history." Three years later, Japanese were asked, "What do you think both China and Japan should do in order to improve the relationship between the two countries?" The modal response (36.7 percent) was "Solve history issues between Japan and China." A full 60 percent answered negatively when asked, "Do you think that the history issue of Japan's compensation to the former victims in the era of colonization has been solved?" The same percentage answered "no" to the question of whether "the issue of Japan's history issue with neighboring countries such as China and South Korea has been solved." The content of these history issues involves material compensation, but they turn on the question of cultural, not monetary, values. The *history* problem is a *memory* problem so far as it centers on moral judgments of the past.

Memory, dignity, and honor

Unlike Western traditions based on "cultures of dignity," Asian traditions are historically rooted in "cultures of honor." Dignity and honor cultures require different kinds of memory. Peter Berger *et al.* explain:

> It is through the performance of institutional roles that the individual participates in history, not only the history of the particular institution but that of his society as a whole. It is precisely for this reason that modern consciousness, in its conception of the self, tends toward a curious ahistoricity. In a world of honor, identity is firmly linked to the past through the reiterated performance of prototypical acts. In a world of dignity, history is the succession of mystifications from which the individual must free himself to attain "authenticity."
>
> (Berger *et al.* 1973: 91)

Honor is almost obsolete in the West and significantly attenuated in Asia, but if we take honor and dignity as concepts—analytic tools—rather than descriptions of reality, we can differentiate societies more precisely. Korea, where defeat and failure are still sources of national shame, is no feudal society, but the remnants of feudal honor distinguish it from America (Schwartz and Kim 2002).

"Honor cultures" maintain order by inducing both guilt and shame among the wayward, but shame does most of morality's heavy lifting. Shame is a reaction to other people's contempt. Thus, when Americans are asked to name the historical events which promote in them a sense of pride, they are most likely to refer to the American founding and World War II, and they do this as a matter of fact, with little concern for the impressions these events make on other peoples. When Koreans are asked the same question, they most often mention the 1988 Olympic Games, which brought them world attention. Japanese name victory in international sports and economic and technological development in almost identical numbers (Schwartz and Kim 2002; Schwartz *et al.* 2005). In China, the 2008 Olympic Games swelled national pride because they impressed the world. Honor rests on achievements that other people notice.

It must be emphasized that the relevance of honor as a standard for thought, action, and feeling is probably fading faster in Asia than in the West, where it is already approaching its plateau. The conviction that every person has a right to respect and protection from arbitrary power, independently of national honor, has advanced more rapidly in some Asian countries than in others, but the direction of change is certain and seemingly relentless. On the other hand, there is a floor, East and West, below which honor cannot descend. This limit, rooted in historical differences, cannot level cultural differences overnight. Before the deep roots of Asian honor are withered as far as the West's, many decades must pass.

Because honor and shame play a more important (albeit receding) role in Asia than in the West (Wallbott and Scherer 1995), new perspectives are required to understand Asian memory. Presentist and traditionalist perspectives are only powerful as long as their empirical equivalents are relevant; as these become less so, fresh problems, hypotheses, and conclusions become more difficult to extract from them. Asia illustrates these limits not through the detail of World War II atrocities but by the spectacle of Japanese officials minimizing them and attributing exculpatory motives to those committing them. These same limits are manifest in the staunch refusal of Chinese and Koreans to accept sincere declarations of regret, to demand in every gesture of apology a level of incontestable "sincerity"—in short, proof of the unprovable. Unrequited demands can be advantageous. Denied recognition of their suffering, victims can draw a sharper line between right and wrong, honorable and dishonorable, "us" and "them."

Many explanations are advanced to account for why Asia's memory problem became so pronounced during the last decades of the twentieth century. Its surge has been linked to new international discourse on justice and human rights, victim nations' rising economic power, self-confidence, nationalism, readiness to criticize rival nations, and, on the other hand, awareness that indignation against former oppressors diverts attention from domestic problems and awareness of the need for political and economic interdependence. These conditions, however, cannot explain why *historical* events are the primary objects of Asian concern. What is it, then, about Asian culture that makes the past resonate so powerfully?

Cultural differences in the memory of trauma

World War II was a watershed of Western history and memory. The ideal of a common humanity emerging from the experience of Nazi Germany's atrocities, observe Michael Schudson and Aleida Assmann, now serves as a common cultural memory for our day. No one can dispute World War II's salience to European memory, but it is even more pivotal to Asian memory. Japanese atrocities of the 1930s and early 1940s, sources of humiliation to postwar generations of Chinese and Koreans, accompany memories of still earlier aggression.

Japan's war against Asia began with Europe's mid-nineteenth-century colonial conquests. Reactions to colonialism, which involved forced modernization, varied: Japan adapted to it and became a world power; China sank in dignity, wealth, and influence; Korea vanished into what proved to be the beginning of a Japanese empire. Meiji elites held China, once the object of unbounded reverence, in contempt, and they adopted toward the rest of Asia an attitude of even sterner superiority. Japan, thus, chose not to resist the Western powers but to become one of them, and the rest of Asia knew it.

China, after millennia of dominance, lost the most. Its "century of humiliation" lasted from the time it submitted to the Nanjing Treaty in 1842 through the 1980s economic expansion under Deng Xiaoping.

During the post–World War II decades, Japan remained Asia's dominant economic and political power. But Japan's neighbors remembered their long disgrace. Japanese officials knew that only the clearest expressions of regret could begin to mitigate their neighbors' resentment. One prime minister after another extended apologies, but China and Korea, under the influence of Confucian ritual formalities, remained too aware of the telltale signs of inauthentic remorse. They were often right. On the other hand, how does any official of any nation act "authentically"? Does not the very consciousness and deliberativeness of enacting a feeling, even if authentic, subvert the impression of sincerity? Here lies a deep perceptual dilemma fueling the memory problem.

Neither in the existing archive of official Japanese apologies nor in public reactions to survey questions about Japanese regret do we find the slightest trace of what is most important to the Chinese and Korean people—efforts to reinstate lost honor. Japan's apologies acknowledge physical suffering but not the humiliation of conquest and subordination. There is no mention of humiliation because there is no vocabulary of apology for the wounding of another's honor.

Such matters are less urgent in dignity cultures. Jewish survivors of the Holocaust, for example, do not condemn Germany for humiliating them. Many captured American and British soldiers died in Japanese prisoner-of-war camps, but the survivors feel no dishonor. Like Holocaust survivors, they condemn their tormentors for murdering their friends and ruining their lives. Violation of rights, not honor, is at stake.

The task of locating the Asian case on the intersecting dimensions of dignity, honor, aggression, and victimhood is simplified in Table 59.1, which places nations along four dimensions and, in parentheses, names the sentiments of aggressor and victim. In dignity culture, aggressors, motivated by guilt, direct their apologies to the rights they have violated, and their victims define those apologies as compensation for physical and mental suffering. In honor cultures, compensation is more difficult. If offenders apologize for physical suffering without acknowledging their own shame, moral inferiority, and humiliation—and doing so convincingly—their victims are deprived of what means most to them. Such sensibilities intensify the memory problem.

New outlooks

Asian memory conforms to both the presentist and traditionalist perspectives. Contemporary Koreans, for example, see their history differently from their parents, while also recognizing that the disagreement has to do with real events. However, presentism

Table 59.1

	Dignity cultures	Honor cultures
Aggression	Germany (guilt)	Japan (formal apology)
Victimhood	Jews and conquered nations of Europe (indignation)	China and Korea (shame)

and traditionalism do not tell us what makes an event memorable or what makes people disagree about it in the first place. Without this knowledge we are at a loss to know why commemoration tells us what it does, for its job, as we recall, is to designate "the significance of events by lifting from the historical record the events embodying a community's cultural values." Presentism and traditionalism are about the *how*, not the *what*, of memory.

The advent of the memory problem reflects both a malleable past, because it is linked to the changing political power of Asian countries, and an obdurate past, because it formulates a century of trauma that will not go away. But the memory problem tells something more, namely the power of culture to make memory resonate, to get under people's skin, to make them take notice when the past is represented in the wrong way. No memory problem exists without a memorable history expressing or violating moral values.

During the past thirty years, the volume of collective memory scholarship has grown rapidly, but the intellectual payoff is leveling. Presentists can only say so much about the way interests distort historical perception, while traditionalists are now more alive to memory's erosion than endurance. Presentist and traditionalist perspectives continue to be elaborated and qualified, but we are reaching the limit of what they can tell us. In Asia, we have reached this limit. To grasp the uniqueness of the Asian memory problem, the concepts of honor and shame have been useful not because they remain dominant aspects of Asian culture but because their residual forms resonate with present experience.

Two statements, accordingly, summarize culture's role in collective memory. First, the perspectives that organize Western scholarship cannot represent Asian memory. The memory problem is central to Asia's current economic and political issues because honor and shame bind individuals to their nation in a way that dignity and guilt cannot. No memory problem afflicts Western societies because their cultural values protect individuals from, rather than subject them to, the demands of the institutions to which they belong. Asia's memory problem would be less consequential, therefore, if its traditions of national honor and shame were less relevant.

Second, Asian cultures, like their Western counterparts, show memory to be dialogic, a mirror and a lamp, a reflector of and guide for the present; but Asia embodies more information about memory as an entity in itself—an ordered system of symbols that make experience, including traumatic experience, meaningful. In few other national or regional settings is the interdependence of past and present, culture and memory, so problematic and consequential, or identification with the past so strong.

Bringing Asia into the field of collective memory studies, not as a site for the testing of Western concepts but as a mine with new concepts and new propositions, widens the existing state of the field, suggesting the contours of a theory that places less emphasis on the interests that distort history and more on the cultural traits that define the meaning of real historical events.

References

Alexander, Jeffrey. 2003. *The Meanings of Social Life: A Cultural Sociology*. New York: Oxford University Press.

Assman, Jan. 1992. *Das kulturelle Gedächtnis: Schrift, Erinnerung und politische Identität in frühen Hochkulturen*. Munich: Beck.

Berger, Peter, Berger, Brigitte, and Kellner, Hansfried. 1973. "On the Obsolescence of the Concept of Honor." Pp. 83–96 in *The Homeless Mind: Modernization and Consciousness*. New York: Vintage.

Bodnar, John. 1992. *Remaking America: Public Memory, Commemoration, and Patriotism in the Twentieth Century*. Princeton, NJ: Princeton University Press.

Coser, Lewis A., ed. 1991. *Maurice Halbwachs on Collective Memory*. Chicago: University of Chicago Press.

Fine, Gary Alan. 2001. *Difficult Reputations: Collective Memories of the Evil, Inept, and Controversial*. Chicago: University of Chicago Press.

Fujitani, Takashi, White, Geoffrey M., and Yoneyama, Lisa, eds. 2001. *Perilous Memories: The Asia-Pacific War*. Durham, NC and London: Duke University Press.

Geertz, Clifford. 1973. *Interpretation of Cultures*. New York: Basic Books.

Halbwachs, Maurice 1952 (1925). *Les Cadres sociaux de la mémoire*. Paris: Presses Universitaires de France.

Jager, Sheila Miyoshi and Mitter, Rana, eds. 2007. *Ruptured Histories: War, Memory, and the Post-Cold War in Asia*. Cambridge, MA: Harvard University Press.

Lyotard, Jean-François 1984 (1979). *The Postmodern Condition*. Minneapolis: University of Minnesota Press.

Mannheim, Karl 1952 (1928). "The Problem of Generations." Pp. 276–320 in Paul Keckemeti, ed., *Essays on the Sociology of Knowledge*. London: Routledge & Kegan Paul.

Nora, Pierre. 1996. *Realms of Memory, Vol. 1*. New York: Columbia University Press.

Olick, Jeffrey K. 1999. "Genre Memories and Memory Genres: A Dialogical Analysis of May 8th, 1945 Commemorations in the Federal Republic of Germany." *American Sociological Review* 64: 381–402.

——. 2007. *The Politics of Regret: On Collective Memory and Historical Responsibility*. New York: Routledge.

Schudson, Michael. 1989. "The Present in the Past versus the Past in the Present." *Communication* 11: 105–113.

——. 1992. *Watergate in American Memory*. New York: Basic Books.

Schwartz, Barry and Kim, Mikyoung. 2002. "Honor, Dignity, and Collective Memory: Judging the Past in Korea and the United States." Pp. 209–26 in Karen Cerulo, ed., *Culture in Mind: Toward a Sociology of Culture and Cognition*. New Brunswick, NJ: Rutgers University Press.

Schwartz, Barry and Schuman, Howard. 2005. "History, Commemoration, and Belief: Abraham Lincoln in American Memory, 1945–2001." *American Sociological Review* 70: 183–203.

Schwartz, Barry, Fukuoka, Kazuya, and Takita-Ishi, Sachiko. 2005. "Collective Memory: Why Culture Matters." Pp. 253–71 in Mark D. Jacobs and Nancy Weiss Hanrahan, eds., *The Blackwell Companion to the Sociology of Culture*. Oxford: Blackwell.

Schuman, Howard and Scott, Jacqueline. 1987. "Generations and Collective Memories." *American Sociological Review* 54: 359–81.

Shils, Edward A. 1981. *Tradition*. Chicago: University of Chicago Press.

Wallbott, Harald G. and Scherer, Klaus R. 1995. "Cultural Determinants in Experiencing Shame and Guilt." Pp. 465–87 in June Price Tangney and Kurt W. Fischer, eds., *Self-Conscious Emotions: The Psychology of Shame, Guilt, Embarrassment, and Pride*. New York: Guilford Press.

Wertsch, James V. 2002. *Voices of Collective Remembering*. Cambridge: Cambridge University Press.

Wirth, Louis. 1936. "Preface." Pp. x–xxx in Karl Mannheim, *Ideology and Utopia*, trans. Louis Wirth and Edward Shils, New York: Harcourt, Brace and World.

Zerubavel, Eviatar. 2003. *Time Maps: Collective Memory and the Social Shape of the Past*. Chicago: University of Chicago Press.

60

From collective memory to commemoration

Hiro Saito

To have "memory" of an event, humans have to experience it themselves. Learning of an event secondhand, humans acquire knowledge, but not memory. Yet, when sociologists speak of "collective memory," they routinely include as agents of memory those who do not have firsthand experience of a past event. This inclusion has been taken for granted ever since Maurice Halbwachs (1992) formulated his Durkheimian theory of the relationship between collective memory and commemoration in terms of group solidarity and identity: collective memory emerges when those without firsthand experience of an event identify with those who have such experience, defining both sets of actors as sharing membership in the same social group. The creation of this affect-laden, first-person orientation to a past event is at the crux of *commemoration*—simply put, a ritual that transforms "historical knowledge" into "collective memory" consisting of mnemonic schemas and objects that define the meaning of a past event as a locus of collective identity. According to Halbwachs's formulation, commemoration is a vehicle of collective memory.

Below, I first elaborate Halbwachs's theory, which has dominated the sociology of commemoration, by drawing on more recent sociological theories of ritual and collective identity. I then critically evaluate the dominant Durkheimian theory of commemoration by examining four empirical phenomena that have not been addressed adequately in the existing literature: (1) commemorations of negative events or difficult pasts, wherein commemoration serves not to produce shared mnemonic schemas, but, rather, to preserve struggles over the meaning of mnemonic objects; (2) the understudied role of political organizations and social movements in the making and remaking of commemorative rituals; (3) the fundamentally temporal nature of commemoration, which calls for a more historical approach to both continuities and discontinuities in the ways actors reiterate commemorative rituals over time; and (4) the incipient rescaling of commemoration from national to transnational arenas and actors, reconfiguring the connection between national identity and collective memory in an increasingly global world.

Commemoration as ritual

Human social life is marked and made meaningful by an array of commemorative practices. Various anniversaries mark our collective calendar—Independence Day, Martin Luther King Jr. Day, and September 11th, to name only a few American examples. When humans commemorate—whatever the scale of commemoration may be—they always do so as members of a social group, be it a family, a school, a city, or a nation. Their membership in these groups does not simply pre-exist this process, but is actually constituted *through* commemoration. By providing actors with objects and performances that narrate a past event as part of a shared group identity, commemoration constitutes social groups. Furthermore, because autobiographical memories are crucial to generating and maintaining individuals' sense of personal identity, commemoration provides people with autobiographical narratives of their purportedly shared past as a group and induces them to feel and accept such narratives as authentic.

The felt authentication of a collective autobiography is made possible by the ritual nature of commemoration. As Randall Collins (2004: 42) has argued, rituals are "occasions that combine a high degree of mutual focus of attention, that is, a high degree of intersubjectivity, together with a high degree of emotional entrainment … [which] result[s] in feelings of membership that are attached to cognitive symbols." The collective effervescence that commemoration generates by virtue of its ritual nature helps participants feel authentic about autobiographical narratives of their purportedly shared past. Alexander (2004a: 527) has further unpacked the nature of rituals as "episodes of repeated and simplified cultural communication in which the direct partners to a social interaction, and those observing it, share a mutual belief in the descriptive and prescriptive validity of the communication's symbolic contents and accept the authenticity of one another's intentions." Commemorations capitalize on this affective power of rituals to prompt participants to generate mutual identifications as members of a social group. Thus Collins's and Alexander's theories of ritual reinforce the Durkheimian point of Halbwachs's theory of commemoration: commemoration is an "alchemy" that transforms historical knowledge into collective memory, making emotionally charged interpretation of past events integral to people's social identities as they shift from a subject position of audience/observers to actors/participants.

This kind of imaginary identification with participants of a past event is most intense and visible in cases of traumatic events (LaCapra 2001), but sociologists have considered such identification a defining feature of "collective memory" in general. What the sociological concept of collective memory is meant to capture is the misrecognition of secondhand knowledge as living memory by virtue of identifications on the part of participants in commemoration. When commemorative rituals succeed in providing people with vicarious experience of a past event, secondhand knowledge begins to be felt as living memory among those who lack firsthand experience. In symbolic–interactionist terms (Fine and Beim 2007), participants of commemorative rituals take attitudes of those who have firsthand experience. Commemorative rituals typically force such symbolic interactions by presenting those who have firsthand experience as the center of the rituals. This setup tends to lead those who lack firsthand experience to fix their attention on those with firsthand experience and induce the former to experience a past event vicariously from the imaginary first-person perspective of the latter. Emotional intensity of commemorative rituals, exemplified by moments of collective effervescence, promotes such misrecognition and imagination of secondhand knowledge as shared living memory.

For commemorative practices to constitute a social group, however, not all members have to be present in the same physical space. As is the case with national anniversaries, mutual awareness that other members of the nation in other places are marking the same occasion helps to produce feelings of group membership and solidarity among individuals. Print capitalism facilitated the formation of national communities (Anderson 1991) partly because it enabled commemorative rituals, such as Independence Day, to extend beyond face-to-face interactions; increasingly distant people were able to imagine their shared participation in commemorative rituals as members of the same social group. Today, mass media play a decisive role in generating collective memories at the national level (Dayan and Katz 1992). Whether and how an event is represented in mass media thus constitutes an important realm for the sociological analysis of commemoration.

Moreover, as implied by Alexander's formulation, "symbolic objects" play an important role in commemorative rituals. Not only do such objects provide focal points for participants' attention, but the contents of symbolic objects shape mnemonic schemas and patterns of thinking and feeling about the purportedly shared past. It is important to emphasize here that symbolic objects are *multimodal*: they generate meaning in multiple registers, including not only the verbal-linguistic, but also visual, auditory, olfactory, gustatory, and tactual registers. Symbolic objects in the context of commemorative rituals thus constitute built environments that operate as gigantic mnemonics, enveloping participants. The disappearance of "*milieux de mémoire*" observed by Pierre Nora (1989) is largely due to the rapid and radical transformation of built environments within modernity. Technological, economic, and demographic changes ushered in by industrialization and urbanization uprooted people from the built environments that had previously served as mnemonics of their past. Creatively rethinking the phrase "out of sight, out of mind" as "out of site, out of mind" nicely captures the constitutive role of built environments in human memory. When the built environments that people inhabit change, what they remember and how they remember it also change. Mnemonic schemas are always mediated by mnemonic objects. From this perspective, "collective memory" is best understood as being "distributed" partly in human actors themselves, and partly in the world of mnemonics (Wertsch 2002).

In sum, following Halbwachs's Durkheimian formulation, sociologists have largely studied commemoration as a vehicle generating group solidarity and collective identity through the distribution and enforcement of shared mnemonic schemas and objects. Although this Durkheimian approach captures important aspects of commemoration, I argue that it fails to pay sufficient attention to key empirical phenomena that need to be addressed by any theory of commemoration. In what follows, I unpack these understudied empirical phenomena and their theoretical implications.

Commemoration of a difficult past

The Durkheimian perspective holds up best in the case of "positive events"—for example the attainment of political independence or a clear-cut military victory—events that generate collective effervescence and reinforce desirable images of collective identity. But what if events present moral ambiguities and controversies, and rituals do not resolve but rather preserve and even foreground such difficulties? Halbwachs's theory of commemoration is ill equipped to analyze such instances. Robin Wagner-Pacifici and Barry Schwartz (1991: 384) were the first to highlight this analytic lacuna when they pointed out the need to study "negative events," that is, moral traumas that "not only result in loss or failure but also evoke disagreement and inspire censure." Their work highlighted the Vietnam War as one such negative event or "difficult past" for Americans: various groups of actors, from veterans to peace activists, not only fail to share a unified mnemonic schema for interpreting the event, but also continue to contest the meaning of key mnemonic objects meant to commemorate it. Here, negative events as moral traumas must be distinguished from "cultural traumas" as theorized by Alexander (2004b). Although both moral and cultural traumas can be triggered by events that psychologically traumatize individual members of a social group, the former divide group members by preserving moral ambiguities of the events, while the latter unify group members by elevating victims to the status of a group totem. Put somewhat differently, moral traumas are the result of *failed* commemorative rituals, in which participants are unable to generate solidarity and mutual identification with one another. In a sense, then, the concept of negative events as moral traumas purports to be anti-Durkheimian.

Although Wagner-Pacifici and Schwartz shed light on an understudied phenomenon, they fail to explore a more fundamental weakness of the Durkheimian theory of commemoration. In their discussion of the Vietnam War, the authors present various groups as disagreeing about the meaning of specific mnemonic objects, yet sharing an implicit understanding that the event is significant for Americans as a collective. There is no discussion of cases in which American citizens dis-identified with the United States itself, or, even more radically, identified with the Vietnamese instead. Whether this character of the analysis is due to nationalism among the historical actors or methodological nationalism in Wagner-Pacifici and Schwartz's analysis is unclear, but the point is that the United States is taken for granted as the scale of commemoration: the nation as master frame of collective identity is never called in question.

The critique offered by Wagner-Pacifici and Schwartz could also be countered with a Durkheimian response that the Vietnam War is only one of many historical events from which Americans can choose to narrate their collective identity. Although every national state is confronted with both "difficult" and "easy" pasts, politicians, intellectuals, and ordinary people tend to over-commemorate past events that are relatively easy to render as triumphant narratives. In light of this preponderance of positive commemorations, the authors' case study of the Vietnam War Memorial does not sufficiently challenge the Durkheimian assertion that commemorations generally facilitate the creation of group identity and solidarity. Arguably the national state can afford to have some failed commemorative rituals and moral traumas, so long as it has other, more high-profile rituals that succeed.

Nonetheless, I find the critique offered by Wagner-Pacifici and Schwartz of Durkheimian theory to be an effective one. However, I would also argue that their real contribution actually lies in another direction. What is most valuable about their study is not so much its focus on the commemoration of negative events or difficult pasts in and of themselves, but its focus on the dynamics of political contention that characterize any commemorative ritual, positive or negative. I elaborate this point in the following section.

Political contentions in commemoration

Functionalist theories are generally weak in accounting for micro interactions and contentions that lead to the emergence and transformation of social institutions.

The Durkheimian theory of commemoration is no exception. Since the ultimate function of commemoration is specified *a priori* as the constitution of collective identity, sociologists of commemoration tend to pay scant attention to social movements and political organizations involved in the production and interpretation of mnemonic objects. Wagner-Pacifici and Schwartz made a novel contribution when they detailed how the construction of the Vietnam War Memorial was initiated by a group of politicians, contested by veterans, and debated by journalists and artists. In a similar vein, Vera Zolberg's (1998) study of controversies surrounding the 1996 Smithsonian exhibit on the bombing of Hiroshima, and Vered Vinitzky-Seroussi's (2002) study of efforts to commemorate the legacy of Yitzhak Rabin capture a strong sense of the political contentions involved in commemoration. These works highlight how different groups mobilize and contest commemorations so as to promote their particular versions of collective memory, thus advancing their own political interests and symbolic legitimacy.

All commemorative rituals, whether they succeed or fail, can be argued to have this undercurrent of dynamic interaction among political organizations and social movements. Consider, for example, postwar Japanese commemoration of the bombing of Hiroshima (Saito 2006). In the immediate aftermath of World War II, there was no national commemoration of the atom bombing: commemorative rituals were fragmented among different groups of actors, such as A-bomb survivors and politicians. Then, the hydrogen-bomb fallout in 1954 caused a cascade of changes in the Japanese commemoration of the atom bombing, elevating "Hiroshima" to the cultural trauma constitutive of postwar Japanese national identity as the pacifist nation of nuclear victims. Importantly, however, such a reframing of Hiroshima as a symbol of Japanese national and moral unity would not have occurred without the mobilization of social-movement organizations and the formation of a coalition among political parties. Moreover, even after national commemoration of the event was institutionalized, the public meaning of "Hiroshima" remained multivocal. Although the initial fragmentation of commemoration was overcome in 1954, different interpretations of mnemonic objects were never unified but rather brought together into dialogue within the shared commemorative ritual.

Categorical distinctions between commemorations of negative or positive events, or between moral or cultural traumas, are less helpful here than a recognition that all commemorative rituals are permeated by dynamics of political contention, albeit to different degrees. The sociology of commemoration thus has much to gain by engaging more extensively with scholarship on political organizations and social movements. In addition to the dominance of Durkheimian functionalism, the sociology of commemoration has been dominated by "endogenous" cultural explanations (Kaufman 2004). That is, sociologists of commemoration have tended to concentrate on the meaning of mnemonic objects without considering the links between such objects and "exogenous" variables such as material resources and political opportunities that may shape their production. The popularity of endogenous cultural explanation in the sociology of commemoration is due, in part, to the topic's resurgence at the same time that a new "cultural sociology" emerged in the 1990s as an alternative to the extant "sociology of culture." The new "cultural turn" took very seriously the autonomy of the symbolic system from social structures, in contrast to an older tradition that tended to explain the symbolic system through reference to exogenous, non-symbolic variables. Sociologists such as Jason Kaufman (2004), however, have recently begun to argue that sociologists should launch a concerted effort to synthesize endogenous and exogenous cultural explanations. Such approaches would enable us to understand how mnemonic objects and their meanings are constituted not only in relation to one another, but also in relation to actors and organizations that produce, use, contest, and transform mnemonic objects under changing historical circumstances.

This is not to suggest that actors and organizations can simply dictate commemorative rituals according to their present political interests. Once a certain form of commemoration is institutionalized, it tends to persist even in the absence of the causes responsible for its initial institutionalization. Conversely, no commemorations remain completely unchanged or locked in over time, for not all elements of institutions are equally durable. This circumstance is an aspect of the third understudied dimension of commemoration—the problem of temporality.

Reiterated commemoration

Rituals, including commemorative ones, are by definition repeated over time to maintain participants' schemas of thinking and feeling about the world, and acting in it. This reiterative nature of commemorative rituals dovetails with the character of memory itself—better understood as a reiterative process than a static thing or state. In reality, what we call "memory" is an act of remembering or a moment of recollection that always involves reconstruction of past experiences. At the individual level, memory of an event persists only as a reiteration of moments of recollection. Similarly, at the group level, collective memory persists only as a reiteration of commemoration.

The reiterative nature of commemoration poses rather complicated conceptual problems of temporality. Like any other institutionalized practices, commemorative rituals are path-dependent in that it becomes increasingly difficult over time to change arrangements adopted at their founding. Under the veneer of path-dependent persistence, however, some parts of institutionalized commemoration may well be undergoing change in response to new political, cultural, and demographic trends. This kind of incremental change may influence the overall trajectory of commemorative rituals gradually over time or transform them dramatically in conjunction with contingent events. Commemorative rituals thus exhibit a seemingly contradictory combination of continuities and discontinuities because of their fundamentally temporal nature. It is analytically useful, then, to parse out some of the implications of this temporality.

First, the reiteration of commemorations of a past event introduces a "period effect." As the historical conditions in which commemorative rituals take place change over time, so too can the ways in which those rituals are organized. Reiterated commemoration also generates a "cohort effect." As older cohorts exit from commemoration of a past event and newer cohorts enter, the overall composition of mnemonic schemas shifts along with the participants themselves. In the same way that different generations remember different historical events as most important to their lives (Schuman and Scott 1989), different cohorts commemorate the same past event differently on the basis of their unique historical and human-developmental trajectories. Finally, period and cohort effects are further compounded by an "age effect": people change how they commemorate a past event as they move through different stages of their own life courses. Overall, one can refer to "age-period-cohort" (APC) effects in commemoration.

Until now, no sociologists have tried to tackle APC effects in the study of commemoration. This is mainly because sociologists have focused primarily on institutional frameworks of commemoration (i.e. the world of mnemonic objects) while bracketing the mnemonic schemas of individual human beings. Within this dominant sociological tradition, researchers have tended to analyze only period effects, while generally ignoring cohort and age effects among individuals who participate in commemorative rituals. I argue, however, that it is time sociologists should take individuals more seriously when thinking about continuities and discontinuities in commemoration. As Andrew Abbott (2005) suggests, human beings are "reservoirs" of mnemonic schemas that encode, preserve, and carry forward from past to present structures from different times and of different trajectories. The diversity of mnemonic schemas that different generations carry inside their bodies can influence existent commemorative rituals towards either continuity or discontinuity. I suggest that APC effects serve as a useful heuristic for sociologists who want to investigate the "wide variety of mnemonic processes, practices, and outcomes, neurological, cognitive, personal, aggregated, and collective" (Olick 1999: 346), that link individuals and institutions in commemorative rituals. If sociologists are to take seriously the reiterative nature of commemoration, they must begin to ask, "How and why do different cohorts of people recollect the same event differently in different periods and over different stages of their lives?" and "How do such age-period-cohort interactions account for continuities and discontinuities in commemorative rituals?"

Furthermore, when tracing APC effects in commemoration, it will be important to contextualize them *vis-à-vis* changes exogenous to the field of commemoration. Although commemorative rituals develop their own internal dynamics over time, they are also structurally articulate with larger demographic, economic, political, and cultural formations. Shifts in these formations can affect the demographic composition of participants in commemorative rituals, change the economic resources available for such rituals, induce actors with particular political interests to enter or exit the field of commemoration, or reconfigure the meanings of mnemonic objects. These exogenous changes all exert effects on commemorative rituals pertaining to the same past event. It is thus imperative for researchers to describe and explain the reiteration of commemoration over time in terms of historical dynamics both internal and external to the field of commemoration itself. This analytical injunction points to the fourth and last set of understudied empirical phenomena—the effects of wider historical conditions on the scale of commemoration.

Nationalism and cosmopolitanism in commemoration

Following Halbwachs, sociologists have continued to study commemorative rituals in terms of the construction of national identity, even though commemoration itself has no intrinsic connection with national identity. The strong, almost quasi-natural association between commemoration and the nation can be linked to the way in which commemorative rituals have been deployed historically as cultural technologies for imagining the nation, as well as to the symbiotic relationship of the discipline of sociology itself to the consolidation of national states at the beginning of the twentieth century. Against the persistent "methodological nationalism" that characterizes studies of commemoration, however, Daniel Levy and Nathan Sznaider explore the question of what they call the "cosmopolitanization" of collective memory at the beginning of the twenty-first century. Levy and Sznaider ask: "Can we imagine collective memories that transcend national and ethnic boundaries? If so, we must ask, how do these transnational memory forms come about, and of what do they consist?" (2006: 2).

To answer these questions, Levy and Sznaider analyze the history of Holocaust commemoration since World War II. They argue that commemorations become cosmopolitan when mnemonic objects are de-territorialized from their original geographical locations and transformed into empty signifiers that can be articulated with the commemoration of other events across national borders. According to the authors, globalization and the transnational circulation of mnemonic objects effect the cosmopolitanization of commemoration. As mnemonic objects traverse national borders through networks of electronic communication and transportation, the collectivities that commemorations may constitute are similarly unbound. Reflecting on the changing scale of communities that are being imagined in a global world, Bruce Robbins makes the following point:

> If people can get as emotional as [Benedict] Anderson says they do about relations with fellow nationals they never see face-to-face, then now that print capitalism has become electronic- and digital-capitalism, and now that this system is so clearly transnational, it would be strange if people did *not* get emotional in much the same way, if not necessarily to the same degree, about others who are *not* fellow nationals, people bound to them by some transnational sort of fellowship.
>
> (Robbins 1998: 7)

Globalization—the increasing interdependency of economic, political, and cultural activities in the world—as well as our awareness of globality, makes it possible for people to incorporate into their commemorative rituals the "cosmopolitan" horizon in which voices of multiple nationalities come to be in dialogue with one another (Beck 2004). Within this cosmopolitan horizon, emotional engagement (e.g. empathy and solidarity) can extend beyond the borders of a single nation.

Again, the Japanese commemoration of the bombing of Hiroshima serves as an illustrative example. In 1991 the Peace Declaration at the Peace Memorial Ceremony held in the city of Hiroshima mentioned for the first time the atrocities and sufferings that Japan had inflicted on other peoples in Asia. The inclusion signaled a sea change, redefining and rearticulating the commemoration of "Hiroshima" from a solely Japanese national trauma to a trauma linked to other Asian national traumas. Unlike the "Holocaust," "Hiroshima" as a signifier always refers to a specific place enclosed within the territory of the Japanese state; however, what it articulates and commemorates has become "cosmopolitanized" through the inclusion of the sufferings of foreign others. Whereas we might say that nationalist commemoration is *monological* in the sense of confining people's emotional engagement within their ascribed national group, cosmopolitan commemoration is *dialogical*, in that people rearticulate national trauma so as to produce forms of solidarity that traverse national borders.

Interestingly, Levy and Sznaider similarly highlight the 1990s as the time when "Holocaust" became an empty signifier and commemorative frame "dislocated from space and time, resulting in its inscription into other acts of injustice and other traumatic national memories across the globe" (2006: 5). How and why did the parallel cosmopolitanization of the "Holocaust" and "Hiroshima" come about during this period? Globalization, coupled with the worldwide diffusion of human-rights discourse through a growing number of international non-governmental organizations (Boli and

Thomas 1999) is undoubtedly part of the story—but only part. Sociologists have not yet begun to systematically investigate the evolving relationship between nationalism, cosmopolitanism, and globalization in commemoration, let alone begun to explore the causal mechanisms through which globalization differentially affects commemorative rituals in different parts of the world.

It is important to point out, however, that cosmopolitanism by no means eliminates nationalism from commemoration. Commemoration of the terrorist attacks on September 11, 2001, for example, can be regarded as cosmopolitan. Victims included not only Americans but also individuals of more than thirty other nationalities, and the unfolding of the attacks was televised in real time across the world. In the immediate aftermath of the attacks, people in different national states commemorated "September 11" as an event relevant to humanity-as-a-whole, although the cosmopolitan commemoration varied regionally in terms of its intensity and expression. This cosmopolitanism in the commemoration of "September 11" still persists today. Nevertheless, some American politicians and publics also framed the event as a cultural trauma specifically and especially constitutive of the American nation, using it as a nationalist justification for subsequent military and political actions. Thus, when studying the cosmopolitanization of commemoration against the backdrop of globalization, sociologists would do well to demarcate carefully the complex articulations between nationalism and cosmopolitanism.

Conclusion

This brief essay offers two take-away messages. The first is that commemoration is a vehicle of collective memory: commemoration is a ritual that emotionally induces people to experience past events vicariously and thereby imagine their secondhand knowledge of those events as living memory that they possess as members of a social group. The second is that sociologists need to address the blind spots of the Durkheimian theory of commemoration by turning their attention to commemorations of difficult pasts, dynamics of political contention within commemoration, problems of temporality, and the incipient decoupling of commemoration from the nation. Commemoration condenses a multiplicity of important theoretical and empirical problems, including but not limited to rituals, traumas, time, nationalism, and globalization. Hopefully, sociological studies of commemoration will expand and develop the multifaceted perspectives necessary to capture this complex and fascinating phenomenon.

References

Abbott, Andrew. 2005. "The Historicality of Individuals." *Social Science History* 29: 1–13.

Alexander, Jeffrey C. 2004a. "Cultural Pragmatics: Social Performance between Ritual and Strategy." *Sociological Theory* 22: 527–73.

——. 2004b. "Toward a Theory of Cultural Trauma." Pp. 1–30 in J.C. Alexander, R. Eyerman, B. Giesen, N.J. Smelser, and P. Sztompka, eds., *Cultural Trauma and Collective Identity*. Berkeley: University of California Press.

Anderson, Benedict. 1991. *Imagined Communities: Reflections on the Origin and Spread of Nationalism*. London: Verso.

Beck, Ulrich. 2004. "Cosmopolitan Realism: On the Distinction between Cosmopolitanism in Philosophy and the Social Sciences." *Global Networks* 4: 131–56.

Boli, John and Thomas, George M., eds. 1999. *Constructing World Culture: International Nongovernmental Organizations since 1875*. Stanford, CA: Stanford University Press.

Collins, Randall. 2004. *Interaction Ritual Chains*. Princeton, NJ: Princeton University Press.

Dayan, Daniel and Katz, Elihu. 1992. *Media Events: The Live Broadcasting of History*. Cambridge, MA: Harvard University Press.

Fine, Gary Alan and Beim, Aaron. 2007. "Introduction: Interactionist Approaches to Collective Memory." *Symbolic Interaction* 30: 1–5.

Halbwachs, Maurice. 1992. *On Collective Memory*, trans. and ed. L.A. Coser. Chicago: University of Chicago Press.

Kaufman, Jason. 2004. "Endogeneous Explanation in the Sociology of Culture." *Annual Review of Sociology* 30: 335–57.

LaCapra, Dominik. 2001. *Writing History, Writing Trauma*. Baltimore, MD: Johns Hopkins University Press.

Levy, Daniel, and Sznaider, Natan. 2006. *The Holocaust and Memory in the Global Age*. Philadelphia: Temple University Press.

Nora, Pierre. 1989. "Between Memory and History: Les Lieux de Mémoire." *Representations* 26: 7–24.

Olick, Jeffrey K. 1999. "Collective Memory: The Two Cultures." *Sociological Theory* 17: 333–48.

Robbins, Bruce. 1998. "Introduction Part I: Actually Existing Cosmopolitanism." Pp. 1–19 in P. Cheah and B. Robbins, eds., *Cosmopolitics: Thinking and Feeling beyond the Nation*. Minneapolis: University of Minnesota Press.

Saito, Hiro. 2006. "Reiterated Commemoration: Hiroshima as National Trauma." *Sociological Theory* 24: 353–76.

Schuman, Howard and Scott, Jacqueline. 1989. "Generations and Collective Memories." *American Sociological Review* 54: 359–81.

Vinitzky-Seroussi, Vered. 2002. "Commemorating a Difficult Past: Yitzhak Rabin's Memorials." *American Sociological Review* 67: 30–52.

Wagner-Pacifici, Robin and Schwartz, Barry. 1991. "The Vietnam Veterans Memorial: Commemorating a Difficult Past." *American Journal of Sociology* 97: 376–420.

Wertsch, James V. 2002. *Voices of Collective Remembering*. Cambridge: Cambridge University Press.

Zolberg, Vera. 1998. "Contested Remembrance: The Hiroshima Exhibit Controversy." *Theory and Society* 27: 565–90.

61

Movement cultures

Francesca Polletta

Many social movements seek to enact in their own operation the society they hope to bring into being. Their members may make decisions by consensus and rotate leadership. They may trade conventional gender roles, swap sexual partners, sign over their paychecks to the group, or refuse to eat animal products. Sometimes, movement groups succeed in creating enduring communities that are nonviolent, egalitarian, self-sustaining, and/or sexually liberated. Often, they collapse, imploding amidst mutual recriminations and charges of bad faith. And occasionally, whether or not they endure, they pioneer organizational forms, interactional styles, and cultural objects that make their way into the mainstream. Food co-ops, blue jeans as a young person's fashion statement, *Ms.* magazine, participatory democratic decision-making, organic food, folk music, and alternative media all began in movements, but each one outlasted the movement and era in which it was born.

It is tempting to see movement cultures as idealistic and expressive, as experiments in alternative living that offer activists a respite from, or alternative to, the more instrumental tasks of engaging opponents, mobilizing support, and negotiating with allies. In recent years, however, scholars have drawn attention instead to the political and instrumental dimensions of movement cultures. Holding hands and singing "Kumbaya" can serve practical functions. At the same time, while not downplaying the experimental character of how movements operate internally, scholars have recognized that movement cultures are rarely created *de novo*. They have therefore probed the institutional *sources* of activists' ideas about how to operate in a feminist or democratic or traditional way. This research, in turn, has shed light on a practical difficulty activists have faced in enacting their countercultural ideals—namely, the limited repertoire of behavioral models that activists have had to draw upon in practicing those ideals.

Along with these two themes, I draw attention to a third that has emerged in recent scholarship. Rejecting the instrumental/expressive duality from the opposite direction, scholars have shown, not only that what often passes as expressive action has instrumental benefits, but that what counts as instrumental action has expressive benefits. In an important sense, instrumental rationality is *performed*. This observation has implications for our understanding of cultural processes outside movements as well as within them.

Movement groups have a stake in subscribing to mainstream ideas where it serves them and refusing them where it does not. The fact that groups sometimes define what is strategic in ways that actually undercut their own aims can help us to understand how mainstream constructions of the rational operate more generally to rule out alternatives.

Not only expressive, experimental but not created out of whole cloth, and not so easily defined in opposition to an instrumental orientation—movement cultures are also less ephemeral than we tend to think of them. They have impact beyond the movements in which they are forged. Surprisingly, there has been little scholarship on this fourth theme. I raise it nevertheless because, like the other three themes, it has implications for cultural processes outside movements as well as within them. In short, studying the conditions in which elements of movement cultures diffuse can shed light on dynamics of cultural change more broadly.

Before I go any further, let me define a few terms. I define a movement as an organized effort to produce institutional or cultural change through the use of non-institutionalized means. Movements are often composed of organizations (such as NOW, the National Organization for Women, and NARAL, the National Abortion Rights Action League, for the American women's movement) but they are also composed of more informal networks and transient groupings. I define culture as shared beliefs, values, ideas, and practices. I emphasize practices, since when we talk about movement cultures colloquially, we are usually referring to styles of action and, especially, interaction that distinguish participation in the movement from participation in institutions outside it. If you go to a meeting of anarchist anti-corporate-globalization activists, you learn rather quickly—or should learn quickly—that wearing a suit or flashing your copy of *Robert's Rules of Order* will elicit suspicion. To be sure, particular movement organizations have norms that are more or less extensive and more or less exigent. Compare, for example, the culture of NOW with that of some radical feminist groups that required their members to live together, renounce intimate relationships with men, and follow strict procedures for ensuring equality. I will argue later that scholars have erred in studying the latter kinds of movement cultures at the expense of the former. For now, though, I simply want to note that when I refer to cultural practices I do not imply that those practices are equally constraining.

At times in the following, I will treat as cultural certain practices that many scholars treat as non-cultural, for example tactics like sit-ins and organizational forms such as bureaucracy. I do so because I want to show that ostensibly brass-tacks, hardnosed, non-ideological practices, just as much as ideologically laden ones, are also cultural insofar as they are animated by shared beliefs (see Hart 2001 for a similar point).

Movement cultures as political and instrumental

When activists in the 1960s sought to make of their organizations experiments in radical egalitarianism and freedom, they were by no means the first activists to try to live out their ideals in the here-and-now. Between two and three hundred socialist and anarchist communities were founded in the US during the second half of the nineteenth century alone. Activists in the abolitionist movement, the women's suffrage movement, and the labor movement in the US all experimented with democratic forms (Polletta 2002). Sociologists studying such experiments in the 1960s, however, tended to assimilate them to a Freudian-tinged theory of collective behavior. Groups like the Student Nonviolent

Coordinating Committee and Students for a Democratic Society were described as acting on the basis of a youthful repudiation of authority that was at odds with the demands of effective political reform. Participatory democratic organizations were conceptualized as "expressive" or "redemptive" in contrast to their "instrumental" and "adversary" bureaucratic counterparts (see Breines 1989; Polletta 2002).

Wini Breines's (1989) account of the 1960s American New Left offered a provocative challenge to that conceptualization. Experiments with egalitarian and co-operative decision-making were a kind of politics—just not the politics of parliamentary maneuver and bureaucratic manipulation. By "prefiguring" within the current practices of the movement the values of freedom, equality, and community that activists wanted on a grand scale, they were helping bring those values into existence.

Breines's notion of prefiguration was valuable in restoring political purpose to under-standings of activists' efforts to live countercultural ideals. Still, her account was ham-pered by a failure to spell out the mechanisms by which prefiguration would have political impact. Was building the new society within the shell of the old aimed at persuading people outside the movement of the viability of radically democratic forms? Or, was its main purpose to transform participants' relationships with each other? Or did activists see themselves as preserving a democratic impulse until a more receptive era? Absent any effort to distinguish among these and other possibilities, and to define what counted as success, prefigurative goals risked sounding very much like expressive ones—defined only by their opposition to considerations of strategy. Likewise, the failure of such efforts seemed inevitable.

The scholarly tendency to contrast prefigurative purposes to strategic ones was not Breines's alone. It ran through numerous analyses of the movement cultures of 1960s anti-Vietnam War activism, 1970s feminism, and 1980s antinuclear activism. It was increasingly challenged, however, by movement scholars who were interested not only in activists' purposes in creating unconventional structures and relationships, but also in the contribution of such efforts to familiar movement tasks such as sustaining members' commitment, developing innovative strategies, managing resources, and delegitimizing opponents.

For example, through a comparison of feminist organizations, Suzanne Staggenborg (1995) showed that decentralized and informal organizational structures generated inno-vative tactics by encouraging group input. Francesca Polletta (2002) showed that col-lectivist decision-making in the southern civil rights movement was a practical way to train activists who had had little prior experience of politics. In an analysis of the National Women's Party—a militant feminist group that remained active after the pas-sage of suffrage legislation—Verta Taylor (1989) demonstrated that the rich affective bonds developed among a cadre of committed women helped to sustain feminism during a period of political inhospitality. American anti-nuclear Plowshares activists were more successful in retaining members than were their European and Australian counterparts because of their deep and extensive movement culture, Sharon Nepstad (2008) argues. Retreats, rituals, intense Bible study, and a discourse of Catholic suffering sustained American members' commitment and faith, even through long prison sentences.

To recognize the instrumental benefits of cultures prized more for their emotional and ideological substance was not to ignore their instrumental liabilities. On the contrary, relinquishing the assumption that organizations built on countercultural values were doomed to fail allowed researchers to probe more carefully the obstacles facing such organizations. For example, some scholars of participatory democratic organizations have argued that the inequalities typical of collectivist decision-making have proved more debilitating than the inefficiencies of the form (Freeman 1973). Others have argued that collectivist decision-making can be both efficient and fair, provided that members have the same basic interests. When that is not the case, however, either members are manipulated into acquiescence or an organizational crisis ensues (Mansbridge 1983).

As scholars of feminist organizations have shown, some of the steepest obstacles to enacting non-mainstream values have come from outside movements. Funders often require explicit job descriptions, assessment criteria, and conventional boards of directors (Matthews 1994). The US Internal Revenue Service's complex standards for retaining tax-exempt status push organizations to hire legal and financial experts (McCarthy *et al.* 1991). These and other similar challenges push movements toward the mainstream.

Just as movement groups that put a premium on equality within the group are both served and disserved by such a commitment, so are those that emphasize the affective quality of group interactions. In the alternative health center studied by Sherryl Kleinman (1996), a focus on interpersonal relations both kept people from leaving a group in which they were underpaid, and, at the same time, frustratingly redefined structural inequities as interpersonal problems. In another mixed assessment, Jeff Goodwin (1997) describes a "libidinal economy" of movements, in which members' affective and erotic attachments to people outside the movement compete with their attachment to the group.

Works like these seem to give empirical flesh to dilemmas of activism that James Jasper (2004) has identified: the "Organization Dilemma," in which activists must decide whether to sacrifice the benefits of informality for those of formal structure; the "Dilemma of Reaching in and Reaching Out," in which appealing to people outside the group jeopardizes the tight intimacy that members have enjoyed; and the "Dirty Hands Dilemma," in which ideologically unsavory means may advance desired goals. However, empirical work suggests that, depending on a group's cultural norms, such dilemmas may not seem especially pressing—may not even seem to be dilemmas—and may not be especially debilitating. For example, in his study of anti-toxics activism, Paul Lichterman (1996) found that a working-class group of activists was just as committed to what it called consensus as a group of college-educated middle-class Greens. However, the working-class group saw no conflict with the fact that the group's de facto leader made all the decisions.

Another example of a tension that in practice may not be much of one: work on feminist organizations suggests that, if few groups today resemble anything like a pure form of participatory democracy (Bordt 1997), many groups have succeeded in introducing elements of more conventional organization without sacrificing their commitment to radical equality (Matthews 1994). For example, they may combine a hierarchy of offices with informal consultation across levels (Disney and Gelb 2000) or divide decisions into those requiring consensus and those not (Iannello 1992).

My point is not to deny that movement groups face common challenges. Such challenges are indeed often rooted in material realities such as the scarcity of resources, the existence of a field of competitors and opponents, the difficulty of sustaining trust in large networks, and so on. My point is rather that cultural norms within the group not only help to handle those challenges (Hall 1988) but do so in part by defining, for example, what even counts as a resource and what trust means and entails. In that sense, the dilemmas that Jasper identifies are better conceived as potential rather than inevitable.

Movement cultures as inherited and emergent

So far, I have treated movement cultures as self-consciously created by their members. They are that, but they are never created out of whole cloth. A number of scholars in recent years have probed the sources of movement cultures. One source of ideas about how the group should operate lies in the networks of activism that predate the group. Movement cultures, like strategies and tactics, are preserved in the "abeyance structures" (Taylor 1989) or "halfway houses" (Morris 1984) that subsist between periods of mass mobilization.

The diffusion of cultural forms and practices from one movement to another can take place much more quickly, of course. Sit-ins, the construction of mock shantytowns characteristic of South African apartheid, affinity group decision-making, and the use of big puppets in marches have all been adopted by groups and movements far removed from the progenitors of these strategies. The proven effectiveness of a strategy, tactic, or style is by no means a precondition for its spread (Soule 2004). Rather, the stature of the initiator movement, perceived similarities between diffusing and adopting groups (Soule 2004), and a group's ability to experiment with new forms (Wood 2007) seem to matter more.

A second source of ideas about how movements should operate can be found in *nonpolitical* structures and relationships. Activists adapt ways of interacting from relationships with which they are familiar, turning those relationships into reference points for abstract concepts like equality, solidarity, care, and authority. For example, in her study of participatory democracy in movements in the 1960s, Polletta (2002) found that although there were older activists on the scene who might have schooled younger ones in Quaker practices of consensus-based decision-making, by and large that did not happen. Instead, student activists invented participatory democracy as they went along— or so they thought. For, in fact, they drew interactional norms from relationships that were already familiar to them—relationships of religious fellowship, tutelage, and, especially, friendship. Treating each other as friends made collective decision-making easy and efficient. It also created problems, however, when newcomers joined the group and felt excluded by a core of insiders.

Familiar relationships have also shaped the culture of racist hate groups, as Kathy Blee (2002) has shown. Such groups delineated a role for women that extended their stereotypically maternal roles. Women's activism was defined as an expression of their nurturing capacities. In this respect, they were not unlike some progressive groups, as Marian Mollin (2006) has documented in her study of gender in the ostensibly egalitarian pacifist movement.

In his study of the anti-vice, abolitionist, and temperance movements of the 1830s US, Michael Young (2006) detailed a similar process of transferring interactional models from a nonpolitical sphere to a political one, although at a larger scale than I have just described. At the same time that Protestant churches were creating a vast network of benevolent societies aimed at eradicating national sins like Sabbath-breaking and drinking, upstart Methodist sects were popularizing a revivalist style that focused on public confession. Schemas of sin and confession joined to produce what Young calls a confessional mode of protest, in which activists fused bids for self- and social transformation.

Note that this movement culture emerged—and emerged widely (temperance societies counted over 1.5 million members)—a century and half before the "lifestyle politics" of the so-called new social movements. I mention this because a third answer to the question of the provenance of movement cultures has come from the study of these more recent movements. Emerging in the 1970s and 1980s, Western European mobilizations around nuclear power, feminism, homosexuality, and local autonomy were middle class in composition and were oriented as much to securing recognition for new identities as to securing political and economic reform. Internal movement culture was a key site of political experimentation. Scholars like Alain Touraine (1981) and Alberto Melucci (1989) linked the new social movements to the rise of a new "postindustrial" social formation, in which information had become at once a key resource, the means of social control, and, in the form of dominant cultural codes, the target of protest. Scholars like Young and others, however, have shown that the new movements' politicizing of the internal lives of movement participants was by no means new. Still, it seems fair to say that in certain historical eras experimentation with interpersonal relations has constituted more or less of a political challenge.

None of the works I have described maintain that movement cultures, once given, are fixed for all time. Each one recognizes that cultures—movement or otherwise—are emergent. But teasing out their roots sheds light on an important obstacle in realizing countercultural ideals. The very *materials* that activists rely on to enact their countercultural ideas—materials such as the interactional norms of familiar relationships and popular role definitions—may operate in ways that reproduce rather than challenge existing structures of power and inequality.

Movement cultures as rational and performative

All of the movement cultures I have described so far have been self-consciously oppositional. They aimed to enact values that were not honored by mainstream institutions. However, few movement organizations have only that as their aim. Most also seek to make instrumental, institutional change. How activists define the latter task—and how they seek to balance it with their commitments to enacting cultural values—is revealing. In an important sense, activists perform rationality as much as they perform normative commitments to democracy, equality, and liberation. By paying attention to those performances, we can better understand the normative force of mainstream constructions of the rational since, at times, activists hew to such constructions in the absence of evidence that they actually produce measurable gains.

Let me illustrate. The middle-class professionals who staffed the alternative health clinic that Sherryl Kleinman (1996) studied in the 1980s saw themselves as bearers of the countercultural impulse of the 1960s. They held hands before meetings and had group hugs after them, strove for consensus in all-night meetings, and were critical of conventional markers of professional accomplishment. But they also insisted that each meeting be recorded in "minutes that had a bureaucratic look—lengthy, well-typed, with lots of headings, subheadings, and underlinings" (Kleinman 1996: 38–39). One staffer created an uproar when she submitted minutes of a previous meeting in longhand and with illustrations, and staffers carefully rewrote the minutes line by line. Kleinman had never seen anyone actually refer to minutes from earlier meetings and there was no evidence that staffers believed that imitating mainstream organizational procedures would get them more clients or funding. Rather, Kleinman argues, minute-taking, in as conventional a way as possible, was associated with "serious" organizations, which this organization also wanted to be.

Another example: the animal rights activists whom Julian Groves (2001) studied discouraged women from serving in leadership positions because they believed that women were seen by the public as prone to the kind of emotionalism that would cost the movement credibility. Activists spent little time debating whether women were in fact prone to emotionalism, however, or whether emotional accounts were more or less effective than rational arguments. Their calculations were strategic but they were based on gendered schemas of reason and emotion.

The anti-Gulf war activists observed by Stephen Hart (2001) offer another example. They relied on a pragmatic, nuts-and-bolts style in their internal discussions, effectively ruling out of order discussions of participants' personal commitments or broad ideological visions. But that "constrained" discursive style served them less effectively than did the "expansive" discourse characteristic of faith-based organizing groups, in which participants' ethical commitments were threaded through all discussions. A discourse valued for its pragmatism, ironically, proved less effective than one valued for its moral depth.

One could describe each of these cases in terms of the familiar dilemma of being at once ideologically consistent and instrumentally rational. But in each case, the hard-nosed, brass-tacks, self-consciously instrumental position was as much a cultural performance—as ideological—as the position to which it was opposed.

This pattern raises an obvious question. Is rationality also a cultural performance in organizations that care little about their alternative identity? How is instrumental rationality performed in the National Organization for Women or the Sierra Club? We don't know. Not knowing, though, leaves intact the perception that such organizations are objectively instrumental and only instrumental. That is unlikely. Similarly, scholars have tended to study "hot" emotions such as anger, love, anxiety, and pride rather than "cool" emotions such as boredom, condescension, and calm. Both kinds of emotions do organizational work, however, and both pose organizational risks. They deserve study.

Movement cultures as evanescent and enduring

"Consciousness-raising," a cultural practice that gained fame in the radical women's movement, has become a familiar political strategy. By contrast, the feminist practice of allocating tasks within the group by lot never really took off. Why? What accounts for why some aspects of movement cultures endure and others fall into disuse?

One might speculate that the movement practices most prone to institutionalization are those that can be detached from their originating movement context in a way that preserves their tone of political idealism without actually encouraging protest. So, for example, participatory democracy as a form of decision-making oriented to consensus has been touted in a variety of mainstream institutions, including for-profit businesses. However, participatory democracy as new leftists meant it—a polity in which ordinary people participated in the decisions that affected them—has dropped out of our political idiom. Current understandings of consciousness-raising, some feminists complain, mistake it for group therapy rather than as preparation for collective action. If it is true that practices and styles that can be detached from their political purposes are prone to institutionalization, then movement objects that can be commercially marketed are even more likely to go mainstream. Blue jeans, peace signs, and rainbow flags fit this category.

Against this analysis, though, one might point out that even today participatory democracy provides tools for naming and challenging inegalitarian practices in organizations. Muslim women's practice of wearing headscarves has been interpreted, at different times and places, as a sign of religious belief or as a political challenge. The political associations of a depoliticized cultural style can be recuperated in a way that gives the style a contentious edge.

Yet another twist is suggested by the changing cultural status of the folk song "Kumbaya." The old spiritual was popularized by Pete Seeger in 1958 and Joan Baez in 1962 and it became closely associated with the civil rights movement. Today, however, the song is most often invoked sarcastically, to refer to naïve romantics who think the world's problems can be solved by "holding hands and singing 'Kumbaya'," in a common phrasing. What accounts for the devaluing of the song? Probably the fact that its association with the civil rights movement led it to be adopted by a range of mainstream groups, including the Boy Scouts, the YMCA, countless summer camps, and Catholic Church folk masses. Thus mainstreamed, the song's movement credentials eroded.

In the absence of empirical research, these possibilities remain speculative. Along with the dearth of research on movement cultures in mainstream and conservative groups, our failure to analyze the impacts of movement cultures on practices outside the movement constitutes a significant gap in the literature.

Conclusion

What can we learn about culture by studying its enactment within movements? One lesson is about the obstacles to enacting countercultural ideals. Those obstacles are in part structural. For example, US Internal Revenue Service codes require a formal organizational hierarchy even in organizations committed to equality. But the obstacles to enacting countercultural values lie also in the very ways in which we make sense of abstract ideals such as freedom or sisterhood. Relying on the norms associated with familiar roles and relationships makes it easier to enact those values, since they let us know what kinds of behaviors are expected. It would be hard to figure out just what equality meant in every interaction without those expectations. But norms derived from familiar roles and relationships also militate against creating new kinds of relationships. They risk promoting intimacy at the expense of inclusivity, respect at the expense of an openness to dissent.

The second thing we can learn about culture from movements is that conventional notions of instrumental rationality have powerful force. Movements are illuminating in this regard because they have a stake in adopting mainstream ideas about rationality when it serves them and ignoring such ideas when it does not. The fact that in the cases I mentioned activists embraced a narrow definition of what counted as strategic even when it hurt their prospects in critical ways points to the truly constraining character of our common sense about strategy.

There is more to be learned about culture from movements. Few scholars have studied the internal culture of conservative organizations. Is prefiguration as important a goal to conservative movement groups? If so, do such groups sacrifice the solidarity that egalitarianism promotes in progressive groups or do they secure solidarity by other means? Even fewer scholars have studied culture in movement groups that see themselves as pragmatic, moderate, and mainstream. What feeling rules (Hochschild 1979) govern interactions in the professionalized, Washington-based organizations that have come to dominate the movement field? Such organizations offer valuable sites in which to investigate the political functions of "cool" emotions.

Finally, although I have mentioned studies of movement cultures in European countries, the vast majority of my examples have come from American movements. This reflects the fact that, with the exception of new social movement theories, most models of social movements have been based on American cases. Where scholars have turned to non-US movements, however, they have found reason to modify the models. This suggests that, should we look outside the United States, we may find very different answers to the questions I have posed about the sources of movement culture and the obstacles to realizing countercultural values.

There is another reason for studying movement cultures outside the US. Scholars of culture have been rightly wary of efforts to delineate national and regional cultures since they seem to imply that such cultures are unitary, along the lines of a Dutch or American or South African "character." However, the coalition work that has become central to transnational protest—coalition work that is often made difficult by so-called "cultural differences"—provides a vital opportunity to see how national and regional cultures are performed and experienced.

References

Blee, K. 2002. *Inside Organized Racism: Women in the Hate Movement.* Berkeley: University of California Press.

Bordt, R. 1997. *The Structure of Women's Nonprofit Organizations.* Bloomington: Indiana University Press.

Breines, W. 1989. *Community and Organization in the New Left, 1962–1968: The Great Refusal.* New Brunswick, NJ: Rutgers University Press.

Disney, J.L. and Gelb, J. 2000. "Feminist Organizational 'Success': The State of U.S. Women's Movement Organizations in the 1990s." *Women and Politics* 21: 39–76.

Freeman, J. 1973. "The Tyranny of Structurelessness." In A. Koedt, E. Levine, and A. Rapone, eds., *Radical Feminism.* New York: Quadrangle Books.

Goodwin, J. 1997. "The Libidinal Constitution of a High-Risk Social Movement: Affectual Ties and Solidarity in the Huk Rebellion, 1946 to 1954." *American Sociological Review* 62: 53–69.

Groves, J. 2001. "Animal Rights and the Politics of Emotion: Folk Constructions of Emotion in the Animal Rights Movement." In J. Goodwin, J.M. Jasper, and F. Polletta, eds., *Passionate Politics: Emotions and Social Movements.* Chicago: University of Chicago Press.

Hall, J.R. 1988. "Social Organization and Pathways of Commitment: Types of Communal Groups, Rational Choice Theory, and the Kanter Thesis." *American Sociological Review* 53: 679–92.

Hart, S. 2001. *Cultural Dilemmas of Progressive Politics: Styles of Engagement among Grassroots Activists.* Chicago: University of Chicago Press.

Hochschild, A. 1979. "Emotion Work, Feeling Rules, and Social Structure." *American Journal of Sociology* 85: 551.

Iannello, K. 1992. *Decisions without Hierarchy.* New York: Routledge.

Jasper, J. 2004. "A Strategic Approach to Collective Action." *Mobilization* 9: 1–16.

Kanter, R.M. 1968. "Commitment and Social Organization: A Study of Commitment Mechanisms in Utopian Communities." *American Sociological Review* 33: 499–517.

Kleinman, S. 1996. *Opposing Ambitions: Gender and Identity in an Alternative Organization.* Chicago: University of Chicago Press.

Lichterman, P. 1996. *The Search for Political Community: American Activists Reinventing Commitment.* New York: Cambridge University Press.

McCarthy, J.D., Britt, D.W., and Wolfson, M. 1991. "The Institutional Channeling of Social Movements by the State in the United States." *Research in Social Movements, Conflicts, and Change* 13: 45–76.

Mansbridge, J. 1983. *Beyond Adversary Democracy*. Chicago: University of Chicago Press.

Matthews, N. 1994. *Confronting Rape: The Feminist Anti-Rape Movement and the State*. New York: Routledge.

Melucci, A. 1989. *Nomads of the Present: Social Movements and Individual Needs in Contemporary Society*. Philadelphia: Temple University Press.

Mollin, M. 2006. *Radical Pacifism in Modern America: Egalitarianism and Protest*. Philadelphia: University of Pennsylvania Press.

Morris, A.D. 1984. *The Origins of the Civil Rights Movement: Black Communities Organizing for Change*. New York: Free Press.

Nepstad, S.E. 2008. *Religion and War Resistance in the Plowshares Movement*. New York: Cambridge University Press.

Polletta, F. 2002. *Freedom is an Endless Meeting: Democracy in American Social Movements*. Chicago: University of Chicago Press.

Soule, S. 2004. "Diffusion Processes within and across Movements." In D. Snow, S.A. Soule, and H. Kriesi, eds., *The Blackwell Companion to Social Movements*. Malden, MA: Blackwell.

Staggenborg, S. 1995. "Can Feminist Organizations Be Effective?" In M.M. Ferree and P.Y. Martin, eds., *Feminist Organizations*. Philadelphia: Temple University Press.

Taylor, V. 1989. "Social Movement Continuity: The Women's Movement in Abeyance." *American Sociological Review* 54: 761–75.

Touraine, A. 1981. *The Voice and the Eye*. Cambridge: Cambridge University Press.

Whittier, N. 1995. *Feminist Generations: The Persistence of the Radical Women's Movement*. Philadelphia: Temple University Press.

Wood, L.J. 2007. "Breaking the Wave: Repression, Identity and the Seattle Tactics." *Mobilization* 12(4): 377–88.

Young, M. 2006. *Bearing Witness against Sin: The Evangelical Birth of the American Social Movement*. Chicago: University of Chicago Press.

62

Cultural movements and the sociology of culture

The case of political consumerism

Sam Binkley

In what follows, I seek to clarify the term "cultural movements," which is often used in a casual and imprecise manner. Cultural movements are not well understood in the field of cultural sociology, and the term is often applied anecdotally to such processes as artistic or style trends, to social changes of various kinds, or to activist movements. In fact, the imprecise use of this term is partly attributable to the considerable attention paid to two neighboring sociological concepts—cultural change and social movements (Rucht and Neidhardt 2002; Melucci 1984; Hall *et al.* 2003: 257). But whereas "cultural change" signals very general patterns of gradual, incremental, and unintended shifts in cultural sensibilities, and "social movements" designates the coordinated efforts of formal collectivities to effect specific legislative and social reforms, cultural movements can be understood as *the generally intentional and loosely collectivized efforts of groups or networks of individuals, to effect gradual and subtle shifts in the habits and sensibilities that shape their own everyday conduct and the everyday conducts of others.* Cultural movements are not unintended processes of cultural change, nor are they intended strategies targeting social or legislative reform through cultural methods. They are intended patterns of cultural transformation resulting from the innovations and disseminations of a group with restricted membership or a cultural vanguard. Participants in such movements foster collective identities around a shared program concerned with the reproduction, innovation, and circulation (and in some cases gatekeeping) of a cultural style, understood as a way of living, a way of acting in and experiencing the world, and a way of relating to oneself and to others.

In this essay, I develop a more complete analysis of cultural movements through the following steps: first, I offer a definition of cultural movements that emphasizes the ideal-typical status of the term and the inevitable blending that occurs between cultural movements and the neighboring concepts already mentioned—social movements and cultural change (pp. 650–51). Next, consideration of one important condition required for the emergence of a cultural movement—that culture itself appear to actors as a flexible rather than fixed feature of social life—will lead to a discussion of one particularly relevant theoretical framework for the study of cultural movements, centered on societal reflexivity as a condition linked to modernization processes themselves (Giddens 1991; Beck 1992) (pp. 651–54). On the basis of this understanding, I will discuss some empirical considerations of cultural movements in relation to more pragmatically oriented social movements, particularly those emerging in the culturally rich fields of consumption and commodity culture (pp. 654–56). The latter phenomena, termed "anti-consumerist movements," variously combine cultural and reformist agendas (Binkley and Littler 2008; Littler 2008). Finally, this chapter will conclude with a reflection on some of the limitations that confront efforts to use the lens of reflexive modernity to understand anti-consumerist cultural movements (pp. 656–57).

What is a cultural movement?

Examples of cultural movements range from the Reformation and Counter-Reformation to the Enlightenment, the New Deal (or at least certain tendencies within it), the student movement of the 1960s, and the lifestyle movements of the 1970s (Turner 2006; Binkley 2007). More contemporary cases might include ravers attempting to reclaim urban space through spontaneous street parties, radical food activists maintaining websites and organizing potlucks, anarchist urban cyclists whose unplanned journeys through busy urban centers are meant to renew civic spirit, and even hate groups attempting to spread their gospel through websites and anonymous graffiti (Duncombe 2007; Levin 2002; Cherry 2006). All of these examples involve the intentional, shared efforts of loosely affiliated individuals to affect the way people live and think, through the production and dissemination of culture.

Having said this, of course, it is necessary to make certain qualifications. The most obvious concerns the ideal-typical status of the term cultural movement: one seldom, if ever, discovers a cultural movement that is not imbricated with other processes and practices, if not formal organizations and institutions. In fact, it is possible to identify, for analytical purposes, three general ways in which cultural movements might be linked with other phenomena. The first concerns overlap with those more formalized and pragmatically oriented social movements mentioned earlier, more recently described as "new social movements" (Melucci 1984). For example, the student movement of the 1960s encouraged large populations to adopt its distinct personal sensibility and way of life, but it also linked to a network of small formal organizations, and trained its mobilizing efforts on a range of concrete policy reforms from the war in Vietnam to civil rights legislation. In this example and more generally, cultural and social movements are only analytically distinguishable.

A second area of empirical overlap concerns how cultural movements can become bound up with the background processes of cultural change against which they emerge. For example, Jackson Lears (1981) has described the emergence, among the American elite classes of the late Victorian period, of an arts-and-crafts movement derived in part from the writings of John Ruskin and William Morris—a development that was linked to a gradual and widespread erosion of the legitimacy of that class across American society, stemming from a rising labor militancy and the encroachment of new technologies. Similarly, Warren Belasco (1989) has studied the emergence of a "counter-cuisine," or a movement for an alternative food culture among counterculturalists of the 1960s, not as a singular episode undertaken by a limited cultural vanguard, but as part of a wider cultural response to the increasing presence of mass-produced goods in American life. As these examples suggest, cultural movements very frequently articulate with not only social movements, but also wider, more gradual processes of cultural change.

A third point of combination makes it even more difficult to tease cultural movements apart from other phenomena. Background cultural processes both create the conditions for cultural movements and explain variations among them. Thus, we have to understand how these changes impact the specific ways in which individuals see culture itself. Background cultural processes must be capable of explaining, not only the sentiments and sensibilities that define the contents of culture, but the deeper social and cultural logics that *make culture conspicuous to individuals*. To understand how it is that individuals come to see culture as something to reflect upon, to innovate, to struggle over, or to proselytize to other groups, we must approach cultural movements with an expanded theoretical and conceptual tool-kit capable of bringing into focus the very general, macro-level processes by which the taken-for-grantedness of everyday lifeworlds is disrupted. One way these processes have been theorized is by way of what sociologists term "reflexive modernity," which describes an incremental and very general process by which the capacity of actors to think and act *reflexively* about culture itself increases alongside other societal processes identified with the spread of modernity. Under reflexive modernization, people tend to consider previously taken-for-granted aspects of their everyday lives and cultural habits not as given, fixed, and inevitable facts, but as pliable, plastic objects, as things to be modified and changed, as the potential stakes of social contests, and therefore as resources in the fashioning of cultural movements (Maffesoli 1996).

However, it would be reductionistic to suggest that reflexivity, as the inclination to examine and modify the seemingly natural features of cultural life and therefore to mobilize culture in the service of a cultural movement, is an effect that follows logically, evenly, and inevitably with the onset of reflexive modernity. Again, we are on the terrain of ideal-typical characterizations: the pure case of a cultural movement resulting from the onset of reflexive modernity might never appear. The value of the concept stems not only from its ability to explain cultural movements, but also from its capacity to enable comparisons between varying cases, and to consider those cases in which such movements remain entirely dormant. To explore these possibilities, I now take up the question of societal reflexivity as a frame through which cultural movements can be understood, before considering articulations of cultural movements, social movements, and cultural change through an empirical discussion of political consumerism.

Cultural movements, cultural change, and reflexivity

Culture, in one of its most widely accepted meanings, describes those commonplace knowledges, habits, and taken-for-granted understandings that enable us to get through everyday social life (Swidler 1998). Culture is, as Raymond Williams put it, "a particular way of life," combining un-thought habits and accepted ways of doing things with those rational and intentional decisions and calculations that orient our actions (Williams 1976: 90). Thus, a significant part of cultural life is contained in those un-thought habits, in those knowledges and competencies that are both intuitive *and* rational, both felt *and* known, and for this reason tend to precede and exclude the kind of conscious, reflexive intentionality we associate with the concept of a "movement." This formulation leaves open the question of how cultural movements come about. For people to become mobilized around culture—around mundane choices in food, dress, music, domestic life, or partner choice—some measure of reflection must be brought to bear on that which

651

typically passes as a pre-reflexive, taken-for-granted aspect of the everyday. Cultural sociologists have offered varying explanations for how such reflection develops.

First we will consider those explanations that stress the denaturalization of the taken-for-grantedness of culture through trauma, crisis, and abrupt social change. Culture remains pre-reflexive under conditions that are sedentary, beyond our control, that demand little thought, that give us fewer choices, and in which we can move along on "automatic pilot." Ann Swidler describes these as the conditions of a "settled life," in which "the undisputed authority of habit, normality, and common sense" remains undisturbed (1998: 181). However, under conditions of societal flux, where people encounter unfamiliar conditions or have their expectations rattled for whatever reason, they become more cognizant of those aspects of their lives that they had previously taken for granted. Where lives become unsettled, Swidler writes: "cultural meanings are more highly articulated and explicit, because they model patterns of action that do not come naturally" (1998: 185). It is under these unsettled conditions that culture itself can become a conspicuous object, something to fight for and fight about, and something around which a cultural movement might take shape.

Pierre Bourdieu has provided one of the best known formulations of this condition in his account of the cultural *habitus*—a set of naturalized habits and competencies that people use to get through life's challenges and tasks, like choosing food, getting dressed, appreciating art or going shopping (Bourdieu 1984; 1977: 93). For Bourdieu, people inhabit these cultural competencies just as they inhabit their bodies, with little self-awareness or reflection. However, there are conditions under which the naturalness of cultural dispositions gives way, and people are forced to adopt a reflexive regard for what had previously passed unreflexively. Under those conditions Swidler described as "unsettled," where the fit between habitus (people's embodied sense of how to get by) and the social fields in which people live and act falls out of synch, people begin to think about and question the way they do things. Cultural styles and taken-for-granted ways of getting by suddenly seem obvious, as things to work on and change, and in some cases to advocate and struggle over (McNay 1999).

Such an account provides tremendous advantage in understanding those episodes in which the stuff of culture emerges as the object of a cultural movement. When global patterns of migration, for example, sweep people from one continent to another, they are likely to become aware of the cultural ways they have been forced to abandon, and perhaps set out to resurrect or preserve these ways, or even to mobilize them in a struggle for dignity and recognition. Bourdieu describes this effect: "Habitus has its 'blips,' critical moments when it misfires or is out of phase: the relationship of immediate adaptation (between habitus and field) is suspended, in an instant of hesitation into which there may slip a form of reflection which ... remains turned towards practice and not towards the agent who performs it" (Bourdieu 2000: 162).

However, many of the "blips" that trouble the habitus of participants in cultural movements do not come from specific traumatic episodes in which lives are unsettled, but are more deeply woven into the social and cultural fabrics of modern societies themselves. Viewed through the macro-sociological lens provided by theorists of reflexive modernization, some measures of reflexivity come part and parcel (if unevenly and in varying and distinct forms) with the wider effects of transition from traditional to modern societies (Beck 1992; Giddens 1991; Beck *et al.* 1994). This general theory can be briefly sketched: under the conditions of traditional society, levels of cultural reflexivity tend to be quite low. Meanings tend to be more fixed and immutable, with fewer opportunities for the production of new meanings or novel interpretations, and thus lower levels of awareness of culture as such. This circumstance likely occurred in medieval Europe, for example, where adherence to church doctrine or allegiance to a monarch was not a question of subjective interpretation or individual choice, but was simply a given characteristic of group life. Similarly, under the conditions of industrial modernity the categories of class membership and the meta-narrative of modern progress instilled a sense of belonging, and certainty and moral coherence seemed like stable facts of daily life. However, with the breakup of industrial modernity and the transition to post-industrial societies, with increasing cosmopolitanism, individualization, social and geo-graphic mobility, the expansion of consumer markets, and what Peter Berger calls the "pluralization of lifeworlds" (all the elements that compose the wider trajectory of social modernization), people experience a greater range of cultural options, and hence wider latitude for the interpretation and practice of culture itself. Citizens of postmodern or late modern societies have to make choices between cultural options, in their clothing styles, television programs, and musical preferences. In short, they become aware of and think about culture *as such* (Bauman 2000). Indeed, as economies and social structures depend more on agreements and group memberships orchestrated around cultural choices than shared material conditions of life, fashionings of such cultural choices become crucial for group membership and personal identity, replacing traditional categories of economic class with new groupings centered on lifestyle and cultural capital.

Such changes, theorists of reflexive modernity tell us, are not localizable within the episodes of "unsettled" lives, though they do impose a similar effect shaking up people's everyday lives, by creating a gap between habitus and field that invites ongoing unease and reflection. Indeed, the state of being constantly compelled to choose—without being furnished or guided by any overarching framework within which such choices might be read as valuable or necessary—yields a sense of permanent anxiety and insecurity. As consumers of culture, people are prey to painful moral ambiguities and to a sense of "ontological insecurity" in everyday life, a truth Giddens has summarized with the maxim "today we have no choice but to choose" (Giddens 1991: 81). In short, reflexivity instituted under conditions of a generalized modernity (as distinct from the unsettling episodic "blips" described by Swidler and Bourdieu) instills a unique emotional quality in the lives of individuals. This quality motivates them and draws them together in ways that cannot be explained as the results of either specific traumatic episodes or their shared structural locations within society. Indeed, the phenomenon of cultural insecurity seems potentially useful for a general explanation of how cultural movements come about and how variations among cultural movements occur.

For Giddens, reflexive modernity is Janus faced: while higher reflexivity undercuts tradition and introduces insecurity, it also frames possibilities for new forms of collective action, this time focused around everyday life choices. It orients individuals toward commonly experienced problems, giving them a common stake around which to mobilize. A generalized experience of insecurity helps to explain why people with no common structural investments or shared history of trauma (such as vegans, animal rights activists or sex radicals, or, to recall earlier examples, anarchist cyclists or even racists) might group together around cultural problems that seem to have no specific structural constituency.

Indeed, the standpoint of reflexive modernity provides an essential part of an explanation for the emergence of cultural movements as specifically collective projects: participants in such a movement purport to attend to a unique crisis of meaning in personal life resulting from pluralization and choice, even as they employ the tactics of cultural choice that are themselves part of the process that produced the crisis of meaning itself. For example, politicized shoppers come together to confront a sense of loss of meaning (though seldom expressed so directly) partly traceable to the expansion of consumer options in everyday life by undertaking specifically politicized patterns of shopping. Giddens develops the term "life politics" to describe such movements, which are fundamentally distinct from traditional emancipatory political movements. Whereas the latter express "a generic outlook concerned above all with liberating individuals and groups from constraints which adversely affect their life chances" (Giddens 1991: 210), life politics begins by assuming the capacity to reflect on and choose among cultural options in daily life, and aims at manifesting possibilities for self-realization and the replenishment of meaning by thinking more carefully about how specifically those choices are to be made: "Life politics does not primarily concern the conditions which liberate us in order to make choices: it is a politics *of* choice" (Giddens 1991: 214).

In short, life politics becomes collective—that is, becomes a cultural movement—as the crisis of meaning resulting from the over-pluralization of life choices in modern society is discovered to be shared among individuals, even though such individuals may share no common structural location in society. Thus, just as it is possible to read sexual politics as a response to the opening up of unprecedented sexual choice, it is also possible to read racist movements as reactions against cultural pluralization. Both movements promote a politics expressed in a unique lifestyle choice, aimed at the enhancement of personal meaning in cultural life.

Together, the ideal-typical categories established by reflexive modernization theory and the discussion of the unsettling of an actor's habitus take us some distance in understanding cultural movements and accounting for their variation: where cultural movements occur, we can explain them by looking for the specific ways in which culture became obvious to participants, as a consequence of either specific trauma or generalized reflexivity. However, neither of these factors alone is sufficient to explain cultural movements, because neither can account for the full range of cultural patterns within the lives of any individual or group that might be said to have become unsettled or reflexive. Reflexivity in one realm does not necessarily imply reflexivity in another. Social life is simply too various and multifaceted to be enfolded within one explanatory scheme. By way of an explanation of this unevenness, I will turn to a discussion of the case of anti-consumerist cultural movements.

Political consumerism as a cultural movement

The realm of consumption defines a broad cultural field: everyday habits of spending, daily provisioning, saving, window shopping, desiring, and fantasizing about goods are mediated by a persuasive and at time phantasmagoric discourse that variously touches on questions of identity, social life, the body, and community. This domain constitutes a field of cultural practice in which social actors employ knowledge and competencies of which they are scarcely aware—judgments, preferences, loyalties, literacies, and powers of interpretation and appropriation that are embodied unreflexively. Or nearly so. The field of consumption (while not alone in this respect) is also the scene of pluralization *par excellence*, fostering unique expressions of reflexivity and the unsettling of personal life, through the sheer magnitude of the choices on offer (Micheletti 2003). How do we explain variation between cases in which reflexivity emergent within fields of consumption develops into a full blown cultural movement, versus others that do not? A speculative and somewhat anecdotal sketch of some anti-consumerist movements will suggest an answer.

In January of 2007, members of the activist group Greenpeace set upon Apple's flagship store in downtown San Francisco with flyers intended to raise public awareness of the hazardous materials used in the manufacture of Apple products. To make their point, the activists flooded the façade of the Apple store with green light from a portable projector, producing an image that was captured and reproduced by news media worldwide (Greenpeace USA 2007). Similar actions were carried out in locations from New York City to Austin, Texas. The group's literature and website highlighted the shortcomings of Apple's environmental policies, which included: the continued use of brominated fire retardants (BFRs) and polyvinyl chloride (PVC) in the manufacture of their products; the product's short lifespan, and the inefficiency of the company's product take-back programs. After continued pressure, Apple CEO Steve Jobs announced a "greener apple," pledging to phase out the use of hazardous materials in all products by 2009 (Martellaro 2006).

In this case, consumers turned activists perceived the givenness of a mundane, everyday choice—the disposal of a worn-out iPod—as the occasion for an intervention intended to change the ways in which others think and live (even as this cultural effort was combined, as previously noted, with the objectives of a social movement). Although it is difficult to argue that they were operating according to any perceived shared interest or common experience of dislocation or trauma, their responses were orchestrated around a more general value: a shared crisis of meaning, which they perceived to be the underlying emptiness and meaninglessness of a cherished commodity icon. This case illustrates how a reflexivity specific to a field of consumption might gain sufficient traction to foster a cultural movement.

Yet the deficits and limitations of a theory of reflexive modernity for the study of cultural movements must also be considered. Such theories have been criticized for essentializing the cultural logics of modernization processes, overlooking local variations of these logics, and falsely universalizing a model of modernization, which may have impacts on the lives of individuals far more uneven than the theories' proponents admit (Alexander 1996). Yet these limitations do not invalidate the reflexive-modernity thesis entirely, but only point out its ultimately ideal-typical status.

To explore these limitations empirically, let us discuss two cases—schematically and for purposes of illustration—in which the highly reflexive realm of consumer culture is combined with the more traditional and less reflexive domains of religion and nationalism.

In 2002, a Dubai-based company launched a new cola beverage, Mecca Cola. Packaged and designed specifically to replicate Coca-Cola, Mecca Cola was created with the intention of challenging US-based beverage dominance—and, with it, US economic dominance more generally—throughout the Arab world (Tagliabue 2002). More innocuous examples of Muslim-themed consumer products can be traced back as far as the 1950s, but the post-9/11 introduction of Mecca Cola signaled a new development in this product category that connected with a renewed sense of anti-Americanism amongst Muslims with the onset of the Iraq war. Moreover, the creator of Mecca Cola, Tawfik Mathlouth, a French entrepreneur of Tunisian heritage, set out specifically with the philanthropic and ideological goal of aiding the people of Palestine, pledging to contribute a portion of all Mecca Cola sales to Islamic Aid, a non-profit group that supports development projects in Palestine. The product currently sells well throughout the Arab world and to Muslim communities throughout Europe, and has since been followed by two popular Muslim cola beverages, Muslim Up and Quibla, all of which are reported to be selling well (*BBC News* 2002). While it is certainly the case that the success of Mecca Cola is partially attributable to the simple logic of capitalist innovation and the savvy of marketing experts, it is important to avoid reducing this phenomenon to such economic forces alone. The success of this product in such a highly competitive category, particularly where the product itself is so clearly identified with the shared political objectives and collective membership of a transnational Islamic community, requires an understanding of lifestyle choice as the site of shared reflexivity and collective efforts to affect cultural meanings.

To take a very different case from a very different time, the word "Swadeshi" indicates a popular movement among Indian nationals during the movement for independence from British rule, centered on new habits of daily provisioning and consumer choice, on the renewal of traditional methods of manufacture, and on the importance of localized markets for commodity exchange (Kumar Dasgupta 1996: 21–30). The term itself suggests a powerful combination of personal ethics and nationalist sentiment: made through the combination of two Sanskrit words, "swa," meaning "self," and "desh," meaning "land our country." The combined connotation of "self-rule" assumed a double meaning, emphasizing personal and local autonomy and self-reliance, but also the independence and self-reliance of the greater Indian state. To practice Swadeshi was to produce and consume goods only for local markets according to pre-colonial, pre-industrial techniques of manufacture, thus affirming Mahatma Gandhi's vision of a modern India composed of self-reliant localized economic hubs (Michelettii 2003: 40–42).

What is distinct about the cases of Swadeshi and Mecca Cola is the emphasis placed not on the highly individualistic concerns with personal anxiety and meaning that are the center of life politics within consumer movements, but on the persistence of traditional cultural themes that, counter to the pronouncements of some proponents of reflexive modernization theory, do not melt into air with the first hint of modernization. This persistence is not limited to non-Western cases (it would have been possible to invoke cases in a developed capitalist country of "Buy American" campaigns among auto-consumers), and it thus suggests a more general limitation of the theory of reflexive modernity. Moreover, the persistence of strong traditional concerns and their deep imbrication with anti-consumerist cultural movements suggest the unevenness with which a macro-level societal process might touch upon any specific life. Thus, no broad-brush approach to the study of cultural movements is possible.

Conclusion

This essay has centered on the use of the concept of cultural movements as a specific ideal type, and has developed an understanding of cultural movements as always con-junctural, always articulated together with social movements, cultural processes, and the effects of macro-level societal transformations. My definition of cultural movements has stressed the reflexive character of such movements, wherein the taken-for-grantedness of culture itself is questioned, denaturalized, and laid open to appropriation and use. I have discussed the specific character of this reflexivity in relation to two principal theoretical approaches. On the one hand, culture may become conspicuous to actors as the focus of a cultural movement when the lives of such actors are unsettled by sudden change, when the taken-for-granted competencies of habitus lose their fit with the objectives of a given social field. Alternately, through the prism of a theory of reflexive modernity, I have highlighted how a more general pluralization of cultural options induces awareness of culture, introducing a crisis in the meaning of culture while creating the conditions for collective action around that perceived lack of meaning through a shared program of "life politics."

I have provided only an overview of the phenomenon of cultural movements, offering only cursory answers to key questions best addressed through careful empirical work. Most importantly, I have said little about variations among cultural movements, or about how specific cultural movements around distinct cultural and political objectives mobilize individuals and groups experiencing disruption of their everyday habitus. Illustrative cases drawn from the field of anti-consumerist cultural movements have pointed toward the need for further analysis of the empirical conditions under which reflexivity emerges, along with the importance of grasping the uniqueness of those conditions if a sociology of cultural movements is to escape theoretical determinism. More empirical research remains to be done before distinct variations among cultural movements can be fully understood.

References

Alexander, Jeffrey. 1996. "Critical Reflections on 'Reflexive Modernization'." *Theory Culture Society* 13: 133.

Bauman, Zygmunt. 2000. *Liquid Modernity*. Cambridge: Polity Press.

BBC News. 2002. "Islamic Cola 'Selling Well in Saudi'." *BBC News World Edition*, August 21. Available at http://news.bbc.co.uk/2/hi/middle_east/2207565.stm (accessed August 22, 2008).

Beck, Ulrich. 1992. *Risk Society*. Thousand Oaks, CA: Sage.

Beck, Ulrich, Giddens, Anthony, and Lash, Scott. 1994. *Reflexive Modernization: Politics, Tradition, and Aesthetics in the Modern Social Order*. Stanford, CA: Stanford University Press.

Belasco, Warren J. 1989. *Appetite for Change: How the Counterculture Took on the Food Industry, 1966–1988*. New York: Pantheon Books.

Binkley, Sam. 2007. *Getting Loose: Lifestyle Culture in the 1970s*. Durham, NC: Duke University Press.

Binkley, Sam and Littler, Jo. 2008. *Cultural Studies*, Special Issue on Anti-Consumerism, 22: 5–6.

Bourdieu, Pierre. 1977. *Outline of a Theory of Practice*. Cambridge: Cambridge University Press.

———. 1984. *Distinction: A Social Critique of the Judgement of Taste*, trans. R. Nice. Cambridge, MA: Harvard University Press.

———. 2000. *Pascalian Meditations*. Cambridge: Polity.

Cherry, Elizabeth. 2006. "Veganism as a Cultural Movement: A Relational Approach." *Social Movement Studies* 5(2): 155–70.

Duncombe, Stephen. 2007. *Dream: Re-Imagining Progressive Politics in an Age of Fantasy*. New York: The New Press.

Giddens, Anthony. 1991. *Modernity and Self-Identity*. Cambridge: Polity.

Greenpeace USA. 2007. "Exposing Apple's Core." Available at http://www.greenpeace.org/usa/news/greening-of-macworld-expo (accessed August 22, 2008).

Hall, John R., Neitz, Mary Jo, and Battani, Marshall. 2003. *Sociology on Culture*. New York: Routledge.

Kumar Dasgupta, Ajit. 1996. *Gandhi's Economic Thought*. New York: Routledge.

Lasch, Scott and Urry, John. 1993. *Economies of Signs and Space*. London: Sage.

Lears, Jackson. 1981. *No Place of Grace: Antimodernism and the Transformation of American Culture 1880–1920*. New York: Pantheon Books.

Levin, Jack. 2002. *The Violence of Hate*. Boston: Allyn & Bacon.

Littler, Jo. 2008. *Radical Consumption: Shopping Change in Contemporary Culture*. London: Open University Press.

McNay, Lois. 1999. "Gender, Habitus, and the Field." *Theory, Culture & Society* 16(1): 95–117.

Maffesoli, Michel. 1996. *The Time of the Tribes: The Decline of Individualism in Mass Society*. London: Sage.

Martellaro, John. 2006. "Greenpeace Demonstrates at Apple's Fifth Avenue Store in NY." *Mac Observer*, December 15. Available at http://www.macobserver.com/article/2006/12/15.9.shtml (accessed August 22, 2008).

Melucci, Alberto. 1984. "An End to Social Movements?" *Social Science Information* 23(4–5): 819–35.

Micheletti, Michele. 2003. *Political Virtue and Shopping: Individuals, Consumerism, and Collective Action*. New York: Palgrave.

Rucht, Dieter and Neidhardt, Friedhelm. 2002. "Towards a 'Movement Society'? On the Possibilities of Institutionalizing Social Movements." *Social Movement Studies* 1: 9–30.

Spillman, Lynette. 2002. *Cultural Sociology*. Malden, MA: Blackwell.

Swidler, Ann. 1998. "Culture in Action: Symbols and Strategies." In Philip Smith, ed., *The New American Cultural Sociology*. Cambridge: Cambridge University Press.

Tagliabue, John. 2002. "Choke On Coke, but Savor Mecca-Cola." *New York Times*, December 31.

Turner, Fred. 2006. *From Counterculture to Cyberculture: Stewart Brand, the Whole Earth Network*. Chicago: University of Chicago Press.

Williams, Raymond. 1976. *Keywords: A Vocabulary of Culture and Society*, revised edition. New York: Oxford University Press.

63

Migration and cultures

Yen Le Espiritu

US immigration studies have been greatly influenced by the historical production of immigrants as bearers of cultural difference. The dominant theories in the field—theories of assimilation (including segmented assimilation), amalgamation, the "melting pot," and cultural pluralism (or multiculturalism)—all conceptualize the immigrants' "original" culture as fundamentally opposed to native and white "American" culture. Though prescribing different outcomes, these immigration theories focus on the degrees of transformations of ethnic consciousness—that is, how much individuals or communities assimilate into American life or retain their community-of-origin ties. The present essay argues that this conceptualization of cultural identity—as bipolar and linear—promotes a discourse of race in which "cultural difference," defined as innate and abstracted from unresolved histories of racial inequality, is used to explain or explain away historically produced social inequalities. Here, I challenge the very authority and authenticity of the term "cultural identity," asserting instead that culture—or, more precisely, culture-making—is a social, historical, and transnational process that exposes multiple and inter-related forms of power relations and that articulates new forms of immigrant subjectivity, collectivity, and practice.

In the American sociology of race relations, Robert Park and the Chicago School of Sociology more generally have been most influential in extending a project of racial knowledge. This project, inaugurated by the science of man and twentieth-century anthropology, explicates the "immigrant problem" as a signifier of cultural difference. Allied with such intellectuals as anthropologist Franz Boas, the Chicago sociologists advocated a cultural rather than a biological definition of race. However, as Henry Yu points out, though University of Chicago sociologists claimed to eliminate biology as a consideration, they merely shifted the importance of the physical body into another realm (2001: 46). Because of their strong interest in the massive immigration in the nineteenth and early twentieth centuries, Chicago theorists such as Robert Park linked "cultural differences" with the foreign origins of certain human bodies: where one came from became an important element of one's cultural consciousness (Yu 2001: 47). This mapping of race reinscribes the "others of Europe" as "absolutely different"—and the cultures and geographies from which they come as fundamentally opposed to modern

American society (Silva 2007: 153; see also Lowe 1996: 5). In other words, when Park appropriates the "stranger" as a spatial metaphor to describe "the problem of race relations," he advances a project of knowledge that is "predicated on a definition of the exotic, of what is absolutely foreign and different about one place and another" (Yu 2001: 6). This approach effectively incarcerates the immigrants in culture, locking them in bounded, timeless, and unchanging "traditions."

Park's early twentieth-century rewriting of racial difference as a signifier of cultural difference is key here: by linking cultural consciousness not with the physical body, but with the body's origins in physical space, Park and his associates literally mapped where "cultural" groups existed in space, fixing their places in the world, *vis-à-vis* white America (Yu 2001: 47). Thus, the perceived origins of one's biological ancestors mattered: "the marginalization of the non-European immigrant is concomitant to the marginalization of the world he or she comes from—a country and culture viewed as alien, backward, poor, and unhappy" (Vassanji 1996: 112). To take an example, in the United States, Asia and America are viewed as mutually exclusive binaries—a primitive and stagnant East versus a modern and mobile West. The Orientalist construction of Asian cultures and geographies as fundamentally antipathetic to modern American society racializes the Asian American as the "foreigner-within"—always-already seen as an *immigrant*, even when born in the United States (Lowe 1996: 5–6). In the same way, anti-immigrant groups have consistently charged that the influx of unwanted immigrants will transform the United States into a Third-World nation. This reference to the "Third World" must be seen as a strategic marker that "metaphorically alludes to social evolution and the threat of immigration leading to a de-evolution of 'American civilization'" (Chavez 1997: 67). It was this tenet of Chicago School of Sociology, which posited the intimate connections between race, culture, and space, that profoundly marked many scholars' understandings of the process of immigrant adaptation and incorporation, informing the logic of both the assimilationist and pluralist perspectives.

Park's Americanization cycle—which theorized that two groups coming into contact always underwent a series of social interactions, beginning with competition and ending with assimilation—established an expectation that immigrants would assimilate and integrate into the dominant culture by shedding their "original" culture. Although this interaction cycle described the trajectory of many European immigrants, it could not explain the experiences of people belonging to subjugated "races and cultures" who simultaneously confronted the political pressure to assimilate and the cultural racism that prevented assimilation. By the 1960s, in light of the new social movements that exposed the material histories of racialization, segregation, and economic discrimination, the prescription of assimilation was revised into "multiculturalism," a new liberal vision that publicly affirmed and celebrated the kaleidoscope of cultures in American society. Scholarly research accordingly shifted from documenting assimilation toward explaining the persistence of ethnic cultures, mainly focusing on the continuing importance of ethnicity among white ethnics of European origin (Novak 1973; Cohen 1977). In an influential article on this topic, Herbert Gans (1979) argued that for the middle-class descendants of European immigrants, "symbolic ethnicity" is all that is left. These later-generation white ethnics, according to Gans, abstract ethnic symbols from the older "original" culture and look for easy and intermittent ways to express their ethnic identity—ways that do not require the rigorous practice of ethnic culture or active participation in ethnic organizations. But the influx of the largely non-European immigrants, precipitated by world upheavals and changes in US immigration law in 1965, raised an important research question: How much can we generalize from the experiences of white European ethnic groups to the experiences of racialized immigrant populations?

The post-1965 increases in racialized immigrant populations in the US—and the new social movements of the 1960s—transformed the academy, ushering in new subjects of social knowledge, but also new critical social knowledges. Contesting the depoliticization of culture, critical scholarship, especially in the emerging field of ethnic studies, rejected assimilation but also critiqued multiculturalism's aim to integrate differences, in the words of Lisa Lowe, as "*cultural* equivalents abstracted from the histories of racial inequality" (1996: 30). According to Lowe, the characterization of the United States as a "polyvocal symphony of cultures" leveled important differences and contradictions within and among racial and ethnic groups, deploying the liberal promise of inclusion to mask the history of exclusion. In other Western societies, where multiculturalism has been widely endorsed, however incompletely, public discourses similarly define the problem of immigrant integration as a cultural one, thus exempting the dominant society from any responsibility toward the "immigrant problem" (Ossman and Terrio 2006; Roggeband and Verloo 2007). Thus, the multiculturalism model, even as it challenges the inevitability and desirability of assimilation, constitutes ethnic cultures as temporally and geographically distant—much like the assimilation model propagated by Robert Park.

As Balibar and Wallerstein (1991) have pointed out, many advocates of multiculturalism, while endorsing cultural diversity, cast culture as primordial, fixed, and homogeneous, thereby ascribing certain immutable traits to the peoples within these presumed cultural groupings. This conception of culture assumes that a natural identity exists between people and places, and that discrete peoples belong to specific, bounded territories, which frame their distinct cultures and local identities. Thus, in a case study of Vietnamese American students in New Orleans, Min Zhou and Carl Bankston (1998) argue that the youth's achievement is rooted in their "core cultural values"—a strong work ethic, high regard for education, and family values, that is, in their "difference." Other scholars have critiqued this essentialization of culture—the idea that it is a bounded and internally consensual system into which one is born and integrated—and warned that the exclusive focus on cultural difference obscures the connections between the cultural and the material (Roggeband and Verloo 2007). In a study of the riots waged by frustrated and disenfranchised suburban immigrant youths in France in 2005, Ossman and Terrio (2006) denounced the discourse of cultural essentialism that undergirded public reaction to the rioting youths. They reported that key French institutions—legal, political, social scientific, and media—linked the causes of "immigrant delinquency" to what they identified as the culture of poverty of immigrant neighborhood enclaves. Noting the influence of the Chicago School of Sociology's cultural-ecology model on this public framing of the riots, Ossman and Terrio (2006) show how Parisian jurists and juvenile judges criminalized the cultural origin of the overwhelmingly poor children and families of non-European ancestry by linking their purported "delinquent" actions to "aberrant cultural norms and dangerous social milieus" (Ossman and Terrio 2006: 12). The Paris officials thus attributed the "immigrant problem" to the hegemony of people's culture of origin rather than to political and economic forces within the "new country." Ossman and Terrio argue that by reifying and criminalizing what was perceived to be the culture of these immigrant youth, culturalist policies set the stage for the deportation of immigrants as a new tool for defending the nation from external threats (2006: 14).

Some advocates of multiculturalism also produce gendered discourses and policies that construct patriarchy as particular to immigrant culture. In line with the global crusade for

661

women's rights, ratified by the 1979 Convention on the Elimination of all Forms of Discrimination against Women (CEDAW), scholars and the larger public became preoccupied with "harmful traditions" that allegedly abuse women in minority immigrant communities (Silva 2004). Over the past decade, in many countries, migrant women have appeared at the top of the political agenda. For example, in the Netherlands, gender equality policies have shifted to an almost exclusive focus on migrant (Muslim) women; and "minority policies" have moved more and more towards gender relations. As Roggeband and Verloo (2007) observe, Dutch official and popular discourses construct patriarchy as a signifier of migrant Muslim culture, which has the effect of shifting the responsibility for Muslim "failure" to fully integrate in Dutch society to Muslim migrants, and away from the dominant culture and society. Anti-immigration agendas in Britain have also become entangled with public initiatives to protect migrant women. Targeting the Muslim migrant community, the media have focused on four "cultural" issues affecting women—forced marriage, honor killing, female genital cutting, and women's Islamic dress. Dustin and Phillips (2008) contend that media treatment of these issues has been problematic, producing discourses that misrepresent Muslim cultural groups as monolithic and naturally oppressive entities. Thus, efforts that purport to address abuses of migrant women simultaneously promote cultural stereotypes, setting up women's rights in false opposition to multiculturalism.

In the United States, academic writings on immigrant family and gender relations, especially as they pertain to Asian and Latino communities, have also emphasized "an ethnically specific patriarchal culture," which freezes immigrant men as subjects who oppress women (Kang 2002: 43–44). For example, literary studies scholars (and the larger public) are fascinated with narratives about young immigrant girls coming to the United States and finding liberation. In her assessment of the critical work produced in response to Julia Alvarez's novel *How the Garcia Girls Lost Their Accent*, Sarika Chandra (2008) argues that the book is read almost exclusively so as to emphasize the girls' identity formation and self-assertion against the perceived overbearing and overprotective patriarchal old world of the Dominican Republic. Chandra argues that the near-exclusive focus on gender politics obscures the novel's engagement with the role of the United States in forcing the Garcias and other Dominicans to flee the island in the first place.

By conceptualizing intergenerational strain as a product of "cultural clash" between "traditional" immigrant parents and their more "modernized" US-born or raised children, rather than as a social, historical, and transnational affair, scholars represent the United States as self-evidently less sexist than the "old country" and they thus fail to expose the multiple and interrelated forms of power relations connecting the two countries.

A more dynamic approach to culture conceptualizes cultural identities not as an essence but as a *positioning*—"the names we give to the different ways we are positioned by, and position ourselves within, the narratives of the past" (Hall 1990: 225). Employing this approach, I have argued elsewhere that Filipino immigrants' cultural claims—that Filipino culture is more family oriented and thus morally superior to white American culture—constitute a strategy of resistance against the colonial racial denigration of their culture, community, and women (Espiritu 2003: 215). Instead of assuming that these cultural claims perfectly correspond to a bounded and static set of practices imported from the home country into the host society, I underscore the immigrants' ability to maneuver and manipulate meanings within the domain of culture in an effort to counter the alternative assumption of inevitable white American superiority. In the same way, Purkayastha (2005) explains young South Asian women's invocation of their homeland culture—specifically the closeness and sense of mutual obligation of their extended family relationships—as an effort to combat their cultural marginalization in the United States, which is based on culturalist stereotypes about arranged marriages and other presumed patriarchal South Asian practices. By stressing what they perceive to be positive South Asian cultural values, these young women manage "to compare their families to that of their peers in ways that *their* families become the norm and those of their peers 'flawed'" (Purkayastha 2005: 67). It is true that the immigrants' gendered discourse of moral superiority often leads to patriarchal calls for cultural "authenticity," which locates family honor and national integrity in its female members and renders them emblematic of the community's cultural survival (Espiritu 2003). However, this critique of patriarchal practices differs from the (multi)culturalist stereotyping of immigrant culture described on pp. 661–62 in that it positions culture in the shifting terrain of histories, economics, and politics. As this line of research shows, the multiculturalist approach to gender outlined on pp. 661–62 is problematic because it misrepresents "patriarchal culture" as indigenous to immigrant communities, rather than as a constantly negotiated strategy deployed by racialized immigrants to claim through gender the power denied them by racism.

In the same way, as numerous case studies of immigrant cultures demonstrate, many immigrants themselves appear to have internalized a definition of culture that is tied to homeland traditions and represented by a fixed profile of shared traits such as language, ethnic food, and folk songs. However, a more critical examination of these cultural claims indicates that the immigrants' seemingly reified comments about their own culture in fact refer to cultural practices that have been reconstituted and transformed in the host society. If we conceptualize culture not as a series of depoliticized and fixed attributes but as a set of evolving practices constituted within webs of power relations, then the immigrants' cultural claims are less about cultural authenticity and more about strategic self-representation, especially in the context of a hostile host society. For example, Nobue Suzuki (2002) reports that Filipina "mail order brides" in Japan respond to their dehumanization and eroticization by eagerly showcasing various aspects of "Filipino lifestyles and culture" at local schools and community events, including giving talks on their history, performing arts and crafts, and displaying their ethnic cuisine and dresses. By showing "the height of their culture," the women strategically tap into the Japanese gendered ideal of housewife and mother, in the hope that the Japanese audience will recognize the "elegance of the Filipinas" and accordingly "reformulate classificatory categories more analogous to their own subjective conceptualizations" (Suzuki 2002: 197). In another study, Sunaina Maira reports that in the post-9/11 racial climate of intensified hostility and scrutiny, South Asian Muslim teens in New England dealt with their liminal positions by fashioning everyday identifications with India or Pakistan through the consumption of popular culture found in Bollywood films, South Asian television programs, and Hindi music websites (Maira 2008: 708–09). Such longing to be more "authentically" tied to the "original" culture continues to be very powerful for immigrant youth because it is directed, in Franz Fanon's words, "by the secret hope of discovering beyond the misery of today, beyond self-contempt, resignation, and abjuration, some very beautiful and splendid era whose existence rehabilitates us both in regard to ourselves and in regard to others" (Fanon 1963: 170). Although these two examples appear to confirm a fixed concept of culture, they in fact demonstrate how immigrants deliberately and strategically memorialize and represent the "original" culture as a form of resistance to places and practices in the host country that are patently anti-immigrant.

In the last twenty-five years, the globalization of labor and capital, the restructuring of world politics, and the expansion of new technologies of communication and transportation all have driven people and products across the globe at a dizzying pace, thus further invalidating the notion of culture as spatially bounded. Recent writings on "transnational sociocultural systems," "the transnational community," "transmigrants," the "deterritorizalized nation-state," and "transnational grassroots politics" have challenged previously conventional notions of *place*, reminding us to think about places not only as specific geographic and physical sites but also as circuits and networks. These writings have contradicted localized and bounded social-science conceptualizations of community and culture, calling attention instead to the transnational relations and linkages among overseas communities, and between them and their homelands (Basch *et al.* 1994; Levitt 2001; Smith 2006). Living between the old and the new, between homes, between languages, and between cultural repertoires, immigrants do not merely insert or incorporate themselves into existing spaces in a given host society; they also transform these spaces and create new ones, for example the "space between" (Small 1997: 193). Transnationalism is thus a valuable concept that can be used as a tool to highlight the range and depth of migrants' lived experiences in multinational social fields, thus disrupting the narrow emphasis on cultural assimilation or cultural diversity characteristic of much of the published scholarship in US immigration studies.

A critical transnational perspective also provokes us to think beyond the limits of the nation-state, that is, to be attentive to the global relations that set the context for immigration and immigrant life. As a rhetorical strategy, multiculturalism, with its focus on culturalist identity politics, obscures the role of the United States and other receiving countries in producing the phenomenon of immigration. Because the framework of multiculturalism is "subordinated to and divorced from the historical and socioeconomic conditions of (im)migration" (Chandra 2008: 847), it cannot take into account the way that a long and continuing history of US imperialism shapes processes of migration, racialization, and marginality. Consider as a case in point the relationship of the Philippines and the United States: its origins lie in a history of conquest, occupation, and exploitation. A study of Filipino immigrant culture must begin with this history, and not with US domestic multicultural identity issues. Coming from a former US colony, Filipinos have long been exposed to US lifestyles, cultural practices, and consumption patterns, so much so that before "the Filipino ... sets foot on the U.S. continent—she, her body, and sensibility—has been prepared by the thoroughly Americanized culture of the homeland" (San Juan 1991: 118). With English as the imposed language of education in the Philippines came a flood, that reached all Filipinos, of US printed materials and mass media—textbooks, novels, news services, magazines, music, and especially movies. These cultural products infected Filipinos with American norms, standards, ideals, values, and viewpoints (Espiritu 2003: 72–73). Thus, in a critically acclaimed 1990 novel, *Dogeaters*, Jessica Hagedorn portrays neocolonial Manila, from about 1956 to 1985, as a world in which American popular culture and local Filipino tradition mix flamboyantly. In other words, Filipino culture is the always-already transnational, thus eliding easy localization.

By the opposite token, Amy Kaplan (1993) reminds us in an important essay that US imperialism contributes not only to the cultural Americanization of the colonized "other" but also to the consolidation of a dominant imperial culture at home.

George Lipsitz has made a similar point: US armed conflicts against "enemies" in Asia "functioned culturally to solidify and reinforce a unified U.S. national identity based in part on antagonism toward Asia and Asians" (1998: 72). These studies suggest that we need to examine migration and cultures not only for what they tell us about the integration of immigrants but more so for what they say about the racialized economic, cultural, and political foundations of the United States. In other words, migrant cultures and US national culture(s) are mutually constituted. By situating US national culture within a globalist framework, these scholars call attention to the deep entanglement of the domestic and the foreign, and thus to how both US national and immigrant cultures are shaping and being shaped by intersecting social and historical relationships. This scholarship suggests that a critical transnational perspective is not just a methodological approach; it is fundamentally a theoretical orientation. That is, it is not necessarily or only about doing multi-sited projects; it is more about linking the study of culture and immigration inextricably to the study of empire—even when the research focus is on the domestic front.

In an influential work on Asian American cultural politics, Lisa Lowe (1996) urges her readers to consider the role that critical cultural works play in exposing the racialized foundations of the nation. Calling attention to the importance of critical remembering, Lowe has argued a position also articulated by others, that "culture is a ... mediation of history, the site through which the past returns and is remembered, however fragmented, imperfect, or disavowed" (1996: x). For participants in racialized immigrant communities who have had to struggle for access to means of representation, she notes, "the question of aesthetic representation is always also a debate about political representation" (Lowe 1996: 4). As Elaine Kim (2003) suggests, many Asian American artists are committed to a cultural politics that challenges, resists, and hopes to transform US nationalized memory and culture. For instance, in recent years, Vietnamese American artists have begun to grapple with the war's disastrous consequences for Vietnam and its people, giving rise to oft-haunting artistic and cultural representations that imagine, remember, and trace the complex genealogies of war and forced displacements that precede and shape Vietnamese resettlement in the United States. In light of the "organized forgetting" of the Vietnam War and its people in US media, these Vietnamese American cultural forms are crucial for what they reveal about US military crimes in Southeast Asia and how they underwrite the tensions, irresolutions, and contradictions of Vietnamese American lives (Espiritu and Nguyen-Vo 2005).

For the most part, migration to the United States "has been the product of specific economic, colonial, political, military, and/or ideological ties between the United States and other countries ... as well as of war" (Ngai 2004: 10). And yet, much of the published work in the field of immigration studies has not situated US immigration history within a transnational or global framework, opting instead to focus on the immigrants' integration into the nation. This framework focused on "modes of incorporation" assesses the assimilability of the immigrants but leaves uninterrogated the racialized and gendered foundations of the United States. In this essay, I have argued that the scholarly focus on immigrants' integration—and the concomitant failure to connect US foreign interventions with US-bound migration—stems from the historical production of the immigrants as bearers of cultural difference. Today, many immigration studies scholars continue to invoke "cultural difference" to individualize and explain (away) immigrants' perceived "lacks," thereby eliding the role that "U.S. world power has played in the global structures of migration" (Ngai 2004: 11). In other words, the

665

essentializing and liberal tendencies of multiculturalism obscure the continuation of racial violence, both physical and symbolic, in the United States and globally. At this moment of reinvigorated US imperialism and soaring immigration to the United States, it is imperative that immigration studies scholars recognize and analyze the intimate connection between US foreign interventions and migration to the United States—to be mindful of what Amy Kaplan (1993) calls the "entanglement of the domestic and the foreign." To do so, we first need to link culture to history, economics, and politics in order to better scrutinize the United States as a historical entity with policies that play a key role in producing (im)migration.

References

Balibar, Etienne and Wallerstein, Immanuel. 1991. *Race, Nation, Class: Ambiguous Identities/Etienne Balibar and Immanuel Wallerstein*. London and New York: Verso.

Basch, Linda, Glick Schiller, Nina, and Szanton Blanc, Cristina. 1994. *Nations Unbound: Transnational Projects, Postcolonial Predicaments, and Deterritorialized Nation-States*. Langhorn, PA: Gordon and Breach.

Chandra, Sarika. 2008. "Re-Producing a Nationalist Literature in the Age of Globalization: Reading (Im)migration in Julia Alvarez's *How the Garcia Girls Lost Their Accents*." *American Quarterly* 60: 829–50.

Chavez, Leo R. 1997. "Immigration Reform and Nativism: The Nationalist Response to the Transnational Challenge." In Perea, ed., *Immigrants Out! The New Nativism and the Anti-Immigrant Impulse in the United States*. New York: New York University Press.

Cohen, Steven M. 1977. "Socioeconomic Determinants of Intraethnic Marriage and Friendship." *Social Forces* 55: 997–1010.

Dustin, Moira and Phillips, Anne. 2008. "Whose Agenda Is It? Abuses of Women and Abuses of 'Culture' in Britain." *Ethnicities* 8: 405–24.

Espiritu, Yen Le. 2003. *Home Bound: Filipino American Lives across Cultures, Communities, and Countries*. Berkeley: University of California Press.

Espiritu, Yen Le and Nguyen-Vo Thu-Huong, eds. 2005. Special issue, "30 Years AfterWARd: Vietnamese Americans & U.S. Empire." *Amerasia Journal* 31: 2.

Fanon, Frantz. 1963. "On National Culture." In *The Wretched of the Earth*. New York: Grove Press.

Gans, Herbert. 1979. "Symbolic Ethnicity: The Future of Ethnic Groups and Cultures in America." *Ethnic and Racial Studies* 2: 1–20.

Hagedorn, Jessica. 1990. *Dogeaters*. New York: Penguin.

Hall, Stuart. 1990. "Cultural Identity and Diaspora." In Jonathan Rutherford, ed., *Identity, Community, Culture, Difference*. London: Lawrence and Wishart.

Kang, Laura Hyun Yi. 2002. *Compositional Subjects: Enfiguring Asian/American Women*. Durham, NC and London: Duke University Press.

Kaplan, Amy. 1993. "'Left Alone with America': The Absence of Empire in the Study of American Culture." In Amy Kaplan and Donald E. Pease, eds., *Cultures of United States Imperialism*. Durham, NC and London: Duke University Press.

Kim, Elaine H. 2003. "Introduction: Interstitial Subjects—Asian American Visual Art as a Site for New Cultural Conversations." Pp. 1–50 in Elaine Kim, Margo Machida, and Sharon Mizota, eds., *Fresh Talk, Daring Gazes: Conversations on Asian American Art*. Berkeley: University of California Press.

Levitt, Peggy. 2001. *The Transnational Villagers*. Berkeley and Los Angeles: University of California Press.

Lipsitz, George. 1998. *The Possessive Investment in Whiteness: How White People Profit from Identity Politics*. Philadelphia: Temple University Press.

Lowe, Lisa. 1996. *Immigrant Acts: On Asian American Cultural Politics*. Durham, NC and London: Duke University Press.

Maira, Sunaina. 2008. "Flexible Citizenship/Flexible Empire: South Asian Muslim Youth in Post-9/11 America." *American Quarterly* 60: 697–720.

Ngai, Mae. 2004. *Impossible Subjects: Illegal Aliens and the Making of Modern America.* Princeton, NJ: Princeton University Press.

Novak, Michael. 1973. *The Rise of Unmeltable Ethnics: Politics and Culture in the Seventies.* New York: Macmillan Company.

Ossman, Susan and Terrio, Susan. 2006. "The French Riots: Questioning Spaces of Surveillance and Sovereignty." *International Migration* 44: 2.

Park, Robert. 1950. *Race and Culture.* Glencoe, IL: The Free Press.

Purkayastha, Bandana. 2005. *Negotiating Ethnicity: Second-Generation South Asian Americans Traverse a Transnational World.* New Brunswick, NJ: Rutgers University Press.

Roggeband, Conny and Verloo, Mieke. 2007. "Dutch Women Are Liberated, Migrant Women Are a Problem: The Evolution of Policy Frames on Gender and Migration in the Netherlands, 1995–2005." *Social Policy & Administration* 41: 271–88.

San Juan, E. Jr. 1991. "Mapping the Boundaries: The Filipino Writer in the U.S." *Journal of Ethnic Studies* 19: 117–31.

Silva, Denise. 2004. "Mapping Territories of Legality: An Exploratory Cartography of Black Female Subjects." In Patricia Truitt and Peter Fitzpatrick, eds., *Critical Beings: Race, Nation, and the Global Subject.* Aldershot, UK: Ashgate.

Silva, Denise Ferreira da. 2007. *Toward a Global Idea of Race.* Minneapolis: University of Minnesota Press.

Small, Cathy. 1997. *Voyages: From Tongan Villages to American Suburbs.* Ithaca, NY: Cornell University Press.

Smith, Robert Courtney. 2006. *Mexican New York: Transnational Lives of New Immigrants.* Berkeley and Los Angeles: University of California Press.

Suzuki, Nobue. 2002. "Women Imagined, Women Imaging: Re/presentation of Filipinas in Japan since the 1980s." In Filomeno V. Aguilar, Jr., ed., *Filipinos in Global Migrations: At Home in the World?* Quezon City: Philippine Migration Research Network and Philippine Social Science Council.

Vassanji, M.G. 1996. "Life at the Margins: In the Thick of Multiplicity." In D. Bahri and M. Vasudeva, eds., *Between the Lines: South Asians and Postcoloniality.* Philadelphia: Temple University Press.

Yu, Henry. 2001. *Thinking Orientals.* New York: Oxford University Press.

Zhou, Min and Bankston, Carl K. III. 1998. *Growing Up American: How Vietnamese Children Adapt to Life in the United States.* New York: Russell Sage.

64

Cultural diffusion

Elihu Katz

I

Long before there were media of mass communication, ideas and practices found ways to traverse vast distances. One would think that broadcasting and the internet would have superseded the interpersonal networks that are implicit here, but they have not; the media, new and old, have a share in the flow of influence, but they are only part of the process, even today. Diffusion research seeks to follow innovations as they spread, within and between social structures, over time and space. Focused on the flow of influence, diffusion research unravels the mix of formal advocacy, informal persuasion, identification, imitation, contagion, resistance, withdrawal, and the like. Thus, the study of diffusion amounts to observing the microdynamics—the "retailing," so to speak—of this more or less voluntary form of social and cultural change that is based on communication—in contrast, say, to simultaneous invention, evolutionary change, or change imposed by fiat or by force.

Interest in how ideas and things travel, and how they aggregate, is integral to most of the social sciences and the humanities, and to some of the natural sciences as well. Early anthropology and cultural history, for example, tried to trace the progress of civilization (monotheism, alphabet, etc.) from its supposed origin in the "fertile crescent." Anthropologists and geographers found interest in the spatial distribution of certain "traits" and in the direction of their movement. Rural sociologists have had a longstanding interest in the diffusion and adoption of new farm practices, and in the role of agricultural extension agencies in their promotion; for a while, they joined with anthropologists in fostering "modernization" overseas. Historians of religion have been fascinated by the rapid diffusion of Christianity and Islam in the old days, and nowadays in the spread of Mormonism and new-age doctrines. Linguists are interested in the geography of speech. Students of fashion, folklore, literature, art, and archeology have investigated the diffusion of style, while social scientists have tracked the diffusion of technical change, and lately of social movements. Social psychologists have long nurtured a passion for ostensibly unstructured forms of "collective behavior" that include news, rumor, gossip, crowds, moral panics, audiences, and public opinion. And, of course, epidemiologists of the flu or of HIV and other infectious diseases are continually occupied with the dynamics of their spread, and with the success of attempts to combat them. Meaning much the same thing, marketing researchers now speak of computer-driven word-of-mouth as "viral marketing." Even terrorist organizations seem to imitate each other's changing tactics.

Several of the classics of sociology have tried to generalize across these domains. Gabriel Tarde (1969 [1890]) went farthest, perhaps, in his *Laws of Imitation*, arguing (against his contemporary, Emile Durkheim), that sociology could ill afford to overlook invention and influence as the pathways of social change. In the same spirit, Georg Simmel (1957 [1904]) saw emulation as the engine of change whereby the symbolic striving for upward mobility led each social class to emulate the class above, thus constraining the upper classes to seek ever new ways to differentiate themselves. Thorstein Veblen's (1899) "conspicuous consumption" is obviously related. In rebuttal, Harvard sociologist Pitirim Sorokin (1941) rejected the idea of "trickle-down" diffusion in favor of a theory of exchange whereby the lower classes export "raw materials" such as cotton or folksongs to be processed and re-exported by the upper classes. Sorokin dwelled on the agents of diffusion such as missionaries, troubadours, traveling salesmen, and the like, on the routes they charted, and on their salesmanship, so to speak, all as part of his larger interest in social and cultural mobility. Innis (1951) studied the tension between media of space (papyrus, printing) and media of time (pyramids, canonic texts), and between custodians of existing knowledge and their challengers. Multiple editions of Everett Rogers's *Diffusion of Innovations* (1994) over a forty-year period catalog the increase in diffusion studies, as if to illustrate the "S-curve" that has come to characterize the trajectory of innovations that "take off." Gladwell's (2000) *The Tipping Point* has popularized the field, as have "small world" studies such as Milgram's (Travers and Milgram 1969), and, even earlier, Pool and Gurevitch (Gurevitch 1961). These classics, it should be noted, are flawed by an over-emphasis on "successful" innovations to the neglect of innovations that fail (cf. Mosse 1975; Strang and Soule 1998).

In spite of the seeming centrality of these concerns, it comes as a surprise that serious sociological studies of diffusion have been so sparse and so sporadic. While anthropologists, archeologists, and linguists may have continued uninterrupted, sociologists, geographers, and others seem to have abandoned the subject between the 1940s and the 1970s. This may be because Durkheim's macro sociological emphasis prevailed over Tarde's, or more likely because the prospect of media influence prevailed over the interpersonal. A still better explanation, however, is that the postwar surge of empirical sociology had not yet forged the tools to cope with the social networks that channel the flow of interpersonal influence. For example, it took some twenty years for Paul Lazarsfeld's Bureau of Applied Social Research at Columbia University to progress from rediscovery of the mediating role of interpersonal influence in the mass communications of change (Lazarsfeld *et al.* 1944) to the incorporation of full-blown social networks in the design of its research (Coleman *et al.* 1966). Methodologically, this amounted to a wedding of sociometry and survey research, made possible by the ever-increasing capacity of the high-speed computer to track the person-to-person transmission of information and influence. Diffusion research is now riding high on the coattails of the explosion of computational research in the social sciences (Watts 2003).

669

II

Given the resurgence of interest, it is all the more surprising that the several domains of diffusion research have shown so little recognition of each other, and of the underlying "accounting scheme" that they share (Katz *et al.* 1963). Yet, it is evident that, whatever the domain, the study of cultural diffusion may be characterized as (1) the reception, or adoption, (2) of some idea or innovation, (3) over time, (4) by units of adoption— individuals, groups, organizations, nations—linked by: (5) channels of communication, internal and external; (6) social structures; and (7) systems of norms and values.

Ostensibly, these components vary so widely from domain to domain that their comparability may be obscured. Who would think that the diffusion of hybrid corn seed among farmers in Iowa (Ryan and Gross 1942) might parallel the diffusion of a new antibiotic among physicians in four Midwestern towns (Katz 1971)? Yet they parallel each other very closely. Both studies aim to show how an innovation was introduced into a professional community, the "reception" it received, and the extent of its saturation. Both aimed to describe the role of the formal media and the extent to which interpersonal influence was active. Both wished to identify the parts played by exogenous influences, the early and late adopters, and the inside influentials, and the rate at which the innovation spread. As if following a shared "accounting scheme," both studies were able to date first use of each adopter (date of first prescription for MDs, season of first planting for farmers), to identify the socio-economic status of each and his/her sociometric location in the web of community relations, and to reconstruct the cognitive and communicative steps in the process of decision-making. In their conclusions, both studies found advertising and salespeople to be harbingers of the innovation, while later stages in the decision-making process were increasingly dependent on professional media and collegial talk. Both studies found evidence of interpersonal influence at work and a positive correlation between social status and time of adoption. However, this correlation is likely limited to innovations that are "compatible" with community norms, implying that innovations that are alien will follow a different trajectory (Menzel 1960).

A study of the diffusion of "nouvelle cuisine" among French restaurants makes similar points (Rao *et al.* 2003). In spite of its ostensible departure from tradition, the innovation was deemed compatible both with the egalitarian turn in the larger French culture and with the professional self-image of the most-highly rated chefs. Thus the path of acceptance proceeded from the highest-starred establishments in the *Guide Michelin* to the lesser-ranking ones, rather than following a revolutionary path. By contrast, the diffusion of jazz in the United States climbed the social ladder from the bottom up (Lopes 2002), while today's fashions, no longer dictated from Paris, have, according to Diana Crane (1999), altogether lost their sense of direction.

Broadly, two interlocking principles are operative here. The first is the principle of compatibility, and the second is social integration. For an innovation to gain acceptance, it must be seen to be compatible with community and personal norms. It must be proposed by trustworthy sources and delivered in culturally acceptable circumstances. It must be capable of operation by the social unit to which it is addressed. If it "takes a village," the village is the unit to address, just as the kibbutz (in the old days) insisted that members take their tea and coffee only in the communal dining hall (Spiro 1956). Reflecting the same principle, Christianity—with its patrilineal symbolism—fared better in patrilineal tribes than in matrilineal ones (Hawley 1946) and, similarly, the expressiveness of Italian culture contributed to the flourishing of early opera in Italy (R. Katz 1986).

When an innovation is perceived to defy group norms, the most marginal members of the group will be early to adopt, if at all. Individuals who are linked to more than one group may often serve as innovators and influentials, however weak their ties (Granovetter 1973; Burt 1999a). Altogether, social location—the boss's secretary, for example—may account for greater influentiality than gregariousness or interest in a particular domain. As a rule, influence is more likely to be exchanged among persons who share the same demographic characteristics (Weimann 1994). However, inasmuch as influentials, or "opinion leaders," require followers, the flow of influence may be asymmetrical. Thus, younger women are more likely than equally interested older women to be sought out for fashion advice. The reverse holds for grocery shopping, where the opinion leadership of older women is more likely to be sought, both by their age-peers and by younger women (Katz and Lazarsfeld 2006 [1955]). Sometimes, "epidemics" originate in certain segments of the population, as when children at school spread the flu virus, or when children serve as agents for linguistic change (Labov 2007).

Extending the channels of influence implicit in social location and social cohesion, relatively newer research has called attention to the imitative influence implicit in "structural equivalence" (Burt 1999b). The idea is that persons or groups situated in similar positions—connected to same or similar constituencies—will keep abreast of each other as far as innovativeness is concerned. One will do what the other does, as noble courts of the seventeenth and eighteenth centuries began to introduce the new medium of opera. This process began with the competitive appointment of resident composers, usually Italian, just as opera was making its way from its "origin" in Florence to other Italian cities (R. Katz 1986). In a similar manner, universities were popping up all over Europe, followed, much later, by football teams (Hobsbawm 1983). The same process is on view today in the parade of self-respecting cities that are clearing their slums to make space for "avenues of the arts." And sociologists are investigating the roles of diffusion and equivalence in the "isomorphism" of organizational structures (Dimaggio and Powell 1983).

Thus, the study of diffusion is well served by the aforementioned "accounting scheme," which contains both a checklist of relevant observations and a set of implicit hypotheses that connect them. Let us consider each of these elements in turn:

1 Reception must be parsed as to whether the potential adopter is aware of the item, is interested in it, has considered its adoption, has tried it, has continued use after trial, etc. The student of diffusion must settle on one of these definitions of acceptance or adoption—for instance, whether an individual has tried to stop smoking, or has actually stopped, or restarted. There is considerable interest in the question of which media are effective at each stage of the decision to adopt (Van den Bulte and Lilien 2004). These "levels" of internalization correspond to those theories of behavior change that posit stages in decision-making and to theories in which change is thought to entail a disconnect from an earlier norm or practice—such as cigarette smoking—before proceeding to another.

2 The attributes of the diffusing item must be scrutinized from the subjective points of view of potential adopters. For example, how "complex" is it (in the sense of how much else has to change if one adopts an innovation such as, say, homosexual "outing," or religious conversion, or vegetarianism)? Is the item packaged as part

of a "pattern" or system, or is it technical and relatively self-contained? Is the proposed change functional or primarily symbolic? Is it aimed to dislodge a competing item? Will it enhance an occupational role? Does it save time or money? Is it easy to operate? Can it be tried in "installments"? Has it found acceptance in positive or negative reference groups (Berger 2007)? Note that the item itself may change its image during the course of its spread; it may become more or less risky, for example, or more or less popular, or be found to serve unanticipated needs. Innovations often also undergo "reframing," as did "organic food" in its early appeal to environmentalism and later appeal to "health." Adopters may also alter the function of an innovation, as when the telegraph and, later, the radio, were transformed from interactive media to broadcast media, thus also changing the orbits of their diffusion (Blondheim 1994). Certain innovations do not succeed in diffusing until they are stripped of unnecessary or unattractive "adhesions" that confound their essence (Mead 1955). In a word, innovations and even the arcs of their diffusion are hard to hold still.

3 Diffusion takes time. The simultaneity of response assumed by advertisers is alien to diffusion research. Obtaining information on time of adoption is often the most daunting problem for the researcher. Archeology employs systems of dating and measurements of distance that make it possible to infer how far an artifact has traveled from its point of origin and how long it took (e.g. Speier 1921). Social science sometimes finds appropriate statistics on time of adoption, as when pharmacists could be asked to date physicians' first prescriptions for a new medication, or municipalities to date their adoption (or rejection) of fluoridation, or producers of music or of automobiles to keep track of how many of each model were sold in a succession of seasons. Bibliometrics were devised to follow the flow of published ideas (Borgman 1990).

4 Unit: not all adopters are individuals. The item itself may dictate the appropriate unit; "it takes two to tango," for example, or to telephone. In the diffusion of fluoridation of water in the United States, which its opponents defamed as "socialized medicine," the unit of adoption was the municipality (Crain *et al.* 1969). Of course, when the adopter is not an individual, there may also be a division of labor in the decision-making process (Dimaggio and Powell 1983). Even ostensibly individual adopters may make joint decisions with others, as when a parent decides for whom the family should vote, or what movie to see.

5 The channels of communication must be accounted for, first of all by distinguishing among the rapidly proliferating media of communication, and the formal and informal modes of interpersonal communication. These channels may then be associated with the different phases of decision-making, and with different types of items. For example, it was once thought that the relative privacy and precision of print, at least in literate societies, was more appropriate and more effective than television for advertising contraceptive practice. The key question, however, is how news of an innovation, and of its attractiveness, reaches a community or network from "outside," and how it circulates "inside" (Stark 1996; Mendels 1999). A missionary, or a salesman, or a magazine may make contact from outside, but there is ample research to show that such intervention, even from friendly sources, is almost never enough to explain non-trivial change or even to ignite interpersonal consideration of a proposed change, without the active initiative and participation of group members.

6   A map of the social structure of a community and the place of potential adopters within it is a key to analyzing diffusion. Such measures range from the density of a community, to the patterns of interaction at different times of the day. Sensational news, for example, may spread interpersonally during the daytime but not at night (DeFleur 1987). Emulation may work in a class-stratified society but not in one based on caste. Social integration will work, positively or negatively, depending on the compatibility of the proposed innovation with the norms of the group. "Structural equivalence," as already noted, may substitute for direct influence. Social, ethnic, and geographic boundaries often block the flow of influence (Hagerstrand 1967). Variations in the structure of such relationships—even between conqueror and conquered peoples, for example—have been associated with different kinds of borrowings, and in both directions (Spicer 1954). Individuals with even weak ties to more than one group may be a source of innovation; consider the role of ship captains in establishing trade between Britain and the East Indies (Erikson and Bearman 2006). Of course, weak ties and low status may also breed dissidence and "reformist" social movements.

7   Culture. The appropriateness of invoking the concept of compatibility is obvious in any discussion of culture change, but that does not make it easy to apply. It involves analysis of the "fit" between potential adopter and diffusing item. It is easy to argue that the music of the Beatles somehow fit the youth culture of the 1960s, but it is very difficult to prove (and even harder to predict). Is there a method that will allow us to confirm Gitlin's (1983) suggestion that the most popular television programs in a given year somehow "fit" the values of the incumbent president? Can it be established that "suicide bombing" will diffuse mostly in cultures that offer a glorious afterlife to their martyrs?

III

It seems fair to say that the cultural sciences, and some of the natural sciences, share an interest in the origin of ideas and practices, and in how they spread. Yet, as has been noted, the several disciplines do not seem to have paid much attention to each other, and there have been only a few now-outdated (but still worthwhile) attempts to generalize across domains. This segmentation must surely result from the academic appeal, to different kinds of scholars, of the telephone, or Marxism, or "impressionism," or the measles. Scholars such as Tarde, Innis, or Sorokin did not overlook their similarities, nor, more recently, do Rogers (1994 [1962]); Brown (1981), or Strang and Soule (1998).

Recently, there appears to be renewed attention to the dynamics of diffusion within the several domains and even across domains. This may be related to the diffusion of interdisciplinarity, or, more likely, to the near-universal diffusion of the computer, and, with it, the relative ease of tracking change across time and space and social networks. For example, anthropologists are studying the diffusion of AIDS (Watkins 2004), sociologists are comparing the diffusion of radical changes of style with the diffusion of contentious politics (Rao *et al.* 2003), and linguists are comparing language change with fashions in children's names (Labov 2007; Lieberson 2000).

It follows that processes of diffusion ought to have a larger share in studies of change—past and present—and that diffusion research must draw its data from a large variety of domains. It is important to overcome the temptation to treat the diffusion of each new item as its very own story. Indeed, items should be compared in terms of the curves of their diffusion. Communications research, in particular, should forgo the specializations that tend to separate media studies from interpersonal communication, rather than to explore the dynamics of their interaction. Students of diffusion must strive to develop a content-analytic scheme to characterize diffusing items (innovations) from the subjective point of view of potential adopters and to stay abreast of how the perception of an item undergoes change even while it is diffusing. The content scheme should be expanded to explore the compatibility of an item with the social, cultural, and communicative contexts in which the potential adopter is embedded.

Diffusion research can contribute to the conceptualization of many different problems. Consider one. We think we know a lot about how opinions are formed, and how they are represented in polls of public opinion. But individual opinions are not "private" property. Circumstances conspire with the media to make an issue salient, and preliminary responses may arise, if they do, from predisposition, thought, and social interaction. But public opinion is not the sum total of individual opinions, as reported in polls. How, we should ask, did a myriad of fuzzy individual inclinations become salient, how did they condense into two opinions—pro-life and pro-choice, for example? Was this the form in which they spread among their constituencies? The aggregation of public opinion is a problem of diffusion, in which the media, social networks, and individuals have a share, as Gabriel Tarde (1969 [1898]) tried to show.

In sum, diffusion research seeks to formalize the role of communications in the study of social and cultural change, past, present, and future, in the spirit of Paul Lazarsfeld's (1964) essay on "The Obligations of the 1950 Pollster to the 1984 Historian." But whereas Lazarsfeld called for periodic portraits of the climate of opinion, diffusion research calls for weather maps of change in action.

References

Berger, J. 2007. "Where Consumers Diverge from Others: Identity Signaling and Product Domains." *Journal of Consumer Research* 34: 121–33.

Blondheim, M. 1994. *News over the Wire.* Cambridge, MA: Harvard University Press.

Borgman, C.L., ed. 1990. *Scholarly Communication and Bibliomertrics.* Newbury Park, CA: Sage Publications.

Brown, L.A. 1981. *Innovation Diffusion: A New Perspective.* London: Routledge.

Burt, R.S. 1999a. "The Social Capital of Opinion Leaders." *Annals of the American Academy of Political and Social Science* 566: 37–54.

——. 1999b. "Social Contagion and Innovation: Cohesion vs. Structural Equivalence." *American Journal of Sociology* 92(6): 1287–1335.

Coleman, J., Katz, E., and Menzel, H. 1966. *Medical Innovation.* Indianapolis, IN: Bobbs Merrill.

Crain, R., Katz, E., and Rosenthal, D. 1969. *The Politics of Community Conflict: The Fluoridation Decision.* Indianapolis, IN: Bobbs Merrill.

Crane, D. 1972. *Invisible Colleges: Diffusion of Knowledge in Scientific Communities.* Chicago: University of Chicago Press.

——. 1999. "Diffusion Models and Fashion: A Reassessment." *Annals of the American Academy of Political and Social Science* 566: 13–24.

DeFleur, M.L. 1987. "The Growth and Decline of Research on the Diffusion of News." *Communication Review* 14: 109–30.

Dimaggio, P.J. and Powell, W.W. 1983. "The Iron Cage Revisited: Institutional Isomorphism and Collective Rationality in Organizational Fields." *American Sociological Review* 48(2): 147–60.

Erikson, Emily and Bearman, Peter S. 2006. "The Structure of English East-Indian Trade 1600–1831." *American Journal of Sociology* 112(1): 195–230.

Gitlin, T. 1983. *Inside Prime Time*. New York: Pantheon.

Gladwell, M. 2000. *The Tipping Point*. New York: Little Brown.

Granovetter, M.S. 1973. "The Strength of Weak Ties." *American Journal of Sociology* 78: 1360–80.

Gurevitch, M. 1961. "The Social Structure of Acquaintanceship Networks." Ph.D. Dissertation, Department of Economics, Political Science Division, Massachusetts Institute of Technology.

Hagerstrand, T. 1967. *Innovation Diffusion as a Spatial Process*. Chicago: University of Chicago Press.

Hawley, F. 1946. "The Role of Pueblo Social Organization in the Dissemination of Catholicism." *American Anthropologists* 448: 407–11.

Hobsbawm, E. 1983. "Mass-Producing: Europe, 1870–1914." Pp. 263–307 in E. Hobsbawm and T. Rangers, eds., *The Invention of Tradition*. Cambridge: Cambridge University Press.

Hornik, R. 2004. "Some Reflections on Diffusion Theory and the Role of Everett Rogers." *Journal of Health Communication* 9(1): 143–48.

Innis, H. 1951. *The Bias of Communication*. Toronto: University of Toronto Press.

Katz, E. 1971. "The Social Itinerary of Technical Change." Pp. 761–97 in W. Schramm and D. Roberts, eds., *Process and Effects of Mass Communication*. Urbana: University of Illinois Press.

Katz, E. and Lazarsfeld, P.F. 2006 (1955). *Personal Influence: The Part Played by People in the Flow of Mass Communication*. Glencoe, IL: The Free Press.

Katz, E., Levin, M.L., and Hamilton, H.H. 1963. "Traditions of Research in the Diffusion of Innovation." *American Sociological Review* 28: 237–53.

Katz, R. 1986. *Divining the Powers of Music*. New York: Pendragon.

Labov, W. 2007. "Transmission and Diffusion." *Language* 83(2): 350–59.

Lazarsfeld, P.F. 1964. "The Obligations of the 1950 Pollster to the 1984 Historian." *Public Opinion Quarterly* 14: 618–638.

Lazarsfeld, P.F., Berelson, B., and Gaudet, H. l944. *The People's Choice: How People Make up Their Minds in an Electoral Campaign*. New York: Columbia University Press.

Lieberson, S. 2000. *A Matter of Taste: New Names, Fashions, and Culture Change*. New Haven, CT: Yale University Press.

Lopes, P. 2002. *The Rise of a Jazz World*. Cambridge: Cambridge University Press.

Mead, M. 1955. *Cultural Patterns and Social Change*. Paris: World Federation for Mental Health, UNESCO.

Mendels, D. 1999. *The Media Revolution of Early Christianity*. Grand Rapids, MI and Cambridge: Eerdmans Publishers.

Menzel, H. 1960. "Innovation, Integration and Marginality." *American Sociological Review* 25: 704–13.

Mosse, G.L. 1975. *Nationalization of the Masses*. New York: H. Fertig.

Rao, H., Monin, P. and Durand, R. 2003. "Institutional Change in Toque Ville: Nouvelle Cuisine as an Identity Movement in French Gastronomy." *American Journal of Sociology* 108(4): 1211–48.

Rogers, E. 1994 (1962). *Diffusion of Innovation*, fifth edition. New York: The Free Press.

Ryan, B. and Gross, N. 1942. "The Diffusion of Hybrid Seed Corn in Two Iowa Communities." *Rural Sociology* 8: 15–24.

Simmel, Georg. 1957 (1904). "Fashion." *American Journal of Sociology* 62: 541–558.

Sorokin, P. 1941. *Social and Cultural Mobility*. Glencoe, IL: The Free Press.

Speier, L. 1921. "The Sundance of the Plains Indians: Its Development and Diffusion." *Anthropological Papers of the American Museum of Natural History* 16: 451–527.

Spicer, E.H. 1954. "Spanish–Indian Acculturation in the Southwest." *American Anthropologist* 56: 663–78.

Spiro, M. 1956. *Kibbutz: Venture in Utopia*. Cambridge, MA: Harvard University Press.

Stark, R. 1996. *The Rise of Christianity: How the Obscure, Marginal Jesus Movement Became the Dominant Religious Force in the Western World in a Few Centuries*. Princeton, NJ: Princeton University Press.

Strang, D. and Soule, S.A. 1998. "Diffusion in Organizations and Social Movements: From Hybrid Corn to Poison Pills." *Annual Review of Sociology* 24: 265–90.

Tarde, G. 1969 (1890). *The Laws of Imitation*. New York: Holt.

——. 1969 (1898). "Opinion and Conversation." In T. Clark, ed., *Gabriel Tarde on Communication and Social Influence*. Chicago: University of Chicago Press.

Travers, J. and Milgram, S. 1969. "An Experimental Study of the Small World Problem." *Sociometry* 32(4): 425–43.

Van den Bulte, C. and Lilien, G.L. 2004. "Two-Stage Partial Observability Models of Innovation Adoption." Working paper, the Wharton School, University of Pennsylvania.

Veblen, T. 1899. *The Theory of the Leisure Class*. New York: Macmillan.

Watkins, S.C. 2004. "Navigating the AIDS Epidemic in Rural Malawi." *Population and Development Review* 30(4): 693–705.

Watts, Duncan. 2003. *Six Degrees: The Science of a Connected Age*. New York: W.W. Norton.

Weimann, G. 1994. *The Influentials*. Albany: State University of New York Press.

65

Cosmopolitanism and the clash of civilizations

Bryan S. Turner

Introduction: alterity, ancient and modern

Inter-civilizational contact invariably creates a sense of the otherness or alterity of different societies and cultures. Any society with a more or less coherent cultural boundary and identity, acting as an inclusionary social force, tends to have an exclusionary notion of membership and hence otherness; the more inclusive the feeling of ethnicity and national membership, the more intense the notion of an outside. With globalization involving the compression of spatial relations between societies, the problem of alterity has been magnified. Thus a paradoxical relationship exists between the growing cultural hybridity, interconnectedness, and interdependency of the world—indeed, the modernization of societies—and the notion of alterity in politics, philosophy, and culture. The emergence of alterity as a theme of inter-civilizational and transnational contact should not, however, be seen as an evolutionary progression, marching in tandem with modernization. The divisive question of alterity has been closely associated with the rise of world religions, the creation of imperial powers, and the history of colonialism and post-colonialism. The question of the other is not easily separated from the "fear of diversity," which can be seen as in fact the foundation of ancient Greek thought (Saxonhouse 1992).

We should be careful to distinguish between a number of separate meanings of the other, otherness, and alterity. The concept of the other has been important in phenomenology and psychoanalysis, where the self as a subject presupposes the existence of a non-self or other. And in existentialism the other often assumes an antagonistic relationship with the self. Because the individual resides in a world of other subjectivities, there exists a mode of existence that is properly referred to as "being-for-others." In the work of Emmanuel Levinas (1998), the other can play a positive role in questioning the confidence and assurance of the subject. The face of the other challenges us to take responsibility for the other, and hence otherness creates the conditions that make ethics possible. Jacques Derrida (2000), playing on the etymological connections between "stranger" and "host" (*hostis* and *hospes*), neatly summarized the issue by saying simply that ethics is hospitality.

This philosophical analysis of the role of the other in modern ethical discourse has an important and obvious relationship to nationalism, ethnic cleansing, and globalization. With the collapse of the Soviet Union between 1989 and 1992, there has been a resurgence of ethnic identity as the basis of political communities, and ethnic violence has largely replaced class conflict as the major arena of political confrontation. The disintegration of Yugoslavia that began in 1991 and the 1992 crisis in Bosnia were tragic illustrations of the importance of ethnicity in international conflicts. Globally there are new and unanticipated conflicts between Sunni and Shi'ite Muslims, often in hitherto harmonious communities. Where globalization weakens the nation-state and promotes identity politics, alterity can play a violent role in ethnic conflict. These modern conflicts thus appear to be a long way removed from what had been relatively successful patterns of social co-operation between Muslims, Jews, and Christians in medieval Spain, for example (Menocal 2002).

By connecting alterity with twentieth-century globalization, we must not ignore the historical roots of the sense of otherness. Fear of the other was fundamental to Greek politics, because endless wars against "barbarians" always involved the threat of capture and enslavement. Slave status entailed the loss of freedom, exclusion from the public arena, and the denial of rationality. Alterity arose out of the growth of international trade and warfare, and it was expressed powerfully in the anthropological writings of Herodotus. However, with the collapse of the ancient world, the question of alterity became closely associated with the Abrahamic religions of Judaism, Christianity, and Islam. Because Yahweh was a jealous God, there was a sacred covenant between God and the tribes of Israel, which excluded those who worshiped idols and false gods. In Christianity, a universalistic orientation that recognized the other was expressed in Paul's letters to the Galatians and Romans, which rejected circumcision as a condition of salvation. Because the uncircumcised (non-Jews) were among the righteous, the message of Jesus had, at least in Pauline theology, a global significance. The righteous were those who were circumcised in the heart, and hence faith came, at least in principle, to be separated from specific cultural practices and ethnic membership. Because Christianity and Islam developed an evangelical faith that stressed human equality, they in a sense denied the problem of alterity. However, the persistence of slavery in both Christendom and the Islamic Household of Faith raises a stubborn problem about the nature and depth of universalism and egalitarianism in both religions (Segal 2001).The competition between Christianity and Islam resulted eventually in the nineteenth-century dominance of Christianity, when the Church often functioned as the civilized veneer of Western colonialism. Because Christian theology treated Islam as a false religion, many in the West imagined Islam as an irrational, stagnant, and licentious sect—thus the origins of what social critic Edward Said (1978) described as "Orientalism."

The Huntington thesis

Samuel Huntington's article on "the clash of civilizations" in *Foreign Affairs* (1993) has defined much of the academic debate about inter-cultural understanding and misunderstanding for over a decade. Huntington's thesis follows Carl Schmitt's *The Concept of the Political* (1996) in terms of seeing the world as a struggle between friend and foe. In retrospect, Said's criticisms of Orientalism and especially his *Representations of the Intellectual* (1994) offered some prospect that intellectuals could cross boundaries between cultures and forged a pathway towards mutual respect and understanding. After 9/11, Huntington's bleak analysis of the development of micro faultline conflicts and macro core state conflicts has more successfully and completely captured the mood of foreign policy in the West in the era of the "war on terror." Huntington of course believes that the major division is between the Christian West and the Muslim world. More recently, he has even more openly written about "the age of Muslim Wars" and the existence of widespread Muslim grievance and hostility towards the United States (Huntington 2003). Any attempt to engage with Islamic civilization is now seen as a "war for Muslim minds" (Kepel 2004).

Opposing the Huntington thesis is not easy, particularly because it is in many respects a self-fulfilling academic prophecy. The more scholars have talked about it, the more it appeared to shape American foreign policy. Much of the criticism of Huntington has been couched at an empirical and practical level in showing, for example, that conflicts within Christianity (such as Northern Ireland) and within Islam (between Sunni and Shi'ite) are as, or more, important than conflicts between religions. In addition, Huntington is said to have no real explanation for the faultline, because the thesis is "an ethnocentric blind to avoid having to discuss the things that Muslim opponents of the US actually care about" (Mann 2003: 169). Although it is important to question the Huntington thesis at the level of empirical social science, his argument opens up the opportunity to engage in a deeper normative and epistemological debate about the moral grounds for recognizing and respecting other cultures. In this discussion, I shall call this normative stance one of "cosmopolitan virtue," by which I mean the ethical imperative for respect, mutual dialogue, recognition, and care (Turner 2008).

From what vantage point can we take up this debate? One starting point might be the early German origins of the Enlightenment, and the work and vision of the philosopher Wilhelm Gottfried Leibniz (1646–1716). In the twentieth century, the Enlightenment became, especially after the attack by the critical theory of Horkheimer and Adorno (1947), a target of critical inspection, precisely because its vision of universal reason was said to be blind to cultural differences. Reading Leibniz on China shows how misguided this interpretation has often been. Leibniz, the (German) precursor of the (French) Enlightenment, is probably best known as a mathematician, who, independently of Newton, developed the calculus, and for his theory of entities (monads). But there is a different, though equally complex, side to Leibniz's philosophy, which appears extraordinarily pertinent to modern times (Perkins 2004). Leibniz lived in a period when European trade with the outside world, including Asia, was expanding rapidly. It was a time of intense commerce of commodities, and, alongside this emerging capitalist enterprise, Leibniz advocated a "commerce of light," namely a trade of mutual enlightenment. Against Spinoza's view that there is only one substance, Leibniz argued that the world is characterized by its infinite diversity and richness. The world is teaming with entities that exist in their fullest capacity and in a state of harmony. According to Leibniz (1989) in his *Discourse on Metaphysics*, God has created the best of all possible worlds (a theodicy), which is "the simplest in hypotheses and the richest in phenomena."

What bearing has this theory of monadology on relations with China? Recognition of the diversity of cultures and civilizations leads us to embrace the inherent value of difference. Leibniz, like Spinoza, advocated a tolerance of diverse views, but went beyond the philosophers of his day to establish a moral imperative to learn from cultural diversity. Applying this ethic to himself and committing much of his life to studying

China from the reports of missionaries and merchants, Leibniz went about establishing a philosophical platform for cosmopolitanism. Differences between entities or monads require exchange, but they also establish a commonality of culture. Leibniz was not, in modern terms, a cultural relativist: If all cultures are equal (in value), why bother to learn from any one of them? Although all knowledge of the outside world is relativistic, Leibniz argued that there are enough innate ideas to make an exchange of enlightenment possible. Leibniz once wrote to Peter the Great, who was at the time engaged in a struggle with Islam to protect Moscovy from being engulfed by Crimean Tartars, to say that he was not one of those "impassioned patriots of one country alone" but a person who works for "the well-being of the whole of mankind, for I consider heaven as my country and cultivated men as my compatriots" (Wiener 1951: 596–97). From the doctrine of blind monads, Leibniz developed a hermeneutics of generosity and hospitality that regarded inter-cultural understanding as not merely a useful tool of anthropological field methods, but an ethical imperative. Leibniz developed an implicit cosmopolitan virtue in his attempt to establish an exchange with China that offers us a guideline for understanding our own times, especially a "commerce of light" with Islam. In this respect, Leibniz provides a sort of rational and moral antidote to Huntington.

Despite Leibniz, the Enlightenment has often been treated as the origin of modern universalism, but a universalism that functions as the basis for cultural domination and exclusion. The Enlightenment notion of universalism set in motion a series of contrasts or binary oppositions between the universalistic world of bourgeois civility and citizenship, and local practices and customs that were considered antithetical to the march of progressive world history. The result was to create a world of minorities who were seen to be in need of education, reform, modernization, and regeneration, leading wherever possible to an eventual assimilation. There is of course much more to this story. In 1793 in *Religion within the Boundaries of Mere Reason* (1998), Immanuel Kant created the modernist division between the moral impulse of Protestant rationalism and the cultic religions that promised to give health and prosperity to ordinary people, provided they surrendered themselves to the gods through the magical powers of the shaman, the wizard, and the witch. He created, at least implicitly, a comparative view of the division between the popular religions of the uncivilized world and the ascetic this-worldly religions. This contrast formed the basis for Max Weber's comparative sociology of the economic ethics of world religions. It was not only or simply a Kantian view of world development, since Hegel in a series of lectures between 1821 and 1831 developed the idea of Christianity as "the consummate religion," namely a religion in which the evolution of the spirit, or *Geist*, of history found its contemporary "consummation" (Hodgson 1985). For Kant, Hegel, and Weber, Judaism did not belong to this world of rational consummate religions.

The Jews were seen to be resistant to the modern Enlightenment, because their passionate commitment to bizarre customs, especially their dietary requirements, was viewed as pre-eminently an example of how "thick" local cultures stood out as a rational offence to the modernizing impulse of the Enlightenment and its political progeny, the French Revolution (Mufti 2007). Weber (1952) adopted a similar view of Jewish dietary culture as an erosion of genuine, rational asceticism in his *Ancient Judaism*. It was on the basis of such reasoning that the revolutionary republican call of Napoleon Bonaparte summoned the Jewish community to assimilate under a banner of rationalist secularism. Progressive secular Jews would leave their ancestral allegiances and throw off their ancient customs to become French or German citizens.

The issues of Jewishness and the Jewish Question are inevitably connected to Karl Marx and his critique of bourgeois capitalist society in his 1843 "On the Jewish Question" (Marx and Engels 1975). Hirschel Levi, Marx's father, was influenced by the secular ideas of the French and German Enlightenment, eventually changing his name to Heinrich Marx and adopting Christianity in 1824. In part Heinrich's conversion to the state religion was designed to avoid the anti-Jewish laws of 1816, which would have undermined his law practice (Berlin 1978). The issue of Jewish identity and the Enlightenment was therefore a concrete rather than abstract issue for the young Marx and it gave rise to his famous argument against Bruno Bauer on liberal political rights. Bauer had argued that political emancipation would give Jews the opportunity to become full citizens, thereby entering the process of modernization by abandoning their medieval religious customs. Marx used the debate about Jewishness to criticize bourgeois liberalism as a shallow political doctrine in which social emancipation was necessary to give political emancipation any substantial content. Genuine citizenship was not possible in capitalism because abstract Man was an alienated creature in which political life had become detached from the real conditions of existence. This discussion in many respects provided the fatal starting point of the long history of the separation of the universal rights of Man from the social transformation of class society by revolutionary action.

Because we cannot escape modernity, we cannot escape the identity conflicts that result in civil disturbance, and we cannot easily guard against the threat of communal violence. Cleaning up the language of discrimination is not going to significantly change the politics of ethnic violence. The current crisis of liberal secularism involves a struggle over claims to identity—a struggle that can no longer be housed within the legacy of the Treaty of Westphalia, in which it was assumed that religion could be simply a matter of private consciousness, not public practice. The Treaty of 1648 came at the end of the Wars of Religion. Separating church and state, it made religion a matter of personal belief rather than public practice and allowed princes to decide which version of Christianity would be hegemonic within their principalities. However, these arrangements are breaking down, partly because, although they may have been relevant to the social characteristics of Christianity in the seventeenth century, they are less relevant to Islam and Hinduism in the modern period. Is there no alternative to this growth of ethnic conflict, especially in societies where the state often appears to take sides with the majority against minorities, for instance in Thailand between a majority Buddhist culture and Muslim minority one, or in Malaysia, where a policy of Islamization of law and education appears to weigh against Buddhists, Hindus, and Christians (McCargo 2007)? What models or metaphors of cosmopolitanism could one appeal to against the homogenizing force of modernity?

One possibility of cosmopolitan inspiration can be illustrated by a story told by Abul Kalam Azad, who confronted a flock of sparrows invading his prison cell during his incarceration by the British at the Ahmednagar Fort in Western India during World War II. After some fruitless confrontation and after many tentative steps of negotiation and persuasion, Azad eventually feeds the birds, and through this "conference of birds" an ethics of coexistence emerges. This little story is in fact based on a twelfth-century Sufi allegory by the Persian poet Fariduddin Attar. Aamir Mufti (2007: 171–72) concludes that these allegorical narratives "reveal the utter human poverty of the politics of separatism and communalism, and constitute perhaps one of the most far-reaching critiques of these corrosive tendencies in India's modern life." Furthermore, "they also contain the elements of a critique of the implicit majoritarianism of 'secular' nationalism itself and its failure ultimately to produce a convincing ethico-political practice of coexistence in an undivided India" (Mufti 2007: 172). This argument is intended to be an attempt "to unravel the assumption of inevitability" that has become attached to the endless cycle of ethnic violence in modern societies. This unraveling represents an important scholarly contribution, but it is also a major contribution to the ethics of hospitality in a world deeply divided between hosts, guests, and strangers.

Cosmopolitan virtue

We can usefully distinguish between negative and positive alterity. Negative alterity exclusively defines the other as dangerous, inferior, and antithetical to the subject's own culture; Orientalism is the classical form of negative otherness. By contrast, positive alterity recognizes the other, embracing the ethical opportunities afforded by global diversity. In contemporary social theory, a variety of authors have defended recognition ethics, multiculturalism, and diversity as positive aspects of globalization. Although successful democracies may require safe—if porous—borders, patriotism can be success-fully distinguished from nationalism. Cosmopolitan virtue—celebrating difference, and promoting the care of the other—is an ethical consequence of globalization and con-stitutes an obligation that complements human rights.

The contemporary philosophical debates about the other have their origins in G.W.F. Hegel's theory of recognition (Williams 1997). The master–slave dialectic sug-gests that neither slave nor master can achieve authentic recognition, and hence, without some degree of social equality, no ethical community—a system of rights and obliga-tions—can function. Rights presuppose relatively free, autonomous, and self-conscious agents capable of rational choice. Recognition is required if people are to be mutually acceptable as moral agents, but life is unequal. Economic scarcity undercuts the roots of solidarity (community), without which conscious, rational agency is difficult. A variety of modern writers, in particular Charles Taylor (1992), have appealed to recognition ethics as the baseline for the enjoyment of rights in multicultural societies. Without recognition of minority rights, no liberal democratic society can function. The growth of human rights is a major index of the growth of juridical globalization, and recognition of the rights of others is an ethical precondition for global governance. Cosmopolitanism now appears as the most articulate alternative to a bleak set of assumptions about the clash of civilizations. Cosmopolitanism has many distinguished supporters—most recently Kwame Appiah (2006). In the West we need to remind ourselves that cosmopolitanism is neither new nor Western as such. We need to recognize the long history of Sanskrit cosmopolitanism as well as Buddhist cosmopolitanism, and more recently various writers have drawn attention to Islamic cosmopolitanism (Marsden 2008). This openness to the alternative versions of cosmopolitanism could be developed as a more general platform for communication between religions and for recognizing opportunities for mutuality that are present in other traditions (Seligman 2004). The search for religious roots of cosmopolitanism can be a useful alternative strategy to the dominant view that cosmo-politanism is an essential secular quest. Religious notions about human vulnerability can be deployed to support the view that human rights are not simply part of a Western juridical tradition (Turner 2006).

Having recognized the possibility of religious roots of cosmopolitanism, we must acknowledge that in the twentieth century much of the burden of cosmopolitan hope was borne on the shoulders of human-rights initiatives, and even here the question of the universality of culture, and thereby the nature and intellectual role of cultural anthropology, became a deeply problematic issue. To counter arguments that humanity is divided by race, it became important to assert the commonality of culture, especially language, in the definition of humanity. The great champion of "culture" as a category and of cosmopolitanism as a moral and political platform was Franz Boas. In *Race and Democratic Society* (1945) and *Anthropology and Modern Life* (1962), he had condemned racism, imperialism, and colonialism as factors that prevented people from openness to the full spectrum of human culture, and he attacked nation and nationalism as artificial and inappropriate receptacles of human cultural production. In almost Kantian terms, Boas embraced a philosophy of cosmopolitanism and international peace as necessary consequences of his belief in the integrating power of human culture. It is ironic that modern anthropology, having had a transfusion of poststructuralism and postmodernism, now deconstructs the Boasian concept of culture, which is considered too essential, bounded, and rigid to cope with the idea of culture as process. Critics of the notion of culture include Lila Abu-Lughod (1991) and Joel Kahn (1989), but without a notion of culture there is another ironic question: Does anthropology still exist (Turner 2008)? This ironic question takes us back to Leibniz and the problems of cultural relativism. While Boas tried to use "culture" in his campaign against nationalism and racism, much of the relativism that fueled the postmodern critique of Enlightenment came from the ethnographic research of anthropology, but with the assault on culture there is little common ground for defending some idea of social justice, human dignity, or human rights (Bauman and Briggs 2003).

Conclusion: terror and *jihad*

In the aftermath of the attacks on the United States in 2001, the social tensions between the West and Islam have been intensified. Political Islam has, in the post-Cold War period, replaced communism as the imaginary enemy of liberal capitalism. As a result, the Huntington thesis of a "clash of civilizations" is compelling and optimism about our political future is in short supply. In this discussion I have explored briefly the case for recognition ethics and cosmopolitan virtue, but the defense of these normative positions is problematic in the light of a civil war in Iraq, and military conflicts in Afghanistan, Thailand, Chechnya, and the Sudan. Huntington's thesis has plausibility because in all of these modern conflicts Islam has been prominent, albeit for a great variety of reasons. Of course there is an equally compelling argument that orthodox Islam does not condone or counsel violence but on the contrary offers the prospects of religious pluralism and mutual respect (Sachedina 2001). One interpretation of Islamic radicalism is that it has involved the re-interpretation of the meaning of *jihad* in response to Western colonialism. Originally meaning a personal struggle against evil, it became under Sayyid Qutb a doctrine of struggle against foreigners to protect the faith, and under Ali Shariati a revolutionary doctrine against state oppression and foreign intervention (Rahnema 2000). By contrast, Olivier Roy (2004: 41) counsels us that all attempts to sort out the "correct" theological interpretation of *jihad* are, especially from a social science perspective, largely sterile, since all of these terms are highly contested within Islam itself and it is not the role of sociology to adjudicate between different theological claims. Western social commentary can make mistakes of interpretation in this particular arena, as we can discover from the journalism of Michel Foucault (Afary and Anderson 2005). Rather, our task is more properly to understand the social forces that sustain these interpretations. For Roy, one crucial issue is that the internet has opened up opportunities for an endless competition between *fatwas*, resulting in a deep crisis of authority within the Muslim community (Turner and Volpi 2007). If there is to be an open dialogue between civilizations, it will not be intellectually adequate to pretend that radical Islam is deeply democratic. Recognition cannot begin with such artificial characterization of difference. Cosmopolitanism must start with the understanding that agreements through dialogue must begin with a recognition of cultural differences, but in the case of *jihad*, Western observers will have also to recognize the parallel role of the notion of crusade and just war in the West.

Finally, much of the intellectual equipment that would be valuable in criticizing the Huntington thesis—such as the idea of a common human culture or a Leibnizian commitment to dialogue—has been compromised or at least brought into question by various intellectual movements such as postmodernism and poststructuralism. Academics who retain a commitment to ideas about universalism, recognition ethics, and cosmopolitanism will need to defend some version of human rights as a transnational movement, some notion of human dignity, and some explication of our common vulnerability if a "commerce of light" is to survive.

References

Abu-Lughod, Lila. 1991. "Writing against Culture." Pp. 137–62 in Richard G. Fox, ed., *Recapturing Anthropology: Working in the Present*. Sante Fe, NM: School of American Research Press.

Afary, Janet and Anderson, Kevin B. 2005. *Foucault and the Iranian Revolution: Gender and the Seductions of Islam*. Chicago: University of Chicago Press.

Appiah, Kwame A. 2006. *Cosmopolitanism: Ethics in a World of Strangers*. New York: W.W. Norton.

Bauman, Richard and Briggs, Charles L. 2003. *Voices of Modernity: Language Ideologies and the Politics of Inequality*. Cambridge: Cambridge University Press.

Berlin, Isaiah. 1978. *Concepts & Categories: Philosophical Essays*. London: Hogarth Press.

Boas, Franz. 1945. *Race and Democratic Society*. New York: J.J. Augustin.

——. 1962. *Anthropology and Modern Life*. New York: W.W. Norton.

Derrida, Jacques. 2000. *Of Hospitality*. Stanford, CA: Stanford University Press.

Hodgson, Peter C., ed. 1985. *Hegel Lectures on the Philosophy of Religion*. Berkeley: University of California Press.

Horkheimer, Max and Adorno, Theodor W. 1947. *Dialectic of Enlightenment*. London: Allen Lane.

Huntington, Samuel P. 1993. "The Clash of Civilizations." *Foreign Affairs* 72(3): 22–48.

——. 1996. *The Clash of Civilizations and the Remaking of World Order*. New York: Simon & Schuster.

——. 2003. "America in the World." *Hedgehog Review* 5(1): 7–18.

Kahn, Joel. 1989. "Culture: Demise or Resurrection." *Critique of Anthropology* 9(2): 5–25.

Kant, Immanuel. 1998. *Religion within the Boundaries of Mere Reason*. Cambridge: Cambridge University Press.

Kepel, Giles. 2002. *Jihad: The Trail of Political Islam*. London: I.B. Tauris.

——. 2004. *The War for Muslim Minds: Islam and the West*. Cambridge, MA: Belknap Press.

Leibniz, G.W. 1989. "Discourse of Metaphysics." In *Philosophical Essays*. Indianapolis: Hackett.

Levinas, Emmanuel. 1998. *Entre Nous: On Thinking-of-the-Other*. London: Athlone Press.

Lyotard, J.-F. 1990. *Heidegger and "The Jews."* Minneapolis: University of Minnesota Press.

McCargo, Duncan, ed. 2007. *Rethinking Thailand's Southern Violence*. Singapore: NUS Press.

Mann, Michael. 2003. *Incoherent Empire*. London: Verso.

Marsden, Magnus. 2008. "Muslim Cosmopolitans? Transnational Life in Northern Pakistan." *Journal of Asian Studies* 67(1): 213–47.

Marx, Karl and Engels, Friedrich. 1975. *Collected Works*, Vol. 3. London: Lawrence & Wishart.

Menocal, Maria Rosa. 2002. *Ornament of the World: How Muslims, Jews and Christians created a Culture of Tolerance in Medieval Spain*. Boston: Little, Brown and Company.

Mosse, George L. 1993. *Confronting the Nation: Jewish and Western Nationalism*. Hanover and London: Brandeis University Press.

Mufti, Aamir R. 2007. *Enlightenment in the Colony: The Jewish Question and the Crisis of Postcolonial Culture*. Princeton, NJ and Oxford: Princeton University Press.

Perkins, Franklin. 2004. *Leibniz and China: A Commerce of Light*. Cambridge: Cambridge University Press.

Rahnema, Ali. 1998. *An Islamic Utopian: A Political Biography of Ali Shariati*. London: I.B. Taurus.

Roy, Olivier. 2004. *Globalised Islam: The Search for a New Ummah*. London: Hurst.

Sachedina, A. 2001. *The Islamic Roots of Democratic Pluralism*. Oxford: University of Oxford Press.

Said, Edward W. 1978. *Orientalism*. New York: Pantheon.

——. 1994. *Representations of the Intellectual*. London: Vintage.

Saxonhouse, Arlene W. 1992. *Fear of Diversity: The Birth of Political Science in Ancient Greek Thought*. Chicago: University of Chicago Press.

Schmitt, Carl. 1996. *The Concept of the Political*. Chicago: University of Chicago Press.

Segal, Ronald. 2001. *Islam's Black Slaves: The History of Africa's Other Black Diaspora*. London: Atlantic Books.

Seligman, Adam. 2004. *Modest Claims: Dialogues and Essays on Tolerance and Tradition*. Notre Dame, IN: University of Notre Dame Press.

Taylor, Charles. 1992. *Multiculturalism and the Politics of Recognition*. Princeton, NJ: Princeton University Press.

Turner, Bryan S. 2002. "Cosmopolitan Virtue: Globalization and Patriotism." *Theory Culture & Society* 19: 45–64.

——. 2006. *Vulnerability and Human Rights*. University Park: Pennsylvania State University Press.

——. 2008. *Rights and Virtues*. Oxford: The Bardwell Press.

——. 2008. "Does Anthropology Still Exist? Towards a Theory of Cultural Survival." *Society* 45(3): 260–266.

Turner, Bryan S. and Volpi, Frederic. 2007. "Introduction: Making Islamic Authority Matter." *Theory Culture & Society* 24(2): 1–21.

Weber, Max. 1952. *Ancient Judaism*. New York: The Free Press.

Wiener, P. 1951. *Leibniz Selections*. New York: Charles Scribner's Sons.

Williams, Robert R. 1997. *Hegel's Ethics of Recognition*. Berkeley: University of California Press.

Index